CHILDREN'S LITERATURE IN THE ELEMENTARY SCHOOL

CHILDREN'S LITERATURE IN THE ELEMENTARY SCHOOL

SECOND EDITION

Charlotte S. Huck
THE OHIO STATE UNIVERSITY

Doris Young Kuhn
UNIVERSITY OF HOUSTON

Holt, Rinehart and Winston, Inc.
New York   Chicago   San Francisco
Atlanta   Dallas   Montreal   Toronto

ACKNOWLEDGMENTS

Grateful acknowledgment is made to the following authors, illustrators, publishers, and agencies for permission to reprint selections from copyrighted material.

AMERICAN HERITAGE   Quotation from *Texas and the War with Mexico* by Fairfax Downey and the Editors of *American Heritage*. Harper and Brothers, 1961, used with the permission of American Heritage.

APPLETON-CENTURY-CROFTS   "I Heard a Bird Sing" by Oliver Herford, from *The Century Magazine*.

ASSOCIATION FOR CHILDHOOD EDUCATION INTERNATIONAL   "Cinderella," from *Told under the Green Umbrella*, Copyright 1930 and 1958, the Macmillan Co., New York, New York. By permission of the Association for Childhood Education International.

ATHENEUM PUBLISHERS   Quotations from "Me, Myself and I" and "Where Is a Poem?" Copyright © 1962 by Eve Merriam. From *There Is No Rhyme for Silver*. Used by permission of Atheneum Publishers; Five lines from "Inside a Poem" and the poems "Thumbprint" and "A Cliché." Copyright © 1964 by Eve Merriam. From *It Doesn't Always Have to Rhyme*. Used by permission of Atheneum Publishers; Four lines from *The Quest of the Gole:* Text copyright © 1966 by John Hollander. From *The Quest of the Gole*. Used by permission of Atheneum House.

BRANDT & BRANDT   Two verses from "Abraham Lincoln" and eight lines from "Indian" from *A Book of Americans* by Rosemary and Stephen Vincent Benét (Holt, Rinehart and Winston, Inc.). Copyright, 1933, by Stephen Vincent Benét. Copyright renewed © 1961, by Rosemary Carr Benét. Reprinted by permission of Brandt & Brandt.

THE BODLEY HEAD LTD.   Canadian rights for selections from: *Beowulf* and *The Hound of Ulster*, both by Rosemary Sutcliff, and from *The Last Battle* by C. S. Lewis. Reprinted by permission of The Bodley Head Ltd.

R. R. BOWKER COMPANY   An excerpt from "Stop Watering Down Biographies" by Fran Martin, *Junior Libraries*, vol. 6 (December 1959). Reprinted from the *School Library Journal*. Copyright by R. R. Bowker Company.

Grateful acknowledgment is made to the following school personnel and photographers:
HORTENSIA DYER, Columbus Public Schools, Ohio
MABEL HEFTY, Punahou School, Honolulu, Hawaii
ALICE BROOKS McGUIRE, Casis School, Austin, Texas
R. E. PETERSON, Lafayette, Indiana
CARL PURCELL, National Education Association

FOREWORD

Many exciting developments have occurred in the field of children's literature since the first and present edition of *Children's Literature in the Elementary School.* Increased emphasis has been placed upon helping children discover the structure of a discipline and its mode of inquiry. The work of Bruner has stressed the necessity of identifying the major concepts of a field and introducing these in a spiral curriculum. Bloom's research has highlighted the importance of the primary grades in a child's learning pattern. Growing out of this emphasis upon the early introduction of a discipline, the English Curriculum Centers at Nebraska and Wisconsin studied the teaching of literature in the elementary grades. The federal government has played a major role in this area by its provision for Institutes for the training of teachers and librarians, and for the funding of libraries and library supervisors through the Elementary and Secondary Education Act of 1965. Such professional organizations as the National Council of Teachers of English have influenced development of elementary school literature programs. The inclusion of children's literature in the National Assessment program will bring increased attention to this discipline. It would appear that at long last, literature was to have an established place in the curriculum of the elementary school.

The authors have played an active role in some of these new developments. They have experimented with different approaches in teaching literature to children and teachers. In working with English scholars, curriculum specialists, and classroom teachers, they have increased their knowledge of literary criticism and its place in the elementary school curriculum.

The second edition reflects these new developments but maintains the authors' original purposes: to help the teacher and the school librarian become familiar with the literature that is available for children, to help them develop criteria for evaluating books, and to create in children a joy and love of good books. The new edition also is designed to help teachers build skill in guiding children's study of literature and to provide a foundation for a sound literature program in the elementary school.

The entire book has been rewritten, updated, and reorganized. In Part 1, criteria for evaluating books have been expanded, and new theories of learning and child development are related to the selection of books and the teaching of literature. The chapters in Part 2 are organized according to types of books rather than interests of children. However, books are consistently related to children's interests. Informational books are discussed in one chapter rather than parts of three chapters as in the first edition. A new chapter is devoted to traditional literature and a complete chapter is given to modern humor and fantasy, whereas these types of books were combined in one chapter previously.

A completely new chapter, titled "Teaching Literature to Children," concludes the new edition. This chapter suggests goals for a literature program, includes a taxonomy of literary skills, and presents examples of literature lessons. Other new features of the second edition include a color section showing various techniques and styles of illustrators. This text provides more information about media and picture book illustrations. The poetry chapter has been expanded to include over seventy poems as illustrative of the various types of poems and elements of poetry that should be considered in a literature program. A new guide for the pronunciation of names of authors, illustrators, characters, and settings has been included in Appendix C.

The authors believe that no text *about* children's books can substitute for *wide reading* of books for children. Descriptions of classroom activities cannot provide the joy and understanding that result from the actual sharing of reading experiences with children. We hope that readers of this text will find the deep satisfactions that come from discovering new books, knowing children's authors and illustrators, and introducing them to boys and girls.

Finally, we wish to express our appreciation to the many children, classroom teachers, librarians, and college students who have shared their enthusiasm for books, their knowledge, and their concerns. Their support has encouraged and influenced the writing of this second edition. We are indebted to Harold G. Shane, Eldonna Everetts, and Carolyn Field for their careful reading and criticism of the manuscript, and to Harriet Price, children's librarian, Bexley Public Library, for her untiring response to our many questions. The authors are particularly grateful to Janet Hickman for her patience, interest, and scholarly research during the preparation of the book, for the arduous task of making the author, illustrator, title index, and typing the final manuscript.

Columbus, Ohio
January 1968

C.S.H.

D.Y.K.

CONTENTS

FOREWORD   xiii

PART I. LEARNING ABOUT CHILDREN AND BOOKS   1

CHAPTER 1. UNDERSTANDING CHILDREN AND LITERATURE   3

Knowing Children's Literature   4

Children's Books Today   4

Big Business   5

What Is Children's Literature?   7

Criteria for Evaluating Children's Fiction   9

Classics in Children's Literature   18

The Award Books   21

Understanding Children and How They Learn   23

Dimensions of Growth   24

Principles of Learning   27

Children's Reading Interests   27

Factors Influencing Reading Interests   28

Guides for Ages and Stages   29

Guides for Studying Children   36

Selecting Books   38

The Need for Good Book Selection   38

Principles of Book Selection   39

Problems of Censorship   42

Aids to Book Selection   43

xv

Suggested Activities   45
Related Readings   46
Chapter References   47

CHAPTER 2. CHILDREN'S BOOKS OF THE PAST   57

Children's Books: Seventeenth and Eighteenth Centuries   59

Background   59
Books of the American Colonial Period   60
Mother Goose   61
Folk Tales and Adventure   62
Newbery Publishes for Children   62
Books of Instruction   63
Didactic Tales   65
Poetry   66

Children's Literature: Nineteenth Century   66

Background   66
Books of Religion and Morals   67
Books of Instruction   69
Folk-Tale Collections   72
Stories of Family Life   72
Stories of Adventure   73
Animal Stories   75
Books of Humor and Fantasy   75
Books of Games and Sports   76
Poetry   77
Magazines   78
Improvements in Book Printing   79
Illustrators of the Nineteenth Century   80
Close of the Nineteenth Century   80

Children's Literature: Twentieth Century   81

Background   81
Technical Improvements   82
Fiction Factories   82
Recognition of Children's Literature   83
Rise of the Picture Book   83
Growth of Informational Books   84
Folk Tales   85
Humor and Fantasy   85
Animal Adventure   86
Books for Personal-Social Development   86
Poetry   87
Translations of Foreign Books   88
Books for Special Interests   88
Summary   88

Children's Books Tomorrow   88

Suggested Activities   89
Related Readings   90

PART 2. KNOWING CHILDREN'S LITERATURE   93

CHAPTER 3. PICTURE BOOKS   95

First Experiences with Books   96
   First Books   96
   "Participation" Books   97
Mother Goose   98
   Appeals of Mother Goose   98
   Different Editions of Mother Goose   100
   Evaluating Mother Goose Books   103
ABC and Counting Books   104
   ABC Books   104
   Counting Books   106
Picture Books   108
   Definitions of Picture Books   108
   Guides for Evaluating Picture Books   109
   Types and Themes of Picture Books   126
Suggested Activities   144
Related Readings   145
Chapter References   146

CHAPTER 4. TRADITIONAL LITERATURE   156

   Theories of Myth   157
Folk Tales   159
   Study of Folk Tales   159
   Types of Folk Tales   159
   Types of Folk Tale Books   180
Fables   185
   Origin of Fables   185
   Single Fables   186
   Modern Fables   187
Epic Literature   188
   Qualities of Epics   188
   Epic Heroes   188
Myths and Mythic Heroes   192
   Studying Myths   192
   Types of Myths   193
   Books of Myths   197

The Bible as Literature   198
    Planning for Study   198
    Books for Study of the Bible   199

Suggested Activities   203
Related Readings   203
Chapter References   204

CHAPTER 5. REALISTIC FICTION   215
    Realism in Children's Literature   216

Finding a Place as a Person   217
    Finding a Place in the Family   217
    Finding a Place in a Peer Group   224
    Finding a Place in Society   228

Meeting Problems of the Human Condition   239
    Physical Handicaps   239
    Poverty   240
    War   244
    Meeting Cultural Change   247
    Loneliness   250
    Death   253

Moving toward Maturity   255
    Gradual Development of Self   255
    Moments of Decision   258

Books and Personal Growth   263
    Bibliotherapy   264

Suggested Activities   265
Related Readings   265
Chapter References   266

CHAPTER 6. BIOGRAPHY AND HISTORICAL FICTION   272

Biography   274
    Criteria for Juvenile Biography   274
    Biographical Series   278
    Well-Known Biographers of Juvenile Literature   283
    Types of Biographies: Lincoln Comparisons   289

Historical Fiction   295
    Criteria for Historical Fiction   295
    Historical Fiction—Prehistoric Times   296
    Historical Fiction—The New World   297
    Historical Fiction—The Old World   313

Suggested Activities   322
Related Readings   323
Chapter References   323

CHAPTER 7. MODERN FANTASY AND HUMOR   331

Modern Fairy Tales   332
The Beginnings of the Modern Fairy Tale   332
Fairy Tales Today   335

New Tall Tales   337
Modern Fantasy   338
Guides to Evaluating Modern Fantasy   338
Strange and Curious Worlds   339
Imaginary Kingdoms   343
Animal Fantasy   346
The World of Toys and Dolls   351
Lilliputian Worlds   353
"Fabulous Flights"   356
Magical Powers   359
Overcoming Evil   360
Time Magic   362

Science Fiction   367
Humorous Books   370
Strange and Amusing Characters   370
Amusing Animals   373
Fun in Everyday Happenings   374

Suggested Activities   376
Related Readings   376
Chapter References   377

CHAPTER 8. POETRY   385

Poetry for Today's Children   386
What Is Poetry?   386
Satisfactions of Poetry   389

Selecting Poetry for Children   396
Forms of Poetry for Children   396
The Content of Poems for Children   400
Poets and Their Books   416
Anthologies of Poems for Children   426

Sharing Poetry with Children   434
Introducing Poetry to Children   434
Children Share Poetry   436

Suggested Activities   438
Related Readings   438
Chapter References   439

CHAPTER 9. INFORMATIONAL BOOKS   445

Guides for Evaluating Informational Books   446

Accuracy and Authenticity   446

Content   454

Style   462

Format and Illustration   469

Organization   473

Summary of Criteria for Informational Books   474

Types of Informational Books   475

Concept Books   475

Informational Picture Books   477

Identification Books   479

Life-Cycle Animal Books   480

Experiment and Activity Books   481

Documents and Journals   483

Geographic Series   484

Survey Books   486

Specialized Books   488

Suggested Activities   492

Related Readings   492

Chapter References   493

CHAPTER 10. BOOKS FOR SPECIAL INTERESTS   507

Animal Stories   508

Appeals of Animal Stories   508

Life-Cycle Stories   508

Children and Animals   510

Horse Stories   512

Dog Stories   516

Mysteries   519

Appeals of the Mystery Book   519

Evaluating Mystery Books   520

Types of Mystery Books   524

Books about Sports   528

Sports in Fiction   529

Biography   531

Informational Books about Sports   531

Books of Adventure   532

Suggested Activities   534

Related Readings   535

Chapter References   535

PART 3. DEVELOPING A LITERATURE PROGRAM   543

CHAPTER 11. CREATING THE LEARNING ENVIRONMENT   545

The School Environment   546

Commitment to Literature   546
Provision of Time and Space   546
School Organization Patterns   547

The Instructional Materials Center   550
Books in the Center   550
Nonprint Materials in the Center   552
Role of the School Librarian   560
Relation of School and Public Library   563

Classroom Reading Environment   564
The Classroom Collection   564
Classroom Arrangement   564
Enticing Children to Read   565

Books in the Elementary Curriculum   571
Books in the Reading Instructional Program   571
Developing Language Skills through Literature   574
Books for Science Education   582
Books for the Social Studies Curriculum   583
Books and Mathematics   585
Books in Art Education   585
Books for the Music Program   587

Working with Parents and the Community   588
Parents and Children's Reading   588
Extending Community Interests   589

Suggested Activities   591
Related Readings   592
Chapter References   594

CHAPTER 12. STIMULATING CREATIVE ACTIVITIES
THROUGH LITERATURE   600

Creative Writing and Literature   602
Developing Sensitivity to Language   602
Literature as Model   604
Literature to Motivate Creative Writing   606
Creative Reporting   610

Art Activities and Literature   613
Flat Pictures and Three-Dimensional Construction   613
Dioramas   614
Table Displays   617
Time Lines   618
Murals   618
Constructing Box Movies   620
Flannel-Board Stories   620
Bulletin Boards   621
Mobiles   622

Wall Hangings   623
Dolls   623
Using Projectors   624

Music and Rhythmic Activities   624
Identifying Background Music for Literature   624
Composing Music   624
Rhythmic Activities   625

Interpreting Books through Creative Dramatics   625
Creative Dramatics Defined   625
An Account of Creative Dramatics   627

Dramatization through Puppetry   631
Value of Puppetry   631
Selecting Stories for Puppetry   631
Constructing Puppets and Marionettes   632

Games Based on Literature   633
Guessing Games and Riddles   633
Table Games   637

Suggested Activities   640
Related Readings   640
Chapter References   642

CHAPTER 13. TEACHING LITERATURE IN THE ELEMENTARY SCHOOL   649

What Literature Does for Children   650
Enjoyment   650
New Perspectives   651
Vicarious Experience   651
Insight into Human Behavior   652
Wisdom of Mankind   652
Beauty and Inspiration   652

Purposes of the Literature Program   652
Experiencing Literature   652
Developing Taste   653
Developing Knowledge   653
Developing Skills of Literary Criticism   656
Fostering Language Skills   657
Enriching Content of Curriculum   657
Stimulating Creative Activities   657
Memorizing Worthwhile Selections   657
Developing Appreciation   658

Presenting Literature to Children   658
Reading to Children   659
Storytelling   661
Using Audio-Visual Media   665

Guiding Literary Criticism   666
   The Process of Literary Criticism   666
   Selecting Materials for Literary Study   667
   The Teacher's Preparation   670

Planning Literature Lessons   671
   Studying a Picture Storybook   671
   Comparing Picture Storybooks with Similar Themes   672
   Identifying Form and Setting of Books   673
   Character Delineation and Development   674
   Discovering Figurative Language in Poetry   676
   Studying a Poem   677
   One Child's Analysis of a Book   678

Children Report Their Reading   680
   Oral Reports   680
   Book Clubs   682
   Written Reports   682
   Evaluating Book Reports   686

Planning the Literature Curriculum   687
   Literary Understandings and Skills   687
   Balance in the Literature Curriculum   692
   Planning the Curriculum Guide   692

Suggested Activities   693
Related Readings   693
Chapter References   695

APPENDIXES   699

   A. Children's Book Awards   701
   B. Book Selection Aids   724
   C. Guide to Pronunciations   735
   D. Publishers' Addresses   740
   E. Book Exhibits and Book Clubs   745

INDEXES   749

   Subject Index   751
   Author, Illustrator, Title Index   761

LEARNING
ABOUT CHILDREN
AND BOOKS

UNDERSTANDING CHILDREN AND LITERATURE

Parents and teachers are pleased and proud when children enter the "world of books." If a cartographer tried to create a map of this elusive world of books, he could include mountain peaks of adventure and valleys shadowed by fears and suspense. There would be broad plains of information, rivers sparkling with laughter, and caves of mystery. Exposed rock strata would reveal life in the past. Snug harbors would indicate comfort and security. New interests would sail forth on exploration of the oceans in that world. This universe stretches toward the unknown where one can meet strange places and different people. The "literature world" is constantly expanding; teachers cannot traverse each road, nor can each child travel to all the corners of that world. But teachers can reveal the "world of books" to the child; they can show him the map, and help him begin his lifetime of exploration.

Children, just as adults, change their purposes for reading according to changing needs. Dad may relax with a James Bond mystery when he is tired and tense; Tim, his ten-year-old son, with a comic book. Later, Tim may want to know all about snakes, and he will read avidly until this curiosity is satisfied. The child may not know why he likes a book or what purpose he is satisfying as he reads it. He only knows that as he reads, he has an enjoyable experience. Children feel good when their mental and emotional skins stretch tautly, then crack and break apart as new concepts are formed. Experiences in reading provide the energizing force for this process of growing, stretching, splitting, and shedding of old ideas as new truths are discovered.

Children seek truth about the world and its people; they want to know themselves and where they belong. To see their own lives clearly, children need to look into the contrasting experiences of others. They want to know what is "right" in their society. Literature communicates these cultural values. Children also sense a need to discover the common elements in human experiences. They search for inner peace and understanding of the universe. These purposes may be satisfied in the world of books.

The adult cannot insist that a child enjoy a book if it does not bring him satisfaction. The adult concept of a good book may not coincide with the child's view, only the reader experiencing the book can make that decision. Children will turn to whatever is available in their search for truth, fun, and beauty. The task of the teacher and librarian is to guide children into the world of books where they will find joy in living through savoring beautiful and interesting words as they satisfy their many purposes for reading. Teachers and librarians are challenged to know children and books so the two may meet in that mystical world in which the child goes beyond himself to better understand the universe and people in it.

KNOWING CHILDREN'S LITERATURE

Children's Books Today

Today, there is a literature for children that has never existed before in the history of mankind. Different kinds of books, vastly increased production of books, and widespread distribution techniques make thousands of books available to children today. Revolving racks in drugstores, supermarkets, train depots, and airports display brightly illustrated books designed to attract young readers. Mother selects a book as she piles groceries into the cart. Encyclopedias are found next to frozen foods. Children cluster in groups to devour comics. Following the adult patterns, selections from children's book-of-the-month clubs and children's magazines find their way into hundreds of homes. With the assistance of the federal government, schools have finally accepted the concept of a central library and trained librarian in every elementary school. Thousands of children visit attractive rooms in public libraries each week where trained librarians give them assistance. They seek information in many books; for, no longer does one school text satisfy children who are eager to learn of their world.

Literature experiences may begin in the grocery store. Photographed by R. E. Peterson.

Big Business

The publication and distribution of juvenile books comprises a big business that is growing ever bigger. While the number of juveniles published has doubled every twenty years from 1920 to 1960, it nearly doubled in the five-year period between 1960 and 1965. Thus, the rate of growth of publications of new juveniles has increased tremendously. In 1966, the *Bowker Annual* reported the number of juveniles published over a forty-five-year period:

JUVENILES PUBLISHED[1]

1920	410
1930	771
1940	852
1950	907
1960	1628
1962	2854
1963	2976
1964	2808
1965	2895

While the number of juveniles published declined slightly in the last two years, this may be accounted for by the increase of paperback editions in the juvenile field. The number of children's book editors has increased from one in 1919 to over one hundred in 1965. Juveniles form an important part of the publishing business and account for about sixteen per cent of the total net sales of all publishers. Two-thirds of the revenue of one firm publishing all types of books is derived from the sale of their juveniles. In many firms, profits from the sale of juveniles subsidize the publication of more esoteric literature.

Once a juvenile has become a "best seller," it is likely to maintain this status for a longer period than books for adults. Sales of successful adult novels tend to reach their peak in six months; sales of outstanding

children's books continue their high levels for many years. For example, Frances Hodgson Burnett's *The Secret Garden* (1909), Marjorie Flack's *The Story about Ping* (1933), E. B. White's *Charlotte's Web* (1952) have steadily sold 10,000 to 20,000 copies a year. Five million copies of *The Poky Little Puppy* were sold in fifteen years.[2] In 1959, Warne sold 24,000 copies of *The Tale of Peter Rabbit*, that was first published in 1902. This firm also sold 3000 copies of *Kate Greenaway's Birthday Book*, which was published in 1880.[3]

Circulation of library books has also increased as more books have become available. For example, in 117 libraries in cities of over 50,000, the circulation increased 4.2 per cent from 1955 to 1956.[4] In 1939, one-third of the total library circulation was juvenile; by 1956 the juvenile circulation accounted for one-half the total.[5] A survey of seventy-three library systems reported in 1960 also indicated increases in library circulation. For example, book borrowing doubled in one city in ten years, whereas its population increased only thirty per cent.[6]

Better Quality and More Variety New developments in printing processes have made possible the publication of more beautiful books. As fine, well-illustrated books received recognition, more talented writers and artists began producing quality books for children. Unfortunately, mass-production techniques have also increased the number of cheap, mediocre books.

A visit to the juvenile book section of a large department store illustrates the wide

[1]Phyllis Steckler, Editor, *Bowker Annual* (New York: Bowker, 1964, 1966).

[2]*Time*, vol. 70 (December 23, 1957), pp. 74–76.

[3]"Currents," *Publishers' Weekly*, vol. 177 (February 19, 1960), p. 83.

[4]U.S. Office of Education, *Statistics of Public Libraries*, Circular No. 505, May 1957.

[5]"Index of American Public Library Circulation," *American Library Association Bulletin*, vol. 51 (September 1957), p. 640.

[6]"Reading on the Rise," *Time*, vol. 76 (July 25, 1960), p. 44.

variety of literature available for children today. On the shelves are books of all sizes and shapes, from Sendak's diminutive *Nutshell Library* books to the tall *A Tree Is Nice* by Udry to the oversized *Iliad and the Odyssey* illustrated by the Provensens. Books of poetry, nonsense, history, science, biography, and fiction are displayed. Illustrations have infinite variety—from Tasha Tudor's quaint drawing to Brian Wildsmith's bright splashes of color, from Marcia Brown's fairy-like *Cinderella* to the realistic photographs in *Visit to a Chief's Son* by Halmi. There are books for adults to read to children, books for the beginning reader, and books for the skilled reader. From these pages, children can experience the near and the far, the exciting and amusing, the real and fantastic—a gamut of human experience. Children's literature has come of age! Selecting books from the vast array now available becomes the challenging task of parents, teachers, and librarians.

Increased Use of Trade Books Emphasis upon individualization of instruction and increased awareness of the need for many materials for learning have been major factors in the trend toward use of trade books in the basic curriculum. Trade books (sometimes called "library books") are those books that are not a part of a graded or developmental series. A textbook is a book designed to meet the needs of all children in a class and to present a sequence of skills or concepts. Supplementary texts have been planned to enrich the content of the basic text and to provide for some individual differences in ability or interest.

The nonfiction series, such as science series, geographical series, and biographical series may appear to be textbooks. However, these books are not designed to provide the basic part of a content area for all children. A recent development in children's books is the publication of "beginning to read" and "easy to read" series books. These books frequently have a controlled vocabulary, but there is no planned development of skills. Some of the trade books in series are very well written; many lack the quality of good material available in some "reading" textbooks. The content and humor of these easy reading books will be useful in the instructional reading program, but few can qualify as literature.

Trade books are increasingly used for instruction as reading programs become more individualized. Educators recommend a minimum of four to six different books for each child in the classroom for individualized reading instruction. It is assumed that this collection would be changed frequently. The science and social studies curricula also draw upon many trade books as children demand more information than can be contained in one textbook. It is difficult for revision of a textbook series to keep pace with new science information, whereas a single trade book containing the most up-to-date material can be easily published.

Publishers of basic readers have recognized the necessity of providing literary material and full length books for the reading program. Sets of trade books to accompany the basic readers are available from several companies. These sets of "library books" include fifteen to twenty-five different titles. Some pamphlet sets include only short selections from longer works with the assumption that children will read the complete book. However, these selections and sets of books should form only a small part of the classroom library.

The current emphasis upon the need for a central library in every elementary school leads to increased use of trade books. With federal funds now available for the purchase of books, elementary schools should be able to provide a balanced selection of the trade books necessary for an effective program of instruction.

What Is Children's Literature?

From the thousands of books now available for boys and girls, how shall teachers, librarians, and parents select that which is literature? How can one distinguish the trees from the forest? In this plethora of books, there is the great danger of overlooking fine literature. The numbers of books published increase the difficulty of book selection and, at the same time, emphasize its need. Two questions need to be considered: (1) What is literature? and (2) What books are appropriate for children?

Literature Defined   The definition of literature is two dimensional, for it includes both the book and the reader. Literature may be viewed as the artistic arrangement of printed symbols, and as the experience of the individual as he interacts with the text according to his own meanings. To formulate a helpful definition of literature, it becomes necessary to think of the *function* of the words and pictures. How do the symbols produce an aesthetic experience; in other words, how do the symbols help the reader perceive pattern, relationships, feelings that produce an inner experience of art? This aesthetic experience may be a vivid reconstruction of past experience, an extension of experience, or creation of a new experience.

> We all have, in our experience, memories of certain books which changed us in some way—by disturbing us, or by a glorious affirmation of some emotion we knew but could never shape in words, or by some revelation of human nature. Virginia Woolf calls such times "moments of being," and James Joyce titles them "epiphanies."[7]

Heilman cites W. H. Auden's definition of second-rate literature as inherent in the reader response that says:

> "That's just the way I always felt." But first-rate literature makes one say: "Until now, I never knew how I felt. Thanks to this experience, I shall never feel the same way again."[8]

The graphic symbols consist of language and illustrations presented in such a way that the reader is made aware of an order, a unity, a balance, or a new frame of reference. Good writing, or effective use of language, on any subject may produce aesthetic experiences. Language used artistically combines both intellectual and emotional responses. It will cause the reader to perceive characters, conflicts, elements in a setting, and universal problems of mankind; it will help the reader to experience the delight of beauty, wonder, and humor; or the despair of sorrow, injustice, and ugliness. Vicariously, he will experience other places and other times; he may identify with others; he may observe nature more closely or from a different perspective; he will encounter the thrill of taking risks and meeting mystery; he will endure suffering; he will enjoy a sense of achievement, and feel he belongs to one segment or all of humanity. He will be challenged to dream dreams, to ponder, and to ask questions of himself.

Children's Literature and Adult Literature   It might be said that a child's book is a book a child is reading, and an adult book is a book occupying the attention of an adult. Before the nineteenth century, only a few books were written for the specific readership of children. Children read books written for adults, taking from them what they could understand. Today, children continue to read some books intended for adults, for example, *The Incredible Journey* and *Rascal*. Children may be able to name the words in many adult books, but this does not mean their background of experience has prepared

---

[7]Frances Clarke Sayers, *Summoned by Books* (New York: Viking, 1965), p. 16.

[8]Robert B. Heilman, "Literature and Growing Up," *English Journal*, vol. 45 (September 1956), p. 307.

them to experience the book as literature. If only vocabulary, syntax, and grammar are considered, Hemingway's *A Farewall to Arms* would be more "readable" for children than the nineteenth century rhetoric of *The Wind in the Willows* by Kenneth Grahame. Yet, children are not ready for Hemingway's characterizations, plot, or theme. It is even more difficult to separate children's poetry from poetry written for adults. Perhaps the poet, less than the writer of fiction, has no particular audience in mind.

The skilled author does not write differently or less carefully for children just because he thinks they will not be aware of style or language. In the introduction to *Hakon of Rogen's Saga*, author Haugaard wrote, "It was not written for 'youth' in the sense that I have blunted my pen before I started."[9] Just as a pediatrician must know the essentials of medicine and then apply this knowledge to his child patients, so the author of children's literature must know the essentials of fine writing and apply this knowledge to children's books. The surgeon and the pediatrician are equally honored. Authors of children's literature and those who write for adults should receive equal approbation. C. S. Lewis maintained that he wrote a children's story because a children's story was the best art form for what he had to say.[10] Lewis wrote both for adults and children as have Rumer Godden, Elizabeth Yates, Pearl Buck, Dorothy Canfield Fisher, and many other well-known authors. They do not "blunt their pens" as they write for boys and girls.

The uniqueness of children's literature lies in the audience that it addresses. Authors of children's books are circumscribed only by the experiences of childhood, but these are vast and complex. For children think and feel; they wonder and they dream. Their lives may be filled with love or terror. Much is known, but little is explained. The child is curious about life and adult activities. He lives in the midst of tensions, of balances of love and hate within the family and the neighborhood. The author who can fill these experiences with imagination and insight, and communicate them to children is writing children's literature.

The modern child is separated from first-hand knowledge of birth and death, yet mass media bring vicarious experiences of crime, war, poverty, violence, and death. Although the child is isolated from many basic activities of life, he is aware of adult anxieties about survival in an atomic age, and he is anxious.

The content of children's literature, then, is limited only by the experience of the reader. Few children have the background to understand psychological probing, political intrigue, or sexual exploits. Mystery stories seldom include murders; most biographies portray the lives of worthy characters. While the realism of adult literature is gradually permeating the literature for children, too gruesome details of violence, war, and crime should still be avoided.

Bruner emphasized the need for literary experience for children:

Man must cope with a relatively limited number of plights—birth, growth, loneliness, the passions, death, and not very many more. They are plights that are neither solved nor by-passed by being "adjusted." An adjusted man must face his passions just as surely as he faces death. I would urge that a grasp of the basic plights through the basic myths of art and literature provides the organizing principles by which knowledge of the human condition is rendered into a form that makes thinking possible, by which we go beyond learning to the

[9]Erik Christian Haugaard, *Hakon of Rogen's Saga* (Boston: Houghton Mifflin, 1963).

[10]C. S. Lewis, "On Three Ways of Writing for Children," *The Horn Book Magazine*, vol. 39 (October 1963), p. 460.

use of knowledge. I am not suggesting that the Greek myths are better than other forms of literature. I urge simply that there be exposure to, and interpretation of, literature that deals with the human condition. I have learned as much from Charley Brown of Peanuts as I have learned from Perseus.[11]

Since many children's books do present the basic plights of mankind, it seems unnecessary to urge children to read, or to read to children, literature designed for adults. Children in the elementary school should discover their own literature before turning to adult literature.

Criteria for Evaluating Children's Fiction

If children are to be helped to become discriminating readers they need to know what constitutes a well-written book. Teachers and librarians, too, must know how to evaluate the literature for children; also, they must take into account such variables as the child's interests, sex, and age. Specialized criteria will be applied to different types of literature, such as picture books, biographies, and informational books. Additional criteria are needed to evaluate certain forms of fiction. For example, criteria for a realistic story would not be the same as those used for modern fantasy. Historical fiction requires the added criteria of authenticity of setting and mood. Perhaps the first task of both the teacher and the children is to identify the kind of book they are reading in order to apply the appropriate criteria for evaluation. In general, however, in reading books of fiction the following factors need to be considered: plot; setting; theme; characterization; style; and format.

Plot Of prime importance in any work of fiction is the plot. Children ask first, "Does the book tell a good story?" The plot is the plan of the story; it tells what the characters do and what happens to them. It is the thread that holds the fabric of the story together and makes the reader want to continue reading.

A well-constructed plot is organic and interrelated. It grows logically and naturally from the actions and the decisions of the characters in given situations. The plot should be credible and ring true rather than depend upon coincidence and contrivance. It should be original and fresh rather than trite, tired, and predictable.

The appeal of the series books is based upon action and happenings. Their stories are always predictable; Nancy Drew never fails to solve a mystery and Tom Swift accomplishes one major feat after another. These books move rapidly from one improbable happening to another. The action is beyond the capabilities of the characters and becomes contrived and sensational.

In books that have substance, obstacles are not quickly overcome, and choices are not always clear-cut. In *The Wild Heart* by Helen Griffiths, a boy must make a cruel decision in order to save the horse he loves. This is not the typical horse story in which the hero finally tames the wild stallion or wins a race, but one that is compellingly different and original.

Books may be exciting, fast-moving, *and* well-written. Sperry's *Call It Courage* gains increasing momentum with each of Mafatu's courageous feats until the climax is reached at the close of the book. Suspense is maintained with the rising action of the story. The climax should be easily identifiable and develop naturally from the story. Children prefer a swift conclusion following the climax, but the dénouement should knit together the loose ends of the story.

Most of the plots in children's literature are presented in a straightforward narration. Usually children do not have the maturity to

[11]Jerome Bruner, "Learning and Thinking," *Harvard Educational Review*, vol. 29 (Summer 1959), p. 186.

follow several plots or many flashbacks in time or place. However, several excellent books do make use of these devices. For example, most of the action in *Berries Goodman* by Neville is reported as a long flashback, and *Home from Far* by Little has a definite subplot. The effectiveness of the structure, then, depends upon the clarity of the author's presentation.

Plot is but one element of good writing. If a book does not have a substantial plot, it will not hold children's interest long. Well-loved books contain indefinable qualities and are memorable for more than plot alone.

Setting The structure of the story pertains to both the construction of the plot and its setting. The setting may be in the past, the present, or the future. The story may take place in a specific locale, or the setting may be deliberately vague to convey the feeling of *all* small towns, large cities, or rural communities.

Both the time and the place of the story should affect the action, the characters, and the theme. The action in *The Perilous Road* by William Steele occurs during a single battle in Tennessee at the time of the Civil War. Caught in the midst of a bitter struggle at dawn between the Confederates and the Yankees, a twelve-year-old boy changes his mind about war and is changed by his grim experience. The theme of the story is the futility of war and obviously requires this kind of background.

Elizabeth Yates has achieved a kind of universality of setting in her quiet pastoral entitled *Mountain Born*. While the actual setting of the story is in New Hampshire, it could take place any time or anywhere that man has watched over flocks of sheep. Life is circumscribed by the shepherd's concern for his sheep:

The year had hinges on which it hung, and every hinge had something to do with the

sheep; but that was the life on Andrew's farm and the living for his family, and it was right that the sheep should mark it for them.[12]

In another well-written story by Elizabeth Yates, the setting both reflects, and helps to create, the strength and quiet dignity of *Amos Fortune, Free Man*. The physical and symbolic presence of Monadnock Mountain looms large in the story of this remarkable man. Always, Amos looks to "his" mountain for fortitude and courage. In return, it is as if "the strength of the hills were his, also." The setting of a story can do much to create the mood and theme of the book.

Setting is not always clearly stated. It may be implied by the mention of a particular building or park. The general locale may be revealed by the dialect or colloquial expressions of the people or by their activities. Natalie Carlson has used language that gives the flavor of the Southern setting in her book, *The Empty Schoolhouse*. The following quotation is an example:

By that time Lullah spotted Oralee in the crowd, and those two were excited as hound dogs under a treed possum.[13]

Whenever a specific period of time or locale is presented, it should be authentic and true to what the author knows of that period, place, or people.

Theme The third point for the evaluation of any story is its *overarching theme*. The theme of a book reveals the author's purpose in writing the story. Most well-written books may be read for several layers of meaning: plot, theme, or metaphor. The story of *Charlotte's Web* by E. B. White on one level is simply an absurd but amusing story of how a spider saves the life of a pig; on another

---

[12]Elizabeth Yates, *Mountain Born* (New York: Coward-McCann, 1943), p. 86.
[13]Natalie Carlson, *The Empty Schoolhouse* (New York: Harper & Row, 1965), p. 17.

level, it reveals the meaning of loneliness and the obligations of friendship. A third layer of meaning can be seen in White's tongue-in-cheek commentary on the absurdity of people who award a prize to a pig for words spelled by a spider. How often society ignores the deserving! The story of *The Yearling* may appear to be the story of a boy and his pet deer; in reality, Marjorie Kinnan Rawlings has described the painful experience of achieving manhood. The theme of Lynd Ward's picture book, *The Biggest Bear*, is similar to *The Yearling*, although its ending is more appropriate for younger children.

Theme provides a dimension of the story beyond the action of the plot. The theme of a book might be the acceptance of self or others, growing up, the overcoming of fear or prejudice. The theme of a story should be worth imparting to young people and be based upon justice and integrity. Sound moral and ethical principles should prevail. Paul Hazard, writing in *Books Children and Men*, made the following comments concerning the kind of children's books that he felt were good:

> . . . *and books that awaken in them not maudlin sentimentality, but sensibility; that enable them to share in great human emotions; that give them respect for universal life—that of animals, of plants; that teach them not to despise everything that is mysterious in creation and in man. . . .*
> *I like books that set in action truths worthy of lasting forever, and inspiring one's whole inner life. . . .*
> *In short, I like books that have the integrity to perpetuate their own faith in truth and justice. . . .*[14]

Characterization True characterization is another hallmark of fine writing. The people portrayed in children's books should be as convincingly real and lifelike as our next door neighbors. Many of the animal characters in modern fantasy have true personalities, also. The credibility of characters will depend upon the author's ability to show their true natures, their strengths, and their weaknesses.

Just as it takes time to know a new friend in all his various dimensions, so, too, does an author try to present many facets of a character. In revealing character, an author may simply (1) tell about the person through narration, (2) record his conversation with others, (3) describe the thoughts of the character, (4) show the thoughts of others about the character, or (5) show the character in action. While children prefer action in their stories and dislike too much introspection, a character that is revealed in only one way is apt to lack depth. In many series books, the characters are stock characters, not realistic human beings. If only one side of a character is presented, or one trait overemphasized, the result is likely to be stereotyped and wooden. In the Tom Swift stories, the reader is always told *how* the hero performs his daring exploits rather than letting the actions and the feelings grow out of the circumstance of the story. Children do not need to be told that Mafatu overcomes his fear of the sea in Sperry's *Call It Courage;* he shows his bravery by his actions.

In addition to realism in characterization, there should be consistency in its portrayal. This consistency should not conform to a pattern but to the true nature of the character as the author has presented him. The characters should be depicted so that everything they do, think, and say will seem natural and inevitable. They should act and speak in accordance with their age, culture, and educational background. This allows authors the freedom to use some slang and even nonstandard English when the authentic speech of a person or region is necessary for true character portrayal. *Smoky* by Will

---

[14]Paul Hazard, *Books Children and Men* (Boston: Horn Book, 1944), pp. 42–44.

Illustrated by Mary Shepard. From *Mary Poppins*, copyright, 1934, 1962, by P. L. Travers. Reproduced by permission of Harcourt, Brace & World, Inc.

Illustrated by Beth and Joe Krush. From *The Borrowers*, copyright, 1953, by Mary Norton. Reproduced by permission of Harcourt, Brace & World, Inc.

From *Rabbit Hill* by Robert Lawson. Copyright 1944 by Robert Lawson. Reprinted by permission of The Viking Press, Inc.

James and *Strawberry Girl* by Lois Lenski are two examples of books in which their authors have made judicious use of slang and colloquialisms. One would hardly expect a cowboy or a Florida "cracker" to speak formal English. Standard speech would be inconsistent with their backgrounds.

Another aspect of sound characterization is growth and development. Do the characters change in the course of the story, or do they remain the undaunted and self-sufficient personalities that they were in the beginning of the tale? Not all characters will change, of course, but many are memorable for their personality development. No girl will ever forget the struggle of headstrong, self-centered Jo of *Little Women* in taming her rebellious ways. Marguerite de Angeli has created a vivid character study of Robin in her outstanding book, *The Door in the Wall*. Robin, crippled son of a great lord, must learn to accept his infirmity and find his useful place in life. The gradual development of his character is made clear as he solves these problems. It is easy to identify with the tomboy, *Caddie Woodlawn*, in her struggle against the inevitable demands of "becoming a lady." When Caddie has finally put away her tomboy ways, she says: "How far I've come! I'm the same girl and yet not the same. I wonder if it's always like this? Folks keep growing from one person into another all of their lives. . . ."[15]

In all these books, and many more, the characters seem real and alive. To be truly human, they must grow and change before the reader's eyes. In keeping with life itself, that change is usually gradual and convincing, rather than mercurial and unrealistic.

A character may be three-dimensional, stand out in sharp relief, and still not change. It is as though the character were frozen at a particular period of time in his

---

[15]Carol Ryrie Brink, *Caddie Woodlawn* (New York: Macmillan, 1936), p. 27.

life, but the many facets of his personality are clearly delineated. Homer Price, Henry Huggins, and Pippi Longstocking show little character development, yet they remain true to their natures in all their adventures. And what interesting characters they are! There is a difference, then, between character delineation and character development.

Long after we have forgotten their stories, we can recall some of the personalities of children's literature. We recognize them as they turn the corner of our memories, and we are glad for their friendship. The line is long; it includes animals and people. It is hard to tell where it begins, and we are happy there is no end. We can distinguish Toad in a new motor car with his loyal friends, Mole and Ratty; Mary Poppins flies by holding tightly to her large black umbrella with one hand and carrying her carpet bag in the other; there's the Potts family and their wonderful magical car, *Chitty-Chitty-Bang-Bang;* Georgie hops down the road looking for "New folks coming"; Janey Larkin walks sedately along holding her cherished Blue Willow plate; Beth, Jo, Amy, and Meg are there; and Mary, Colin, and Dickon are in their Secret Garden. If one looks closely, he can see tiny Arrietty and Pod, out for a Borrowers holiday; Stuart Little paddles his souvenir canoe along the drainage ditch, and our favorite Hobbit, Bilbo Baggins, outwits the terrifying Gollum. School appears to be out, for here come Henry Huggins and Ribsy followed by Beezus and Ramona: Roosevelt Grady is still pondering the meaning of the "opportunity class," and Pippi Longstocking has completed her first and only day of school. Wilbur has just discovered his wonderful new friend, Charlotte A. Cavatica, a spider, and he is sleeping peacefully in the barnyard. There are many more in this procession of real persons in children's literature. We know them well because their authors created them and blew the breath of life into each one of them.

Illustration by Garth Williams from *Stuart Little* by E. B. White. Harper & Row, 1945.

From *Roosevelt Grady* by Louisa R. Shotwell, illustrated by Peter Burchard. Copyright © 1963 by Louisa R. Shotwell.

These characters came alive on the pages of their books, and they live forever in our memories.

Style   An author's style of writing is simply his selection and arrangement of words in presenting his story. Good writing style is appropriate to the plot, theme, and characters of the story, both creating and reflecting the mood of the story. An author's style is individual and unique. Compare the different ways in which DeJong and O'Dell have described characters who have been left alone:

The dog had no name. For a dog to have a name, someone must have him and someone must love him, and a dog must have someone. The dog had no one, and no one had the dog. . . . The dog had only himself, so the dog had nothing, and he was afraid.[16]

The thought of being alone on the island while so many suns rose from the sea and went slowly back into the sea filled my heart with loneliness. . . Now I was really alone. I could not eat much, nor could I sleep without dreaming terrible dreams.[17]

DeJong has presented many dimensions of aloneness and makes the reader empathize with the plight of the lost dog. O'Dell, on the other hand, has used economy of expression as Karana, the Indian girl, states her feelings with simplicity and in a style reflecting the basic stoicism of the Indian of her day.

The style of writing should mirror the setting of the story and the background of the characters. In *Hakon of Rogen's Saga*, Haugaard uses objects common to the daily life of the Vikings to make his comparisons, for example:

A plan should be whole and tight like a cooking pot, and ours seemed to me to resemble a fishing net.[18]

In retelling an Hawaiian legend, Marcia Brown uses figurative language that is appropriate to the setting of this ancient tale:

The wounded bird left lying on the path shames the hunter. By now the two steersmen who had wronged Pakaá hated the sight of him and wished to destroy him.[19]

The big wave swamps even the strong canoe. Pakaá felt his heart almost go under in the flood of aloha for the boy and relief at his words. He held his son to him and wept.[20]

Children do not enjoy a story that is too descriptive, but they can appreciate figurative language, provided the comparisons are within their background of experience. Children in the middle grades can also comprehend symbolic meanings. Literary symbols are recurring concrete objects or events that represent an abstract idea. Children in the fourth grade, for example, were able to understand DeJong's use of a broom as a symbol of all that had frightened the little dog in *Hurry Home, Candy*. The significance of the title, *The Cabin Faced West* by Fritz was clearly grasped by another group of middle graders.

The language pattern utilized by the author will reflect the action or setting of the story. Again, in *Backbone of the King*, Marcia Brown has captured the rhythmical pattern of the ancient Hawaiians by her skilled use of parallel construction:

It was too late to regret the untrue word said and the true word unsaid, the cruel deed done and the kind deed undone.[21]

---

[16]Meindert DeJong, *Hurry Home, Candy* (New York: Harper & Row, 1953), p. 1.
[17]Scott O'Dell, *Island of the Blue Dolphins* (Boston: Houghton Mifflin, 1960), p. 60.
[18]Haugaard, p. 96.
[19]Marcia Brown, *Backbone of the King* (New York: Scribner, 1966), p. 44.
[20]Brown, p. 149.
[21]Brown, p. 121.

Language patterns should change with the action of the story. Short staccato sentences will help create the feeling of excitement. The language patterns of *Time of Wonder* change from long, lazy sentences describing the childhood joys of summer living to short, jerky sentences that relate the onslaught of the storm:

> *. . . in the afternoon, when the tide is out, they build a castle out of the rocks and driftwood below the spot where they had belly-whopped and dog-paddled during the morning. . . .*
>
> *Suddenly the wind whips the water into sharp, choppy waves. It tears off the sharp tops and slashes them in ribbons of smoky spray. And the rain comes slamming down. The wind comes in stronger and stronger gusts. A branch snaps from a tree.*[22]

The author's choice of the point of view of the story will necessarily influence the style. Is the story told in the first person, the third person, or from a standpoint of an omniscient author who knows the thoughts of all the characters involved? *Hakon of Rogen's Saga* and *Island of the Blue Dolphins* are told in the first person, while *Backbone of the King* and *The Cabin Faced West* are told in the third person. *Time of Wonder* is one of the few children's books told in the second person. In evaluating these books, we need to ask why the author chose his particular point of view, how this choice influenced the style of writing, and how the story might have been different if another point of view had been used.

The tastes of children place some demands upon the writer's style. Children tend to want action in their stories and prefer a style that has movement rather than too much description or contemplation. Children also demand conversation in their stories. They feel as Alice did when she looked into her sister's book and said, "What's the use of a book without pictures or conversation?" Master craftsmen at writing conversation that is natural and amusing are A. A. Milne in *Winnie the Pooh* and E. B. White in *Charlotte's Web.*

The best test of an author's style is through oral reading. Did it read smoothly and effortlessly? Was the conversation stilted or natural sounding? Did the author introduce variety in his sentence patterns and use of words? Several years ago, the expression "Tom Swifties" was coined to characterize the kind of writing in series books in which every verb was modified by a descriptive adverb, for example: "Tom said earnestly," "Tom fought gallantly." In one recent children's book, which received some excellent reviews, the author used the word "said" some eighty times in just one chapter. Read aloud, this book would seem very repetitious and dull.

Although it is difficult for children to analyze a particular author's style, they do react to it. Children are quick to detect the patronizing air of an author who talks down to them. They dislike a story that is too sentimental, and they see through the disguise of the too moralistic tale of the past. Adults respond to the cute, the clever, the slyly written, and the sarcastic; children do not. Frequently, a child is better able to identify what he dislikes about an author's style than to identify what he likes. However, the matter of style is important in evaluating books for children.

Format   The format of a book includes size, shape, design of pages, illustrations, typography, quality of paper, and binding. Frequently, some aspect of the format will be an important factor in a child's decision to read the book. Books today are more attractive than ever before. A new point of view in art and technical progress in printing and picture reproduction have produced some

---

[22]Robert McCloskey, *Time of Wonder* (New York: Viking, 1957), pp. 24, 44.

THE DOOR IN THE WALL

BY MARGUERITE DE ANGELI

Unity of format and content are illustrated by this well-designed title page, which suggests the illuminated manuscripts of the medieval setting of the book. From *The Door in the Wall* by Marguerite de Angeli. Courtesy of Doubleday & Company, Inc., 1949.

startling results in book illustrating.

Not only do we have beautiful picture books[23] for young children, but books for older boys and girls are becoming increasingly well designed and attractive. While pictures are not essential in books for older children, they may enrich the interpretation of the story and should be carefully planned and integrated with the text. Garth Williams has captured the real, human expressions on the faces of Wilbur, a pig, and Templeton, a rat, in E. B. White's wonderful American fantasy, *Charlotte's Web*.

[23]Chapter 3 presents special criteria for evaluating picture books and discusses outstanding examples.

The rough line drawings of the individual animals and the barnyard scenes perfectly complement the humor, pathos, and homespun philosophy of the text. Beth and Joe Krush have made the miniature world of *The Borrowers* series seem quite believable with their captivating illustrations. The black and white sketches are detailed and intricate. Frequently, Pod, Homily, and Arrietty are almost camouflaged by leaves, curtains, or bric-a-brac. The artists have skillfully portrayed some of the perils and delights of being six inches high in our "normal" sized world. Mary Norton has written a charming, humorous fantasy; the illustrations give it an added dimension of enchantment.

The total format of Marguerite de Angeli's *The Door in the Wall* complements the medieval background of this beautifully written piece of historical fiction. Her many black and white pictures realistically portray the castle, churches, and people of that period. Three illustrations are as rich in color and detail as an original illuminated manuscript. The design of the title and dedication pages remind the reader that fine books can be works of artistic as well as literary merit.

There are factors other than illustrations that need to be considered in the total format of the book. Typography is very important. The type should be large enough for easy reading by the age level for which it was intended. At the same time, if the type is too large, children will consider the book "babyish." The space between the lines (leading) should be sufficient to make the text clear. The quality of the paper must be considered. A cream-tinted, dull-finished paper that is thick enough to prevent any penetration of ink is most desirable. The binding should be durable and practical, one that can withstand the use of many interested, but frequently grimy, hands. For library and classroom use, books that are bound in cloth, side sewn, with soil-resistant washable covers are recommended. A book should never be selected on the basis of format alone without an accompanying evaluation of its content. No book is better than its text.

Additional Considerations   A book should not be considered in isolation, but as a part of the body of literature. Books should be compared with other books on the same subject or theme. Is this just another horse story, or does it make a distinctive contribution? Every teacher and librarian should know books so well that each has developed a personal list of books of excellence that can serve as models for comparison. How does this adventure story compare with Sperry's *Call It Courage*, this family story with *Meet the Austins* by L'Engle, or this historical fiction with *Johnny Tremain*? These reference points of outstanding books will help to sharpen evaluations.

An author's new book should be compared with his previous works. Contributions by the same author are often uneven and inconsistent in quality. What is the best book DeJong has written? Is *The Last Little Cat* as good as *Hurry Home, Candy*? How does *Shadrach* compare with *Far Out the Long Canal*? Too frequently, books are evaluated on the basis of the author's reputation rather than for their inherent worth.

Many informational and biographical series are written by different authors. The quality of the book will vary with the ability of the writer, despite similarity in approach and format. Rather than condemning or approving an entire series, each book should be evaluated on its own merits.

A book needs to be compared with outstanding prototypes, with other books written by the same author, and with other books in the same series. What have reputable reviewers said about this book? Where have they placed it in relation to others of its type? A comparison of reviews of one book would probably reveal more similarities than differences, but the elusive factor of personal preference of both adults and children should be respected.

In summary, the basic considerations for the evaluation of fiction for children are a well-constructed plot, a significant theme, authentic setting, convincing characterization, appropriate style, and attractive format. Not all books will achieve excellence in each of these areas. Some books are remembered for their fine characterizations, others for their exciting plots, and in others, the quality of the setting looms large. The following list of questions may help the reader evaluate a book more carefully. Not all questions will be appropriate for each book.

GUIDES FOR EVALUATING CHILDREN'S LITERATURE

Before Reading
- What kind of book is this?
- What does the reader anticipate from:
  Title
  Dust jacket illustration
  Size of print
  Illustrations
  Chapter headings
  Opening page?
- For what age range is this book appropriate?
- Does the book appear to be for either boys or girls?

Plot
- Does the book tell a good story? Will children enjoy it?
- Is the plot original and fresh?
- Is it plausible and credible?
  Is there preparation for the events?
  Is there a logical series of happenings?
  Is there a basis of cause and effect in the happenings?
- Is there an identifiable climax?
- How do events build to a climax?
- Is the plot well constructed?

Setting
- Where does the story take place?
- How does the author indicate the time?
- How does the setting affect the action, characters, or theme?
- Does the story transcend the setting and have universal implications?

Theme
- Does the story have a theme?
- Is the theme worth imparting to children?
- Does the theme emerge naturally from the story or is it stated too obviously?
- Does the theme overpower the story?
- Does it avoid moralizing?

Characterization
- How does the author reveal characters? Through narration?
  In conversation?
  By thoughts of others?
  By thoughts of the character?
  Through action?
- Are the characters convincing and credible?
- Do we see their strengths and their weaknesses?
- Does the author avoid stereotyping?
- Is the behavior of the characters consistent with their age and background?
- Is there any character development or growth?
- Has the author shown the causes of character behavior or development?

Style
- Is the style of writing appropriate to the subject?
- Is the style straightforward or figurative?
- Is the dialogue natural and suited to the characters?
- Does the author balance narration and dialogue?
- What are the main characteristics of the sentence patterns?

- How did the author create a mood? Is the overall impression one of mystery, gloom, evil, joy, security?
- What symbols has the author used to communicate meaning?
- Is the point of view from which the story is told appropriate to the purpose of the book?

Format
- Do the illustrations enhance the story?
- Are the illustrations consistent with the story?
- How is the format of the book related to the text?
- What is the quality of the paper?
- How sturdy is the binding?

Other Considerations
- How does the book compare with other books on the same subject?
- How does the book compare with other books written by the same author?
- How have other reviewers evaluated this book?

Classics in Children's Literature

Knowledge of children's classics, those books that have stood the test of time, may provide further guidance for evaluating children's books. What makes a book endure from one generation to another? Alice Jordan states: "Until a book has weathered at least one generation and is accepted in the next, it can hardly be given the rank of a classic. . . . "[24] Many books and poems have achieved an honored position among the best of children's literature through a combination of adult adoration, parent perpetuation, and teacher requirements. Most adults remember with nostalgia the books they read as children. They tend to think that what they read was best, and ignore the possibility

---

[24]Alice M. Jordan, *Children's Classics* (Boston: Horn Book, 1947), p. 4.

of the production of any better books. It is easy to forget that every "classic" was once a new book; that some of today's new books will be the classics of tomorrow. Times have changed, but adults seem unaware of the change in children's reading interests. Teachers and librarians should begin with the modern child and his interests, not his parents' interests when they were children.

Certain books became classics when there were very few books from which children could choose. In fact, many classics were not children's books at all, but were written for adults. In their desire to read, children claimed these adult books, struggled through the difficult parts, and disregarded that which they did not understand. They had no other choice. Today's child is not so persevering because he sees no reason for it. The beginning of *Robinson Crusoe* presents difficult vocabulary and sentence structure. In fact, the introductory sentence runs the length of the entire first page. Defoe wrote this story in 1719 for adult readers, but children quickly discovered its excitement and plunged into it. Some children may still enjoy this wonderful story of shipwreck and adventure. However, they can find the same tingling excitement and more readable prose in Sperry's *Call It Courage* or Steele's *Winter Danger*.

The classics should not be excused from evaluation by virtue of their past veneration. They should be able to compete favorably with modern-day books. Unimpressed with vintage or lineage, children seldom read a book because they think they should. They read more for enjoyment than edification. Some books have been kept alive from one generation to the next by common consent; these are the true classics of children's literature. No teacher or parent has to cajole a child into reading them. These books can hold their own amid the ever-increasing number of new and beautiful books of today.

What is the continuing appeal of these well-loved books for the contemporary child? First and foremost, they are magnificent stories. There are adventure and suspense in *Treasure Island, Robinson Crusoe, Swiss Family Robinson, Tom Sawyer,* and *Huckleberry Finn. Hans Brinker, or the Silver Skates* and *The Secret Garden* are filled with mystery and excitement. The characterization in most of the classics is outstanding. There is very little plot in the story of *Little Women,* but what reader can forget the March sisters? They could have been next-door neighbors. This is also true of Tom and Aunt Polly and Huck. The animal personalities of Christopher Robin's stuffed toys are unmistakable. Even adults have known a Bear of little brain and a gloomy Eeyore!

The appeal of many of the classics is based upon the type of story they represent. Family chronicles such as *Little Women* give the reader a sense of warmth and security. A feeling of place and atmosphere is skillfully developed in the well-loved *Heidi.* Animal stories are represented by *Black Beauty, The Jungle Book,* and *Bambi. Black Beauty* is a sentimental story filled with short essays on the prevention of cruelty to animals. The theme was timely in 1877 when Anna Sewell wrote this story. However, the genuine emotion in *Black Beauty* appears to be timeless, for it remains popular despite its Victorian airs. Boys and girls still love the beautifully written story of Mowgli who was adopted by the wolf pack when he was a baby and taught the law of the jungle by Bagheera, the panther, and Baloo, the bear. Other favorites in Kipling's *The Jungle Book* include "Rikki-Tikki-Tavi," the story of a mongoose, and "Toomai of the Elephants." Most children respond favorably to Felix Salten's sensitively written, if somewhat sentimental, life story of *Bambi,* a deer of the Danube forest.

Many classics are fantasies. Children's reactions to fantasy are like those of many adults who seem to thoroughly enjoy or completely reject them. For some people, *Alice in Wonderland, Peter Pan, The Wind in the Willows, Winnie the Pooh,* and *The Wizard of Oz*

Shepard's pen-and-ink drawings capture the joy and companionship of Mole and Ratty on a picnic by their beloved river. From *The Wind in the Willows* by Kenneth Grahame. Illustrated by E. H. Shepard. Courtesy of Charles Scribner's Sons, 1908, 1933, 1953.

have never been surpassed in the field of children's literature. Others actively dislike these books. Many readers do not "discover" these fantasies until they are adults, and then they applaud them as excellent fare for children! True classics appeal to both children and adults. As one father reported: "I've learned one important thing in three years. It's possible to read to a young child without boring either child or parent. I think parent's boredom is just as important as the child's."[25]

[25]Edward Eager, "A Father's Minority Report," Reprinted in *A Horn Book Sampler* (Boston: Horn Book, 1959), p. 166.

Some cautions need to be observed when presenting classics to children. It should be remembered that the so-called classics are not fare for all children and frequently appeal to the exceptional child. Many classics are more thoroughly appreciated if they are read aloud and shared with an adult rather than read by the child alone. It is important that timing be considered if children are to enjoy these books. Frequently, the classics are introduced before children are ready for them; most five-year-olds are not ready for the whimsy of *Winnie the Pooh*, nor are the eight-year-olds ready for *Treasure Island*. There is a readiness in appreciation that needs to be developed. Before reading *The Wind in the Willows*, introduce children to Lawson's *Rabbit Hill* and White's *Charlotte's Web*. Today's child needs to know Cleary's *Henry Huggins*, Butterworth's Nate Twitchell, and McCloskey's *Homer Price* before he is ready for *Tom Sawyer*. Young readers should be introduced to *Mary Poppins* by Travers, *The Borrowers* by Norton, and *The Phantom Tollbooth* by Juster before meeting the complex *Alice in Wonderland*. Students who have been intrigued with the stories of isolation found in *Island of the Blue Dolphins* by O'Dell and *My Side of the Mountain* by George are more likely to be interested in reading *Robinson Crusoe*. Adults should reread the "wonderful books we read as children" to see if they were that wonderful! Finally, the practice of compelling children to read certain books should be questioned. Children's literature should provide enjoyment and lead to a deeper understanding of life. These purposes are not served by "forced feeding" of classics. Boys and girls should enjoy reading; they should be exposed to the fine writing that may be found in both the classics and the new books. Today, there are some 25,000 juvenile books in print; we have no right to confine children's reading to a list of so-called classics.

The Award Books

Teachers and librarians will find it helpful to be familiar with books that have won awards.[26] These awards have been established for various purposes and provide criteria for what experts consider to be the best in children's literature. Such awards have helped to counteract the judgment of the market place by focusing attention upon beautiful and worthwhile books. In an age of mass production, they have stimulated artists, authors, and publishers to produce books of distinction and have helped children's literature achieve a worthy status.

Occasionally, one hears the criticism that the award books are not popular with children. This is true of some of the award books. However, most of the awards are not based upon popularity but upon recognized excellence. They were never intended to rubber stamp the tastes of children, but to raise them. Children's reactions to books are significant, but it is important to remember that they are not the final test of distinction. Likewise, adult praise of a book is no assurance of children's praise.

Newbery and Caldecott Awards   The two most coveted awards in children's literature are the Newbery and Caldecott Awards,[27] determined every year by a committee of twenty-three members of the Children's Services Division of the American Library Association. A candidate for either of the awards must be a citizen or resident of the United States. The book must have been first published in the United States.

The John Newbery Medal is the oldest award for children's books, having been es-

tablished in 1922. It is named for John Newbery, a British publisher and bookseller of the eighteenth century. Appropriately called the "father of children's literature," he was the first to conceive the idea of publishing books expressly for children. The Newbery Medal is awarded to the author of the most distinguished contribution to American literature for children published the preceding year.

The Randolph J. Caldecott Medal is named in honor of the great English illustrator of the nineteenth century, Randolph Caldecott. Caldecott was well known for his gay picture books depicting the country life of England. The Caldecott Medal was established in 1938 and is awarded to the most distinguished American picture book for children chosen from those first published in the United States during the previous year. The text should be worthy of the illustrations, but the award is made primarily for the art work.

Students of children's literature would do well to acquaint themselves with the winning books and their authors and illustrators. It is also interesting to review the runners-up for these awards. In 1939, the Newbery Award was made to *Thimble Summer*, a story that has limited appeal for girls only. However, a runner-up for that year was the still popular and dearly loved *Mr. Popper's Penguins*. Likewise, the highly praised *Charlotte's Web* was a runner-up in 1953 to the winner, *Secret of the Andes*, a beautifully written and sensitive story that, unfortunately, is not popular. It is interesting to see the number of times a particular author has been nominated and still has failed to win. Books by Laura Ingalls Wilder were runners-up for five different years, but never received the Award. Final restitution was made, perhaps, by the establishment of the Laura Ingalls Wilder Award, which serves a different purpose. Since the selection for the Newbery Award must be

---

[26]A list of all the various children's book awards, criteria, conditions, and winners is given in Appendix A.

[27]A list of the winners and runners-up for both the Newbery and Caldecott Medals is included in Appendix A.

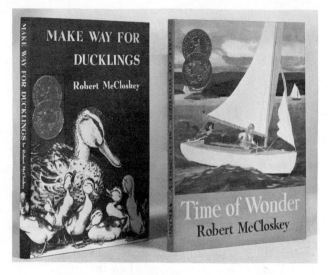

Two Caldecott winners by Robert McCloskey.
From *Make Way for Ducklings* by Robert McCloskey,
copyright 1941 by Robert McCloskey, and *Time of
Wonder* by Robert McCloskey, copyright © 1957
by Robert McCloskey. Both reprinted by permission of The Viking Press, Inc.

limited to books published in one year, the
quality of the Award books varies, for certain years produce a richer harvest than others. The selection in 1936 must have been
very difficult to make. How could one choose
among *Caddie Woodlawn, Honk the Moose,* and
The Good Master? It must have been equally
difficult in 1957 to make a choice among *Old
Yeller, House of Sixty Fathers, Mr. Justice
Holmes,* and *Miracles on Maple Hill.* In the
majority of cases, the years have shown the
choices to have been wise ones. Many age
ranges are represented, but most of the
Newbery books are for able, mature readers.
Frequently, these books have to be read
aloud and discussed with an adult before
children develop a taste for their excellence.

There has been less controversy over the
choices for the Caldecott Award. The list
again shows variety as to type of art work,
media used, age appeal, and subject matter.
The range of art work includes the realistic

paintings of Berta and Elmer Hader in *The
Big Snow,* the childlike, primitive work of
Leo Politi, the bright modern design of Will
and Nicolas, the delicate pictures of Marcia
Brown's *Cinderella,* and the stylized work of
Sidjakov. Various media are represented
among the winners, including collage, wood
block printing, watercolor, opaque paints,
and various combinations of pen and ink
and paint. Both Robert McCloskey and
Marcia Brown have won the Caldecott Award
twice. Joseph Krumgold and Elizabeth
Speare have received two Newbery Awards;
Robert Lawson is the only person who has
won both the Newbery and Caldecott Awards.

Lifetime Contributions To honor an author or illustrator for a substantial and lasting contribution to children's literature, *The
Laura Ingalls Wilder Award* was established in
1954 by the Children's Services Division of
the American Library Association. It was
presented first to Laura Ingalls Wilder herself, for her "Little House" books. Awarded
every five years, it makes no requirement
concerning the number of books that must
be produced, but a body of work is implied,
and the books must be published in the
United States. The Award was presented
posthumously to Clara Ingram Judson in
1960. In 1965, Ruth Sawyer received this distinctive honor.

In 1959, The Catholic Library Association established a somewhat similar award to
be presented annually for "continued distinguished contribution to children's literature." The Regina Medal "is not limited to
one creed, nor one country, nor to one criterion, other than excellence." It may be
given to writers, illustrators, editors, and
others who have given unstintingly of their
creative genius to the field.

International Award The Hans Christian
Andersen Medal was established in 1956 as
the first international children's book award.

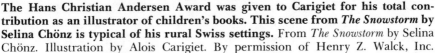

The Hans Christian Andersen Award was given to Carigiet for his total contribution as an illustrator of children's books. This scene from *The Snowstorm* by Selina Chönz is typical of his rural Swiss settings. From *The Snowstorm* by Selina Chönz. Illustration by Alois Carigiet. By permission of Henry Z. Walck, Inc.

The Medal is given every two years by the International Board on Books for Young People to a living author who has made an outstanding contribution to juvenile literature. Meindert DeJong is the only American author to have achieved this distinction. In 1966, plans were made to give a medal to an outstanding illustrator of children's books.

No one but the most interested follower of children's literature would want to remember all the awards that are given for children's books. Like the coveted "Oscars" of the motion picture industry, and the "Emmys" of television, the awards in children's literature focus attention not only upon the winners of the year but also upon the entire field of endeavor. They recognize and honor the best and also point the way to improved writing, illustrating, and producing of worthwhile and attractive books for children.

UNDERSTANDING CHILDREN AND HOW THEY LEARN

Child development has contributed knowledge about children that provides guideposts for selecting books. Recent years have brought new approaches to child study; new theories are evolving; research reveals new evidence regarding the forces affecting the growth and learning of the child. Teachers and librarians must continually seek information about these developments and search for implications for practice. The following section can only highlight some of the recent findings of research that should influence the selection of books and teaching of literature.[28] It is not enough to recall information and concepts from a course in child development or educational psychology, nor is it enough to rely upon observation of one child or a group; adults responsible for planning school experiences must continue to learn about children and the learning process.

Dimensions of Growth

Parents, teachers, and librarians need to be aware of the dimensions of growth of each child as they guide his selection of books and his reading. In the early decades of child study, emphasis was placed upon discovery of normal behavior patterns for each age. Growth studies revealed similarities in patterns of physical, mental, and emotional growth. More recently, longitudinal studies have shown wide variables in individual rates of growth. Within one child, growth may be uneven, and a spurt in one aspect of development may precede a spurt in another. Age trends continue to be important in understanding the child, but recent research has been more concerned with the interaction of biological, cultural, and life experience forces. It now appears that development does not result as a process of

maturation of neural cells, but evolves as new experience reshapes existing structures. Experience affects the age at which development may appear. The child-development point of view begins with the recognition and the acceptance of the uniqueness of childhood. Children are not miniature adults, but individuals with their own rights, needs, interests, and capacities. This concept suggests a need for literature that captures the wonders, humor, and disappointments of childhood.

Physical Development A graded school organization falsely appears to provide homogeneous classroom groups. Not only may there be a two-to-three-year chronological age range within one class, but children of the same age will reflect varied levels of development. The teacher will need to be aware of the widely varying rates of development as well as levels of development. To meet these needs, the school must provide an extensive collection of books covering a large range of topics and varying reading levels.

Physical appearance, in addition to size and muscle coordination, is influential in development, not so much for its innate value, but because of the way others react to the individual. Such reactions influence the child's perception of himself, and his behavior is, therefore, changed in response.

Early maturing has been found to be a significant factor in development. The child who is given tasks and privileges earlier because he is larger, tends to increase his skill, and thus, derives personal satisfaction if he meets the challenges successfully.

Many children, especially girls, reach puberty during the elementary school years. Physical maturity and social forces have led to earlier heterosexual interests. American society seems to be placing a premium upon early maturity and pushing children through

---

[28]Ira J. Gordon, "New Conceptions of Children's Learning and Development," in *Learning and Mental Health in the School*, 1966 Yearbook, Association for Supervision and Curriculum Development (Washington, D.C.: National Education Association, 1966).

childhood at a faster pace. As C. S. Lewis so aptly said in *The Last Battle:*

> *She wasted all her school time wanting to be the age she is now, and she'll waste all the rest of her life trying to stay that age.*[29]

Environmental Influences on Growth   Recent research has increased the understanding of environmental influences of culture and the family on the growth of the child. Studies of infant deprivation have indicated the importance of the pre-school years in total personality development. Lack of maternal love, limited social experiences, and little tactile stimulation inhibit development. Inadequate language development among disadvantaged children handicaps their further learning. In Durkin's studies of children who learned to read before entering school, family respect for reading was found to be a significant factor. All the children had been read to from the age of three.[30] Literature experience should form a significant part of the pre-school program.

Moral judgments, prejudice, and achievement motivation are some examples of behavior that are determined by social class and family. The conflicting values of middle class teachers and lower class children may create problems in teaching. The social expectations demanded by the child's environment often lead to anxieties. Through literature, the child may gain understanding of himself and others. The child learns who he is, whether he is loved and respected, as others respond to him. He identifies first with his parents, and then, with other models. Teachers must be aware of the socialization process in order to understand the basic needs and concerns of childhood.

Cognitive Development   Psychology and education are on the leading edge of truly significant studies of intellectual processes. One important idea proposed by Piaget[31] is that intelligence develops as a result of interaction of environment and maturation of the child. Piaget's findings suggest distinct stages in the development of logical thinking. Some Russian psychologists[32] suggest instruction can influence the stages of development; psychologists in the United States believe experiences in a rich environment may affect the rate of intellectual development. Other investigators hold the view that children develop different styles of thinking, and that personality influences the style accepted by the child. Bruner's[33] work suggests children are ready to discover structures of a problem at a far earlier age than was formerly expected. This idea implies the study of literature as a discipline need not be delayed until the high school.

Research in language development has emphasized linguistic patterns rather than size of vocabulary. It has been found that children use varied sentence structures at rather early ages. This suggests there is little need for repetitive use of subject-predicate form of sentence structure in writing for children.

The cognitive field theory of learning,[34] or perceptual field theory, is based upon the

---

[29]C. S. Lewis, *The Last Battle* (New York: Macmillan, 1956), p. 127.

[30]Dolores Durkin, "Children Who Read before Grade One," *The Reading Teacher*, vol. 14 (January 1961), pp. 163–166.

[31]Bärbel Inhelder and Jean Piaget, *The Growth of Logical Thinking* (New York: Basic Books, 1962). John Flavell, *The Developmental Psychology of Jean Piaget* (Princeton, N.J.: Van Nostrand, 1963).

[32]For example, see L. S. Vygotsky, *Thought and Language* (Cambridge, Mass.: Massachusetts Institute of Technology Press, 1962).

[33]Jerome Bruner, *The Process of Education* (Cambridge, Mass.: Harvard University Press, 1960).

[34]See Arthur W. Combs and Donald Snygg, *Individual Behavior* (New York: Harper & Row, 1959). Donald Snygg, "A Cognitive Field Theory of Learning," *Learning and Mental Health in the School*, 1966 Yearbook of the Association for Supervision and Curriculum Development (Washington, D.C.: National Education Association, 1966), pp. 77–96.

assumption that the learner behaves according to his perception of the situation. The learner perceives the problem situation and continually reinterprets it until a solution is found. Through the process of discovery, the learner becomes more aware of details and subproblems. Mistakes are necessary in order that the child reorder his perception. Recently, it has been proposed that the motivation of behavior may be the satisfaction of a drive for competence. The organism seeks stimulation and the mastery of the environment. Therefore, materials and questions should provide enough difficulty to lead to success after some effort. Given a rich environment of books, the child can be trusted to make his own selection.

The discovery theory changes the teacher's role from one of giving information to one of guiding children in their discovery of data and generalizations. For example, the teacher would not tell a child the theme of Wojciechowska's *Shadow of a Bull;* rather the teacher's questions and comments would challenge the child to formulate his own statement of the theme.

Creativity The development of the creative individual has gained increasing significance as an educational objective. Although there are many gaps in present knowledge about the nature of creativity, it seems clear that this quality is not necessarily equated with intelligence. Creativity is characterized by sensitivity to problems, curiosity, fluency of ideas, flexibility, originality, and ability to enter the world of fantasy. Divergent thinking (seeking new responses) rather than convergent thinking (seeking the one correct answer) should be emphasized in order to foster creativity. The adequacy of the self-concept and openness to new experience appear to be related to creativity. Teachers will encourage children to give their unique interpretations of literature. They will also provide books which present several points of view about a problem. For example, Chakoh in *Walk the World's Rim,* by Baker, changes his point of view about slavery when he learns that not all slaves are to be despised, and that there are many forms of slavery.

Personality Development To become a "fully functioning" person the child's basic needs must be met. He needs to feel he is loved and understood; he must feel he is a member of a group significant to him; he needs to feel he is achieving and growing toward independence. Behavior is consistent with the child's perception of the environment at the moment and with his continuing purpose of enhancing self. The concept that the individual is continually "becoming" is a more positive view than the notion that little change can take place in personality.

Erikson[35] has noted eight stages in this process of becoming: a sense of *trust* must be gained during the first year; a sense of *autonomy* should be realized from twelve to fifteen months; between four and five years the sense of *initiative* is needed; and a sense of *duty and accomplishment* occupies the period of childhood from six to twelve years. In adolescence, a sense of identity is built; a sense of intimacy, a parental sense or productivity, and a sense of integrity are tasks of adulthood.

Havighurst[36] has identified certain developmental tasks for growing up in the American culture. Some of the developmental tasks with which the elementary school child needs assistance are:

- Developing a satisfactory self-concept
- Learning to get along with peers
- Learning his appropriate sex role
- Developing skills in reading, communicating, and using numbers

---

[35]Erik H. Erikson, *Childhood and Society,* Revised edition (New York: Norton, 1964).
[36]Robert J. Havighurst, *Developmental Tasks and Education* (New York: McKay, 1955).

- Developing scientific and social concepts necessary for effective everyday living
- Developing values, attitudes, and conscience
- Developing self-direction

Books alone cannot bring satisfaction of basic needs. Literature may provide opportunities for identification and for understanding self and others. Books may contribute to feelings of success as children satisfy their desires for new experiences, gain new insights into their behavior and that of others, or "try on" new roles as they identify with various characters.

Principles of Learning

Investigations of the learning process have yielded general agreements on conditions that facilitate learning. The following guides will aid teachers and librarians in planning the literature program in the elementary school:

- The learner reacts as a whole. Anxiety and interest are involved in learning.
- A single experience may result in multiple learnings, including development of values and attitudes.
- Learning and behavior result as the behaver perceives the situation. Total development, including level of aspiration, influences learning.
- Readiness is influenced by the child's perception of the value and meaning of the task as well as the interplay of biological and environmental factors. Instruction can foster readiness.
- Rewards include the satisfactions of new experience and feelings of accomplishment.
- Learning through intrinsic motivation is preferable to learning through extrinsic motivation.
- Learning is facilitated as the learner is clued into the structure of the content and the learning process itself.
- Active participation in selecting and planning the learning activity increases interest.
- Each learner is unique in his perception. He interprets experience according to his own "set."
- Achievement is an interaction between the inner growth potential of the child and the experiences, learning or nurture he has been given.

Children's Reading Interests

Literature can both develop and extend children's interests. Understanding the development of interest in the cultural matrix will help parents, teachers, and librarians study interests of individual children. This knowledge will help them to effectively guide children's reading.

Rousseau[37], at the close of the eighteenth century, emphasized the place of interest in the education of Emile; since that time, educators have been concerned about developing, expanding, and utilizing children's interests. Interest is an elusive factor, but teachers know that this subtle element that focuses attention is essential to the learning process. Interests have been defined as preferences, drives, feelings of satisfaction, or mental excitations. Although there have been many studies of children's preferences, their wishes, their favorite activities, and their reading choices, there is still uncertainty about this channeling force which causes an individual to seek particular objects or activities.

Children have decided reading interests, and in many instances, they can articulate them. In a conference with her teacher, this third grader revealed her likes and dislikes about the books by one author:

[37]J. J.Rousseau, *Emile*, Translated by Barbara Foxley (New York: Dutton, 1925).

I didn't like this book like some of the other Bulla books. I especially liked The Sword in the Tree. *This book,* Surprise for a Cowboy, *didn't have very many exciting and interesting things in it. It seemed sort of easy. It got sort of boring because it was the same thing all the time.*

The Sword in the Tree *was so exciting. I read it in a quarter of a day. It wasn't boring at all. I've read a lot of other Bulla books and I liked them. They were real exciting. The people in the books found out so many interesting things that I've never seen or about things that have never happened to me before or maybe about things that happened in the olden days. This book,* Surprise for a Cowboy, *kept talking—just a boy, just a ranch, and just the same old thing all over. Nothing really, really exciting happened, you know, that would teach you something.*[38]

Children's reading interests reflect the pattern of their general interests. Stories of animals, real boys and girls, adventure and exploration, biographies, and stories of the past all have appeal for children. Humor, make-believe, suspense and action are the qualities that children enjoy most in their reading. Non-fiction books are growing in acceptance: children seek specific information about space, underwater life, and animals.

Factors Influencing Reading Interests

AGE AND SEX There have been many investigations of children's reading preferences, and the elements that attract children to books. Huus reviewed the literature on children's reading interests and found rather consistent results in some eight studies reported over a period of twenty years. She listed seven conclusions that point up age and sex differences in children's preferences for books:

- Interests of children vary according to age and grade level.
- Few differences between the interests of boys and girls are apparent before age nine.
- Notable differences in the interests of boys and girls appear between ages ten and thirteen.
- Girls read more than boys, but boys have a wider interest range and read a greater variety.
- Girls show an earlier interest in adult fiction of a romantic type than do boys.
- Boys like chiefly adventure and girls like fiction, but mystery stories appeal to both.
- Boys seldom show preference for a "girl's" book but girls will read "boy's" books to a greater degree.[39]

More recent studies have indicated that boys and girls have definite reading interests that differ as early as the first grade.

MENTAL AGE Besides sex and age, reading interests have also been linked to mental ability. Russell came to three major conclusions after comparing the studies of reading interests and intelligence:

- Bright children like books that dull children two to three years older like.
- Bright children read three or four times as many books as do average children and do not taper off in reading at thirteen as most children do.
- There is little variation in the reading interests of bright, average, and dull

[38]Esther Schatz, *et al.*, *Exploring Reading in the Primary Grades*, Study of Independent Reading, Bulletin No. 2 (Columbus, Ohio: College of Education, Ohio State University, 1960), p. 35.

[39]Helen Huus, "Interpreting Research in Children's Literature," in *Children, Books and Reading* (Newark, Del.: The International Reading Association, 1964), p. 125.

children, except bright children have a wider range of interests.[40]

FORMAT OF BOOK Illustrations, color, format, type of print, and style are all factors that influence children's choice of books. In a study of 2500 kindergarten children, Cappa found that illustrations were the most important source (thirty-four per cent) of appeal for these children. Story content (thirty per cent) was second, followed by information in content, humor, the surprise element, and refrain.[41]

Children in the middle grades may decide a book is too babyish because of the size of the print. Boys frequently will not choose a book if a girl is pictured on the cover or if a girl's name is in the title. Foreign words in a title may discourage both boys and girls from selecting the book.

ENVIRONMENT Environmental factors such as availability and accessibility of reading materials in the home, school, public and school libraries determine and affect the development of reading interests. Children's reading interests do not seem to vary greatly according to their geographical location. Rural, urban, and metropolitan children have somewhat similar tastes in reading.

Cultural expectations are influential factors in determining individual interests. For example, girls may be interested in dolls, but are not expected to express interest in mechanics. The child acquires interests that bring approval through conformity to social expectations. A sixth-grade girl may not be "interested" in horses or horse stories, but if most of the girls in her group express these interests, she will also ask for books related to this theme. Boys in the group may reject horse stories because "those are just for girls."

As the child identifies with parents and teachers who are enthusiastic readers, he develops his own interests. Getzels pointed out that "One cannot so much *teach* interests as *offer appropriate models* for *identification* [sic]."[42]

The child cannot be interested in something that does not exist for him; therefore, the school, home, and community must provide opportunities for children to have many first-hand, multisensory experiences. Through a background of meaningful experience he can build interests. As Dora V. Smith so ably pointed out:

> The reading interests with which pupils come to school are the teacher's opportunity — the reading interests with which children leave school are the teacher's responsibility.[43]

Guides for Ages and Stages

Adults who are responsible for children's reading need to be aware of the guides from child development, learning theory, and children's interests. They will also recognize characteristics and needs of children at different ages and stages of development. At the same time, it is important to remember that each child has his unique pattern of growth. The following outline describes some characteristic growth patterns, suggests implications for selection and use of books, and provides examples of suitable books for that particular stage of development.

[40]David Russell, *Children Learn to Read* (Boston: Ginn, 1961), pp. 394–395.

[41]Dan Cappa, "Sources of Appeal in Kindergarten Books," *Elementary English*, vol. 34 (April 1957), p. 259.

[42]Jacob W. Getzels, "Psychological Aspects," in *Developing Permanent Interest in Reading*, Helen Robinson, Editor, Supplementary Educational Monographs No. 84 (Chicago: University of Chicago Press, 1956), p. 9.

[43]Dora V. Smith, "Current Issues Relating to Development of Reading Interests and Tastes," in *Recent Trends in Reading*, W. S. Gray, Editor (Chicago: University of Chicago Press, 1939), p. 300.

BOOKS FOR AGES AND STAGES

Preschool and Kindergarten

CHARACTERISTICS	IMPLICATIONS	EXAMPLES
Rapid development of language.	Interest in words, enjoyment of rhymes, nonsense and repetition. Enjoys retelling stories.	*Mother Goose* Brooke, *Johnny Crow's Garden* Carroll, *What Whiskers Did* Gag, *Millions of Cats* Krauss, *A Very Special House*
Continuous activity, short attention span.	Requires books that can be completed "in one sitting." Enjoys participation through naming, touching, and repeating phrases.	Brown, *Where Have You Been?* Garten, *The Alphabet Tale* Francoise, *The Things I Like* Kunhardt, *Pat the Bunny* Kunhardt, *Tickle the Pig* Munari, *Who's There? Open the Door!* Rey, *Where's My Baby?* *The Three Billy Goats Gruff* (Il. by Marcia Brown)
Interests and behavior are egocentric.	Likes stories in which he is clearly identified. In telling a story, teacher or parent may substitute his name for the main character.	Brown, *Good Night Moon* Buckley, *Grandfather and I* Ets, *Just Me* Krauss, *The Growing Story* Rand, *I Know a Lot of Things*
Curious about *his* world.	Stories about everyday experiences, pets, playthings, home, people in his immediate environment are enjoyed.	Flack, *Angus and the Ducks* Hoban, *Bedtime for Frances* Janus, *Teddy* Keats, *The Snowy Day* Lenski, *Papa Small* Yashima, *Umbrella* Zolotow, *Do You Know What I'll Do?*
Building concepts through many first-hand experiences.	Books help the child explore the various dimensions of a single concept.	Budney, *A Kiss Is Round* Showers, *The Listening Walk* Steiner, *Listen to My Seashell*
Enjoys imaginative play.	Likes stories that personify the inanimate. Enjoys talking animals.	Burton, *Mike Mulligan and His Steam Shovel* De Regniers, *May I Bring a Friend?* *Goldilocks and the Three Bears* Gramatky, *Little Toot* Holl, *The Rain Puddle*

CHARACTERISTICS	IMPLICATIONS	EXAMPLES
Seeks warmth and security in relationships with adults.	Likes to be close to the teacher or parent during storytime. The ritual of the bedtime story begins literature experiences at home. Requires poetic justice and happy endings in his stories.	Buckley, *The Little Boy and the Birthdays* Flack, *Ask Mr. Bear* Massie, *The Baby Beebee Bird* Minarik, *Little Bear* Potter, *The Tale of Peter Rabbit*
Beginning to seek independence from adults.	Books can help children adjust to new and frightening experiences.	Brown, *The Runaway Bunny* Kauffman, *What's That Noise?* Lexau, *Benjie* MacDonald, *The Little Frightened Tiger* Sauer, *Mike's House*

Early Elementary, 1–2

CHARACTERISTICS	IMPLICATIONS	EXAMPLES
Attention span increasing.	Prefers short stories, or may enjoy a continued story provided each chapter is a complete incident.	Bishop, *The Five Chinese Brothers* Brown, *Cinderella* Flack, *Walter, the Lazy Mouse* (revised edition) MacDonald, *Mrs. Piggle Wiggle* Newell, *The Little Old Woman Who Used Her Head*
Striving to accomplish skills demanded by adults.	Child is expected to learn the skills of reading and writing. Needs to accomplish this at his own rate and feel successful. First reading experiences should be enjoyable.	Duvoisin, *Petunia* Felt, *Rosa-Too-Little* "Easy reading materials": Hoff, *Danny and the Dinosaur* Minarik, *Little Bear* Series Palmer, *Do You Know What I'm Going to Do Next Saturday?* Seuss, *The Cat in the Hat*
Continued interest in the world around him—eager and curious. Insatiable curiosity.	Needs wide variety of books. Interests in home and neighborhood, but mass media have extended his interests to include other lands and outer space.	Bemelmans, *Madeline* Branley, *A Book of Astronauts For You* Burton, *The Little House* Fisher, *In the Middle of the Night* Hawes, *Fireflies in the Night* Merrill, *Tell about the Cowbarn, Daddy*
Developing greater imagination.	Enjoys books about imaginative play. Likes to dramatize simple stories.	Craig, *Boxes* Craig, *Dragon in the Clockbox* Sawyer, *Journey Cake, Ho!*

CHARACTERISTICS	IMPLICATIONS	EXAMPLES
		Scheer, *Rain Makes Applesauce*
		Tresselt, *The Mitten*
		Zolotow, *Someday*
Has a growing sense of justice. Demands applications of rules, regardless of circumstances. Frequently a tattletale.	Equal opportunities to read and share books should be provided. Expects poetic justice in his books.	Caudill, *A Pocketful of Cricket* Flack, *Wait for William* Joslin, *What Do You Say, Dear?* Udry, *Let's Be Enemies* Zion, *The Meanest Squirrel I Ever Met*
Vague concepts of time.	Books may help children begin to understand time concepts. Simple biographies and historical fiction may give a feeling for the past but accurate understanding of chronology is beyond this age group.	Aliki, *William Penn* Dalgliesh, *The Columbus Story* Zolotow, *Over and Over*
Humor is developing, enjoys incongrous situations, misfortune of others, and slapstick.	Encourage appreciation of humor in literature. Reading aloud for pure fun has its place in the classroom. Enjoys books that have surprise endings, play on words, and broad comedy.	Kahl, *The Duchess Bakes a Cake* Krasilovsky, *The Man Who Didn't Wash His Dishes* Kuskin, *Just Like Everyone Else* Parish, *Amelia Bedelia* Ressner, *August Explains* Rey, *Curious George Gets a Medal* Vogel, *The Don't Be Scared Book*
Beginning sexual curiosity.	Teachers need to accept and be ready to answer children's questions about sex.	Gruenberg, *The Wonderful Story of How You Were Born* Selsam, *All about Eggs* Zolotow, *The White Marble*
Physical contour of the body is changing. Permanent teeth appear. Learning to whistle and develop other fine motor skills.	Books can help the child accept physical changes in himself and differences in others.	Beim, *Two Is a Team* Keats, *Whistle for Willie* McCloskey, *One Morning in Maine*
Continues to seek independence from adults. By end of this period, children forming clubs and cliques.	Needs opportunities to select books of his own choice. Should be encouraged to go to the library on his own.	De Regniers, *A Little House of Your Own* Myrick, *The Secret Three* Petrides, *Hans and Peter* Zolotow, *A Tiger Called Thomas*
Continues to need warmth and security in adult relationships.	Books can provide examples of good family relationships. Individual conferences with the child about his reading will	Flack, *The New Pet* Hoban, *The Sorely Trying Day* Kumin, *The Beach before Breakfast*

CHARACTERISTICS	IMPLICATIONS	EXAMPLES
	provide feelings of security and interest.	Lexau, *Maria* Zolotow, *The Quarreling Book*

Middle Elementary, 3 — 4

CHARACTERISTICS	IMPLICATIONS	EXAMPLES
Attention span longer. Attaining independence in reading skill, may read with complete absorption.	Discovers reading as an enjoyable activity or hobby. Prefers an uninterrupted block of time for independent reading. By end of this period, many children have become avid readers.	BOOKS FOR GIRLS Anderson, *Thumbelina* Carlson, *The Happy Orpheline* Enright, *Zeee* Fritz, *The Cabin Faced West* Godden, *Miss Happiness and Miss Flower* Haywood, *"B" Is for Betsy* Series Lovelace, *Betsy-Tacy* Series
Wide variation in ability and interest. Differences in interests of boys and girls are now evident. By age 9 many activities are sex-typed.	Many books are needed to meet interests and abilities. Teacher needs to be aware of sex preferences for books.	BOOKS FOR BOYS Cleary, *Henry Huggins* Series Cone, *Mish-Mash* Corbett, *The Lemonade Trick* Haywood, *Little Eddie* Series Lord, *Quarterback's Aim* Slobodkin, *Space Ship under the Apple Tree* Williams, *Danny Dunn, Time Traveler*
Peer group acceptance becomes increasingly important. Very sensitive to criticism. Seeking standards of right and wrong, developing a conscience.	Children need opportunities to recommend and discuss books. Book choices may be influenced by leaders in the peer group. Reading certain books may provide status.	Cleary, *Ellen Tebbits* Estes, *The Hundred Dresses* Lenski, *Shoo-Fly Girl* Lionni, *Tico and the Golden Wings* Matsuno, *Taro and the Tofu* Yashima, *Crow Boy*
Is more able to cooperate and work in groups.	Books may be interpreted through group projects. Group discussions and comparisons of books, murals, puppetry, dramatization provide for development of skills in working with groups.	Caudill, *The Best-Loved Doll* (Compared with:) Reyher, *My Mother Is the Most Beautiful Woman in the World* *Aesop's Fables* (various editions) Haviland, *Favorite Fairy Tales Told in France* Sherlock, *Anansi, The Spider Man* Agle, *Three Boys* Series
Interest in collections is high.	Quantity of books read becomes important. Enjoys series books. Likes to collect and trade paperback books. Seeks identification and hobby books.	*Beginning-to-Read* Biographies *Childhood of Famous Americans* Series Cormack, *The First Book of Stones*

CHARACTERISTICS	IMPLICATIONS	EXAMPLES
		Kettelkamp, *Kites*
		Lopshire, *How to Make Flibbers*
		MacGregor, *Miss Pickerell* Series
Enjoys the challenge of solving puzzles and mysteries. Likes secret codes and languages.	Enjoys creating guessing games about books. Beginning interest in mysterious, spooky stories.	Coombs, *Dorrie's Magic* Epstein, *First Book of Codes and Ciphers* Hicks, *Alvin's Secret Code* Steele, *The Spooky Thing*
Improved coordination makes proficiency in games possible. Success in team sports becomes a developmental task of this age.	Interest in sports books.	Brewster, *First Book of Baseball* Renick, *Nicky's Football Team* Schiffer, *First Book of Swimming*
Expanding interest in others, less egocentric. Deepened interest in the past. Seeks adventure.	Interest in biographies, life in the past, people of other lands. Prefers fastmoving and exciting stories, biographies of men of action.	d'Aulaire, *Abraham Lincoln* Bulla, *The Sword in the Tree* Bulla, *Viking Adventure* Carlson, *The Letter on the Tree* Coatsworth, *Jon the Unlucky* DeJong, *Far Out the Long Canal*
Seeks specific information to answer his questions.	Needs guidance in locating information. Needs help in use of library, card catalog, and reference books.	Earle, *Crickets* McClung, *Sphinx* Zim, *Golden Hamsters*
Enjoys slapstick humor in everyday situations. Appreciates imaginary adventure.	Teachers need to recognize the importance of books for releasing tension and providing enjoyment.	Atwater, *Mr. Popper's Penguins* Du Bois, *The Alligator Case* Lawson, *Mr. Twigg's Mistake* Lindgren, *Pippi Longstocking* Sharp, *Miss Bianca* Travers, *Mary Poppins*
Interested in books beyond his reading ability.	Poses a necessity for the teacher to continue to read aloud each day.	Alexander, *The Book of Three* Colum, *Children of Odin* DeJong, *Hurry Home, Candy* Henry, *King of the Wind* McNeer, *America's Abraham Lincoln* White, *Charlotte's Web*

Later Elementary, 5–6

CHARACTERISTICS	IMPLICATIONS	EXAMPLES
Rate of physical development varies widely. Rapid growth	Continued sex differentiation in reading preferences. Guide	L'Engle, *A Wrinkle in Time* Sorensen, *Miracles on Maple Hill*

CHARACTERISTICS	IMPLICATIONS	EXAMPLES
precedes beginning of puberty. Girls about two years ahead of boys in development and reaching puberty. Increasingly aware of body changes.	understanding of growth process and help children meet personal problems.	Sperry, *Call It Courage* Levine, *A Baby Is Born* Selsam, *Animals as Parents* Zim, *How Things Grow*
Understanding and accepting the sex role is a developmental task of this period. Girls display interests in boys.	Books may provide impetus for discussion and identification with others meeting this task.	Brink, *Caddie Woodlawn* Harnden, *The High Pasture* Krumgold, *And Now Miguel* L'Engle, *Moon by Night* Robertson, *Henry Reed's Journey* Seredy, *The Good Master* Steele, *The Lone Hunt*
Sustained, intense interest in specific activities.	Children spend more time in reading at this age than any other. Tend to select books related to one topic, for example horses, mysteries, and science fiction.	Farley, *Black Stallion* Series Heinlein, *Orphans of the Sky* Henry, *Misty of Chincoteague* Martel, *City under the Ground* Meader, *River of the Wolves* Trease, *No Boats on Bannermere*
Increased understanding of the chronology of past events. Beginning sense of his place in time. Able to see many dimensions of a problem.	Literature provides the opportunity to examine issues from different viewpoints. Needs guidance in being critical of biased presentations.	Bradley, *Meeting With a Stranger* Hunt, *Across Five Aprils* Sommerfelt, *Miriam* Speare, *The Bronze Bow* Steele, *The Perilous Road* Yates, *Amos Fortune, Free Man*
Increased understanding of reality makes possible projection into the world of fantasy.	May need to be enticed to read fanciful literature.	Boston, *The Treasure of Green Knowe* Dahl, *Charlie and the Chocolate Factory* Du Bois, *The Twenty-One Balloons* Lewis, *The Lion, the Witch, and the Wardrobe*
Family relationships changing. Highly critical of siblings. By end of period may challenge parents' authority.	Books may provide understanding of these changing relationships.	Burch, *D. J.'s Worst Enemy* Cleary, *Beezus and Ramona* Krumgold, *Onion John* Neville, *It's Like This, Cat* Stolz, *The Bully of Barkham Street*
Increased emphasis upon peer group and sense of belonging. Deliberate exclusion of others. Expressions of prejudice.	Emphasize unique contribution of all. In a healthy classroom atmosphere, discussion of books can aid individual and group adjustment.	Burch, *Queenie Peavy* Farmer, *The Summer Birds* Graham, *South Town* Ish-Kishor, *A Boy of Old Prague* Neville, *Berries Goodman*

CHARACTERISTICS	IMPLICATIONS	EXAMPLES
Begins to have models other than parents. May draw them from TV, movies, teachers, and books. Beginning interest in future vocation.	Books may serve to provide appropriate models and information concerning various careers.	Faber, *Robert Frost, America's Poet* George, *Gull 737* Judson, *Mr. Justice Holmes* Kugelmass, *Ralph J. Bunche, Fighter for Peace* Simon, *All Men Are Brothers, A Portrait of Albert Schweitzer*
Awareness of self and seeking identity. Interest in feelings of self and others. Search for values. Interest in problems of the world.	Help children relate reading to current events. Provide opportunities for discussion of books and their significance to individuals.	Bloch, *The Two Worlds of Damyan* DeJong, *The House of Sixty Fathers* Houston, *Tiktá Liktak* Mirsky, *Nomusa and the New Magic* Sommerfelt, *The White Bungalow* Wojciechowska, *Shadow of a Bull*

Guides for Studying Children

The teacher or librarian may be very familiar with general characteristics and interest patterns of children at various age levels and understand the basic principles of learning. Such knowledge is of value only as it is applied to guiding each child as a unique individual. It is important to know that most six-year-olds enjoy folk tales and that many sixth-graders are interested in career books. However, the teacher will find wide variations from the norms established for particular age groups. Only after studying each child can the teacher say, "David will like this book. Philip will be challenged by this one. Just now, Beth will enjoy this fantasy." Several techniques may be used to collect evidence of the child's interests and needs. These records may be shared with the elementary school librarian who is in a unique position to study the child over a period of years. The librarian can share invaluable information about children.

Understanding of the child and the accumulated effect of past experiences is gained through observing him in many situations. The teacher or librarian observes the child as he studies or reads alone, as he reacts to others in work and play situations, and as he meets problems. The teacher will note what he does not do or say as well as his active behavior responses. The teacher seeks to understand the child's perception of himself, for this self-concept influences his behavior, his choices, his achievement.

Observation provides many clues regarding the reading interests and habits of children. Watching the child as he selects a book will help determine his interests in books. Does he go directly to a specific book section? Does he know where he will find science books, poetry, biography, or fiction? Does he look at the chapter headings or illustrations before he selects a book? Does he ask for help in locating books? Does he seem to follow the leadership of one or two other children, selecting in accordance with their choice? Is he really browsing and getting to know books, or is he engaged in aimless wandering? Does he select books that are too difficult to read because he seeks status?

Observing the child during the classroom library period reveals other helpful information. Does he begin quickly? Can you sense his appreciation of the illustrations? Does the position of his body reflect relaxation and interest in the book? If a child becomes absorbed in the book, he is not easily distracted by movements or sounds in the classroom. The teacher may find it helpful to record these brief observations for a part of the continuous anecdotal record. If such a brief observation is made of two or three children during each library period, a systematic observation record can be maintained.

A record of each child's reading should be kept and added to his cumulative folder. There are various ways in which children may help to keep these records. For example, slips of paper with the book title or a number assigned according to the teacher's list may be placed in the book pocket or fastened with a rubber band around the back cover. As the first- or second-grader looks at the book or reads it, he removes a slip and places it in his own pocket on a reading chart. Similarly, the younger child may write his name on a slip of paper and place it in a pocket or envelope in the book when he finishes. Another method involves attaching a large card to the back of the book. When the child completes the story, he writes his name on the card.

A plan for individual reading records can be arranged so that competition among individuals is reduced. A gaily painted or covered box can hold the children's file folders. As a book is read, the child may write the title or use one of the teacher-made record slips in his folder. Older children may write brief comments about the book. If books are read aloud at home, mother or father may complete a simple record form that can be placed in the folder.[44]

When children are involved in planning and recognize the purpose for such records, they will assume more responsibility for the process. Records should not be kept to determine who reads the most books. Reading records help the child answer the following questions: What kind of books do I enjoy? Am I reading different kinds of books? Am I reading books which are usually too easy, often too difficult, or usually just right for me? Am I spending enough leisure time in reading? Children can participate in evaluation through use of such records.

The teacher also gains clues regarding children's reading interests by noting books that are brought for the sharing period. Does the child bring books that are on his level? What type of book does he prefer? What books does he receive at home or obtain at the public library?

In addition to expressed reading interests, the teacher needs to determine the other interests of children in the group. Among the children in one class, some interests may persist. For example, nine-year-old Bruce has been enthralled with insects, especially moths and butterflies, since he was a toddler. Diana, now ten, is engrossed in dancing. Ballet lessons and daily practice are deeply satisfying. Although they are no longer actively engaged in a class study of prehistoric life, several children in the third grade have continued their excitement over dinosaurs. Current interests are developed through family trips, news items, visitors from other countries to the school or community, and through television programs. Teachers should provide books that will capitalize on children's outside interests and anticipate new areas of interest.

To wisely select books for children in the class, the teacher also uses cumulative records. These school records should include the child's special interests. The standardized test data will show the present reading achievement level and the progress he has made. At times, a child may push beyond the reading level indicated by tests when he really wants the information in a

---

[44]Suggestions for book reports are in Chapter 13.

more difficult book. For his recreational reading, he may choose books that are somewhat below his level of achievement on the reading tests.

Cumulative records, achievement and intelligence test scores, and anecdotal records may be supplemented by other devices to help understand the child. Children's original stories based upon such titles as "My Happiest Day," "What I Like about Week Ends," and "Favorite People I Have Known" will often yield helpful clues in understanding the child's interests.

Through parent conferences, the teacher may learn about the child's interests, previous experiences, and present reading habits. Do parents read aloud to the child? Is there a quiet time for reading? Does the child have a library card and use it regularly? What are his interests and hobbies? Do parents purchase books for his library? Are there newspapers, magazines, encyclopedias available at home? Has he traveled, visited museums, or enjoyed concerts? More significant than these environmental factors, however, are the attitudes of parents toward reading. Is reading scorned, looked down upon, or encouraged as a worthwhile, important phase of living? In the conference, the teacher will become aware of the parent's expectations of the child. Parent conferences help the teacher understand the many forces that affect the child's reading.

SELECTING BOOKS

The Need for Good Book Selection

Good book selection not only requires a thorough knowledge of children and their individual needs, interests, and abilities, but it demands an equal understanding of the field of children's literature. Knowing children and knowing books are two sides of the coin of good book selection.

Unfortunately, we cannot rely solely upon the choices of children. They are not born with inherent good taste in literature, any more than with good taste in art and music, or in their choice of clothes and food. This does not mean that they do not like good literature; they do. But like Browning's "My Last Duchess" they are indiscriminate and tend to like "what ere they look upon." A typical ten-year-old girl is capable of enjoying Doris Gates' *Blue Willow* and a *Nancy Drew* mystery with the same relish. Children's reactions to books are important, however, for a book that is not read by children cannot be considered a good children's book. At the same time, the most popular children's books are not necessarily the best books, any more than the best sellers of today represent great literature for adults.

Many adults can remember a period when they were completely engrossed in the Bobbsey Twins, the Hardy Boys, the Nancy Drew mysteries, or the Sue Barton stories. These books did not harm the readers who went on to read other well-written literature. Why, then, should there be concern about children's choices today? There is concern for three reasons.

First, children read comparatively few books. Assuming that a child reads one book every two weeks from the time he is seven (when he may begin to read independently) until he is fourteen (when he may start reading adult books), he will read about twenty-five books a year or some 200 books during this period of childhood. Currently, there are 25,000 or more children's books in print. A child may have read widely and *never have read a significant book.*

Second, the time of childhood is limited; most children's books have to be read at the appropriate age and stage in the development of a child's life or they will *never be read.* The eight-year-old does not read *The Tale of Peter Rabbit*, the twelve-year-old may think *The Courage of Sarah Noble* by Alice Dalgliesh is "babyish," and the junior high school student has outgrown Lawson's *Rabbit Hill.* Introduced at the right time, these books would have provided rich and satisfying experiences with literature.

Third, it appears that not only is the time of childhood limited, it is decreasing, as boys and girls are growing up faster today than twenty years ago. In their sophistication, they are beginning to read adult books at an earlier age than ever before. For example, one sixth-grade class recently voted *Gone with the Wind* and *The Diary of Anne Frank* as their favorites. In turning to these adult books too quickly, it is likely that these children have missed the well-written books of such authors as Sutcliff, L'Engle, and Stolz. At the same time, one wonders how much even sophisticated twelve-year-olds understand of the meaning of *Gone with the Wind*! Unfortunately, children in sixth grade who read this book and others such as *To Kill a Mockingbird* will feel they have "read" the book and may not read it later when maturity of living could produce a much richer experience. Since the number of books that children read is greatly limited, and the period of time in which they are interested in children's books appears to be decreasing, it becomes even more imperative that the books they do read are worthwhile.

Principles of Book Selection

Evaluation of an individual book involves literary criticism; evaluation of a particular book for a particular child entails an understanding of literature and the background of the individual child; but evaluation of many books for many children who will use them for a variety of purposes requires knowledge of some basic principles of good book selection. The term "book selection" also may refer to the selection of books for a classroom unit of study. Since the process of book selection is broader than the evaluation of a single book, it usually refers to obtaining books for a library collection. It is important for each school to develop a written statement concerning policy for book selection. Factors to be considered in such a policy would include: (1) who selects the books, (2) quality of books, (3) needs and interests of the children, (4) appropriateness of content, (5) school curriculum needs, (6) balance in the collection, and (7) present collection. A statement regarding the review of books and a plan for considering complaints is helpful in the event self-appointed censors or pressure groups attempt to remove particular books from library shelves.

Who Selects the Books? Teachers and students may recommend particular titles, but the final selection of books for the library should be determined by the librarian. Frequently, librarians will appoint interested teachers and, occasionally, a parent to serve on a book selection committee, but the final responsibility should rest with the professionally trained librarian.

In schools where there is no librarian, a teacher committee with an interested chairman appointed by the principal could make the selections.

Quality of Books Books for the school library collection should meet the criteria of fine writing described earlier in this chapter. Every book should be read and evaluated on its own merits prior to purchase, whenever possible. With the abundance of excellent materials available for children, librarians should make no compromise with mediocrity. However, a single book may not meet all recommended criteria. The decision for selection, then, becomes a matter of judgment in terms of its value in the school curriculum. For example, a work of fiction may have a contrived plot; yet, its theme is of value for discussion in social studies. A science book may have some anthropomorphism in its text, but the facts are accurate. The book selection committee will have to weigh the merits of the total effect of the book, its use in the curriculum, and the availability of other materials for instructional purposes against the weaknesses of the book.

The familiar cry of "but children are reading the series books" should not prompt the purchase of them. Perhaps, they are reading them because they know nothing else. Well-stocked libraries may provide substitutes for both the comics and the mediocre series books. A decision should be made about adaptations and abridgments of books. To adapt or condense a book usually destroys the style or richness of the language that made it great in the first place. The actual story or plot of *Tom Sawyer* is not outstanding, only the way in which Mark Twain wrote it. If children cannot read it in the original, it is usually better that they wait for the time when they can. In a few instances, a book has been abridged without changing the style of the author. Kathleen Lines' abridgment of Kingsley's *Water Babies* eliminated long, mid-Victorian moralizing passages that were extraneous to the story. Elizabeth Yates skillfully edited *Sir Gibbie* by George MacDonald, changing many of the difficult Scottish words, but still retaining the flavor of the original. Adaptations of an author's works are usually unacceptable; abridgments must be judged on their own merits.

A written policy concerning the criteria by which books are evaluated will aid the librarian, who may need to be protected from the well-intentioned parent who decides to clean the attic and "reward" the library with all the outdated, frequently poor, books that have accumulated through the years.

Needs and Interests of Children   Books should always be purchased in terms of the children who will be using them. The chart on pages 30–36 showing needs of children at various stages of their growth should guide book selection. Particular groups of children in an elementary school may have special needs; for example, a partially sighted class will require library books with large type. The background and abilities of the school population should be considered when selecting books. For example, children in a culturally disadvantaged area may need more easy reading materials at all levels, while children who have had more educational advantages may demand young adult materials. It is a mistake, however, to assume that city children need books with urban settings and multiethnic characters any more than suburban children. All children need books that will give them insight into their own lives, but they also need books to take them out of those lives to help them see the world in its many dimensions. Suburban children need to read of life in the slums; it may be their only contact with it. And slum children need to be introduced to the best literature we have. We cannot tolerate the notion that somehow it is all right to give poor children poor books. Regardless of their background, good book selection should provide a wide range of quality books for all children.

Appropriate Content   Librarians and teachers will want to be aware of the appropriateness of the content of the book for children. Some plots and themes are beyond the maturity levels of many elementary school children. Also, portions of certain books may not seem appropriate reading for children. Some children's books do contain objectionable language, grim horror, or sordid situations. However, it is the total effect of the book that determines its appropriateness. If these elements are necessary to the theme of the book and grow naturally from the situations and the characters, they are acceptable. For example, the word "nigger" is used by the white rabble-rouser in Carlson's *The Empty Schoolhouse*. In this situation, the use of the epithet creates the realism of prejudice, and it was made quite clear that a despicable character spoke the ugly word. However, if the author described Lullah as a "nigger who longed for a better education," it would be entirely inappropriate. In *The Long Secret* by Fitzhugh, twelve-year-old Norman collects toilets from an old hotel and sells them for a small profit. The purpose for using this device as a sex symbol seems contrived and unrelated to the total story. On the other hand, the discussion of menstruation is not objectionable because the onset of puberty is a part of Beth Ellen's total development, and the misconceptions given by her grandmother serve to describe their relationship. Most girls reading this story will be going through adolescence and will find meaning in this frank discussion of menstruation.

Controversy about horror in children's tales has long been a subject for discussion. After protests by some psychologists, fairy tales were rewritten to temper the grim details that were once included. However, folk tales represent the plight of the human condition and are symbolic of good and evil. The horror may serve as catharsis for fears and anxieties that may be larger than those depicted in the stories. In Grimm's story of *The Seven Ravens*, the little girl must cut off her finger in order to enter the crystal palace and save her brothers. Neither pain nor blood is described. In the broad context of the story, the action represents the sacrifice of the girl who was partially responsible for the original curse placed upon her brothers. The rewards of the fairy tale are not easily won, and something must be given for each favor received. The monsters in *Where the Wild Things Are* by Sendak have been criticized for being too grotesque and frightening to children. The critics do not really understand the theme of the story, nor do they understand that children have their own private horrors. After his wild dream,

Max "returns" home to find the reality of love and warmth.

In some instances, books may be the very instruments by which children first learn to meet the hardships of life. Hopefully, few American children will ever know the terror, pain, and hunger suffered by Tien Pao in *The House of Sixty Fathers* by DeJong. They may never know the personal horrors of war that he faced alone. This book, with its starkly vivid writing, contains a message that attacks the very roots of survival in the twentieth century. It is not a book that all children are fortified to withstand. There is no reason to overprotect or coddle the child's mind. However, there is no reason to shock or deliberately frighten the child until such time as he may have developed the maturity and inner strength to face the tragedies of life, even vicariously. This is a matter of age and experience, and points up the importance of a teacher knowing children.

School Curriculum Needs   Librarians will need to consider particular needs of the school curriculum when ordering books. If the Initial Teaching Alphabet is used for beginning reading, the library should include i/t/a editions of trade books. If anthropology is introduced in the social studies, for example, teachers and the librarian will want to make certain that enriching materials are available. Intensive study of the local region will require additional copies of books about the particular state, industries, and people of the region. Multiple copies of books recommended for literature study may be required. In contrast to the public library, one of the major functions of the school library is to provide a wide range of informational books specifically chosen to meet the demands of the school curriculum.

Balance in the Collection   As more funds become available for library purchases, it is important to maintain a balanced collection. Keeping in mind the total needs of the school, the librarian will consider the following balances: book and nonbook material (including tapes, records, filmstrips, and other materials), reference books and trade books, fiction and nonfiction, poetry and prose, classics (both old and "new"), realistic and fanciful stories, books for younger and older children, books for poor and superior readers at each grade level, and books for teachers to read to students and use for enrichment purposes.

The librarian must always select materials in terms of the present library collection. What are the voids and needs in the collection now? What replacements should be considered? How many duplicate copies of a particularly popular book should be ordered? Every book added to a collection should make some distinct contribution to it. Just because children are interested in magnets does not mean that all new books on magnets should be ordered. What is unique about this book? Perhaps, it presents new information; perhaps the experiments are more clearly written than similar books, or it may be for a different age group. Only the person who knows the total collection can make these decisions.

Many elementary school libraries do not meet the standards established in 1960 by the American Library Association for the size of the book collection. This recommendation suggests that all schools enrolling 200–999 students should have between 6000–10,000 books. Schools that are larger than this should maintain ten books per child. While quality of books is essential, quantity is important also. All children should be served by the best books available for them.

Problems of Censorship

There is a fine line between appropriate selection of books for children and censorship. Selection is made upon the basis of quality and appropriateness for children. Censorship, however, would curtail the purchase of books that represented conflicting religious, political, or social points of view. The "School Library Bill of Rights" lists six functions of the school library. The last three assert that the library has a responsibility:

> To provide materials on opposing sides of controversial issues. . . .
> To provide materials representative of the many religious, ethnic, and cultural groups. . . .
> To place principle above personal opinion and reason above prejudice in the selection of materials. . . .[45]

Almost every school librarian has faced some criticism of books in the school collection, although junior and senior high schools often receive more attacks than do elementary schools. Some of the criticism is well-intentioned and may be quite justified. Occasionally, self-appointed censors with specific axes to grind, attempt to have certain books removed from the library. More serious are the concerted attacks on particular books by organized groups. Books dealing with particular social, religious, or political problems, books using "objectionable" language, or books by a particular author have all come under attack. Because some groups questioned his political persuasion, the excellent poetry by Langston Hughes was quietly removed from many library shelves. An innocent, homey, little folk tale titled *My Mother Is the Most Beautiful Woman in the World*, retold by Becky Reyher, has been the center of several controversies. The book was published just at the close of World War II, when relations between the United States and Russia were peaceful and respectful. No

---

[45]School Library Bill of Rights, endorsed by the Council of American Library Association, July 1955, Quoted in *Standards for School Library Programs* (Chicago: American Library Association, 1960), p. 75.

one objected to the sentences in the middle of this Russian folk tale that stated:

The Russian sun shines with a warm glow that makes Russia's wheat the most nourishing in the world, her fruit and vegetables the most delicious that ever grew. The cherries are the reddest, largest and juiciest, the apples the firmest and crunchiest to the teeth, the cucumbers the most plentiful on the vine. As for the watermelons, only someone who has seen a Ukranian watermelon really knows what a watermelon should be.[46]

These boasts in no way represented political propaganda, but are typical of the literary hyperbole of folklore. Critics who knew little about the style of writing folktales misinterpreted these words as Communist propaganda and demanded the removal of the book.

Every school should be ready for such an attack *before* it happens. Complainants should be asked to file a written report citing the specific objections to the books in question.[47] A panel that might include outside experts as well as local parent and teacher representatives should be selected to deal with the criticism. Adequate time should be allowed for reviewing the problem and making recommendations. Frequently, the objection is dropped when such a procedure is calmly suggested.

A more subtle and frightening kind of censorship is that which is practiced voluntarily by librarians and teachers. If a book has come under scrutiny in a nearby town, it is carefully placed under the librarian's desk until the controversy dies down. Or, perhaps the librarians or the teachers just do not order controversial books. "Why stir up trouble when there are so many other good books available"? they falsely reason. One teacher feared the possibilities of a frank discussion of restricted real estate sales that might accompany reading Neville's book, *Berries Goodman.* Although sensitive to community feeling, this teacher denied children the opportunity to evaluate a social problem.

It is not always easy to stand firm in the face of pressure and publicity. But careful preparation with the assistance of the administration should strengthen the professional position of the librarian. A very large principle is at stake; the principle of freedom to read, to inquire, to know all sides. The student has this right, the librarian and teacher must guarantee it.

Aids to Book Selection

Teachers and librarians are faced with seemingly overwhelming problems in selecting books for classroom studies, buying books for new libraries, planning a literature curriculum, and in adding books to already established libraries. The number of books published each year makes it increasingly difficult to read all the books before ordering, and teachers cannot know all of the books available for every topic of study. In order to make wise decisions about these problems, teachers and librarians need to know the values of the selection aids that are available. The following anecdote illustrates the uses of some of the resources teachers and librarians may consult. These and other selection aids are listed and annotated in Appendix B.

Using Book Selection Aids *In Sandburg Elementary School, recommendations for new books come from children, teachers, and consultants, but it is the librarian who makes the final decision regarding purchase. Miss Shipley, the librarian, continuously evaluates the collection, and orders books as needed throughout the year.*

---

[46]Becky Reyher, *My Mother Is the Most Beautiful Woman in the World* (New York: Lothrop, 1945), unpaged.

[47]Sample forms and other helpful materials are available from both the American Library Association and the National Council of Teachers of English.

Teachers, consultants, and children look at many new books during the annual Fall Book Fair. The children in each class compile a recommended list and give it to Miss Shipley who is aware of their special interests. The teachers and consultants who attend professional conferences bring back suggestions for new materials. The county school system obtains an annual book exhibit that gives teachers an opportunity to examine new books. Also, children tell their teachers and the librarian about books they see in book stores or books that they find in the public library. Miss Shipley's "openness" has created the feeling that all are responsible for extending the library collection.

Miss Shipley is alert to needs created by current events, film productions of children's books, and new curriculum studies. She urges the teachers to inform her before their classes begin a new area of study and when special assignments will be made. Recalling the problems that developed when one fourth grade teacher required children to use four trade books to write reports about the Eskimo, Miss Shipley reminds the teachers that it is well nigh impossible to provide suitable books for twenty-six children on such a limited topic.

Miss Shipley also replaces the worn, faded copies of books. Rows of dark, dingy books do not invite reading.

Three teachers who are especially interested in children's books and the language arts consultant serve on a book selection committee with Miss Shipley. They meet regularly during the year to discuss new books and to compare their evaluations to those of the reviewers who write for various periodicals. All of the teachers, as well as the selection committee, use several journals in selecting books they may want to order. The Booklist and Subscription Books Bulletin, *published semi-monthly by the American Library Association, recommends recent children's books and gives concise annotations. By checking the regular column "Suggested for the Small Library," Miss Shipley is aware of the outstanding books among those listed. The teachers on the committee are becoming familiar with the* School Library Journal *published by R. R. Bowker, September through May. The reports of the librarians who write the reviews are sometimes extended by the editorial staff. These additional comments or different opinions are presented in italics. Miss Shipley especially notes the titles that are double-starred for first purchase and those receiving one star for being above average. Regular columns in journals for teachers,* Elementary English *and* Childhood Education, *present reviews of children's books. The evaluations in* Elementary English *tend to be more provocative of discussion and analysis than do the* Childhood Education *reviews. A wider range of books is apparently considered by* Elementary English.

The reviews of The Horn Book Magazine, *published six times a year, give dependable summaries of recommended books. Regular reviews of science books and books for able, mature readers are special features of value to the committee. The articles related to literature for children, authors, and illustrators have been very helpful in establishing criteria and in teaching literature. The teachers in Sandburg School have liked the detailed reviews in* The Bulletin of the Center for Children's Books *published at the University of Chicago. These teachers find it very helpful to know which books are recommended, as well as books not recommended. In addition to giving reasons why some are not recommended, the reviewers indicate books they consider to be of marginal value, books for the special reader or special collection, and those that are accepted but would be purchased only if the library needed more books of this type. They also appreciate the frank criticism of the reviews in* The Young Reader's Review, *a monthly magazine devoted to children's books. The reviewers in this relatively new journal frequently compare the book being evaluated to others by the same author and previous publications of similar theme or content. Book reviews of children's books are also presented in the weekly magazine,* Saturday Review.

In the spring and fall, Miss Shipley orders copies of The New York Times *and the* Chicago Tribune *so their special children's book sections will be available. Articles by critics as well as by author and illustrators are often included. The brief reviews of new books, and the publishers' advertisements, give the selection committee suggestions of books they would like to check further.*

Miss Shipley is aware that not all books that are published are reviewed in these selection aids. For this reason she consults the publishers' catalogs to see if there are other books that would meet the special needs of the school.

The staff finds the Children's Catalog *published by H. W. Wilson Company very useful in selecting books for a particular class study. Grade level indications, subject categories, and starred recommendations are helpful. The an-nual supplement provides another reviewing source.*

The selection aids listed and described in Appendix B are regularly used by the librarian and teachers.

There is no shortage of tools for the selection of books. Faithful and consistent reading of one of the publications that reviews books for children will lead the interested person to those titles that he will want to read and appraise for himself. The experts cannot give a complete presentation of any book in a six-line review. They can only help the teacher decide if this is a book he would like to consider. Book selection aids should help eliminate the *number* of books that most librarians and teachers must read, but they do not eliminate reading. Whether it is for a seven-year-old or a seventy-year-old, there is no substitute for the personal reading of a book you recommend.

SUGGESTED ACTIVITIES

1. Write an autobiographical account of the development of your reading interests. What factors facilitated your interests; what were inhibiting factors? What were your favorite books?
2. If possible, interview one child concerning his reading habits, likes, and dislikes. Also interview one of his parents to determine the reading environment in the home. What relationships can you identify?
3. If you can meet with a class of children, ask them to submit names of their ten favorite books. How do their choices reflect their particular age and stage of development?
4. Can you think of any one book that you read and reread as a child? What particular qualities of the story appealed to you? Reread it and evaluate it according to the criteria established in this chapter. Would you still recommend it for children?
5. Read one of the series books, the Bobbsey Twins, the Hardy Boys, the Sue Barton, or Nancy Drew series. Analyze this book for plot, content, theme, characterization, style, and format.
6. Review the winners and runners-up for the Newbery Award or the Caldecott Award for one year. Do you agree with the judges? Be prepared to state your reasons.
7. Analyze the art work of the Caldecott winners as to style, media, color, and subject.
8. Read several acceptance speeches of either the Caldecott or Newbery winners. How has the author's or illustrator's style been influenced by his concepts of childhood?
9. If possible, visit a printing shop or bindery. What can you learn about binding, typography, and general format?
10. Compare reviews of two books in at least three sources.

RELATED READINGS

1. Almy, Millie. *Ways of Studying Children.* New York: Bureau of Publications, Teachers College, Columbia University, 1959.

Using materials from Cunningham and others, the author presents many suggestions for collecting evidence for child study through observation, discussion, interviews, and records. Chapter 5, "Study the Ways Children Express Themselves," is particularly related to use of literature in studying children.

2. Arbuthnot, May Hill. *Children and Books.* Third Edition. Glenview, Ill.: Scott, Foresman, 1964.

A comprehensive and detailed study of children and their books. Primarily a college textbook for children's literature courses; it would also be valuable for parents. Includes an annotated bibliography of books for each chapter with age grading. Chapter 1 presents children's needs that are satisfied through books. Chapter 2 discusses criteria for children's books.

3. Cunningham, Ruth. *Understanding Group Behavior of Boys and Girls.* New York: Bureau of Publications, Teachers College, Columbia University, 1951.

Descriptions of techniques used for determining the social relationships within a class group are presented in this study.

4. Fenner, Phyllis. *The Proof of the Pudding, What Children Read.* New York: John Day, 1957.

Out of some thirty-two years' experience, a librarian writes with enthusiasm about the books children like to read and how to encourage them to read more. Contains annotated lists of books in many fields. Chapter 15 is entitled "My Father Says to Get a Classic."

5. Fisher, Margery. *Intent upon Reading.* Leicester, England: Brockhampton Press, 1961.

An English critic includes evaluative criteria in her analysis of books. She identifies age levels as she writes of the appeals and values of selected books. The book is organized according to genre and content, such as picture books, fairy tales, and animal stories. The chapter bibliographies will be especially useful to the student seeking books of a particular type.

6. Kingman, Lee, Editor. *Newbery and Caldecott Medal Books: 1956–1965* with Acceptance Papers, Biographies, and Related Material chiefly from *The Horn Book Magazine.* Boston: Horn Book, 1964.

The origin of the medals, an analysis of the themes of the medal books, and critical appraisals of the Newbery and Caldecott books are included with the information outlined in the title. Reproductions of illustrations from the Caldecott books help the student contrast the styles of the picture books.

7. Miller, Bertha Mahony, and Elinor Whitney Field, Editors. *Caldecott Medal Books: 1938–1957.* Horn Book Papers, Volume II. Boston: Horn Book, 1957.

This is a companion volume to the *Newbery Medal Books.* It contains the acceptance speeches of the artists, their biographies, and a brief format and book note for each winning book. There is a biographical sketch of Randolph Caldecott and an interesting article by Esther Averill entitled "What Is a Picture Book?" A center signature includes one picture from each award book. Unfortunately, the limitation of black and white reproductions cannot convey the rich colors of many of the award winners.

8. Miller, Bertha Mahony, and Elinor Whitney Field, Editors. *Newbery Medal Books: 1922–1955.* Horn Book Papers, Volume I. Boston: Horn Book, 1955.

This book presents a brief history of the Newbery Award and a biographical sketch of John Newbery. It includes a book note, excerpt from the book, biographical note, and acceptance speech of each award winner from the inception of the award. The winning books are presented in chronological arrangement. Some illustrations from the award books are included.

9. Sayers, Frances Clarke. *Summoned by Books.* New York: Viking, 1965.
   A collection of speeches and essays by an outstanding critic of children's literature. "Lose Not the Nightingale" and "Books That Enchant: What Makes a Classic?" are particularly appropriate reading for this chapter.
10. Smith, Irene. *A History of the Newbery and Caldecott Medals.* New York: Viking, 1957.
    The author reviews the events that led to the founding of the awards, describes the selection proceedings, appraises the winning books, and points out the far-reaching influence of the awards. Chapter 9 is one of the most interesting—it discusses the popularity of the award books.
11. Smith, Lillian. *The Unreluctant Years: A Critical Approach to Children's Literature.* Chicago: American Library Association, 1953.
    "The Case for Children's Literature" discusses the qualities of literature that satisfy children's needs and places children's literature in the body of literature. In "An Approach to Criticism," the author establishes standards for good writing and gives an excellent analysis of the process of literary criticism.
12. Stone, L. Joseph, and Joseph Church. *Childhood and Adolescence.* New York: Random House, 1957.
    Chapters 8 and 9 discuss the middle years—development and needs of elementary school children.
13. Viguers, Ruth Hill. *Margin for Surprise, about Books, Children, and Librarians.* Boston: Little, Brown, 1964.
    Ruth Hill Viguers has been a children's librarian, teacher, parent, and editor of the well-known *Horn Book.* These papers present her various points of view as she reflects on children's literature. Her first paper, "Margin for Surprise" discusses the problems involved in reviewing children's books. Mrs. Viguers discusses the librarian's role in utilizing children's interests to motivate reading in "Invitation to the Feast."
14. Walsh, Frances. *That Eager Zest: First Discoveries in the Magic World of Books.* Philadelphia: Lippincott, 1961.
    An anthology of selections about books written by authors and critics of books for children and adults. Each person recalls his introduction to books and the qualities that made books endearing and essential in his life.

CHAPTER REFERENCES[48]

1. Agle, Nan H., and Ellen Wilson. *Three Boys* Series. New York: Scribner.
   Three Boys and a Helicopter, 1958.
   Three Boys and a Lighthouse, 1952.
   Three Boys and a Mine, 1954.
   Three Boys and a Train, 1956.
   Three Boys and a Tugboat, 1953.
   Three Boys and Space, 1962.
   Three Boys and the Remarkable Cow, 1952.
2. Alcott, Louisa M. *Little Women.* Illustrated by Barbara Cooney. New York: Crowell, 1955, 1868.
3. Alexander, Lloyd, *The Book of Three.* New York: Holt, Rinehart and Winston, 1964.
4. Aliki, pseud. (Aliki Brandenberg). *The Story of William Penn.* Englewood Cliffs, N.J.: Prentice-Hall, 1964.
5. Andersen, Hans Christian. *Thumbelina.* Illustrated by Adrienne Adams. New York: Scribner, 1961.

---

[48]The list of books at the end of each chapter cite title references and does not constitute a recommended buying list.

6. Asbjørnsen, P. C., and J. E. Moe. *The Three Billy Goats Gruff.* Illustrated by Marcia Brown. New York: Harcourt, 1957.
7. Atwater, Richard and Florence. *Mr. Popper's Penguins.* Illustrated by Robert Lawson. Boston: Little, Brown, 1938.
8. d'Aulaire, Ingri and Edgar Parin. *Abraham Lincoln.* New York: Doubleday, 1957.
9. Baker, Betty. *Walk the World's Rim.* New York: Harper & Row, 1965.
10. Barrie, James M. *Peter Pan.* Illustrated by Nora S. Unwin. New York: Scribner, 1949, 1911.
11. Baum, L. Frank. *The Wizard of Oz.* Illustrated by W. W. Denslow. Chicago: Reilly & Lee, 1956, 1900.
12. Beim, Lorraine and Jerrold. *Two Is a Team.* Illustrated by Ernest Crichlow. New York: Harcourt, 1945.
13. Bemelmans, Ludwig. *Madeline.* New York: Viking, 1939.
14. Bishop, Claire Huchet. *Five Chinese Brothers.* Illustrated by Kurt Wiese. Coward-McCann. 1938.
15. ————*Twenty and Ten,* as told by Janet Joly. Illustrated by William Pène du Bois. New York: Viking, 1964.
16. Bloch, Marie. *The Two Worlds of Damyan.* New York: Atheneum, 1966.
17. Boston, L. M. *The Treasure of Green Knowe.* New York: Harcourt, 1958.
18. Bradley, Duane. *Meeting with a Stranger.* Illustrated by E. Harper Johnson. Philadelphia: Lippincott, 1964.
19. Branley, Franklyn. *A Book of Astronauts for You.* Illustrated by Leonard Kessler. New York: Crowell, 1963.
20. Brewster, Benjamin. *The First Book of Baseball.* Illustrated by Jeanne Bendick. New York: F. Watts, 1963.
21. Brink, Carol Ryrie. *Caddie Woodlawn.* Illustrated by Kate Seredy. New York: Macmillan, 1936.
22. Brooke, Leslie. *Johnny Crow's Garden.* New York: Warne, 1963, 1903.
23. Brown, Marcia. *Backbone of the King.* New York: Scribner, 1966.
24. ————*Cinderella.* New York: Scribner, 1954.
25. Brown, Margaret Wise. *Goodnight Moon.* Illustrated by Clement Hurd. New York: Harper & Row, 1947.
26. ————*The Runaway Bunny.* Illustrated by Clement Hurd. New York: Harper & Row, 1942.
27. ————*Where Have You Been?* Illustrated by Barbara Cooney. New York: Hastings, 1963, 1952.
28. Brown, Myra Beery. *The First Night Away from Home.* Illustrated by Dorothy Marino. New York: F. Watts, 1960.
29. Buckley, Helen E. *Grandfather and I.* Illustrated by Paul Galdone. New York: Lothrop, 1959.
30. ————*The Little Boy and the Birthdays.* Illustrated by Paul Galdone. New York: Lothrop, 1965.
31. Budney, Blossom. *A Kiss Is Round.* Illustrated by Vladimir Bobri. New York: Lothrop, 1954.
32. Bulla, Clyde Robert. *Surprise for a Cowboy.* Illustrated by Grace Paull. New York: Crowell, 1950.
33. ————*The Sword in the Tree.* Illustrated by Paul Galdone. New York: Crowell, 1956.
34. ————*Viking Adventure.* Illustrated by Douglas Gorsline. New York: Crowell, 1963.
35. Burch, Robert. *D.J.'s Worst Enemy,* Illustrated by Emil Weiss. New York: Viking, 1965.
36. ————*Queenie Peavy.* Illustrated by Jerry Lazare. New York: Viking, 1966.
37. Burnett, Frances Hodgson. *The Secret Garden.* Illustrated by Tasha Tudor. Philadelphia: Lippincott, 1938, 1909.

38. Burnford, Sheila. *The Incredible Journey.* Illustrated by Carl Burger. Boston: Little, Brown, 1961.
39. Burton, Virginia Lee. *The Little House.* Boston: Houghton Mifflin, 1942.
40. ———*Mike Mulligan and His Steam Shovel.* Boston: Houghton Mifflin, 1939.
41. Carlson, Natalie Savage. *The Empty Schoolhouse.* Illustrated by John Kaufmann. New York: Harper & Row, 1965.
42. ———*The Happy Orpheline.* Illustrated by Garth Williams. New York: Harper & Row, 1957.
43. ———*The Letter on the Tree.* Illustrated by John Kaufmann. New York: Harper & Row, 1964.
44. Carroll, Lewis, pseud. (Charles L. Dodgson). *Alice's Adventures in Wonderland and Through the Looking-Glass.* Illustrated by John Tenniel. New York: Macmillan, 1963 (first published, separately, 1865 and 1872).
45. Carroll, Ruth. *What Whiskers Did.* New York: Walck, 1965.
46. Caudill, Rebecca. *The Best-Loved Doll.* Illustrated by Elliott Gilbert. New York: Holt, Rinehart and Winston, 1962.
47. ———*A Pocketful of Cricket.* Illustrated by Evaline Ness. New York: Holt, Rinehart and Winston, 1964.
48. *Childhood of Famous Americans* Series. Indianapolis: Bobbs-Merrill.
Examples:
Frisbee, Lucy Post. *John F. Kennedy: Young Statesman,* 1964.
Mason, Miriam E. *Dan Beard: Boy Scout,* 1953.
Stevenson, Augusta. *Sitting Bull: Dakota Boy,* 1956.
49. Clark, Ann Nolan. *Secret of the Andes.* Illustrated by Jean Charlot. New York: Viking, 1952.
50. Cleary, Beverly. *Beezus and Ramona.* Illustrated by Louis Darling. New York: Morrow, 1955.
51. ———*Ellen Tebbits.* Illustrated by Louis Darling. New York: Morrow, 1951.
52. ———*Henry Huggins.* Illustrated by Louis Darling. New York: Morrow, 1950.
53. Coatsworth, Elizabeth. *Jon, the Unlucky.* Illustrated by Esta Nesbitt. New York: Holt, Rinehart and Winston, 1964.
54. Colum, Padraic. *The Children of Odin.* Illustrated by Willy Pogany. New York: Macmillan, 1920.
55. Cone, Molly. *Mishmash.* Illustrated by Leonard Shortall. Boston: Houghton Mifflin, 1962.
56. Coombs, Patricia. *Dorrie's Magic.* New York: Lothrop, 1962.
57. Corbett, Scott. *The Lemonade Trick.* Boston: Little, Brown, 1960.
58. Cormack, M. B. *The First Book of Stones.* Illustrated by M. K. Scott. New York: F. Watts, 1950.
59. Craig, M. Jean. *Boxes.* Illustrated by Joe Lasker. New York: Norton, 1964.
60. ———*The Dragon in the Clock Box.* Illustrated by Kelly Oechsli. New York: Norton, 1962.
61. Dahl, Roald. *Charlie and the Chocolate Factory.* Illustrated by Joseph Schindelman. New York: Knopf, 1964.
62. Dalgliesh, Alice. *The Columbus Story.* Illustrated by Leo Politi. New York: Scribner, 1955.
63. ———*The Courage of Sarah Noble.* Illustrated by Leonard Weisgard. New York: Scribner, 1954.
64. De Angeli, Marguerite. *The Door in the Wall.* New York: Doubleday, 1949.
65. Defoe, Daniel. *Robinson Crusoe.* Illustrated by N. C. Wyeth. New York: Scribner, 1920, 1719.
66. DeJong, Meindert. *Far Out the Long Canal.* Illustrated by Nancy Grossman. New York: Harper & Row, 1964.
67. ———*The House of Sixty Fathers.* Illustrated by Maurice Sendak. New York: Harper & Row, 1954.

68. ————*Hurry Home, Candy.* Illustrated by Maurice Sendak. New York: Harper & Row, 1956.

69. ————*The Last Little Cat.* Illustrated by Jim McMullan. New York: Harper & Row, 1961.

70. ————*Shadrach.* Illustrated by Maurice Sendak. New York: Harper & Row, 1963.

71. De Regniers, Beatrice Schenk. *A Little House of Your Own.* Illustrated by Irene Haas. New York: Harcourt, 1954.

72. ————*May I Bring a Friend?* Illustrated by Beni Montresor. New York: Atheneum, 1964.

73. Dodge, Mary Mapes. *Hans Brinker, or The Silver Skates.* Illustrated by George Wharton Edwards. New York: Scribner, 1915, 1865.

74. Du Bois, William Pène. *The Alligator Case.* New York: Harper & Row, 1965.

75. ————*The Great Geppy.* New York: Viking, 1940.

76. ————*The Twenty-One Balloons.* New York: Viking, 1947.

77. Duvoisin, Roger. *Petunia.* New York: Knopf, 1950.

78. Earle, Olive L. *Crickets.* New York: Morrow, 1956.

79. Enright, Elizabeth. *Thimble Summer.* New York: Holt, Rinehart and Winston, 1938.

80. ————*Zeee,* Illustrated by Irene Haas. New York: Harcourt, 1965.

81. Epstein, Sam and Beryl. *The First Book of Codes and Ciphers.* Illustrated by Laszlo Roth. New York: F. Watts, 1956.

82. Estes, Eleanor. *The Hundred Dresses.* Illustrated by Louis Slobodkin. New York: Harcourt, 1944.

83. Ets, Marie Hall. *Just Me.* New York: Viking, 1965.

84. Faber, Doris. *Robert Frost, America's Poet.* Illustrated by Paul Frame. Englewood Cliffs, N.J.: Prentice-Hall, 1964.

85. Farley, Walter. *The Black Stallion.* Illustrated by Keith Ward. New York: Random House, 1941.

86. Farmer, Penelope. *The Summer Birds.* Illustrated by James Spanfeller. New York: Harcourt, 1962.

87. Felt, Sue. *Rosa-Too-Little.* New York: Doubleday, 1950.

88. Fisher, Aileen. *In the Middle of the Night.* Illustrated by Adrienne Adams. New York: Crowell, 1965.

89. Fitzhugh, Louise. *The Long Secret.* New York: Harper & Row, 1965.

90. Flack, Marjorie. *Angus and the Ducks.* New York: Doubleday, 1930.

91. ————*Ask Mr. Bear.* New York: Macmillan, 1932.

92. ————*The New Pet.* New York: Doubleday, 1943.

93. ————*The Story about Ping.* Illustrated by Kurt Wiese. New York: Viking, 1933.

94. ————*Wait for William.* Pictures by author and R. A. Holberg. Boston: Houghton Mifflin, 1935.

95. ————*Walter the Lazy Mouse.* Illustrated by Cyndy Szekeres. New York: Doubleday, 1963, 1937.

96. Forbes, Esther. *Johnny Tremain.* Illustrated by Lynd Ward. Boston: Houghton Mifflin, 1946.

97. Francoise, pseud. (Francoise Seignobosc). *The Things I Like.* New York: Scribner, 1960.

98. Fritz, Jean. *The Cabin Faced West.* Illustrated by Feodor Rojankovsky. New York: Coward-McCann, 1958.

99. Gág, Wanda. *Millions of Cats.* New York: Coward-McCann, 1928.

100. Garten, Jan. *The Alphabet Tale.* Illustrated by Muriel Bartherman. New York: Random House, 1964.

101. Gates, Doris. *Blue Willow.* Illustrated by Paul Lantz. New York: Viking, 1940.

102. George, Jean. *Gull 737.* New York: Crowell, 1964.

103. ————*My Side of the Mountain.* New York: Dutton, 1959.

104. Gipson, Fred. *Old Yeller.* Illustrated by Carl Burger. New York: Harper & Row, 1956.

105. Godden, Rumer. *Miss Happiness and Miss Flower.* Illustrated by Jean Primrose. New York: Viking, 1961.

106. Graham, Lorenz. *South Town.* Chicago: Follett, 1959.

107. Grahame, Kenneth. *The Wind in the Willows.* Illustrated by E. H. Shepard. New York: Scribner, 1908.

108. Gramatky, Hardie. *Little Toot.* New York: Putnam, 1939.

109. Greenaway, Kate. *Kate Greenaway's Birthday Book.* New York: Warne, 1880.

110. Griffiths, Helen. *The Wild Heart.* Illustrated by Victor Ambrus. New York: Doubleday, 1963.

111. Grimm, Jacob and Wilhelm. *The Seven Ravens.* Illustrated by Felix Hoffman. New York: Harcourt, 1963.

112. Gruenberg, Sidonie Matsner. *The Wonderful Story of How You Were Born.* Illustrated by Hildegard Woodward. New York: Doubleday, 1959.

113. Hader, Berta and Elmer. *The Big Snow.* New York: Macmillan, 1948.

114. Halmi, Robert. *Visit to a Chief's Son.* New York: Holt, Rinehart and Winston, 1963.

115. Harnden, Ruth. *The High Pasture.* Illustrated by Vee Guthrie. Boston: Houghton Mifflin, 1964.

116. Haywood, Carolyn. *"B" Is for Betsy* Series. New York: Harcourt.
"B" Is for Betsy, 1939.
Back to School with Betsy, 1943.
Betsy and Billy, 1941.
Betsy and the Boys, 1945.
Betsy and the Circus, 1954.
Betsy's Busy Summer, 1956.
Betsy's Little Star, 1950.
Betsy's Winterhouse, 1958.
Snowbound with Betsy, 1962.

117. ———*Little Eddie* Series. New York: Morrow.
Annie Pat and Eddie, 1960.
Eddie and Gardenia, 1951.
Eddie and His Big Deals, 1955.
Eddie and Louella, 1959.
Eddie and the Fire Engine, 1949.
Eddie Makes Music, 1957.
Eddie's Green Thumb, 1964.
Eddie's Pay Dirt, 1953.
Little Eddie, 1947.

118. Haugaard, Erik Christian. *Hakon of Rogen's Saga.* Boston: Houghton Mifflin, 1963.

119. Hawes, Judy. *Fireflies in the Night.* Illustrated by Kazue Mizumura. New York: Crowell, 1963.

120. Heinlein, Robert. *Orphans of the Sky.* New York: Putnam, 1964.

121. Henry, Marguerite. *King of the Wind.* Illustrated by Wesley Dennis. Skokie, Ill.: Rand McNally, 1948.

122. ———*Misty of Chincoteague.* Illustrated by Wesley Dennis. Skokie, Ill.: Rand McNally, 1947.

123. Hicks, Clifford. *Alvin's Secret Code.* Illustrated by Bill Sobol. New York: Holt, Rinehart and Winston, 1963.

124. Hoban, Russell. *Bedtime for Frances.* Illustrated by Garth Williams. New York: Harper & Row, 1960.

125. ———*The Sorely Trying Day.* Illustrated by Lillian Hoban. New York: Harper & Row, 1964.

126. Hoff, Syd. *Danny and the Dinosaur.* New York: Harper & Row, 1958.

127. Holl, Adelaide. *The Rain Puddle.* Illustrated by Roger Duvoisin. New York: Lothrop, 1965.

128. Hope, Laura Lee, pseud. *The Bobbsey Twins.* New York: Grosset & Dunlap, 1910.

129. Houston, James. *Tiktá Liktak*. New York: Harcourt, 1965.
130. Hunt, Irene. *Across Five Aprils*. Chicago: Follett, 1964.
131. Ish-Kishor, S. *A Boy of Old Prague*. New York: Pantheon, 1963.
132. James, Will. *Smoky, the Cow Horse*. New York: Scribner, 1965, 1926.
133. Janus, Grete. *Teddy*. Illustrated by Roger Duvoisin. New York: Lothrop, 1964.
134. Joslin, Sesyle. *What Do You Say, Dear?* Illustrated by Maurice Sendak. New York: W. R. Scott, 1958.
135. Judson, Clara Ingram. *Mr. Justice Holmes*. Illustrated by Robert Todd. Chicago: Follett, 1956.
136. Juster, Norton. *The Phantom Tollbooth*. Illustrated by Jules Feiffer. New York: Random House, 1961.
137. Kahl, Virginia. *The Duchess Bakes a Cake*. New York: Scribner, 1955.
138. Kauffman, Lois. *What's That Noise?* Illustrated by Allan Eitzen. New York: Lothrop, 1965.
139. Keats, Ezra Jack. *The Snowy Day*. New York: Viking, 1962.
140. ————*Whistle for Willie*. New York: Viking, 1964.
141. Keene, Carolyn, pseud. *Nancy Drew* Series. New York: Grosset & Dunlap. *The Message in the Hollow Oak*, 1935, etc.
142. Kettelkamp, Larry. *Kites*. New York: Morrow, 1959.
143. Kingsley, Charles. *The Water-Babies*, Kathleen Lines, Editor. Illustrated by Harold Jones. New York: F. Watts, 1961, 1863.
144. Kipling, Rudyard. *The Jungle Book*. Illustrated by Philip Hays. New York: Doubleday, 1894.
145. Krasilovsky, Phyllis. *The Man Who Didn't Wash His Dishes*. Illustrated by Barbara Cooney. New York: Doubleday, 1950.
146. Krauss, Ruth. *The Growing Story*. Illustrated by Phyllis Rowand. New York: Harper & Row, 1947.
147. ————*A Very Special House*. Illustrated by Maurice Sendak. New York: Harper & Row, 1953.
148. Krumgold, Joseph. *. . . And Now Miguel*. Illustrated by Jean Charlot. New York: Crowell, 1953.
149. ————*Onion John*. Illustrated by Symeon Shimin. New York: Crowell, 1959.
150. Kugelmass, J. Alvin. *Ralph J. Bunche, Fighter for Peace*. New York: Messner, 1962.
151. Kumin, Maxine W. *The Beach before Breakfast*. Illustrated by Leonard Weisgard. New York: Putnam, 1964.
152. Kunhardt, Dorothy. *Pat the Bunny*. New York: Golden Press, 1962, 1940.
153. ————*Tickle the Pig*. New York: Golden Press, 1964.
154. Kuskin, Karla. *Just Like Everyone Else*. New York: Harper & Row, 1959.
155. Lawson, Robert. *McWhinney's Jaunt*. Boston: Little, Brown, 1951.
156. ————*Rabbit Hill*. New York: Viking, 1945.
157. L'Engle, Madeleine. *Meet the Austins*. New York: Vanguard, 1961.
158. ————*Moon by Night*. New York: Farrar, Straus, 1963.
159. ————*A Wrinkle in Time*. New York: Farrar, Straus, 1962.
160. Lenski, Lois. *Papa Small*. New York: Walck, 1951.
161. ————*Shoo-Fly Girl*. Philadelphia: Lippincott, 1963.
162. ————*Strawberry Girl*. Philadelphia: Lippincott, 1945.
163. Levine, Milton, and Jean H. Seligmann. *A Baby Is Born: The Story of How Life Begins*, Illustrated by Eloise Wilkin. New York: Golden Press, 1949.
164. Lewis, C. S. *The Last Battle*, Illustrated by Pauline Baynes. New York: Macmillan, 1956.
165. ————*The Lion, the Witch, and the Wardrobe*. Illustrated by Pauline Baynes. New York: Macmillan, 1950.
166. Lexau, Joan. *Benjie*. Illustrated by Don Bolognese. New York: Dial, 1964.
167. ————*Maria*. Illustrated by Ernest Crichlow. New York: Dial, 1964.
168. Lindgren, Astrid. *Pippi Longstocking*. Translated from the Swedish by Florence Lamborn. Illustrated by Louis S. Glanzman. New York: Viking, 1950.

169. Lionni, Leo. *Tico and the Golden Wings.* New York: Pantheon, 1964.

170. Little, Jean. *Home from Far.* Boston: Little, Brown, 1965.

171. Lopshire, Robert. *How to Make Flibbers.* New York: Random House, 1964.

172. Lord, Beman. *Quarterback's Aim.* Illustrated by Arnold Spilka. New York: Walck, 1960.

173. Lovelace, Maud Hart. *Betsy-Tacy* Series. New York: Crowell.
Betsy and Joe, 1948.
Betsy and Tacy Go Downtown. Illustrated by Lois Lenski, 1943.
Betsy and Tacy Go over the Big Hill. Illustrated by Lois Lenski, 1942.
Betsy and the Great World. Illustrated by Vera Neville, 1952.
Betsy in Spite of Herself. Illustrated by Vera Neville, 1946.
Betsy-Tacy. Illustrated by Lois Lenski, 1940.
Betsy-Tacy and Tib. Illustrated by Lois Lenski, 1941.
Betsy Was a Junior. Illustrated by Vera Neville, 1947.
Betsy's Wedding. Illustrated by Vera Neville, 1955.
Heaven to Betsy. Illustrated by Vera Neville, 1945.

174. Lowrey, Janette. *The Poky Little Puppy.* Illustrated by Gustaf Tenggren. New York: Golden Press, 1945.

175. McCloskey, Robert. *Homer Price.* New York: Viking, 1943.

176. ———*One Morning in Maine.* New York: Viking, 1952.

177. ———*Time of Wonder.* New York: Viking, 1957.

178. McClung, Robert M. *Sphinx.* New York: Morrow. 1949.

179. MacDonald, Betty. *Mrs. Piggle Wiggle.* Illustrated by Hilary Knight. Revised edition; Philadelphia: Lippincott, 1957.

180. MacDonald, George. *Sir Gibbie.* Elizabeth Yates, Editor. New York: Dutton, 1963.

181. MacDonald, Golden, pseud. (Margaret Wise Brown). *Little Frightened Tiger.* Illustrated by Leonard Weisgard. New York: Doubleday, 1953.

182. MacGregor, Ellen. *Miss Pickerell* Series. Illustrated by Paul Galdone. New York: McGraw-Hill.
Miss Pickerell and the Geiger Counter, 1953.
Miss Pickerell Goes to Mars, 1951.
Miss Pickerell Goes to the Arctic, 1954.
Miss Pickerell Goes Undersea, 1953.

183. McNeer, May. *America's Abraham Lincoln.* Illustrated by Lynd Ward. Boston: Houghton Mifflin, 1957.

184. Martell, Suzanne. *The City under Ground.* Illustrated by Don Sibley. New York: Viking, 1964.

185. Massie, Diane. *The Baby Beebee Bird.* New York: Harper & Row, 1963.

186. Matsuno, Masako. *Taro and the Tofu.* Illustrated by Kazue Mizumura. Cleveland: World Publishing, 1962.

187. Meader, Stephen W. *River of the Wolves.* Illustrated by Edward Shenton. New York: Harcourt, 1948.

188. Merrill, Jean. *Tell about the Cowbarn, Daddy.* Illustrated by Lili C. Wronker. New York: W. R. Scott, 1963.

189. Milne, A. A. *The House at Pooh Corner.* Illustrated by Ernest H. Shepard. New York: Dutton, 1928.

190. ———*Winnie the Pooh.* Illustrated by Ernest H. Shepard. New York: Dutton, 1926.

191. Minarik, Else Holmelund. *Little Bear.* Illustrated by Maurice Sendak. New York: Harper & Row, 1957.

192. Mirsky, Reba. *Nomusa and the New Magic.* Chicago: Follett, 1962.

193. Munari, Bruno. *Who's There? Open the Door!* Cleveland: World Publishing, 1957.

194. Myrick, Mildred. *The Secret Three.* Illustrated by Arnold Lobel. New York: Harper & Row, 1963.

195. Neville, Emily. *Berries Goodman.* New York: Harper & Row, 1965.

196. ———*It's Like This, Cat.* New York: Harper & Row, 1963.

197. Newell, Hope. *The Little Old Woman Who Used Her Head.* Illustrated by Margaret Ruse. Camden, N.J.: Nelson, 1962.

198. North, Sterling. *Rascal.* Illustrated by John Schoenherr. New York: Dutton, 1963.

199. Norton, Mary. *The Borrowers* Series. Illustrated by Beth and Joe Krush. New York: Harcourt.
The Borrowers, 1953.
The Borrowers Afield, 1955.
The Borrowers Afloat, 1959.
The Borrowers Aloft, 1961.

200. O'Dell, Scott. *Island of the Blue Dolphins.* Boston: Houghton Mifflin, 1960.

201. Palmer, Helen. *Do You Know What I'm Going to Do Next Saturday?* Photos by Lynn Fayman. New York: Random House, 1963.

202. Parish, Peggy. *Amelia Bedelia.* Illustrated by Fritz Siebel. New York: Harper & Row, 1963.

203. Petrides, Heidrun. *Hans and Peter.* New York: Harcourt, 1963.

204. Potter, Beatrix. *The Tale of Peter Rabbit.* New York: Warne, 1902.

205. Rand, Ann and Paul. *I Know a Lot of Things.* Illustrated by Paul Rand. New York: Harcourt, 1956.

206. Rawlings, Marjorie Kinnan. *The Yearling.* Illustrated by N. C. Wyeth. New York: Scribner, 1961, 1939.

207. Renick, Marion. *Nicky's Football Team.* Illustrated by Marian Honigman. New York: Scribner, 1951.

208. Ressner, Phil. *August Explains.* Illustrated by Crosby Bonsall. New York: Harper & Row, 1963.

209. Rey, Hans A. *Curious George Gets a Medal.* Boston: Houghton Mifflin, 1957.

210. ————*Where's My Baby?* Boston: Houghton Mifflin, 1956.

211. Reyher, Becky. *My Mother Is the Most Beautiful Woman in the World.* Illustrated by Ruth Gannett. New York: Lothrop, 1945.

212. Robertson, Keith. *Henry Reed's Journey.* Illustrated by Robert McCloskey. New York: Viking, 1963.

213. Salten, Felix. *Bambi.* New York: Grosset & Dunlap, 1929.

214. Sauer, Julia L. *Mike's House.* Illustrated by Don Freeman. New York: Viking, 1954.

215. Sawyer, Ruth. *Journey Cake, Ho!* Illustrated by Robert McCloskey. New York: Viking, 1953.

216. Scheer, Julian. *Rain Makes Applesauce.* Illustrated by Marvin Bileck. New York: Holiday, 1964.

217. Schiffer, Don. *The First Book of Swimming.* New York: F. Watts, 1960.

218. Selsam, Millicent. *All about Eggs.* Illustrated by Helen Ludwig. New York: W. R. Scott, 1952.

219. ————*Animals as Parents.* Illustrated by John Kaufmann. New York: Morrow, 1965.

220. Sendak, Maurice. *The Nutshell Library.* New York: Harper & Row, 1962.

221. ————*Where the Wild Things Are.* New York: Harper & Row, 1963.

222. Seredy, Kate. *The Good Master.* New York: Viking, 1935.

223. Seuss, Dr., pseud. (Theodor S. Geisel). *The Cat in the Hat.* New York: Random House, 1957.

224. Sewell, Anna. *Black Beauty.* Illustrated by John Beer. New York: Dodd, Mead, 1941, 1877.

225. Sharp, Margery. *Miss Bianca.* Illustrated by Garth Williams. Boston: Little, Brown, 1962.

226. Showers, Paul. *The Listening Walk.* Illustrated by Aliki. New York: Crowell, 1961.

227. Simon, Charlie. *All Men Are Brothers, A Portrait of Albert Schweitzer.* New York: Dutton, 1956.

228. Slobodkin, Louis. *The Space Ship under the Apple Tree.* New York: Macmillan, 1952.

229. Sommerfelt, Aimée. *Miriam*. New York: Criterion, 1963.
230. ———*The White Bungalow*. Illustrated by Ulf Aas. New York: Criterion, 1963.
231. Sorensen, Virginia. *Miracles on Maple Hill*. Illustrated by Beth and Joe Krush. New York: Harcourt, 1956.
232. ———*Plain Girl*. Illustrated by Charles Geer. New York: Harcourt, 1955.
233. Speare, Elizabeth George. *The Bronze Bow*. Boston: Houghton Mifflin, 1961.
234. Sperry, Armstrong. *Call It Courage*. New York: Macmillan, 1941.
235. Spyri, Johanna. *Heidi*. Translated by Helen B. Dole. Illustrated by William Sharp. New York: Grosset & Dunlap, 1945, 1884.
236. Steele, William O. *The Lone Hunt*. Illustrated by Paul Galdone. New York: Harcourt, 1956.
237. ———*The Perilous Road*. Illustrated by Paul Galdone. New York: Harcourt, 1958.
238. ———*The Spooky Thing*. Illustrated by Paul Coker. New York: Harcourt, 1960.
239. ———*Winter Danger*. Illustrated by Paul Galdone. New York: Harcourt, 1954.
240. Steiner, Charlotte. *Listen to My Seashell*. New York: Knopf, 1959.
241. Stevenson, Robert Louis. *Treasure Island*. Illustrated by N. C. Wyeth. New York: Scribner, 1939, 1883.
242. Stolz, Mary. *The Bully of Barkham Street*. Illustrated by Leonard Shortall. New York: Harper & Row, 1963.
243. Stong, Phil. *Honk the Moose*. Illustrated by Kurt Wiese. New York: Dodd, Mead, 1955, 1935.
244. Travers, Pamela L. *Mary Poppins*. Illustrated by Mary Shepard. New York: Harcourt, 1934.
245. Trease, Geoffrey. *No Boats on Bannermere*. Illustrated by Richard Kennedy. New York: Norton, 1965.
246. Tresselt, Alvin. *The Mitten*. Illustrated by Yaroslava. New York: Lothrop, 1964.
247. Twain, Mark, pseud. (Samuel Clemens). *The Adventures of Huckleberry Finn*. New York: Harper & Row, 1884.
248. ———*The Adventures of Tom Sawyer*. New York: Harper & Row, 1876.
249. Udry, Janice May. *Let's Be Enemies*. Illustrated by Maurice Sendak. New York: Harper & Row, 1961.
250. ———*A Tree Is Nice*. Illustrated by Marc Simont. New York: Harper & Row, 1956.
251. Vogel, Ilse-Margaret. *The Don't Be Scared Book*. New York: Atheneum, 1964.
252. Ward, Lynd. *The Biggest Bear*. Boston: Houghton Mifflin, 1952.
253. Watson, Jane Werner. *The Iliad and the Odyssey*. Illustrated by Alice and Martin Provensen. New York: Golden Press, 1956.
254. White, E. B. *Charlotte's Web*. Illustrated by Garth Williams. New York: Harper & Row, 1952.
255. Wilder, Laura Ingalls. *Little House* Series. Illustrated by Garth Williams. New York: Harper & Row, 1953.
    By the Shores of Silver Lake, 1939.
    The Little House in the Big Woods, 1932.
    Little House on the Prairie, 1935.
    Little Town on the Prairie, 1941.
    The Long Winter, 1940.
    On the Banks of Plum Creek, 1937.
    These Happy Golden Years, 1943.
256. Williams, Jay, and Raymond Abrashkin. *Danny Dunn, Time Traveler*. Illustrated by Owen Kampen. New York: McGraw-Hill, 1963.
257. Wojciechowska, Maia. *Shadow of a Bull*. New York: Atheneum, 1964.
258. Wyss, Johann. *The Swiss Family Robinson*. Illustrated by Lynd Ward. New York: Grosset & Dunlap, 1949, 1913.
259. Yashima, Taro, pseud. (Jun Iwamatsu). *Crow Boy*. New York: Viking, 1955.

260. ———*Umbrella*. New York: Viking, 1958.

261. Yates, Elizabeth. *Amos Fortune, Free Man*. Illustrated by Nora Unwin. New York: Dutton, 1950.

262. ———*Mountain Born*. Illustrated by Nora Unwin. New York: Coward-McCann, 1943.

263. Zim, Herbert. *Golden Hamsters*. Illustrated by Herschel Wartik. New York: Morrow, 1951.

264. ———*How Things Grow*. Illustrated by Gustav Schrotter. New York: Morrow, 1960.

265. Zion, Gene. *The Meanest Squirrel I Ever Met*. Illustrated by Margaret Bloy Graham. New York: Scribner, 1962.

266. Zolotow, Charlotte. *Do You Know What I'll Do?* Illustrated by Garth Williams. New York: Harper & Row, 1958.

267. ———*Over and Over*. Illustrated by Garth Williams. New York: Harper & Row, 1951.

268. ———*The Quarreling Book*. Illustrated by Arnold Lobel. New York: Harper & Row, 1963.

269. ———*Someday*. Illustrated by Arnold Lobel. New York: Harper & Row, 1964.

270. ———*A Tiger called Thomas*. Illustrated by Kurt Werth. New York: Lothrop, 1963.

271. ———*The White Marble*. Illustrated by Lilian Obligado. New York: Abelard-Schuman, 1963.

2

CHILDREN'S BOOKS OF THE PAST

"Boy, we had a good time," Ken exclaimed as he bounced into the Dryden living room with eleven-year-old energy. "See the neat books I bought with my birthday money from Grandmother!" Ken opened the package to show *Retreat to Glory: The Story of Sam Houston* and two paperbacks, *The Incredible Journey* and *Science in Your Back Yard.* Ken's grandmother Dryden, aged sixty, and his eighty-two-year-old Great Aunt Marian admired his choices.

"Children today do have wonderful books compared to those in my time," said Great Aunt Marian. "Just look at this living room! No, I don't mean the mess, Elizabeth, I mean the books you and John read, the books the children own, and the books you bring home from the library."

The adults looked around the pleasant room with sudden awareness of the wide variety of reading material. Three-year-old Nancy had her new picture books from the library. Janey at seven had her own shelf of favorites and made independent trips to the neighborhood library. There were news magazines, women's magazines, a journal about records and music, a gardening magazine, and two literary periodicals in addition to John Dryden's professional journals. The book shelves contained old favorites and some of the new novels, poetry, history, biography, and an encyclopedia for the children.

"But this has always been a 'reading' family," said Grandmother Dryden. "John and his brothers and sisters read a great deal when they were young — actually more than these children do because they didn't have television."

"But John's children do read a great deal, I've noticed," Aunt Marian remarked. "The books are certainly wonderful, compared to the ones I had — and

57

they're even much better than the literature you and Elizabeth had, John."

"What were some of your favorites, Aunt Marian?" Ken's mother asked. "What kinds of books did you read when you were Janey's and Ken's age?"

"They were certainly not attractive," she reminisced. "Oh, there were a few black and white sketches, but little action—very seldom any color. I can recall *Robinson Crusoe, Treasure Island*, and *Alice in Wonderland*, of course. I loved *Swiss Family Robinson* when Father read it aloud. Then I read things my brothers liked, too—*Hans Brinker, Tom Sawyer, Black Beauty*."

"Why we are still reading some of those books!" exclaimed Ken. "What else did you have in the olden days, Aunt Marian?"

She chuckled and went on, recalling books at the turn of the century. "I remember reading some of the 'penny dreadfuls' as they were called. Jack Harkaway had exciting adventures in those cheap books. Then there was the *Five Little Peppers* series—oh, yes, we had series books, too. And fantasy, I liked *The Water Babies* and the fairy tales by Grimm. Ken, we had a marvelous science fiction book, *Twenty Thousand Leagues Under the Sea. Heidi* and *Little Women* were favorites—you have them on your shelf, too."

"The wonderful part is that the good books of our days live on. But there are so many now," added Grandmother Dryden. "John enjoyed the same *Johnny Crow's Garden* and *The Tale of Peter Rabbit* which Mother read to me, and now my grandchildren enjoy them."

"What did you like to read when you were a little girl, Grandma?" asked Janey.

"Many of the books Aunt Marian named were my favorites, too," she answered. "I liked *The Secret Garden* and *The Wonderful Adventures of Nils.* Mother read *The Wind in the Willows* aloud, and I loved it. And I liked *The Wizard of Oz* books, too. Then, we all looked forward to *St. Nicholas* magazine each month."

"I was just thinking how many you have mentioned were books I enjoyed, too, but I don't feel I had nearly the opportunities to enjoy picture books," Ken's mother added. "I loved *The Secret Garden* and *Winnie the Pooh*. Later there were the *Little House* books. My copies of *Caddie Woodlawn* and *The Good Master* are being saved for Janey. And I read series books, too, *The Bobbsey Twins*, for example. But I'm sure we didn't have lovely picture books like these Nancy can enjoy before going to school."

"And we didn't have your exciting books of science or paperbacks, Ken," said his father.

Through this discussion of books that had been enjoyed by three generations of one family, it is easy to note changes in literature for children. The Drydens were aware of changes in the quantity of books and general format. They were also aware of the heritage of good literature that children in each generation continue to enjoy.

The elementary teacher can better appreciate the richness of children's literature today by tracing the development of these varied types of books for children. Meigs wrote of the importance of knowledge of the development of literature:

> To be aware of the greatness of a literature is not always to understand it fully, since to have interest and regard for it does not imply entire knowledge of what it is and how it came to be. But if thinking people are to have any part in shaping the literature of the present and the future, they should have a fuller understanding of it as a whole and of its past.[1]

Children's literature developed in accordance with the changing attitudes of society toward children and changing cultural values. The literature available for children reflects the attitudes of society in that period. Books for children have always been viewed as instruments for transmitting the mores of the culture and for inculcating attitudes and values. For example, colonial children were treated as miniature adults, not as developing personalities, important in their own right. When Joseph Downing published the first catalog of books for children and young people, *The Young Christians Library* (1710), he stressed the idea that the purpose of such books was to foster the health of the child's soul. Children were admonished to avoid "books, ballads, songs, sonettes, and ditties of dalliance."

Today, as in the past, adults write the books; adults print the books; teachers, librarians, parents, and gift-givers review and select most of the books children read. Hazard says children defend themselves, ". . . when they have singled out a work that they like and have decided to take possession of it, nothing can make them change their minds. . . . It is that book there that they want, that very one and not its neighbor."[2] Children *are* the final arbiters of books

they will read, but Sloane reminds us that "It is impossible to determine precisely how much of the change that occurred in children's literature was due to increasing sagacity of adults and how much was due to increasing demands of children."[3] As society changed its attitude toward children, the didactic and dour became the fanciful and "precious." Adults became more aware of children's demands for informational books and adventure. In addition, the changing attitudes, values, philosophies, and concepts of man and the universe are reflected in children's books. An understanding of the growth of children's literature as part of a developing culture will enable the classroom teacher to better evaluate children's books of today.

CHILDREN'S BOOKS: SEVENTEENTH AND EIGHTEENTH CENTURIES

Background

To that "stern and rock-bound coast" the early colonists brought old-world concepts and philosophies that would yield to new-world pressures and needs. Traditional Christian theism held that children were born in sin, that eternal salvation could come only to the elect, and that eternal punishment would be meted out to the sinner. Voting rights and office-holding privileges were reserved for members of the church. Children were viewed as miniature adults who learned obedience to authority through fear.

By the middle of the eighteenth century, there was a shift from knowledge based upon religious sanctions to knowledge derived from human investigation. Newton, Bacon, Copernicus, Kepler, and Galileo had

---

[1]Cornelia Meigs, Editor, *A Critical History of Children's Literature* (New York: Macmillan, 1953), p. 3.
[2]Paul Hazard, *Books Children and Men* (Boston: Horn Book, 1947), p. 51.

[3]William Sloane, *Children's Books in England and America in the Seventeenth Century* (New York: Kings Crown, 1955), p. 17.

challenged the divine laws and authoritarian reasoning, and had shown the way toward a method of science. Apparent natural laws suggested the study of nature and human nature. Locke stated that human nature was at least partially the result of the environment; Rousseau emphasized the natural unfolding of a child nature which he believed to be inherently good.

Concurrently, an agrarian feudalism was changing to commercial capitalism. There was a growing middle class; the emphasis upon trade led to new educational needs. Some of the religious sects introduced social reform and emphasized teaching children through love. Colonial government had been based upon the view that only the few "godly" men should rule; the changing eighteenth-century view held that government should be based upon the natural rights of all men.

By the end of the century, the idea of individual rights of the child was being recognized. Life was often uncomfortable and rigorous in this new land, and there were few books for adults or children to relieve the drabness of living.

Books of the American Colonial Period

What books were packed in the chests that came across the Atlantic with the early colonists? The Bible was a treasured book of those who could afford to have one. Perhaps a copy of William Caxton's 1497 book, *The Book of Courtesye* was owned by some colonists. This was a description of the typical day of the well-bred English child. Another book of manners was *Youth's Behavior*, translated from the French in 1636. Here one could read how to dress properly, how to walk, how to remove fleas tactfully, how to dispose of bones neatly, and other niceties of life. *Properties of Things*, printed by Wynken de Worde in 1495, gave the names of parts of the body, plants, mountains, and diseases. Caxton also printed *Aesop's Fables* in 1484, using many woodcuts.

Probably some of the colonists owned at least one of the bestiaries, animal tales that combined elements of fable and scripture. Topsel's *The History of Four-Footed Beasts* (1658) is an example of these books about dragons, unicorns, and other strange creatures. The first picture book planned for children was written by Comenius in 1657. Perhaps a few colonists brought the 1658 English translation of this book, *Orbus Pictus*, with its woodcuts illustrating everyday objects.

Just before sailing, a colonist might have purchased a chapbook from a peddler. These were very small, inexpensive paper booklets sold by peddlers or chapmen. "A ballad of a most strange wedding of the froggee and the mouse" had been licensed in 1580. In a collection published in the 1680s, may be found *Tom Thumb, Guy of Warwick,* and accounts of crimes and executions, descriptions of the art of making love, and riddles. The earliest known edition of *Jack the Giant Killer* seems to be a chapbook printed in 1711.

The religious leaders could give approval to the moral and religious instruction in John Bunyan's *Pilgrim's Progress,* first printed in 1678. No doubt children skipped the long theological dialogues as they found adventure by traveling with the clearly defined characters.

Early writers and educators often thought that words of wisdom and lectures instilling good manners and a righteous way of life could best be given children in verse form. Their recognition of the child's delight in rhythm and rhyme was a step toward a literature for children. This trend was exemplified by the eight pages of rhymed couplets describing the wares of the peddler-author, Thomas Newbery, entitled, *A Booke in Englysh Metre, of the great Marchante Man called Dives Pragmaticus, very preaty for children to reade* (1563). John Bunyan gave emblematic lessons in his verses about everyday objects and nature, *A Book for Boys and Girls or Country Rhymes for Children* (1696). The emblem books provided examples of the good and dutiful life through symbols:

This bee an Emblem truly is of Sin,
Whose Sweet unto many a Death hath been.

A 1679 title reflects the purpose of such books, *The Prodigal Son Sifted, or the lewd life and lamentable end of extravagant persons emblematically set forth, for a warning to unexperienced youth.*

Mother Goose

There is reassurance in the knowledge that children who experienced the hardships of the seventeenth and eighteenth centuries had access to the nonsense and gaiety of Mother Goose. The Mother Goose verses apparently originated in the spoken language of the common folk and royalty. Some have been traced as far back as the pre-Christian era. A few writers hold the theory that "Jack and Jill" refers to the waxing and waning of the moon. It is believed that many of the verses were written as political satires or told of royal tragedy. "Pussycat, Pussycat," for example, was based upon an incident in Queen Elizabeth's court. "Three Wise Men of Gotham" reflects stories of the foolish inhabitants of Gotham before the days of King John. Thomas cites the account of a deed in the possession of a Horner family signed by Henry VIII that was a "plum" pulled out of the pie—the King's collection of deeds.[4] However, other scholars have found little evidence of these relationships.[5]

The name of Mother Goose was first associated with folk tales rather than the verses known today. In 1697, Charles Perrault published in France a collection of nursery tales that included "Cinderella," "Red Riding

Forerunner of cartoon style in a woodcut used to illustrate an early chapbook of *Sir Richard Whittington*. From *Illustrators of Children's Books, 1744–1945*, by Bertha E. Mahony, *et al.* Courtesy of Horn Book, 1947.

Hood," "Puss in Boots," and "Sleeping Beauty." The frontispiece showed an old woman spinning and telling stories to children. The caption read, "Contes de ma Mere l'Oye" (Tales of Mother Goose). These tales were brought to England and translated about 1729.[6] According to French legends, two Berthas may have been Mother Goose. One, called goose-footed, was known to tell stories to children. Another was rumored to have borne a child with the head of a goose.

While the Revolutionary War was in progress, an American publisher, Isaiah Thomas, somehow obtained Newbery's books for children. These smuggled books were reprinted with few changes; thus, *Mother Goose, The History of Little Goody Two Shoes,* and *Robinson Crusoe* became available for children of the new country. No copies of this 1785 edition of Mother Goose are now extant, but a reproduction by W. H. Whitmore was published in 1889.

[4]Katherine Elwes Thomas, *The Real Personages of Mother Goose* (New York: Lothrop, 1930).
[5]Iona and Peter Opie, *The Oxford Nursery Rhyme Book* (London: Oxford University Press, 1952). William S. and Ceil Baring-Gould, *The Annotated Mother Goose* (New York: Charles N. Potter, 1962).

[6]Baring-Gould, p. 149.

The legend that Dame Goose is buried in Boston is kept alive for tourists and children who visit the Boston burying ground, but it has created confusion regarding the origin of the verses. Even the publication of *Songs for the Nursery; or Mother Goose's Melodies* by the son-in-law of Dame Goose has become a legend. According to the story, Thomas Fleet tired of the good woman's frequent renditions of the ditties as she cared for his children, so he decided to collect and publish them. There has been no actual evidence of this 1719 edition.

The Comic Adventures of Old Mother Hubbard and Her Dog, by Sarah Martin, first appeared in 1805. In that same year, *Songs from the Nursery Collected by the Most Renowned Poets* was published. For the first time, "Little Miss Muffet" and "One, Two, Buckle My Shoe" appeared in print.

Folk Tales and Adventure

Handed down by word of mouth for centuries, folk tales were among the first types of literature to be printed. It is difficult to find the point at which they were considered suitable *only* for the young. In France, Charles Perrault recorded eight fairy tales for adults at court. *Puss in Boots, Sleeping Beauty, Cinderella*, and *Little Red Riding Hood* were included. For the first time, tales were written so children, too, could hear them over and over in exactly the same words.

The Arabian Nights is another collection of old tales that came from India, Persia, and North Africa. Galland published these tales in 1704, and it appears they were available in English translation in 1712. Ridley also published a series of tales modeled after the Arabian Nights under the title, *The Tales of the Genii* (1766).

In the first half of the seventeenth century, stories of St. George, St. Patrick, and other knights were roughly printed on 12-by-18-inch sheets. Also, small gilt books were popular with children and adults. For example, *The History of Cajanus, The Swedish Giant*, was printed in 1742 on $3\frac{1}{4}$-by-$2\frac{1}{4}$-inch sheets and bound in floral Dutch gilt boards.

Defoe did not write his account of the eighteenth-century hero, Robinson Crusoe, for children, but they made his story part of their literature. *The Life and Strange and Surprising Adventures of Robinson Crusoe* (1719) was later printed in an abridged and pocket-sized volume that became a "classic" of children's literature. *Gulliver's Travels* was a scathing satire of high society, yet young and old alike enjoyed this tale published in 1726. Perhaps children recognized themselves as dwarfs or giants. The forerunner of the modern superman may be identified in the stories of *Tommy Trip* written by John Newbery in 1759. In one story, Tommy Trip, the size of Tom Thumb, challenges and defeats a giant who tormented a child.

Newbery Publishes for Children

Although there was strong emphasis upon religious literature, it is apparent that the colonists and their children enjoyed the chapbooks. These little books of sixteen, thirty-two, or sixty-four pages were small, folded booklets that might be compared to modern comics. Ballads about Guy of Warwick, Bevis of Southhampton, and Robin Hood brought adventure to drab lives. Although children took these books for their own, it was not until 1744 that John Newbery published a book especially designed for children. The title page notes, *A Little Pretty Pocketbook*, "Intended for the Instruction and Amusement of Little Master Tommy and Pretty Miss Polly, with an agreeable Letter to read from Jack the Giant Killer, as also a Ball and a Pincushion, the use of which will infallibly make Tommy a good Boy, and Polly a good Girl." The advertisement in his shop, The Bible and Sun, said, "The books are to be given away, only the binding is to be paid for." For parents, the book included Locke's advice on children.

No documentary evidence is available to determine whether John Newbery or Oliver Goldsmith wrote *The History of Little Goody Two Shoes*, published by Newbery in 1766. Records do show that Newbery gave Goldsmith lodging above his shop, and it is probable that Goldsmith was author of some of the two hundred books published by Newbery. In this story of righteousness, Margery Meanwell, turned out of her own home by a grasping villain, became a teacher who moralized as she taught children to read. Eventually, she married a rich gentleman and carried on her good works.

Newbery's books emphasized love rather than the wrath and punishment of God. The gilt-paper covers of his small books were gay, but the moral lessons were still plain to the young readers who came to this first juvenile bookstore operated by Newbery from 1745 to 1767.

Books of Instruction

With the invention of the Horn book, English and Colonial children were able to handle their own books. A sheet of paper printed with the alphabet, vowels, the Lord's prayer, and Roman numerals was fastened to a small board about 2¾ by 5 inches. The parchment was covered with transparent horn and bound with strips of brass. Sometimes, a hole in the handle made it possible for the child to carry the book on a cord around his neck or waist. Colonial children learned to read from the Horn book.

Shortly after the middle of the eighteenth century, the battledore was developed. This consisted of a cardboard folded with three leaves. There were no religious teachings, but alphabets, numerals, easy reading lessons, and woodcuts of animals were included. Probably these were the first books

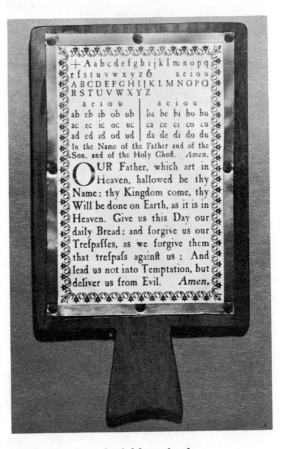

Facsimile of a colonial horn book.

of pictures that could be handled by children themselves. Battledores were still being used in the nineteenth century.

Children were expected to memorize John Cotton's catechism, *Spiritual Milk for Boston Babes in either England, drawn from the Breasts of both Testaments for their Souls' nourishment.* Originally published in England in 1646, it was revised for American children, and was the first book written and printed for children in America. Later books followed its question-and-answer approach with such questions as, "How did God make you?" The accompanying answer, "I was conceived in sin and born in iniquity" was memorized by the child. Even alphabet rhymes for the youngest emphasized the sinful nature of

Facsimiles of cardboard battledores.

man. For example, the *New England Primer*, first recorded in 1683, includes, "In Adam's fall We sinned all." The rhyming alphabet did change with the times. For example, "The Judgment made *Felix* afraid" was used instead of "The idle *Fool* is whipt at school." This primer also provided a catechism, the Ten Commandments, and verses about death. The 1781 edition included the prayer, "Now I Lay Me Down to Sleep." Approximately three million copies of this primer were sold.

Early in the eighteenth century, James Janeway's book, *A Token for Children, Being an Exact Account of the Conversion, Holy, and Exemplary Lives and Joyful Deaths of Several Young Children*, was published in England. Before it was printed in America, Cotton Mather

added life histories of New England children.

In the latter half of the seventeenth century, informational books were published. One of the first geographies appeared in 1665. The author, Henry Winstanly, considered California a South Sea island and noted that Virginia lay directly south of New England, but his book titled *All the Principal Nations of the World Presented in their Habits of Fashions of Dressing . . .* was a milestone leading to modern travel and informational books.

In the first part of the eighteenth century, several "science" books were published. Isaac Watts presented *The Knowledge of the Heavens and the Earth Made Easy, or the First Principles of Geography and Astronomy Ex-*

plained (1726). Ten years later, Thomas Breman introduced the idea that learning should be fun in his title, *A Description of a Great Variety of Animals and Vegetables . . . especially for the Entertainment of Youth.* In America, Isaiah Thomas reprinted books pirated from England, including *Jack Dandy's Delight: or The History of Birds and Beasts,* a juvenile natural history. *The Circle of the Sciences* (1745), *Tommy Trip's History of Beasts and Birds* (1779), and *Juvenile Rambles* (1786) were some of the informational books published by John Newbery.

Religious history had been part of the fare for children before the eighteenth century — many read descriptions of the horrors in John Foxe's *Book of Martyrs* written in 1563. Nathaniel Crouch edited *The Young Man's Calling,* a collection of stories for youth that included engravings of beheadings, burnings of martyrs, and information about proper behavior.

After the Revolution, several distinctly American histories appeared. In the 1795 book, *The History of America,* six woodcuts were used over and over (the same woodcut was used for Christopher Columbus and General Montgomery). *Cooper's History of America abridged for the Use of Children of All Denominations* appeared in 1795.

Textbooks for subject matter areas were introduced to the American schools near the end of the eighteenth century. Noah Webster's *Blue Backed Speller, Simplified and Standardized American Spelling,* published in 1783, was used widely for spelling bees. Webster's *Third Part* of the series, published in 1785, was the first secular reader. In 1789, Jedediah Morse introduced the first American geography with his *American Universal Geography.* Nicholas Pike's *Arithmetic* (1793) and Root's *Introduction to Arithmetic* (1796) were two of the first arithmetic texts. The influence of the rising commercial classes made such textbooks necessary. Consequently, these textbooks constituted a major

Woodcuts illustrate an alphabet page in the *New England Primer*.

portion of the books available for children during the period.

Didactic Tales

In the last half of the eighteenth century, women writers entered the field of juvenile literature with the purpose of teaching through stories. In *Mrs. Teachem's School for Girls,* Sarah Fielding published stories that emphasized character development. *Easy Lessons for Children,* published in 1760 by Mrs. Barbauld, presented lessons for children of different ages. Mrs. Sarah Trimmer apparently agreed with Locke, who had approved of fables for children, for she created a family of robins who could talk of problems in day-to-day family life. She gave some information about nature by weaving facts into conversations in her *Fabulous Histories* (1786). Meigs quotes a sample of the conversation, "I am delighted, my dear children, with your humane behavior toward the animal creation . . . but though it is a most commendable propensity, it requires regulation."[7] One wonders what meaning children derived from such difficult and unnatural vocabulary.

As the eighteenth century drew to a close, the influence of Rousseau was felt in children's literature. Following Rousseau's theory of accompanying the child in his natural search for knowledge, parents, relatives, or teachers were always at hand to seize upon every comment made by a child or to call attention to objects of interest so that the incident might be used as a means of instruction. Books frequently contained dialogues and conversations. Instead of long lists of rules, the lessons were now concealed in didactic tales and juvenile biographies.

Thomas Day utilized the conversational approach in *The History of Sandford and Merton*, a didactic tale that appeared in three sections (1783, 1786, 1789). Harry Sandford and Tommy Merton were six-year-old boys who were tutored together, although Harry was the son of a farmer. It was Harry who exemplified the just and righteous for the spoiled Tommy Merton. Day after day, lecture after lecture, the tutor presented long lessons that interrupted the narrative. These priggish children served as models of behavior for nearly one hundred years.

Poetry

In this period, poetry for children also emphasized religion and instruction. Although Isaac Watts spent most of his time writing hymns, he did devote some of his energy to writing poetry for children. *Divine Songs Attempted in Easy Language for the use of Children* (1715) made religious instruction more pleasant for children.

Play was still seen as an occasion for mischief and a time when children might come under the influence of Satan. In 1785, children were told to use play as a time for introspection. The verses in *A Present to Children* suggested thoughts for play:

> *Now on the Ice I shape the Slide,*
> *And smoothly O'er the Surface glide,*
> *I learn amidst the slipp'ry Play*
> *Most dangerous is the easiest way.*

John Newbery printed *Pretty Poems for Children Three Feet High* and added the inscription, "To all those who are good this book is dedicated by their best friend."

An engraver and artist, William Blake, wrote poetry that children enjoyed, but the poems of *Songs of Innocence,* 1789, were not specifically written for children. The poetry was filled with imagination and joy, and made the reader aware of beauty without preaching. One artist emerged during this period as an illustrator of books for boys and girls. Thomas Bewick's white-line wood engravings for *A Pretty Book of Pictures for Little Masters and Misses: or Tommy Trip's History of Beasts and Birds* (1767) were interesting and of excellent workmanship.

As the century terminated, most of the stories for children were about how to live the "good life." Information about the natural world was peddled in didactic lectures sugar-coated with a conversational style. Little prigs were models for young people to follow. However, there was now a literature for children. Authors and publishers were aware of a new market for books. Parents and teachers were beginning to recognize the importance of literature for children.

CHILDREN'S LITERATURE: NINETEENTH CENTURY

Background

The nineteenth century brought tremendous changes to the western world as powerful nations arose. The Industrial Revolu-

---

[7]Meigs, p. 78.

tion, use of agricultural machinery, and improved communication and transportation, brought technological changes that influenced men's values and attitudes. In America, the Westward Movement led to emphasis upon individualism, and a growing nationalism emphasized freedom and enlightenment for all peoples. Education came to be viewed as a *natural right* for all children. With the influx of immigrants, the school became the institution to mold new Americans. In science, there was emphasis upon fact-finding and classified knowledge. Psychology was beginning to be considered a science as Wilhelm Wundt, William James, and G. Stanley Hall observed and recorded human behavior. This led to more emphasis on life in the present. With Darwin's work in biological evolution and the findings of LaPlace and other astronomers, the world and its life were increasingly viewed as products of natural forces. However, the basic school texts continued to reflect the view of God's will influencing all of life. Transcendentalism pushed even further the idea of nonsectarian religion; it was deemed possible to be a good citizen yet not a member of a religious sect.

In the last three decades of the nineteenth century, teaching children through objects in nature was emphasized. Experimental schools were based on the idea of the child as the center of the school curriculum. Near the end of the century, the pragmatists, Peirce, James, and Dewey, asserted that knowledge arises out of experience, and theories must be tested. Dewey's new philosophy held that education was a social process; the child's interests were significant and should be channeled; thinking was viewed as problem-solving. These ideas were in the growing stages; neither schools nor books actually changed very much, but there was an optimistic, expanding feeling—a young nation progressing. Art and music reflected classical traditions. Realism in art was emphasized, although the Impressionists were beginning to create new styles of painting.

These changes of the nineteenth century were slowly reflected in books for children. Libraries were established; the Sunday School Movement led to distribution of tracts and books. The didactic stories that preached good behavior continued to be of major importance during this period, but some books were written with a child audience in mind. The school curriculum was broadened to include natural science, history, geography, and citizenship training. Science and technology made possible travel to far places, and realistic accounts of these journeys became popular. A growing nationalism led to books of American history and geography. Pioneer adventures and stories of the War of 1812 and the Civil War provided exciting plots for boys.

The emphasis upon individual rights and freedom for all seemed to influence attitudes toward children. Conditions created a climate in which a son's opinions were as valid as his father's. Children were considered individuals with unique rights. The attitudes toward religion gave way to secularism and to recognition of play as an acceptable part of child life. Each type of book reflected these social, political, and economic changes. By the end of the century, there was a growing body of literature expressly written for children.

Books of Religion and Morals

In the first half of the nineteenth century, the didactic school of writing for children flourished as women writers wielded influential pens. They condemned fairy stories and relentlessly dispensed information in lengthy dialogues between parent and child. Martha Sherwood, a prolific writer, produced about 350 moralizing books and tracts. While living in India, she wrote *The*

History of Little Henry and His Bearer (1814). The story of little Henry's conversion illustrates her missionary theme. St. John notes that the advertisement of a later edition read, "Upwards of two hundred and fifty thousand copies have been sold . . ."[8]

Mrs. Mary Sherwood wrote a series of stories about *The Fairchild Family*, beginning in 1812. It opens with a funeral, as many of the tales of that period were wont to begin. The religious tone is still present, and moral lessons are provided through stilted dialogue. For example, one evening Papa tells about the globe. After a long discourse, Lucy asks, "Papa may we have some verses about mankind having evil hearts?" Each child then quotes scripture. Little Henry exclaims, "Oh, I wish I could love the Lord Jesus Christ more than I do; but my wicked heart will not let me!" In another part of one of the early editions, Mr. Fairchild takes the children to see the body of a man who had been hanged for the murder of his brother. Mrs. Sherwood also wrote of taking children to visit a dying farmer boy. The lad had prepared for his approaching death by inspecting the family vault and visiting the cemetery. In these ways, children were urged to prepare for death.

Biographies of pious children who experienced premature death were favorites in the early nineteenth century. A collection of such biographies by Mary Pilkington was titled *Biography for Girls: or Moral and Instructive Examples for the Female Sex.*

The horrible-example technique was also employed by some writers for children. In one book published near the end of the eighteenth century, children were given animal bodies, as "Jacky Idle turned into the body of an Ass," "Master Greedyguts into a Pig," and "Miss Dorthy Chatterfast became a Magpie."

[8]Judith St. John, *The Osborne Collection of Early Children's Books 1566–1910* (Toronto, Canada: Toronto Public Library, 1958).

John Locke's essays on education had wide influence on children's literature. He suggested combining learning and pleasure, recommended the use of fables, and encouraged use of illustrations. At the same time, he urged educators and parents to set a good example for children. These influences may be seen in Maria Edgeworth's *Easy Lessons* that contained examples of children who always obeyed their parents. Maria Edgeworth was determined to educate young readers, but she did add suspense to her stories. Usually a gracious lady or nobleman appeared to make an award or point out a moral. *The Parent's Assistant: or Stories for Children* (1796) included "The Purple Jar," "Waste Not, Want Not," and "Lazy Lawrence." In this series of essays, she incorporated the story of *Rosamund and the Purple Jar.* Little Rosamund learned that a purple jar she desired instead of new shoes was only a clear glass bottle colored by the bad smelling liquid it contained.

During the early part of the century, parents were exhorted to set examples of good behavior. Educators were beginning to assert that children went astray because they did not receive enough love. However, authors continued to reflect rigid attitudes toward youthful misdemeanors. In *My Teacher's Gem*, a collection of moralistic stories, the dire results of stealing a bird's nest are righteously pronounced:

CRUEL BOYS

"O, what a shame!" a kind child may be ready to say on looking at this picture. You see these boys, little as they are, have hard and cruel hearts. They have been robbing a happy little bird family of one of the young ones; and now they will so hurt it that it will die, or they will let it starve to death. And they have robbed another pair of birds of their nest and eggs. How unhappy must all these birds be! and how wicked it is to give such needless pain to any of

The Grief of Little Jack, at his Mother's Funeral.

THE

INTERESTING HISTORY

OF

LITTLE JACK.

A MORAL TALE.

EMBELLISHED WITH

SEVERAL NEAT ENGRAVINGS ON WOOD.

LONDON:

PRINTED AND SOLD BY

DEAN & MUNDAY, THREADNEEDLE-STREET.

1821

Jack, with his Father and Brother, visiting the
Mother's Grave.

The frontispiece and title page of this 1821 book illustrate the preoccupation of children's literature with death. Reproduced from *The Osborne Collection of Early Children's Books, 1566–1910, A Catalogue* (1958). Courtesy of the Toronto Public Library.

God's creatures! No kind child can think of hurting a dear, innocent little bird. But those who delight in such sport will very likely grow up to be capable of injuring their fellow-men in the various ways of which we so often hear and read. Let us be kind to everything that lives.

And this isn't the whole story about these wicked boys. Don't you see they are in a quarrel, how they shall divide what they have so cruelly stolen from the poor birds? Ah, that is the way in doing wrong—one wrong step leads on to another; and robbing birds' nests does not usually go alone—a quarrel, or some other wickedness, usually follows it. Beware, then of the beginnings of cruelty and wickedness.[9]

Books of Instruction

By 1800, the *New England Primer* reflected the changing social purposes and interests of the new nation. The alphabet became less pious:

A was an angler and fished with a hook
B was a Blockhead and ne'er learned his book.

---

[9]Asa Bullard, *Sunnybrook Stories: My Teacher's Gem* (Boston: Lee and Shepard, 1863), pp. 22–24.

A picture of George Washington was substituted for the woodcut of George III. Adaptations of the Primer were made by several educators. "A Mother" added space and large print for *Lessons for Children from Two to Four Years Old.* Another revision included such little stories as:

> Bring the tea things. Bring the little boy's milk. Where is the bread and butter? Little boys do not eat butter. Sop the bread in your tea.

The illustrations were crude, and size relationships were of little importance. In Mathew Carey's 1813 edition of *The American Primer,* for example, the illustration of a mouse was the same size as that of a horse.

Rhymes to help children learn the multiplication tables were presented in *Marmaduke Multiply's Merry Method of Making Minor Mathematicians* by Harris in 1816. *The Multiplication Table,* in verse, printed in 1819, included this verse:

> Twice one are two sweet little cats
> One black, the other gray,
> Twice two are four as pretty mice
> That from them ran away.[10]

Nonsense about parts of speech and punctuation was the basis for *Punctuation Personified.* Mr. Stop, who was shown in accompanying illustrations, told the reader how to use punctuation marks.

Reading for patriotism, good citizenship, and industry was the purpose of the well-loved *Eclectic Readers* by William H. McGuffey. They were used so widely from 1834 to 1900 one could almost say these readers comprised the elementary curriculum in literature. A glance at the *Fifth Reader* reflects the type of material included in these readers: speeches by Daniel Webster, essays by Washington Irving, selections from Shakespeare (although the play is often not identified), narrative, sentimental and patriotic poetry, and many didactic essays with such titles as "Advantages of a Well-educated Mind," "Impeachment of Warren Hastings," and "Eulogy on Candlelight."

Although compulsory education was being extended, and the publicly supported common school was being established, parents were also expected to teach children at home. The parent's role was established through stories in which mothers embroidered, sipped tea, and dispensed information to *sweet* children. The following conversation was in *A Key to Knowledge,* published in 1822:

> Louisa—*By the by, when I come to think of it, what a dirty thing honey is; first swallowed by bees, and then by us.*
>
> Mother—*Your description is certainly not very inviting. Suppose rather that we should call the honey, the syrup of flowers, drawn from the opened buds by the trunk, or proboscis, of the industrious bee.*
>
> Louisa—*Now I like honey again. But Mamma, if honey is the juice of flowers, what then is wax?*
>
> Mother—*Wax has been determined by an attentive naturalist (Reamer) to be the farina, or pollen of flowers. . . . But we have done tea, and must now begin our evening amusements.*
>
> Louisa—*Mamma, we have been already delightfully amused.*[11]

In the early nineteenth century, nature study and contemplation of the universe was encouraged to develop an admiration of God's works. In this period, Samuel Goodrich was chiefly responsible for eliminating the British background in books for American children. History, geography, and science were included in his *Tales of Peter Parley about America* (1827). As Goodrich tried to satisfy children's curiosity in an 1839 edition of *Peter Parley's Farewell,* the idea of a series of informative books was initiated.

---

[10]St. John, p. 131.

[11]"19th Century Juvenilia," *Times Educational Supplement,* 2262:1412 (September 26, 1958).

Peter Parley told tales of Europe and Africa and of the Sun, Moon, and Stars. Isaac Taylor wrote a series of *Scenes* "for little tarry-at-home travellers." *Scenes in Africa,* was printed in 1820, while *Scenes of Commerce, by Land or Sea; or, "Where Does It Come from?" answered* was published ten years later. Jacob Abbott also followed this plan as he wrote about *Little Rollo* learning to talk, Rollo learning to read, and of Rollo's travels to Europe. In the first books of the series, published in 1834, Rollo was a natural little boy, but as he became older and traveled about the world he became another little prig. There was no plot, merely a series of incidents as Rollo and his uncle viewed city and country. Rollo frequently gave lectures about the places of interest. In *Rollo in Holland*, the demanding wife of a friend is the "horrible example" of the American traveler. Two or three pages of the small (4 by 6 inches) book were devoted to relatively unimportant details of travel arrangements such as orders to waiters and costs of guided tours. The modern reader wonders what elements really maintained the interest of the child reader.

The Bodley Family, conceived by Horace Scudder, explored New England, Holland, and other countries (1857). In *Seven Little Sisters Who Live on the Big Round Ball that Floats in the Air* (1861), Jane Andrews told of little girls who lived in the far north, in the desert, in China, and in Switzerland. Through a dramatic family story, *Hans Brinker: or The Silver Skates,* Mary Mapes Dodge gave accurate glimpses of Dutch life in 1865. The skating race is actually less important than the daring brain surgery performed on father Brinker, who had been nearly an idiot for several years after an accident. The bravery and courage of Hans and his sister in facing poverty, scorn, and their father's illness provided further examples for child behavior. To make another country seem real, Johanna Spyri wrote *Heidi* in 1884. Not only did readers share the joys and sorrow in Heidi's life; they "breathed" the clear mountain air and "lived" in Switzerland.

Problems of war, temperance, and slavery were topics in histories in the first half of the nineteenth century. Samuel Wood discussed the miseries of the world as he gave information in *The Seven Wonders of the World* (1814). Biographies of churchmen published by the American Tract Society gave children some historical background. Thomas Higginson's *A Young Folk's History of the United States* (1875) marks the beginning of history-writing for American children. Famous battles were described by Charles Coffin in *Boys of '76* and *Boys of '61*. In 1880, George Henty wrote a military history for boys, *The Young Buglers*. This book was only one of his many stories of adventure and war. History in the form of biographies was written by George Towle in an 1883 publication, *Young Folk's Heroes of History. Ten Boys Who Lived on the Road from Long Ago to Now* by Jane Andrews gave young readers information about Puritans, Horatius, and other heroes (1886).

Most of the science books were about flowers and gardens. Mrs. Margaret Gatty's *Parables from Nature, Worlds Not Realized*, gave accurate information as well as moral instruction. One writer who did not "write down" to children was Mrs. Ewing, who published a series of nature lessons under the title *Mary's Meadow* (1886). The science of astronomy was presented to children in an 1805 publication, *The Wonders of the Telescope*.

Only a few writers and publishers seemed to realize that children want to learn about their world. Children had to plod through pages of tiresome conversations with moralistic overtones to gain the information they sought. It was not until much later that informational books on almost every subject were placed on bookshelves for boys and girls.

Folk-Tale Collections

Early in the nineteenth century, two German brothers went about asking servants and peasants to recall stories they had heard. In 1812, Jacob and Wilhelm Grimm published the first volume of *Kinder-und Hausmauchen* (Household Stories). These serious scholars tried to preserve the form as well as the content of the old tales that were translated and published in England by Edgar Taylor in 1823–1826. "The Elves and the Shoemaker," "Rumplestiltskin," and "Snow White," in addition to many others, became part of the literature of childhood.

In America, Washington Irving included "Rip Van Winkle" and "The Legend of Sleepy Hollow" in the 1819 *Sketch Book*. These tales, written mainly for adults, were enjoyed by older children.

The origin of *The Three Bears* has been questioned by various authorities. Meigs[12] noted it was published in Robert Southey's *Doctor*, 1834–1837. Muir reported there was some evidence that it was written by an anonymous author in 1831 and retold by Southey. Lexau identified this author as Eleanor Mure whose 1831 manuscript was located by Edgar Osborne, English collector of children's books.[13] Mure's story was written in verse. In the early version of the story, a wicked old woman comes to visit the bears who are pictured as wee, middle-sized, and huge. Through many retellings, the story has been changed to the more familiar fair-haired child visiting a bear family.[14]

In 1846, Mary Howitt translated a book of tales called *Wonderful Stories for Children*.

---

[12]Meigs, p. 157.

[13]Joan Lexau, "The Story of the Three Bears and the Man Who Didn't Write It," *The Horn Book Magazine*, vol. 40 (February 1964), pp. 88–94.

[14]Lexau suggests comparing versions in *English Fairy Tales* by Joseph Jacobs, *The Green Fairy Book* by Andrew Lang, Leslie Brooke's *The Story of the Three Bears*, and "Scrapefoot" in *Told under the Green Umbrella* by the Association for Childhood Education.

Hans Christian Andersen's stories came to England and America, and children were enthralled by "The Tinder Box," "The Princess and the Pea," and "The Ugly Duckling." In these stories, inanimate objects and animals come alive. The values and foibles of human life were presented in stories with action and rich language.

In the last half of the nineteenth century, folk tales and fairy tales were given new importance as well-known authors contributed their versions. John Ruskin retold *The King of the Golden River* in 1851 and Charles Dickens' *The Magic Fishbone* was written as a serial in 1868. *The Wonderbook for Boys and Girls* was published by Nathaniel Hawthorne in 1852 and was followed by *Tanglewood Tales* in 1853. Sir George Dasent translated *Popular Tales from the North* in 1859, making it possible for children to enjoy more tales from Scandinavia. *The Nürnberg Stove* was another favorite, first published by Louise de la Ramee in a collection of children's stories in 1882. Joel Chandler Harris collected stories from the South for *Uncle Remus, His Songs and Sayings* (1881).

Collections of folk tales were made by Andrew Lang in his famous series beginning with *The Blue Fairy Book*. The Red, Green, and the Yellow fairy books followed the 1889 publication of the first volume of folklore. Joseph Jacobs was also interested in retelling folk tales for children. *English Fairy Tales* (1892), *Celtic Fairy Tales* (1893), and *Indian Fairy Tales* (1892) were important contributions to the realm of folklore. As the merits of folklore were recognized everywhere, there was increasing interest in such volumes as Howard Pyle's *Pepper and Salt* (1886) and *Wonder Clock* (1888).

Stories of Family Life

Some authors felt that the joys of realistic children should be portrayed in lifelike situations. In England, Charlotte Yonge's *The*

Daisy Chain (1856) described the daily life and learning of a family of eleven children. Somewhat later, series books about families appeared. The *Dotty Dimple* series and the *Little Prudy* series were written by Rebecca Clarke under the name of Sophie May. *Little Prudy's Captain Horace* centered on the Clifford family during the Civil War. Eight-year-old Horace is described as a very naughty boy; yet, the reader sympathizes with him. Horace's sister Grace keeps a record of all his misdeeds and such bad words as "shucks," "gallus," and "by George." Cousin Prudy exerts a good influence on the boy who pretends to be a captain after his father joins the Union Army. There is great sorrow and pages of grief when they receive news that Horace's father is killed. An interesting advertisement appears on the last page; it shows Red Riding Hood meeting the wolf, and a doggerel verse tells how she tames the beast by sharing her Jello.

Harriet Lathrop (under the pseudonym Margaret Sidney) presented a lively family in the *Five Little Peppers* in a series starting in 1880. Popular through the years, a new edition appeared as late as 1962. Under the name of Farquharson, Martha Finley initiated the *Elsie Dinsmore* series in 1867. Pools of tears were shed over the life of this character. By 1894, Elsie had become a grandmother and accompanied her growing family to the World's Fair. Several chapters included long discussions of the Bible.

The most familiar and well-loved family described in series books is probably the March family. Written by the irrepressible Jo, Louisa May Alcott, this series about a warm, human family remains an American classic. *Little Women* (1867) and *Little Men* (1871) are still the favorites of the series.

Frances Hodgson Burnett described family conflict within the English aristocracy in *Little Lord Fauntleroy* (1886). Her second book, *Sara Crewe* (1888), told of the pitiful plight of a wealthy pupil who is orphaned and reduced to servitude in a boarding school. Mrs. Burnett's best-known book is *The Secret Garden* (1910), which presents an exciting plot in a mysterious setting.

Stories of Adventure

The pioneer spirit sought stories of adventure. *Swiss Family Robinson* by J. H. Wyss was translated in 1814, bringing excitement to many children. In America, daily life was full of adventure as conceived by children today. A few writers recognized the value of recording some of the incidents and also realized the growing demand for such literature. Although written for adults, *The Last of the Mohicans*, by James Fenimore Cooper, interested children when it was published in 1826. Its bloody incidents and tragedy gave tingling adventure. Captain Frederick Marryat began a series of sea adventures with *Adventures of a Naval Officer; or, Frank Mildmay* in 1829. *Mr. Midshipman Easy* and *Masterman Ready* were juvenile adventures that followed in 1836 and 1844. In 1856, Robert Ballantyne began his series of nearly eighty books, with an account of his fur trading experiences, *The Young Fur Trader*. Ballantyne was a writer for boys who related exciting stories based upon events in the world. *The Battery and the Boiler; or Adventures in the Laying of Submarine Electric Cables* would have been of great interest to boys in 1883. Boy readers also found adventure in W. H. G. Kingston's *Peter the Whaler* and in the short stories in *Kingston's Magazine for Boys*.

Ragged Dick (1867) was the first of the series of stories by Horatio Alger. Over one hundred of these stories of triumph over difficulties in the climb from rags to riches were published by this American writer. The final paragraph of *Struggling Upward* presents the theme:

So closes an eventful passage in the life of Luke Larkin. He has struggled upward from a

"Good bye, feet!" Carroll's drawing of Alice from his original manuscript shows how he visualized Alice growing taller. From *Alice's Adventures Underground* by Lewis Carroll. Courtesy of Dover Publications.

boyhood of privation and self-denial into a youth and manhood of prosperity and honor. There has been some luck about it, I admit, but after all he is indebted for most of his good fortune to his own good qualities.[15]

Oliver Optic was the pen name of William Adams, a teacher who wrote such series as *The Boat Club Series* (1855), *The Army and Navy Series*, and *The Starry Flag Series*. There were many scenes of excitement and adventure, but Oliver's readers also learned some geography as they traveled with the heroes. *Outward Bound* told of reckless boy sailors, but stilted speeches and the incidents of drinking and gambling led librarians to eliminate these books from their shelves. *All Aboard*, for example, relates the story of a boating club whose members were indeed "noble fellows." They accept Tim, a boy who promised to reform after release from a reformatory, but Tim brings great trouble. When Tim organizes a gang and steals the boat, the author digresses to give one of his many lectures:

> *The whole scheme was one of the natural consequences of reading bad books, in which the most dissolute, depraved, and wicked men are made to appear as heroes, whose lives and characters are worthy of emulation. . . . My young readers will see where Tim got his ideas, and I hope they will shun books which narrate the exploits of pirates and robbers.*[16]

In 1860, the first dime novel was published by Beadle and Adams, beginning the tremendous business of cheap books for the ten- to sixteen-year-old. Ann S. W. Stephens' *Malaeska, the Indian Wife of the White Hunter* was the first of the avalanche to be written by hacks. William S. Patten created the red-blooded Frank Merriwell in 1896. Travel, rescue of helpless women, and success were the ingredients in more than 800 books of this stereotyped character.

In the latter half of the century, there appeared the first great school story, *Tom Brown's School Days* (1885), by Thomas Hughes. In this book, sports were of great interest to the pupils, and excitement

---

[15]Horatio Alger, Jr., *Struggling Upwards; or Luke Larkin's Luck* (New York: Superior Printing, n.d.), p. 280.

[16]Oliver Optic, *All Aboard; or Life on the Lake* (Chicago: M. A. Donohue, 1855), pp. 143–144.

was provided in accounts of team events.

Many of the series books provided adventure, but the characters tended to be rather superficial. In 1882, a serial intended for boys was acclaimed by adults as well. Robert Louis Stevenson published it as *Treasure Island* in 1883. Not only were there tense, thrilling moments, the characters were convincingly and consistently drawn.

Mark Twain combined realism, humor, and adventure in his classic accounts of the Missouri boys, Tom Sawyer and Huckleberry Finn. *Adventures of Tom Sawyer*, published in 1876, was followed by *Adventures of Huckleberry Finn* in 1884. The author's imagination and understanding made possible this realistic portrayal of American boyhood.

The beginning of science fiction and adventure can surely be found in Jules Verne's *Twenty Thousand Leagues under the Sea* (1870) and *Around the World in Eighty Days* (1872). Modern readers may be surprised to note the early date of these books.

Animal Stories

A Dog of Flanders (1872) by Louise de la Ramee has been considered the first modern dog story. *Black Beauty* appeared in 1877 as a protest against cruel treatment of horses. Some children today continue to enjoy Anna Sewell's rather overdrawn and sentimental tale. Kipling's *Jungle Books* (1894–1895) were exciting animal stories. Many children know the story of Mowgli, a child raised by a wolf family, a bear, and a panther.

Ernest Thompson Seton's sketches added much to the children's enjoyment of *Wild Animals I Have Known* (1898). This book with "personal" histories of animals was a forerunner of the modern books written about one animal.

Books of Humor and Fantasy

Although many of the early titles of books for children included the word "amusing," the main purpose was to instruct or moralize. Undoubtedly, children enjoyed the broad humor in some of the folk tales and the nonsense in Mother Goose, but few books brought humor or nonsense before the middle of the nineteenth century.

The early steps toward a literature for children's enjoyment led naturally to the development of fantasy. Charles Kingsley's story of Tom's adventures with the sea creatures in *The Water-Babies* (1863) represents the beginning of modern fantasy. This story of a chimney sweep who became a wa-

"Curioser and Curioser." Tenniel's Alice seems more sturdy and surprised at her sudden growth. From *Alice in Wonderland* by Lewis Carroll, 1865. Illustrated by Tenniel.

ter baby with gills might have amused adults, but children would find it difficult to understand some of the hidden meanings. Mrs. Bedonebyasyoudid teaches her lessons:

> . . . *for you must know and believe that people's souls make their bodies just as a snail makes its shell (I am not joking, my little man; I am in serious, solemn earnest). And therefore, when Tom's soul grew all prickly with naughty tempers, his body could not help growing prickly too, so that nobody would cuddle him, or play with him, or even like to look at him.*[17]

On a summer day in 1862, a professor of mathematics, Charles Dodgson, told a story to three little girls at a picnic. In response to their request that he record the story, Dodgson wrote *Alice's Adventures Underground* and presented it to his young friends as a Christmas gift in 1864. At the insistence of others, he decided to have it published. By 1865, the artist, Tenniel, completed the drawings, and *Alice's Adventures in Wonderland* was ready for the host of readers to come.

Although the Duchess tells Alice, "Everything's got a moral if you can only find it," there is no moralizing in this fantasy. Indeed, children can appreciate her pattern of giving good advice that she never takes. *Alice in Wonderland* is a book that must be read aloud, for it is the inflection of the voice, the pause before the parenthetical explanation, the tonal change for conversation that make it fun for children. The teacher's or librarian's enjoyment is a key, for effective reading is essential. Alice falls and falls, talking to herself constantly. The scenes at the Mad Hatter's tea party, the croquet game, and the court scene are enjoyed more by adults than children for their nonsense and play on words. For example, the phrase "was immediately suppressed by the court" is ex-

plained to Alice when the guinea pig who cheered in court was stuffed into a bag. Now she "understood" that phrase! Her second adventure occurs as she goes through the looking glass to fairyland. Children who are beginning to play chess may enjoy hearing some of these incidents.

Other well-known fantasies were published near the end of the century. *At the Back of the North Wind*, George MacDonald's fantasy, appeared in 1871. From Italy came *The Adventures of Pinocchio* (1892) by Carlo Lorenzini (pseudonym, C. Collodi). While she was in India and homesick for her children, Helen Bannerman wrote *The Story of Little Black Sambo* (1899). In this fantasy, one absurd incident after another occurs, excitement is high, and the ending is satisfying.

In the category of books for fun, the books with movable parts might also be included. Harlequinades or turnups, first appeared in 1766. They consisted of a page of pictures covered with flaps that could be raised or lowered to create other scenes. Doggerel verse on each section told a simple story. In 1810, stories in rhyme were printed on sheets with slots, and pockets were fastened to the reverse side. Cut-out figures could be slipped through the slot and were held in the pocket. A hero or heroine could appear in a number of different costumes in this way. From 1840 until about 1900, a variety of books with flaps and movable parts was published. By pulling tabs, various pictures appeared to illustrate the verse or story.

Books of Games and Sports

Essays on proper conversation, manners, drawing, and music were included with games in Lydia Child's 1858 edition, *The Girl's Own Book: A Course of Geography, by means of instructive games . . .* published in 1829. It included maps and counters for locating the places. Craft books, too, were

---

[17]Charles Kingsley, *The Water-Babies* (New York: Platt & Munk, 1900), p. 149.

available. *Papyroplastics, or The art of modelling in paper; being an instructive amusement for young persons of both sexes* was translated from the German by D. Boileau, and printed in 1825. Another title that suggested fun for children appeared about 1800, *The Whim Wham; or Evening Amusement for All Ages and Sizes . . . .*

Poetry

In the nineteenth century, a wide variety of poetry was written for children. The Taylor sisters, Ann and Jane, emphasized polite behavior in their volume published in 1804, *Original Poems for Infant Minds.* Their poems about lifelike young people in everyday life were translated and published on the continent. Morals, death, and justice were emphasized in the poems, as in this example:

> *You are not so healthy and gay*
> *So young, so active and bright,*
> *That death cannot snatch you away,*
> *Or some dread accident smite.*
>
> *Here lie both the young and the old,*
> *Confined in the coffin so small*
> *The earth covers over them cold,*
> *The grave-worms devour them all.*

Jane Taylor wrote the oft-parodied, "Twinkle Twinkle Little Star" for this collection. The entire poem, with its original illustrations, is reproduced in *Flowers of Delight* by De Vries.

Fantastic verse and brightly colored pictures were introduced in 1807 with *The Butterfly's Ball and the Grasshopper's Feast* by William Roscoe.

Clement Moore, a professor who wrote to please his own children, gave the world the Christmas classic, *A Visit from St. Nicholas.* One of the first American contributions to a joyous literature for children, it was published with this title in 1822, but is now known as *The Night before Christmas.* In 1846,

Movable parts give a venetian-blind effect in this early book for children. From *Pleasant Surprises: A Novel Mechanical Book for the Little Ones* (*circa* 1880). Courtesy of P. K. Thomajan Collection of Animated Juvenilia.

They all laughed at the snail who came to dance at *The Butterfly's Ball* by William Roscoe. Illustrated by Mulready. 1807. From *Flowers of Delight* by Leonard De Vries. Reprinted by permission of Pantheon Books, a Division of Random House, Inc. All rights reserved under International and Pan-American Copyright Conventions. Also published by Dennis Dobson, London.

an author appeared who wrote verse solely to entertain. Edward Lear's nonsense poems brought joy to both children and adults as they met fantastic Pobbles and Quangle Wangles. In the 1872 volume, *More Nonsense,* the owl and the pussy cat went out to sea in their pea-green boat, and other impossibles appeared to delight young and old alike.

Christina Rossetti's poetry for children is reminiscent of Mother Goose, but she also wrote verse that brought to children vivid descriptions of the beauty around them. *Sing Song* (1872) continues to delight young children with such verses as:

> Mix a pancake
> Stir a pancake,
> Pop it in the pan;
> Fry the pancake,
> Toss the pancake,
> Catch it if you can.

Modern children enjoy the rhythm and mood of:

> Who has seen the wind?
>   Neither I nor you;
> But when the leaves hang trembling
>   The wind is passing thro'.
>
> Who has seen the wind?
>   Neither you nor I;
> But when the trees bow down their heads
>   The wind is passing by.

In the latter half of the nineteenth century, young people were also enjoying William Allingham's *Ballad Book* (1865). John Greenleaf Whittier wrote many of the fine poems of the period in *Child Life, A Collection of Poems* (1871). Kate Greenaway is known as an illustrator, but her verses were enjoyed as much as the drawings in *Under the Window* (1878) and *Marigold Garden* (1885).

The century ended with the appearance of a volume of poetry for children that told of everyday life and the child's own world as he views it. This volume by Robert Louis Stevenson was originally titled *Penny Whistles*

(1885) and later changed to *A Child's Garden of Verses.* He was a poet who could recapture a child's imaginings for all to enjoy. "My Shadow," "My Bed Is a Boat," "Windy Nights," and "Good Play" tell of fun, and bring rhythm to the child's world.

The close of the nineteenth century found two American poets writing for children. Eugene Field's *Poems of Childhood* (1896) included "The Sugar Plum Tree" and "The Duel." In *Rhymes of Childhood* (1891), James Whitcomb Riley employed dialect as he described local incidents and Indiana farm life. His "Little Orphant Annie" and "The Raggedy Man" continue to be favorites.

Magazines

Magazines formed a significant part of the literature for children in the last half of the nineteenth century. In keeping with the philosophy of the times, a French teacher, Madame Beaumont, published a magazine titled *Magasin des infants.* Madame Beaumont also wrote seventy books, including *Beauty and the Beast.* The chapbooks sold by peddlers in England might be considered forerunners of magazines, but they were really books. The comic hero and adventurer, Jack Harkaway, of one of the chapbooks, closely resembled the modern comic-book figure.

The first true magazine for English children appeared in 1852 under the title, *The Charm.* It was not until the 1860s that children's magazines gained importance. Many of the best stories for children first appeared in such form. Charlotte Yonge's own stories appeared in her magazine, *The Monthly Packet.* Mrs. Gatty and Mrs. Ewing were among the early writers who contributed to *Aunt Judy's Magazine* initiated in 1868.

The first magazine planned for children in America, *The Juvenile Miscellany,* 1827, emphasized American history and biography. Other magazines resulted from the Sunday School Movement. Horace Scudder, editor of *The Riverside Magazine,* published several of Hans Christian Andersen's stories. He was also one of the earliest editors to discuss selection of books for children. *The Youth's Companion,* 1827–1941, engaged such writers as Tennyson, Gladstone, Kipling, Oliver Wendell Holmes, and Mark Twain.

In 1873, Mary Mapes Dodge became editor of one of the most famous magazines for children, *St. Nicholas.* Meigs writes of the editorial policy, "With the advent of St. Nicholas didacticism as the chief element in reading for children fled away forever."[18] Stories, verse, a "How to Do and Make" section, and letters from children were included in the magazine. Such well-known writers for children as Alcott, Stevenson, Kipling, Burnett, Lucretia Hale, and Laura E. Richards wrote for this magazine that guided children's reading for over half a century.

Magazines provided new outlets for children's authors and illustrators. It was now respectable for children to read purely for pleasure. Juvenile magazines of the nineteenth century made a significant contribution to the total development of a literature for children.

Improvements in Book Printing

The printing process dates back to the seventh century in China when paper was rubbed over inked wood blocks. Today, ink is still rubbed from varied surfaces onto paper. During the nineteenth century, improvements in the printing process made possible publication of a larger quantity of books, and books of a better quality. In 1803, a method for making paper by machinery was invented, and the process of making paper from wood pulp was developed in 1840. Type had been set by hand; each block was cut and fastened in place, until the linotype was patented in 1884. In

mid-century, the cylinder type press and steam power made printing large quantities much easier.

The student of children's literature should be familiar with the three basic methods of printing. *Relief printing* is done by moving the ink roller over the plate that has blocks with letters or illustrations raised above the surface. Only the high ridge receives ink that can then be transferred to paper. *Intaglio printing* results when designs are scratched below the surface by using an engraving tool or etching with acid. The ink is rolled on the plate, sinking into the low areas; another roller wipes it off the higher surface. As the paper is pressed against the plate, it absorbs the ink. The *planographic method* uses a repellent on areas that are not to be printed. Lithography is an example of the planographic method of printing. The artist drew directly on a porous limestone with a grease pencil. Water was added to the other areas. When the ink was rolled over the stone it would adhere only to the grease. Later, zinc or aluminum plates were used. Today, the plate prints the design on a rubber roller that applies the ink to the paper. This offset method makes quantity printing possible. Photo-offset printing has come to be termed lithography, but it does not refer to the original process of printing with stone.

Another significant development in the latter part of the nineteenth century was the halftone process. By taking a photograph of the illustration through a fine screen, a series of tiny dots is created. The negative is used to etch the plates, with lighter areas having smaller dots and darker areas having larger dots.

Early illustrations were made by relief designs in woodcuts. To withstand the pressure of steam presses, copper plates were used. In the early part of the century, groups of children or families colored the sheets by hand. Later, one color could be added on the copper plate. Today, three-

---

[18]Meigs, p. 280.

George Cruikshank's illustration from *The Brownies* **by Mrs. Ewing.** Reproduced from *The Osborne Collection of Early Children's Books, 1566 – 1910, A Catalogue* (1958). Courtesy of the Toronto Public Library.

and four-color processes make possible the lovely illustrations in children's books.

Technological developments of the nineteenth century were the basis for the vast improvements in the process of printing in the century ahead.

Illustrators of the Nineteenth Century

In the nineteenth century, several outstanding artists emerged as illustrators of children's books. George Cruikshank was an engraver who illustrated *Grimm's Fairy Tales* in 1820 with gay, cheerful people instead of the solemn prigs children had known earlier. A cartoonist, his work appeared in newspapers and journals as well as the children's periodical, *Aunt Judy's Magazine.* His elves and fairies were especially appealing.

Walter Crane used flat, bright colors and bold outlines in his first picture books, *The House That Jack Built,* and *History of Cock Robin and Jenny Wren.* Delicate, fairy-like pencil drawings illustrated *The First of May.*

He especially enjoyed drawing animals and outdoor scenes, and his pages were decorated with elaborate borders.

The picture books by Randolph Caldecott established new standards of illustration for children's books. His drawings were filled with action, joy of living, and good fun. His love of animals and the English countryside is reflected in the illustrations that seem to convey much meaning through a few lines. On the Caldecott medal, there is a reproduction of John Gilpin's famous ride, reminder of this famous illustrator of the nineteenth century.

Kate Greenaway's name brings visions of English gardens, delicate, prim figures, and the special style of costume on her rather fragile children. Her flowers in *The Language of Flowers* and *Marigold Garden* (1885) were beautifully drawn.

Crane, Caldecott, and Greenaway created a happy world and reflected the English countryside, but expressed little individuality or emotion in the faces of their children. Crane and Greenaway seemed to decorate rather than to extend the text through visual images.

Howard Pyle created *real* people for his collection of folk tales and legends. His characters from the Middle Ages were strong; the life of the times was portrayed with interesting, clear detail. Pyle also illustrated for the popular magazines of his day, *St. Nicholas* and *Scribner's Monthly.* He made a further contribution by establishing classes for illustrators of children's books.

Close of the Nineteenth Century

With the steady decline of Puritanism, there came a gradual realization that the morbid tone of many of the books was actually harmful. The make-believe accounts of impossible children and perfect parents were no longer being written. Fairies were finally accepted, and by the end of the century, literature was expressly designed for children to give them happiness rather than moral lectures.

CHILDREN'S LITERATURE: TWENTIETH CENTURY

Background

In the rapidly changing world of the twentieth century, the child became an important individual in the family, school, and community. The importance of early childhood was emphasized by Freudian psychology, social anthropologists, and students of child development. The emerging concepts of child development emphasized continuous growth, uniqueness of the individual, and the interrelationship of physical, emotional, and social growth. Kindergartens became an accepted part of many school systems. Needs for love, affection, and belonging were stressed in the many books and articles for parents and teachers. Television producers and advertisers became aware of a vast new market as the infant population boomed in the 1940s. The "world of childhood" was recognized as a unique and significant world.

Historians of the twenty-first century will see even more clearly the influences of events in the United States and the world on books for boys and girls. Two world wars and the development of atomic power forced the nation to turn from isolation to participation and leadership among world powers. Conflicting ideologies marshaled forces in a continuing cold war, and a new impetus for world understanding was recognized. Individualism in industry changed as large businesses merged into huge corporations, and as social forces led to increased government control and protection. Subur-

Lucy Locket, lost her pocket,
Kitty Fisher found it :
There was not a penny in it,
But a ribbon round it.

Tiny, quaint figures in old-fashioned dress are characteristic of Greenaway's children. From *Mother Goose or the Old Nursery Rhymes* by Kate Greenaway. Used by permission of the publisher, Frederick Warne and Company.

ban developments mushroomed around cities, changing patterns of family life. Air and water pollution, beautification, and conservation received new concern. Travel by jet plane and the mass media of radio and television provided much more information, and led to a new awareness of people of the world. Problems of integration continued despite the massive protests that increased civil rights for Negroes. Technology ushered in the Space Age with its new frontiers for modern pioneers.

Art of the twentieth century was now experimental. After the 1919 Armory Show in New York, there was an awareness of new styles of painting. Freedom, light, and color marked the abstract designs of cubism, surrealism, and other new art forms. In the 1960s, Op art and Pop art influenced design. Early in the century, jazz reflected distinctly American rhythms. A new realism in literature was followed eventually by starkly realistic film portrayals of human problems. The philosophy of existentialism led to reexamination of age-old questions regarding the meaning of life. To some, there was no purpose; life was an absurdity. From the influences of such writers as Sartre and Camus came the literature of despair.

In the United States of the 1960s, the federal government played an increasing role in education. Preschool programs were established with federal funds as part of the attack on poverty. Under the Elementary and Secondary Education Act of 1965, federal financial assistance became available for experimental programs, new materials, and libraries. Schools were seeking ways to provide for the wide range of individual differences among children. Creativity and development of productive thinking were now deemed major goals of education.

The types of literature published for the expanding child's world reflected the changes and challenges of life in the twentieth century. The new philosophy held that childhood was to be enjoyed. It is, perhaps, one of the finer commentaries of our times that as adult literature has reflected the disillusionment of depression, wars, and materialism by becoming more sordid, sensational, and psychological, children's literature has produced books of outstanding beauty and quality. It is almost as if publishers, authors, and illustrators have conspired to give this generation the very best in the world of books in order to compensate for a very uncertain future in the adult world.

Technical Improvements

The printing improvements initiated in the nineteenth century were fully realized in the next four decades. Photo-offset lithography made it possible to print many more books at a lower cost. Bindings were more durable, often washable, and bright and gay. It was possible to create beautiful, fine books for children and just as easy to mass produce shoddy, cheap editions. Paperback editions of good books for children became available early in the latter half of the twentieth century.

Fiction Factories

The dime novel had been initiated in the nineteenth century, and the series books of George Henty, Oliver Optic, Sophie May, and Horatio Alger had introduced the repetitive incident plot and stereotyped character.[19] "Fiction factories" were developed by Edward Stratemeyer, who wrote literally hundreds of books under a variety of pseudonyms.[20] *The Motor Boys, Tom Swift,* and *Nancy Drew* all came from this manufacturer of plots. Stratemeyer would give a three-page outline of characters and plot to hack writers to complete. In the biography of Howard Garis, *My Father Was Uncle Wiggly,* Roger Garis tells how his father worked for the Stratemeyer syndicate. Garis wrote *The Motor Boys* under the name of Clarence Young, *Tom Swift* books as Victor Appleton, and with Mrs. Garis, created *The Bobbsey Twins.* Garis could produce a book every eight or ten days. *Tom Swift* (1910), *The Rover Boys* (1899), *The Bobbsey Twins* (1904), and *Nancy Drew* continue to be "best sellers." The plots and characters have remained the same, although the modern versions deal

---

[19]"The Grinch & Co.," *Time,* vol. 70 (December 23, 1957), pp. 74–76.
[20]"For It Was Indeed He," *Fortune Magazine,* vol. 9 (April 1934), pp. 86–89.

with nuclear war, space flights, and submarines. The hero remains a child or adolescent, but partakes of adult adventure and acts with adult wisdom. A representative of good, he triumphs over all obstacles.

Recognition of Children's Literature

Disturbed by the influence of the fifty-cent juvenile, Franklin K. Mathiews, Chief Scout Librarian, sought to raise the level of reading. His suggestion for establishing a Children's Book Week was promoted in 1919 by Frederick Melcher as a project of the American Booksellers Association. Schools, libraries, newspapers, and book stores supported the event that became a significant stimulant to the development of children's literature. In 1945, the Children's Book Council was established to promote Book Week and to distribute information throughout the year.

Mr. Melcher also promoted another event that has encouraged the development of children's literature. He proposed the presentation of an annual award for the most distinguished book for children. Since 1922, the Newbery Award and the Caldecott Medal for picture books, awarded first in 1938, have had great influence in raising the standards of writing and illustrating children's books. Recent years have seen the establishment of other awards that encourage writers and illustrators of children's books.[21]

The addition of children's departments to publishing firms indicated the growing importance of literature for the young. In 1919, Macmillan made Louise Seaman children's editor, and other companies were soon to follow. May Massee became editor of children's books at Doubleday in 1922. The first critical reviews of children's books appeared in *The Bookman* in 1918. Anne Carroll Moore continued this influential work in her *New York Herald Tribune* column, "The Three Owls." *The Horn Book Magazine*, a publication solely devoted to children's literature, was first published in 1924 under the editorship of Bertha Mahony.

Public libraries instituted children's rooms and many elementary schools had libraries. By 1915, the American Library Association had established a School Library division. However, in 1963 nearly two-thirds of the elementary schools were still without school libraries. Federal funds gave impetus to development of instructional materials centers.

The National Council of Teachers of English was influential in promoting children's literature through articles about authors of children's books, reviews of books, and book lists. In the 1960s, the Council gave leadership in the movement to teach literature in the elementary school.

The Junior Literary Guild was established in 1929 and was the first to send children selected books each month. In the late 1950s, paperback book clubs made it possible for more children to own books and increased their enthusiasm for reading. Currently, many book clubs offer selections of children's literature.

Rise of the Picture Book

The importance of early childhood made it imperative that books be designed for young children. Technological progress made it possible to produce picture books for the preschoolers and picture storybooks for children in primary grades. C. B. Falls' *ABC Book* of 1923 presented woodcuts of high quality. *Clever Bill*, written and illustrated by William Nicholson, was published in England in 1926. Wanda Gág's delightful tale, *Millions of Cats,* published in 1928, has been called the first American picture storybook. In that same year, Boris Artzybasheff

---

[21]See Appendix A.

illustrated *The Fairy Shoemaker and Other Poems*, beginning his outstanding work. In England, Arthur Rackham was drawing his grotesque people and trees, often evoking an eerie atmosphere with his skilled lines. His illustrations of *Aesop's Fables, Gulliver's Travels*, and *Mother Goose* show fine detail, imaginative elves and gnomes, and excellent use of color. Leslie Brooke's animals in *Johnny Crow's Garden* were costumed and personified with facial expressions conveying feeling, humor, and charm.

The production of American picture books not only benefited from improved techniques in the field of graphic arts, but also from the influx of many fine European artists who, for one reason or another, sought refuge in this country. These artists found a legitimate outlet for their creative talents in the field of children's literature. Picture books were greatly enriched through their unique contributions. A glance at a roster of some of the names of well known illustrators will indicate the international character of their backgrounds: Charlot, d'Aulaire, Duvoisin, Eichenberg, Galdone, Mordvinoff, Petersham, Rojankovsky, Simont, Slobodkin, Yashima, and many more. The variety of their national backgrounds has added a cosmopolitan flavor to our picture books that is unprecedented both in time and place. American children have become the beneficiaries of an inheritance from the whole artistic world.

Growth of Informational Books

Lucy Sprague Mitchell utilized knowledge of child development in her *Here and Now Story Book* first published in 1921. She pointed out the young child's preoccupation with himself and his interest in daily experiences. Other writers recognized that such simple themes as taking a walk, planting a carrot, or listening to night sounds represented adventure for the three- to five-year-old. Books helped the preschool child

interpret experience; they were not designed to funnel information into his head. E. Boyd Smith's *The Farm Book* and *The Chicken World*, published in 1910, were among the first illustrative informational books.

The child's natural curiosity was extended through realistic stories or through straightforward text. The Lucy Fitch Perkins *Twins* series, beginning in 1911, gave information through stories. In *The Japanese Twins*, for example, Taro and Take are always "nice" children having a "nice" time in the series of incidents described. The inferior place of woman symbolized in the scene in which the new male baby's foot is placed on his big sister's neck was realistic. Most children would miss the meaning of this incident that ends as the mother sighs and turns her face to the wall. Unfortunately, stereotyped characters prevailed. Maud and Miska Petersham, who used rich colors to illustrate informational books about oil, wheat, food, clothing, and other products, were the first to give children in the early 1930s information about such processes. Reed's *The Earth for Sam* and Fenton's *Along the Hill* (1935) exemplify the beginning of accurate informational books.

Since the 1940s quantities of informational books have rolled from the presses to give children facts on almost every conceivable subject. Series books in the areas of science and social studies were important developments in this period. The *First Books, All About Books*, and the *True Books* series are examples of the trend. Many books of experiments by such authors as the Schneiders and Freemans have stimulated children's science activities. Developments in the fields of atomic energy and exploration of space have been reflected in books for children. Lewellen, Zim, Ley, Selsam, and Gallant have made significant contributions. Science books for younger children were increasingly available through such series as *Let's Read and Find Out* and *Junior Research*. Biographies appeared to satisfy children's interest in national heroes. Daugherty's *Daniel Boone*, published in 1930, was outstanding. The *Childhood of Famous Americans* series initiated the trend to publish biographies for boys and girls in series form. By the 1960s, biographies gave less emphasis to the early years of great men and women. More biographies for young children were available. Civil rights and world leaders and women were among the newer biographies for children.

Early in the twentieth century, historical fiction was written for children. Laura Richards quoted from diaries and letters as she wrote *Abigail Adams and Her Times* (1909). *The Horsemen of the Plains* (1910) by Altsheler related exciting frontier stories. The legendary approach to history was utilized by MacGregor in *Story of Greece* (1914). *When Knights Were Bold* brought another period of history to life when Tappan published this book in 1911. The sweep of history was shown in Van Loon's *The Story of Mankind* (1921). Coatsworth's historical fiction about America was initiated with *Away Goes Sally* in 1934. Long selections from original diaries and journals were presented in the historical accounts of Smith's *Pilgrim Courage* (1962) and *The Coming of the Pilgrims* (1964).

In the 1950s, factual books about rockets satellites, and space almost seemed to be fantasy, but by the 1960s such books were an accepted fact of daily life. Accounts of space flights and detailed descriptions of the work of the astronauts have helped children understand the technology of the new age. Concurrently, science books have pointed up problems of modern life. In *Clean the Air!, Fighting Smoke, Smog and Smaze across the Country* (1965), Lewis shows one of the problems and some possible solutions.

Folk Tales

A famous storyteller, Gudrun Thorne-Thomsen, recorded stories from Norway in *East O' the Sun and West O' the Moon* in 1912. Kate Douglas Wiggin edited tales from the *Arabian Nights* and Ellen Babbitt brought forth a collection of *Jataka Tales* from India. From 1900 to 1920 many collections of folk tales were purchased. Serious scholars recognized the value of these tales, and storytellers in schools and libraries brought them to the lives of children. Padraic Colum, Kate Douglas Wiggin, Parker Fillmore, and others contributed significant collections. Tales from the Far East and Africa were also added in the 1940s and 1950s. Wanda Gág illustrated single tales, but it was Marcia Brown who developed the trend to illustrate single tales by the publication of *Stone Soup* (1947). *Cinderella* (1954) and *Once a Mouse* (1961) won Caldecott Medals, while her other fairy tales, *Puss in Boots, Dick Whittington and His Cat,* and *The Steadfast Tin Soldier* were runners-up for the award.

Humor and Fantasy

Fantasy for children in the first half of the twentieth century seemed to come mainly from English writers. The *Just So Stories* (1902) stimulated children's imaginations as Kipling gave delightful accounts of the origin of animal characteristics. The boy who refused to grow up and lose the beauties of Never Never Land, Peter Pan, appeared in a London play in 1904 by J. M. Barrie, who made the play into a story titled *Peter Pan and Wendy* in 1911.

Another storyteller, Kenneth Grahame, wrote installments of adventures of a water rat, a mole, and a toad for his small son who was on a vacation. Thus, *The Wind in the Willows* was written and published in 1908.

Selma Lagerlöff had been commissioned to write a geographical reader on Sweden. She decided to present the information in the form of fantasy in which a boy is changed into an elf who flies over Sweden on a gander's back. Thus, *The Wonderful Adventures of Nils* appeared in 1907.

E. Nesbit's fantasies of magic rings, wishes, and invisible children mix humor, the real, and the unreal. Written in the early 1900s, *The Treasure Seekers* tells of the Bastable family that tries to recover a fortune. These magic tales were forerunners of the Mary Poppins stories.

In 1900, the Cowardly Lion and the Tin Woodsman met Dorothy in the Land of Oz. Although its merits have been debated by librarians and teachers, *The Wizard of Oz* by Baum, has been enjoyed by thousands of children and adults. The first book of the series might well have sufficed, for the others in the series are repetitious and not as well written.

One of the most delightful books of humor appeared in 1926. A. A. Milne created such believable characters as Eeyore, Piglet, and Pooh for young Christopher Robin, his son. The stuffed animals in *Winnie the Pooh* have many adventures that are true fantasy.

Perhaps books of humor and fantasy reflected the need for escape from the shadows of world tensions and war. New theories of child development recognized the rights of children to be themselves; the mental-health movement pointed up the values of recreation and fun for wholesome personality development. McCloskey's *Homer Price*, Cleary's *Henry Huggins*, and Atwater's *Mr. Popper's Penguins* brought humor in realistic stories. Dr. Seuss, Lawson, du Bois, and Norton are well-known writers of twentieth-century fantasy for children.

Animal Adventure

One of the most famous animals in literature is Peter Rabbit, who appeared in Mr. MacGregor's garden at the turn of the century. Two privately published editions preceded the book that was published by Warne in 1902 as *The Tale of Peter Rabbit*. Beatrix Potter introduced other animals, *Jemima Puddleduck* and *Benjamin Bunny*, but the cottontail family is best known and loved. While younger children were enjoying Peter

Rabbit, older boys and girls turned to Jack London's *Call of the Wild* (1903).

Although many teachers would place Hugh Lofting's *The Story of Doctor Dolittle* (1920) with the books of fantasy, children usually think of it as an animal story. Boys and girls read and reread Terhune's story of the faithful collie, *Lad: A Dog* (1919). *Smoky the Cowhorse* (1926) by Will James was an exciting story of the early decades of the century. This moving story of an intelligent horse who was mistreated by a series of owners brought a new realism to younger readers.

In the 1940s, Anderson wrote the Blaze stories, Henry delighted children with Misty and Brighty, and Farley's *Black Stallion* series gained popularity.

Many realistic, informational books about specific animals appeared in the 1950s, representing a new type of literature to meet children's interests.

Books for Personal-Social Development

The shadows of religious austerity and didacticism were reduced with the light of understanding of children. Also, the changing attitudes toward religion were reflected in books for children. Religious books were designed to help the child appreciate his religion and that of others. Dorothy Lathrop's *Animals of the Bible* was the first Caldecott Award book. The Petershams illustrated a beautiful story, *The Christ Child*, in 1931. Helen Sewell's effective, sculptured drawings enriched selections from the Bible in *A First Bible*, published in 1934. Elizabeth Orton Jones interpreted Bible verses in *Small Rain* (1943). She drew realistic, charming children engaged in everyday activities to illustrate Bible verses. The gay rhythm band for the text, "Make a joyful noise unto the Lord" is especially appealing. Miss Jones shows children of all races happily playing together. *One God: The Ways We Worship Him* by Fitch

(1944) explained religious beliefs and rituals of Protestants, Jews, and Catholics.

Emphasis on books of manners continued into the twentieth century as Gelett Burgess initiated the cartoon approach in *"A Manual of Manners for Polite Infants Inculcating Many Juvenile Virtues Both by Precept and Example."* The main title was *Goops and How to Be Them* (1900). This was a forerunner of Munroe Leaf's book, *Manners Can Be Fun* (1958).

Realistic fiction often reflected war, depression, and social problems in the contemporary scene. Just as in the past, children's books mirrored adult concerns and interests. Intercultural education took on new significance. Lois Lenski pioneered in presenting authentic, detailed descriptions of life in specific regions of the United States. By living in the community, observing the customs of the people, and listening to their stories, she was able to produce a significant record of American life from the 1930s into the 1960s. Problems of the migratory worker were dramatized by Gates in *Blue Willow* (1940). Eleanor Estes was one of the first to write about poverty and children's interrelationships in their closed society. Her book, *The Hundred Dresses* (1944), enabled teachers to guide frank discussions of the problem of being "different."

Very few books dealt with racial problems. Books that portrayed Negroes, for example, showed stereotypes of the bandana-covered, fat mammy and the kinky-haired, thick-lipped "funny" boy. This stereotype was eptomized in the Nicodemus series written by Hogan in the late 1930s with such titles as *Nicodemus and the Gang* (1939). The jacket of this book quotes part of a *New York Herald Tribune* review that said, "A story that will get itself remembered when some longer and louder ones are forgotten." Fortunately, Nicodemus with his gang who have such stereotyped names as Rastus, Obadiah, and Petunia have been forgotten. "I'se a

comin'," "Yas'm Mammy," and "nex' time, I spec you better stan' on de groun' fo' speech makin'" exemplified the stereotyped dialect used in this series. The segregation of Negroes was clearly shown in *Araminta* (1935) by Evans and the photographic essay, *Tobe* (1939), by Sharpe. It was nearly ten years later that Negroes and whites were shown participating in activities together. The theme of *Two Is a Team* by the Beims is revealed in both the title and the action as a Negro boy and a white boy play together. Prejudice was openly discussed for the first time in Jackson's *Call Me Charley* (1945) and Marguerite de Angeli's *Bright April* (1946). *Mary Jane* (1959) by Sterling told of the new social problems caused by school integration. By the mid-1960s, a few books showed Negro characters through the illustrations, but the fact was not mentioned in the text. Examples include *The Snowy Day* by Keats, *Mississippi Possum* by Miles, and Shotwell's *Roosevelt Grady.*

A tremendous increase in series books about other lands followed World War II, and beautiful photography books about other lands appeared in the late 1950s. The importance of security in early family relationships led to books about new babies, adopted children, and good family relationships. Other books dealt with such problems as fear, adjustment to new situations, and acceptance in the peer group. Some of these books moralized, as did the old didactic stories. Unfortunately, many overemphasized the theme and failed to meet criteria of good books for children.

Poetry

"Liquid liveliness," "rare charm," "exquisite mastery of words"—these phrases have been used to describe the beauty in the poems of and for children by Walter de la Mare. *Songs for Childhood* appeared in 1902, beginning the new century with a work that helped young and old alike perceive infinite beauty and enchantment. Eleven years later *Peacock Pie* brought new melodies, nursery rhymes, and fairy poems.

The fun and gaiety of the child's everyday world was interpreted by such poets as A. A. Milne, Rachel Field, Dorothy Aldis, and Aileen Fisher. The transition in children's poetry from the didactic to the descriptive, from moralizing to poems of fun and nonsense had at last been achieved.

Translations of Foreign Books

An exciting development in children's literature was the appearance of a large number of translations of foreign books. *Pippi Longstocking* by Lindgren had arrived from Sweden in 1950. The same author wrote *Rasmus and the Vagabond,* published in Sweden in 1956 and in the United States in 1960. From Germany came *Emil and the Detectives* first published in 1930 by Erich Kästner. Both Lindgren and Kästner have received the International Hans Christian Andersen Award. American editions of books written by British authors have been made by changing some of the spelling and words. When children realize they are reading the same stories read by children in other countries, they develop a sense of companionship in the wide world of literature.

Books for Special Interests

Another trend in the twentieth century was the increase in the number of special-interest books. "How-to-do-it" books, books about art, music, and dance, sports stories, and mysteries were produced rapidly. Books about all kinds of hobbies were available in the 1950s. There were books to guide young collectors, from *Stamp Collecting* by Lewis (1952), to *Catch a Cricket* by Stevens (1961), to *Birds Will Come to You* by Fox (1963). If parents and teachers guide children's interests toward satisfying hobbies, they are laying a foundation for leisure time resulting from automation.

Summary

When the twentieth century opened, the young reader could find on his bookshelf many books primarily intended for adults, didactic tales aimed at instruction, some informational books, and a few stories written purely for his pleasure. By mid-century books no longer had to teach, preach, or patronize! Fun was now acceptable; the child's natural curiosity was both extended and satisfied through informational books.

Forerunners of modern books have been identified in this chapter. Part 2 will describe each of the types of books available today and establish criteria for selection. The tremendous development in children's book publishing in the first half of the twentieth century has created a "golden age" of children's literature.

CHILDREN'S BOOKS TOMORROW

Literature for children has reflected changing cultural patterns throughout the centuries. In an era of rapid social change, it is difficult to predict adult purposes for publishing and selecting books for children, but it is possible to discern trends that will influence children's books of tomorrow. The concern about conformity, social problems, mental health, commitment to democratic values, and world understanding will continue to be reflected in future offerings.

Science books for children will draw upon man's rapidly growing knowledge of outer space, biological principles, and underwater life. Younger children will find more informational books and biographies geared to their reading levels. More nonfiction books will have controlled vocabularies.

Books about anthropology, economics, and government may be written to help children understand their complex world.

The interest in the culturally disadvantaged in rural and urban areas may well lead to books about children in these unfortunate circumstances. More realistic family patterns may be portrayed, with mother working, or parents divorced, for example. Racial problems will continue to form the basis of many plots. As publishers see the increased need for these kinds of books, there is a danger that authors will be commissioned to write socially oriented books in which the theme overrides the plot.

Picture books will continue to reflect increased experimentation with new media and art forms. More picture books will be designed for older children. Beautifully illustrated editions of one song or poem will be created, just as individual fairy tales were given outstanding treatment.

The trend toward special packages of literature as part of the basic reading program may encourage teachers to promote wide reading of good books. More paperback editions will be used in schools for individual and small group study.

As educators use varied materials to meet the wide range of individual differences, the "grade" labels will tend to disappear. A book may serve the needs of a child in second grade as well as the needs of another child, working at a different level, in a sixth grade. The sharp division between texts and trade books for use in gaining information will decrease.

With the advent of foreign languages in elementary curricula and the possibilities for world-wide television, children should be given the opportunity to enjoy books from other countries. In addition to increasing numbers of translated books, the trend toward a simultaneous publication of books in English and another language probably will continue.

Books for children will continue to deal with the "human condition," the problems of fear, loneliness, and isolation from others. Perhaps more allegories will find their place on bookshelves for boys and girls. The "sick literature" written for adults may infect writing for children as authors express their views of life.

There is now a recognized body of children's literature. The number of mediocre books published each year may increase; at the same time, a number of books of lasting quality will also be written each year. We can expect juvenile writers of the next decade to give to children the light of humor and understanding as well as vicarious experiences in the joys and sorrows of human relationships.

SUGGESTED ACTIVITIES

1. Recall your reading experiences from childhood. What were your favorite books? What books were read to you as a child?
2. Look at some copies of the earliest books for children. Compare content, type, and illustrations of these early examples with modern books.
3. Identify adult purposes in several recent books for children.
4. Begin your reading of children's books by reviewing a modern book of each type— humor, information, picture, folk tale, biography, animals, or other lands.
5. If possible, bring your favorite book to class and discuss it with others. What parts did you like best as a child? Do you enjoy the book now upon re-reading?
6. Interview five adults of different ages. Inquire about their favorite books and childhood reading interests.

RELATED READINGS

1. Arbuthnot, May Hill. *Children and Books*. Third edition. Glenview, Ill.: Scott, Foresman, 1964.
Chapter 3 emphasizes the puritanical influence and describes the didactic literature through the years. Chapter 4 traces the development of illustration, and origins of Mother Goose are presented in Chapter 5.

2. Blanck, Jacob. *Peter Parley to Penrod*. New York: Bowker, 1938.
This is really a guide for collectors of children's books, but will be of interest to the student of the series books and adventures of this period. Authors, titles, sizes of books, and colors of covers are given. Little information about the content of the books is included.

3. Darton, F. J. Harvey. *Children's Books in England: Five Centuries of Social Life*. Cambridge, England: Cambridge University Press, 1932.
This volume includes a detailed study of the fables and romances of the Middle Ages, a discussion of the work of John Newbery, and an analysis of books published before 1900. The influence of the social attitudes of the period on books for children is clearly shown in this study.

4. De Vries, Leonard. *Flowers of Delight: An Agreeable Garland of Prose and Poetry 1765–1830*. New York: Pantheon, 1965.
The editor selected books and poems from the Osborne collection of early children's books, and has published them with the original illustrations. It is especially valuable because the story or poem is printed in its entirety. Reproductions of illustrations are excellent.

5. Epstein, Sam and Beryl. *The First Book of Printing*. Pictures by Laszlo Roth. New York: F. Watts, 1955.
This book for children will be useful to the teacher in explaining various printing processes.

6. Folmsbee, Beulah. *A Little History of the Horn Book*. Boston: Horn Book, 1942.
A tiny volume, the size of the early hornbooks, gives the recipe for making sheets of horn and tells how the hornbook was made.

7. Garis, Roger. *My Father Was Uncle Wiggly, The Story of the Remarkable Garis Family*. New York: McGraw-Hill, 1966.
An entertaining biography of Howard Garis, one of the "hack" writers who created series books for the Stratemeyer syndicate.

8. Hazard, Paul. *Books Children and Men*. Boston: Horn Book, 1947.
Glowing prose illuminates the relationship of literature to life and stresses the values of providing opportunities to bring literature to children. Criteria for good books for children are established.

9. Jordan, Alice M. *From Rollo to Tom Sawyer*. Boston: Horn Book, 1948.
Biographies of authors of children's books of the latter half of the nineteenth century help the teacher understand books of this period.

10. Kiefer, Monica. *American Children through Their Books 1700–1835*. Philadelphia: University of Philadelphia Press, 1948.
The significance of the changing status of children in the development of literature is clearly delineated. Influences of educational philosophers are illustrated in this reference. Descriptions of children's clothing and customs are interesting.

11. Mahony, Bertha E., Louise Latimer, and Beulah Folmsbee. *Illustrators of Children's Books 1744-1945*. Boston: Horn Book, 1947.
Part I traces the history of picture books in England and America. Reproductions of early illustrations are excellent. Graphic processes in children's books are clearly explained.

12. McKendry, John J., Editor. *Aesop: Five Centuries of Illustrated Fables*. The Metropolitan Museum of Art. Greenwich, Conn.: New York Graphic Society, 1964.
Through the pages of this book, a reader can trace the development of many

types of illustrations, from German woodcuts of the fifteenth century, to engravings of the nineteenth, and modern woodcuts of the twentieth century. The introduction provides a good summary of the development of the fables and their varied illustrations.

13. Meigs, Cornelia, *et al. A Critical History of Children's Literature.* New York: Macmillan, 1953.
    An interesting survey of books for children from earliest times to the middle of the twentieth century. The organization by chronological periods emphasizes influences upon children's literature and trends. Many examples of books for children in each period of history provide details regarding the development of children's literature.

14. Muir, Percy. *English Children's Books 1600 to 1900.* London, England: Batsford, 1954.
    The development of literature for children in England is outlined in detail. The section describing the work of early illustrators of children's books is particularly useful.

15. Personn, Lisa-Christina, Editor. *Translations of Children's Books.* Lund, Sweden: Bibliotekstjanst, 1962.
    Several papers read at international conferences present problems of translating children's books. A list of books recommended for translation will interest students of children's literature.

16. Pitz, Henry C. *Illustrating Children's Books.* New York: Watson-Guptill, 1963.
    Technical aspects of illustration are emphasized in this book that includes information about illustration in books in England, Europe, and America. Many examples of modern illustration are included in the book to illustrate techniques and influences of artists from many countries.

17. Sloane, William. *Children's Books in England and America in the Seventeenth Century.* New York: Kings Crown, 1955.
    A valuable account of folk material, books of good advice, and religious books available for children in the seventeenth century is presented.

18. Smith, Dora V. *Fifty Years of Children's Books 1910–1960: Trends, Backgrounds, Influences.* Champaign, Ill.: National Council of Teachers of English, 1963.
    This book presents the author's choices of best books in the fifty-year period. It recognizes the influence of foreign writers and illustrators, awards and organizations, as well as social concerns and changes in educational practice.

19. Smith, Elva S. *The History of Children's Literature.* Chicago: American Library Association, 1937.
    This book gives an outline of influences and types of books of each period from 1659–1900. The list of representative writers of each period would be useful to the serious student of the history of children's literature.

20. St. John, Judith. *The Osborne Collection of Early Children's Books 1566–1919: A Catalogue.* Toronto, Canada: Toronto Public Library, 1958.
    This catalogue describes approximately 3000 books in the Osborne collection. The books are classified according to interests such as nursery and fairy tales, poetry, instruction, and stories. The reproductions from these early books are excellent.

21. Thwaite, M. F. *From Primer to Pleasure: An Introduction to the History of Children's Books in England, from the Invention of Printing to 1900.* London, England: Library Association, 1963.
    A very readable history of children's literature, this volume shows developments in each period, and lists a number of books not found in other references. The analysis of the influence of American writing on English books is interesting.

22. Turner, E. S. *Boys Will Be Boys.* Castle Hedingham, Essex, England: Daiman Press, 1962.
    This paperback book traces the development of the comic book and "fifty-center" in England. Such characters as Sweeney Todd, Deadwood Dick, and Dick Barton are described.

2

KNOWING CHILDREN'S LITERATURE

3

PICTURE BOOKS

Annie, aged two and one-half, returned home from a morning visit with her four-year-old playmate. While waiting for her lunch, Ann looked thoughtfully at her mother and said, "Do you know, Robin can't read." There was a mixture of pity and amazement in her voice, for Annie could "read." True, she could not identify the printed words, but she could read pictures with understanding. In fact, her favorite entertainment was "reading" books or magazines by herself, with her mother, or any other willing interpreter of the printed page. Although only two and a half, Annie had discovered the joys and pleasure that can be derived from reading. She was amazed and a little sad to learn that all children actually did not share her favorite pastime.

FIRST EXPERIENCES WITH BOOKS

Children cannot be introduced to books too soon. At age two and one-half, Annie had already entered the world of literature. To know exactly why she enjoyed books and Robin did not, would require an intimate knowledge of their family backgrounds. We know that Annie came from a home in which books were a part of her natural environment. She saw her mother, father, and sister reading. She frequently went to the library with them. After they had selected their books, Annie was taken to the children's room for her books. The bedtime story was a ritual for her. But enjoyment of books was not limited to just this time; rainy days meant reading days; the quiet and lonely time right after her daddy had gone to work and her sister had gone to school; a few moments before her naptime; at dusk when the family was waiting dinner for father; these were all times when Annie could say, "Read to me, please."

Annie is learning to love books, as she has many opportunities to snuggle up close to her mother and father for a story time. She is also increasing her vocabulary as she points to pictures and names them, or hears new words used in the context of the story. The language development of children of this age is phenomenal; preoccupation with words and the sounds of words is characteristic of the very young child. Books help to fulfill this insatiable desire to learn new and more words.

The young child who has the opportunity to hear and enjoy many stories is also getting ready to learn how to read. The process of learning to read should hold no terror for Annie, only the opportunity to become independent in a skill that she knows gives pleasure. Her experiential background has been widened as a result of exposure to many books. Research has shown that the nature and extent of children's past experiences influence their progress in learning to read. The meaning and comprehension of the printed page depends upon the meaning and understanding that the reader brings to that page. Annie's background of experience is rich and not limited to books alone. However, her enjoyment and appreciation of the world of literature will facilitate the transition from *hearing* stories to *reading* stories independently.

First Books

Frequently, young children's "first books" are the family magazines. Toddlers can look at these, find pictures of "mother," "daddy," "sister," and even themselves. If pages are bent or torn, no serious damage has been done. Recognizing this need of the young child to identify objects, publishers have produced simple "first books." These are usually constructed with heavy, durable pages and portray such familiar objects as favorite toys, clothing, and animals. "First books" may have an accompanying text, but there is little or no continuity of plot to these stories. The fun is in the naming of the pictures. The illustrations should be simple, uncluttered, and easily identifiable, with usually only one object, or a group of two or three on a page. *Baby's First Book,* illustrated by Garth Williams, is an excellent example of this type of book. *Teddy* by Janus uses the accumulative approach, first showing a teddy bear, then his clothes, his special dishes, and finally, his bed. Francoise has written a "naming book" for the preschool child entitled *The Things I Like.* In her usual peasant-like style of art, the author-illustrator has a little girl, a boy, and a dog tell the things they like: animals, people (this is the dog's preference), good things to eat, picnics, vacations, books, parties, the circus, Easter, and Christmas. The ending of this book invites the reader's participation with the question, "What do *you* like?"

After naming objects, children enjoy telling their own stories. Some books have no text and encourage the child to tell the story from the pictures only. *The Good Bird* by Wezel presents the story of a bird who shares his worm with an unhappy goldfish. The pictures are simple and childlike, but the action and plot are clearly illustrated. *What Whiskers Did* by Carroll has a more complex plot. The pictures show a little dog chasing some rabbits. In turn, the dog is chased by a larger one and must seek refuge in the same rabbit hole as his former victims. The subtle irony of the story is understood by many four- and five-year-olds. While all children enjoy telling a story, these books are particularly useful with children who need opportunities for language experiences.

"Participation" Books

The secret of sharing any book or picture with very young children is to involve the child in some way. In looking at a picture in Friskey's *Seven Diving Ducks,* the adult will say, "Show me the ducks that are in the water. Show me the ducks that are on the land. Where is the little duck who wouldn't dive?" Young children enjoy riddle-like questions. For example, when sharing Slobodkina's *Caps for Sale,* the child can be asked, "Find the monkey—not the one in the red hat, not the one in the blue hat, but the one in the green hat!" Such questioning will help children develop visual discrimination, but, more importantly, it will make storytime fun.

Some books have "built-in participation" as part of their design. These books may well serve as the transition between toys and real books. Two books by Kunhardt entitled *Pat the Bunny* and *Tickle the Pig* encourage fun and participation. In *Pat the Bunny,* the child is invited to use senses other than sight and sound. A "pattable" bunny made of flannel is on one page, flowers that really smell on another, and daddy's unshaven face, repre-

A whole family enjoys a new edition of Mother Goose. Photographed by Francis Haar, Honolulu, Hawaii.

sented by sandpaper roughness, is on still another. Young children literally wear out this "tactile" book.

H. A. Rey has provided for participation in some of his books by the simple device of placing a surprise picture under a flap of each page. In *Where's My Baby?* children are asked to look for the young kangaroo—lift the flap, and there he is all cozy in his mother's pocket! Similarly designed books by the same author-illustrator include the titles *Anybody at Home?* and *Let's Feed the Animals.* The sophisticated cut-out books by Bruno Munari have immediate appeal for young children. In *Animals for Sale,* a tall gentleman is walking a flamingo. The text asks if the reader would like a flamingo and the reply is given, "No, it might peck at the wallpaper. Show me another animal."[1] By lifting a

---

[1]Bruno Munari, *Animals for Sale,* Translated by Maria Cimino (Cleveland: World Publishing, 1957).

smaller page, the reader sees a porcupine attached to the same leash and walking with the same tall gentleman. An armadillo, bat, and centipede are discovered under subsequently smaller pages. In *Who's There? Open the Door!*, the first double-page spread shows Lucy, the giraffe, having arrived all the way from Lisbon, with a crate. Open the crate (which is a page) and there is Peggy, the zebra, from Paris with a trunk (a smaller page) and so the story continues. One three-year-old was first introduced to this book by knocking at the cover and repeating the title of *Who's There? Open the Door!* It became a book that he requested again and again. The preliminary participation of knocking on the cover became an established ritual.

The Birthday Present, also by Munari, has a similar format. A truck driver is taking a birthday present home to his three-year-old son. When he is ten miles from home, his truck breaks down, and the various means of transportation by which he reaches home are presented on smaller and smaller-sized pages. The design of this book is original and the book is well constructed for three-year-olds' use. Sturdy construction is an essential requirement for books for the youngest. Simplicity of format and clear, recognizable pictures are equally important. Books with cloth pages and manipulative devices may appear to be "toys" rather than books, but two- and three-year-olds derive pleasure and build concepts as they identify objects, tell stories from pictures, and open "surprise flaps" on books. First experiences with books should be enjoyable.

MOTHER GOOSE

For many children, Mother Goose[2] is their first introduction to the world of literature. Even a one-year-old child will respond

with delight to "Pat-a-Cake! Pat-a-Cake!" or "This Little Pig Went to Market." Many of the Mother Goose rhymes and jingles continue to be favorites among the fours and fives. What is the attraction of Mother Goose that makes her so appealing to these young children? What accounts for her survival through these many years? Much of the language in these rhymes is obscure. For example, no modern-day child has any understanding of curds and whey, yet he delights in Miss Muffet. Nothing in current literature has replaced the venerable Mother Goose for the nursery-school age.

Appeals of Mother Goose

Language Pattern Much of the appeal of Mother Goose is in the varied language pattern; the rhythm and rhyme of the verses; the alliteration of such lines as: "Wee Willie Winkie runs through the town," or "Deedle, deedle, dumpling, my son John." Children love the sound of the words, for they are experimenting with language in this period of their development. The greatest growth in language development is achieved between the ages of two and six years. The child learns new words every day; he likes to try them out, to chant them in his play. Chukovsky, a Russian poet, refers to the tremendous "speech-giftedness of the preschool child" and maintains that "beginning with the age of two, every child becomes for a short period of time a linguistic genius."[3] Mother Goose rhymes help the young child satisfy his preoccupation with language patterns.

Participation Mother Goose rhymes offer young children many opportunities for active participation and response. Most of the verses are short and easily memorized;

[2]See Chapter 2 for the development and background of Mother Goose.

[3]Kornei Chukovsky, *From Two to Five,* Translated by Miriam Morton (Berkeley, Calif.: University of California Press, 1963), pp. 7, 9.

they can be chanted in unison, or children may join in the refrains. Some of the rhymes, such as "Pease Porridge Hot," "London Bridge," or "Ring a Ring o'Roses," are games or involve direct action from the child. Other verses include counting, as in "1, 2, buckle my shoe/3, 4, shut the door." Children of five and six enjoy answering the riddles in some of the Mother Goose rhymes or attempting to say their favorite tongue twisters. Every child likes to fool someone with the well-known riddle, "As I was going to St. Ives, I met a man with seven wives." Older children never fail to delight in successful recitation of the entire verse of "Peter Piper picked a peck of pickled peppers."

Narrative Quality   Another attraction of many of the Mother Goose rhymes is their narrative quality; they tell a good story. In just six lines, "Little Miss Muffet" proves to be an exciting tale with action, a climax, and a satisfying conclusion. This is also true of "Simple Simon," "Sing a Song of Sixpence," "The Old Woman in the Shoe," and "Three Blind Mice." These stories in Mother Goose are characterized by their quick action. They are not moralistic, but justice does prevail, as in the ending of "The Queen of Hearts."

Characters   Many of the characters in Mother Goose are interesting, likeable people. Old King Cole *is* a merry old soul, Old Mother Hubbard tried to find her poor dog a bone, and although Tommy Lynn put the pussy in the well, Johnny Stout pulled her out! "The Crooked Man" has a crooked smile, and Mary did love her lamb. Unpleasant character traits are suggested by "Crosspatch" and "Tom, Tom, the piper's son." Teachers might hope that their pupils would not emulate the "Ten O'clock Scholar." The behavior of the "Little Girl with a Curl" is all too familiar, and children like the line "But when she was bad she was horrid."

Content   The content of the verses reflects the interests of young children. Many favorites are rhymes about animals, such as "The Three Little Kittens," "The Cat and the Fiddle," "The Mouse Who Ran Up the Clock," "Old Mother Hubbard," "Mary Had a Little Lamb," and "Pussy Cat, Pussy Cat." While many of the animals are personified, some are not. For example, the kitten in "I Love Little Pussy" is very real.

Some of the verses are about simple every-day experiences and include such incidents as "Lucy Locket" losing her purse, "The Three Little Kittens" losing their mittens, and "Little Bo Peep" who lost her sheep. Children's pranks are seen in "Ding, Dong, Bell!" and "Georgie Porgie." Everyday misfortunes are included in "Jack and Jill" and "Humpty Dumpty." "Peter, Peter, Pumpkin-Eater" had a housing problem, as did the "Old Woman in the Shoe." There are several verses about the weather, a concern of both young and old. The pleading request of one boy for "Rain, Rain Go Away" reflects the feelings of all children.

Humor   A major appeal of Mother Goose is the varied humor. There is the jolly good fun of a ridiculous situation in:

One misty, moisty morning
When cloudy was the weather,
I chanced to meet an old man
Clothed all in leather;
He began to compliment
And I began to grin—
"How do you do" and "How do you do"
And "How do you do" again!

Two seven-year-olds interpreted this verse in action by pretending to pass each other; as one moved to the left, the other moved in the same direction. Their movements were perfect for this amusing and familiar situation.

Young children's rather primitive sense of humor that delights in other people's misfortune is satisfied by the verses about "Jack and Jill" and "Dr. Foster":

> Doctor Foster went to Gloucester
> In a shower of rain;
> He stepped in a puddle up to his middle
> And never went there again.

When this kind of humor is exaggerated it is apt to become sadistic. Children's humor can be cruel, however, and they are quite insensitive to the dire punishment of the "old man/Who would not say his prayers/I took him by the left leg/And threw him down the stairs." For children, such action is fun and thoroughly relished.

Finally, there is much pure nonsense in Mother Goose that tickles children's funny bones. Chukovsky reminds us, however, that there is sense in nonsense;[4] a child has to know reality to appreciate the juxtaposition of the strawberries and the herrings in the reversed order of the following verse:

> The man in the wilderness asked me
> How many strawberries grew in the sea.
> I answered him as I thought good,
> As many as red herrings grew in the wood.

Different Editions of Mother Goose

Today's children are fortunate to be able to choose among many beautifully illustrated Mother Goose editions. There is no *one* best Mother Goose book, for this is a matter of individual preference. The children in every family deserve at least one of the better editions, however.

English Editions Three English editions of Mother Goose have been treasured classics for many generations. While they are, perhaps, not the most appropriate selections for the modern American child, they still appeal to children. They are important for

the student of children's literature for they are the forerunners of many of our present editions. *Mother Goose, or The Old Nursery Rhymes*, illustrated by Kate Greenaway, is tiny in format, with quaint, precise, and old-fashioned pictures. Her children have a quiet decorum that is in keeping with their nineteenth century finery. However, there is action in these tiny pictures and a feeling for the English rural countryside and villages.

Quite different in feeling is the edition by Arthur Rackham entitled *Mother Goose, Old Nursery Rhymes*. Rackham uses three different types of illustrations for his verses; pen-and-ink sketches, silhouettes, and colored pictures. The latter are painted in the typical Rackham fashion with eerie trees and weird little men peering from under their mushroom hats.

Leslie Brooke's *Ring O'Roses* presents a very different impression from that of the Rackham edition. His pictures are delightfully humorous and gay. The pigs in "This Little Pig Went to Market" are happy and complacent except for the poor dejected fellow who had no roast beef. Even Brooke's crooked man has a gay crooked smile.

More recent English editions of Mother Goose are equally outstanding. *Lavender's Blue* was compiled by Kathleen Lines and illustrated by Harold Jones. The colored pictures are in muted tones of blue, green, and brown and are unmistakably English in setting, costume, and mood. "Old King Cole," "I Had a Little Nut Tree," and "Sing a Song of Sixpence" are more richly colored scenes with settings in palaces or royal courtyards. Other settings include the rural English countryside with winding lanes and thatched roofed houses, English villages, and a beautifully composed picture of all the steeples in London for "Gay go up and gay go down, to ring the bells of London town."

Raymond Briggs chose only twenty-three rhymes to illustrate in his first book of Mother Goose entitled *The White Land*. The

---

[4]Chukovsky, p. 95.

rhymes are illustrated with paintings that combine color and a chalky white in a most unusual way. Briggs later produced a more comprehensive edition titled *The Mother Goose Treasury* including over 400 rhymes and more than twice as many illustrations. Almost all of the verses are from the authentic Opie collection and include most of the well-loved rhymes, plus some that are less well known. The book appears crammed with many vivid little scenes, objects, and comic people. Each rhyme has its own illustrations, and in some instances, each verse or line has an accompanying picture. Pages of black and white drawings alternate with pages of brilliant color. Occasionally, a beautiful full-page picture will illustrate one verse such as the picture of the dark blue fish leaping from the blue seas into the blue sky for the verse of "Terrence McDiddle." Usually, however, four or five verses with their separate illustrations appear on one page. This gives a feeling of clutter, although it does provide much for the child to enjoy.

Probably the most striking and unusual Mother Goose edition is *Brian Wildsmith's Mother Goose.* Painted in brilliant watercolors, these pictures capture the gaiety of Mother Goose for twentieth-century children. The typical Wildsmith trademark is seen in the harlequin designs on the clothing of his characters. Another unusual characteristic of Wildsmith's style is the frequency with which he shows just the backs of people. By illustrating the back of "Tom, Tom, the Piper's Son" and that of the "Ten O'clock Scholar," Wildsmith makes the reader a witness to the scene. The careful planning of this book is reflected in the combination of rhymes that are presented on a single page. For example, "Little Boy Blue" is shown opposite "Diddle, Diddle, Dumpling"; both boys are sleeping, one in the haystack and the other in his bed. A contrast of rich and poor is seen in the placement on facing pages of the rhymes that say "Ride a cock horse to Banbury Cross/

A self-satisfied pig goes to market as depicted by Brooke's humorous style. From *A Nursery Rhyme Picture Book,* Number Two, by L. Leslie Brooke. Reproduced by the permission of the publisher, Frederick Warne & Company.

To see a fine lady upon a white horse," and "Hark, hark, the dogs do bark/The beggars have come to town." Mindful of the medieval origin of some of the Mother Goose rhymes, Wildsmith has used this period as the setting for many of his verses.

American Editions Counterparts of the English editions may be seen in some of the newer American editions. The good humor that is so characteristic of Brooke is equally characteristic of Rojankovsky's illustrations in *The Tall Book of Mother Goose.* His pictures are bright and gay; his children are natural looking, sometimes homely and disheveled. It is one of the few editions that portray children in today's dress; for example, his "Jack Be Nimble" is dressed in a cowboy suit. Rojankovsky is particularly skilled in capturing children's expressions—for example, his "Little Miss Muffet" is terrified; "Lucy Locket" is thoughtful and pensive; "Jack Horner" is a picture of greedy innocence. Rojankovsky has been criticized for moralizing in his pictures. For example, little Johnny Green, who was responsible for pushing the pussy in the well, is shown smoking. A large "X" is drawn through his face in order to leave no doubt in the reader's mind as to the kind of boy who would do such a thing. Rojankovsky has portrayed his Humpty Dumpty as Hitler. Since one theory maintains that the first nursery rhymes were really political satire, this portrayal seems quite appropriate, particularly in 1942 when this edition was first published.

The Real Mother Goose by Blanche Fisher Wright has long been an established favorite in American nurseries. The large traditional pictures remind one of Brooke's work, but they lack his delightful humor. First published in 1916, the golden anniversary edition was printed in 1965. Although old-fashioned in appearance, it continues to be a favorite and is passed from one generation to another.

The Tenggren Mother Goose by Gustaf Tenggren is more stylized than any of the other books. Children will enjoy his fat rounded figures that have a certain similarity to Walt Disney's cartoons. Tenggren uses bright, rich colors. Unfortunately, many tiny, extraneous decorations appear throughout the text. One page includes a picture of a windmill, when there is no mention of one in the verses given; another pictures a black lamb that does not relate to any of the rhymes on the page. Such details might prove confusing to young children.

The *Mother Goose* by Tasha Tudor is reminiscent of the work of Kate Greenaway. Her soft pastel pictures are quaint and charming; her characters, lovable. The costumes of the characters represent many periods: American colonial, pioneer, Kate Greenaway, and Elizabethan. The settings of the interiors are as authentic as the costumes. The rural scenes portray the changing seasons delightfully. The miniatures in flowered frames on the endpapers and title page add to the period feeling of this book.

A quaint, old-fashioned feeling is also conveyed in Anglund's *In a Pumpkin Shell.* This is a combination Mother Goose and ABC book in which each letter is introduced with a Mother Goose rhyme. Limited to twenty-six, the illustrations are in pen and ink and rich watercolors. Anglund's style of illustrating is easily recognizable, portraying cherubic faces without noses or mouths, and rather amusing caricatures of adults. Costumes and setting are frequently nineteenth-century American

One of the most beautiful editions of Mother Goose is *The Book of Nursery and Mother Goose Rhymes* by Marguerite de Angeli. This is a large book containing nearly 250 pictures, some of which are full-page illustrations painted in soft watercolors. No one could ever forget the lovely picture that illustrates the fine lady on her beautiful horse. The rich detail of the English countryside is similar to *Lavender's Blue.* Marguerite de Angeli's children and babies are beautifully portrayed.

Carefully designed wood engravings in six colors illustrate Philip Reed's *Mother Goose and Nursery Rhymes.* His rustic human characters and spirited animals provide humor and charm. The total format of this book represents superb bookmaking. The fine paper and well-designed use of space give a feeling of quality and richness. This selection of Mother Goose rhymes includes several that are less well known than the usual verses, for example, "Guy Fawkes Day."

Single-Verse Editions   A recent trend has been the publication of picture books portraying only one Mother Goose rhyme. Paul Galdone has illustrated five of these books, including *The Old Woman and Her Pig, The House That Jack Built, Old Mother Hubbard and Her Dog, Tom, Tom, the Piper's Son,* and *The History of Simple Simon.* These narrative verses have action and humor and lend themselves well to individual presentations. Galdone's pictures have much sly humor and his animal "personalities" are delightful.

A handsome edition of *The House That Jack Built* has been presented in two languages with bold woodcuts by Antonio Frasconi. While this verse does not regularly appear in Mother Goose books, it is a well-known traditional nursery rhyme. Frasconi's four-color woodcuts have a strength and a rusticity appropriate for this old rhyme.

Maurice Sendak chose to illustrate two less well-known rhymes in *Hector Protector* and *As I Went over the Water.* His illustrations greatly expand the original text of four lines into a story of their own. Sendak has told the tale of Hector, a small rebellious boy who hates green *and* the queen, in twenty-four pictures! In the second rhyme, a little boy conquers a boat-swallowing dragon with the greatest of aplomb.

Barbara Cooney has illustrated in minute detail *The Courtship, Merry Marriage, and Feast of Cock Robin and Jenny Wren, to which is added the Doleful Death of Cock Robin.* For her wedding, Jenny Wren wears a white dress with train, pearls, and a hat with a beautiful plume. Later, in a widow's veil, she stands quite apart from the other mourners by Cock Robin's grave. Barbara Cooney has captured both the gaiety of the marriage and the solemnity of the funeral in this distinguished little book.

In *Lady Bird, Quickly,* Juliet Kepes has given an unusual twist to the ending of the verse "Lady Bird, Lady Bird, fly away home." The message that her house is on fire is re-

If wishes were horses, beggars would ride.
If turnips were watches, I would wear one by my side.
And if *ifs* and *ands* were pots and pans,
There'd be no work for tinkers!

Reed's wood engravings express a rustic humor.
Copyright © 1963 by Philip Reed. From *Mother Goose and Other Nursery Rhymes.* Used by permission of Atheneum Publishers.

layed by one insect after another. Lady Bird quickly flies home to find her children quite safe but dancing with thousands of fireflies all flashing and sparkling in the night. The brilliantly colored backgrounds of the illustrations become darker and darker as the lady bug hastens home.

Evaluating Mother Goose Books

With so many editions of Mother Goose, what factors should be considered when evaluating them? The following six points may be useful in studying various editions.

- *Coverage:* How many verses are included? Are they well-known rhymes or are there some fresh and unusual ones?
- *Illustrations:* What medium has been used? What colors? Are the illustrations realistic, stylized, varied? Are the illustrations consistent with the text? Do they elaborate the text? Are they extraneous? What is the mood of the illustrations (humorous, sedate, contemplative)?
- *Period:* Is the setting modern or in the past? What period do the costumes, houses, furnishings, activities represent?
- *Setting:* What background is presented, rural or urban? Do the characters portray multiethnic types or only Caucasians?
- *Arrangement:* Is there a thematic arrangement of the verses? Is there a feeling of unity to the whole book rather than just separate verses?
- *Format:* What is the quality of the paper and the binding? Is the title page well designed? Is there an index or table of contents? Is there harmony between endpapers, cover, and jacket? Are pictures and verses well spaced or crowded?

No matter what edition is selected, however, children should be exposed to the rhythm and rhyme of Mother Goose. It is part of their literary heritage and may serve as their first introduction to the realm of literature.

ABC AND COUNTING BOOKS

ABC Books

Parents and teachers frequently use alphabet and counting books in a similar fashion to "first books" and participation books.

Certain factors need to be considered in selecting alphabet books, however. Only one or two objects should be presented on a page and they should be easily identifiable and meaningful for the age level of the child for whom the book was planned. It is best to avoid portraying those objects that might have several correct names. For example, if a rabbit is presented for "R," the very young child might refer to it as a "bunny." Similarly, the more common sounds of the letter should be represented, rather than blends or even silent letters. To present a "gnu" for a "G" is most confusing. Parents who use alphabet books to teach children their letters prefer both upper and lower case letters. Since the text is necessarily limited, the pictures usually "carry" the story. For this reason they should be both clear and consistent with the text, reflecting and creating the mood of the book.

One of the earliest ABC books, by Edward Lear, was filled with nonsense rhymes for each letter. A new edition of this book has been reproduced in Lear's own handwriting under the title *Lear Alphabet: ABC.* Two almost classic alphabet books are C. B. Falls' *An ABC Book* with its simple illustrations of animals from the zoo and farmyard, and Fritz Eichenberg's *Ape in a Cape,* a humorous alphabet book that is liked by young children. They will remember his amusing pictures of a "Goat in a Boat" and "Fox in a Box," along with the rhyming captions. Another earlier, but beautifully designed alphabet book, is Wanda Gág's *ABC Bunny.* Here, a little rabbit provides the continuity and slight story line for each letter. The illustrations are woodcuts and the large capital letters stand out in scarlet color.

Vivid, full-color photographs of single objects illustrate *ABC An Alphabet Book* by Matthiesen. The simple, clear photographs of common objects make this a book for the youngest child. A touch of whimsy in the simple, direct text would amuse children, for

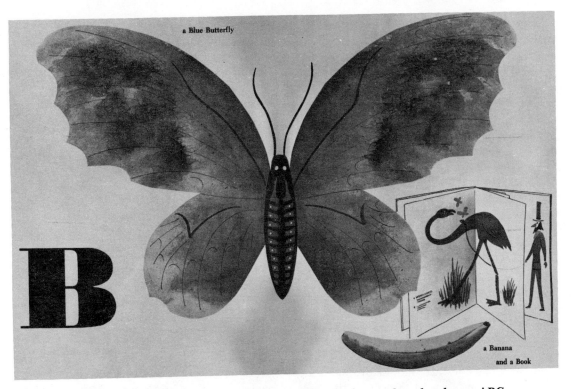

a Blue Butterfly

B

a Banana
and a Book

Large objects, uncluttered design, and brilliant colors make a handsome ABC book. From *Bruno Munari's ABC* by Bruno Munari. Copyright © 1960 by Bruno Munari. By permission of The World Publishing Company.

example, "It is not good to drop an egg unless you like to mop the floor."[5]

Three handsome new alphabet books have come to us from artists abroad. The current trend of including the illustrator's name in the title can be noticed in these books: *Bruno Munari's ABC, Brian Wildsmith's ABC,* and *Celestino Piatti's Animal ABC.* Munari, an Italian artist, has created a book that is notable for its simple but beautiful design. Objects are clearly presented with a fly adding a touch of humor at intervals throughout the text. Each letter of the alphabet is represented by a painting of one animal in *Brian Wildsmith's ABC.* Background colors provide stunning contrast, for example, a calm, regal lion, painted a vivid tangerine color with flecks of lemon in his coat, is pictured lying down against a deep purple background. Celestino Piatti is a Swiss artist and graphic designer. His ABC book shows unusual animals in striking, bold colors. Using a heavy black outline, his artwork resembles that of Rouault. The book lacks unity because the four-line verses fail to interpret the action in the picture.

A novel alphabet book that allows for some participation is *The Alphabet Tale* by Jan Garten. Each letter is introduced on the preceding page by showing just the tail of an animal. Turning the page, you see the whole animal. Children have four clues by which they may determine each animal; the content of the verse referring to the animal's characteristics, the sound of the rhyme, the

[5]Thomas Matthiesen, *ABC An Alphabet Book* (New York: Platt & Munk, 1966), unpaged.

picture of the tail, and the beginning letter. The letter "G" is introduced with this verse: "A neck so long it makes you laugh/This tail is the tail of the tall _____ (giraffe)."[6]

Two other animal ABC books for older children are *A for the Ark* by Duvoisin and *All in a Suitcase* by Morse, illustrated by Barbara Cooney. Duvoisin's book is based on the Old Testament story of the flood in which Noah decides to call all the animals to the ark in alphabetical order. On large double-page spreads, the animals march through this book in a continuous kind of picture frieze. The drama of the impending deluge is indicated as the clouds grow darker and more ominous on each page. *All in a Suitcase* is a witty and sophisticated ABC book. In verse form, it describes the many rare animals that a traveler intends to pack in his suitcase and take to Boston. The suitcase bulges larger and larger with such animals as an eccentric echidna, an ibex, a limpet, and a mandrill. The Boston scenes are delightful, including the houses on Beacon Street with their famous panes of lavender glass and shiny brass door knockers. Primary children might enjoy planning a similar alphabet trip to a different city (perhaps their own).

Not all ABC books are about animals. *Puptents and Pebbles* by William Jay Smith presents a miscellany of alphabetical objects in gay nonsense verse. The pictures by Juliet Kepes are bright and lively. A favorite of many little girls is Tasha Tudor's *A Is for Annabelle* that uses an old-fashioned doll with all her belongings to present the alphabet.

Several alphabet books present various aspects of city or country living. *A Big City* by Grossbart shows brightly colored silhouettes of such familiar city objects as *F*ire escape, *G*arbage can, and *H*ydrant. The simplicity and clarity of the graphic design make this an excellent book for the preschool child. A

novel design is seen in *The City-Country ABC* by Marguerite Walters. The first half of the book describes *My Alphabet Walk in the Country;* turn the book over and begin again with *My Alphabet Ride in the City.* The text does not always present the correct sound of the letter, however. The letter "G" is introduced with the "gr" sound rather than the "g" sound: "Why a great/green grasshopper/where the tall grass grew."[7] Phyllis McGinley's *All around the Town* contains lively, gay verse about city sights and sounds. The illustrations by Helen Stone reflect busy city life. An example of the alliterative verse that is given for "E," follows:

> E is an Escalator
>   That gives an elegant ride
> You step on the stair
> With an easy air
>   And up and up you glide.[8]

Children's interest in technological and scientific advances is met by Zacks' *Space Alphabet,* Shuttlesworth's *ABC of Buses,* and Alexander's *ABC of Cars and Trucks.* There is no lack of ABC books, both general and specialized. Each should be evaluated for its own merit and for the purpose for which it will be used.

Counting Books

In order to teach boys and girls correct mathematical concepts, counting books need to be carefully planned. Objects to be counted should stand out clearly on the page. Various groupings of objects may help avoid a cluttered look. Illustrations and page design are most important in evaluating counting books. Accuracy is essential.

Many of the same author-illustrators who have published alphabet books have also written counting books. Eichenberg's *Danc-*

---

[6]Jan Garten, *The Alphabet Tale,* Illustrated by Muriel Batherman (New York: Random House, 1964), unpaged.

[7]Marguerite Walters, *The City-Country ABC,* Illustrated by Ib Ohlsson (New York: Doubleday, 1965), unpaged.
[8]Phyllis McGinley, *All around the Town,* Illustrated by Helen Stone (Philadelphia: Lippincott, 1948), unpaged.

ing in the Moon explains the numbers 1 through 20 in one-line rhymes. Tasha Tudor's book, *1 Is One,* is artistically illustrated in her old-fashioned, dainty style. Numbers 1 through 20 are explained in verse form. Garth Williams' soft, fuzzy-looking animals illustrate Moore's *My First Counting Book* and account for much of its appeal. Duvoisin's *Two Lonely Ducks* includes numbers from 1 through 10 in a simple but amusing story. Charlotte Zolotow's *One Step, Two . . .,* also illustrated by Duvoisin, shows a little girl taking a walk with her mother and discovering wonderful things like daffodils, a white pebble, and a blue jay. She counts her steps as she goes along.

John Langstaff's *Over in the Meadow* is based upon the old counting rhyme and song of that title. Children love Rojankovsky's full-page colored illustrations of the sunny meadow and the cool pond where the frogs and beavers live. They enjoy the lilt and rhyme of the poem and chant the refrain at the end of each verse.

Brian Wildsmith's 1, 2, 3's is handsome but confusing. He utilizes basic abstract forms, the circle, triangle, and rectangle in combination with a kind of patchwork design. The designs within the basic shapes are distracting and might well be miscounted. For example, the picture for number ten is an engine. The two black circles of smoke are difficult to discern against the dark navy background, yet they are essential for the development of the concept of ten. The smoke stack is a rectangle made of two squares of different color. Most children will count these squares as two objects rather than see it as one. This is an exciting, brilliantly designed book that is too complex for most young children.

Most counting books present a cumulative procession of objects with a thread of a story to hold them together. *One Snail and Me* by McLeod is described in the subtitle as "A Book of Numbers, and Animals and a Bathtub." With amusing verse and pictures, it tells of the different animals who join in the sloshing fun of a big, old-fashioned bathtub. Francoise's book, *Jeanne-Marie Counts Her Sheep,* is an amusing story that involves much counting. Jeanne-Marie dreams of the many lambs that her pet sheep, Patapon, will have, and what she may purchase from their sale. At the conclusion, Patapon has only one lamb, and Jeanne-Marie can make only a very small purchase.

Two counting books present both the cumulative story of many objects and the concept of subtraction or deletion. In Alain's *One, Two, Three, Going to Sea,* one fisherman is added to another until the boat sinks. Maurice Sendak's counting book, *One Was Johnny,* is a part of the very small Nutshell Library; however, it may be ordered for school use in a size of approximately 5 by 7 inches. Typically Sendak in humor, it is the story of "Johnny who lived by himself" until he is disturbed by one noxious animal after another. Not knowing what to do, he starts counting backward with the threat "'and when/I am through—/if this house isn't empty/I'll eat/all of you!!!!'"[9] Needless to say the house is emptied and Johnny is left all alone to enjoy his solitude.

James Krüss has utilized the mathematical concept of grouping in his brilliantly illustrated book, *3 × 3 Three by Three.* Three hunters, three foxes, three dogs, three cats, three mice, and three chickens chase each other in and out of a very busy house. The excitement of the chase is good fun and children enjoy the simple three-line verses. One double-page spread may be confusing, however, for it pictures *six* hens.

Two books by Ipcar provide information about farms and number concepts. *Brown Cow Farm* presents easy lessons in counting, adding, and multiplying, and pictures the story of the life cycle on a farm. *Ten Big Farms* gives children practice with ordinal numbers as a family visits first, a poultry

---

[9]Maurice Sendak, *One Was Johnny* (New York: Harper & Row, 1962), unpaged.

farm; second, a fruit farm; third, a horse farm; and seven other kinds of farms. The specialization of farming today is shown in large stylized pictures of the ten different farms.

The folk tales, *Six Foolish Fishermen* by Benjamin Elkin, and *Nine in a Line* by Kirn, are not really counting books, but their stories revolve around the ability to count. Six brothers go out to fish in various places. When it is time for them to go home, each counts the others, neglecting himself, and decides that one must have drowned. A small boy counts the brothers and assures them that they are all there. *Nine in a Line* is based upon an Arabic tale with the same theme. Each time Amin counts his camels he has only eight, until he is convinced that "the Evil One" has taken a camel. A shepherd, two women, and three children count them and find he has nine camels each time. The children discover that Amin has forgotten to count the camel on which he was riding! Both of these books give children an opportunity to participate in counting several times plus the added fun of being "in" on the joke.

PICTURE BOOKS

Picture books are very important for young children whose appreciation and interest level far surpass their reading ability. Pictures not only make the book more attractive, but they must convey the same message as the written word. The child "reads" the picture as the adult reads the accompanying text. Story and illustrations should be so unified that a child may get the "sense" of the story through the pictures alone. In accepting the Caldecott Award for 1965, Beni Montresor defined a picture book in this way:

For me a picture book is a book whose content is expressed through its images. . . . The story

told with pictures has a language all its own: the visual language.[10]

Definitions of Picture Books

A picture book is a book in which the pictures are designed to be an integral part of the text. The fusion of both pictures and text is essential for the unity of presentation. This fusion does not exist in the illustrated book. In the latter, the pictures are mere extensions of the text. They may enrich the interpretation of the story, but they are not necessary for its understanding. Beth and Joe Krush have illustrated *The Borrowers* by Mary Norton. Their intricate line sketches greatly add to the fantastic nature of this delightful book, but they are not essential for its understanding. Illustrated books are usually written for those children who have already achieved considerable fluency in reading skills.

Some authorities differentiate between the picture book and the picture storybook. The difference is one that is contingent upon the development of plot and characters. A picture book may be an alphabet book, a counting book, a first book, or a concept book. In these books the pictures must be accurate and synchronized with the text; however, it is not essential that they provide the continuity required by a book with a story line. The illustration in a "first book" for children or an alphabet book may depict a different object or animal on each page providing for much variety in the pictures. Examples of such a picture book would be *Bruno Munari's ABC* or Weisgard's *The Important Book*. In a picture storybook, however, the same characters and settings are frequently drawn, while variety is achieved through the action of the characters. The author must consider plot and character development in the picture storybook rather

[10]Beni Montresor, "May I Bring a Friend?" in *Newbery and Caldecott Medal Books: 1956–1965*, Edited by Lee Kingman (Boston: Horn Book, 1965), pp. 262, 264.

than just the theme required for a picture book. An example of a picture storybook would be Freeman's *Dandelion*. The picture storybook probably places a greater demand on the talent of both author and illustrator than does the picture book. It is important to recognize the different requirements of these two types of books. In many instances, however, the two terms are used interchangeably to refer to that large group of books in which pictures and text are considered to be of equal importance.

Picture books are not to be confused with beginning reading books. Most picture storybooks require reading ability of at least third-grade level, and are read *to* children by adults. They are written for the young child's interest and appreciation level and not his reading-ability level. There is a new genre of picture books that has been written for the young child to read independently. This type of book is still a trade book, but it is written with a controlled vocabulary and becomes a transition book between the basic reading text and "library books." Examples of this type of book include *The Cat in the Hat* by Seuss, *Nobody Listens to Andrew* by Guilfoile, and *Little Bear* by Minarik. Some of these books are well written and can take their place in children's literature. Others are hampered by the necessity for a controlled vocabulary and remind one of a stilted primer.

The number of picture books designed for older children is growing rapidly. This trend merely reflects the greater role of visual presentation in books and magazines for all ages. Many of these picture books for older boys and girls may be classified as informational books in the science or social studies areas and are reviewed in Chapter 9. Occasionally, however, a picture storybook designed for somewhat older children is shelved with other picture books and consequently, is, lost to the age level for which it was intended. This may easily happen to such beautiful but oversized books as Valens'

Wingfin and Topple or the d'Aulaires' *Abraham Lincoln*. The humor and subtle commentaries on human nature as presented in Thurber's *Many Moons* are completely wasted on very young children. It is also well to remember that some picture books are ageless—appealing to a wide age range of children. A sixteen-year-old boy from Kentucky enjoyed Lynd Ward's wonderful story of *The Biggest Bear* as much as do second and third graders. The slapstick humor of the many books by Dr. Seuss appeals to all ages.

Guides for Evaluating Picture Books

Probably the best way to learn to judge a picture storybook is to look searchingly at the finest that have been produced. The following questions will help direct attention to the factors that should be considered.

- *The content of the book:* What is the story or content of the book? In what genre of literature does it belong? Where does it take place? When does it take place? What theme is presented? Is the text well written? For what age group does it seem most appropriate?
- *The illustrations:* How are the pictures made an integral part of the text? How is action in the text reflected by action in the pictures? How do the pictures help create the mood of the story? How do the pictures show character delineation and development? Are the pictures accurate and consistent with the text? Are the pictures authentic?
- *The media and style of illustrations:* What medium or combinations of media have been used (watercolor, chalk, crayon, woodcut, collage, ink)? How many colors have been used? Are the colors bright, soft, varied? How would you describe the style of illustrating (delicate, vigorous, realistic, stylized, decorative)? How has the illustrator varied style and technique? What techniques

Rhythmical curves reflect the repetitive text.
From *Millions of Cats* by Wanda Gág (1928).
By permission of Coward-McCann, Inc.

seem to create movement or rhythm? How has the artist created balance in composition?

- *The format of the book:* What is the size of the book? Does the jacket design express the theme of the book? Does the cover design convey the spirit of the book? How do the endpapers portray the general character of the book? How does the title page add to the book? Is the type design well chosen for the theme and reader of the book? What is the quality of the paper? How durable is the binding?

- *Comparison with others:* How is this work similar to or different from other work of the artist? How is this book similar to or different from other books with the same subject or theme? What comments have other reviewers made about this book? What has the artist said about his work?

The Content of the Book   In evaluating a picture book, one first looks at the story or content of the book. What kind of book is it? Does it have a story or is it giving informa-

tion? Informational books are evaluated differently from picture books (see Chapter 9). Within the genre of picture books, a reader must still determine if the purpose of the book is identification of objects, such as an ABC book; the exploration of a single concept such as "roundness" or "redness"; or the telling of a story. If the book does tell a story, this must be evaluated. Criteria developed in Chapter 1 for all fiction apply equally well to picture storybooks. However, the age and ability of the audience for picture books does demand that the story be presented much more quickly, usually in some thirty-two or sixty-four pages. Since most of these books will be read to children rather than by them, there is no reason to oversimplify the content or talk down to today's knowledgeable and sophisticated children. The television screen has extended their horizons to encompass the universe. They have a right to the joys of childhood, but they should never be treated as childish.

The Illustrations   The picture storybook is one that conveys its message through two media, the art of illustrating and the art of writing. Both media must bear the burden of narration. It is difficult to think of Wanda Gág's *Millions of Cats* without hearing its frequent refrain about the millions and billions and trillions of cats. At the same time, the rhythmical picture of the gnomish little old man wandering over the rolling hills and down the winding roads followed by all those cats is inseparable from the repetitive text. The action in the text is reflected by the action in the illustrations. One can almost hear the howls of the terrific cat fight and the subsequent silence when only one little kitten remains. Although one of our earliest picture books,[11] it still serves as an outstanding example of a book in which text and illustrations seem to flow together.

---

[11]First published in 1928 (New York: Coward-McCann).

Another outstanding picture storybook is *Blueberries for Sal* by Robert McCloskey. This is a story that children can tell by themselves just by looking at the clear blue and white pictures. The illustrations help the "reader" anticipate both the action and climax as Sal and her mother are seen going berry picking up one side of Blueberry Hill, and Little Bear and his mother are seen coming up the other side. McCloskey uses a false climax, a good storytelling technique. Sal hears a noise and starts to peer behind an ominously dark rock; the reader is expecting her to meet the bears, but instead, she sees a mother crow and her children. On the next page, she calmly meets Mother Bear and tramps along behind her. A parallel plot gives Little Bear a similar experience, but Sal's mother is not so calm about meeting him! The human expressions of surprise, fear, and consternation on the faces of both mothers express emotion as well as action.

Lynd Ward has used another technique to show the climax in his well-loved story, *The Biggest Bear.* In order to dramatize the growth of Johnny's bear, he shows him first as a lovable but mischievous cub. The next four pictures illustrate the chaos the bear created in the kitchen during the summer, Mr. McCarroll's trampled cornfield in the fall, the half-eaten and ruined bacon and hams in the smokehouse during the winter, and the overturned sap buckets in the spring. The bear is not shown in any of these pictures; only the results of his destructive actions are portrayed. The text suggests the passage of time, but in no way prepares the reader for the shock of the next picture of a gigantic bear, standing on his hind legs gorging himself on the McLeans' maple syrup! This adventure story has moments of real pathos, compassion, and humor. The illustrations create these feelings as well as the text.

Pictures should not only reflect the action of the plot, they should help to create the

Illustrations help build climax as Johnny's lovable, mischievous cub grows—to become *The Biggest Bear!* From *The Biggest Bear* by Lynd Ward (1952). By permission of Houghton Mifflin Company.

basic mood of the story. Weisgard has created a rainy world in his illustrations for *Where Does the Butterfly Go When It Rains?* by Garelick. In order to achieve the textured haziness of a light summer rain, soft blue chalk was sponged on paper that had been placed on a rough grained board. Scratching with a needle added the slanting rain lines. The general conception of this book is one of misty wonder.

In a perfection of words and watercolors, Robert McCloskey has captured the changing mood of the Maine coast in his *Time of Wonder*. Using soft grays and yellow, he has conveyed the warmth and mystery of the early morning fog in the woods. His ocean storm scene, on the other hand, is slashed with streaks of dark blues and emerald greens, highlighted by churning whites. The text is no longer quiet and poetic, but races along with "the sharp choppy waves and slamming rain." The storm subsides, the summer ends, and it is time to leave the island. The beauty of this book will not reach all children; but it will speak forever to young and old alike who have ever intensely loved a particular place on this earth. Words and pictures so complement each other that the reader is filled with quiet wonder and nostalgia when he sees the family's boat slip into the sunset and reads the poetic prose:

> Take a farewell look
> At the waves and sky.
> Take a farewell sniff
> Of the salty sea.
> A little bit sad
>   about the place you are leaving,
> A little bit glad
> About the place you are going.
> It is a time of quiet wonder—
>   for wondering, for instance:
> Where do hummingbirds go in a hurricane?[12]

---

[12]Robert McCloskey, *Time of Wonder* (New York: Viking, 1957), p. 62.

Both text and pictures should convey the fun and humor of a story. It is difficult to imagine the hilarious stories of Dr. Seuss without his fantastically absurd pictures. Children and adults alike delight in the pictures of the faithful elephant, Horton, sitting in a tree on an egg in a nest. The story of *Horton Hatches the Egg* is ridiculous and so are the pictures.

Illustrations not only aid in creating the basic mood of a story, but they also help portray convincing character delineation and development. The characterization in the pictures must correspond to that of the story. There is no mistaking the devilish quality of the incorrigible *Madeline* as she balances herself on the ledge of the Pont des Arts in Paris, or says "pooh-pooh to the tiger in the zoo." Following her bout with appendicitis, a quiet subdued Madeline is shown propped up in bed watching her friends play with her gifts. It is with real relief that the reader sees her in the next picture proudly exhibiting her scar to the envious eyes of her eleven friends. Madeline has recovered and is very much herself again. She is always the roguish Madeline in the four other books that Bemelmans wrote about her. She shows little or no character development, but the delineation of her character is unmistakable. Madeline is a real personality.

One of the few picture storybooks that portrays character development is *Crow Boy* by Yashima. In the very first picture of that wonderfully sensitive story, "Chibi" is shown hidden away in the dark space underneath the schoolhouse, afraid of the schoolmaster, afraid of the children. In subsequent pictures, he is always alone while the other children come to school in twos and threes. With the arrival of the friendly schoolmaster and his discovery of Chibi's talent to imitate crows, Chibi grows in stature and courage. On graduation day, he is pictured standing tall and erect, having been the only one honored for perfect attendance at school for six years. Chibi does not completely change with his new name of Crow Boy, for this story has the integrity of life itself. He remains aloof and independent as he assumes his increased adult responsibilities. He has lost the gnawing loneliness of Chibi, however, as the final pages of text and pictures combine to tell us of his character development:

> Crow Boy would nod and smile as if he liked the name. And when his work was done he would buy a few things for his family. Then he would set off for his home on the far side of the mountain, stretching his growing shoulders proudly like a grown-up man. And from around the turn of the mountain road would come a crow call—the happy one.[13]

Another requirement of the excellent picture book is one of accuracy and consistency with the text. If the story states, as Bemelmans does in *Madeline*, that "In an old house in Paris that was covered with vines lived twelve little girls in two straight lines,"[14] children are going to look for the vines, they are going to count the little girls, and they are going to check to see that the lines are straight. Bemelmans was painstakingly careful to include just eleven little girls in his pictures after Madeline goes to the hospital. He failed in one small picture that shows twelve girls breaking their bread, even though Madeline was still hospitalized. A seven-year-old child noticed the error and called attention to it one day during a story hour.

Pictures and text must be synchronized, for as the adult reads the text, the child is reading the pictures. For this reason, children prefer that the picture be on the same page or facing the part of the story that it illustrates.

Many picture books today are quite authentic and show the result of hours of research. Barbara Cooney spent much time studying rare, illuminated manuscripts before she illustrated *Chanticleer and the Fox* adapted from *The Canterbury Tales*. The results of her research are to be seen in every picture. For example, the book begins in the style of an illuminated manuscript with a strawberry plant placed inside the capital letter of the first word. The thatched roof cottage, the wattle fence, and every flower and grass shown in the book are indigenous to the England of Chaucer's time. True to the superstitions of the day, she placed a magpie, thought to be an evil omen, on the second page of the story to foretell the disaster that was to befall the proud rooster.

Not only are settings in the past carefully documented, but settings of today are faithfully presented in children's picture storybooks. Every young American may visit the public gardens of Boston in McCloskey's almost classic story of *Make Way for Ducklings*. Don Freeman has illustrated the magnificent beauty of San Francisco in his *Fly High, Fly Low*, the story of two pigeons. Leo Politi has captured the excitement and beauty of a Mexican Christmas procession in Los Angeles in his book *Pedro, the Angel of Olvera Street*. In *Piccolo's Prank*, Politi has preserved a part of old Los Angeles known as Bunker Hill. Since the quaint old houses on top of this hill are destined to be torn down, this is a labor of love for young and old to appreciate.

Foreign settings have been authentically represented in Bemelmans' books about *Madeline* and *Madeline's Rescue*. In these stories, Bemelmans has used well-known landmarks of Paris such as Notre Dame, the opera building, Sacre Coeur, the Tuileries, and the Pont Neuf as background for his striking colored pictures of Madeline and her eleven friends. In brilliant blues, pinks, and lavender, Marcia Brown has recreated the charm

---

[13]Taro Yashima, *Crow Boy* (New York: Viking, 1955), p. 37.
[14]Ludwig Bemelmans, *Madeline* (New York: Viking, 1939, 1962), unpaged.

She had only three large sows, three cows, and also a sheep called Molly.

Authentic details of the English countryside enrich the setting of Chaucer's story. Illustration by Barbara Cooney (copyright © 1958 by Thomas Y. Crowell Company) in *Chanticleer and the Fox,* adapted by Barbara Cooney from Robert Mayer Lumiansky's translation of Chaucer's *Canterbury Tales.* Thomas Y. Crowell Company, New York, Publishers.

of Venice in her book *Felice,* the story of a young gondolier's cat. Her pictures recall the extravagant beauty of St. Mark's Square, the Grand Canal swarming with barcas and gondolas, and the intriguing narrow, back canals.

The authenticity of the setting of a story is not as important to boys and girls as it is to adults. Where a specific setting is suggested, it should be accurate and authentic. Children will not like a particular story just because it is laid in a different city or country. It still must have a good story to hold their interest. However, young children's horizons are widened by these occasional glimpses of other worlds that may serve as background for favorite stories.

The Media and Style of the Illustrations

Children accept and enjoy a variety of media in the illustrations of their picture books. Many artists today are using the picture book as a vehicle for their experimentation with new and interesting media. Since the primary purpose of an illustration is to reflect, interpret, and extend the text of the book, only two questions need to be asked about the medium used: (1) How appropriate is this particular medium to the theme of the story? and (2) How effectively has the artist used it?

WOODCUTS AND SIMILAR TECHNIQUES   In the beginning of printing, the woodcut was the only means of reproducing art. It is still used effectively today. In making a woodcut, the nonprinting areas are cut away, leaving a raised surface, which, when inked and pressed on paper, duplicates the original design. If colored overlays are to be used, the artist must prepare as many woodcuts as colors. Woodcut illustrations produce a bold simplicity and have a power that is not found in any other media. Marcia Brown has used woodcuts superbly in her fable of India, *Once a Mouse.* Taking full advantage of the use of her medium, she has allowed the texture or grain of the wood to show through, adding depth and interesting patterns to these dramatic illustrations. The woodcuts by Evaline Ness capture the color and spirit of Haiti in her book, *Josefina February.* These illustrations are both bold and compassionate as they portray the poverty and richness of native life in Haiti. Antonio Frasconi is equally well known for his well-designed woodcuts in such books as *See Again, Say Again.*

Wood engravings are cut on the end grain of hardwood, rather than with the grain as are woodcuts. This process gives a delicate, finer line to the illustrations. Not many picture books have been illustrated with wood engravings. Boris Artzybasheff's illustrations for *Aesop's Fables* are fine examples of this medium as are Philip Reed's for his Mother Goose book.

Linoleum block prints also give a finer line than woodcuts. The simple, direct story of *Dick Whittington and His Cat* was illustrated by Marcia Brown with linoleum block prints. Clement Hurd has placed linoleum block prints on a background of a print made from the grain of weathered wood. This intriguing technique of print on print produced an effect of water for *Wingfin and Topple* and a forest fire in *Wildfire.* Both of these books were written by Valens.

Cardboard cuts resemble wood or linoleum cuts except that a less permanent material is used. Blair Lent has produced some striking art work using this medium in illustrating *The Wave* by Hodges and his own amusing books, *Pistachio* and *John Tabor's Ride.* Lent is able to adapt this particular medium to express many moods. In *The*

Brilliant splashes of yellow and red with heavy black line make a handsome rooster. The crude, bold woodcuts give the effect of different textures. From *The House that Jack Built,* © 1958, by Antonio Frasconi. Reproduced by permission of Harcourt, Brace & World, Inc.

Wave, he created a delicate, almost fragile Japanese village that was completely engulfed by a mighty tidal wave. There is a wonderful circus atmosphere in the story of the green cow, *Pistachio*; and action and wild humor are captured by his pictures for John Tabor's ride on a whale. In skilled hands, this technique has infinite possibilities.

STONE LITHOGRAPHY[15] Another very old method of illustrating is that of drawing directly on stone. Using a greased crayon or pencil, the artist transfers his designs to the surface of the stone. The stone is dampened with an ink-repellent. When the ink is placed on the stone, it will

[15]Today "lithography" is a term that has come to be synonymous with photo-offset, which is a printing process. The term "offset" merely means that the original plate does not touch the paper; it first makes an impression on another, or "blanket" roller, which, in turn, prints the illustration. Stone lithography, however, refers to the old-fashioned method of printing from an image that has been drawn directly on stone.

adhere only to the greased area. In this country, all the Currier and Ives prints were made from stone lithography. McCloskey used this method in illustrating his well-known *Make Way for Ducklings* and the d'Aulaires have utilized it in their books, *Ola, Abraham Lincoln, Pocahontas*, and so forth. The fine subtle grain of the stone can be easily discerned in these pictures.

SCRATCHBOARD ILLUSTRATIONS Scratchboard illustrations may be confused with wood engravings since their appearance is similar. However, the process of making them is very different. In making scratchboard illustrations, a very black ink is usually painted on the smooth white surface of a drawing board or scratchboard. When it is thoroughly dry, the picture is made by scratching through the black-inked surface with a sharp instrument. Color may be added with a transparent overlay, or it may be painted on the white scratchboard prior to the black ink. Scratchboard technique produces crisp black and white illustrations. Barbara Cooney has achieved a dramatic effect with this technique in *Chanticleer and the Fox*. Handsome illustrations for Prokofieff's *Peter and the Wolf* were made with scratchboard by Frans Haachen of Germany.

COLLAGE The use of collage for illustrating children's books is a comparatively new medium. Collage is derived from the French verb *coller* meaning "to paste," and refers to the kind of picture that is made by cutting out a variety of different kinds of materials, newspaper clippings, patterned wallpaper, and the like, and assembling them into a unified harmonious illustration. Ezra Jack Keats has proven himself a master of this technique with his award-winning *The Snowy Day*. Using patterned and textured papers and pen and ink, Keats has captured young Peter's delight in a snowy day.

Leo Lionni has used collage with patterned crayon shapes to create the grass, the leaves, and the birds in his highly original *Inch by Inch*. Circles torn from colored paper convey his story of *Little Blue and Little Yellow*.

Frequently, collage is used in the new art form, pop art. In *Jennie's Hat*, Keats combined old valentine cards, flowers, lace paper doilies, fans, and a nest of birds to make an extraordinary hat for Jennie. While the story is delightful, one is not quite prepared for the sudden flight into the fanciful. The pictures are not as original as in *The Snowy Day* or *Whistle for Willie*. The illustrations by McMullan for *Kangaroo & Kangaroo* by Braun are really a form of pop art. Here photographs of many objects are reduced in size to represent the "junk" that two kangaroos collected in their house. Gramaphones, telescopes, and boats are all stored by these two compulsive collectors. The "art" is to be seen in the arrangement and conception of the unusual ways that these objects may be put together to tell a story.

PAINTS, CRAYON, PEN AND INK The vast majority of illustrations for children's books are done in paint, crayon, pen and ink, or combinations of these media. The creation of new materials, such as plastic paints, and new techniques, frequently make it very difficult to determine the medium used.

Generally, paint may be divided into two kinds, that which is translucent and has a somewhat transparent quality such as watercolor; and that which is opaque and is impenetrable to light such as tempera, gouache, and oils. The English illustrator, Edward Ardizzone, is a master of both watercolors and pen-and-ink sketches. He is best known for his seascapes in his Little Tim books, but his vertical mountain scenes of the Pyrenees for *The Land of the Right Up and Down* by Wuorio are breathtaking. Other artists who have successfully employed the use of watercolors are McCloskey in *Time of Wonder*, Burton for *The Little House*, Slobodkin in all his picture books including *Many Moons*, Bemelmans' *Madeline*, and all of Marguerite de Angeli's work.

One winter morning Peter woke up and looked out the window. Snow had fallen during the night. It covered everything as far as he could see.

A collage of red patterned paper conveys the warmth of Peter's room in contrast to the snowy city roofs. From *The Snowy Day* by Ezra Jack Keats. Copyright © 1962 by Ezra Jack Keats. Reprinted by permission of The Viking Press, Inc.

Opaque paint may give a brilliant sparkling look such as Weisgard achieved in *The Little Island* and *Little Lost Lamb*, or it may produce the rather somber colors of Politi's *Song of the Swallows*. Sidjakov has created a stained-glass quality for his story of *Baboushka and the Three Kings* by using bright blue, red, and yellow tempera paints and a black felt pen to outline his wooden, doll-like figures. Sendak has chosen dark green and blue tempera contrasted with shades of purple to create Max's weird fantasy world in *Where the Wild Things Are*. Texture and shading are achieved with pen-and-ink crosshatching strokes.

Crayons and soft pencils are frequently employed in illustrations for children's books. The subtle texture of crayon is easily discernible. Rojankovsky used crayon, brush, and ink to make his delightful illustrations for *Frog Went A-Courtin'*. Marcia Brown combined gouache and crayon for her dazzling picture of that handsome feline, *Puss in Boots*. The textured quality of Yashima's colored penciled trees is always recognizable. These can be seen in his *Village Tree*, *Plenty to Watch*, and *Crow Boy*.

Pen and ink are more generally used in combinations with other media. In *May I Bring a Friend?*, Montresor has combined pen-and-ink drawings with overlays of brilliant colors. By using a fractured pen line, Montresor achieves the effect of a shimmering sunset in his illustrations for *Sounds of a Summer Night* written by Garelick. Nonny Hogrogian illustrated an old Scottish song entitled *Always Room for One More* with intriguing pen-and-ink illustrations combined with a heathery colored wash. Using crosshatching and parallel lines, her figures appear as misty as the Scottish moors themselves.

PHOTOGRAPHY Photographs are less likely to find favor with children than other types of media. However, the popular books by one of the world's foremost animal photographers, Ylla, have proved exceptions to this statement. Although she died in 1955, others are contributing the text for some of her entrancing photographs. Her pictures for *The Sleepy Little Lion*, *Two Little Bears*, and *Animal Babies* (words by Gregor) are simple, large, and beguiling. The subjects for her photographs are always in sharp focus with uncluttered backgrounds. These character- istics are also true of *The Red Balloon,* photo- graphed in France by Lamorisse. While the pictures of Dare Wright's *The Lonely Doll* books meet these criteria, the stories seem slightly contrived and sophisticated. Children appear to enjoy photographic stories pro- vided they are presented with simplicity and skill by a camera artist.

EVALUATING MEDIA The question of eval- uating media still remains one of harmony between text and illustrations. Occasionally, there will be a book whose illustrations are superb and whose story is a good one, but story and pictures do not belong together. *The Happy Owls* is a rather quiet story of two old owls who never quarrel. It is illustrated by Piatti with bold, beautifully colored pic- tures heavily outlined in black in a fashion similar to Rouault. The pictures alone are magnificent; the story alone is peaceful and quiet. The choice of opaque paints, rich heavy colors, and a bold style of illustration seems inappropriate for the theme of this story.

THE USE OF COLOR Children generally pre- fer brightly colored illustrations, although they readily accept pastels and black and white, provided the pictures and text tell a good story. Many perennial favorites do not use color in their illustrations; the sepia pictures of McCloskey's *Make Way for Duck- lings* and Ward's *The Biggest Bear,* the black and white humorous illustrations by Lawson for *The Story of Ferdinand* and *Wee Gillis* by Leaf, and the well-loved black and white il- lustrations of *Millions of Cats* by Wanda Gág. The use of color alone is no guarantee of success. The appropriate use of color is significant.

The choices of color or colors depend on the theme of the book. Certainly, the choice of blue for both pictures and text for *Blue- berries for Sal* by McCloskey was appropriate. Golden yellow and black were the natural choices for Don Freeman's wonderfully funny story of the lion who suddenly decided

to live up to the double meaning of his name, *Dandelion.* Quiet stories, such as *Play with Me* and *Gilberto and the Wind* by Marie Hall Ets are quietly illustrated with pastels of white, browns and pale yellow against a soft gray background. Brian Wildsmith has used vibrant jewel-like colors to illustrate the fable *The North Wind and the Sun* by La Fontaine. In cool greens and blues, he shows the wind blowing violently to make a man remove his new cloak. In rich oranges, yellows, and reds, Wildsmith shows that the sun is able to achieve by warmth what the wind could not achieve by coldness!

In her acceptance speech for the Calde- cott Award for *Cinderella,* Marcia Brown tells how she selects the color combination for a picture book:

> Gold of the summer fields, gold of a small boy's thatch of hair, gold of his dream of London, the sunrise when he heard his destiny ring out in Bow Bells, gold of his treasure and of the chain of his office of Lord Mayor,—gold was the color for Dick Whittington.
>
> When I was in the Virgin Islands, the unbe- lievable turquoise water of the Caribbean, the mahogany-skinned people, brilliant white sand, coral-colored houses and bougainvillea, deep green of welcome shadow, chartreuse of leaves filtering sunlight—the colors for Henry- Fisherman *chose themselves.*[16]

Certain artists have made effective use of color to show the change in mood of the story. In order to convey the loneliness of *Swimmy* after the tuna fish had gulped down all of his friends, Lionni places the tiny black fish on a large double page spread of watery gray. In *White Snow, Bright Snow,* Duvoisin has utilized a gray-blue to give the feeling of cold. The reader sees the day grow darker as the snow becomes thicker and heavier. The next morning the storm is over. With bril- liant splashes of red, yellow, and dazzling

[16]Marcia Brown, "Integrity and Intuition" in *Caldecott Medal Books: 1938–1957,* Edited by Bertha Miller and Elinor Field (Boston: Horn Book, 1957), p. 274.

white, Duvoisin emphasizes the contrast of this weather change. Leonard Weisgard's colored pictures reveal the beauty of the mountains and the tender concern of the boy shepherd for his *Little Lost Lamb.* In the first half of this book by Golden Macdonald, the sparkling color of the pictures almost makes the reader feel the warmth of the sun-drenched mountains in the springtime. The illustrations for the last half of the book are in shades of brown and add to the growing concern for the little black lamb lost in the mountains that are now cold, dark, and treacherous in the night. In order to signify danger, Marcia Brown has added red to her pictures for *Once a Mouse.* Starting with cool forest green, mustard yellow, and a trace of red, the red builds up in increasing amounts until the climax is reached and the tiger is changed back to a mouse. The last picture is without any reds and shows the hermit is once again "thinking about big — and little . . . ."

THE STYLE OF THE ILLUSTRATIONS   Occasionally, the question is raised as to what style of illustration is best for children's books. There can be only one answer to that question: there is no *one* style that is most preferred by all children. Many different types of paintings and drawings: realistic, stylized, near-abstract, and caricatures appear to be enjoyed by children. The primary question concerning the style of a picture book is again one of harmony with the text. The style of art should be judged solely by its appropriateness to the story.

Children should be exposed to a wide variety of art styles in picture books. Since appreciation is learned, opportunity to view some of the best talents in children's literature might well have a lasting effect on children's taste in art. Marcia Brown emphasizes this point:

Perhaps exposure to good picture books in childhood will not assure an adult taste capable of appreciating fine art, but I do believe that a child unconsciously forms an approach to his visual world of order, rhythm and interesting arrangements of color from the books he sees when young. The clearness and simplicity of a well-designed page may start a chain of reactions that will continue into adulthood. If the child is accustomed to seeing varied and interesting shapes in his picture books, abstract art will not have the terrors for him that it seems to have for some adults. His discrimination along with whatever of his individuality he can manage to preserve, will be his main defense against the bombardment of visual materials on his eyes in most of his waking hours.[17]

Style is the arrangement of line, color, and mass into a visual image. The style of an illustrator will be influenced by the content of the story that he is interpreting. One cannot imagine the style of Dr. Seuss for illustrating *Time of Wonder,* for example. Style is also determined to a certain degree by choice of media used. Tasha Tudor could never create old-fashioned, delicately illustrated children by using woodcuts.

The age of the child for whom the book is intended places a few restrictions on style. Young children's eyes are not fully matured until age seven or eight. Distracting backgrounds may confuse them. It is difficult for them to grasp the idea of perspective. One young child of three looked at a picture that showed a man in the distance and remarked "That's a funny tiny man down there." Just as many young children have difficulty comprehending perspective, so, too, are they bothered by the incomplete picture of a hand, part of an animal, or other object. They want to know where the missing parts are and tend to become confused. Imagine the concept of a flamingo that a very young child might derive from Lionni's picture of

[17]Marcia Brown, "Distinction in Picture Books," in *Illustrators of Children's Books: 1946–1956,* Compiled by Bertha Mahony Miller, *et al.* (Boston: Horn Book, 1958), pp. 9–10.

an inchworm measuring just the neck of a flamingo! If the child had seen a flamingo, or if a complete flamingo was pictured before showing only a partial illustration of it, he could fill in the rest of the bird. With increased experience and visual maturity, children are ready for more complex and varied art styles.

Another limitation on the artist may be his knowledge of his audience. Some artists "paint down" to children, showing a kind of patronization of children conveyed in pictures as well as words. Books that always picture children as sweet and cherubic, rolling in green meadows of blooming flowers are guilty of doing just this. Adults say they are "cute"; children know that they are basically dishonest.

Some artists' styles have stabilized to the point that they are quite recognizable. They frequently persist in their preference for one style, one medium, and even in their choice of content. Thus, we have come to associate quaint and quiet pastel illustrations with Tasha Tudor's work. Lois Lenski's rounded adult personages in five-year-old bodies are quite different from Tasha Tudor's, but equally distinctive. Whether Mr. Small is *Cowboy Small* or *Policeman Small,* he is easily identified as he gaily goes about the important details of his daily life. Slobodkin's work is almost always in water colors with figures that are sketchy and incomplete. With only a few lines, he is able to suggest the throne of the king, or the huge bed of Princess Lenore in *Many Moons.* His illustrations seem almost to float on the page and complement the fairy-tale quality of this modern fantasy. Such an "airy style" seems less appropriate for his own story of *Yasu and the Strangers,* the adventure of a modern Japanese boy who helps some Americans find their way back to their tourist buses. The peasant art style of Francoise for her *Jeanne Marie* books is most appropriate for her stories and the nursery school children who enjoy them.

All her little doll-like people have pink, rosy circles on their cheeks, and the pages frequently contain decorative folk designs of hearts and flowers. This same peasant art is used with more brilliant colors by Virginia Kahl for her amusing story of the Duke and Duchess and their thirteen daughters in *The Duchess Bakes a Cake.* Politi's panoramic views of villages or missions in Mexico, California, and Italy are childlike and delightful. His people have large hands and feet, showing a somewhat primitive style. He has written many regional stories with characters of various nationalities and ethnic groups. James Daugherty's powerful and vigorous illustrations portray movement and action with large swirls of color. His style of art seems more appropriate for the biographies and pioneer stories he has illustrated than for his two picture books, *Andy and the Lion* and *The Loudest Noise in the World.* Some illustrators are cartoon-artists such as H. A. Rey, Jean de Brunhoff, and Dr. Seuss. Their illustrations of *Curious George,* the monkey, Babar, the French elephant, and all the zany animals of Dr. Seuss are refreshing and amusing.

Several artists are experimenting with both style and media. Sendak's droll little whimsical characters are as recognizable as the white sealyham terrier that appears in many of his books. However, his pictures for *The Moon Jumpers, Mr. Rabbit and the Lovely Present,* and *Where the Wild Things Are* vary, despite the fact that each has a moonlight setting. The luminous illustrations for *The Moon Jumpers* give a dreamy effect for the children's dance in the night. The children are not caricatures but have a look of almost arrested motion. The impressionistic Monet-like pictures for *Mr. Rabbit and the Lovely Present* by Zolotow are easily identifiable. The little girl looks like an old woman in the way she walks and by the worried look on her face; the rabbit, however, is a very sophisticated rabbit; at times smug, puzzled, or pleased but always in complete control of the situation. The trees and end papers of *Where the Wild Things Are* have been compared to Henri Rousseau's paintings. However, Max, with his roguish smile, and the big ludicrous beasts with their "terrible eyes and terrible teeth" are very much Sendak. Leo Lionni is also experimenting with style and media. His collage pictures for both *Inch by Inch* and *Little Blue and Little Yellow* were most successful. The ocean background of *Swimmy* is watercolor, but he has also used collage and linoleum block print in this book. Textured fish swim by seaweed that has been made by imprinting with lace doilies. Despite the many techniques that have been used to make this lovely book, it has a unity of theme and harmony with the text. Hopefully, this experimentation with new art forms will continue and foster a better understanding of their place in art among our younger generation.

Marcia Brown's sensitivity to the varying requirements of different stories has lead her to use different media and styles of illustrating. One feels that she is master of them all. Look at the movement of her wonderful *The Three Billy Goats Gruff* as they come prancing over that bridge in the Norwegian fjord country. Her troll is a muddy, ugly one that you are glad to see crushed to bits! Compare these vigorous crayon and gouache drawings to the fluff and frills of *Cinderella* or to the bold, vigorous concentration of lines and design in the woodcuts for *Once a Mouse*. Barbara Cooney displays some of this same versatility as she moves easily from the realistic portrayal of *Peter's Long Walk* by Kingman, to the brilliant scratchboard illustrations for *Chanticleer and the Fox,* to the sophisticated French version of "The Owl and the Pussycat" by Lear (*Le Hibou et La Poussiquette*). Marie Hall Ets has used at least three different approaches to illustrating. Her *Play with Me* and *Gilberto and the Wind* present a quiet mood both by the text and the pastel illustrations. The black and white effect of Ets' "paper batik" illustrations for the *Little Old Automobile* and *Mr. Penny's Race Horse* is most appropriate for the folk-tale quality of these stories. The brilliant and unusual combination of color in her Caldecott winner, *Nine Days to Christmas*, is a departure from both of these latter approaches. Garth Williams is another artist who varies his style with the text. He is well known for his soft, furry-looking animals in such books as *The Rabbits' Wedding* and *Wait Till the Moon Is Full*. His brightly colored illustrations of the little girl in *Over and Over* reflect a tenderness towards childhood as do the delicate pictures for *Do You Know What I'll Do?* by Zolotow.

Style, then, is an elusive quality of the artist changing and varying over the years and with the particular demands of the work. There is, perhaps, more freedom to experiment in illustrating children's books than ever before. Many of our contemporary artists are taking advantage of this new freedom and producing fresh and original art.

The Format of the Book   The actual format of the book is important in creating its total impact. Today, picture books have many sizes and shapes. Children enjoy large and beautiful books, but the continuous popularity of Potter's *The Tale of Peter Rabbit* and her other well-loved books shows they like small-sized books also. Sendak's *The Nutshell Library* consisted of four tiny books measuring $2\frac{1}{2}$ by $3\frac{5}{8}$ inches that fitted in their own small case. In addition to liking the size of these tiny books, children love Sendak's humor, particularly his "I don't care, Pierre" who was eaten by a lion!

The shape of some books suggests their very content; for example, *A Tree Is Nice* by Udry is vertical in shape. The horizontal shape of McCloskey's *Blueberries for Sal* is quite appropriate for portraying Sal and her mother on one side of a long, sloping hill

A Pocketful of Cricket

REBECCA CAUDILL

Illustrated by Evaline Ness

Holt, Rinehart and Winston
New York / Chicago / San Francisco

This well-designed title page includes all of the objects a boy found on his walk. Interesting shapes and lines focus attention upon the cricket. From *A Pocketful of Cricket* by Rebecca Caudill. Illustrated by Evaline Ness. Copyright © 1964 by Evaline Ness. Reproduced by permission of Holt, Rinehart and Winston, Inc.

and the bear cub and his mother on the other. Armies march easily across one page and onto the next in the horizontally shaped book of *Yankee Doodle* by Schackburg. Row upon row of tents and bands of soldiers add to the effect of military cadence in this pictorial presentation of a patriotic song.

Both the cloth cover and dust jacket of a book should receive careful attention. The primary purpose of the jacket is to call attention to the book. It should not be just a duplicate of an illustration from the book, but should be carefully designed to express the general character or mood. Too often the binding design or cloth cover of a book is just a repeat of the jacket; yet, the cloth material will not take the color of an illustration in the same way as the paper of the jacket. Good cloth designs are usually small and symbolic of the content. For example, a

small single white cricket is stamped on the gray cover of *A Pocketful of Cricket* by Caudill. The jacket design shows Jay standing with his hands in his overalls and a satisfied look on his face, some leaves and branches of the hickory nut tree, and the cricket that he took to the first day at school. Most library bindings do incorporate the jacket design on the cloth since these covers are washable and will take color as well as paper. This type of binding preserves the gay attractiveness of the jacket for children to enjoy in a permanent form.

The endpapers of a picture book may also add to its attractiveness. These are the first and last pages of the book, one of which is glued to the back of the cover while the other is not pasted down. Endpapers are usually of stronger paper than the printed pages. In picture books, they are usually a color that harmonizes with the cover or other pictures in the book, and frequently they are illustrated. Again, their patterns usually give a hint of the general theme of the book. The striking endpapers of Marcia Brown's *Felice* with their design of interlacing black and white gondolas against a dark blue background suggest the setting of the story. The brilliant red and blue design on the endpapers of *Chanticleer and the Fox* by Cooney represents the eye of that proud rooster. The endpapers of *Crow Boy* by Yashima show a flower and butterfly alone against a dark background. They seem to symbolize the emergence of Crow Boy's life from one of dark despair to brilliant hope.

Even the title page of a picture book may be beautiful and symbolic. Rajankovsky has filled the title page of *Over in the Meadow* by Langstaff with flowers that seem to sparkle with the very warmth of sunshine. The title page of *The Happy Lion* by Louise Fatio introduces the reader to the tame nature of this wise beast. On a double-page spread,

Duvoisin has drawn a golden, serene lion peacefully sleeping while a small bird eats a meal not more than a paw away from his mouth.

Attention should be given to the spacing of pictures and text so that they do not appear monotonously in the same place. Frequently, full-color illustrations are alternated with two-color or black and white ones. This provides variety and saves the publisher the cost of color reproductions. In Margaret Wise Brown's book *The Dead Bird*, the text of the story appears on separate white pages interspersed between full-colored pictures painted in subdued blues and greens. Both the pictures and plain white pages with their brief text help to express the sadness, simplicity, and beauty of this book. Variety in size of pictures may reflect the increasing tempo of the story. As Max's fantasy becomes greater and greater in the story of *Where the Wild Things Are*, the pictures become larger and larger. Finally when the "mad rumpus begins," three double-page

The text flows in the same rhythmical pattern as the road. The little house is personified with details in windows and door. From *The Little House* by Virginia Lee Burton (1942). By permission of Houghton Mifflin Company.

He was afraid of the children and could not make friends with them at all.

Yashima's use of space conveys Chibi's loneliness and isolation. From *Crow Boy* by Taro Yashima. Copyright 1955 by Mitsu and Taro Yashima. Reprinted by permission of The Viking Press, Inc.

spreads illustrate the action with no text at all. Then, the illustrations are gradually reduced in size until Max is back home again in his own room. A similar technique was used in Marcia Brown's *Stone Soup*. As the French villagers help the soldiers with the soup, more double-page spreads are used as if to emphasize the greatness of the project. The variety of the spacing of the sentences adds movement to the format of Burton's *The Little House.*

The appropriate choice of type design is also a matter for consideration. Type is the name given to all printed letters, and typeface refers to the over 6000 different styles available today. These typefaces vary in legibility and the feeling they create. Some seem bold, others delicate and graceful, some crisp and businesslike. Sidjakov describes the difficulty he and his editor had in finding a suitable typeface for his *Baboushka and the Three Kings*. When they did find one they liked, it was obsolete and not easily available. They finally located enough fonts to hand-set *Baboushka* a page at a time![18]

Other details contribute to the making of a quality picture book. Sometimes, the very margins and blank space within a book add to the total impact of the story. In illustrating *Crow Boy*, Yashima has made skillful use of space to help create the feeling of isolation. In the picture of the schoolroom, Chibi looms large in a foreground with empty space separating him from the children across the room. The wide margins of clear white paper in *Time of Wonder* give a rich spacious feeling to this book. Only in the storm scene is the text placed over the illustration in order to have a full page of a dark, violent storm.

Other factors of a picture book are necessary considerations from the utilitarian standpoint. The paper should be dull so that it does not easily reflect light, opaque to prevent print showing through, and strong to withstand heavy usage. Its color, texture, and receptivity to ink must be considered. Picture books should be bound in cloth and side sewn, with soil-resistant, washable covers. Careful planning for side sewing should make it possible for pictures to meet correctly at the center seam. If the book is a tall narrow one, side sewing is undesirable since the pages will not lie flat when the book is open. Unfortunately, many of our children's books are not bound with a durable binding and have to be rebound for library use. Librarians and teachers have to consider durability of books along with many other aspects that go into the making of fine picture books.

Comparison with Other Picture Books   To understand the art of the picture book, teachers and librarians need to examine many of them. Thorough study of the work of one artist will reveal the media and style he used in various books, and show changes in his art through the years. Leonard Weisgard, for example, has changed his style of illustrating from one of very realistic, beautifully colored pictures to one of almost monochromatic, subdued art forms.

A second method of study is to compare different artists' styles. The excellent film, *The Lively Art of Picture Books*[19] compares the various ways artists have portrayed cats, trees, Notre Dame, and small towns. A similar comparison could be made by an individual of other subjects.

Comparing books with the same theme or subject can be interesting and give understanding of different art techniques. Marcia Brown's *Stone Soup* may be compared with Zemach's *Nail Soup;* Lent's illustrations

---

[18]Nicolas Sidjakov, "Caldecott Award Acceptance" in *Newbery and Caldecott Medal Books: 1956–1965*, Edited by Lee Kingman (Boston: Horn Book, 1965), pp. 223–225.

[19]"The Lively Art of Picture Books" produced by Morton Schindel, Weston Woods Studios, Weston Woods, Conn. 06883.

for *The Wave* with those of Funai for *The Burning Rice Fields.* Various editions of Mother Goose, ABC, and counting books might be contrasted.

Comments by different reviewers help the teacher and the librarian become more aware of significant aspects of a book. Frequently, reviewers emphasize content, giving little attention to style and media. Gradually publishers are including more information about the artists in their advertising copy on the jacket flap or back fly leaf. Unfortunately, publishers include little information about media when giving notes about the artists on the fly leaf or jacket flap.

Another way of enriching one's knowledge of the artist's purposes and techniques is reading what the artists themselves have to say about their work. The acceptance speeches for the Caldecott Awards are interesting in their own right and contain a wealth of information about the illustrating of children's books.[20]

Types and Themes of Picture Books

Young children have many and varied interests. They are filled with "insatiable curiosity" about their world. As boys and girls reach out for richer and wider experiences, they are ready for many different types of picture books.

Family Stories The young child's world revolves around himself and his immediate family. To meet these interests, Lois Lenski has written six "Davy" books about a child's daily experiences and growth. *Big Little Davy* gives a complete story of Davy's life from the time he was a baby until he is five and ready for school. It shows growth in terms of physical size, accomplishments, and responsibilities, such as taking care of his pets and

crossing the street alone. With simple vocabulary and her typical little rounded figures, Lenski has told "every child's" experience in a way that puts him in the center of the story.

The Bundle Book by Ruth Krauss describes a game played between a mother and her young child as the mother guesses what is in the strange bundle under the blanket on her bed. She guesses "a bundle of laundry," "carrots," "a monkey," and so on. Each time "the bundle" replies vociferously, "No, no, no." Finally "the bundle" can stand it no longer and announces "It's me." His mother is delighted and assures him he is just what she needs. This book shows warmth and family love. Young children enjoy knowing the secret of what is in the bundle before it is revealed in the book.

The arrival of a new baby is portrayed by Flack in *The New Pet.* Dreaming of the animal they might receive, the children are surprised and delighted when the "pet" turns out to be a new baby. A more recent book on this same subject is *Amy and the New Baby* by Myra Brown. Here, understanding parents help a big sister accept her new baby brother.

Several humorous books reflect children's frustrations of parental controls. In *When I Am Big,* Robert Paul Smith describes a small boy who looks forward eagerly to the time when he will be the one to pick up pieces of broken glass, insert plugs into sockets, and climb ladders to put up the storm windows. With her keen perception of children, Charlotte Zolotow has written two books about young children's secret desires. In the first book, one little girl lets her readers know that things are going to be quite different when she has a little girl. She announces that *When I Have a Little Girl* she can have a party every week, answer the phone first, and let her hair grow as long as she wants to! The illustrations by Hilary Knight have captured the tongue-in-cheek humor of this book. In

---

[20]These speeches are printed annually in the August issue of *The Horn Book Magazine.* See related readings for collections of speeches.

Someday, Zolotow describes such improbable wishes as:

> *Someday, I'm going to come home and my brother will introduce me to his friends and say, "This is my sister." Instead of "Here's the family creep."*[21]

Zolotow also has skillfully portrayed different sibling relationships in her books *Big Brother, Do You Know What I'll Do?*, and *If It Weren't for You.* In the first book, a big brother delights in his sister's howls when he teases her. When the little girl finally understands that her brother just pretended to put tacks in her bed or break an egg in her hair, she stops her crying. Mary Chalmers' illustrations capture the irritation, the humor, and the companionship of the two children. In the second book, *Do You Know What I'll Do?*, an older sister lovingly tells her little brother of all the thoughtful things that she wants to do for him. Some of her promises are beautiful and include "I'll bring you a shell to hold the sound of the sea." and "I'll remember my dreams and tell them to you.[22] The softly shaded illustrations by Garth Williams reflect the dignity and deep feelings of the little girl's promises. In *If It Weren't for You*, Zolotow realistically presents an older brother's feelings of jealousy of his younger brother. For example, if it weren't for his little brother he could have a room of his own, a treehouse of his own, sit in the front seat, and be an only child! The ending shows that being a big brother does have some compensations, however.

Helen Buckley has written several books about the joy of the extended family. Her book, *Grandfather and I* is a favorite with many children. Here, she describes the leisurely pace of a walk with grandfather in contrast to the way mothers and fathers and big sisters and brothers race along. Young children enjoy the rhythm and repetition of the lines "But Grandfather and I never hurry. We walk along and walk along And stop . . . And look . . . just as long as we like."[23] Others in this series include *Grandmother and I* and *My Sister and I,* all illustrated with Galdone's refreshingly modern illustrations.

Buckley has also written *The Little Boy and the Birthdays* that has the theme of forgetting self in concern for others. A boy worries that no one will remember his fifth birthday until his mother suggests a way for him to remember all the birthdays that come before his.

In *The Sky Was Blue*, Zolotow has conveyed the feeling of the continuity of life and the everlasting quality of such important things as the blueness of the sky, the greenness of grass, and constancy of mothers' love. This difficult theme is introduced as a mother and her little girl are looking at the pictures in a family album. Even though her ancestors' dresses, dolls, houses, cars, and buggies were different, the little girl found that they all *felt* very much as she did. It is good to have a book that emphasizes the enduring qualities of life.

Familiar Everyday Experiences   Books can help children keep alive the wonder of first-time experiences. All too frequently, the familiar grows commonplace and the excitement of daily living is lost. Myra Brown appears to be able to see the "big things" that happen in the lives of small children. In *First Night Away from Home*, she shows Stevie packing such essential things as his rock collection and his squirt gun and walking to Davie's house, five houses away from home. After Stevie gets ready for bed, he finds the room looks quite different at night and he

[21]Charlotte Zolotow, *Someday*, Illustrated by Arnold Lobel (New York: Harper & Row, 1965), unpaged.

[22]Charlotte Zolotow, *Do You Know What I'll Do?*, Illustrated by Garth Williams (New York: Harper & Row, 1958), unpaged.

[23]Helen Buckley, *Grandfather and I*, Illustrated by Paul Galdone (New York: Lothrop, 1959), unpaged.

cannot get to sleep. The doorbell rings and his mother has sent his forgotten Teddy Bear. Now Stevie has something familiar and he snuggles up close to his bear and goes to sleep. In *Benjy's Blanket,* Brown tells the story of a little boy who carries his blanket with him wherever he goes. Finally, he finds a better use for it! Brown also describes a child's anticipation and enjoyment in helping his mother prepare for guests in *Company's Coming for Dinner.*

Other "firsts" may include the first time a child learns how to do something such as whistle or print his name. In *Whistle for Willie,* Ezra Jack Keats has captured a small boy's delight in learning how to whistle. With colorful collage pictures, Keats has suggested a hot city afternoon, but not too hot or noisy for Willie, the dog, to hear Peter's first whistle and come running. Sue Felt has written of *Rosa-Too-Little* who loved to go to the library, but she was too little to write her name and thus be allowed the privilege of her own library card. There is a moment of pride and joy when she learns to write her name and can borrow books from the library.

Robert McCloskey has caught the excitement of every-day living in his wonderful book, *One Morning in Maine.* When Sal loses her first tooth and discovers she is growing up, it is a very big moment. She makes general announcements about her tooth to a hawk, a loon, a seal, and her father—only her father appeared interested! She drops her tooth while helping her father dig clams, but she makes her wish on a gull's feather instead, and the wish comes true. This is a joyous story that should be shared with five- and six-year-olds who may be losing more teeth than Sal.

The first day of school is always a milestone in the path of childhood. In *A Pocketful of Cricket,* Rebecca Caudill tells what happens to Jay, a farm boy, who takes his cricket to school. When Jay refuses to put his very noisy cricket out of the classroom, his percep-

tive teacher realizes that the cricket gives Jay the security of the familiar in an unfamiliar situation. She allows him to keep it and show it to the class. Jay is so pleased that he starts planning what he can share with the class the next day. The quality of the pictures by Evaline Ness complements the beauty of this quiet story.

Some children are shy about any encounter with grown-ups. Joan Lexau has written understandingly about a little boy, *Benjie,* who was too frightened to talk to any adults. One day, however, his granny loses one of her earrings and Benjie has to overcome his shyness in order to find it for her. Yashima has described the growing relationship of trust between a little two-year-old, Bobby, and his ten- or eleven-year-old neighbor, Momo, in *Youngest One.* At first, Bobby hides behind his grandmother's skirt when Momo talks to him, but gradually his gaze meets hers, and they become friends.

Books may also help children to see their everyday world in a new perspective. A boy and his father get up early to explore the changing seashore in Kumin's book, *The Beach Before Breakfast.* They dig clams and watch the sea gulls fish for food. But there is a kind of joy in recalling similar previous experiences and in doing the unusual at an early hour alone with your father. Weisgard's horizontal lines and luminous color convey a feeling of space and peace of the beach at dawn. In lovely poetry form, Aileen Fisher tells of a little girl's desire to go out *In the Middle of the Night* to see what it was like. Her father agrees to take her for her birthday present, and they make wondrous discoveries. It becomes a peak moment for both of them:

> *The world seemed so wide and high*
> *and so full of wonder,*
> *with a piece of moon in the sky*
> *and a cloud to go in and out of*
> *and under.*

It was even better
than I had dreamed;
and my Father seemed
not tall, and me small,
but as if we'd become
sort-of-the-same size,
looking with surprise
through the same kind of eyes.[24]

Janice Udry and Maurice Sendak captured a mood of gay abandon rather than quiet wonder as they portrayed children playing in the moonlight in *The Moon Jumpers*. The beautiful illustrations reflect the exhilarating magic of a pale moon on a summer evening.

The White Marble by Zolotow is the simple story of a little boy and girl going to a city park on a hot summer night. It contains a fragile and lovely moment when the two experience a flickering understanding of human companionship. At the park, John Henry meets Pamela from school and the two run and lie in the soft grass enjoying the feel of the wind and being together. He shows her his white marble; they run to the fountain for water; they go back to their parents to have icy pineapple sticks before returning home. Pamela skips back to say goodbye to John Henry—he in turn gives her his white marble. This, in a sense, is a love story. Some will say that it is not true behavior of children; others will recognize its beauty and universal qualities.

Daily experiences can be dismal as well as joyous. Recently, authors have shown all sides of children's behavior including their nastier moods. Udry's story, *Let's Be Enemies,* is a tongue-in-cheek parody on children's quarrels. The illustrations by Sendak are uproariously funny. John announces in a very formal four- or five-year-old way that

James is now his enemy. It seems James always carries the flag, and besides that, he throws sand. Using a direct approach, John marches over to James' house in the rain to tell him that he is now his enemy. By the time he has delivered his message, the sun has symbolically appeared, and they are fast friends again. *The Quarreling Book* by Zolotow recounts the cumulative effect of a rainy gray morning and the fact that Mr. James forgot to kiss Mrs. James goodbye. Mrs. James is then quite cross with Jonathan who, in turn, is nasty to his sister, who hurts her best friend's feelings and so forth, until the chain is broken by Eddie's little dog who plays with him and licks his face until he laughs. Then the whole dismal process is reversed and the day is saved. *Two Is a Team* by Beim also begins with a quarrel between Ted and Paul, who are building a wagon together. After the quarrel, each decides to make his own wagon. However, the wagon race down the hill results in real trouble that can only be solved by working together. The larger message of this book is revealed only through the pictures which show that one child is dark skinned and the other is white.

Learning to give something up for the first time, particularly something loved and cared for, can be a heart-rending experience for a youngster. In Simon's story of *Benjy's Bird*, Benjy finds a robin who has fallen out of its nest. He cares for it, and it becomes a pet, free to come and go as it wishes. However, in the autumn the pet joins the migrating birds and Benjy's mother explains that when "he is growing up there are many goodbyes."

All children encounter the fact of death while they are growing up. The quiet explanation and serenity of the lovely blue, green and yellow oil paintings give reassurance about the mystery of death in *The Dead Bird* by Margaret Wise Brown. The children pick up a dead bird, feel no heart beating. "That was the way animals got when they had been dead for some time—cold dead and stone

---

[24]Aileen Fisher, *In the Middle of the Night,* Illustrated by Adrienne Adams (New York: Crowell, 1965), unpaged.

Simple, stylized figures create unity in the double-page illustrations colored in bright blues, greens, and yellows. From *The Dead Bird* by Margaret Wise Brown. Illustrated by Remy Charlip. Copyright 1958 by Roberta B. Rauch. William R. Scott, Inc.

still with no heart beating."[25] They have a typically childlike funeral, make a stone marker, and carry flowers to the grave. But the children soon return to their play and forget the bird. Life goes on — we need not feel guilty if we forget; the cycle continues.

Stories of the Country and City Young children should be ever extending their horizons, not forever roaming within them. Books about the city may give the city child a review of familiar experiences, but they will offer new experiences to the rural or suburban child. Likewise, books about the farm may be enjoyed for their familiarity by the country child and appreciated for their newness by the urban child. In *A Thousand Lights and Fireflies,* Tressel has contrasted city life with country life while emphasizing the universal qualities of both. He compares the settings of city and country in rich descriptive prose:

In the city everything is squeezed together.
The buildings are so close they have to stretch up into the sky to find room.
The country is stretched out for miles and

miles, rolling over hills and valley and broad flat farms.
The houses sit apart so they can look at one another.[26]

Other differences are noted, such as city noises, "the shriek of the fire engines," and country noises, "Brooks gossiping with the pebbles;"[27] but similarities include mothers and fathers, children playing and going to school.

In *Wake Up, City!* Tressel describes how morning comes to the city from the first chirping of the sparrow to the honking of the bus that picks the children up for school. In a companion book, *Wake Up, Farm!,* he tells how the animals waken one by one, the horse, the baby colt, the roly-poly pig, the lambs, and last of all, the little boy in the farm house. *Sun Up,* also by Tressel and illustrated by Duvoisin, traces a hot midsummer day on the farm from the cock's early morning crow through a late afternoon's sudden storm to the peacefully cool coming of the night.

[25]Margaret Wise Brown, *The Dead Bird,* Illustrated by Remy Charlip (New York: W. R. Scott, 1958), unpaged.

[26]Alvin Tressel, *A Thousand Lights and Fireflies,* Illustrated by John Moody (New York: Parents' Magazine Press, 1965), unpaged.
[27]Tressel.

A stifling hot day in the city is described by Bourne in *Emilio's Summer Day.* The writing is as realistic as the drab brown pictures of the slums, for example:

He felt his damp shirt sticking to his damp back. He smelled orange peel in an open garbage can. Around the corner he heard a car start. Music floated out of the windows across the street. A baby cried. But nothing moved.[28]

Relief and fun do come in the form of the street washer that sprays the children with icy water. This book would be interesting to compare with *A Snowy Day* by Keats, which describes a city child's delight in the new-fallen snow.

Margaret Wise Brown has emphasized the sound of the city and the country in her two well-loved books, *The City Noisy Book* and *The Country Noisy Book.* Both books relate the sounds heard by a little dog, Muffin, and involve the reader in guessing what the sounds are.

The hard contrasts of luxury and alley life of city cats are humorously described in Waber's book, *Rich Cat, Poor Cat.* The story of a city cat that has four names and four owners is told in *Galumph* by Lansdown. Unwittingly, each owner shares in the care and feeding of this golden cat until she is trapped in a tenement fire and the multi-ownership is discovered. While this story is somewhat contrived, it does provide an opportunity to show the varied ethnic character of city neighbors. In *The Two Reds* by Will and Nicolas, a day in the life of a city boy with red hair and a red cat is portrayed. Both Reds are involved in trouble; one for stealing a fish from the fish market, the other for spying on the Seventh Street Signal Senders. Each escapes his pursuers and finds refuge and friendship on the boy's front stoop. A little Puerto Rican boy finds friends and help as he searches the city for his beloved dog in *My Dog Is Lost* by Keats.

The encroachment of the city on the country is portrayed in Burton's classic story of *The Little House* that stood on the hill and watched day and night and the seasons pass. Gradually, a road is built, cars come, and soon the city grows up around the little house. Elevated cars speed by her, subway trains speed under her, and people rush to and fro in front of her. One day, the great-great-granddaughter of the original owner saw the little house, bought her, and had her moved back to the country where she could once again see the stars. The little house is personified to the extent that she appears to have an expression that changes from happiness to sorrow and dismay, and back to happiness and contentment.

Hello-Goodbye by Felt is a story that tells of the mobility of our population. The process of moving, the long ride to the new home, and the enforced stay at a motel until the furniture arrives are vividly described. This book evokes the feelings of the excitement of moving, the exhaustion of parents, and the strangeness of a new home.

Second and third graders will enjoy the story of *Hans and Peter,* two ingenious boys who make an old builder's shack into a house. Hans lived in an attic room where he could see only the roofs of houses; Peter lived in a basement where he could see only paving stones, feet, and legs. Their new house had a window through which they could see trees and bushes, meadows, fields, and a stream. Heidrun Petrides, a German girl of fifteen, wrote and illustrated this story for her little brother.

Weather and the Seasons   Weather and seasonal changes are important events in a young child's life, often more significant than they are for adults. Tresselt and Duvoisin have presented this contrast of adults' and children's reactions to weather in *White Snow,*

[28]Miriam Anne Bourne, *Emilio's Summer Day,* Illustrated by Ben Shecter (Harper & Row, 1966), p. 23.

Bright Snow and *Hide and Seek Fog.* In the first book, the discomfort of adults brought about by a snow storm is compared with the children's joy over its arrival. Repeating this same pattern, Tresselt has described the children's ready response to a fog that came and stayed for three days in a little seaside village on Cape Cod, while their parents grumbled about spending their vacations in the middle of a cloud. Duvoisin's hazy pearl gray illustrations effectively convey the mystery of a fog-shrouded day. In *Josie and the Snow* by Buckley, Josie found her family much more willing to go out in the deep snow than her cat, her dog, or little mouse. After a "lovely, blowy, snowy day," the family comes home, builds a fire, and goes to sleep. The brilliant pinks, oranges, and aqua colors contrasted with crisp black and white drawings by Evaline Ness make this a handsome book. *The Big Snow* by the Haders realistically pictures the plight of woods' animals facing real discomfort and danger as a result of a big snow.

In *The Storm Book* by Zolotow, children may follow the progress of a storm from the oppressive dry stillness broken by the first faint rumble of thunder to the last graceful arch of the rainbow. *Rain Drop Splash* by Tresselt catches the cadence of the raindrops in telling of the raindrops that "dripped from the shiny leaves, dropped from a rabbit's nose, splashed from a brown bear's tail.[29] The raindrops form a puddle that drains into a pond, a lake, a river, and at last joins the sea. Francoise has told the story of Jeanne-Marie and her family caught in a flood in *The Big Rain.* When the water goes down, Jeanne-Marie and her friends help clean their little French village. *James and the Rain* by Karla Kuskin is an accumulative rhyme about a small boy who goes out in the rain and is joined by one cow, two ducks,

three toads, and so on, all of whom enjoy the rain as much as the little boy. In *Umbrella* by Yashima, Momo is impatient for rain so that she can wear her new red rubber boots and carry her new umbrella to nursery school. At last the rain comes, and Momo walks straight like a lady, listening to the rhythmic patter of the raindrops on her new umbrella. Yashima's pictures are consistent with the text, yet they also add information to it. For example, the reader is not told that this is a city story, but the illustrations show Momo's home and her nursery school are at least on the third floor or higher. A little Mexican boy pretends that Wind is his playmate in *Gilberto and the Wind* by Marie Hall Ets. Some days Wind is good company for Gilberto, sometimes he whispers to him, at other times he roars and tears things from his hands, still other days he is all tired out and says nothing at all. The quiet pictures of Gilberto's expressive face, even his very stance, reflect his response to this changeable playmate.

Children sometimes confuse seasonal changes with weather changes. Lois Lenski has written four little books for the young child describing the various activities and delights of each season. Written in verse form, these books include *Spring Is Here, On a Summer Day, I Like Winter,* and *Now It's Fall.* Although it still feels like winter, a robin shows a small boy the many signs of spring in *"Hi, Mister Robin!"* by Tresselt. The animals' joy over the end of the winter has been beautifully illustrated by Marc Simont in *The Happy Day* by Ruth Krauss. The Hurds also have portrayed the restless woodland animals eagerly awaiting the coming of spring in their book, *The Day the Sun Danced.* Using his unusual wood printing technique, Clement Hurd progresses from stark black and white scenes to a radiating sunrise in brilliant colors. The varied soft-colored pictures of Adrienne Adams are in perfect harmony with Aileen Fisher's singing verse that de-

---

[29]Alvin Tresselt, *Rain Drop Splash,* Illustrated by Leonard Weisgard (New York: Lothrop, 1946), unpaged.

scribes a young child's longing for the days of June when he could go barefoot.

> *How soon*
> *how soon*
> *is a morning in June*
> *a sunny morning or afternoon*
> *in the wonderful month*
> *of the Barefoot Moon?*
> *I can go barefoot*
> *like kittens and dogs*
> *bears and beetles*
> *and hoppity frogs*
> *as soon*
> *as it's June.*[30]

This same author-artist team has written a book about fall and winter in *Where Does Everyone Go?* These books will heighten children's awareness of the beauty of the changing seasons. Tasha Tudor's *First Delights* helps very young children experience the changing seasons through their five senses. Sally smells spring in the daffodils and damp earth, tastes summer in wild strawberries warm in the sun, hears autumn in the call of the wild geese, and sees winter in the new-fallen snow. Zolotow has caught a young child's feelings about all the seasons in her book *Over and Over.* Time concepts are explained in meaningful terms to the young child through the exciting events of each season of the year—the first snowfall, Christmas, Valentine's Day, Easter, summer vacation, Halloween, Thanksgiving, a birthday, and it begins "over and over" again.

Concept Books A concept book is one that describes the various dimensions of an abstract idea through the use of many comparisons. These books seldom have plots but hold the child's interest through skilled questioning and by relating the familiar to the unfamiliar. Well-defined concepts are nec-

essary for the young child's cognitive and language development. For this reason, the book that is conceptual rather than narrative should be accurate and concise in expressing true relationships.

One of the earliest examples of a concept book was Budney's *A Kiss Is Round*, that explored the various aspects of "roundness" through such verses as:

> *Round is the moon*
> *When it's bright and full,*
> *Round is a ball*
> *Of knitting wool,*
> *A kiss is round,*
> *And so is a hug;*
> *The rim of a glass,*
> *And the lid of a jug;*
> *The top of a hole*
> *When it's carefully dug.*[31]

Square shapes, round shapes, fat and thin shapes are part of the fun of the book, *Are You Square?*, by Ethel and Leonard Kessler. With provocative questions and illustrations, the Kesslers help children become aware of the various shapes around them. In *The Wing on a Flea*, Emberley presents the basic concepts of a triangle, rectangle, and circle and suggests that children look to see how many examples of these shapes they can find. Comparative size is examined by Ramirez in her book, *Small as a Raisin Big as the World.* She describes relative sizes of familiar objects at the child's level of experience. Miriam Schlein's books, *Heavy Is a Hippopotamus* and *Fast Is Not a Ladybug* are both concept books that discuss comparative values of weight and speed. They give more specifics than most concept books and are more appropriate for second or third-graders.

The concept of a direction is given in Zion's book, *All Falling Down,* by describing how leaves, the snow, and a house of blocks

---

[30]Aileen Fisher, *Going Barefoot,* Illustrated by Adrienne Adams (New York: Crowell, 1960), unpaged.

[31]Blossom Budney, *A Kiss Is Round,* Illustrated by Vladimir Bobri (New York: Lothrop, 1954), unpaged.

fall down. This book also includes the ideas of night and shadows as objects that fall downward. Such a sudden switch from the development of a concept to the use of metaphor would be confusing to the young child. Relative degrees of difficulty are explored in the book *Is It Hard? Is It Easy?* by Mary Green. Respect for others' capabilities and weaknesses might be developed by reading this book.

All the different uses and delights to be had in, with, or under a tree are described in the award-winning book, *A Tree Is Nice,* by Udry. The joyous illustrations by Marc Simont picture children, adults, and animals enjoying trees in various ways. *Night's Nice* for many reasons and the Emberleys have thought of a good number of them in their story of that title. Margaret Wise Brown's *The Important Book,* illustrated by Leonard Weisgard, helps children to make generalizations concerning the most significant aspects of such different objects as a spoon or an apple. Children could be encouraged to develop their own "Important Books" after hearing this one. Critical thinking would be stimulated by such an activity.

Realistic Animal Stories   There are more animal stories, including realistic and fanciful tales, than any other kind for young children. Scientific accounts of particular species are included in Chapter 9 ("Informational Books"). Picture stories of animals that are true to their own animal nature are included here. Because young children tend to humanize animals, many of these stories do ascribe speech and human thoughts to their animal characters, however.

Four- and five-year-olds still enjoy the simple but exciting adventures of a young curious Scottish terrier in the Angus stories by Marjorie Flack. A new edition of Friskey's *Seven Diving Ducks* has just recently been issued. Long a favorite, it tells the story of the shy little duck who was afraid to learn to swim and dive. The story of *Make Way for Ducklings* by Robert McCloskey has become a classic for primary children. No child worries about the vintage of the cars in this story, for he is too concerned with the safety of Mrs. Mallard and her ducklings in the bustle of Boston traffic. Will and Nicolas have written and illustrated two amusing stories of farm animals. In *The Little Tiny Rooster,* a much-maligned rooster compensates for his size by warning the henhouse of the coming of a fox. *Billy the Kid* is a story of a little goat with as many questions as a pumpkin has seeds. No one has time for him and he wanders from animal to animal until he finally finds a friend in a young, incorrigible horse and both become easier to live with. The bold illustrations and humor of these books appeal to children.

Clare Newberry's many books about cats have a slight story line, but the beautiful pictures of soft cuddly kittens and sleek shiny cats appeal to children. In *April's Kittens,* Father finally agrees to move to a "two-cat" apartment rather than a "one-cat" one. *Marshmallow* is the story of a furry white bunny who comes to live in the same house as Oliver, a cat; and *Mittens* tells of a search for a lost cat who has six toes on each front paw. Wesley Dennis has used rich black and white pictures to illustrate his horse stories of *Flip* and *Flip and the Cows,* which are most popular with second and third graders.

The lilting narrative poem *Listen, Rabbit* by Aileen Fisher portrays a realistic story of a wild rabbit and a boy who wanted it for a pet. Patiently the boy watches for his rabbit all year until finally in the spring he discovers a wonderful surprise, "a nest/like a fur-lined cup/and *five baby rabbits*/to watch grow up!"[32] This same author has described all the various little houses that insects and animals build in *Best Little House.* The parallel stories

---

[32] Aileen Fisher, *Listen, Rabbit,* Illustrated by Symeon Shimin (New York: Crowell, 1964), unpaged.

of a family and a possum caught in a flood are presented in *Mississippi Possum* by Miles. The stunning black and white pictures by John Schoenherr show Rose Mary gradually taming the little possum while both wait in the tent city for the flood waters to go down. When the family returns to its shack at the bottom of the hill, the possum goes home with them. This same author and artist have written and illustrated *The Fox and the Fire* telling of a fox that seeks refuge under a barn during a forest fire. True to his nature, the fox does not become a pet, but steals a chicken after searching for days for something to eat in his fire-blackened world. One of the best-loved realistic animal stories is Lynd Ward's *The Biggest Bear*. This is the story of Johnny's lovable little pet cub that grows into an enormous droll creature quite impossible for Johnny to lose. While Ward has pictured the bear with amazingly human expressions, Johnny, his family, and neighbors are all rugged men of the land. Reminiscent of *The Biggest Bear* is *Nic of the Woods*, Lynd Ward's story of a cocker spaniel who becomes lost in the Canadian woods. Dark gray, blue, and black pictures emphasize the despair of Davey and the vast wilderness faced by Nic. This is a story that reveals Ward's deep childhood love of the Canadian woods and his sensitive understanding of the relationship between a boy and his dog.

Fanciful Animal Stories Ever since the day Peter Rabbit disobeyed his mother and squeezed through Mr. MacGregor's garden fence, children have enjoyed stories in which animals act like people, frequently like small children. Children can easily see their own behavior mirrored in *Bedtime for Frances*, the story of an engaging badger who finds as many excuses to avoid going to sleep as any five-year-old. In *A Baby Sister for Frances*, also by the Hobans, Frances decides that Gloria is receiving entirely too much attention, so she packs her knapsack, says goodbye to

Charcoal drawings create the texture of sleek, soft fur and show realistic movement and postures. Illustration from *April's Kittens* by the author-artist Clare Turlay Newberry. Harper & Row, 1940.

her parents, and runs away—under the dining room table. Her parents cure her of wanting just *Bread and Jam for Frances*, by literally serving her only bread and jam. In *Nothing to Do* by the same authors, a small possum serves as the child substitute and persists in bothering his father. His father gives him a magical "Something-to-do-Stone" that helps him to look and see something to do all by himself. Diane Massie has told the story of *The Baby Beebee Bird* who was new to the zoo and sang his song all night long much to the dismay of the sleepy animals. The next day the animals decided to teach him a lesson, and they sang every time the Beebee bird tried to take a nap. The very next night, "not an ear or a tail or a whisker moved," for every animal in the zoo was fast asleep. In *The Secret Hiding Place* by Bennett, a baby hippo is overprotected by all the big hippos and constantly warned about such dangers as going in the tall grass where the zebras hide for fear he might get stripes! Little Hippo decides what he needs is a nice safe hiding place. The lion offers to take him to his cave, but the hippo does not want to be alone that much! Finally, he discovers the top of a nice small hill where "he could be alone, but not too alone."

The warmth of a mother's love is portrayed in Margaret Wise Brown's book *The Runaway Bunny.* When the bunny warns his mother that he is going to run away, she says that she will follow him. The bunny imagines many things that he will become, and his mother tells him how she can find him. For example, when he says he will become a bird and fly away, she replies that she will be the tree that he comes home to. Finally, the bunny decides to stay and just be his mother's little bunny.

Many animal characters in children's literature have real personalities of their own. All first graders love the stories of a silly goose, *Petunia,* who thinks she has acquired wisdom when she finds a book. Duvoisin's gay pictures show Petunia holding her head higher and higher with pride until it stretches off the page. Another lovable creation of Duvoisin is *Veronica,* the hippopotamus who longed to be conspicuous and made a trip to the city to achieve her wish. Duvoisin also has illustrated his wife's many stories about that sophisticated French lion, *The Happy Lion.* One day, this king of the beasts finds his cage door open and observes that anyone could walk in. It then occurs to him that he could take a stroll himself. He is completely mystified by the strange antics of his friends, the townspeople, when he walks into their village. Only the zookeeper's son, Francois, calls out "Bonjour, Happy Lion" and seems glad to see him as he calmly walks him back to the zoo. Another sophisticated French "animality" is Tomi Ungerer's *Crictor,* a most affectionate boa constrictor pet of Madame Bodot, who teaches school in a peaceful French village—peaceful until a burglar breaks into her apartment only to meet Crictor! *Anatole* by Eve Titus is a cheese-

tasting mouse who is as French as his little beret and bicycle. He saves M'sieu Duval's cheese factory from financial ruin and becomes first Vice-President in charge of cheese-tasting! Other books tell of further adventures of this resourceful French mouse. *The Story of Babar* by Jean de Brunhoff is the story of a little elephant who runs away from the jungle and goes to live with an understanding lady in Paris. His cousins, Arthur and Celestine, come to visit and persuade him to return to Africa where his poise and elegant wardrobe are so impressive that he is made King of the Jungle. The popular Babar stories are now being continued by Jean de Brunhoff's son, Laurent.

Other favorite animal personalities include the *Curious George* stories by H. A. Rey. This comical monkey has one escapade after another, but the man in the yellow hat always manages to save him from real danger. H. A. Rey also illustrated *Katy No-Pocket* by Payne, the sad and amusing tale of a poor kangaroo who had no pocket for her baby until she solved her dilemma with a carpenter's apron! When the Primm family move into their apartment in *The House on East 88th Street,* they find Lyle, a performing crocodile, in the bathtub. They become fast friends and live happily together. The sequel to this book by Waber is *Lyle, Lyle, Crocodile,* in which Lyle is put in a zoo by a cross neighbor. Lyle is finally freed and before running away to Australia, he pays a last visit to the house on East 88th Street just in time to save the neighbor from a fire. The preposterous animals of Dr. Seuss need little introduction to children. They love the story of *Horton Hatches the Egg* that tells of the good-natured elephant who helps the ungrateful lazy bird, Mazie, to hatch her egg. The incongruity of a great big elephant sitting on a nest in a tree tickles the funny bone in all of us. Another lovable Seuss animal is *Thidwick, the Big-Hearted Moose,* whose generosity nearly costs him his life.

The theme of being true to one's own

1

EARLY
ILLUSTRATORS

2

1 Randolph Caldecott was one of the first illustrators for children to show action in his pictures. One can almost hear the squawking geese, the barking dogs, and the squalling child as John Gilpin's horse dashes madly through a peaceful English village. From "John Gilpin," *Picture Book Number 1,* illustrated by Randolph Caldecott. Reproduced by the permission of the publisher, Frederick Warne & Company.

2 Rackham's illustration for "The Man in the Wilderness" shows one tree with a kindly face and long grotesque arms combing another tree's branches! A wistful little girl seems unafraid of the weird elfman with his pointed ears. From *Mother Goose* by Arthur Rackham. Copyright, 1913, Arthur Rackham, 1941 by Edyth Rackham. By permission of Appleton-Century-Crofts, an affiliate of Meredith Press.

3 A tiny sketch in pale watercolor shows a self-confident Peter setting out for Mr. MacGregor's garden. From *The Tale of Peter Rabbit* by Beatrix Potter, 1902. Reproduced by the permission of the publisher, Frederick Warne & Company.

3

INTERPRETERS
OF
MOTHER GOOSE

ucy Locket
lost her pocket,
Kitty Fisher
found it;
There was not a penny in it,
But a ribbon round it.

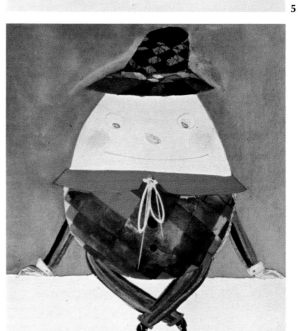

Humpty Dumpty sat on a wall;
Humpty Dumpty had a great fall.
All the king's horses and all the king's men
Couldn't put Humpty Dumpty together again.

3

7

4 Rojankovsky has pictured "Lucy Locket" in a pensive mood as she considers the contents of her purse. Lucy is a sturdy-looking child dressed in warm play clothes. The rich red of the purse is repeated in the small design of the initial letter. Art work by Feodor Rojankovsky for *The Tall Book of Mother Goose* (copyright 1942 by Artists and Writers Guild, Inc.). Reprinted by permission.

5 Tasha Tudor's old-fashioned children lightly dance around a mulberry bush in the warm glow of autumn sunlight. From *Mother Goose* illustrated by Tasha Tudor, 1944. By permission of Henry Z. Walck, Inc.

6 Brian Wildsmith has dressed his Humpty Dumpty in a brilliant array of geometrical patterns. From *Brian Wildsmith's Mother Goose,* illustration by Brian Wildsmith, published 1963 by Franklin Watts, Inc.

7 A little boy on his cock-horse and a little girl with her doll stand in awed wonder at the fine lady riding in medieval splendor. Marguerite de Angeli has provided the authentic background of an English cathedral and Banbury Cross for this verse. From *Book of Nursery and Mother Goose Rhymes,* by Marguerite de Angeli. Copyright 1954 by Marguerite de Angeli. Reprinted by permission of Doubleday & Company, Inc.

8 Dressed in bridal finery, Jenny Wren emerges from her elegant limousine to greet the groom, Cock Robin. Barbara Cooney has added a dimension of humor to this book of a single verse by drawing such details as the bird radiator cap, the red carpet, and the vintage car. Reproduced with the permission of Charles Scribner's Sons from *Cock Robin,* illustrated by Barbara Cooney (copyright © 1965 Barbara Cooney).

8

A little while after came the second
Billy Goat Gruff to cross the bridge.
"Trip, trap! trip, trap! trip, trap!"
went the bridge.

One day a hermit
sat thinking about
big and little—
Suddenly,
he saw a mouse

11

12

THE WORK
OF ONE ILLUSTRATOR

9 10 11 12

These illustrations by Marcia Brown show the great versatility of one artist in adapting style, media, and color to meet the demands of each story. The Norwegian origin of *The Three Billy Goats Gruff* is reflected in the rugged strength of the landscape. The well-designed woodcuts of jungle colors are most appropriate for the Indian fable of *Once a Mouse. . . .* The ethereal illustrations in delicate blues and pinks are faithful to the French origin of *Cinderella*. Gondolas, pigeons, cats, and the famed columns of the Doge's Palace are portrayed in brilliant watercolors that reflect the sparkling light of Venice in the modern story of *Felice*. © 1957 by Marcia Brown, reproduced from *The Three Billy Goats Gruff* by P. C. Asbjørnsen and J. E. Moe, with pictures by Marcia Brown, 1957, by permission of Harcourt, Brace & World, Inc. Reproduced with the permission of Charles Scribner's Sons from: *Once a Mouse*, page 3, by Marcia Brown (copyright © 1961 Marcia Brown); *Cinderella*, page 16, by Marcia Brown, copyright 1954 Marcia Brown; and *Felice* by Marcia Brown (copyright © 1958 Marcia Brown).

14   13

The salt spray stung John Tabor's face. He shivered with fear and excitement. His teeth chattered and he held on with all his strength.

The whale bounded from wave to wave, faster than any ship, fairly flying through the sea.

"Look below, John Tabor, look below!" said the old man leaning over the side of the whale, "and you'll see a pretty sight."

15

16

13 Sharp contrasts in black and white and. red are achieved with scratchboard technique in illustrating *Peter and the Wolf*. Excellent composition is seen in these strong vertical and horizontal lines that lead the eye to Peter as he cautions the bird. From *Peter and the Wolf* by Serge Prokofieff, illustration by Frans Haacken, published 1961 by Franklin Watts, Inc.

14 Blair Lent has used cardboard cuts to portray the humor of John Tabor's wild ride on a whale. Action is expressed by the angle of the boats, the swirling waves, and the flying hat. Copyright © 1966 by Blair Lent, Jr. Illustration from *John Tabor's Ride* by Blair Lent, by permission of Atlantic-Little, Brown and Co.

15 Clement Hurd has created an effect of a quiet sea with the unusual technique of stamping blockprints on top of a print made from the grain of weathered wood. From *Wingfin and Topple* by Evans G. Valens, Jr., illustrated by Clement Hurd. Text copyright © 1962 by Evans G. Valens, Jr. Illustrations copyright © 1962 by Clement Hurd. Reprinted by permission of The World Publishing Company.

16 The little fish, *Swimmy,* is almost lost in a forest of seaweed made by stenciling of lace paper doilies. Leo Lionni has used collage, paper stamping, and many muted watercolors to create this watery world of fantasy. From *Swimmy* by Leo Lionni. © Copyright 1963 by Leo Lionni. Reprinted by permission of Pantheon Books, a Division of Random House, Inc.

17 Soft gray and green watercolors portray a foggy morning in a forest so quiet you could hear "the sound of growing ferns." From *Time of Wonder* by Robert McCloskey. Copyright © 1957 by Robert McCloskey. Reprinted by permission of The Viking Press, Inc.

18 Realistic wash drawings and watercolors reflect the tenderness of the moment a boy discovers a nest of baby rabbits. Fine draftsmanship is evident in Shimin's natural sketches of people and animals. Illustration by Symeon Shimin (copyright © 1964 by Symeon Shimin) in *Listen, Rabbit!*, by Aileen Fisher. Thomas Y. Crowell Company, New York, publishers.

18

19

20

THE
EFFECTIVE
USE
OF
COLOR

19 Harald Wiberg, a famous Swedish painter, has created a feeling of stillness and mystery as *The Tomten* walks about the lonely farm on a snowy night. The deep blue shadows and sparkling white snow give the effect of a bitter cold moonlit night. Illustration by Harald Wiberg from *The Tomten* by Astrid Lingren, 1961. Reprinted by permission of Coward-McCann, Inc.

20 Heathery colored wash and pen-and-ink sketches are combined to portray the misty Scottish moors in *Always Room for One More*. The wide expanse of sky and hills makes the wee house appear even smaller than it is. From *Always Room for One More* by Sorche Nic Leodhas. Illustrated by Nonny Hogrogian. Copyright © 1965 by Nonny Hogrogian. Reproduced by permission of Holt, Rinehart and Winston, Inc.

21 Using only shades of blue chalk, Weisgard has created a wet misty world as seen through the gentle slanting rain. From *Where Does the Butterfly Go When It Rains?* by May Garelick. Illustrated by Leonard Weisgard. Copyright 1961 by May Garelick. William R. Scott, Inc.

21

22

23

24

COLOR IN POSTER STYLE

22 and 23   In *White Snow, Bright Snow,* color is effectively used to show the change in the weather from the darkening sky, through a night of snow, to a dazzling white winter day. The curving road leads the eye into the poster-like village of bright red and yellow buildings. Illustration from *White Snow, Bright Snow* by Alvin Tresselt, illustrated by Roger Duvoisin, copyright © 1956 by Lothrop, Lee & Shepard Co., Inc. By permission of Lothrop, Lee & Shepard Co., Inc.

24   Bold black outlines, abstract forms, and poster colors are characteristic of Piatti's style of illustrating. Copyright © 1963 by Artemis Verlag. From *The Happy Owls* by Celestino Piatti. Used by permission of Atheneum Publishers.

The King said. "Hello."
He said. "How do you do?"
The Queen said. "Well!
Fancy meeting you!"

25

SETTINGS
OF
REALISM
AND
FANTASY

25 Montresor designs each incident in his nonsense story of *May I Bring a Friend?* like a stage setting with curtained entrances, many arches, and a patterned floor. Unusual color combinations are highlighted with many black lines to create an effect of brilliance. Pictures copyright © 1964 by Beni Montresor. From *May I Bring a Friend?* by Beatrice Schenk de Regniers. Used by permission of Atheneum Publishers.

26 Paris is suffused with yellow in Bemelmans' story of *Madeline's Rescue.* Authentic landmarks are seen as Miss Clavel and her twelve charges cross the Pont des Arts in front of the Institute of France. From *Madeline's Rescue* by Ludwig Bemelmans. Copyright 1951, 1953 by Ludwig Bemelmans. First appeared in *Good Housekeeping.* Reprinted by permission of The Viking Press, Inc.

27

FANTASY
AND IMPRESSIONISM

27 Max triumphantly rides one of his dream monsters in the "Wild Rumpus." The ponderous creatures dance riotously across the page. Muted greens, blues, and browns create this eerie fantasy world *Where the Wild Things Are*. Illustration on pp. 29–30 of *Where the Wild Things Are* by the author-artist Maurice Sendak. Harper & Row, 1963.

28 A sophisticated rabbit and a serious-minded little girl wander through impressionistic landscapes while selecting appropriate presents for her mother. Sendak has extended this text by adding little details and creating definite characters in these luminous watercolors. Illustration by Maurice Sendak from *Mr. Rabbit and the Lovely Present* by Charlotte Zolotow. Harper & Row, 1962.

basic nature is frequently presented in fanciful animal stories. Moore's Harriet, *The Unhappy Hippopotamus*, searches vainly for enjoyment and finally discovers she is happiest when wallowing in the mud. *Dandelion* by Freeman is the story of a lion who becomes such a "dandy" in order to go to a party that his hostess does not recognize him. Freeman has also used this same theme for his story of *Cyrano, the Crow* who could imitate all the other birds but could not crow like a crow! Waber's book *"You Look Ridiculous" Said the Rhinoceros to the Hippopotamus* is as funny as its title. Each animal that the sensitive hippopotamus meets tells her that she looks ridiculous without the distinctive characteristic of his particular species. In a dream she sees herself with a giraffe's neck, a leopard's spots, an elephant's ears, a lion's mane, a monkey's tail, a turtle's shell, and a nightingale's voice; but the animals are laughing at her even more. She falls into the proverbial mudhole and from that day to this, she is quite happy to be just what she is—a big fat wonderful hippopotamus. Discontentment with one's features is also the theme of *The Little Rabbit Who Wanted Red Wings* by Bailey, and Lawson's amusing story of *Robbut, A Tale of Tails*. One of the best-loved tales of children's literature is Leaf's *The Story of Ferdinand*, the bull who, contrary to his nature, prefers smelling flowers to bull fighting. When he sits on a bee, his ferocious behavior causes him to be chosen for the bull fight. Once in the arena, he sits—smelling the flowers!

Humorous and Fanciful Picture Books
Young children's humor is simple and obvious. They enjoy the pure nonsense found in the books on manners by Joslin, *What Do You Say, Dear?* and *What Do You Do, Dear?*, that give the proper behavior for ridiculous situations. For example, if you have gone downtown shopping and happen to bump into a crocodile, what do you say? The obvious answer is "Excuse me." Maurice

Sendak's illustrations have added to the hilarity of these encounters. Joslin has used a similar pattern for the appropriate time to say useful phrases in French, Italian, and Spanish in her books *There Is a Dragon in My Bed, Spaghetti for Breakfast,* and *There Is a Bull on My Balcony*. Again, funny, unexpected situations are used to demonstrate a variety of appropriate phrases.

Both slapstick and nonsense are a part of the good fun of *May I Bring a Friend?* by Beatrice Schenck de Regniers. A little boy is invited by the King and Queen to tea and each time he goes he takes a friend: a giraffe, monkeys, lions, and hippos, not all of whom are very polite. The monkeys swing on the chandeliers, the hippopotamus puts his foot in the cake, the lions roar, and the seal plays "Long Live Apple Pie" on his bugle. Through it all, their royal majesties retain their equanimity. The brilliant purple, pink, and yellow illustrations by Beni Montresor resemble stage settings for the passing parade of incongruities. *Harold and the Purple Crayon* by Crockett Johnson combines humor with fantasy in this highly amusing tale of a small boy who "draws" himself in and out of exciting adventures.

Nonsense can only be funny when it is contrasted with sense. Marvin Bileck has made the nonsense of *Rain Makes Applesauce* by Scheer, visible in his lovely, ethereal illustrations. Hidden in each fantastic picture is a small sequence showing the proper way to make applesauce, beginning with the planting of an apple tree. The humorous manipulation of language patterns is also a part of the delight of this book. For when the text says "The wind blows backwards all night long," the reader can join in the refrain of "Oh, you're just talking silly talk."

Ruth Krauss has capitalized upon children's enjoyment of the sound of words in *A Very Special House*. Part of the fun of this book is the thought of a very special house where you can do all the things you cannot do in a regular house. The fact that this is a

There's a bed that's very special
and a shelf that's very special
and the chairs are very special
—but it's not to take a seat—
and the doors are very special
and the walls are very special and
a table very special where to put your feet feet feet.

Sendak's droll figures are as much fun as the amusing text. From *A Very Special House* by Ruth Krauss, illustrated by Maurice Sendak. Harper & Row, 1953.

pretend house is finally admitted "in very special language" on the last page:

I know a house—
and it's not up in a tree
or underneath the bed—
Oh it's right in the middle—
Oh it's ret in the meddle—
Oh it's root in the moodle of my head head head.[33]

Slapstick is also a characteristic of young children's humor. They thoroughly enjoy the part in Freeman's story of *Mop Top* where a near-sighted lady mistakes the little boy who would not get his hair cut for a floor mop. They laugh at the silly antics of the boy in Ruth Krauss' book who decides to spend *The Backward Day* by putting his coat on first, then his suit and underwear, walking backwards to breakfast and saying "Goodnight" to his father and mother! Krasilovsky's story of *The Man Who Didn't Wash His Dishes* continues to be a favorite as children giggle over the idea of using flower pots and a soap dish for plates. They delight in the novel way the man finally gets his dishes clean.

Surprise endings frequently appeal to the young child's sense of humor. They love Karla Kuskin's repetitious story of *Just Like Everyone Else* that describes how Jonathan James gets up in the morning, how he gets dressed, what he has for breakfast, and how he says goodbye to his mother, father, dog, and little sister, just like everyone else. Then, "Jonathan James flew off to school." One kindergarten child, on hearing this story, said, "It sounded just like a broken record, but I knew it had to end funny." The sur-

[33]Ruth Krauss, *A Very Special House*, Illustrated by Maurice Sendak (New York: Harper & Row, 1953), unpaged.

prise ending of *The Camel Who Took a Walk* by Tworkov intrigues children. Their excitement grows as the gentle young camel walks down the path toward the place where the tiger plans to pounce upon her, and then they feel a surge of relief as the camel stops, yawns, and says, "I think I'll return now."

Young children are past masters at exaggeration so they appreciate the humor of the tall tale. Dr. Seuss' stories, *And to Think That I Saw It on Mulberry Street* and *McElligot's Pool*, are models of humorous tall tales. In *The Long and Dangerous Journey* by Craig, a small boy's imagination turns a walk to the ice cream store into a series of exciting adventures. The postman becomes a giant; a puppy, a wolf; and a striped moving van looks like a tiger. James Flora has told four very funny tall tales in *Grandpa's Farm*, including the story of the "Terrible Winter of '36" when Grandpa's and Grandma's words froze in the air and had to be thawed in a frying pan before they knew what they were saying to each other! *Burt Dow, Deep Water Man* by McCloskey is a tall tale of an old fisherman who catches a whale by the tail and then binds the wound with a candy-striped bandage. The grateful whale swallows him whole, boat and all, in order to protect him from a storm. With the help of some bilge water and the giggling gull, Burt Dow is burped back into the ocean and home to his sister Leela, but not before he has put candy-striped band-aids on a whole school of whales. Blair Lent has told the wonderful tale of *John Tabor's Ride* on a whale from the South Seas where he was shipwrecked, to Nantucket where he watched the whale swim out of sight, and then "went home to finish bowl after bowl of clam chowder and almost all of a big plum duff."[34]

Many picture storybooks portray children's dreams or fantasies. Some of these

Vigorous action is shown by splashing water, teetering gull, and the angle of the boat in this tall tale of the sea. From *Burt Dow: Deep-Water Man* by Robert McCloskey. Copyright © 1963 by Robert McCloskey. Reprinted by permission of The Viking Press, Inc.

are humorous, such as *A Very Special House*, while others may convey deeper meanings, such as Sendak's *Where the Wild Things Are*. *The Dragon in the Clock Box* by Craig tells of a small boy's imaginary dragon. For days, Joshua carried a clock box that he claimed contained a dragon's egg. Later, he announced that it had hatched and a baby dragon was in the box. No one in his family was allowed to peek, however, since Joshua said the dragon was shy. Then one day, his mother found the clock box open and empty, and she asked Joshua where his

[34]Blair Lent, *John Tabor's Ride* (Boston: Little, Brown, 1966), p. 48.

dragon was. He replied calmly that it had flown away to "where dragons go." An equally quiet but very believable fantasy is *Tigers in the Cellar* by Carol Fenner. Each night, a little girl dreams that she hears tigers in the basement. One night, she goes to the head of the stairs and smells a tiger smell and sees the yellow eyes of two tigers. One of them moves "like water over stones" and comes up the stairs until the little girl can see he is crying. She pets him and then crawls on the sad tiger's back while the other one sings "rumbly tumbly" songs in a funny tiger voice. She tries to tell her mother about the tiger ride, but her mother will not believe her. Yet, how did the little girl still know the tiger's song? *Andy and the Lion* by Daugherty is a wonderful mixture of fantasy and reality. Andy is re-

Gay color and cartoon-like style personify the little tugboat. Reprinted by permission of G. P. Putnam's Sons from *Little Toot* by Hardie Gramatky. Copyright 1939 by Hardie Gramatky.

turning the story of "Androcles and the Lion" to the library when he meets his own lion. Andy extracts a thorn from his paw and thereby becomes his friend for life. The vigorous black and white illustrations reflect the power and strength of this favorite story.

Another form of fantasy for young children is the personification of inanimate objects such as toys and machines. All children know and love Watty Piper's story of *The Little Engine That Could,* . . . and did, get the toys over the mountain. Most of the books written by Virginia Lee Burton contain personification; *Mike Mulligan and His Steam Shovel, Katy and the Big Snow,* and *The Little House.* The modern problem of obsolescence is solved easily in the story of Mike and his beloved steam shovel, Mary Ann. After proving that Mary Ann could dig a basement for the new town hall in a day, Mike was forced to convert her into a furnace since he had neglected to plan a way for Mary Ann to get out of the excavation. Katy is a snowplow who saves the day by plowing out a whole village. No child should miss the lovely rhythmical pictures of Virginia Lee Burton that so clearly reflect her early interest in ballet. Hardie Gramatky has written several books that personify the inanimate. *Little Toot* is the story of a headstrong tugboat in the New York harbor who refuses to accept his tugboat responsibilities until a time of crisis makes him a hero. *Hercules* by the same author-illustrator tells of the last run of a horse-drawn engine, while *Loopy* is a disobedient airplane. Gramatky's illustrations have action and the same engaging humor that characterizes his stories. However, they do reflect the years Gramatky worked for Walt Disney. *The Little Old Automobile* by Ets was incorrigible and said "I won't" just once too often. The moral of this story is almost too pointed. Lynd Ward's illustrations personify the George Washington Bridge and a little lighthouse in Swift's story of *The Little Red Lighthouse and the Great Gray Bridge.* This theme, like that of Mike Mulligan, is one of usefulness despite obsolescence.

One of the earliest stories to personify toys was *The Velveteen Rabbit* by Margery Williams. Any child who has loved a stuffed animal of his own will understand the conversation between the old skin horse and the velveteen rabbit on the subject of becoming real. The skin horse tells the rabbit, "Real isn't how you are inside. . . . It's a thing that happens to you when a child loves you for a long long while." When the rabbit asks how it happens, he replies, "It doesn't happen all at once. . . . you become. It takes a long while."[35]

Many picture storybooks are written in the traditional folk-tale style. These stories are original and modern, yet they have the rhythm, repetition, and refrains of the old tales. Wanda Gág's stories of *Millions of Cats* and *Nothing at All* ring of the oral tradition. So, too, does the ever popular *Caps for Sale* by Slobodkina. In this story, a peddler who is selling caps tries vainly to recover his merchandise from some mischievous monkeys. Only after he becomes very angry and throws his own cap on the ground do the imitating monkeys return his caps. The story of *Finders Keepers* by Will and Nicolas has a touch of both folklore and fable in it. Two dogs quarrel over a bone and so they ask a farmer, a goat, an apprentice barber, and a big dog, whose bone it is. When the big dog threatens to take it from them, they quickly resolve their quarrel and work together to save the bone. Marjorie Flack also has used this accumulative style of writing in her popular *Ask Mr. Bear.* Cooperative action is the theme of several modern folk tales by Marie Hall Ets. *Mr. T. W. Anthony Woo* is the story of the combined efforts of a mouse, a dog, and a cat to rid a kindly cobbler of his interfering sister. *Mister Penny* and *Mister Penny's Race Horse* relate the amusing incidents of Mister Penny, Limpy, his horse, and his three barnyard friends.

The stories by Virginia Kahl have a decided folktale flavor to them. *Maxie* is the repetitive tale of a very small dachshund who passes three tests to prove he is the biggest, fastest, and fiercest dog in the village and therefore qualified to belong to the Baron. Kahl's first book, *The Duchess Bakes a Cake,* is written in rhyme and gives an account of the duchess who is determined "to make a lovely light luscious delectable cake." The results of her cooking are disastrous, but she tries all over again in *Plum Pudding for Christmas.* Cooking is again the theme in Kahl's original *The Perfect Pancake.*

The Five Chinese Brothers by Bishop is an ingenious tale of the unique abilities of five identical brothers; one can swallow the sea, one has an iron neck, one can stretch his legs to any height, one cannot be burned, and the last can hold his breath indefinitely. Each of these skills saves the first brother from fearful punishment, much to the amusement and delight of young children. The Joji stories by Betty Lifton tell of the most famous scarecrow in all Japan, whose best friends were the crows. They loved Joji so much that they ate worms instead of rice and helped him guard the rice paddies. In *Joji and the Dragon,* the crows help frighten the dragon that the farmer had substituted for Joji. *Joji and the Fog* describes Joji's success in scaring away the fearsome Fog who had decided to take up residence in the farmer's bathtub. The blurry drawings of Mitsui add to the humor and the Japanese flavor of these modern tales.

The Tomten by Lindgren is a beautifully illustrated picture book of a little Swedish troll who walks around a lonely old farm on a cold winter's night reassuring the animals of the coming of spring. *The Tomten and the Fox* is a sequel to this book.

[35] Margery Williams, *The Velveteen Rabbit* (New York: Doubleday, 1926), p. 17.

Curving lines lead the eye over a hilly landscape. Tiled roofs, oxen, women washing in a stream are authentic details of an Italian hill town. Reproduced with the permission of Charles Scribner's Sons from *Little Leo*, pages 27–28, by Leo Politi. Copyright 1951 Charles Scribner's Sons.

Picture Books of Other Lands Many beautiful picture storybooks of today emphasize the universal qualities of childhood while they provide an early familiarity with cultures in all parts of the world. Picture books, then, may contribute to making that which is foreign seem familiar.

Certain picture books create only the flavor and feeling of a country, while others vividly portray recognizable scenes. Leo Politi gives the feeling of the warmth and gaiety of the Italian hill towns in his autobiographical picture book of *Little Leo*. While this book portrays such unfamiliar scenes as hillside vineyards, olive trees, and white oxen teams, it shows the love of play in children throughout the world. *Tamarindo!* by Marcia Brown is a story of a lost Sicilian donkey and the adventures of the boys who

find him. Her village and country scenes capture the flavor of Sicily. Lisl Weil's book, *I Wish, I Wish,* tells the story of Francesca, who regularly visited the Galleria Pitti in Florence to watch an American lady paint miniatures. How she obtained both a painting and a kitten makes a story children enjoy. Bettina pictures the bustling confusion of market day in the little town of Grado, Italy, in her amusing story about a small dog named *Pantaloni. A Bell for Ursli* and *The Snowstorm* by Chönz vividly portray village children's preparations for two Swiss festivals. *Florina and the Wild Bird* is the story of Ursli's sister who rescues a wild ptarmigan and raises the bird over the summer in the mountain hut where the brother and sister have come to pasture the goats. These stories are told in verse form with brilliant watercolors of the Swiss mountains by Carigiet. In Krasilovsky's story of *The Cow Who Fell in the Canal,* children may see lovely detailed pictures of the Dutch countryside and market day in the town. While the story of *Ola* by the d'Aulaires is fantasy, the pictures of the interior scenes of Norwegian houses and the Norwegian stave churches provide an authentic background for the setting. Duvoisin, in his illustrations for *Red Bantam* by Fatio, has portrayed a beautiful French farm scene. This is the story of a brave little banty rooster who saves his favorite hen, Nanette, from the fox and so proves his courage and superiority over the Big Rooster. It would be interesting to compare the illustrations and this story with *The Little Tiny Rooster* by Will and Nicolas.

Paris has been variously pictured in children's books. Francoise has shown a brightly-colored, stylized Paris in her story of Nanette's search for her lost cat, *Minou.* It is difficult, however, to surpass the distinctive watercolors of Paris by Bemelmans for *Madeline* and *Madeline's Rescue.* Just before his death, Bemelmans wrote and illustrated *Madeline in London* and so presented that lovely city to his many Madeline fans. Shulman has written the story of *Preep, The Little Pigeon of Trafalgar Square* who is kidnapped by a cook who has just lost his job in a Soho restaurant and wants to make a pigeon pie. All the London pigeons refuse to be photographed with humans until Preep is found. The cook returns him and the sun comes out over Westminster Abbey. Lawson's black and white illustrations of the lowlands and the highlands of Scotland in *Wee Gillis* capture the flavor of the country and the humor of this well-loved story by Munro Leaf.

Marie Hall Ets has carefully portrayed both the old Mexico in her market scene and the new modern Mexico showing Dairy Queens, supermarkets, and TV aerials in *Nine Days to Christmas.* Using bright yellows, fuchsia pinks, and orange against a pearl gray background, Ets has created a modern child's delight in the Christmas *Posada* and piñata party. Politi has shown Mexican children in a more traditional manner in his two well-illustrated books, *Lito and the Clown* and *Rosa.* The story of Paco, a little Peruvian Indian shepherd who is tired of taking care of his flock of llamas and wants to become a fisherman, is told by Surany in *Ride the Cold Wind.* After Paco tries it once, he agrees that fishing is man's work, and he is quite content to herd the llamas. Leonard Fisher's rather stiff, stylized figures are shown in ochres and orange against a midnight blue background. The sharp contrasts present a crisp, clear look that seems most appropriate for this story that takes place in the blue shadows of the giant peaks of the Andes Mountains. The sparkling turquoise of the Caribbean provides the background for the story of another small boy who wants to become a fisherman in Marcia Brown's *Henry-Fisherman; A Story of the Virgin Islands.* The flavor of Haiti has been accurately conveyed by Evaline Ness in her story of *Josefina February.* Like the little burro that she finds, Josefina seems to be all skinny arms and legs with a thatch of unruly hair atop her head.

Oasis of the Stars is a hauntingly beautiful story of Abu and his family, nomads of the desert. Abu has one abiding wish, to find an oasis where his family might make a permanent home. Night after night, Abu digs a hole in hopes of finding water. His father sighs, "The child is a dreamer and sometimes dreams hurt, . . . But dreams, like water and food, make boys grow into men."[36] But the next day when the camels are all packed and ready to go, Abu finds his well of "shimmering stars" at the bottom of the hole. The handsome cardboard cuts in blue, black, green, and yellow by Blair Lent give a feeling of powerful dignity to this

[36]Olga Economakis, *Oasis of the Stars,* Illustrated by Blair Lent. (New York: Coward-McCann, 1965), unpaged.

Pride in new shoes is the same in any language. With a few sketchy lines the artist conveys the emotion of each character. From *A Pair of Red Clogs.* Text copyright © by Masako Matsuno, 1960, illustrations copyright © 1960 by Kazue Mizumura. By permission of The World Publishing Company.

story of a little boy's search for the living well of water.

Yashima's stories of *Crow Boy, The Village Tree,* and *Plenty to Watch* recall his childhood in rural Japan. The pictures of the lovely sweeping branches of the village willow tree and the patterned hills of the countryside give a distinctive picture of Japan. Matsuno tells, in *A Pair of Red Clogs,* the story of Mako, a little Japanese girl who cracks her brand new red clogs by playing the weather-telling game. She tries to deceive her mother by walking in the mud, but, like all mothers, Mako's seems to know the whole story. The illustrations by Mizumura express the little girl's pride in her new shoes and her misery over trying to deceive her mother. In *Chie and the Sports Day,* Matsuno relates a modern story of how a Japanese girl finds an unsual way to help her brother run in the races.

There are, of course, no picture stories of modern China. Children continue to love Flack's classic *The Story about Ping,* the little Chinese duck and his adventure on the Yangtze River. The handsome, black-and-white illustrations for *Mei Li* by Handforth tell the story of the Chinese girl who went all alone to the New Year's Fair in the city.

Picture storybooks of other lands can enlarge children's lives and enhance their living. The phenomenal growth of beautiful picture books for young children is an outstanding accomplishment of the past twenty-five years of publishing. Children may not always recognize the beauty of these books, but early impressions do exert their influence on the development of permanent tastes.

SUGGESTED ACTIVITIES

1. Read a story to a three-year-old. See how many different ways you can provide for his participation in the story.
2. Using the criteria established in this chapter, compare three different editions of Mother Goose, or three ABC, or counting books.
3. Ask a four-year-old to tell you a story from a picture storybook before you read it to him. Note what he is able to derive from the pictures compared to the narrative told by the text.
4. Present several books that use different styles of illustrations and different media to a group of primary children. Which ones do they seem to prefer? Why?
5. Study the work of one illustrator. Is it possible to identify his particular style of art? Does he vary it with different content? How has his style changed over the years?
6. Begin to develop a card file on well-known illustrators. What is their particular style of illustrating? Do they tend to illustrate a particular subject (cats, for example)? Do

they prefer working in a certain medium? What books have they illustrated previously? Find interesting anecdotes to tell to children about these illustrations, which will make their art work more interesting and vital to students.

7. Study additional examples of the types and themes of picture books developed in this chapter.

8. Find examples of picture books with well-designed endpapers or title pages and share them with the class.

9. Find three or four examples of the use of one medium and bring to class to share.

10. Find examples of picture books in which color has been used effectively and share these.

11. Read and report on one of the acceptance speeches for the Caldecott Award. Bring examples of the illustrations to class.

12. Observe children during a story hour either at school or during the library story hour. Record their reactions—either verbal comments, facial expressions, or body movement.

RELATED READINGS

1. Colby, Jean Poindexter. *Writing, Illustrating and Editing Children's Books.* New York: Hastings, 1967.
   This book covers all phases of juvenile publishing from techniques of writing, illustration, and production, to the duties of the editor. Part Two includes a clear discussion of illustrating books, printing methods, topography, and book design. Based on some twenty years' of experience in the children's book business, this account is written from the point of view of an editor.

2. Foster, Joanna. *Pages, Pictures, and Print.* New York: Harcourt, 1958.
   This is the story of a book in the making: It describes the process of selecting manuscripts, editing them, setting type, preparing pictures and binding. Certain chapters could be read by interested sixth-graders. Gives an interesting over-all account of publishing.

3. Heffernan, Helen, and Vivian E. Todd. *The Kindergarten Teacher.* Boston: Heath, 1960.
   Chapter 12, "Introducing Children to Literature," describes the place of picture books in the kindergarten program. The authors discuss the selection of books, storytelling, interpretation of literature, and developing appreciation for books.

4. Kingman, Lee, Editor. *Newbery and Caldecott Medal Books: 1956–1965.* Boston: Horn Book, 1965.
   This is the most recent volume of the acceptance papers, biographies, and related materials concerning the Newbery and Caldecott Awards for the past ten years. Norma R. Fryatt's excellent article "Picture Books Today" is a critical review of the award winners.

5. Klemin, Diana. *The Art of Art for Children's Books.* New York: Potter, 1966.
   A contemporary survey of those artists who have illustrated children's books for a decade or more. Sixty-four artists are represented through examples, eight of these in full color. Under the name of each artist is the title of the book illustrated, the technique used, and the size of the original illustration. A most useful reference.

6. Mahony, Bertha E., *et al. Illustrators of Children's Books: 1744–1945.* Boston: Horn Book, 1947.
   This book includes the history and development of illustrated books. The article by Helen Gentry titled "Graphic Processes in Children's Books" gives a detailed, clear description of the various methods and processes used in printing illustrations. Lynd Ward's article, "The Book Artist: Yesterday and Tomorrow," de-

scribes the importance of picture books for children, the contributions of artists from abroad, and the variety of character and style of illustrating.

7. ———*Illustrators of Children's Books: 1946–1956.* Boston: Horn Book, 1958.
This book is a supplement to the above reference. It contains many short biographical sketches of illustrators and several excellent discussions of the art in children's books. Marcia Brown's article, "Distinction in Picture Books" and Lynd Ward's "The Book Artist: Ideas and Technique" are both highly recommended.

8. Miller, Bertha Mahony, and Elinor W. Field. *Caldecott Medal Books: 1938–1957.* Boston: Horn Book, 1957.
This volume includes a biography and the acceptance speech of each artist who has won the Caldecott Award up to 1957. Their acceptance papers frequently reveal their convictions about illustrating for children; they are fascinating reading. In a final article titled, "What Is a Picture Book," Esther Averill candidly evaluates the award-winning books.

9. Pitz, Henry C. *Illustrating Children's Books.* New York: Watson-Guptill, 1963.
Pitz describes the history of illustrating books, the techniques of the process, and actual production. This book is profusely illustrated; unfortunately, many of the illustrations are from a single press. Useful index and bibliography are included.

10. Simon, Irving B. *The Story of Printing.* Illustrated by Charles E. Pont. Irvington-on-Hudson, N.Y.: Harvey House, 1965.
A most useful and detailed book on the story of printing, from wood blocks to today's electronics. The chapters on "Relief Picture Printing" and "Offset Lithography" are very helpful. The book includes pictures of various kinds of printing presses and many black and white diagrams. It could be used for research on the printing process. An index and glossary of printing terms are included.

11. Smith, Lillian H. *The Unreluctant Years.* Chicago: American Library Association, 1953.
Lillian Smith considers five picture books in a depth analysis of the criteria for fine illustrating for young children. Her chapter, "Picture Books," is a discriminating appraisal of contemporary picture books.

CHAPTER REFERENCES

Mother Goose and Nursery Rhymes

1. Anglund, Joan Walsh. *In a Pumpkin Shell.* New York: Harcourt, 1960.
2. Briggs, Raymond. *The Mother Goose Treasury.* New York: Coward-McCann, 1966.
3. ———*The White Land.* New York: Coward-McCann, 1963.
4. Brooke, Leslie. *Ring O'Roses.* New York: Warne, 1923.
5. Cooney, Barbara. *The Courtship, Merry Marriage, and Feast of Cock Robin and Jenny Wren, to which is added the Doleful Death of Cock Robin.* New York: Scribner, 1965.
6. De Angeli, Marguerite. *Book of Nursery and Mother Goose Rhymes.* New York: Doubleday, 1954.
7. Frasconi, Antonio. *The House That Jack Built.* New York: Harcourt, 1958.
8. Galdone, Paul. *The History of Simple Simon.* New York: McGraw-Hill, 1966.
9. ———*The House That Jack Built.* New York: McGraw-Hill, 1961.
10. ———*Old Mother Hubbard and Her Dog.* New York: McGraw-Hill, 1960.
11. ———*The Old Woman and Her Pig.* New York: McGraw-Hill, 1960.
12. ———*Tom, Tom, the Piper's Son.* New York: McGraw-Hill, 1964.
13. Greenaway, Kate. *Mother Goose, or The Old Nursery Rhymes.* New York: Warne, n.d.
14. Kepes, Juliet. *Lady Bird, Quickly.* Boston: Little, Brown, 1964.
15. Lines, Kathleen. *Lavender's Blue.* Illustrated by Harold Jones. New York: F. Watts, 1964.
16. Rackham, Arthur. *Mother Goose.* New York: Appleton, 1913.

17. Reed, Philip. *Mother Goose and Nursery Rhymes.* New York: Atheneum, 1963.
18. Rojankovsky, Feodor. *The Tall Book of Mother Goose.* New York: Harper & Row, 1942.
19. Sendak, Maurice. *Hector Protector* and *As I Went over the Water.* New York: Harper & Row, 1965.
20. Tenggren, Gustaf. *The Tenggren Mother Goose.* Boston: Little, Brown, 1940.
21. Tudor, Tasha. *Mother Goose.* New York: Walck, 1944.
22. Wildsmith, Brian. *Mother Goose.* New York: F. Watts, 1963.
23. Wright, Blanche Fisher. *The Real Mother Goose.* Skokie, Ill.: Rand McNally, 1944.

ABC Books

24. Alexander, Anne. *ABC of Cars and Trucks.* Illustrated by Ninon. New York: Doubleday, 1956.
25. Duvoisin, Roger. *A for the Ark.* New York: Lothrop, 1952.
26. Eichenberg, Fritz. *Ape in a Cape.* New York: Harcourt, 1952.
27. Falls, Charles Buckles. *An ABC Book.* New York: Doubleday, 1923.
28. Gág, Wanda. *The ABC Bunny.* New York: Coward-McCann, 1933.
29. Garten, Jan. *The Alphabet Tale.* Illustrated by Muriel Batherman. New York: Random House, 1964.
30. Grossbart, Francine. *A Big City.* New York: Harper & Row, 1966.
31. Lear, Edward. *ABC.* New York: McGraw-Hill, 1965.
32. McGinley, Phyllis. *All Around the Town.* Illustrated by Helen Stone. Philadelphia: Lippincott, 1948.
33. Matthiesen, Thomas, *ABC An Alphabet Book.* New York: Platt & Munk, 1966.
34. Morse, Samuel French. *All in a Suitcase.* Illustrated by Barbara Cooney. Boston: Little, Brown, 1966.
35. Munari, Bruno. *Bruno Munari's ABC.* Cleveland: World Publishing, 1960.
36. Piatti, Celestino. *Celestino Piatti's Animal ABC.* New York: Atheneum, 1966.
37. Shuttlesworth, Dorothy. *ABC of Buses.* Illustrated by Leonard Shortall. New York: Doubleday, 1965.
38. Smith, William Jay. *Puptents and Pebbles.* Illustrated by Juliet Kepes. Boston: Little, Brown, 1959.
39. Tudor, Tasha. *A Is for Annabelle.* New York: Walck, 1954.
40. Walters, Marguerite. *City-Country ABC.* Illustrated by Ib Ohlsson. New York: Doubleday, 1966.
41. Wildsmith, Brian. *Brian Wildsmith's ABC.* New York: F. Watts, 1963.
42. Zacks, Irene. *Space Alphabet.* Illustrated by Peter Plasencia. Englewood Cliffs, N.J.: Prentice-Hall, 1964.

Counting Books

43. Alain, pseud. (Emile Chartier). *One, Two, Three, Going to Sea.* New York: W. R. Scott, 1964.
44. Duvoisin, Roger. *Two Lonely Ducks.* New York: Knopf, 1955.
45. Eichenberg, Fritz. *Dancing in the Moon.* New York: Harcourt, 1955.
46. Elkin, Benjamin. *Six Foolish Fishermen.* Illustrated by Katherine Evans. Chicago: Childrens Press, 1957.
47. Francoise, pseud. (Francoise Seignobosc). *Jeanne-Marie Counts Her Sheep.* New York: Scribner, 1951.
48. Ipcar, Dahlov. *Brown Cow Farm.* New York: Doubleday, 1959.
49. ————*Ten Big Farms.* New York: Knopf, 1958.
50. Kirn, Ann. *Nine in a Line.* New York: Norton, 1966.
51. Krüss, James. *3 X 3 Three by Three.* Translated by Geoffrey Strachan. Illustrated by Johanna Rubin. New York: Macmillan, 1965.

52. Langstaff, John. *Over in the Meadow.* Illustrated by Feodor Rojankovsky. New York: Harcourt, 1957.

53. McLeod, Emilie W. *One Snail and Me: A Book of Numbers and Animals and a Bathtub.* Illustrated by Walter Lorraine. Boston: Little, Brown, 1961.

54. Moore, Lilian. *My First Counting Book.* Illustrated by Garth Williams. New York: Golden Press, 1956.

55. Sendak, Maurice. *One Was Johnny* (*Nutshell Library,* vol. 3). New York: Harper & Row, 1962.

56. Tudor, Tasha. *1 Is One.* New York: Walck, 1956.

57. Wildsmith, Brian. *Brian Wildsmith's 1, 2, 3s.* New York: F. Watts, 1965.

58. Zolotow, Charlotte. *One Step, Two . . . .* Illustrated by Roger Duvoisin. New York: Lothrop, 1955.

Picture Books

59. Ardizzone, Edward. *Little Tim* Series. New York: Walck.
    Little Tim and the Brave Sea Captain, 1955.
    Tim All Alone, 1957.
    Tim and Charlotte, 1951.
    Tim and Ginger, 1965.
    Tim and Lucy Go to Sea, 1958.
    Tim in Danger, 1953.
    Tim to the Rescue, 1949.
    Tim's Friend Towser, 1962.

60. Artzybasheff, Boris. *Aesop's Fables.* New York: Viking, 1933.

61. Asbjørnsen, P. C., and J. E. Moe. *The Three Billy Goats Gruff.* Illustrated by Marcia Brown. New York: Harcourt, 1957.

62. d'Aulaire, Ingri and Edgar. *Abraham Lincoln.* New York: Doubleday, 1939, 1957.

63. ———*Ola.* New York: Doubleday, 1932.

64. ———*Pocahontas.* New York: Doubleday, 1946.

65. Bailey, Carolyn Sherwin. *The Little Rabbit Who Wanted Red Wings.* Illustrated by Dorothy Grider. New York: Platt & Munk, 1945.

66. Beim, Lorraine and Jerrold. *Two Is a Team.* Illustrated by Ernest Crichlow. New York: Harcourt, 1945.

67. Bemelmans, Ludwig. *Madeline.* New York: Viking, 1939.

68. ———*Madeline in London.* New York: Viking, 1961.

69. ———*Madeline's Rescue.* New York: Viking, 1953.

70. Bennett, Rainey. *The Secret Hiding Place.* Cleveland: World Publishing, 1960.

71. Bettina, pseud. (Bettina Ehrlich). *Pantaloni.* New York: Harper & Row, 1957.

72. Bishop, Claire Huchet. *The Five Chinese Brothers.* Illustrated by Kurt Wiese. New York: Coward-McCann, 1938.

73. Bourne, Miriam Anne. *Emilio's Summer Day.* Illustrated by Ben Shecter. New York: Harper & Row, 1966.

74. Braun, Kathy. *Kangaroo & Kangaroo.* Illustrated by Jim McMullan. New York: Macmillan, 1965.

75. Brown, Marcia. *Cinderella.* New York: Scribner, 1954.

76. ———*Dick Whittington and His Cat.* New York: Scribner, 1950.

77. ———*Felice.* New York: Scribner, 1958.

78. ———*Henry-Fisherman.* New York: Scribner, 1949.

79. ———*Once a Mouse.* New York: Scribner, 1961.

80. ———*Puss in Boots.* New York: Scribner, 1952.

81. ———*Stone Soup.* New York: Scribner, 1947.

82. ———*Tamarindo.* New York: Scribner, 1960.

83. Brown, Margaret Wise. *The City Noisy Book.* Illustrated by Leonard Weisgard. New York: Harper & Row, 1939.

84. ————*The Country Noisy Book.* Illustrated by Leonard Weisgard. New York: Harper & Row, 1940.

85. ————*The Dead Bird.* Illustrated by Remy Charlip. New York: W. R. Scott, 1958.

86. ————*The Important Book.* Illustrated by Leonard Weisgard. New York: Harper & Row, 1949.

87. ————*The Runaway Bunny.* Illustrated by Clement Hurd. New York: Harper & Row, 1942.

88. ————*Sleepy Little Lion.* Photographs by Ylla. New York: Harper & Row, 1947.

89. ————*Wait Till the Moon Is Full.* Illustrated by Garth Williams. New York: Harper & Row, 1948.

90. Brown, Myra Berry. *Amy and the New Baby.* Illustrated by H. Hurwitz. New York: F. Watts, 1965.

91. ————*Benjy's Blanket.* Illustrated by Dorothy Marino. New York: F. Watts, 1962.

92. ————*Company's Coming for Dinner.* Illustrated by Dorothy Marino. New York: F. Watts, 1959.

93. ————*The First Night Away from Home.* Illustrated by Dorothy Marino. New York: F. Watts, 1960.

94. Bryant, Sara Cone. *The Burning Rice Fields.* Illustrated by Mamoru Funai. New York: Holt, Rinehart and Winston, 1963.

95. Buckley, Helen E. *Grandfather and I.* Illustrated by Paul Galdone. New York: Lothrop, 1959.

96. ————*Grandmother and I.* Illustrated by Paul Galdone. New York: Lothrop, 1961.

97. ————*Josie and the Snow.* Illustrated by Evaline Ness. New York: Lothrop, 1964.

98. ————*The Little Boy and the Birthdays.* Illustrated by Paul Galdone. New York: Lothrop, 1965.

99. ————*My Sister and I.* Illustrated by Paul Galdone. New York: Lothrop, 1963.

100. Budney, Blossom. *A Kiss Is Round.* Illustrated by Vladimir Bobri. New York: Lothrop, 1954.

101. Burton, Virginia Lee. *Katie and the Big Snow.* Boston: Houghton Mifflin, 1943.

102. ————*The Little House.* Boston: Houghton Mifflin, 1942.

103. ————*Mike Mulligan and His Steam Shovel.* Boston: Houghton Mifflin, 1939.

104. Carroll, Ruth. *What Whiskers Did.* New York: Walck, 1965.

105. Caudill, Rebecca. *A Pocketful of Cricket.* Illustrated by Evaline Ness. New York: Holt, Rinehart and Winston, 1964.

106. Chönz, Selina. *A Bell for Ursli.* Illustrated by Alois Carigiet. New York: Walck, 1953.

107. ————*Florina and the Wild Bird.* Illustrated by Alois Carigiet. New York: Walck, 1953.

108. ————*The Snowstorm.* Illustrated by Alois Carigiet. New York: Walck, 1958.

109. Cooney, Barbara. *Chanticleer and the Fox.* New York: Crowell, 1958.

110. Craig, M. Jean. *The Dragon in the Clock Box.* Illustrated by Kelly Oechsli. New York: Norton, 1962.

111. ————*The Long and Dangerous Journey.* Illustrated by Ib Ohlsson. New York: Norton, 1965.

112. Daugherty, James. *Andy and the Lion.* New York: Viking, 1938.

113. De Brunhoff, Jean. *The Story of Babar.* New York: Random House, 1960.

114. Dennis, Wesley. *Flip.* New York: Viking, 1941.

115. ————*Flip and the Cows.* New York: Viking, 1942.

116. De Regniers, Beatrice Schenk. *May I Bring a Friend?* Illustrated by Beni Montresor. New York: Atheneum, 1964.

117. Duvoisin, Roger. *Petunia.* New York: Knopf, 1950.

118. ————*Veronica.* New York: Knopf, 1961.

119. Economakis, Olga. *Oasis of the Stars.* Illustrated by Blair Lent. New York: Coward-McCann, 1965.

120. Elkin, Benjamin. *The Loudest Noise in the World.* Illustrated by James Daugherty. New York: Viking, 1954.

121. Emberley, Barbara and Ed. *Night's Nice.* New York: Doubleday, 1963.
122. Emberley, Ed. *The Wing on a Flea.* Boston: Little, Brown, 1961.
123. Ets, Marie Hall. *Gilberto and the Wind.* New York: Viking, 1963.
124. ———*Little Old Automobile.* New York: Viking, 1948.
125. ———*Mister Penny.* New York: Viking, 1963.
126. ———*Mister Penny's Race Horse.* New York: Viking, 1956.
127. ———*Mr. T. W. Anthony Woo.* New York: Viking, 1951.
128. ———*Play with Me.* New York: Viking, 1955.
129. Ets, Marie Hall, and Aurora Labastida. *Nine Days to Christmas.* Illustrated by Marie Hall Ets. New York: Viking, 1959.
130. Fatio, Louise. *The Happy Lion.* Illustrated by Roger Duvoisin. New York: McGraw-Hill, 1954.
131. ———*Red Bantam.* Illustrated by Roger Duvoisin. New York: McGraw-Hill, 1962.
132. Felt, Sue. *Hello-Goodbye.* New York: Doubleday, 1960.
133. ———*Rosa-Too-Little.* New York: Doubleday, 1950.
134. Fenner, Carol. *Tigers in the Cellar.* New York: Harcourt, 1963.
135. Fisher, Aileen. *Best Little House.* Illustrated by Arnold Spilka. New York: Crowell, 1966.
136. ———*Going Barefoot.* Illustrated by Adrienne Adams. New York: Crowell, 1960.
137. ———*In the Middle of the Night.* Illustrated by Adrienne Adams. New York: Crowell, 1965.
138. ———*Listen, Rabbit.* Illustrated by Symeon Shimin. New York: Crowell, 1964.
139. ———*Where Does Everyone Go?* Illustrated by Adrienne Adams. New York: Crowell, 1961.
140. Flack, Marjorie. *Ask Mr. Bear.* New York: Macmillan, 1932.
141. ———*The New Pet.* New York: Doubleday, 1943.
142. ———*The Story about Ping.* Illustrated by Kurt Wiese. New York: Viking, 1933.
143. Flora, James. *Grandpa's Farm.* New York: Harcourt, 1965.
144. Francoise, pseud. (Francoise Seignobosc). *Jeanne-Marie* Series. New York: Scribner.
    The Big Rain, 1961.
    Jeanne-Marie at the Fair, 1959.
    Jeanne-Marie Counts Her Sheep, 1957.
    Jeanne-Marie in Gay Paris, 1956.
    Noel for Jeanne-Marie, 1953.
    Springtime for Jeanne-Marie, 1955.
    What Time Is It, Jeanne-Marie? 1963.
145. ———*Minou.* New York: Scribner, 1962.
146. ———*The Things I Like.* New York: Scribner, 1960.
147. Frasconi, Antonio. *See Again, Say Again.* New York: Harcourt, 1964.
148. Freeman, Don. *Cyrano the Crow.* New York: Viking, 1960.
149. ———*Dandelion.* New York: Viking, 1964.
150. ———*Fly High, Fly Low.* New York: Viking, 1957.
151. ———*Mop Top.* New York: Viking, 1955.
152. Friskey, Margaret. *Seven Diving Ducks.* Illustrated by Jean Morey. Chicago: Childrens Press, 1965.
153. Gág, Wanda. *Millions of Cats.* New York: Coward-McCann, 1928.
154. ———*Nothing at All.* New York: Coward-McCann, 1941.
155. Garelick, May. *Sounds of a Summer Night.* Illustrated by Beni Montresor. New York: W. R. Scott, 1963.
156. ———*Where Does the Butterfly Go When It Rains?* Illustrated by Leonard Weisgard. New York: W. R. Scott, 1961.
157. Gramatky, Hardie. *Hercules.* New York: Putnam, 1940.
158. ———*Little Toot.* New York: Putnam, 1939.
159. ———*Loopy.* New York: Putnam, 1941.

160. Green, Mary McBurney. *Is It Hard? Is It Easy?* Illustrated by Lucienne Bloch. New York: W. R. Scott, 1960.

161. Guilfoile, Elizabeth. *Nobody Listens to Andrew.* Illustrated by Mary Stevens. Chicago: Follett, 1957.

162. Hader, Berta and Elmer. *The Big Snow.* New York: Macmillan, 1948.

163. Handforth, Thomas. *Mei Li.* New York: Doubleday, 1938.

164. Hoban, Russell. *A Baby Sister for Frances.* Illustrated by Lillian Hoban. New York: Harper & Row, 1964.

165. ————*Bedtime for Frances.* Illustrated by Garth Williams. New York: Harper & Row, 1960.

166. ————*Bread and Jam for Frances.* Illustrated by Lillian Hoban. New York: Harper & Row, 1964.

167. ————*Nothing to Do.* Illustrated by Lillian Hoban. New York: Harper & Row, 1964.

168. Hodges, Margaret. *The Wave.* Illustrated by Blair Lent. Boston: Houghton Mifflin, 1964.

169. Hurd, Edith. *The Day the Sun Danced.* Illustrated by Clement Hurd. New York: Harper & Row, 1965.

170. Janus, Grete. *Teddy.* Illustrated by Roger Duvoisin. New York: Lothrop, 1964.

171. Johnson, Crockett. *Harold and the Purple Crayon.* New York: Harper & Row, 1958.

172. Joslin, Sesyle. *Spaghetti for Breakfast.* Illustrated by Katharina Barry. New York: Harcourt, 1965.

173. ————*There Is a Bull on My Balcony.* Illustrated by Katharina Barry. New York: Harcourt, 1966.

174. ————*There Is a Dragon in My Bed.* Illustrated by Irene Haas. New York: Harcourt, 1961.

175. ————*What Do You Do, Dear?* Illustrated by Maurice Sendak. New York: W. R. Scott, 1961.

176. ————*What Do You Say, Dear?* Illustrated by Maurice Sendak. New York: W. R. Scott, 1958.

177. Kahl, Virginia. *The Duchess Bakes a Cake.* New York: Scribner, 1955.

178. ————*Maxie.* New York: Scribner, 1956.

179. ————*The Perfect Pancake.* New York: Scribner, 1960.

180. ————*Plum Pudding for Christmas.* New York: Scribner, 1956.

181. Keats, Ezra Jack. *Jennie's Hat.* New York: Harper & Row, 1966.

182. ————*The Snowy Day.* New York: Viking, 1962.

183. ————*Whistle for Willie.* New York: Viking, 1964.

184. Keats, Ezra Jack and Pat Cherr. *My Dog Is Lost.* New York: Crowell, 1960.

185. Kessler, Ethel and Leonard. *Are You Square?* Illustrated by Leonard Kessler. New York: Doubleday, 1966.

186. Kingman, Lee. *Peter's Long Walk.* Illustrated by Barbara Cooney. New York: Doubleday, 1953.

187. Krasilovsky, Phyllis. *The Cow Who Fell in the Canal.* Illustrated by Peter Spier. New York: Doubleday, 1957.

188. ————*The Man Who Didn't Wash His Dishes.* Illustrated by Barbara Cooney. New York: Doubleday, 1950.

189. Krauss, Ruth. *The Backward Day.* Illustrated by Marc Simont. New York: Harper & Row, 1950.

190. ————*The Bundle Book.* Illustrated by Helen Stone. New York: Harper & Row, 1951.

191. ————*The Happy Day.* Illustrated by Marc Simont. New York: Harper & Row, 1949.

192. ————*A Very Special House.* Illustrated by Maurice Sendak. New York: Harper & Row, 1953.

193. Kumin, Maxine W. *The Beach Before Breakfast.* Illustrated by Leonard Weisgard. New York: Putnam, 1964.

194. Kunhardt, Dorothy. *Pat the Bunny*. New York: Golden Press, 1962, 1940.
195. ———*Tickle the Pig*. New York: Golden Press, 1964.
196. Kuskin, Karla. *James and the Rain*. New York: Harper & Row, 1957.
197. ———*Just Like Everyone Else*. New York: Harper & Row, 1959.
198. La Fontaine, Jean de. *The Lion and the Rat*. Illustrated by Brian Wildsmith. New York: F. Watts, 1964.
199. ———*The North Wind and the Sun*. Illustrated by Brian Wildsmith. New York: F. Watts, 1964.
200. Lamorisse, Albert. *The Red Balloon*. New York: Doubleday, 1956.
201. Langstaff, John. *Frog Went A-Courtin'*. Illustrated by Feodor Rojankovsky. New York: Harcourt, 1955.
202. Lansdown, Brenda. *Galumph*. Illustrated by Ernest Crichlow. Boston: Houghton Mifflin, 1963.
203. Lawson, Robert. *Robbut, a Tale of Tails*. New York: Viking, 1949.
204. Leaf, Munro. *The Story of Ferdinand*. Illustrated by Robert Lawson. New York: Viking, 1936.
205. ———*Wee Gillis*. Illustrated by Robert Lawson. New York: Viking, 1938.
206. Lear, Edward. *Le Hibou et La Poussiquette*. Translated by Francis Steegmuler. Illustrated by Barbara Cooney. Boston: Little, Brown, 1961.
207. Lenski, Lois. *Cowboy Small*. New York: Walck, 1949.
208. ———*I Like Winter*. New York: Walck, 1950.
209. ———*Little Davy* Series. New York: Walck.
     Big Little Davy, 1956.
     Davy and His Dog, 1957.
     Davy Goes Places, 1961.
     Davy's Day, 1943.
     A Dog Came to School, 1955.
     Surprise for Davy, 1947.
210. ———*Now It's Fall*. New York: Walck, 1948.
211. ———*On a Summer Day*. New York: Walck, 1953.
212. ———*Policeman Small*. New York: Walck, 1962.
213. ———*Spring Is Here*. New York: Walck, 1945.
214. Lent, Blair. *John Tabor's Ride*. Boston: Little, Brown, 1966.
215. ———*Pistachio*. Boston: Little, Brown, 1964.
216. Leodhas, Sorche Nic. *Always Room for One More*. Illustrated by Nonny Hogrogian. New York: Holt, Rinehart and Winston, 1965.
217. Lexau, Joan. *Benjie*. Illustrated by Don Bolognese. New York: Dial, 1964.
218. Lifton, Betty Jean. *Joji and the Dragon*. Illustrated by Eiichi Mitsui. New York: Morrow, 1957.
219. ———*Joji and the Fog*. Illustrated by Eiichi Mitsui. New York: Morrow, 1959.
220. Lindren, Astrid. *The Tomten*. Adapted from a poem by Viktor Rydberg. Illustrated by Harald Wiberg. New York: Coward-McCann, 1961.
221. ———*The Tomten and the Fox*. Adapted from a poem by Karl-Erik Forsslund. Illustrated by Harald Wiberg. New York: Coward-McCann, 1966.
222. Lionni, Leo. *Inch by Inch*. New York: Obolensky, 1960.
223. ———*Little Blue and Little Yellow*. New York: Obolensky, 1959.
224. ———*Swimmy*. New York: Pantheon, 1963.
225. McCloskey, Robert. *Blueberries for Sal*. New York: Viking, 1948.
226. ———*Burt Dow, Deep-Water Man*. New York:Viking, 1963.
227. ———*Make Way for Ducklings*. New York: Viking, 1941.
228. ———*One Morning in Maine*. New York: Viking, 1952.
229. ———*Time of Wonder*. New York: Viking, 1957.
230. MacDonald, Golden, pseud. (Margaret Wise Brown). *The Little Island*. Illustrated by Leonard Weisgard. New York: Doubleday, 1946.
231. ———*Little Lost Lamb*. Illustrated by Leonard Weisgard. New York: Doubleday, 1945.

232. Massie, Diane. *The Baby Beebee Bird.* New York: Harper & Row, 1963.

233. Matsuno, Masako. *Chie and the Sports Day.* Illustrated by Kazue Mizamura. Cleveland: World Publishing, 1965.

234. ———*A Pair of Red Clogs.* Illustrated by Kazue Mizamura. Cleveland: World Publishing, 1960.

235. Miles, Miska. *The Fox and the Fire.* Illustrated by John Schoenherr. Boston: Little, Brown, 1966.

236. ———*Mississippi Possum.* Illustrated by John Schoenherr. Boston: Little, Brown, 1965.

237. Minarik, Else. *Little Bear.* Illustrated by Maurice Sendak. New York: Harper & Row, 1957.

238. Moore, Nancy. *The Unhappy Hippopotamus.* Illustrated by Edward Leight. New York: Vanguard, 1957.

239. Munari, Bruno. *Animals for Sale.* Cleveland: World Publishing, 1957.

240. ———*The Birthday Present.* Cleveland: World Publishing, 1959.

241. ———*Who's There? Open the Door!* Cleveland: World Publishing, 1957.

242. Ness, Evaline. *Josefina February.* New York: Scribner, 1963.

243. Newberry, Clare Turlay. *April's Kittens.* New York: Harper & Row, 1940.

244. ———*Marshmallow.* New York: Harper & Row, 1942.

245. ———*Mittens.* New York: Harper & Row, 1936.

246. Payne, Emmy. *Katy No-Pocket.* Illustrated by H. A. Rey. Boston: Houghton Mifflin, 1944.

247. Petrides, Heidrun. *Hans and Peter.* New York: Harcourt, 1963.

248. Piatti, Celestino. *The Happy Owls.* New York: Atheneum, 1964.

249. Piper, Watty. *The Little Engine That Could.* Illustrated by George and Doris Hauman. New York: Platt & Munk, 1954, 1930.

250. Politi, Leo. *Lito and the Clown.* New York: Scribner, 1964.

251. ———*Little Leo.* New York: Scribner, 1951.

252. ———*Pedro, the Angel of Olvera Street.* New York: Scribner, 1946.

253. ———*Piccolo's Prank.* New York: Scribner, 1965.

254. ———*Rosa.* New York: Scribner, 1963.

255. ———*Song of the Swallows.* New York: Scribner, 1949.

256. Potter, Beatrix. *The Tale of Peter Rabbit.* New York: Warne, 1902.

257. Prokofieff, Serge. *Peter and the Wolf.* Illustrated by Frans Haacken. New York: F. Watts, 1961.

258. Ramirez, Carolyn. *Small as a Raisin Big as the World.* Illustrated by Carl Ramirez. New York: Harvey, 1961.

259. Rey, Hans Augusto. *Anybody at Home?* Boston: Houghton Mifflin, 1958.

260. ———*Curious George* Series. Boston: Houghton Mifflin.
Curious George, 1941.
Curious George Gets a Medal, 1957.
Curious George Learns the Alphabet, 1963.
Curious George Rides a Bike, 1952.
Curious George Takes a Job, 1947.

261. ———*Let's Feed the Animals.* Boston: Houghton Mifflin, n.d.

262. ———*Where's My Baby?* Boston: Houghton Mifflin, 1956.

263. Robbins, Ruth. *Baboushka and the Three Kings.* Illustrated by Nicolas Sidjakov. New York: Parnassus, 1960.

264. Schackburg, Richard. *Yankee Doodle.* Illustrated by Ed Emberley. Notes by Barbara Emberley. Englewood Cliffs, N.J.: Prentice-Hall, 1965.

265. Scheer, Julian. *Rain Makes Applesauce.* Illustrated by Marvin Bileck. New York: Holiday, 1964.

266. Schlein, Miriam. *Fast Is Not a Lady Bug.* Illustrated by Leonard Kessler. New York: W. R. Scott, 1953.

267. ———*Heavy Is a Hippopotamus.* Illustrated by Leonard Kessler. New York: W. R. Scott, 1954.

268. Sendak, Maurice. *The Nutshell Library.* New York: Harper & Row, 1962.
   Alligators All Around.
   Pierre.
   One Was Johnny.
   Chicken Soup with Rice.
269. ———*Where the Wild Things Are.* New York: Harper & Row, 1963.
270. Seuss, Dr., pseud. (Theodor S. Geisel). *And to Think That I Saw It on Mulberry Street.* New York: Vanguard, 1937.
271. ———*The Cat in the Hat.* New York: Random House, 1957.
272. ———*Horton Hatches the Egg.* New York: Random House, 1940.
273. ———*McElligot's Pool.* New York: Random House, 1947.
274. ———*Thidwick, the Big-Hearted Moose.* New York: Random House, 1948.
275. Shulman, Milton. *Preep, the Little Pigeon of Trafalgar Square.* Illustrated by Dale Maxey. New York: Random House, 1964.
276. Simon, Norma, *Benjy's Bird.* Illustrated by Joe Lasker. Racine, Wis.: Whitman, 1965.
277. Slobodkin, Louis. *Yasu and the Strangers.* New York: Macmillan, 1965.
278. Slobodkina, Esphyr. *Caps for Sale.* New York: W. R. Scott. 1947.
279. Smith, Robert Paul. *When I Am Big.* Illustrated by Lillian Hoban. New York: Harper & Row, 1965.
280. Surany, Anico. *Ride the Cold Wind.* Illustrated by Leonard Everett Fisher. New York: Putnam, 1964.
281. Swift, Hildegarde H. *The Little Red Lighthouse and the Great Gray Bridge.* Illustrated by Lynd Ward. New York: Harcourt, 1942.
282. Thurber, James. *Many Moons.* Illustrated by Louis Slobodkin. New York: Harcourt, 1943.
283. Titus, Eve. *Anatole.* Illustrated by Paul Galdone. New York: McGraw-Hill, 1956.
284. Tresselt, Alvin. *Hi, Mr. Robin.* Illustrated by Roger Duvoisin. New York: Lothrop, 1950.
285. ———*Hide and Seek Fog.* Illustrated by Roger Duvoisin. New York: Lothrop, 1965.
286. ———*Rain Drop Splash.* Illustrated by Leonard Weisgard. New York: Lothrop, 1946.
287. ———*Sun Up.* Illustrated by Roger Duvoisin. New York: Lothrop, 1949.
288. ———*A Thousand Lights and Fireflies.* Illustrated by John Moodle. New York: Parents, 1965.
289. ———*Wake Up, City!* Illustrated by Roger Duvoisin. New York: Lothrop, 1957.
290. ———*Wake Up, Farm!* Illustrated by Roger Duvoisin. New York: Lothrop, 1955.
291. ———*White Snow, Bright Snow.* Illustrated by Roger Duvoisin. New York: Lothrop, 1956.
292. Tudor, Tasha. *First Delights.* New York: Platt & Munk, 1966.
293. Tworkov, Jack. *The Camel Who Took a Walk.* Illustrated by Roger Duvoisin. New York: Dutton, 1951.
294. Udry, Janice May. *Let's Be Enemies.* Illustrated by Maurice Sendak. New York: Harper & Row, 1961.
295. ———*The Moon Jumpers.* Illustrated by Maurice Sendak. New York: Harper & Row, 1959.
296. ———*A Tree Is Nice.* Illustrated by Marc Simont. New York: Harper & Row, 1956.
297. Ungerer, Tomi. *Crictor.* New York: Harper & Row, 1958.
298. Valens, Evans G. *Wildfire.* Illustrated by Clement Hurd. Cleveland: World Publishing, 1963.
299. ———*Wingfin and Topple.* Illustrated by Clement Hurd. Cleveland: World Publishing, 1962.
300. Waber, Bernard. *The House on East 88th Street.* Boston: Houghton Mifflin, 1962.
301. ———*Lyle, Lyle, Crocodile.* New York: Houghton Mifflin, 1965.

302. ———*Rich Cat, Poor Cat.* New York: Houghton Mifflin, 1963.

303. ———*You Look Ridiculous Said the Rhinoceros to the Hippopotamus.* Boston: Houghton Mifflin, 1966.

304. Ward, Lynd. *The Biggest Bear.* Boston: Houghton Mifflin, 1952.

305. ———*Nic of the Woods.* Boston: Houghton Mifflin, 1965.

306. Weil, Lisl. *I Wish, I Wish.* Boston: Houghton Mifflin, 1957.

307. Wezel, Peter. *The Good Bird.* New York: Harper & Row, 1964.

308. Will and Nicolas, pseud. (William Lipkind and Nicolas Mordvinoff). *Billy the Kid.* New York: Harcourt, 1961.

309. ———*Finders Keepers.* New York: Harcourt, 1951.

310. ———*The Little Tiny Rooster.* New York: Harcourt, 1960.

311. ———*The Two Reds.* New York: Harcourt, 1950.

312. Williams, Garth. *Baby's First Book.* New York: Golden Press, 1955.

313. ———*The Rabbits' Wedding.* New York: Harper & Row, 1958.

314. Williams, Margery. *The Velveteen Rabbit.* Illustrated by William Nicholson. New York: Doubleday, 1958, 1922.

315. Wright, Dare. *Lonely Doll* Series.
The Doll and the Kitten. New York: Doubleday, 1960.
Edith and Mr. Bear. New York: Random House, 1964.
Holiday for Edith and the Bears. New York: Doubleday, 1958.
The Lonely Doll. New York: Doubleday, 1957.
The Lonely Doll Learns a Lesson. New York: Random House, 1961.

316. Wuorio, Eva-Lis. *Land of the Right Up and Down.* Illustrated by Edward Ardizzone. Cleveland: World Publishing, 1964.

317. Yashima, Taro, pseud. (Jun Iwamatsu). *Crow Boy.* New York: Viking, 1955.

318. ———*Umbrella.* New York: Viking, 1958.

319. ———*The Village Tree.* New York: Viking, 1953.

320. ———*Youngest One.* New York: Viking, 1962.

321. Yashima, Taro and Mitsu. *Plenty to Watch.* New York: Viking, 1954.

322. Ylla, pseud. (Camilla Koffler). *Animal Babies.* Text by Arthur Gregor. New York: Harper & Row, 1959.

323. ———*Two Little Bears.* New York: Harper & Row, 1954.

324. Zemach, Harve. *Nail Soup.* Illustrated by Margot Zemach. Chicago: Follett, 1964.

325. Zion, Gene. *All Falling Down.* Illustrated by Margaret Bloy Graham. New York: Harper & Row, 1951.

326. Zolotow, Charlotte. *Big Brother.* Illustrated by Garth Williams. New York: Harper & Row, 1960.

327. ———*Do You Know What I'll Do?* Illustrated by Garth Williams. New York: Harper & Row, 1958.

328. ———*If It Weren't for You.* Illustrated by Ben Shecter. New York: Harper & Row, 1966.

329. ———*Mr. Rabbit and the Lovely Present.* Illustrated by Maurice Sendak. New York: Harper & Row, 1962.

330. ———*Over and Over.* Illustrated by Garth Williams. New York: Harper & Row, 1951.

331. ———*The Quarreling Book.* Illustrated by Arnold Lobel. New York: Harper & Row, 1963.

332. ———*The Sky Was Blue.* Illustrated by Garth Williams. New York: Harper &
333. Row, 1963.
———*Someday.* Illustrated by Arnold Lobel. New York: Harper & Row, 1964.

334. ———*The Storm Book.* Illustrated by Margaret Bloy Graham. New York: Harper & Row, 1952.

335. ———*When I Have a Little Girl.* Illustrated by Hilary Knight. New York: Harper & Row, 1965.

336. ———*The White Marble.* Illustrated by Lilian Obligado. New York: Abelard-Schuman, 1963.

4

TRADITIONAL
LITERATURE

After hearing one of the stories from *Little One Inch,* which her mother said were favorites of Japanese children, six-year-old Lissa said, "I know why these stories are favorites of Japanese children. I think they're just wonderful. Don't you think children all over the world are sort of alike?"

The adults who discussed this spontaneous comment of a child recognized her unconscious wisdom. Children everywhere do respond to stories with action and suspense, heroes who surmount obstacles to achieve good, the portrayal of just rewards for those who express virtues of compassion and love, as well as deserved punishment for cruelty, dishonesty, or greed.

Scholars who study the folklore of different cultures have made discoveries similar to the six-year-old awareness of common bonds in literature. Man in all times and places has responded to his world through chants, poetry, drama, and imaginative narrative. Literature today continues to express man's concern about his human strengths, weaknesses and his relationships to the world and to other people. Traditional literature forms the foundation of understandings of life as expressed in modern literature.

Traditional literature consists of the literature that has its origin in the primitive ritual, drama, poetry, and storytelling of human society. Parables, fables, proverbs, sacred writings, classical myth, and folklore constitute the traditional literature of mankind. Folklore includes songs, tales, and legends connected with historical persons. The study of myth and folklore is a special field of literature, anthropology, and psychology. In the preservice or in-service program of preparation, the elementary teacher and librarian should devote time to a deeper study than can be included in a survey of children's literature. However, the teacher can become familiar with general theories of myth and the development of the types of traditional literature. Knowledge of basic themes, plots, devices, and characters of traditional literature is an essential part of the background of the elementary teacher and librarian. Familiarity with the types of materials available and criteria for written forms of traditional literature will aid educators in selecting books for the literature curriculum.

Theories of Myth

It is difficult to arrive at a clear definition of myth, for the term is used by literary critics, anthropologists, psychoanalysts, and folklorists in different ways. In *Quest for Myth,* Chase quotes an eighteenth-century *Encyclopédie,* "a myth is whatever one's interests lead one to think it is."[1] The title of Chase's book expresses modern literary study—a quest for myth. In this sense, myth refers to the ideas, the meanings held by a group of people. Myths comment on the world and man. When myth is defined as "imagined event" or "pagan falsehood" as opposed to "historical fact" or "Christian truth," the term may receive an undesirable connotation. In literary study, however, *myth* does not mean "untrue"; rather, the term refers to a generalized meaning or universal idea, a significant truth about man and his life. A single myth is a narrative that tells of origins,[2] explains natural or social phenomena, or suggests the destiny of man through the interaction of man and supernatural beings. A *mythology* is a group of myths of a particular culture. Myth-making[3] is continuous and in process today. Usually, myth is a product of society rather than a single author.

According to some early mythologists, the myths originated in India and were carried to Europe. Müller held that the Aryan language consisted only of metaphors, and in this language one could not say, "the sun rises"; instead, "Night gives birth to a brilliant child" would necessarily be the expression used to convey the idea. As the Aryans migrated, the original meaning was lost, and the myths were told to explain figures of speech. This approach has little significance today. Many specialists believe that myths originated in all cultures.

Another group of mythologists explained myths in terms of movements of the sun or moon. All the myths and folk tales expressed the basic plot of the sun or sun hero battling against the powers of darkness. Little Red Riding Hood, for example, was viewed as the sun being devoured by the wolf (night) only to be disgorged to reappear.

Anthropologists study myths of primitive peoples in order to determine values, religions, customs, and taboos. To these scholars, myth is viewed as the religion of the people, derived from rituals that were recounted in drama and narratives. Some writers, such as the Grimms, held that myth preceded the folk tale, while others, such as Lang, thought the folk tales came first. Anthropologists have identified recurrent themes in myths of different cultures.

[1] Richard Chase, *Quest for Myth* (Baton Rouge, La.: Louisiana State University Press, 1949), p. 105.
[2] See Sylvan Barnet, Morton Berman, and William Burto, *The Study of Literature* (Boston: Little, Brown, 1960), pp. 315–316.
[3] Jerome Bruner, "Myth and Identity," in Richard M. Ohrmann, *The Making of Myth* (New York: Putnam, 1962), pp. 159–170.

Kluckhohn's study[4] of myths of fifty cultures revealed such recurring themes as the flood, slaying of monsters, incest, sibling rivalry, and castration. He also found several patterns repeated in the myth of the hero. In these stories, there is something special about the birth of the hero; he often receives help from animals; near relatives express hostility; eventually the hero returns and receives recognition. One of the major influences was Sir James Frazer's twelve-volume analysis of ritual, taboos, and myths in *The Golden Bough*.[5] This anthropological study, written in the form of a quest, gave sexual symbolic meaning to primitive myths and greatly influenced modern literature.

Freud's analysis[6] of myth as dream, or disguised wish fulfillment, was the beginning of psychological literary criticism. This interpretation is based on the idea that a distressful stimulation leads an individual to dream of an object, situation, or an act. If the dream is felt to be sinful, it will include punishment and serve as a deterrent. Freud held the view that all myths expressed the Oedipus theme with its incest motive, guilt and punishment. Another psychiatrist, Rank,[7] agreed that myth is the dream of the masses of people, and the imaginative faculty of humans is the source of all myth. He traced the common elements in mythic births of such heroes as Moses, Oedipus, Judas, Tristan, Jesus, Zoroaster, and Buddha. Jung's basic concept held that a "collective unconscious" is "inherited in the structure of the brain."[8] These unconscious,

recurring images created the primitive mythic heroes and still exist as individual fantasies for the civilized man. Murray[9] presented the psychiatrist's view of myth as an imagined situation or series of events in which extraordinary persons and supernatural beings are involved in a basic or crucial plot. He noted that myths served to show a better way to satisfy needs, to convince people of universal truth, to create an emotional effect, and to unify society.

The recurring patterns or symbols in myths are called archetypes.[10] Poetry, prose, or drama becomes more significant emotionally because both the artist and the reader or listener possess these unconscious aspects of human experience. The hero who is a savior, the cruel mother, the flood, the psychological need to die and be reborn are archetypes found in literature. Northrop Frye, literary critic, showed the relationship between the solar cycle of the day, the seasonal cycle of the year, and the birth-mating-death cycle of human life.[11] Frye insists that understanding of archetypes is essential because they unify and integrate literary experience.

The folklorist, however, may disagree with the psychological interpretations. Dorson notes that "folk literature cannot all be prettily channeled into the universal monomyth," and "the folklorist looks with jaundiced eye at the excessive straining of mythologists to extort symbols from folk tales."[12] Whether or not the folk tales and myths express symbolic images or unconscious dreams, they are literature derived from human imagination and should be an important part of the elementary school literature curriculum.

[4]See Clyde Kluckhohn, "Recurrent Themes in Myth and Mythmaking," in Ohrmann, pp. 52–65.

[5]Sir James Frazer, *The Golden Bough*, Third edition (London, England: Macmillan, 1911–1915).

[6]Stanley E. Hyman, *The Armed Vision*, Revised edition (New York: Vintage, 1955).

[7]Philip Freund, Editor, *The Myth of the Birth of the Hero and Other Writings by Otto Rank* (New York: Vintage, 1959).

[8]Carl C. Jung, "On the Relation of Analytic Psychology to Poetic Art," in O. B. Hardison, Jr., Editor, *Modern Continental Literary Criticism*. (New York: Appleton, 1962), pp. 267–288.

[9]Henry A. Murray, "Definitions of Myth," in Ohrmann, pp. 7–37.

[10]Maud Bodkin, *Archetypal Patterns in Poetry* (Oxford, England: Oxford University Press, 1934).

[11]Northrop Frye, "The Archetypes of Literature" in James E. Miller, Editor, *Myth and Method* (Lincoln, Neb.: University of Nebraska Press, 1960).

[12]Richard Dorson, "Theories of Myth and the Folklorist," in Ohrmann, p. 45.

FOLK TALES

Study of Folk Tales

Folk tales have been defined as "all forms of narrative, written or oral, which have come to be handed down through the years."[13] This definition would include epics, ballads, legends, folk songs, as well as myths and fables. For the purpose of the elementary literature curriculum, folk tales will include the German *Märchen* or household tales, the French *Conte populaire*, the romance narratives of many lands, and local legends.[14] The term, "fairy tale," is popularly applied to the folk tale although many stories do not include fairies, elves, or gnomes. Modern, fanciful stories created by a known writer are often called fairy tales. Hans Christian Andersen's *Fairy Tales* are becoming part of the heritage that might be described as folk tales, but they originated in written rather than oral form. Thus, they are distinguished from the stories told by the common folk that were finally collected and recorded.

Types of Folk Tales

FORMULA TALES   "Formula tales" are folk tales that follow a distinct pattern. Catch tales usually have no plot, but are used to end a storytelling session or to tease. In *I Saw a Rocket Walk a Mile* (117), Withers cites the example of the storyteller who promises to tell a million stories. The first one is to be about three men on a boat—Harry, Larry and Shut-up. After telling that Harry and Larry jumped into the sea, the narrator asks, "Who was left?" Of course the audience replies, "Shut-up," and the storyteller responds that

Rhythm and balance characterize the illustrations of Wanda Gág. Her elfish fun is in keeping with folk-tale humor. From *Tales from Grimm* by Wanda Gág. Copyright © 1936 by Wanda Gág. By permission of Coward-McCann, Inc.

he cannot continue with his million stories. The "endless stories" are based upon repetition. Again, Withers reports a Japanese endless story, "The Rats of Nagasaki" (117). These endless story patterns are found throughout the world. The "chain tale" may be based on numbers or objects or events. "Solomon Grundy" links days of the week in a chant. The dialogue pattern in which one comment leads to the next is another type. In a story, "Good or Bad?" (117) two pilots talk of a motor failure. One says "That's bad." The other replies "No, that was good. They had a parachute." When the first says, "Oh, that's good," the other replies, "No, that was bad. It didn't open."[15] The pattern of the recent book, *Fortunately* by Charlip, is based on this formula. Children thoroughly enjoy the chain of events as they hear "The Old Woman and Her Pig" (224) with its "Rat! rat! gnaw rope; rope won't hang butcher; butcher won't kill ox; ox won't drink water; water won't quench fire; fire won't burn stick; stick won't beat dog; dog won't bite

[13]Stith Thompson, *The Folktale* (New York: Holt, Rinehart and Winston, 1951), p. 4.

[14]The numbers in parentheses following the title of a folk tale will indicate the number of the collection reference where the tale may be found. The collections are listed in a separate section, "Folk Tales," according to the country of their origin, at the end of this chapter.

[15]Carl Withers, *I Saw a Rocket Walk a Mile,* Illustrated by John E. Johnson (New York: Holt, Rinehart and Winston, 1965), p. 32.

pig; piggy won't get over the stile; and I shan't get home tonight." "The House That Jack Built" (222) and "Johnny-Cake" (159, 248) are based upon accumulation and repetition of detail. These are called "cumulative tales." Henny Penny thinks the sky is falling and shouts to animals who join the chorus until a wise one shows the truth. The same pattern is found in "Plop!" (117), a Tibetan story of six rabbits who heard ripe fruit fall into a lake and started to flee from "Plop." A deer, pig, buffalo, rhinoceros, elephant, and other animals run wildly until a lion traces the origin of the fear.

WISE BEAST – FOOLISH BEAST The complex folk tale has a plot with a conflict to be resolved through several episodes. It may be an animal tale of the wise beast—foolish beast pattern. The Anansi stories from West Africa (119) or Jamaica (132) often tell how Anansi, the spider, tricks other animals. In Nigerian folk tales, Zomo (127), the rabbit, cleverly outwits hyena, leopard, and other friends.

ROMANCE Many folk tales are romances in which the hero must journey forth to meet a monster or prove his bravery or ability. Romantic love is sudden, glamorous, and idealized, with no indication of lovemaking as emphasized in modern romances. In "The White Bird" (113), which exemplifies this type of folk tale romance, the youngest brother sets out to get the golden apple from the tree of happiness. Whereas his two elder brothers choose to remain in the house where life is gay and easy, he chooses an humble cottage where you pay for what you need. The old man he helps gives him a barley straw that becomes a magic horse and a magic egg. When he fails to heed the advice in the book of knowledge, new tasks are set. Eventually, he recovers the sword of brightness, the white bird becomes a beautiful girl, and he receives the golden apple. Honesty, humility, patience, and courage are the virtues that bring happiness.

POURQUOI Some of the folk tales are "why" stories or *pourquoi* stories explaining certain animal traits or characteristics or customs of people. These are closely allied with myth, for a god often delivers the punishment. In *The Adventures of Spider* (120), Arkhurst presents West African tales explaining "How Spider Got a Bald Head," "How Spider Got a Thin Waist," and "Why Spider Lives in Ceilings." Courlander relates a Haitian tale about why dogs chase cats, "Sweet Misery" (130). When a woman spilled a calabash of syrup she cried, "Oh misery, oh misery." Dog lapped it up, saying, "Oh, misery is sweet!" The envious cat went to God to get some misery. God gave cat a sack, and when cat opened it, a dog jumped out and began to chase him. And so it is that cat received misery and is still chased by dogs.

Teachers can help children begin to identify types of folk tales by the end of their elementary school experience.

Plot Structure of Folk Tales The plot structure of the longer folk-tale narrative is usually simple and direct. A series of episodes maintains a quick flow of action. If it is a wise beast—foolish beast story, the characters are quickly delineated, the action shows the inevitable conflict and resolution, and the ending is usually brief. If the tale is a romance, the hero sets forth on his journey, often helps the poor on his way, frequently receives magical power, overcomes the obstacles, and returns to safety. The plot that involves the weak or innocent child going forth to meet the monsters of the world is another form of the "journey-novel." "Hansel and Gretel" (142) go out into a dark world and meet the witch, but goodness and purity triumph.

Repetition is a basic element in many folk-tale plots. Frequently, three is the magic number for building suspense. There are three little pigs whose three houses face the puffing of the wolf. Then the wolf gives three challenges to the pig in the brick house—to get turnips, apples, and to go to the fair. *The Three Billy Goats Gruff* (212) face the troll under the bridge, and the repetition of the trip, trap, trap, the troll's demands, and the goats' responses are essential elements in this well-loved tale.

Repetition of responses, chants, or poems is frequently a part of the structure of the tale. In the Russian story, "The Straw Ox" (176), an old woman insists that her old man make an ox of straw and tar. Each day, she takes the ox to the pasture, repeating, "Graze away, little ox, while I spin my flax! Graze away, little ox, while I spin my flax." While she sleeps, an animal comes to get some of the tar and becomes hopelessly enmeshed. Through this ruse, they catch a bear, rabbit, and fox, who bring gifts when they are freed. "Mirror, mirror on the wall, who is fairest of them all" and "Fee, fi, fo, fum" are other familiar repetitive verses.

In the folk tales, action takes place very quickly. The hero may be transplanted to another setting with economy of words. In "The Water of Life" (113), a faithful servant seeks a cup of the water. "On he went and on, until his shoes were dusty, and his feet were sore, and after a while he came to the end of the earth and there was nothing more over the hill."[16] Time passes quickly in the folk tale. The woods and brambles encircle Sleeping Beauty's (247) palace in a quarter of an hour and "when a hundred years were gone and passed," the prince appears at the moment the enchantment ends. The setting of the folk tale is not specific, but in some faraway land, in a cottage in the woods, in a beautiful palace. The plots of folk tales are credible in terms of their stereotyped characters and events. The reader is fully aware that the folk tale will usually have a "happy ending," that the hero will be successful in his quest, the children will be saved, the

prince will marry the princess. If the foolish younger son appears to be an unlikely character to achieve success, it seems logical that his kindness or basic cleverness helps him overpower stupidity, social status, or wealth. This economy of incident, the summarizing of action or events in one or two sentences is an important characteristic of the folk tale structure.

The introduction to the folk tale usually presents the conflict, characters, and setting in a few sentences. In "Wolf Wisdom," a Chippewa tale recounted by Leekley, the first four sentences reveal the characters and tension to be developed:

> *Manabozho knew that he should learn the wisdom of the animals, the birds, and the fishes. From time to time he had tried to learn from every other creature. But he usually made the mistake of thinking that for a manitou like him, one who had already brought fire to the wigwam of Nakomis, learning the lore of the beasts would be quite easy. This was the cause of the whole series of mistakes he made about the wolves.*[17]

In one sentence, a storyteller can establish setting: "There was once upon a time a Fisherman who lived with his wife in a miserable hovel close by the sea, and every day he went out fishing." The listener knows the conflict immediately, and that one will get the better of the other, when he hears, "Once there was and was not in ancient Armenia a couple who could not get along with one another." With few details, the storyteller goes to the heart of his story, capturing the interest of his audience.

The conclusion of the story follows the climax very quickly and includes few details. After Sleeping Beauty was awakened by the Prince, there is a fine dinner. "After supper, without losing any time, the Prince and

---

[16]Howard Pyle, *The Wonder Clock* (New York: Harper & Row, 1887, 1915), p. 22.

[17]Thomas B. Leekley, *The World of Manabozho*, Illustrated by Yeffe Kimball (New York: Vanguard, 1965), p. 20.

The atmosphere of medieval France is re-created in Duvoisin's patterned and stylized drawings. Illustrations copyright © 1959 by Roger Duvoisin. Illustration by Roger Duvoisin from *Favorite Fairy Tales Told in France* by Virginia Haviland, by permission of Little, Brown and Co.

Princess were married in the chapel of the palace. In two years, the Prince's father died. The Prince and Princess became the new King and Queen, and were given a royal welcome at the capital."[18] Even this is a long ending compared with, "and so they were married and lived happily ever after." Some of the endings lead to wonder, as in the Swedish tale, "The Boy and the Water-

sprite." A boy very cleverly frightens the water-sprite when he says he plans to tie up the lake with the rope he received as his only inheritance. When he obtains gold, his jealous brothers give him the cottage and ask for the rope so they, too, may make money by catching animals. "To this day they may still be doing this. But whether they have become richer or not, no one knows.[19]

The *pourquoi* stories end with the summarizing statement of the reason for the characteristic that was developed in the story. For example, a California Indian tale, "The Theft of Dawn" tells how the animals were disturbed by the sudden appearance of the sun. When Blue Jay and Ground Squirrel go to steal dawn, Ground Squirrel takes a large piece of obsidian that can be used for tools. His back was blistered from carrying it, "And it is for this reason that Ground Squirrel has stripes upon his back, for where the blisters had been, his fur grew as black as obsidian."[20] Stories that point out a moral often conclude with a direct statement. *The Black Heart of Indri* is a Chinese tale adapted by Hoge. Indri was an ugly fellow who had webbed feet and hands and the face of a toad. He controlled the stream of the water of life, so he had much power over the people. Told that his ugliness would vanish if he would live in the presence of virtue for nine days and nights, he learns that it is only when he tries to make others happy that ugliness disappears. The story ends, "It is said by the wise ones that greed is at the base of all evil. As for the water of life, happy are they who shall drink of it and never grow old, for their love shall last forever."[21]

[18]Virginia Haviland, *Favorite Fairy Tales Told in France*, Illustrated by Roger Duvoisin (Boston: Little, Brown, 1959), p. 75.

[19]Virginia Haviland, *Favorite Fairy Tales Told in Sweden*, Illustrated by Ronni Solbert (Boston: Little, Brown, 1966), p. 13.
[20]Jane Louise Curry, *Down from the Lonely Mountain*, Illustrated by Enrico Arno (New York: Harcourt, 1965), p. 47.
[21]Dorothy Hoge, *The Black Heart of Indri*, Illustrated by Janina Domanska (New York: Scribner, 1966), unpaged.

The structure of the folk tale, with its quick introduction, economy of incident, logical and brief conclusion, maintains interest through suspense and repetition. Because the storyteller has to keep the attention of his audience, each episode must contribute to the theme of the story. Written versions, then, should follow the oral tradition, adding little description, and avoiding lengthy asides or admonitions.

Characterization in Folk Tales Characters in folk tales are shown in flat dimension, being symbolic of the completely good or entirely evil. Character development is seldom depicted. The beautiful girl is usually virtuous, humble, patient, and loving. Stepmothers are ugly, cross, and mean. The hero, usually fair-haired or curly-haired, is strong, virile, brave, kind, and sympathetic. The poor are often kind, generous and long suffering, while the rich are imperious, hard-hearted and often conniving, if not actually dishonest. Physical characteristics may be described briefly, but the reader forms his own picture as he reads: "Pretty children they all were, but the prettiest was the youngest daughter, who was so lovely there was no end to her loveliness."[22] In describing "The Daughter of the Dragon King" the Chinese grandmother says, "Now this young woman was poorly dressed, but her face was as fair as a plum blossom in spring, and her body was as slender as a willow branch."[23] Star Gazer, who was told in a dream that he would marry a princess, was given physical characteristics:[24] "As he had a white skin, blue eyes, and hair that curled all over his head, the village girls used to cry

An oriental feeling is conveyed by delicate lines of plants and the posture of the girl shaded by the happy frog, Indri. Illustration by Janina Domanska is reproduced with the permission of Charles Scribner's Sons from *The Black Heart of Indri,* page 33, by Dorothy Hoge. Copyright © 1966 by Janina Domanska.

after him. . . ." The beast in "Beauty and the Beast" is not described, only the fact that Beauty felt terror when she beheld him.

Qualities of character or special strengths or weaknesses of the characters are revealed quickly, because this factor will be the cause of conflict, or lead to resolution of the plot. The stepmother and stepsister of Marushka are contrasted with the pretty girl in the Czechoslovakian story, "The Twelve Months." Marushka was made to do all the hard work, "But Marushka never com-

[22]P. C. Asbjørnsen and Jorgen E. Moe, *East of the Sun and West of the Moon and Other Tales,* Illustrated by Tom Vroman (New York: Macmillan, 1963), p. 1.

[23]Frances Carpenter, *Tales of a Chinese Grandmother.* Illustrated by Malthe Hasselriis (New York: Doubleday, 1949), p. 75.

[24]Andrew Lang, *The Red Fairy Book,* Illustrated by Marc Simont (New York: McKay, 1950), p. 1.

plained. Patiently she bore the scoldings and bad tempers of the mother and daughter. Holena's ugliness increased, while Marushka became even lovelier to look at.[25] A rich merchant in Addis Ababa was characterized in one sentence: "Haptom Hasei was so rich that he owned everything that money could buy, and often he was very bored because he had tired of everything he knew, and there was nothing new for him to do.[26]

Seeing folk-tale characters as symbols of good, evil, power, wisdom, and other virtues, children begin to understand the basis of literature that distills human experience.

Style of the Folk Tale   The folk tales offer many opportunities for linguistic study and appreciation of different language patterns.

Different forms of story introductions could be listed by middle-grade children. "There was once . . .", "Once there lived . . .," "Many dry seasons ago, before the oldest man in the village can remember . . .," "Once there was and was not in ancient Armenia . . .," "Long, long ago . . .," and "Once upon a time . . ." are familiar beginnings. Persian tales beginning "There was a time and there wasn't a time in the long ago . . ." could be compared with similar patterns from Russia and Armenia. Sometimes, the tale begins with a proverb or statement that will be explained in the story. Courlander begins an Arabian tale, "The Spotted Rug" in this way: "There is a saying among the people, 'He has spotted the rug.' This expression is heard when a person who has performed a kind service receives bad treatment in return."[27] Some of the collec-

tors begin with the storyteller's introduction that gives background for the story; for example, Guillot introduces "The Children of the Wind" in this way:

This is a tale of the fishermen of Maca and of one of their daughters who married the Wind and bore him three fine sons. They tell it in the lands along the Senegal river and down by the coast where the sea breaks in surf.[28]

A unique method to introduce stories appears in *Tales from the Story Hat* (118). The storyteller wears a hat from which tiny wood and ivory carvings dangle. A member of the audience chooses an object that the storyteller uses as a basis for his tale. After hearing these tales, children could make their own story hats and create stories for their peers.

The language of the folk tale should maintain the "flavor" of the country but still be understood by its audience. Folk tales should not be "written down" to children, but they may need to be simplified. Wanda Gág states her meaning of simplification in adapting folk tales for children:

By simplification I mean:
(a) freeing hybrid stories of confusing passages
(b) using repetition for clarity where a mature style does not include it
(c) employing actual dialogue to sustain or revive interest in places where the narrative is too condensed for children
However, I do not mean writing in words of one or two syllables. True, the careless use of large words is confusing to children; but long, even unfamiliar words are relished and easily absorbed by them, provided they have enough color and sound value.[29]

[25]Virginia Haviland, *Favorite Fairy Tales Told in Czechoslovakia*, Illustrated by Trina Hyman (Boston: Little, Brown, 1966), p. 3.

[26]Harold Courlander and Wolf Leslau, *The Fire on the Mountain* (New York: Holt, Rinehart and Winston, 1950), p. 7.

[27]Harold Courlander, *The Tiger's Whisker and Other Tales and Legends from Asia and the Pacific*, Illustrated by Enrico Arno (New York: Harcourt, 1959), p. 100.

[28]René Guillot, *Guillot's African Folk Tales*, Illustrated by William Papas (New York: F. Watts, 1965), p. 11.

[29]Wanda Gág, *Tales from Grimm* (New York: Coward-McCann, 1936), p. ix.

Rather than interrupt the flow of the story with explicit definitions, the teacher might reread the following sentence after completing the tale: "The three princes were delighted at the thought of so felicitous and high-placed an alliance. So each in turn expressed his pleasure."[30] Children will also grasp the meaning of unfamiliar words in the context of the story. After hearing or reading a story of Sorche Nic Leodhas, children might discuss "pawkiest piece," "cosseted," and "in a taking." Since "gobha" is not immediately explained, the teacher might tell the children in introducing the story that he was a blacksmith.

An old laird had a young daughter once and she was the pawkiest piece in all the world. Her father petted her and her mother cosseted her till the wonder of it was that she wasn't so spoiled that she couldn't be borne.[31]

When the laird's daughter stops at the blacksmith's to look over the gobha's sons she says she must go: "'Oh, nay!' said the laird's daughter. 'I just stopped by. They'll be in a taking if I'm late coming home.'"[32]

When the tales are written as though the storyteller is speaking directly to the reader, the oral tradition is more clearly communicated. Arkhurst uses this style effectively in *The Adventures of Spider*: "So spider threw his hat on his head, and, of course, you can guess what happened." Again the storyteller says, "My friends, can you imagine what happened? I don't think so, so I will tell you."[33] The vigorous style of Evaline Ness'

Broad humor is expressed by the awkward, angular pose of the miller's daughter. Crude woodcuts are appropriate for the "gatless girl" of the folk tale. Reproduced with permission of Charles Scribner's Sons from *Tom Tit Tot* by Evaline Ness. Copyright © 1965 Evaline Ness.

version of *Tom Tit Tot* reflects this old form of storytelling:

Well, she was that frightened, she'd always been such a gatless girl, that she didn't so much as know how to spin, and what was she to do tomorrow with no one to come nigh her to help her? She sat down on the stool and LAW, HOW SHE DID CRY![34]

In *Puss in Boots*, Hans Fischer interpolates explanations of the cat's reactions:

What the story does not tell is that it is not at all easy for a cat to stand in boots and to walk on two legs. This he had first to learn. He practiced secretly during the night: first standing, then walking—until it worked.[35]

Fischer's illustrations show the cat falling, twisting, and teetering in his boots. He ends the story by remarking that the cat was glad he could take off the boots. This version is

[30]Elizabeth Jamison Hodges, *The Three Princes of Serendip*, Illustrated by Joan Berg (New York: Atheneum, 1964), p. 44.

[31]Sorche Nic Leodhas, *Thistle and Thyme*, Illustrated by Evaline Ness (New York: Holt, Rinehart and Winston, 1962) p. 17.

[32]Leodhas, p. 20.

[33]Joyce Cooper Arkhurst, *The Adventures of Spider: West African Folk Tales*, Illustrated by Jerry Pinkey (Boston: Little, Brown, 1964), pp. 26, 10.

[34]Evaline Ness, *Tom Tit Tot* (New York: Scribner, 1965), unpaged.

[35]Hans Fischer, *Puss in Boots* (New York: Harcourt, 1959), unpaged.

quite different from Marcia Brown's, for her last picture shows the cat gloating with pleasure over his finery and the attentive service of a monkey valet.

The comments of the storyteller also enrich the meanings. Pyle writes, "After he had done all these things, he and the old man sat down to supper together, and, if it was not the finest, why the prince had a good appetite, and one can have no better sauce to a crust than that."[36] Such asides must be skillfully written, however, or they will appear to be talking down to the reader.

Although there is a minimum of description in the folk tale, similes and imagery are used by effective narrators. When Zomo's trick frightens the cock he has "a feeling in his belly as if the hairy caterpillar that he had swallowed earlier that morning has come to life and is going on a tour of inspection."[37] A comparison of the rich prose of Walter de la Mare with that of an oversimplified version of Cinderella illustrates the importance of style in folk tales:

> Indeed, all was so hushed at last in the vacant kitchen that the ashes, like pygmy bells in a belfry, tinkled as they fell; a cricket began shrilly churring from a crevice in the hob, and she could hear the tiny tic-a-tac-tac of the mice as they came tippeting and frisking 'round her stool. Then, suddenly, softly, and without warning, there sounded out of the deep hush a gentle knock-knocking at the door.[38]

> After the sisters had gone, Cinderella went into the kitchen and sat before the fire crying silently.
> Suddenly, her fairy godmother appeared. . . .[39]

Syntax in authentic folk-tale style could be compared with other prose. Children in primary grades can notice differences in sentence patterns in these two introductions To "The Elves and the Shoemaker":

> Once upon a time there was a poor shoemaker. The poor shoemaker had a wife. The poor shoemaker had a shop. He made shoes. He made little shoes. He made big shoes. He made long shoes. He made short shoes.[40]

> There once was a shoemaker who made shoes and made them well. Yet luck was against him for, although he worked hard every day, he became poorer and poorer until he had nothing left but leather for one pair of shoes.[41]

The following description could be used to illustrate inverse syntax:

> Blue was the sky and rich was the earth. The woods were filled with sweet wild berries and colorful flowers. Green were the grasses and tall were the trees in the hills and the valleys. . . .[42]

Unusual phrases appear in many folk tales. In the *Russian Wonder Tales* (178), the narrative includes "whether the way was long or short," "across three times nine kingdoms," and "the morning is wiser than the evening." Ekrem writes "They sailed a short way, they sailed a long way . . ." in *Turkish Fairy Tales* (166). Some folk tales include proverbs of the country. For example, in the silly Turkish tale, *Hilili and Dilili*, Walker adds "The poor have empty pockets but full hearts," "Trust in God, but first tie your camel," and "A good companion shortens the longest road."[43]

Names given characters often reveal their special characteristics. Marcia Brown calls

[36]Howard Pyle, *The Wonder Clock* (New York: Harper & Row, 1915, 1887), p. 110

[37]Hugh Sturton, *Zomo the Rabbit*, Illustrated by Peter Warner (New York: Atheneum, 1966), p. 22.

[38]Walter de la Mare, *Tales Told Again* (New York: Knopf, 1927), p. 49.

[39]Association for Childhood Education, *Told Under the Green Umbrella* (New York: Macmillan, 1930), p. 114.

[40]Frances Pavel, *The Elves and the Shoemaker*, Illustrated by Joyce Hewitt (New York: Holt, Rinehart and Winston, 1961), p. 1.

[41]Grimm, Jacob and Wilhelm, *More Tales from Grimm*, Retold and Illustrated by Wanda Gág (New York: Coward-McCann, 1947), p. 251.

[42]Henry Chafetz, *Thunderbird and Other Stories,* Illustrated by Ronni Solbert (New York: Pantheon, 1964), p. 27.

[43]Barbara K. Walker, *Hilili and Dilili*, Illustrated by William Barss (Chicago: Follett, 1965), pp. 5, 9, 14.

Puss in Boots (245) "master cat," "sly rogue," "Master Slyboots," and "great lord" as well as "Puss."

Stories that are retold in modern English should omit modern colloquialisms. A popular style is reflected in Hornyansky's retelling of *The Golden Phoenix.* One must read the entire story to realize how sentences, words, and pacing differ from the traditional pattern. This example shows the modern idiom:

> *"Oh, you wouldn't want that old thing," he said. "Let me offer you three chests of treasure instead."*
> *"I couldn't possibly take your treasure," said Petit Jean. "The cage is quite enough."*
> *The Sultan turned purple with rage. But at last he agreed that Petit Jean had won the cage fair and square. . . .*[44]

In most of the stories about *Zomo the Rabbit,* Sturton's style seems appropriate for the Nigerian tales. However, one colloquialism seems entirely out of place for this region: "Bushiya says that fifty thousand is a whale of a lot of money. . . ."[45]

Dialect enhances the story, but it is difficult for children to read. The teacher will need to practice reading or telling a story with dialect, but it is worth the effort. The following very long sentence from Uncle Remus illustrates the difficulty:

> *One day, w'en Brer Rabbit, en Brer Fox, en Brer Coon, en Brer B'ar, en a whole lot un um wuz clearin' up a new groun' fer ter plant a roas' n' year patch, de sun 'gun ter get sorter hot, en Brer Rabbit he got tired; but he didn't let on, kaze he feared de balance un um'd call 'im lazy, en he keep on totin' off trash en pilin' up bresh, twil bimeby he holler out dat he gotter brier in his han' en den he tak' en slip off, en hunt fer cool place fer ter res.*[46]

Richard Chase recorded stories from the Appalachian mountain folk in *The Jack Tales.* He notes, "The dialect has been changed enough to avoid confusion to the reading eye; the idiom has been kept throughout."[47] In this dialogue from "The Heifer Hide," the mountaineer vocabulary and dialect are clear:

> *"Well, now," she says, "hit's just a little I was a-savin' for my kinfolks comin' tomorrow."*
> *"Me and Jack's your kinfolks. Bring it on out here for us."*
> *So Jack and him eat a lot of them good rations. Jack was awful hungry, and he knowed she hadn't brought out her best stuff yet, so he rammed his heifer hide again, says, "You blabber-mouthed thing! I done told you to hush. You keep on tellin' lies now and I'll put you out the door."*[48]

The use of dialogue makes a folk tale more readable and interesting, and few folk tales are written without conversation. The words of the characters convey the action and tone. Some writers omit "he said" or "she said" and merely write the words of the speakers. Most writers use little description in expressing the feelings of the characters, but let the dialogue itself convey emotion. In *The Goose Girl,* the princess is indeed very sad, but when she speaks to the magical horse, the narrator, de Angeli, merely says:

> *. . . the princess said:*
> "Alas! dear Falada, there thou hangest."
> *Falada answered:*
> "Alas! Queen's daughter, there thou hangest.
> If thy mother knew thy fate,
> Her heart would break with grief so great."[49]

[44]Michael Hornyansky, *The Golden Phoenix* by Marius Barbeau, Illustrated by Arthur Price (New York: Scholastic, 1965), p. 20.

[45]Sturton, p. 33.

[46]Richard Chase, Compiler, *The Complete Tales of Uncle Remus* by Joel Chandler Harris (Boston: Houghton Mifflin, 1955), p. 51.

[47]Richard Chase, *The Jack Tales* (Boston: Houghton Mifflin, 1943), p. xi.

[48]Chase, p. 165.

[49]Marguerite de Angeli, *The Goose Girl* (New York: Doubleday, 1964), p. 21.

Other writers use brief, descriptive phrases to indicate emotion. Ernest Small's expressive language adds to the tension in *Baba Yaga*:

She clawed at the air with her long bony fingers, gnashed her iron teeth and snarled, "I think I smell a bad Russian child." . . .
Then she turned to Marusia and hissed, "You say nothing!"
"I don't dare," said Marusia timidly. . . .[50]

The major criteria for style of the written folk tale are that it maintain the atmosphere of the country from which it originated, and that it truly seems to be a tale *told* by a storyteller.

Themes in Folk Tales The basic purpose of the folk tale was to tell an entertaining story, yet these stories do present themes. Some tales may be merely humorous accounts of foolish people who are so ridiculous that the listeners see their own foolish ways exaggerated. Many of the stories provided an outlet for feelings against the kings and nobles who oppressed the poor. Values of the culture were expressed in folklore. The virtues of humility, kindness, patience, sympathy, hard work, and courage were invariably rewarded. These rewards reflected the goals of man—long life, a good husband or loving wife, beautiful homes and fine clothing, plenty of food, freedom from fear of the ogre or giant. The power of love, mercy, and kindness is one of the major themes of the folk tales. "The Pumpkin Child" (171), a Persian tale, was a little girl born to a woman who expressed a deep wish for a daughter even if she looked like a pumpkin. When a prince agreed to marry the girl, love released her from the enchantment and she became "as beautiful as the moon on its fourteenth night." A Japa-

nese folk tale, *The Dwarf Pine Tree* (235), suggests that pain is essential to achieve beauty. A little pine tree who loves a princess learns she will recover from an illness if she receives a beautiful, dwarf pine. A tengu, or spirit, grants the wish of the pine, but he brings pain as roots are cut and the branches bound. The tree dies in happiness, and his shape may still be seen on a mountain at the time of the full moon. The thematic wisdom of *Beauty and the Beast* (220) is that one should not trust too much to appearances. The lesson that inner qualities of love and kindness are more important than the outer semblance is clearly presented.

A tale written in China in 350 B.C. is the basis of Jean Merrill's story, *The Superlative Horse*. When the Chief Groom and trusted adviser of the Duke Mu nears retirement age, the Duke tries to find someone to take his place. A peasant boy is suggested by the old man, Po Lo, as his successor. Accompanied by the Chief Minister, a rather gross character who was unaware of deeper values, the boy journeys forth to locate a superlative horse. Duke Mu speaks wisely: "'There are two kinds of men,' he said, 'those who ask 'What is the value?' and those who ask "What is the price?'"[51] The lesson of the story is that external details have little to do with the heart or spirit.

Parents, teachers, and some psychologists have expressed concern about a theme of cruelty and horror in folk tales. "Little Red Riding Hood" (159), for example, has been rewritten so that the wolf eats neither the grandmother nor the heroine. These deeds occur very quickly with no sense of pain and no details of the action. No blood drips from the Ravens' sister's hand when she cuts off a finger; not an "ouch" escapes her lips (226). The wolf is cut open so the six kids can escape, and the mother goat sews the stones

---

[50]Ernest Small, *Baba Yaga*, Illustrated by Blair Lent (Boston: Houghton Mifflin, 1966), pp. 9, 22.

[51]Jean Merrill, *The Superlative Horse*, Illustrated by Ronni Solbert (New York: Scholastic, 1961), p. 27.

into his stomach without any suggestion that the wolf is being hurt (98). Children accept these stories as they are—symbolic interpretations of life in an imaginary land of another time. Long ago, young children heard the stories within the reassuring circle of family and friends. This is one reason why it is good to tell or read the stories so that the child can sense the adult's communication of security in this moment. Three- to five-year-olds who have not distinguished the real world from the imaginary world are not ready for many folk tales. By the time children can read the folk tales for themselves, they can enter the land of make-believe where the horror is not horror as adults think of it in the world of reality.

Motifs in Folk Tales Folklorists analyze folk tales according to motifs or patterns, numbering each tale and labeling its episodes.[52] This kind of analysis is for the specialist, yet the teacher and librarian need to become familiar with motifs as a way of studying traditional literature. As they tell stories and guide children's study, they should help children become aware of common elements and variants of a motif. Thompson pointed out the frequent inclusion of one tale within another. He reported 770 versions of *The Two Brothers* and 368 variants of *The Dragon Slayer*.[53]

A comparison of the variants of Cinderella (98, 141, 143, 148, 160, 239, 240, 244) illustrates differences in theme and motif. Scholars have found versions of this story in ancient Egypt, in China in the ninth century, and in Iceland in the tenth century. Cinderella receives the magic objects in different ways; in one version, a dove appears from a tree that grew from the tears she had shed on her mother's grave; the fairy godmother is most familiar; in the English "Tattercoats" she receives the gifts from a herdboy. Cleaning peas, or retrieving peas thrown into the fire by the stepmother, are obstacles to her attendance at the ball. She attends three balls in some variants; for example, in the Italian version, Cenerentola throws coins as she leaves the first night, pearls on the second escape, and loses her slipper on the third night. The treatment of the stepsisters varies from blinding them to inviting them to live with her at the palace. An Indian Cinderella (98) wins Strong Wind by giving an honest answer to his sister's questions, for he is truly invisible. Her sisters are changed into aspen that still shake and tremble at the approach of Strong Wind.

ENCHANTED PEOPLE Enchantment of tiny people is exemplified in the Japanese tale, "Little One Inch" (153) or "Isun Bashi, the One-Inch Lad" (155). He is born to older parents who want a child, and comes from a bamboo reed. One-Inch saves a princess from an ogre or a giant with his needle sword. He becomes a normal size through the wish granted by the magic hammer (153) or good-luck charm. (155). Andersen's well-known story, "Thumbelina," is based upon this same theme.

The long sleep is another form of enchantment. A Russian collection includes "The Sleeping Tsarevna and the Seven Giants" (179), which is very similar to "Snow Drop" (104) or "Snow White and the Seven Dwarfs" (229). "The Sleeping Beauty in the Wood" (146, 247) was apparently first recorded by Perrault and has been considered a French fairy tale. However, the Grimms included the similar "Briar Rose" in their German collection.

Other kinds of enchantment appear in many tales. In "The History of Dwarf Long Nose" (101) young Jean is enchanted for seven years. He awakens one day in the form of a dwarf with a long nose. With the aid of a

---

[52]See Stith Thompson, *Motif Index of Folk-Literature* (Bloomington, Ind.: Indiana University Press, 1955–1958), 6 vols.

[53]Stith Thompson, *The Folktale* (New York: Holt, Rinehart and Winston, 1961).

Goose Girl, he finds the hero that restores him to normalcy. A Japanese story, "Urashima Taro and the Princess of the Sea" (155) tells of a boy who remains under the sea in a beautiful palace for three years, only to discover he was gone three hundred years. The New England whaling captain. "Ichabod Paddock" (206), is bewitched by a mermaid in the belly of the Crooked Jaw whale he has pursued for years. His wife releases him by killing the whale with a silver harpoon.

Magic powers are often given. In "Six Servants" (143), the characters, the Fat One, the Long One, the Looker, the Listener, Shatter Eyes, and Frosty-hot, use their special powers to help the prince win the princess. Invisibility is a kind of enchantment often employed. The old soldier in "The Dancing Princesses" (102) is given a clock of invisibility so he may discover where the twelve princesses go each night, for although locked in their room, their dancing shoes are worn thin. In another version (211, 146), the young gardener becomes invisible and learns of the secret castle.

The Indians of Wisconsin told the story of "Little Bear" (199) who threw the sun back up in the sky after it was stolen by an old woman. As a reward, Little Bear marries the chief's son. She asks him to throw her in the fire, whereupon she emerges as a beautiful girl.

In some of the stories, changes of form are effected rapidly. "Niilo and the Wizard" (185) is a Finnish story of a boy who earns money by changing himself into a horse that is sold; then he escapes in another form and is sold again. The wizard tries to catch him by changing to a rooster to eat him in the form of peas; the boy then changes to a fox to catch the rooster whom he eats. "Mywhat" (177) is a tale from Russia that has a similar pattern. In this story, the wizard becomes a thread destroyed by a fire, but the boy had cleverly changed himself into a needle that survived the fire.

In a Spanish story, "Three Golden Oranges" (136), Diego cannot wait to open the oranges. He has no bread for the first girl who comes out of the orange so she disappears; there is no water for the second. The third is changed to a dove, but a wise woman he once helped changes the dove back to human form.

MAGICAL TRANSFORMATIONS   The transformation of an animal to a person, or vice versa, is a part of many folk tales. "Beauty and the Beast" (146, 220) is one of the most familiar. A lovely, young girl named Beauty is given to a beast as a punishment for her father who picked a rose for Beauty in the beast's garden. While visiting her sisters, she thinks of the beast and returns to find him dying. When she promises to marry the creature, he emerges as a prince. "East of the Sun and West of the Moon" (180, 181, 183) is similar, but the girl's curiosity leads her to look at the beast. A drop of tallow from her candle causes him to disappear. Eventually, she frees him from his enchantment by being the only one who can wash the tallow from his shirt. In "Snow White and Rose Red" (143, 228), a bear plays with the two girls. By saving a gnome whose beard catches in a log or is held by a fish, they discover a treasure. The bear overpowers the gnome and changes to a prince.

A Swiss tale, "The Flaxen Thread" (139), and a Finnish tale, "The Mouse Bride" (182), have a similar plot and theme. Three sons seek brides, and of course the youngest meets the greatest difficulty. Accepting his fate, he agrees to marry the mouse he meets in the deep woods. She proves her skill in weaving and baking and becomes a beautiful girl. In "The Flaxen Thread" (139), Hans, the simple brother, is helped by a frog who spins fine thread. His faith is rewarded when the frog changes to a beautiful girl coming down the aisle of the church.

"The Frog Prince" (143) is one of the stories collected by the Grimm brothers. A frog retrieves the princess's ball in exchange for her promise that he can eat from her plate and sleep with her. He becomes a prince when allowed on her pillow. *The Seven Ravens* (226), another of the Grimms' tales, is a transformation story. Seven boys are changed into ravens by the wish of their father who was angry because they broke a jug when they went to get water to christen the new baby sister. When she is older, the sister seeks her brothers, cuts off her finger to use as a key to open the door to the glass mountain and releases her brothers. Some scholars interpret this as symbolic of the castration fear; others believe it represents the theme of sacrifice to receive forgiveness and love. *The Wild Swans* by Andersen is a much more complex version derived from this tale.

MAGIC OBJECTS Magic objects are essential aspects of many tales that also reflect other themes. From Japan, comes *The Dancing Kettle* (155) that makes a fortune for a junkman. A different version appears in *The Old Old Teakettle* (154). As a reward for helping him, badger changes himself into a teakettle for an old man and suggests the farmer sell it to the priest. When it is put on the fire, it changes back to badger.

The magic tablecloth is a frequent device for providing food. In "Little One-Eye, Two-Eyes, and Three-Eyes" (137) the magic cloth appears when Two-Eyes says, "Little goat bleat, Little table appear!" Other magical objects are the hen that laid the golden eggs in "Jack and the Beanstalk" (159) and the magic harp. Aladdin's magic lamp is familiar to boys and girls. Although usually included in *The Arabian Nights*, it was not originally in this collection. Lang (169) tells the story in its most familiar form. Among the *Legends of the United Nations* (103) by Frost is "The Magic Lamp," a story from India. The incidents are similar to those in the Arabian tale.

A magic doll saves a Russian maiden in "Vasilissa the Beautiful" (178). The doll does much of the work assigned by the cruel stepmother and saves the maiden from the witch. A magical flying ship is a feature of "The Flying Ship" (103) and "The Ship That Sailed by Land and Sea" (182). In these stories from Russia, Norway, and Finland, the youngest son is given the magic ship, and helpers arrive so that he may accomplish his tasks.

A magic ring is given "Martin the Peasant's Son" (178) after he chooses a bag of sand instead of silver or gold. The ring could bring him the wife he wanted; however, she resented this and had it hidden. The cat and dog whom he had befriended recapture the ring with the assistance of the mice and lobster kingdoms. Similarly, in the Yugoslavian tale, "The Magic Ring" (137), a boy gets a wife through the power of a ring won after slaying a dragon. He, too, loses the ring and is put in a pit, but mice help him recover the magic ring.

TASKS AND TRIALS Tasks and trials may be to win a maiden, to free oneself of sorcery, or to improve status. Sometimes the tasks are penalties for bragging or misbehavior. For example, in the English "Tom-Tit-Tot" (104, 241), a woman boasts her daughter could spin five skeins in a day. The king marries the girl, but insists she must live up to her mother's boast. A little man does her spinning, but she must guess his name or become his bride. Unwittingly, the king tells his wife of seeing a tiny man spinning and singing a verse about his name. This story is similar to "Rumpelstiltskin" (99). "Spin, Weave, Wear" is a Scotch variant in which the girl is helped by her cat who says. "every self-respecting cat has a friend or two among the witches."[54] Spinning is also involved in "The Bad Old Woman" (139), a Swiss tale. A mistreated stepdaughter finds a cow that helps her spin the assigned amount, yet the cow

[54]Sorche Nic Leodhas, *Heather and Broom*, Illustrated by Consuelo Joerns (New York: Holt, Rinehart and Winston, 1960), p. 98.

steps on the flax of the stepsister who tries the same task. The girl receives jewels when she combs an old woman's hair for her, but frogs and bugs drop in the lap of the stepsister performing the same task.

The firebird theme is expressed in various ways in Russian stories. It usually begins with the three sons being charged to find the thief who steals the golden apple from a certain tree. The youngest gets the feathers of the firebird and sets out to find it. He shows kindness to a wolf and is given much help by this animal. Each time the boy has a task, he disregards the wolf's advice and has an even more difficult task assigned. In "The Wolf Who Knew How to Be a Friend" (177), he returns to save his brothers who lost when gambling in parcheesi games, but they put him in a well. The wolf digs a tunnel to the well and saves his friend. The prince is also tested by the girl he wins, in another tale, "The Fire-Bird, the Horse of Power, and the Princess Vasilissa" (101). "The Golden Phoenix" (128) is a French-Canadian tale of a golden bird and the trials of Petit Jean to obtain it and the fair princess.

Yurick, the king's servant, wins "Zlatovlaska the Golden-Haired" (101) by carrying out her assignments—gathering pearls of a necklace, finding a ring on the ocean floor, and obtaining the water of life and death. Because he helped them, the ants, ravens, and fish give assistance with these tasks. Beheaded by the king, Yurick is brought to life when the princess sprinkles him with the water of life. When the old king allows himself to be killed so he can "return" as a young man, the girl conveniently forgets the procedure and is able to marry Yurick.

In some stories, the task involves going to an imaginary land and finding an imaginary person. A Skaski tale, "Whither No One Knows" (179), relates the trials of Yuri in getting a goat with golden horns and finding Schmat-Razum or "no-one-knows-what." "Schmat-Razum" (178) is the title of a variant

in which an archer saves a white duck who becomes a beautiful bride. The envious Tsar tries to get rid of the archer by sending him to get the impossible. Schmat-Razum is an invisible servant who is found. "I Know-Not-What of I Know-Not-Where" (175) is a very similar story, although a frog is added as a helper in finding "Nobody."

The Norwegian Cinderlad achieves the task of riding up the mountain to get the three golden apples from "The Maid on the Glass Mountain" (182).

A Southern Blue Ridge tale, "Old Bluebeard" (199), includes the trials of Jack who follows the old man down a hole where he finds a magic ring and three beautiful girls.

WIT PREVAILS   The cleverness of wives, little people, and imps provides gay humor in many folk tales. The clever wife of Fin McCaul so frightened the Giant Cucullin he never returned. In "A Legend of Knockmany" (158), Fin gets in the cradle and pretends to be a baby while the wife has Cucullin turn the house around "since Fin isn't home to do it." He breaks his teeth on the griddle placed in the center of the pancake, yet the "baby" eats one easily. The "baby" also squeezes water from a rock by squeezing whey from curds held in his hand with the rock. "Molly Whuppie" (102) also outwits a giant, returning to steal a sword, a purse, and a ring. She gaily escapes over the bridge of one hair.

A hungry soldier obtains food by creating "Nail Soup" (137, 256) in a Yugoslavian folk tale. Placing a nail in water, he asks for vegetables to give it flavor. In *Stone Soup* (216), a group of soldiers trick an entire village into providing ingredients for their soup.

The faith of a wife in her husband is illustrated in the Norwegian tale "Gudbrund on the Hillside" (183). The old man swaps a cow for various animals until he returns home empty-handed. A neighbor wagers the wife will be very angry, but she gives praise for each of her husband's unwise dealings, and Gudbrund wins the one hundred dollars.

"The Tiger's Minister of State" (152), a Burmese tale, provides a good example of wit. Tiger tests the applicants for the position of minister by asking each if his breath is sweet. The boar denies the truth and is rejected as a flatterer. The monkey agrees the tiger's breath is very offensive. He is rejected because he will speak without regard for the feelings of others. But the rabbit twitches his nose and says he has such a cold he can't smell anything. So he is chosen minister of state, and to this day he twitches his nose to show he cannot smell. The lesson that politicians must ignore certain acts has meaning today.

FOOLS AND SIMPLETONS Acceptance of the simpleton is reflected in most folk tales. His antics may provide humor, but it is usually neither cruel nor barbed. Frequently, fools win prizes or are rewarded. In several stories, the fool's literal interpretation of advice leads to dire results. "Silly Jean" (139), told by his mother to be friendly to people as he goes to the mill and to answer politely if someone asks the way, offers the advice but is rebuffed. His mother tells him he should have commented, "So you're leading your goat to the fair." When he makes this remark to the bride and groom he next meets, he is beaten. And so it goes, until his mother decides he can not go out into the world.

Just Say Hic! (253) (pronounced "heech") is a Turkish tale with a similar motif. Sent by his master to buy some salt, a servant boy repeated the word for salt, "Hic, hic, hic." In Turkey, "hic" also meant "nothing." He repeated the word as he watched a fisherman who told him to say, "May there be five or ten of them," instead of "nothing." This phrase he then repeats as he sees a funeral procession. And so it goes, as Hasan creates amusing scenes with his right phrases in the wrong places. Finally, he is given the original

word, and he goes to buy the salt. This would be a very amusing story to dramatize, and it could involve many children.

In his collection, *Zlateh the Goat* (115), Singer tells about Chelm, a village of fools where the seven elders are the most foolish of all. One night, they planned to gather the pearls and diamonds of the snow so the jew-

Sendak has captured both the humor and sadness of European Jewish folklore. Illustration by Maurice Sendak from *Zlateh the Goat* by Isaac Singer. Harper & Row, 1966.

els could be sold. They decided that the messenger should be carried on a table supported by four men so his feet would not spoil the snow as he went from house to house to tell the people to stay inside. The story of Lemel, a silly bridegroom who follows advice in the wrong way, is in the Epaminondas pattern. When Lemel's child was born, an Elder asked if it were a boy. To Lemel's response of "no," the Elder inquired if it were a girl. "'How did you guess?' Lemel asked in amazement. And the Elder of Chelm replied, 'For the wise men of Chelm there are no secrets.'"[55]

A tale of the Grimms, "Goose Hans" (144), is about the foolish boy who receives gifts from a prospective bride. He puts the needle in a haystack, the knife in his sleeve, a goat in his pocket — following literally his mother's directions. Left alone, he causes havoc in the house but ends the day by rolling in honey and goose feathers to sit on the eggs, replacing the goose he kills.

"Clever Elsie" (143) is also a tale from the Grimms in which Elsie cries because the baby she might have someday could be cut by the axe in the cellar. When she cuts her clothes instead of the rye she asks, "Am I myself?" Upon returning to the house, she asks her husband if Elsie is at home. Thinking his wife is upstairs, her husband answers, "Yes." Elsie runs away, "but is probably getting along all right because she is so clever."

"Rusty Jack" (199) is a fool who receives good fortune. This American folk tale is about a farmer's son who is wise enough to trick a woodsman into believing his crow talks. The crow points out treasure Jack has already seen when spying through the window. Jack wins the beautiful girl who has also been hiding in the house.

An amusing Swiss story is that of "The

---

[55]Isaac Bashevis Singer, *Zlateh the Goat and Other Stories*, Illustration by Maurice Sendak, Translated by the author and Elizabeth Shub (New York: Harper & Row, 1966), p. 50.

Three Sneezes" (139). A man tells Jean Marie he will fall, for he is sawing the very limb he is sitting on. Of course Jean falls, so he asks the man to predict his future. Jean is told he will die when his donkey sneezes three times. Soon the donkey sneezes thrice, and Jean Marie falls over "because it isn't proper for a dead man to stand up!" In "The Shepherd Who Laughed Last" (136), a play on words provides fun. Teasing a simple shepherd, an innkeeper tells him they call a bottle a Fat Boy; a pudding, Johnny; a rooster is Singer; a hen, the Woman; the cat, our Neighbor; the bed, St. Sebastian; the fire, Happiness; the master, Holy Lord; the chimney chain, Forbearance. After all are in bed, the cat comes in and her tail catches on fire. The shepherd takes the pudding and wine and calls out, "Arise, Holy Lord, from the heights of St. Sebastian. For there goes our Neighbor up Forbearance pursued by Happiness. As for the Fat Boys, Johnny, the Singer, and the Woman, they go along with me!" The innkeeper rolls over wondering, "What can the simpleton be saying?"

Foolish people are the central figures in such single tales as *Hilili and Dilili* (252), a Turkish couple, and *Seven Silly Wise Men* (214), the cautious and simple-minded elders of Holmolaiset.

WISHES Many stories are told of wishes granted but used in anger or without thought. "The Three Wishes" (160) tells how a woodsman wished for a pudding that is wished on the end of his nose. Of course, the last wish must be used to remove it.

The story *The Fisherman and His Wife* (258) illustrates the lesson that we often possess that for which we wish, but it lies unrecognized. A kind fisherman throws a fish back into the sea when the fish says he is an enchanted prince. The domineering wife makes her husband ask the fish to grant her wishes for a cottage and a mansion. Next she asks to be king, emperor, and pope. Her final wish to be God causes her to be returned to the original hut.

TRICKERY Both animals and people trick their friends and neighbors in folk literature. Hansel and Gretel trick the old witch into crawling into the oven, thus overcoming the symbol of evil. Children love the witch's call, "Nibble, nibble little mouse, Who's nibbling at my house?" and the reply, "'Tis Heaven's own child, the tempest Wild."

After "The Brave Little Tailor" (105) killed seven flies at once, he embroidered the words "Seven at one blow" on his girdle. Impressed by his prowess, the king sends him out to kill giants. By trickery, he overpowers the giants and wins a kingdom. "Nazar the Brave" (173), who was really a coward, killed many flies at one blow and persuaded the priest to make a banner proclaiming he killed "a thousand at a single blow." When he appears at a feast, a few pretend to remember the hero and his deeds. Rather than face such a hero, seven giants bow to him. Shaking with fear, Nazar climbs a tree when sent to kill a tiger. He falls on the back of the tiger, and the villagers kill it. In battle, his horse bolts, and Nazar is credited with a victorious ride. The American tale, "Jack in the Giant's Newground" (198), employs similar tricks.

Anansi, from West Africa, is a famous trickster. In "Anansi and the Old Hag" (132), there is an account of the way Anansi tricked people to give him food by saying he dreamed the Old Hag was coming if people didn't stop talking about their neighbors. Frequently, however, Anansi is caught by his own tricks.

The Uncle Remus (197) stories abound with tricks by Rabbit and Fox. The Tar Baby in this collection is well known, but it is also found in an Indian tale, "How Rabbit Deceived Fox" (129).

Scheherazade tricks the sultan by continuing her stories for one thousand and one nights. These tales are presented in several versions of *The Arabian Nights* (164).

The Coconut Thieves (221) is an African bush story based upon the trickery of Turtle

Curving lines of stylized trees and plants create the feeling of a Near Eastern folk tale. Jewel-like colors make the pages glow. Illustrations copyright © 1966 by Nonny Hogrogian. Illustration by Nonny Hogrogian from *Once There Was and Was Not* by Virginia Tashjian, by permission of Little, Brown and Co.

and Dog. When they go to steal Leopard's coconuts, Dog fails to keep his promise to help Turtle, so Turtle must save himself by trickery. Turtle forgives Dog and again they go to gather coconuts. This time, Dog tricks Leopard by making a fearful noise, and he and Turtle remain fast friends.

In many folk tales, trickery plays a part in races held by the animals. The pattern of the fable "The Hare and the Tortoise" is found in several tales. In "Crafty Crab," (188) the fox and crab plan a race. It is won by crab who hangs onto fox's tail, then drops off at the finish line. "This would be a race in-deed—a race between a turtle and a hare!"[56] is a statement made by Little Mukra when he races the king's messengers. If a child had not first heard the fable of the turtle and the rabbit, he would not understand this com-ment in an Arabian tale, "The Story of Little Mukra."

An Hawaiian story, *Punia and the King of the Sharks* (238), shows a human tricking the animals. The king of the sharks refused to allow fishermen to get lobsters, but Punia tricks him by diving in one spot, although he announces his intention to dive at another place. At last, Punia tricks the shark into swimming into such shallow water that he dies.

REALISTIC EVENTS The realistic motif re-fers to stories that could have happened, but have been embellished with exaggeration. Magic plays no part in these stories. "Dick Whittington and His Cat" (159, 215) is a clas-sic example of the rags-to-riches story. Dick's cat, Thursday, brings him wealth while Dick is serving as a cabin boy. His reward for rid-ding an island of mice is used wisely when Dick returns to London. With wealth and his continuing goodness, he becomes Lord Mayor.

The Steel Flea (233) is a story of national pride and cleverness. After the Russians de-feated Napoleon, the Emperor took his chief, Platov, and visited many lands. When the English presented a microscopic, danc-ing steel flea, Platov begged to do something to show Russian gunsmiths could equal this skill. They surpassed the English by putting shoes on the minute flea.

LOCAL LEGENDARY HEROES Stories of local heroes who are given legendary characteris-tics become part of folklore. North Amer-ica has produced many men of action who

helped create the country and have been assigned legendary qualities. Davy Crockett and Daniel Boone actually lived, but stories about them have been embroidered or in-vented. They swagger, exaggerate, and play tricks, yet solve problems with good humor. Paul Bunyan was a huge lumberjack who bossed a big gang of lumbermen in Michi-gan, Wisconsin, and the Northwest. Children will enjoy stories of Paul's birth, and of his school problems, for "Just to write his name Paul had to put five copy books one on top of the other, and even then the teacher would only see part of each letter and he would mark him wrong."[57] Paul's light lunch one day was "three sides of barbecued beef, half a wagon load of potatoes, carrots and a few other odds and ends."[58] Shephard's story-telling style is especially good for these tall tales. Describing Babe the Blue Ox, she says, "I've forgot most of the other figures, but I remember he measured forty-two ax-handles between the eyes—and a tobacco box—you could just fit in a Star Tobacco Box after the last axhandle."[59]

Tony Beaver (205) was a Southern lum-berjack. His buildings were huge water-melons. During a flood, he built a dam of peanuts, molasses, and vinegar. In this way, peanut brittle was invented! *Pecos Bill* (196) was a famous cowboy who established many of the cowboy customs. *Old Stormalong* (209) was a sailor whose size made life on ship, on a ranch, or on a farm quite uncomfortable, but his adventures are exciting. *John Darling* (205) also lived on a boat, but on the Erie Canal. Another famous boatman who lived on the Mississippi was Mike Fink. In his words:

[56]Charles Mozley, *The First Book of Tales of Ancient Araby* (New York: F. Watts, 1960), p. 66.

[57]Roberta Strauss Feuerlecht, *The Legends of Paul Bun-yan,* Illustrated by Kurt Werth (New York: Macmillan, 1966), p. 17.
[58]Glen Rounds, *Ol' Paul the Mighty Logger* (New York: Holiday, 1949), p. 28.
[59]Esther Shephard, *Paul Bunyan,* Illustrated by Rockwell Kent (New York: Harcourt, 1924), p. 33.

I'm thunder and lightnin' and hurrycane all rolled into one! With a mite o' earthquake throwed in for good measure. I'm a Mississippi whirlpool! I'm a river snag! I'm half hoss and half alligator! I'm all that and a long chalk more! I can outrun, outjump, knock down and mud waller any man as wants to try me! Whoopee! Make way for the king of the keel-boatmen![60]

Industry has its heroes, too. "Joe Magarac" (205, 208) is a man of steel who came to Hunkietown. Magarac means Jackass, and Joe works like a mule and eats like a mule. He can stir molten iron with his arm, but when there is no more work to be done, he melts himself and becomes part of a new steel mill. "John Henry" (201, 204) is a powerful man who swings his hammer mightily to build the transcontinental railroad. His contest with a steam drill is a dramatic story. Ezra Jack Keats (204) created huge, bold figures to tell of this legendary figure.

Stories of New York City are presented in *The Ghost of Peg-Leg Peter* (203). In addition to the story of Stuyvesant's ghost, there are several tales about a brave Quaker named John Bowne who fended off a giant bear and defied Stuyvesant by holding meetings in his house. There is a story of the "Greatest Hoax in New York City," a plan to cut the island in half because too many houses were on one end. The story of Macy's store and the Hope tree of Harlem reveal other local legends.

Daugherty's vigorous illustrations are very appropriate for "John Henry" and "Joe Magarac" in Shapiro's collection, *Heroes in American Folklore* (208). McKay's Casey Jones and Old Stormalong are also rugged, exaggerated characters. The more complete story of John Henry who came back to operate a

[60]Zachary Ball, *Young Mike Fink* (New York: Holiday, 1958), p. 196.

Houston's pictures capture the action and strength of this Eskimo legend. The rounded figures give the effect of the sculpture of Eskimo artists. From *Tiktá Liktak: An Eskimo Legend,* written and illustrated by James Houston, copyright © 1965 by James Houston. Reproduced by permission of Harcourt, Brace & World, Inc.

steam drill after people thought he was dead suggests man's fear of machines.

Tiktá Liktak (192), a legendary Eskimo hunter, was isolated when an ice pan broke away. In desperate hunger, he became obsessed with the idea that the island he reaches is his grave. He builds a coffin and climbs into it to die. The dreams of the past bring refreshment of spirit, and he wakens saying, "I will not die." Still living in the dream, he kills a seal, and gains the strength to survive. He demonstrates skill and bravery in fighting a bear, making a boat, and finding his way home. Tiktá Liktak feels the keen edge of loneliness, as well as the triumph over nature.

TALKING ANIMALS In all the types of folk tales discussed, animals have been given human characteristics including the power of speech. Fish are often found in English, German, and South Sea stories. Goats and blackbirds appear in Italian tales; rabbits, badgers, monkeys, or bees are represented in Japanese stories; wolves, foxes, bears, and horses are often found in Russian folklore.

Puss in Boots (245, 246) is one of the well-known animal helpers. Puss tells the king about an imaginary Marquis of Carabas, his master, who is only a miller's son. Dashing ahead of the royal carriage, the cat tells the peasants to say the land belongs to the Marquis of Carabas or he will make mincemeat of them. Reaching the castle, he tricks the ogre into changing into a mouse whom he promptly eats. The castle becomes his master's, and Puss remains the dashing hero in boots and plumed hat.

Two stories follow a similar pattern in which a fowl carries other animals in his bill, throat, or under his wing. As "Drakestail" (137) goes to collect money from the king or fox, a ladder, a river, and wasps go along in his throat or gizzard. Each helps him escape from chickens, a well, and a furnace. "Red-chicken" (139), a Swiss animal, takes a fox, wolf, and a pond to collect a debt in Florimont.

"The Musicians of Bremen" (143, 230) are the donkey, dog, cat, and rooster who frighten robbers away from their den. The same story is told in a Celtic tale, "Jack and His Comrades" (158).

The Cock and the Ghost Cat (234) is a Japanese tale presented in a single book by Lifton. The cock is brave and faithful to the poor farmer with whom he lives. When a small kitten changes itself to a huge ghost cat, the cock crows to warn his master, Gam-bei. However, the villagers are disturbed by the crowing cock and demand that he be drowned in the river. At last, a monk who can understand animal talk understands the peril of the ghost cat and saves Gambei. The cock dies but is immortalized by a bronze statue erected in the village. Akino's watercolor illustrations show village life and portray the vigorous action of the story.

POURQUOI STORIES The "why" stories may be mythical or more closely related to folktale style. Folk tales may explain the recurring movements of sun and moon. An Eskimo story, "The Extraordinary Black Coat" (188), includes the motif of the sun as well as the origin of one animal. A boy who has a black coat recovers the lost ball of fire and throws it out piece by piece. Thus, day returns. His children's children never remove their black coats and become ravens.

A Mexican tale, "The Rabbit in the Moon" (135), describes the sacrifice of two gods who leap into a fire to create the sun and the moon. The first to leap into the fire was poor, but honest and good, whereas the second was a coward, at first. The sun appeared as the first spirit, and the moon was the second spirit. Because the moon should not shine as brightly as the sun, a god threw a rabbit to the moon to knock out some of the light, and you can still see the rabbit's outline!

"Why Wisdom Is Found Everywhere" (131) is an explanation of the distribution of wisdom. The animals are competing to collect wisdom, but they have no good place for it. Terrapin suggests that they put it all together in his pot. He upsets the pot, and the animals scramble for "sense." Today, terrapin still looks in the grass for wisdom.

The custom of wearing golden caps with lace covers is explained in a story of how Christianity came to Frisia in the Netherlands (138). A princess was forced to wear a crown of thorns when she accepted the story of Jesus as it was first told by minstrels whom she freed despite the anger of the people. The caps resemble her helmet of gold.

Physical characteristics of animals are explained in many folk tales. The bear who fished with his tail until it froze in the lake and broke off is familiar to most children. This story, "The Bear Goes Fishing" (182), is found in a Finnish collection. Rabbit, chief guide in the forest, loses his tail by helping a man pull himself out of a pit. In the story, "How Rabbit Lost His Tail" (129), this helpful rabbit splits his lip on his way to a wedding. The bride, in this Glooskap story of Canada, gives him a white coat for winter. Why bats sleep upside down and in the daytime is explained in an Indian story, "Tale of Bat" (187). Bat disobeys the Great Spirit by eating of a white lily. He feels miserable and speaks to a blackbird crossly. This starts a chain of unkindness, so he is punished by being made to sleep in the day, hiding his shame.

Land formations are also explained by folk tales. Mount Pilatus in Italy was supposedly named after "Pontius Pilate" (139) Glooskap (129, 191) shaped the eastern coast of Canada. For example, when two girls laughed at him, they became rocks that can be seen today. "Paul Bunyan" (207) dug Puget Sound by hitching Babe to an Alaskan glacier. *Pecos Bill* (196) created the Grand Canyon and Death Valley. "Why the Sea Is Salt" (105) is the story of a hand mill that could grind out any kind of food. The owner's brother who took the mill didn't know how to stop it when he asked for salt. He threw it in the ocean, where it continues to grind out salt today. Zemach's book, *Salt* (257), gives authentic Russian settings for this story.

SUPERNATURAL CREATURES The term "fairy tale" is often used for folk tales, yet only part of the stories have fairy folk, giants, ogres, or witches. Palmer has published two "references," *Fairy Elves: A Dictionary of the Little People with Some Old Tales and Verses about Them* (110) and *Dragons, Unicorns and Other Magical Beasts* (109). The dictionary lists the places where fairy folk live. For example, giants are everywhere, tengus are in Japan, the tomte are found in Sweden, and rusalkas are in Russia. The animals of folklore are pictured in pen-and-ink sketches, and brief descriptions include their characteristics.

"Farmer Grigg's Boggart" (112) was an ill-tempered imp who could be seen only when it was cold. He played such tricks that the Griggs family decided they must move, but the boggart went to the new place. By laying out fine clothes for him to wear, the farmer frightened the imp away. Similar boggarts appear in the modern stories by Jean Fritz, *Magic to Burn,* and William Mayne, *Earthfasts* (see Chapter 7).

Bogles are ghosts that inhabit old houses in Scotland. "The Bogles from the Howff" (161) are sent on their way by a red-haired

Zemach's typical cartoon-like peasant figures add humor to this Russian tale. Ivan the fool is nearly lost in swirling waves. Illustration by Margot Zemach from *Salt* by Harve Zemach. Copyright © 1965. Reprinted courtesy of Follett Publishing Company.

Details of the traditional costume, hair, and facial expression represent the demure character of a princess who accepted "The Shepherd's Nosegay." Illustrations copyright © 1966 by Trina Schart Hyman. Illustration by Trina Schart Hyman from *Favorite Fairy Tales Told in Czechoslovakia* by Virginia Haviland, by permission of Little, Brown and Co.

lass who thoroughly cleans a doctor's house. Of course he marries the girl, and the house is filled with bairns instead of Bogles. In *Gaelic Ghosts* (161), Sorche Nic Leodhas relates humorous, mysterious, and sad ghost stories. These ghosts are friendly; for example, one old lady returned to insist her husband continue to give grain from one field to the poor. This author also has published *Ghosts Go Haunting* (108) that includes such tales as "The Wicked House of Duncan McBain," "The Man Who Didn't Believe in Ghosts," and "The Man Who Helped Carry the Coffin." A glossary helps with pronuncia-

tion and meaning of such Scottish words as "bothan" (a cottage), "liefer" (rather), and "hauld your whisht" (hold your tongue). These are tales for the children in upper grades to read aloud or tell.

A Book of Dwarfs (107) includes stories of dwarfs in Germany, Denmark, Ireland, Japan, and Arabia. Some are like humans, as Mukra is, but others are magic, as is Katto, who changed himself into a cat. "Maia" is a Danish story very much like Andersen's "Thumbelina." A little girl is born in a flower and has many difficulties avoiding marriage to a frog and a mole.

Types of Folk Tale Books

Collections of Folk Tales Early collectors of folk tales were the Brothers Grimm in Germany, Joseph Jacobs in England, and Joel Chandler Harris in the United States. Andrew Lang was a folklorist of the late nineteenth century whose collections under the titles of *The Blue Fairy Book, The Red Fairy Book, The Yellow Fairy Book* extended through several volumes. The unabridged versions of the Blue, Brown, and Green books are available in paperback, so children today may enjoy the prose and unaltered versions of the tales. Modern collections are most frequently made according to country. Virginia Haviland's series, *Favorite Fairy Tales Told in Germany, . . . in Italy, . . . in Russia,* and several other countries are very good sources. The Oxford press series includes Curcija-Prodanovic's *Yugoslav Folk Tales* (137) and *West Indian Folk Tales* (133) by Sherlock. Frances Carpenter has written a series as though a grandmother is telling stories to the children. Customs of the people are included as she introduces a story. Her titles include *Tales of a Chinese Grandmother* (150), *African Wonder Tales* (121), and *The Elephant's Bathtub, Wonder Tales from the Far East* (151).

Sorche Nic Leodhas has established a reputation for collections of Scottish tales with *Heather and Broom* (162), *Thistle and Thyme* (163), and *Gaelic Ghosts* (161). Harold Courlander has made a distinctive contribution with his collections of folk tales from West Africa, the West Indies, and Asia (122, 130, 131, 152).

Once upon a Totem (190) is an example of the good collections presented by serious scholars. The five stories reveal customs, rituals, and taboos as well as information about homes, clothing, and food. The problem faced by Du'as in the story "The One Horned Mountain Goat" is as difficult as any modern problem. What is the value of old laws and traditions? How can one person stand alone against the feelings of the tribe?

The First Book of Tales of Ancient Egypt (126) gives children stories of Isis and Osiris, mortals and immortals who lived along the Nile.

A collection that includes stories from all countries of the United Nations is *Ride with the Sun* (100); Courlander's style keeps the traditional tone, yet it is very readable. The Middle East is represented with collections by Larson, *Palace in Bagdad* (170), Downing's *Tales of the Hodja* (165), and Ekrem's *Turkish Fairy Tales* (166).

James Reeves' *Three Tall Tales* (114) provides gay nonsense. One story includes:

Last Sunday morning at six o'clock in the evening, as I was sailing over the tops of the mountains in my little boat, I met two men on horseback riding on one mare: so I asked them, Could they tell me whether the little woman was dead yet who was hanged last Saturday week for drowing herself in a shower of feathers?[61]

A collection of unusual stories is Picard's *The Faun and the Woodcutter's Daughter* (111). Unfortunately, the author does not cite the sources for the tales. Each story presents a different theme and often has an unpredictable ending. The title story tells how a girl meets a faun in the forest. When the faun appears at her wedding, she flees with him.

Several collections of American folk tales should be a part of the elementary-school child's literary background. Malcolmson's *Yankee Doodle's Cousins* (206) is full of humor, and McCloskey's illustrations complement the text. In *The Rainbow Book of American Folk Tales and Legends* (205), Leach records lore from each state. Billy the Kid and Jesse James are included among the "Bad Men." The "Strange Tales" tell of ghostly hitchhikers. There are also tales of Indians from North America, Central America, and South America in this interesting volume. Credle's *Tall Tales from the High Hills* (200) are told through the voice of Mr. Huggins. One of these stories is about the "Blizzard of '98." He insisted Ma didn't warn him of the approaching storm, but when her words thaw out and come back to his ears, Mr. Huggins believes her. Middle- and upper-grade children will chuckle delightedly over these whoppers! Chase has recorded stories told to him by Cumberland mountaineers. *The Jack Tales* (198) illustrate American variations of familiar themes. Cothran's group of American stories, *With a Wig, With a Wag* (199), will be of interest to older boys and girls.

Single Tales The number of folk tales published as single books and illustrated as picture books has increased tremendously since Wanda Gág's *Snow White and the Seven Dwarfs* (220) appeared in 1938. Marcia Brown's beautiful picture books, *Stone Soup* (216), *Cinderella* (244), *Dick Whittington and His Cat* (215), *The Three Billy Goats Gruff* (212), and *Puss in Boots* (245) were published in the 1950s. The artist retained the style of the traditional text as she enriched the stories with her pictures. Adrienne Adams has created a delicate, gay, fairy world in her illustrations for *The Shoemaker and the Elves*

---

[61]James Reeves, *Three Tall Tales*. Illustrated by Edward Ardizzone (New York: Abelard-Schuman, 1964), p. 26.

Snow White and Rose Red free a cantankerous dwarf. Adams achieves an effect of brilliance with delicate, clear watercolors. Illustration by Adrienne Adams is reproduced with the permission of Charles Scribner's Sons from *Snow White and Rose Red* by Brothers Grimm, translated by Wayne Andrews. Copyright © 1964 Adrienne Adams.

(227) and *Snow White and Rose Red* (228). The costumes portrayed in *The Shoemaker and the Elves* are authentic for the period in which the Grimms were collecting their tales.

Felix Hoffman has illustrated several single tales, including *The Sleeping Beauty* (247), *Rapunzel* (225), and *The Seven Ravens* (226). The eerie, twisted briars truly encircle the castle where the princess sleeps. Hoffman's Rapunzel is fat and quite ugly, as the text suggests. His humor is evident in the pictures of the seven boys in *The Seven Ravens* who •

are shown at different times emerging into the new form—a figure may be half raven, half boy. In his books, the pictures are carefully planned to flow from one page to the next.

The Mitten (251), a Ukrainian tale retold by Tresselt and illustrated by Yaroslava, exemplifies the picture-book folk tale. When a boy drops his mitten in the forest, the animals decide to make it their home. One by one, a mouse, frog, owl, rabbit, fox, wolf, boar, and a bear snuggle into the mitten. When a black cricket tries to wriggle into the mitten, it pops apart. Young children enjoy the repetition and the suspense of this story told in modern language.

An accumulative counting rhyme, *All in the Morning Early* (242), is also appropriate for younger children. Sandy is joined by one huntsman, two ewes, three gypsies, four farmers, and finally, ten bonny lasses. The children will soon join the chorus:

> *Over the burn and over the hill,*
> *And down the road that leads to the mill,*
> *Where the old mill wheel is never still—*
> *Clicketty—clicketty—clicketty—clack!*
> *All in the morning early.*[62]

The woodcuts by Ness create the humor of the characters. The turquoise, brown, and olive colors give the atmosphere of the Scottish landscape.

Some of the folk tales presented in single volumes are more complex but are richly illustrated and printed in the size of the picture book. However, they are more appropriate for children in the middle grades. *Rakoto and the Drongo Bird* (236) by McKown tells of Madagascar in the days of the slave trade. When slave traders appear, Rakoto courageously warns the people, and the bird tricks the foreigners by imitating a baby's cry

---

[62]Sorche Nic Leodhas, *All in the Morning Early*, Illustrated by Evaline Ness (New York: Holt, Rinehart and Winston, 1963).

A father's curse turns his seven sons into seven ravens. Notice the boots and hats of the boys as the transformation occurs. From *The Seven Ravens* by The Brothers Grimm, with pictures by Felix Hoffmann, © 1962 by H. R. Sauerländer & Co., Aarau. Reproduced by permission of Harcourt, Brace & World, Inc.

so they follow another route. The illustrations convey the jungle atmosphere and the excitement of the story. *Baba Yaga* (249), another, longer story, tells of the Russian witch who lives in a house that stands on chicken legs. Baba Yaga rides in a mortar, steers with a pestle, and sweeps away her traces with a broom. The colorful Russian towers, swooping air currents as the witch rides, and the fiendish Baba Yaga tell much more of the story than does text alone.

Yamaguchi's Japanese story, *The Golden Crane* (255), tells of Toshi, a deaf-and-dumb child who was befriended by an old fisherman. Each day, golden cranes fly over the shore, but one is wounded. Toshi is able to speak as he defends the crane. On the day the bird is to be caged, there is a flash of golden wings and the bird, boy, and old man are borne away. Only the fluttering of the wings is pictured as the birds descend, so the reader can create his own image of the birds. The unstated message of freedom could be introduced in a discussion with middle grade children.

A Jewish folk tale, *The Magic Top* (254), is based on the theme of faith and love. A very poor boy had only three coins to buy candles for Hannukah, but he gave them to beggars who gave him very peculiar blessings. The last beggar presented Avrum with a magic

The crowded mitten has been re-created by a teacher's table display. Constance Pennington, student, University of Maine.

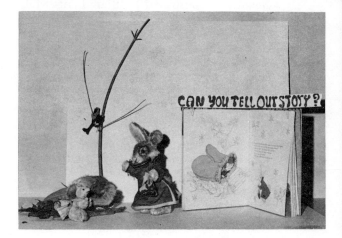

top that transported him to another land. The blessings he had received proved to be the answers needed by a beautiful maiden who had been imprisoned because she refused to marry a sorcerer. With her release, her entire family won freedom. Avrum had proved himself by his simple acts of kindness.

The Fast Sooner Hound (213) is an example of a tall tale recorded by Bontemps and Conroy. Called "Sooner" because he would sooner run than eat, a hound belonging to an itinerant train fireman races ahead of every train because he is not allowed to ride with his master. Burton's illustrations add to the exaggerations of the story. A Japanese tall tale by Stamm, *Three Strong Women* (250), is about a daughter, mother, and grandmother who taught a strong wrestler a thing or two before he went to a wrestling contest at court. For example, it was easy for them to pick up a tree and toss it over a mountain.

An adaptation of "The Pancake" (98) is told by Ruth Sawyer in *Journey Cake, Ho!* (248). McCloskey's illustrations in browns and blues add much to the humor of this tale.

A comparison of a tale presented in two versions helps children become aware of the variations in content, language, and illustration. *The Wave* (231) is a Japanese legend retold by Hodges from Lafcadio Hearn's version and illustrated by Blair Lent, while *The Burning Rice Fields* (217) was told by Sara Cone Bryant. An old man burns his rice, or the rice of all the villagers, in order to draw the people away from the shore village that is engulfed by a tidal wave. Hodges' version brings richer description, for Bryant's is rewritten for primary children to read. However, the reader must infer the reason for burning the fields in the Bryant version, while Hodges' text makes it explicit.

Folk Song Books Folk songs are also part of the folklore of a culture, and artists have presented some fine folk song books for children. John Langstaff's edition of the Southern mountain song, *Frog Went A-Courtin'* (261) is beautifully illustrated by Rojankovsky. Langstaff has also published *The Swapping Boy* (262), illustrated by Beth and Joe Krush. The endpaper quilt design is very appropriate. The humor in the sketches, such as a dog scratching fleas and the flowered hat on the horse in the field, makes this a very enjoyable book. Glen Rounds portrays the surprise and simple-mindedness of *Billy Boy* (259), another Appalachian song. Richard Chase collected the verses, including some less familiar lines such as "Did she set for you a chair? Yes, she set for me a chair but the bottom wasn't there." The sunbonnet hides the face of the "young thing" who cannot leave her mother, but she is indeed a vigorous woman!

Always Room for One More (263) is a Scotch song about a poor man who welcomed all travelers. At last, there wasn't room for one more and all came tumbling out. Optimistically, they rebuild the house for the man, his wife, ten bairns, and *more*. Hogrogian's heathery purples and greens convey the atmosphere in misty beauty, and the people with rugged faces and bowed legs are as individual as Scots can be. Nic Leodhas wrote the text in story form with a repeated refrain. The music is found at the end of the book.

In red and blue, Emberley's stiff soldier figures march across the pages of *Yankee Doodle* (265). Children and teachers will be surprised to learn that the author of the song was a surgeon in the British army. The British sang it to make fun of the revolutionaries, but soon it was the rebels who were singing it to taunt the British.

May Justus adapted a folk song, *Tale of a Pig* (260), and the illustrations by Aloise are hilarious. The details in the room reflect a "pig" culture: portraits of ancestor pigs on the wall and a book shelf with pig figures for book ends. Children will delight in these details as they sing the song.

In times when there is so much pressure upon children, laughter is needed. What better way to release tension than to enjoy these songs? There are many collections of folk songs, such as Seeger's *American Folk Songs for Children* (266) and Ritchie's *Swapping Song Book* (264) with interesting photographs. Teachers and librarians will want to consult with music specialists to select these books.

FABLES

Origin of Fables

Fables are brief, didactic tales in which an animal or inanimate object speaks as a human. In a few fables, as in "The Milkmaid and Her Pail," the characters are human. The story usually encompasses only one incident, and the lesson may be implied or stated directly. In some cases, the same fable has been given different interpretations. For example, in the fable of the fox and the grapes, the fox in most versions pretends his unattainable goal was really not desirable; therefore, the term "sour grapes" is used to express the idea of self-delusion. Other interpretations consider the fox wise to recognize that his goal could not be reached and limitations should be accepted.

Fables are usually associated with the name Aesop, a Greek slave who is said to have lived about 600 B.C. Some scholars doubt his actual existence. Evidence has been found that a Greek, Demetrius Phalereus, recorded about two hundred fables that were later translated into Latin, about A.D. 30, by a slave named Phaedrus. Some fables apparently appeared in Greek literature two centuries before Aesop's birth. Thus, it seems clear that the fables came from many sources. William Caxton translated and printed the first English edition in 1484.

In India, the early Buddhists used beast tales to teach moral lessons. Several of these tales were included in the *Jatakas* that tell of the previous births of the Buddha. The Buddha appears as a crane, a lamb, and other animals. These stories are known to have existed in A.D. fifth century. Later, a guide for princes was composed as a series of animal stories known as the *Panchatantra*. Many of the lessons were told in verse. Another version is titled *The Fables of Bidpai*.

In France, La Fontaine, the poet, wrote his fables in verse form, but he drew largely upon the collections of Aesop's fables that were available in the seventeenth century.

James Reeves, the English writer for children, noted that people like the fables because they are simple, easy to remember, and they are true to humanity since the animals represent different aspects of human nature.

> *The lion stands for kingliness, the ass for obstinate stupidity, the fox for cunning, the sheep for simplicity, the wolf for greed and savagery towards the defenceless. In this way, the various sides of our nature can be seen to be at war with one another; the weak and simple are the victims of the strong and cunning; pride goes before a fall, meddlers often come to harm; patience and skill triumph over life's difficulties. We read Aesop's Fables, not to discover these truths, nor just for the neatness and simplicity of the stories; we read them because, through our pleasure in the stories, we recognize the truths we have always known, but which we delight to meet again in novel form.*[63]

Comparison of a Fable   The fables are stories with few, usually no more than three, characters and single incidents. Differences in the texts of the fable, "The Ass in the Lion's Skin," reveal differences in the interpretation. Richard Scarry's adaptation of La

---

[63]James Reeves, *Fables from Aesop*, Illustrated by Maurice Wilson (New York: Walck, 1962), introduction.

Dramatic woodcuts illustrate such fables as "The Tortoise and the Hare" in Artzybasheff's collection. From *Aesop's Fables* by Boris Artzybasheff. Copyright 1933 by Boris Artzybasheff. All rights reserved. Reprinted by permission of The Viking Press, Inc.

Fontaine's fable portrays a lion-donkey carrying bags of wheat toward a windmill:

> *A donkey dressed himself in a lion's skin and pretended that he was a ferocious lion.*
> *All the townsfolk ran in fear from him.*
> *But Tom, the miller's son, saw an ear sticking out and grabbed the donkey.*
> *Later the townsfolk were astonished to see a lion carrying bags of grain to the mill.*
> One may fool people by appearances, but not for long.[64]

James Reeves has added details and uses modern conversational style in telling this story of how a donkey used a lion's hide to frighten all the animals. The following quotation shows Reeves' interpretation:

> *So Reynard only laughed and ran right up to Donkey; he lifted the corner of Lion's skin and*

saw Donkey's dusty grey hair.
> *"Good day, Your Majesty," said Reynard slyly. "I shouldn't be surprised to see a pair of long ears under that mane of yours. Why, what a donkey you are, to think you could frighten me! Whoever heard a lion bray like that?"*
> *And he ran off to tell all the other animals what a donkey Donkey was, and how silly they had been to be scared of him.*
> If you play a part you are not fitted for, you're sure to give yourself away.[65]

Artzybasheff's collection is illustrated by his fine woodcuts. The text is brief, and he uses the term "application" instead of "moral":

> *An Ass, finding the skin of a Lion, put it on and roamed about frightening all the silly animals he met with. Seeing a Fox, he tried to alarm him also, but the Fox, having heard his voice before said, "Well, to be sure! And I should have been frightened, too; if I had not heard you bray."*
> *Application: They who assume a character that does not belong to them generally betray themselves by overacting it.[66]*

Children might write their version of a fable after comparing various interpretations; in this way they will become more sensitive to style and to possible meanings. Another value of comparison is the study of the art work. The woodcuts of Artzybasheff, watercolors of Wilson for the Reeves collection, and the imaginative paintings of the Provensens offer fine examples of different approaches to illustration.

Single Fables

Brian Wildsmith's glowing colors and geometric patterns distinguish his illustrations for oversize books based on a single

---

[64]Richard Scarry, *The Fables of La Fontaine* (New York: Doubleday, 1963), p. 55.

[65]Reeves, p. 24.
[66]Boris Artzybasheff, *Aesop's Fables* (New York: Viking, 1933), pp. 40–41.

Cartoon figures and the imaginative conversation of animals that are given human qualities extend the meaning of the fables. From *Aesop's Fables* illustrated by Alice and Martin Provensen, copyright © 1965 by Golden Press, Inc.

fable. *The Rich Man and the Shoemaker, The North Wind and the Sun,* and *The Lion and the Rat* portray the characters in interesting designs. Squares, triangles, and trapezoids are repeated in designs of clothing, towns, or houses. The rat in *The Lion and the Rat* fairly bristles. He is painted in greyed blues, greens, and browns with purple eyes and orange ears.

Barbara Cooney's *Chanticleer and the Fox* has a medieval flavor, with delicate flowers and grasses that actually grow in England. This fable with its lesson of the dangers of flattery was part of Chaucer's *Canterbury Tales.*

A Caldecott winner, *Once a Mouse* by Marcia Brown, is a fable from India concerning a hermit who pondered big and little. A mouse was nearly caught by a crow and then a cat. Using magic, the hermit changed the mouse to a cat, and as he was

threatened, to a dog, and then a tiger. When the hermit reprimanded the tiger for being so proud, the tiger decided to kill the hermit. Alas! He was changed back to a mouse. The artist uses shadows effectively. For example, the shape of the hills form the shadow of a beak snatching the mouse; the tiger's shadow is shaped like the dog of his previous existence; the jungle pattern is shaped like a tiger leaning toward the final mouse form.

John Ciardi wrote *John J. Plenty and Fiddler Dan,* an amusing verse based on the fable of an ant and grasshopper. The ant nearly starves because he is afraid to eat his stored food, and even in the winter the grasshopper enjoys singing and romancing.

Modern Fables

Modern writers use old themes to create stories, and they also write fables for today.

In Chapter 3, the examples of picture stories that illustrate the theme of being true to yourself were presented. *Andy and the Lion* by James Daugherty was based upon "Androcles and the Lion," an old story derived from "The Lion and the Mouse." His robust illustrations are humorous, yet tell the story with conviction.

Tico and the Golden Wings by Lionni is a story based on a Hindu fable. Born without wings, Tico is given help by the other birds. Tico's wish for wings, even golden wings, is granted. But now his friends think he is conceited, and Tico is shunned. The bird helps others by giving away his golden wings; in their place, he receives black feathers like those of his friends. Finally, Tico is accepted because they are "all alike," but Tico knows he is different, "for his own memories, and his own invisible golden dreams."[67] Lionni's Indian designs add an authentic flavor, and children gasp with delight when they see the shimmering golden wings.

Children enjoy fables if only one or two are read at a time. Continued moralizing can become dull. Older children may try to create fables after discussing the basic pattern—one or two characters that represent qualities of personality, some action that illustrates the point, and a statement of the moral. As they write, they will learn to use animal characters as symbols for greed, wisdom, vanity, or other qualities. In this way, a deeper understanding of the fable as a form of literature will be reached.

EPIC LITERATURE

Qualities of Epics

The epic form is a long, narrative poem that expresses the moral values of a society through the action of a single hero. Tales of

the heroic, ideal man of the culture were woven into a complete cycle, birth to death of the hero, by the bards and poets. Since the hero may combat the gods or have their help, there is a quality of myth in the songs, sagas, or ballads. The epic will recount the trials, joys, sorrows, successes, and failures of the man who is frequently portrayed as one who fulfills the destiny decreed by the gods. Children today can understand that the epics have come down through the years and illustrate the history of man's thoughts about goals and values of human life. Modern dragons may be the computers with blinking lights and whirring wheels, or napalm bombs instead of scaly animals breathing smoke and flame. The epic heroes show courage, fortitude, patience, and wisdom; yet, they exhibit human weaknesses. Through experiences in meeting these heroes, the child may receive glimpses of the possibilities of common men in an alien, hostile world.

The teacher and librarian will read some of the epics to upper grade classes, and will suggest others to the more mature child who is ready for this part of his literary heritage. The translations used should keep the poetic rhythm, for the epics were sung in measured dignity with rich images and acknowledgement of emotions. In many epic poems, set phrases were repeated. Such tales should not be rewritten in a "thin" style, nor should they omit the dangers, horrors, or man's faults.

Epic Heroes

Greece: *Iliad* and *Odyssey* According to tradition, a blind minstrel named Homer composed the epic poems, the *Iliad* and the *Odyssey*, about 850 B.C., but scholars generally believe that parts of the stories were sung by many persons and that they were woven into one long narrative before they were written. The *Iliad* is an account of the Trojan War fought by the Greeks to recover Helen, the most beautiful woman in the world. Paris,

---

[67]Leo Lionni, *Tico and the Golden Wings* (New York: Pantheon, 1964), unpaged.

son of King Priam of Troy, had taken her away from the Greek king, Menelaus. After a siege of nine years, Agamemnon and Achilles, Greek leaders, quarrel bitterly over the spoils of the war, and Achilles asks his mother, who was related to the gods, to intervene to help him win back honor from Agamemnon. The gods and goddesses have their favorites and also quarrel among themselves. This complex story is difficult to read, although specific incidents intrigue some upper grade boys. The *Odyssey* is an account of the ten-year journey of Odysseus, called Ulysses by the Romans, from Troy to his home in Ithaca after the end of the war. He meets the challenges of the Lotus Eaters, defeats the one-eyed Cyclops, spends a year with Circe who directs him to Hades, makes his way past the Sirens, and steers safely between the whirlpool of Charybdis and the monster, Scylla, and is forced to remain with Calypso for seven years. A loyal servant and his son aid the returned hero in assuming his rightful throne and saving his wife, Penelope. Straightforward accounts of the incidents are given in encyclopedias and in Asimov's chapter, "The Siege of Troy," in *Words from the Myths.* These guides may help children understand the plot and relationships of characters, but they do not convey the dramatic action nor the sense of man meeting his fate as do other translations.

The Iliad and the Odyssey by Watson is enriched by the powerful illustrations of the Provensens. The modern text maintains the flow of action, but it does not recall the stately language of more traditional translations. A pronunciation guide is very helpful. Picard's *The Odyssey of Homer* gives more emphasis to development of characters. De Selincourt's *Odysseus the Wanderer* gives a definite view of Odysseus as a man who loved danger, was too curious, liked to be alone, and really did not want to go home. The slang in this version, for example, "he cared not a rap for Helen" and "here we are, still alive and kicking," seems inappropriate.

The two books written by Church in 1906 and 1907 have been reprinted under the titles, *The Iliad of Homer* and *The Odyssey of Homer.* The style includes such phrases as "Come hither," "You speak truly, fair lady," and "We beseech thee," yet suspense is maintained and the prose depicts events in an appropriate style. Padraic Colum's version, *The Children's Homer,* keeps the essence of the traditional poem, and Pogany's illustrations distinguish this book.

England: *Beowulf* Scholars do not know the origins of the Anglo-Saxon *Beowulf,* but they believe it was sung in the eighth century before the Saxons came to England. The only manuscript known today was written in the tenth century, and is important because it is the oldest epic in English. In *The Golden Treasury of Myths and Legends,* White employs a vocabulary and style that can be understood by most ten-year-olds. Beowulf went from Sweden to help the Danes conquer the fierce monster, Grendel. When Grendel's mother seeks revenge, Beowulf follows her to the bottom of a lake and battles her to death in her lair. After serving as king for fifty years, Beowulf is summoned again to kill a dragon, but this time he loses his life. Many more details are included in E. V. Sandys' account, *Beowulf.*

Serraillier maintains the poetic form in *Beowulf the Warrior.* Note the alliteration in these lines about King Hrothgar's worry:

> . . . *his heart bleak as a ruin*
> *Where the wind makes riot while in the wintry wood*
> *The night-owl cries. . . .*[68]

The meter gives the effect of marching men as Beowulf goes forward:

> . . . *Beside him in shining armour*
> *Strode Beowulf and his warriors. And the wild moor*

---

[68]Ian Serraillier, *Beowulf the Warrior,* Illustrated by Severin (New York: Walck, 1961), p. 18.

Was stunned with their tramping, the hills and the wolf crags
Rang as they marched with the clink of mailed men.[69]

Sutcliff's prose version, *Beowulf*, is another excellent source. The descriptions include details of life of another era and her prose keeps the majestic quality of the epic poem:

Long and gloriously he ruled, holding his people strongly and surely as in the hollow of his great sword hand. Fifty times the wild geese flew south in the autumn, fifty times the birch buds quickened in the spring. . . .[70]

It is true that there is horror in these adventures. Beowulf tears an arm from Grendel; he cuts off the head of the Sea Hag; the death of Beowulf is a brief but painful scene. However, the themes of nobility, virtue, justice, and loyalty to friends are as needed today as at any time.

Ireland: *Cuchulain*   Beowulf is a human who performed heroic deeds; Cuchulain and his companions "have the blood of the Gods and the Fairy Kind (almost the same thing in Irish legend) running fiery in their veins."[71] He earned the name "Hound of Ulster" because he killed a ferocious guard dog with his bare hands when he was a boy. His strength was increased when angered in battle, and a kind of insanity overcame him. Cuchulain loves Emer, daughter of a Druid, but he also turns to other women. Brief references to these affairs of heart are overshadowed by his bravery in battle. When he halted Queen Maeve's drive to conquer all of Ireland, he received her evil wishes. Times became bad, Cuchulain was no longer recognized as a hero, and witchcraft over-

came the brave man, who was fated to die in battle.

Finland: *Vainamoinen*   In the middle of the nineteenth century, a Finnish country doctor named Lönmot collected old songs and poems and created a poem called the *Kalevala*. Vainamoinen, a minstrel and magician, is the hero of the North Country, probably Lapland. Described as "lusty old Vainamoinen," he goes to the North Country and meets the Mistress of that land who wants a magic Sampo and releases him with a warning not to look up. Forgetting the warning, he looks up to find a maid of the rainbow who demands such tasks as splitting a horsehair, peeling a stone, and tying an egg in knots. These loosely connected tales, retold by Deutsch, deal more with romance and nature myths than with battles and heroic action.

Scandinavia: *Sigurd*   The Norsemen of Sweden, Norway, and Denmark were entertained by *skalds*, or professional storytellers. With the advent of Christianity, the tales were discouraged, but the skalds in Iceland continued the tradition. During the twelfth and thirteenth centuries, the Icelandic tales were written and called Eddas; the Older or Poetic Edda had no specific author, but the Younger, or Prose Edda, was written by Sturluson. The prose epic literature was called a saga. The Volsunga Saga was based upon the Elder Edda and tells how Sigurd, one of the Volsungs, killed the dragon Fafnir, married Brynhild after riding through a ring of fire, left for adventure, and married Gudrun while under the influence of a love potion. Forgetting his love of Brynhild, he helps Gudrun's brother, Gunnar, win and marry her. She causes Sigurd to be killed and joins him in death. Sigurd's mighty sword, Gram, and his horse, Grani, help him in his journeys. The gods enter their lives only in that Brynhild was punished by Odin

---

[69]Serraillier, p. 22.

[70]Rosemary Sutcliff, *Beowulf*, Illustrated by Charles Keeping (New York: Dutton, 1962), p. 74.

[71]Rosemary Sutcliff, *The Hound of Ulster*, Illustrated by Victor Ambrus (New York: Dutton, 1963), p. 7.

for keeping a warrior instead of taking him to Valhalla.

Padraic Colum includes the saga of Sigurd in *The Children of Odin,* and it is retold in Hosford's *Sons of the Volsungs.* In *The Sword of Siegfried,* Scherman begins with the ancestry of Sigurd, called Siegfried here, and the story of the golden treasury hoarded by Fafnir the dragon. The format and text make this version easier to read. Coolidge's *Legends of the North* includes the saga of the Volsungs and how Sigurd joined the Nibelungs. The illustrations in this book convey more hatred and horror than seems necessary for the text.

The German epic, *The Nibelungenlied,* was based on the Volsunga Saga. Emphasis in this epic is on the hoard of gold possessed by the Nibelungs and the story of the widow who married Attila. In *The Treasure of Siegfried,* Almedingen makes the political intrigue clear. Wagner based his four operas about the magic ring on the Icelandic Edda.

France: *Roland* The French epic, "Chanson de Roland," dates from the eleventh century and was a combination of many tales about a hero who served Charlemagne. The major part of the poem is concerned with a battle with the Saracens as Charlemagne's troops were returning from wars in Spain. Because of treachery, a part of the force is trapped at a mountain pass. Roland blows his enchanted horn so mightily that Charlemagne, many miles distant, hears it and comes to the rescue. The tremendous effort, however, caused Roland's death.

Roland is included in White's *The Golden Treasury of Myths and Legends. The Story of Roland* is the title given retellings by Baldwin and Sherwood. Clark's version (same title) gives much information about medieval life.

England: *King Arthur* Some historians believe there was a King Arthur who became famous about the sixth century. Defeated by the invading Saxons, his people fled to Wales and Brittany and told stories of his bravery and goodness. Other stories became attached to these, and the exploits of Tristram, Gawain, and Lancelot were added to the "Arthurian cycle." The religious element of the quest of the Holy Grail, the cup used by Christ at the Last Supper, was also added. Whether or not the chalice actually existed, it remains as a symbol of purity and love. In the fifteenth century, Sir Thomas Malory's *Morte d'Arthur* was one of the first books printed in England and became a major source of later versions.

Sidney Lanier's edition of *The Boy's King Arthur* first appeared in 1880 and has remained on the list of classics. It is difficult to read, and boys and girls need much background information to understand these stories. Words such as anon, withal, leech, sieges (seats at the Round Table) need to be explained. Howard Pyle's *The Story of King Arthur and His Knights* is another older, but very fine edition. Picard's *Stories of King Arthur and His Knights* includes the deceit of Guinivere. The style is in the old form. Robinson's version, *King Arthur and His Knights,* written for the Landmark series is easy to read, for it is written in modern style. MacLeod's retelling is also designed for easier reading. The story of Gareth or Fairhands, one of King Arthur's court, is retold by Schiller in *The Kitchen Knight.* Placed in the kitchen, the boy volunteers to help a lady whose sister is besieged. She taunts the lad, but he overcomes the Indigo, Green, and Red Knights. This book may be an introduction to other tales of knighthood.

England: *Robin Hood* It is possible that Robin Hood did live at the beginning of the thirteenth century. It is also possible that this mythical character was derived from festival plays given in France at Whitsuntide. By the fifteenth century, Mayday celebrations in England were called "Robin Hood's Festivals." The old ballads tell how the gay hero lived in Sherwood Forest, outwitted the Sheriff of Nottingham, and shared his stolen goods with the poor. Others in the band were the tall Little John, Friar Tuck, the minstrel Alan-a-Dale, and Robin's sweetheart, Maid Marian. According to one story, Richard the Lionhearted comes in a disguise, hears of their loyalty, and gives them pardon. Other stories tell how Robin was killed by treachery. Robin Hood represents the desire for justice and rights of people under tyranny. Children need to hear these tales read aloud to build understanding of such words as "prithee," "quoth," "forbear," and "blithely." They enjoy the action and relish Robin Hood's tricks on the symbol of authority, the Sheriff of Nottingham.

Howard Pyle's *Some Merry Adventures of Robin Hood* is a shorter version of his classic, *The Merry Adventures of Robin Hood*. Music is included for the ballads in *Songs of Robin Hood*. Virginia Lee Burton's illustrations in this book, edited by Malcolmson and Castagnetta, convey the medieval atmosphere and resemble illuminated manuscripts with elaborate initial letter designs.

Other Epic Heroes   Twelve stories based on the Kiev cycle sung for nearly 1000 years were collected by Almedingen in *The Knights of the Golden Table*. Vladema was a cruel ruler who became a Christian. Anyone, even a peasant, could become one of his knights by deeds of bravery. Each chapter tells of the deeds of a knight who received special power: Ilya received a magic cudgel; Dobryna, a magic handkerchief; Aliosha's beautiful harp music overpowered his foes; Samson's cross overcame an evil doll.

Gaer relates *The Adventures of Rama*, an epic of India. He killed giants and demons and won Sita, his wife, because he was able to bend the great bow of Siva. Mukerji's version, *Rama, the Hero of India*, tells how Hindus memorize these stories. Surely Western children should know this hero who was the god Vishnu born as a man. Monkeys figure prominently in these stories of man's acceptance of his destiny.

Havelock the Dane by Crossley Holland is based upon a thirteen century narrative romance. In England, Goldborough, daughter of the dead king, is imprisoned. Across the sea in Denmark, Havelock's father dies when the boy is ten. Unfortunately, each regent is hungry for power. Ordered to drown Havelock, a fisherman named Grim decides to flee the country with the prince, and he settles on the English coast. Havelock is chosen to marry Goldborough. With great physical strength, courage, and cleverness they regain their kingdoms. Accustomed to the brilliant colors of Wildsmith's illustrations, the reader is pleasantly surprised to find his pen-and-ink sketches introducing each chapter.

MYTHS AND MYTHIC HEROES

Studying Myths

Because so much literature and art have been derived from Greek mythology, it is wise to introduce children to many of these myths; however, a "world view" demands that we include myths of people in non-Western cultures. Myths may be a part of the study of a culture, African, Indian, Japanese, or Eskimo, or they may be studied as literature. Both kinds of experiences should be included in the elementary curriculum.

Children can learn about the nature of myth—that it evolved as primitive man searched his imagination and related events to forces as he sought explanation of the earth, sky, and human behavior. These explanations moved slowly through the stages of a concept of one power or force in human form who controlled the phenomena of nature; to a complex system in which the god or goddess represented such virtues as wisdom, purity, or love; to a worshipping of the gods in organized fashion. Gods took the form of man, but they were immortal and possessed supernatural powers.

Myths deal with men's relationships with their gods, with the relationship of the gods among themselves, with the way men accept or fulfill their destiny, and with the struggle of man between good and evil forces both within and without himself. The myths are good stories, too, for they contain action, suspense, and basic conflicts. Usually, each story is short and can be enjoyed by itself, without deep knowledge of the mythology.

Types of Myths

Nature Myths   The nature myths include the stories of creation and the explanations of seasonal changes, animal characteristics, earth formation, constellations, and movements of the sun and earth. Indian nature myths are appropriate for children in the primary grades. Belting's collection, *The Long-Tailed Bear,* is a good source for such stories as "How the Birds Came to Have Many Colors," "How Duck Got His Bill," and "How Frogs Lost Their Tails." In most of the stories, the stronger, or more clever, beast causes the change and no god interferes. In *Tales the Muses Told,* Green organizes myths according to tales of flowers, trees, stars, birds and beasts, and great lovers and true friends. The familiar stories of Narcissus and Echo, and Baucis and Philemon, are in this collection as well as the less familiar "The Two Bears," that tells how the constellations of the Great Bear and Little Bear were put into the sky. The story of Baucis and Philemon illustrates the virtues of kindness to strangers, but it may be difficult for children to understand why the couple wanted to die at the same moment.

"Demeter and Persephone" explains the change of seasons. Hades, god of the underworld, carried Persephone off to his land to be his bride, and Demeter, her mother, who made plants grow, mourned for her daughter. When she learned of Persephone's fate, she asked Zeus to intercede, and it was granted that the girl might return if she had eaten nothing in Hades. Since she had eaten of a Pomegranate, she was compelled to return for four months each year.

A good source for creation myths is the book by Fahs and Spoerl, *Beginnings: Earth Sky Life Death.* The creation of man by Coyote as told by the Miwok Indians of California could be compared with the idea of the Wintu of northern California that people were created first, and then they were changed into animals, trees, and flowers. Curry tells another California Indian tale of Coyote's part in making the mountain ranges. Her book, *Down from the Lonely Mountain* (189), includes stories of the theft of fire and dawn. According to a Hawaiian myth related by Thompson, Kane, God of creation, tossed a calabash into the air to make sky. Pieces broke off to become sun, moon, and stars. Other gods made animals and plants. Kane made man and later made a woman from man's shadow. The African bush myth, "Aziza" (125), tells how the god came down from the moon and fashioned animals. In Norse mythology, a giant, Ymir, emerged from fire and mist. As the cow, Audhumbla, fed the giant, she licked salt from the icy stone and shaped a god who was the grandfather of Odin. Ymir's sons were the frost giants who were enemies of the gods. Odin created man from an ash tree and made woman of an alder.

Mythic Heroes   Many myths tell of heroes, but they differ from the epic in form and usually do not relate the entire life of the hero. One hero was Jason, a handsome, young Greek who was challenged to recover the Golden Fleece in order to regain his title as King. Jason asked brave young men to

Stobbs' woodcut shows the terrible features of the minotaur who faced Theseus at Crete. Illustration by William Stobbs from *The Way of Danger.* © Ian Serraillier 1962. By permission of Henry Z. Walck, Inc. and Oxford University Press.

accompany him on the ship *Argo,* from which they derived the name "Argonauts." Jason slays the dragon and obtains the fleece, an object of worship. Medea, a beautiful but evil woman, assists him, and they marry. The story ends in sadness, for the fleece turns black, and both Jason and Medea create evil. Kingsley pointed the moral: "it stands forever as a warning to us, not to seek for help from evil persons, or to gain good ends by evil means. For if we use an adder even against our enemies, it will turn again and sting us."[72] To realize the importance of language, compare the terse, modernized version of *The Golden Fleece* by Gunther with the rich language and rhythmic style of the version by Kingsley.

Perseus is another Greek hero that upper grade children should meet. The birth and life of Perseus follows the pattern of many heroes. Foretold that his grandson would kill

him, Acrisius imprisoned his daughter, but Zeus came to her, and a child was born. Acrisius put mother and child in a wooden chest and pushed it into the sea. They are found by a fisherman who accepts the child as his son. Perseus rashly promises to bring the king the head of a terrible gorgon, Medusa. Her hair is made of snakes, and anyone who looks at her turns to stone. With Athena's help, and his own courage and strength, he slays the monster. An accidental misthrow of the discus does cause the death of his grandfather. Both the stories in Kingley's *The Heroes* and Serraillier's *The Gorgon's Head* are told with vigor. Serraillier's well-written edition is available in paperback. This British author-poet has also written *The Way of Danger, The Story of Theseus.* Theseus slays the bull at Marathon, the Minotaur in the labyrinth at Crete, and returns from a terrible journey to the underworld. Theseus ends life in sadness and is murdered, but his bravery endured. *Greek Gods and Heroes* by Graves is a collection of myths about the heroes. The author writes in a news report style that seems to omit the sense of conflict within each person.

Maui is a Polynesian hero who was a human with supernatural power. Because he was deformed when he was born, his mother cast him into Moana, the ocean. After he was cared for by the god of the sky, he returned to earth. Maui changes himself into a dove and seeks his parents in another world. To help the people get their work done, Maui snared the sun and exacted its promise to cross the sky more slowly. New Zealand was created from a giant fish caught by Maui, but it is mountainous because his brothers did not wait for him to give thanks to the gods. Stories of Maui are found in books by Hill, Colum, and Thompson.

Backbone of the King, The Story of Pakáa and His Son Ku is Marcia Brown's dramatic retelling of a legend of Hawaii. Another hero whose father deserts him, Pakáa shows great intelligence in making a sail that enables him

---

[72]Charles Kingsley, *The Heroes,* Illustrated by Vera Bock (New York: Macmillan, 1954), p. 43.

to defeat the men in a race to shore. This feat proves he is ready to search for his father, the chief guardian, or backbone of the king. Given a magic calabash and the mantle and loincloth of his father, he sets forth and wins recognition as son of the king's guardian. When his father dies. Pakáa takes his place, but enemies cause trouble, and he must leave. Eventually, the king searches for him, but Pakáa now has trained his son Ku so he can meet the king. Ku carries out his father's wishes and takes revenge upon his enemies. As Ku returns to tell his father that the king wants him again, the boy ponders the relationships of king and servant, for he now realizes a king can be weak and suffer the hungers and tears of men. "Might it not even be easier to love a man-king who falters than a god-king who cannot? Might there not be a better way to settle a wrong than to give weeping to a man's family?"[73] The many Hawaiian words and difficult chants suggest this is a book to read aloud. An authentic quality is given the legends by inclusion of these chants.

A legend of Hungary is the basis of Seredy's beautiful story, *The White Stag*. Hadur, god of the tribe, spoke and led the people toward the promised land through two sons of Nimrod, Hunor and Magyar. In a time of trouble they call out, "'Where is Hadur? Why does he let hatred between brothers poison our souls?'" The doubt of the next leader, Bendeguz, expressed the lack of faith of many men, and he vows that his son, Attila, will become the Scourge of God. The Huns carry out this scourge — led by Attila "who from the moment of his tragic birth had been deprived of love, tenderness, and comfort, grew hard as steel in body and soul."[74] After years of battle, Attila and his father reach a low point of despair, and Bendeguz says, "Pray, but do not challenge!"

Linoleum block prints in gray-green reflect the legendary strength of these ancient Hawaiians. Reproduced with the permission of Charles Scribner's Sons from *Backbone of the King*, page 35, by Marcia Brown. Copyright © 1966 Marcia Brown.

The older man finally comes to believe and to trust Hadur, their god. At that moment, the White Stag appears to the people and leads them through the mountains to a beautiful valley. As he stoops to comfort a child, Attila finds a sword embedded in the soil and discovers it was the sword of Hadur. This story of people who always wanted a sign to maintain their faith speaks to man today.

Gods Punish Men In several of the myths, the gods punish men. One of the best known examples is the story of King Midas or *The Golden Touch*. Nathaniel Hawthorne's version in *The Wonder Book* probably is read most frequently, but the style is indeed inappropriate, for he talks down to the readers. For example, the narrator interrupts the flow of the story to say, "And truly, my dear little folks, did you ever hear of such a pitiable use in all your lives?"[75] Sewell's selection

---

[73]Marcia Brown, *Backbone of the King* (New York: Scribner, 1966), p. 147.

[74]Kate Seredy, *The White Stag* (New York: Viking, 1937), p. 75.

[75]Nathaniel Hawthorne, *The Golden Touch*, Illustrated by Paul Galdone (New York: Whittlesey, 1959), p. 44.

from Bulfinch gives the more accurate version, for it is the god, Bacchus, who granted his wish for gold. Then Midas became a worshipper of Pan and supported his claim that Pan's music was greater than that of Apollo. In anger, Apollo gave Midas ears in the shape of a donkey's ears. The story continues with the way the barber of Midas whispered the secret into a hole, but the reeds overheard, and to this day whisper, "Midas has ass's ears." In this version the greed of Midas was not as great a sin as his continual defiance of the gods.

Daedalus was a great architect who constructed the labyrinth for King Minos of Crete, but he fell into disfavor and was imprisoned. Daedalus fashioned wings so he and his son, Icarus, could fly from the island. Icarus made the mistake of trying to approach the home of the gods in the sky, and the sun melted his wings, so he was plunged to his death. Punishment was given for trying to be like the gods.

Relationships among the Gods Many of the myths are concerned with conflicts and loves of the gods. Jealousy and the struggle for power often cause trouble for the humans. The loves and quarrels of the immortals, however, are generally inappropriate for children.

The Greek mythology includes the creation story that Earth and Sky were the first gods. Their children were giant Cyclops and the Titans, one of whom was Cronus who drove his father away with a scythe (thus, the picture of father time). Cronus swallowed each of his children so they would not usurp his place, but his wife gave him a stone instead of her last child, Zeus. Of course, Zeus overthrew his father and made him disgorge his brothers and sisters, who were still alive. Zeus married Hera, a very jealous woman, who caused a great deal of trouble. Prometheus was a Titan who defied the other gods to give man fire. Zeus then chained him to

Mount Caucasus where an eagle devoured his liver each day, for it was renewed at night. Zeus also sent Pandora, with her box of trouble, as a punishment for Prometheus and man. However, another story is that Pandora was sent in good faith to bless man, but she opened the box, and all the blessings, except hope, escaped.

The Norse myths are mainly stories of relationships among the gods. Derived from the Poetic and Prose Eddas already mentioned, these myths tell of the gods in Asgard, which can be reached by crossing a rainbow bridge. Valhalla is the great hall of Odin where the Valkyrie bring the fallen heroes. The Aurora Borealis was seen as the light coming from the armor of the maidens. Thor, the thunderer, used his magic hammer, a belt of strength, and iron gloves to perform many heroic deeds against the giants. Loki was a mischief maker among these gods, and it was Baldur, god of light, who was most loved. Frigga, his mother, neglected to get a promise from the mistletoe when she made all other creatures and objects promise they would never harm Baldur. Loki learns of this weakness and causes Baldur's death. The best collection of these myths remains *The Children of Odin* by Colum. It was reissued in a modern format in 1962. Hosford's *Thunder of the Gods* is easier to read and maintains a style in keeping with the serious themes of struggle.

Children should not be required to learn all the names of the gods and goddesses, nor their family relationships. In addition to the stories cited above, they should have the opportunity to enjoy such myths as the story of true friends, Damon and Pythias, and stories that explain the constellations such as Bellerophon and Pegasus. It is especially important that they become familiar with myths from many cultures. Discussion of similarities and differences would focus upon ways men have considered the human condition.

The figures on the endpapers of *The Iliad and the Odyssey* seem to have emerged from Greek vases. From *The Iliad and the Odyssey* illustrated by Alice and Martin Provensen. Copyright © 1956 by Golden Press, Inc.

Books of Myths

Several fine books of myths have been discussed as the stories were presented. Probably, the most complete collection of myths is that of Thomas Bulfinch who selected myths to help readers understand literature. His *Age of Fables* was first published in 1855 and is currently available in paperback. This is an excellent resource for teachers and advanced readers.

Hawthorne's treatment of the myths in *A Wonder Book and Tanglewood Tales* has been questioned by several authorities. Cousin Eustace is a priggish young man who relates the stories to "good little people" in a rather sentimental, sugary style typical of the last half of the nineteenth century. A more serious criticism is the way he adapted the sto-

ries, often changing the gods to children and actually changing the meaning. The use of conversation in the stories does add interest, and Hawthorne's tales are often used in school readers. These are recommended only as works for comparison with other versions.

Helen Sewell illustrated a Bulfinch collection, *A Book of Myths*, in 1942. Her pictures resemble Greek sculpture and are beautifully composed. This book gives an excellent, readable background of mythology. The style and vocabulary are difficult in these books, for example, "to insure a meeting, repair to a well-known edifice standing without the city's bounds. . . ."

Alexander's collection, *Famous Myths of the Golden Age* includes the "Wanderings of Ulysses." The color in the stylized illustrations by Florian is pleasing. Kingsley included only tales of such heroes as Perseus and Theseus in *The Heroes, Greek Fairy Tales.* In the drawings, the lines, which are probably intended as symbols, seem to create confusion. Neither of these books includes a pronunciation guide, which is essential for use by children.

Sellew's *Adventures with the Gods* is written in simple, interesting style and includes a pronunciation guide. Elgin wrote *The First Book of Mythology* in a modern style, presenting a selection of myths appropriate for children. It has an excellent guide to pronunciation, using a phonetic form as Persephone — per-SEF-o-nee. The reds and blues combined with bold, black figures form dramatic illustrations for this good introduction to mythology. In *Stories of the Gods and Heroes,* Benson has kept the flavor of the older storyteller, but has presented the tales in very readable style. Conversation is used wisely to create interest. The pronunciation of a word or name follows immediately in the text. The language is realistic, but not gory. In *The Adventures of Ulysses,* Gottlieb uses sensational language.

The Provensens' illustrations are outstanding features of two Golden Books, *The Golden Treasury of Myths and Legends* by White and *The Iliad and the Odyssey* by Watson. The design is outstanding, and colors create the mood. A mask-like quality of the faces painted in charcoal, grey, or brown is in keeping with the myths. There is no pronunciation guide, but the style is readable.

Words from the Myths by Asimov is a fascinating book, for the author illustrates the use of names and meanings from Greek mythology in modern life. For example, he tells that the gods saw to it that Nemesis, goddess of retribution, made sure that a person had equal amounts of good fortune and bad fortune. "Since most of the Greek myths involve matters evened out by bad fortune, rather than by good fortune, 'nemesis' has come to mean, in our language, an

unavoidable doom."[76] Asimov's explanations of science terms related to mythology are especially good.

The d'Aulaires' organization of their *Book of Greek Myths* according to stories about Zeus and his family, minor gods and nymphs, and mortal descendants of Zeus helps children clarify relationships of the mythical beings. The full page lithographs convey the sense of power of the gods. The text is written in modern language, but it is not colloquial. Whereas Sewell uses no dialogue, the d'Aulaires include conversation that makes the book more interesting.

Several paperback books now make myths available at low cost. One of these, *The Greek Gods,* by Evslin, and others, gives the accounts of the Pantheon, Zeus and his family, and nature myths. A helpful list of word origins is included. The pace of the text will appeal to today's child, yet some of the sentences create a jarring note. For example, in the story of Phaethon, the son of Apollo, who brought destruction by his disobedience, the underlined phrases seem out of place in mythical literature:

> *Sometimes I visit my father . . . he teaches me and gives me presents. Know what he gave me last time? . . .*
> *Bring him here in comfort. Round up some of your companions. . . .*
> *Yes, of course. Must get over that way and visit them all one of these seasons.*[77]

THE BIBLE AS LITERATURE

Planning for Study

A literature curriculum designed to acquaint children with their literary heritage and develop understandings and skills that

[76]Isaac Asimov, *Words from the Myths,* Illustrated by William Barss (Boston: Houghton Mifflin, 1961), p. 126.
[77]Bernard Evslin, Dorothy Evslin, and Ned Hoopes, *The Greek Gods,* Illustrated by William Hunter (New York: Scholastic, 1966), pp. 66, 68, 70.

will enable them to make continued progress in appreciating fine literature must include study of the Bible. Other literature cannot be fully understood unless children are familiar with the outstanding characters, incidents, poems, proverbs, and parables of this literature of the Western world of thought. It is time we clarified the difference between the practice of religious customs and indoctrination of one viewpoint, and the study of the Bible as a great work of literature. In 1963, the Supreme Court asserted that "religious exercises" violated the First Amendment, but the Court also encouraged study:

> In addition, it might well be said that one's education is not complete without a study of comparative religion or the history of religion and its relationship to the advancement of Civilization. It certainly may be said that the Bible is worthy of study for its literary and historic qualities.
>
> Nothing we have said here indicates such a study of the Bible or of religion, when presnted objectively, as part of a secular program of education may not be effected consistent with the First Amendment. . . .[78] The problem

that may arise is suggested by the phrase "when presented objectively." Some critics may feel that such study will undermine faith in the Bible as an infallible revelation from God to man. The reporter who interviewed church leaders and educators in schools where programs of study of the Bible as literature were underway summarized the difficulty:

> In a pluralistic society with divergent views about the Bible, "it will be very hard to teach the way the Supreme Court has asked," Rabbi Gilbert says.
>
> "We will have to give up some romanticized notions about why we are teaching this material," he stresses. "Religious people will have to say, 'Yes, in a secular public school system

> you can teach the Bible as literature but not as the word of God.'
>
> "There may be some danger in this, but we have to be willing to take the risk in order to have a better informed and more literate citizenry. If we are not prepared to say this, then we can't give the Bible over to the public school to teach."[79]

The literary scholar, Northrop Frye, believes it essential to teach the Bible, for it presents man in all his history. "It's the *myth* of the Bible that should be the basis of literary training, its imaginative survey of the human situation which is so broad and comprehensive that everything else finds its place inside it."[80] Some critics would be disturbed by use of the term *myth,* for they would not understand myth as defined in its larger sense, as man's search for and expression of his truth and meanings.

The school staff would need to consider the purposes of such study, approaches to use, and materials. First of all, the teacher or librarian must be well prepared to teach literature. Emphasis should not be on details of incident or setting; the major concern is man's response to his world, his questions about it, and his dilemmas in facing the problems of living with himself and others (see Chapter 13).

Books for Study of the Bible

Stories from the Bible   When a school staff agrees that children should read or hear stories from the Bible, it faces the task of selecting materials. As with other ancient works, there have been many translations of the Bible. Lampe and Daniell present an excellent summary of the difficulties and dangers encountered by men who translated the Bible into English, *Discovering the Bible.* It includes fictionalized accounts of the writing

[78]Quoted by Betty D. Mayo, "The Bible in the Classroom," *The Christian Science Monitor* (September 30, 1966), p. 9.

[79]Mayo.

[80]Northrop Frye, *The Educated Imagination* (Bloomington, Ind.: Indiana University Press, 1964), p. 111.

A taut figure of the young Moses strains toward the voice of God. The sandals are placed symbolically in the foreground. From *The Old Testament* by Marguerite de Angeli. Copyright © 1959, 1960, 1966 by Marguerite de Angeli. Reprinted by permission of Doubleday & Company, Inc.

of the gospels and stories of the men who made English translations. The second part of the book describes the content of the Bible and the different versions. The same text is presented from Tyndale's version (1525), the King James version (1611), the Revised Standard Version (1946), and the New English Bible (1961).

Walter de la Mare's introduction to *Stories from the Bible* provides an excellent background for understanding the problems of translation. He compares versions of the story of Ruth in the Geneva Bible (1560), the Douai Bible (1609), and the Authorized Version (1611). The old form of spelling is used in his quotations from Wycliffe of 1382, John Purvey of 1386, and Miles Coverdale of 1536. He clearly explains the differences between literal, allegorical, moral, and analogical meanings given words and phrases. This book presents the Creation, the flood, and stories of Moses, Joseph, Samson, Samuel, Saul, and David. The text combines

modern style with imagery in description and a Biblical form in conversation. For example, "As Joseph grew older, and in all that he was and did showed himself more and more unlike themselves, jealousy gnawed in their hearts like the fretting of a cankerworm."[81] When Joseph tells his brothers his dream, the author uses the archaic form:

> *"Meaning, forsooth!" they said. 'Who art thou that we should bow ourselves down before thee, and that thou shouldst have dominion over us? The place for thee is with the women and sucklings in the tents." And they hated him the more.*[82]

Nancy Barnhart's sketches of scenes in Egypt and Israel contribute a feeling for the setting and an awareness of the people. Titled *The Lord Is My Shepherd*, her selections include Elijah, Elisha, Jonah, Nehemiah, and Isaiah as well as the creation, flood, and stories of Moses, Joseph, and Solomon. Parts of the New Testament are also included with text references to the King James Bible. The language is stately and has the rhythm of the King James version; yet, it is easy to read.

The Old Testament was arranged in an interesting and helpful way by Marguerite de Angeli. Noting that "it is a library of thirty-nine books, written in the course of a thousand years or more," Samuel Terrien introduces this edition. It is organized in the sequence of the Hebrew Bible. From the creation to the birth of Israel to the prophets, the exile, restoration and Greek rule, a sense of continuity is achieved. Psalms are added in each section. The soft, watercolor illustrations are superb, and the pencil character studies are especially fine. The text is similar to the King James version.

Glowing color in Rojankovsky's illustrations for *The Golden Bible*, arranged by Wer-

---

[81]Walter de la Mare, *Stories from the Bible*, Illustrated by Edward Ardizzone (New York: Knopf, 1961), p. 62.
[82]de la Mare, p. 63.

ner, gives quite a different tone. Illuminated initial letters and many small pictures on a page sometimes make the book appear cluttered, but there are many well-designed, full-page, exciting pictures. Parts of the Bible are summarized in italic type, and the story continues in modern language. Psalms 23, 24, 100, and 121 are included.

The Rainbow Book of Bible Stories by Gwynne is more nearly a complete Old and New Testament. Written in today's language patterns, this book is beautifully illustrated by Steele Savage. *The First Seven Days* is a picture book by Paul Galdone telling the story of creation in rich color. Several of the double-page spreads appear to be overcrowded. The text is slow and dignified, in keeping with the story.

Heroes of the Bible   Individual picture book stories of heroes of the Old Testament are especially useful for teaching literature in the school. Wynants has created fascinating collage and textured illustrations for *Noah's Ark*. Color spreads alternate with black and white, but all use varied shapes of textured material overlaid to form the figure or design. An unusual picture shows life inside the ark with a mother holding a baby and a child teasing a cat with a ball of yarn. The pictures will interest all ages, but the simplified text is more appropriate for younger children.

Another handsome book is Galdone's *Shadrach, Meshach and Abednego*. Nebuchadnezzar's golden image is pictured as a huge creature, and the figures of the characters are powerful. Although the story is simplified, the author retains the rhythm of the chant and uses repetition effectively. The three loyal, courageous boys are portrayed as quietly determined in their faith.

In *A Basket in the Reeds* by Saporta, the illustrations are patterned after Egyptian wall paintings. Moses is given a family, with names for his father, mother, and sister. In

Wynants' collage of texture and brilliant colors create a stylized figure of Noah and the dove. Copyright © 1965 by Miche Wynants. Reproduced from his volume, *Noah's Ark*, by permission of Harcourt, Brace & World, Inc.

this book, incidents are invented to create interest. For example, they hide the baby in different places, and the children play tricks on the soldiers. The text includes a poetic description of the river as the basket floats in the reeds. Children should be made aware of the way this author used his imagination to extend the brief account in the Bible. This picture book could be used with very young children, but by age eight, they would be ready for the complete life of Moses.

David and Goliath by De Regniers is a very good retelling of the story of the youngest son going forth to meet the monster. The folk-tale pattern is used; for example, David passes the tests before his father consents to his journey. The longer part of his life is concluded briefly, noting he fought battles, married the king's daughter, and took Saul's place as king. Two Psalms are skillfully added within the text. Brilliant oranges and pinks contrast with blue and green tones in the illustrations by Powers. This artist uses space very effectively to create distance and a sense of power. This would be an excellent book for children in grades two to five.

The picture stories of Bible heroes by the Petershams reflect the Old World atmosphere. Although the characters are robed, the strength of muscles is revealed through transparent material. Costumes and artifacts are authentically presented. In addition to the excellent art, the texts keep the syntax and movement of the traditional language, yet are quite easy to read. *Moses, David, Ruth, Joseph,* and *Jesus* are books by this talented team. In *The Shepherd's Psalm,* Maud Petersham gives information about the life of the shepherd as it relates to each part of the 23d Psalm.

Continuing her "Adventures" series, Sellew published *Adventures with Abraham's Children.* The titles give a clue to the theme she presents: Jacob, a Clever Adventurer; Joshua, a Great General; Saul, a Disobedient King; David, a Beloved King; Rehoboam, a Foolish King. A vigorous text, dialogue without archaic forms, and descriptive detail make these stories interesting and appropriate for children in the middle grades.

Proverbs and Psalms   A tiny, delicately illustrated book by Joan Walsh Anglund, *A Book of Good Tidings,* brings children selected Bible verses. "By their fruits ye shall know them" is illustrated by a scene in which children harvest apples. The burial of a bird illustrates "God is our refuge and strength."

Tony Palazzo's sensitive interpretations of *The Lord Is My Shepherd* and *A Time for All Things* make these sections of the Bible meaningful for children. Animals and birds in their natural behavior illustrate the words.

A colt lies in a green pasture; as a gay rooster crows, his soul is restored; a squirrel finds a table prepared; a polar bear licks her cub, anointing it with love; and a dove promises hope. To illustrate "a time to break down, and a time to build up," he shows a beaver at work. A puppy at any empty swing experiences "a time to mourn." The wise use of space contributes to the sense of calm and dignity in each book.

Related Literature   *Animals of the Bible,* a picture book by Dorothy Lathrop, has won recognition as the first Caldecott book. However, the text selected from the King James Bible by Helen Fish should also be considered for its literary value. The creation, flood, and serpent are presented, as well as selections titled "Abraham's Ram," "Isaac's Camels at Rebekah's Well," and "The Ravens Who Fed Elijah." The selections from Job would be difficult for most children in elementary school.

A Hebrew legend, *The Carpet of Solomon,* by Ish-Kishor, tells how Solomon dared to compare himself with God. Solomon recognizes that the carpet was made by the Devil, but his desire for power overwhelms him. As he flies, he says he is now like God himself, and he starts to fall. Finally, he realizes he has encountered a force stronger than his, but he cannot recall the Almighty name. When a third eagle appears and says he must brush off a "speck of dust" from his castle window sill, Solomon cries out "I am a man—a living man!" At that moment he is taken into the castle. He is given visions of his false judgments. In a vision, he sees an untrustworthy servant try to kill his son, and he cries the word he had forgotten, "O God!" Although this legend is not from the Old Testament, it is necessary to read the story of Solomon in order to understand the legend.

In *Words in Genesis,* Asimov gives information about the translations of the Bible and shows how modern words have been derived from words in the Old Testament. He points out that "Although the Bible includes, among other things, a history of all mankind's existence, it is particularly interested in those parts of history where man's relationship to God is at a crisis."[83] Use of

[83]Isaac Asimov, *Words in Genesis,* Illustrated by William Barss (Boston: Houghton Mifflin, 1962), p. 73.

books about the Bible and literary study should lead the student to independent reading of the Bible in the version accepted by the child's family.

Children who have rich experiences with traditional literature in a balanced curriculum are given the keys to pleasure in their cultural heritage and to understanding of man and all his literature.

SUGGESTED ACTIVITIES

1. Compare several folk tales from one country. Note the theme, motifs, characters, and style.
2. Compare several folk tales from different countries that are based upon similar themes. Note the differences in introduction, characters, incidents, and conclusion.
3. Try to identify local, community, or campus legends.
4. Prepare a transparency for the overhead projector to show the relationships among the gods and goddesses of the Greeks, Romans, or Norse.
5. Write a modern fable using present-day objects, animals, or people.
6. Read folk tales or myths of Indians who lived in your region. Identify motifs of these tales.
7. Compare several collections of folk tales, fables, or myths. Note the differences in content, information given by the editor, style of writing, and illustration.
8. Tell a cumulative tale, endless story, romance, fable, or myth to children or peers.
9. Compare variants of one tale, for example, the different versions of "Little Red Riding Hood," "The Three Bears," "Rumpelstiltskin," and "The Firebird."
10. Make a list of titles or literary allusions, of any literature, that were derived from myth or scriptural writings.

RELATED READINGS

1. Arbuthnot, May Hill. *Children and Books.* Third edition. Glenview, Ill.: Scott, Foresman, 1964.
   Chapter 10 gives folk tale sources according to countries. Theories of folk-tale origins are discussed. Chapter 11 includes examples of fables, myths, and epics.
2. ————*Time for Fairy Tales Old and New.* Illustrated by John Averill, and others. Glenview Ill.: Scott, Foresman, 1952.
   An excellent collection of folk tales, fables, and myths, legends, and modern fairy tales. The introductions provide background information concerning origins.
3. Brean, Herbert, and editors of *Life. The Life Treasury of American Folklore.* Illustrated by James Lewicki. New York: Time, 1961.
   Picture maps would be of interest to children. Includes lesser-known American heroes and such unsavory characters as Jesse James.
4. Bulfinch, Thomas. *The Age of Fable or Beauties of Mythology.* New York: New American Library, 1962.
   This classical survey of mythology is presented in paperback. Notes and references are very helpful.
5. Chase, Richard. *Quest for Myth.* Baton Rouge, La.: Louisiana State University Press, 1949.
   An historical account of many theories of myth.

6. Colum, Padraic. *Myths of the World.* Illustrated by Boris Artzybasheff. New York: Grosset & Dunlap, 1930.
Creation myths and myths of Egypt are included as well as Greek and Norse mythology.

7. Frye, Northrop. *The Educated Imagination.* Bloomington, Ind.: Indiana University Press, 1964.
A literary critic develops a theory of literature and presents a plan for literary study in the school that includes intensive study of the Bible and other traditional literature.

8. Hamilton, Edith. *Mythology.* Illustrated by Steele Savage. Boston: Little, Brown, 1944.
The introduction summarizes the emergence of Greek ideas. Genealogical tables are helpful. A very readable source presenting Creation, Stories of Love and Adventure, and Heroes of the Trojan War.

9. Hollowell, Lillian. *A Book of Children's Literature.* Third edition. New York: Holt, Rinehart and Winston, 1966.
This anthology provides a sampling of folk tales, fables, myths, and legends.

10. McKendry, John J. *Aesop: Five Centuries of Illustrated Fables.* New York: Metropolitan Museum of Art, 1964.
An excellent introduction gives information about the origins of fables. Illustrations give a history of printing with examples of work from Bewick to Calder.

11. Miller, James E., Editor. *Myth and Method, Modern Theories of Fiction.* Lincoln, Neb.: University of Nebraska Press, 1960.
A series of essays for the advanced student. Frye's discussion of archetype is especially helpful.

12. Ohrman, Richard, Editor. *The Making of Myth.* New York: Putnam, 1962.
Viewpoints of the anthropologist, psychologist, and folklorist are presented. Bruner's essay, "Myth and Identity" discusses myth-making today.

13. Smith, Lillian. *The Unreluctant Years.* Chicago: American Library Association, 1953.
The teacher will find the analysis of introductions, plot, and conclusions of folk tales in Chapter 4, "The Art of the Fairy Tale," a valuable guide to studying the tales.

14. Thompson, Stith. *The Folktale.* New York: Holt, Rinehart and Winston, 1951.
Various theories of the origins of folk tales and folk-tale themes are thoroughly presented in this book.

15. Webber, F. E. "Children Glory in the Gory," *Progressive Education,* vol. 32 (March 1955), p. 48.
The author holds the view that children should not be protected from the evil or the gory in folk tale literature.

16. Whitman, R. S. "Folksongs for Elementary School Children," *Elementary English,* vol. 40 (November 1963), pp. 724–728.
The values of folksongs in literary study are presented. Bibliographies of books for teachers, children, and recordings are included.

CHAPTER REFERENCES

Bible

1. Anglund, Joan Walsh. *A Book of Good Tidings.* New York: Harcourt, 1965.

2. Asimov, Isaac. *Words in Genesis.* Illustrated by William Barss. Boston: Houghton Mifflin, 1962.

3. Barnhart, Nancy. *The Lord Is My Shepherd.* New York: Scribner, 1949.

4. De Angeli, Marguerite. *The Old Testament.* New York: Doubleday, 1959.

5. De la Mare, Walter. *Stories from the Bible.* Illustrated by Edward Ardizzone. New York: Knopf, 1961.
6. De Regniers, Beatrice. *David and Goliath.* Illustrated by Richard M. Powers. New York: Viking, 1965.
7. Galdone, Paul. *The First Seven Days.* New York: Crowell, 1962.
8. ————*Shadrach, Meshach, and Abednego.* New York: McGraw-Hill, 1965.
9. Gwynne, John H. *The Rainbow Book of Bible Stories.* Illustrated by Steele Savage. Cleveland: World Publishing, 1956.
10. Ish-Kishor, Sulamith. *The Carpet of Solomon.* Illustrated by Uri Shulevitz. New York: Pantheon, 1966.
11. Lampe, G. W. H., and David S. Daniell. *Discovering the Bible.* Illustrated by Steele Savage. Nashville, Va.: Abingdon, 1966.
12. Lathrop, Dorothy. *Animals of the Bible.* Text selected by Helen Fish. Philadelphia: Lippincott, 1937.
13. Palazzo, Tony. *The Lord Is My Shepherd.* New York: Walck, 1965.
14. ————*A Time for All Things.* New York: Walck, 1966.
15. Petersham, Maud. *The Shepherd Psalm.* New York: Macmillan, 1962.
16. Petersham, Maud and Miska. *David.* New York: Macmillan, 1958.
17. ————*Jesus' Story.* New York: Macmillan, 1942.
18. ————*Joseph and His Brothers.* New York: Macmillan, 1958, 1938.
19. ————*Moses.* New York: Macmillan, 1958, 1938.
20. ————*Ruth.* New York: Macmillan, 1958, 1938.
21. Saporta, Raphael. *A Basket in the Reeds.* Illustrated by H. Hechtkopf. New York: Lerner, 1965.
22. Sellew, Catherine E. *Adventures with Abraham's Children.* Illustrated by Steele Savage. Boston: Little, Brown, 1964.
23. Werner, Elsa J., Editor. *The Golden Bible.* Illustration by Feodor Rojankovsky. New York: Golden Press: 1946.
24. Wynants, Miche. *Noah's Ark.* New York: Harcourt, 1965.

Epics, Myths, and Legends

25. Alexander, Beatrice. *Famous Myths of the Golden Age.* Illustrated by Florian. New York: Random House, 1947.
26. Almedingen, E. M. *The Knights of the Golden Table.* Illustrated by Charles Keeping. Philadelphia: Lippincott, 1964.
27. ————*The Treasure of Siegfried.* Illustrated by Charles Keeping. Philadelphia: Lippincott, 1964.
28. Asimov, Isaac. *Words from the Myths.* Illustrated by William Barss. Boston: Houghton Mifflin, 1961.
29. d'Aulaire, Ingri and Edgar Parin. *Book of Greek Myths.* New York: Doubleday, 1962.
30. Baldwin, James. *The Story of Roland.* Illustrated by Peter Hurd. New York: Scribner, 1930.
31. Belting, Natalia. *The Long-Tailed Bear and Other Indian Legends.* Illustrated by Louis Cary. Indianapolis: Bobbs-Merrill, 1961.
32. Benson, Sally. *Stories of the Gods and Heroes.* Illustrated by Steele Savage. New York: Dial, 1940.
33. Brown, Marcia. *Backbone of the King, The Story of Pakáa and His Son Ku.* New York: Scribner, 1966.
34. Bulfinch, Thomas. *The Age of Fable.* New York: New American Library, 1962.
35. ————*A Book of Myths.* Illustrated by Helen Sewell. New York: Macmillan, 1942.
36. Church, Alfred J. *The Iliad of Homer.* Illustrated by John Flaxman. New York: Macmillan, 1935.

37. ————*The Odyssey of Homer*. Illustrated by John Flaxman. New York: Macmillan, 1951.
38. Clark, Eleanor. *The Song of Roland*. Illustrated by Leonard Everett Fisher. New York: Random House, 1960.
39. Colum, Padraic. *The Children of Odin*. Illustrated by Willy Pogany. New York: Macmillan, 1920.
40. ————*The Children's Homer: The Adventures of Odysseus and the Tale of Troy*. Illustrated by Willy Pogany. New York: Macmillan, 1962.
41. ————*Legends of Hawaii*. Illustrated by Don Forrer. New Haven, Conn.: Yale University Press, 1937.
42. Coolidge, Olivia. *Legends of the North*. Illustrated by Edouard Sandoz. Boston: Houghton Mifflin, 1951.
43. Crossley-Holland, Kevin. *Havelok the Dane*. Illustrated by Brian Wildsmith. New York: Dutton, 1965.
44. De Selincourt, Aubrey. *Odysseus the Wanderer*. Illustrated by Norman Meredith. New York: Criterion, 1956.
45. Deutsch, Babette. *Heroes of the Kalevala*. Illustrated by Fritz Eichenberg. New York: Messner, 1940.
46. Elgin, Kathleen. *The First Book of Mythology*. New York: F. Watts, 1955.
47. Evslin, Bernard, Dorothy Evslin and Ned Hoopes. *The Greek Gods*. Illustrated by William Hunter. New York: Scholastic, 1966.
48. Fahs, Sophia Lyn, and Dorothy T. Spoerl. *Beginnings: Earth, Sky, Life, Death*. Boston: Starr King Press, 1958.
49. Gaer, Joseph. *The Adventures of Rama*. Illustrated by Randy Monk. Boston: Little, Brown, 1954.
50. Gottlieb, Gerald. *The Adventures of Ulysses*. Illustrated by Steele Savage. New York: Random House, 1959.
51. Graves, Robert. *Greek Gods and Heroes*. Illustrated by Dimitris Davis. New York: Doubleday, 1960.
52. Green, Roger L. *Tales the Muses Told*. Illustrated by Don Bolognese. New York: Walck, 1965.
53. Gunther, John. *The Golden Fleece*. Illustrated by Ernest Kurt Barth. New York: Random House, 1959.
54. Hawthorne, Nathaniel. *The Golden Touch*. Illustrated by Paul Galdone. New York: McGraw-Hill, 1959.
55. ————*A Wonder Book and Tanglewood Tales*. Illustrated by Maxfield Parrish. New York: Dodd, Mead, 1910.
56. Hill, W. M. *Tales of Maui*. Illustrated by Jacques Boullaire. New York: Dodd, Mead, 1964.
57. Hosford, Dorothy G. *Sons of the Volsungs*. Illustrated by Frank Dobias. New York: Holt, Rinehart and Winston, 1949.
58. ————*Thunder of the Gods*. Illustrated by Claire and George Louden. New York: Holt, Rinehart and Winston, 1952.
59. Kingsley, Charles. *The Heroes, Greek Fairy Tales*. Illustrated by Vera Bock. New York: Macmillan, 1954.
60. Lanier, Sidney. *The Boy's King Arthur*. Illustrated by N. C. Wyeth. New York: Scribner, 1880.
61. MacLeod, Mary. *King Arthur, Stories from Sir Thomas Malory's* Morte D'Arthur. Illustrated by Herschel Levit. New York: Macmillan, 1963.
62. Malcolmson, Anne, Editor. *Songs of Robin Hood*. Illustrated by Virginia Lee Burton. Boston: Houghton Mifflin, 1947.
63. Mukerji, Dhan Gopal. *Rama, the Hero of India*. Illustrated by Edgar Parin d'Aulaire. New York: Dutton, 1930.
64. Picard, Barbara Leonie. *The Odyssey of Homer Retold*. New York: Walck, 1952.
65. ————*Tales of the British People*. New York: Criterion, 1961.
66. Pilkington, F. M. *The Three Sorrowful Tales of Erin*. Illustrated by Victor Ambrus. New York: Walck, 1966.

67. Pyle, Howard. *The Merry Adventures of Robin Hood.* New York: Scribner, 1946, 1883.
68. ————*Some Merry Adventures of Robin Hood.* New York: Scribner, 1954.
69. ————*The Story of King Arthur and His Knights.* New York: Scribner, 1933, 1903.
70. Robinson, Mabel L. *King Arthur and His Knights.* Illustrated by Douglas Gorsline. New York: Random House, 1953.
71. Sandys, E. V. *Beowulf.* Illustrated by Rolf Klep. New York: Crowell, 1941.
72. Scherman, Katherine. *The Sword of Siegfried.* Illustrated by Douglas Gorsline. New York: Random House, 1958.
73. Schiller, Barbara. *The Kitchen Knight.* Illustrated by Nonny Hogrogian. New York: Holt, Rinehart and Winston, 1965.
74. Sellew, Catharine. *Adventures with the Gods.* Illustrated by George and Doris Hauman. Boston: Little, Brown, 1945.
75. Seredy, Kate. *The White Stag.* New York: Viking, 1937.
76. Serraillier, Ian. *Beowulf the Warrior.* Illustrated by Severin. New York: Walck, 1961.
77. ————*The Gorgon's Head: The Story of Perseus.* Illustrated by William Stobbs. New York: Scholastic, 1961.
78. ————*The Way of Danger: The Story of Theseus.* Illustrated by William Stobbs. New York: Walck, 1963.
79. Sherwood, Merriam. *The Song of Roland.* Illustrated by Edith Emerson. New York: McKay, 1938.
80. Spenser, Edmund. *Saint George and the Dragon.* Adapted by Sandol Warburg. Illustrated by Pauline Baynes. Boston: Houghton Mifflin, 1963.
81. Sutcliff, Rosemary. *Beowulf.* Illustrated by Charles Keeping. New York: Dutton, 1962.
82. ————*The Hound of Ulster.* Illustrated by Victor Ambrus. New York: Dutton, 1963.
83. Thompson, Vivian. *Hawaiian Myths of Earth, Sea, and Sky.* Illustrated by Leonard Weisgard. New York: Holiday, 1966.
84. Watson, Jane Werner. *The Iliad and the Odyssey.* Illustrated by Alice and Martin Provensen. New York: Golden Press, 1956.
85. White, Ann Terry. *The Golden Treasury of Myths and Legends.* Illustrated by Alice and Martin Provensen. New York: Golden Press, 1959.

Fables

86. Artzybasheff, Boris. *Aesop's Fables.* New York: Viking, 1933.
87. Babbitt, Ellen C. *Jataka Tales.* Illustrated by Ellsworth Young. New York: Appleton, 1912.
88. Brown, Marcia. *Once a Mouse.* New York: Scribner, 1961.
89. Ciardi, John. *John J. Plenty and Fiddler Dan.* Illustrated by Madeleine Gekiere. Philadelphia: Lippincott, 1963.
90. Cooney, Barbara. *Chanticleer and the Fox.* Adapted from Geoffrey Chaucer. New York: Crowell, 1958.
91. Daugherty, James. *Andy and the Lion.* New York: Viking, 1938.
92. La Fontaine, *The Fables of La Fontaine.* Adapted and illustrated by Richard Scarry. New York: Doubleday, 1963.
93. ————*The Lion and the Rat.* Illustrated by Brian Wildsmith. New York: F. Watts, 1963.
94. ————*The North Wind and the Sun.* Illustrated by Brian Wildsmith. New York: F. Watts, 1963.
95. ————*The Rich Man and the Shoemaker.* Illustrated by Brian Wildsmith. New York: F. Watts, 1965.
96. Lionni, Leo. *Tico and the Golden Wings.* New York: Pantheon, 1964.
97. Reeves, James. *Fables from Aesop.* Illustrated by Maurice Wilson. New York: Walck, 1962.

FOLK TALES

General Collections

98. Arbuthnot, May Hill. *The Arbuthnot Anthology of Children's Literature*. Illustrated by Arthur Paul, and others. Glenview, Ill.: Scott, Foresman, 1952.

99. Association for Childhood Education. *Told Under the Green Umbrella*. Illustrated by Grace Gilkison. New York: Macmillan, 1957, 1930.

100. Courlander, Harold. *Ride with the Sun*. Illustrated by Roger Duvoisin. New York: McGraw-Hill, 1955.

101. Dalgliesh, Alice. *The Enchanted Book*. Illustrated by Concetta Cacciola. New York: Scribner, 1947.

102. De la Mare, Walter. *Tales Told Again*. Illustrated by Alan Howard. New York: Knopf, 1946, 1927.

103. Frost, Frances. *Legends of the United Nations*. Illustrated by Karl Schultheiss. New York: McGraw-Hill, 1943.

104. Hutchinson, Veronica. *Chimney Corner Fairy Tales*. Illustrated by Lois Lenski. New York: Minton, Balch (Putnam), 1926.

105. Lang, Andrew. *The Blue Fairy Book*. Illustrated by Reisie Lonette. New York: Random House, 1959.

106. ———*The Red Fairy Book*. Illustrated by Marc Simont. New York: McKay, 1950.

107. Manning-Sanders, Ruth. *A Book of Dwarfs*. Illustrated by Robin Jacques. New York: Dutton, 1963.

108. Nic Leodhas, Sorche. *Ghosts Go Haunting*. Illustrated by Nonny Hogrogian. New York: Holt, Rinehart and Winston, 1965.

109. Palmer, Robin. *Dragons, Unicorns and Other Magical Beasts*. Illustrated by Don Bolognese. New York: Walck, 1966.

110. Palmer, Robin, and Pelagie Doane. *Fairy Elves: A Dictionary of the Little People with Some Old Tales and Verses about Them*. Illustrated by Pelagie Doane. New York: Walck, 1964.

111. Picard, Barbara Leonie. *The Faun and the Woodcutter's Daughter*. Illustrated by Charles Stewart. New York: Criterion, 1964.

112. Pyle, Howard. *Pepper and Salt; or, Seasoning for Young Folk*. New York: Harper & Row, 1913, 1885.

113. ———*The Wonder Clock*. New York: Harper & Row, 1915, 1887.

114. Reeves, James. *Three Tall Tales*. Illustrated by Edward Ardizzone. New York: Abelard-Schuman, 1964.

115. Singer, Isaac Bashevis. *Zlateh the Goat*. Illustrated by Maurice Sendak. New York: Harper & Row, 1966.

116. Spicer, Dorothy Gladys. *13 Monsters*. Illustrated by Sofia. New York: Coward-McCann, 1964.

117. Withers, Carl. *I Saw a Rocket Walk a Mile*. Illustrated by John E. Johnson. New York: Holt, Rinehart and Winston, 1965.

Collections of Tales from Regions and Countries

AFRICA

118. Aardema, Verna. *Tales from the Story Hat*. Illustrated by Elton Fax. New York: Coward-McCann, 1960.

119. Appiah, Peggy, *Ananse the Spider, Tales from an Ashanti Village*. Illustrated by Peggy Wilson. New York: Pantheon, 1966.

120. Arkhurst, Joyce Cooper. *The Adventures of Spider, West African Folk Tales*. Illustrated by Jerry Pinkney. Boston: Little, Brown, 1964.

121. Carpenter, Frances. *African Wonder Tales*. Illustrated by Joseph Escourido. New York: Doubleday, 1963.

122. Courlander, Harold, and George Herzog. *The Cow Tail Switch and Other West African Stories*. Illustrated by Madye Lee Chastain. New York: Holt, Rinehart and Winston, 1947.

123. Courlander, Harold, and Wolf Leslau. *The Fire on the Mountain and Other Ethiopian Stories*. Illustrated by Robert W. Kane. New York: Holt, Rinehart and Winston, 1950.

124. Gilstrap, Robert, and Irene Estabrook. *The Sultan's Fool and Other North African Tales*. Illustrated by Robert Greco. New York: Holt, Rinehart and Winston, 1958.

125. Guillot, René. *René Guillot's African Folk Tales*. Illustrated by William Papas. New York: F. Watts, 1964.

126. Mozley, Charles. *The First Book of Tales of Ancient Egypt*. New York: F. Watts, 1960.

127. Sturton, Hugh. *Zomo the Rabbit*. Illustrated by Peter Warner. New York: Atheneum, 1966.

CANADA

128. Barbeau, Marius. *The Golden Phoenix and Other French-Canadian Fairy Tales*. Retold by Michael Hornansky. Illustrated by Arthur Price. New York: Scholastic, 1958.

129. Macmillan, Cyrus. *Glooskap's Country and Other Indian Tales*. Illustrated by John A. Hall. New York: Oxford, 1955.

CARIBBEAN

130. Courlander, Harold. *The Piece of Fire and Other Haitian Tales*. Illustrated by Beth and Joe Krush. New York: Harcourt, 1964.

131. ————*Terrapin's Pot of Sense*. Illustrated by Elton Fax. New York: Holt, Rinehart and Winston, 1957.

132. Sherlock, Philip M. *Anansi the Spider Man, Jamaican Folk Tales*. Illustrated by Marcia Brown. New York: Crowell, 1954.

133. ————*West Indian Folk Tales*. Illustrated by Joan Kiddell-Monroe, New York: Walck, 1966.

CENTRAL AND SOUTH AMERICA

134. Finger, Charles. *Tales from Silver Lands*. Illustrated by Paul Honoré. New York: Doubleday, 1924.

135. Jordan, Philip D. *The Burro Benedicto and Other Folk Tales and Legends of Mexico*. Illustrated by R. M. Powers. New York: McKay, 1960.

EUROPE

136. Boggs, Ralph Steele, and Mary Gould Davis. *Three Golden Oranges and Other Spanish Folk Tales*. Illustrated by Emma Brock. New York: McKay, 1936.

137. Curcija-Prodanovic, Nada. *Yugoslav Folk Tales*. Illustrated by Joan Kiddell-Monroe. New York: Oxford, 1957.

138. De Leeuw, Adele. *Legends and Folk Tales of Holland*. Illustrated by Paul Kennedy. Camden, N.J.: Nelson, 1963.

139. Duvoisin, Roger. *The Three Sneezes and Other Swiss Tales*. New York: Knopf, 1941.

140. Grimm, Jacob and Wilhelm. *Fairy Tales by Jacob and Wilhelm Grimm*. Translated by Lucy Crane. Illustrated by Jean O'Neill. Cleveland: World Publishing, 1947.

141. ————*Grimm's Tales*. Illustrated by Helen Sewell and Madeleine Gekiere. New York: Oxford, 1954.

142. ————*More Tales from Grimm*. Retold and illustrated by Wanda Gág. New York: Coward-McCann, 1947.

143. ———*Tales from Grimm.* Translated and illustrated by Wanda Gág. New York: Coward-McCann, 1936.

144. ———*Three Gay Tales from Grimm.* Translated and illustrated by Wanda Gág. New York: Coward-McCann, 1943.

145. Haviland, Virginia. *Favorite Fairy Tales Told in Czechoslovakia.* Illustrated by Trina Schart Hyman. Boston: Little, Brown, 1966.

146. ———*Favorite Fairy Tales Told in France.* Illustrated by Roger Duvoisin. Boston: Little, Brown, 1959.

147. ———*Favorite Fairy Tales Told in Germany.* Illustrated by Susanne Suba. Boston: Little, Brown, 1959.

148. ———*Favorite Fairy Tales Told in Italy.* Illustrated by Evaline Ness. Boston: Little, Brown, 1965.

149. Jagendorf, M. A. *The Priceless Cats and Other Italian Folk Stories.* Illustrated by Gioia Fiammenghi. New York: Vanguard, 1956.

FAR EAST

150. Carpenter, Frances. *Tales of a Chinese Grandmother.* Illustrated by Malthe Hasselriis. New York: Doubleday, 1949.

151. ———*The Elephant's Bathtub: Wonder Tales from the Far East.* Illustrated by Hans Guggenheim. New York: Doubleday, 1962.

152. Courlander, Harold. *The Tiger's Whisker and Other Tales and Legends from Asia and the Pacific.* Illustrated by Enrico Arno. New York: Harcourt, 1959.

153. Sakade, Florence. *Little One-Inch and Other Japanese Children's Favorite Stories.* Illustrated by Yoshisuke Kurosaki. Rutland, Vt.: Tuttle, 1958.

154. Scofield, Elizabeth. *A Fox in One Bite and Other Tasty Tales from Japan.* Illustrated by K. Wakana. Tokyo: Kodanska International, 1965.

155. Uchida, Yoshiko. *The Dancing Kettle and Other Japanese Folk Tales.* Illustrated by Richard C. Jones. New York: Harcourt, 1949.

GREAT BRITAIN

156. Haviland, Virginia. *Favorite Fairy Tales Told in England.* Retold from Joseph Jacobs. Illustrated by Bettina. Boston: Little, Brown, 1959.

157. ———*Favorite Fairy Tales Told in Scotland.* Illustrated by Adrienne Adams. Boston: Little, Brown, 1963.

158. Jacobs, Joseph. *Celtic Fairy Tales.* Illustrated by John D. Batten. New York: Putnam, n.d.

159. ———*English Fairy Tales.* Illustrated by John D. Batten, third revised edition. New York: Putnam, n.d.

160. ———*More English Fairy Tales.* Illustrated by John D. Batten. New York: Putnam, n.d.

161. Nic Leodhas, Sorche. *Gaelic Ghosts.* Illustrated by Nonny Hogrogian. New York: Holt, Rinehart and Winston, 1963.

162. ———*Heather and Broom, Tales of the Scottish Highlands.* Illustrated by Consuelo Joerns. New York: Holt, Rinehart and Winston, 1960.

163. ———*Thistle and Thyme, Tales and Legends from Scotland.* Illustrated by Evaline Ness. New York: Holt, Rinehart and Winston, 1962.

MIDDLE EAST

164. Colum Padraic. *The Arabian Nights.* Illustrated by Lynd Ward. New York: Macmillan, 1953, 1923.

165. Downing, Charles. *Tales of the Hodja.* Illustrated by William Papas. New York: Walck, 1965.

166. Ekrem, Selma. *Turkish Fairy Tales.* Illustrated by Liba Bayrak. Princeton, N.J.: Van Nostrand, 1964.
167. Hodges, Elizabeth Jamison. *The Three Princes of Serendip.* Illustrated by Joan Berg. New York: Atheneum, 1964.
168. Kelsey, Alice Geer. *Once the Hodja.* Illustrated by Frank Dobias. New York: McKay, 1943.
169. Lang, Andrew. *Arabian Nights.* Illustrated by Vera Bock. New York: McKay, 1951.
170. Larson, Jean Russell. *Palace in Bagdad.* Illustrated by Marianne Yamaguchi. New York: Scribner, 1966.
171. Mehdevi, Anne Sinclair. *Persian Folk and Fairy Tales.* Illustrated by Paul E. Kennedy. New York: Knopf, 1965.
172. Mozley, Charles. *The First Book of Tales of Ancient Araby.* New York: F. Watts, 1960.
173. Tashijan, Virginia A. *Once There Was and Was Not.* Based on stories by H. Toumanian. Illustrated by Nonny Hogrogian. Boston: Little, Brown, 1966.

RUSSIA

174. Almedingen, E. M. *Russian Folk and Fairy Tales.* Illustrated by Simon Jeruchim. New York: Putnam, 1963.
175. Downing, Charles. *Russian Tales and Legends.* Illustrated by Joan Kiddell-Monroe. New York: Oxford, 1957.
176. Haviland, Virginia. *Favorite Fairy Tales Told in Russia.* Illustrated by Herbert Danska. Boston: Little, Brown, 1961.
177. Papashvily, George and Helen. *Yes and No Stories: A Book of Georgian Folk Tales.* Illustrated by Simon Lissim. New York: Harper & Row, 1946.
178. Wheeler, Post. *Russian Wonder Tales.* Illustrated by Bilibin. New York: Yoseloff, 1957.
179. Zeitlin, Ida. *Skazki Tales and Legends of Old Russia.* Illustrated by Theodore Nadejen. New York: Farrar, Straus, 1926.

SCANDINAVIA

180. Asbjørnsen, P. C., and Jorgen E. Moe. *East of the Sun and West of the Moon and Other Tales.* Illustrated by Tom Vroman. New York: Macmillan, 1963.
181. ————*Norwegian Folk Tales.* Illustrated by Erik Werenskiold and Theodor Kettelsen. New York: Viking, 1960.
182. d'Aulaire, Ingri and Edgar Parin. *East of the Sun and West of the Moon, Twenty-One Norwegian Folk Tales,* New York: Viking, 1938.
183. Bowman, James Cloyd, and Margery Bianco. *Tales from a Finnish Tupa.* Illustrated by Laura Bannon. Racine, Wis.: Whitman, 1936.
184. Haviland, Virginia. *Favorite Fairy Tales Told in Sweden.* Illustrated by Ronni Solbert. Boston: Little, Brown, 1966.
185. Owen, Ruth Bryan. *Picture Tales from Scandinavia.* Illustrated by Emma Brock. Philadelphia: Frederick A. Stokes, 1939.
186. Thorne-Thomsen, Gudrun. *East O' the Sun and West O' the Moon, with Other Norwegian Folk Tales.* New York: Harper & Row, 1946.

UNITED STATES: INDIAN

187. Chafetz, Henry. *Thunderbird and Other Stories.* Illustrated by Ronni Solbert. New York: Pantheon, 1964.
188. Cothran, Jean. *The Magic Calabash, Folk Tales from America's Islands and Alaska.* Illustrated by Clifford N. Geary. New York: McKay. 1956.
189. Curry, Jane Louise. *Down from the Lonely Mountain.* Illustrated by Enrico Arno. New York: Harcourt, 1965.

190. Harris, Christie. *Once upon a Totem.* Illustrated by John Frazer Mills. New York: Atheneum, 1963.
191. Hill, Kay. *Glooscap and His Magic.* Illustrated by Robert Frankenberg. New York: Dodd, Mead, 1963.
192. Houston, James. *Tiktá Liktak: An Eskimo Legend.* New York: Harcourt, 1965.
193. Leekley, Thomas B. *The World of Manabozho, Tales of the Chippewa Indians.* Illustrated by Yeffe Kimball. New York: Vanguard, 1965.
194. Reid, Dorothy. *Tales of Nanabozho.* Illustrated by Donald Grant. New York: Walck, 1963.

UNITED STATES: LEGENDARY HEROES

195. Ball, Zachary. *Young Mike Fink.* Illustrated by Paul Lantz. New York: Holiday, 1958.
196. Bowman, James Cloyd. *Pecos Bill.* Illustrated by Laura Bannon. Racine, Wis.: Whitman, 1937.
197. Chase, Richard, Compiler. Joel Chandler Harris. *The Complete Tales of Uncle Remus.* Illustrated by Arthur Frost, and others. Boston: Houghton Mifflin, 1955.
198. ————Editor. *The Jack Tales.* Illustrated by Berkeley Williams. Boston: Houghton Mifflin, 1943.
199. Cothran, Jean. *With a Wig with a Wag and Other American Folk Tales.* Illustrated by Clifford Geary. New York: McKay, 1954.
200. Credle, Ellis. *Tall Tales from the High Hills.* Illustrated by Richard Bennett. Camden, N.J.: Nelson, 1957.
201. Felton, Harold W. *John Henry and His Hammer.* Illustrated by Aldren A. Watson. New York: Knopf, 1950.
202. Feuerlecht, Roberta Strauss. *The Legends of Paul Bunyan.* Illustrated by Kurt Werth. New York: Macmillan, 1966.
203. Jagendorf, M. A. *The Ghost of Peg-Leg Peter.* Illustrated by Lino S. Lipinsky. New York: Vanguard, 1965.
204. Keats, Ezra Jack. *John Henry, An American Legend.* New York: Pantheon, 1965.
205. Leach, Maria. *The Rainbow Book of American Folk Tales and Legends.* Illustrated by Marc Simont. Cleveland: World Publishing, 1958.
206. Malcolmson, Anne. *Yankee Doodle's Cousins.* Illustrated by Robert McCloskey. Boston: Houghton Mifflin, 1941.
207. Rounds, Glen. *Ol' Paul, the Mighty Logger.* New York: Holiday, 1949.
208. Shapiro, Irwin. *Heroes in American Folklore.* Illustrated by Donald McKay and James Daugherty. New York: Messner, 1962.
209. ————*How Old Stormalong Captured Mocha Dick.* Illustrated by Donald McKay. New York: Messner, 1942.
210. Shephard, Esther. *Paul Bunyan.* Illustrated by Rockwell Kent. New York: Harcourt, 1924.

Single Tales

211. Adams, Adrienne. *The Twelve Dancing Princesses.* New York: Holt, Rinehart and Winston, 1966.
212. Asbjørnsen, P. C., and Jorgen E. Moe. *The Three Billy Goats Gruff.* Illustrated by Marcia Brown. New York: Harcourt, 1957.
213. Bontemps, Arna and Jack Conroy. *The Fast Sooner Hound.* Illustrated by Virginia Lee Burton. Boston: Houghton Mifflin, 1942.
214. Bowman, James Cloyd, and Margery Bianco. *Seven Silly Wise Men.* Illustrated by John Faulkner. Racine, Wis: Whitman, 1964.

215. Brown, Marcia. *Dick Whittington and His Cat.* New York: Scribner, 1950.

216. ————*Stone Soup.* New York: Scribner, 1947.

217. Bryant, Sara Cone. *The Burning Rice Fields.* Illustrated by Mamoru Funai. New York: Holt, Rinehart and Winston, 1963.

218. Ciardi, John. *John J. Plenty and Fiddler Dan.* Illustrated by Madeleine Gekiere. Philadelphia: Lippincott, 1963.

219. De Angeli, Marguerite. *The Goose Girl.* New York: Doubleday, 1964.

220. De Beaumont, Marie Leprince. *Beauty and the Beast.* Translated by Richard Howard. Illustrated by Hilary Knight. New York: Macmillan, 1963.

221. Fournier, Catharine. *The Coconut Thieves.* Illustrated by Janina Domanska. New York: Scribner, 1964.

222. Frasconi, Antonio. *The House That Jack Built.* New York: Harcourt, 1958.

223. Galdone, Paul. *The House That Jack Built.* New York: McGraw-Hill, 1961.

224. ————*The Old Woman and Her Pig.* New York: McGraw-Hill, 1960.

225. Grimm, Jacob and Wilhelm. *Rapunzel.* Illustrated by Felix Hoffman. New York: Harcourt, 1961.

226. ————*The Seven Ravens.* Illustrated by Felix Hoffman. New York: Harcourt, 1963.

227. ————*The Shoemaker and the Elves.* Illustrated by Adrienne Adams. New York: Scribner, 1960.

228. ————*Snow White and Rose Red.* Illustrated by Adrienne Adams. New York: Scribner, 1964.

229. ————*Snow White and the Seven Dwarfs.* Translated and illustrated by Wanda Gág. New York: Coward-McCann, 1938.

230. ————*The Traveling Musicians.* Illustrated by Hans Fischer. New York: Harcourt, 1955.

231. Hodges, Margaret. *The Wave.* Illustrated by Blair Lent. Boston: Houghton Mifflin, 1964.

232. Hoge, Dorothy. *The Black Heart of Indri.* Illustrated by Janina Domanska. New York: Scribner, 1966.

233. Leskov, Nicholas. *The Steel Flea.* Adapted by Babette Deutsch and Avrahm Yarmolinsky. Illustrated by Janina Domanska. New York: Harper & Row, 1964.

234. Lifton, Betty Jean. *The Cock and the Ghost Cat.* Illustrated by Fuku Akino. New York: Atheneum, 1965.

235. ————*The Dwarf Pine Tree.* Illustrated by Fuku Akino. New York: Atheneum, 1963.

236. McKown, Robin. *Rakoto and the Drongo Bird.* Illustrated by Robert Quackenbush. New York: Lothrop, 1960.

237. Merrill, Jean. *The Superlative Horse.* Illustrated by Ronni Solbert. New York: W. R. Scott, 1961.

238. Mohan, Beverly. *Punia and the King of the Sharks.* Illustrated by Don Bolognese. Chicago: Follett, 1964.

239. Montresor, Beni. *Cinderella.* From the opera by Gioacchino Rossini. New York: Knopf, 1965.

240. Moore, Marianne. *Puss in Boots, The Sleeping Beauty, and Cinderella.* Retold from Perrault. Illustrated by Eugene Karlin. New York: Macmillan, 1963.

241. Ness, Evaline. *Tom Tit Tot.* New York: Scribner, 1965.

242. Nic Leodhas, Sorche. *All in the Morning Early.* Illustrated by Evaline Ness. New York: Holt, Rinehart and Winston, 1963.

243. Pavel, Frances K. *The Elves and the Shoemaker.* Illustrated by Joyce Hewitt. New York: Holt, Rinehart and Winston, 1961.

244. Perrault, Charles. *Cinderella.* Illustrated by Marcia Brown. New York: Scribner, 1954.

245. ————*Puss in Boots.* Illustrated by Marcia Brown. New York: Scribner, 1952.

246. ———*Puss in Boots.* Illustrated by Hans Fischer. New York: Harcourt, 1959.
247. ———*The Sleeping Beauty.* Illustrated by Felix Hoffman. New York: Harcourt, 1959.
248. Sawyer, Ruth. *Journey Cake, Ho!* Illustrated by Robert McCloskey. New York: Viking, 1953.
249. Small, Ernest. *Baba Yaga.* Illustrated by Blair Lent. Boston: Houghton Mifflin, 1966.
250. Stamm, Claus. *Three Strong Women, A Tall Tale from Japan.* Illustrated by Kazue Mizumura. New York: Viking, 1962.
251. Tresselt, Alvin. *The Mitten.* Illustrated by Yaroslava. New York: Lothrop, 1964.
252. Walker, Barbara. *Hilili and Dilili, A Turkish Silly Tale.* Illustrated by Bill Barss. Chicago: Follett, 1965.
253. ———*Just Say Hic!* Illustrated by Don Bolognese. Chicago: Follett, 1965.
254. Welcher, Rosalind. *The Magic Top.* New York: Panda Prints, 1965.
255. Yamaguchi, Tohr. *The Golden Crane.* Illustrated by Marianne Yamaguchi. New York: Holt, Rinehart and Winston, 1963.
256. Zemach, Harve. *Nail Soup.* Illustrated by Margot Zemach. Chicago: Follett, 1964.
257. ———*Salt.* Illustrated by Margot Zemach. Chicago: Follett, 1965.
258. Zemach, Margot. *The Fisherman and His Wife.* New York: Norton, 1966.

Folk Songs

259. Chase, Richard. *Billy Boy.* Illustrated by Glen Rounds. San Francisco, Calif.: Golden Gate Junior Books, 1966.
260. Justus, May. *Tale of a Pig.* Illustrated by Frank Aloise. Nashville, Tenn.: Abingdon, 1963.
261. Langstaff, John. *Frog Went A-Courtin'.* Illustrated by Feodor Rojankovsky. New York: Harcourt, 1955.
262. ———*The Swapping Boy.* Illustrated by Beth and Joe Krush. New York: Harcourt, 1960.
263. Nic Leodhas, Sorche. *Always Room for One More.* Illustrated by Nonny Hogrogian. New York: Holt, Rinehart and Winston, 1965.
264. Ritchie, Jean. *The Swapping Song Book.* New York: Oxford, 1952.
265. Schackburg, Richard. *Yankee Doodle.* Illustrated by Ed Emberley. Engelwood Cliffs, N.J.: Prentice-Hall, 1965.
266. Seeger, Ruth C. *American Folk Songs for Children.* New York: Doubleday, 1948.

5

REALISTIC FICTION

The children in Miss Winston's sixth-grade class had flitted restlessly from one activity to another, interrupted each other and the teacher. Finally, Miss Winston took a book from her desk and suggested they relax for a time and listen to a story.

As she read, her shoulders lost some of their tenseness, her voice became an instrument to communicate the feelings of Aunt Anne portrayed in a selection from *Cheaper by the Dozen*.[1] The classroom became quiet. As she finished reading the incident, one boy said, "You really felt like Aunt Anne this morning, didn't you, Miss Winston? You were just as mad at us."

Miss Winston smiled as she replied, "Yes, Pete. I was really irritated. You haven't worked well this morning. The whole class was unwilling to help. There were arguments, clenched fists, and an undercurrent of anger."

"But, Miss Winston," interjected Emmy Lu, "Didn't Aunt Anne in the story *like* the children? She was very cross with them, but they liked her."

The discussion of adult-child relationships continued until one lanky pre-adolescent shifted to ask, "But you get mad at us sometimes. Do you *love* us, Miss Winston?"

The noon dismissal bell rang. A stillness hovered over the group. Miss Winston looked at the boys and girls—their eyes pleading for the answer. Unkempt, some not very intelligent, many over-age—fat, listless, the potential delinquents from this sordid neighborhood—they listened for her answer.

---

[1]Frank B. Gilbreth and Ernestine G. Carey, *Cheaper by the Dozen* (New York: Crowell, 1948), pp. 175–181

A book had made it possible to bring a feeling of unity to the classroom once more. By means of a story, the teacher relieved tensions—her own and the children's. More important, an atmosphere of warm friendliness and acceptance had made it possible for these children to ask the question all humans ask of each other and of those persons important to them. "Do you love me? Can you love me even though I live in a crowded tenement? Even though I don't wash very often? Even though I lose my temper and lash out at others in my hurt? Even though I still can't subtract very well? Does anybody *know* the kinds of problems I am experiencing?"

Realism in Children's Literature

Realistic fiction serves children in the process of understanding and coming to terms with themselves as they acquire "human-ness" and understand the nature of being human. In speaking of the function of literature for children, Emily Neville commented, "They need to know that an adult understands—that someone knows these problems exist. Final answers are not essential."[2]

It is not easy to grow up to face the realities of the human condition. There are shadows on the sunny landscape of the world of childhood. Speaking of this darkness, Madeleine L'Engle said,

> . . . to pretend there is no darkness is another way of extinguishing light. In literature, children and adults can find the heroes, the uncommon men who face these same dark clouds but show what a man can do. They do not always show the way, but serve as a point of reference.[3]

Although literature does function to provide these points of reference and to give insight, the major function is to provide entertainment.

Reality in literature is something more than "reality of presentation" defined by Lewis as "the art of bringing something close to us, making it palpable and vivid, by sharply observed or imagined detail."[4] But "reality" is more than details of the weather, locale, clothing, or food.

> Truth to life or reality is not to be judged by factual accuracy of this or that detail. . . . This world or Kosmos of a novelist—this pattern or structure or organism, which includes plot, characters, setting, world-view, "tone"—is what we must scrutinize when we attempt to compare a novel with life or to judge, ethically or socially, a novelist's work.[5]

However, the question of what is "true to life" is even more significant. C. S. Lewis described three types of "realism of content":

> But when we say, "The sort of thing that happens," do we mean the sort of thing that usually or often happens, the sort of thing that is typical of the human lot? Or do we mean "The sort of thing that might conceivably happen or that, by a thousandth chance, may have happened once"?[6]

Lewis points out that the early stories presented exceptional deeds; he suggests that fantasy may present the human lot realistically; and he notes that some fiction, even with a realistic setting, such as school stories, may present life unrealistically. Other critics maintain that the essential reality of a work of fiction is "its effect on the reader as a convincing reading of life."[7]

---

[2]Discussion at the University of Chicago Graduate Library School Conference, August 1966.

[3]Madeleine L'Engle in a speech before the Florida Library Association, Miami, May 1965.

[4]C. S. Lewis, *An Experiment in Criticism* (Cambridge, England: Cambridge University Press, 1961), p. 57.

[5]René Wellek and Austin Warren, *Theory of Literature*, Second edition (New York: Harcourt, 1956) pp. 202, 203.

[6]Lewis, p. 61.

[7]Wellek and Warren, p. 202.

Although this illusory "true to life" quality may exist in folk tales and fantasy, "realistic" fiction includes those stories that could have happened to real people living in the natural, physical world and social environment as experienced or imagined by the author. Usually the protagonist is a child, but an animal may be given qualities of patience, endurance, and courage so that it becomes a character overcoming conflicts or challenges in its environment. These stories are included in Chapter 10. Many humorous stories could be defined as realistic fiction. However, their humor is usually based on exaggeration or distortion of everyday experiences, and for this reason, they have been included in Chapter 7. Realistic stories based on the reconstruction of past events are discussed in Chapter 6.

The realistic fiction discussed in this chapter provides an entertaining story, is related to the developmental tasks of childhood, gives insight into human behavior, and helps the reader build his own values and concept of self. These narratives present man's universal problems of finding a place for himself in a family, in the peer group, and the larger society. The characters become universal figures who meet the human problems of cultural change, loneliness, physical handicaps, the social evils of war and poverty, the problems of growing toward creative and responsible adulthood, and death. Realistic fiction, in this chapter, is defined as prose narrative that presents universal problems of human beings in the twentieth century.

FINDING A PLACE AS A PERSON

Finding a Place in the Family

Within the family, the human personality is nurtured; here the growing organism learns of love and hate, of fear and courage, of joy and sorrow. Some books portray family life without these moments of anger or hurt; they present a "slice of life," but select the happy or adventurous moments. A few authors dwell on the times of tension, while others show a balance of sun and shadow in family life.

In many stories, the parents recede into the background as cardboard figures, and emphasis is upon the children. The more effective story includes the adults with their strengths and weaknesses and shows children interacting with them.

Happy Family Life   Eleanor Estes creates believable children of the pre-television era in her books, *The Moffats, The Middle Moffat,* and *Rufus M.* Despite their economic hardships, these very independent children have fun and share each other's problems. The Halloween stunt they devise is especially amusing. There is adventure as Rufus Moffat rides the freight train to get little Hughie Pudge back in school; there is laughter and drama as Joe is unwillingly catapulted into a dance recital. These books recapture life of another time, a time when kerosene lamps are used, Mama "shakes down the fire" before bed, and travel is by trolley. The teacher or librarian should take time to talk about this period—after the "pioneer days," but before electricity and automobiles. These books tend to be episodic, with little character development; however, they do provide an opportunity for the vicarious experience of warm family relationships.

Another book in which a somewhat aloof father and unusually patient housekeeper seem relatively unimportant is *The Saturdays* by Enright. New York in the early 1940s was quite different from today, and the Melendy children seem amazingly close knit despite their age range. Their plan to pool their allowances so that each child, in turn, may enjoy a special Saturday excursion brings humor and pathos. Randy goes to an art museum, Rush to the opera, and Oliver goes alone to the circus. When Mona returns with haircut and curls from the beauty salon she feels guilty; yet, she feels secure in this process of emerging into an adolescent:

> She was safe in her bed, the house enclosed her in a shell of warm security and all about, on every side, were the members of her own family who loved and understood her so well. She felt calm and happy.[8]

This is, essentially, the plot of the journey. In each episode one child leaves the home, ventures forth to meet the "monsters," and returns safely to the security of the family.

Family life in a Lower East Side Jewish home is portrayed in Taylor's *All-of-a-Kind Family* books. Although published nearly two decades ago, the books recreate life in the 1930s, a life much slower than the modern tempo. Titled "All-of-a-Kind" because all are girls until a baby boy is born, the children also understood that all-of-a-kind meant they were Jewish and "we're all close and loving and loyal—and our family will always be that." Children will better understand their parents' point of view after reading the incident in which Sarah refuses to eat her soup before the meat and vegetables. Mama holds to the rule, and the soup appears at Sarah's plate for two meals. The entire family aches with the tension. This incident, as many others, is as modern as the newest cereal, and could well be used for role playing and discussion of parental roles. The descriptions of the Jewish feasts and holy days contribute much to understanding of a religious faith. Librarians might well read the opening chapter of *All-of-a-Kind Family* to see an example of a librarian who recognizes that children's needs may be more important than library needs. *More All-of-a-Kind Family* and *All-of-a-Kind Family Uptown* continue the family chronicle and show the girls growing up.

All too frequently, children feel left out because parents refuse to explain the troubles that come to the family. Marly felt shut out, afraid, and insecure when her father returned from the war, emotionally spent and withdrawn. Sorensen's characterizations of the family in *Miracles on Maple Hill* are well portrayed. The family draws strength from each other and from kind neighbors as they rebuild their lives in the country.

Families in other countries have close relationships, too. Meindert DeJong sensitively interprets childhood in *Far Out the Long Canal* and *Shadrach*. Moonta of *Far Out the Long Canal* is the only son of two champion ice skaters, but he has not learned to skate although he is nine years old. DeJong has captured Moonta's desperate anxiety to achieve skill in skating after his understanding mother gives up her skating tour in order to teach him. Although he disobeys and goes off alone to the far place where his father had promised to take him, Moonta heroically warns his father and grandfather of melting ice and all return to the warmth of the home where the inner warmth of understanding glows as brightly as the fire.

In *Shadrach*, DeJong demonstrates his fine literary skill in his interpretation of a small boy's deep emotional attachment to a pet rabbit. This story also portrays Davie's secure place in a family that loves him all the more because he had been desperately ill. His Grandpa and Dad try to make the boy physically and emotionally well by giving him work, providing a pet to care for, and urging him to grow up. Davie's mother is overprotective, yet very understanding. To his father, Davie says, "You want to make me big all of a sudden, but Mother wants to keep me sort of sick, and sort of a baby."[9]

---

[8]Elizabeth Enright, *The Saturdays* (New York: Holt, Rinehart and Winston, 1941), p. 102.

[9]Meindert DeJong, *Shadrach,* Illustrated by Maurice Sendak (New York: Harper & Row, 1953), p. 104.

Davie's older brother helped him when the boy nearly fell in the canal, but he teases with exaggerations about the rabbit's care. Davie's overwhelming fears about the skinniness of the rabbit are finally revealed to his father. The boy's thoughts express the needs of all children:

> *Off and on he almost cried a little as he talked, but that wasn't because of his worries. That was because Dad listened so seriously. Then he was finished with all he had to say, but his father didn't have a quick grown-up's answer ready for him the moment he was finished. He didn't make a joke. He sat and thought! He thought about it!*[10]

Natalie Carlson's Canadian families are economically poor, but are rich in love and faith. In *The Letter on the Tree*, Carlson creates a very believable boy, ten-year-old "Bebert" (rhymes with Gray Bear), who tells a first person story of a family's struggles to improve a dairy farm. Desperately wanting an accordion, he attaches a letter to a Christmas tree being shipped to the United States. His father's pride is deeply hurt by the implied accusation that he cannot take care of his family:

> *My son it is not important to be rich. It is only important that we give something in return for what we receive. Then we can stand straight and hold our heads up. And if we need more money to bring the ends together, we must look for extra ways to earn it. Only the sick and weak have a right to charity.*[11]

There is typical boy-mischief in this book, as when Bebert and another altar boy fight in the church with candle wax. The Christmas scene would be an excellent chapter to read aloud at holiday time. Bebert helps find a way to make money by befriending a tramp who, in turn, helps repair a shed, so it can be rented to the Americans for a fishing lodge. As Bebert and Spike, the boy who found his letter on the tree, become friends, Bebert learns to see Americans as individuals.

Joan Phipson has written several stories of the Barker family who live on a sheep station in Australia. In *The Family Conspiracy*, the children work to earn money for an operation for their mother. Their successes and failures unite this family in which each member has his place. In *Threat to the Barkers*, there is a mystery; *The Boundary Riders* shows the development of courage in a crisis. Each story makes the Australian countryside and work on the station very real. These books present more than the facts about another land; the characters are well worth knowing.

Acceptance in his family was not easy for Sammy Agabashian, for he was a baseball player in a "musical" family. In *All Except Sammy*, Cretan describes the efforts of the boy to learn to play the piano or violin and to sing. His mother expressed her disgust, "How can this happen in this family? . . . Can the fruit fall so far from the tree?"[12] Sammy's brother and sister give comfort, but he is still different. When carrying out a homework assignment, Sammy discovers a painting that truly delights him. He decides to enroll in art class, but also maintain his interest in baseball. His talent in drawing wins his parents' respect, and he becomes an accepted member of an "artistic" family. Not all children are able to achieve a solution to the problem of meeting the family's expectations as well as did Sammy.

One of the outstanding family stories of recent years is *Meet the Austins* by Madeleine L'Engle. No one character stands above the others, although the narrative is told in first person from the point of view of twelve-

---

[10]DeJong, pp. 131–132.

[11]Natalie Savage Carlson, *The Letter on the Tree*, Illustrated by John Kaufman (New York: Harper & Row, 1964), p. 39.

[12]Gladys Yessayan Cretan, *All Except Sammy*, Illustrated by Symeon Shimin (Boston: Little, Brown, 1966), p. 10.

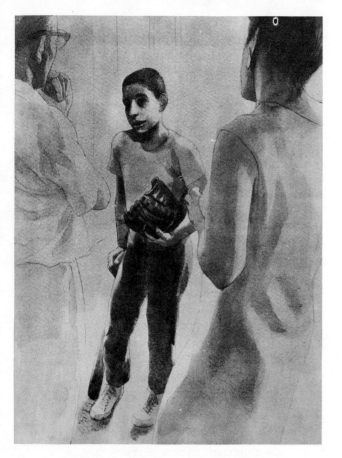

A baseball player is a misfit in his musical family. Shimin's sensitive faces and expressive postures communicate the tension of the moment. Illustration copyright © 1966 by Symeon Shimin. Illustration by Symeon Shimin from *All Except Sammy* by Gladys Yessayan Cretan, by permission of Atlantic-Little, Brown and Co.

year-old Vicki. It is a "happy family" in the sense that each person is an individual, respected, loved, and expected to assume his share of the work. It is not the typical "happy story" in the sense that it is a series of episodes in which the children have fun and adventure. The parents are very much a part of the story and do not recede into the background while the children seem to manage their lives alone. Many difficult problems are faced by the Austins during one year.

The quiet way in which the parents and children show their sympathy for Aunt Elena when her husband dies demonstrates the faith and security of the family. When Maggy, an orphan, comes to live with the Austins, her behavior corrodes the fine family unity. Vicki's accident creates another problem. When mother takes the older children to a hilltop to look at the stars after they learn of Uncle Hal's death, the children express their curiosity about growing up and having things change. This mother's response will inspire many children:

> ". . . We can't stop on the road of Time. We have to keep on going. And growing up is all part of it, the exciting and wonderful business of being alive. We can't understand it, any of us, any more than we can understand why Uncle Hal and Maggy's father had to die. But being alive is a gift, the most wonderful and exciting gift in the world. And there'll undoubtedly be many other moments when you'll feel this same way, John, when you're grown up and have children of your own."[13]

Children in this family are included in serious discussions; grown-ups respect their difficult questions and share their knowledge with the younger generation. When John, the eldest with the scientific bent, says Einstein didn't believe in God, his grandfather reads Einstein's own words to him. The author reflects this same kind of respect for children who read the book. Perhaps parents will say that Dr. and Mrs. Austin are just too good to be true. However, there are adults whose inner convictions are sure, whose sights are set on the future for their children's values instead of their own temporary convenience. In a sophisticated era when material things and fast-paced activity seem to take precedence in many families, it is good to "Meet the Austins."

---

[13]Madeleine L'Engle, *Meet the Austins* (New York: Vanguard, 1960), p. 40.

Children without Parents   Children who have no parents or who have been adopted do not necessarily want to read books about children in similar situations. Yet, they may find reassurance in these stories, and children in secure families may gain understanding as they consider the problems of others.

Several books portray the problems of orphans. The warmth of life in a poverty-stricken orphanage is illustrated in Natalie Carlson's books about the French orphans, *The Happy Orpheline* and *A Brother for the Orphelines.* In the latter, the incident in which resourceful Josine wins the boys' best marbles would be fun to dramatize. Deeper concern for unwanted children is expressed as these orphelines accept a new baby left on their doorstep.

An orphaned boy from Tennessee must return to live with his great-uncle on the *Big Blue Island.* Wilson Gage and Glen Rounds create a boy whom the reader will dislike, yet have compassion for his loneliness. The gnarled old spirit of the uncle is smoothed as the boy slowly responds and accepts his situation. Told he can have a dollar for each heron he can catch, Darrell tries several methods unsuccessfully. He becomes angry because he thinks the old man wants him to be caught by the conservationist and sent to jail. Later, his uncle reveals it was his way of keeping him interested in something. When he buys a boat so the boy can go to school, Darrell thinks of escape, but realizes his island is not a jail; it is a refuge. The authors attempt to create believable dialogue, but are not always careful to maintain consistent speech patterns. The old man says, "Make haste. *Git* in. It's fixing to *get* dark." Probably he would say *fixin'* and *git* in each instance.

The deep and tender love of a brother and sister form the theme of a story of two Greek children left homeless by an earthquake. *The Orphans of Simitra,* a French prize book by Bonzon, describes the search of a boy for his sister after she had run away from the Dutch people to whom they had been taken as refugees. It was not that the Dutch family was unkind; Mina, the girl, could not stand the gray, cold days. Porphyras, only two years older, searches for her in France, and finally makes his way to Marseilles where the land and climate seem more like Greece. It seems improbable that a boy would reach Paris, find a Greek restaurant where he could work, or that the two children would eventually be reunited. Yet, as the story unfolds, it does seem believable; patience, courage, and faith do overcome the evils the children have faced. Porphyras realizes that "In spite of all the disasters that had overtaken him, he had kept his trust in life."[14] Children today need stories of people who have deep inner resources.

Skinny is one of the most engaging optimists we can meet in children's fiction. Robert Burch tells of a boy who was left alone when his alcoholic father died. He finds a place working at Miss Bessie's hotel and hopes he can stay there when it seems Miss Bessie and Daddy Rabbit, foreman of a highway construction gang, might marry. But at the last moment Daddy Rabbit's itching feet take him away; Miss Bessie and Skinny accept their situation without bitterness. Skinny does have to go to the orphanage, but the young man who comes for Skinny gives a reassuring picture when he offers to let the boy bring his dog. Skinny's maturity is revealed when he decides to leave the pet to console Miss Bessie. There are some excellent and amusing scenes showing Skinny's methods to "save face" in situations where reading is required. He doesn't know how to read, but quotes passages from the Bible in Sunday School to cover up his illiteracy. Skinny accepts people as they are—

---

[14]Paul-Jacques Bonzon, *The Orphans of Simitra,* Illustrated by Simon Jeruchim, Translated by Thelma Niklaus (New York: Chilton, 1962), p. 160.

Roman, the ex-convict, who works at the hotel, Peachy, the bossy cook, Miss Bessie who gives him some feeling of being wanted — most of all, he accepts himself.

Another delightful orphan is Rasmus, a Swedish boy who escapes the orphanage and joins a tramp named Oscar, God's Friend. Lindgren's book, *Rasmus and the Vagabond*, won the Hans Christian Andersen Prize in 1958. There are poignant scenes in the orphanage when the stern matron comes and Rasmus aches for her touch, when a couple comes and chooses a child, leaving the others. Fear of punishment for a series of mistakes causes the homely, forlorn boy to run away. There is much excitement and mystery as Oscar and Rasmus become involved with two robbers. Given an opportunity to stay with a good farm couple, Rasmus realizes he loves Oscar, so remains a wanderer. As it turns out, Oscar does have a wife, Martina, so Rasmus finds a home, but the reader knows he and Oscar will one day be back on the open road.

Relationships with One Parent Many children have only one parent because of death or divorce or desertion. Others find an emotional gulf separates them from one parent or another. These life situations are encountered by children in fine books.

In the book, *The Grizzly*, David has been reared by his mother after she separated from his father. When he is eleven, the boy, who has less than average physical skill and endurance, is taken on a camping trip by Mark, his rugged, outdoorsman father. The book opens with a description of David's fear of his father expressed in nightmares:

Fear . . . sometimes it is a swift thing. But there are times when it is more like a great dark clock, ticking. To David it came that way, out of long-ago years he could hardly remember. For months it would be quiet inside him as his

own heartbeat. Then he would have one of the nightmares.[15]

The reader is immediately intrigued. What will a grizzly have to do with a boy's fear of his father? The authors give details of his father's prowess and skill in chopping a tree, casting for fish, and cooking. David fears that his father will leave him alone to test him. He recalls the way Mark was always trying to make him strong when he was small, and so he is still afraid. The authors build a sense of threat in a rising crescendo. Even the description of the setting heightens the anxiety. For example, dawn is painted in taut prose:

The fire made a small pinch of warmth in the vastness of the fog. . . . Around him out there in the haze the valley seemed to crouch, waiting. Even the mutter of the river was hushed in the ghostly white of dawn. David felt threatened.[16]

As the day wears on, Mark and David meet the unexpected—a grizzly that chases David and attacks Mark. David proves he does have skill, endurance, and courage in a crisis. His father experiences for the first time fear for himself and his boy. Each learns from the other as respect and understanding grow between father and son.

Run, Westy, Run is a story by Gudrun Alcock of a boy who runs away from the prison of his windowless, crowded bedroom, from a life of work with no opportunity for play, from isolation, from his overworked parents who are struggling to save for a better home "sometime." The last time he ran away Westy took money, so he was brought to court for truancy and delinquency. At the juvenile home, Westy is fortunate in having

---

[15]Annabel and Edgar Johnson, *The Grizzly*, Illustrated by Gilbert Riswold (New York: Harper & Row, 1964), p. 3.

[16]Johnson, p. 41.

skilled and compassionate help from the truant officer and chaplain. Some readers may doubt that the typical boy in Westy's situation would "unload" his burdens as quickly as Westy did, yet the need to have someone listen was real and overpowering. Teachers will wonder why no one at the school had recognized the symptoms or found out about the reasons why Westy was truant. The realism of the court scene will give children a picture of justice in action. Westy's father relates the story of his life—of being poor on a farm where there was no fun, no freedom, just work. As an adult, he faced more struggles when he was laid off work and placed on relief. Suddenly, Mr. Weston realizes Westy is behaving just as he did, has the same needs, and Westy begins to see his father in a new light. The window for his bedroom becomes a symbol of need for space and companionship; when his parents exchange rooms so he can see the sky, he realizes he is also receiving their love and encouragement.

In his second Newbery Award book, Krumgold writes of Andrew Rusch who wants to be like his father, a hardware merchant in the small town of Serenity. However, Mr. Rusch hopes to realize his own dreams of becoming a scientist through his son. When Andy discovers he has an ability to communicate with an immigrant town bum, *Onion John*, he transfers his loyalty and resents his father's interference with the superstitions and rituals of Onion John. He is hurt by the way his father and the townspeople try to change Onion John into a "proper citizen" by building an acceptable home for him. Finally, Andy is freed from his father's dominance and the superstition of Onion John. Each of these men contributes to Andy's growing independence. The closing scene is a beautifully written description of the communication of a father and son through gesture and smiles.

Another Newbery Award book, *It's Like This, Cat,* describes a boy's relationship with his father. Dave's insistence upon having a pet cat despite his father's disapproval symbolizes his growing independence. The opening scene in which Dave's father roars at him about a record he is playing is repeated in countless homes. Dave has some understanding of reasons for his father's raving and realizes their arguments cause his mother's asthma. Dave's encounters with Nick, with girls, with Mary, whose intellectual parents seem to care little about her, Aunt Kate, the eccentric who liked cats, and the school are depicted in realistic first person style. Dave sees his father in a new light when he helps Tom, an older boy who gets into trouble. Dave and his father do not settle all their quarrels; there is the beginning of tolerance, but the author leaves the family still struggling to attain some degree of harmony.

Gull 737 is the title derived from the number given a sea gull chick being studied by a biologist, Dr. Rivers. Author Jean George includes fascinating information about gulls and the procedures of research in this narrative that portrays a boy growing up and a father realizing he has a responsibility to his family as well as to science. When there is a plane crash caused by gulls on a runway, Dr. Rivers is called in to help solve the problem. His son Luke's suggestions are accepted by another scientist, and Luke becomes excited about his own investigation—not for money or for fame, but *to find out for himself.* Luke realizes his father is self-centered and close-minded, so he defies his father by leaving to begin his own study. "He had just stepped out of his father's image of him . . . a nice little boy . . . and he was finding the new suit of manhood a loose garb to wear."[17] Luke's father finally recog-

[17]Jean George, *Gull 737* (New York: Crowell, 1964), p. 169.

nizes the value of his son's creative ideas and is able to communicate his feeling to the boy, who is beginning to understand his father.

Three stories about girls and their relationships with parents are well written for middle and upper grade girls. *Home from Far* by Little is described in full in Chapter 13. *Lotte's Locket* by Sorensen tells of the problems of a Danish girl who found it difficult to accept her mother's marriage to a Texan. She did not object so much to the marriage as to the necessity for moving away from her friends and the family traditions represented by the locket that was handed down from one generation to the next. For one who had visited Copenhagen, the descriptions of the city, the Little Mermaid, and Tivoli are a real treat, but children will find them tedious. A subplot is developed through a contest for the best essay on Danish participation in World War II. Here, too, there is more historical detail than many children will accept. Lotte's passionate jealousy and desire to win are important to the story, and illustrate fine characterization.

The theme of *My Daughter, Nicola* by Arthur is a daughter's struggle for acceptance by her father and herself. The setting is a Swiss village, but the relationships are universal. Nicola's father leaves the village after her mother dies, and she is raised by her grandmother. The story is told as though an old lady is recalling her childhood. She points out the root of her trouble, her tempers and fights, as caused by her small size. Thinking that people despised her, she "felt impelled to show everyone that I was a person of consequence in spite of my small stature. This I did by hurtling myself into battle, fighting with my fists, my feet, and even my teeth, whenever I imagined myself slighted."[18] It is in the Italian home of her friend Carlotta that Nicola learns she has

talent and that she wants to be a singer. Before that dream is realized, she must show her father she is as good as the son he did not have by meeting the challenge of the mountain. Instead of climbing up, she descends into an abandoned mine. Friends save her from the foolhardy venture, but she is able to win her father's praise and apology for being blind to her needs. The author recreates the calm village life of Switzerland sixty years ago.

D. J. Madison's story of his relationship with his parents, his sister, and little brother, Renfroe, is told in first person by Robert Burch in *D. J.'s Worst Enemy*. Set in the rural South in the 1930s, this is also a story of poverty. D. J. simply refused to help the family in any way and was always "spoiling for a fight." D. J. feels remorse for the behavior that led to the infection in his little brother's foot which nearly cost him his life. Getting even for Clara May's bossiness, D. J. mixes the labels so his sister loses a ten-dollar reward during the peach harvest. Realizing that he is his own worst enemy, D. J. begins to change by accepting himself. This is a happy family despite the pinch of poverty, and the reader comes to like D. J.

Finding a Place in a Peer Group

Three- and four-year-olds have momentary concern for their sand-box companions, but it is not until children go to school that the peer group becomes important. By age nine, what other children think is often more significant than what parents or teachers think, and by thirteen, the place in the peer group is *all*-important. A few authors are especially sensitive to the patterns of childhood society.

Finding Acceptance by Peers In *The Smallest Boy in the Class*, Beim accurately portrays the behavior of a small boy who tried to prove he was big by telling big tales, shout-

---
[18]Ruth M. Arthur, *My Daughter, Nicola,* Illustrated by Fermin Rocker (New York: Atheneum, 1965), p. 5.

ing in a loud voice, painting big things, and by trying to be first. This child grows when he shares his lunch and receives the accolade, "You have the biggest heart in the class."

The need to belong to a closely knit group of peers is emphasized in *The New Boy*. On the first day in the new school, Jack asks himself, "Would he ever again be as these boys were, together, good pals, belonging?"[19] After a continuous quarrel with one boy erupts into a fight in the museum, Jack evaluates his own behavior:

Perhaps he had been too anxious to make the right impression on his fellows, to become one of them all in a moment, even to be recognized as a leader, as had been his place in his old school. These things did not come all in a moment, his common sense knew. It took time and trying to earn a place in a new group. For most people it did.[20]

There is humor and action in the story; the analysis does not merge into moralizing. This book would provide the basis for discussion of problems that boys and girls face in new situations.

One of the best-known works of realistic fiction for children is *The Hundred Dresses* by Eleanor Estes. Wanda Petronski, a Polish girl from a poor, motherless family, attempts to win a place in the group by telling of the hundred dresses she owns. Of course, she wears the same faded dress to school day after day, and is taunted by the other girls because she has a "funny" name and appears to be very stupid. After she moves away, her hundred dresses are presented in an art contest—one hundred fine drawings. The girls understand, too late, but it is Maddie who worries the most. Maddie is also poor, and as she recalls the way the taunting game started, she realizes her own cowardice:

She had stood by silently, and that was just as bad as what Peggy had done. Worse, she was a coward. At least Peggy hadn't considered they were being mean, but she, Maddie, had thought they were doing wrong.[21]

Peggy and Maddie's letter to Wanda does not really contain an apology, but Wanda does reply with a friendly note. There is not a happy ending, for Maddie will always have the burden of memory, and we can imagine Wanda will still have problems. Teachers will wonder what the teacher's role should have been, and ponder their responsibilities as they read this book.

The need for at least one good friend is expressed by Mary Stolz in *The Noonday Friends*. Franny and her only friend Simone stop speaking to each other, yet Franny can hardly recall the reason for the quarrel. The two girls were noonday friends because Franny had to care for her five-year-old brother after school and had much housework. They regularly eat lunch together and occasionally have time to make scrapbooks and talk. While Simone wants the world and people in it to be beautiful, Franny realizes that one has to see ugliness and admit it is there. More than a story of the friends, this is an account of a family struggling against poverty.

A more complex and controversial book is *Harriet, the Spy* by Fitzhugh. This book has the theme of the precocious child who finds difficulty in relating to her parents and her peers. The author presents the story in first person narrative and through the device of Harriet's diary. A nurse, Ole Golly, had been Harriet's sole source of security; when she leaves, Harriet is very lonely. The sophisticated parents are too busy to give more than superficial attention to Harriet's "spy" activities in her New York neighborhood. The people Harriet observes are particularly ec-

[19]Mary Urmston, *The New Boy* (New York, Doubleday, 1950), p. 41.
[20]Urmston, p. 176.

[21]Eleanor Estes, *The Hundred Dresses*, Illustrated by Louis Slobodkin (New York: Harcourt, 1944), p. 49.

centric. There are excellent descriptions of the couple who are only concerned with material things, the strange man who keeps cats but builds bird cages, the family that operates a small grocery, and a disillusioned movie "actress." These profiles are of more interest to adults than to children, although some children find them somewhat amusing. It is Harriet's relationships with other children and the alienation that occurs when they discover her journal that is of most interest to young readers. Sport, the boy who has to care for his writer-father, and Janey, who hopes to be a scientist, do represent children's problems. Fitzhugh has given a very accurate study of the way children respond to teachers, to their cliques, and to their cruelty. Most children like Harriet, but many adults dislike her. Children know the Harriets and recognize her qualities in themselves. They would often like to have the courage to do what she does. However, Fitzhugh has suggested a questionable solution to Harriet's problems when Ole Golly mentions that it is sometimes necessary to lie in order to get along with people. Harriet's visit to the psychiatrist has little effect on her behavior. Basically, Harriet remains unchanged by her traumatic experience, but she has grown in understanding. Whether Harriet lives on in children's literature will depend upon the way children and teachers discuss the implications of this book for their lives.

Two books by Mary Stolz should be read together, but the sequence of reading *A Dog on Barkham Street* and *The Bully of Barkham Street* seems unimportant. The same characters and events are treated in each book, but from a different point of view. Edward is frightened of the bully next door because he is two years younger and smaller. He teases Martin by calling him "Fatso" and "Plump Pudding" and then running to safety. Envious of the parental love Edward receives, and angry because his parents seem unin-

terested in him and partial to his sister, Martin becomes aggressive and sullen. In *A Dog on Barkham Street*, Edward and his friend recall that Marty had owned a dog briefly but had not taken care of it, and it had mysteriously disappeared. In the other book, *The Bully of Barkham Street*, the reader learns the details of the incident and the intensity of Martin's loss when the dog was peremptorily removed by his parents. There are moments of understanding between his teacher, his sister, his mother, and his neighbors. Martin says to his mother, "I think that if people listened to their children it might be easier, for both parties. . . ."[22] Martin goes on a diet and tries to ignore the other boys, but reform is neither easy nor smooth. Edward's father goes to Marty after his son and a friend run away and are nearly caught in a refrigerator car. His understanding and recall of Martin's good sportsmanship at a school program give Martin hope. He remarks, "Someday, when you're grown, Martin, you'll find that things can't be as simple as children would like them to be. The human being is extremely complicated, with the good and the bad all mixed up."[23] Mary Stolz's books show these mixtures in an interesting style that brings humor, adventure, and insight to boys and girls.

Life in a Gang   Children today form gangs at earlier ages than in former years. By the second grade, they seek independence from adults, yet need the security of the peer group. The gangs are often just groups having fun. Sometimes, the gangs express a group hostility through stealing or violence.

The title of Emily Neville's book about children on one block in New York would lead to the expectation of a story about the

---

[22]Mary Stolz, *The Bully of Barkham Street,* Illustrated by Leonard Shortall (New York: Harper & Row, 1963), p. 143.

[23]Stolz, p. 190.

typical, organized gang. However, *The Seventeenth-Street Gang* is composed of younger children who still get parental permission before venturing very far. Leadership of this group shifts frequently. In flashbacks, the author shows how the friendships within the gang were formed. A girl nicknamed Minnow, the most imaginative of the group, leads in attacks on the "flots," people who are stuffy, who talk down to children, and who are bossy to children. Minnow also organizes a plot to torment the new boy, Hollis. Hollis wants to be friendly, but has used his big dog to frighten the children because he is afraid he will not be accepted. When Minnow falls in the river and is rescued by Hollis, the plan against him backfires. The children reject Minnow because they feel she betrayed them. Each child's relationship with his parents is revealed as he reacts to the newspaper account of the rescue. The need of children for love and attention from adults is made clear in these brief, realistic sketches.

In *Trouble After School*, Beim has depicted the way a boy becomes involved with a leather-jacket gang. This story of a junior-high group points out the rebellion of these young adolescents. The reaction to his mother's questions about after-school activities brings forth a torrent of words from Lee:

> *"Golly, parents just don't want kids to grow up! they want to treat them like infants, wrap them in cotton-wool, and keep them that way forever! . . . I'll get along all right on my own—you'll see—you'll see!"*[24]

When he discovers the boys steal from the store and the gang decides to destroy the high-school canteen, Lee stands against them although it is hard to hear the words, "You're yellow!"

---

[24]Jerrold Beim, *Trouble After School* (New York: Harcourt, 1957), p. 93.

A boy's love for his dog is the only light in Jamie's dull, bleak existence in crowded London. From the book *The Greyhound*, by Helen Griffiths, illustrated by Victor Ambrus. Copyright © 1964 by Hutchinson & Co. (Publishers). Reprinted by permission of Doubleday & Company, Inc.

The Greyhound by Griffiths is a dog story, but it is far more than a story of a boy's need and the development of love for an old dog. Jamie's loneliness, the poverty of the London home, the bullies at the cheerless, dull school seem more than one boy can bear. Into this bleak existence comes a greyhound, at first only observed walking with an old man, then "borrowed" for walks, and at last owned by Jamie. That ownership costs Jamie much more than the five pounds he borrows from an older boy at school! He buys the dog when the man has to go to an old people's home, for "he knew that Silver Streak must feel like him; empty and sometimes afraid."[25] When he cannot return the money, Jamie is forced to help the gang steal. Knowing he cannot have the dog at home, Jamie has made a hideaway in a bombed-out building. Jamie becomes more isolated from his mother when he lashes out at her after her refusal to let him keep the dog. "He was more lonely now than he had ever been — trapped on an island of his own creation — and in the gathering darkness of his confusion his love for Silver offered him the only gleam of light."[26] He has hurt his mother, continues to tell lies, and has to leave his dog for long periods of time in a dark damp cellar. He goes without food and works so he can get money to feed the dog. Jamie is utterly trapped into the gang activities. The time comes when he refuses to help rob an old lady, and finally confesses the whole sordid predicament to his mother. The authorities accept his story, but do not apprehend the gang. When Jamie goes to get Silver there is an ugly, brutal scene as the gang enters the basement and attacks the dog to take revenge on Jamie. Worry, lack of food, and exposure lead to a severe illness, but Jamie recovers. There is a happy ending for the reader who can withstand the shock of the beating of the dog. The poverty of Jamie's environment looms larger than one boy's inner resources. This book is a dog story, but it is also a commentary on life in the slums. It raises important questions. Do the means justify the end? What is the limit of endurance, or loyalty, or honesty when one you love is alone, cold, and hungry?

The torments of a gang can be cruel, even though their acts are merely verbal. In *You Have a Friend, Pietro,* by Grund, a Sicilian village gang harasses Pietro because his father is in prison. An old stonecutter comes to the village and prepares his own monument with a broken dagger on the top. The boys go to Emilio, planning to force him to talk. Surprised by his acceptance of their behavior, they are soon engrossed in his story of a vendetta that he tells in parts over a period of time. Through these weeks, Emilio is also teaching Pietro to cut stone. He suggests Pietro draw pictures of the boys who are cruel to him. The behavior of the boys changes as they hear the tragic story of hatred being told by Emilio. There is exciting mystery, as well as suspense, in this narrative of a chain of hate that is finally broken by expressions of love.

Frank Bonham's social documentary, *Durango Street,* centers upon Negro gangs in California. A Negro teenager returns from the reformatory to the same environment that caused him to be sent there. Poverty, no father, a mother who doesn't understand him, and the gangs continue to plague this boy. To be safe from one gang, he must join another. There is brutality, fear, constant danger. A young social worker joins the gang, but is merely tolerated. The book ends on a note of slight hope, but one realizes there will be many more fights, more trouble in the years ahead. This book is more appropriate for junior or senior high school, but some children in sixth grade may have the emotional security to withstand the grim details of gang violence and the interest in boy-girl relationships described in this book.

Finding a Place in Society

Both the family and peer group exist in a larger society that influences the behavior of adults and children. Finding a place in the wider social group in the United States today is dependent upon one's economic status, education, religion, and racial background. Juvenile literature presents these conflicts as they are encountered by children in the modern world.

Racial Differences Teachers and librarians have sought books that present natu-

---

[25]Helen Griffiths, *The Greyhound,* Illustrated by Victor G. Ambrus (New York: Doubleday, 1964), p. 35.
[26]Griffiths, p. 87.

ral wholesome characters with whom the minority-group child could identify. All children need to understand the prejudice experienced by minority-group children. Unfortunately, few books faced the problems of Negroes or others in minority groups, and many presented major or minor characters as stereotyped figures. A stereotype is a characterization of an individual with common, generalized traits believed to be possessed by all members of his group. For example, the mental image of a "farm boy" as a red-haired, freckled-faced lad in a torn shirt trudging barefoot down a dusty lane with a fishing pole over his shoulder is a stereotype. All people should be viewed as individuals, as the vast diversity of human characters should be presented.

Many of the early books about Negroes presented stereotyped characters (see page 87). Written in the 1930s, *Sad-Faced Boy* by Bontemps describes the adventures of three Negro boys who visit Harlem for the first time. The illustrations in this book are stereotypes showing the kinky-headed, grinning Negro who is hard working, but mainly seeks fun. Although their trip to New York is plausible, their confidence in exploring the city seems somewhat improbable. This was one of the first books, however, to show the poor conditions where the Negroes lived.

A book of photographs of Negro farm life in North Carolina, *Tobe*, by Sharpe, was published in 1939. The large photographs are sharp and detailed; the text is easy to read, but is written in a trite, primer style. The photographs are out-of-date, for ankle-length dresses are worn by the women going to church, the farm machinery is very old, and the boys' caps and overalls are out of fashion. Unfortunately, this book, which gives an inaccurate picture of the Negro today, still appears on some recommended lists.

In the books published before World War II, the Negroes lived segregated lives. Pictures of city streets and schoolrooms did not show Negroes as part of society. The Negro was still "in his place." By the end of World War II, several books appeared that openly faced the problem of prejudice, and some showed integration. The illustrations in one picture book published by the Beims in 1945, *Two Is a Team*, showed a Negro boy and white boy playing together, quarreling, and reuniting to rebuild their wagon, but the skin color was not mentioned in the text. *Melindy's Medal* by Faulkner and Becker and *Call Me Charley* by Jackson were published in 1945, while de Angeli's *Bright April* followed in 1946. *Skid* was published by Hayes in 1948. A Boston housing development is the setting of *Melindy's Medal*. The illustrations are natural; the reader hardly realizes Melindy is a Negro, as race is rarely mentioned. In one incident, prejudice is clearly suggested, however, as people comment about those who were to move into the project:

> *This man made a speech in which he told how lots of people said the project was foolish because it was built for colored people and how lots of colored people had never owned property so they wouldn't know how to take care of fine property and would make it dirty and destroy it.*[27]

The pride of these people is clearly demonstrated as they enjoy a private bathroom, clean space for living, and gardens. Medals had been won by Melindy's great grandfather, grandfather, and father in times of war. Being a girl, she could hardly carry on the tradition, but she does receive a medal for bravery in playing the piano to maintain order while the children escaped during a school fire. The plot of this story is more important than the racial theme.

Jackson presented the conflict experienced by the white boy who befriends Charley, a Negro. It is to be hoped no school principal would speak to a student as does the one in this book. The conflicting values

[27]Georgene Faulkner and John Becker, *Melindy's Medal* New York: Messner, 1945), p. 23.

expressed in school and community were openly presented:

> *"It's like the real estate man told father when we looked at our house, before we bought it. He said, 'No nigger or Jews or Dagos live in Arlington Heights. It's only for Americans.' You see? Charley doesn't really live here. He only stays at Doctor Cunningham's because his parents work there."*
> *"That kind of stuff ain't what we say at school."*
> *"What do you mean?" George asked.*
> *"You know when we have the flag raising. You know. . . ." Tom looked at the floor. "All that stuff about liberty and justice for all."*[28]

For several years, *Bright April* was considered a good book to use for development of racial understanding. A closer study of the book today reveals its weaknesses of moralizing and a "pat" solution. A repetition of such platitudes as "Do your best" reduces its effectiveness for children. April faces prejudice in her Brownie scout troop; her older sister and brother meet the problem in their attempt to enter professions. The plot seems too thin to bear the burden of so many problems. Fine family relationships are described in the text. The soft illustrations show warmth and humor, although they do not portray the handsome, distinctive quality of Negro characteristics. Instead, the Negroes resemble dark-skinned whites. A comparison of these illustrations with those by Crichlow for *South Town* and *Mary Jane* will reveal startling differences.

In the preface to *Skid*, Florence Hayes writes, "Boys are boys no matter what their race or language." No mention is made of the characters as Negroes, although in the description of the teacher, her "brown skin" is noted. The illustrations by Elton Fax show *natural*-appearing boys and girls. When the family moves north so Skid can have a better education, this ten-year-old suffers the pangs of being new in a school.

By the mid-1960s, books emphasizing the problem of school integration were available for classroom discussion. A book for young children was *New Boy in School* by Justus. Seven-year-old Lennie does not like the new, integrated school in Nashville. As the only Negro in the room, he is sure the others are laughing at him. Soon he accepts invitations to play and wins a place for himself by singing for a parents' program. The unchildlike dialogue, lack of action, and moralizing statements combine to make this book of questionable value for the classroom.

Three books with girls as central characters present the problems of school integration. *Mary Jane* by Sterling was based upon a junior high school situation in Arkansas. As one of the first Negroes to attend a former all-white school, Mary Jane realizes she is truly a pioneer. The taunting crowd calls forth her courage, and the reader feels the impact of the scene:

> *The policemen went first, clearing a path through the crowd, leading the way. It was as if they were marching in a parade.*
> *Heads up. Eyes front. One-two-three-four.*
> *Only instead of drums to keep time, there were screams.*
> *A man, angry. "Go back to Africa!"*
> *Mary Jane turned her head, trying to see who it was. What did he mean?*
> *A woman, high-pitched—could it have been a woman? "Pull her black curls out."*
> *A group of boys chanting, for all the world as if they were at a football game:*
> > *Two, four, six, eight*
> > *We ain't gonna integrate.*[29]

Her academic ability, friendship with a white girl who is also a misfit, care of a pet squirrel,

---

[28]Jesse Jackson, *Call Me Charley*, Illustrated by Doris Spiegel (New York: Harper & Row, 1945), p. 5.

[29]Dorothy Sterling, *Mary Jane*, Illustrated by Ernest Crichlow (New York: Doubleday, 1959), p. 51.

and the reputation of her scientist grandfather combine to win her a place at school. However, the two girls cannot be friends outside the school.

Natalie Carlson presents the story of Lullah, who continued to go to *The Empty Schoolhouse* after the white children were sent to the public school. When the first Louisiana parochial school was integrated, Lullah and her white friend, Oralee, enjoyed their experiences. Two agitators from the outside threaten both whites and Negroes and cause hostile feelings. The poignant scene when Oralee refuses to include Lullah in her party will remind all children of moments when they have failed to do what is "right." When Lullah is shot in the ankle, the community is aroused, the white ladies come to see Lullah, and all ends on a falsely happy note.

Patricia Crosses Town by Baum deals with the problems of city children who enter a previously all-white school. Pat had not been a good student, and had won a place for herself by playing the clown. Now the teacher seems to *expect* her to learn and also turns her interest in drama to constructive activity. Friendship with a white girl is acceptable at school, but the children are told they cannot play together. The contrived plot weakens the value of the book, but the classroom scenes might well be discussed.

Some books are now appearing that present Negroes as main characters without mentioning the problems of prejudice. *A Summer Adventure* by Lewis is a description of a Negro boy's first summer on a farm. No reason is given for the move to the farm, nor do we know how Ross was accepted at school, or why he has no friends. He collects tadpoles, insects, turtles, and tames a crow for his "zoo." When he breaks an arm and is "imprisoned" in the hospital he realizes what it is to be caged. Ross gives his animals their freedom, with the implied theme of freedom for all. A story for younger children is *Mississippi Possum* by Miles. When the Mississippi

Lullah feels left out as her white friend plays on the swings in a segregated playground. Illustration by John Kaufmann from *The Empty Schoolhouse* by Natalie Savage Carlson. Harper & Row, 1965.

River floods their farm, a Negro family stays in a tent on high ground. The possum symbolizes those who will accept Negroes as he willingly joins them.

For older children, two books by Graham present the problems of change as a family is forced to leave the south and adjusts to life in the North. *South Town* shows the fear of the white community after World War II and Korea as Negroes seek more education and gain some measure of skill that becomes of economic value. In order to make more money, David's father has gone to the city to work in a factory. When the factory closes, he refuses to return to work for low wages as a mechanic in a local garage. To show them "their place" and to frighten all the Negroes, the whites put David's father in jail without

A handsome Negro lad is deeply troubled by the injustice of a small Southern community. From *South Town* by Lorenz Graham. Jacket design by Ernest Crichlow. Copyright 1958. Reprinted courtesy of Follett Publishing Company.

cause and try to terrorize his family. A white veteran who had been saved in Korea by Negro medics is shot while staying with the family through a long night of tension. There are some signs of hope; those whites in the town who had remained quiet, protest, and the son of the white leader comes to David to express his feeling of sympathy. In *North Town* there are many incidents showing Northern prejudice—in housing, the hospital, and the court. David gets in trouble and refuses to trust the whites who try to

help. One of the values of this book is that it reveals the various points of view of different Negroes and helps readers understand the folly of generalizing about a "Negro attitude."

A book that may be said to represent "literature of despair" for children is *The Jazz Man* by Weik. Zeke is a lonely, crippled boy living in Harlem. His parents love him, but both work during the day. The fact that Zeke was nine and had never been to school is never fully explained in the text. Zeke and his parents find moments of happiness when a new neighbor, a jazz man, plays the music that talks to Zeke:

> . . . about all the things that nobody in the world had ever talked to him about before, that explained everything that had happened in his whole life.
>
> It was wonderful what he could do. He could play a table of food right down in front of you when you were hungry. He could play your Mama's worries right off her head, when the rent man was nagging her for the rent money she didn't have. He could play the sad look off her mouth, and shiny silver slippers onto her feet—just like that—and zip her into a party dress with silver stars all over it, smelling of violet perfume (the kind she loved!), and start her dancing like she used to do.
>
> He could play your Daddy out of his no-job blues, play the dreams right out of his old brown bottle, and make him feel like the king of the universe.[30]

His Daddy loses his job, drinks, and his mother leaves them both. Then Daddy stays away, too. Zeke finally refuses the food left grudgingly by neighbors; he becomes colder and hungrier; at last he sleeps. The jazz man has gone, too. Zeke wakens, in pain, and feverish. He goes out—seeking somebody:

> He was trying to find somebody—just who, he didn't know. Somebody he knew better than himself. Who knew all about him too—who he

[30]Mary Hays Weik, *The Jazz Man*, Illustrated by Ann Grifalconi (New York: Atheneum, 1966), p. 17.

was, what he looked like, how mixed-up he was. And who still loved him.[31]

Zeke crosses a street and views a heaven—a room filled with the music of the jazz man, smell of food, and his Daddy and Mama. The reader will not be sure whether Zeke wakens to reality with the return of his parents and all the old fear and worry, or whether death has taken him to meet the symbolic jazz man. At any rate, the author leaves no hope of escape in Harlem. She expresses the spiritual hunger of a child, of all men, for understanding and love.

We can hope that in a few years literature will be less self-conscious, that there will be stories of Negroes with plots and themes chosen for reasons other than problems created by the color of their skin.

The books about Puerto Ricans and Cubans tend to be written with less character development, more contrivance of plot, and more limited imagery in language than the books about Negroes. A book that describes the adjustment problems of a Puerto Rican child in New York is *Candita's Choice* by Lewiton. How fortunate for Candita that the school provided a special class with an understanding teacher! This book makes clear the importance of social workers in a community and sympathetically portrays the problems of immigrants.

In *That Bad Carlos,* Lewiton narrates the story of a boy who is irresponsible, who accepts ideas of others without thinking for himself, and who seems to be earning a bad reputation in the neighborhood. The contacts with the policemen in this book would indicate that the police respect Puerto Ricans and are not prejudiced. These people live in their own section of the city, speak Spanish, and seem to have few contacts with the "outside" world.

The warmth of family love in the Santos family is chilled by the prejudice these Puerto Ricans find in New York. In *The Spi-*

The music of the jazz man brings fleeting happiness to a Negro family of Harlem. Copyright © 1966 by Mary Hays Weik. From *The Jazz Man,* illustrated by Ann Grifalconi. Used by permission of Atheneum Publishers.

der Plant by Speevack, life seems more difficult in the new housing development than it was in the crowded tenement torn down for urban renewal. When Carmen and Pedro go to a park to get soil for her spider plants, a policeman, thinking all Puerto Ricans look alike, insists he told them last month not to take dirt. This brief encounter with the law leads other children and parents to avoid the family. Carmen does win acceptance by sharing her plants, however. Unfortunately, the ending is contrived; the details of the party and games are "padding" beyond the climax.

Acceptance in society may be a problem in other countries, too. In *Blue in the Seed,* Kim Yong Ik writes of a Korean boy's problems because he was different. Bok's blue eyes bring teasing from the boys in a new

---

[31]Weik, p. 37.

school, yet they try to help him. He attempts to hide the problem by buying dark glasses; he runs away and finds peace in a monastery where a Monk speaks to him of the "inner eye." Bok's pet, his ox, disappears and is recovered because a man remembered the boy's blue eyes. When Bok is bitten by a poisonous snake, he finally accepts help from other children. Recalling the love in his mother's blue eyes, Bok realizes he must think of the inner eye of love. Although the theme of the book is concerned with prejudice, it also asks why it is sometimes difficult to accept love.

In these books, children will find a kind of courage "to be" that will serve as a beacon toward the day when it is no longer necessary to question a man's place in society because of his race.

Regional Differences The term "region" may refer to a very large geographical area, such as the Northwest, to a type of land, as the desert region, or to an economic area, as the farming region. In another sense, it may be a smaller section, such as the Tennessee mountains, or a locale where immigrants have continued to live in closed communities, such as the Amish region in Pennsylvania. Also, a city or suburb might be considered a region when discussing books that are specifically intended to show the influence of locale upon the characters and theme of the book. In realistic fiction, the setting plays a part, but in regional books, it exerts a stronger influence. *Harriet, the Spy* by Fitzhugh reflects one aspect of life in New York, but the purpose is not to show the influence of the city. Life does revolve around the raising of sheep in New Mexico in *. . . And Now Miguel,* in Montana in *The Loner,* and in New England in *Mountain Born.* Each of these books might be called a regional book, yet their themes are universal.

Leo Politi's picture books are regional in the sense that they show the life of people who live in one section of a city. *Pedro, the Angel of Olvera Street* tells of a little Mexican boy who played the part of an angel in a pageant of the people who live on this street in Los Angeles. *Juanita* by the same author-illustrator carries a dove in the Mexican Procession of the Blessing of the Animals on the Saturday before Easter. These books have a slight story, but are intended to show customs of cultural groups.

Credle's picture storybook, *Down, Down the Mountain,* portrays mountain life in Depression days. Two children raise turnips to sell to buy shoes, but give away all but one of the vegetables as they go down the mountain. The remaining turnip wins a prize at the fair, so they have five dollars to buy two pairs of shoes. The language is stilted; the children are unbelievably optimistic! Although frequently cited as a book about mountain life, this story conveys little of the isolation and hard life of the mountaineers. Caudill's Christmas story, *A Certain Small Shepherd,* and Musgrave's *Robert E.* give more details of life in this region.

The name of Lois Lenski is closely associated with the term "regional fiction." Lenski goes to live in a community, observes as an anthropologist would observe, listens to the people, asks them to tell what has happened in their lives. Then she weaves the facts into an interesting plot centered upon one family. Lenski writes of the purposes of her books:

> *I am trying to introduce the children of one region to another, thus widening their horizons. I want to tell how they live and why, to point out details in backgrounds, occupations and customs peculiar to each region. But along with these differences, I show also the inward likenesses—the same universal love of family and kinfolk, the same devotion to or longing for one's homeplace, the same universal struggle for the things we all hold dear—truth, security and happiness. My stories emphasize*

not the things that hold us apart, but all those things that bring and hold us together in the one great human family.[32]

In *Strawberry Girl*, a Newbery Award book, she describes life in the central Florida backwoods early in the twentieth century. In *Coal Camp Girl*, the West Virginia family experiences hunger during a winter when there is no food; they know the agony of waiting for the rescue of men trapped in a mine and the hard economic lesson of being paid "scrip" in advance of the salary and buying at the high-cost company store.

Texas Tomboy is about a young girl who wants to become a ranchwoman. Riding over the plains with her father, "Charlie Boy" learns the lore of ranching. Strong and fearless, her imagination and energy sometimes cause problems. Charlie Boy is often thoughtless, sometimes cruel, and frequently disobedient. The child who reads this book learns about problems of ranch life; he also gains insight into the conflicting demands of society and the individual, as a little girl rebels against her expected sex role. In *Prairie School*, Lenski has written a modern story of prairie life. The trials of life on a snowbound prairie of South Dakota are arduous. Miss Lenski realistically portrays the snowbound days in the school, the dramatic episode when the teacher takes Dolores through the storm for an appendectomy, and the hay drop by helicopter to save the cattle. In these stories, children and adults face their problems and eke out a living, but characters seldom make value choices or grow up as a result of experience. Although the children show little character change, they do effect change. Frequently, it is the child who improves the lot of the family.

Lenski's observations have included language patterns that have been accurately recorded. For example, when Birdie Boyer, in *Strawberry Girl*, is accused of being a Yankee she explains:

> *Shucks, no! . . . We're shore 'nough Crackers. We was born in Marion County. We're just the same as you-all . . . I done tole you we ain't Yankees.*[33]

This may be one of Lenski's greatest contributions, for some regional dialects are being lost with the advent of television and greater mobility of population. In *Corn Farm Boy*, Dick says "He just don't like hogs, Dad," but these characters seldom use "yeah," "git," or omit the "g" sound in verbs as do many rural Iowans today. This illustrates the problem of attempting to portray an entire region with one book. Northern Iowa speech may be different from that of southern Iowa.

Teachers also need to help children who read these books to become aware of the time period. Lenski portrays changes coming to the region at the time she writes, but the reader needs to realize that the San Francisco of 1953 is not San Francisco in 1968. A further problem is that the people in these books are poor or from the lower middle class. Teachers need to remember that each book presents only one small aspect of life in a particular region. Children need to be reminded of the danger of generalizing about all people of a region, class, or occupation.

This Boy Cody, by Wilson, presents a series of incidents in the life of a Cumberland Mountain family, including a house raising, a hunt for bees, and the house warming. The chapter about riddles would intrigue children in middle grades. The pervading atmosphere of contentment and fun ignores the hard work, lack of balanced diets, poor health, and other hardships usually associated with such a region.

George Harmon Smith describes life in Louisiana in *Bayou Boy*. Jean LeBlanc had

[32]Lois Lenski, "My Purpose," *Lois Lenski: An Appreciation*, Charles Adams, Editor (Durham, N.C.: Christian Printing Company, 1963), pp. 40–41.

[33]Lois Lenski, *Strawberry Girl* (Philadelphia: Lippincott, 1945), p. 29.

never gone to school, but his father had taught him the lore of the swamp and the skills needed to exist by farming, hunting, and trapping. While Jean's father goes to work on the off-shore oil rig, the boy is left in charge. He proves his ability to help his mother solve the problems of an invasion of wild hogs, a sick mule, and helping to find an alcoholic neighbor who went off to Wilderness Island. Jean is also brave and clever in meeting the challenge of an escaped convict, but he nearly loses his own life when he goes in search of his dog, taken by the escapee. Jean and his family realize change will come with the building of the road. After proving himself, Jean feels he can now go to school, even though he will have to begin with little children. The grimness and poverty of life near the swamp is presented in this exciting story.

Different Religious Backgrounds Although the United States was founded upon a belief in freedom of religion, misunderstanding and religious prejudice have persisted in our society. Some historical fiction shows these conflicts. For example, *Thee, Hannah* by de Angeli describes the escapades and restlessness of a little Quaker girl just before the Civil War. Hannah and the boys wince at the taunting, "Quaker, Quaker, mashed pertater!" Hannah yearns for pretty dresses, but she learns the value of the plain Quaker bonnet when a runaway slave recognizes it as a symbol of help. In *Skippack School*, this author shows the religion of the Mennonites as a joy rather than a burden.

Three books present the lives of girls who belong to the "plain people." Adjustment to conflicting values of her Amish home and the school "outside" is difficult for Esther, the central character in *Plain Girl*. Sorenson sensitively writes of a father's disappointment when his son leaves the religious community and his fear when his daughter goes to the public school. Esther

grows up as she realizes that one step away from the values of home leads to other temptations. She also discovers that people who wear pink, blue, and red may be as kind and good as those who wear plain clothing. When her brother finally returns, the young people recognize they may need to change outward symbols, such as hair cuts and use of machinery, but they can keep the inner values of their religion.

Hannah Elizabeth by Rich is the quiet story of a year in the life of a ten-year-old Indiana Mennonite. She has to learn to accept taunts of schoolmates because her father refused to fight in the war. Many quotations from the Bible and parts of sermons are included as well as accounts of fun in family life. Hannah Elizabeth attends a movie and party with her music teacher, but realizes she was not being a good Mennonite. Faced with conflicting values, she has no difficulty in choosing. This book lacks action, but the warm relationships of the family life will appeal to many middle-grade girls.

Shoo-Fly Girl by Lenski portrays life in an Amish family in Pennsylvania. The Foreword is an important part of this book and should be read by the teacher to the children. This book paints a detailed picture of a different culture—the homes, language, work of the children, church, and values. Shoo-Fly's encounters with the outside world bring confusion, and she prefers home. She accepts the answer of her Great-Grossomommy, who explained why women used pins instead of buttons:

> . . . *To keep humble, to avoid false pride. We are the plain people. We eat plain, we live plain, we dress plain, to show that our hearts are not set on the things of this world, but above. We are Amish. These things we have always done. So we will always do.*[34]

---

[34]Lois Lenski, *Shoo-Fly Girl* (Philadelphia: Lippincott, 1963), pp. 117–118.

In *A Promise Is a Promise,* Cone helps children understand the Jewish faith. Essentially, this is the story of Ruth Morgen's growing understanding of the meaning and history of her religion. Ruthy's preparation for her Bas Mitzvah is interwoven with the decisions she must make about daily relationships with people. Ruth is concerned about an eccentric, lonely neighbor whose cats bother another neighbor. Ruthy promises Mr. Hainey she will care for his cats when he goes to the hospital, and when he returns briefly to close his house forever, she promises to find a home for them. This would have been easy except for the complication of the neighbor who wants to get rid of the cats and Ruthy's father's directive that she must not become involved. "We don't want to quarrel with our neighbors. Do you understand? We are not going to stick our noses into other people's business. They don't both us; we're not going to bother them."[35] Ruth's problems become intertwined with her questions about the meaning of Judaism. The Rabbi does not preach; his comments are brief, but they help readers understand, too:

> . . . *You are old enough to recognize the responsibility of your religion: To act justly, to love mercy, and to keep for your good the commandments of the Lord . . . To a Jew there are no endings. There are only beginnings. . . .*[36]

The customs of the Jewish holidays and religious service are described in this sensitive story of a girl growing up.

The effect of anti-Semitism is realistically presented in *Berries Goodman* by Emily Neville. The book begins with a meeting of two high school boys, one of whom is defying his mother by going away from home on a holiday. The other, Berries, thinks about causes

Stiff figures are typical of Lenski's drawings that present realistic details of Amish life. From *Shoo-Fly Girl* by Lois Lenski, J. B. Lippincott Company, 1963; copyright by the author; used by permission of the author.

of behavior and begins a reminiscence of his relationship with Sidney, his Jewish friend. The rest of the book is a flashback to a New York suburb and the development of their friendship. Berries' parents provide love and interest in him, although his mother has little interest in cooking or keeping house. Sandra, next door, has to prove herself to others because her parents really give her little time. It is Sandra and her family who introduce Berries to prejudice against Jews. Berries learns that parents can be weak when his mother acquiesces to "agreements" made by the real estate agency for which she

---

[35]Molly Cone, *A Promise Is a Promise,* Illustrated by John Gretzer (Boston: Houghton Mifflin, 1964), p. 111.
[36]Cone, p. 141.

works. When Sidney is hurt because Sandra taunted him into skating in a dangerous area, his mother refuses to let Berries see him. In a discussion of the accident Sidney said, "The trouble was, Mom couldn't see that your family were any different from Sandra's. If your Mother had called up or anything. . . ."[37] Berries' father makes no protest when Sidney's father insists that the boys must stop their clandestine meetings.

In discussing realistic writing, Neville has expressed the view that an author should show that parents can be "nice cowards" and there should be a puzzlement; ". . . and this may make a child look a little more closely, a little more acutely at the people around him."[38]

The Impact of Government   Two books by Bloch show clearly the impact of the communistic government of Russia upon lives of individuals. *Aunt America* is the story of the effect on a Ukrainian family, especially eleven-year-old Lesya, of the visit of her aunt from America. Lesya has admired her uncle who gets along so well with the authorities, and she has questioned her father who was forced to abandon her when she was young. As her father's story is related, she sees him in a new light. The visit of the American aunt brings special privileges to show life is good, but the villagers realize the truth. Lesya's new understanding of courage and freedom prompt her to independent action to save her aunt from possible trouble.

In *The Two Worlds of Damyan*, the influence of the family is brought out strongly in the story of a boy's conflict with the values in a dictatorship. Damyan's two worlds are the home, where his grandmother expresses the values of respect for the individual and love for others and God, and the school and

society, where materialism and glory of the state are emphasized. Recognized as a good swimmer, Damyan is given an opportunity for training that might lead him to the Olympics. However, Fedya, the older boy who made this possible, insists that Damyan will succeed only if he joins the Komsomols. Damyan is further tempted by a new friend, Igor, whose parents have position in the Party and money for a large apartment, a maid, television, a car, and chocolates. Damyan's dream now includes these wonders. When he is urged to accompany the Komsomols to harass people who worship on Christmas, he decides he is obligated, despite the nagging doubts created by his grandmother's preparation for Christmas. Before the plan is executed, he goes alone to the church where Igor enters, smoking a cigarette. Igor knocks down the cleaning woman who had protested this sacrilege. Damyan is shocked and runs away to think:

> *Anguish on his face, Damyan stared out across the river. His two worlds were not a million miles apart, after all. On the contrary, the world outside surrounded the world of home on every side and with relentless might tried to worm its way in.*
> *Damyan took a deep breath. Then how did one think or stand alone? That was a question too big for him, he told himself. It was even too big for many grownups to find the answer to. Too big.*
> *Once he had dreamed of rescuing his grandmother, his father. . . . And wasn't that impudent of him? They could both stand alone, firm in their own beliefs. It was not they who needed rescuing but he.*[39]

Damyan decides he must give up the swimming lessons in order to be free. When he confesses the plan and his decision, his grandmother says she now believes those

[37]Emily Neville, *Berries Goodman* (New York: Harper & Row, 1965), p. 177.
[38]Emily Neville, "Social Values in Children's Literature," *Library Quarterly* (January 1967), p. 46.

[39]Marie Halun Bloch, *The Two Worlds of Damyan*, Illustrated by Robert Quackenbush (New York: Atheneum, 1966), p. 160.

who have the dream of freedom must not shut themselves away from the other world. Bloch expresses hope as the grandmother says, "You will need courage, much wisdom. But I have faith in you, faith in my teaching. For the things that one learns in childhood are the things that abide."[40] The author's descriptions of the crowded living quarters, the poverty, the school, and the market are indeed realistic. No factual book could present so well the impact of Communism upon daily life.

MEETING PROBLEMS OF THE HUMAN CONDITION

Men in all times and places face the human condition—loneliness, illness, poverty, war, and death. Individual responses to life are also determined by physical appearance, size, ability, and physical handicaps. Children do not escape these human problems; literature can give them windows for looking at different aspects of life, show them how some characters have met universal crises, and help them ask and answer questions about man as a human being.

Physical Handicaps

Understanding of the difficulties faced by a family in helping a baby who is handicapped by cerebral palsy is sensitively portrayed by Killilea in her book *Wren*. When the parents learn that Karen may never walk, they help the older child understand and accept her sister. When Karen gets braces and struggles to walk, Marie is told that it is no kindness to do things for her, or she will not learn to do them for herself. The faith expressed by the family and Karen herself is culminated in a beautiful moment at Christmas when she balances on one foot to lean toward the crèche.

In another story of a child who has cerebral palsy, a family has to learn to give love, but not to help too much. Jean Little's characterizations in *Mine for Keeps* are believable portraits. When Sally returns from a school for the handicapped to live at home, she attends regular school and meets many problems. A dog that may be hers "for keeps" helps her gain physical skill and emotional courage. Through Sally, a Dutch boy who has been ill and also has many problems, finds new confidence. This book will give new perspective on the problems of the emotionally or physically handicapped.

Another story of courage is told in *Follow My Leader* by James Garfield. Jimmy tried to duck an exploding firecracker, but it was too late. "The world exploded in a white flash. Deafening thunder smashed against his ears. Then the light was gone, and the sound was gone. Everything became very dark, very quiet."[41] Eleven-year-old Jimmy's world was to remain dark forever, but it is far from quiet as he learns to eat, to walk, to read, and to use the dog, Leader, as his constant guide and companion. At the guide school, Jimmy receives a warning about the sharp corner on a mantelpiece. When he suggests they put a piece of sponge on it the director asks, "Do you expect the world to pad its corners for you, just because you're blind?" The details of learning braille and of the training received at the guide-dog school are fascinating. Overcoming his hatred toward Mike, the boy who threw the firecracker, is very difficult for Jimmy. However, Jimmy visits Mike and they agree, "You can't be happy until you quit hating." Here is a good story, one that communicates feelings of those who must learn to live without sight.

The Dark of the Cave by Rydberg tells of three darknesses. One darkness is Ronnie's sight, but there is hope that an operation will

---

[40]Bloch, p. 168.

[41]James B. Garfield, *Follow My Leader* (New York: Viking, 1957), p. 14.

restore his vision. Ronnie's independence in his blindness, his sensitivity to life around him, and his courage shed a light of their own. The second darkness is the color of his new neighbor's skin. Ronnie wondered why the reporter didn't take his picture as he had planned after the news spread that Ronnie had carried a boy with an injured ankle down a treacherous hill. He wondered about other incidents, too. When the successful operation makes it possible for him to see the picture of Garth, he is not surprised to learn that his friend is a Negro. The third darkness was the cave where the bully, Butch, and another boy were lost. Garth and Ronnie play an important part in the rescue. The suspense is good, but the moralizing paragraphs at the conclusion really detract from the story.

All too frequently, the handicap of deafness is forgotten. Robinson's *David in Silence* is a good story that tells of a boy who learns to live with this problem. Set in modern England, there is plenty of action as the children make overtures to a new boy who can only make grunting noises. David is delighted when Michael learns sign language so he can communicate through his wall of silence. The absence of the sounds of life, and what it might mean is made clear in the description of David's silent world. When David's actions in playing football are misinterpreted and he doesn't read lips clearly, the other boys become confused and angry:

> *He can't hear. He can't hear. He makes noises like an animal. The creepiness was frightening. Fear, mistrust, and ignorance combined to arouse the mob instinct in them, and they drew close together. . . .*[42]

When the boys give chase David runs away and hides. Tension mounts as he moves into a dark tunnel of a canal and is overcome by the mirage of ugly faces. When he emerges he is lost, becomes hopelessly confused and cannot tell anyone his problem.

> *Suddenly he was swept by a wave of terror and desolation. People everywhere who could help him so easily if they were able to; ordinary homely people who looked kind until the moment they realized he was deaf, and then they would become frightened by their own ignorance of how to talk to him.*[43]

The other boys come to accept David and have a new awareness of the joy of hearing, but David remains in his silent world.

Other examples of children's courage in facing physical handicaps may be found in books of historical fiction, such as de Angeli's *The Door in the Wall* and *Johnny Tremain* by Forbes. Biographies of Helen Keller, Annie Sullivan, and other handicapped people portray individual strength in overcoming obstacles (see Chapter 6).

Poverty

Despite the picture of an affluent society in the United States, hundreds of children live in poverty, joining with the thousands in other lands who are in want. There are heroes in children's literature who meet this poverty with rare courage, humor, and fortitude. All children are richer for having known these characters.

Migrant Workers The people who follow the crops have been portrayed in several books, beginning with Lenski's *Judy's Journey* in 1947. Conditions were so bad for these sharecroppers that they had to sell some of their possessions and begin following the crops. Papa spends the money as he makes it; he does not want to work inside a factory:

> *". . . Machine's a big monster tryin' to gobble a feller up and break his spirit. . . . A little*

---

[42]Veronica Robinson, *David in Silence*, Illustrated by Victor Ambrus (Philadelphia: Lippincott, 1966), p. 66.

[43]Robinson, p. 86.

piece of land is all I want. . . . This country's always been a place where a man has a right to own a little piece of land.[44]"

Judy's more practical mother notes, "So many big companies buy it up, a lone man ain't got a chance."[45] As the family works in Florida and up the coast, they learn there are few opportunities for the migrant. Too proud to accept help from the Salvation Army or the women's welfare society, they struggle on. "We're not destitute, and we don't take *charity* off nobody. We still got our pride."[46] Lenski seldom uses metaphor in her writing; she builds detail upon detail until the reader receives the total impression of the scene. She describes Judy's work in the fields:

> *Potatoes — potatoes — nothing but potatoes. . . . The sun got hotter and hotter. Her ragged overalls stuck to her, and she was red with sunburn and prickly heat. Her back ached badly — she must rest for a minute. She stretched out full length in the dirt.*[47]

At school Judy fought the town kids, learned to read, and to care for the cuts and bruises of others. She learned from her parents: "'People are what you think they are,' said Papa. 'If you think they're good and treat 'em right, they'll *be* good and treat *you* right. But first, you got to be plumb good your own self.'"[48] No matter where they live, or what their economic status, children need to ponder this idea of life.

Published a year after Lenski's book, *Blue Willow* by Doris Gates has become a modern classic. Janey Larkin, however, does not work in the fields. She longs for a permanent home, and sacrifices her only treasure,

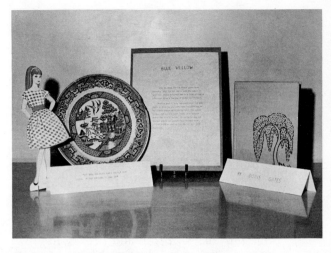

A teacher's table display calls attention to the symbolic meaning of Janey's Blue Willow plate. Dorothy Kidney, student, University of Maine.

a blue willow plate, to keep the home her family has found.

> *Janey stood staring helplessly at the closed door. It was gone. The only beautiful thing they owned. The thing that for Janey had had the power to make drab things beautiful and to a life of dreary emptiness bring a sense of wonder and delight. She felt as if her heart had been plucked from her. Now she knew how Dad had felt when he had lost the ranch in Texas. Now she knew what he had meant that day he had said it took courage not to lose your grip on things. She didn't have to wait, after all until she was grown up to learn that there are at least two kinds of courage in the world.*[49]

Janey has courage to prevent the overseer from killing ducks; she is brave enough to go for the doctor when her mother is dangerously ill; she is brave enough to tell the truth about the unscrupulous rent collector. Most of all, Janey expresses a kind of persistent courage in meeting adversity and injustice that is an example for all.

[44]Lois Lenski, *Judy's Journey* (Philadelphia: Lippincott, 1947), p. 31.

[45]Lenski, p. 31.

[46]Lenski, p. 58.

[47]Lenski, p. 167.

[48]Lenski, p. 186.

[49]Doris Gates, *Blue Willow,* Illustrated by Paul Lantz (New York: Viking, 1948), pp. 140–141.

Johnny Bill is another migrant child who hopes for a permanent home. Juline's book, *A Place for Johnny Bill,* describes the realities of hunger more vividly and the physical discomfort in more detail than do the previous books. Although they refused help at first, the family was glad to have the assistance of the minister when Mama had to go to the hospital. Papa is given a permanent job, but bad luck strikes again when he is injured. Johnny Bill becomes a hero when he struggles through a raging storm to warn the stationmaster that a railroad bridge has washed out. This incident is overdramatic, perhaps, but provides suspense and proves Johnny's courage. Even more realistic is his courage in fighting the daily battle for existence.

Mario by Garthwaite is the story of a Mexican boy who joins the "wetbacks" who come across the border to work in the fields. The terrible working conditions, the danger of the crossing, and the occasional flashes of kindness present another picture of poverty. Mario is finally given help by the rancher and a juvenile officer who had been in Mario's village. This rather unlikely turn of events does not limit the impact of the book. To see a modern city, with its television, telephone, and running water through the eyes of a boy from a primitive village would be a worthwhile experience for the middle grade child.

One of the outstanding recent books of children's literature is *Roosevelt Grady* by Shotwell. There is a warm family relationship among the Gradys despite their hard life. The illustrations show the family is Negro, but the text does not indicate their dark skin, nor that they receive any different treatment because of race. They share the same poor housing and drudgery as the whites who follow the crops. Roosevelt's experience in the "Opportunity Class" provides food for thought for all educators, for he never stays long enough to learn about "putting into." Forced to give up their place as tenant farmers because of new machines, the Gradys continue to fear that machines will replace them again. When Roosevelt is ill, they go to a doctor who gives advice that would be impossible to carry out. Mamma's explanation is a telling account of their poverty. She said:

> *"Doctor Bates, I think I'd best tell you something. We follow the crops for a living. Right now we're living in one room, all six of us. We got no clock to measure taking medicine by. We got no icebox. What we eat with, it isn't silver, it's tin, but we keep it clean. We fetch our water from a community spigot and I heat it on an oil stove."*[50]

Roosevelt and a friend, Man o'War, plan a way to get a more permanent job for Mr. Grady so they can stay long enough in one place for Roosevelt's brother to have surgery on a crippled foot. "Providence" did make these dreams come true, and finally Roosevelt can go to a school "with everybody who belongs." However, when Mamma hangs the red velvet curtains in the bus that will be home for three months, the reader fears she will have to take them down all too soon.

More mature readers who are beginning to be interested in the opposite sex will enjoy *Wanderers of the Field* by Smith. At age sixteen, Jack O'Neal assumes a man's role when his father dies. This responsibility includes repaying a debt of more than two hundred dollars, driving the truck from crop to crop, working long hours in fields and orchards. He is attracted to a pretty girl, but they must always go their separate ways. Jack was resigned to his life:

> *"A man's life is set—that's what my daddy always said,"* he answered. *"You can't do anything to stop the way you're going, no more than you can look up there at that big ole sun and command it to quit shining so hot."*[51]

---

[50]Louisa Shotwell, *Roosevelt Grady,* Illustrated by Peter Burchard (Cleveland: World Publishing, 1963), p. 71.
[51]George Harmon Smith, *Wanderers of the Field* (New York: John Day, 1966), p. 79.

The theme that "'fiddlefoots' don't have no choice" changes when Jack's diligence in paying off the debt is rewarded with land he can call his own. Probably the "fiddlefoots" would say, "It could only happen in a story—tain't real."

The Velvet Room by Snyder is a novel concerned with the development of an imaginative girl who must choose between security with a new family and hardship with her own parents who are migratory workers. Robin "wanders off" both literally and in her imagination. Given a key to a mysterious old house, she discovers the beautiful library hung with velvet draperies. Although Robin's feelings for books and beauty are partially satisfied here, her longing for loveliness grows more intense. The mystery of the life of an old woman who has befriended Robin is solved. Bridget tells Robin, "belonging to a place isn't nearly as necessary as belonging to people you love and who love and need you."[52] Robin realizes that the room was indeed "a quiet core in the middle of confusion"; at the same time, she knows "what it wasn't, was what Robin had tried to make it—an enchanted refuge, a strictly private world of dreams."[53] Discussion of Robin's decision will help boys and girls establish their own values.

The books written twenty years after *Judy's Journey* have the same ingredients —warm family relationships, the struggle to exist in poor housing, under blazing heat in dirty fields, with empty stomachs, and with a feeling of rejection from society. Through all these books, the reader will ponder the problems that persist, the changes that will come with the machine and larger companies holding more and more land, and the part of individual courage in a hostile world.

Poverty in Many Places   Relatively few books have described the life of children in city slums. In *A Tree for Peter* by Seredy, a mystical theme overshadows the realism of Shantytown's poverty. When a man asks a famous builder what changed Shantytown from dirty, bleak houses with "half-blind old windows" and "crooked roofs that looked like shapeless hats," Peter Marsh replied it was a kind of magic, and the magic wand was a spade. The remainder of this tender, moving book is a flashback to the boyhood of Peter. When Peter was almost six he found a friend, a man who taught him courage. Young Peter calls his new friend King Peter and believes he brought the spade that turned the earth that started a garden. This small beginning led to the entire change in the neighborhood! Like magic, the friend came to bring a tiny tree on Christmas Eve. The boy's friendliness and his tree lighted the hearts and kindled the dreams of Shantytown.

One might consider "those Bunkers" a shiftless, irresponsible set of parents. As indeed they are! In *Maggie Rose, Her Birthday Christmas*, the reader realizes that although they may be lazy and social parasites, the Bunker parents, as described by Ruth Sawyer, give much to their brood. Somehow they produce a child who is different, who "hankers" for a clean house, jobs like other people, and a real Christmas celebration on her birthday. When Maggie Rose's money is stolen, she loses spirit, but the family rouses itself and goes to work to do for Maggie what she wanted to do for them. Their pride shines as brightly as the Christmas candles!

The poverty of other countries has also been described in literature for children. In Paris the poor huddle under the bridges, and cold winds bite the French family who "adopt" the hobo, Armand. Loyalty and the joy of simple things is emphasized by Carlson in *The Family under the Bridge*.

Two books by the Norwegian writer, Aimée Sommerfelt, describe the sharp edges of poverty in India. *The Road to Agra* won the Norwegian State Prize for Children's Litera-

[52]Zilpha Keatley Snyder, *The Velvet Room*, Illustrated by Alton Rauble (New York: Atheneum, 1965), p. 181.
[53]Snyder, p. 185.

ture, the Jane Addams Book Award, and several other awards. It is the story of a village boy, Lalu, who walks nearly three hundred miles with his seven-year-old sister to take her to a hospital where her blindness may be cured. On the way, the children face hunger, danger from a cobra and jackals, and evil men. Lalu and his pretty sister, Maya, do meet a few kind people, but their exhaustion often leads to despair. When they learn that their grand-uncle has moved, and when the guard at the hospital gate turns them away, all hope disappears. They decide they must return home. Fortunately, they join a group of lepers and poor children at a jeep health station where the World Health Organization doctors examine Maya and agree to operate on her eyes. Lalu's fortitude and courage are to be admired, and the change in his purpose for the journey gives a fine example of character development. Lalu's story is continued in *The White Bungalow*. Maya's eyes are well and the children have returned to the village. Lalu is able to go to school, but his friend, Ram, must learn by crowding with others outside the door of the school tent. The Monsoon does not come and food becomes even more scarce. When his father's back is injured, Lalu's desires for education conflict with the needs of his family. It is difficult to give up the chance to go to boarding school and to become a doctor. His grandmother understands that Lalu really does want to save others, but she says, "others can save them, Lalu. Only you can save us." His dream of the doctor's white bungalow where he had lived and hoped to live in the future disappears as a storm breaks. Even his envy of Ram, who will have his place at school, is washed away in the rain, and he begins to plan to sow the new wheat. In another way, Lalu will contribute to a new India through his strength and values.

Sommerfelt has also written a book about slum life in Mexico titled *My Name Is Pablo*.

This is a narrative of contrasts—the contrast of the color of flowers and sun with the grey, dark hovels, and the contrast of the life of Pablo with that of Frederik, son of the Norwegian engineer. Pablo has earned a few pesos by shining shoes, but he does not have a license, so he is sent to the reformatory where conditions are unbelievably bad. Pablo's loyalty to the family that befriends him and his courage are revealed in his trouble with the bully, Manuel. Over and over, Pablo is caught by the circumstances of slum life. With the help of the Harbos, his life will be better, "'But what about all the others?' said Mrs. Harbo. 'Yes, what about all the others?' said Frederik."[54] The question remains unanswered and the reader is left to ponder the problem.

War

While War Rages Modern warfare does not exclude children from its danger, hunger, separation, and death of loved ones. Children, as well as adults, have shown bravery in facing the enemy. Twentieth-century writers have used these themes in books for children, both to show the futility of war and to present stories of individual courage.

Some stories take place away from the battle but describe conditions at the time. McSwigan's *Snow Treasure* is an exciting story based upon an actual incident in World War II. During the Nazi occupation of Norway, children helped to remove the gold bullion so it could be shipped to the United States. Under the stern eyes of the commandant, children transported the bullion by sledding down the hill to the port. At a crucial point, the self-discipline and courage of these children saved them and the entire venture.

---

[54]Aimée Sommerfelt, *My Name Is Pablo*, Translated by Patricia Crampton, Illustrated by Hans Norman Dahl (New York: Criterion, 1965), p. 143.

In *Pancakes-Paris,* by Bishop, a French boy receives a box of pancake mix from a World War II G.I. To get help in reading the directions, he goes to the American Embassy, meets the G.I. again, and a wonderful party is held in the drab apartment. The poignant discussions of BEFORE (before the war) make clear the effect of war:

> . . . *"There was no BEFORE. It's all kidding."*
> *Louise and Reme said both together, "No kidding. I remember BEFORE. It was warm in the school . . . . BEFORE. It was nice and warm at home. We had fires. . . ."*
> *"There was never any fire. Anywhere. Ever,"* said Jules darkly, "they are just making it up."
> *"Oh, shut up," said Louise. "There was fire, and shoes, and clothes, and thread, and pencils, and paper, and meat, and milk, and eggs . . . and chocolate . . . and oranges! . . . and bananas!!!"*
> *"She is crazy," said Paul, shrugging his shoulders.*[55]

Another book by Bishop, *Twenty and Ten,* tells of Jewish children who are given refuge in a Catholic French orphanage. They, too, talk wistfully of *before.* This book portrays the bravery of all the children as they maintain silence under Nazi investigation. Their dramatization of "The Flight into Egypt" finally saved them and was symbolic of the whole situation.

Daily life in occupied Netherlands during World War II is realistically presented by Van Stockum in *The Winged Watchman.* War comes closer when Joris finds and protects an English pilot who was shot down. An ever-present danger is the neighbor boy who is a "landwatcher" working with the Germans. It is hard to accept the teaching of the priest who says a lie is always bad, when lies are necessary. Joris' mother explains:

> *"It is bad when you hide the truth from someone who has a right to it, and in a normal world, where people try to obey God, everyone has a right to truth. But when you know that the other person is going to use the truth to rob and maim and kill, do you think he still has a right to it? . . . You are right to hate lies, my dear. But remember that truth itself becomes a lie in the twisted minds of our conquerors."*[56]

Joris' brother, Dirk Jan, proves his endurance and wit by delivering an important message to the underground who would send it on by setting the arms of the windmills. This is a tremendously exciting book, but the theme is concern for others: "All the same, we did have one thing during the war that kept us going: we felt responsible for our neighbors, and I don't think we need lose that. It's up to us."[57]

Silence over Dunkerque by Tunis tells of the heroic evacuation in 1940 and the silent days that followed. Sergeant Williams stays with his men instead of accepting a boat ride back to his home at Dover. Because of the courage of a fourteen-year-old French Girl Scout and her grandfather, the Sergeant and his buddy, Fingers, make their escape to England. Tunis maintains a breathless suspense until the men and the faithful dog that has attached himself to them are safe in Dover. The deeper meaning of the story, that "courage wears many uniforms, or none," is applicable to life in peace as well as war. The author himself has the courage to show that some English were less than brave in this battle. This book might be a springboard to discussion of the momentary weakness or courage of men.

The Silver Sword by Ian Serraillier might well be subtitled "an incredible story," yet the author's note says that it is based upon fact. Father, mother, and children of the

[55]Clarie Huchet Bishop, *Pancakes-Paris,* Illustrated by Georges Schreiber (New York: Viking, 1947), pp. 10–11.

[56]Hilda Van Stockum, *The Winged Watchman* (New York: Farrar, Straus, 1962), p. 111.
[57]Stockum, p. 203.

Polish Balicki family are separated in early 1940. The father escapes from the Nazi prison and meets Jan, an orphan, when he returns to Warsaw to search for the family. He gives Jan a carved letter opener in the shape of a tiny sword in order to help him remember a message for his children in case he should ever meet Ruth, Edek, and Bronia. A slim chance, but Jan does meet the children who escaped the bombing of their house and had lived in the woods and bombed-out cellars for two years. Together, they undertake the journey to Switzerland as their father had directed. Jan, the wily, clever boy keeps the sword as a talisman of hope. Edek is sent to a German farm and escapes by holding himself under the carriage of a truck. With the aid of kind farmers, a helpful Russian soldier, and friendly Americans, the children at last reach Switzerland's border. Their father is to come for them, but tragedy stalks their path—a fierce, sudden storm sweeps Edek out into the lake. Convalescing from tuberculosis, he is nearly lost before Ruth and Jan save him. The last chapter is anticlimactic, yet the reader is glad to know what happened to this family that continued to suffer the effects of their years of hardship.

To the south, in Greece, the Nazi invasion brought war from *The Skies of Crete*. Forman's war story describes the conflict between a boy, who has endured the horror of modern warfare as he made his way south, and his grandfather who lives on memories of the heroism and glory of the Turkish wars of the past. To Penelope, the granddaughter, war was: "the private possession of her grandfather who brought it out on wintry nights with its curved swords and flapping flags like pictures carefully etched in a history book."[58] When their home is bombed and they are unable to reach the refugee boat, she realizes her cousin, Alexis,

was right, for war is fear, weariness, "and a hopelessness mute beyond communication."[59] Alexis is haunted by his guilt of killing a soldier, and says this guilt is worse than bombing. Penelope and Alexis follow their old warrior grandfather over a tortuous mountain, accompanied by El Greco, a shepherd who symbolizes the truth. After recounting the history of Crete, he comments, "it's hard to be angry or sure of anything when you look back over thousands of years."[60] They eventually reach a port where Penelope and her mother escape to Alexandria. Alexis remains behind to help the partisans protect the refugees. True to his word that he will never shoot another man, he gives Penelope the cartridges from his gun. Forman's writing is filled with images. As they reach the shore, "Searchlights swept the beach, etched boats and figures of Partisans and soldiers as colorful cardboard cut-outs against the sand. The machine gun began knocking the cut-outs down while the partisans fired back slowly."[61] This well-written book will help mature readers understand true heroism and the terror of war. Forman's book for teen-agers, *Ring the Judas Bell*, reiterates the theme of the futility of war.

The House of Sixty Fathers by DeJong is an example of a book that does not glorify war; it clearly, vividly tells of the horror of bullets coming in your direction and of the pains of hunger. DeJong's description of Tien Pao's fear, loneliness, and hunger are starkly realistic. The Chinese boy and his family flee before the Japanese invasion, but they are separated. Clutching his pet pig, Tien Pao struggles on, not knowing where to go. He finds an American flier, and helps him survive. The boy is taken to the barracks and becomes a mascot of the soldiers, his sixty fathers. Although it seems impossible, he continues to believe his parents will be

---

[58]James Forman, *The Skies of Crete* (New York: Farrar, Straus, 1963), p. 20.

[59]Forman, p. 25.
[60]Forman, p. 70.
[61]Forman, p. 179.

found. The reunion of the family is a beautiful scene. Children see the effects of war in television newscasts and dramas. This book helps them to identify with the personal experiences of a child.

Citizens of the United States can take no pride in our treatment of the Japanese-Americans at the beginning of the war against Japan. In *The Moved Outers,* Florence Means has recorded this unpleasant chapter of our history. Opening with family life typical of any American household, the text soon reveals that the Oharas, Emily, Sue, and Kim, are different:

> *Here they were, Americans from their hearts out to their skins. But their skins were not American. Their skins were opaque, their hair was densely black, their eyes were ever so little slanted, and their names were Sumiko and Kimio.*[62]

When Japan attacked Pearl Harbor, all persons who fit this description were ordered to camps where they were crowded behind barbed wire. The reader shares the sorrow of the families as they give up businesses, pack their treasures, and are separated from each other. They look forward to the day when they will be "going back to America." One son is killed in the war; the spirit of the other is nearly broken by the humiliating treatment they receive. Although the characters are in their teens, sixth-graders can understand their disillusionment and hopes for a future place. Discussion of the irrationality of human behavior during a war might follow the reading of this book.

Aftermath of War   Peace does not always bring surcease of pain and trouble. Many children's lives remained twisted because of unhappy war experiences.

Readers of *The Secret Garden* by Burnett will also like *Nobody's Garden* by Cordelia Jones. Two girls in postwar England remake a garden at a bombed-out house. They are an unusual pair, talkative, outgoing Hilary and quiet, unresponsive Bridget. Orphaned by the war, Bridget feels unwanted by the aunt who is frustrated by Bridget's silence. Bridget is tormented by feelings of guilt that an inadvertent comment she made during the Nazi occupation of the island of Jersey had led to her mother's death. Her emotional problems lead to truancy, and she hides in the garden where she is found by Hilary and her mother. The book pictures middle-class life in London and helps children see that behavior is caused by past experiences.

A quiet story of a German family after World War II is told by Margot Benary-Isbert in *The Ark.* Housing problems, labor office edicts, food rationing, and cold rooms are challenges met by a mother and four children. Two of the children go to work on a farm where they make a home from an old railroad car—truly an ark, a refuge for the family that is finally reunited. Two sequels, *Rowan Farm* and *Castle on the Border,* continue the story of this family.

In *The Happy Days,* Kim Yong Ik tells of the sacrifices of a family and a Korean village after the war. Before she died, Song Chun's mother had said, "When the happy days come, you can go back to the mainland and start to school."[63] The customs, daily life, and values of another culture are clearly described as Song Chun returns to his grandparents. This is a story of sacrifice and sorrow, a story of a boy who grows up and realizes that "the happy days" will always be shadowed with sadness.

Meeting Cultural Change

Literature for children has reflected the impact of cultural change upon family life and individuals. The migrant workers feel the change brought by machines; people

---

[62]Florence Means, *The Moved Outers,* Illustrated by Helen Blair (Boston: Houghton Mifflin, 1945), p. 14.

[63]Kim Yong Ik, *The Happy Days,* Illustrated by Artur Marokvia (Boston: Little, Brown, 1960), p. 26.

move from farms to cities to work in factories; primitive peoples must learn to accept new ideas in technology, health, and education.

In the United States   Moving to a northern city from the southern mountains brought a tremendous fear to *Robert E.* His grandfather decided to live in his daughter's home, for he hated to leave the boy he had reared for ten years. The new world of shiny appliances, speed, and television are fascinating to the boy and old man. When Robert E. goes to school, he receives the mountain code: "'And don't you take nothin' from nobody,' Grandpap told him once more. 'You stick up for yourself. That's the only way to get along.'"[64] Robert E. has to learn that fighting is not the accepted way of establishing yourself in this community. Group work, activities, conferences—all these aspects of the new school create confusion and insecurity. One of the most amusing incidents is Grandpap's conference with the teacher. An understanding mother and teacher help the boy face his changed world.

New ways come to *The Tomahawk Family* who live on a Sioux reservation in South Dakota. "They lived in a log cabin with corners like clasped fingers—as if they were holding the family tightly together. But logs were not strong enough to hold the Tomahawks together because they were a divided family."[65] There is a conflict between Alice and her brother, Frankie, because she wants to learn "civilized ways" while Frankie prefers his dream of being like an Indian of the past. Grandma lives in her own world of games, unconcerned about the two children. Alice wants to follow the teacher's advice to "help our parents become good citizens. She's the

only parents we have now." Frankie's reply is one for all who want to bring change: "You can't help people if they don't want to be helped."[66] Carlson's pictures of life at home and school are authentic portraits. Frankie runs away after his pet raccoon gets the boy into trouble. He returns to warn the school that a buffalo really is coming, and proves his courage as a warrior of old. Frankie's ruse and an understanding teacher lead Grandma to school, and she is even elected PTA president! The author uses the same metaphor as the book ends, "But it was cozy and comfortable inside the cabin. Its logs clasped the Tomahawks like fingers, holding them tightly together."[67]

A book with a similar theme is *Quiet Boy* by Waltrip. This twelve-year-old boy lives on an Indian reservation in Arizona where old and new ways conflict. Before his father was killed in World War II, he wrote his son a letter urging him to obtain as much education as possible. Despite the conflict with the older generation, he decides to attend the government boarding school.

In Other Lands   To understand the changes that are coming to the Zulus in Africa, children should read first Mirsky's *Thirty-One Brothers and Sisters.* Life in the kraal is authentically presented in this story of Nomusa and her chieftain father's family of six wives and thirty-one children. Cultural expectations, roles each person plays, customs, and taboos show the old patterns of living. In *Nomusa and the New Magic,* the girl, now fourteen, goes to school to learn to be a nurse. Zitu, her father, accepts new ways, but Damasi, a boy who likes her, is afraid she will not want him and will cost him too many cows to marry. When Buselapi, the nurse, and Nomusa go to treat a wounded man, it is clear to Nomusa that the witch doctor treated

[64]Florence Musgrave, *Robert E.,* Illustrated by Mary Stevens (New York: Hastings, 1957), p. 59.

[65]Natalie Savage Carlson, *The Tomahawk Family,* Illustrated by Stephen Cook (New York: Harper & Row, 1960), p. 3.

[66]Carlson, p. 8.

[67]Carlson, p. 170.

the fears of the wives while the nurse's penicillin made the man well. Damasi leaves his work in the mines to go to the agricultural school. Thus Damasi and Nomusa, who recognize their love, prepare to bring a change to their people.

It is good for Americans to look at themselves through the eyes of the people who are receiving their assistance. In *Meeting with a Stranger,* Duane Bradley helps the reader understand the problems faced by a proud primitive tribe in Ethiopia when an American comes to give agricultural aid. Teffera is a boy who was injured and taken to a modern hospital by his uncle who accepted modern ways. At the uncle's home, he meets Mr. Sam Jones. Teffera is shocked by the strange customs:

> *Teffera watched as they shook hands, instead of bowing deeply to each other as was proper. . . . His astonishment grew as Mr. Sam Jones took off his coat. . . . It was not proper to undress in front of others. . . .*[68]

Mr. Jones sends white powder to give the sick sheep, but Teffera distrusts him. When Teffera's father goes to the foreign hospital to cure his eyes, the boy is left in charge of the farm. Jones understands Teffera's concern and agrees to leave the best sheep of the flock where Teffera had hidden them. However, Teffera continues to be suspicious of the stranger and devises a test by placing his best ram with the culls that are to be killed. If Jones is evil, he will also kill the prize ram. In a tense scene, one of the village men makes sure that Jones examines the good ram. The American's surprise proves to all that he was truly trying to help. When he learns of Teffera's trick, he does not blame the boy:

> *Life is difficult in your country now, Teffera, because so many things are changing, and you*

A young African distrusts the friendly American agricultural advisor. Illustration by E. Harper Johnson for *Meeting with a Stranger* by Duane Bradley. Copyright © 1964 by Duane Bradley. Published by J. B. Lippincott Company.

> *do not know what to believe. It would be wrong for your people to shut their eyes to the outside world and to refuse to have anything to do with the new knowledge and ideas, but it would be equally bad if they tried to be like the rest of the world.*[69]

In his skepticism, Teffera asks, "'If their own country is so wonderful, why did they come

[68]Duane Bradley, *Meeting with a Stranger,* Illustrated by E. Harper Johnson (Philadelphia: Lippincott, 1964), p. 16.

[69]Bradley, p. 128.

here?'" The answer is given in this excellent book about a continuing problem.

A boy in India is the first in his village to learn to read. *What Then, Raman?* is the title of the book that tells how the boy worked to achieve his dream and how he found an answer to the question posed by the (American) Merkin lady who befriended him. It becomes necessary for his father to go to the city to get work and for Raman to leave school to work for the family. He is isolated from the other boys, for school has made him different. One day, he tells the Merkin lady he will be a great scholar and read shelves of books.

> *"Good," the Merkin lady nodded. "And then what?"*
> *Again Raman stopped short, puzzled. He shifted feet a trifle uncomfortably.*
> *"What will you do then, after you have learned so many things? . . ."*
> *"Why—why then I shall know them, that's all," he answered, stammering a little.*[70]

Raman discovers the joy of teaching when he begins to teach his sister to read. He also discovers he has courage when he goes to the jungle to find an orchid for the Merkin lady. It required even greater courage to buy things for his family instead of the beautiful book he had dreamed of owning. When Raman agrees to teach the boys of the village, he knows he is answering the Merkin lady's question. Change will come to this village more quickly because one boy had been sent to school by a woodcutter, and that boy accepted his responsibility.

Loneliness

Loneliness is one of the plights of man, for each individual lives alone, within himself, finding few moments of real communi-cation and sharing. In a time when too many people try to escape this loneliness through restless seeking, literature may help children understand the difference between being alone and being lonely. Books can help children become aware of the inner resources each person has in order to accept loneliness as a necessary condition of being human. Creative solitude is essential for achievement; moreover, each man must learn how to be alone as an individual in a world of conformity.

Characters Who Lived Alone   The hero of *Nuvat the Brave* was labeled a coward by the people of his tribe because of his momentary panic on a bear hunt. Feeling worthless, he volunteers to go out to hunt during a storm and time of hunger. The ice breaks away, and Nuvat is alone for over two years. His exciting adventures in hunting the seals and walrus and his victorious encounters with polar bears prove his bravery. Nuvat had only a knife and spear, but he survived the dangers and lonely hours for "in his heart he had great courage and determination and a store of the instinctive wisdom of his people. . . ."[71] Also, he had the companionship of his own dog, Kakk, and the other dogs of the team. The details of his survival—making a lamp, a house, a sled—make fascinating reading. Here, too, is anthropological material, information about customs and beliefs of the Eskimo tribe. There are few references to the loneliness he must have felt. When he thought of home "a great tightness came in Nuvat's chest." In moments of failure he would feel despair, "But there was work to be done that would not let him brood long."[72] He becomes the epic hero—an Eskimo Ulysses who faced and overcame the dangers of his hostile environ-

[70]Shirley L. Arora, *"What Then, Raman?"*, Illustrated by Hans Guggenheim (Chicago: Follett, 1960), p. 115.

[71]Radko Doone, *Nuvat the Brave*, Illustrated by Hans Axel Walleen (Philadelphia: Macrae, 1934), p. 68.
[72]Doone, p. 125.

ment and the dangers of man's sense of human smallness.

A more recent story of an Eskimo boy who survived when he drifted out to sea on an ice floe is *Tiktá Liktak: An Eskimo Legend* by Houston (see page 177).

Another boy who was called a coward was Mafatu, a boy of the South Sea Islands who had been frightened of the sea when his mother drowned. In *Call It Courage,* Sperry relates the narrative of the boy's chosen voyage and his life on an island. After he had explored the island briefly, he thought of home.

> *And he was swept by a sudden wave of loneliness, a longing for the sound of his father's deep voice. . . . He shut his lips tight and fought it back, then leaped to his feet and set about his tasks with a great show of business. He would not think of those things.*[73]

His days are filled with the work—making a canoe, fighting a wild boar, and preparing to return to prove his courage. Mafatu eases his loneliness by talking to his dog, Uri. The days of drifting on the sea must have been very lonely, but his thoughts were occupied when he was not sleeping. Never again would the boy feel lonely after he returned to his home! Here is a story of finding one's inner resources (see pages 674–676).

Why did Scott O'Dell choose *Island of the Blue Dolphins* for the title of the story of Karana, an Indian girl who for eighteen years lived alone on an island off the California coast? After most of the men of her tribe are overcome by Aleuts who came to hunt otters, all her people leave their island home by boat. When Karana realizes her young brother is left on the island, she jumps overboard and returns to him. Within a few hours, the island becomes a land of sadness; the boy is killed by wild dogs, and

memories of the tribe are all she has left. The author does express Karana's feelings of deep loneliness when she realizes the boat will not return. Despite these feelings, she creates a life for herself. The island provides its resources, and the twelve-year-old draws upon her memories to build a house, to make utensils, and to make weapons, although in so doing, she violates a taboo. When she has weapons, she is able to hunt the wild dogs that killed her brother. For some deep reason, she cannot bring herself to kill the leader of the pack although she had wounded him. It is this act of mercy that saves Karana both physically and emotionally; as she gives love, she receives protection and companionship. Naming the dog Rontu, she talks to him. "Because of this I was not lonely. I did not know how lonely I had been until I had Rontu to talk to."[74]

Karana's days are filled with work, and the authentic details of her "Crusoe" efforts are interesting. There is excitement in her encounters with animals and her continuing battle against the elements. There is poignance—sharpest in her brief contact with an Aleut girl and in the death of the dog Rontu. Spanish priests at last find Karana, and her final parting from the island is sad with memories of her family, her pets, "and of all the happy days." The reader may ponder whether she found as much happiness at the mission with human companionship as she had known alone on her island.

My Side of the Mountain by Jean George is a book about a city boy who chooses to spend a winter alone on land in the Catskills once farmed by his ancestors. The crowded apartment, the pressures all around him, impel Sam to prove he can live off the land. Armed with knowledge from reading about how to survive on the land, he makes a home in a hollow tree, makes buckskin clothing,

---

[73]Armstrong Sperry, *Call It Courage* (New York: Macmillan, 1940), p. 53.

[74]Scott O'Dell, *Island of the Blue Dolphins* (Boston: Houghton Mifflin, 1960), p. 101.

and lays up stores for winter. The meals are described in mouth-watering fashion even though acorn flour, bulbs, and strange herbs are the ingredients. A professor discovers the boy while on a mountain hike and respects his wish to be alone. At Christmas "Bando" returns, and also Sam's father finds him. His pet falcon and a weasel provide Sam with entertainment, and work keeps his days busy. There are only occasional glimpses of loneliness. "I did not become lonely. Many times during the summer I had thought of the 'long winter months ahead' with some fear. . . . The winter was as exciting as the summer—maybe more so."[75] He writes in his journal, observes the birds, and keeps busy with the chores of living. In the early spring, a young news reporter discovers him, and Sam talks freely about the "wild boy" as Matt writes his story. Sam realizes he is now ready to be found. Matt spends a week with him, and Bando returns for a visit. The professor tells Sam what he has already learned: "You can't live in America today and be quietly different. If you are going to be different, you are going to stand out, and people are going to hear about you. . . ."[76] This seems an implausible story, yet the details are so vividly related, the reader feels he is on the mountain with Sam. A naturalist, Jean George has drawn upon her background to provide authentic facts of nature. This boy found himself in an unusual way; children may consider how one can maintain individuality in today's world.

Loneliness Amid People   The title of Ester Wier's book, *The Loner,* immediately tells the reader it is about a person who felt alone. The great loneliness of this boy is that he had no family, not even a name. His code of living is that he should look out for himself and not blame others when they think only of themselves, even though he is left sick and alone in a deserted camp. The grimness of life of the migrant is shown in the scene in which a service-station owner refuses to allow the migrants to drink at the water tap. The first person to show concern for the boy is a girl, Raidy, who plans to give him a name. Just as she is ready to say it, her long hair is caught in the potato digging machine. With stark realism, yet avoiding details of the horror, Wier describes the accident: "Leaping forward he saw that her yellow hair was caught in the whirring moving parts of the machine. Powerless to help, he stood and watched in cold horror while the machine ripped and tore."[77]

David's first reaction was one of anger, "Why wasn't she taking care of herself?" He finishes the day's work in the fields and wanders until he is exhausted. The boy is found by Boss, a huge, stern woman, who manages a Montana sheep ranch. She is a loner, too, for she was always unlike other women and found it difficult to express her feelings. Tex, the herder, explains that he, too, had been a loner:

> . . . *One of those who didn't believe anyone cared about them or wanted to help. I figured it was up to me to take care of myself and I didn't need help from anyone. . . . Somebody will care if you just give 'em a chance. . . . There's always people who need you as much as you need them. . . . All you got to do is find 'em, and when you do, you find you're happier carin' about someone else than just about yourself all the time.*[78]

The boy receives his name, David, from the Bible, and he tries to live up to the Biblical example by working and learning. He makes mistakes as he learns the big lesson Boss is trying to teach—the lesson of responsibility for the sheep. David tries to take the place of Ben, Boss's son who had been killed by a

---

[75]Jean George, *My Side of the Mountain* (New York: Dutton, 1959), p. 121.

[76]George, p. 170.

[77]Ester Wier, *The Loner,* Illustrated by Christine Price (New York: McKay, 1963), p. 13.

[78]Wier, pp. 34–35.

bear. He helps rescue Tex from a trap, nurses Boss when she is ill, and, in a final dramatic scene, he kills the grizzly. David has proved his courage, and has learned to give and accept love, to "throw in his lot with others and work for everyone, not just himself."[79] Wier's realistic descriptions of the work in caring for the sheep make this an outstanding regional book, with a message of deep impact for boys and girls.

Boy Alone by Ottley takes place on an isolated Australian cattle station. The protagonist is given no name, nor do we know why he is there, a boy alone without family or friends. The realistic language will interest readers, for example, "Cor" is used as an exclamation, a man weighs "fifteen stone," he carries water in a "billy," food is "tucker." The very size of the ranch influences the boy's feelings. "It's the bigness that makes you lonely."[80] The boy cares for a dog and her pup although he knows the hard-bitten master of the dog pack, Kanga, will take them away. The boy searches for meaning as he questions the destruction of animals. Kanga kills six of the pups, keeping only one to be trained as "king dog"; sheep are killed for food; the dog, Brolga, dies when Kanga makes her go back with the pack although the dog wants to stay with the boy. In despair, he goes out to the desert to save the pup, Rags. When he is lost in the sand, he realizes "He needed someone human — someone to help and guide."[81] All the men search, but it is Kanga who finds the boy. Kanga gives him the pup although the boy now realizes that Kanga needs the dog to lead the pack. The author's descriptions of the heat and scorched earth make the reader's throat feel parched. Without being sentimental, he conveys the love of boy and man for the dogs. More than this, he shows that inability to communicate real feelings

brings a sense of loneliness: "He wished there was more he could say to Kanga—some way to thank him. 'But there ain't,' he thought. 'Words ain't much, whichever way you use them. An' they couldn't pay for Rags.'"[82]

Waterless Mountain, by Armer, was a Newbery Award book of 1932. The author tells of the growth of a young Navajo who is destined to become a medicine man. The beliefs of his people and many folk tales are woven into the narrative. Younger Brother never questions his destiny; he is given understanding and encouragement by his uncle, a medicine man, and the Big Man who runs the trading post. He is vitally alive, sensitive to beauty, and able to develop a mystic oneness with nature. His journey to the West, encounters with a white boy, and a family trip to the Pacific Coast where they demonstrate crafts at a museum, provide interest. Although he ". . . felt the power and the peace that comes through fellowship with men and gods," Younger Brother knows a kind of loneliness of spirit that is different from others:

> *At times he was lonely, but not for any particular person. The loneliness came when he was the happiest. Then he felt the old longing to share his joy with someone, as he had wanted to share the secret of the cave when he was a little boy.*[83]

Waterless Mountain symbolizes the life of the individual, the secret pool in the heart of the mountain, the secret of inner strength and creativity.

Death

Adults may wish to protect children from knowledge of death, but the mysterious shadow comes into their lives as pets die and

[79]Wier, p. 152.
[80]Reginald Ottley, *Boy Alone,* Illustrated by Clyde Pearson (New York: Harcourt, 1965), p. 55.
[81]Ottley, p. 178.
[82]Ottley, p. 188.
[83]Laura Adams Armer, *Waterless Mountain,* Illustrated by Sidney and Laura Armer (New York: McKay, 1931), p. 106.

as disease, accident, or war claims lives of classmates, adult friends, or parents. Vicarious experience through literature can help them realize death is a part of life. In some books, death is only a small part of the story; in others, the response of a child to death becomes the central theme. For young children, *The Dead Bird* expresses this theme (see page 129).

Middle grade children will come to understand the feeling of a twin when her brother is killed in an accident as they read *Home from Far* by Little (see page 678). This story tells of a girl's misunderstanding of her mother's attempt to keep only happy memories. The need of children to talk about their feelings is illustrated in this book. In many of the books about war, as *The Skies of Crete* by Forman, children meet death. So, too, in *Island of the Blue Dolphins, The Loner,* and *Boy Alone* does loneliness follow loss of a brother, friend, or dog. The description of the death of the grandmother in *Bond of the Fire* by Fon Eisen is perhaps too detailed for some children, yet such realism may remove the veil of mystery that often concerns them. In *Meet the Austins,* the parents show calm acceptance of the death of their good friend and express faith when their children's questions must remain unanswered (see page 219).

Children in upper grades will find *The High Pasture,* by Harnden, an exciting, moving book. When his mother is taken to the hospital, Tim is sent to his great-aunt's ranch in Colorado. He learns to be patient and faithful as he tries to tame a "ghost dog" that had remained in the high pasture where his master had been killed by an avalanche. Tim has to face learning about death when his Aunt Kate's dog died:

It was entirely different when it was someone you knew. Death was real when it happened to someone you knew. It was as real as life! Was this one of the things he'd been sent out here to learn? O. K. he thought angrily. So he'd

learned. And he just hoped his father knew how much he hated it! He hoped he'd never learn any more, too![84]

As they bury the dog, Aunt Kate talks about the dog as a puppy and all the things he did. Tim decides, "It was a kind of *remembering*— that's what it was. He guessed it was necessary, and he thought it was nice."[85] But he was denied this part of the end of his mother's life, and he resented his father for sending him away while his mother was in the hospital. Tim rides away when he hears his father is coming, for he knows now that his mother is dead. He is injured when the horse bucks him off and the "wild" dog, Lobo, comes to him. Lobo overcomes his own fears to go to the ranch for help. Tim's father arrives and explains that his mother wanted him to be away, to learn to be independent; Tim begins to understand. His father shares the sense of loss he feels:

. . . it isn't the quantity that counts, it's the quality. The quality of your Mother was something beautiful—and if she'd lived to be a hundred years old it couldn't have been any greater. . . . We have to talk about her as time goes by and remember all the fine, lovely things she was.[86]

Pearl Buck's account of *The Big Wave* is a classic that conveys courage and understanding of death. Kino, a farmer's son, and Jiya, son of a fisherman, live in a Japanese village where there is always fear of death from the earth's volcanic eruptions or the tidal waves of the sea. Kino asks his father, "'Must we always be afraid of something?'" His reply, "'We must say, someday I shall die, and does it matter whether it is by ocean or volcano, or whether I grow old and weak?'"[87] reflects the wisdom of these peo-

[84]Ruth Harnden, *The High Pasture,* Illustrated by Vee Guthrie (Boston: Houghton Mifflin, 1964), p. 51.
[85]Harnden, p. 56.
[86]Harnden, p. 164.
[87]Pearl Buck, *The Big Wave* (New York: John Day, 1947), p. 30.

ple. When a big wave does come, it engulfs the homes and the people who live on the beach. The compassion toward the boy, Jiya, who is numbed by the loss of his family is beautifully expressed. Kino's father describes death as a great gateway and reminds Kino that he did not want to be born. He explains that a baby does not know about the happy life that awaits it.

> *"You are afraid only because you don't know anything about death," his father replied. "But someday you will wonder why you were afraid, even as today you wonder why you feared to be born."*[88]

Again, Kino's father tries to help him understand how to console his friend Jiya:

> *"Ah, no one knows who makes evil storms," his father replied. "We only know that they come. When they come we must live through them as bravely as we can, and after they are gone, we must feel again how wonderful is life. Every day of life is more valuable now than it was before the storm."*[89]

Jiya chooses to remain with the poor farmer instead of accepting the wealthy Old Gentleman's offer to make him his son. He does "live" again, returns to work, and laughs, because he does not want others to feel sad because he is sad. Eventually, he decides to return to the sea as a fisherman and builds a house down on the beach. Life goes on.

MOVING TOWARD MATURITY

In building his concept of self, each person comes to answer such questions as "What kind of person am I?" "What are my roles in society to be?" "What do others think of me?" The self is built through the mirrored reactions and interactions with people,

places, and things. The child creates the concept of what he is: that he is a worthy person, a person who can succeed, a person who is loved, who can, in turn, respect and love others as he receives these impressions from others.

As children grow toward adulthood, they may experience brief moments of awareness of this growth process. A conversation, an experience, or a book may bring the sudden realization that a step has been taken to a new level of maturity, and there is no turning back. This step may be toward adult responsibility, acceptance of sex roles, or vocational choice. Often, there is a definite decision to make—a decision that gives direction for the future development of self. This process of "becoming," of finding the unique core of self, is not easy. In literature, there are models of ordinary boys and girls who find the courage "to be," to stand firm despite pressures.

Gradual Development of Self

The gradual development of self is a process of which we are usually unaware. Seeing stages of development in a literary figure may help the child realize he, too, is becoming a unique person.

Kate, who was sent by her father to his brother, was gradually tamed by *The Good Master*. Seredy's story of a spoiled girl who comes from Budapest to the Hungarian farm is told from the viewpoint of Jansci, her cousin. The author does not reveal Kate's inner feelings; the reader can only surmise her sorrow at her mother's death and her fear of the strange surroundings. Each chapter is an incident in the life of the peasants shortly after the turn of the century. Children thoroughly enjoy Kate's naughtiness when she climbs the rafters and eats the sausages. Her bravado is proven true bravery at the round-up and when she is kidnapped by gypsies. Kate's personality is

[88]Buck, p. 37.
[89]Buck, p. 30.

gradually changed through the gentle discipline of her uncle and aunt, the opportunity to observe the miracle of growth on the farm, and learning through the folk tales and traditional festivals.

Dobry is a Bulgarian boy whose story by Monica Shannon won the 1935 Newbery Medal. This book is a slow-paced narrative of the discovery and development of creativity in a peasant boy. Dobry's grandfather helps him respect his own uniqueness as he points out that no two things are exactly alike: "people study how to be all alike instead of how to be as different as they really are."[90] Dobry's mother finds it difficult to accept a son who is always drawing pictures. The scenes of nineteenth century life in Bulgaria are sometimes amusing, always interesting. Folk tales are woven into the narrative. When Dobry creates a beautiful ice sculpture of the Nativity, his mother accepts his talent, and the village joins to help send him to art school. The theme of this book is "to be true to oneself" as it portrays the development of a boy's confidence in his own ability, his trust in his inner need to create.

Nkwala is the beautiful story of an Indian boy's search for personal identity as he seeks his place in tribal life. As the Salish Indians migrate northwestward from the Columbia Plateau, his understanding parents help Nkwala find courage and peace with himself. The mother expresses her understanding of Nkwala's impatience to grow up, "His childhood itches him like a goatskin robe!"[91]

Both boy and sheep are *Mountain Born* in Elizabeth Yates' pastoral by this title. This is a short, slow-paced story of a boy's growing understanding of life as he assumes more responsibility for the sheep. Biddy, the little black lamb that Peter's mother restored to life, becomes his pet. Biddy shows unusual curiosity, endurance, and sensitivity and becomes leader of the flock. Peter accepts his pet's death with the realization that her ewe lamb will take her place. This book will not have immediate appeal to children, but once it is introduced and discussed, they will find pleasure in the account of rural life.

Brooklyn, at the time that the Dodgers played at Ebbets Field, is indeed a different setting for growing up. In *Brooklyn Girl*, Karen Rose presents one year of Kay's life. Kay changes in that year from a tomboy who races everywhere creating currents of noise around her, to a responsible girl who walks slowly downstairs instead of leaping. The author has created a very believable girl and gives authentic pictures of school, home, and neighborhood. Many girls will say, "Kay's just like me."

Vicky Austin is another girl who grows toward maturity in one summer as her family drives across the United States. *The Moon by Night* continues L'Engle's story of the fine family introduced in *Meet the Austins*. On this trip, Vicky meets a rather obnoxious older boy who is wealthy, has been kicked out of school, and expresses the despair of many teen-agers. Only fourteen, Vicky pretends she is older and is pleased with Zachary's attentions as they meet at different campgrounds. Vicky is disturbed by the boy's attitudes and the knowledge that her family disapproves of him. Vicky learns that Zachary has a heart condition but refuses to see doctors or to care for himself. She reaches a crisis in her thinking when Zachary takes her to see the play, *The Diary of Anne Frank*, and says to her:

> *"What's the point of believing in God when nothing makes any sense? . . . You're so darned good, Vicky, you dope! Don't you know it doesn't make any sense to be good?"*[92]

Vicky's uncle helps her look at the unfairness of life and broadens her concept of

---

[90]Monica Shannon, *Dobry,* Illustrated by Atanas Katchamakoff (New York: Viking, 1934), p. 7.

[91]Edith Lambert Sharp, *Nkwala* (Boston: Little, Brown, 1958), p. 35.

[92]Madeleine L'Engle, *The Moon by Night* (New York: Farrar, Straus, 1963), p. 137.

God. He points out that growing up isn't a particular point in time, "It goes right on being rough forever. But nothing that's easy is worth anything. You ought to have learned that by now. What happens as you keep on growing is that all of a sudden you realize that it's more exciting and beautiful than scary and awful."[93] Vicky meets a very different boy, Andy, who is fun and approved by the family. The Austins are in Yellowstone Park when an earthquake causes havoc. Vicky and Zachary are caught in a rock slide and are alone in a long night lit by a cold moon. Zachary decides life is worth living and Vicky knows that she doesn't understand God, but "there was something there to be *understood*." Many exciting events before the earthquake and fine character sketches are given throughout. Girls in grades five through eight will grow with Vicky as she learns who she is and what she believes.

Boys and girls in the middle grades find Miguel, the middle brother of a family on a New Mexico sheep ranch, a character with whom they can identify. Pedro, the younger brother, seems satisfied with what he has, but Miguel thinks his nineteen-year-old brother, Gabriel, can do everything and has everything he wants. Miguel expresses the problem of all who feel "in between":

> *Both of them, they are happy.*
> *But to be in between, not so little any more and not yet nineteen years, to be me, Miguel, and to have a great wish—that is hard.*[94]

Miguel is told, "To become something different from what you are, it takes more than being strong. Even a little time is needed as well."[95] Miguel does work hard, but he is not recognized for his individual contribution at lambing time. A moment of joy is reached when he is invited to eat with the men and the shearers. However, it is apparent that he will not be given the opportunity to go with the men when they take the sheep to the Sangre de Cristo Mountains. His prayers are answered, but not as Miguel wished. Gabriel is drafted into the Army, and Miguel is allowed to take his place. Miguel confesses his guilt feelings to Gabriel who helps him understand the meaning of prayer. Although Miguel has been growing all the time, he is suddenly aware that he is "no longer me."

Secret of the Andes by Clark appears to be realistic fiction, yet elements of legend and fantasy are included in this story of an Indian boy who is chosen to be the one who shall know of the secret gold and llama herd of the Incas. When Cusi is eight, he discovers other people; until this time, he has known only old Chuto who has taught him his language, care of the llamas, and to be satisfied with little. Life is monotonous. "He was always a little hungry, always a little cold, always a little lonely."[96]

Cusi's mystical, mute acceptance gives the element of fantasy: "All this had happened before. It must have happened, because it was what he was waiting for and he was ready."[97] The fantasy develops as Cusi's llama leads him down a hidden trail to an ancient temple. There he discovers golden sandals that are his, says his "heart." Now, Chuto says, he has received the sign; he must go to Cuzco to seek his heart's desire. Encounters there with strangers who seem to recognize him only leave him with more questions. Attempting to realize his secret desire, Cusi does join a family. When the father talks of sharing, Cusi feels he could never share his golden sandals. He returns to the mountains, for only in the hidden valley can he feel secure. Chuto shows him the cave where the gold is hidden, and Cusi swears he will never reveal the secret and

---

[93]L'Engle, p. 139.
[94]Joseph Krumgold, . . . *And Now Miguel*, Illustrated by Jean Charlot (New York: Crowell, 1953), p. 9.
[95]Krumgold, p. 31.

[96]Ann Nolan Clark, *Secret of the Andes*, Illustrated by Jean Charlot (New York: Viking, 1952), p. 31.
[97]Clark, p. 69.

that he will train another to take his place.

The pace of the book is as slow as the climb up the mountain trails, but the author's descriptions provide moments of beauty. The mystery of Cusi's identity supplies the suspense of the *Secret of the Andes*.

Moments of Decision.

In many books for children, there are moments of crisis when the protagonist makes a decision that leads him toward conformity or individuality, toward responsibility or complacency, toward concern for others or preservation of self, in sum, toward good or evil.

A relatively short, but dramatic, incident is the moment of decision for Jim, a young sheepherder who must overcome tribal superstition to save his sheep by entering *The Cave*. Although he feels that Fernando, the man in charge, is an enemy and senses the restlessness of the sheep, Jim goes with the flock to the summer pasture. A sudden storm makes it imperative that they find shelter. Jim knows about a cave where his ancestors are buried, but he is afraid to enter. "Wasn't it better for sheep to die than for something terrible to happen to men?"[98] But Jim's concern for the animals and the example of bravery of one of the sheep lead him on. He wins the respect of the older man and comes to understand why Fernando spoke in anger as he did.

In *The Wheel on the School*, a Newbery winner, DeJong shows the growth of each of six children in a school in a Netherlands village. The only girl, Lina, wrote an unassigned essay about storks, asking why no storks came to Shora. Excellent teaching is demonstrated by the sensitive teacher who takes the opportunity to develop creativity and to teach more than facts from a text-book. He tells the children to wonder about storks:

> *We can't think much when we don't know much. But we can wonder! . . . Will you wonder why and wonder why? Will you wonder why storks don't come to Shora to build their nests on the roofs, the way they do in all the villages around? For sometimes when we wonder, we can make things begin to happen.*[99]

When they discuss their findings the next day, he encourages them to dream, and then helps them identify a practical problem they can solve. To get a pair of storks, they can try placing a wheel on a roof. Each child grows in understanding or responsibility as he searches for a wheel. Through their efforts and courage, the legless man in the village who had isolated himself in bitterness becomes a part of the social group. Excitement mounts as legless Janus, the teacher, and three of the children make a daring rescue of two storks exhausted by a storm. All have learned that dreams can come true when each person works with others.

Manolo was a Spanish boy who had to decide whether to follow his own conscience or to conform to the expectations of the community. *Shadow of a Bull*, by Wojciechowska, describes the darkening shadow of Manolo's fear of failure to be like his father, a famous bullfighter. Everything and everybody in Arcangel reminds Manolo of his destiny to face his first bull at the age of twelve. A group of nameless men hover over him, their shadows like vultures, constantly teaching as they take him to bullfights. At night he practices the passes, trying to be ready, even though he knows he will fail. When only a year remains before his test, he asks Juan, an older boy who truly wants to fight bulls, if he can try to cape a bull at

---

[98]Elizabeth Coatsworth, *The Cave*, Illustrated by Allan Houser (New York: Viking, 1958), p. 55.

[99]Meindert DeJong, *The Wheel on the School*, Illustrated by Maurice Sendak (New York: Harper & Row, 1954), p. 6.

night in order to test himself. Such practice is forbidden, but Juan does it because he is given no other chances. Manolo saves Juan by facing the bull, but he is overcome by fear. To Juan, Manolo confesses his fear that he will not do well, that he does not have the *afición* for bull fighting. He suggests Juan take his place, but Juan refuses. On the night before his test, Manolo's mother tells him how tired his father had been after the bullfights, but she also tells him his father did what he wanted to do. "That was the great thing about your father: his own will to do what he was doing. What he did was for himself, most of all for himself."[100] Manolo's prayer is for bravery to stand his ground, not to be saved from wounds or death. When he meets a famous critic before the bullfight, Manolo hears the words he should have heard earlier:

> "*A man's life is many things. Before he becomes a man, he has many choices: to do the right thing, or to do the wrong thing; to please himself, or to please others; to be true to his own self, or untrue to it. . . . Real courage, true bravery is doing things in spite of fear, knowing fear. . . . Be what you are, and if you don't yet know what you are, wait until you do. Don't let anyone make that decision for you.*"[101]

Manolo proves his physical and spiritual courage, and the town receives a new bull-fighter hero. Above all, Manolo's decision is what *he* really wanted. Many boys and girls know the shadows Manolo faces; all will have deeper insight as they discuss it.

Queenie Peavy, by Robert Burch, is the story of an eighth-grade girl living in a small Southern town during the depression. Queenie is a big tomboy who can hit any target with a rock and shows off at school to prove she is better than the children who

Manolo's life is haunted by the deep shadows of his own fear, memories of his dead father's fame as a bullfighter, and the community expectations. Illustration by Alvin Smith. Copyright © 1964 by Maia Wojciechowska. From *Shadow of a Bull*. Used by permission of Atheneum Publishers.

torment her because her father is in prison. The author depicts other aspects of her personality, too. She has ability and does her homework well. Queenie's mother is a drab, wishy-washy person too exhausted by the struggle to keep food in their mouths to be concerned about her daughter's life. If she would even scold, Queenie would feel someone cared. The girl's tenderness and imagination are revealed in her play with the Negro neighbor children. Relationships with this Negro family whose economic status is better than Queenie's are very pleasant. Called to court, Queenie expresses extreme

---

[100]Maia Wojciechowska, *Shadow of a Bull*, Illustrated by Alvin Smith (New York: Atheneum, 1965), p. 128.
[101]Wojciechowska, pp. 145–146.

hostility. Her savage humor is shown as she spits tobacco on the stove and says to the judge, "I might or I might not." Queenie shows kindness to a classmate who faints from hunger, and while calmly aiding the doctor, finds his encouragement helpful. She feels guilty when it appears that she caused a boy to break his ankle, and fully expects to be sent to the reformatory. Her father returns on parole, but her joy turns to sadness when he ignores her. One of the most dramatic scenes occurs when he drives off in a truck so quickly that she is knocked down. Queenie finally sees the man as he is—irresponsible, not put upon by others, but making his own choices. Because he violates parole by carrying a gun, he is sent back to prison. Queenie realizes that she had tried to make her father into something that he wasn't. "She loved him still, but she would never again pretend anything was true that wasn't."[102] Queenie proves she can behave properly during an entire day when she thought she would be sent to reform school. Frequently, the author does not allow the reader to think for himself; he tells Queenie's inner thoughts in detail and in a somewhat moralizing style. For example, Queenie is ready to hurl another rock, "But her own voice nagged . . . Go wild if you want to, see if I care! But who are you hurting in the long run?"[103] Alone, she makes the choice to become a better person, and "Queenie Herself" is the title of the last chapter that shows her changed personality. Robert Burch's descriptions of the cabin, the school, the life of the depression period are stark portraits. This book helps children understand the causes of behavior and holds hope that the "incorrigible child" can change.

A boy in Europe finds his identity as he goes *North to Freedom*. This excellent novel by Holm won the 1965 prize for the Best Scan-

dinavian Children's Book. David knows only the blacks, greys, and browns of the concentration camp where he was born. The "man," a guard whom he hates, and who he is sure hates him, tells David the current will be off long enough for him to climb the electric fence. He will find a package, and should go to Salonika, then north to Denmark. David expects to be tricked, but an inner force pushes him on to escape. The food is there; in addition, the man left the soap David requested. The act of washing away the smell of the prison is symbolic of his movement toward freedom. David had learned seven languages from the prisoners and he had been taught by Johannes, but so much of his learning was without the essential experience to bring meaning that it was difficult to relate to the world. His tentative gestures toward human relationships, his fears, and his values are depicted in a series of taut scenes. One, for example, shows how David expressed his new-found freedom. David had helped an Englishman who had lost his glasses. He refused the offer of money because it was a decision *he* could make. David decides to accept God, but is concerned that he does not know what to do in return for God's help. The opportunity comes when he saves a little girl from a burning shed. The grateful family take him to their home, accepting his story that he was in a circus and making his way north to join the troupe. But David does not smile, and he cannot learn to play. He tells the children of evil and discusses the "truth" of life. When he overhears the parents talking of their concern about his influence on their children, he decides he must leave. Taken in by a mean farmer in the mountains, he is once again a prisoner. He tunnels out of the barn, comes near a prison where the old fear returns. His dog is killed while the boy escapes. An incredible, yet possible, meeting with a Danish artist gives him a clue that his mother is still alive.

[102]Robert Burch, *Queenie Peavy*, Illustrated by Jerry Lazare (New York: Viking, 1966), p. 145.
[103]Burch, p. 155.

Although David doubts God and criticizes Him, he realizes that he chose his God, just as the dog had chosen to meet death to save his friend, and as David himself had made a choice when he entered the fire to save the child. That he did not have to go north to find freedom or achieve identity of self is the theme of the book. Incredibly, he did find his mother in Copenhagen, but this ending is actually an anticlimax in contrast to the self-understanding and the individual freedom he had received. As David thinks of the dog, he raises another question—did the dog choose? Or had God entered the dog and made him do it? The questions raised in this book are universal questions for all ages.

A controversial book tells of a boy's growing toward maturity as he changes his concepts of security and freedom. *Dorp Dead* expresses Gilly Ground's hostility, and the misspelling of the word "drop" shows that he has not changed completely at the end of the story when he scrawled the words on the door of the man who took him from the orphanage. Told in the first person, the style of the narrative is unrealistic, for most children would not use such beautiful language. This is one clue that indicates the book goes beyond mere "reality of presentation." Gilly keeps his intelligence a secret: "It is a weapon for defense as comforting as a very sharp knife worn between the skin and the shirt."[104] He describes himself: "Anyone can see why I am never very popular or sought after: A stuffed bear in school, from whom infrequent and inaccurate grunts of nonknowledge are extracted, and a true clunk at sports, besides offering nothing in the way of malice or inventiveness in between. This is the way I want it and have it."[105]

A maker of ladders, Master Kobalt takes Gilly to his house which is, at first, a haven to the boy. He relishes the quiet and the order,

An intelligent, lonely boy expresses inner turmoil as he ponders the meaning of security and conformity. From *Dorp Dead* by Julia Cunningham, illustrated by James Spanfeller. © Copyright 1965 by Julia Cunningham. Reprinted by permission of Pantheon Books, a Division of Random House, Inc.

but he is puzzled by the dog, Mash, who cannot respond to friendly gestures. Gilly had another place of refuge, a stone tower where he could be alone. There he had met the hunter who carried a gun although it had no bullets. When Gilly describes his orderly life with Kobalt, the hunter asks, "Are you bewitched, boy?" and gives Gilly an envelope containing his name and address.

[104]Julia Cunningham, *Dorp Dead,* Illustrated by James Spanfeller (New York: Pantheon, 1965), p. 4.
[105]Cunningham, p. 12.

After Kobalt beats the dog, Gilly revengefully messes up the ladders in the workshop. Furiously, Kobalt makes him sit on a ladder for hours. Gilly discovers a cage in Kobalt's room—just the size for a boy. When Kobalt knows he has turned his ankle, the sadist seems pleased. Gilly says, "My insides leap alive. I shovel my grief for Mash under as many layers of consciousness as I can. I recognize the danger now and it is as keen edged as the blade that kills."[106] Gilly escapes by using one of the ladders to crawl up the chimney. Kobalt finds him at the tower and tries to kill him. Gilly is saved by Mash, who has survived, and is able to show his response to the love Gilly had given him. Gilly goes to the hunter, apparently finds security, and begins to use his intelligence wisely. The allegorical nature of this book is discussed on page 361.

The universal search for truth, contentment, and security is presented in *The Most Beautiful Place* by Ruck-Pauquet. In his home village of Igane, the orphan Joschko was cared for by all the people. At age fourteen, he sets out to see the world, to find the most beautiful place. An old gypsy gives advice all should consider:

> "You must know that people are weak. They would like to be good, but they are weak. All people in the whole world. When someone has been good to you, then you must remember it. Think about it again and again! But if someone has treated you badly, Joschko, forget it. Forget it quickly and so thoroughly that it is as if it never happened. You owe it to them."[107]

Joschko meets the weak people, yet he learns they also have moments of strength. For example, the owner of a cafe who is a smuggler gives money for a sick child. Joschko begins

to discover his own weakness. When his beloved donkey is killed by a wolf, he asks, as do so many, "Why does that have to be?" The response of the old woman is both harsh and comforting:

> "Because there is light and there is darkness . . . happiness and sorrow. And only he who feels both can say that he lives and that he is a human being."[108]

Joschko realizes that Igane is the most beautiful place, and returns to the warmth of his village, a wiser, more human, boy. There is suspense in the book, for the villagers have asked the police to search for him. Each of the people Joschko meets is interesting, each incident teaches that behavior has no single cause. The vivid descriptions of the sea, wind, sun, and the mountains enrich this dramatic story that contains several layers of meaning.

> That is the story they tell of the old days in the valley of Kurtal; of the conquest of the great mountain called the Citadel; and of how Rudi Matt, who was later to become the most famous of all Alpine guides, grew from a boy into a man.[109]

So ends the book titled *Banner in the Sky*, a book based upon the actual events of the first climbing of the Matterhorn. Rudi is a character of fiction, but he is indeed real. At age sixteen, this rugged son of a famous guide is relegated to the kitchen of a hotel to learn the hotel business. Rudi's burning desire is to climb the mountain that claimed his father's life, the peak that no other guide has dared to climb. An old guide, now chef at the hotel because he was injured at the time Rudi's father died, gives the boy help and understands his deep need to scale the peaks. Rudi often runs away, although his

---

[106]Cunningham, p. 71.
[107]Gina Ruck-Pauquet, *The Most Beautiful Place*, Translated by Edelgard von Heydekampf Bruehl, Illustrated by Sigrid Heuck (New York: Dutton, 1965), p. 40.

---

[108]Ruck-Pauquet, p. 160.
[109]James Ramsey Ullman, *Banner in the Sky* (Philadelphia: Lippincott, 1954), p. 252.

mother and uncle have forbidden him to climb. On one excursion, he saves an English climber. When Rudi learns the Englishman plans to climb the Citadel, he leaves work and goes to join the climber and his guide from another village. Rudi goes alone to find a way around a difficult rock face, and reaches a point where man has never been. The book is filled with vivid descriptions of the climb: the hazardous inching along rock ledges, of being nearly smothered in an avalanche, of planning deliberate movements. For example, when Rudi achieves the highest point man has reached, he searched for a way to go on, the path his father had sought. The suspense of moments like this is breathtaking:

> . . . *Stepping out from the ledge, he inched out onto the bulge, using not only hands and feet, as in ordinary climbing, but all of his body that he could bring into play.* . . . *Space wheeled beneath him.* . . . *His clothing scraped against the granite; his knees and elbows churned; his fingers clawed and kneaded. Once he slipped—and once more—.* . . .[110]

After proving one could go on around the rock face called the Fortress, he could not return because of darkness. Spending a lonely, freezing night in the cave where his father had died, he faces terror, and then finds faith in memory of his father as well as in the Father to Whom he prayed. Meanwhile, Rudi's uncle agrees to climb with the Englishman and Saxo, the guide from another village. Rivalries and prejudice shadow the four, however, as they set out to reach the summit. Captain Winters, the Englishman, becomes ill, and according to the code of the mountains, the guide must remain with his "Master" if he becomes ill or is injured. Saxo cannot resist his own ambition and sets out alone to reach the top. Realizing what Saxo has done, Rudi leaves his uncle

and Winters to pursue the guide. Saxo insists Rudi must return, for he alone will be the first to the top. In anger, the man turns, falls, and is injured. At that moment, Rudi faces a terrible decision—to go on to the top and leave an injured man, even an enemy, or to help Saxo. There was a way out, but it was down, not up. The descent is dangerous and exhausting, but Rudi and the injured man reach safety. Winters had recovered and with Rudi's uncle did reach the top. When the climbers return, Rudi looks through the telescope and sees his father's shirt flying from a pole at the summit. The shirt which he had hoped to carry to the top had been placed there by Winters, who tells the people it should now be called Rudi's mountain. Most young people will not climb mountains, but they will have other dreams, other challenges, and their own moments of decision in becoming men.

BOOKS AND PERSONAL GROWTH

Folk tales and moralistic stories long have been viewed as sources for character training of the young. In modern times, such sociologists as Riesman[111] have analyzed the influence of literature in establishing cultural expectations. A few psychologists have explored the impact of literature upon the emotional development of children. Four editions of a volume titled *Reading Ladders for Human Relations* testify to the belief of educators that books are a significant force in developing social sensitivity. Throughout this text, the values of literature for interpretation and extension of experience have been stressed. The process of guiding children to read with insight and awareness has been emphasized. Concurrently, it has been recognized that literature is only one part of

---

[110]Ullman, p. 133.

[111]David Riesman, Nathan Gleazer, and Reuel Denney, *The Lonely Crowd* (New Haven, Conn.: Yale University Press, 1950), pp. 86–112.

a child's experience in home, school, and community. The specific effect of a particular book, or of all his reading, upon a child's attitudes, values, or feelings cannot be accurately assessed.

Bibliotherapy

The use of books to develop understanding of specific personal problems has been termed *bibliotherapy*. To many educators and psychologists, however, the term refers to the process of providing therapy through books for those who have emotional or mental illness.

Three processes in bibliotherapy correspond to the three phases of psychotherapy: identification, catharsis, and insight. The process of identification is association of self, through projection, with another person. Catharsis refers to release of emotion or removal of suppressed desires, while insight is the emotional awareness of motivation. The definition of bibliotherapy may be considered:

> . . . *A process of dynamic interaction between the personality of the reader and literature. This interaction may be utilized for personality assessment, adjustment, and growth.*[112]

The kind of guided reading and discussion proposed for a literature curriculum, described in this text, would lead to this goal. However, if bibliotherapy is considered to be the prescription of books for emotionally disturbed children, neither the classroom teacher nor the librarian is qualified. It is unwise to probe too deeply or to encourage expression of raw emotion in a large-group situation, for the child may feel guilty later on, and the teacher may be unable to cope with the feelings expressed. Individual conferences or small group discussions in an atmosphere of acceptance can facilitate expression of feeling, however, and the flow of the child's responses should not be stopped. Books may help the child (1) acquire information and knowledge about the psychology and physiology of human behavior, (2) learn what it means to "know thyself," (3) find an interest outside himself, (4) relieve conscious problems in a controlled manner, (5) utilize an opportunity for identification and compensation, and (6) illuminate difficulties and acquire insight into his own behavior.[113] However, "Stories are not like mustard plasters to be applied for immediate relief where deep-seated problems of behavior, attitudes, and values exist."[114]

Literature, and especially realistic fiction, makes it possible to use the imagination to enter other lives in other places, to know more of the world in which we live. Literature provides identification with humanity as it reveals other children facing universal problems. As C. S. Lewis noted, this process involves the extension of self:

> But in reading great literature I become a thousand men and yet remain myself. Like the night sky in the Greek poem, I see with myriad eyes, but it is still I who see. Here, as in worship, in love, in moral action, and in knowing, I transcend myself; and I am never more myself than when I do.[115]

---

[112]David Russell and Caroline Shrodes, "Contributions of Research in Bibliotherapy to the Language Arts Program," *School Review*, I, vol. 68 (September 1950), pp. 335–342; II, vol. 68 (October 1950), pp. 411–420.

[113]Patricia Cianciolo, "Children's Literature Can Affect Coping Behavior," *Personnel and Guidance Journal*, vol. 43 (May 1965), pp. 897–901.

[114]Margaret M. Heaton and Helen B. Lewis, *Reading Ladders for Human Relations*. Revised edition (Washington, D.C.: American Council on Education, 1955), p. 35.

[115]C. S. Lewis, *An Experiment in Criticism* (Cambridge, England: Cambridge University Press, 1961), p. 141.

SUGGESTED ACTIVITIES

1. Prepare a comparative analysis of several books dealing with one racial or religious group.
2. Read five of the books suggested in this chapter. Prepare a list of questions you might ask about each book to guide children's discussion and interpretation.
3. Compare the treatment of fear, loneliness, or death in several books for children.
4. Read books about one country or region and compare characters and situations.
5. Make a list of books that could be used for a study of the individual versus conformity. List the questions that you would ask to guide children's discussion of these books.
6. Read some of the books in which characters have to make major decisions. Identify the forces that affect the way the decisions are made.
7. Compare the relationships of the parents and children in the following families: the Moffats, the Austins, the Barkers, the Gradys, the Goodmans.

RELATED READINGS

1. Arbuthnot, May Hill. *Children and Books.* Third edition. Glenview, Ill.: Scott, Foresman, 1964.
   Chapter 15 includes "Realism for the Youngest" and books for older readers organized according to outstanding authors.
2. Baker, Augusta. *Books about Negro Life for Children.* New York: New York Public Library, 1963.
   Criteria for these books are established. The annotated list includes books about Negroes in the United States and other lands. Frequently revised.
3. Boyd, Jennemary. "Passports to the Promised Land," *Elementary English,* vol. 35 (November 1958), pp. 441–449.
   A teacher describes books she would use with children in her classes that are predominantly Negro. Although selections are personal, she suggests criteria other teachers might well consider.
4. Cianciola, Patricia. "Children's Literature Can Affect Coping Behavior," *The Personnel and Guidance Journal,* vol. 43 (May 1965), pp. 897–903.
   Books can help children by providing new insights for therapy and prevention of emotional problems. Research is reviewed, and a list of children's books is appended. Caption comments indicate the problem theme of each book.
5. Combs, Arthur, Editor. *Perceiving, Behaving, Becoming.* 1962 Yearbook of the Association for Supervision and Curriculum Development. Washington, D.C.: National Education Association, 1962.
   The implications of papers by Earl Kelley, Carl Rogers, A. H. Maslow, and Arthur Combs are related to educational practice by the yearbook committee. The process of becoming is defined and related to views of self, creativity, motivation, values, and practices that would facilitate development of the "fully functioning" or "adequate" personality.
6. Crosby, Muriel, Editor. *Reading Ladders for Human Relations.* Fourth edition. Washington, D.C.: American Council on Education, 1963.
   The presentation of the role of books in human relations education and suggestions for classroom discussion of these books will help teachers plan for their effective use. Annotated lists are organized according to such topics as "How It Feels to Grow Up" and "The Search for Values."
7. Kircher, Clara J., Compiler. *Behavior Patterns in Children's Books: A Bibliography.* Washington, D.C.: Catholic University Press, 1966.
   An annotated bibliography of 507 books organized under twenty-two different

headings of behavioral patterns such as honesty, intercultural understanding, and kindness to animals.

8. Larrick, Nancy. "The All-White World of Children's Books," *Saturday Review* (September 11, 1965).

   An analysis of the pressures and problems related to publishing books about Negroes.

9. Lewis, C. S. *An Experiment in Criticism.* Cambridge, England: Cambridge University Press, 1961.

   The discussion of realism in literature provides background for understanding "realistic" fiction.

10. Little, Jean. "The People in Books," *The Horn Book Magazine,* vol. 42 (April 1966), pp. 159–162.

    An author expresses her views of literature that will help children understand the human condition.

11. Mandel, R. L. "Children's Books: Mirrors of Social Development," *Elementary School Journal,* vol. 64 (January 1964), pp. 190–199.

    An analysis of books and social-emotional development of children.

12. Newell, E. "At the North End of Pooh: A Study of Bibliotherapy," *Elementary English,* vol. 34 (January 1957), pp. 22–25.

    The author notes that Pooh asked that a sustaining book be read to him while he was stuck. The question of identification with the hero is raised. A good list of books for personal problems is included.

13. Overstreet, Bonaro W. "The Role of the Home," in *Development in and through Reading,* 16th Yearbook, Part I, National Society for the Study of Education. Chicago: National Society for the Study of Education, 1961.

    Books are viewed as mediators (between the individual and other environments), makers of an atmosphere, and builders of inner resources.

14. Stendler, Celia B., and William B. Martin. *Intergroup Education in Kindergarten-Primary Grades.* New York: Macmillan, 1953.

    The need for intergroup education is clearly presented. Suggestions for many experiences in the school and community could be adapted.

15. Wolfe, Ann G. *About 100 Books, a Gateway to Better Intergroup Understanding.* Fifth edition. New York: The American Jewish Committee, Institute of Human Relations, 1965.

    Annotations of books from 1962–1965 give enough information to guide teachers and librarians seeking books for study of human relations.

CHAPTER REFERENCES

1. Alcock, Gudrun. *Run, Westy, Run.* Illustrated by W. T. Mars. New York: Lothrop, 1966.

2. Armer, Laura Adams. *Waterless Mountain.* Illustrated by Sidney and Laura Armer. New York: McKay, 1931.

3. Arora, Shirley. *"What Then, Raman?".* Illustrated by Hans Guggenheim. Chicago: Follett, 1960.

4. Arthur, Ruth M. *My Daughter Nicola.* Illustrated by Fermin Rocker. New York: Atheneum, 1965.

5. Baum, Betty. *Patricia Crosses Town.* Illustrated by Nancy Grossman. New York: Knopf, 1965.

6. Beim, Jerrold. *The Smallest Boy in the Class.* Illustrated by Meg Wohlberg. New York: Morrow, 1949.

7. ———*Trouble After School.* Illustrated by Don Sibley. New York: Harcourt, 1957.

8. Beim, Lorraine and Jerrold. *Two Is a Team.* Illustrated by Ernest Crichlow. New York: Harcourt, 1945.

9. Benary-Isbert, Margot. *The Ark*. Translated by Clara and Richard Winston. New York: Harcourt, 1953.

10. ————*Castle on the Border*. New York: Harcourt, 1956.

11. ————*Rowan Farm*. New York: Harcourt, 1954.

12. Bishop, Claire Huchet. *Pancakes-Paris*. Illustrated by Georges Schreiber. New York: Viking, 1947.

13. ————*Twenty and Ten*, as told by Janet Joly. Illustrated by William Pène du Bois. New York: Viking, 1964.

14. Bloch, Marie Halun. *Aunt America*. Illustrated by Joan Berg. New York: Atheneum, 1963.

15. ————*The Two Worlds of Damyan*. Illustrated by Robert Quackenbush. New York: Atheneum, 1966.

16. Bonham, Frank. *Durango Street*. New York: Dutton, 1965.

17. Bontemps, Arna. *Sad-Faced Boy*. Illustrated by Virginia Lee Burton. Boston: Houghton Mifflin, 1937.

18. Bonzon, Paul-Jacques. *Orphans of Simitra*. Illustrated by Simon Jeruchim. New York: Criterion, 1962.

19. Bradley, Duane. *Meeting With a Stranger*. Illustrated by E. Harper Johnson. Philadelphia: Lippincott, 1964.

20. Brown, Margaret Wise. *The Dead Bird*. Illustrated by Remy Charlip. New York: W. R. Scott, 1958.

21. Buck, Pearl S. *The Big Wave*. Illustrated with prints by Hiroshige and Hokusai. New York: John Day, 1948.

22. Burch, Robert. *D. J.'s Worst Enemy*. Illustrated by Emil Weiss. New York: Viking, 1965.

23. ————*Queenie Peàvy*. Illustrated by Jerry Lazare. New York: Viking, 1966.

24. ————*Skinny*. Illustrated by Don Sibley. New York: Viking, 1964.

25. Burnett, Frances Hodgson. *The Secret Garden*. Illustrated by Tasha Tudor. Philadelphia: Lippincott, 1938, 1909.

26. Carlson, Natalie Savage. *A Brother for the Orphelines*. Illustrated by Garth Williams. New York: Harper & Row, 1959.

27. ————*The Empty Schoolhouse*. Illustrated by John Kaufmann. New York: Harper & Row, 1965.

28. ————*The Family under the Bridge*. Illustrated by Garth Williams. New York: Harper & Row, 1958.

29. ————*The Happy Orpheline*. Illustrated by Garth Williams. New York: Harper & Row, 1957.

30. ————*The Letter on the Tree*. Illustrated by John Kaufmann. New York: Harper & Row, 1964.

31. ————*The Tomahawk Family*. Illustrated by Stephen Cook. New York: Harper & Row, 1960.

32. Caudill, Rebecca. *A Certain Small Shepherd*. Illustrated by William Pène du Bois. New York: Holt, Rinehart and Winston, 1965.

33. Clark, Ann Nolan. *Secret of the Andes*. Illustrated by Jean Charlot. New York: Viking, 1952.

34. Coatsworth, Elizabeth. *The Cave*. Illustrated by Allan Houser. New York: Viking, 1958.

35. Cone, Molly. *A Promise Is a Promise*. Illustrated by John Gretzer. Boston: Houghton Mifflin, 1964.

36. Credle, Ellis. *Down, Down the Mountain*. Camden, N.J.: Nelson, 1934.

37. Cretan, Gladys Yessayan. *All Except Sammy*. Illustrated by Symeon Shimin. Boston: Little, Brown, 1966.

38. Cunningham, Julia. *Dorp Dead*. Illustrated by James Spanfeller. New York: Pantheon, 1965.

39. De Angeli, Marguerite. *Bright April*. New York: Doubleday, 1946.

40. ————*The Door in the Wall.* New York: Doubleday, 1949.
41. ————*Thee, Hannah!* New York: Doubleday, 1949.
42. ————*Skippack School.* New York: Doubleday, 1961.
43. DeJong, Meindert. *Far out the Long Canal.* Illustrated by Nancy Grossman. New York: Harper & Row, 1964.
44. ————*The House of Sixty Fathers.* Illustrated by Maurice Sendak. New York: Harper & Row, 1956.
45. ————*Shadrach.* Illustrated by Maurice Sendak. New York: Harper & Row, 1963.
46. ————*The Wheel on the School.* Illustrated by Maurice Sendak. New York: Harper & Row, 1954.
47. Doone, Radko. *Nuvat the Brave.* Illustrated by Hans Axel Walleen. Philadelphia: Macrae, 1934.
48. Enright, Elizabeth. *The Saturdays.* New York: Holt, Rinehart and Winston, 1941.
49. Estes, Eleanor. *The Hundred Dresses.* Illustrated by Louis Slobodkin. New York: Harcourt, 1944.
50. ————*The Middle Moffat.* Illustrated by Louis Slobodkin. New York: Harcourt, 1942.
51. ————*The Moffats.* Illustrated by Louis Slobodkin. New York: Harcourt, 1941.
52. ————*Rufus M.* Illustrated by Louis Slobodkin. New York: Harcourt, 1943.
53. Faulkner, Georgene, and John Becker. *Melindy's Medal.* Illustrated by Elton C. Fax. New York: Messner, 1945.
54. Fitzhugh, Louise. *Harriet the Spy.* New York: Harper & Row, 1964.
55. Fon Eisen, Anthony. *Bond of the Fire.* Illustrated by W. T. Mars. Cleveland: World Publishing, 1965.
56. Forbes, Esther. *Johnny Tremain.* Illustrated by Lynd Ward. Boston: Houghton Mifflin, 1946.
57. Forman, James. *Ring the Judas Bell.* New York: Farrar, Straus, 1965.
58. ————*The Skies of Crete.* New York: Farrar, Straus, 1963.
59. Gage, Wilson. *Big Blue Island.* Illustrated by Glen Rounds. Cleveland: World Publishing, 1964.
60. Garfield, James B. *Follow My Leader.* Illustrated by Robert Greiner. New York: Viking, 1957.
61. Garthwaite, Marion. *Mario, a Mexican Boy's Adventure.* New York: Doubleday, 1960.
62. Gates, Doris. *Blue Willow.* Illustrated by Paul Lantz. New York: Viking, 1940.
63. George, Jean. *Gull 737.* New York: Crowell, 1964.
64. ————*My Side of the Mountain.* New York: Dutton, 1959.
65. Gilbreth, Frank B. Jr., and Ernestine G. Carey. *Cheaper by the Dozen.* Revised edition. New York: Crowell, 1963, 1949.
66. Graham, Lorenz. *North Town.* Chicago: Follett, 1965.
67. ————*South Town.* Chicago: Follett, 1959.
68. Griffiths, Helen. *The Greyhound.* Illustrated by Victor G. Ambrus. New York: Doubleday, 1966.
69. Grund, Josef Carl. *You Have a Friend, Pietro.* Translated by Margaret Mutch. Illustrated by Kurt Schmischke. Boston, Little, Brown, 1966.
70. Harnden, Ruth. *The High Pasture.* Illustrated by Vee Guthrie. Boston: Houghton, Mifflin, 1964.
71. Hayes, Florence. *Skid.* Illustrated by Elton C. Fax. Boston: Houghton Mifflin, 1948.
72. Holm, Anne. *North to Freedom.* New York: Harcourt, 1965.
73. Houston, James. *Tiktá Liktak.* New York: Harcourt, 1965.
74. Jackson, Jesse. *Call Me Charley.* Illustrated by Doris Spiegel. New York: Harper & Row, 1945.
75. Johnson, Annabel and Edgar. *The Grizzly.* Illustrated by Gilbert Riswold. New York: Harper & Row, 1964.
76. Jones, Cordelia. *Nobody's Garden.* Illustrated by Victor Ambrus. New York: Scribner, 1966.

77. Juline, Ruth. *A Place for Johnny-Bill*. Illustrated by Georgeann Helms. Philadelphia: Westminster, 1961.
78. Justus, May. *New Boy in School*. New York: Hastings, 1963.
79. Kililea, Marie. *Wren*. Illustrated by Bob Riger. New York: Dodd, Mead, 1954.
80. Kim Yong Ik. *Blue in the Seed*. Illustrated by Artur Marokvia. Boston: Little, Brown, 1964.
81. ————*The Happy Days*. Illustrated by Artur Marokvia. Boston: Little, Brown, 1960.
82. Krumgold, Joseph. . . . *And Now Miguel*. Illustrated by Jean Charlot. New York: Crowell, 1953.
83. ————*Onion John*. Illustrated by Symeon Shimin. New York: Crowell, 1959.
84. L'Engle, Madeleine. *Meet the Austins*. New York: Vanguard, 1961.
85. ————*The Moon by Night*. New York: Farrar, Straus, 1963.
86. Lenski, Lois. *Coal Camp Girl*. Philadelphia: Lippincott, 1959.
87. ————*Corn Farm Boy*. Philadelphia: Lippincott, 1954.
88. ————*Judy's Journey*. Philadelphia: Lippincott, 1947.
89. ————*Prairie School*. Philadelphia: Lippincott, 1951.
90. ————*Shoo-Fly Girl*. Philadelphia: Lippincott, 1963.
91. ————*Strawberry Girl*. Philadelphia: Lippincott, 1945.
92. ————*Texas Tomboy*. Philadelphia: Lippincott, 1950.
93. Lewis, Richard W. *A Summer Adventure*. New York: Harper & Row, 1962.
94. Lewiton, Mina. *Candita's Choice*. Illustrated by Howard Simon. New York: Harper & Row, 1959.
95. ————*That Bad Carlos*. Illustrated by Howard Simon. Harper & Row, 1964.
96. Lindgren, Astrid. *Rasmus and the Vagabond*. Illustrated by Eric Palmquist. New York: Viking, 1960.
97. Little, Jean. *Home from Far*. Boston: Little, Brown, 1965.
98. ————*Mine for Keeps*. Illustrated by Lewis Parker. Boston: Little, Brown, 1962.
99. McSwigan, Marie. *Snow Treasure*. Illustrated by Mary Reardon. New York: Dutton, 1964, 1942.
100. Means, Florence. *The Moved Outers*. Illustrated by Helen Blair. Boston: Houghton Mifflin, 1945.
101. Miles, Miska. *Mississippi Possum*. Illustrated by John Schoenherr. Boston: Little, Brown, 1965.
102. Mirsky, Reba. *Nomusa and the New Magic*. Illustrated by W. T. Mars. Chicago: Follett, 1962.
103. ————*Thirty-One Brothers and Sisters*. Illustrated by W. T. Mars. Chicago: Follett, 1952.
104. Musgrave, Florence. *Robert E.* Illustrated by Mary Stevens. New York: Hastings, 1957.
105. Neville, Emily. *Berries Goodman*. New York: Harper & Row, 1965.
106. ————*It's Like This, Cat*. New York: Harper & Row, 1963.
107. ————*The Seventeenth-Street Gang*. Illustrated by Emily McCully. New York: Harper & Row, 1966.
108. O'Dell, Scott. *Island of the Blue Dolphins*. Boston: Houghton Mifflin, 1960.
109. Ottley, Reginald. *Boy Alone*. Illustrated by Clyde Pearson. New York: Harcourt, 1965.
110. Phipson, Joan. *The Boundary Riders*. Illustrated by Margaret Horder. New York: Harcourt, 1963.
111. ————*The Family Conspiracy*. Illustrated by Margaret Horder. New York: Harcourt, 1962.
112. ————*Threat to the Barkers*. Illustrated by Margaret Horder. New York: Harcourt, 1965.
113. Politi, Leo. *Juanita*. New York: Scribner, 1948.

114. ————*Pedro, the Angel of Olvera Street.* New York: Scribner, 1946.
115. Rich, Elaine Sommers. *Hannah Elizabeth.* Illustrated by Paul Kennedy. New York: Harper & Row, 1964.
116. Robinson, Veronica. *David in Silence.* Illustrated by Victor Ambrus. Philadelphia: Lippincott, 1966.
117. Rose, Karen. *Brooklyn Girl.* Chicago: Follett, 1963.
118. Ruck-Pauquet, Gina. *The Most Beautiful Place.* Translated by Edelgard von Heyde-kampf Bruhl. Illustrated by Sigrid Heuck. New York: Dutton, 1965.
119. Rydberg, Ernie. *The Dark of the Cave.* Illustrated by Carl Kidwell. New York: McKay, 1965.
120. Sawyer, Ruth. *Maggie Rose, Her Birthday Christmas.* Illustrated by Maurice Sendak. New York: Harper & Row, 1952.
121. Seredy, Kate. *The Good Master.* New York: Viking, 1935.
122. ————*A Tree for Peter.* New York: Viking, 1941.
123. Serraillier, Ian. *The Silver Sword.* Great Meadows, N.J.: S. G. Phillips, 1959.
124. Shannon, Monica. *Dobry.* Illustrated by Atanas Katchamakoff. New York: Viking, 1962, 1934.
125. Sharp, Edith Lambert. *Nkwala.* Boston: Little, Brown, 1958.
126. Sharpe, Stella G. *Tobe.* Photos by Charles Farrell. Durham, N.C.: University of North Carolina Press, 1939.
127. Shotwell, Louisa. *Roosevelt Grady.* Illustrated by Peter Burchard. Cleveland: World Publishing, 1963.
128. Smith, George H. *Bayou Boy.* Chicago: Follett, 1965.
129. ————*Wanderers of the Field.* New York: John Day, 1966.
130. Snyder, Zilpha Keatley. *The Velvet Room.* Illustrated by Alton Raible. New York: Atheneum, 1965.
131. Sommerfelt, Aimée. *My Name Is Pablo.* Translated by Patricia Crampton. Illustrated by Hans Norman Dahl. New York: Criterion, 1965.
132. ————*The Road to Agra,* Illustrated by Ulf Aas. New York: Criterion, 1961.
133. ————*The White Bungalow.* Translated by Evelyn Ramsden. Illustrated by Ulf Aas. New York: Criterion, 1964.
134. Sorensen, Virginia. *Lotte's Locket.* New York: Harcourt, 1964.
135. ————*Miracles on Maple Hill.* Illustrated by Beth and Joe Krush. New York: Harcourt, 1956.
136. ————*Plain Girl.* Illustrated by Charles Geer. New York: Harcourt, 1955.
137. Speevack, Yetta. *The Spider Plant.* Illustrated by Wendy Watson. New York: Atheneum, 1965.
138. Sperry, Armstrong. *Call It Courage.* New York: Macmillan, 1941.
139. Sterling, Dorothy. *Mary Jane.* Illustrated by Ernest Crichlow. New York: Double-day, 1959.
140. Stolz, Mary. *The Bully of Barkham Street.* Illustrated by Leonard Shortall. New York: Harper & Row, 1963.
141. ————*A Dog on Barkham Street.* Illustrated by Leonard Shortall. New York: Harper & Row, 1960.
142. ————*The Noonday Friends.* Illustrated by Louis S. Glanzman. New York: Harper & Row, 1965.
143. Taylor, Sydney. *All-of-a-Kind Family.* Illustrated by Helen John. Chicago: Follett, 1951.
144. ————*All-of-a-Kind Family Uptown.* Illustrated by Mary Stevens. Chicago: Follett, 1958.
145. ————*More All-of-a-Kind Family.* Illustrated by Mary Stevens. Chicago: Follett, 1954.
146. Tunis, John R. *Silence Over Dunkerque.* New York: Morrow, 1962.

147. Twain, Mark, pseud. (Samuel Langhorne Clemens). *The Adventures of Huckleberry Finn*. New York: Harper & Row, 1884.

148. Ullman, James Ramsey. *Banner in the Sky*. Philadelphia: Lippincott, 1954.

149. Urmston, Mary. *The New Boy*. Illustrated by Brinton Turkle. New York: Doubleday, 1950.

150. Van Stockum, Hilda. *The Winged Watchman*. New York: Farrar, Straus, 1962.

151. Waltrip, Lela and Rufus. *Quiet Boy*. Illustrated by Theresa Kalab Smith. New York: McKay, 1961.

152. Weik, Mary Hays. *The Jazz Man*. Illustrated by Ann Grifalconi. New York: Atheneum, 1966.

153. Wier, Ester. *The Loner*. Illustrated by Christine Price. New York: McKay, 1963.

154. Wilson, Leon. *This Boy Cody*. Illustrated by Ursula Koerning. New York: F. Watts, 1950.

155. Wojciechowska, Maia. *Shadow of a Bull*. Illustrated by Alvin Smith. New York: Atheneum, 1964.

156. Yates, Elizabeth. *Mountain Born*. Illustrated by Nora S. Unwin. New York: Coward-McCann, 1943.

6

BIOGRAPHY
AND HISTORICAL
FICTION

Mac was waiting at the door when Miss Harper came down the hall to open the school library. He was small for a ten-year-old, but what he lacked in size was compensated for by his sparkling personality. He gave Miss Harper one of his disarming smiles and said, "Gee, I'm glad you're here. Today is *the day,* isn't it?" Miss Harper laughed and nodded. She had no difficulty understanding his question; he had visited the library every day last week to see when the service committee would be finished preparing the new books for circulation. She had promised him that they could be checked out today. He literally bolted to the shelf of new books and looked eagerly through the titles until he came to the one he wanted. With a sigh of relief he wrote his name on the card and stamped on the due date. He looked up at Miss Harper and his big brown eyes were shining with accomplishment. "Well, I got it before Jim did. Guess he didn't think I'd get up early and catch a ride with Dave and his Dad—but it is worth it. You know, Miss Harper, sometimes I'm afraid to start another book by Steele for fear it won't be as good as the last one. Guess I've read almost all he's ever written—funny, and I didn't use to like books about the olden days at all."

Miss Harper watched him settle himself in one of the large comfortable chairs in the reading section of the library. Miss Harper knew she'd probably have to remind him when the last bell rang; absorbed in reading, he sometimes didn't hear it. She thought of his last remark, "Funny, and I didn't use to like books about the olden days at all." She could remember him when he didn't like *books* of any kind. He had loved story hours in first grade. She recalled how disturbed she was that any child who enjoyed stories so much should have difficulty learning to read. When his second and third grade class came to the library for recreational reading, he could never settle down and enjoy a book. Then he'd been assigned Lucille Harris for his fourth-grade teacher. Lucille had had more success with nonreaders than any other teacher she knew; she always thought that it was because Lucille loved books so much herself. Anyway, she made special trips to the library with four boys who were her "late bloomers" as she called them. They selected some of the easy informational books to read to each other; then she weaned them on some of the books by Bulla, and *The Childhood of Famous Americans Series.* Mac had wanted to read just the informational books, and so she had let him. But in connection with their study of the Westward Movement, Miss Harper had read them Edmonds' *The Matchlock Gun* and told them it was a true story. Mac checked it out four times, and that had been the beginning of his interest in reading and "the olden days." Mac did everything with intensity; both Miss Harper and his fifth-grade teacher hoped his interest in reading became permanent.

Children are creatures of the here and now. They have not developed an appreciation for their historical heritage. Their time concepts are inadequate and inaccurate; "the olden days" are likely to be "back when there wasn't any television." For young children, understanding of the time between the arrival of Columbus and the Pilgrims in the New World is in direct proportion to the calendar time between Columbus Day and Thanksgiving! The development of the understanding of time concepts is a gradual growth process that extends throughout the years in the elementary school.

Children establish their own frame of reference for time relationships by relating past events to their personal experiences. Teachers should help children see their present place in time as part of a *living past.* They should help them understand that the way of life today is a result of what people did in the past, and that the present will influence the way people live in the future. The study of history can be the vantage point for observing the panoramic view of all that has happened and will happen to mankind.

Man would not be man without his historical heritage; everything he does is built on the lives and thoughts of people he never saw or knew. Man is the only creature who can build on the past, who can profit from the experiences of others, and begin where others left off. The wisdom of the ages may be accumulated, refined, and transmitted. Korzybski[1] has identified this time-binding capacity of man to utilize and profit by the past as something that is uniquely human.

Even though children have difficulty establishing exact time concepts, they can develop an appreciation of their historical heritage. Enthusiastic teachers can make the past live for children, and a wide variety of materials also will create interest. Although history textbooks have been improved in recent years, no single text can ever give children an appreciation and feeling for their historical heritage. Children's literature provides three types of books that enrich and extend children's study of history. These

---

[1]Alfred Korzybski, *Manhood of Humanity* (New York: Dutton, 1921), p. 186.

books include factual presentations of history, biographies of great men of the past, and historical fiction. Informational books are discussed in Chapter 9; biography and historical fiction, in this chapter.

BIOGRAPHY

While contemporary children appear to enjoy factual accounts of their past, they prefer history when it is told as a living story. The biographical narrative fulfills this need for the story "that really happened." Biography for children has reached a new, high level of popularity; children in first and second grades are clamoring for true stories about "people who really lived," while boys and girls in the middle grades continue to find satisfaction in reading of the lives and accomplishments of people in all walks of life. These children are beginning to develop "crushes" on favorite teachers, camp counselors, sports figures, and movie stars. It is only natural that their reading choices would reflect this hero worship. Biographies extend the child's opportunity for identification, not only with those who are great today, but with those who have lived greatly in the past.

Biography fulfills children's needs for identification with someone "bigger" than they are. In this day of mass conformity, it may give them new models of greatness to emulate. The reading of biography serves another function, however, and that is to make the past live. Carlyle has said that "biography is the only true history." By consistent reading of fine biographies, children will develop an appreciation and understanding of our heritage that may not be obtained in any other manner.

Publishers have been quick to recognize and capitalize upon children's interest in biographies. Series has followed series until the proliferation of titles overwhelms teachers, children, and parents. We begin to lose sight of a single biography of outstanding quality amidst the shelves of mass-produced ones. Children, and even teachers, ask for books by the publisher's trade name or the color of the cover, rather than by author or title. There are some fine biographies that have been written for children; there are many mediocre ones. The task of the teacher and librarian is to help children to distinguish between them.

Criteria for Juvenile Biography

The criteria for evaluating biographies for boys and girls differ somewhat from those established for juvenile fiction. They also diverge from generally accepted patterns for adult biography. Children read biography as they read fiction—for the story or *plot*. Children demand a fast-moving narrative. In biography, events and action become even more exciting because "they really happened." Thus, children want biography to be written as a story with continuity; they do not want a collection of facts and dates. The encyclopedia gives them facts in a well-organized fashion; biography must do more than this, it must help them to *know* the person as a living human being.

Choice of Subject Most of the biographies for children are about the more familiar American figures of the past, particularly those whose lives offer the readiest action material. It is more difficult to interest children in a biography of Thomas Jefferson, who made his greatest contributions to the world of ideas, than the action-packed story of Daniel Boone or Kit Carson. The past five years, however, have seen an increase in biographies of poets, authors, artists, musicians, and humanitarians. Perhaps children are beginning to appreciate the challenges to the mind and spirit as well as heroic physical accomplishments.

Writers generally accept the principle that children's biography should be limited to those subjects whose lives are worthy of emulation. These may be the famous and great leaders of our nation such as Washington, Lincoln, and Jefferson; or they may be unknown common people who have lived great lives as represented by the story of *Amos Fortune, Free Man* by Yates. A few biographies of such unsavory characters as Hitler and Mussolini have been written for older students. With grim pictures and biting text, Benjamin Appel has recorded the story of *Hitler From Power to Ruin.* The infamy of this man should not be forgotten, nor the factors that allowed for his rise to supreme power, for history can repeat itself. As long as such books are balanced against those that show mankind's struggle to achieve decency, justice, and peace, perhaps they may serve as a useful contrast and warning.

Certain liberties are allowed authors of juvenile biographies that would not be accorded to writers in the adult field. For example, in some instances, dark shadows in a person's life may be omitted from biographies for children. In writing the biography of Hamilton, authors Anna and Russel Crouse did not emphasize the fact that Alexander Hamilton was an illegitimate child. They did not deliberately alter any facts of his life, but simply never referred to his parents as husband and wife. Another liberty allowed biographers in the field of juvenile literature is the presentation of a portion of the subject's life. Frequently, the stories will end before tragedy or an unsavory incident occurs. In writing about Abraham Lincoln for primary children, the d'Aulaires omitted his assassination and closed the book with the end of the Civil War. The authors' purpose was to present the greatness of the man as he *lived,* for too frequently, they believed, children remember only the manner of his death.

For many years, it was thought that children were only interested in reading about the childhood of great men and women, and that the complexities of adult activities would hold no interest for them. For this reason,

many earlier biographies focused primarily on childhood pranks and legends that suggested future accomplishments but neglected, or oversimplified, real achievement. Today the trend is towards a more complete presentation of the subject's entire life. Boys and girls in the middle grades who want to read of the fascinating story of Heinrich Schliemann, the man who discovered the ancient city of Troy, are more intrigued by the stories of his excavations and archaeological discoveries than his early childhood as a grocer's apprentice. Thus, Marjorie Braymer wisely begins her excellent biography *The Walls of Windy Troy* when Schliemann was nineteen.

Characterization Characterization of the subject must be true to life. The reader should have the opportunity not only to know *about* him but to *know* him as a human being with both shortcomings and virtues. There is danger in overdramatizing greatness. The result will be the story of a man who never emerges from his accomplishments as a vibrant living person, but remains a shallow, overly glamorous hero. Martin suggests that many of the characters in biographical series are cut from the same pattern:

> There is a convention that great men and women invariably started out as normal and likeable youngsters, good mixers, and good sports. There is no inkling of the fact that loneliness and oddity often bear a dark fruit of their own. By pushing these books, we muff our best chance to show children that the awkward child, the poor athlete, the boy who comes to school in funny clothes may be the Lincoln or the Thomas Edison of the future.[2]

Biography must not degenerate into mere eulogy; neither should it include "debunking." Worthy subjects should be selected and

[2]Fran Martin, "Stop Watering Down Biographies," *Junior Libraries,* vol. 6 (December 1959), p. 9.

portrayed so that they come alive for the reader. The background of their lives, their conversations, their thoughts, and their actions should be presented as faithfully to the facts as possible. The subject should be seen in relationship to his times, for no man can be "read" in isolation.

Style Three kinds of biography are presented in children's literature: (1) authentic biography, (2) fictionalized biography, and (3) biographical fiction. Authentic biography corresponds to that written for adults. It is a well-documented and researched account of a man's life. Only those statements that are actually known to have been made by the subject are included in conversation. *Invincible Louisa, the Story of the Author of "Little Women"* by Cornelia Meigs is authentic biography with its photographs of the homes of the Alcotts and old daguerreotypes of Louisa herself. *America's Abraham Lincoln* by May McNeer is another example of superb biography based only upon recorded facts.

Fictionalized biography is the generally accepted form for juveniles, however. This type of biography is grounded in thorough research but allows the author more freedom to dramatize certain events and personalize the subject than does the straight reporting of authentic biography. It makes use of the narrative rather than the analytical approach. Children do not want detailed interpretations and explanations. They come to know the character of the subject as presented through his actions, deeds, and conversations. In fictionalized biography, the author may invent dialogue and even include the unspoken thoughts of the subject. These conversations are usually based upon actual facts taken from diaries and journals of the period. Clara Ingram Judson, a well-known biographer in the juvenile field, emphasized the importance of authentic conversation in the foreword of her book,

Abraham Lincoln, Friend of the People. She states:

> As I began writing, I saw that life is not a mere tale to be told: it includes talk as well as action. Talk is a kind of alchemy that brings reality. So parts of my story are told through conversations. When actual words are a matter of authentic record, those words are used. When such record is lacking, but the incident is true, talk is reconstructed — much as the cabins are — from records and letters and the well-known manner of talk of each time and place.[3]

When dialogue is invented, it should make the scenes more effective and move the narrative forward. Some dialogue is unbelievably stilted and creates an impression of wooden characters. Listen to the following unnatural conversation among Abe Lincoln, his sister Sarah, and their cousin Dennis when Abe's father had left the three of them alone in Indiana.

> At last Sarah said, "It's lonesome here."
> "It's mighty lonesome," said Abe.
> "I guess you miss your mother," said the older boy kindly.
> "Yes, I do, Cousin Dennis," said Sarah.
> "So do I," said Abe.
> "I miss her, too," said Dennis. "Look how she had me come here and live when my mother died. And she was always good to me, too."
> "She was good to everyone," said Sarah.
> "No one else could be so good," said Abe.[4]

When the biography consists entirely of imagined conversation and reconstructed action, it becomes biographical fiction. Some authors intend to write this type. An example of the best of this form is Lawson's hilarious *Ben and Me*, the story of Benjamin

[3]Clara Ingram Judson, in "Author's Note," *Abraham Lincoln, Friend of the People* (Chicago: Follett, 1950), p. ii.
[4]Augusta Stevenson, *Abe Lincoln, Frontier Boy,* Illustrated by Jerry Robinson (Indianapolis: Bobbs-Merrill, 1932), p. 99.

Franklin as told by his good friend Amos, the mouse who lived in Franklin's old fur cap. The facts of Franklin's life are truly presented, but Amos takes the credit for most of his accomplishments! Lawson used the same tongue-in-cheek pattern for his readable *Mr. Revere and I,* the story of Paul Revere as told by his horse, Scheherazade.

In all biographies, the biographical and background materials should be integrated into the narrative with smoothness and proportion. The judicious use of quotes from letters or journals may add to the authenticity of the biography, but it should not detract from the absorbing account of the life of the subject. Children enjoy a style that is clear and vigorous with a fast-moving narrative that reads like fiction. The research must be there, but it should be a natural part of the presentation.

Theme   Underlying all biography, whether it be authentic biography, fictionalized biography, or biographical fiction, is the author's interpretation of his subject. No matter how impartial an author may be, he cannot write a life story without some interpretation. The very selection of facts that a biographer chooses to present may limit the dimensions of his portraiture, or highlight certain features. The quality of a person's character (particularly one who is no longer living) must be deduced from known deeds, letters, diaries, pictures, canceled checks, and others' memories of him. Outward facts must always be interpreted. For example, the simple detail of Elizabeth holding the christening robe of Edward has been the subject of various interpretations. Geoffrey Trease in *The Seven Queens of England* maintains that Elizabeth "was taken to the church and made to hold up the christening robe of the baby brother who had come to displace her."[5] Jeannette Nolan, on the other hand,

in her biography of *Queen Elizabeth* implies that Elizabeth held the edge of the christening robe, not because she had been made to do so, but because "I have always loved him—as he loves me."[6] A single fact, but interpreted so differently!

These various interpretations are usually made in terms of the way the author sees the life style of his subject. This emphasis becomes the theme of the biography. Frequently in juvenile biography, the theme will be identified in the title as in *Retreat to Glory, the Story of Sam Houston,* or *Young Man in a Hurry, the Story of Cyrus W. Field,* both by Jean Lee Latham. The remarkable story of Annie Sullivan, Helen Keller's teacher, is told in a biography appropriately titled *The Silent Storm.* Annie's early life had left permanent scars on her spirit:

> *On the surface, at least, she became more sure of herself, more poised, but underneath there was still the silent storm. Her own beginnings, the almshouse, the nightmare of losing Jimmie, the aloneness, her utter lack of the simplest opportunities, the great gaps in her education —all these, in her own mind, set her apart and made her inadequate.[7]*

Yet these adversities prepared her to face and understand the wild tornado that was young Helen Keller. Her whole life seemed one of continual turmoil until Helen graduated from Radcliffe, and Annie met John Macy. "The silent storm" was finally stilled.

There is a danger in oversimplifying and forcing all facts to fit a single mold. An author must not recreate and interpret a life history in terms of one fixed picture. The most common man has several facets to his personality; the great are likely to be multidimensional. The perceptive biographer

---

[5]Geoffrey Trease, *The Seven Queens of England* (New York: Vanguard Press, 1953), p. 78.

[6]Jeannette Nolan, *Queen Elizabeth,* Illustrated by Marie Lawson (New York: Harper & Row, 1951), p. 4.

[7]Marion Brown and Ruth Crone, *The Silent Storm,* Illustrated by Fritz Kredel (Nashville, Tenn.: Abingdon, 1963), p. 189.

concentrates on those items from a full life that helped to mold and form that personality. It is this selection and focus that creates the theme of the biography.

Authenticity Authenticity is the hallmark of good biographical writing, whether it is for adults or children. More and more writers of juvenile biography are acknowledging primary sources for their materials either in an introductory note or an appendix. Conscientious authors of well-written children's biography frequently travel to the locale of the setting in order to get a "feeling" for a place. They will visit museums to study actual objects that were used by their subjects; they will spend hours poring over original letters and documents. Much of this research may not be used in the actual biography, but its effect will be evidenced by the author's true insight into the character of his subject, by the accuracy of the historic detail, and by his respect for verifiable reporting. Parson Weems was successful in perpetuating the unrealistic myth of George Washington and his cherry tree upon generations of Americans. Modern biographers have more respect for fact and do not have to resort to the invention of moralistic stories to emphasize the worthy attributes of their subjects. They are much more concerned with presenting a true and accurate picture of a human being who once lived in a certain period and place, but who can live again in a child's imagination and appreciation.

When writing dialogue or a first-person account, careful attention should be given to the authenticity of the language. What words were in use in that particular period? How can an author give the language a seventeenth-century flavor without resorting to the cumbersome use of "thee's" and "thou's"? The Beattys[8] write amusingly of

the research they conducted while writing their first-person historical narrative, *At the Seven Stars.* At one point of the story, they spoke of a door knob to a secret passage. On checking both *The Shorter Oxford English Dictionary on Historical Principles* and a concordance of the King James version of the Bible, they found that door knobs were very newfangled contrivances and that "button" would have been the term that their heroine would have used in the seventeenth century. Such painstaking care in writing both biography and historical fiction is beginning to be reflected in more and more books for children.

Many modern biographies for children are illustrated. The same kind of careful research should be reflected in the accuracy of the illustrations that convey the time, place, and setting. The costumes of the period, the interiors of the houses, the very utensils that are used must be authentic representations. Most difficult of all, perhaps, is the actual portrayal of the subject. There are many paintings and even photographs of some of our national heroes. Usually, their features were recorded for posterity after they had achieved their fame. What did George Washington, or Thomas Jefferson, or Abraham Lincoln look like as a child? Here the artist must attempt to paint the child with his future appearance in mind. The d'Aulaires in their book, *Abraham Lincoln,* have pictured the transition of Abe from boy to man in a most believable fashion. His buckskin breeches always seem too short and his gangling awkwardness becomes increasingly apparent as he reaches adolescence. Abraham Lincoln grows up, matures, is happy, worried, and saddened in the d'Aulaires' pictures as well as their text.

Biographical Series

Biographical series continue to spawn at such a rapid pace that they threaten to engulf readers of juvenile biography. Recent

---

[8]John and Patricia Beatty, "Watch Your Language —You're Writing for Young People," *The Horn Book Magazine,* vol. 41 (February 1965), pp. 34–40.

developments include many series written especially for the primary child who is not yet an accomplished reader. Certain figures in American history have been presented too many times by too many books in the same stereotyped manner. Sometimes, authors have written books to fill gaps in publishers' lists of proposed titles rather than to fulfill their own consuming desire to portray for children the life of a certain worthy man. The quality of the books within each series varies with the ability and interest of the author. This calls for an individual evaluation of the merits of each book, plus the added consideration of the need for another title about this particular subject. These decisions and selections must be made personally by librarians and teachers on the basis of the school library collection. A knowledge of the distinguishing characteristics of each series will be helpful in selecting biographies.

The Beginning-to-Read Series   Just before Clara Ingram Judson died, she wrote three books for this series, published by Follett, *Abraham Lincoln, George Washington,* and *Christopher Columbus.* Another title in the series is *Paul Revere* by Gladys Saxon. These are simply written, complete biographies, describing the boyhood and the accomplishments of these famous men. The vocabulary and length of the sentences is controlled for independent reading in first and second grade. However, the narratives read smoothly and do give the child a feeling for the man. Small, four-color illustrations appear on every page. This series does satisfy the young child's desire to read biography himself.

See and Read Biographies   Written for children six-to-eight years old, these books are published by Putnam and are based upon a second-grade word list. The series contains stories of the most popular "big three" with primary children: Washington, Lincoln, and Columbus, plus biographies of

Johnny Appleseed, Ben Franklin, and Davy Crockett. The narratives are written in a stilted style, with nonsentences, for example:

> *One night George went to a party*
> *And he danced with a young woman.*
> *Her name was Martha.*
> *"How pretty you are!" said George.*
> *He went to see her many times.*
> *"Will you marry me?" he said.*
> *"Will you be my wife?"*
> *"Yes," said Martha, "I will be your wife."*[9]

The pastel illustrations are in two colors, brown and soft gold and black and gold. The endpapers, covers, and print make a harmonious format.

The See and Read Beginning-to-Read Biographies   Also published by Putnam, the title of this series is confusing since these books are longer and somewhat more difficult than the "See and Read" series described above. Their controlled vocabulary is based upon a second-grade word list. Again, biographies of the "big three" are included, plus one on *Pocahontas* by Patricia Martin. Well-known incidents in Lincoln's and Washington's lives are incorporated in these narratives, but the child is given little help in understanding the causes of some of the historical events. For example, two pages are devoted to Lincoln's rescue of a pig, but the Civil War is announced by two words, "War came"—[10]no explanation, even as to *what* war. Can we assume that second graders will necessarily know? The text is certainly more natural-sounding than in the other Putnam series. The illustrations, unfortunately, are rather garish poster art.

The Discovery Books   Garrard was the first to publish a set of stories of historical

---

[9]Gertrude Norman, *A Man Named Washington*, Illustrated by James Caraway (New York: Putnam, 1960), unpaged.

[10]Patricia Miles Martin, *Abraham Lincoln*. Illustrated by Gustav Schrotter (New York: Putnam, 1964), p. 53.

personages that was written especially for children in the primary grades. The series currently contains over sixty titles including stories of presidents, explorers, pioneers, scientists, reformers, famous women, and war heroes. Different authors and different artists prepare each of these books, although the format remains much the same. Each book is about eighty pages in length, and the illustrations are usually in two colors. Again, certain cause-and-effect relationships are omitted as being too complex for young children to comprehend. On the whole, however, the writing style is natural, and children are given a feeling for the accomplishments of the man. For example, the Epsteins definitely capture the enthusiasm of *George Washington Carver* for learning; they detail his perseverance in the face of unbelievable obstacles, and they emphasize his unselfish dedication to his own people. His story is told through well-selected and occasionally amusing incidents.

The Step-Up Books The announced purpose of the "Step-Up" books from Random House was to provide a series that had more substance and information than the usual limited-vocabulary biographies. While vocabulary is not tightly controlled, writing style is. Most sentences follow a noun-verb pattern and are more repetitious than many primers, for example:

> *In 1732, Virginia was an English colony. It belonged to England. And it was ruled by the Kind of England. The people of Virginia felt they were Englishmen.*[11]

There is enough available research to show that children can and do understand a well-constructed complex sentence; in fact, such a sentence is usually easier for them to interpret than a series of such short simple

sentences as quoted above. The biographies in this series include Heilbroner's *Meet George Washington, Meet Abraham Lincoln* by Cary, and *Meet John F. Kennedy* by White. The first two are realistically illustrated while the last one contains many photographs.

The Childhood of Famous Americans Series Started in 1932, this series, published by Bobbs-Merrill, was one of the first to popularize biography for children. These books are really more fictional than biographical as they attempt to reconstruct the childhood of real persons. The emphasis in all these stories is upon the "growing-up" of famous people. Usually, only the last chapter is devoted to their accomplishments as adults. For example, in the story of *Eleanor Roosevelt, Courageous Girl* by Weil, one full chapter is devoted to Eleanor's midnight trip to the ice house for some ice for her sick aunt, while all of her contributions to the United Nations are related in a single chapter of the same size. Such portrayals distort facts and become oversimplified success stories. There are over 150 titles in this series representing a wide variety of American men and women who left an imprint in our history and culture. The books contain much dialogue, and the stories move quickly. Designed for self-reading by eight-to-twelve-year-olds, this particular series of books has probably lured more children into becoming independent readers of library books than any other series. The format now has undergone revision to include colored illustrations and more attractive covers. Although many authors have written these books, the names of Augusta Stevenson, Miriam Mason and Guernsey Van Riper, Jr. have been identified with several titles in the series.

Initial Biographies Genevieve Foster has written the life stories of George Washington, Abraham Lincoln, Andrew Jackson, and Theodore Roosevelt in a series of books sub-

---

[11]Joan Heilbroner, *Meet George Washington*, Illustrated by Victor Mays (New York: Random House, 1965), p. 4.

titled "Initial Biographies," published by Scribner. These books are characterized by the same high quality of writing and accuracy of detail that distinguishes Foster's *George Washington's World* and *Abraham Lincoln's World*. The initial biographies are more simplified than the documentary "world" books. They do include, however, much information concerning the lives of these four men. They are good stories that may be easily read by fourth and fifth graders. The two-color illustrations by the author are as clear as her text, and reflect the action and humor of the stories.

The Landmark Series   This popular series, first published by Random House in 1950, is probably the most advertised and well known of all the series books. These books are written about events, places, personalities, and movements that are landmarks in history. Some of the books emphasize events more than particular people, and are not biographical. Thus, the series may include two books on a similar subject but with a different emphasis, for example, *George Washington, Frontier Colonel* by Sterling North and *The Winter at Valley Forge* by Van Wyck Mason. The addition of "World Landmark" books has widened the variety of subjects considerably. The books in this series, for the most part, are written by well-known authors of adult works. The list of writers for this series includes such outstanding names as Margaret Cousins, Pearl S. Buck, Thomas Costain, MacKinlay Kantor, Dorothy Canfield Fisher, and many others. Some prominent authors in the juvenile field have also written for this series, for example, Armstrong Sperry, Jim Kjelgaard, May McNeer, and James Daugherty. The books are checked by consulting historians for authoritative information in text, illustrations, and maps. Designed for a reading level from age ten through sixteen, this series requires greater reading skill than the others mentioned.

North Star Books   This is a popular series that deals with exciting events and famous people of America's past. Published by Houghton Mifflin, the authors include such well-known writers as John Dos Passos, Helen Papashvily, and Sterling North, the general editor of the series. These biographies are well researched and documented with entries from journals, letters, and newspapers. The subjects include authors, such as Louisa May Alcott and Mark Twain; naturalists, John Muir and Thoreau; inventors, Edison; and doctors, the Mayo brothers for example. Illustrated with pictures and maps, each book contains an index. This series is appropriate reading for grade levels five through seven.

Breakthrough Books   The purpose of this series, published by Harper & Row, is to identify major breakthroughs in battles, exploration, science, and social relations. Written by various authors, these books are designed for children ten to fourteen. Jeannette Mirsky's authentic biography of *Balboa, Discoverer of the Pacific* represents an historical biography in the series. *Breakthrough to the Big League, the Story of Jackie Robinson* by Robinson and Alfred Duckett represents another kind of milestone in the history of race relations. Others in this series include *Peary to the Pole* by Lord, *The Triumph of the Seeing Eye* by Putnam, and *The Lion in the Gateway* by Mary Renault.

Lives to Remember Series   Putnam publishes this series of biographies for students ages ten to fourteen. Perhaps because the series is directed at more mature students, quite objective reporting is used. For example, in the biography of *Zebulon Pike, Young America's Frontier Scout* by Bern Keating, accurately presented facts show that Pike *deliberately* altered some of his entries in his journal to suit his purposes. This does not detract from his accomplishments, but does show an explorer who was very courageous and very human in both his strengths and weaknesses. We need more such accurate presentations in biographical series.

Horizon Caravel Books and American Heritage Junior Library   Both of these series are published by American Heritage and distributed by Harper & Row. The first series is edited by the *Horizon Magazine* and the second by the editors of *American Heritage*. They are similar in format, each utilizing outstanding pictorial materials in full color, including paintings, photographs, drawings, maps of the period, and newspaper clippings. Similar in some respects to the *American Heritage Magazine*, the "Junior Library" series focuses upon such Americans as *Abraham Lincoln in Peace and War* by Miers, *The Many Worlds of Benjamin Franklin* by Donovan, and *Commodore Perry in Japan* by Reynolds. The "Caravel" books have a world perspective and include such titles as *Caesar* by Isenberg, *Marco Polo's Adventures in China* by Rugoff, *The Universe of Galileo and Newton* by Bixby, and *Alexander the Great* by Mercer. Pictorially, these are fascinating books with accurate photographs of actual scenes and wide use of documentary material. The texts are smoothly written, using a straight biographical reporting style. Children in the middle grades may have difficulty reading the rather adult text, but the superb pictorial material will help them visualize the man in his surroundings.

Specialized Series   Certain authors and publishers are focusing upon particular groups of subjects and producing such specialized biographies as Elizabeth Ripley's lives of famous artists, originally published by Walck and now published by Lippincott. Illustrated with black-and-white photographs of the artists' works, this series includes biographies on *Goya, Leonardo da Vinci, Michelangelo, Rembrandt, Rubens, Van Gogh, Titian, Botticelli, Winslow Homer, Rodin*, and others.

These well-written biographies focus on the artist's works in relation to his life. The only disappointment is that the photographs of the works of art are not in color. These books are written for students aged twelve and up.

Children from seven to eleven who are in the throes of beginning piano lessons may enjoy the biographies of musicians written by Opal Wheeler and Sybil Deucher and published by Dutton. At first, these authors collaborated on their writing of *Joseph Haydn, the Merry Little Peasant* and *Mozart, the Wonder Boy*. Later, they worked individually but used the same format established by their early books. Their pattern usually focuses upon the childhood of the musicians and their later accomplishments. Emphasis is frequently placed upon escapades and pranks, such as Haydn's cutting off the pigtail of one of the boys in the Vienna Boys Choir. These books are almost too gay in their accounts of composers' lives. No suggestions of the tragedy of Mozart's life or the deafness of Beethoven are given. These realities are not beyond the understanding of young children and would present a more truthful and rounded picture of their greatness. The books are illustrated by simple black-and-white drawings. Excerpts from the music of the composers are included for the reader who may wish to play some of their easier compositions.

Reba Paeff Mirsky gives a more balanced picture of the composers in her series of books on *Johann Sebastian Bach, Beethoven, Haydn, Mozart*, and *Brahms*, published by Follett. These books have a lively style but they do present an understanding of the times and the major influences on the composer's life. Disappointments, hard work, and poverty are not glossed over in these accounts. Well-illustrated with attractive format, these books are written for children ten-to-fourteen years of age.

The "Great Composers" series published by Crowell is for this same age group. In this series, each book is written by a different author: Joan Chissell has written the story of the life of *Chopin,* and Imogen Holst has told the story of *Bach.* Both books contain pieces of music composed by these men. Photographs and reproductions of engravings illustrate this carefully researched series.

These are only a few of the many series that specialize in biographies. Others include the *Makers of America* series by Abingdon, the *Immortals of History and Science* series by Watts, the *Junior Research Books* by Prentice-Hall, and the *Julian Messner Shelf of Biographies,* an excellent, but more advanced, series for teenagers. Only the general characteristics of each series may be described. Individual books should be evaluated on their own merit, for within each series are excellent and mediocre books.

Well-Known Biographers of Juvenile Literature

Some of the best biography for children has been written by individual writers not necessarily connected with series books. While mention cannot be made of all the writers who have contributed to this special area of juvenile biography, students of children's literature will want to become acquainted with some of the books by the following authors:

Aliki   Aliki (Brandenberg) has written and illustrated some outstanding easy-vocabulary picture biographies for the beginning reader. Her texts are brief and simple, but they avoid the pitfalls of too much repetition and stilted language patterns. The childlike pictures create a feeling of true colonial primitives. In *The Story of Johnny Appleseed,* this author-illustrator has captured the humor and simplicity of the legendary Johnny Appleseed. Delicately illustrated period pictures reflect the warmth and gentleness of the Quakers in *The Story of William*

Penn. Their belief in the simple life is shown in the sharp contrast of William's plain dress with the King of England's curls and frills. William Penn practiced what he believed, and his fairness in treating the Indians proved to the world that men can live as brothers if they choose. This quiet picture biography somehow conveys the dignity and greatness of the man. The same dignity and simplicity is communicated in *A Weed Is a Flower, the Life of George Washington Carver.* Again, Aliki has made meaningful for the youngest reader, the inspiring story of the man who was born a Negro slave but lived to become one of America's greatest research scientists. Unfortunately, in *George and the Cherry Tree,* Aliki perpetuates the old Parson Weems myth of the ever-truthful George and his cherry tree.

Ingri and Edgar Parin d'Aulaire   This husband-and-wife team has written and illustrated beautiful picture book biographies. Their titles include *George Washington, Abraham Lincoln* (for which they received the Caldecott Award in 1940), *Buffalo Bill, Pocahontas, Columbus, Benjamin Franklin,* and *Leif, the Lucky.* Full-page, colored lithographs printed from the old stone process appear on every other page. Large black-and-white pictures are on the alternate pages and many small pictures are interspersed throughout the books. The illustrations match the text beautifully. The d'Aulaires, who were not born in this country, bring a fresh perspective to their writing and illustrating of these American heroes. In *Abraham Lincoln,* they have captured the homespun humor and philosophy of the man. One seven-year-old child having just heard the d'Aulaires' *Abraham Lincoln,* commented that she thought it was an honest book. When she was asked why she used that word, she replied, "The pictures look honest, they look *real!*"

The d'Aulaires' story of Columbus is one of the few for younger children that includes his discouraging last voyages. They picture his bitterness with sympathetic understanding but do not gloss over the facts. These books are authentic in both text and illustration. Teachers in kindergarten and first grade will want to show the pictures as they tell certain portions of these stories to children. Second and third graders enjoy hearing the stories read aloud. More mature readers of the third and fourth grades can read them independently.

Alice Dalgliesh   Alice Dalgliesh has written two outstanding picture biographies for younger children: *The Columbus Story* illustrated by Leo Politi, and *Ride on the Wind* illustrated by Georges Schreiber. *The Columbus Story* is a straightforward account of his boyhood, his difficulties obtaining support for his venture, and his successful first voyage. The pictures by Politi are striking in their simplicity and clarity and seem perfectly suited to this dignified biography of the discoverer of the New World. *Ride on the Wind* is another picture biography for somewhat older children based upon the book *The Spirit of St. Louis* by Charles A. Lindbergh. Some background of Lindbergh's childhood is related, but the major portion of the story is devoted to the actual experience of the first nonstop solo flight across the Atlantic. A dramatic account is given of Lindbergh's greatest struggle—his effort to fight drowsiness.

May McNeer and Lynd Ward   This husband-and-wife team has produced several fine biographies. They have written two life stories of outstanding religious leaders, namely, *Martin Luther* and *John Wesley*. Their stories are told with dignity and simplicity and are illustrated with striking, full-page pictures by Ward. The large illustrations are in color, while black-and-white illustrations appear on almost every page.

A similar format is used in their *America's Abraham Lincoln* and *America's Mark Twain*, two of the most handsome biographies written for young people. Thorough research is reflected in both May McNeer's perceptive texts and Lynd Ward's magnificent pictures. Ward visited Lincoln's birthplace in Kentucky, the store he kept in New Salem, Illinois, and Samuel Clemens' hometown, Hannibal, Missouri, in preparing the many illustrations for these books. *America's Mark Twain* includes the life story of Samuel Clemens interspersed with reviews and pictures of some of the books he wrote.

The Wards have produced another type of biography in their book entitled *Armed with Courage*. Here they present the biographies of seven men and women who are similar only in their physical and spiritual courage: Florence Nightingale, Father Damien, George Washington Carver, Jane Addams, Wilfred Grenfell, Mahatma Gandhi, and Albert Schweitzer. It is always difficult to portray a complete picture of a person in a few pages. However, in this collection of seven biographical sketches the Wards have been eminently successful. With sensitive text and dramatic black-and-white illustrations, they capture the self-sacrifice and determination of these great men and women who were "armed with courage."

Clara Ingram Judson   All of the biographies by Clara Ingram Judson are characterized by scholarly research. She visited the places where the stories were located and used primary sources for her information, poring over letters, journals, and first-hand accounts. Then she wrote the facts in a vivid, interesting style that holds the attention of boys and girls from age ten to sixteen.

Frequently, the theme of Mrs. Judson's books can be seen in their titles, for example, *George Washington, Leader of the People; Andrew Jackson, Frontier Statesman; Thomas Jefferson, Champion of the People; Abraham Lincoln, Friend of the People;* and *Theodore Roosevelt, Fighting Patriot.* Many biographies have been written about these famous men, but it appeared to Mrs. Judson that the only justification for writing more would be the presentation of a different interpretation of their lives. Her intensive research frequently revealed facets of the lives of these great men that had not been included in the more stereotyped biographies for children. For example, while reading the diary of a private soldier who served with Washington at Valley Forge, she came upon these words: "The General came by and pitched. The General is a good pitcher." Few biographies of Washington ever pictured him as a good ballplayer! And yet this side of his character would be much more appealing to children than the priggish presentation of the cherry-tree story. Clara Ingram Judson's *George Washington* emerges as a real person, the Commander-in-Chief, the first President, but also as a farmer, father, and the man who loved his family as dearly as he loved his country.

When Judson began writing *Abraham Lincoln, Friend of the People,* she journeyed to the little cabin on Knob Creek in Kentucky. As she looked at the little home, Judson decided that Lincoln's poverty had been overstressed. It was true that his family had few possessions, but no one else living on the frontier had many either. Mrs. Judson makes the reader feel that the Lincolns were rich in their family relationship.

Mr. Justice Holmes is a more difficult book to read than the others by Mrs. Judson, but it tells a fascinating story. Even when Wendell Holmes was a judge and six feet four inches tall, his famous father, Doctor Oliver Wendell Holmes, called him "my little boy." Though Wendell often wondered if he could ever really grow up in his father's opinion, he became one of the greatest men America has produced. This fine and penetrating biography for the more mature reader was the winner of one of the Thomas A. Edison mass-media awards in 1956. Unfortunately, Mrs. Judson died just four weeks before she was to receive the 1960 Laura Ingalls Wilder Award for her lasting contributions to children's literature. Her last book on *Andrew Carnegie* was published posthumously.

Ronald Syme Syme has written a biographical series about explorers that is particularly enjoyed by boys. These biographies are written in an easy flowing style without being written down or simplified. The author includes an amazing number of facts in these concise and clearly written books; yet he manages to portray his subjects realistically with their strengths and weaknesses. In *John Smith of Virginia,* Syme has drawn a picture of Smith that shows the leadership qualities which made men his willing followers, and also portrays those qualities which made men hate and envy him. Syme's account of *Cortés of Mexico* is somewhat different from the one usually given. He emphasizes Cortés' desire to explore and map the new world and blames the greedy men under him for his troubles with the Aztecs.

Despite the magnificent seamanship of *Vasco da Gama,* Syme points out in his biography that he was unable to make friends with the natives. The author has shown the dark side of da Gama's character, his violent temper and revengeful nature. His demands and reprisals against the Arabs and natives of Africa made too many enemies for his little country of Portugal. He discovered the sea route to India, but he failed miserably in his attempt to use it. It is easy to understand why the Portuguese empire was shortlived as one reads Syme's description of da Gama's departure from India. The vigorous black-and-white drawings of William Stobbs add greatly to the forcefulness of Syme's writing. The artist always includes an excellent map showing the routes of the different explorers.

Syme has also written two fine biographies of adventurous women; *African Traveler, the Story of Mary Kingsley* and *Nigerian Pioneer, the Story of Mary Slessor.* Mary Kingsley was the first woman to explore Africa, armed with nothing but curiosity, a sense of humor, and a British parasol. Syme has included some delightfully funny incidents in his account of this intrepid traveler. One of these describes the time that Mary, having carefully concluded her dignified inspection of a village, decided to climb a steep green hillside to get a better view of the Ogowe River. She slipped and fell down the hill, crashing through the roof of one of the huts. "In time to come, the natives acquired the habit of saying that so-and-so event occurred either before or after the great day the white woman jumped through the roof of a house."[12]

Catherine Owens Peare   Peare has told *The Helen Keller Story* with much warmth and insight into the character of this remarkable woman. Children have always been fascinated by Helen Keller's accomplishments, but they are particularly drawn to this interesting and authentic biography of her life. Catherine Owens Peare does more than just tell her story, she makes the reader feel and "see" as Helen Keller did:

> She [Helen Keller] wrote about the subjects that she understood best: how she "saw" with her hands and how her imagination helped her hands to see; how the hands of others felt to her and how she judged character by a handclasp. She could remember that Bishop Brooks had had hands that were "brimful of tenderness and a strong man's joy." And Mark Twain's hand was "full of whimsies and the drollest humors." Some people's hands were weak, some strong, some fidgety, some brave, some timid.[13]

Peare's biography of *Mary McLeod Bethune* is told with the same warmth and respect for the accomplishments of this amazing Negro leader as is reflected in *The Helen Keller Story*.

---

[12]Ronald Syme, *African Traveler, the Story of Mary Kingsley,* Illustrated by Jacqueline Tomes (New York: Morrow, 1962), p. 72.
[13]Catherine Owens Peare, *The Helen Keller Story* (New York: Crowell, 1959), p. 92.

In her presidential biographies for older students, only Franklin Roosevelt comes alive as a personality in *The FDR Story. The Woodrow Wilson Story* and *The Herbert Hoover Story* give an accurate record of the times and the accomplishments of the man, but the men themselves seem lifeless.

Jean Lee Latham   The biographies by Jean Lee Latham are highly fictionalized and fascinating. Most authors would be dubious about writing an interesting biography for children about a mathematician; Miss Latham was challenged. She studied mathematics, astronomy, oceanography, and seamanship. Then she went to Boston and Salem to talk with descendants of Nathaniel Bowditch and to research the geographical and maritime backgrounds of her story. The result of all of this painstaking preparation was the Newbery Award winner for 1956, *Carry On, Mr. Bowditch.* This is the amazing story of Nat Bowditch who had little chance for schooling, but mastered the secrets of navigation for himself. Denied the education for which he yearned, Nathaniel was apprenticed to a ship chandler for nine long years. However, he taught himself everything he could learn about the sea and ships, mathematics, astronomy, and even Latin. Before he was thirty, Nat Bowditch had written *The American Practical Navigator,* which is still used some 150 years later as a standard text in the United States Naval Academy! Jean Lee Latham has also written the biographies of Matthew Fontaine Maury, the founder of the Naval Academy, in *Trail Blazer of the Seas,* and *Retreat to Glory, the Story of Sam Houston.* For somewhat younger readers, she has written *Medals for Morse* and *Young Man in a Hurry, the Story of Cyrus Field.* Miss Latham is a gifted storyteller who also respects accuracy and authenticity.

Dorothy Sterling   Dorothy Sterling has written many different kinds of books for various age levels. Several of her titles are well-written biographies of Negroes or those who aided the cause of the slaves in the 1850s. *Freedom Train, the Story of Harriet Tubman* is a fast-moving biography of the amazing slave who brought freedom to more than 300 of her race. In this account of her life, Harriet Tubman emerges as a strong, fearless woman with only one thought in mind, to lead her people out of slavery. No wonder the slaves called her "Moses." For *Captain of the "Planter,"* Dorothy Sterling has told the story of a less well-known slave, Robert Smalls. All of his life Robert Smalls was called "boy," even after he had married and had children of his own, and was recognized as one of the best pilots of the steamer boats. One day he saw a way to escape being called "boy." He took the steamer, "Planter," over to the Northern forces and freed himself and his family. Later, he fought for freedom in the United States Army, and as Congressman, he worked for it through the hopes and bitter disillusionment of the Reconstruction. His name was Robert Smalls, but he was a big man in all that he did. Sterling has written the story of *Lucretia Mott, Gentle Warrior* for more mature readers. This is the story of the diminutive Quaker who fought gallantly for the abolition of all inequalities. She preached against slavery and incited women to assert their rights. Although a "gentle warrior," she was a most formidable foe as this well-researched account shows. *Lift Every Voice* is a collection of short biographies of four Negroes; Booker T. Washington, W. E. B. DuBois, Mary Church Terrell, and James Weldon Johnson. Bibliographies and acknowledgments indicate the careful research that has gone into all of Dorothy Sterling's absorbing biographies.

Hildegarde Swift Two fascinating biographies of naturalists are Hildegarde Hoyt Swift's story of John Muir, *From the Eagle's Wing,* and *The Edge of April, a Biography of John Burroughs.* The story of John Muir, father of our national parks, is perhaps the most exciting of the two. The restless, adventurous spirit and boundless energy that characterized all of John Muir's life bursts forth from this book. A geologist, Muir had an intense curiosity to explore the vast wilderness of the West. Determined to prove his glacial theory, he made frequent trips to explore glaciers. Swift has told the moving story of the rescue of his little dog Stickeen from near-death on a glacier. Still exploring at seventy-four, John Muir's life was one of complete dedication to the preservation of the natural beauty of our West. Lynd Ward's black-and-white illustrations add strength and artistry to these fine biographies.

James Daugherty The name of James Daugherty seems almost synonymous with that of biographer and illustrator of the American scene. With singing, swinging, pictures and rhythmical prose he has portrayed Daniel Boone, Abraham Lincoln, Lewis and Clark, Benjamin Franklin, and Marcus and Narcissa Whitman. His story of *Daniel Boone* received the Newbery Award for the most distinguished contribution to children's literature. Here, in almost epic prose he has portrayed the rigor and humor of pioneer life. He tells of Boone's early explorations, the building of the Wilderness Road, and the grim nine-day siege of Boonesborough. It was during this siege that the Indians offered friendship in exchange for a peaceful surrender. Boone welcomed this delay and explained that his people would give an answer in two days. Daugherty describes their answer in the following words:

Inside the fort the chances were talked over and argued and weighed after the democratic way of the backwoods. The odds were ten to one and worse against defense, and not a man, woman, or child would be spared if—But the

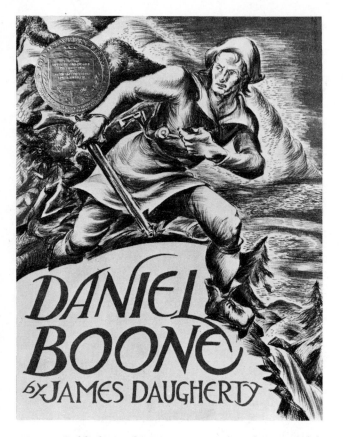

Bold, lusty figures express the pioneer spirit of early Americans. Cover from *Daniel Boone* by James Daugherty. Copyright 1939, © 1967 by James Daugherty. Reprinted by permission of The Viking Press, Inc.

tough cantankerous spirit of the frontier urged: "Go ahead or bust." They would not have been where they were if they had not been stubborn survivors of a rough, tough, restless race who lived and died in their own independent way by the rifle, the ax, the Bible, and the plow. So they sent back the eagle's answer: "No surrender," the answer of the sassy two-year-old baby democracy, the answer of Man the Unconquerable to the hosts of darkness —"No surrender."[14]

---

[14]James Daugherty, *Daniel Boone* (New York: Viking, 1939), p. 59.

Daugherty's illustrations depict the lusty good fun of the frontier life as readily as the terror of an Indian capture. There is joy, horror, courage, and action in his swirling turbulent scenes. His powerful pictures are not pretty, but they are a perfect complement to his vigorous prose.

The books by James Daugherty are for the superior reader. His biographies of Lincoln, Franklin, and Lewis and Clark are more appropriately written for the teenager. Teachers in intermediate grades may want to read parts of these books aloud to their classes; their prose invites oral presentation.

Other Biographers It is impossible to include all of the biographers of well-known children's books. Some authors have only written one or two, and yet, these are excellent biographies. Clyde Bulla has written two very popular biographies for primary readers, *Squanto, Friend of the White Man* and *John Billington, Friend of Squanto*. The true story of Squanto is one that has always appealed to children, for it is filled with adventure, anxiety, and pathos. They identify readily with this Indian who was kidnapped by English explorers and spent some eight years in England. At last, Squanto has the opportunity to return home, but once again he is captured and sent back across the Atlantic to be sold as a slave in Spain. Clyde Bulla tells this moving tale with simplicity and dignity. The pictures by Peter Burchard are as forceful as the text.

Older boys and girls are equally entranced by *Dark Pilgrim, the Story of Squanto* written by Ziner. In this imaginative biography, Mrs. Ziner develops a plausible explanation for Squanto's acceptance of the Pilgrims. The research that went into this book is apparent and the author's notes carefully distinguish between fact and fiction.

Amos Fortune, Free Man by Elizabeth Yates is a moving account of a common man who lived simply and greatly. Born free in Africa, he was sold as a slave in America. In time, he purchased his own freedom and that of several others. Not until he was eighty years old did Amos Fortune spend money for himself; then he purchased twenty-five acres of land in the shadow of his beloved mountain, Monadnock, Indian for "the mountain that stands alone." Like Monadnock, Amos Fortune stood alone, a rock of strength and security for all those he loved.

Only five biographies have won the Newbery Award; *Amos Fortune, Free Man* was one of these. *I, Juan de Pareja* by Elizabeth Borten de Treviño is the most recent biography to win this coveted award. It, too, is the story of a Negro slave. Juan tells his own pitiful story of the change in his life in seventeenth-century Spain when his indulgent mistress dies. Placed in the charge of a cruel gypsy muleteer, Juan must steal or beg for his food on the long trip to Madrid, where he is delivered to his mistress's nephew and heir, Diego Velázquez, the famous painter. Once again, his life changes as he becomes the artist's indispensable assistant and companion. Little is known about Velázquez or his slave, so the author has had to invent a great deal. She has been faithful to the period, the known facts about the artist, and her feeling for this man. In her afterword, the author states:

> My story about Juan de Pareja will, I hope, be forgiven the liberties I have taken with known facts and the incidents I have invented. It will appeal, I hope, to young people of both white and Negro races because the story of Juan de Pareja and Velázquez foreshadows, in the lifetime of the two men, what we hope to achieve a millionfold today. Those two, who began in youth as master and slave, continued as companions in their maturity and ended as equals and as friends.[15]

---

[15]Elizabeth Borten de Treviño, *I, Juan de Pareja* (New York: Farrar, Straus, 1965), pp. 179–180.

Nardi Campion has written an exciting, perceptive biography of *Patrick Henry, Firebrand of the Revolution*. Skillfully, the author shows the important role that each of our great leaders played in the formation of this country. Washington was ever ready to serve in action, but he never spoke in public; Jefferson was best when he was writing; and so it fell to Patrick Henry with his gift for oratory to be the "Voice of the Revolution." Campion describes his famous "Liberty or Death" speech in a way that makes the reader feel he were witnessing it.

The names of Jeannette Eaton, Miriam Gurko, Marguerite Vance, and Aylesa Forsee are also associated with fine biography. Most of their works are written for the teenager, however. Their books serve the useful purpose of bridging the gap between biographies for children and adults.

As teachers and parents guide children's reading, it will be helpful to know the limitations and outstanding characteristics of biography for children. There are biographies to meet almost all interests and levels of reading, from fare for the reluctant reader to historical research for the avid one.

Types of Biographies: Lincoln Comparisons

Probably there have been more adult biographies written about Abraham Lincoln than any other American. The same statement can be made about the number of juvenile biographies that have portrayed his life. Children enjoy reading stories about this famous American hero the year around and not just during the month of his birth. A comparison of the many biographies about him will illustrate the wide range of biographical types for children.

Picture Books   In describing Lincoln, the late Carl Sandburg said he was like something out of a picture book for children. Yet

Brightly colored lithographs depict a fun-loving gawky Lincoln. Illustration from *Abraham Lincoln* by Ingri and Edgar Parin d'Aulaire, copyright 1939, by Doubleday & Company, Inc. Reprinted by permission of Doubleday & Company, Inc.

there have not been many picture books about Lincoln. The d'Aulaires' *Abraham Lincoln* is the best example of this type of biography. In full-page lithographs of glowing color, these artists have presented the picture book story of Lincoln from childhood through the Civil War. Children will delight in the story and picture of Abe holding a little boy upside down to make muddy tracks on the whitewashed ceiling in order to fool his stepmother. Another full-page illustration shows Abe stretched out on the carpet in the parlor of his Springfield house reading a book, oblivious to the antics of his three noisy sons. The reflection of Mary Todd Lincoln in the mirror suggests an unhappy ending to the day's fun. The d'Aulaires have captured the homespun qualities of this gawky, great man in both

their text and illustrations. This book serves as a perfect introduction of Abraham Lincoln for seven-, eight-, and nine-year-olds.

Another picture book titled *Lincoln, a Big Man* emphasizes Lincoln's "bigness" of stature and nature. Helen Kay has painted wonderful word pictures in this text that are complemented by the slightly distorted black and white sketches of this tall, awkward man. Lincoln's height is stressed in the author's description of a marble game among Willie Slemmons, a nine-year-old, and two friends.

Suddenly a shadow fell across the marble ring and a pair of very large feet appeared beside him. Willie looked up the very long legs and even higher up to the large kindly, smiling face. And as if put there to make him look even taller, on his head sat a plug hat—half a foot high![16]

Lincoln took time to play with the boys. He won all their marbles and then returned them! Abraham Lincoln was frequently inconvenienced by his height. An amusing picture of him in bed in one of the many hotels at which he stayed while riding the Circuit shows his long feet sticking out from under the footboard. This book includes many other references to his size, but also tells many of the anecdotes that showed his bigness of heart. As his wife, Mary, once remarked, "People are not aware that his heart is as large as his arms are long." The author and illustrator have carefully blended the outward appearances of this man with his inner character. Younger children will enjoy the humorous stories and pictures, but they may also gain an insight into the greatness of his spirit.

Beginning-to-Read Books   In the past six years many easy-reading biographies with controlled vocabularies have been written

---

[16]Helen Kay, *Lincoln, a Big Man,* Illustrated by Arthur Polonsky (New York: Hastings, 1958), pp. 8–9.

about Lincoln. Clara Ingram Judson's *Abraham Lincoln* is a straight narrative account that includes favorite anecdotes of his life. While simplified, this book does suggest multiple causes for the Civil War, including the right of secession and slavery. *A Man Named Lincoln* by Norman recounts the story of his life in a more condescending way. The author frequently interrupts the story to interject her reactions. Thus, after Lincoln's mother dies, the text states, "Poor Abe! That was a bad time for him."[17] The sentences are set up line by line for ease of reading, rather than in paragraph form. Unfortunately, this creates a choppy effect, for example:

> *Both men made good speeches,*
> *But they did not think the same way*
> *About the slaves.*[18]

In another "See and Read" biography of *Abraham Lincoln* by Patricia Miles Martin and also published by Putnam, this jerky sentence pattern is avoided. The reasons for the Civil War are not clearly stated, however. The first five words of the Gettysburg speech are given, and then the reader is told it was a speech that will always be remembered! This same kind of oversimplification is characteristic of *Abraham Lincoln for the People* by Colver. Little explanation of the Civil War is given, and war is introduced with this very brief sentence: "When the Civil War began the President was even busier."[19] Credence is given to the now disproved story that Lincoln composed the famous Gettysburg address while riding on the train. When the Lincolns go to the theater the text states: "The President and Mrs. Lincoln sat in a box."[20] No picture shows the Lincolns in their box seats, so one wonders what images second- and third-graders who are not familiar with the legitimate theater will derive from this statement! In *Meet Abraham Lincoln* by Cary, a greater attempt has been made to present cause and effect relationships. However, this objectivity is offset by the repetitive style of writing. For example:

> *Douglas was a small man. People called him the "Little Giant." They called Lincoln the "Big Giant." They said the debates were a battle of the giants. They called them the "Great Debates."*[21]

Generally, then, beginning-to-read biographies only give a superficial picture of the man without ever focusing on the depth, the height and the breadth of the man, Abraham Lincoln.

Biographical Episode There are many stories for children that are based upon a single biographical incident in Lincoln's life. In *Abe Lincoln's Birthday*, Wilma Pitchford Hays has reconstructed his thoughts and the events of his twelfth birthday. This is a quiet story, but one that reflects Abe Lincoln's personality and the depths of his mind. Primary children will come away from this book knowing something of the man's spirit.

Henry's Lincoln by Louise Neyhart tells of the Lincoln-Douglas Debate at Freeport, Illinois. Henry, a ten-year-old, is finally allowed to drive Prince, his spirited white horse, into town to hear the two men speak. The author has made this debate and the issues involved in it come alive for boys and girls of the twentieth century. They will identify with Henry's indecision as to which man to support. Finally, he is won over to Lincoln's side and waits to speak to him after the debate. Mr. Lincoln sees him wearing his Douglas badge and remarks that he is glad

[17]Gertrude Norman, *A Man Named Lincoln*, Illustrated by Joseph Cellini (New York: Putnam, 1960), unpaged.
[18]Norman, unpaged.
[19]Anne Colver, *Abraham Lincoln for the People*, Illustrated by William Moyers (Champaign, Ill.: Garrard, 1960), p. 60.
[20]Colver, p. 72.

[21]Barbara Cary, *Meet Abraham Lincoln* Illustrated by Jack Davis (New York: Random House, 1965), p. 61.

to have a Douglas man on his side. In this small, exciting book, the issues of this famous occasion are presented clearly and forcefully.

Ruth Painter Randall has collected many of the incidents relating to Abraham Lincoln's encounters with animals and presented them in her book *Lincoln's Animal Friends.* Each chapter tells a separate story. One of the most moving is the tale of six-year-old Abe's pet pig. On the unbelievably horrible day of hog-killing, Abe hid with his pet in the woods. However, the next day, his father rose early and caught the hog. Lincoln always remembered this "awful tragedy," as he termed it, and once made the comment that sadness comes harder to the young "because it takes them unawares."

Partial Biography   One of the liberties allowed juvenile biographers is the writing of partial or incomplete biography. Carl Sandburg wrote a partial biography for children titled *Abe Lincoln Grows Up.* It was made from the first twenty-seven chapters of the longest and most definitive of biographies for adults, Sandburg's *Abraham Lincoln, the Prairie Years.* In his juvenile biography, Sandburg included Lincoln's birth and boyhood, until he was nineteen and "grown up." It was written in singing prose that at times seems more like poetry. Sandburg told not only the story of Lincoln's early life, but described the monotony of daily living in those times. He described Lincoln's desire for learning and knowledge in these words:

> *He wanted to learn, to live, to reach out; he wanted to satisfy hungers and thirsts he couldn't tell about, this big big boy of the backwoods. And some of what he wanted so much, so deep down, seemed to be in books. Maybe in books he would find the answers to dark questions pushing around in the pools of his thoughts and the drifts of his mind. He told Dennis and other people, "The things I want to*

> *know are in books; my best friend is the man who'll git me a book I ain't read." And sometimes friends answered, "Well, books ain't as plenty as wildcats in these parts o' Indianny!"* [22]

The rhythm of Sandburg's prose begs to be read aloud and shared. It is perhaps best read orally by the teacher, although more mature readers in the fifth and sixth grade could read it independently.

Frances Cavanah's book, *Abe Lincoln Gets His Chance,* covers a somewhat longer period than the Sandburg book, ending with Lincoln's departure for the White House. Cavanah has made good use of dialogue in this well-written book. The theme that she emphasizes is that Abe Lincoln made opportunities from what others would have considered handicaps. The end papers show an interesting map of the locations of the various homes of Abraham Lincoln. The black-and-white sketches seem almost too modern, the women too chic and attractive in their poke bonnets, and the men too handsome. Children will enjoy the conversation, the humor, and the inclusion of many interesting anecdotes in this book. It is easily read by middle-graders.

Complete Biography   A few of the many complete biographies of Lincoln are outstanding. One of these is Clara Ingram Judson's *Abraham Lincoln, Friend of the People.* In this beautifully written account, Mrs. Judson portrays Lincoln as a boy, father, lawyer, and President—but always human. She plays up his ability to tell good stories and entertain his listeners. Her description of his early campaign speeches is delightful:

> *Lincoln's first chance to speak came at an auction nearby. He arrived early, dressed in his best—a coat of mixed jeans, cut clawham-*

[22]Carl Sandburg, *Abe Lincoln Grows Up,* Reprinted from *Abraham Lincoln: the Prairie Years,* Illustrated by James Daugherty (New York: Harcourt, 1928), p. 135.

mer fashion (with sleeves and coattails too short), tow and flax pantaloons, and a straw hat without a band. He visited with the men and made a campaign speech. His statement of principles got attention, and his backwoods tales delighted them. A favorite yarn was about a preacher who during a long sermon felt a lizard crawling up inside his breeches. Abe Lincoln's gifted mimicry as he acted out the preacher's frantic misery had the men rocking with laughter.[23]

Robert Frankenberg has produced clear, forceful black-and-white line drawings for this book. In addition, colored photographs of the Lincoln dioramas from the Chicago Historical Society provide interest and authenticity.

May McNeer and her husband, Lynd Ward, have collaborated to produce one of the most moving and beautiful biographies of Abraham Lincoln. From a literary and pictorial standpoint, this book is superb. The only dialogue that is used are those words which are known to have been Lincoln's. Yet the story moves rapidly from a "shirttail boy" of seven walking to school with his sister, Sarah, to a single shot during the third act of a play at Ford's Theatre. The events of Lincoln's childhood are described in well-chosen words against a backdrop of black-and-white pictures and vividly colored ones glowing with the rich greens of the wilderness.

The Wards have pictured the many sides of the moody, good-natured, studious young man. They emphasize his grief at the death of Ann Rutledge with poetic prose and a forceful picture:

Lincoln's long face, where sadness seemed to make its home, grew lined and etched with grief. In his twenty-six years he had lost his mother, his sister, and now the girl Ann. . . .

A soft pink sunset provides contrast for the grief-stricken figure of Lincoln. From *America's Abraham Lincoln* by May McNeer. Illustrated by Lynd Ward. Houghton Mifflin Company, 1957. Reprinted by permission of Houghton Mifflin Company.

lost in grief, wandering about unable to think, unable to work. Nancy and Bowling Green took him to their home and put an axe in his big hands. Out under the sky, sinking his axe blade in a log, stripping the ripened ears of corn, and driving a team, he found help while their friendship gave him comfort.[24]

The fun-loving side of Lincoln is portrayed by Ward in a picture of Lincoln with his three boys. He is holding the youngest

---

[23]Clara Ingram Judson, *Abraham Lincoln, Friend of the People,* Illustrated by Robert Frankenberg (Chicago: Follett, 1950), pp. 89–90.

[24]May McNeer. *America's Abraham Lincoln,* Illustrated by Lynd Ward (Boston: Houghton Mifflin, 1957), p. 48.

while the other two are hugging him. Even the cat is purring and rubbing against one of his long legs. Mary Todd Lincoln stands quietly at the door with loving admiration in her eyes and a somewhat wistful expression on her face. She would never tolerate such hilarious "goings-on" herself, but Lynd Ward's picture suggests a longing to enter into this world of open-hearted joy. Children will be the richer for meeting him through the media of May McNeer's flowing prose and Lynd Ward's detailed and expressive illustrations.

James Daugherty has written a complete and comprehensive biography, also titled *Abraham Lincoln*. Again, this is a book that requires mature reading ability. Daugherty's prose has a distinctive swing and vigor that is repeated in the lines of his powerful illustrations. Some of his writing reminds the reader of the same poetic quality in the Sandburg biography of Lincoln. The following passage is typical of Daugherty's rhythmical prose:

> *Long after the lights had gone out forever in the deserted cabins on the New Salem bluff, and when a tragic glory hung about his name and fame, recorders came to the old scenes seeking out the men and women Lincoln had known and loved in the vanished cabins and the haunted paths where he had walked asking Why was he sad? What was he like? What made him weep? What made him laugh? What was his secret? Whom did he love? What did he hate?*
>
> *Men and women, searching in the twilight attic of past years, dusted off daguerreotypes of memory, and repeated the echoes of his remembered phrases, recalling the old jests and laughter, and restoring the colors of pictures faded and darkened by time.*[25]

Daugherty's pictures of Lincoln vary from the tall, gawky, almost grotesque, young man telling stories in the New Salem store, to the powerful wrestler who defeated Jack Armstrong, to the brooding, somber, war-weary President. All of the illustrations have the vitality so typical of Daugherty's work.

Documentary Biographies   A new kind of biography has been prepared under the direction of the editors of the *American Heritage Magazine*. Profusely illustrated in color and black and white, *Abraham Lincoln in Peace and War* by Earl Schenck Miers gives the reader a visual knowledge of the man and his times. Paintings, drawings, maps, cartoons, and photographs all contribute to a feeling of immediacy. The straightforward, readable biography presents Lincoln from his boyhood to his assassination. Our visually minded children of today will find this book a rich source for reports and enjoyment.

Lincoln's America by Adele Nathan is also richly documented with many authentic photographs in black and white of the man and his times. Engravings of the period and a facsimile of Lee's surrender note to Grant add to the straight reporting of this visual presentation.

Mary Kay Phelan has written an extensively detailed book about the drafting, writing, and delivery of the Gettysburg Address in *Mr. Lincoln Speaks at Gettysburg*. Included in the many photographs of the occasion, are illustrations of the five manuscript versions of the address. Newspaper coverage and press reaction to the speech are also a part of this documentary. In *The First Book Edition of the Gettysburg Address, the Second Inaugural*, Leonard Everett Fisher has illustrated with striking black-and-white scratchboard pictures both of these famous speeches. The introduction is from Carl Sandburg's volumes, *The Prairie Years* and *The War Years*.

---

[25]James Daugherty, *Abraham Lincoln* (New York: Viking, 1943), p. 48.

Related Biographies The greatness of Lincoln seems to have increased rather than diminished with time. As people become more interested in finding out about this enigmatic man, they have focused their attention on his background, upon his parents, and his relations with members of his own family. Children's books have also reflected this interest as indicated by such titles as Le Sueur's *Nancy Hanks of Wilderness Road,* Margaret Friskey's *Tad Lincoln and the Green Umbrella,* Frances Cavanah's *They Knew Abe Lincoln,* and Randall's *I, Mary,* the story of Mary Todd. Aileen Fisher has written an interesting biography of Lincoln told from the point of view of his cousin, Dennis Hanks. It is titled *My Cousin, Abe.* There are many of these related biographies, but in the juvenile field they appear to be restricted to the subject of Abraham Lincoln.

The biographies about Abraham Lincoln have revealed six main types: picture biographies, beginning-to-read biographies, biographical incidents or episodes, partial biographies, complete biographies and "documentary" biographies. For the subject of Abraham Lincoln, there are also related biographies. Most of these biographies use a fictionalized form; some represent the factual reporting of the authentic biography (McNeer's *America's Abraham Lincoln* and *Abraham Lincoln in Peace and War* by Miers are the truest to this form); while some of the biographical episodes, such as the story of *Henry's Lincoln* are biographical fiction.

HISTORICAL FICTION

America's awakened interest in the historical novel is clearly reflected in the increasing number of fictional books for children that have an historical background. These books supplement the information obtained from factual books and biographies. Historical fiction for children seeks to reconstruct the life and thought of an age or period of time other than that of the present generation. The characters, settings, and events are drawn from the past, or the author may invent plots, characters, and events provided he does not alter basic historical fact. Real personages, actual events, and places are frequently introduced into the historical novel along with fictional characters and plot.

There is a difference between historical fiction that is written as historical fiction, and those books that take on historical significance with the passage of time. It is sometimes difficult to understand that what may be a vivid memory for an adult is history for children. Such books as *Snow Treasure* by Marie McSwigan and *Twenty and Ten* by Bishop are historical stories in the sense that today's child has no recollection of the Nazi occupation of Norway and France. However, in the 1940s when these books were written, they were stories of contemporary life. They are stirring, well-written tales that recapture the anxiety and courage of the people of their time, but they are not historical fiction in the usual definition of the term. These are stories that have endured, and in the process of this endurance they have acquired an historical value. In historical fiction, the author deliberately attempts to reconstruct the life of an age other than that of the present. Both historical fiction and books written at the actual time of an historical event may convey the life and spirit of the period to children.

Criteria for Historical Fiction

Books of historical fiction are not exempt from the requirement of telling a good story. They should not just sugar-coat history, but tell a story that is interesting in its own right.

Second, these stories must make the period come alive for their readers by recreating both the physical environment of the times and capturing the spirit and feelings of the age. Third, these stories must be historically accurate and authentic, both in presenting the everyday life of their characters and the events of the period, for the author cannot falsify the fundamental record of history. In this sense, then, the historical record does impose a certain limited framework on the author. Fourth, well-written books of historical fiction contain a theme just as do other distinguished books of fiction. The theme may be an historical one based on the issues of the time; or a universal one such as growing up, as portrayed in *Caddie Woodlawn* by Brink. Too much attention to historical detail may overpower the theme and make dull reading. Finally, historical fiction for children usually has a central character who is a boy or girl experiencing the life of his time as a child. This character should be believable and meaningful to the contemporary child. Places and events may be different, but human nature tends to remain constant.

Historical Fiction—Prehistoric Times

Just as children are fascinated with the thought of being the first man on the moon, so too are they intrigued with the idea of what life must have been like for the first men on earth. While no one can be certain of the exact ways that prehistoric man lived, anthropologists and geologists are providing scientific data that make it possible to imagine how life in prehistoric times might have been. *One Small Blue Bead* by Schweitzer is a poetic picture book that describes prehistoric times among a tribe that is convinced it is the only people in the world. One man thinks differently and yearns for others of his kind. His chores are willingly assumed by a boy to enable the old man to roam free in

quest for knowledge. As the boy goes about his daily chores, he wonders, too:

> *I wonder . . . I wonder*
> *If on some far hillside*
> *There is a boy*
> *who sits alone.*
> *And thinks the same thoughts*
> *As my own.*
> *I wonder if he wonders if*
> *There's a boy with thoughts like his.*
> *I'd like to tell him that there is*
> *And I'm that boy.*[26]

The boy's faithfulness is rewarded as the man returns with a boy from another tribe, who gives him one small blue bead. This is a moving story of loneliness and man's quest of the unknown that will be understood and appreciated by children as young as seven.

In *Beyond the Gorge of Shadows*, Harvey tells the story of Gahyaz, a sixteen-year-old boy who lived in the American Southwest some 10,000 years ago. Finding strange spearpoints in a cave, he dared to defy the Hunt Chief's lifelong belief that the only men on earth are those in their tribe. Banished from the tribe, he sets out with Seska, the Hunt Chief's son, who alone had the courage to stand by him in the council and was banished also. Maitsoh was the least convinced of the three, but he accompanied his friends out of a feeling of friendship and loyalty. Gahyaz is killed in a fight with a lion, but Seska and Maitsoh continue the search for others of their own kind. At last they do find other men, but they meet with the same disbelief from them as they had faced in their own tribe; they could not have come from the East, they are told, for no men lived there. Slowly, the boys prove that they did come from this direction and they return

---

[26]Byrd Baylor Schweitzer, *One Small Blue Bead,* Illustrated by Symeon Shimin (New York: Macmillan, 1965), p. 18.

to their own tribe with living proof of other men. This book has a tightly knit plot, excellent characterization, and a theme as meaningful today as 10,000 years ago: the age-old conflict between the questing mind and the closed one. *Fire Hunter* by Kjelgaard is the story of Hawk, a sixteen-year-old boy who also dared to ignore the tribal rites and try something new. He was put out of the tribe but survived through his own resourcefulness.

This same theme runs through a remarkable story of primitive men entitled *And the Waters Prevailed* by Barringer. When Andor, the Little, journeyed to the ocean he saw that at what is now the Straits of Gibraltar, the water would some day break through the fragile natural dam and flood the valley that was his people's home. No one shares his vision, and Andor spends his life trying to convince the tribe of the impending danger. Andor is finally rejected by all except his loyal wife, Bardis, and his children, who are somewhat embarrassed and ashamed of their father's fanaticism. When the flood does come, Bardis has died, and Andor is an old man, too old to make the long journey to the caves in the Pyrenees that he had long ago found as a suitable refuge. The tribe delays in their preparation, and only Andor's family are saved. Andor is not vindicated, however, for he had wanted to lead his whole tribe to safety. Even as the flood comes, it is called "Andor's Flood" and he is blamed for it. Only the reader knows the vision of the man and senses his frustration at being unable to convince his people of their impending doom.

No one can recreate the life and times of early Britain as believably as Rosemary Sutcliff. In *Warrior Scarlet,* she tells the story of Drem, a Bronze Age boy, who must kill a wolf singlehanded in order to win his right to wear the scarlet of manhood. Drem is determined to become a warrior rather than be forced to live with the Earth people and be a shepherd. His task would be a difficult one for most boys; it seemed almost impossible for a fifteen-year-old boy who had only the use of one arm. This story not only accurately presents the life of these primitive peoples, it also shows the hurt, loneliness, and defiance of the handicapped.

In *The Faraway Lurs,* Harry Behn has created a hauntingly beautiful story of the love between a young Stone Age girl, Heather, and Wolf Stone, son of the chieftain of the Sun People. One morning Heather hears the great bronze trumpets (called lurs) of the Sun People who have camped beside a lake near her village. Later, she meets Wolf Stone in the forest as he searches for the mighty tree that her Forest People worship. Heather's people are peaceful forest dwellers, while the Sun People are fierce warriors. The two fall in love, but there is no solution for them other than death in this Romeo-and-Juliet story of the Bronze Age. The author was inspired to tell Heather's tale after a journey to Denmark to visit the birthplace of his mother. An important archeological find had been made on this farm when they discovered the "wet grave" of an eighteen-year-old girl perfectly preserved for some 3000 years. Harry Behn listened to the details of her burial and then wrote his own interpretation of what might have happened. In his foreword, Behn points out the relative brevity of man's history and his slow progress in human relations since Heather's time.

Historical Fiction—The New World

American Indians The point of view of the historical fiction portraying American Indians has gradually changed. In the earlier stories, the Indians were seen as cruel, bloodthirsty savages attacking small groups of helpless settlers. The provocation for the attacks was seldom given. Thus, in Edmond's exciting story, *The Matchlock Gun,* a mother and two small children outwit three savages, but not before the Indians burn their house and wound the mother. In Field's *Calico Bush,* the Indians are equally cruel as they burn the settler's house. Other stories, however, such as *Sword in the Wilderness* and *Moccasin Trail* portray the Indian in three-dimensional terms; showing his cruelty as a part of his culture, his amazing generosity in certain stiuations, and the white man's treatment of him. Finally, in such fine books as Baker's *Killer-of-Death, The Raven's Cry* by Harris, and *Ishi, Last of His Tribe* by Kroeber, the terrible story of the white man's destruction of the Indians' way of life is told.

Many stories that reveal the complex character of the Indian nature are stories of white captives who observe, and occasionally, learn to appreciate the Indian way of life. Boys and girls in third and fourth grades will like *Bread and Butter Indian* by Anne Colver. Too young to understand her parents' fear of Indians, Barbara befriends a hungry Indian, offering him the bread and butter with which she was having a tea party for her imaginary friends. Although they cannot communicate, they look for each other every day, and always Barbara shares her sandwich with him. While following her pet crow one evening at dusk, Barbara is kidnapped by a strange Indian. How her "bread and butter" Indian comes to her rescue is the climax of a warm, exciting story. Garth Williams' illustrations portray the simple joys of a pioneer child as she listens to her mother tell a story, makes new friends at a picnic, and plays dress-up in her aunt's fine clothes. His illustration of Barbara's "bread and butter Indian" are as warm and reassuring as this story of an incident that really happened.

Two books for children in the middle grades tell the stories of a white prisoner and an Indian prisoner. Sometimes listed under biography, *Indian Captive, the Story of Mary Jemison* by Lois Lenski is the highly fictionalized account of a real twelve-year-old girl who was captured by the Indians and taken to live with the Senecas. The theme of this story is the basic conflict between Indian and white culture. Mary is treated kindly by the Indians as they adopt her into their tribe, but she is determined to remember her white ways. Almost without realizing it, she begins to understand the Indians and to love them. When the time comes for her to decide whether she will remain with them or go with the English, she chooses to stay.

Wayah of the Real People was not captured and imprisoned by the whites, but being sent to the Brafferton School for Indians at Williamsburg seemed like prison to him. The white men had promised the Cherokees lead, powder, knives, and blankets if they would send one of their boys to school for a year. Wayah did not want to go, for his Grandfather had warned him of the whites, saying:

> *"An Indian who takes on white man's ways is like an oak tree struck by lightning. . . . As lightning splits the oak's trunk in two, so the white man's touch splits the red man. He is no longer one good tree, but two worthless ones, part white, part Indian, no good to either tribe."*[27]

For a year, Wayah endures hostility, sickness, loneliness, and cruelty from his classmates. He does make friends with red-haired Duncan and he learns much from his schoolmaster. At last, he returns home to find that his experience has not split his spirit but rather strengthened him, so that now he is better able to serve his tribe by interpreting the white man's ways.

A story of Indian capture for more mature readers is *Calico Captive* by Elizabeth

[27]William Steele, *Wayah of the Real People,* Illustrated by Isa Barnett (New York: Holt, Rinehart and Winston, 1964), p. 6.

Speare. Based upon real people and events, this is a fictionalized account of the experiences of young Miriam Willard who had just been to her first dance when she was captured by the Indians. Her sister, brother-in-law, three children, and a neighbor are captured with her, taken to Montreal, and sold as slaves. Their hardships and ordeals are taken from a diary kept by a real "captive" in 1754. Speare tells this story with her usual fine characterizations and attention to authentic detail.

Two stories of whites brought up as Indians lend themselves well for purposes of comparison: *Moccasin Trail* by Eloise McGraw and *The Light in the Forest* by Conrad Richter. In the first book, Jim Heath is rescued from a grizzly bear by the Crow Indians and brought up to think and feel like an Indian. When the braves return with a blond scalp, just the color of his mothers hair, Jim has a sudden longing to be with his own kind and leaves the Indians to search for some whites. He joins forces with a trapper and learns some of the white man's ways, when his long-lost family contacts him. His mother and father have both died, but the three younger children have come West to claim land and find him. Jim pitches in to help the family make a home, but at the same time, he clings to his strange Indian ways. His long braids, long feathers, and trapping smell are offensive to his sister, Sally, puzzling to his brother, Jonnie, and acceptable only to his little brother, Daniel, who worships and admires everything he does. Jim longs for the sensible Indian ways, but more than that, he wants to be accepted by all his family. Everything that he does seems to be wrong. He steals a horse for Jonnie, the grandest present a Crow Indian can give, and is rebuffed in front of the other settlers and made to return the horse. A loner, Jim decides to leave. Daniel is heartbroken and runs away only to be captured by the Umpqua Indians who keep

slaves. Jim rescues him but knows that for his sake and his brother's he must forsake the moccasin trail forever. He cuts his braids and is at peace with himself and his family at last. Richter's book was written for adults but has been enjoyed by older children. In this story, True Son, a white boy, reared by an Indian chief, is forced to return to his original home. His love and loyalty to his Indian parents and his rejection of the white man's civilization arouse inevitable conflicts. At last, he runs away and rejoins the Indians. However, he betrays the tribe when at the last moment he will not be a part of tricking a boatload of whites into the Indians' ambush. Instead of calling for help as planned, he sees a small boy who reminds him of his brother, and he shouts a warning. Condemned to die by the Indians, he is rescued by his Indian father who imposes the most severe punishment of all—banishment from the tribe and the forest forever. Forced back to the white man's trail, the boy, who truly felt he was Indian, faced unbearable loneliness:

> *Ahead of him ran the rutted road of the whites. It led, he knew, to where men of their own volition constrained themselves with heavy clothing like harness, where men chose to be slaves to their own or another's property and followed empty and desolate lives far from the wild beloved freedom of the Indian.*[28]

A moving story of the Apache rivalry with the white man is paralleled by an inner story of conflict between two young boys in *Killer-of-Death* by Betty Baker. The long feud between the medicine man's son and Killer-of-Death quickly disappeared when they saw most of their people killed like rabbits at the feast the white trader had planned so carefully. Broken and disheartened, the remnants of the tribe are moved to a reservation.

---

[28]Conrad Richter, *The Light in the Forest* (New York: Knopf, 1963), 179.

In *Raven's Cry*, **Christie Harris has described the Haida Indian not as a blood-thirsty savage, but as a member of an art-oriented culture. The illustrations were done by Bill Reid, one of the few artists capable of working in the authentic Haida tradition.** Copyright © 1966 by Christie Harris. Illustrations by Bill Reid. From *Raven's Cry.* Used by permission of Atheneum Publishers.

The missionary asks Killer-of-Death to send his son to the white man's school. For two days the father fasted and then went to a hill on which stood a single pine tree split by lightning. He waited for the spirits to speak his name and to provide the answer. Finally, the sign came in the brilliant dawn of the new day. Might there be a renewal of the people in the same way? Killer-of-Death

made his decision: He would send his son to school.

Mature readers will enjoy the highly fictionalized biography of *Ishi, Last of His Tribe* by Theodora Kroeber. Most of the Yana Indians of California had been killed or driven from their homes by the invading gold seekers and settlers during the early 1900's. A small band of the tribe called Yahi resisted their fate by living in concealment. They covered every footprint, jumped from rock to rock, and cut tunnels in the underbrush, but everywhere it seemed the Saldu (white people) had come. One by one his family die, and at last, Ishi is the lone survivor of his tribe. Hungry and ill, he allows himself to be found in a corral outside Oroville. Haltingly, he tells his story to an anthropologist who takes him to live in the University of California's museum. Here he lives happily for five years helping to record the language and ways of the Yahi world.

In one hundred and fifty years, the once proud and powerful Haidas, lords of the western waters of Canada were gone. The people themselves were reduced to a mere handful. *Raven's Cry* by Christie Harris tells the dramatic story of these doomed people and their great heritage to the world—the art of the Haida.

> *"Critics don't quite believe Haida art,"* its *modern disciple says. "It's so refined and highly evolved that they can't believe it emerged from an Indian culture."*
>
> *After all, as the old fur traders told their shipmates, these were only savages; they hadn't fine feelings like civilized human beings.*
>
> *Maybe a more enlightened generation will know better.*[29]

Hopefully, such well-documented human stories about the American Indian may help to produce this more enlightened generation.

---

[29]Christie Harris, *Raven's Cry*, Illustrated by Bill Reid (New York: Atheneum, 1966), p. 193.

The Explorers Most of the children's books about the early explorers are biographical. However, Betty Baker has told the dramatic story of the epic journey through the American Southeast and Mexico by Cabeza de Vaca and three other Spaniards in her book titled *Walk the World's Rim.* The story is primarily that of Esteban, a Negro slave of one of the Spaniards, and Chakoh, a Pima Indian boy who accompanies the men on their long trek. Chakoh is faced with conflicting values when he discovers that Esteban, his friend, is a slave. For among the Pima Indians, a slave is a man without honor, a man who has allowed himself to be captured. And yet this slave is the only one of the four Spaniards who has honor. Only when Chakoh sees his friend forfeit his life for others, does he understand the true meaning of courage and honor and realize that slavery, rather than the slave, is to be despised. This fictional account of de Vaca's long journey is based upon the same source materials as the biography by Maia Wojciechowska titled *Odyssey of Courage;* yet the interpretation is different indeed. A comparison of the two books would be most worthwhile.

In *The King's Fifth,* Scott O'Dell has told the exciting story of the Conquistadores' search for gold in the New World. Six men and Zia, an Indian girl, their guide and interpreter, left Coronado's summer camp to search for the golden cities of Cibola. Only Esteban de Sandoval returns to tell their story in a series of flashbacks as he stands trial for having defrauded the King of Spain of his rightful share of one-fifth of the treasure. His story is the story of the greed of men and what they will sacrifice for the lust for gold—blood, honor, sanity, and life itself. Only when he realizes that he is responsible for the death of his friend, Father Francisco, does Esteban come to his senses and dispose of the gold in such a way that prevents anyone from having it. In prison, he is at last free from the evil that had nearly cost him his sanity and the love of Zia. Honor and greed are contrasted in this complex but powerful story.

Colonial America All children in the United States know the story of the Pilgrims and the first Thanksgiving. Many informational books tell us what these people did, but there are few records that tell how the Pilgrims felt about what they did. Meadowcroft's book *The First Year* tells of the hardships of these Pilgrims in a way that makes them real people to second and third graders. Two books by Hays, *Christmas on the Mayflower* and *Pilgrim Thanksgiving* are enjoyed by this same age group. Weisgard's simple and attractive illustrations enrich these texts. Only in *John Billington, Friend of Squanto* by Clyde Bulla does any one Pilgrim assume much individuality, however. Young John Billington is always in trouble and considered the bad boy of the colony, but he is instrumental in effecting a friendship between the settlers and the Cape Cod Indians. Younger readers enjoy this simple, straightforward account of mischief in Plymouth.

According to Love Brewster, John Brewster's young son, all of the Billingtons were a trial to the Pilgrims. *I Sailed on the Mayflower* by Pilkington is the young boy's quite candid account of the Mayflower voyage and the first year in the new land. Love describes their seemingly endless weeks at sea. He tells about their cramped quarters, and how they had to take turns sleeping because there were only half as many bunks as people. When they finally landed at Plymouth on a cold and dreary day in December, Love went along on the exploration party to find a suitable place to settle. He describes many hardships in their first months on the land. Sickness struck the settlement and the time of the "Great Dying" came. Many of Love's close friends died, but work went on just the same. The day-to-day activities of the settlers as seen through the eyes of a young boy make fascinating reading.

The terrible ordeal of Jamestown is realistically told for middle graders by Jean Lee Latham in *This Dear Bought Land*. This is the story of scrawny, coddled David Warren, the Jamestown colony, and its brave and wily captain, John Smith. Reluctantly at first, David's respect and admiration for Smith grew and strengthened as he watched him save Jamestown time and again. Severely burned by an explosion, Smith is returned to England. Only sixty of the five hundred men survived the "time of starving" when at last, the ships of Lord Delaware sailed up the James River. David receives a letter from John Smith who had recovered from his burns. His words of advice to David provided Jean Latham with the title to this exciting book:

> . . . *Men like you will keep England alive in America.*
> *Wherever fate casts my lot, I shall work for it, and fight for it. It is my life. It has been my hawk, my hounds, my wife, my child, the whole of my content—this dear-bought land.*[30]

The Puritans soon forgot their struggle for religious freedom as they persecuted others who did not follow their beliefs or ways. Older girls will thoroughly enjoy the superb story of *The Witch of Blackbird Pond* written by Elizabeth Speare. Flamboyant, high-spirited Kit Tyler was a misfit in the Puritan household of her aunt and stern-faced uncle. For Kit was as different from her colorless cousins as the bleak barren shore of Wethersfield, Connecticut, differed from the shimmering turquoise bay of Barbados that had been her home for sixteen years. Before Kit ever landed on shore, she had cast suspicion on herself by diving over-

board to rescue a small child's doll. Only witches were supposed to know how to swim in New England in the 1680's! The only place that Kit feels any peace or freedom is in the meadows near Blackbird Pond. And it is here that she meets the lonely bent figure of Quaker Hannah, regarded as a witch by the colonists. Here, too, she meets Nathaniel Eaton, the sea captain's son, with his mocking smile and clear blue eyes. Little Prudence, whose doll Kit had rescued, also comes to the sanctuary in the meadows. One by one, outraged townspeople put the wrong things together and the result is a terrifying witch hunt and trial. The story is fast-paced and the characters are drawn in sharp relief against a bleak New England background that shows a greening of promise for spring and Kit at the close of this magnificent story.

Although the subject is the same, the tone of *Tituba of Salem Village* by Petry is as forbidding as the rotten eggs found on the steps of the bleak parsonage the day that the Reverend Samuel Parris, family, and slaves, John and Tituba, arrived in Salem Village in 1692. Tituba, too, had come from sunny Barbados and then been sold as a slave to a self-seeking, pious minister. The fact that Tituba was both a slave and Negro made her particularly vulnerable to suspicion and attack from the obsessed witch hunters in Salem. A sense of foreboding, mounting terror, and hysteria fill this story of great evil done in the name of God. A comparison of *The Witch of Blackbird Pond* and *Tituba of Salem Village* would provoke much critical thinking by mature readers.

Other settlers followed the Pilgrims. One, in particular, has been immortalized for younger children by Alice Dalgliesh in her popular book *The Courage of Sarah Noble* This is the true and inspiring story of eight-year-old Sarah who accompanies her father into the wilderness to cook for him while he builds a cabin for their family. Many times, Sarah has to remind herself of

[30]Jean Lee Latham, *This Dear Bought Land*, Illustrated by Jacob Landau (New York: Harper & Row, 1957), p. 246.

her mother's final words to her when she left home, "Keep up your courage, Sarah Noble!" Sarah has reason to remember when she hears the wolves howl outside the campfire, or when alone one day, she is suddenly surrounded by Indian children. The real test of her courage is faced when her father tells her that he must leave her with Tall John, a friendly Indian, while he returns to Massachusetts for the rest of the family. Symbolic of Sarah's courage is the cloak that Sarah's mother had fastened on her just before leaving home. When her family are finally reunited in their new home in the wilderness, Sarah is secure in the knowledge that she has "kept up her courage."

> That night Sarah slept under the quilts. On a peg near by hung her cloak—and she did not need it. She had kept up her courage and it was something that would always be with her. Always—even when the cloak was all worn out.[31]

This book might be compared with Jean Fritz's poignant story of lonely ten-year-old Ann Hamilton who was the only girl in the wilderness of early western Pennsylvania. Ann, too, kept a diary filled with her longing for her cousin Margaret and the girl-fun she had enjoyed on the other side of the Allegheny Mountains in Gettysburg. The title of this book, *The Cabin Faced West,* characterizes Ann's father's attitude towards the family's new adventure. They were not to look back to the past, but forward, and so he built his cabin facing in that direction. Ann grows to hate the word "someday" as she hears it again and again. Someday she would have books to read, someday they would have windows in the cabin, and someday there would be a special occasion to use the linen table cloth and the lavender flowered plates that her mother kept in her chest. All the

"somedays" seemed so very far away to Ann. At last, however, a special occasion did happen. George Washington stopped at the Hamilton cabin for dinner. Ann wore ribbons in her hair and set the table in the way she had longed to do. This final episode is based upon fact and really happened to Ann Hamilton, who was the author's own great-great grandmother.

Marguerite de Angeli is known for her many books about religious or regional minorities. Some of these have an historical background. *Elin's Amerika* describes the life of children in the settlement of New Sweden on the Delaware in 1648. The unique contributions of the Swedish pioneers are emphasized throughout the story. *Skippack School* is the story of Eli Shrawder, who came from across the sea to make a home in the Mennonite Settlement on the Skippack River in Pennsylvania. Eli was a mischievous lad who preferred to go fishing, chase squirrels, and carve wood than go to school. However, with a schoolmaster such as Christopher Dock who is remembered in the history of Germantown of the 1750s as one of the most beloved and far-seeing schoolmasters of our country, Eli soon mended his ways and found himself anxious to go to school.

Indian raids instigated by the French were of grim concern for the Dutch settlers living in the Hudson Valley in 1756. In *The Matchlock Gun,* Walter D. Edmonds tells the true story of the Van Alstyne family. Hearing that the Indians are raiding Dutch homes, Teunis, the sturdy Dutch father, is summoned to watch for marauding Indians. Before leaving, he takes the great matchlock gun down from the wall and shows young Edward how to fire it. When the Indians do come, Edward's mother gives the command to fire the matchlock gun. The shot kills the Indians but does not save the mother from a flying tomahawk that pierces her shoulder. Edward drags his unconscious mother from the step of the burning cabin and waits with

---

[31]Alice Dalgliesh, *The Courage of Sarah Noble,* Illustrated by Leonard Weisgard (New York: Scribner, 1954), p. 54.

Trudy for their father to return with the militia. When Teunis rides in with his friends, he finds his wife still unconscious, the baby asleep, and Edward with the matchlock gun in his lap aimed at three dead Indians.

This is much more than an exciting adventure story. The characters are very real and true to life. The reader and the children sense the fear and the anxiety of the parents when they hear of the Indian raid. After their father had gone, the children are alone in the loft.

> There was only the note of the wind in the chimney and the feeling of it on the roof, like a hand pressed down out of darkness. It was easy to think of it passing through the wet woods, rocking the bare branches where only the beech trees had leaves to shake.[32]

This is a book that pleases both the critics and the children. It won the Newbery Award for the most distinguished contribution to literature in 1941, and it has won the interest and devotion of boys in the middle grades ever since it was published.

The winds of war may brush children lightly but still stir them deeply. In *Adam and the Golden Cock*, Dalgliesh has told the story of a boy during the American Revolution. Added to the excitement of the arrival of the regiments of Rochambeau is the new doubt and suspicion that Adam feels for his friend Paul, a Tory's son. This book provides a clear sense of history in the making, but the plot is not as interesting or well-defined as in *The Courage of Sarah Noble* by the same author.

As boys and girls in the middle grades read *The Scarlet Badge* by Wilma Pitchford Hays, they may learn that there was justification for different points of view concerning the American Revolution. Rob Roberts was a Virginian, and fiercely proud of the colony in which his forebears had lived for more than 150 years. Now the flames of the revolution blazed, and the Roberts family could no longer hope for a peaceful settlement of the wrongs imposed on the Colonies by King George III; they had to choose between the Rebels and the Loyalists. They made their choice, and Rob soon learned the price of that choice—the courage needed to stand fast in an unpopular cause. In a world turned upside down, he saw revolution and rebellion become patriotism, loyalty to his king called treason, and friends and neighbors become strangers and enemies. Well-documented, this book from the Colonial Williamsburg press will help children see the Revolution in a different perspective and value the importance of standing up for what one believes to be right.

Leonard Wibberly has written a series of four books about the Revolutionary War, *John Treegate's Musket, Peter Treegate's War, Sea Captain from Salem,* and *Treegate's Raiders.* John Treegate was a solid citizen of Boston who had fought for his king and country in the Battle of Quebec on the Plains of Abraham. He was loyal to his British king, and had taught his son, Peter, to be loyal, too. However, he could not tolerate a country that marched armed troops of 700 men through a peaceful countryside to seize two men. John and Peter Treegate, father and son, arm themselves for the battle against the British that would go down in history as the Battle of Bunker Hill. The first year of the Revolution as seen through Peter's eyes is recorded in *Peter Treegate's War.* The *Sea Captain from Salem* is the story of a raider ship that cruises around the British Isles attacking British ships, sinking them or taking them as prizes. The final book of the series, *Treegate's Raiders,* describes the Revolution in the South in the highlands of the Carolinas. This story ends with the surrender of Cornwallis at Yorktown.

Probably no story for children of the

---

[32]Walter D. Edmonds, *The Matchlock Gun,* Illustrated by Paul Lantz (New York: Dodd, Mead, 1941), p. 14.

American Revolution is better known than the fine juvenile novel of *Johnny Tremain* by Esther Forbes. The story grew out of the research that the author had done for her adult biography of Paul Revere. Johnny Tremain is a silversmith's apprentice, a conceited, cocky young lad who is good at his trade and knows it. The other apprentices are resentful of his overbearing manner and determine to get even with him. Their practical joke has disastrous results, and Johnny's hand is maimed for life. Out of a job and embittered, Johnny joins his friend, Rab, and becomes involved in pre-Revolutionary activities. As a dispatch rider for the Committee of Public Safety, he meets such men as Paul Revere, John Hancock, and Samuel Adams. Slowly, gradually, Johnny regains his self-confidence and overcomes his bitterness. His friend, Rab, is killed in the first skirmish of the Revolution, and Johnny is crushed, but not completely. Somehow, this greatest of blows toughens his fiber and he becomes a man—a man of fortitude and courage—a new man of a new nation.

Tree of Freedom by Rebecca Caudill describes the Revolution from the backwoods settlers' point of view. In the year 1780, thirteen-year-old Stephanie Venable made the long trek from North Carolina to Kentucky where her family had a tract of rich new land waiting for them. Each child of the family is allowed to take one prized possession. Stephanie takes an apple seed because that is what her grandmother had brought from France. Stephanie plants her little tree by the side of their cabin door and calls it her "Tree of Freedom," a symbol of the new way of life the pioneering families meant to have in the fresh green land. Kentucky was full of promise and hardship. After they had built their cabin and planted their crops, a Britisher arrived with rival claims to their land. Now the Revolution became more important than ever, for the legality of their claim depended upon belonging to a new

nation. One by one, their father, Noel, and Jonathan left to serve their country, leaving the back-breaking care of the crops to resourceful Stephanie, her mother, and young Rob. Always, Stephanie had time to prune and care for her little tree. When her family returned from war and the quarrel between Noel and her father is resolved, Stephanie tells herself:

> *Everything was all right then. . . . A body couldn't kill freedom any more than he could kill a tree if it had good, strong roots growing, she reckoned. No matter what passed over the land and possessed the people, you couldn't kill freedom if somebody gave it uncommon good care.*[33]

The American Frontier   No other period in United States history has been more dramatized by films and television than that of the Westward Movement of the American pioneer. For this reason, even seven-year-olds ask for books about "the pioneers." One favorite for younger children is *Caroline and Her Kettle Named Maud* by Miriam E. Mason. Caroline is a pioneer tomboy who longs for a real gun for her birthday just like her seventeen uncles. Instead, she receives a copper kettle that proves just as effective as a gun in capturing the wolf that threatens the family cows.

Carolina's Courage is the well-written story by Elizabeth Yates of one family's journey from New Hampshire to Nebraska. Carolina, her brother, Mark, and her father and mother were leaving their farm in New Hampshire for the West. Each member of the family could take only one personal possession in the crowded covered wagon. Carolina chose her beloved doll, Lydia-Lou, with her painted china face, black, buttoned shoes, and layers of petticoats and party dresses. All across that endless prairie,

[33]Rebecca Caudill, *Tree of Freedom,* Illustrated by Dorothy Morse (New York: Viking, 1947), p. 263.

Carolina proudly displays her doll's many petticoats to her Indian visitor. The Indian girl's delight and desire are portrayed in her hands and posture. Her own doll lies partially hidden in her lap, giving little clue to the dramatic role it will play in the story. From the book *Carolina's Courage* by Elizabeth Yates. Illustrated by Nora S. Unwin. Copyright, ©, 1964 by Elizabeth Yates McGreal and Nora S. Unwin. Reproduced by permission of E. P. Dutton & Co., Inc.

Lyddy was good company for Carolina. As they neared their claim, rumors of unfriendly Indians stirred their hearts with fear, and her father sat all night by the fire, his gun across his knees. But the night passed without incident and morning came:

> It was good to be alive on such a morning. They had been walking into the future for four months. Now it seemed that the future was at last coming to meet them. Fears felt during the night had shrunk to daylight size, and the family talked together easily and naturally.[34]

However, the trip was not finished, for the family came to an encampment of wagons waiting for an interpreter before going any further into Indian territory. Carolina found a green, mossy place in the woods, quite perfect for a tea party with Lyddy. Startled by a noise, Carolina looked up to find that an Indian girl carrying a doll made of hide

---

[34]Elizabeth Yates, *Carolina's Courage,* Illustrated by Nora S. Unwin (New York: Dutton, 1964), p. 64.

had joined her. After they exchanged dolls, the Indian girl made many strange motions with her hands and darted away still holding Lyddy. Truly courageous, Carolina remembered that her father had said that pioneers had to share. That evening her parents found her asleep clutching the greasy Indian doll as closely as she had slept with Lyddy. When she poured out her story to her father, he slowly interpreted the Indian girl's signs as promising a safe passage through the mountains. So with "Safe Conduct," as they named the Indian doll, sitting on Carolina's knees, the Putnams headed the wagon train. At different times during the day Indians rode down, circled the wagon and pointed the way for the friend of the Indian chief's daughter who had a new china doll with many petticoats.

No books of historical fiction are more loved than the eight "Little House" books by Laura Ingalls Wilder. These stories tell of the growing up of the Ingalls girls and the Wilder boys. In the first book of the series, *Little House in the Big Woods,* Laura is only six years old; the last two books, *Little Town on the Prairie* and *These Happy Golden Years,* tell of Laura's teaching and her marriage. Based upon the author's own life, these books portray the hardships and difficulties of pioneer life in the 1870s and 1880s, and describe the fun and excitement that was a part of the daily living. Throughout the stories, the warmth and security of family love runs like a golden thread that binds the books to the hearts of their readers. There are floods, blizzards, grasshopper plagues, bears and Indians, droughts and the fear of starvation; but there is the wonderful Christmas when Laura receives her rag doll, the new house with real windows, trips to town, and dances. Best of all, there are the long winter evenings of firelight and the clear singing of Pa's fiddle. These mean love and security whether their home is in Wisconsin, the wild Kansas country as described in *Little House on* the *Prairie,* in the Minnesota of *On the Banks of Plum Creek,* or *By the Shores of Silver Lake* in Dakota Territory. Children who read these books sense the same feelings of love and family solidarity as experienced by Laura in the closing pages of *Little House in the Big Woods:*

> But Laura lay awake a little while, listening to Pa's fiddle softly playing and to the lovely sound of the wind in the Big Woods. She looked at Pa sitting on the bench by the hearth, the firelight gleaming on his brown hair and beard and glistening over the honey-brown fiddle. She looked at Ma, gently rocking and knitting.
> She thought to herself, "This is now."
> She was glad that the cosy house, and Pa and Ma and the firelight and the music, were now. They could not be forgotten, she thought, because now is now. It can never be a long time ago.[35]

A uniform edition of all eight of Mrs. Wilder's books was published in 1953 and profusely illustrated by Garth Williams' black-and-white sketches. He has captured the excitement and terror of many of the episodes in the books, but he also conveys the tenderness, love, amusement, and courage that were necessary requisites to the life of the early settlers.

Another favorite book of pioneer days is *Caddie Woodlawn* by Carol Ryrie Brink. While this story takes place in the Wisconsin wilderness during the 1860s, it is primarily the story of the growing up of tomboy Caddie. She had been a frail baby, and her father had persuaded her mother to allow her to be raised more freely than her older sister, Clara, who was restricted by the rules of decorum for young ladies. So, Caddie was free to run about the half-wild Wisconsin frontier with her two brothers. Their escapades and

A tender Christmas scene exemplifies the warmth and simple joy of pioneer living. Cover illustration by Garth Williams from *Little House in the Big Woods* by Laura Ingalls Wilder. Harper & Row, 1953.

adventures read like a pioneer "Tom Sawyer." However, the pranks they played on their cousin Annabelle from the city were harder on Caddie than Annabelle. Gradually, but surely, Caddie grows up.

Not all pioneer stories are about girls. William Steele's many exciting books of frontier life are almost always about boys. In *The Lone Hunt,* he writes vividly of a boy's yearning to take a man's part in the last buffalo hunt held in Tennessee in 1810. Ever since his father died, Yance Caywood had had to help his mother with fetching, carrying, and hoeing, while his older brother did the plowing and hunting. At last, he is al-

[35]Laura Ingalls Wilder, *Little House in the Big Woods,* Illustrated by Garth Williams (New York: Harper & Row, 1953), p. 238.

lowed to go on the buffalo hunt, taking along his well-loved hound dog, Blue. It is a long trail, and one by one, the men drop out. When the snow begins, the last one turns back, but not Yance. His lone hunt through the wilderness takes courage, amazing ingenuity, and fortitude. Yance kills his buffalo but loses his dog to the frozen river. Pride in his accomplishment is overshadowed by his grief for his dog. Yance is grown up when he returns from his lone hunt.

William Steele is not afraid of realism for children. Frontier living had its terror and horror, and Steele recreates it with authentic detail. In *The Year of the Bloody Sevens,* eleven-year-old Kelsey Bond decided to go west to Kentucky to join his father at Logan's Fort. He joins two "woodsies" for safety and companionship, but one day they are ambushed by Indians. Kel knows he should go to their aid but he can't make his legs move. When he does return to the campsite, he finds both of them dead. Kel runs away, but he brands himself as a coward. Even after he reaches the Fort and finds his father, the knowledge of his cowardice festers inside of him. At last, he tells his father, who reassures him that it took much courage for Kel to come to Kentucky. Kel had known that it would be wrong to give up, but he had never thought that he was brave. "But maybe it had been. Maybe the bravest things were the things you did without knowing you were being brave, without expecting other people to know you were brave."[36] Realism, excitement, and much backwoods wisdom that contains a ring of truth for the twentieth century characterize Steele's writing. His other pioneer stories include *Winter Danger, The Buffalo Knife, Tomahawks and Trouble, Flaming Arrows,* and *Trail Through Danger.*

Fourteen-year-old Jim Fraley was the only boy to go along with Colonel Zane and his eleven men to blaze the Ohio Trail in 1796. *Trace through the Forest,* written by Robinson, is an exciting account of the Zane Expedition from Wheeling, West Virginia, to Maysville, Kentucky. Jim was allowed to go in order to search for his father and older brother, Jeb, who had been away for over a year looking for a place to settle in the Ohio Territory. The party of men meet a lone Indian named Wapanucket who offers to be their scout and becomes Jim's friend. After many adventures, Jim finally finds his father, held captive by a warring tribe; his brother had died of a fever. Jim manages to rescue his father who then plans to bring the rest of his family west to farm on the land he selected. Farming is not for Jim, so he joins forces with his friend, Wapanucket, to trap and live in the woods. Woven into the many exciting adventures of this story is the graphic presentation of what the opening of the new territory meant to both Indians and white men.

Two Logs Crossing, John Haskell's Story is an absorbing and moving account of a sixteen-year-old boy who goes fur trading with an Indian in the northern woods of New York State in order to pay back his father's debt and support his widowed mother, brothers, and sisters. Determined to amount to something, John bravely faces the loss of his first year's trapping. This is the story of the growing up of John Haskell and at the same time the story of America. For, as the author states in his foreword:

> *To be able to do for oneself in one's own way was the dream which first brought some people to this land. There are a few people who confuse it with becoming rich, but money is not the American Dream and never has been. Money can be made of anything you choose, but a man's life is made of courage, independence, decency and self-respect he learns to use.*[37]

---

[36]William O. Steele, *The Year of the Bloody Sevens,* Illustrated by Charles Beck (New York: Harcourt, 1963), p. 184.

[37]Walter D. Edmonds, In the author's foreword to *Two Logs Crossing, John Haskell's Story,* Illustrated by Tibor Gergely (New York: Dodd Mead, 1943).

When Adam Crane finished school in 1850, there seemed only two career choices open to him; the sea or the land. Although his father was a sea captain, Adam had always planned on starting the new farm that had long been his family's dream. In *I, Adam* by Jean Fritz, Adam precedes the family to the farm and meets with treachery from the former owner, friendship of neighbors, and inspiration from the schoolmaster. Adam proves his physical stamina and courage by making a success of the farm in the face of many hardships. His moral courage is tested when his father returns from his last trip at sea with only one leg. Adam had decided to tell his father that farming was not for him, he wanted to go on to school. Now, he felt he could never reveal this desire. However, his understanding father senses Adam's restlessness and maintains that he would much prefer to have a scholar for a son than a farmer. Besides portraying an excellent father-son relationship, this book vividly recreates the details of farm, city, and village life in the 1850s.

The great westward trek continued as the frontier was pushed back further and further each year. The moving story of the Sager children is told by A. Rutgers van der Loeff in *Oregon at Last!* When both their parents die on the westward trail, the rest of the settlers want to divide the family of seven children among them, but they had not counted on the determination of thirteen-year-old John. When the men decide to go to California rather than tackle the difficult trail over the mountains to Oregon, John plans secretly with the rest of the children and they quietly steal away from camp. How they survive bears, fire, quicksand and a walk over one thousand miles of mountainous trails to reach Oregon is an incredible story. Always driving them on was the unquenchable spirit of young John Sager who was determined to fulfill their father's dream of settling in the Columbia River Valley. At

last they reach the Whitman mission, and John begs Marcus and Narcissa Whitman to take them in. The baby, Indepentia, was near death from starvation and exposure, but when Mrs. Whitman pressed a few drops of warm milk between her blue lips, she swallowed. That night John leaned his thin, shaking body against Marcus and sobbed:

"Take the load off me . . . I can't go on, I can't. They don't love me any more, they couldn't understand, and I love them so much. I've beaten them, I've dragged them along . . . and now we've got here, and they don't love me any more! Please won't you help me? I can't go on!"[38]

Later he repeated his question, and with the plea of a boy grown man before his time he said, "'Won't you take care of us? I want to . . . play with them again.' The last had been spoken very softly. Like an admission of guilt."[39]

Civil War Fiction of the Civil War period may be valuable in helping children understand a period of history in which brothers fought against brothers and our nation was divided. Many stories of the Civil War revolve around the activities of the Underground Railroad when men faced the moral issue of breaking laws out of their compassion for mankind. In Marguerite de Angeli's book, *Thee, Hannah*, a young girl is able to help a Negro mother and her child who were sick and weary from days of walking and hiding. Hannah was a Quaker, but she did not willingly wear the clothes that were necessary to fulfill her family's religious expectations. She particularly despised her stiff, drab bonnet that did not have flowers and a brightly colored lining like that of her friend, Cecily. Yet, it was her bonnet that

---

[38]A. Rutgers van der Loeff, *Oregon at Last!*, Illustrated by Charles Geer, Translated from the Dutch by Roy Edwards (New York: Morrow, 1961), p. 217.
[39]Van der Loeff, pp. 217–218.

identified her as a Quaker and one who could be trusted to give aid to a runaway slave. Later, when the Negro is safe and tells Hannah this, Hannah's feelings toward her hated bonnet change.

In *Brady*, Jean Fritz tells the story of a very believable boy who discovers his father is an agent for the Underground Railway. His parents had not told Brady of their forbidden activities, for Brady just could not keep a secret. However, Brady, always curious, discovers the secret for himself. On the very night that had been set to transfer a slave to the next station, Brady's father's barn is burned, and his father suffers a broken leg during the fire. Unbeknown to his father, Brady carries out the plan for moving the slave and earns his father's respect. When his father hears of his son's resourcefulness, he asks for the family Bible and painstakingly writes the following inscription on the page reserved for significant events of family history:

> On this day the barn burned down and Brady Minton did a man's work.[40]

By Secret Railway by Meadowcroft is another popular story about the work of the Underground Railway. David Morgan brings a young Negro boy home with him one day after he had gone down to the wharf to find a job. David's family welcome Jim, but he is with them only a short while. After Jim's freedom papers were destroyed, he was kidnapped and sold again as a slave. From runaway slaves, the Morgans learn that Jim is in Missouri. David is determined to rescue him and eventually finds him. The suspense is high when the boys are captured on their way home. They work their way out of their difficulties and finally reach Chicago, where Jim decides to stay with the Morgans.

Thomas Fall has told the moving story of the friendship of a young Scottish indentured boy and a former slave in his book *Canalboat to Freedom*. Benja did not know that indenture was illegal when he became a "hoggee" for Captain Roach in return for his passage to America. It was Benja's exhausting and lonely job to walk miles along the towpaths each day leading the horses that pulled the canalboat. His only friend was the deckhand Lundius, a former slave, who patiently taught him the ways of nature and protected him from the bullying captain. Benja joins Lundius in helping two fugitive slaves to escape. One frightening morning Lundius loses his life, and Benja must carry out the escape of the slave with only the help of Kate and Mrs. Robbins. Heartsick at the loss of their loyal friend, Kate and Benja climb to the crest of the mountain and recall his goodness:

> They sat in silence—a strangely satisfying silence that was filled with Lundius and a sense of what they had learned from him. He had been a slave, treated as an animal, brutally disfigured by the hands of men—and he had come into their lives and by his strength and gentleness had taught them to love.[41]

The Perilous Road is a superb story of a boy caught between the divided loyalties of the Civil War. Chris Brabson, not quite twelve, lived in Tennessee, and was certain he hated the Union troops. When the Yankee raiders steal his family's newly harvested crops, the Brabsons' only horse, and his new deerskin shirt, Chris is determined to have revenge and sets out singlehandedly to achieve it. He reveals the position of a Union wagon train to a person he believes is a spy. Too late, he realizes his brother, who is with the Union troops, could be with the group. Chris tries to find him to warn him and finally spends the night with the Union troops who have befriended him. He is caught in a bitter battle at dawn when the Confederates make a surprise attack. Chris realizes that

[40]Jean Fritz, *Brady*, Illustrated by Lynd Ward (New York: Coward-McCann, 1960), p. 219.

[41]Thomas Fall, *Canalboat to Freedom*, Illustrated by Joseph Cellini (New York: Dial, 1966), p. 160.

even a Union soldier may "be a good and decent man." He understands the full meaning of his father's words, "Like I told you before, war is the worst thing that can happen to folks and the reason is it makes most everybody do things they shouldn't."[42]

Joanne Williamson portrays the Civil War as seen through the eyes of a young immigrant boy recently arrived in New York from Germany. At first, the struggle between the states does not seem as important to Martin Hester as the internal strife among various national and political groups within New York City. But then he meets Aaron, a fugitive slave, and the battle for an individual's right to be free, becomes Martin's consuming interest. As a young news reporter for the *Tribune*, he has ample opportunity to debate the issues of the day and even covers the Battle of Gettysburg. Few history or trade books for children present the intense feelings against Civil War, President Lincoln, and the Abolitionists that was felt by many Political groups in Northern cities. This dimension of the many-faceted struggle of the Civil War is effectively recreated in this book, *And Forever Free* . . . .

In *Orphans of the Wind*, Erik Haugaard has told the story of the Civil War from the various points of view expressed by an English crew when they discover that the ship they are sailing is a blockade runner. The men are divided in their hatred of slavery. Finally, a crazed carpenter sets fire to the old brig, and the men rush for the life boats. Four of the young sailors who land on the Southern coast are determined to walk north until they could join the Union cause. They decide it would be easier to hide *in* the Southern army than to hide *from* it, so they enlist and move rapidly to the North. They are caught in the Battle of Bull Run, and one of them is killed. The other two do join

the Union Army, while Jim, the twelve-year-old boy, sails once again, but this time on an American ship. There is much strength and sensitivity in any story that Haugaard tells. Many of the passages are poetic in nature. For example, when the boys part, the twelve-year-old can not stop his flow of tears.

Yet tears will stop and cheeks bathed in sorrow will dry. Those who are capable of loving will feel the pain of parting so hard that sometimes they will curse their gift; for they know not and cannot imagine the horror of the world of those who are locked in themselves, hidden in those icy caverns where a brother's laughter or his tears cannot be heard.[43]

The effect of the war on a frontier family in Illinois has been told by Irene Hunt in the fine historical novel, *Across Five Aprils*. Jethro Creighton is only nine years old at the outbreak of the war that first seemed so exciting and wonderful. But one by one, Jethro's brothers, cousins, and his beloved schoolteacher enlist in the Northern army. His favorite brother, Bill, after a long struggle with his conscience, joins the South. As the war continues, Jethro learns that it is not glorious and exciting but heartbreaking and disruptive of all kinds of relationships. Although the many letters used to carry the action of the story to different places and provide historical detail make difficult reading, this is a beautifully written, thought-provoking book.

Rifles for Watie by Harold Keith tells of the life of a Union soldier and spy engaged in the fighting of the Western campaign of the Civil War. Jefferson Davis Bussey, a young farm boy from Kansas, joins the Union forces, becomes a scout, and quite accidentally, a member of Stand Watie's Cherokee Rebels. Jeff was probably one of the few soldiers in the West to see the Civil War from

---

[42]William O. Steele, *The Perilous Road*, Illustrated by Paul Galdone (New York: Harcourt, 1958), pp. 188–189.

[43]Erik Haugaard, *Orphans of the Wind*, Illustrated by Milton Johnson (Boston: Houghton Mifflin, 1966), p. 182.

both sides. This is a fast-paced novel, rich in detail, with fine characterizations.

The United States through 1900 Stories of the Civil War and Westward Expansion constitute the settings for the bulk of children's historical fiction of the nineteenth century. The few stories of the late nineteenth and early twentieth centuries are frequently nostalgic reminiscences that create a feeling for the period, but have little historical significance.

Patricia Beatty has told a fine family story of the Kimballs, who lived in 1886 on the coast of Washington Territory. *The Nickel-Plated Beauty* was the Sunshine Stove that thirteen-year-old Whit had ordered for Mother from the Montgomery Ward catalogue without realizing the meaning of C.O.D. All seven of the children go to work digging clams and picking berries; Whit works at the general store and Hester at the Palace Hotel until at last they have enough saved to redeem the nickel-plated beauty from the miserly Mr. Willard. There is much fun in this lively story of a family's determination to buy a present for their hardworking mother.

Good fun and tongue-in-cheek humor enliven the story of *Mr. Mysterious and Company* by Fleischman. In this book, a delightful family of traveling magicians journey to California in the 1880s in their gaily painted wagon, making one-night stands in many frontier towns. All the children share a part in the magic show: Jane as a floating princess, Paul as a Sphinx who knows all the answers including the identity of the Badlands Kid, and Anne as the little girl who is transformed from a big rag doll. Pa trades his cherished chiming watch for a maltreated dog for the children, and the children, in turn, decide to spend their reward money to buy their father another watch. This is a fine family story that gives a feeling for life in the frontier towns of the West. *By the Great Horn Spoon!*, also written by Fleischman, tells of the Gold Rush days. It is more correctly a tall tale rather than historical fiction.

The Great Wheel by Robert Lawson is the story of Conn Kilroy who helped to build the first Ferris wheel for the World's Columbian Exposition of 1893. When Conn was twelve years old, his Aunt Honora had read his fortune in the tea leaves of his cup and told him: "Your fortune lies to the west. Keep your face to the sunset and follow the evening star, and one day you'll ride the greatest wheel in all the world."[44] This is the story of the fulfillment of that prophecy. It conveys the flavor of the lusty life of Chicago as the many immigrants poured into this melting pot. Some children may not like the slight romantic thread in this plot. *The Great Wheel* is the last book that Robert Lawson wrote and illustrated with his humorous pictures that so complement the wit and deft characterizations of this amusing tale.

Roller Skates by Ruth Sawyer is autobiographical rather than historical, but it does give a rich picture of New York City in the 1890s. Left with an understanding teacher when her family went to Europe, ten-year-old Lucinda was gloriously free to explore New York City on her roller skates. She made friends with Patrick Gilligan and his hansom cab, with Policeman M'Gonegal, with the fruit vendor, Vittore Coppicio, and his son, Tony, and with many others. Much of the gaiety and sorrow of that year are recorded in the perceptive entries of Lucinda's diary. A comparison of Lucinda's New York with that of Harriet's in *Harriet, the Spy* by Fitzhugh (see Chapter 5) might be most worthwhile. Both Harriet and Lucinda kept diaries but for very different purposes, and both girls had personalities that were not afraid to express their opinions—but here the comparison ends. No psychiatrist

---

[44]Robert Lawson, *The Great Wheel* (New York: Viking, 1957), p. 12.

could help Harriet achieve the sensitivity and zest for living that were a natural part of Lucinda's personality.

Libby Fletcher was told that you have to get used to *The Taste of Spruce Gum* which, to most non-Vermonters, tastes like turpentine. But Libby had to get used to a whole new way of life; a new Papa, a lumpy, straw mattress in a new house, and living up on a mountain in a lumber mill filled with rough characters. Formerly sheltered, Libby is spared little in this strange new environment. The lumberjacks get drunk and beat their wives; she helps as her mother is called upon to be midwife for the birth of a baby girl; she watches their home burn down on Christmas night; and she overhears her mother quarreling with her new husband about the dishonesty of his oldest brother. It is almost too much for an eleven-year-old to bear, but Libby has as much gumption as her mother, and, like the taste of spruce gum, she gets used to her new Vermont home and comes to love it *and* her new Papa. Jacqueline Jackson has told a realistic story of life in a lumber camp in 1903. The plot is fast-paced, occasionally melodramatic, but with characters that live and speak of their time.

Barrie & Daughter by Rebecca Caudill is the story of one man's determined fight to right certain wrongs in the Black Mountains of southeastern Kentucky in the early 1900s. When the Scollards, who owned the only store in town, began taking advantage of the farmers, Peter Barrie decides that competition might bring justice, and opens a store in his smokehouse. A mountain feud seethes, and Barrie finds that victory, as always, belongs to the stout at heart. Not alone in his battle, Peter Barrie has the loyal support of Fern, his enterprising daughter, Blanche Barrie, his firm but understanding wife, George Wooten, a teacher ahead of his times, and others who would fight for integrity and justice. The characters are beautifully drawn in this convincing story of one

man's struggle for democratic principles. The author creates a poignant moment as Fern watches her little sister joyously go off for her first day of school with the beloved schoolmaster, and she finds herself envying Letty.

> *She remembered how the soft, hot dust squished between her toes the first day she went to school, how George had led her as he was leading Letty now, how he had taught her to love books and all things of which books are made—the sky, the earth, running water, the seasons, and the ways of people.*[45]

This is a story that has sustained action and substance. It is a moving tribute to the thousands of little-known Americans who have made this country great by their determination to strike out against injustice.

Historical Fiction—The Old World

There are fewer stories with Old World settings than those of the New World. Increasingly, however, American children have access to books published in England and Europe. These books, plus those written in the United States, have produced a growing body of fine historical fiction of the Old World. Some of the most distinguished are described in the following pages.

Ancient Times   The ancient world of Egypt with all of its political intrigue provides a rich background for Eloise McGraw's story of a slave girl, *Mara, Daughter of the Nile.* Mara, the mistreated slave of a wealthy jewel trader, is bought by a mysterious man who offers her luxury in turn for her services as a spy for the queen. On a Nile riverboat, Mara meets Lord Sheftu, who employs her as a spy for the king! In this exciting and

---

[45]Rebecca Caudill, *Barrie & Daughter,* Illustrated by Berkeley Williams, Jr. (New York: Viking, 1943), p. 76.

sinister story of espionage and counterespionage, Mara endures torture for her love of Lord Sheftu and her loyalty to Egypt and its rightful king. The transformation of Mara from a selfish, deceitful slave to a loyal and courageous young woman is made slowly and believably. Plot and characterization are just as skillfully developed in McGraw's second book about Egypt, *The Golden Goblet*. In this fast-paced story, Ranofer finds that his cruel and grasping half-brother has been stealing gold scraps from the goldhouse. The discovery of a golden goblet leads Ranofer to suspect the worst—his brother is plundering the sacred tombs of the Pharaohs. Both these books with their intricate plots and excellent characterizations make the life and times of ancient Egypt come vividly alive for mature readers from twelve to fifteen.

Daniel Bar Jamin had but one all-consuming purpose in his life, to revenge the cruel death of his father and mother by driving the Romans out of his land of Israel. First with an outlaw band, and then with a group of boy guerrillas, Daniel nurses his hatred and waits for the hour to strike. He takes comfort in the verse from II Samuel 22:35—"He trains my hands for war, so that my arms can bend a bow of bronze." Seen as a symbol for what *no man* can do, *The Bronze Bow* is the title of the story of Daniel's tormented journey from blind hatred to his acceptance and understanding of love. Only after he has nearly sacrificed his friends and driven his sister, Leah, deeper into mental darkness, does he seek the help of Simon's friend, Jesus. After he has poured out his troubles to this gentle teacher, Jesus speaks to him and tells him:

> . . . *it is hate that is the enemy, not men. Hate does not die with killing. It only springs up a hundredfold. The only thing stronger than hate is love.*[46]

The healing strength of Jesus cures Leah and, at that moment, Daniel can forgive the Romans. He understands at last that only love can bend the bow of bronze. Each character stands out in this startling story of the conflict of good and evil, of love overcoming hate.

In *The Iron Charm*, Joanne Williamson has told another story in which revenge dies slowly. This time a young Roman patrician, Marcus Malcius, is kidnapped and sold into slavery during the sixth century. While on a slave ship bound for Constantinople, Marcus receives an iron charm from another dying slave—it is an amulet to the old god, Lugh. Marcus tries to return to Rome and his father, but he is tricked once again and sent to Briton as a seaman. In his pilgrimage, Marcus touches the lives of people who became the rulers of their century—Justinian, and Arthur and Guinevere. Before he reaches Rome again, Marcus has experienced all of the vagaries of life which sixth-century Europe could offer. No longer a slave, Marcus finds contentment in being a good shoemaker and forgives Joseppi, who first betrayed him into slavery. Joanne Williamson has a remarkable ability to create a feeling for the place and people of this early Christian era.

The Romans did not rule the ancient world without bloody conflict. In Baumann's *I Marched with Hannibal*, an old man relives his experiences as a twelve-year-old elephant driver with Hannibal on his march across the Alps to Rome with 45,000 men, 6000 horses and 39 elephants. In this first-person narrative, the reader learns much about this intrepid young general, the tortuous journey, and the ways of war. Primarily, however, this is the story of Suru, Hannibal's favorite elephant, and the last to survive. Upon Suru's death, the boy deserts the army and returns to the ruins of Saguntum where Suru had first found him, the only living person in those smoldering ruins. This is a grim but powerful story of the ruthlessness of war.

---

[46]Elizabeth George Speare, *The Bronze Bow* (Boston: Houghton Mifflin, 1961), p. 224.

Viking Adventures While ancient civilizations flourished and decayed in Egypt, Greece, and Rome, the beginnings of European history were just stirring in England, Scotland, and the Scandinavian countries. The stories of the Vikings are a part of the eerie half-light of the predawn of history when facts were recorded only in legend and song. Historians and archeologists gradually have added to our knowledge of these people, but it remained for the creative writer to breathe life into each fact and clothe these rugged adventurers with purpose and being. In *Viking Adventure*, Clyde Bulla has made the Vikings live for the children in third and fourth grades. This is the story of young Sigurd who joins the crew of a ship that sails to verify Leif Ericson's discovery of Wineland a century earlier. After enduring the hardships of the voyage, and witnessing the treacherous murder of the captain, Sigurd escapes from the ill-fated ship and is the only survivor of the trip to the New World. Returning home at last, he asks the old bard to instruct him in writing and reading, so he may record for others what he has seen. In *Beorn the Proud* by Madeleine Polland, the Vikings go on an expedition to plunder rather than to explore. While sacking an Irish village, twelve-year-old Ness is taken captive by Beorn, the willful son of Anlaf, the Sea King. The dramatic story recounts Ness's experiences as Beorn's slave on the doomed ship on which Beorn's father dies. When they finally return to Denmark, Beorn's pride and fiery temper lead him close to disaster time and time again, but the wisdom and gentle Christian ways of Ness help him to overcome his worst enemy, himself. Banished from Denmark with his small band of faithful followers, Beorn swallows his pride and returns to the islands off Ireland, to Ness's former home. Her family forgives him in the joy of her return, and Beorn finds a new life and a new God. The characterization is excellent in this stirring story of individual and tribal conflict placed

Powerful woodcuts portray the evil and heroic Norsemen. Here Eirik, the Fox, hunts not for his namesake, but for Hakon, a thirteen-year-old boy, owner of Rogen—as long as he lives. From *Hakon of Rogen's Saga* by Erik Haugaard. Illustrated by Leo and Diane Dillon. Houghton Mifflin Company. 1963. Reprinted by permission of Houghton Mifflin Company.

against the larger conflict of paganism and Christianity.

Erik Haugaard has written two superb stories of the Vikings that sing with the cadences of the traditional sagas: *Hakon of Rogen's Saga* and *A Slave's Tale*. In the first story, Hakon felt his island home, Rogen, was indestructible—had it not been in his family for nine generations? But his widowed father had rashly kidnapped an earl's daughter for his new bride. With the spring thaws came vengeance, and Hakon was an orphan at the mercy of his evil uncle. Treated as one of his uncle's slaves, Hakon hides in the mountains while Rark and others loyal to his father come to his aid. At last, Hakon, grown wise beyond his years, achieves his birthright along with his manhood. Having tasted the bitter gall of enslavement, if only briefly, his first act is to free Helga, the slave girl with whom he had been raised, saying:

> That is everyone's birthright, his freedom, and the gods have only one message for us, that we must live.[47]

A Slave's Tale continues the story of Hakon and Helga. Anxious to keep his word to Rark, to return the former slave to his homeland, Hakon embarks for Brittany. Helga, determined not to be left alone, stows away on board the ship. All goes well on the trip until they reach their destination and find that Rark's wife has remarried and Rark's friends, the priests, have been killed by a Norse raid. The new priests do not trust the Vikings and unknowingly aid in a tragic plot to kill Rark and the others. Only Hakon, Helga, and two others make their escape to the ship and the handful of men left to guard it. The basic theme of A Slave's Tale is still freedom. Haugaard explores the various dimensions of enslavement; the slavery of the mind that will not let Helga forget that she was *once* a slave, or the slavery of power, the desire to possess all. These books speak to all ages, as profound in the depth of their darkness as in the extent of their light.

Viking's Dawn, The Road to Miklagard, and Viking's Sunset form a trilogy of the life of Harald Sigurdson as told by a well-known English writer, Henry Treece. When he was but a boy Harald went a-viking on the fine new long ship, the Nameless. Disasters followed early fortune, and treachery boarded the ship with looted treasure. Harald at last found his way home, wiser for the hardships and suffering of this voyage of which he was the only survivor, but ready to go again. Henry Treece, like Haugaard, has written these stories with the violent poetic terseness of the old Norse sagas. They do require older, more mature readers.

Tales of Early Britain   The Vikings' control over Great Britain was not to last for long. In Escape to King Alfred, Geoffrey Trease (another excellent English writer) has told the exciting story of three English hostages held by the Danes in Gloucester. After a hazardous escape, they survive a long winter and the battles that restore English control. Some of the Danes were baptized and remained in England. With the marriage of Judith and Olaf, the author shows that the English became part of each group they conquered and were conquered by.

No one has surpassed Rosemary Sutcliff in her ability to recreate the life and times of early Britain. The Eagle of the Ninth, the Silver Branch, and The Lantern Bearers form a trilogy that tells of the period when Britain was ruled by Romans. In the third book, the last of the Roman auxiliaries set sail in their galleys and abandon Britain to the internal strife and menace of invasion by the Saxons. At the last moment, one Roman officer decides that his loyalties lay with Britain rather than the Legions. Aquila returns to his family villa only to have all that he loves destroyed within two days. His father is killed, his sister captured, and he is tied to a tree to be killed by the wolves. In the morning, however, another band of invaders capture him and enslave him. Three years later, he escapes his thralldom, but it is many years before he can rid himself of the black bitterness of his sister's marriage to a Saxon. At last, he finds a measure of contentment: a contentment partly learned from the kind

---

[47]Erik Haugaard, *Hakon of Rogen's Saga,* Illustrated by Leo and Diane Dillon (Boston: Houghton Mifflin, 1963), p. 132.

and gentle Brother Ninnias, partly from the loving loyalty of his British wife, Ness, lastly for his part in saving his sister's son, an enemy Saxon. His life has come full circle; free of bitterness and revenge, Aquila can look to the future. His old friend reflects his thoughts and the theme of this fine book:

> I sometimes think that we stand at sunset. . . . It may be that the night will close over us in the end, but I believe that morning will come again. Morning always grows again out of the darkness, though maybe not for the people who saw the sun go down. We are the Lantern Bearers, my friend; for us to keep something burning, to carry what light we can forward into the darkness and the wind.[48]

Both light and the stirring of the wind symbolize the beginning of a new era in Sutcliff's *Dawn Wind*. The story begins at the end of the Britons' last battle against the Saxons. Defeated fourteen-year-old Owain regains consciousness on a corpse-strewn field—wounded and alone in the world. He starts for home and is joined by a half-starved hound who shields him through his first dreadful night. An old man and woman care for him when he collapses at their door. When he is well enough to travel, he returns home to find his town a gutted shell, deserted except for a ragged orphan girl, Regina. The two decide their only hope lies in Gaul and they head for the coast. Regina becomes desperately ill and Owain takes her to a Saxon settlement knowing that it will mean his freedom. The Saxons help Regina and care for her, but Owain is sold into thralldom. His next eleven years are spent among the conquerors, first as a slave, and later as a free man serving a promise to his dead master as binding as any iron ring. At last, he is free to search for Regina, and he finds her waiting for him in the deserted town where they had first met. She asks, as though eleven years had not interrupted their flight, if they are still going to Gaul. Owain replies, "No. That was for the dark; now, there's a dawn wind stirring. . . ."[49]

Such fine historical fiction may cast a light into the shadows of the past and illuminate the path ahead. For always there is hope in Rosemary Sutcliff's books—hope for the future and the eventual triumph of courage, compassion, and love.

Medieval Times The Dark Ages had two windows to the light, the learning of the monks and the chivalrous deeds of the knights. Even young children in the second grade are intrigued with stories of the days of knighthood. They can easily read Bulla's *Sword in the Tree*, which is the story of a boy who saved his father and Weldon Castle by bravely going to King Arthur. Through treachery, Shan's uncle makes his own brother a captive and takes control of the castle. By remembering where he hid his father's sword in a tree, Shan establishes his identity as the rightful owner of Weldon Castle. This is an easy-reading book with excitement on every page. It has more than just a lively plot, however, for it presents an interesting picture of the justice of the times.

Marguerite de Angeli has written many books, but her finest is *The Door in the Wall*, Newbery Award winner for 1950. Set against a background of fourteenth-century England, de Angeli has painted in words and pictures the dramatic story of Robin, crippled son of Sir John de Bureford. Robin's father has gone off to the Scottish wars, his mother is in service to the Queen, and Robin is to go to the castle in the north to serve as a page to Sir Peter de Lindsay. He becomes ill with a strange malady, however, and is taken to the monastery by Brother Luke. There

---

[48]Rosemary Sutcliff, *The Lantern Bearers*, Illustrated by Charles Keeping (New York: Walck, 1959), pp. 250–251.

[49]Rosemary Sutcliff, *Dawn Wind*, Illustrated by Charles Keeping (New York: Walck, 1962), p. 240.

A mural of textured cloth interprets medieval life as described in historical fiction. Created by Ann Ritchie, student, Purdue University.

Robin learns many things: to whittle, to swim, to read, to write, and above all to have patience—all "doors in the wall," according to Brother Luke. For:

> Whether thou'lt walk soon I know not. This I know. We must teach thy hands to be skilled in many ways, and we must teach thy mind to go about whether thy legs will carry thee or no. For reading is another door in the wall, dost understand, my son?[50]

Robin does learn to walk but only with the aid of the crutches that he makes with his own hands. When he is well enough to travel, Brother Luke takes him to Sir Peter's castle. Robin is fearful of the reception a crippled page might receive, but Sir Peter, like Brother Luke, assures him that everyone has his place in the world and that there are many ways to serve. It is during a seige of the castle that Robin finds his way to aid the king. Finally, Robin, or Sir Robin as he becomes for his exploits, is reunited with his father and mother. This is a beautiful book, in format and text. Mrs. de Angeli visited England and saw many of the churches, castles, and inns that she has portrayed in the background of her pictures. The pageantry of the medieval days and the hardships of living in that period are all conveyed in *The Door in the Wall*.

A well-written story of thirteenth-century Ireland is *Children of the Red King* by Madeleine Polland. In one of their raids on the castle Cormacht, the Normans take the two children of Cormac, the Red King, and hold them as hostages. Well treated, the children stay with Sir Jocelin and his wife for several years. When King John of England arrives,

---

[50]Marguerite de Angeli, *The Door in the Wall* (New York: Doubleday, 1949), p. 28.

he is displeased with Sir Jocelin's determination to make a peaceful settlement with the Red King. Grania and her brother make an exciting trip to the secret hiding place of Cormac and effect the reconciliation of their proud father with Sir Jocelin before the king can demand a final battle.

Barbara Leonie Picard has written some of the best stories of life in the medieval days. The lawlessness of the period when King Richard was away fighting the Crusades is described in the story of *Lost John.* Fifteen-year-old John Fitzwilliam was given the name of Lost John when he was found wandering about in the Forest of Arden by outlaws whose leader was the notorious Ralf the Red. John had left home when he could no longer bear the taunts of the stepfather who had usurped his father's castle and John's rightful fortune. He and a loyal servant set out to revenge the man who had killed his father. Robbers kill the servant, and John is captured by a band of Ralf's outlaws. John joins the outlaw band and comes to worship Sir Ralf as a substitute father. Ralf himself grows to love John with a father's love, for his own son, Alain, reminded him too much of his wife whom he killed when he found she had betrayed him. It was neither to John's liking nor Ralf's, then, when Alain runs away from the monastery where his father had placed him and finds the outlaws' hideout. John still retained Ralf's favor, however, and Alain was assigned to help in the kitchen. Quite by accident, Alain reveals the identity of his last name, and John discovers that Sir Ralf is the murderer of his father—the man he has sworn to kill. The knowledge is almost too painful for John to bear, for he knows he can never fulfill his sworn promise. Only Alain understands the pain of loving a parent who has killed another, but John wants none of his sympathy. In the end, John is the cause of Sir Ralf's death, for he is mortally wounded while protecting John in battle. The two boys, who have in common

their love for Sir Ralf, leave Arden Woods together. Each of these characters stands out in clear relief against an authentic background of the customs and grisly horrors of the period. The interrelationships of the characters and the skillful plot development make this an exciting story of the Middle Ages.

The haunting story of *One Is One* by Picard derives its name from the lines of an English folk song, "One is one and all alone and evermore shall be so." When Miss Picard was asked what happened to the misfits in medieval society, she promptly replied that they were sent to the monastery, for there would have been nowhere else for them. This was the destiny of Stephen de Beauville, a gentle, sensitive boy who had been branded a coward by his many half-brothers and sisters and considered unfit for the life of a knight. Sent to the monastery at thirteen, Stephen finds some comfort in learning to paint, a skill in which he has remarkable talent, but the gruff Brother Ernulf refuses to praise him. Still dreaming of knighthood, Stephen runs away from the monastery. Quite by chance, he is found half-starved by a wise and valiant knight, Sir Pagan Latourelle, who takes Stephen on as his squire. Sir Pagan tutors Stephen in the arts of knighthood, jousting, riding and archery. Stephen comes to love his friend, the first who ever accepted him just as he is. In an unsuccessful attempt to free the king, Sir Pagan is captured. Just before his grim execution, Stephen contrives to visit him and Pagan gives him advice that he follows for the remainder of his life:

"Above all, always be yourself. Do not be afraid to do what you want to do, as long as it hurts no one else. We are each of us as God made us, and if God has seen fit to make you in an uncommon mould, be brave enough to be different. Promise me that, Stephen."[51]

---

[51]Barbara Leonie Picard, *One Is One* (New York: Holt, Rinehart and Winston, 1966), p. 169.

When Stephen sees Sir Pagan's severed head raised above the crowd, he no longer wants to live. But time heals wounds of anguish as well as pain. Stephen wins his knighthood as well as the devotion of an incorrigible young squire. When young Thomas dies of the plague, Stephen remembers Pagan's words and returns to the solace of his painting at the monastery. He had found sorrow that he could have avoided if he had never run away, but he had also found happiness, two friends to love, and himself. Children who read *One Is One* will have lived most intensively with Stephen de Beauville—they will have experienced literature.

Again, Rosemary Sutcliff has recreated the period and people of feudal England in her book, *Knight's Fee.* This is the story of an orphaned dog-boy who was won at a chess game by a minstrel who, in turn, gave him to Sir Everard as varlet for his son, Bevis. Bevis and Randall grow up together on the Dean land, the grassy downs that reached back into the very roots of time. Randall is as faithful to Bevis as the dogs that first knew his care. When Bevis kept his lonely all-night vigil in the church before the day of his knighting, Randall knelt quietly outside in the shadows. Such devotion was rewarded but in a way that Randall would never have chosen—Bevis made him a knight just before he died of a wound received at the Battle of Tenchebrai. Randall, the mistreated dog-boy became Sir Randall, to hold the Dean land by knight's fee. Life was cheap and of little value in the Middle Ages. A boy could be won in a game of chess—but given a chance, that same boy could develop qualities of loyalty and courage that were unsurpassed. In her characteristic fashion, Rosemary Sutcliff has dramatized the potential for goodness in mankind in this story of knighthood and friendship.

Thirteenth-century England is the setting for the Newbery Award winner, *Adam of the Road*, by Elizabeth Janet Gray. It is the story of Adam, his minstrel father, and Adam's devoted dog, Nick. On their way to the great Fair of St. Giles, Nick is stolen. In the frantic chase that follows, Adam is separated from his father. It takes a whole long winter to find both Nick and Roger again. Adam has many adventures and some disasters, but he learns that the road is home to the minstrel and that people, generally, are kind. In *I Will Adventure*, Elizabeth Gray tells the story of Master Talbot against the authentic background of Shakespeare's England. The title of the book comes from the page's speech in *Romeo and Juliet:* "I am almost afraid to stand alone/Here in the churchyard; yet I will adventure." This was the first play Andrew Talbot had ever seen, and the words struck a particularly responsive note for him. He resolved that he, too, would "adventure." But somehow London life fell short of his expectations, and Andrew was homesick. The only person who really understood how he felt was Master Shakespeare, and he had no need for an apprentice. When Andrew decides to run away, his uncle remembers his responsibility to the lad and takes a day off to enjoy a play with him. After the play, they go to the tavern "The Freckled Lily," where Shakespeare and his uncle determine Andrew's future.

Another book that makes the colorful life and times of Shakespeare's England come alive for children is *The Wonderful Winter* by Marchette Chute. It is the story of young Sir Robin Wakefield who runs away from three strict, unbending aunts to spend the winter in London. He is saved from near starvation by John Heminges, the famous actor. Robin is welcomed into his home and treated as a member of his family. In return for the warmth and affection that he receives from her, Robin helps Mrs. Heminges with her garden, carries wood, and takes bit parts in some of Shakespeare's plays. He has an opportunity to get to know the famous playwright and he delights in his company. In fact, "They talked of many things, and Robin could not follow all that Mr. Shakespeare said. But it felt like sitting in the sun. You do not have to understand sunlight in order to enjoy it."[52] Sir Robin returns to Suffolk, a happier, more mature boy, who is quite capable of melting the frigid hearts of his aunts after knowing the warmth and joy of his wonderful winter.

The life of the peasants under the feudal system of Europe in the sixteenth century was a far cry from Shakespeare's England. In *Boy of Old Prague*, Ish-Kishor has told the grim story of a sensitive, intelligent, but quite uneducated peasant boy, Tomas. Tomas grows up accepting without question the harshness of the feudal system in which the lord of the manor owns both the land and its wealth and his people as well. Tomas is equally accepting of all that he hears about the Jews in the Ghetto, believing them to be the foredoomed property of the Devil. Imagine his horror, then, when caught stealing a roast chicken from the kitchen for his ill and starving mother, to be sentenced to serve as a bond servant to an old Jew in the Ghetto. He would rather have faced public excution. However, Reb Pesach and his beautiful granddaughter Rachel were kind to Tomas. The sensitive boy was confused. How could he admire the young lord of the manor who starved his family and nearly killed him for the theft of a chicken, yet fear and despise these kind and gentle people? Gradually, Tomas allows himself to think and feel as his heart tells him. While home on a visit, Tomas escapes the cruel pogrom of the Jews instigated by the young lord whose affections Rachel had rejected. Tomas searched for "his family" amidst the bodies on the streets and those left charred by the human bonfire in the marketplace. He clings to the hope that some of the Jews escaped

and ends his story with a moving plea for understanding that speaks as forcefully to our times as to sixteenth-century Prague:

Perhaps some day I shall find them again, little Joseph, and my gentle maiden, Mademoiselle Rachel, and the old man who taught me from his Hebrew soul the loving-kindness which I had never known. I shall find them, and I shall help them and work for them with my two strong hands, and among us we shall learn that the God of mercy is the same God, no matter where we find Him.[53]

Modern Europe There are few stories for elementary school children of the period designated as modern Europe. In *The Emperor and the Drummer Boy*, Ruth Robbins has told a simple tale of Napoleon based upon a true incident that occurred at the port of Boulogne in July of 1804. Jean and Armand were two drummer boys who so distinguished themselves in the parade for Napoleon that Admiral Bruix gave them each a special assignment for the next day. Jean was put in the Admiral's special service and Armand was to be the drummer on a gunboat. The next morning the skies were dark and ominous, and Admiral Bruix refused to send his men out to sea. Napoleon was furious and ordered the Vice-Admiral to carry out his command. The disaster that followed was everything that Admiral Bruix had feared, the ships foundered, and the gunboats were flung against the rocks. All night, Napoleon watched the hopeless rescue teams, and Jean watched for Armand. Drummer boy and Emperor kept vigil together. At dawn, Napoleon viewed the wreckage wrought by his pride, but amid the floating timbers, Jean saw his friend Armand safely clinging to a bobbing red and blue drum. The striking stylized pictures by Sidjakov give a feeling of

---

[52]Marchette Chute, *The Wonderful Winter*, Illustrated by Grace Golden (New York: Dutton, 1954), p. 193.

[53]Sulamith Ish-Kishor, *A Boy of Old Prague*, Illustrated by Ben Shahn (New York: Pantheon, 1963), p. 90.

the old parchment pages of the journals that contained the account of the original incident.

Geoffrey Trease has written an absorbing historical novel for older boys and girls titled *Victory at Valmy.* The early days of the French Revolution are brought to life in this first-person story of Pierre Mercier, an artistic young peasant who becomes a protegé and pupil of the aristocratic but liberal-minded Madame de Vairmont. While painting her portrait, Pierre falls in love with a nobleman's niece, someone outside his rank until the Revolution makes equals of them all. This story reveals the issues and the excesses of the day. Trease has written another historical adventure of a little-known period, that of the time of Garibaldi's struggle to unify Italy. *Follow My Black Plume* tells this story through the experiences of Mark Apperley, an English lad sent to study in Rome.

The English struggle for freedom of speech is presented in Hester Burton's story, *Time of Trial.* When a London bookstore owner protests against the neglect of a tenement, he is imprisoned and the very people he tried to befriend turn against him. Each character is well drawn, but the integrity and trust of Mr. Pargeter stand out in sharp relief against the injustices of his time.

Such well-written historical fiction as has been reviewed in this chapter can enable a child to see the continuity of life and his place in the vast sweep of history. It can broaden his horizon to encompass the events of the past and to make him wonder about the future. Hopefully, such books will help him see that history is not a sterile subject only to be studied in school, but that it can be an exciting encounter with the events of the past. Well-written biographies and fine historical fiction may give boys and girls a perspective by which they can come to realize that men make and shape their destinies by the decisions and actions of each individual. The events that happen today do become the history of tomorrow.

SUGGESTED ACTIVITIES

1. Using the criteria established in this chapter, (a) compare three biographies of the same person; (b) compare three historical fiction books of the same period.
2. Assume you were guiding a study of the pioneers in the third grade. Make an annotated list of the biographies and fictional books you would want to use.
3. Compare *America's Paul Revere* by Esther Forbes and *Johnny Tremain* by the same author. What are the values of each book? Which one gives a better picture of the times? Which one would children prefer?
4. Compare and contrast *Ben and Me* by Lawson, Judson's *Benjamin Franklin,* and Daugherty's *Poor Richard.* What are the strength and appeals of each book? What is the approximate age level of each?
5. Make an annotated bibliography for biographies of a special group of people; for example, Negro leaders, scientists, writers, artists, musicians, nurses, physicians, and others.
6. Choose a particular period in United States history, such as Colonial, Revolutionary, Westward Movement, Civil War, World War I, or World War II and prepare an annotated list of both biographies and historical fiction that would illuminate the period.
7. Ask a group of fourth- or fifth-graders each to make a list of their ten favorite books. What percentage of these can be classified as historical in nature?
8. What insights and understandings of child development may be derived from reading the Wilder books?

RELATED READINGS

1. Arbuthnot, May Hill. *Children and Books*. Third edition. Glenview, Ill.: Scott, Foresman, 1964.
   Chapter 17 of this book gives a comprehensive account of biography for children. Historical fiction is discussed in Chapter 16. Both these sections of Mrs. Arbuthnot's book are well written and clearly organized.
2. Beatty, John and Patricia. "Watch Your Language—You're Writing for Young People!" *The Horn Book Magazine*, vol. 41 (February 1965), pp. 34–40.
   The Beattys tell of the careful research they do to obtain authentic language for their historical fiction. All words used in conversation or a first-person account are checked to see if they were in usage at the time of the setting of the novel. Interesting examples are given.
3. Jarolimek, John. *Social Studies in Elementary Education*. Third edition. New York: Macmillan, 1967.
   In this edition of a popular text, more attention is focused upon the disciplines of the social sciences, the inquiry method, and learning resources. Chapter 3 gives guidance for the development of social studies units, while Chapter 4 deals with the selection and use of learning resources.
4. Michaelis, John U. *Social Studies for Children in a Democracy,* Third edition. Englewood Cliffs, N.J.: Prentice-Hall, 1963.
   This book presents a sound point of view on the teaching of social studies. One chapter is devoted to the use of reading materials and literature in the social studies program. Specific techniques are given for guiding children's reading in this field.
5. Miller, Bertha Mahony, and Elinor Whitney Field. *Newbery Medal Books: 1922–1955*. Boston: Horn Book, 1955.
   The acceptance speech of Elizabeth Janet Gray for her award-winning book *Adam of the Road* is well worth reading. Titled "History is People," the speech describes her philosophy of writing historical fiction for young people. May Massee's biographical sketch of Elizabeth Janet Gray is also interesting reading.
6. Smith, Lillian H. *The Unreluctant Years*. Chicago: American Library Association, 1953.
   Historical fiction is discussed in Chapter 11. Careful analysis of some of the classics of historical fiction for children reveals criteria for evaluation of today's literature.
7. Sprague, Rosemary. "Biography: The Other Face of the Coin." *The Horn Book Magazine*, vol. 42 (June 1966), pp. 282–289.
   Rosemary Sprague compares the task of the biographer with that of the historical novelist and finds them both much alike. She discusses possible solutions to the "factual gap" in the record of any man. The relevance of well-written biography and historical fiction to modern living is emphasized.

CHAPTER REFERENCES

Biography

1. Aliki, pseud. (Aliki Brandenberg). *George and the Cherry Tree*. New York: Dial, 1964.
2. ————*The Story of Johnny Appleseed*. Engelwood Cliffs, N.J.: Prentice-Hall, 1963.
3. ————*The Story of William Penn*. Engelwood Cliffs, N.J.: Prentice-Hall, 1964.
4. ————*A Weed Is a Flower, the Life of George Washington Carver*. Engelwood Cliffs, N.J.: Prentice-Hall, 1965.
5. Appel, Benjamin. *Hitler, From Power to Ruin*. New York: Grosset & Dunlap, 1964.
6. d'Aulaire, Ingri and Edgar. *Abraham Lincoln*. Revised edition. New York: Doubleday, 1957.

7. ————*Benjamin Franklin*. New York: Doubleday, 1950.
8. ————*Buffalo Bill*. New York: Doubleday, 1952.
9. ————*Columbus*. New York: Doubleday, 1955.
10. ————*George Washington*. New York: Doubleday, 1936.
11. ————*Leif, the Lucky*. New York: Doubleday, 1951.
12. ————*Pocahontas*. New York: Doubleday, 1949.
13. Bixby, William, and editors of *Horizon Magazine. The Universe of Galileo and Newton*. New York: Harper & Row, 1964.
14. Braymer, Marjorie. *The Walls of Windy Troy*. New York: Harcourt, 1960.
15. Brown, Marion, and Ruth Crone. *The Silent Storm*. Illustrated by Fritz Kredel. New York: Abingdon, 1963.
16. Bulla, Clyde Robert. *John Billington, Friend of Squanto*. Illustrated by Peter Burchard. New York: Crowell, 1956.
17. ————*Squanto, Friend of the White Man*. Illustrated by Peter Burchard. New York: Crowell, 1954.
18. Campion, Nardi Reeder. *Patrick Henry, Firebrand of the Revolution*. Illustrated by Victor Mays. Boston: Little, Brown, 1961.
19. Cary, Barbara. *Meet Abraham Lincoln*. Illustrated by Jack Davis. New York: Random House, 1965.
20. Cavanah, Frances. *Abe Lincoln Gets His Chance*. Illustrated by Paula Hutchison. Skokie, Ill.: Rand McNally, 1959.
21. ————*They Knew Abe Lincoln*. Illustrated by Harve Stein. Skokie, Ill.: Rand McNally, 1952.
22. Chissell, Joan. *Chopin*. New York: Crowell, 1965.
23. Colver, Anne. *Abraham Lincoln for the People*. Illustrated by William Moyers. Champaign, Ill.: Garrard, 1960.
24. Crouse, Anna and Russel. *Alexander Hamilton and Aaron Burr*. Illustrated by Walter Buehr. New York: Random House, 1958.
25. Dalgliesh, Alice. *The Columbus Story*. Illustrated by Leo Politi. New York: Scribner, 1955.
26. ————*Ride on the Wind*. Illustrated by Georges Schreiber. From *The Spirit of St. Louis* by Charles A. Lindbergh. New York: Scribner, 1956.
27. Daugherty, James. *Abraham Lincoln*. New York: Viking, 1943.
28. ————*Daniel Boone*. New York: Viking, 1939.
29. ————*Marcus and Narcissa Whitman, Pioneers of Oregon*. New York: Viking, 1953.
30. ————*Of Courage Undaunted, Across the Continent with Lewis and Clark*. New York: Viking, 1951.
31. ————*Poor Richard*. New York: Viking, 1941.
32. Donovan, Frank R., and editors of *American Heritage. The Many Worlds of Benjamin Franklin*. New York: Harper & Row, 1963.
33. Epstein, Sam and Beryl. *George Washington Carver: Negro Scientist*. Illustrated by William Moyers. Champaign, Ill.: Garrard, 1960.
34. Fisher, Aileen. *My Cousin Abe*. Illustrated by Leonard Vosburgh. Camden, N.J.: Nelson, 1962.
35. Foster, Genevieve. *Abraham Lincoln, an Initial Biography*. New York: Scribner, 1950.
36. ————*Abraham Lincoln's World*. New York: Scribner, 1944.
37. ————*Andrew Jackson, an Initial Biography*. New York: Scribner, 1951.
38. ————*George Washington, an Initial Biography*. New York: Scribner, 1949.
39. ————*George Washington's World*. New York: Scribner, 1941.
40. ————*Theodore Roosevelt, an Initial Biography*. New York: Scribner, 1954.
41. Friskey, Margaret. *Tad Lincoln and the Green Umbrella*. Illustrated by Lucia Patton. New York: Oxford, 1944.
42. Hays, Wilma Pitchford. *Abe Lincoln's Birthday*. Illustrated by Peter Burchard. New York: Coward-McCann, 1961.

43. Heilbroner, Joan. *Meet George Washington*. Illustrated by Victor Mays. New York: Random House, 1965.

44. Holst, Imogen. *Bach*. New York: Crowell, 1965.

45. Isenberg, Irwin, and editors of *Horizon Magazine*. *Caesar*. New York: Harper & Row, 1964.

46. Judson, Clara Ingram. *Abraham Lincoln*. Illustrated by Polly Jackson. Chicago: Follett, 1961.

47. ————*Abraham Lincoln, Friend of the People*. Illustrated by Robert Frankenberg. Chicago: Follett, 1950.

48. ————*Andrew Carnegie*. Illustrated by Steele Savage. Chicago: Follett, 1964.

49. ————*Andrew Jackson, Frontier Statesman*. Illustrated by Lorence F. Bjorklund. Chicago: Follett, 1954.

50. ————*Christopher Columbus*. Illustrated by Polly Jackson. Chicago: Follett, 1960.

51. ————*George Washington*. Illustrated by Polly Jackson. Chicago: Follett, 1961.

52. ————*George Washington, Leader of the People*. Illustrated by Robert Frankenberg. Chicago: Follett, 1951.

53. ————*Mr. Justice Holmes*. Illustrated by Robert Todd. Chicago: Follett, 1956.

54. ————*Theodore Roosevelt, Fighting Patriot*. Illustrated by Lorence F. Bjorklund. Chicago: Follett, 1953.

55. ————*Thomas Jefferson, Champion of the People*. Illustrated by Robert Frankenberg. Chicago: Follett, 1952.

56. Kay, Helen. *Lincoln: A Big Man*. Illustrated by Arthur Polonsky. New York: Hastings, 1958.

57. Keating, Bern. *Zebulon Pike*. New York: Putnam, 1965.

58. Latham, Jean Lee. *Carry On, Mr. Bowditch*. Illustrated by John O'Hara Cosgrave II. Boston: Houghton Mifflin, 1955.

59. ————*Medals for Morse*. Illustrated by Douglas Gorsline. New York: Aladdin, 1954.

60. ————*Retreat to Glory, the Story of Sam Houston*. New York: Harper & Row, 1965.

61. ————*Trail Blazer of the Seas*. Illustrated by Victor Mays. Boston: Houghton Mifflin, 1956.

62. ————*Young Man in a Hurry*. Illustrated by Victor Mays. New York: Harper & Row, 1958.

63. Lawson, Robert. *Ben and Me*. Boston: Little, Brown, 1951, 1939.

64. ————*Mr. Revere and I*. Boston: Little, Brown, 1953.

65. LeSueur, Meridel. *Nancy Hanks of Wilderness Road*. Illustrated by Betty Alden. New York: Knopf, 1949.

66. Lincoln, Abraham. *The First Book Edition of the Gettysburg Address, The Second Inaugural*. Illustrated by Leonard Everett Fisher. New York: F. Watts, 1963.

67. Lord, Walter. *Peary to the Pole*. New York: Harper & Row, 1963.

68. McNeer, May Yonge. *America's Abraham Lincoln*. Illustrated by Lynd Ward. Boston: Houghton Mifflin, 1957.

69. ————*America's Mark Twain*. Illustrated by Lynd Ward. Boston: Houghton Mifflin , 1962.

70. ————*Armed with Courage*. Illustrated by Lynd Ward. New York: Abingdon, 1957.

71. ————*John Wesley*. Illustrated by Lynd Ward. New York: Abingdon, 1951.

72. ————*Martin Luther*. Illustrated by Lynd Ward. New York: Abingdon, 1953.

73. Martin, Patricia Miles. *Abraham Lincoln*. Illustrated by Gustav Schrotter. New York: Putnam, 1964.

74. ————*Pocahontas*. Illustrated by Portia Takakjian. New York: Putnam, 1964.

75. Mason, Van Wyck. *The Winter at Valley Forge*. Illustrated by Harper Johnson. New York: Random House, 1953.

76. Meigs, Cornelia. *Invincible Louisa.* Boston: Little, Brown, 1961, 1933.
77. Mercer, Charles and editors of *Horizon Magazine. Alexander the Great.* New York: Harper & Row, 1963.
78. Miers, Earl Schenck and editors of *American Heritage. Abraham Lincoln in Peace and War.* New York: Harper & Row, 1964.
79. Mirsky, Jeannette. *Balboa Discoverer of the Pacific.* Illustrated by Hans Guggenheim. New York: Harper & Row, 1964.
80. Mirsky, Reba Paeff. *Beethoven.* Chicago: Follett, 1957.
81. ————*Brahms.* Illustrated by W. T. Mars. Chicago: Follett, 1966.
82. ————*Haydn.* Illustrated by W. T. Mars. Chicago: Follett, 1963.
83. ————*Johann Sebastian Bach.* Illustrated by Steele Savage. Chicago: Follett, 1965.
84. ————*Mozart.* Illustrated by W. T. Mars. Chicago: Follett, 1960.
85. Nathan, Adele Gutman. *Lincoln's America.* New York: Grossett & Dunlap, 1961.
86. Neyhart, Louise A. *Henry's Lincoln.* Illustrated by Charles Banks Wilson. New York: Holiday, 1958.
87. Nolan, Jeannette. *Queen Elizabeth.* Illustrated by Marie Lawson. New York: Harper & Row, 1951.
88. Norman, Gertrude. *A Man Named Lincoln.* Illustrated by Joseph Cellini. New York: Putnam, 1960.
89. ————*A Man Named Washington.* Illustrated by James Caraway. New York: Putnam, 1960.
90. North, Sterling. *George Washington, Frontier Colonel.* Illustrated by Lee Ames. New York: Random House, 1957.
91. Peare, Catherine Owens. *The FDR Story.* New York: Crowell, 1962.
92. ————*The Helen Keller Story.* New York: Crowell, 1959.
93. ————*The Herbert Hoover Story.* New York: Crowell, 1965.
94. ————*Mary McLeod Bethune.* New York: Vanguard, 1951.
95. ————*The Woodrow Wilson Story.* New York: Crowell, 1963.
96. Phelan, Mary Kay. *Mr. Lincoln Speaks at Gettysburg.* New York: Norton, 1966.
97. Putnam, Peter. *The Triumph of the Seeing Eye.* New York: Harper & Row, 1963.
98. Randall, Ruth Painter. *I, Mary.* Boston: Little, Brown, 1959.
99. ————*Lincoln's Animal Friends.* Illustrated by Louis Darling. Boston: Little, Brown, 1958.
100. Renault, Mary. *The Lion in the Gateway.* Illustrated by C. Walter Hodges. New York: Harper & Row, 1964.
101. Reynolds, Robert L. and editors of *American Heritage. Commodore Perry in Japan.* New York: Harper & Row, 1963.
102. Ripley, Elizabeth. *Botticelli.* Philadelphia: Lippincott, 1960.
103. ————*Goya.* New York: Walck, 1956.
104. ————*Leonardo da Vinci.* New York: Walck, 1952.
105. ————*Michelangelo.* New York: Walck, 1953.
106. ————*Rembrandt.* New York: Walck, 1955.
107. ————*Rodin.* Philadelphia: Lippincott, 1966.
108. ————*Rubens.* New York: Walck, 1957.
109. ————*Titian, a Biography.* Philadelphia: Lippincott, 1962.
110. ————*Vincent Van Gogh.* New York: Walck, 1954.
111. ————*Winslow Homer, a Biography.* Philadelphia: Lippincott, 1963.
112. Robinson, Jackie, and Alfred Duckett. *Breakthrough to the Big League, the Story of Jackie Robinson.* New York: Harper & Row, 1965.
113. Rugoff, Milton, and editors of *Horizon Magazine. Marco Polo's Adventures in China.* New York: Harper & Row, 1964.
114. Sandburg, Carl. *Abe Lincoln Grows Up.* Reprinted from *Abraham Lincoln, the Prairie Years.* Illustrated by James Daugherty. New York: Harcourt, 1956, 1928.
115. Saxon, Gladys. *Paul Revere.* Illustrated by Jo Kotula. Chicago: Follett, 1965.

116. Sterling, Dorothy. *Captain of the Planter*. Illustrated by Ernest Crichlow. New York: Doubleday, 1958.
117. ————*Freedom Train, The Story of Harriet Tubman*. Illustrated by Ernest Crichlow. New York: Doubleday, 1954.
118. ————*Lucretia Mott, Gentle Warrior*. New York: Doubleday, 1964.
119. Sterling, Dorothy, and Benjamin Quarles. *Lift Every Voice*. Illustrated by Ernest Crichlow. New York: Doubleday, 1965.
120. Stevenson, Augusta. *Abe Lincoln, Frontier Boy*. Illustrated by Jerry Robinson. Indianapolis: Bobbs-Merrill, 1932.
121. Swift, Hildegarde Hoyt. *The Edge of April: A Biography of John Burroughs*. Illustrated by Lynd Ward. New York: Morrow, 1957.
122. ————*From the Eagle's Wing*. Illustrated by Lynd Ward. New York: Morrow, 1962.
123. Syme, Ronald. *African Traveler, the Story of Mary Kingsley*. Illustrated by Jacqueline Tomes. New York: Morrow, 1962.
124. ————*Cortes of Mexico*. Illustrated by William Stobbs. New York: Morrow, 1951.
125. ————*John Smith of Virginia*. Illustrated by William Stobbs. New York: Morrow, 1951.
126. ————*Nigerian Pioneer*. Illustrated by Jacqueline Tomes. New York: Morrow, 1964.
127. ————*Vasco da Gama, Sailor toward the Sunrise*. Illustrated by William Stobbs. New York: Morrow, 1959.
128. Trease, Geoffrey. *The Seven Queens of England*. New York: Vanguard, 1953.
129. Treviño, Elizabeth Borton de. *I, Juan de Pareja*. New York: Farrar, Straus, 1965.
130. Weil, Eleanor. *Eleanor Roosevelt, Courageous Girl*. Indianapolis: Bobbs-Merrill, 1965.
131. Wheeler, Opal, and Sybil Deucher. *Joseph Haydn, the Merry Little Peasant*. Illustrated by Mary Greenwalt. New York: Dutton, 1936.
132. ————*Mozart, the Wonder Boy*. Illustrated by Mary Greenwalt. New York: Dutton, 1941.
133. White, Nancy Bean. *Meet John F. Kennedy*. New York: Random House, 1965.
134. Yates, Elizabeth. *Amos Fortune, Free Man*. Illustrated by Nora S. Unwin. New York: Dutton, 1950.
135. Ziner, Feenie. *Dark Pilgrim, the Story of Squanto*. Chilton, 1965.

Historical Fiction

136. Baker, Betty. *Killer-of-Death*. Illustrated by John Kaufmann. New York: Harper & Row, 1963.
137. ————*Walk the World's Rim*. New York: Harper & Row, 1965.
138. Barringer, D. Moreau. *And the Waters Prevailed*. Illustrated by P. A. Hutchinson. New York: Dutton, 1956.
139. Baumann, Hans. *I Marched with Hannibal*. Illustrated by Ulrik Schramm. New York: Walck, 1962.
140. Beatty, John and Patricia. *At the Seven Stars*. Illustrated by Douglas Gorsline. New York: Macmillan, 1962.
141. Beatty, Patricia. *The Nickel-Plated Beauty*. Illustrated by Liz Dauber. New York: Morrow, 1964.
142. Behn, Harry. *The Faraway Lurs*. Cleveland: World Publishing, 1963.
143. Bishop, Claire Huchet. *Twenty and Ten*. Illustrated by William Pène du Bois. New York: Viking, 1952.
144. Brink, Carol Ryrie. *Caddie Woodlawn*. Illustrated by Kate Seredy. New York: Macmillan, 1936.

145. Bulla, Clyde Robert. *The Sword in the Tree*. Illustrated by Paul Galdone. New York: Crowell, 1956.

146. ———*Viking Adventure*. Illustrated by Douglas Gorsline. New York: Crowell, 1963.

147. Burton, Hester. *Time of Trial*. Illustrated by Victor Ambrus. Cleveland: World Publishing, 1964.

148. Caudill, Rebecca. *Barrie & Daughter*. Illustrated by Berkeley Williams, Jr. New York: Viking, 1943.

149. ———*Tree of Freedom*. Illustrated by Dorothy Morse. New York: Viking, 1949.

150. Chute, Marchette. *The Wonderful Winter*. Illustrated by Grace Golden. New York: Dutton, 1954.

151. Coatsworth, Elizabeth. *Sword in the Wilderness*. New York: Macmillan, 1936.

152. Colver, Anne. *Bread and Butter Indian*. Illustrated by Garth Williams. New York: Holt, Rinehart and Winston, 1964.

153. Dalgliesh, Alice. *Adam and the Golden Cock*. Illustrated by Leonard Weisgard. New York: Scribner, 1959.

154. ———*The Courage of Sarah Noble*. Illustrated by Leonard Weisgard. New York: Scribner, 1954.

155. De Angeli, Marguerite. *The Door in the Wall*. New York: Doubleday, 1949.

156. ———*Elin's Amerika*. New York: Doubleday, 1941.

157. ———*Skippack School*. New York: Doubleday, 1961.

158. ———*Thee, Hannah!* New York: Doubleday, 1949.

159. Edmonds, Walter D. *The Matchlock Gun*. Illustrated by Paul Lantz. New York: Dodd, Mead, 1941.

160. ———*Two Logs Crossing, John Haskell's Story*. Illustrated by Tibor Gergely. New York: Dodd, Mead, 1943.

161. Fall, Thomas. *Canalboat to Freedom*. Illustrated by Joseph Cellini. New York: Dial, 1966.

162. Field, Rachel. *Calico Bush*. Illustrated by Allen Lewis. New York: Macmillan, 1946, 1931.

163. Fleischman, Sid. *By the Great Horn Spoon!* Illustrated by Eric von Schmidt. Boston: Little, Brown, 1963.

164. ———*Mr. Mysterious and Company*. Illustrated by Eric von Schmidt. Boston: Little, Brown, 1962.

165. Forbes, Esther. *Johnny Tremain*. Illustrated by Lynd Ward. Boston: Houghton Mifflin, 1946.

166. Fritz, Jean. *Brady*. Illustrated by Lynd Ward. New York: Coward-McCann, 1960.

167. ———*The Cabin Faced West*. Illustrated by Feodor Rojankovsky. New York: Coward-McCann, 1958.

168. ———*I, Adam*. Illustrated by Peter Burchard. New York: Coward-McCann, 1963.

169. Gray, Elizabeth Janet. *Adam of the Road*. Illustrated by Robert Lawson. New York: Viking, 1944.

170. ———*I Will Adventure*. Illustrated by Corydon Bell. New York: Viking, 1962.

171. Harris, Christie. *Raven's Cry*. Illustrated by Bill Reid. New York: Atheneum, 1966.

172. Harvey, James O. *Beyond the Gorge of Shadows*. New York: Lothrop, 1965.

173. Haugaard, Erik. *Hakon of Rogen's Saga*. Illustrated by Leo and Diane Dillon. Boston: Houghton Mifflin, 1963.

174. ———*Orphans of the Wind*. Boston: Houghton Mifflin, 1966.

175. ———*A Slave's Tale*. Illustrated by Leo and Diane Dillon. Boston: Houghton Mifflin, 1965.

176. Hays, Wilma Pitchford. *Christmas on the Mayflower*. Illustrated by Roger Duvoisin. New York: Coward-McCann, 1956.

177. ———*Pilgrim Thanksgiving*. Illustrated by Leonard Weisgard. New York: Coward-McCann, 1955.

178. ————*The Scarlet Badge.* Illustrated by Peter Burchard. New York: Holt, Rinehart and Winston, 1963.
179. Hunt, Irene. *Across Five Aprils.* Chicago: Follett, 1964.
180. Ish-Kishor, Sulamith. *A Boy of Old Prague.* Illustrated by Ben Shahn. New York: Pantheon, 1963.
181. Jackson, Jacqueline. *The Taste of Spruce Gum.* Illustrated by Lilian Obligado. Boston: Little, Brown, 1966.
182. Keith, Harold. *Rifles for Watie.* New York: Crowell, 1957.
183. Kjelgaard, Jim. *Fire-hunter.* Illustrated by Ralph Ray. New York: Holiday, 1951.
184. Kroeber, Theodora. *Ishi, Last of His Tribe.* Illustrated by Ruth Robbins. New York: Parnassus, 1964.
185. Latham, Jean Lee. *This Dear Bought Land.* Illustrated by Jacob Landau. New York: Harper & Row, 1957.
186. Lawson, Robert. *The Great Wheel.* New York: Viking, 1957.
187. Lenski, Lois. *Indian Captive, the Story of Mary Jemison.* Philadelphia: Lippincott, 1941.
188. McGraw, Eloise Jarvis. *The Golden Goblet.* New York: Coward-McCann, 1961.
189. ————*Mara, Daughter of the Nile.* New York: Coward-McCann, 1953.
190. ————*Moccasin Trail.* New York: Coward-McCann, 1952.
191. McSwigan, Marie. *Snow Treasure.* Illustrated by Mary Reardon. New York: Dutton, 1942.
192. Mason, Miriam E. *Caroline and Her Kettle Named Maud.* Illustrated by Kathleen Voute. New York: Macmillan, 1951.
193. Meadowcraft, Enid. *By Secret Railway.* Illustrated by Henry C. Pitz. New York: Crowell, 1948.
194. ————*The First Year.* Illustrated by Grace Paull. New York: Crowell, 1946.
195. O'Dell, Scott. *The King's Fifth.* Illustrated by Samuel Bryant. Boston: Houghton Mifflin, 1966.
196. Petry, Ann. *Tituba of Salem Village.* New York: Crowell, 1964.
197. Picard, Barbara Leonie. *Lost John.* Illustrated by Charles Keeping. New York: Criterion, 1963.
198. ————*One Is One.* New York: Holt, Rinehart and Winston, 1965.
199. Pilkington, Roger. *I Sailed on the Mayflower.* Illustrated by Douglas Bisset. New York: St. Martins, 1966.
200. Polland, Madeleine. *Beorn the Proud.* Illustrated by William Stobbs. New York: Holt, Rinehart and Winston, 1961.
201. ————*Children of the Red King.* New York: Holt, Rinehart and Winston, 1961.
202. Richter, Conrad. *The Light in the Forest.* New York: Knopf, 1953.
203. Robbins, Ruth. *The Emperor and the Drummer Boy.* Illustrated by Nicolas Sidjakov. New York: Parnassus. 1962.
204. Robinson, Barbara. *Trace through the Forest.* New York: Lothrop, 1965.
205. Sawyer, Ruth. *Roller Skates.* Illustrated by Valenti Angelo. New York: Viking, 1964, 1936.
206. Schweitzer, Byrd Baylor. *One Small Blue Bead.* Illustrated by Symeon Shimin. New York: Macmillan, 1965.
207 Speare, Elizabeth George. *The Bronze Bow.* Boston: Houghton Mifflin, 1961.
208. ————*Calico Captive.* Illustrated by W. T. Mars. Boston: Houghton Mifflin, 1957.
209. ————*The Witch of Blackbird Pond.* Boston: Houghton Mifflin, 1958.
210. Steele, William O. *The Buffalo Knife.* Illustrated by Paul Galdone. New York: Harcourt, 1952.
211. ————*Flaming Arrows.* Illustrated by Paul Galdone. New York: Harcourt, 1957.
212. ————*The Lone Hunt.* Illustrated by Paul Galdone. New York: Harcourt, 1956.
213. ————*The Perilous Road.* Illustrated by Paul Galdone. New York: Harcourt, 1958.

214. ————*Tomahawks and Trouble.* Illustrated by Paul Galdone. New York: Harcourt, 1955.
215. ————*Trail Through Danger.* New York: Harcourt, 1965.
216. ————*Wayah of the Real People.* Illustrated by Isa Barnett. New York: Holt, Rinehart and Winston, 1964.
217. ————*Winter Danger.* Illustrated by Paul Galdone. New York: Harcourt, 1954.
218. ————*The Year of the Bloody Sevens.* Illustrated by Charles Beck. New York: Harcourt, 1963.
219. Sutcliff, Rosemary. *Dawn Wind.* Illustrated by Charles Keeping. New York: Walck, 1962.
220. ————*The Eagle of the Ninth.* Illustrated by C. W. Hodges. New York: Walck, 1954.
221. ————*Knights's Fee.* Illustrated by Charles Keeping. New York: Walck, 1960.
222. ————*The Lantern Bearers.* Illustrated by Charles Keeping. New York: Walck, 1959.
223. ————*The Silver Branch.* Illustrated by Charles Keeping. New York: Walck, 1959.
224. ————*Warrior Scarlet.* Illustrated by Charles Keeping. New York: Walck, 1958.
225. Trease, Geoffrey. *Escape to King Alfred.* New York: Vanguard, 1959.
226. ————*Follow My Black Plume.* New York: Vanguard, 1963.
227. ————*Victory at Valmy.* New York: Vanguard, 1961.
228. Treece, Henry. *Road to Miklagaard.* Great Meadows, N.J.: S. G. Phillips, 1957.
229. ————*Viking's Dawn.* Great Meadows, N.J.: S. G. Phillips, 1956.
230. ————*Viking's Sunset.* New York: Criterion, 1960.
231. Van der Loeff, Anna Rutgers. *Oregon at Last!* Illustrated by Charles Geer. New York: Morrow, 1962.
232. Wibberley, Leonard. *John Treegate's Musket.* New York: Farrar, Straus, 1959.
233. ————*Peter Treegate's War.* New York: Farrar, Straus, 1960.
234. ————*Sea Captain from Salem.* New York: Farrar, Straus, 1961.
235. ————*Treegate's Raiders.* New York: Farrar, Straus, 1962.
236. Wilder, Laura Ingalls. *By the Shores of Silver Lake.* Illustrated by Garth Williams. New York: Harper & Row, 1953, 1939.
237. ————*The Little House in the Big Woods.* Illustrated by Garth Williams. New York: Harper & Row, 1953, 1932.
238. ————*Little House on the Prairie.* Illustrated by Garth Williams. New York: Harper & Row, 1953, 1935.
239. ————*Little Town on the Prairie.* Illustrated by Garth Williams. New York: Harper & Row, 1953, 1941.
240. ————*On the Banks of Plum Creek.* Illustrated by Garth Williams. New York: Harper & Row, 1953, 1937.
241. ————*These Happy Golden Years.* Illustrated by Garth Williams. New York: Harper & Row, 1953, 1941.
242. Wojciechowska, Maia. *Odyssey of Courage.* Illustrated by Alvin Smith. New York: Atheneum, 1965.
243. Williamson, Joanne S. *And Forever Free . . . .* New York: Knopf, 1966.
244. ————*The Iron Charm.* Illustrated by Brian Wildsmith. New York: Knopf, 1964.
245. Yates, Elizabeth. *Carolina's Courage.* Illustrated by Nora S. Unwin. New York: Dutton, 1964.

MODERN FANTASY
AND HUMOR

*O*nce upon a time there was a child who did not believe in dreams.
*He did not believe in fantasy, or make-believe, or anything that was imaginary. When
other boys played pirate, he studied botany in his garden. When other boys went exploring,
he conducted chemistry experiments in his attic. And at night, when other boys were sound
asleep, he sat on the roof of his house, observing the stars.*
His name was Andrew Peterson Smith.[1]

Imagine Andrew's reaction when he comes upon an old
"Book of Beasts" describing obviously impossible creatures, like the unicorn or
the manticore, as though they were real. Andrew decides he must report this
unscientific book to the proper authorities in the library. Reading further to
tabulate all the untruths, he finally falls asleep. In his dreams he enters *The
Land of Forgotten Beasts* and saves from the oblivion of being forgotten, the
beautiful, brave—and once believable—inhabitants.

How many children and adults today are like Andrew Peterson Smith,
engrossed in reading only facts and ignoring books that can exercise their
imaginations! Yet the development of the imagination is one of the most profound of all activities and should be a major goal of education. For engineers,
inventors, doctors, and other scientists must first dream dreams before they
can bring them into reality. Paul Fenimore Cooper once wrote an essay in which
he had this to say on the importance of nourishing the child's imagination:

---

[1]Barbara Wersba, *The Land of Forgotten Beasts,* Illustrated by Margot Tomes (New York: Atheneum,
1964), p. 3.

Fancy is to the imagination what the seed is to the tree. Let it lie in barren ground and it will not grow. But nourish it and care for it through the years and it will grow into imagination, (as dear a possession for the man as fancy is for the child). He who lacks imagination lives but half a life. He has his experiences, he has his facts, he has his learning. But do any of these really live unless touched by the magic of the imagination? So long as the road is straight he can see down it and follow it. But imagination looks around the turns and gazes far off into the distance on either side. And it is imagination that walks hand in hand with vision.[2]

MODERN FAIRY TALES

The traditional folk or fairy tale had no identifiable author but was passed by word of mouth from one generation to the next. While the names of Grimm and Jacobs have become associated with some of these tales, they did not *write* the stories but compiled the folk tales of Germany and England. The modern fairy tale utilizes the form of the old but has an identifiable author.

The Beginnings of the Modern Fairy Tale

Hans Christian Andersen is generally credited with being the first *author* of modern fairy tales, although even some of his stories, such as *The Wild Swans*, are definite adaptions of the old folk tales. (Compare Andersen's *The Wild Swans* with Grimm's *The Seven Ravens*, for example.) Every Anderson story bears his unmistakable stamp of gentleness, melancholy, and faith in God. Even his adaptations of old tales were embellished with deeper hidden meanings, making them very much his creations.

Two of Andersen's tales are said to be autobiographical, *The Ugly Duckling* and *The Steadfast Tin Soldier*. The little ugly duckling was the jest of the poultry yard until he became the beautiful swan. Andersen himself

suffered all kinds of indignities as a young boy and youth, but later he was honored by his King and countrymen—truly, a duckling

A unicorn, manticore, and cockatrice accompany Andrew Peterson Smith on his explorations of *The Land of Forgotten Beasts*. Pictures copyright © 1964 by Margot Tomes. From *The Land of Forgotten Beasts* by Barbara Wersba. Used by permission of Atheneum Publishers.

[2]Paul Fenimore Cooper, "On Catching a Child's Fancy," in *Three Owls,* Third Book, Annie Carroll Moore, Editor (New York: Coward-McCann, 1931), pp. 56–57.

turned into a swan. The sad tale of the painfully shy but loyal tin soldier and his love for the cold and unbending toy ballerina is said by some authorities to represent Andersen's rejection by the woman he loved.

Many of Andersen's fairy tales are really commentaries on the false standards of society. In "The Princess and the Pea," sometimes called "The Real Princess," Andersen laughs at the snobbish pride of the princess who claimed she could feel a pea through twenty mattresses and twenty eider-down beds. The farce of *The Emperor's New Clothes* is disclosed by the young child who had no reason to assume the hollow pretense of his elders and said what they all knew—that the Emperor was stark naked! Both of the stories, *The Nightingale* and *The Swineherd,* show the foolishness of preferring the mechanical and the spurious over that which is real.

Andersen was not afraid to show children cruelty, morbidity, sorrow, and even death. In the long tale, "The Snow Queen," the glass splinter enters Kay's eye and stabs his heart, which becomes cold as ice. He then becomes spiteful and angry with Gerda, his former friend. Gerda is hurt by the changed behavior of her companion but still loving him, searches for him in the Snow Queen's palace. At last she finds him, and her tears melt the splinter and his icy coldness. "The Little Mermaid" suffers terribly for her selfless love of a mortal prince. She dies on the night of his marriage, unwilling to kill him as her sisters had planned and unable to speak to him of her love. Her goodness brings a promise of immortality, however. The story of "The Little Match Girl" ends in the gentle death of a little frozen girl who had seen a vision of her grandmother in the last flicker of her matches. A few stories, such as the tender *Thumbelina,* end happily, but most of Andersen's tales contain a thread of tragedy.

Many of Andersen's stories have been beautifully illustrated in single editions. Marcia Brown has captured the mystical beauty of *The Wild Swans* with her subdued

A child's interpretation of Thumbelina. Illustrated by children of eighteen nations. From Andersen's *Fairy Tales.* Orion Press (1958).

pen and wash drawings in black and gray tones with the shyest touch of coral for warmth. She used a proud red and blue for *The Steadfast Tin Soldier,* gold for the little dancer's spangle (all that was left of her), and charcoal for the charred little breast of the soldier. Adrienne Adams has portrayed *Thumbelina* and her enchantingly small world with delicate details and bright water colors. Her drawings for *The Ugly Duckling* are, more properly, subdued and somber. Before making these illustrations, Adrienne Adams paid a special visit to Denmark to become familiar with Andersen's native land. Erik Blegvad also revisited his native Denmark before he illustrated the small but amusing

Nancy Burkert has captured various reactions of awe, delight and doubt to the Emperor's marvelous mechanical nightingale. Rich colors illuminate these illustrations painted in the style of traditional Chinese art. Illustration by Nancy Burkert from Hans Christian Andersen's *The Nightingale,* translated by Eva Le Gallienne. Harper & Row, 1965.

The Swineherd. Nancy Burkert has richly portrayed the Chinese setting of *The Nightingale* in the Oriental tradition. Many of her pictures resemble paintings on old Chinese silk screens. Andersen's stories are melancholy, and children should not hear too many at one time. These handsome single editions will serve to introduce many children to at least one or two of Andersen's fairy tales. They are more appropriate for children in the middle grades than for the primary grades.

Oscar Wilde wrote two fairy tales, *The Happy Prince* and "The Selfish Giant." The first one has been illustrated by Gilbert Riswold in a striking single edition. This is a somewhat sentimental story of the love of a swallow and the golden statue of a prince. In real life, the prince had been happy, for he had known nothing of the misery of his people. Now from his high pedestal, he could look out over his city and see all the suffering that existed. Making the swallow his emissary of mercy, he sends the great ruby of his sword to a poor seamstress for her sick son. One by one, he asks the swallow to pluck out his sapphire eyes and give them to the poor. Now the happy prince is blind, so the swallow stays with him, flying over the city and relieving suffering by stripping the statue of its gold leaf and giving it away. No longer able to live in such a cold climate, the bird kisses his friend goodbye and falls dead at his feet. The town councilors, on seeing the shabbiness of the statue, pull it down and melt its lead. All will burn except its heart, which is thrown on the same ash heap as the dead bird. Together, the two are received in Heaven as the most precious things of the city. "The Selfish Giant" has even more religious symbolism and is less appropriate for children.

Many of George MacDonald's fairy tales also had religious overtones. However, *The Light Princess* is pure fun and even more appropriate for this generation, who have heard of weightlessness, than for the children of the nineteenth century for whom Mac-Donald wrote. Bewitched at her christening by an uninvited aunt, the princess of Lagobel lost her gravity. She became a most perplexing princess—she weighed nothing at all and had to be tied down to keep from floating away. One day, when she was swimming, a prince, hearing her laughter, thought she was in distress and rescued her. Given a strong lift from the water, the weightless princess rose quickly and was saved only by clutching a pine tree. In a perfect fury, she demanded: "What business had you to pull me down out of the water and throw me to the bottom of the air?"[3] Such twists of phrases and the humorous pictures by du Bois in a recent single edition make this a wonderfully fresh and amusing fairy tale.

Fairy Tales Today

In many instances, modern writers have written farcical versions of the old fairy tale form. The settings will be medieval in the days of kings and queens and beautiful princesses, the language will reflect the manners of the period, and the usual "Once upon a time" beginning and "They lived happily ever after" ending will be present, but the conflict may have a modern twist. True to all fairy tales, virtue will be rewarded and evil overcome. An example of one of these modern literary fairy tales is the fresh and original story by Phyllis McGinley of *The Plain Princess,* who owns the handsomest two-wheeled bicycle in the world. Yet the story of the transformation from a plain to a beautiful princess has a familiar ring. The proud

and spoiled Esmeralda is sent to live with Dame Goodwit and her five daughters for nine months. When Esmeralda discovers that there are others who are as clever as she, her nose no longer tilts in the air; when she bakes muffins for the family, her mouth begins to turn up; and when she gives her locket to little Echo in her first unselfish act, her eyes begin to glow. Esmeralda's appearance has grown as beautiful as her character!

Three other popular modern fairy tales are Thurber's *Many Moons* and *The Great Quillow* and Slobodkin's *The Amiable Giant. Many Moons* is the story of a petulant princess who desires the moon. The characterizations of the enraged king, the perplexed wise men, and the understanding jester are well drawn. Princess Lenore solves the problem of obtaining the moon in a completely satisfying and childlike manner. Louis Slobodkin received the Caldecott Medal for his illustrations of *Many Moons. The Great Quillow* is the story of an insignificant toy-maker who cleverly saves his town from Hunder, the giant. Slobodkin wrote and illustrated *The Amiable Giant,* which is a disarming tale of a friendly, but misunderstood, giant. As in *Many Moons,* a child solves the problem, for Gwendolyn is the only one who hears the giant's message. She convinces the villagers that they are being fooled by the wicked wizard's interpretations of the giant's conversations. The giant is so grateful that he gives Gwendolyn a birthday party, baking the cake himself. All three stories lend themselves to interpretation through creative dramatics.[4]

The 13 Clocks and *The Wonderful O* by James Thurber are more sophisticated and mature fairy tales. A cold duke who was afraid of "now" had frozen time in Coffin Castle where he kept the beautiful Princess Saralinda. Of course, a prince in the disguise of a ragged minstrel accomplishes the im-

[3]George MacDonald, *The Light Princess,* Illustrated by William Pène du Bois (New York: Crowell, 1962), p. 117.

[4]See Chapter 12.

possible tasks set by the Duke and wins her hand. However, it is only with the bungling and amusing help of the Golux that the Prince is able to obtain the one thousand jewels and start the thirteen clocks so that the time is Now and he may marry his Princess. This is an imaginative spoof on fairy tales and one that middle graders thoroughly enjoy. *The Wonderful O* is the story of what happens to an island when a black-hearted pirate in search of a treasure banishes the use of the letter "o." He had a hatred for it ever since his mother became wedged in a porthole. Terrorizing the islanders to produce a treasure they do not own, the pirate eliminates not only words beginning with "o", but the objects they represent. Finally, he is overcome when the people of the island find and use four words that contain "o," hope, love, valor, and freedom. *The Wonderful O* is restored to its rightful place, and a monument is erected to commemorate the time when it did not exist. The play on words in this book is clever but requires considerable maturity.

For fun in a fantastic manner, *The 500 Hats of Bartholomew Cubbins* by Dr. Seuss has not been surpassed. This is the hilarious tale of a small boy who is commanded to take off his hat for the king. Bartholomew complies, only to find that another hat has appeared on his head in its place. The king is enraged and takes the boy to court. Sir Snipps, the royal hat maker, cannot remove Bartholomew's hat; his wise men have no practical suggestions, and the royal magicians cannot even charm it off his head. Finally, he is sent to the executioner, who is a very proper kind of person and refuses to execute anyone wearing a hat. The king's horrid nephew, The Grand Duke Wilfred, suggests that he be allowed to push poor Bartholomew off the highest parapet of the castle. As they climb the stairs, Bartholomew desperately tears off his hats that become more and more elaborate. The 500th hat is so "be-

feathered and bejeweled" that the king offers to spare Bartholomew's life in exchange for his gorgeous hat. Bartholomew gladly removes it. Much to his relief, his head remains bare. *Bartholomew and the Oobleck* is a sequel to the magical medieval tale of Bartholomew Cubbins.

Kenneth Grahame's *The Reluctant Dragon* is the droll tale of a peace-loving dragon who is forced to fight St. George. The dragon's friend, called simply the Boy, arranges a meeting between St. George and the dragon, and a mock fight is planned. St. George is the hero of the day, the dragon is highly entertained at a banquet, and the Boy is pleased to have saved both the dragon and St. George. The pictures by Ernest Shepard add to the subtle humor of this book.

Jack of Dover by Richard Garnett, a wonderful spoof on many of the common fairy tale motifs, includes a handsome prince, a fearful dragon, and the biggest fool of all Christendom, Jack himself. But this didn't bother Jack because he knew every tale of a lucky fool that had ever been told—and he believed them all. So Jack sets out for London town to make his fortune, and the comedy of errors begins. In his first adventure, he falls for the old pebble-soup trick, but Garnett gives it a new twist. With the help of friendly Prince Sadi, Jack naively survives a series of adventures. Trapped into marrying the horrid Princess Matilda or losing his life, Jack finally uses his wits and defeats the prosecutor at his trial. The tongue-in-cheek style and play on words should make this witty story popular with middle graders. Graham Oakley's drawings add to the flavor and fun of this fantasy. Like the book, they imitate the old form of illuminated manuscripts with little figures enclosed in decorative frames.

A popular fairy tale of our time for adults and children is the haunting story of *The Little Prince* by Antoine de Saint-Exupéry. Written in the first person, the story tells of the author's encounter with the Little

Prince on the Sahara desert when he made a forced landing with his disabled plane. Bit by bit, he learns the strange history of the Little Prince. He found that the Little Prince lived all alone on a tiny planet no larger than a house. He possessed three volcanoes, two active and one extinct, and one flower, unlike any other flower in all the galaxy. However, when he saw a garden of roses, he doubted the uniqueness of his flower until a fox showed him that what we have loved is unique to us. This gentle story means many things to different people, but its wisdom and beauty are for all.

NEW TALL TALES

Tall tales are one of the few forms of folk tales that are indigenous to our North American culture. The stories of Paul Bunyan, Mike Fink, Pecos Bill, John Henry and others grew out of America's lusty braggadocious frontier life. It is only natural that authors should continue this form in writing stories today.

William Steele is a master at creating modern tall tales in the tradition of American folklore. *Daniel Boone's Echo, Davy Crockett's Earthquake,* and *Andy Jackson's Water Well* are stories about famous persons, but any resemblance to their real lives is purely coincidental! Nervous, quaking Aaron Adamsale reluctantly accompanied Daniel Boone to Kentucky although he was terrified of the Sling-Tailed Galootis and the One-Horned Sumpple that lay in wait for him. How Daniel helped Aaron overcome his fears is a succession of hilarious tall tales. *Davy Crockett's Earthquake* is a tongue-in-cheek account of Davy's adventures on a hunting trip in 1811. Davy had only intended to go bear hunting, but he ran into both a comet and an earthquake that changed the course of the Mississippi River. How he masters these two phenomena provides much more ex-

citement than a bear hunt. Andy Jackson and his friend, Chief Ticklepitcher, set out for East Tennessee to relieve the monstrous bad drought in Nashville. They bring back a water well in spite of ferocious land pirates, snapping turtles, and a hoopsnake that finally wore down to the size of a caterpillar. *Andy Jackson's Water Well* is indeed a tall tale! *The Spooky Thing* is a terrifying tale of the mountains. Two brothers who are as ornery and mean as rattlesnakes set off for town to do some trading for their father who couldn't stand hearing them fight with each other. On their way back through the woods, the boys are chased by a Thing, an awesome creature they couldn't see but could only hear. The Thing chases them throughout the book, coming closer and closer until finally a rabbit saves them. Based on an old Tennessee folk tale, this story will delight and terrify children at the same time. *The No-Name Man of the Mountain* is a tall tale about a younger brother who had no name because his twin brothers, Creel and Huckabuck, had taken it away from him for safekeeping. He was so ugly that his brothers made him wear an onion sack over his head and live on a no-account farm on the top of a mountain. The farm was so small that there wasn't enough air to go around and younger brother and his animals had to take turns breathing! At last, younger brother sets out with his crooked horse Filkin to find a better place to live and to get his name back. The way he finds his name is comic indeed. This tale has more humor than *The Spooky Thing.* Third and fourth graders love these hilarious tall tales.

Sid Fleischman is also becoming a master at creating modern tall tales. *Chancy and the Grand Rascal* is the story of a young orphan who sets out to find his brothers and sisters but first meets his uncle, the Grand Rascal, who can out-talk, out-laugh, and out-fox any man on the river. Uncle Will accompanies Chancy on his search, and what hilarious adventures they have! The free and easy style of this tale is exemplified by the Grand Rascal's account of his winter in Dakota:

> *"I had nothing to eat but my belt and my boots. They don't taste half bad, boiled. After that there was nothing to do but start in on the tree bark. There are places up in that country where it's twenty miles between trees, but I was lucky. I had all the aspens I could eat and some bur oak too. I didn't go hungry. Chancy, you won't believe it, but when spring came along I'd eaten so much wood that the sap began to rise in my veins — and I broke into bud. That's the almighty truth! And that's not even the worst of it. For three months after that I couldn't scratch my back without givin' myself splinters!"*[5]

Fleischman has also written *McBroom Tells the Truth*, a tall tale about a wonderful one-acre farm in Iowa that produces several crops daily. Once the owners had to wait as long as three hours for the field to produce a shade tree from an acorn! This tall tale is told in a matter-of-fact manner that contrasts suberbly with the gross exaggerations of the story.

Children need the humor and inventiveness of modern tall tales. Such tales are a healthy, robust sign of a country and people that can continue to laugh at themselves.

MODERN FANTASY

Books of fancy give an extra dimension to life, for they help push back the usual horizons of everyday living and encourage the child's creative powers. Children vary in their capacity for this imaginative thinking. The literal-minded child finds the suspension of reality a barrier to enjoyment of fantasy; other children relish the opportunity to enter the world of enchantment. Children's reactions to books of modern fantasy are seldom predictable or mild; they appear to be either vehemently for or against them. Frequently, taste for fantasy may be developed by reading aloud such books as Milne's *Winnie the Pooh* or Merrill's *The Pushcart War*.

Guides to Evaluating Modern Fantasy

Books of modern fantasy are usually longer than fairy tales and may take a variety of forms. All contain some imaginary elements that are contrary to reality as we know it today; for example, they may personify animals or toys, create new worlds, change the size of human beings, give humans unusual powers, or manipulate time patterns. Some fantasies utilize several of these approaches. Characteristic of most fantasy, like the fairy tales of old, is the presentation of a universal truth or a hidden meaning — love overcomes hate, the fools may be wiser than the wise men, the granting of wishes may not bring happiness. Well-written fantasy, like other fiction, will have a well-constructed plot, convincing characterization, worthwhile theme, and appropriate style. However, additional considerations need to guide the evaluation of fantasy.

The primary concern is the way the author made his fantasy believable. A variety of techniques may be used to create belief in the unbelievable. Many authors firmly ground a story in reality before gradually moving into the fantasy. Not until Chapter Three in *Charlotte's Web* does author E. B. White suggest that Fern can understand the farm animals as they talk. And even then, Fern never talks to the animals, she only listens to them. By the end of the story, Fern is growing up and really is more interested in listening to Henry Zuckerman than to the animals.

Another method for creating belief is the careful attention to the detail of the setting.

[5]Sid Fleischman, *Chancy and the Grand Rascal*, Illustrated by Eric von Schmidt (Boston: Little, Brown, 1966), p. 43.

Mary Norton's graphic description of the Borrowers' home beneath the clock enables the reader to visualize this domestic background and to feel what it would be like to be as small as *The Borrowers.* The well-written fantasy includes details of sensory imagery helping the reader to experience the sounds, smells, and tastes of this new world.

The characters' acceptance of the fanciful nature of the book is another device for developing credibility. In *Earthfasts,* Mayne has portrayed David and Keith as two rather mature scientific children. Therefore, their acceptance and horror of an eighteenth century drummer rising out of the earth create the same kind of reaction from the reader. Max could very easily have picked up the twelve toy soldiers and taken them to the Haworth Museum in *The Return of the Twelves* by Clarke. However, he respected the integrity of the little soldiers and helped them in their march to safety. The reader, too, comes to think of these soldiers as being alive.

Documentation, real or imagined, will give a feeling of truth to a statement. Merrill's constant references to verified statements or pictures make *The Pushcart War* of 1976 seem as if it actually happened. Hollander has used a similar technique as he refers to the lost manuscripts in presenting his story of *The Quest of the Gole.* The use of appropriate language adds a kind of documentation to fantasy. Underground for nearly two hundred years, the drummer uses such obsolete words as "arfish" for "afraid" in *Earthfasts,* and his lack of understanding of such modern words as "breakfast" seems very authentic, indeed.

The proof of real objects gives an added dimension of truth. How can one explain the origin of Greta's kitten or her father's penknife, if not from Blue Cove in Julia Sauer's story of *Fog Magic.* When elderly Mrs. Oldknow mends a quilt, she reminisces over pieces from Susan's dresses as she tells Tolly about the little blind girl in *The Treasure of Green Knowe.* All these devices may increase the reader's belief in the fantasy.

Another point to be considered when evaluating fantasy is the consistency of the story. Each fantasy should have a logical framework and an internal consistency within the rules that the author has developed. Characters cannot become invisible whenever they face difficulty, unless invisibility is a well-established part of their nature. The laws of fantasy may be strange indeed, but they must be obeyed.

Finally, while all plots should be original, the plots of fantasy must be ingenious and creative. A contrived or trite plot seems more obvious in a fanciful tale than in a realistic story.

In summary, the following specific questions might guide evaluation of modern fantasy:

- What are the fantastic elements of the story?
- How has the author made the story believable?
- Is the story logical and consistent within the framework established by the author?
- Is the plot original and ingenious?

Strange and Curious Worlds

When Alice followed the White Rabbit down his rabbit hole and entered into a world that grew "curiouser and curiouser," she established a pattern for many modern books of fantasy. Starting in the world of reality, they move quickly into the world of fantasy where the everyday becomes extraordinary in a believable fashion. The plausible impossibilities of *Alice's Adventures in Wonderland* include potions to drink and edibles to eat that make poor Alice grow up and down like an elevator. At the famous "Mad Hatter's Tea Party," there is no room nor tea. The Mad Hatter, the Dormouse, and the Rabbit are just a few of the individuals whom Alice meets in her wandering. Other characters include the Red Queen, who has to keep running in order to stay "in the same place"; the hurrying White Rabbit, who keeps murmuring that he'll be late—yet no one knows where he is going; the terrifying Queen of Hearts, who indiscriminately shouts, "Off with her head." Alice's matter-of-fact acceptance of these nonsensical statements makes them seem believable. Alice herself maintains her own personality despite her bizarre surroundings. She becomes the one link with reality in this amazingly fantastic world.

Not all children enjoy *Alice's Adventures in Wonderland*, for many of them do not have the maturity or imagination required to appreciate this fantasy. Teachers and librarians might read certain popular selections from the story and then encourage those who enjoy the stories to read the entire book.

The cyclone that blew Dorothy into the Land of Oz continues to blow swirling controversies around this series of books by L. Frank Baum and others. Some maintain that *The Wizard of Oz* is a skillfully written fantasy, a classic in its own right. Others condemn the first book because of some of the poorly written volumes that followed. Altogether, there are some forty Oz books, of which Baum himself wrote nineteen. *The Wizard of Oz* was the first book and is the most popular. In this story, Dorothy, her dog, Toto, the Scarecrow, the Tin Woodman, and the Cowardly Lion make the long, hazardous trip to the Emerald City to seek special gifts of the Wonderful Wizard. The Scarecrow wishes for brains, the Tin Woodman, a heart, and the Lion wants to be brave. Dorothy only wants to go back to Kansas to her Aunt Em and Uncle Henry. The book contains some satire, for example, the "heartless" Tin Woodman is really very thoughtful, refusing even to step on ants.

> *The Tin Woodman knew very well he had no heart, and therefore he took care never to be cruel or unkind to anything.*
>
> *"You people with hearts . . . have something to guide you, and need never do wrong; but I have no heart, and so I must be very careful. When Oz gives me a heart of course I needn't mind so much."*[6]

Eventually each of the characters achieves his particular wish, but the wizardry is in the way they think of themselves rather than anything that the Wizard does for them. For the most part, this fantasy depends upon the strange situations and creatures that Dorothy and her companions meet rather than anything that they do or say. One never doubts that the four will overcome all odds and achieve their wishes. Even the Wizard holds no fear for practical, matter-of-fact Dorothy. This lack of wonder and awe, the basic ingredients of most fantasy, makes *The Wizard of Oz* seem somewhat pedestrian when compared with other books of its kind.

Mary B. Palmer has created another very forthright little girl, Andulasia, the heroine of *The Teaspoon Tree*. The author firmly grounds this story in reality, before she moves into the fanciful. Notice the transition that is made in the first two paragraphs of the book:

> *Andulasia had parents like anyone else, but much of the time she might just as well not have. Whole delicious slices of the day belonged entirely to her. The afternoon was particularly her own. And this, since she was a determined, inquisitive, and adventurous type, was spent beyond the First Hill.*
>
> *Once over the hill, she entered a different world. There, arithmetic and spelling didn't matter. Nor scales. Nor punctuality, school spirit, tidying-up, finishing-everything-on-your-plate, washing behind both ears, getting*

---

[6]I. Frank Baum, *The Wizard of Oz*, Illustrated by W. W. Denslow (New York: Dover, 1960, 1900), p. 72.

sweaters on frontwards, and closing the front door QUIETLY. The people and animals she met treated her as a person, not somebody who was going to be one later on. They never asked her how old she was, exclaimed at how much she had grown, or made her play a piece on the piano. They didn't fuss about whether or not she would ever learn to sew or acquire the graces of a "little lady." They just seemed to take her the way she was on the particular day she turned up.[7]

As Andulasia marches along with her pop gun, in quest of the teaspoon tree, she meets an amazing assortment of characters—the Lady Who Names Things, the Commuting Animal who's terribly busy coming and going "between," the terrifying Melifflua, the Antiquarian with the extra long beard, and others. At last, Andulasia reaches the tree that had thirty-one silver and red teaspoons on it shimmering and jingling in the breeze. Andulasia intends to take the tree home with her until she realizes that it was the only beautiful thing in the owl's life. Like all quests, the seeking was greater than the prize, and the joy lay in telling of the adventure.

For many years, the Moomintroll family has delighted children of Sweden. Now American children are taking to these strange but endearing creatures that look slightly like hippopotamuses. The Moomin live in a lonely valley with various peculiar friends, the Snork Maiden, restless Snufkin, and the moody stamp-collector, Hemulen, who comes to visit and never leaves, and, of course, the horrid Hattifatteners. Each member of the Moomin family is an individual and remains faithful to his characterization throughout the series of books. *Tales from Moominvalley* is the first, and perhaps, best of this fantastic series. Each episode is stranger and more frightening than the last in these fantasies, but the inner life of the characters is what gives them depth. Tove Jansson won the 1966 Hans Christian Andersen International Award for her contribution to the literature of children. Not all American children react favorably to these strange creatures, but those who do, become enthusiastic "Moominfans."

A popular fantasy of today is Roald Dahl's marvelous morality tale, *Charlie and the Chocolate Factory*. Mr. Willie Wonka, owner of the mysterious, locked chocolate factory, suddenly announced that the five children who find the gold seal on their chocolate bars will be allowed to visit his fabulous factory. And what an assortment of children win—Augustus Gloop, a greedy fat pig of a boy; Veruca Salt, a spoiled, little rich girl whose parents always buy her what she wants; Violet Beauregarde, the world's champion gum chewer; Mike Teevee, a fresh child who spent every waking moment in front of television; *and* Charlie Bucket, the Hero, who was honest, brave, trustworthy, obedient, poor, and starving. One by one, the children are disobedient and meet with horrible accidents in the chocolate factory. Nothing, of course, happens to the virtuous Charlie. At the end of the story, Charlie and Mr. Wonka fly an elevator back to Charlie's house to pick up his starving family and take them to live at the chocolate factory while Charlie learns all of Mr. Wonka's secrets in order to become the future owner of this marvelous place. The play on words in this highly creative story is not forced but certainly provides much of the humor.

Going through *The Phantom Tollbooth*, Milo discovered a strange and curious world indeed. Norton Juster, the author, created "The Lands Beyond," which included The Foothills of Confusion, the Mountains of Ignorance, the Lands of Null, the Doldrums, and the Sea of Knowledge. Here Milo meets King Azoz the Unabridged, the unhappy

---

[7]Mary B. Palmer, *The Teaspoon Tree*, Illustrated by Carlota Dodge (Boston: Houghton Mifflin, 1963), pp. 1–2.

ruler of Dictionopolis, the Mathemagician who served them subtraction stew and increased their hunger, and the watchdog, Tock, who keeps on ticking throughout all their adventures. Among the many funny episodes in the book is the Royal Banquet where the guests must eat their words! But the substance of this fantasy is in its play on words rather than its characters or situations. Its appreciation is dependent upon the reader's knowledge of various meanings of words. For this reason, it is funny only for children with mature vocabularies.

Rather than create their own imaginary worlds, many authors have successfully blended fantasy with reality to produce strange elements in the known world. A hauntingly beautiful fantasy is a story of the Appalachian mountains titled *You Better Come Home with Me* by John Lawson. No one saw the Boy come down the mountains, he just appeared on Main Street one Saturday night and joined the men as they sat around the stove at Nagles' store. As they got up to leave, the Scarecrow said, "You'd better come home with me," which, as everyone in the mountains knows, is a way of saying goodbye. But the Boy, who had no home and did not know who he was, accepted it for the welcome it offered. At the Scarecrow's house, he met the clever Mr. Fox, the witch, and the wise Snowman who thought he recognized the Boy, but melted before he could tell him who he was. The Boy felt at home at the Scarecrow's house and he savored the beauty of the woods and the hay fields—somehow he belonged here. All the while, the Boy was drawn to the Old Man, who had told him to get off his property. This mystical story of the Boy's quest for his identity blends reality with fantasy. Lawson's descriptions of the coming of the Appalachian spring are superb:

Sometimes the thaw came suddenly. You smell it first, warm and sweet. Then the rain came. It was almost as if just then he felt a drop. Then

he did hear it coming softly in the mountains—ten thousand million thousand drops falling on bare branches, onto the snow, each drop making a dent.[8]

The cherry tree was reaching, and where its branches had been bare the night before because it had lost last year's leaves, now the branches were bare because this year's leaves had not yet come.[9]

For *A Grass Rope*, William Mayne has created belief in Mary's unicorn by acknowledging everyone else's disbelief. Nan, her older sister, did not believe in the legend at all. Adam, however, tried to find rational explanations behind the old story of a unicorn and a treasure. Mary was too young to bother about science, she simply believed and wove a grass rope to catch the unicorn. The old sign at the Unicorn Inn gave the children their first clues. The rest of the story is told almost entirely through conversation until the very end when Mary's action frightens everyone. She doesn't find her unicorn at the bottom of the old mine shaft, but she does find the nine silver collars that had belonged to the dogs in the legend and a genuine unicorn's skull! The Yorkshire setting of this story is made more vivid by old Charlie's dialect. However, Mary's childlike expressions are characteristic of all children who still wonder—for example, "What colour is a thing you can't see?"[10]

The Sea Egg by L. M. Boston is the haunting story of two young boys and their magical summer on the Cornish coast. The boys buy an unusual egg-shaped rock from a lobsterman and place it in a sheltered pool of sea water that could be reached only at low tide through a tunnel. They hoped that whatever it might be—sea serpent, sea horse

---

[8]John Lawson, *You Better Come Home with Me,* Illustrated by Arnold Spilka (New York: Crowell, 1966), p. 68.

[9]Lawson, p. 70.

[10]William Mayne, *A Grass Rope,* Illustrated by Lynton Lamb (New York: Dutton, 1962), p. 54.

or genii—could hatch in secrecy and safety in this hidden spot. The egg hatches into a baby triton (a merman), with whom they swim and play most of the day. On the last night of the boys' holiday, their companion shared the most remarkable experience of all—a magical night swimming with the seals through the underwater tunnels of Seal Island. L. M. Boston evokes an eerie beauty in this strange, suspenseful sea adventure.

The private world of dreams can be a strange and curious blend of reality with the fanciful. For Calpurnia, *The Secret River* was real, but Mother Albirtha told her she would never see it again. The background for this simple and beautiful story by Marjorie Kinnan Rawlings is Florida. When hard times come to the back woods, Calpurnia wants to make the "hard times, soft times." She asks Mother Albirtha where she might catch some fish. The old lady tells her to follow her nose to the Secret River. Following her nose, which had followed a rabbit and a blue jay, Calpurnia finds a beautiful river that she had never seen before. She finds a boat along the shore and fills it with fish. When next she looks for the secret river, it is gone. Mother Albirtha tells her that the secret river is in her mind, and that she may go there by simply closing her eyes. Did Calpurnia dream her secret river? If so, how do you account for the fish? This story is well illustrated by Leonard Weisgard. It is appropriate for young children in second or third grade.

Ben wished for a dog so intensely that he began to dream he had one in the story of *A Dog So Small* by Philippa Pearce. His grandfather had promised him a dog for his birthday, but his parents had said it was impossible to have a dog in London. Instead, his grandparents gave him a little wool-embroidered picture of a chihuahua. Ben lost the picture on the train, but he didn't lose the one he carried in his mind, Chiquitito, the little dog that always came in his dreams and responded to his call. Ben drifted into his dream world more and more, closing his eyes to see his dog. One day Ben closed his eyes and stepped into the street—following Chiquitito—and was struck by a car. After his recovery, Ben's parents allowed him to have a puppy. He is overwhelmingly disappointed because it is so big, not small like his dream dog. His grandmother wisely comments: "People get their heart's desire . . . and then they have to begin to learn to live with it."[11] Finally, Ben learns that it's best to be satisfied with possible things rather than dream of the impossible. The intensity of the feeling of loneliness in this story is similar to that created by DeJong in *Shadrach*, the realistic story of a little boy and his black rabbit.

Imaginary Kingdoms

Frequently, authors have created long fairy tales about mythical kingdoms. Carefully detailing the settings, even providing maps of these strange lands, the authors have made them seem very real. The laws of the kingdom and the customs of the people are described—they may be very different from ours, but once stated they do not deviate.

Elizabeth Enright has presented a detailed description of the kingdom of Tatrajan in her story of *Tatsinda*, the lovely little girl who had golden hair and brown eyes. All the animals in the kingdom had names that began with "ti," like the racing tidwell prized by the Tatran children. The people had names that began with "Ta," as well as white hair that glittered like snow crystals and greenish blue eyes—all except Tatsinda. On the other side of the wall of mist that surrounded Tatrajan, lived a tribe of ugly troll-like giants—the Gadblangs, who spent all their lives digging for greb, a precious metal. Johrgong, their leader, discovered Tatrajan and, attracted by the gold color of

---

[11]Philippa Pearce, *A Dog So Small*, Illustrated by Antony Maitland (Philadelphia: Lippincott, 1962), p. 138.

The little people of Tatrajan raise their lanterns to behold the awesome spectacle of Johrgong, the giant. Illustration from *Tatsinda,* © 1963 by Elizabeth Enright and Irene Haas. Reproduced by permission of Harcourt, Brace & World, Inc.

Tatsinda's hair, seized her as a hostage. Prince Tackatan rescues Tatsinda, and with her help, rids the kingdom of the evil Johrgong forever. Enright has created a gracious, fragile world in this believable fairy tale. Irene Haas has illustrated magical pictures with delicate lines to complement the beauty of the story.

Many children know the land of Narnia as well as their own backyards or city blocks. C. S. Lewis, a well-known English scholar and theologian, created seven fantasies about the country of Narnia. The best of the series is the first published, *The Lion, the Witch, and the Wardrobe,* although it was the second in the sequence according to the history of Narnia. Beginning quite realistically in our time and world, four children find their way into the land of Narnia through the back of a huge wardrobe in one of the large rooms of an old English house. They find Narnia wrapped in a blanket of snow and ice, under the wicked Snow Queen's spell that controls the weather so it is "always winter and never Christmas." The children and the Narnians pitch themselves against the evil witch and her motley assortment of ghouls, boggles, minotaurs, and hags. With the coming of the great Aslan, the Lion, signs of spring are seen in the land. The children successfully aid the lion king in destroying the evil forces in his land, and he crowns them Kings and Queens of Narnia. Narnia has its own history and time, and in *The Magician's Nephew,* the reader is told of the beginnings of Narnia born from the Lion's song of creation. Narnian time is brief as measured against our time, so in each visit of the children, several hundred Narnian years have passed. In the seventh and last of the books of Narnia, King Tirian remembers the stories of his ancestors about the Earth Children and calls on them to come to his aid in this, *The Last Battle.* Narnia is destroyed, yet the real Narnia, the inner Narnia, is not. The children learn that no good thing is ever lost, and the real identity of the Great Lion, Aslan, is finally revealed to them. These stories are mysterious, intriguing, and beautifully written. If children do not always understand their religious allegory, they may appreciate them as wondrous adventures that somehow reveal more than they say.

Welsh legends and mythology are the inspiration for the intriguing chronicles of the imaginary land of Prydain as told by Lloyd Alexander. In *The Book of Three,* the reader is introduced to Taran, an assistant pigkeeper who dreams of becoming a hero. With a strange assortment of companions, he pursues Hen Wen, the oracular pig, and struggles to save Prydain from the forces of evil. Probably no one was less prepared for this role than Taran, but he grew as he erred, and matured under stress. Dalben later tells him, "the seeking counts more than the finding." The chronicles are continued in the most exciting of all of the books, *The Black Cauldron.* Once again, the faithful companions fight evil as they seek to find and destroy the great cauldron in which are created the dread Cauldron-Born, "mute and deathless warriors" made from the stolen bodies of those slain in battle. Taran is proud to be chosen to fight for Lord Gwydion, for now he will have more opportunity to win honor than when washing pigs or weeding a garden. His wise and sensitive companion Adaon answers him thus:

"I have marched in many a battle host . . . . but I have also planted seeds and reaped the harvest with my own hands. And I have learned there is greater honor in a field well plowed than in a field steeped in blood."[12]

The perceptive Adaon also opens Taran's eyes to the natural beauty round about him as he says:

"There is much to be known . . . . and above all much to be loved, be it the turn of the seasons or the shape of a river pebble. Indeed, the more we find to love, the more we add to the measure of our hearts."[13]

Gradually, Taran learns what it means to become a man among men—the sacrifice of his gentle Adaon, the final courage of the proud Ellidyr, and the faithfulness of his companions. He experiences treachery, tragedy and triumph, yet a thread of humor runs throughout this sinister tale to lighten its tension. Good does prevail, and Taran has matured and is ready for his next adventure. In the third book of the series, *The Castle of Llyr,* Taran escorts Princess Eilonwy to the Isle of Mona, where Queen Teleria is expected to teach the temperamental Eil-

onwy to behave as a proper princess. Eilonwy is kidnapped by the wicked Chief Steward and the faithful companions of Prydain pursue him to fight with might and magic. The story is enlivened by a faint trace of love and delightful humor. In the fourth book of the Prydain Cycle, *Taran Wanderer,* Taran goes questing in search of his identity. His search takes him through awful marshes at Morva, the rugged wastelands, and at length to the Llawgadarn Mountains where in a moving climax, he looks into the Mirror of Llunet. More important than the identity of his parentage, however, is Taran's self-discovery of who he is and what he dares to become. Each of these titles may be read independently, but together they represent an exciting adventure in some of the best-written fantasy of our time.

John Hollander has given a feeling of authenticity and credibility to his tale of *The Quest of the Gole* by constant reference to an old manuscript, part of which is in unrhymed poetry, and parts from other sources that are rhymed. The story has the mark of an old Norse saga as it begins:

Way to northwest, where the water whispers
As the cold sea slips up into the saltmarshes
And frost forms at the foot of the trees,
There was a high hall. Hrimhaegl it was
called. . . .[14]

When the good king of Hrimhaegl came to die, he told his sons of a curse that was laid upon his land that had kept it so wet and cold. No one could become king until one discovered a mysterious something called the "Gole." Each of the brothers saw his search in a different light, and only Moad, the third brother, persevered until finally:

. . . he beheld a picture of fulfillment; of the end of all quests that do not merely lead to new ones; of what would always lie beyond wanting and doing and getting; but what was more

[12]Lloyd Alexander, *The Black Cauldron* (New York: Holt, Rinehart and Winston, 1965), p. 43.

[13]Alexander, p. 43.

[14]John Hollander, *The Quest of the Gole,* Illustrated by Reginald Pollack (New York: Atheneum, 1966), p. 7.

A loyal Charlotte spins her opinion of her friend Wilbur. Garth Williams has captured the expressive feelings and humor of the animals in this story. Illustration by Garth Williams from *Charlotte's Web* by E. B. White. Harper & Row, 1952.

clearly and certainly there *than anything outside of himself that Moad had ever known.*[15]

Moad and his wife Sophia return to their land and see the towns of Hrimhaegl glistening in the sun—the curse has been lifted. This is a strange and deeply moving tale filled with adventure, wanderings, and wisdom.

Animal Fantasy

Many authors create fantasy by personifying animals and imagining their thoughts and conversations. Sometimes humans can converse with these animals, and sometimes

they cannot. In E. B. White's delightful fantasy, *Charlotte's Web*, eight-year-old Fern can only understand the geese who always speak in triplicate ("certainly-ertainly-ertainly"), the wise old sheep, and Templeton, the crafty rat. The true heroine of the story is Charlotte A. Cavatica, a beautiful, large, gray spider who befriends Wilbur, a humble, little pig. The kindly old sheep inadvertently drops the news that as soon as Wilbur is nice and fat, he will be butchered. When Wilbur becomes hysterical, Charlotte promises to save him. By miraculously spinning words into her web that describe the pig as "radiant," "terrific," and "humble," she makes Wilbur famous. The pig is saved, but Charlotte dies alone on the fairgrounds. Wilbur manages to bring Charlotte's egg sac back to the farm so the continuity of life in the barnyard is maintained. Wilbur never forgets his friend Charlotte, though he loves her children and grandchildren dearly. Because of her, Wilbur may look forward to a secure and pleasant old age:

> *Life in the barn was very good—night and day, winter and summer, spring and fall, dull days and bright days. It was the best place to be, thought Wilbur, this warm delicious cellar, with the garrulous geese, the changing seasons, the heat of the sun, the passage of swallows, the nearness of rats, the sameness of sheep, the love of spiders, the smell of manure, and the glory of everything.*[16]

This is a story that has humor, pathos, wisdom, and beauty. Its major theme speaks of the web of true friendship and life. All ages find meaning in this most popular fantasy. Much of our fantasy is of English origin. *Charlotte's Web* is as American as the Fourth of July and should be just as much a part of our children's heritage. An earlier book by E. B. White tells the story of *Stuart Little*, the

---

[15] Hollander, p. 115.

[16] E. B. White, *Charlotte's Web*, Illustrated by Garth Williams (New York: Harper & Row, 1952), p. 183.

mouse son of the Frederick C. Littles. Children are intrigued by Stuart's many exciting aventures. Adults are somewhat disturbed by the calm acceptance of a mouse born to human parents, but this in no way bothers children.

The Mousewife by Rumer Godden is a tender story of the friendship between a small, industrious, mousewife and an encaged turtledove. At first, the mouse is only interested in the dried peas in the bird's cage; but later, she comes to know the dove as a friend. The dove tells her about dew, about night, and the glory of flying. It is with wonder and awe that the little mousewife learns of the outside world. At last, she can no longer stand to think of her friend imprisoned in a cage and she jumps on the catch, releasing the dove. As she sees him fly away, she cries tears the size of millet seeds. But she knows now what it means to fly, for she has seen the stars, and some of the world beyond. There is a gentle sadness in this story that reminds the reader of some of Andersen's tales. William Pène du Bois has captured mouse expressions of wonder and compassion in his soft gray and white illustrations that are so appropriate for this animal fantasy.

Robert Lawson has written a gay and gentle story about all the little animals who live on *Rabbit Hill.* The story opens with excitement and wonder about the new folks who are moving into the big house on the hill. Will they be planting folks who like small animals, or shiftless, mean people? Each animal character responds in his own unique way to this sudden bit of news. Mother Rabbit is a worrier and tends to be pessimistic; Father Rabbit, stately and always eloquent, feels that there are many auspicious signs (he is a Southern gentleman and always speaks in such a fashion), and young Georgie delightedly leaps down the hill chanting, "New folks coming, new folks coming!" Uncle Analdas, who comes to visit

his sister on Rabbit Hill, is somewhat disinterested but debonair, as befitting a worldly bachelor. Although on probation for several days after their arrival, the new folks win the approval of all the animals of Rabbit Hill by putting up a large sign that says "Please Drive Carefully on Account of Small Animals." They plant a garden without a fence, provide much garbage for Phewie, the skunk, and do not permit the use of poison or traps. Little Willie, the fieldmouse, is rescued from drowning in the rain barrel and Georgie is saved from an automobile accident. Finally, on Midsummer's Eve, the animals on Rabbit Hill have an opportunity to return the kindnesses of the gentle Folks who live in the house. *The Tough Winter* is a sequel to *Rabbit Hill* and describes the plight of all the animals when the "Folks" go away for the winter and leave a neglectful caretaker and mean dog in charge. Both these books are more thoroughly enjoyed by fourth and fifth graders if they can be savored together during story time.

The urban counterpart of *Charlotte's Web* and *Rabbit Hill* is *The Cricket in Times Square* by Selden. A fast-talking Broadway mouse named Tucker and his pal, Harry the Cat, initiate a small country cricket called Chester into the vagaries of city living. Chester spends only one summer in New York City, having been transported in someone's picnic lunchbasket. The climax of Chester's summer adventures comes when the cricket begins giving nightly concerts from the Bellinis' newsstand, saving his benefactors from bankruptcy. On his last night before his return to Connecticut, Chester brings traffic in New York City to a standstill as he chirps the sextet from *Lucia di Lammermoor.* After his friends, Tucker and Harry, find him a small corner out of the wind on the Late Local Express, they return to Tucker Mouse's home in the drain pipe and plan their vacation for next summer in the country in Connecticut! The incongruous friendship of these three companions, their comments on city life, and their sophisticated dialogue make this a memorable fantasy. Garth Williams has captured the human expressions of these animals in such a way as to picture each of their personalities.

Dear Rat by Julia Cunningham is a tremendous spoof on a hard-boiled detective story. Andrew is a tough-talking but tender-hearted rat from Humpton, Wyoming. Andrew knows his way around the world and can usually take care of himself in any company. He nearly meets his match in Chartres, France, however, in the person of a villainous rat named Groge, head of an underworld mob. Andrew finds himself caught in a wicked scheme to steal the jewels from the cathedral and dispose of the loot in Paris. Plots, counterplots, and a wild chase through the sewers of Paris keep Andrew running for his life. But in the end, the jewels are restored, and Andrew has gained the love of the royal Princess Angelique. The line pictures and typeface are printed in deep purple—a most appropriate touch.

Macaroon, by the same author, is a more subtle and gentle animal fantasy. It is the story of a raccoon, a fox, and a very naughty, lonely little girl. In the fall when the leaves turned to scarlet and the air became crisp, the raccoon knew it was time for him to adopt a child. Each year, he allowed himself to be hugged and loved in return for soft rugs in front of a fire and his meals delivered in a special saucer. It was a good arrangement, the raccoon felt, far better than a cold hole in a tree, except for the leaving. Each year, it became increasingly difficult to abandon his adopted children on the first day of spring. This year, therefore, he had decided to adopt the most impossible of all impossible children, so the spring departure would be a relief. The raccoon did find such a girl, named Erika, living at the big house. The relationship was perfect—she called him old macaroon and threw food at him. Slowly

and quite believably, Macaroon reforms Erika and loses his heart to her in the process. Evaline Ness has portrayed the temperament and tenderness of this story with her most unusual illustrations. *Viollet* is a rather sinister animal fantasy also by Julia Cunningham. It combines some elements of both *Dear Rat* and *Macaroon,* but does not have the humor of the first or the loving compassion of the second. An old count in France is threatened by danger from Tressac, his foreman of the vineyard. Oxford, the count's faithful dog, Warwick, the old wise fox, and Viollet, a timid thrush, all know of the evil plans but can do little to thwart them. At last, it is Viollet who overcomes her timidity to distract the aim of Tressac as he tries to kill the count. Fantasy and realism become too mixed in this story for believability. While the characters are clearly drawn, they lack focus. It is Viollet's story, yet the reader only meets her at the beginning and the end. One's sympathies are directed more towards Oxford, the hound, and Warwick, the old fox.

Margery Sharp's sinister stories of *Miss Bianca,* the pure and beautiful white mouse, are melodrama at its best. The first story is titled *The Rescuers* and tells of the breathtaking adventure of three mice, Miss Bianca, Bernard, and Nils as they rescue a Norwegian poet from the grim, windowless Black Castle. *Miss Bianca* is the exciting story of the rescue of a little girl, Patience, from the clutches of a hideous wicked duchess who lives in the Diamond Palace. She has twelve mechanical ladies-in-waiting who regularly bow to her every hour and say "as your Grace pleases." The fiendish duchess wants at least one human being who will react to her cruelty, however, so Patience was kidnapped for this purpose. The beautiful and gracious Miss Bianca and the humble and resolute Bernard effect her rescue with the aid of the mouse members of the Ladies Guild! Once again, Garth Williams has drawn the illustrations for this animal fantasy. No one can quite picture such varied human expressions on animals as Garth Williams. Also, he has portrayed the intricacies and atrocities of the Diamond Palace consistent with the vivid description of Margery Sharp. *The Turret* and *Miss Bianca in the Salt Mines* continue the adventures of these intrepid mice.

Two very small mice are the heroes of *Belling the Tiger,* a parody by Mary Stolz on the fable "Belling the Cat." In this version, the two smallest mice are "elected" to be the heroes who will bell the cat. As they attempt to obtain a collar and bell, they are chased by a waterfront cat onto a ship. After a long ocean voyage, the boat docks, and the two mice find themselves at the jungle's edge. The rest of the story is told by the title. Some of the tongue-in-cheek humor is adult, although most middle-graders would recognize the satire in the whispered conversation of the twin mice following Portman's announcement that a Steering Committee had come up with a solution to the question of the cat:

> *"What's a Steering Committee?" said Asa, one of the two smallest mice, to his brother, Rambo, the other smallest mouse.*
> *"It's Portman and his friends deciding before the meeting starts what we're going to decide in the meeting," said Rambo.*
> *"Is that fair?" said Asa.*
> *"It's customary," said Rambo.*[17]

The adventures of these engaging mice are continued in *The Great Rebellion, Siri the Conquistador,* and *Maximilian's World.*

Probably no one has recreated the animal world as magnificently as has Kenneth Grahame in his *The Wind in the Willows.* For sheer beauty of description and characterization, it has never been surpassed. This is the incomparable tale of Water Rat, Mole,

The evil duchess takes perverse delight in whipping little Patience. Garth Williams' pictures exaggerate the ugliness of the duchess and her hideous diamond palace as befitting this Victorian melodrama. From *Miss Bianca* by Margery Sharp, illustrated by Garth Williams. Little, Brown and Company, 1962.

Toad, and Badger. Kindly Badger is the oldest and wisest of the quartet, the one they all seek when they are in trouble. Rat is a practical soul, good-natured and intelligent. Mole is the appreciative, sometimes gullible one. The comic relief of the story is provided by Toad who develops one fad after another. He is always showing off and becoming involved in situations from which Rat, Mole, and Badger are forced to rescue him. The quiet adventures of Rat and Mole along their river bank evoke the beauty and mood of *The Wind in the Willows.*

Each chapter tells a complete adventure of these four friends. The most wonderful

---

[17]Mary Stolz, *Belling the Tiger,* Illustrated by Beni Montresor (New York: Harper & Row, 1961), p. 11.

episode in the story comes during the search by Rat and Mole for the baby otter, Portly. The two set out before dawn, Mole rowing, and Rat sitting in the stern of the boat. Suddenly Rat sits up and listens to the "thin, clear, happy call of distant piping." On they glide with the piping becoming clearer. At last, as if in a dream, they come before an august Presence, Pan, and between his hooves nestles the round pudgy form of the baby otter. Mole expresses his awe and wonder as he asks Rat if he is afraid:

> *"Afraid?" murmured the Rat, his eyes shining with unutterable love. "Afraid! Of* Him? *O, never, never! And yet—and yet—O, Mole, I am afraid!"*
> *Then the two animals, crouching to the earth, bowed their heads and did worship.*
> *Sudden and magnificent, the sun's broad golden disc showed itself over the horizon facing them; and the first rays, shooting across the level water-meadows, took the animals full in the eye and dazzled them. When they were able to look once more, the Vision had vanished, and the air was full of the carol of birds that hailed the dawn.*[18]

Kenneth Grahame has created a world of mirth, quiet beauty, and enchantment. All children will not have the background of experience to appreciate its beauty, but those who do, love this book above all others. It is best read aloud a chapter at a time, just as Grahame wrote it for his son.

The mystical quality of *The Wind in the Willows* is also found in a moving allegory by Agnes Smith, *An Edge of the Forest*. A small, black lamb whose mother had died, wandered into the forest and was saved from death by a young black leopardess. Trusting and innocent, the lamb brought love into the forest and received only love in return. In fact, the black leopardess, the doe, and the owls became friends as they protected and cared for him. But all except the smallest mouse are fearful of the black lamb—what was he doing to the forest, and who was the black lamb? A parallel story of a farmer's third son and his love for his grandmother is woven into the plot. The black lamb and his mother had belonged to the boy's flock. After their loss, the boy tells his father that he does not want to be a shepherd for he thinks only of the sheep, not the flock.

> *"I love the flock," he said, "but, Father, I'm no shepherd. I'm a lamb and a wolf and grass and the grazer. I can't give my life to the multitudinous. I'm a lover of singularity, of multiplicity. I'm a master fool."*[19]

At the end, the black lamb leaves his friends in the forest who fear his love and returns to the young man and his grandmother. Not all children will understand the symbolism of this beautifully written book.

Randall Jarrell, the late poet, wrote two fanciful animal tales, *The Bat Poet* and *The Animal Family*. Of the two, the story of the small brown bat that turns poet is more appropriate for children than *The Animal Family*. Once a bat, for some reason, couldn't sleep during the days, so he opened his eyes and saw squirrels and chipmunks, the sun and the mockingbird. He tried to get the other little bats to open their eyes and see the world, but they refused. Admiring the mockingbird's many songs, the little bat makes up some of his own. However, he can't sing, he can only squeak, so he just tries saying the words. He tries his poems out on the bats, but they aren't interested. The mockingbird deigns to listen, but comments only on the form, not the content of his poem. At last, he finds the perfect listener, the chipmunk who is delighted with his

---

[18]Kenneth Grahame, *The Wind in the Willows*, Illustrated by E. H. Shepard (New York: Scribner, 1940, 1908), p. 136.

[19]Agnes Smith, *An Edge of the Forest*, Illustrated by Roberta Moynihan (New York: Viking, 1959), p. 109.

poems and believes in them. The fine pen-and-ink drawings by Maurice Sendak give the impression of steel engravings. *The Animal Family* tells of man's longing for a family. A man and woman and their son are ship-wrecked on an uninhabited coast where they live an isolated life. The boy's mother and father grow old and die, and the boy, now a man, is left completely alone. His loneliness is intensified by his desire to share beauty. The hunter's loneliness is assuaged as a mermaid, bear, lynx, and finally, a ship-wrecked baby become his family. This is a strange and haunting story of man's need to create a family relationship. Sendak has wisely illustrated the original home of each member of the family, the hunter's cabin, the sea, the tree where the bear was found, the cave of the baby lynx, and the empty boat of the boy. The hunter, the mermaid, the boy, and the animals he has left to the reader's imagination.

The World of Toys and Dolls

Just as authors have endowed animals with human characteristics, so too have they personified toys and dolls. Young children enjoy stories that personify the inanimate, such as a tugboat or a steamshovel.[20] Seven-, eight-, and nine-year-olds still like to imagine that their favorite playthings have a life of their own. Hans Christian Andersen utilized this approach in his stories of "The Steadfast Tin Soldier," "The Fir Tree," and many others. One of the most popular of all children's stories, *The Adventures of Pinocchio*, by Collodi, is a personification type of story. The mischievous puppet that old Geppetto carves out of wood becomes alive and has all kinds of adventures. He plays hookey from school, wastes his money, and tells lies. Each time he lies to the Blue Fairy his nose grows longer, until it is so long that he has difficulty turn-

ing around in a room. When Pinocchio at last does something for someone else, he becomes a real boy. Written in Italy in 1880, this story has been translated into many different languages and is a universal favorite.

Probably no one has made toys seem quite so much like people as has A. A. Milne in his well-loved Pooh stories. Each chapter contains a separate adventure about the favorite stuffed toys of Milne's son, Christopher Robin. The good companions include *Winnie-the-Pooh*, a bear of little brain; doleful Eeyore, the donkey; Piglet, the happy follower and devoted friend of Pooh; and Rabbit, Owl, Kanga, and little Roo. A bouncy new friend, Tigger, joins the group in Milne's second book, *The House at Pooh Corner*. They all live in the "100 Aker Wood" and spend most of their time getting into, and out of, exciting and amusing situations. One time, Pooh becomes wedged in a very tight place and has to abstain from eating his "hunny" for a whole week until he grows thin again. Eight- and nine-year-olds thoroughly enjoy the humor of the Heffalump story and appreciate the self-pity of gloomy Eeyore on his birthday. They like kindly, but forgetful, Pooh who knocks at his own door and then wonders why no one answers. They are delighted when Piglet and Roo exchange places in Kanga's pocket and even more pleased when Piglet gets a dose of Roo's medicine! The humor in these stories is not hilarious but quiet and subtle, with a gentle touch of whimsy. Such humor is usually lost on primary children but greatly appreciated by children in the middle grades. However, younger children may enjoy the Pooh stories when they are read within a family circle. Parents' chuckles are contagious, and soon the whole family has become Pooh admirers. Some children and some adults see no humor in these fanciful stories. They are to be pitied, for they have missed much, but their preferences should be respected. Not everyone likes whimsy.

---

[20]See Chapter 3.

Rumer Godden makes the world of dolls seem very much alive in several of her books, *The Dolls' House, Impunity Jane, The Fairy Doll, Candy Floss, The Story of Holly and Ivy,* and *Home Is the Sailor.* The idea expressed in all Godden's doll books is stated best by Toddie in *The Dolls' House.* She says, "It is an anxious, sometimes a dangerous thing to be a doll. Dolls cannot choose; they can only be chosen; they cannot 'do;' they can only be done by."[21] Another characteristic of Godden's stories is that many of them are stories about boy dolls or even boys who enjoy playing with dolls. For example, Impunity Jane, so named because the salesclerk said she could be dropped "with impunity," belongs to a boy named Gideon. She pilots his airplane, rides his bicycle, and sails his boat. No doll could have more exciting or wonderful adventures. *Home Is the Sailor* is the story of a doll family's house that had for many years stood by a window in a house in Wales overlooking the sea. A touch of sadness pervaded this household of dolls, for there was not a male doll left, except for Curly, who was only a boy. Curly's chance meeting with Bertrand, a lonely French boy visiting Wales for the summer, gives him an opportunity for a marvelous adventure. Part of this unusual doll's story is the way Curly helps Bertrand grow up.

Another unique fantasy about dolls that appeals to both boys and girls is *The Return of the Twelves* by Pauline Clarke. Eight-year-old Max finds twelve wooden soldiers under an attic floor in a Yorkshire farmhouse not far from Haworth, the village where the Brontë family once lived. Warmed by his delight, the little soldiers come to life and talk to him of a time past when four "genii," Branwell, Charlotte, Emily, and Anne, loved them and played with them. Max and his sister learn that an American has offered 5000 pounds for Branwell Brontë's soldiers in order to give them to an American museum. The children reason that the toys belong in their ancestral house at Haworth, which is now the Brontë Museum. However, they respect the sturdy independence of the Twelves and help them make their last march to Haworth rather than carry them there. Various persons report having seen the soldiers and the modern-day search closes in on the Twelves. Their flight is an exciting story even without knowing the background of the soldiers.

The children in Edward Eager's story, *Knight's Castle,* did not have the good sense to leave the toy castle and soldiers the way they found them; they built their own magic city of cars, electric trains, tin cans, and cookie cutters around the castle. When the "old one" granted their wish to be a part of the doll castle, they saw the results of their creations. Knights were riding motorcycles, and crashes occurred regularly — mechanization cannot take place overnight!

> *Traffic was now hopelessly snarled, and all the knights and ladies were blowing their horns. A factory whistle screamed, and more knights and ladies emerged for lunch hour, reading comic books and movie magazines. One of the knights jostled against Roger.*
> *"I crave thy pardon, gentle sir," said Roger.*
> *"Get outa the way, stoopid," said the knight, shoving past. From somewhere nearby a band started playing, "Sh-Boom, Sh-Boom."*
> *"This is awful," said Roger. "We might just as well not have come. It's not like magic at all. It's just like ordinary times back home."*[22]

Ivanhoe had lost interest in the siege and was reading science fiction. When he hears that the evil Brian de Bois-Guilbert has kidnapped Rebecca, he goes to the Dolorous Tower in his flying saucer to save her. Dur-

[21]Rumer Godden, *The Dolls' House,* Illustrated by Tasha Tudor (New York: Viking, 1962, first published in 1947), p. 13.

[22]Edward Eager, *Knight's Castle,* Illustrated by N. M. Bodecker (New York: Harcourt, 1956), p. 67.

ing the fight, Ivanhoe is nearly killed and the children cry out the magic words—"You're nothing but a lead soldier." The soldiers became toys again, the castle its normal size, and the children are back at their aunt's house in Baltimore. But magic happens in threes, and the children restore the castle to its "yeomanly nature" and have many other adventures on their next trips. The blending of fantasy, reality, and humor make this a highly entertaining story. The children's belief and concern for the soldiers increase the credibility of the plot.

Miss Hickory by Bailey is the story of a unique country doll whose body is an applewood twig and whose head is a hickory nut. Miss Hickory has all the common sense and forthright qualities that her name implies. She survives a severe New Hampshire winter in the company of her friends, Crow, Bull Frog, Ground Hog, and Squirrel. It was Squirrel who ended it all when he ate Miss Hickory's head; but then some might say that was just the beginning—and so it was. The Newbery Medal was awarded to Carolyn Sherwin Bailey for this book in 1947. Ruth Gannett illustrated it with beautifully clear black and white pictures.

Another book with a New England flavor is the story of *Hitty, Her First Hundred Years* by Rachel Field. The imagined memoirs of Hitty and her adventures are recorded by the author. Hitty is a doll of great charm and real character who prefers to tell her own story of a sailing trip on a whaler that takes her to many strange and interesting ports. This is a long story that is rather difficult to read.

Lilliputian Worlds

Man has always been intrigued with the possibility of little people. Gulliver explored the land of the Lilliputians in *Gulliver's Travels,* and Andersen left us the tale of the lovely *Thumbelina.* Boys and girls in the middle grades enjoy Winterfeld's *Castaways in Lilliput,* which is the story of three modern children who drift away from the Australian coast while playing with a rubber raft and land in a strange country. They discover that they are in Lilliput and, like Gulliver, are giants and curiosities. After the Lilliputians have determined that they mean no harm, they take the children to Gulliver Square and finally deliver them a "snack" in truck loads! Their adventures are ingenious, although their actions are quite predictable. Jim's impulsiveness makes it necessary for the children to leave. The Lilliputs send out an SOS giving the children's location at sea. Ralph wisely denies the whole adventure in order to save the Lilliputs. The fast-paced plot makes this a very popular story.

In the great tradition of English fantasy, Mary Norton has told a fascinating story about tiny people, *The Borrowers,* and their miniature world under the grandfather clock. There are not many borrowers left, for the rush of modern life does not suit them. They derive their names from their occupation, which is "borrowing" from human "beans," those "great slaves put there for them to use." "Borrowing" is a dangerous trade, for if one is seen by human beings, disastrous things may happen. Therefore, it is with real alarm that Pod and Homily Clock learn of their daughter, Arrietty's, desire to explore the world upstairs. Finally, Pod allows her to go on an expedition with him. While Pod is borrowing fibers from the hall doormat to make a new brush for Homily, Arrietty wanders outside where she meets the boy. Arrietty's disbelief about the number of people in the world who are the boy's size compared to those of her size is most convincing:

"Honestly—" began Arrietty helplessly and laughed again. "Do you really think—I mean, whatever sort of world would it be? Those great chairs . . . I've seen them. Fancy if you

Arrietty meets a "human bean." The artists have skillfully shown comparative sizes of the tiny borrower and the boy. Illustrated by Beth and Joe Krush. From *The Borrowers*, copyright, 1953, by Mary Norton. Reproduced by permission of Harcourt, Brace & World, Inc.

had to make chairs that size for everyone? And the stuff for their clothes . . . miles and miles of it . . . tents of it . . . and the sewing! And their great houses, reaching up so you can hardly see the ceilings . . . their great beds . . . the food *they eat . . . great smoking mountains of it, huge bags of stew and soup and stuff.*"[23]

In the end the Borrowers are "discovered" and have to flee for their lives. This surprise ending leads directly to the sequel called *The Borrowers Afield. The Borrowers Afloat* and *The Borrowers Aloft* complete the series. The characterizations in these stories are particularly well drawn. Homily *is* a worrier and Pod is her solid, kindly husband. Prim and properly brought-up, Arrietty still cannot control her natural curiosity. These are real people that Mary Norton has created. Her apt descriptions of setting, and the detailed

illustration by Beth and Joe Krush, make the world of the Borrowers come alive.

Jean Fritz has created a lively little character in her delightful fantasy, *Magic to Burn*. His name is Blaze and he is a boggart—a small, mischievous creature with a pair of horns on his head and a definite mind of his own. Ann and Stephen first met him in England, where their father was doing research on Chaucer. Blaze decided that America would be just the answer to his problems —an uncrowded land of deer and Indians. Blaze was well-read—Livy, Johnson and Shakespeare—his information on America was somewhat outdated, coming from Raleigh's reports! When Ann and Stephen found Blaze a "stowaway" in their cabin aboard ship, they felt a mixture of delight and dismay. It was soon quite apparent that America was a real disappointment to Blaze. He didn't feel safe going out in the city to make mischief, for it was far more populated than England. Blaze insisted that Stephen

---

[23]Mary Norton, *The Borrowers*, Illustrated by Beth and Joe Krush (New York: Harcourt, 1952), p. 78.

play with him each night. This interfered with Stephen's football training. Stephen worried about Blaze:

> . . . it was clear that America was not for Blaze and Blaze was not for America. There was no place on the whole continent that was like Twillington-on-the-Twine, and when Stephen thought about the possibility of setting Blaze free in the country, he knew this wouldn't work either. Boggarts needed a small cozy country—not a big rambling one where the farmhouses were miles apart, where there were mountains instead of hills, prairies instead of heaths, and where some states were as large as the whole island of Britain. When he came to think of it, Stephen had never heard stories about little guys the size of Blaze living in America; they had all been big guys, great giants of men like Paul Bunyan and Mike Fink who were looking for trees to pull up, not blackberry bushes to hide under.[24]

Finally they return to England, but the boggart is not content with just returning home. He expects Stephen to save all the boggarts by finding them a less built-up spot than Twillington. Stephen does produce a very workable plan that saves both the mischief and magic of the boggarts. Jean Fritz always writes a good story, but this, her first venture into fantasy, seems particularly fine.

Another very readable American fantasy is *The Gammage Cup* by Carol Kendall. For 880 years the Minnipins had lived securely in their villages along the Watercress River in the Land Between the Mountains. Revering their relics, their traditions (and mistaken notions), and their first family, the Periods, most of the Minnipins are conformists who wear green cloaks and have green front doors to their homes—"the proper color for Minnipins." A few of the Minnipins rebel against this stuffy tradition and paint their doors red and wear orange sashes. This can no longer be tolerated, for the village of Slipper-on-the-Water is preparing to enter a contest for the "best village" in The Land Between the Mountains. At a town meeting it is decided that in order to win the Gammage Cup all homes must be painted green and have scalloped roofs—and of course all Minnipins must wear green. Muggles, uncertain and embarrassed to speak before the whole village, had the courage to try to explain her reasons for nonconformity:

> "Well, I don't think it's doors or cloaks or . . . or orange sashes. It's us. What I mean is, it's no matter what color we paint our doors or what kind of clothes we wear, we're . . . well, we're those colors inside us. Instead of being green inside, you see, like other folk. So I don't think it would do any good if we just changed our outside color."[25]

Muggles' explanation was not accepted, however, and the five friends were outlawed to the mountains. Here, the little group of exiles establish a house for themselves and make the startling discovery that the Minnipins' ancient enemies, the Mushrooms, have found a way into the valley and are preparing to attack! Sounding the alarm, the five save the village and are welcomed back as heroes. The tart commentary on the false values of a society and the timely theme of the individual versus the group give an added dimension to this well-written fantasy. *The Whisper of Glocken* continues the adventures of the Minnipins but tells of another village and a new set of heroes. This time five unlikely adventurers set out to find why the Watercress River has reversed its flow. What they discover on the other side of the mountains is no more amazing than the resources that they discover within each of them.

---

[24]Jean Fritz, *Magic to Burn*, Illustrated by Beth and Joe Krush (New York: Coward-McCann, 1964), p. 137.

[25]Carol Kendall, *The Gammage Cup*, Illustrated by Eric Blegvad (New York: Harcourt, 1959), pp. 91–92.

Perhaps the best-known fantasy of little people in our time is *The Hobbit* by J. R. R. Tolkien, a retired professor of Oxford and a scholar of the folk tale and myths of Northwest Europe. With his background, it seems only natural that he should choose to create a world in which the little folk, dwarfs, elves, and hobbits dwell. And what is a hobbit?

> *They are (or were) small people, smaller than dwarves (and they have no beards) but very much larger than lilliputians. There is little or no magic about them, except the ordinary everyday sort which helps them to disappear quickly when large stupid folk like you and me come blundering along making a noise like elephants which they can hear a mile off. They are inclined to be fat in the stomach; they dress in bright colors (chiefly green and yellow); wear no shoes, because their feet grow natural leather soles and thick warm brown hair like the stuff on their heads (which is curly); have long clever brown fingers, good-natured faces, and laugh deep fruity laughs (especially after dinner, which they have twice a day when they can get it).*[26]

Generally, the hobbits are very respectable creatures who never have any adventures or do anything unexpected. This is the story of one hobbit, Bilbo Baggins, who has an adventure and finds himself doing and saying altogether unexpected things. He is tricked by the dwarfs and the elves into going on a quest for treasure when he would much rather stay at home where he could be sure of six solid meals a day rather than be off fighting dragons. On the way, he is lost in a tunnel and nearly consumed by a ghoulish creature called Gollum, who is "dark as darkness except for his two big round pale eyes." Gradually the hobbit's inner courage emerges as he struggles on through terrifying woods, encounters with huge hairy spi-

ders, battles with goblins to a somewhat enigmatic victory over the dragon (a more heroic figure is allowed to slay it). *The Hobbit* gives children an introduction to middle-earth and its creatures. As adults they may pursue this interest in Tolkien's vastly expanded view of middle-earth in *Lord of the Rings,* a 1300-page trilogy.

"Fabulous Flights"

Before the age of seven, Peter Peabody Pepperell III was a perfectly normal boy. But shortly after his seventh birthday, he stopped growing, in fact he started shrinking! By the time Peter was thirteen, he had "grown down" to almost four inches. Both Peter and his family had adjusted to this reversal of growth, and Peter had a wonderful time training an army of small animals, riding a rabbit, and sailing in a model sailboat. One day Peter met Gus, an uneducated seagull with a great deal of common sense. Gus offered to give him a ride, the first of many wonderful flights. *The Fabulous Flight,* which Robert Lawson titled his tongue-in-cheek story, was a dangerous mission across the Atlantic Ocean to steal a small capsule more deadly than any atom bomb. Peter was sure that he and Gus might fly into the heavily guarded castle completely unnoticed. His father thought the plan had possibilities. Finally, they convinced the Secretary of State, and Gus and Peter made their flight. Upon reaching Zargonia, they discovered that the "professor" involved was really an American crook who had taken over when the scientist had died. At a dramatic moment, Peter obtained the capsule, and Gus dived to safety. Halfway over the ocean, Peter decided that no country should own such an explosive and he and Gus agreed to unload the capsule. The terrific force of the explosion restored Peter's "sacropitulianphalangic gland" to its normal functioning and his growth once again became

---

[26]J. R. R. Tolkien, *The Hobbit* (Boston: Houghton Mifflin, 1938), p. 12.

normal. Although written nearly twenty years ago, this story of *The Fabulous Flight* is as fresh and timely a fantasy as any being published today.

No one ever had a more fabulous flight than did James in the book, *James and the Giant Peach*, by Roald Dahl. James is one of the saddest and loneliest boys in the world, living with two wicked aunts, Aunt Sponge and Aunt Spiker, in a strange, ramshackle-house on a high hill in the south of England. James met a queer old man who thrust a bag of green crystals into his hands and told him to mix them with water and drink them and he'd never be miserable again. After cautioning James not to let them escape, he disappeared. James was so excited and so intent upon getting to the kitchen without being seen by his aunts that he slipped and fell, and all of the magic crystals disappeared into the ground right under the old peach tree. In no time at all, an enormous peach grew on the tree, bigger than a house. The aunts immediately capitalized on this phenomenon and sold tickets to people to view the peach—James was locked in his room so he would not be in the way. That night when his aunts had freed him, James walked down to the peach and discovered a door in its side. Within he found six amazing creatures who said they had been waiting for him—a grasshopper the size of a large dog, a giant ladybug, an enormous spider, a centipede, an earthworm, and a silkworm. Early the next morning, the centipede gnawed off the stem and the huge peach started rolling down the hill, incidentally smashing Aunt Spiker and crushing Aunt Sponge on its mad dash to the sea. The marvelous adventure had begun! Threatened by sharks, James saved the peach by throwing strands of silk and spider webbing over 502 seagulls who gently lifted the peach from the ocean and sailed away across the sea. This is a wonderful spoof on the Victorian morality tales. The characters are well drawn and their grumbling conver-

sations very believable. The plot is original and ingenious. The illustrations by Nancy Burkert are beautifully detailed and reflect the pathos and joy of James' "fabulous flight."

The Pott family had a very different kind of flight in their amazing car, *Chitty-Chitty-Bang-Bang*. This sophisticated spoof on a detective story is the only children's book written by the late Ian Fleming, the creator of the well-known James Bond mysteries. Commander Caractacus Pott was a famous inventor, but he couldn't account for all the magical abilities of his mysterious green car. Chitty-Chitty could be an airplane or a boat whenever she wanted to. So the Potts took a sea voyage from their English home and accidentally found a gangsters' hidden cave across the Channel in France. The cave contained all the ammunition of a mob of gangsters—Joe the Monster, Man-Mountain Fink, Soapy Sam, and Blood-Money Banks. With the help of the great green car, Commander Pott and his family blew up the cave, but not before the gangsters had seen them. The children are kidnapped and held as hostages. However, by this time the reader is certain that Chitty-Chitty will use the marvelous radar scanner on her hood and find the twins. And she does! The gangsters are properly turned over to the police. At the very end of the book Chitty-Chitty soars up to the sky, and the Potts are off on an unknown adventure. Part of the fun of this book is its obvious farcical nature. Just when the family is safely at rest and seems relaxed, the author will say

But! But! But!
And again, But![27]

The reader does not have to surmise that the family is in danger, rather, he is told, usually in capital letters, reminiscent of an old silent

---

[27]Ian Fleming, *Chitty-Chitty-Bang-Bang*, Illustrated by John Burningham (New York: Random House, 1964), p. 77.

The wonderful car, Chitty-Chitty-Bang-Bang, flies off with Commander Pott and his family on another fabulous adventure. From *Chitty-Chitty-Bang-Bang* by Ian Fleming, illustrated by John Burningham. Illustrations © Copyright, 1964, by Jonathan Cape, Ltd. Reproduced by permission of Random House, Inc.

movie or dime-store detective. The tongue-in-cheek humor is maintained throughout this most popular fantasy.

Another fabulous flight is recorded in the story of *The Twenty-One Balloons* by William Pène du Bois. Professor Sherman left San Francisco on August 15, 1883 in a giant balloon, telling reporters that he hoped to be the first man to fly across the Pacific Ocean. He was picked up three weeks later in the Atlantic Ocean clinging to the wreckage of a platform which had been flown through the air by twenty-one balloons. The story is told as the Professor's speech at the Explorers' Club. On the seventh day of his voyage, a sea gull plummeted through the Professor's balloon, and he was forced to land on the island of Krakatoa. Professor Sherman discovered that he was to be a *permanent* visitor, since the twenty families who lived over the most fabulous diamond mine in the world

wished to remain unknown. They were extremely gracious to the Professor and escorted him on a tour of their amazing island that heaved like the ocean from the volcanic activity. However, each of the houses was built on a diamond foundation and so did not move. The houses were amazing; they included a replica of Mount Vernon, a British cottage with a thatched roof, the Petit Trianon, a Moroccan house, and so on. Mr. F. told him the story of the discovery of the mines and the selection of the twenty families to come and live on the island.

Each family was required to have two things in order to be chosen. They had to have: a) one boy and one girl between the ages of three and eight; and b) they had to have definite creative interests, such as interests in painting, writing, the sciences, music, architecture, medicine. These two requirements would not only assure future generations of Krakatoa citizens; but he assumed that people with creative interests are not liable to be bored on a small desolate island; and people with inventive interests can more easily cope with unusual situations and form a stronger foundation for a cultured heredity.[28]

The Professor describes with graphic detail the houses, the amazing inventions, and customs of Krakatoans and their escape when the volcano erupted. As usual, the detailed description of William Pène du Bois' text is matched only by the meticulous perfection of his pen and ink drawings.

Magical Powers

The folk tales are replete with characters or objects that possess particular magical powers of enchantment. Modern authors, too, have been quick to utilize this motif in many of their fanciful tales. "Zak," an eight-year-old girl, had a terrible power and a highly developed sense of righteous indignation. When she became irate at her neighbors for hunting, she put *The Magic Finger* on them. The next morning when Mr. and Mrs. Gregg awaken, they find that they have shrunk to the size of the ducks they were shooting and have grown wings where their arms were. Imagine their consternation when they are out in their back yard trying out their wings, to see a family of enormous ducks with long arms instead of wings moving into their house! Sizing up the situation, Mr. Gregg builds a nest for the night. They awaken after a damp, rainy night to find themselves peering down the ends of three doublebarreled shotguns. The Greggs promise the ducks that they shall never go hunting again, at which point they are suddenly standing in their own yard once more with arms instead of wings. Their reform is complete. At the end of the story, Zak hears more guns, and once again, her magic finger begins to grow very hot—the pictures by William Pène du Bois are in keeping with the somewhat macabre humor of this story by Roald Dahl.

The children in the many books of fantasy by Edward Eager frequently possessed a magic object, knew a magic saying, or had magical powers themselves. In *Half Magic*, Jane finds what she believes to be a nickel, but it is a magic charm, or at least half of a magic charm, for it provides half of all their wishes. For example, Katherine wished that their cat would talk, but no one could understand its garbled language. Thereafter, the children learned to double their wishes, so that half of them would come true. Each

Amazing things happened to Mr. and Mrs. Gregg when their eight-year-old neighbor put *The Magic Finger* on them! Illustration by William Pène du Bois from *The Magic Finger* by Roald Dahl. Harper & Row, 1966.

---

[28]William Pène du Bois, *The Twenty-One Balloons* (New York: Viking Press, 1947), pp. 83–84.

child in the family has an exciting adventure including a trip to the Sahara Desert and one through time to the days of King Arthur! Another of Eager's stories, *Seven-Day Magic,* tells of a magic book that the children borrowed from the library. When they opened the book, they found it was about themselves; everything they had done that morning was in the book and the rest of the book was shut tight waiting for them to create it. The children all agree that the best kind of book is a magic one, where:

> . . . *the people in the book would be walking home from somewhere and the magic would start suddenly before they knew it. . . .*
> . . . *and then they'd have to tame the magic and learn its rules and thwart it.*[29]

When their wonderful book is due at the library at the end of seven days, they return it. Logic and humor are characteristic of the many books of fantasy that were Edward Eager's legacy of modern magic for today's children.

The Summer Birds by Penelope Farmer tells of the strange boy who meets Charlotte and Emma in the lane one morning. One by one, he teaches the village children how to fly like birds, and all enjoy a magical summer of enchantment. There was an eerie and exciting moonlight flight, day-long expeditions to a remote and lovely lake, and Charlotte's daring swoop like a gull from a cliff top. Yet, running throughout the children's excitement and pleasure was the brooding, ominous question as to the boy's identity. The climax occurs when the boy attempts to take the children with him to a special island, and the children learn who and what he is. He is a bird, the last of his race, who has been given the summer to come and restore his kind with any creatures he can find, for they would become his form once on the

island. Charlotte, who was attracted to the boy more than any of the others, had the courage to demand that he tell them where they were going. In the end, Maggot, an orphan with no ties, joins the bird and the two fly off, leaving the rest of the children desolate and without the power to fly. An intriguing part of the story is the closed child-society that is formed and the boy's struggle for leadership within it. The characterization is excellent, and the eerie mood of the story is sustained throughout. *Emma in Winter* is a sequel to *The Summer Birds.* With her sister, Charlotte, away at boarding school, the lonely Emma began to dream of the joyous summer when the strange boy had taught them to fly. When fat Bobby Fumpkins, even lonelier and more friendless than Emma, began to appear in her dreams, Emma treated him with the same cruel mockery as she did when she was awake, until she learned that they actually were sharing the same dreams. Emma's growing companionship with Bobby in her dreams affects her relationship with him in real life. Conflict and friendship are also the theme of another of Farmer's books, *The Magic Stone.* Alice, the oldest daughter of a family recently moved to the country from the London slums, meets Caroline, who has lived all of her life in the country and is planning to go off to boarding school. The two girls are immediately antagonistic toward each other until they find the magic stone. Because of the stone, they become more sensitive to nature and to each other. Finally, they surrender their stone so that their two brothers, hostile to each other, may have the same experience.

Overcoming Evil

Many fantasies employ the good versus evil theme, frequently in combination with wicked enchantments or time magic. *Tistou of the Green Thumbs* by Maurice Druon is a most

---

[29]Edward Eager, *Seven-Day Magic,* Illustrated by N. M. Bodecker (New York: Harcourt, 1962), p. 25.

unusual story of a small French boy who lives in a castle with his beautiful mother and a handsome father who is a munitions manufacturer. One day, Tistou discovers he has the remarkable ability to make flowers grow anywhere. He uses his green thumb in astonishing ways to grow flowers on prison walls, to conceal slums, to sprout flowers inside a hospital, and even to take root in the cannons in his father's factory. The secret of Tistou's real identity is held until the last page when it is revealed by his pony, Gymnast. Children will enjoy Tistou's magical ability to grow plants, but they will miss much of the satire and serious overtones of this strange allegory.

The controversial *Dorp Dead* by Julia Cunningham is also allegorical in nature. Gilly Ground represents all youth caught between its need to be non-conforming and its need for security; Kobalt, the ladder-maker, *is* evil, the epitome of all evil that would control and damage basic personalities. The Hunter whose gun has no bullets may represent love or the meaning of life. In an article for *The Horn Book*, Miss Cunningham explains him in this way:

> I think the Hunter is no more or less than that person or, if one is lucky, persons who pass through every life for a moment, or sometimes longer, and give it strength and meaning. Why didn't he have a name? I guess I did not give him a name because he has so many.[30]

The plot of this story is sinister, but evil is overcome, and the integrity of Gilly Ground's personality preserved. Viewed as realistic fiction, this story seems too evil and unbelievable. Seen as allegory, *Dorp Dead* becomes an exceptional book indeed.

L. M. Boston has created a sinister mood for her story, *An Enemy at Green Knowe*. Granny Oldknow tells Tolly and his Chinese friend, Ping, about a mad alchemist who lived as a tutor at Green Knowe in the year 1630. In order to gain power and wealth, he practiced witchcraft. Soon after hearing this story, a Miss Melanie Powers, an oddly unattractive woman who had rented a house nearby, comes to call on Granny in search of some of the alchemist's books that she believes might still be in the house. Drawn into the search, the boys find themselves fighting evil as mysterious and dark as it was in the 1600s. The plagues of maggots, birds, and snakes are as repulsive as Miss Powers herself. The suspense and imagination of this eerie story quite captivate middle graders.

> Better sometimes not to know the powers ranged against you, who is your enemy, and how heavy the odds.[31]

So begins the chilling story of Andrew Badger, a lonely orphan who lives with his unfeeling stepmother as the only boy in a girls' boarding school in England. Andrew makes one friend in the girls' school, Ronnie Peters, a self-sufficient, matter-of-fact girl. The two of them discover the Annerlie ring of power although they do not guess its significance. However, the ring made Andrew feel braver, somehow, and much more aware of the beauty around him. He also was sure that there was some relationship between the ring and his dreams of *The Cloud Forest* — that mystical place where he met the other Andrew, his true self. And yet he didn't understand the connection of the ring with Sir Edward Annerlie, the proud and contemptuous owner of Annerlie Hall. Ronnie overhears the headmistress and Sir Edward discussing the ring and Andrew. She suspects his true identity and also realizes the danger they are in. Enlisting the aid of a rather timid rector, Ronnie's over-protective mother, and an ineffective teacher, Andrew

---

[30]Julia Cunningham, "Dear Characters," *The Horn Book Magazine*, vol. 43 (April 1967), p. 234.

[31]Joan North, *The Cloud Forest* (New York: Farrar, Straus, 1966), p. 1.

and Ronnie attempt to fight the forces of evil that include Sir Edward, a neuropsychologist who wants the ring for the power it will give him, the headmistress, and a social scientist with a strange program of Self-Development. The good do overcome the evil forces, but the latter are not completely eliminated, for evil is never completely vanquished. This is a strong story with a theme that gives warning of the ruthless men of science who would try to control men's minds.

Both mystery and fantasy combine in Jane Langton's spellbinding tale of *The Diamond in the Window*. Edward and Eleanor live with their aunt and uncle in a strange old turreted house in Concord, Massachusetts. Their Uncle Freddy had been a world-renowned authority on Emerson and Thoreau until the mysterious disappearance of his younger brother and sister had left him slightly deranged. In the tower room, the two beds were made up in vain hope of the return of the two children. Edward and Eleanor move to the tower room and search in their dreams for the two missing members of the family. Their dreams include excitement, terror, and romance. Finally, the two children overcome their adversaries and free the lost children and their Prince from a spell cast upon them by the Prince's evil uncle. The magnificent star diamond of India is returned to its rightful owner and even Uncle Freddy regains his senses! *The Swing in the Summerhouse* is an exciting sequel to *The Diamond in the Window*, and once again, the children must thwart the powers of darkness.

In *Steel Magic* by Norton, three modern-day children are off for a picnic and a day of exploration when they come upon a miniature castle. Going through the "Gate of the Fox," they are astonished to find that they are in the legendary land of Avalon where an armor-clad knight begs for their help. Dark powers of evil threaten Avalon, and the people cannot fight back for they have lost three magic talismans: King Ar-

thur's sword, Excalibur, Merlin's iron ring, and Huon's silver horn. What is even worse, Avalon and the world are mirrors for each other, and if the sword, ring, and horn are not recovered, not only Avalon but the world will be doomed by an evil enchantment. Each of the children agrees to find one of the talismans. On their separate journeys they meet weird, frightening men and creatures. Their only weapons and ties to reality are their stainless steel cutlery and the food in their picnic baskets. Each child performs his exciting task courageously. Merlin meets them at the "Gate of the Fox" and grants them "iron of spirit and iron of courage" forever.

A story with a somewhat similar theme is *Over Sea, Under Stone* by Susan Cooper. The three Drew children on a holiday in Cornwall had found an old map and were hunting for an ancient treasure linked with King Arthur. The treasure, which lay "over sea, under stone," if found by the right people, would keep at bay the ancient forces of evil. The children soon find themselves faced with deadly danger somehow connected with the local vicar and a curiously menacing man and his sister. The children turn for help to their Great-Uncle Merry, a known scholar of ancient lore. They find the treasure in a cave along the coast only to be trapped by the rising tide and their enemies. They save what they call "The Grail," but lose the manuscript that was the key to the cup's inscriptions. Simon discovers the clue to Great-Uncle Merry's real identity and he has no doubts as to the authenticity of the grail.

Time Magic

Probably every human being at one time or another during his lifetime has wondered what it would be like if he could visit the past. Children's authors have been particularly skilled at creating different worlds of time in their stories.

Julia Sauer's *Fog Magic* is a tender, moving story of Greta Addington, a little girl of Nova Scotia. One day, while walking in the fog, Greta discovers a secret world, the village of Blue Cove. This fishing village is only there in the fog; on sunny days there are just empty cellar holes of houses of the past. Midst the fog magic, she meets a girl her own age named Retha Morrill. Retha's mother senses that Greta is from "over the mountain" and quietly reminds her each time the fog is lifting that it is time for her to go home. Some occasional knowing looks and comments from Greta's father make her realize that he, too, has visited Blue Cove. Greta is particularly anxious that her twelfth birthday be a foggy day. It isn't; but that evening when she is on the way home from a church picnic with her father, the fog comes in. She runs back to enter Blue Cove where Retha's mother gives her a soft gray kitten as a birthday present and quietly wishes her a "Safe passage for all the years ahead." Greta realizes that this will be the last time that she will be able to visit Blue Cove. She walks slowly down the hill to find her father waiting for her. As she shows him her kitten, he reaches into his pocket and pulls out an odd little knife that he had received on his twelfth birthday at Blue Cove. This is a hauntingly beautiful story that should appeal to girls in the middle grades.

No one is more skillful in mingling the past with the present than L. M. Boston in her stories of Green Knowe, that mysterious old English house in which the author still lives. In *The Children of Green Knowe*, the first in this series, Mrs. Boston tells the story of a small boy called "Tolly" who is sent to live with his great-grandmother. Over the great fireplace in the drawing room hangs a picture of three children who grew up at Green Knowe in the seventeenth century. His great-grandmother tells Tolly stories about them: of Toby and his pony Festi, of Linnet and her birds, of Alexander and his flute.

The children seem so real that Tolly is convinced they often play hide and seek with him. His great-grandmother believes him, and soon the reader does too! In *The Treasure of Green Knowe*, Boston has included a mysterious search for lost jewels, but the real interest of the book is the story-within-a-story of blind Susan Oldknow's life at Green Knowe some two centuries ago. Children may appreciate the problems and joys of the blind after hearing Susan's story of misunderstanding and mistreatment. Even Tolly, in another generation, becomes concerned that Susan had never seen the stars. His grandmother reminds him that she could smell the spring night and maybe even the stars:

> *"I nearly can myself tonight. She could certainly smell the kind of things that stars belong to and happen in. Sometimes you make things smaller by giving them a name to themselves, like 'star.' Imagine Susan taking a breath of it and just thinking all that!"*
> *Tolly took a lungful of star and cherry blossom and fresh-water river and yew and sleeping violets, and then leaped into bed.*[32]

The old house at Green Knowe is again the setting for the story of *The River at Green Knowe*. New characters are introduced, but the reader misses Tolly and his great-grandmother who just naturally belong to Green Knowe.

Nan Chauncy's memorable fantasy, *The Secret Friends*, won the award for the best Australian children's book for 1961. It is the story of a little fair-haired girl of Tasmania who meets and plays with Merrina, an "abo" girl. But the aborigines had all been cruelly killed or died years ago when Lexie's great-great-aunt Rita had known and played with one. Lexie was nine when she first felt someone watching her.

[32]L. M. Boston, *The Treasure of Green Knowe*, Illustrated by Peter Boston (New York: Harcourt, 1958), p. 93.

Her glance rested on the great grey rock like the letter 'A' with a blackness in the middle — Ooh, it was here the eyes were watching! She could feel *the blackness was not just an empty hole. A* something *was inside watching.*[33]

In growing curiosity, trust and affection, the children meet almost daily, unknown to anyone. Merrina is fascinated with Lexie's clothes, her zipper, and the fact that she can "unpeel" her shoes and socks. Merrina wears no clothes. One day the "fathers" had invited her to a kangaroo feast — never before had she joined in the tribal festivals. The feast ended in terror, however, as two escaped starving convicts found the tribe and shot them. Merrina got Lexie safely away both from the convicts and her tribe, who thought she had betrayed them. While hurrying over the rocks, Lexie fell and was found unconscious and in deep shock by her father and Andy. Gradually, she recalled part of the story and only confided in Kent, her brother. The dream was gone, and Lexie would never again play with Merrina. But Merrina had told her that she would always know when she wanted her. Years later, she kept that promise when she mysteriously appeared and guided Lexie to her brother who had fallen down the cleft of the same valley and hurt his knee. Lexie wants to thank her, and finds her as Kent said she would be, huddled over her "yearning fire," calling back all her loved ones — for Merrina was all alone. The unusual setting of this story, the convincing characterization, and the smooth stepping back and forth in time make this an outstanding fantasy.

An English fantasy that deals with time as its major theme is the mysterious and exciting *Tom's Midnight Garden* by Philippa Pearce. Forced to spend part of a summer with a rather boring aunt and uncle, Tom's visit is quite dull until he hears the grandfather clock in the hall strike thirteen. That is the time for him to slip into the most exciting garden in the world and play with Hatty, a child of the past. Hatty and the gardener, Abel, are the only ones who can see Tom in his pyjamas; he is invisible to everyone else. Tom becomes so absorbed in his midnight visits when "there is time no longer," that he does not wish to return home. One fateful night, Tom opens the back door and sees only the paving and the fences that stand there in daylight — Hatty and her garden have vanished. When Tom meets the real Hatty, a little old lady who has been dreaming about her past, he understands why the weather in the garden has always been perfect, why some nights it has been one season and the next night a different one, why Hatty was sometimes young and sometimes older; it all depended upon what old Mrs. Bartholomew had chosen to remember. Lonely and bored, Tom had joined her in her dreams. This is a fascinating story that should please both boys and girls in the middle grades. It won the Carnegie Medal as the outstanding English children's book written in 1958.

Time at the Top by Edward Ormondroyd is a refreshingly different time fantasy. It had been a windy, wretched day when everything went wrong, and then Susan had met a funny little old lady who had lost her hat, had her umbrella blown inside out, and had her bag of groceries ripped. After Susan helped her, the "Mary Poppins-ish" woman had said she'd give her three, and off she went. That had started it, for when Susan pushed the elevator button for the top floor where she and her father lived, the elevator had kept right on going to the eighth floor — except there was no eighth floor. Susan got off and found herself in a different time and a different place. How she made friends with Victoria and her brother, Robert, solved their financial difficulties, and their widowed mother's marital problems

---

[33] Nan Chauncy, *The Secret Friends,* Illustrated by Brian Wildsmith (New York: F. Watts, 1962), p. 34.

makes for a fast-paced, amusing story that girls in the middle grades will particularly enjoy.

Some authors have made history particularly vivid as they shift modern characters to interesting historical periods. *Time Cat* by Lloyd Alexander tells of the remarkable journeys of Jason and his cat, Gareth. Contrary to tradition, Gareth had only one life, but he had the power to visit nine different lives and take his fortunate human friend with him as he visited famous people and eras of the past. Their travels through time include an exciting adventure in Egypt; they are mascots of a Roman legion invading Britain; they meet St. Patrick in Ireland; they continue their travels in Japan, Renaissance Italy, Peru, the Isle of Man, Germany, and the colony of Massachusetts.

A Traveler in Time is based upon the dream experiences of its author, Alison Utley. Penelope, who is visiting her aunt and uncle at an old manor house, The Thackers, in Derbyshire, steps through a door and finds herself talking to her great-aunt who is kneading dough in an Elizabethan kitchen. At first, her visits are brief, but then, she finds herself caught up with the old tragedy of Anthony Babington and his plot to save Mary Queen of Scots. Knowing Mary's fate, Penelope tries to communicate the dangers involved, but no one will listen to her pathetic pleas. Penelope slips back and forth in time, but she sadly realizes that she will outgrow her visions.

Earthfasts by William Mayne is a chilling story that combines many of the elements of fantasy, legend, and science fiction. David and Keith meet at dusk at the place where Keith had seen a swelling in the earth the day before. Tonight it was larger, and the ground was vibrating with the sound of drumming. The boys speculated as to the cause. Could it be water, a giant mushroom, or badgers? As the noise increased, the boys were frozen in terror as a person emerged from the ground beating a drum and clutching a steady, cold white flame. David identifies this stranger as Nellie Jack John, who according to legend went underneath the castle more than 200 years ago to seek the treasure of King Arthur. The boys protect him and feed him, but Nellie Jack John only stays above the earth for two days leaving his strangely cold candle behind him. Fascinated by the glow of the taper, David realizes that the many strange things occurring over the countryside are related to Nellie Jack John's disturbance of time. The ancient stones, called earthfasts, work up in a farmer's ploughed field, a family's boggart returns after an absence of many years, and one terror-filled night David vanishes in what looks like a flash of lightning. Trying to find a clue to David's disappearance, Keith stares at the brilliant cold flame of the candle. Suddenly he understands:

> *On the skyline, where lightness filled the air, stood a row of huge stones, or giants. Keith was not sure which they were, but it did not matter, because standing stones were giants, and giants became standing stones whilst the King's time was standing still. And the King's time stood still when the candle Keith held was in its proper place under the ground, because King Arthur's time was not yet come. . . . When Nellie Jack John took up this candle and brought it out from its place he disturbed the time that slept and the King that slept with it, and he woke what was asleep before, and things that slept since, like giants that had become standing stones, and the boggart; and the things that whirled.*[34]

This is an unforgettable book that creates belief in the inexplicable.

Silverberg does not manipulate time, as much as history, in his fascinating book *The Gate of Worlds*. He describes the world that

---

[34]William Mayne, *Earthfasts* (New York: Dutton, 1967), p. 140.

THE PUSHCART WAR

By JEAN MERRILL

ILLUSTRATED BY *Ronni Solbert*

Frank, the Flower, shoots down another truck during the Pea Shooter Campaign of The Pushcart War of 1976 between the trucks of New York City and the pushcart peddlers. From *The Pushcart War* by Jean Merrill, illustrated by Ronni Solbert. Copyright 1964 by Jean Merrill. William R. Scott, Inc.

might have come into existence if the Black Death of 1348 had killed three-fourths of the European population rather than one-fourth. As the story opens in 1963, Dan Beauchamp, late of the city of New Istanbul which was formerly London, sets out for the Western world in a paddle-wheeler owned by the world's leading maritime nation, the Aztecs. He is shown to the steerage section of course, since he is of pale complexion. The Turks ruled Europe; the Incas, Lower Hesperides (South America); the Aztecs the

rest of the New World; and the Russians, Asia. Dan saves the life of an official of the court of Montezuma who repays him by insisting that they drive together to Terrochtitlan. All goes well until the boiler of the car they are driving blows up! It is Quequex, the official, who describes what he means by the Gate of Worlds:

> *"The Gate of Worlds . . . is the gate beyond which all our futures lie. For each of us at any time many futures lie in wait. And for each possible future, there is a possible world beyond the Gate."*[35]

He then goes on to describe today's world as one that might have happened if the Plague had not been so severe and the Turks had been defeated. Don finds adventure in the New World, but he finally boards ship for Africa where he hopes to find freedom, culture, and to marry Takinoktu.

The Pushcart War by Jean Merrill is a delightful satire written from the point of time of 1986 and is a documented report of the famous Pushcart War of 1976. Believing that we cannot have peace in the world unless people understand how wars start, the "author-historian" proceeds to describe the beginning of the war between the giant trucks of New York City and the Pushcarts. The Daffodil Massacre has been established as taking place on the afternoon of March 15, 1976, when Mack, driver of the Mighty Mammoth, rode down the cart of Morris the Florist. Like the Minutemen, the 509 pushcart peddlers unite to fight the three largest trucking firms in the city, known simply as The Three. At first, their fragile carts are crushed like matchboxes, but then the loyal band of defenders developed the old-fashioned pea-shooter into a highly effective weapon. The straight-faced account that provides details of the progress of the war

[35]Robert Silverberg, *The Gate of Worlds* (New York: Holt, Rinehart and Winston, 1967), p. 64.

and the eventual triumph of the pushcart peddlers is both a funny and pathetic commentary on modern life today. Children thoroughly enjoy this satire; in fact, one fifth-grade class returned for their report cards on the last day of school and stayed one extra hour while their teacher completed the book. Few books can claim such devotion!

The City Under Ground by Suzanne Martel also deals with future time. This compelling story takes place one century after a great atomic explosion had eliminated all human life except for a small group of scientists who had built a fully functioning city under ground. One of their descendants, Luke 15-P9, finds and explores a secret passage to the surface of the earth, disobeying strict laws of the group never to leave. Luke discovers a small colony of friendly people living above the ground, while at the same time a group of hostile people are discovered in another underground city. This book might well be compared with the beliefs of the primitive peoples of *Beyond the Gorge of Shadows* by James O. Harvey.

SCIENCE FICTION

Science fiction, as the name implies, is fiction based upon scientific fact or scientific possibilities that have not yet been proven. This does not alter the possibility of their being tested in the future. A century ago, Jules Verne wrote of atomic submarines and rocket ships taking passengers to distant places. Atomic submarines have been in active use since 1954, and with each new space probe, the possibility of space travel becomes more assured.

The science-fiction writer uses his imagination and constructs a future world in which these unknowns have been proven. As in modern fantasy, his detailed descriptions of these "scientific facts" and the characters' acceptance of them make the story believable. Science-fiction writers should do more than create adventure stories with the trappings of the 21st century, just as historical fiction must be more than coonskin caps, buckskin clothing, and encounters with the Indians. The science-fiction writer of today will try to detail the interaction of science upon every aspect of society from politics to warfare, from religion to sports. Few science-fiction writers for children have been able to rise above the scientific novelty to see the human dimension of this new knowledge.

One of the values of science fiction for children is its ability to develop imagination, speculation, and flexibility in the minds of its readers. Most literature offers a static picture of society; whereas, science fiction assumes a future that is vastly different from the one we know today. In his introduction of *Worlds to Come*, Damon Knight makes this statement:

> *What science fiction has been doing for the last forty years is to shake up people's thinking, make them skeptical of dogma, get them used to the idea of change, let them dare to want new things. Nobody will ever know for sure how much effect these stories have had, but it is almost impossible to believe they have had none.*[36]

Some of the easiest science fiction for young readers includes the two tales by Slobodkin of Marty, the Martian who visits Eddie Blow on earth in *The Space Ship Under the Apple Tree* and *The Space Ship Returns to the Apple Tree*. In the latter tale, Marty and Eddie travel over the country in the Interspacial Superphotic Astral Rocket Disk. Marty saves the Fourth of July fireworks before he departs again for outer space.

Felsen's *The Boy Who Discovered the Earth* is equally amusing and appropriate for younger readers. A Feorian family has to make a forced landing on earth to repair its space ship. TexSon wanders off and

---

[36]Damon Knight, Editor, in the introduction to *Worlds to Come* (New York: Harper & Row, 1967), p. xi.

meets an earthen by the name of Tommy Taplinger. At first, he thinks TexSon is kidding him in a play space suit, but when he helps him find his parents and sees their spaceship, Tommy is terrified. TexSon convinces him that they mean no harm, and they become friends. Each decides that the other's planet sounds more interesting than his own, so they agree to exchange places. However, when Tommy observes TexSon's delight in earth games and realizes that Feorian children are supposed to spend their time in thinking, he changes his mind, and TexSon returns to his own planet, Feor. The Prince and the Pauper twist to this simple story gives added intrigue and interest.

Children in the middle grades continue to enjoy the four books by Ellen MacGregor about that intrepid traveler, Miss Pickerell. Returning from her vacation, the elderly Miss Pickerell is amazed to find a spaceship parked in her pasture. In a rage, she endeavors to remove the trespassers, but instead finds herself involved in a flight to Mars where she becomes a heroine in spite of her lack of knowledge about space. The story of her trip is told in *Miss Pickerell Goes to Mars*. *Miss Pickerell and the Geiger Counter* is the second in the series, followed by *Miss Pickerell Goes Undersea* and *Miss Pickerell Goes to the Arctic*. The mixture of humor and scientific facts delights children who are just discovering science fiction.

Eleanor Cameron's series about the people who visit Basidium, the Mushroom Planet, are exciting and convincingly written. The names of the characters are intriguing: Tyco Bass, a scientist who is actually one of the space people and is old enough to have known Galileo; Prewyt Brumblydge, who has invented the Bumblitron that can make sea water fresh; and King Ta who comes to visit earth. In *The Wonderful Flight to the Mushroom Planet*, two extraordinary California boys go by space rocket to Basidium where they save the people by restoring an essential food to their diet. *Stowaway to the Mushroom*

Planet, Mr. Bass's Planetoid, and *A Mystery for Mr. Bass* continue the fascinating story with moments of suspense and fast action. *Time and Mr. Bass* has more elements of fantasy than science fiction.

The Forgotten Door by Alexander Key is a fascinating science-fiction story with an unusual theme. Little Jon wakens in a mossy cave and finds himself cold and bruised. He cannot remember who he is or where he came from. Little Jon allows himself to be found by the kindly Beans, who gradually discover some amazing facts about the quiet, sensitive boy. He cannot speak English, but he understands what they are thinking and gradually translates it into words. He can communicate with animals, even their cross dog. He eats only vegetables and knows nothing of money, guns, robbery, murder, war, or other evils. It soon becomes apparent to the Beans that he is not from our world. They protect Jon, taking him into their home and making secret trips with him back to the cave where he remembers awakening. Vaguely, he recalls the memory of a door that opened and glorious shining stars. They discover only an unusual gash in the rocks of the cave—nothing more.

The local folk call Jon a wild boy and are afraid of his extraordinary powers. "He ain't natural," they say. Accused of a robbery, Jon demonstrates his innocence in an exciting scene in the closed session of the judge's chambers. Rumors continue to spread, however, and soon the federal government demands custody over Little Jon. Other political groups would like to use Jon's powers, and the Beans are desperate for help. Finally, Jon is able to hear his parents calling him and communicates his concern for his friends, the Beans. He is told to bring them with him. As the various forces close in on the tiny cabin, Jon and the Beans disappear through the Forgotten Door to the world Jon had described to them—a world so simple as to need no laws, no leaders, or money, where intelligent people work together and are friends with the deer. The pace of the plot of the story is breathtaking. In addition, the characters have substance and the theme is thought-provoking.

Another well-written story of a visitor from outer space is *Down to Earth* by Patricia Wrightson. When Cathy and George discovered the space boy living in an old abandoned house, they didn't believe his story until they saw him curled up asleep in an old stove glowing with a strange green color. They also found that he bounced when he fell. Falling into the role of his protectors, the children's greatest difficulty was to keep Marty, the Martian, as they called him, from announcing he was a space man to everyone they met. He couldn't understand why, when he was just visiting the country until the next new moon, he couldn't make his presence known. Finally, Marty realizes some of the problems when he is put in custody in the child welfare home. Hiding in the meter box until the children come to save him, Martin is most indignant at his treatment at the hands of the adults. He is grateful for the friendship of the children and as he awaits his space ship on the night of the new moon he comments:

> *"A pity about all the trouble; the police, and the ships and rockets. A great pity. But I'll remember the people, and you and Cathyn . . . Strange, all the same . . . that the sum should be so much smaller than its parts."*[37]

If there is a classic that emerges from this field of writing, it may be Madeleine L'Engle's *A Wrinkle in Time,* the Newbery Award winner for 1962. This is the exciting story of Charles Wallace, a five-year-old boy brilliant beyond his age and time; Meg, his twelve-year-old sister, whose stubbornness becomes an asset in space encounters; and Calvin O'Keefe, a fourteen-year-old friend upon whose stability the others often rely.

The three become involved in a frenzied search for Meg and Charles' missing father, a scientist who had been working for the government. The children are helped in their search by three ladies who appear to have supernatural powers, Mrs. Whatsit, Mrs. Who, and Mrs. Which. To accomplish the rescue, the children must travel in space by the fifth dimension, a tesseract, which reduces the distance between two points by creating a wrinkle in time. Their first tesser takes the children to a friendly planet where they learn that their father is being held prisoner on the distant planet, Camazotz. Camazotz had surrendered to the Power of Darkness, a giant black cloud that represents all evil in the universe. On their second tesseract, the children go alone to Camazotz to rescue their father. Here, they find that the people have given up their identity and do everything in a mechanical robot fashion. Charles Wallace attempts to overcome the Prime Coordinator of the Central Intelligence Building with his superior reasoning and is hypnotized instead into another dehumanized citizen of Camazotz. By using Mrs. Who's glasses, Meg is able to pass through a transparent wall and rescue her imprisoned father. In a frightening scene, she is nearly brainwashed by the disembodied, pulsating brain named It. Her father saves her only by tessering her and Calvin to another planet, leaving Charles Wallace behind. Still under the influence of the Black Thing of hate, Meg is furious with her father and Calvin for leaving Charles. She slowly recovers from her ordeal, nursed back to love and peace by one of the planet's strange, faceless inhabitants whom she calls Aunt Beast. The three ladies return and tell Meg that she alone has the necessary power to save her brother. Meg is frightened but agrees to go. When she confronts Charles Wallace, she suddenly realizes what she has what It does not. She saves Charles from the power of It by repeating her love for him. Together, they rejoin Mr. Murray and Cal-

[37]Patricia Wrightson, *Down to Earth,* Illustrated by Margaret Horder (New York: Harcourt, 1965), p. 201.

vin, and with one more tesser, they are all back safe on Earth. This story has many layers of meaning. It may be read for its exciting science-fiction plot alone, or it may be read for its themes of love conquering evil and the need to respect individual differences. It is a strange and wonderful combination of science fiction, modern fantasy, and religious symbolism.

Older readers will enjoy the books by Heinlein, one of the first writers of space fiction for boys and girls. The problem of peace and freedom is the theme of *Between Planets.* Don Harvey, born in a space ship, is a citizen of neither Earth nor Venus. *Red Planet, A Colonial Boy on Mars* tells of life in a colony on Mars. Excitement is provided by the plot to gain independence from the Earth. Background knowledge of time and light-years is needed to appreciate *Time for the Stars.* Mind-reading twins are used to maintain contact with ships sent to other star systems, one twin remaining on earth. Tom goes on the journey and ages little. He returns to find Pat a great-grandfather. Heinlein's books meet the criteria of good fiction, and the description of details gives them credence.

The many science-fiction books by Andre Norton also appeal more to the mature reader. *The Night of Masks* is a spellbinding story of a young man who finds that actions are more important than looks in determining the value of a man. *Key Out of Time* describes the time trip of Ross Murdock back some 10,000 years to a primitive world ravaged by warfare. These stories are imaginative and well-written science fiction for teen-age readers.

HUMOROUS BOOKS

Children and adults need to have fun, for it is essential for the development of a healthy personality. The increased tensions of modern living are frequently dissolved by laughter. Fun is therapeutic, and laughter can be the safety valve that releases tension and anxieties.

Children and adults do not always agree on what is funny. Research indicates a marked change in ideas of the humorous as children grow.[38] Usually slapstick and the juxtaposition of incongruous ideas are the most frequent stimuli for laughter. The child must have had certain experiences to know what is proper, before he can laugh at the improper. Only as he acquires a grasp of size relationships, for example, does he find amusement in the picture distortion of a man with an exaggeratedly long nose. Concepts of humor are developmental, ranging in ascending order from the grossly absurd, to the incongruous, to whimsy or satire.[39] Just as fanciful literature may stretch a child's imagination, books of fun may develop his sense of humor. Frequently, there is a very thin line between the fantastic and the humorous. *Charlotte's Web* by E. B. White contains much humor, but children find this animal fantasy both humorous and sad. Travers' story of that unpredictable nursemaid, *Mary Poppins,* is pure fancy, yet children always think of this book as a "funny" one. There is no true classification of humorous books, for humor can be found in all types of children's literature. The books discussed in this section[40] are those which children themselves usually refer to as "funny books."

Strange and Amusing Characters

Many humorous books for children are based upon amusing episodes concerning eccentric characters. The forerunner of all

---

[38]David H. Russell, *Children's Thinking* (Boston: Ginn, 1956), p. 152.
[39]Russell, pp. 150–152.
[40]See Chapter 3 for a discussion of humorous picture books for the young child.

American nonsense stories was Lucretia Hale's *The Peterkin Papers*. One of these stories, "The Lady Who Put Salt in Her Coffee," first appeared in a juvenile magazine in 1868. Over one hundred years later, children continue to be amused by the tales of the Peterkin family and their friend, the lady from Philadelphia, who offered a simple, sensible solution to whatever problem perplexed them.

The humor in the story of *Lazy Tommy Pumpkinhead* by William Pène du Bois is pure slapstick. Lazy Tommy lives in an all-electric house with an electric bed that wakes him up in the morning and slides him into a nice warm bathtub. An electric contraption dries and powders him, while another brushes his teeth and combs his hair. He is then dressed by a machine, fed by a machine, and entertained by a machine. After such a tiring day, Lazy Tommy is ready to crawl back into his electric bed that will rock him to sleep. But one night, there is a violent storm and a power failure. When Tommy falls into his bathtub, the water is icy cold; Tommy screams and moves too fast, so he then goes through his day head first. His head goes into his trousers, his toes are brushed, and his feet are fed scrambled eggs! As usual, the detailed pictures by the author add to the fun of this hilarious short story.

Amelia Bedelia by Peggy Parish is the literal-minded maid of the Rogers. Amelia follows Mrs. Rogers' instructions to the letter. She can't understand why Mrs. Rogers wants her to dress the chicken or draw the drapes, but she cheerfully goes about making a pair of pants for the chicken and drawing a picture of the drapes. Her wonderful lemon-meringue pie saves the day and Amelia's job. Amelia Bedelia continues to do things in her own special way in *Thank You, Amelia Bedelia*.

A riotously funny character in children's literature is *Pippi Longstocking*, created by a Swedish writer, Astrid Lindgren. Pippi is an orphan who lives alone with her monkey and her horse in a child's utopian world in which she tells herself when to go to bed and when to get up! Pippi takes care of herslf most efficiently and has a wonderful time doing it. When she washes her kitchen floor, she ties two scrubbing brushes on her bare feet and skates over the boards. She is a tidy housekeeper—in her fashion, as witnessed by the way she cleaned the table at her own birthday party:

> *When everybody had had enough and the horse had had his share, Pippi took hold of all four corners of the tablecloth and lifted it up so that the cups and plates tumbled over each other as if they were in a sack. Then she stuffed the whole bundle in the woodbox.*[41]

Although she is only a little girl she can hold her own with anyone, for she is so strong that she can pick up a horse or a man and throw him into the air. Her "logical thinking" delights children. For example, she decides to go to school because she feels it really isn't fair for her to miss Christmas and Easter vacation by not attending! However, one day at school is sufficient for both Pippi *and* her teacher. Children love this amazing character who always has the integrity to say what she thinks even if she shocks adults; actually, children are quite envious of Pippi's carefree existence. Eight-, nine-, and ten-year-olds enjoy her hilarious adventures in the two sequels to the original Pippi book, *Pippi Goes on Board,* and *Pippi in the South Seas.*

Betty MacDonald, the author of the humorous adult book, *The Egg and I,* gave children four amusing books about an eccentric woman named *Mrs. Piggle-Wiggle.* Mrs. Piggle-Wiggle has no family but is the widow of a pirate, which accounts for the buried treasure in her back yard. One of the most

---

[41] Astrid Lindgren, *Pippi Longstocking,* Illustrated by Louis S. Glanzman (New York: Viking, 1950), p. 150.

remarkable things about Mrs. Piggle-Wiggle is her upside-down house. Every child in town is a friend of Mrs. Piggle-Wiggle. Although she knows few of their parents, they are her friends, also, but for different reasons than the children. Mrs. Piggle-Wiggle has the amazing ability to cure every childish bad habit imaginable. For example, she had to use "The Won't-Pick-up-Toys Cure" on Hubert Prentiss and "The Answer-Backer Cure" on Mary O'Toole. These stories are reminiscent of some of the lectures on good manners and morals of the nineteenth century. However, their popularity proves that they are served in a more hilarious and palatable fashion than the earlier moralistic stories.

Third and fourth graders thoroughly enjoy the fun of *Miss Osborne-the-Mop* by Wilson Gage. One very dull summer Jody discovers that she has the power to change people and objects into something else and back again. Complications arise when Jody turns a dust mop into a person who strongly resembles her fourth-grade teacher, and then finds that she cannot turn the tireless, spindly-legged Miss Osborne back into an ordinary dust mop.

When the east wind blew *Mary Poppins* into the Banks' house in London to care for Michael and Jane, it blew her into the hearts of many thousand readers. Wearing her shapeless hat and white gloves, carrying her parrot-handled umbrella and a large carpet bag, Mary Poppins is as British as tea, yet many American children love this nursemaid with strange magical powers. Probably their favorite story is that of the laughing-gas party. Jane, Michael, and Mary Poppins visit Mary Poppins' uncle for tea only to be overcome by fits of uncontrollable laughter. Filled with laughter, they all blow right up to the ceiling. Mary Poppins raises the table in some way, and they have birthday tea suspended in midair! Nothing seems impossible for this prim autocrat of the nursery to per-

form in her matter-of-fact, believable fashion. Not all children enjoy the British flavor of this book, but many adore her as much as did Michael and Jane. Mary Poppins goes serenely on her way through other excruciatingly funny adventures in *Mary Poppins Comes Back, Mary Poppins Opens the Door,* and *Mary Poppins in the Park.* Children hope that the west wind will never blow her away permanently, for she has become a classic character in many a family's reading. While the movie of Mary Poppins by Walt Disney introduced her to thousands more children, it also destroyed some of the acerbity of the character created by P. L. Travers. For Walt Disney's Mary Poppins was beautiful, gay, and fun, while the original was unpredictable, abrupt, and mysterious.

Not all of the strange and amusing characters in children's literature are women. Robert Lawson has created the droll and inimitable character of Professor Ambrose Augustus McWhinney, inventor of Z-Gas. In fact, it is this same Z-Gas in his bicycle tires that takes him on *McWhinney's Jaunt,* a kind of gliding trip across the country. With Z-Gas, the professor's bicycle tires just won't stay on the ground. He soars westward from the George Washington Bridge, wins $500 in a professional bike race, and is given $1000 for crossing the Grand Canyon on a kite string. Boys in the middle grades enjoy this serious account of the professor's hilarious adventures. Lawson's illustrations of the comic professor in his tall hat, protected by a large umbrella from which he hangs his socks to dry, are as droll and as amusing as Professor McWhinney himself.

Mr. Twigg's Mistake is another humorous story by Robert Lawson. This is the amazing tale of what happens to a mole when he eats pure vitamin X instead of Bita-Vita breakfast food. It is all Mr. Twigg's fault because, as a scientist for a breakfast-food company, he pulled the wrong lever and put all of the vitamins intended for thousands of packages into one. It was quite by accident that Squirt Appleton fed this box of "Bities" breakfast food to his pet mole, named General Charles de Gaulle. The results of this mixup are amazingly funny.

Amusing Animals

Ever since Kipling told his humorous *Just-So Stories* about the origins of certain animal characteristics, authors have been writing imaginative tales of amusing animals. The humor of the *Just-So Stories* is based upon Kipling's wonderful use of words and his tongue-in-cheek asides to the reader. The favorite with children is the story of *The Elephant's Child* who originally has a nose no bigger than a bulgy boot. His "satiable curtiosity" causes him all kinds of trouble *and* spankings. To find out what the crocodile has for dinner, he departs for the "banks of the great grey-green, greasy Limpopo River, all set about with fever trees. . . ." Here he meets the crocodile who whispers in his ear that today he will start his meal with the Elephant's Child! The Elephant's Child is finally freed from the crocodile, but only after his nose has been badly pulled out of shape. As he waits for it to shrink, the Bi-Colored-Python-Rock-Snake points out all of the advantages of having an elongated nose. It is convenient for eating, for making a "cool-schloopy-sloshy mud-cap all trickly behind his ears," but most of all it would be wonderful for spanking! Some of these stories such as *The Elephant's Child, How the Camel Got His Hump, How the Leopard Got His Spots,* and others have been published in single editions.

The amazing *Story of Dr. Dolittle* and his animal friends, Dab-Dab, the duck, and Gub-Gub, the pig, is recorded in a whole series of twelve books by Hugh Lofting. The humor, swift-paced episodes, and realistic dialogue make them particular favorites of nine- and ten-year-olds. The film

version of these stories has generated new interest in this character that was created over forty years ago.

The story of *Mr. Popper's Penguins* by Richard and Florence Atwater has long been the favorite funny story of many school children. This is the tale of Mr. Popper, a mild little house painter whose major interest in life is the study of the Antarctic. An explorer presents Mr. Popper with a penguin that he promptly names Captain Cook. In order to keep Captain Cook from becoming lonely, Mr. Popper obtains Greta from the zoo. After the arrival of ten baby penguins, Mr. Popper has a freezing plant put in the basement of his house and his furnace moved upstairs to the living room. The Atwaters' serious accounting of a highly implausible situation adds to the humor of this truly funny story.

Michael Bond has written a series of books about a very endearing *Bear Called Paddington,* because the Brown family found him in Paddington Station in London, obviously looking for a home. Paddington earnestly tries to help the Browns but invariably ends up in difficulty. His well-meaning efforts produce a series of absurdities that make amusing reading. One of the funniest incidents is in the book, *More about Paddington,* and describes the day Paddington decided to wallpaper his room. He covers over the doors and windows and then can't find his way out! Other adventures of this lovable bear are included in *Paddington at Large, Paddington Helps Out,* and *Paddington Marches On,* all amusingly illustrated by Peggy Fortnum.

William Pène du Bois has written and illustrated an intriguing and funny mystery that is solved by *The Great Geppy,* a red-and-white striped horse, who is a most efficient detective. Sent by Armstrong and Trilby detective agency, Geppy must resolve the mystery of the stolen circus money. He works with each suspect and then writes quite formal reports of his findings to the agency. The number of possible robbers is gradually limited until finally *The Great Geppy,* in a flash of insight, discovers the "robber." This is a well-written "Scotland Yard" story that will interest boys in the middle grades.

One of the truly humorous stories for children in the middle grades is Butterworth's *The Enormous Egg.* Nate Twitchell, a twelve-year-old boy living in Freedom, New Hampshire, takes over the care of an enormous egg laid by a hen and helps the hen turn it regularly during its six-week incubation period. The egg finally hatches into a baby Triceratops. Trying to raise a dinosaur in a small New Hampshire town provides many hilarious situations. Finally, Washington, D.C., is consulted about the problem, and members of the Congress attempt to have "Uncle Beazley" (the dinosaur) destroyed since he is extinct and probably un-American! Nate Twitchell tells the story of his efforts to save Uncle Beazley's life with a manner of gravity and sincere earnestness that makes this book seem even funnier. The satire on American politics is a delightful mixture of humor and truth. The anachronism of a dinosaur in today's world greatly appeals to children's sense of the ridiculous.

Fun in Everyday Happenings

Some very funny American juveniles derive their humor primarily from situational factors rather than from peculiar characters. The characters themselves are usually very realistic all-American boys (occasionally, a girl) who live in small modern communities. They become involved in all kinds of funny, amazing, and exaggerated predicaments. The story line is built around the solution to these problems. Many of these humorous books are episodic—each chapter representing a complete story.

Third-graders can read Carolyn Haywood's *Little Eddie* stories independently —much to their delight. Eddie Wilson is a typical American boy with a passion for collecting all kinds of "valuable property" (junk in the eyes of his parents). There are nine *Little Eddie* books now, and in each one, Eddie turns his collecting instinct into profit. One of the funniest of the books, *Eddie and His Big Deals,* involves a rival collector, a girl, which makes matters even worse. Eddie starts a long and involved process of swapping in order to obtain an old printing press from her. Boys will laugh uproariously at Eddie's humiliation in trying to repair a dilapidated old doll to use in his trading. Carolyn Haywood has also written a series of books for girls, the *Betsy* series. These stories are filled with the everyday activities of Betsy and her friends. Some of the episodes are amusing, but they do not match her *Little Eddie* books for humor. However, girls in second and third grade find them completely satisfying.

Another genuinely funny series of books about a very natural and normal boy are the *Henry Huggins* stories by Beverly Cleary. Mrs. Cleary's intimate knowledge of boys in the middle grades is very evident as she describes their problems, adventures, and hilarious activities. In the first book, Henry's problems center on a stray dog, named Ribsy, and his efforts to keep him. In *Henry and Beezus,* Henry's major interest is in obtaining a new bicycle. At the opening of the Colossal Market, he is delighted when he wins one of the door prizes and then horrified to find out it is fifty dollars worth of Beauty Shoppe permanent waves, facials, and false eyelashes! Beezus (really Beatrice), the girl Henry finds least obnoxious among girls, offers to buy some of the coupons to have her hair waved. Soon Henry sells most of the coupons, and he obtains the shiny red bicycle of his desire. At the end of the book, he casually pedals by Scooter McCarthy's house with his spokes twinkling in the sunshine and the snap-on tail of his coonskin cap fluttering from the handle bars—a moment of complete triumph and joy!

Beverly Cleary has followed the adventures of Beezus in the book, *Beezus and Ramona,* to make one of the funniest stories ever written for girls. In this book, four-year-old Ramona becomes a real trial to both Beezus and her mother. Probably, the funniest episode is the day Ramona casually invites her entire kindergarten class to a party at her home without mentioning it to her mother. Girls with younger brothers and sisters will find this story hilarious. They certainly will sympathize with Beezus and may be helped to understand their own feelings toward the youngest members of their families.

Another book that portrays real boys is Corbett's *The Lemonade Trick.* When an eccentric lady gives Kerby a magic chemistry set, strange things begin to happen. One sip from a special vial, and Kerby becomes frighteningly good; in fact, he can't keep himself from mowing the lawn, cleaning the cellar, and the garage. Luckily, the spell wears off, and Kerby becomes the typical boy who hates all manner of household chores. When Kerby adds the mysterious liquid to a pitcher of lemonade for the boys who are practicing the Sunday School pageant, the effects are riotous. Corbett has written a truly humorous book in which Kerby and his friend, Fenton, are real boys. Their gradual understanding of the town bully makes this more than just an amusing story. Five other "trick" books continue the adventures of Kerby. These include the amusing *The Limerick Trick* in which Kerby only speaks in limericks and *The Turnabout Trick* in which Kerby uses his chemistry set again and has such disastrous results as making the cat bark and the dog meow.

A delightfully humorous story is Butterworth's *The Trouble with Jenny's Ear.* When six-year-old Jenny discovers she has extrasensory perception, her older brothers immediately become her managers. Jenny uses her new-found ability for quiz shows, for court evidence, and even to further her uncle's romance. Some of the schoolroom scenes and those in the broadcasting studio are hilarious. The author neatly resolves the moral issue of the prize money that Jenny receives in the quiz show. Jenny herself is a quaint and sensitive child; her brothers are real boys of the electronic age. Fifth- or sixth-grade readers would enjoy this spoof of the false values of our society.

Probably the classic of modern humorous stories is McCloskey's *Homer Price.* The six chapters of this book present extravagant yarns about life in Centerburg as aided and abetted by Homer and his friends. One story tells how Homer captured four robbers singlehanded with the help of Aroma, his pet skunk. "The Case of the Cosmic Comic" is pure satire, on the child's level, however. Probably the favorite Homer Price story is that of the doughnuts. Homer helpfully offers to make some doughnuts in his uncle's new doughnut machine. A rich customer volunteers to make the batter, and Homer is doing beautifully until he realizes he can't stop the machine! The shop becomes full of doughnuts and then, after his uncle finally stops their manufacture, there is the problem of how to dispose of them. The missing bracelet of the woman who had helped to make the doughnuts, supplies the answer. The story of *Lentil* by McCloskey is really a picture story book for all ages. It is the story of Lentil's inability to sing for which he compensates by his remarkable playing of the harmonica. *Centerburg Tales* continues the adventures of Homer Price. The stories of the preposterous happenings in this small town are told in the American tradition of the tall tale. Homer Price has almost become the legendary hero of all modern American boys.

Robert McCloskey has illustrated the story of *Henry Reed, Inc.,* written by Keith

Robertson. This book is recorded as the journal of Henry Reed, who has come to spend the summer with his aunt and uncle at Grover's Corner, Princeton, New Jersey. Henry is planning to use the journal as part of a report, for his teacher had asked that they do something that can be used to illustrate free enterprise. Henry establishes a business firm named "Reed and Glass, Inc., Pure and Applied Research." Although Henry has a poor opinion of girls in general, he recognizes business ability and accepts Margaret Glass as a partner. He gravely records the side-splitting details of his undertakings in the great American tradition of free enterprise. His sober comments let the reader have the satisfaction of seeing the humorous side to his adventures without telling him that they are funny. Boys and girls from fifth grade through the seventh thoroughly enjoy this story.

More adventures of Henry are recorded in the stories of *Henry Reed's Journey,* which includes his observations and adventures on a cross-country trip and *Henry Reed's Baby-Sitting Service,* where Henry and Margaret collaborate on a money-making scheme.

Books of humor and fantasy need no justification. They may stretch the child's imagination or increase his sense of humor, but they are primarily for enjoyment. They provide a healthy balance for a reading diet that may be overburdened with too many books dealing with the social problems of our day. They form an important part of the child's literary heritage.

SUGGESTED ACTIVITIES

1. Compare the chronicles of Narnia by C. S. Lewis with Lloyd Alexander's chronicles of Prydain. In what ways are they similar; how are they different?
2. Make an informal survey to determine reactions of your friends to several well-known fantasies such as *Alice in Wonderland, Winnie the Pooh,* and *The Wonderful Wizard of Oz.*
3. Write a modern fairy tale, fable, or tall tale using the old forms with twentieth-century content.
4. What universal truths can you discover in such fantasies as *Charlotte's Web, The Wind in the Willows, The Gammage Cup,* and *The Pushcart War?*
5. Read five fantasies suggested in this chapter. Prepare a list of the questions you might ask about each book to guide children's discussion and interpretations.
6. Read and contrast several books of science fiction. In what ways has the author shown the impact of the scientific advancements on the total lives of the people in the future?
7. Read some of the books by Jules Verne, such as *Mysterious Island, Twenty Thousand Leagues Under the Sea, Journey to the Center of the Earth,* or *Dr. Ox's Experiment.* How many of the scientific inventions that he assumed as fact have become realities today?
8. Read a humorous story to a group of children and record the situations that bring smiles, chuckles, and laughter.

RELATED READINGS

1. Alexander, Lloyd. "The Flat-Heeled Muse," *The Horn Book Magazine,* vol. 41 (April 1965), pp. 141–146.
   The author of the chronicles of Prydain discusses the craft of writing good fantasy.
2. Arbuthnot, May Hill. *Children and Books.* Third edition. Glenview, Ill.: Scott, Foresman, 1964.

Chapter 12, "New Magic," includes a critical analysis of both modern fantasy and humor.

3. Fisher, Margery. *Intent upon Reading.* Market Place, Leicester, England: Brockhampton Press, 1961.

Nearly half of the fifteen chapters in this critical appraisal of modern fiction for children is devoted to a discussion of fanciful and humorous books. Although Mrs. Fisher is English, she includes both English and American books in her reviews.

4. Frye, Northrup. *The Educated Imagination.* Bloomington, Ind.: Indiana University Press, 1964.

Dr. Frye stresses the social utility of developing the imagination and sees literature as one way in which man reaches out to his environment and finds his place in it.

5. Heinlein, Robert. "Ray Guns and Rocket Ships," in *Readings about Children's Literature,* Evelyn R. Robinson, Editor. New York: McKay, 1966.

One of the leading science fiction writers defines and evaluates good science fiction writing.

6. Kappas, Katherine H. "A Developmental Analysis of Children's Responses to Humor," *Library Quarterly,* vol. 37 (January 1967), pp. 67–77.

Kappas identified different categories of humor and related these to children's development. She found that visual forms of humor amused all ages but that verbal humor increased with age. It would be interesting to try to find books that represented her various categories of humor and appealed to different developmental levels of children.

7. Lewis, C. S. "On Three Ways of Writing For Children," *The Horn Book Magazine,* vol. 39 (October 1963), pp. 459–469.

The well-known author of the Narnia Series discusses writing for children. An article by Lillian H. Smith in the same issue is titled "News From Narnia." Both articles give much insight into the writing of the late C. S. Lewis.

8. Tolkien, J. R. R. *Tree and Leaf.* Boston: Houghton Mifflin, 1965.

The author of *The Hobbit* has written a critical essay on the technique and purposes of writing "On Fairy Stories." This discussion is followed by a short story, "Leaf by Niggle," which is an illustration of the points Tolkien made in his essay.

CHAPTER REFERENCES

1. Alexander, Lloyd. *The Black Cauldron.* New York: Holt, Rinehart and Winston, 1965.

2. ———*The Book of Three.* New York: Holt, Rinehart and Winston, 1964.

3. ———*The Castle of Llyr.* New York: Holt, Rinehart and Winston, 1966.

4. ———*Taran Wanderer.* New York: Holt, Rinehart and Winston, 1967.

5. ———*Time Cat, The Remarkable Journeys.* Illustrated by Bill Sokol. New York: Holt, Rinehart and Winston, 1963.

6. Andersen, Hans Christian. *The Emperor's New Clothes.* Illustrated by Virginia Lee Burton. Boston: Houghton Mifflin, 1949.

7. ———"The Fir Tree" in *Seven Tales.* Translated by Eva Le Gallienne. Illustrated by Maurice Sendak. New York: Harper & Row, 1959.

8. ———"The Little Match Girl" in *Thumbelina and Other Fairy Tales.* Illustrated by Sandro Nardini and Ugo Fontana. New York: Macmillan, 1962.

9. ———"The Little Mermaid" in *Fairy Tales of Hans Christian Andersen.* New York: Orion, 1958.

10. ———*The Nightingale.* Translated by Eva Le Gallienne. Illustrated by Nancy Ekholm Burkert. New York: Harper & Row, 1965.

11. ———"The Princess on the Pea" in *Seven Tales.* Translated by Eva Le Gallienne. Illustrated by Maurice Sendak. New York: Harper & Row, 1959.

12. ————"The Snow Queen" in *Fairy Tales*. Illustrated by Janusz Grabianski. New York: Duell, Sloan, 1963.

13. ————*The Steadfast Tin Soldier*. Translated by M. R. James. Illustrated by Marcia Brown. New York: Scribner, 1953.

14. ————*The Swineherd*. Translated and Illustrated by Erik Blegvad. New York: Harcourt, 1958.

15. ————*Thumbelina*. Illustrated by Adrienne Adams. New York: Scribner, 1961.

16. ————*The Ugly Duckling*. Illustrated by Adrienne Adams. New York: Scribner, 1965.

17. ————*The Wild Swans*. Illustrated by Marcia Brown. New York: Scribner, 1963.

18. Atwater, Richard and Florence. *Mr. Popper's Penguins*. Illustrated by Robert Lawson. Boston: Little, Brown, 1938.

19. Bailey, Carolyn Sherwin. *Miss Hickory*. Illustrated by Ruth Gannett. New York: Viking, 1962, 1946.

20. Baum, L. Frank. *The Wonderful Wizard of Oz*. Illustrated by W. W. Denslow. Chicago: Reilly & Lee, 1956, 1900.

21. Bond, Michael. *A Bear Called Paddington*. Illustrated by Peggy Fortnum. Boston: Houghton Mifflin, 1960.

22. ————*More about Paddington*. Illustrated by Peggy Fortnum. Boston: Houghton Mifflin, 1962.

23. ————*Paddington at Large*. Illustrated by Peggy Fortnum. Boston: Houghton Mifflin, 1963.

24. ————*Paddington Helps Out*. Illustrated by Peggy Fortnum. Boston: Houghton Mifflin, 1961.

25. ————*Paddington Marches On*. Illustrated by Peggy Fortnum. Boston: Houghton Mifflin, 1965.

26. Boston, L. M. *The Children of Green Knowe*. Illustrated by Peter Boston. New York: Harcourt, 1955.

27. ————*An Enemy at Green Knowe*. Illustrated by Peter Boston. New York: Harcourt, 1964.

28. ————*The River at Green Knowe*. Illustrated by Peter Boston. New York: Harcourt, 1959.

29. ————*The Sea Egg*. Illustrated by Peter Boston. New York: Harcourt, 1967.

30. ————*The Treasure of Green Knowe*. Illustrated by Peter Boston. New York: Harcourt, 1958.

31. Butterworth, Oliver. *The Enormous Egg*. Illustrated by Louis Darling. Boston: Little, Brown, 1956.

32. ————*The Trouble with Jenny's Ear*. Illustrated by Julian de Miskey. Boston: Little, Brown, 1960.

33. Cameron, Eleanor. *Mr. Bass's Planetoid*. Illustrated by Louis Darling. Boston: Little, Brown, 1958.

34. ————*A Mystery for Mr. Bass*. Illustrated by Leonard Shortall. Boston: Little, Brown, 1960.

35. ————*Stowaway to the Mushroom Planet*. Illustrated by Robert Henneberger. Boston: Little, Brown, 1956.

36. ————*Time and Mr. Bass*. Illustrated by Fred H. Meise. Boston: Little, Brown, 1967.

37. ————*The Wonderful Flight to the Mushroom Planet*. Illustrated by Robert Henneberger. Boston: Little, Brown, 1954.

38. Carroll, Lewis, pseud. (Charles Dodgson). *Alice's Adventures in Wonderland and Through the Looking-Glass*. Illustrated by John Tenniel. New York: Macmillan, 1963 (published separately, 1865 and 1872).

39. Chauncy, Nan. *The Secret Friends*. Illustrated by Brian Wildsmith. New York: F. Watts, 1962.

40. Clarke, Pauline. *The Return of the Twelves*. Illustrated by Bernarda Bryson. New York: Coward-McCann, 1963.

41. Cleary, Beverly. *Beezus and Ramona*. Illustrated by Louis Darling. New York: Morrow, 1955.

42. ————*Henry and Beezus*. Illustrated by Louis Darling. New York: Morrow, 1952.

43. ————*Henry and Ribsy*. Illustrated by Louis Darling. New York: Morrow, 1954.

44. ————*Henry and the Paper Route*. Illustrated by Louis Darling. New York: Morrow, 1957.

45. ————*Henry Huggins*. Illustrated by Louis Darling. New York: Morrow, 1950.

46. ————*Ribsy*. Illustrated by Louis Darling. New York: Morrow, 1964.

47. Collodi, C. *The Adventures of Pinocchio*. Illustrated by Naiad Einsel. New York: Macmillan, 1963, 1892.

48. Cooper, Susan. *Over Sea, Under Stone*. Illustrated by Margery Gill. New York: Harcourt, 1966.

49. Corbett, Scott. *The Baseball Trick*. Illustrated by Paul Galdone. Boston: Little, Brown, 1965.

50. ————*The Disappearing Dog Trick*. Illustrated by Paul Galdone. Boston: Little, Brown, 1963.

51. ————*The Lemonade Trick*. Illustrated by Paul Galdone. Boston: Little, Brown, 1960.

52. ————*The Limerick Trick*. Illustrated by Paul Galdone. Boston: Little, Brown, 1964.

53. ————*The Mailbox Trick*. Illustrated by Paul Galdone. Boston: Little, Brown, 1961.

54. ————*The Turnabout Trick*. Illustrated by Paul Galdone. Boston: Little, Brown, 1967.

55. Cunningham, Julia. *Dear Rat*. Boston: Houghton Mifflin, 1961.

56. ————*Dorp Dead*. Illustrated by James Spanfeller. New York: Pantheon, 1965.

57. ————*Macaroon*. Illustrated by Evaline Ness. New York: Pantheon, 1962.

58. ————*Viollet*. Illustrated by Alan E. Cober. New York: Pantheon, 1966.

59. Dahl, Roald. *Charlie and the Chocolate Factory*. Illustrated by Joseph Schindelman. New York: Knopf, 1964.

60. ————*James and the Giant Peach*. Illustrated by Nancy Ekholm Burkert. New York: Knopf, 1961.

61. ————*The Magic Finger*. Illustrated by William Pène du Bois. New York: Harper & Row, 1966.

62. DeJong, Meindert. *Shadrach*. Illustrated by Maurice Sendak. New York: Harper & Row, 1953.

63. Druon, Maurice. *Tistou of the Green Thumbs*. Illustrated by Jacqueline Duheme. New York: Scribner, 1958.

64. Du Bois, William Pène. *The Great Geppy*. New York: Viking, 1940.

65. ————*Lazy Tommy Pumpkinhead*. New York: Harper & Row, 1966.

66. ————*The Twenty-One Balloons*. New York: Viking, 1947.

67. Eager, Edward. *Half Magic*. Illustrated by N. M. Bodecker. New York: Harcourt, 1954.

68. ————*Knight's Castle*. Illustrated by N. M. Bodecker. New York: Harcourt, 1956.

69. ————*Seven-Day Magic*. Illustrated by N. M. Bodecker. New York: Harcourt, 1962.

70. Enright, Elizabeth. *Tatsinda*. Illustrated by Irene Haas. New York: Harcourt, 1963.

71. Farmer, Penelope. *Emma in Winter*. Illustrated by James Spanfeller. New York: Harcourt, 1966.

72. ————*The Magic Stone*. Illustrated by James Spanfeller. New York: Harcourt, 1964.

73. ————*The Summer Birds*. Illustrated by James Spanfeller. New York: Harcourt, 1962.

74. Felsen, Gregor. *The Boy Who Discovered the Earth*. Illustrated by Leonard Shortall. New York: Scribner, 1955.

75. Field, Rachel. *Hitty, Her First Hundred Years*. Illustrated by Dorothy P. Lathrop. New York: Macmillan, 1962 (1929).

76. Fleischman, Sid. *Chancy and the Grand Rascal*. Illustrated by Eric von Schmidt. Boston: Little, Brown, 1966.

77. ————*McBroom Tells the Truth*. Illustrated by Kurt Werth. New York: Norton, 1966.

78. Fleming, Ian. *Chitty-Chitty-Bang-Bang, the Magical Car*. Illustrated by John Burningham. New York: Random House, 1964.

79. Fritz, Jean. *Magic to Burn*. Illustrated by Beth and Joe Krush. New York: Coward-McCann, 1964.

80. Gage, Wilson. *Miss Osborne-the-Mop*. Illustrated by Paul Galdone. Cleveland: World Publishing, 1963.

81. Garnett, Richard. *Jack of Dover*. Illustrated by Graham Oakley. New York: Vanguard, 1966.

82. Godden, Rumer. *Candy Floss*. Illustrated by Adrienne Adams. New York: Viking, 1960.

83. ————*The Dolls' House*. Illustrated by Dana Saintsbury. New York: Viking, 1948.

84. ————*The Fairy Doll*. Illustrated by Adrienne Adams. New York: Viking, 1956.

85. ————*Home Is the Sailor*. Illustrated by Jean Primrose. New York: Viking, 1964.

86. ————*Impunity Jane*. Illustrated by Adrienne Adams. New York: Viking, 1954.

87. ————*The Mousewife*. Illustrated by William Pène du Bois. New York: Viking, 1951.

88. ————*The Story of Holly and Ivy*. Illustrated by Adrienne Adams. New York: Viking, 1958.

89. Grahame, Kenneth. *The Reluctant Dragon*. Illustrated by Ernest H. Shepard. New York: Holiday, 1938.

90. ————*The Wind in the Willows*. Illustrated by E. H. Shepard. New York: Scribner, 1908.

91. Grimm, Jacob and Wilhelm. *The Seven Ravens*. Illustrated by Felix Hoffman. New York: Harcourt, 1963.

92. Hale, Lucretia P. *The Complete Peterkin Papers*. Boston: Houghton Mifflin, 1960.

93. Harvey, James O. *Beyond the Gorge of Shadows*. New York: Lothrop, 1965.

94. Haywood, Carolyn. *Annie Pat and Eddie*. New York: Morrow, 1960.

95. ————*"B" Is for Betsy*. New York: Harcourt, 1939.

96. ————*Back to School with Betsy*. New York: Harcourt, 1943.

97. ————*Betsy and Billy.* New York: Harcourt, 1941.

98. ————*Betsy and the Boys*. New York: Harcourt, 1945.

99. ————*Betsy and the Circus*. New York: Harcourt, 1954.

100. ————*Betsy's Busy Summer*. New York: Harcourt, 1956.

101. ————*Betsy's Little Star*. New York: Harcourt, 1950.

102. ————*Betsy's Winterhouse*. New York: Harcourt, 1958.

103. ————*Eddie and Gardenia*. New York: Morrow, 1951.

104. ————*Eddie and His Big Deals*. New York: Morrow, 1955.

105. ————*Eddie and Louella*. New York: Morrow, 1959.

106. ————*Eddie and the Fire Engine*. New York: Morrow, 1949.

107. ————*Eddie Makes Music*. New York: Morrow, 1957.

108. ————*Eddie's Green Thumb*. New York: Morrow, 1964.

109. ————*Eddie's Pay Dirt*. New York: Morrow, 1953.

110. ————*Little Eddie*. New York: Morrow, 1947.

111. ————*Snowbound with Betsy*. New York: Harcourt, 1962.

112. Heinlein, Robert. *Between Planets*. Illustrated by Clifford Geary. New York: Scribner, 1957.

113. ————*Red Planet, A Colonial Boy on Mars*. Illustrated by Clifford Geary. New York: Scribner, 1949.

114. ———*Time for the Stars.* New York: Scribner, 1956.
115. Hollander, John. *The Quest of the Gole.* Illustrated by Reginald Pollack. New York: Atheneum, 1966.
116. Jansson, Tove. *Exploits of Moominpappa.* Translated by Thomas Warburton. New York: Walck, 1966.
117. ———*Finn Family Moomintroll.* Translated by Elizabeth Portch. New York: Walck, 1965.
118. ———*Moominland Midwinter.* Translated by Thomas Warburton. New York: Walck, 1962.
119. ———*Moominsummer Madness.* Translated by Thomas Warburton. New York: Walck, 1961.
120. ———*Tales from Moominvalley.* Translated by Thomas Warburton. New York: Walck, 1964.
121. Jarrell, Randall. *The Animal Family.* Illustrated by Maurice Sendak. New York: Pantheon, 1965.
122. ———*The Bat Poet.* Illustrated by Maurice Sendak. New York: Macmillan, 1964.
123. Juster, Norton. *The Phantom Tollbooth.* Illustrated by Jules Feiffer. New York: Random House, 1961.
124. Kendall, Carol. *The Gammage Cup.* Illustrated by Erik Blegvad. New York: Harcourt, 1959.
125. ———*The Whisper of Glocken.* Illustrated by Imero Gobbato. New York: Harcourt, 1965.
126. Key, Alexander. *The Forgotten Door.* Philadelphia: Westminster, 1965.
127. Kipling, Rudyard. *The Elephant's Child.* Illustrated by Feodor Rojankovsky. New York: Garden City Books, 1942.
128. ———*How the Camel Got His Hump.* Illustrated by Feodor Rojankovsky. New York: Garden City Books, 1942.
129. ———*How the Leopard Got His Spots.* Illustrated by Feodor Rojankovsky. New York: Garden City Books, 1942.
130. ———*Just-So Stories.* Illustrated by Nicolas. New York: Doubleday, 1952, 1902.
131. Knight, Damon, Editor. *Worlds to Come, Nine Science Fiction Adventures.* New York: Harper & Row, 1967.
132. Langton, Jane. *The Diamond in the Window.* Illustrated by Erik Blegvad. New York: Harper & Row, 1962.
133. ———*The Swing in the Summerhouse.* Illustrated by Erik Blegvad. New York: Harper & Row, 1967.
134. Lawson, John. *You Better Come Home with Me.* Illustrated by Arnold Spilka. New York: Crowell, 1966.
135. Lawson, Robert. *The Fabulous Flight.* Boston: Little, Brown, 1949.
136. ———*McWhinney's Jaunt.* Boston: Little, Brown, 1951.
137. ———*Mr. Twigg's Mistake.* Boston: Little, Brown, 1947.
138. ———*Rabbit Hill.* New York: Viking, 1945.
139. ———*The Tough Winter.* New York: Viking, 1954.
140. L'Engle, Madeleine. *A Wrinkle in Time.* New York: Farrar, Straus, 1962.
141. Lewis, C. S. *The Horse and His Boy.* Illustrated by Pauline Baynes. New York: Macmillan, 1962, 1954.
142. ———*The Last Battle.* Illustrated by Pauline Baynes. New York: Macmillan, 1964, 1956.
143. ———*The Lion, the Witch, and the Wardrobe.* Illustrated by Pauline Baynes. New York: Macmillan, 1961, 1950.
144. ———*The Magician's Nephew.* Illustrated by Pauline Baynes. New York: Macmillan, 1964, 1955.
145. ———*Prince Caspian, the Return to Narnia.* Illustrated by Pauline Baynes. New York: Macmillan, 1964, 1951.
146. ———*The Silver Chair.* Illustrated by Pauline Baynes. New York: Macmillan, 1962, 1953.

147. ———*The Voyage of the "Dawn Treader."* Illustrated by Pauline Baynes. New York: Macmillan, 1962, 1952.
148. Lindgren, Astrid. *Pippi Goes on Board.* Translated by Florence Lamborn. Illustrated by Louis S. Glanzman. New York: Viking, 1957.
149. ———*Pippi Longstocking.* Translated by Florence Lamborn. Illustrated by Louis S. Glanzman. New York: Viking, 1950.
150. ———*Pippi in the South Seas.* Translated by Florence Lamborn. Illustrated by Louis S. Glanzman. New York: Viking, 1959.
151. Lofting, Hugh. *Dr. Dolittle and the Green Canary.* Philadelphia: Lippincott, 1950.
152. ———*Dr. Dolittle and the Secret Lake.* Philadelphia: Lippincott, 1948.
153. ———*Dr. Dolittle in the Moon.* Philadelphia: Lippincott, 1928.
154. ———*Dr. Dolittle's Caravan.* Philadelphia: Lippincott, 1926.
155. ———*Dr. Dolittle's Circus.* Philadelphia: Lippincott, 1924.
156. ———*Dr. Dolittle's Garden.* Philadelphia: Lippincott, 1927.
157. ———*Dr. Dolittle's Post Office.* Philadelphia: Lippincott, 1923.
158. ———*Dr. Dolittle's Puddleby Adventures.* Philadelphia: Lippincott, 1952.
159. ———*Dr. Dolittle's Return.* Philadelphia: Lippincott, 1933.
160. ———*Dr. Dolittle's Zoo.* Philadelphia: Lippincott, 1922.
161. ———*The Story of Dr. Dolittle.* Philadelphia: Lippincott, 1920.
162. ———*The Voyages of Dr. Dolittle.* Philadelphia: Lippincott, 1922.
163. McCloskey, Robert. *Centerburg Tales.* New York: Viking, 1951.
164. ———*Homer Price.* New York: Viking, 1943.
165. ———*Lentil.* New York: Viking, 1940.
166. MacDonald, Betty. *Hello, Mrs. Piggle-Wiggle.* Philadelphia: Lippincott, 1957.
167. ———*Mrs. Piggle-Wiggle.* Illustrated by Hilary Knight. Revised edition. Philadelphia: Lippincott, 1957, 1947.
168. ———*Mrs. Piggle-Wiggle's Farm.* Illustrated by Maurice Sendak. Philadelphia: Lippincott, 1954.
169. ———*Mrs. Piggle-Wiggle's Magic.* Philadelphia: Lippincott, 1957.
170. MacDonald, George. *The Light Princess.* Illustrated by William Pène du Bois. New York: Crowell, 1962.
171. McGinley, Phyllis. *The Plain Princess.* Illustrated by Helen Stone. Philadelphia: Lippincott, 1945.
172. MacGregor, Ellen. *Miss Pickerell and the Geiger Counter.* Illustrated by Paul Galdone. New York: McGraw-Hill, 1953.
173. ———*Miss Pickerell Goes to Mars.* Illustrated by Paul Galdone. New York: McGraw-Hill, 1951.
174. ———*Miss Pickerell Goes to the Arctic.* Illustrated by Paul Galdone. New York: McGraw-Hill, 1954.
175. ———*Miss Pickerell Goes Undersea.* Illustrated by Paul Galdone. New York: McGraw-Hill, 1953.
176. Martel, Suzanne. *The City Under Ground.* Illustrated by Don Sibley. New York: Viking, 1964.
177. Mayne, William. *Earthfasts.* New York: Dutton, 1967.
178. ———*A Grass Rope.* Illustrated by Lynton Lamb. New York: Dutton, 1957.
179. Merrill, Jean. *The Pushcart War.* Illustrated by Ronni Solbert. New York: W. R. Scott, 1964.
180. Milne, A. A. *The House at Pooh Corner.* Illustrated by Ernest H. Shepard. New York: Dutton, 1928.
181. ———*Winnie the Pooh.* Illustrated by Ernest H. Shepard. New York: Dutton, 1926.
182. North, Joan. *The Cloud Forest.* New York: Farrar, Straus, 1966.
183. Norton, Andre. *Key Out of Time.* Cleveland: World Publishing, 1963.
184. ———*Night of Masks.* New York: Harcourt, 1964.
185. ———*Steel Magic.* Illustrated by Robin Jacques. Cleveland: World Publishing, 1965.

186. Norton, Mary. *The Borrowers*. Illustrated by Beth and Joe Krush. New York: Harcourt, 1953.

187. ———*The Borrowers Afield*. Illustrated by Beth and Joe Krush. New York: Harcourt, 1955.

188. ———*The Borrowers Afloat*. Illustrated by Beth and Joe Krush. New York: Harcourt, 1959.

189. ———*The Borrowers Aloft*. Illustrated by Beth and Joe Krush. New York: Harcourt, 1961.

190. Ormondroyd, Edward. *Time at the Top*. Illustrated by Peggy Bach. New York: Parnassus, 1963.

191. Palmer, Mary. *The Teaspoon Tree*. Illustrated by Carlota Dodge. Boston: Houghton Mifflin, 1963.

192. Parish, Peggy. *Amelia Bedelia*. Illustrated by Fritz Siebel. New York: Harper & Row, 1963.

193. ———*Thank You, Amelia Bedelia*. Illustrated by Fritz Siebel. New York: Harper & Row, 1964.

194. Pearce, Philippa, *A Dog So Small*. Illustrated by Antony Maitland. Philadelphia: Lippincott, 1962.

195. ———*Tom's Midnight Garden*. Illustrated by Susan Einzig. Philadelphia: Lippincott, 1959.

196. Rawlings, Marjorie Kinnan. *The Secret River*. Illustrated by Leonard Weisgard. New York: Scribner, 1955.

197. Robertson, Keith. *Henry Reed, Inc.* Illustrated by Robert McCloskey. New York: Viking, 1963, 1958.

198. ———*Henry Reed's Baby-Sitting Service*. Illustrated by Robert McCloskey. New York: Viking, 1966.

199. ———*Henry Reed's Journey*. Illustrated by Robert McCloskey. New York: Viking, 1963.

200. Saint-Exupéry, Antoine de. *The Little Prince*. Translated by Katherine Woods. New York: Harcourt, 1943.

201. Sauer, Julia. *Fog Magic*. Illustrated by Lynd Ward. New York: Viking, 1943.

202. Selden, George. *The Cricket in Times Square*. Illustrated by Garth Williams. New York: Farrar, Straus, 1960.

203. Seuss, Dr., pseud. (Theodor S. Geisel). *Bartholomew and the Oobleck*. New York: Random House, 1950.

204. ———*The 500 Hats of Bartholomew Cubbins*. New York: Vanguard, 1938.

205. Sharp, Margery. *Miss Bianca*. Illustrated by Garth Williams. Boston: Little, Brown, 1962.

206. ———*Miss Bianca in the Salt Mines*. Illustrated by Garth Williams. Boston: Little, Brown, 1967.

207. ———*The Rescuers*. Illustrated by Garth Williams. Boston: Little, Brown, 1959.

208. ———*The Turret*. Illustrated by Garth Williams. Boston: Little, Brown, 1963.

209. Silverberg, Robert. *The Gate of Worlds*. New York: Holt, Rinehart and Winston, 1967.

210. Slobodkin, Louis. *The Amiable Giant.* New York: Macmillan, 1955.

211. ———*The Space Ship Returns to the Apple Tree*. New York: Macmillan, 1958.

212. ———*The Space Ship Under the Apple Tree*. New York: Macmillan, 1952.

213. Smith, Agnes. *An Edge of the Forest*. Illustrated by Roberta Moynihan. New York: Viking, 1959.

214. Steele, William O. *Andy Jackson's Water Well*. Illustrated by Michael Ramus. New York: Harcourt, 1959.

215. ———*Daniel Boone's Echo*. New York: Harcourt, 1957.

216. ———*Davy Crockett's Earthquake*. New York: Harcourt, 1956.

217. ———*The No-Name Man of the Mountain*. Illustrated by Jack Davis. New York: Harcourt, 1964.

218. ———*The Spooky Thing*. Illustrated by Paul Coker. New York: Harcourt, 1960.

219. Stolz, Mary. *Belling the Tiger*. Illustrated by Beni Montresor. New York: Harper & Row, 1961.

220. ———*The Great Rebellion*. Illustrated by Beni Montresor. New York: Harper & Row, 1961.

221. ———*Maximilian's World*. Illustrated by Uri Shulevitz. New York: Harper & Row, 1966.

222. ———*Siri, the Conquistador*. New York: Harper & Row, 1963.

223. Swift, Jonathan. *Gulliver's Travels*. Illustrated by Hans Baltzer. Edited by Elaine Moss. New York: Duell, Sloan, 1961, 1726.

224. Thurber, James. *The Great Quillow*. Illustrated by Doris Lee. New York: Harcourt, 1944.

225. ———*Many Moons*. Illustrated by Louis Slobodkin. New York: Harcourt, 1943.

226. ———*The 13 Clocks*. Illustrated by Marc Simont. New York: Simon & Schuster, 1950.

227. ———*The Wonderful O*. Illustrated by Marc Simont. New York: Simon & Schuster, 1957.

228. Tolkien, J. R. R. *The Hobbit*. Boston: Houghton, Mifflin, 1938.

229. ———*The Fellowship of the Ring*. Boston: Houghton, Mifflin, 1954.

230. ———*The Return of the King*. Boston: Houghton, Mifflin, 1956.

231. ———*The Two Towers*. Boston: Houghton, Mifflin, 1955.

232. Travers, Pamela L. *Mary Poppins*. Illustrated by Mary Shepard. New York: Harcourt, 1934.

233. ———*Mary Poppins Comes Back*. Illustrated by Mary Shepard. New York: Harcourt, 1935.

234. ———*Mary Poppins in the Park*. Illustrated by Mary Shepard. New York: Harcourt, 1952.

235. ———*Mary Poppins Opens the Door*. Illustrated by Mary Shepard and Agnes Sims. New York: Harcourt, 1943.

236. Uttley, Alison. *A Traveler in Time*. Illustrated by Christine Price. New York: Viking, 1964, 1939.

237. Wersba, Barbara. *The Land of Forgotten Beasts*. Illustrated by Margot Tomas. New York: Atheneum, 1964.

238. White, E. B. *Charlotte's Web*. Illustrated by Garth Williams. New York: Harper & Row, 1952.

239. ———*Stuart Little*. Illustrated by Garth Williams. New York: Harper & Row, 1945.

240. Wilde, Oscar. *The Happy Prince*. Illustrated by Gilbert Riswold. Engelwood Cliffs, N.J.: Prentice-Hall, 1965.

241. ———"The Selfish Giant" in *Complete Fairy Tales*. New York: F. Watts, 1961.

242. Winterfeld, Henry. *Castaways in Lilliput*. Translated by Kyrill Schabert. Illustrated by William M. Hutchinson. New York: Harcourt, 1960.

243. Wrightson, Patricia. *Down to Earth*. Illustrated by Margaret Horder. New York: Harcourt, 1965.

POETRY

Sharing time was nearly over in Mrs. Hill's first grade when Jeannie shyly raised her hand and said, "I have a pair of new shoes."

"Of course you do, Jeannie," responded Mrs. Hill, "and they are very special shoes, too. Will you come up here and show them to us?"

Her new sandals brought admiring comments from the rest of the children. Mrs. Hill encouraged Jeannie to tell the group about buying them by asking: "Did you look at other shoes? Did you have a hard time choosing these? How did you decide?" Then the teacher and the children talked about how new shoes made them feel. Mrs. Hill told them that new shoes had made one person feel this way:

> NEW SHOES
> *I have new shoes in the Fall-time*
> *And new ones in the Spring.*
> *Whenever I wear my new shoes*
> *I always have to sing!*
> ALICE WILKINS (7)[1]

This poem reminded the children of another favorite, "Choosing Shoes" (182) by Ffrida Wolfe. Mrs. Hill asked the children to stand around the edge of

---

[1]The numbers following the poems in this chapter refer to the number of the book listed in Chapter References where the poem may be found. Many of the poems are in several anthologies, however.

the rug and say this poem together. As each of the four verses was chanted, the children on each side of the rug went back to their seats. All the children joined in the last verse as the group on the far side of the rug went back to their places, stamping to the rhythm of the last verse, "Flat shoes, fat shoes, Stump-along-like-that-shoes." . . .

Poetry was a natural part of these children's lives. Mrs. Hill enjoyed it herself and was alert to the various opportunities in the school day in which poetry could extend and enrich children's experiences. She had memorized many poems so they could be readily recalled for that "teachable moment." In addition to those poems she knew, she had her own personal collection filed on four-by-six cards in categories that complemented her knowledge of six-year-olds' interests. Hardly a day passed in her classroom when there were not a few moments to share a poem. Sometimes, the children joined her in saying the poem as they did in "Choosing Shoes." More frequently, they just listened and enjoyed the poem for its own sake.

POETRY FOR TODAY'S CHILDREN

What Is Poetry?

There is an elusiveness about poetry that defies definition. It is not so much what it is that is important as how it makes us feel. Eleanor Farjeon tells us that "Poetry" (65) is "not a rose, but the scent of the rose. . . . Not the sea, but the sound of the sea." Fine poetry is this distillation of experience that captures the essence of an object, feeling, or thought. Such intensification requires a more highly structured patterning of words than prose. Each word must be chosen with care, both for its sound and meaning; for poetry is language in its most connotative and concentrated form.

Poetry may both broaden and intensify experience. It may present a range of experiences beyond the realm of possibility for the individual listener. It may also illuminate, clarify, and deepen an every-day occurrence in a way the reader never considered before. For poetry does more than mirror life, it reveals life in new dimensions. Robert Frost stated that a poem goes from delight to wisdom. Poetry does delight chil-

dren, but it also should help them develop new insights, new ways of sensing their world.

Poetry communicates experience by appealing to both the thoughts and feelings of its reader. It has the power to evoke in its hearers rich sensory images and deep emotional responses. Poetry demands total response from the individual—his intellect, senses, emotion, and imagination. It does not tell *about* an experience as much as it invites its hearers to *participate in* the experience. Emily Dickinson defined poetry in terms of this total involvement:

> *If I read a book and it makes my whole body so cold that no fire can ever warm me, I know that is poetry. If I feel physically as if the top of my head were taken off, I know that is poetry. These are the only ways I know it. Is there any other way?*[2]

Much of what poetry says is conveyed by suggestion, by indirection, by what is not said. Carl Sandburg made the statement that "What can be explained is not poetry." And

---

[2]Quoted in "Emily Dickinson Herself" by Helen Plotz, in *Poems of Emily Dickinson*, selected by Helen Plotz (New York: Crowell, 1964), p. ix.

quoting Ken Nakazawa, he noted, "The poems that are obvious are like the puzzles that are already solved. They deny us the joy of seeking and creating."[3] A certain amount of ambiguity is characteristic of poetry, for more is hidden in it than in prose. The poet does not tell the reader "all" but invites him to go beyond the literal level of the poem and discover its deeper meanings for himself.

Robert Frost playfully suggested that poetry is what gets lost in translation—and translation of poetry into prose is as difficult as translation of poetry into a foreign language. To paraphrase a poem is to destroy it. Would it be possible to reduce Frost's "Mending Wall" to prose? The scene, the situation, the contrast of the two men's thoughts about the wall they are repairing may be described, but the experience of the poem cannot be conveyed except by its own words.

Poetry and Verse Teachers frequently ask how to differentiate between real poetry and verse or mere rhyme. Imagination and depth of emotion are both qualities that help distinguish poetry from verse. Elizabeth Coatsworth, who has written superb poetry and verse for children, refers to rhyme as "poetry in petticoats" in the preface to her recent book, *The Sparrow Bush:*

> . . . *Rhymes are made up of such things as jingles repeated to amuse children, lullabies, old saws, counting-out games, limericks, anything informal and easy-going with a rocking-horse rhythm and a simple versification. One doesn't look for beauty in rhymes, though sometimes one may find a little. One may even find a sudden shaft of strangeness. But mostly what one will find are playfulness and good humor.*
>
> *Rhyme is poetry in petticoats.*[4]

Mother Goose, jump-rope rhymes, tongue twisters, and much of modern verse for children is not poetry. Its rhythm and rhyme provide delight, however, and a background of readiness for the acceptance and presentation of true poetry.

Poetry for Children Poetry for children differs little from poetry for adults, except that its content appeals directly to children. Its language should be poetic and its subject meaningful to children. Eve Merriam has identified what makes a poem in terms that children will understand in the following lines:

> . . .
>
> *What makes a poem?*
> *Whatever you feel:*
> *The secrets of rain*
> *On a window pane,*
> *The smell of a rose*
> *Or of cowboy clothes,*
> *The sound of a flute*
> *Or a foghorn hoot,*
> *The taste of cake*
> *Or a fresh water lake,*
> *The touch of grass*
> *Or an icy glass,*
> *The shout of noon*
> *Or the silent moon,*
> *A standstill leaf*
> *Or a rolling wheel,*
> *Laughter and grief:*
> *Whatever you feel.*
>
> EVE MERRIAM (130)

Children are keenly aware of these sensory experiences and poetry may intensify them. Young persons experience emotions that are similar to those of adults; only the stimuli may differ. The scope of poetry for children encompasses all the feelings and experiences of childhood.

The limitations on poetry for children are surprisingly few. Poems of passion, bitterness, hate, and nostalgia have little place. Literary allusions are necessarily limited, and

---

[3]Carl Sandburg, "Short Talk on Poetry," in *Early Moon* (New York: Harcourt, 1930), p. 27.
[4]Elizabeth Coatsworth, *The Sparrow Bush*, Illustrated by Stefan Martin (New York: Norton, 1966), p. 8.

metaphors must be related to meaningful reference points within children's experiences. Figures of speech are frequently confusing to children unless they are based on well-known objects. Young children readily respond to the figures of speech in the following poem, however:

DECEMBER LEAVES

The fallen leaves are cornflakes
That fill the lawn's wide dish,
And night and noon
The wind's a spoon
That stirs them with a swish.

The sky's a silver sifter
A-sifting white and slow,
That gently shakes
On crisp brown flakes
The sugar known as snow.

KAYE STARBIRD (171)

The freshness of the comparison between brown leaves and breakfast food will have immediate appeal for today's young child. The poet has helped children see two common, disparate objects in a new relationship. She has reinforced her visual image with the use of appropriate sound. The words "dish" and "swish" are onomatopoetic, suggesting the sound of the leaves being blown by the wind, while the repetition of the initial "s" in the words of the last stanza creates the sensation of the soft falling snow. Capitalizing upon children's interests, this poem helps the child to view the world of nature in a new way, through the language of poetry. Its metaphor is childlike, but not "childish." Another poet speaks to older children and adults as she compares thoughts to wrapped cocoons:

DAYS

Some days my thoughts are just cocoons — all cold,
and dull and blind,
They hang from dripping branches in the grey
woods of my mind;

And other days they drift and shine — such free
and flying things!
I find the gold-dust in my hair, left by their brushing wings.

KARLE WILSON BAKER (6)

Little symbolism is used in poetry for children, but the symbols used should be understandable. With adroit questioning, children can see that the bird in Herford's poem represents more than just the return of spring:

I heard a bird sing
  In the dark of December
A magical thing
  And sweet to remember.

"We are nearer to Spring
  Than we were in September,"
I heard a bird sing
  In the dark of December.

OLIVER HERFORD (6)

Older children are responsive to the symbolic content of Frost's "The Road Not Taken" (85), and they easily transfer the choice of roads to decision-making in general. A symbol does not state a particular relationship, but only suggests it in the mind of the reader. Most children have not established the reference points needed to interpret symbolism.

Poetry that is cute, coy, nostalgic, or sarcastic may be *about* children, but it is not *for* them. Whittier's "The Barefoot Boy" (166) looks backward upon childhood in a nostalgic fashion characteristic of adults, not children. "The Children's Hour" (66) by Longfellow is an old man's reminiscences of his delight in his children. Some poems patronize childhood as a period in life when children are "cute" or "naughty." Even the best of children's poets occasionally have been guilty of this. For example, "Vespers" (132) by A. A. Milne appeals more to adults who are amused and pleased by this sweet description of a child's desultory thoughts during prayer. Children, however, find little humor in this poem that makes them the object of laughter. John Ciardi has written many poems that make children laugh; he has also written many poems that laugh at children. Frequently, he appears to be talking to parents when he refers to children as "monsters," "the little dears" or the "Sillies." Exasperated parents or teachers may occasionally think of children in this way; but do children? Eugene Field's "Little Boy Blue" (66) describes an adult's reaction to the loss of a child—it, too, is inappropriate fare for children. Many poems are didactic and preachy. Some teachers will accept moralizing in poetry that they would never accept in prose. Sentimentality is another adult emotion, seldom felt by children. The poem "Which Loved Best," frequently quoted before Mothers Day, drips with sentiment and morality. Poems, then, that are *about* childhood or aim to instruct are usually disliked by children. Excellence in poetry for children should meet the same criteria of excellence as poetry for adults. In some instances, it is difficult to distinguish between the two.

There are two schools of thought concerning what is appropriate poetry for children. Some would disallow any poetry written by the so-called children's poets and present only poems of recognized poets who write for adults. They would search for the few poems of Tennyson, Shakespeare, and Dickinson, for example, that might be appropriate fare for children. Others have limited poetry in the classroom to such childhood poets as Stevenson, Farjeon, and Aldis. This argument seems to draw an unnecessary dichotomy. In evaluating a poem for children, it makes little difference who the author is, provided the poem speaks *to children* in the *language* of poetry. The most illustrious poet may not be able to relate to children. However, children's experiences with poetry should not be limited to works written only by children's poets but should include acquaintance with some of the poems by Frost, Hopkins, and Whitman, for example, that speak on subjects meaningful to childhood. Children deserve excellence in poetry regardless of its source, but it must speak to them at their point of time in living.

Satisfactions of Poetry

Poetry is as personal as one's religion. What is poetry for one person does not necessarily call forth the same responsive chord in another. In his preface to *Early Moon,* Carl Sandburg reinforced this point in his characteristically vivid style:

> *That is, what is poetry for any given individual depends on what the individual requires as poetry. Beauty depends on personal taste. What is beauty for one person is not for another. What is poetry for one person may be balderdash or hogwash for another.*[5]

Children, too, respond differently to poetry, and they derive various satisfactions from it.

Rhythm   The young child is naturally rhythmical. He beats on the tray of his highchair, kicks his foot against the table, and chants his vocabulary of one or two words in a singsong fashion. He delights in the rhythm of "Pat-a-cake, pat-a-cake, baker's man," or "Ride a cock-horse to Banbury Cross" before he understands the meaning of the words. This response to a measured beat is as old as man himself. Primitive man had his chants, his hunting and working songs, his dances, and his crude musical instruments. Rhythm is a part of the daily beat of our lives; the steady pulse rate, regular breathing, and pattern of growth. The inevitability of night and day, the revolving sea-

---

[5]Carl Sandburg, "Short Talk on Poetry," in *Early Moon,* Illustrated by James Daugherty (New York: Harcourt, 1930), p. 30.

sons, and birth and death provide a pattern for every man's life. The very ebb and flow of the ocean, the sound of the rain on the window, and the pattern of the rows of corn in a field reflect the rhythm of the world around us.

Poetry satisfies the child's natural response to rhythm. Eve Merriam has described the importance of rhythm in the first verse of the title poem of her book, *It Doesn't Always Have to Rhyme:*

INSIDE A POEM

It doesn't always have to rhyme,
but there's the repeat of a beat, somewhere
an inner chime that makes you want to
tap your feet or swerve in a curve;
a lilt, a leap, a lightning-split:—

                              EVE MERRIAM (130)

It is this built-in rhythm or meter that helps to differentiate poetry from prose. A poem has a kind of music of its own, and the child responds to its melody.

The very young child enjoys the monotonous rocking-horse rhythm of Mother Goose and looks for it in other poems. Mary Ann Hoberman has matched the rhythm of swinging with the rhythm of the daily and seasonal changes in a child's life:

Hello and good-by
Hello and good-by

When I'm in a swing
Swinging low and then high
Good-by to the ground
Hello to the sky.

Hello to the rain
Good-by to the sun,
Then hello again sun
When the rain is all done.

In blows the winter,
Away the birds fly.
Good-by and hello
Hello and good-by

     MARY ANN HOBERMAN (92)

The lilt and the rhythm of Stevenson's "The Swing" (175) suggest the physical sensation of swinging with a different meter than "Hello and Good-by." The galloping rhythm of Stevenson's "Windy Nights" compares the sound of the wild wind to a mysterious horseman riding by. The refrain of the last four lines may be read loudly and then softly to give the effect of the wailing wind:

. . . .

By, on the highway, low and loud,
By at the gallop goes he:
By at the gallop he goes, and then
By he comes back at the gallop again.

        ROBERT LOUIS STEVENSON (174)

Stevenson has captured the fast pace of a train with the clipped rhythm of his poem "From a Railway Carriage" (174). The sliding, gliding movement of "Skating" is well portrayed by the rhythm of Herbert Asquith's poem. (6). The rhythm of a poem, then, should be appropriate to its subject matter, reinforcing and creating its meaning.

In some poems, both the rhythm and the pattern of the lines are suggestive of the movement or mood of the poem. The arrangement of these poems forces the reader to emphasize a particular rhythm. The words of Farjeon's "Mrs. Peck-Pigeon" have the same bobbing rhythm as the pigeon herself:

MRS. PECK-PIGEON

Mrs. Peck-Pigeon
Is picking for bread,
Bob — bob — bob
Goes her little round head.
Tame as a pussy-cat
In the street,
Step — step — step
Go her little red feet.
With her little red feet
And her little round head,
Mrs. Peck-Pigeon
Goes picking for bread.

        ELEANOR FARJEON (65)

In Dorothy Baruch's "Merry-Go-Round" (6), the pattern of the line and the rhythm suggest the increasing and decreasing speed of a merry-go-round. The somewhat pensive mood of A. A. Milne's "Halfway Down" (132) is heightened by the arrangement of the words and lines. The reader has to interpret the slow descent of a little boy going down the stairs until he stops—half-way down.

A change of rhythm is indicative of a new element in the poem: a contrast in mood, a warning, or a different speaker, for example. Mary Austin has contrasted the ominous movement of "The Sandhill Crane" (6) as he goes "slowly solemnly stalking" with the fast scuttling movements of the frogs and minnows who fear for their lives. A similar warning is seen in the change of rhythm of the following poem:

> The sea gull curves his wings,
> The sea gull turns his eyes.
> Get down into the water, fish!
> (If you are wise.)
>
> The sea gull slants his wings,
> The sea gull turns his head.
> Get down into the water, fish!
> (Or you'll be dead.)
>
>   ELIZABETH COATSWORTH (6)

The first two lines of each verse soar with the flight of the gull, but the last two lines change the pace of the poem and issue a fearful warning.

While children naturally enjoy the rhythm of poetry, they need guidance in seeing how the poet uses rhythm and variations of rhythmical patterns to reinforce and intensify the movement, the mood, and meaning of the poem.

Rhyme and Sound In addition to the rhythm of a poem, children respond to its rhyme. For rhyme helps to create the musical qualities of a poem, and children enjoy the "singingness of words." Although Mer-

riam maintains "It doesn't always have to rhyme," most poetry for children has a strong rhythm and regular rhyme. In order to avoid developing the notion that all poetry must rhyme, it is well to introduce children to some free verse or haiku.

Rhyme is one aspect of sound; alliteration or the repetition of initial consonant sounds is another, while assonance or the repetition of particular vowel sounds is still another. The repetition of the hard "g" sounds in "Godfrey Gordon Gustavus Gore" (6) adds to the humor of this poem about the boy who would never shut the door. Younger children delight in the "splishes and sploshes and slooshes and sloshes" which Susie's galoshes make in Rhoda W. Bacmeister's poem "Galoshes" (182). The quiet "s" sound and the repetition of the double "o" in "moon" and "shoon" suggest the mysterious beauty of the moon in "Silver" (6). Onomatopoeia is a term that refers to the use of words that make a sound like the action represented by the word, such as "crack," "hiss," and "sputter." Occasionally, a poet will create an entire poem that resembles a particular sound. David McCord has successfully imitated the sound of hitting a picket fence with a stick in this chant:

> The pickety fence
> The pickety fence
> Give it a lick it's
> The pickety fence
> Give it a lick it's
> A clickety fence
> Give it a lick it's
> A lickety fence
> Give it a lick
> Give it a lick
> Give it a lick
> With a rickety stick
> Pickety
> Pickety
> Pickety
> Pick
>
> DAVID McCORD (123)

Another way that the poet may add to the music of his poem is through the use of repetition. He may repeat a particular word or phrase for emphasis, for sound effects, or to create a recurring theme as in a symphony. The repetition of the last line "miles to go before I sleep" in Frost's famous "Stopping by Woods on a Snowy Evening" (85) adds to the mysterious element in that poem. In "Night Song" (128) by Merriam, the repetition of the last stanza and the word "hushaby" makes a particularly effective lullaby poem for young children. The repetition of the words "how far" in a poem by that title emphasizes the evanescence of time, particularly when you are young:

> How far
> How far
> How far is today
> When tomorrow has come
> And it's yesterday?
>
> Far
> And far
> And far away.
> MARY ANN HOBERMAN (92)

Children are intrigued with the sounds of language and enjoy unusual and ridiculous combinations of words. The gay nonsense of Laura Richards' "Eletelephony" (6) is as much in the sound of the ridiculous words as in the plight of the poor elephant who tried to use the "telephant." Children love to trip off the name of "James James Morrison Morrison Weatherby George Dupree," who complained about his mother's "Disobedience" (132). Harry Behn's "Tea Party" is a delightful mumble of scolding:

> Mister Beedle Baddlebug,
> Don't bandle up in your boodlebag
> Or numble in your jumblejug,
> Now eat your nummy tiffletag
> Or I will never invite you
> To tea again with me. Shoo!
> HARRY BEHN (16)

Poets use rhyme, rhythm, and the various devices of alliteration, assonance, repetition, and coined words to create the melody and sound of poetry loved by children.

Imagery Poetry draws on many kinds of language magic. To speak of the imagery of a poem refers to direct images of sight, sound, touch, smell, or taste. This sensory aspect of poetry appeals to children, for it reflects the way they explore their world.

Poetry is a way of seeing as well as hearing. Since most children are visual-minded, they respond readily to the picture-making quality of poetry. Adults frequently are blind to the beauty of the commonplace. Children, however, are capable of seeing "the dearest freshness deep down things" described in Gerard Manley Hopkins' poem "God's Grandeur" (70). Children's senses have not been dulled, and they see with the eyes of the poet. Even very young children appreciate the vivid picture of snow created in the following poem:

> SNOW
> The fenceposts wear marshmallow hats
> On a snowy day;
> Bushes in their nightgowns
> Are kneeling down to pray—
> And all the trees have silver skirts
> And want to dance away.
> DOROTHY ALDIS (3)

Winifred Welles has painted an exquisite word picture of the pale green Luna moth in her poem "The Green Moth." Older children can easily visualize the mysterious beauty of this night-time creature in the first stanza of her poem:

> The night the green moth came for me,
>   A creamy moon poured down the hill,
> The meadow seemed a silver sea,
> Small pearls were hung in every tree,
>   And all so still, so still—.
> WINIFRED WELLES (6)

Some poets are so skilled in presenting a particularly vivid picture that they can direct "eye movements" and change the reader's focus on a certain scene. Harry Behn has done this in the following poem:

FAR AND NEAR
Farther away than a house is a lawn
  A field and a fence and a rocky hill
  With a tree on top, and farther still
  The sky with a cloud in it gold at dawn.

Closer than dawn in the sky is a tree
  On a hill, and a fence and a field and a green
  Lawn and a house and a window screen
  With a nose pressed against it—and then me.
                                  HARRY BEHN (17)

Did you stand at the house and see a panoramic view of the lawn, the field, the hill, and the tree silhouetted against the sunrise; and then did you see the picture in reverse, as gradually you shifted your focus from the sky to the tree, to the field, to the lawn, the house, and yourself? The poet created these shifting images without the use of any figurative language, relying solely upon his picture-making ability.

Appreciation for descriptive poetry is developed gradually in children and is directly related to their experiences. The child who has been awed by the elegant beauty of a Luna moth will respond quite differently to the Winifred Welles poem than the child who has never had an opportunity to see one. Poetry helps us recapture or intensify the memory of a beautiful experience. The child poet, Hilda Conkling, expresses this thought:

LOVELINESS
Loveliness that dies when I forget
Comes alive when I remember.
                        HILDA CONKLING (6)

Most poetry depends on visual and auditory imagery to evoke a mood or response, but imagery of touch, taste, and smell is also used. Children readily agree with Polly Chase Boyden's enjoyment of "Mud":

Mud is very nice to feel
All squishy-squash between the toes!
I'd rather wade in wiggly mud
Than smell a yellow rose.

Nobody else but the rosebush knows
How nice mud feels
Between the toes.
                        POLLY CHASE BOYDEN (6)

Aileen Fisher has created a vivid sensory impression by contrasting the various textures of the skins of fruits in this poem:

SKINS
Skins of lemons are waterproof slickers.
Pineapple skins are stuck full of stickers.
Skins of apples are skinny and shiny
and strawberry skins (if any) are tiny.

Grapes have skins that are juicy and squishy.
Gooseberry skins are vinegar-ishy.
Skins of peaches are fuzzy and hairy.
Oranges' skins are more peely than pare-y.

Skins of plums are squirty and squeezy.
Bananas have skins you can pull-off-easy.

. . . .

I like skins that are thin as sheeting,
so what-is-under is bigger for eating.
                        AILEEN FISHER (79)

This same poet displays an unfaltering ear for the sound of footsteps in the dry snow characteristic of an extremely cold day:

ZERO WEATHER
When we walked home
on Friday for lunch
the crisp white snow
had a soda-cracker crunch
                        AILEEN FISHER (79)

Older children will enjoy "The Noise of Waters" (66) by James Joyce. Christopher

Morley's poem "Smells (Junior)" (6) amuses and pleases children. Zhenya Gay's poem that begins "The world is full of wonderful smells" (88) tells of the luscious smell of hot bread and cake, of a haymow, and a warm dog lying in the sun. Much of children's poetry evokes this rich sensory response from its hearers and serves to sharpen children's perceptions.

Heightened Emotional Response Poetry not only helps a child recapture the beauty of a scene, it may also increase his sensitivity to an idea or mood. Children, just as adults, have their moments of sadness, gaiety, and loneliness. The causes for these moods will be very different from those of adults, but the feelings are the same. Many poems express pure feeling; joy, sorrow, longing, excitement, pain. The essence of joy in living is seen in the following haiku:

> Just simply alive,
> Both of us, I
> And the poppy.
> ——ISSA (108)

Harry Behn's poem, "This Happy Day" (15), portrays a child's zest and joy in living as he simply says "good morning to the sun." This same exhilaration is found in Rose Fyleman's "Singing Time" (6) and Blake's "Laughing Song" (19). Fatigue and boredom are reflected in the description of "Tired Tim":

> Poor Tired Tim! It's sad for him.
> He lags the long bright morning through.
> Ever so tired of nothing to do;
> He moons and mopes the livelong day,
> Nothing to think about, nothing to say;
> Up to bed with his candle to creep,
> Too tired to yawn, too tired to sleep;
> Poor Tired Tim! It's sad for him.
> WALTER DE LA MARE (60)

Dorothy Aldis is always a true interpreter of children's moods. Her "Lazy Day" (4) tells of a young child's restless half-hearted attempts to amuse herself. "Bad" (3) reflects remorse and a certain amount of self-pity by a boy who had been so bad, he was now in bed. In "Quarreling" (65), Eleanor Farjeon describes a brother-sister squabble, and in "Brother" (92) by Mary Ann Hoberman, a small child complains of a "little bother of a brother" and wants to trade him in on another! Myra Cohn Livingston details the despair of an older sister who is tired of her "Little Brother" (115) and queries "Do you think when he is grown/I might go somewhere alone?"

Deeper emotions are evoked by more serious poems. In "Asleep" (44), Coatsworth described the reactions of a child who was unable to sleep so sought comfort in her mother's room. Peeking in the door, she sees her mother asleep, a stranger to her:

> . . .
> It seemed to me some enemy
> Was lying in my mother's place
> With eyes closed tight to shut
> me out,
> and a forgetting face.
> ELIZABETH COATSWORTH (44)

Two poignant poems by Gwendolyn Brooks reveal the pride of the poor and the quiet ache of a frightened child:

> OTTO
> It's Christmas Day. I did not get
> The presents that I hoped for. Yet
> It is not nice to frown or fret.
>
> To frown or fret would not be fair
> My Dad must never know I care
> It's hard enough for him to bear.
> GWENDOLYN BROOKS (29)

> CHARLES
> Sick-times, you go inside yourself,
> And scarce can come away
> You sit and look outside yourself
> At people passing by.
> GWENDOLYN BROOKS (29)

With the dignified simplicity of understatement, Langston Hughes has described the sorrow of a broken relationship in this poem:

> I loved my friend.
> He went away from me.
> There's nothing more to say.
> The poem ends,
> Soft as it began—
> I loved my friend.
>> LANGSTON HUGHES (127)

Poetry has the power to create feelings of wonder and awe in both children and adults. The young child is filled with questions and demands that his parents "Tell me, tell me everything!" (16) As children grow older, they continue their search for they know not what. Coatsworth has described man's natural attraction for water as a place for contemplation. After listing all the possibilities one can see by a pond, she flatly states that she is not looking for ducks, but goes on to reaffirm her faith that "Some Day" she shall find the object of her search:

> Whenever I go down to the shore
> There's something I am looking for.
> I don't think it can be the pond;
> It's not the low green hills beyond;
> . . .
> Sometimes I think the ducks might be
> The thing I'm waiting there to see,
> But it's not ducks.
>
> Yet more and more,
> I'm sure that some day by the shore
> I'll see what I am waiting for.
>> ELIZABETH COATSWORTH (44)

Children will respond to poems of quiet wonder such as Farjeon's lovely description of the ephemeral quality of night:

> THE NIGHT WILL NEVER STAY
> The night will never stay.
> The night will still go by,
> Though with a million stars
> You pin it to the sky;
> Though you bind it with the blowing wind
> And buckle it with the moon,
> The night will slip away
> Like sorrow or a tune.
>> ELEANOR FARJEON (65)

The best poems are those that suggest more than they tell; that cause a child to go beyond himself in the search for wondrous things to be felt and warm hopes to come true. Hope needs to be held high in a world sick with despair. Langston Hughes has expressed this desire in his poem:

> DREAMS
> Hold fast to dreams
> For if dreams die
> Life is a broken-winged bird
> That cannot fly.
> Hold fast to dreams
> For when dreams go
> Life is a barren field
> Frozen with snow.
>> LANGSTON HUGHES (99)

Enjoyment of the Story Element in Poetry Many favorite poems of children tell a story. The story may be a humorous one as A. A. Milne's amusing tales of "The King's Breakfast" and "Bold Sir Brian" (132), or the mysterious romantic story of "The Highwayman" (187) by Alfred Noyes. American boys particularly enjoy the well-known "Casey at the Bat" (179), Stephen Vincent Benet's "The Mountain Whipporwill" (53), and the grisly tale by W. S. Gilbert of "The Yarn of the 'Nancy Bell'" (53). Many narrative poems for children are not great poetry. Children do enjoy them, however, and frequently they have been the catalyst necessary to bring children and poetry together. Many teachers introduce poetry to children by sharing a popular narrative poem with them.

SELECTING POETRY FOR CHILDREN

In selecting poetry for children, the teacher will want to consider their interests and needs, their previous experience with poetry, and the types of poetry that appeal to them. A sound principle to follow when selecting poetry for children is to begin where they are. If children of primary age have not heard much poetry, the teacher might begin with some of the chants of childhood. Carl Withers has collected children's jump-rope jingles, riddles, and tongue twisters in *A Rocket in My Pocket*. These chants and some modern verse will help convince children that poetry is fun. Older children who have not been introduced to poetry may be reached through humorous or narrative poems. The poetry presented should be appropriate in theme and mood to the maturity of the group. Appreciation for many a lovely poem has been destroyed by its too early introduction to a group not ready for it.

The poetry selected also should have relevance for today's child. "The Village Blacksmith" (66) was a favorite of our grandfathers, but it has little meaning for the child whose heroes work in space rather than under the spreading chestnut tree. It is best to avoid poems with forbidding or archaic vocabulary, those that "talk down" to children, nostalgic poems about childhood, and those that try to teach a lesson. Poetry should be appropriate to the background of the child, the age level of the child, and the age in which he lives.

A teacher's prime purpose should be to increase enjoyment of poetry. However, taste needs to be developed, too, and children should go beyond their delight in humorous and narrative poetry to develop an appreciation for other various types of poetry. As children have increased experiences with poetry, they will grow in their enjoyment and understanding of finer poems.

Forms of Poetry for Children

Children are more interested in the "idea" of a poem than in knowing about the various forms of poetry. However, one of the literary understandings to develop in the elementary school is knowledge of types of poetry. These understandings grow gradually as children are exposed to different forms. The teacher will provide balance in the selection of forms of poetry according to children's readiness for them. Do children enjoy lyrical poems more than free verse? Does this class like limericks? Are these children ready for the simple, yet highly complex, form of haiku? These and similar questions may be answered by noting children's reactions to the various forms of poetry.

Ballads   Ballads are narrative poems that have been adapted for singing or give the effect of a song. Originally, they were not made or sung for children, but were the literature of all the people. Characteristic of the ballad form is frequent use of dialogue in telling the story, repetition, marked rhythm and rhyme, and refrains that go back to the days when the ballads were sung. The popular ballads have no known authors, as they were handed down from one generation to the next; the literary ballad, however, does have a known author. Ballads usually deal with heroic deeds and include stories of murder, unrequited love, feuds, and tragedies. For this reason, many are not appropriate fare for children in the elementary grades. Those that are shared need to be selected carefully.

Children in the middle grades thoroughly enjoy the amusing story of the stubborn man and his equally stubborn wife in "Get up and Bar the Door" (20). As in many ballads, the ending is abrupt, and the reader never does find out what happened to the two sinister guests, other than that the good husband finally locked them all in the house together! "The Outlandish Knight" (187) and "Robin Hood and the Widow's Sons" (187) will appeal to youngsters' sense of poetic justice, while "Sir Patrick Spens" (20) and the "Raggle Taggle Gypsies" (187) may make them question injustices. Shrewdness is honored in "King John and the Abbot of Canterbury" (187), and true love reigns in "The Bailiff's Daughter of Islington" (187) and "Robin Hood and Allan-a-Dale" (187).

Literary ballads that are appropriate for use with children include "A Legend of the Northland" (187) by Phoebe Cary and "Beth Gêlert" (187) by William Spencer. The first ballad tells of the origin of a red-headed woodpecker from a selfish old woman, while the latter ballad is the appealing story of a faithful dog. Older children will enjoy the poignant tale of "The Ballad of the Harp-Weaver" (6) by Edna St. Vincent Millay.

The revival of interest in folk songs with guitar accompaniments will help children see that ballad-making is still in process. Carl Sandburg collected and classified many ballads of our cowboys, lumberjacks, and railroad workers in his book, *The American Songbag*. Most of our native ballads are not as well polished as the Scotch and English ones, however, and depend upon their musical arrangements for their full beauty. "The Ballad of the Green Beret" is ample evidence of the fact that men are still creating ballads (see Chapter 4).

Narrative Verse The narrative poem relates a particular event or episode, or tells a long tale. It may be a lyric, a sonnet, or written in free verse, but its one requirement is that it *must* tell a story. Many of children's favorite poems are these so-called story poems. Two classics that are loved by all are Browning's "The Pied Piper of Hamelin" (32) and "A Visit from St. Nicholas" (66) by Clement Moore, known to children as "'Twas the Night before Christmas." Moore created the American Santa Claus in this poem that was published in 1823. Other well-known favorites include Laura E. Richards' ironic tale of "The Monkeys and the Crocodile" (6), Eugene Field's "The Duel" (6), and that swashbuckling "Pirate Don Durk of Dowdee" (6).

One of the favorite narrative poems of young children is the simple story of the parents who lovingly pretend to look for their son in the poem "Hiding" (3) by Dorothy Aldis. The triumphant ending of "The Little Turtle" (6) who caught a mosquito, a flea, and a minnow, "But he didn't catch me," always delights younger children. They appreciate the ingenuity of the elf who made the first umbrella in "The Elf and the Dormouse" (6), and they love A. A. Milne's poems of a lost mouse in "Missing" (132) and the disappearing beetle in "Forgiven" (131).

Seven- and eight-year-olds delight in "The King's Breakfast" (132) and "King John's Christmas" (133), and they are old enough to enjoy Christopher Robin's humorous deception of adults in "Sneezles" (133). The long narrative verses of the many books by Dr. Seuss have their greatest appeal for this age group, as does the humorous story of "Custard the Dragon" (187) by Ogden Nash.

While many of children's favorite narrative poems are humorous, some are not. Older children respond to the pathos of "Nancy Hanks" (18) and the irony of "Abraham Lincoln" (18) by the Benéts. They are stirred by the galloping hoofbeats in *Paul Revere's Ride* (119) and the courageous sacrifice of the six hundred in Tennyson's "Charge of the Light Brigade" (178). Their favorite romantic tale is the dramatic "The Highwayman" (187) by Alfred Noyes.

One of the best ways to capture children's interest in poetry is to present a variety of narrative poems. Teachers will want to build a file of story-poems appropriate for the age level of the children in their classes and read them often.

Lyrical   Most of the poetry written for children is lyrical. The term is derived from the word "lyric" and means poetry that sings its way into the minds and memories of its listeners. It is usually personal or descriptive poetry with no prescribed length or structure, other than its melody.

Much of William Blake's poetry is lyrical, beginning with the opening lines of his introductory poem to *Songs of Innocence:* "Piping down the valley wild/Piping songs of pleasant glee" (19). Stevenson's poems have a singing quality that makes them unforgettable. Everyone knows the poem "The Swing" (174), and "The Wind" (174), and the mysterious "Windy Nights" (175). In his poem "Where Go the Boats?" the tempo of the words reminds one of the increasing swiftness of the flow of the river toward the sea:

> Dark brown is the river,
>   Golden is the sand.
> It flows along forever,
>   With trees on either hand.
>
> Green leaves a-floating,
>   Castles of the foam,
> Boats of mine a-bloating—
>   Where will all come home?
>
> On goes the river
>   And out past the mill,
> Away down the valley,
>   Away down the hill.
>
> Away down the river,
>   A hundred miles or more,
> Other little children
>   Shall bring my boats ashore.
>   ROBERT LOUIS STEVENSON (174)

The music-making quality of Christina Rossetti's poems is unmistakable. All children should know her poem that begins: "Who has seen the wind?" (6). Her delight in a rainbow is captured in the poem "Boats sail on the rivers" (6). The singing, soaring flight

of a "Kite" (16) is described by Harry Behn, as is its sudden fall into a tree. Older children love the lyrical beat of Masefield's "Sea-Fever" (6) or Allan Cunningham's "A Wet Sheet and a Flowing Sea" (20). Boys, particularly, respond to the strong beat and internal rhyme scheme of the lone dog that will have no master but himself:

> THE LONE DOG
> I'm a lean dog, a keen dog, a wild dog, and lone;
> I'm a rough dog, a tough dog, hunting on my
>   own;
> I'm a bad dog, a mad dog, teasing silly sheep;
> I love to sit and bay the moon, to keep fat souls
>   from sleep.
>   IRENE RUTHERFORD McCLEOD (6)

Lyrical poetry is characterized by this singingness of words that gives children an exhilarating sense of melody.

Limerick   A nonsense form of verse that is particularly enjoyed by children is the limerick. This is a five-line verse with the first and second line rhyming, the third and fourth agreeing, and the fifth line usually ending in a surprise or humorous statement. Freak spelling, oddities, and humorous twists characterize this form of poetry. David McCord in his book, *Take Sky,* suggests that "a limerick, to be lively and successful, *must* have *perfect* riming and *flawless* rhythm."[6] He gives an excellent example of a limerick about limericks!

> A limerick shapes to the eye
> Like a small very squat butterfly,
>   With its wings opened wide,
>   Lots of nectar inside,
> And a terrible urge to fly high.
>   DAVID McCORD (124)

---

[6]David McCord, *Take Sky,* Illustrated by Henry B. Kane (Boston: Little, Brown, 1961), p. 55.

Although Edward Lear did not originate the limerick, he did much to popularize it. A modern book of intriguing limericks is William Jay Smith's *Typewriter Town*. This poet combines limericks with pictures that are made by using the typewriter. Middle-grade children who enjoy creating original limericks would be challenged by this approach.

Free Verse   Free verse does not have to rhyme but depends upon rhythm or cadence for its poetry form. It may use some rhyme, alliteration, and pattern. It frequently looks different on a printed page, but it sounds very much like other poetry when read aloud. Children who have the opportunity to hear this form of poetry will be freed from thinking that all poetry must rhyme. Read them some of the descriptive and arresting poems written by Hilda Conkling when she was a child. Boys and girls enjoy listening to the way another child described a "Mouse" (55) in his "gray velvet dress," or the "Hills" (55) that are "going somewhere." When Hilda Conkling was six years old, she wrote the following poem:

> The world turns softly
> Not to spill its lakes and rivers.
> The water is held in its arms
> And the sky is held in the waters.
> What is water,
> That pours silver,
> And can hold the sky?
>
> *HILDA CONKLING (55)*

Langston Hughes' melodic "April Rain Song" (146) is another example of the effective use of free verse. Probably one of the best-known poems of our day is "Fog" (146) by Carl Sandburg. This metaphorical description of the fog characterized as a cat is written in free verse.

Haiku   Haiku is an ancient Japanese verse form that can be traced back to the

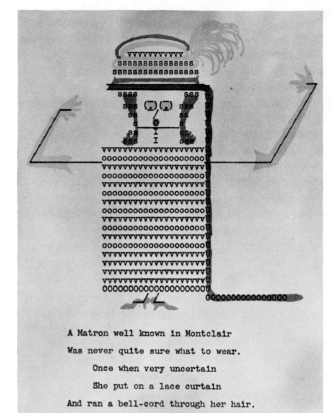

A Matron well known in Montclair
Was never quite sure what to wear.
Once when very uncertain
She put on a lace curtain
And ran a bell-cord through her hair.

Smith's unusual typewriter designs add to the enjoyment of his humorous limericks. From the book *Typewriter Town* written and illustrated by William Jay Smith. Copyright, ©, 1960 by William Jay Smith. Reproduced by permission of E. P. Dutton & Co., Inc.

thirteenth century. There are only seventeen syllables in the haiku; the first and third lines contain five, the second line, seven. Almost every haiku may be divided into two parts; first, a simple picture-making description that usually includes some reference, direct or indirect to the season, and second, a statement of mood or feeling. A relationship between these two parts is implied, either a similarity or a telling difference.

The greatest of haiku writers, and the one who crystallized the style, was Basho. In his lifetime, Basho produced more than 800 haiku. He considered the following poem to be one of his best:

> *An old silent pond . . .*
> *A frog jumps into the pond,*
> *splash! Silence again.*
> BASHO (12)

The silence reverberates against the sudden noise of the splash, intensified by the interruption. Another poet has contrasted destruction of material things with the everlasting beauty of nature in this haiku:

> *Ashes my burnt hut . . .*
> *But wonderful the cherry*
> *Blooming on my hill.*
> HOKUSHI (101)

The meaning of haiku is not expected to be immediately apparent. The reader is invited to add his own associations and meanings to the words, thus completing the poem in his mind. Each time the poem is read, new understandings will be developed. Harry Behn has written a haiku to explain the deeper meanings of this form of poetry:

> *A spark in the sun,*
> *this tiny flower has roots*
> *deep in the cool earth.*
> HARRY BEHN (12)

The Content of Poems for Children

Children derive certain satisfactions from hearing and reading poetry, but their preference for particular poems is often based upon the idea or content of the poem. Form may influence choice, but it does not necessarily determine it. Teachers will want to become familiar with a wide range of poetry so they may select the appropriate poem for the appropriate moment. Acquaintance with the work of individual poets is important, but knowledge of the subject matter of poetry will prove more helpful. In making a choice, the teacher does not think, "What poem by Elizabeth Madox Roberts should I read to the group?" Instead, "The Woodpecker" (6) by Roberts is selected because the class has seen this bird eating the suet at their bird-feeding station.

Young children want their poems to be simple, vivid, and to the point, much the same pattern that they demand of their stories. Each poem should present one clear thought or image, or a succession of such thoughts. Children will accept poems they do not completely understand, such as the mysterious poems by Walter de la Mare, for the very appeal of these poems lies in their enigma. Children are not as tolerant about poetry that is vague and deliberately confusing; they cannot "take" too many figures of speech, long descriptions, or philosophizing.

Children's tastes for poetry are very similar to their preferences for prose. The young child enjoys poems of every day occurrences. His interest in animals, both comical and real, is reflected in many poems. The changes in the weather and the seasons continue to be a source of wonder to him. All children enjoy humorous poetry, whether it be gay nonsense or an amusing story. Poems about fairies and elves are not for the youngest, but are more appropriately read to eight- and nine-year-olds. Poems of wonder, wisdom, and beauty or of adventure, romance, and historical interest are best delayed until children are older and have the background of experience to appreciate them.

My Family and I   The young child is egocentric and views the world as revolving about himself. He has an innate desire to retain his individuality—to be unique. Dorothy Aldis reflects this wish in her poem:

> EVERYBODY SAYS
> *Everybody says*
> *I look just like my mother.*

Everybody says
I'm the image of Aunt Bee.
Everybody says
My nose is like my father's
But I want to look like me.
　　　　　DOROTHY ALDIS (3)

Aileen Fisher describes a child's frustration with the questions he is asked at his "Mother's Party" (182). Every lady asked "What's your age?" and "What's your name?" They paid no attention to his boots, his studded belt, his glider game; worst of all, they paid no attention to him!

Eve Merriam ponders the stability of self from the child's point of view in her poem:

ME MYSELF AND I

Isn't it strange
That however I change,
I still keep on being me?

Though my clothes get worn out,
Though my toys are outgrown,
I never grow out of me.

. . . .

If I say 'Yes,' or if I say 'no';
If I go fast, or if I go slow;
When I'm at work, or when I'm at play:
Me I stay.

I may lose many things and frequently do.
I never lose me.
Does that happen to you?

　　　　　EVE MERRIAM (130)

Children and adults are frequently confused about who they really are. Gwendolyn Brooks has described this bewilderment of an older child in "Robert, Who Is Often a Stranger to Himself" (29). The conflict between outward appearances and inward desires is depicted by Rachel Field in her poem, "My Inside-Self" (66). Girls in the awkward stage of development will respond to this poem. Older children, too, are interested in the potentialities of self. Eve Mer-

MY OTHER NAME

Jennifer's my other name
　　(It's make-believe
　　and just a game.)

I'm really Anne,
But just the same
I'd much
　　much
　　rather
　　have a name
　　like Jennifer.

　　(So, if you can
　　don't call me Anne.)

A changing concept of self is expressed in this poem about a preadolescent. Illustration by Jacqueline Chwast. From *Whispers and Other Poems*, © 1958 by Myra Cohn Livingston. Reprinted by permission of Harcourt, Brace & World, Inc.

riam describes the uniqueness of the individual in:

THUMBPRINT

In the heel of my thumb
are whorls, whirls, wheels
in a unique design:
mine alone.
What a treasure to own!
My own flesh, my own feelings.
No other, however grand or base,
can ever contain the same.

My signature,
thumbing the pages of my time.
My universe key,
my singularity.
Impress, implant,
I am myself,
of all my atom parts I am the sum.
And out of my blood and my brain
I make my own interior weather,
my own sun and rain.
Imprint my mark upon the world,
whatever I shall become.

                    EVE MERRIAM (129)

Some mature students who have responded to "Thumbprint" may wish to consider the continuity of self through time as expressed in Hardy's poem:

HEREDITY

I am the family face;
Flesh perishes, I live on,
Projecting trait and trace
Through time to times anon,
And leaping from place to place
Over oblivion.

The years-heired feature that can
In curve and voice and eye
Despise the human span
Of durance—that is I;
The eternal thing in man,
That heeds no call to die.

                    THOMAS HARDY (148)

Family relationships have been described simply and naturally in poetry for young children. "Little" (3) by Dorothy Aldis tells of a little girl who shows her favorite toys to her baby brother, and each day he is too tiny to look. Several psychologically oriented poems about family relationships are "Satellite, Satellite" (130) by Eve Merriam, "Portrait" (34) by Marchette Chute, and "My Mother's Cross Afternoon" (10) by Dorothy W. Baruch. The first one tells of a little brother who "orbits" around his older brother all day, while the second one reflects on a small sister who is "always on the go." The last poem tells of the day "Mother got the growls" and paid no attention to her child. "Andre" (29) by Gwendolyn Brooks describes a dream in which a boy had to pick out parents and much to his surprise, he found he chose the same ones. Alfred Noyes' story of the day "Daddy Fell in the Pond" (66) never fails to amuse children. Walter de la Mare has immortalized the delightful "fat grandmamma with a very slippery knee" who is the keeper of "The Cupboard" (6) filled with lollipops and Banbury Cakes!

Such Interesting People   Children also enjoy poems about people outside their families. Dorothy Baruch has written about the "Barber's Clippers" (89), Rose Fyleman about "The Dentist" (89), and Rachel Field tells about "The Ice-Cream Man" (67). Probably one of Rachel Field's best-known poems is the one called "Doorbells" (67), in which she describes all the possible people who might be at the door when the doorbell rings. Rose Fyleman has written a monologue of questions that a young child asks "The New Neighbor" (6). His final query concerns an invitation to tea! Harry Behn treats the same situation quite candidly in "The New Little Boy."

A new little boy moved in next door
So I climbed a tree and bounced on a limb
And asked where he used to live before
And he didn't know but his name was Tim,
So I told all three of my names to him.

When he didn't say anything after that
I hung by my knees to see if he scared
And meowed and made my face like a cat,
But he only stood in his yard and stared,
He only watched like he never cared.

Well, all I know is his name is Tim
And I don't think very much of him.

                    HARRY BEHN (16)

Poetry for children is filled with interesting individual characters. Mary Austin describes "A Feller I Know" (66) whose name is "Pedro-Pablo-Ignacio-Juan-Francesco Garcia y Gabaldon," but fortunately, the boys just call him Pete! "My Friend, Leona" by Mary O'Neill describes an imaginative child who has a special way of seeing her world:

. . .
Leona makes over
Things she can't bear
All ugly streets
And ratted hair
All frightened things
And things that glare
The hole in the carpet
And the chair.
All broken ones
Who sit and stare
From window sills in
Their underwear.

Listen to her
And you'll see
Everything as it
Wants to be . . .
Leona's tall and her eyes are blue
And if you knew Leona you'd love her, too!
MARY O'NEILL (141)

All children should know a "Goody O'Grumpity" (66) who lives up to her first rather than her last name as she bakes delicious spice cakes and shares them with the children in the neighborhood. Edna St. Vincent Millay has given children her "Portrait by a Neighbor" (146) that tells of an eccentric lady who suns before she does her dishes and weeds her lettuce by the light of the moon! Children's world of poetry is populated with as realistic, kind, and erratic characters as they will find in their own lives.

Everyday Happenings Poetry may help children see a familiar object or interpret an everyday experience in a fresh, meaningful way; for poetry has the capacity of making the commonplace seem distinctly uncommon. Dorothy Aldis has playfully described the fun of brushing your teeth in "See, I Can Do It" (3). In "Not That" (3), this same poet has identified the young child's wish to be independent in every respect except one; he hopes he won't have to tuck himself in bed! Children who plead for "five minutes more" before going to bed will see themselves in "Bedtime" (65) by Farjeon.

Many other common experiences of children have been portrayed in poetry. The difficulty of "Choosing Shoes" (7) has been described in the poem used in the introduction of this chapter. The special joy of "Animal Crackers" (6) and cocoa for tea will provoke a familiar response from any child who has enjoyed the loving attention of a favorite food prepared just for him. One poet has shown that even such a routine experience as watering flowers and washing dishes can be new and exciting if done "At Josephine's House" (182). The joy of a picnic coupled with the minor disaster of dropping a jelly sandwich in the sand is ably described by Dorothy Aldis in "The Picnic" (3). In "Beach Fire" (6), Frances Frost has pictured a moment of a family's togetherness as they linger after a picnic on the beach to watch the sparks from their fire and the stars and moon lighten the evening darkness. Some poems tell of the delight of doing things alone. Winifred Welles' poem, "Skipping Along Alone" (6), enumerates the joys of isolated play. Everyone has had a special or favorite place of his own. No one has described the quiet peace of such a spot quite so well as David McCord in:

THIS IS MY ROCK
This is my rock,
And here I run
To steal the secret of the sun;
This is my rock,
And here come I

Before the night has swept the sky;
This is my rock,
This is the place
I meet the evening face to face.
            DAVID McCORD (123)

This poem may be compared with "Solitude" (131) by A. A. Milne, "The Secret Place" (3) by Dorothy Aldis, and "Keziah" (29) by Gwendolyn Brooks.

Other poems record children's delight in first-time experiences or accomplishments. In "A Year Later" (92), Mary Ann Hoberman tells of a little boy who could not swim at all and then, suddenly, he could! All children empathize with the frustrated young lad who is trying to learn to "Whistle" (3) in the Dorothy Aldis poem by that name.

Poetry can help children see their daily surroundings in a new way. The child who lives in the city may see his world anew when he views it through Langston Hughes' eyes:

CITY
    In the morning the city
    Spreads its wings
    Making a song
    In stone that sings.

    In evening the city
    Goes to bed
    Hanging lights
    About its head.
    LANGSTON HUGHES (66)

Rachel Field has personified the "Skyscrapers" (67) when she wonders if they ever "grow tired of holding themselves up high" or if they ever "shiver on frosty nights." This same poet has captured the busy rush of the city in her popular poem "Taxis" (69). The exciting sound of the "Trains" (89) as they rush through the dusk and the dawn has been re-created by James Tippett. Dorothy Baruch has recorded some of the sounds of the city in her poem "Funny the Way Different Cars Start" (89) and described

traffic patterns in "Stop-Go" (89). In her poem, "Motor Cars" (6), Rowena Bennett suggests that from a high window, cars look like "burnished beetles, black" and at night "grope their way with golden feelers of their lights."

Emotional response to one's environment has been the subject of several poems for children. Gwendolyn Brooks describes a boy's reaction to the city in the first verse of her poem:

RUDOLPH IS TIRED OF THE CITY
    These buildings are too close to me.
    I'd like to PUSH away.
    I'd like to live in the country,
    And spread my arms all day.
    GWENDOLYN BROOKS (29)

Aileen Fisher, who formerly lived in Chicago and now lives in the Rocky Mountains, contrasts the perspectives these different surroundings have given her:

UNTIL WE BUILT A CABIN
    When we lived in a city
    (three flights up and down)
    I never dreamed how many stars
    could show above a town.

    When we moved to a village
    where lighted streets were few,
    I thought I could see All *the stars,*
    but, oh, I never knew—

    Until we built a cabin
    where hills are high and far,
    I never knew how many
                many
                stars there really are!
    AILEEN FISHER (79)

Weather and the Seasons   The child is alive to the wonder and beauty of night and day, the weather, and the seasons. Poems about these phenomena have a distinctive place in the growing body of children's po-

etry because they capture and recall the eva-
nescent loveliness of the revolving seasons,
the changing weather, and variable moods of
the day. Beginning with Emily Dickinson's
"I'll tell you how the sun rose,/a ribbon at a
time" (149), there are poems for almost
every hour of the day. Elizabeth Coatsworth
uses personification to contrast the speeds at
which "Morning and Afternoon" pass:

The morning runs on nimble feet,
it's gone before you see
more than a ripple in the grass,
a flutter in the tree.

The afternoon is more inclined
to drowse along the wall;
some days it seems to close its eyes
and scarcely move at all.
ELIZABETH COATSWORTH (43)

Robert Francis has likened the passage of
time to the slow nibbling-away of a mouse in
his poem, "The Mouse Whose Name Is
Time" (91). Harry Behn describes the
coming of evening for younger children in
this way:

EVENING
Now the drowsy sunshine
Slides far away

Into the happy morning
Of someone else's day.
HARRY BEHN (182)

In "Check" (6) James Stephens personifies
night: "The Night was creeping on the
ground!/She crept and did not make a
sound." Even though she throws her shawl
of blackness all around, she is "checked"
from extinguishing a candle. Elizabeth
Coatsworth also personifies night in a rather
eerie poem:

SONG TO NIGHT
Night is something watching
something that is unseen,

something that moves a little,
patient and fierce and lean.

Night comes close to the window,
breathing against the pane,
and follows the lonely traveler
swiftly down the lane.
ELIZABETH COATSWORTH (125)

Sara Teasdale's poem "Night" (177) contains
the well-known line: "Look for a lovely thing
and you will find it." Her poem, "The Falling Star" (177), is also a favorite.

Robert Louis Stevenson has given children two of their favorite poems about the
"Wind" (174), the one that begins, "I saw
you toss the kites on high," and "Windy
Nights" (174), with its galloping rhythm and
mystery. Another much-loved favorite is
Christina Rossetti's "Who has seen the
wind? (6). "Voice of the Sky" (75) by Aileen
Fisher proclaims that "The sky has the oldest
voice/that ever has been heard." In free
verse, Adrien Stoutenberg describes the
wind in a storm.

STORM
In a storm
the wind talks
with its mouth wide open.
It yells around corners
with its eyes shut.
It bumps itself
and falls over a roof
and whispers
Oh . . . . oh . . . . oh . . . .
ADRIEN STOUTENBERG (176)

"The Storm" (3) by Dorothy Aldis is described by a little child from the security of
her safe, warm bed. Harry Behn portrays
the golden summer day that follows "The
Storm" (13), and he has also pictured a quiet
and lovely "Spring Rain" (15). Rachel Field
has described "City Rain" (67) with its
"streets of shiny wetness" and "umbrellas
bobbing to and fro." In a poem called "Rain

Sizes" (38), John Ciardi depicts rain as small mist that tickles, and as big as a nickel that "comes down too heavy to tickle." In "April Rain Song" (146), Langston Hughes conveys delight and joy in the rain that "plays a little sleep-song on our roof at night." James Tippett has captured the staccato sound of rain turned to ice in his "Sleet Storm" (23). The next morning the cold sun shines on a glittering world, still at last. Lew Sarett has painted a similar picture for older children in his "Brittle World":

> Brittle the snow on the gables,
>   The sleet-hung pines, the night
> Sprinkled with stars that quiver
>   Over the waste of white.
>
> Fragile the earth in the moonlight,
>   The glassy sheet of lake;
> If I tapped it with a hammer,
>   The brittle world would break.
>   LEW SARETT (181)

Snow intrigues children both for its beauty and its fun. Children who have just made a snowman will enjoy hearing Aileen Fisher's "The Snowman's Resolution" (89). "Snow" (6) by Alice Wilkins, "The First Snow" (89) by Mary Louise Allen, and "Snow" (3) by Dorothy Aldis present different childlike pictures of new-fallen snow, and are interesting to read and compare. "Snow Color" (79) by Aileen Fisher suggests the variety of colors that snow may reflect. Harry Behn's description of "Morning in Winter" (16) begins: "Shadows blue, sun bright/And everything else in the world white." His "Winter Night" (13) falls with the cadence of softly drifting snow. Some children in the middle grades will appreciate the silent world of new-fallen snow in Wylie's "Velvet Shoes" (146). If children have developed an appreciation for such quiet poems, they may be introduced to Robert Frost's contemplative "Stopping by Woods on a Snowy Evening" (85). Too early intro-

duction to this poem may destroy children's appreciation of it forever.

Changing seasons are a never-ceasing wonder to children. Myra Cohn Livingston has extracted the major differences between winter and summer as seen from a child's point of view:

> WINTER AND SUMMER
> The winter
>   is an ice-cream treat,
>   all frosty white and cold to eat.
> But summer
>   is a lemonade
>   of yellow sun and straw-cool shade.
>   MYRA COHN LIVINGSTON (117)

There are many spring and summer poems. Children might walk with Harry Behn and his friend Joe as they discover spring:

> DISCOVERY
> In a puddle left from last week's rain,
>   A friend of mine whose name is Joe
> Caught a tadpole, and showed me where
>   Its froggy legs were beginning to grow.
>
> Then we turned over a musty log,
>   With lichens on it in a row,
> And found some fiddleheads of ferns
>   Uncoiling out of the moss below.
>
> We hunted around, and saw the first
>   Jack-in-the-pulpits beginning to show,
> And even discovered under a rock
>   Where spotted salamanders go.
>
> I learned all this one morning from Joe,
>   But how much more there is to know!
>   HARRY BEHN (13)

Older children will appreciate Sara Teasdale's "April" (6) and Lew Sarett's touching "Four Little Foxes" (66) that tells of tragedy and the new little foxes who are left shivering in the March rain. Children who have enjoyed "Stopping by Woods on a Snowy Evening" (85) might want to compare it to this twelfth-century Oriental poem that contemplates the fragile beauty of spring:

Whose are this pond and house?
I lean on the red door, yet dare not knock.
But a fragment of sweet spring cannot be hidden,
As over the colored wall there peeps the tip of
*   an apricot branch.*

                    CHANG LIANG-CH'EN (110)

Rachel Field has personified summer in her well-known "A Summer Morning" (6). Kaye Starbird's poem about "Summer" (171) is refreshing and childlike in its point of view.

The birds proclaim the approach of fall even sooner than the brilliant coloring of the leaves. In "The Last Word of a Bluebird" (85) by Robert Frost, a young crow relays a bluebird's message to his daughter, Lesley, that "He just had to fly/But he sent his 'Good-by'" and a promise to return in the spring. Perhaps the best-known fall poem is the rather ominous warning contained in:

SOMETHING TOLD THE WILD GEESE
Something told the wild geese
*   It was time to go.*
Though the fields lay golden
*   Something whispered, "Snow."*
Leaves were green and stirring,
*   Berries, luster-glossed,*
But beneath warm feathers
*   Something whispered "Frost."*
All the sagging orchards
*   Steamed with amber spice,*
But each wild breast stiffened
*   At remembered ice.*
Something told the wild geese
*   It was time to fly—*
Summer sun was on their wings,
*   Winter in their cry.*

                    RACHEL FIELD (6)

The first two stanzas of "The Mist and All" (146) by Dixie Willson provoke a similar response as "Something Told the Wild

Geese," but the last verse provides a decided contrast.

Animal Poems   Poems about animals are always favorites with children. The behavior of wild animals is so closely linked to seasonal changes that it is sometimes difficult to distinguish between animal and seasonal poetry. Lew Sarett's poem about the "Four Little Foxes" (66) is as much about animals as it is about spring. Coatsworth's poem, "The Song of the Rabbits Outside the Tavern" (43), contrasts the plight of the rabbits out in the bitter cold with the warmth of the interior of the tavern. The poet tells us that those who seek the warmth of the fire have never known the rabbits' delight in their wild and hungry dance in the light of the moon. In "Cold Winter Now Is in the Wood" (6), this same poet compares the condition of the favored cat and dog with the horses and cows in the dark barn and the hungry fox and lean hawk. Frances Frost notes the effect of the season on the changing pelt of the rabbit in this picture:

WHITE SEASON
In the winter the rabbits match their pelts to the
*   earth.*
With ears laid back, they go,
Blown through the silver hollow, the silver
*   thicket,*
Like puffs of snow.

                    FRANCES FROST (83)

In "Green Hill Neighbors" (81), this poet tells about the little creatures who have their homes in one small hill. "The House of a Mouse" (89) has been described by Lucy Sprague Mitchell in words young children love to hear, particularly the ending that goes: "This sweet little, neat little, wee little green little cuddle-down hide-away house in the grass." Aileen Fisher contrasts the huge darkness of the night with the size of a mouse "In the Dark of Night" (71). "Night

Variety is the key word for both the poetry and the illustrations in this handsome book of *Cats and Bats and Things with Wings*. Milton Glaser has used different media and various colors to capture the many moods of these animal poems. Illustrations copyright © 1965 by Milton Glaser. From *Cats and Bats and Things with Wings* by Conrad Aiken. Used by permission of Atheneum Publishers.

of the Wind" (6) by Frances Frost pictures a little lost fox "caught by the blowing cold of the mountain darkness." In "Little Things" (6), James Stephens asks for forgiveness for mankind from the little creatures that have been trapped and must die in silence and despair. In "The Snare," he makes the reader *feel* the pain and cruelty inflicted by man as he describes the cries of the little rabbit caught in a trap. Note the mounting intensity of the poem as the poet becomes more frustrated in his search for the wounded rabbit:

THE SNARE
I hear a sudden cry of pain!
There is a rabbit in a snare;

Now I hear the cry again,
But I cannot tell from where.

But I cannot tell from where
He is calling out for aid!
Crying on the frightened air,
Making everything afraid!

Making everything afraid!
Wrinkling up his little face!
As he cries again for aid;
—And I cannot find the place!

And I cannot find the place
Where his paw is in the snare!
Little One! Oh, Little One!
I am searching everywhere!
        JAMES STEPHENS (6)

Mary Austin's lovely poem about "The Deer" (190) has a chanting refrain of "Follow, follow/By hill and hollow." Older students will appreciate Millay's delicate description of her unexpected meeting with a "Fawn" (47), and the mysterious mood created by Thomas Hardy in his picture of "The Fallow Deer at the Lonely House" (20). In *Cats and Bats and Things with Wings* (2), Conrad Aiken has written sixteen poems about various animals including "The Fallow Deer," "The Elephant," and "The Lion" —"who has a beauty unsurpassed." William Jay Smith has described "The Lion" (47) as having "a royal coat of brushed and beaten gold." Older children may want to ponder the question posed by Blake's haunting poem "The Tiger" (66).

In *The Dreaming Zoo* (192), John Unternecker presents fourteen dreams of zoo animals who reveal their desires to be free and in their natural habitat. For example, the hippopotamus dreams of "a steaming river" where he can soak himself in the mud and become "a brown island with eyes." *Prayers from the Ark* is a collection of twenty-seven poems, each one representing a prayer from a particular animal. The prayers reveal the distinctive characteristic of each animal and speak profoundly of their place in the world, for example:

THE PRAYER OF THE COCK

Do not forget, Lord,
it is I who make the sun rise.
I am Your servant
but, with the dignity of my calling,
I need some glitter and ostentation
Noblesse oblige . . . .
All the same,
I am Your servant,
only . . . do not forget, Lord,
I make the sun rise.
                    Amen
CARMEN BERNOS DE GASZTOLD (87)

Frances Frost has described the proud rooster in a similar fashion in "Rise, Sun!" (81) for younger children. The "Prayer of the Foal" (87) might be read to middle-grade children and compared with Robert Frost's "The Runaway" (85), the little Morgan colt, who is skittish at the sight of his first snow. Young children readily accept Robert Frost's invitation in his poem "The Pasture" (85) to go out and clean the spring and fetch the little calf. Children continue to enjoy Stevenson's friendly "The Cow" (174), "all red and white." Anyone who has heard the muffled clucking in a hen house at twilight will appreciate Elizabeth Madox Roberts' description of "The Hens" (161). Young children who have been to a farm will respond to the sensory imagery of Kim Worthington's poem, "I Held a Lamb" (182) and Zhenya Gay's "Did You Ever Pet a Baby Goat?" (182). Dorothy Aldis has captured children's universal delight in new baby animals in her poem, "In Spring in Warm Weather" (182).

Cats are well represented in poetry for children. Eleanor Farjeon describes "A Kitten" (6) who "has a giant purr and a midget mew." Mary Britton Miller depicts the movements of a "Cat" (6) in her poem by that title. "The Mysterious Cat" (6) by Vachel Lindsay is written in his characteristically rhythmical style. Roselle Moore's "Catalog" (187) proclaims that "cats sleep fat and walk thin." T. S. Eliot has written two amusing story poems about cats that older boys and girls like. One is called "The Rum Tum Tugger" (66) and the other is about "Macavity" (125), "A fiend in feline shape, a monster of depravity." In "The Cat and the Moon" (21), William Butler Yeats describes a dance between the cat, Minnaloushi, and the moon.

It does not seem that there are as many good poems about dogs as there are about cats. Milne's "Puppy and I" (133) is a favorite, of course. "The Hairy Dog" (127) by Herbert Asquith presents an amusing picture. James Reeves sings a song to "Mick" (47), his "mongrel-O." The ending is no surprise to anyone who has ever owned a dog! The origin of "The Dog's Cold Nose" (47) is explained in a poem with the same title by Arthur Guiterman. "The Prayer of the Dog" (87) in *Prayers from the Ark* reflects the dog's sense of responsibility "to keep watch."

These represent only a few of the poems about wild animals, barnyard animals, and pets. Children should be encouraged to bring their favorite animal poems and begin a class collection of them.

Poems of Fantasy and Make-Believe   For many years, poets have written of creatures who belong to fairyland. These poems were considered particiularly appropriate for children, until there was almost a surfeit of "fairy poems for little ones." American children who play with dump trucks that work, fire engines, holsters and guns, or dolls that "wet" and to which they can give permanents, usually have no appreciation for the "little people." Some believe in Santa Claus and the fairy who puts a dime under their pillow when they leave a tooth there — others pretend to believe so as not to hurt their parents' feelings. This is an "enlightened" generation that accepts the possibilities of space travel and investigates UFO's, but generally rejects the existence of fairies.

What should be done, then, with the large number of poems about fairies? Read some of them to children, particularly those that tell a story. Seven-year-olds enjoy Rose Fyleman's "The Best Game the Fairies Play" (6) that describes the joys of steeple-sliding. They laugh at the scolding, cross "Stocking Fairy" (6) by Winifred Welles. The characterization of this fairy is so well done that the poem can be pantomimed or pictures can be drawn of this crabby little person.

Children accept elves better than fairies—somehow boys think elves are not "sissy." "The Little Elf" (6) by John Bangs lends itself to dramatizations. The lyrical poem, "The Fairies" (51) by Allingham, is really about elves and has a narrative quality that children enjoy. They also like the story of "The Elf and the Dormouse" (6) by Herford, which tells of the origin of umbrellas.

"Overheard on a Saltmarsh" (6) by Monro depicts an imaginary conversation between a nymph and a goblin who covets her green glass beads. It is a wonderful poem for two children to take the parts of the nymph and the goblin. "A Goblinade" (6) by Florence Page Jaques tells the delightful story of a small goblin who was quite concerned when he found that instead of being alarming, he was amusing. He solved his problem by changing from a green goblin to an elf. With rare perception, Elizabeth MacKinstry has told the story of "The Man Who Hid His Own Front Door" (6). The neighbors, the Banker, and the Mayor went to call upon this elvish man and could not find his door, but a little girl in fading calico found the wandering door easily and entered the strange and mossy hall. A similar story is told by Winifred Welles in her mysterious poem, "Behind the Waterfall" (6). Here, a little old woman beckoned a child to come through a waterfall and into the crystal city that lay behind the misty spray. "Musetta of the Mountains" (158) by James Reeves is the hauntingly beautiful tale of a golden-haired girl who lives in the snowy mountains and rides a white doe. Though her thin voice cries "follow me," none will ride with Musetta to her mountainside.

The eerie quality of Walter de la Mare's "Someone" (60) captures children's interests and may motivate creative expression as they talk or write about the mysterious visitor. Less well known, but just as haunting, is:

NOTHING

Whsst, *and away, and over the green,*
Scampered a shape that never was seen.
It ran without sound, it ran without shadow.
Never a grass-blade in unmown meadow
Stooped at the thistledown fall of its foot.
I watched it vanish, yet saw it not—
A moment past, it had gazed at me;
Now nought but myself and the spindle tree:
A nothing. Of air? Of earth? Of sun?—
From emptiness come, into vacancy gone! . . .
Whsst, *and away, and over the green,*
Scampered a shape that never was seen.
                    WALTER DE LA MARE (56)

Poems of fantasy or make-believe can stretch children's imaginations and help them to dream dreams. Harry Behn suggests that "Childhood daydreams are often experimental journeys into subjective time":[7]

DAY DREAMS

In some far other time than here
Are forests full of dappled deer.

Where wandering minstrel winds awake
Shadows across a misty lake,

Shadowy ripples rippling away
To dreams of a still more distant day

---

[7]Harry Behn, "Poetry For Children," *The Horn Book Magazine*, vol. 42 (April 1966), p. 165.

*Where gardens greener than my own
Grow round a mossy tower of stone,*

*Where prancing steeds and knights of old
Wear coats of armor bright with gold,*

*And children dream, as still they do
Remembering what they never knew.*

HARRY BEHN (17)

If children have not been exposed to much poetry, it is better to start with content other than fantasy or make-believe. Gradually, the teacher may read a few of the suggested poems of elves, fairies, and other spirits, and begin to build an appreciation for this magical world of the imagination.

Humorous Poetry The humor in children's poems is derived from many sources. Fun-tickling words and nonsense provide one avenue of amusement. Children chant nonsense rhymes as they bounce their balls, skip rope, and count each other out for games. Carl Withers has collected some four hundred children's chants, riddles, tongue twisters, and others in his book, *Rocket in My Pocket.* When first introduced to this book, one third grader was enthralled and kept her family and friends amused as she recited, "Theophilus, the thistle sifter"; or "Of all the saws I ever saw saw, I never saw a saw saw like that saw saws." Her interest was aroused; she went on to enjoy other humorous poetry, and later, sensitive lyrical poems. Charles Potter has compiled two books of *Tongue Tanglers* that contain hilarious rhymes. The Petershams collected and beautifully illustrated similar folk sayings in their book, *The Rooster Crows.* Other favorites have been compiled by Ray Wood in *The American Mother Goose.* Older girls will enjoy Lillian Morrison's *Touch Blue,* a collection of love charms, chants, and rhymed superstitions. These books contain the verbal nonsense that is current in the United States. A teacher who wishes to develop an interest in po-

etry among children might do well to begin with the "stuff" children chant in their everyday lives.

Edward Lear was master of the limerick, but he also produced many narrative poems based on nonsensical words. In "Calico Pie" (20), "The Little Birds fly/Down to a Calico tree," and "The little Fish swam/Over the syllabub sea." A syllabub sea is as meaningless as a calico ·tree, but the words have a pleasant ring. He also wrote "The Jumblies" (106), those amazing creatures who went to sea in a sieve and "The Owl and the Pussy Cat" (187) who preferred a pea-green boat. Lewis Carroll carried on the gay tradition of nonsense with his amusing "Father William" (187), "The Walrus and the Carpenter" (66), and his tongue-twisting "Jabberwocky" (187).

**"How much wood would a woodchuck chuck. . . ."
One of the humorous illustrations by the Petershams for their collection of folk rhymes.** Reprinted with permission of The Macmillan Company from *The Rooster Crows* by Maud and Miska Petersham. Copyright 1945 by The Macmillan Company.

Younger children relish the words of Laura E. Richards' "Eletelephony" (6) and "Bobbily Boo and Wollypotump" (159). Recent poets have also enjoyed playing with words. David McCord in his poem "Glowworm" suggests that you never talk down to a glowworm —"Just say/Helloworm!" (124). Eve Merriam has fun playing with the word "Schenectady" (128) in a nonsense poem by that title, while Mary Ann Hoberman provides a similar kind of humor in her poem "Riding to Poughkeepsie" (92).

Preposterous animals are the subject of many humerous poems for children. Eleanor Farjeon tells of "Three Little Puffins" who "were partial to muffins" (121); Mary Austin gives advice for meeting a "Grizzly Bear" (6) and Gelett Burgess describes a "Purple Cow" (121). Sophisticated children today delight in the humor of Ogden Nash's "The Octopus" (139), "The Porcupine" (139), and the sage advice given in:

THE PANTHER
The Panther is like a leopard
Except it hasn't been peppered.
Should you behold a panther crouch
Prepare to say OUCH!
Better yet if called by a panther
Don't anther.

OGDEN NASH (139)

Charles Carryl's "The Plaint of the Camel" (146) who is most unhappy with his "bumpy humpy lumpy shape," is another favorite with children in the middle grades. Palmer Brown informs the reader that "The Spangled Pandemonium" (6) is missing from the zoo, but reveals little else about him. For this reason, the poem would be excellent for creative interpretations. The clues given in "How to Tell the Wild Animals" (6) by Carolyn Wells please children's somewhat sadistic humor. Many of the poems by John Ciardi are descriptions of weird imaginary animals, for example, "The Saginsack" (38) or the "Bugle-Billed Bazoo" (38). One of his best poems for children is about the "grin-cat":

THE CAT HEARD THE CAT-BIRD
One day, a fine day, a high-flying-sky day,
A cat-bird, a fat bird, a fine fat cat-bird
Was sitting and singing on a stump by the highway.
Just sitting. And singing. Just that. But a cat heard.
A thin cat, a grin-cat, a long thin grin-cat
Came creeping the sly way by the highway to the stump.
"O cat-bird, the cat heard! O cat-bird scat!
The grin-cat is creeping! He's going to jump!"

—One day, a fine day, a high-flying-sky day,
A fat cat, yes, that cat we met as a thin cat
Was napping, cat-napping on a stump by the highway.
And even in his sleep you could see he was a grin-cat.
Why was he grinning?—He must have had a dream.
What made him fat?—A pan full of cream.
What about the cat-bird?—What bird, dear?
I don't see any cat-bird here.

JOHN CIARDI (35)

Much of the humor in children's poetry revolves around the description of funny, eccentric characters with delightful sounding names. Laura E. Richards immortalized "Mrs. Snipkin and Mrs. Wobblechin" (6), "Little John Bottlejohn" (159), and Antonio (139), who was tired of living "alonio." A contemporary English poet, James Reeves, introduces children to such funny people as "Mrs. Golightly," "Little Minnie Mystery," and "Mrs. Gilfillan" (156), who "when troubled with troubles" goes to the kitchen and blows bubbles! "Jonathan Bing" (6) by Beatrice Brown is another favorite with eight- and nine-year-olds. They enjoy the inconsistencies of this strange character who in "A New Song to Sing about Jonathan Bing" (30) has "a curious way/Of trying to walk into yesterday."

Many humorous poems are based upon ludicrous situations and funny stories. A. A. Milne writes of "King John's Christmas" (133) and "The King's Breakfast" (133). Both are delightful tales of petulant kings, one of whom wants only a "little bit of butter" for his bread, while the other desires only a big red India-rubber ball! "Bad Sir Brian Botany" (133) relates the metamorphosis of bold Sir Brian to plain Mr. Botany B. in a story that is the epitome of poetic justice. In "The Monkeys and the Crocodile" (159), Laura Richards has also portrayed poetic justice in a tale of a monkey's "comeuppance." Eve Merriam's poem, "Teevee" (128), is a satire of Mr. and Mrs. Spouse who never spoke to each other until the day their television set was broken. They were just in the process of introducing themselves when the TV came back on! Third- and fourth-graders love the story of the "Alligator on the Escalator" (128) in the same book. Other funny tales in poetry include "A Tragic Story" (48), "The Twins" (66), and "After the Party" (66). A longer story that has become quite the favorite is Ogden Nash's "The Tale of Custard the Dragon" (187).

Dozens of nonsense rhymes and humorous narrative tales are available for school-age children. Frequently these are the poems that will open the door to poetry that may have become rusty with neglect.

Poems of Adventure and Accomplishment Many narrative poems are historical in nature—they tell of the accomplishments of great men and small. Included in this group are the well-known poems of "Paul Revere's Ride" (119) by Longfellow, Whittier's "Barbara Frietchie" (195), and "Columbus" (6) by Miller. This latter poem could be compared with Squire's "The Discovery" (125), which is told from an Indian's point of view as he watches the arrival of the

"huge canoes with bellying cloths." In "Indian" (18), the Benéts have ironically described the white man's treatment of the Indian. One stanza provides an example:

. . .

He knows his streams are full of fish,
His forests full of deer,
And his tribe is the mighty tribe
That all the others fear.
—And, when the French or English land,
The Spanish or the Dutch,
They'll tell him they're the mighty tribe
And no one else is much.
ROSEMARY AND STEPHEN VINCENT BENÉT (18)

Both Annette Wynne's "Indian Children" (6) and Elizabeth Coatsworth's lovely "The Wilderness Is Tamed" (45) tell of the changes that have been wrought in our country. Stephen Vincent Benét helps children appreciate the origin and excitement of "American Names" (125). He and his wife, Rosemary, have written the stirring, rhythmical "Western Wagons" (18). Older boys respond to the exhilaration and the challenge expressed in "The Coming American" by Foss (125). John T. Alexander has presented an ironical twist in his "The Winning of the TV West" (125), a poem that could stimulate much discussion about new frontiers.

Children in the middle grades enjoy biographical poetry as much as they appreciate biographies. Rosemary and Stephen Vincent Benét's verses about great Americans give capsule biographies and summarize the events in which men and women played a part. *A Book of Americans* includes "Miles Standish," "Aaron Burr," "Andrew Jackson," "Thomas Jefferson" as well as poems of "Clipper Ships and Captains" and "Pilgrims and Puritans." The latter poem portrays the self-righteousness of our forefathers as well as their resolute character in face of difficulties. The authors suggest that as "punishment for sinners/They invented New England dinners!" Although many of their poems are humorous, most present a serious theme. One about Abraham Lincoln quietly comments on the inability of people to recognize greatness when it is before their eyes:

. . .

"Need a man for troubled times?
Well, I guess we do.
Wonder who we'll ever find?
Yes—I wonder who."

That is how they met and talked,
Knowing and unknowing.
Lincoln was the green pine
Lincoln kept on growing.
ROSEMARY AND STEPHEN VINCENT BENÉT (18)

Boys in middle and upper grades become intensely interested in battle. They read avidly of battles of the Civil War, Naval battles, air battles of World War II. Too often, the bright uniform, the stirring song, the parade, the excitement and adventures of war are emphasized. Poetry can bring to the preadolescent and adolescent another view of war—its pain, loneliness, and horror. In "Epitaph for a Concord Boy" (125), the poet describes the death of a young, sleepy lad, routed from his bed by his father, who died at Concord without knowing why he had fought. Southey's poem, "The Battle of Blenheim" (187), tells of an old man's memory of a battle in the early eighteenth century. When the children find a skull and question him about it, he recalls how the English won a "famous victory." But he cannot tell "what good came of it at last." When children study the Civil War, they learn of the conflictng loyalties of many individuals. Girls like Woolson's narrative poem, "Kentucky Belle" (187) that tells how a Southern woman living in Ohio helped a rebel soldier by giving him her horse, Kentucky Belle. Inner struggles of the fighting man are revealed by Yeats who writes "Those that I fight I do not hate,/Those that I guard I do

not love," in his poem "An Irish Airman Foresees His Death" (21). Robert Nathan's long poem "Dunkirk" is a moving story of two British children who sailed their patched sailboat, *The Sarah P*, across the English Channel to rescue fourteen soldiers; 600 small boats sailed that night and reached Dunkirk:

. . .

They raised Dunkirk with its harbor torn
By the blasted stern and the sunken prow;
They had raced for fun on an English tide,
They were English children bred and born,
And whether they lived, or whether they died,
They raced for England now.

. . . .

For Nelson was there in the Victory,
With his one good eye, and his sullen twist,
And guns were out on the Golden Hind,
Their shot flashed over the Sarah P.
He could hear them cheer as he came about.

By burning wharves, by battered ships,
Galleon, frigate, and brigantine,
The old dead Captains fought their ships.
And the great dead Admirals led the line.
It was England's night, it was England's sea.
ROBERT NATHAN (188)

Some mature students will be ready for Robert Frost's well-known poem, "The Gift Outright" (125), that suggests that deeds of war were necessary for Americans to psychologically accept the land that, in truth, was ours before we recognized it.

Modern accomplishments of both the mean and the great have been recorded in poetic form. Children may be brought to understand the dignity of their own worth when they hear Mary Austin's "A Song of Greatness" (6). In this poem, an Indian boy hears of the heroic feats of his forefathers and knows that when his time comes, he too, "Shall do mightily." Mature students with scientific interests may be amused by "Lines to Dr. Ditmars" (148). They will appreciate the moving poem, "The Gift to Be Simple"

(148), which was written at the time of Einstein's death. In his beautiful and reverent poem, "High Flight" (125), the poet-pilot, John Gillespie Magee, has captured the sense of accomplishment and exhilaration that flying can produce. Poetry can help children realize that there are still frontiers and achievements to be won—these may be of the mind or the spirit.

Poems of Beauty and Wisdom   It is a mistake to introduce poetry to children with poems of beauty and wisdom, but it is also a mistake never to get to these poems. For poetry should illuminate and celebrate even simple experiences. Much of the poetry of Robert Frost reflects the glory of daily living. When a crow has to remind him of the joy of living, the poet laughs at himself:

DUST OF SNOW
The way a crow
Shook down on me
The dust of snow
From a hemlock tree

Has given my heart
A change of mood
And saved some part
Of a day I had rued.
ROBERT FROST (85)

William Henry Davies reminds us of the importance of "Leisure" (187), of taking small moments to do nothing more than "to stand and stare." Children's eyes need to be opened to the natural beauty around them. Even in the squalor of a tenement, there is joy in laughter, the delight of a smile, the warmth of love, and the beauty of neon signs against a summer's black night. Teacher and children might well follow Sara Teasdale's advice in her poem:

NIGHT
Stars over snow
And in the west a planet

Swinging below a star—
Look for a lovely thing and you will
*   find it,*
It is not far—
*   It never will be far.*
SARA TEASDALE (177)

In "The Coin" (177), this same poet suggests that each lovely sight be tucked away into the heart's treasury, for far better than money "Is the safe-kept memory/Of a lovely thing." Elizabeth Coatsworth's best-known poem contrasts the beauty of swift things with those that are slow and steady. Her message is much the same as Sara Teasdale's "Night"; namely, look for beauty in all living things:

POEM OF PRAISE
Swift things are beautiful:
Swallows and deer,
And lightning that falls
Bright-veined and clear,
Rivers and meteors,
Wind in the wheat,
The strong-withered horse,
The runner's sure feet.

And slow things are beautiful:
The closing of day,
The pause of the wave
That curves downward to spray,
The ember that crumbles,
The opening flower,
And the ox that moves on
In the quiet of power.
ELIZABETH COATSWORTH (43)

Poems may be about the concept of beauty or quicken children's responses to that which is beautiful. Such poetry should make children see more clearly and feel more deeply.

Poems of wisdom should teach rather than preach. While children reject the didactic, they do appreciate poems that make them think. Flashes of Carl Sandburg's keen wisdom penetrated all his poems, as in:

CIRCLES

The white man drew a small circle in the sand
*   and told the red man,*
"This is what the Indian knows,"
And drawing a big circle around the small one,
"This is what the white man knows."

The Indian took the stick
And swept an immense ring around both circles:
"This is where the white man and the red man
*   know nothing."*

CARL SANDBURG (165)

Sandburg frequently gave advice that is palatable to most children. His "Primer Lesson" speaks directly to boys and girls in terms they can understand:

Look out how you use proud words.
When you let proud words go, it is not easy to
*   call them back.*
They wear long boots, hard boots; they
*   walk off proud; they can't hear you calling—*
Look out how you use proud words.

CARL SANDBURG (127)

Emily Dickinson is more ambiguous than Sandburg, but certainly the following poem could be compared with "Primer Lesson":

A WORD

A word is dead
When it is said,
*   Some say.*

I say it just
Begins to live
*   That day.*

EMILY DICKINSON (6)

Dickinson's poem "Hope is the thing with feathers" (6) appeals to older boys and girls, as does Victor Hugo's "Be Like the Bird" (6). In the first, hope is metaphorically represented as a bird, while in the second, the confident action of the bird implies hope and faith.

The wisdom of the Bible and the poetic beauty of many of the Psalms should be a part of children's heritage (see Chapter 4). Proverbs and certain portions from both the Old and New Testament are truly poetic. For example, listen to the poetic quality of the following verses from Isaiah:

But they that wait upon the Lord shall renew
*   their strength;*
They shall mount up with wings as eagles;
They shall run, and not be weary;
And they shall walk, and not faint.

ISAIAH 40:31

Paul's advice to the Philippians in Chapter 4:8 sings with poetry in the well-known admonition "Whatsoever things are true/whatsoever things are honest/whatsoever things are just/whatsoever things are pure/whatsoever things are lovely . . . think on these." The Bible may be considered both a source of wisdom and a source of great literature.

Poets and Their Books

Recent years have seen an increase in the number of writers of verse for children and the number of poetry books published for the juvenile market. The poetry itself has changed, becoming less formal, more spontaneous, and imitative of the child's own language patterns. The range of subject matter has expanded with the tremendous variation of children's interests. It is difficult to categorize the work of a poet on the basis of the content of his poems, for many poets interpret various areas of children's experience. However, an understanding of general subject matter of the works of each poet will help the teacher select poems and make recommendations to children.

Interpreters of the World of Childhood

William Blake was the first poet to discover

the world of childhood, which he celebrated in his *Songs of Innocence,* published in 1789. Many of these poems are symbolic and religious in tone, and have little meaning for today's child. Some, however, sing with joy, for example "The Laughing Song," "Infant Joy," and "Piping Down the Valleys Wild." Ellen Raskin has illustrated a new edition of *Songs of Innocence* with strikingly modern woodcuts.

Robert Louis Stevenson was the first poet to write of childhood from the child's point of view. *A Child's Garden of Verses,* published in 1885, continues its popularity today. Stevenson was a frail child and spent much of his early life in bed or confined indoors. His poetry reflects a solitary childhood, but a happy one. In "Land of Counterpane" and "Block City," he portrays a creative, inventive child who can make his own amusement. He found playmates in his shadow, in his dreams, and in his storybooks. Occasionally, Stevenson lapsed into the moralistic tone of his time with such poems as "System," "A Good Boy," and "Whole Duty of Children." "Foreign Children" presents a narrow, parochial point of view that is contrary to the goals of modern social studies. However, the rhythm of Stevenson's "The Swing," "Where Go the Boats," and "Windy Nights" appeals to children today as much as to the children of nearly a century ago.

Currently, some fifteen illustrated editions of *A Child's Garden of Verses* are in print. They range in interpretation from Tasha Tudor's quaint pastel pictures that portray Stevenson as a young child, to Brian Wildsmith's edition that is a brilliant kaleidoscope of color. In this latter edition, the pictures almost overpower the poetry. For example, the illustration for "At the Seaside" depicts a large oceanside pavilion and pier, which dwarf the central character and action of the poem. The reader must search to find the little boy who is digging holes in the sand and watching the sea fill them up. On the other hand, "Land of Counterpane" is effectively illustrated by Wildsmith's characteristic geometrical shapes of color that make a handsome bed quilt. Overly profuse illustrations may destroy the picture-making power of the poem itself. It is wise to remember that something needs to be left to the imagination, both in the text of poetry and its illustration.

Perhaps the best-loved of children's poets is A. A. Milne. Some of his poems show perceptive insight into the child's mind, such as "Halfway Down" and "Solitude." "Happiness" captures a child's joy in such delights as new waterproof boots, and raincoat and hat. Told in the first person, "Hoppity" reveals a young child's enjoyment of the state of perpetual motion! The majority of A. A. Milne's poems are delightfully funny. His Christopher Robin is an only child, whose playmates are toys or adults. Perhaps this is why he has to resort to entertaining his adult friends with "Sneezles." In the poem "Missing," the reader never does hear Aunt Rose's reply to the query concerning a mouse with a "woffelly nose"—we hope the lady liked mice, however. A. A. Milne's solitary child is so engrossed in his play and himself, that he never seems lonely—only creatively busy. His activities include the well-known trip to "Buckingham Palace" where they are changing guards, or walking on just the "Squares" of the sidewalks. The poetry from both of Milne's poetry books has now been collected into one volume titled *The World of Christopher Robin.* The illustrations by Ernest Shepard seem as much a part of A. A. Milne's poetry as Pooh belongs to Christopher Robin; it is hard to imagine one without the other.

Another well-loved British poet for children is Eleanor Farjeon. Her knowledge and understanding of children's thoughts and behavior are reflected in her books, *Eleanor Farjeon's Poems for Children* and *The Children's Bells.* The simple poem, "New Clothes and Old," tells of a child's preference for his old things. "Over the Garden Wall" is a hauntingly beautiful poem that makes the reader feel as lonely as the child who is left out of the ball game on the other side of the wall. This poet also wrote the lovely nature poem "The Night Will Never Stay" and the popular description of "Mrs. Peck-Pigeon." Some of her poems are fanciful; others are pure nonsense. Her versatility defies classification other than that of the approbation of children.

Before her death in 1965, Eleanor Farjeon had received notable recognition for her poetry and prose. She was the first recipient of the International Hans Christian Andersen Medal in 1956, and in 1959 she received the Regina Medal for her life's work. No other poet who has written exclusively for children has received such recognition.

Dorothy Aldis gives realistic pictures of the child's everyday experiences and expresses so very touchingly the thoughts and personal reactions of young children to their environment. She catches the young child's delight in the simple routines of home life as expressed in "Ironing Day," "After My Bath," "The Windy Wash Day," and "Going to Sleep." This poet shows sensitivity to the child's emotions in "Bad," "The Secret Place," and "Alone." Family relationships are lovingly portrayed in "Little," "My Brother," and "Hiding." Poems from the first four books by Dorothy Aldis have been collected in a single volume entitled *All Together*. Two other books are *Hello Day* and *Quick As a Wink*. Dorothy Aldis died in 1966, but her poetry lives on to celebrate the simply joys of childhood.

Primary children also enjoy Rachel Field's poems. The book, simply titled *Poems*, includes her first book of poetry, *Pointed People* (1924) and *Taxis and Toadstools* (1926). Many of these poems are written from the city child's point of view, including "Skyscrapers," "Taxis," "City Rain," and "Snow in the City." However, Rachel Field spent four months of every year on an island off the coast of Maine, hence the "toadstools" part in the title of one book. She has immortalized the experience of sleeping on an island for the first time in the lines of her poem: "If once you have slept on an island/You'll never be quite the same" (69). Other favorite country poems are "Roads" with its surprise ending, and "General Store" with its "tinkly bell" and "drawers all spilly." The warning conveyed in "Something Told the Wild Geese" may have provided the signal for Rachel Field to return to the city and her "Taxis."

James Tippett has written poems about the city and traveling in his books *I Go A-Traveling, I Spend the Summer*, and *I Live in the City*. His poem "Sh" deals with one of the problems of a boisterous child who lives in an apartment. "Ferry-Boats" dramatizes the constant shuffling to and fro of the boats, and the increasing speed of engines is reflected in the tempo of "The Trains."

A Pulitzer Prize winner, Gwendolyn Brooks, has written some poignant poetry about children who live in the inner city. *Bronzeville Boys and Girls* contains thirty-four poems, each bearing the name and thoughts of an individual child. There is Gertrude's joyous reaction to hearing Marian Anderson sing, Beulah's quiet thoughts at church, and Michael's fear of the storm. Lyle thinks about a tree that is rooted to its "first and favorite" home, while he has been uprooted seven times. Maurice's feelings of importance about his family's move change when he realizes that he may take his belongings, but not his friends.

Myra Cohn Livingston is a comparative newcomer to the scene of young children's poetry, and she brings a charm and freshness that is delightful. Her book, *Whispers and Other Poems*, is filled with laughter, curiosity, gaiety, and tenderness. Some of the imagery is as delicate as her title poem:

WHISPERS

Whispers
  tickle through your ear
  telling things you like to hear.
Whispers
  are as soft as skin
  letting little words curl in.
Whispers
  come so they can blow
  secrets others never know.
  MYRA COHN LIVINGSTON (117)

Other books of poems by Livingston include *Wide Awake* and *The Moon and a Star*. *I'm Hiding, See What I Found, I'm Not Me, Happy Birthday,* and *I'm Waiting* are written in simple rhythmic prose that approaches poetic form. Erik Blegvad's detailed black and white illustrations are completely harmonious with the mood of these texts.

Mary Ann Hoberman's book, *Hello and Good-by,* has many lyrical, amusing, and happy poems. The rhythmical title poem gives the motion of swinging. Amusing nonsense poems such as "The Llama Who Had No Pajama" and "The Folk Who Live in Backward Town" are included. Her "Halloween" poem is reminiscent of Dorothy Aldis' "Hiding," but children will enjoy it thoroughly.

The childlike verses of Karla Kuskin's *In the Middle of the Trees* are a welcome addition to poetry for younger children. Some of her poems are musical, as the lines "And I'm the one who woke the Sun/and kissed the stars good night" in the poem "Very Early." In "Spring," she describes a child's hilarious joy over the return of this season. The poems in *Sand and Snow* contrast two children's responses to summer and winter. Gay nonsense characterizes her poems in *Alexander Soames, His Poems*. Karla Kuskin illustrates her own books with amusing stylized pictures.

Beatrice Schenk de Regniers has presented ten childlike poems in a little volume called *Something Special,* which Irene Haas has illustrated gaily. These poems have a bouncing rhythm and wonderful nonsense. The title poem includes the chant "What did you put in your pocket/in your pockety pockety pocket . . .?" A quiet poem with charming imagery includes the line "a feather is a letter from a bird." Children of all ages might well heed her advice in the following poem:

Keep a poem in your pocket
and a picture in your head
and you'll never feel lonely
at night when you're in bed.
BEATRICE SCHENK DE REGNIERS (62)

Other recent poets who interpret the world of childhood include Patricia Hubbell and Kaye Starbird. From *8 A.M. Shadows,* the title poem, to "Bedtime," the last poem in Hubbell's book, lies a full day of a young child's thoughts, games, and encounters with nature. The imagery is fresh and childlike in these poems. For example, "Squirrels" are described as having tails "like dandelion down," and in "The Shepherd," "The wind is a shepherd/That herds the clouds/across the summer sky." An earlier volume, *The Apple Vendor's Fair,* includes forty-one poems dealing with everything from clouds to dinosaurs.

Kaye Starbird's first book of poems for children was *Speaking of Cows*. Two more recent books are: *Don't Ever Cross a Crocodile* and *A Snail's a Failure Socially*. Most of these poems include amusing observations of animals and people from a child's point of view. (See "December Leaves") The problem of visiting a friend who is interested only in reading is the subject of a poem titled "Masie." "Minnie Morse" is a typical fourth-grade girl who is so engrossed with the subject of horses she might as well be one. The most outstanding camper by far was "Eat-It-All Elaine" who swallowed birch bark, prune pits, and stink bugs with quiet aplomb. Third-and fourth-graders who are beginning to read poetry independently will find these verses hilarious.

Poets of Nature   Children, like the poets, are fascinated with the constant changes and beauties of nature and enjoy poems that communicate a sense of wonder and appreciation.

Christina Rossetti was a contemporary of Stevenson, and some of her poetry has the distinctive lyrical quality that characterizes his poems. In her only book, *Sing Song,* she sings of the wind, the rain, the rainbow, and small creatures. Her best-known poems are "Boats Sail on the Rivers," "Who Has Seen the Wind?" and the lovely color poem, "What is Pink?"

Elizabeth Madox Roberts also wrote only one book of poetry for children, *Under the Tree.* Her poems show keen insight into the child mind as she writes about digging for worms, the fun of wading, and listening to "Water Noises." Children enjoy the staccato rhythm of "The Woodpecker" and the description of "The Hens" going to roost and speaking their little "asking words." The poem, "Crescent Moon," might well be compared with the prose story of *The Moon Jumpers* by Udry. Many of Roberts' poems are written in the first person and give the child's thoughts as he encounters some aspect of his natural world.

Frances Frost has described nature as seen through the eyes of a child in her two books, *The Little Whistler* and *The Little Naturalist.* Fox cubs, otters, a chubby woodchuck, and a wren that made its nest in a mailbox are a few of the small creatures that parade through these books. The poet uses such vivid phrases as "my heart is a grasshopper wild in my chest" in the tale of the "Little Fox Lost." Frances Frost's poems are based on accurate observations and are filled with warmth and tenderness for the creatures of the natural world.

Aileen Fisher is equally adept at observing nature and children. In "Butterfly Tongues," for example, she accurately describes how the butterfly uncoils his tongue to sip the nectar from the flowers, but then observes, as a child would, that if humans only had tongues like that we'd never need straws! Her poems are filled with sensory imagery, as in the following verse:

> PUSSY WILLOWS
> *Close your eyes*
> *and do not peek*
> *and I'll rub Spring*
> *across your cheek—*
> *smooth as satin,*
> *soft and sleek—*
> *close your eyes*
> *and do not peek.*
>   AILEEN FISHER (75)

Some of Aileen Fisher's books of poems are *Runny Days, Sunny Days, Cricket in a Thicket,* and *In the Woods In the Meadow In the Sky.* Her longer narrative poems are told in lilting verse and include *Listen, Rabbit, Going Barefoot, Where Does Everyone Go?, Like Nothing at All, I Like Weather,* and *In the Middle of the Night.* Beautifully illustrated by such well-known artists as Adrienne Adams, Symeon Shimin, and Leonard Weisgard, these books are usually presented to children as picture storybooks (see Chapter 3).

Each new book by Harry Behn proves his versatility and increases his stature as a major poet for children. His most recent book, *The Golden Hive,* reflects this poet's joy in the natural world. "The Lake," "Summer," "The Storm," "Winter Night," and "September" exemplify titles of nature poems. The depth of his poetry is revealed in "River's Song" as he describes the everlasting river:

> *Here am I where you see me*
> *Strong and brown.*
> *Still, I am far away*
> *Where yesterday I was.*

Here am I, shouting
And tossing my feathers.
Still, I am far away
Where I have not yet gone.

I am a drop of dew
Dripping to earth from a leaf.
I am a Sea.

Here am I
Where I was,
Where someday I will be.
HARRY BEHN (13)

The poetry of Elizabeth Coatsworth reflects the moods and perceptions of an astute observer of nature. Her delicate and beautiful verse reveals a deep love of nature and animals. She frequently employs a pattern of comparison in her poems. For example, she contrasts the beauty of swift things with that of slow in "Poem of Praise," and again in "January," when snow is described as coming as quietly as a cat or with "windy uproar and commotion." Elizabeth Coatsworth's poems are included in the following books: *Poems, Summer Green,* and *The Sparrow Bush.* The third volume is illustrated with delicate wood engravings by Stefan Martin. Thirteen poems about mice comprise *Mouse Chorus.* Three narrative poems of a religious nature are included in her book, *The Peaceable Kingdom.*

Mary Austin has described the beauties of the Southwest in, *The Children Sing in the Far West.* Her most popular poems include the amusing "Grizzly Bear" and "A Feller I Know." Children also enjoy "Prairie-Dog Town" and "The Sandhill Crane." Her Indian poems reflect the quiet dignity of that ancient race, particularly "A Song of Greatness."

Known mostly for her poetry for adults, Sara Teasdale has given children some exquisite poems in her book, *Stars To-Night.* Although she writes of the changing seasons, the sea, and birds, her favorite subject, stars,

gleams through most of her poetry. Her poems, "Night," "Stars," and "The Falling Star" reflect a reverence and awe for the beauties of nature.

Some of the strong, quizzical poetry of Carl Sandburg is appropriately used with children in the middle grades. They enjoy the humor of "Phizzog," the finality of "Buffalo Dusk," and the wisdom of "Circles." Sandburg had made two collections of his verse particularly suited to young people, *Early Moon* and *Wind Song.* In *Wind Song,* available in paperback, the vivid imagery of "Haystacks," "Night," and "River Moons" will help children see with the eyes of a poet.

NIGHT

Night gathers itself into a ball of dark yarn.
Night loosens the ball and it spreads.
The lookouts from the shores of Lake Michigan
  find night follows day,
    and ping! ping! across sheet gray
    the boat lights put their signals.
Night lets the dark yarn unravel,
Night speaks and the yarns change
  to fog and blue strands.
CARL SANDBURG (165)

Many poems of Robert Frost are simple enough for a child to understand and complex enough for graduate study. Before his death, he selected some of his poems to be read to, or by, young people. Interestingly, the title of this collection, *You Come Too,* was taken from a line of "The Pasture," the first poem in this book and the introductory poem of the very first book of Frost's to be published. At first reading, this poem seems no more than a literal invitation to join someone as he cleans the pasture spring. However, the poem takes on more complexity when viewed in the context of its placement; the trip to the pasture to clean the spring may mean an invitation to the enjoyment of poetry itself — "you come too!" Robert Frost seemed to have had a preoccupation with clearing muddied waters, and it seems significant that his last book was titled *In the Clearing*. Let children enjoy "The Runaway," "Dust of Snow," "The Last Word of a Bluebird," and "The Pasture" on their level of understanding. Older children will begin to understand the deeper meanings in "Mending Wall," "The Road Not Taken," and "The Death of the Hired Man." The poetry of Robert Frost is for all ages. Frost himself gave us the best reasons for introducing it to children:

> *People keep saying it's not good*
> *To learn things by heart,*
> *But pretty things well said—*
> *It's nice to have them in your head.*
> ROBERT FROST[8]

Weavers of Magic and Fantasy Children love eerie "spooky" poetry. The master craftsman in creating mysterious moods is Walter de la Mare. Children enjoy the hushed mystery of "Someone," which ends with the enigmatic lines: "So I know not who came knocking, at all, at all, at all." The poem "Nothing" intrigues children with the same kind of eeriness. The "Ride-by-Nights" is a vividly descriptive poem about witches who "surge pell-mell down the Milky Way." Even when Walter de la Mare is describing a kitchen cupboard, it is "a little cupboard with a teeny tiny key." Two of his best-known poems are "Silver" and "The Listeners." Both create a mood of sustained stillness and mystery. Walter de la Mare's most popular poems are found in *Peacock Pie*, first published in 1913. A new edition has been illustrated by Barbara Cooney. A collection of all his poems has been published in one book, *Rhymes and Verses, Collected Poems for Young People*. A selected group of poems have been delicately illustrated by Dorothy Lathrop for *Bells and Grass*.

---

[8]Quoted in Chester Morrison, "A Visit with Robert L. Frost," *Look* (March 31, 1959), p. 81.

Fyleman's four books each contain the word "fairy" in their titles. Her fairies are believable persons precisely because Rose Fyleman introduced them in such modern settings as a bus on Oxford Street or sliding down steeples. Although Rose Fyleman is primarily known for these fairy poems, her poem about "Mice" continues to be one of children's favorites.

Some of the poems in *Skipping Along Alone* by Winifred Welles portray the supernatural. Her crotchety old "stocking fairy" contrasts sharply with Fyleman's dainty fairies with gossamer wings. In both "The Green Moth" and "Behind the Water Fall," a compelling and mysterious invitation is issued.

James Reeves' books, *The Blackbird in the Lilac* and *The Wandering Moon*, contain a wide variety of poems. Many of them are funny verses about strange people; some are thoughtful and quiet; and some are eerie fantasies of myth and legend, such as "Little Fan," "Pat's Fiddle," and "Queer Things." Children will enjoy "The Old Wife and the Ghost," which is the amusing tale of a deaf woman who refuses to be frightened by a ghost. "A Garden at Night" and "The Toadstool Wood" paint ghostly scenes. Imaginative and pleasantly scary for younger children are the poems in *Prefabulous Animiles* illustrated by Edward Ardizzone. Reeves has invented such creatures as the fearsome Hippocrump with a hundred teeth and the forty-legged Snyke. These verses are fun to illustrate.

Harry Behn bridges the world of reality and enchantment with equal adroitness. Many of his poems in *The Wizard in the Well* cast a mysterious spell on the reader with tales of elves, fairies, and wizards. Seven long poems, in *The House Beyond the Meadow*, weave a story of a little boy's visit to fairyland. A silky, black crow sitting on a weathervane is described in *Windy Morning* as "A Gnome." In a conversation between "The Fairy and the Bird," the fairy reminds the bird of the "land of marvelous moonful magical ever" but the bird refuses to return, and the very next day "a cold wind blew." It is easy to believe in the fanciful when Harry Behn leads the way.

Writers of Humorous Verse Almost all poets have written some humorous poetry, but only a few have become noted primarily for this form. In the nineteenth century, the names of Edward Lear and Lewis Carroll became almost synonymous with humorous nonsense poems. Although Lear did not create the limerick, he was certainly master of the form. His narrative verse includes the well-known "The Owl and the Pussycat," "The Jumblies," "The Quangle Wangle's Hat," and "The Duck and the Kangaroo." His limericks, alphabet rhymes, and narrative poems have been compiled into one book, *The Complete Nonsense Book*. Each absurd verse is illustrated by the poet's grotesque drawings, which add greatly to Lear's humor.

Most of Carroll's nonsense verse is included in *Alice's Adventures in Wonderland* and *Through the Looking-Glass*. Many of Carroll's poems were parodies of the popular poems of the time. "The Lobster Quadrille" mimics Mary Howitt's "The Spider and the Fly"; "Father William" copies Southey's "The Old Man's Comforts," while "How Doth the Little Crocodile" parodies Watt's "How Doth the Busy Bee." Interest in the original poems has all but disappeared, but the parodies continue to delight. "Jabberwocky" is a "made language" of portmanteau words; namely, combining the meaning and parts of two words to create a new one. "Brunch," for example, carries the combined meaning and sound of both breakfast and lunch. The sound and play of words must have fascinated Lewis Carroll, for his poems and books abound with puns, double meanings, coined words, and wonderful nonsense.

Laura E. Richards' rhythmical nonsense poems are presented in her book, *Tirra Lirra*. Much of the humor of Richards' poems is

There was a Young Lady whose chin
Resembled the point of a pin;
So she had it made sharp, and purchased a harp,
And played several tunes with her chin.

Lear's illustrations frequently exaggerate a portion of the body and are as zany as his limericks. Used by permission of Dodd, Mead & Company, Inc., from *The Complete Nonsense Book* by Edward Lear.

based upon the manufacture of delightful sounding words; her children go fishing for "pollothywogs" and get stuck in "bogothybogs," a frog lives on the banks of "Lake Okeefinokee," and a "Wiggledywasticus" is in the museum with the "Ploodlecumlumpsydyl." Many of her poems are humorous narratives such as "The Seven Little Tigers and the Aged Cook" and "The Monkeys and the Crocodile." Funny characters and situations pervade the poetry of this prolific writer.

Following the tradition of Lear are several modern poets. William Jay Smith has written and illustrated his unique limericks for *Typewriter Town*. His *Laughing Time* and *Boy Blue's Books of Beasts* include some fresh and spontaneous nonsense verse. Some of his poems are lyrical as the interesting "Over and Under" and "When Candy was Chocolate."

The sophisticated light verse and limericks of Ogden Nash appeal to both adults and children. They delight in "The Panther," "The Centipede," and "The Eel." Younger children enjoy his longer narrative poems including "The Adventures of Isabel," who eats a bear, and the sad demise of "The Boy Who Laughed at Santa Claus." These poems appear in his book *The Moon Is Shining Bright as Day.*

E. V. Rieu, an English classicist, finds relaxation in writing nonsense verse for children. These have been collected in a book titled *The Flattered Flying Fish and Other Poems.* Several of these, such as "A Dirge for a Bad Boy" and "Two People," are about children's misbehavior and consequent punishment, a subject that never fails to amuse children.

The originator of poems about mischievous children and their grim punishments was Heinrich Hoffman in "Slovenly Peter." Harry Graham continued the tradition with his *Ruthless Rhymes for Heartless Homes* first published in 1899, with such gems as:

THE STERN PARENT
Father heard his Children Scream
So he threw them in the stream
Saying, as he drowned the third,
"Children should be seen, not heard!"
HARRY GRAHAM (90)

John Ciardi appears to be following the Hoffman-Graham tradition in some of his poems. The first verse of "Children When They're Very Sweet" is an example:

Children when they're very sweet,
Only bite and scratch and kick
A very little. Just enough
To show their parents they're not sick.
JOHN CIARDI (36)

His book, *You Know Who,* is filled with sly descriptions of different "someones" and their behaviors. *The Monster Den* is the title of the book about his own children, and has more appeal for parents than children. Many of Ciardi's poems are enjoyed by boys and girls with enough sophistication to appreciate their tongue-in-cheek humor. His poems about imaginary animals such as the "Shiverous Shreek" or the "Saginsack" are well liked. One fourth grade's favorite was the disastrous custard made by "Some Cook." In *The Reason for the Pelican,* there are some fine lyrical poems including "There Once Was an Owl," "The River Is a Piece of Sky" and "Rain Sizes." Humorous poetry characterizes his other books, which include *I Met a Man, The Man Who Sang the Sillies,* and *You Read to Me and I'll Read to You.* Sophisticated Victorian illustrations by Edward Gorey perfectly complement Ciardi's spoof on parent-child relations of today.

"Of Cabbages and Kings"   It is difficult to characterize the great variety of poems by David McCord. Much of the poetry in his first book, *Far and Few, Rhymes of Never Was and Always Is,* is about simple country sights or walking in the woods with his father. The unusual verse arrangement in "The Grasshopper" pleases children. An exasperated parent questions the tardiness of the children for dinner in the poem "At the Garden Gate," while a pleading child begs her parents to let her stay up late in "Conversation." Both poems reveal McCord's knowledge of children and his ability to capture the intonations of an argument in poetry. David McCord has written fifty more "Rhymes of Never Was and Always Is" in *All Day Long.* These include songs of nature, a trip to the laundromat, and other humorous verse. Some poems reflect his persistent interest in language such as "Figures of Speech," "Ptarmigan," and "Says Tom to Me." This special delight in words was the subject of most of the poems in his book *Take Sky.* The long "Write Me a Verse" contained Professor Swigly Brown's talk on "four kinds of Rime."

WHAT IS RED?

Red is a sunset
Blazy and bright.
Red is feeling brave
With all your might.
Red is a sunburn
Spot on your nose,
Sometimes red
Is a red, red rose.
Red squiggles out
When you cut your hand.
Red is a brick and
A rubber band.
Red is a hotness
You get inside
When you're embarrassed
And want to hide.

A brilliant red ribbon and rose frame the sensitive face of a young girl bravely meeting her world. Weisgard's illustrations reflect the imagery and symbolism of O'Neill's popular poems about color. From *Hailstones and Halibut Bones*, by Mary Le Duc O'Neill. Illustrated by Leonard Weisgard. Copyright © 1961 by Mary Le Duc O'Neill. Copyright © 1961 by Leonard Weisgard. Reprinted by permission of Doubleday & Company, Inc.

Eve Merriam has written a trilogy of books for children about the nature of poetry including *There Is No Rhyme for Silver, It Doesn't Always Have to Rhyme,* and *Catch a Little Rhyme.* Her poetry has a lilt and a bounce that will capture the most disinterested child's attention, beginning with "How to Eat a Poem." Such poems as "Metaphor," "Cliché," "Simile," and "Onomatopoeia" are excellent for the language class. The poems in *Catch a Little Rhyme* are for children in the primary grades. City boys and girls who are accustomed to slum clearance will appreciate "Bam Bam Bam." They will also enjoy the ironic twist to "The Stray Cat." Humor is found in "Teevee" and "Alligator on the Escalator." The poet would refer to these as "Rhymes for reasons and for none/Mainly just for having fun" (130).

Children of all ages have responded with enthusiasm to Mary O'Neill's poems about color in *Hailstones and Halibut Bones, Adventures in Color.* Using fresh imagery, the poet has explored the various sensory and emotional dimensions of each color, for example, "Green is an olive and a pickle. The sound of green is a water-trickle" and "Brown is cinnamon and morning toast and the good smell of the Sunday roast." This same poet has used a similar approach in her books *Words, Words, Words* and *What Is That Sound!* The first book contains poems about the history of the language, parts of speech, punctuation, and reflections upon particular meanings of words, for example, "Imagination is a new idea beginning to grow/In the warm, soft earth of all we know." The book on sounds is not up to her usual standard of work.

Anthologies of Poems for Children

General Anthologies Every teacher and family will want to have at least one excellent anthology of poetry for children. Before purchasing an anthology, the following questions should be considered in terms of your purposes for using the book:

- What is the age level appeal of this book?
- How many poems are included?
- What types of poems are included?
- How many poets are represented?
- What is the quality of the poetry?
- Are recent poems included as well as old favorites?
- What is the subject matter of the poems?
- How are the poems arranged and organized?
- How adequate are the indices in helping the reader find a poem?
- How helpful are the introduction and commentaries?
- Has the compiler achieved his stated or implied purpose in making the collection?
- Are the illustrations and format appropriate for the poems and age appeal of the collection?

Sung Under the Silver Umbrella includes some 200 choice poems for young children that were selected by a committee of the Association for Childhood Education International. A more recent and distinctive collection for young children appears in Thompson's *Poems to Grow On.* The format of this book and the selection of poems achieve a remarkable unity. It is unfortunate that in this collection the poets' names are only included in the table of contents and not directly under each poem. Even primary children should begin to associate poets with particular poems. Kindergarten and primary teachers find the Geismer and Suter book, *Very Young Verses,* quite useful. Prepared by two teachers, it supplies many poems that have proven appeal.

All the Silver Pennies incorporates two old favorites, *Silver Pennies* and *More Silver Pennies,* edited by Blanche Jennings Thompson. The commentaries on each of these poems contain excellent suggestions for either a teacher or children reading these poems. *Away We Go* contains 100 poems selected by Catherine McEwen to meet the needs of today's young child. The black and white illustrations by Barbara Cooney are as fresh and contemporary as the poems. *The Big Golden Book of Poetry* (by Werner) contains eighty-five childhood favorites including many of Stevenson, Walter de la Mare, Roberts, Rossetti, Aldis, and others equally well known. Some large, full-page color illustrations make this an attractive book for primary children to read themselves.

Nancy Larrick recently compiled a group of favorites for boys and girls in her collection *Piper, Pipe That Song Again!* Before she included any poem, she tested it in a school classroom to determine children's responses. It includes such favorites as "Isabel" by Ogden Nash, Austin's "Grizzly Bear" and "Daddy Fell into the Pond" by Alfred Noyes, as well as selections by de la Mare, Fisher, Field, Sandburg, Frost, and others. Another book that contains the tested favorites of children is *The First Book of Poetry* compiled by Peterson, a teacher in the Laboratory School of the University of Chicago. *The First Book of Short Verse* by Howard contains short poems by Frost, Sandburg, and many poems by children. The introduction on "Why People Write Poetry" and the discussion of various forms of poetry in the postscript would make this an extremely useful book for helping children in the middle grades write poetry. Nine- and ten-year-olds who may have just discovered the pleasure of reading poetry for themselves will appreciate both the price and the selection of poems in the *Arrow Book of Poetry*. This paperback collection was chosen by Ann McGovern and sells for only thirty-five cents. It contains poems about wishes and feelings, animals, weather and seasons, long ago, and town and city. Langston Hughes, Ciardi, Stephens, and McCord are a few of the poets represented in this excellent collection.

Teachers find Arbuthnot's *Time for Poetry* almost indispensable. This book contains an unexcelled collection of poems for all ages. Suggestions are given for the interpretation of some of the poems. *Favorite Poems Old and New* by Helen Ferris is another excellent general anthology for boys and girls. It does not include many poems for the very young child, but middle-grade children enjoy the narrative poems that are in this collection. Louis Untermeyer's anthology of poems, *The Golden Treasury of Poetry,* is beautifully illustrated by Joan Walsh Anglund. Untermeyer has written a commentary on each poem as he did in his other, older collections of *Stars to Steer by, This Singing World,* and *Rainbow in the Sky*. Untermeyer's collections rely upon many of the ballads, narrative poems such as "The Pied Piper of Hamelin," "Annabel Lee," and other old favorites. Few contemporary poets are included. This same criticism may be directed at the *Oxford Book of Poetry for Children* compiled by Edward Blishen and brilliantly illustrated by Brian Wildsmith. Here one may find the classic poetry for children: poems by Lear, Carroll, de la Mare, Masefield, Stevenson, even Shakespeare, Thackeray, and Shelley. Beautiful, quaint, old-fashioned illustrations harmonize with the rather nostalgic poetry selected by Tasha Tudor for *Wings from the Wind*. Blake's "Infant Joy," Longfellow's "The Children's Hour" and "The Village

Blacksmith," and Wordsworth's "Daffodils" are represented in this collection. However, poems by McCord, Coatsworth, Frost, and Field are included also. Walter de la Mare looked to the past as he selected poetry "that wears well" for his two anthologies *Tom Tiddler's Ground* and *Come Hither*. The first one ranges from a few Mother Goose rhymes to Tennyson, Keats, and Poe; while the second contains imaginative poems for young people and adults.

A discerning and most unusual collection of poems is McDonald's book, *A Way of Knowing*. These poems were selected particularly for boys. The book is not overloaded

The Golden Treasury of Poetry **is profusely illustrated by Joan Walsh Anglund, a versatile artist whose drawings change with the mood of the poem. In this sketch she conveys the excitement and danger of "The Highwayman."** From *The Golden Treasury of Poetry* compiled by Louis Untermeyer. Illustrated by Joan Walsh Anglund. Golden Press, 1959. © Copyright 1959 by Golden Press, Inc.

Tasha Tudor's quaint illustration reflects the old-fashioned feeling of Rachel Field's poem "The General Store" in *Wings from the Wind.* Illustration by Tasha Tudor for *Wings from the Wind* by Tasha Tudor. Copyright © 1964 by Tasha Tudor. Published by J. B. Lippincott Company.

with narrative poems; rather, the collection is varied, including light and serious, old and some very modern poetry. It is a book that speaks to girls and adults as well as boys. *An Inheritance of Poetry* by Adshead and Duff is a comprehensive volume of unusual poems. Its appeal will be for adolescents, however. An excellent collection, *This Way, Delight,* compiled by Herbert Read, will interest young people and also adults. It is for those discerning few who have developed a keen appreciation for poetry. Another anthology for this group is *Lean Out of the Window* by Hannum and Reed. It includes well-known poetry of the twentieth century.

The Golden Journey is a distinguished anthology compiled by two poets, Louise Bo-

gan and William Jay Smith. The title is derived from a modern poem entitled the "Golden Journey to Samarkan." In the introduction, the authors liken "the poet to a traveler whose itinerary covers every area of human experience from birth to death."[9] This "golden journey" is a lovely trip, and teachers and children will find much pleasure among the two hundred or so selections. The poems are arranged from the simplest to the more difficult and from the light, happy poems to the more serious. Categories include such interesting titles as "A Pea-Green Gamut/Country Poems," "The Dark Hills/War Poems," and "Lyrebird Country/Dreams and Fancies." Padraic Colum has selected poems for "those whose twentieth birthday is still before them" in his *Roofs of Gold, Poems to Be Read Aloud.* These include such well-known poems as "Ozymandias," "Kubla Khan," "Fern Hill," and "The Solitary Reaper." Except for the unusual child, these poems are more appropriate for junior high school. An exciting modern anthology for this age level is *Reflections on a Gift of Watermelon Pickle and Other Modern Verses* by Dunning, Lueders, and Smith. Illustrated with superb photographs, many of the poems would appeal to the middle-grade child; for example "Sonic Boom" by John Updike, "Ancient History" by Arthur Guiterman, "Dreams" by Langston Hughes, and "Valentine" by Donald Hall, to mention but a few. Elinor Parker has made a notable collection for young people in *The Singing and the Gold, Poems Translated from World Literature.* Taken from thirty-four languages, these poems show that man's thoughts and emotions are basically the same wherever he lives. He is a worshipping being, he venerates his country or tribe, cares for his friends, falls in love, responds to the beauties of nature and changing seasons, seeks solitude, and finally dies. Poetry celebrates it all.

---

[9]Louise Bogan and William Jay Smith, Compilers, *The Golden Journey, Poems for Young People,* Illustrated by Fritz Kredel (Chicago: Reilly & Lee, 1965), p. xvii.

Specialized Anthologies American genius for organization is apparent in the number of specialized anthologies of particular types of poems. They are most useful for reference and libraries, but teachers may want to own some of them.

William Cole has compiled many specialized anthologies. A poetry-picture book for younger children is his *I Went to the Animal Fair, A Book of Animal Poems.* It contains some thirty-five poems about animals. The fine-line illustrations on pale green pages by Colette Rosselli add much to the attractiveness of this book. Three humorous collections by Cole include *Oh What Nonsense!, Beastly Boys and Ghastly Girls,* and *Humorous Poetry for Children.* Cole deliberately left out the poems of Lear and Carroll in his nonsense book because they were so readily available in other books. Thus, he was able to include many contemporary poets not found in other collections. Illustrated by Tomi Ungerer, this book is guaranteed to tickle the funny bone of most readers from eight to eighty. Ungerer also illustrated *Beastly Boys and Ghastly Girls,* a collection of poems about children's misbehavior, a most popular subject with third and fourth graders. His *Humorous Poetry for Children* contains many amusing narrative poems. Cole has also edited *Story Poems New and Old, Poems of Magic and Spells, Poems for Seasons and Celebrations,* and *The Birds and Beasts Were There.* These books are attractively illustrated and focused around themes that have much appeal for children in the middle grades.

The Brewtons have made seven excellent anthologies that specialize in animals, people, joy and beauty, Christmas, seasons, and birthdays. The titles of their books are: *Under the Tent of the Sky, Gaily We Parade, Bridled with Rainbows, Christmas Bells Are Ringing, Sing a Song of Seasons, Birthday Candles Burning Bright,* and *Laughable Limericks.* These are discriminating collections that can prove to be particularly useful for teachers and librarians.

A PEA-GREEN GAMUT

Country Poems

Handsome green woodcuts decorate the section headings and suggest the views that may be seen on *The Golden Journey* through the land of poetry. Woodcut by Fritz Kredel, *The Golden Journey,* Reilly & Lee, Chicago.

Helen Siegl's distinguished woodcuts complement the selection of some 300 animal poems. Woodcut by Helen Siegl for *The Birds and the Beasts Were There* by William Cole, copyright © 1963 by William Cole. Reprinted by permission of The World Publishing Company.

Outstanding wood engravings illustrate a discriminating collection of poems about music and dance. Illustration by Clare Leighton (copyright © 1957 by Clare Leighton) in *Untune the Sky,* compiled by Helen Plotz. Thomas Y. Crowell Company, New York, publishers.

Ogden Nash has collected a sparkling group of humorous poems for his two anthologies for older children: *The Moon Is Shining Bright as Day* and *Everybody Ought to Know.* These include both contemporary poems and the old favorites.

Lillian Morrison has made three collections of popular "school verse" in *A Dillar, A Dollar, Yours Till Niagra Falls,* and *Touch Blue.* The first includes folk sayings about school, the second consists of verses usually found in autograph albums, and the third presents rhymes of spells and belief. In *Sprints and Distances, Sports in Poetry and Poetry in Sport,* she captures children's interest in distinctive poetry through their interest in sports. Almost every sport is represented, from baseball to falconry. Arranged by the sport, the collection includes poems culled from ancient and modern writers such as Virgil, Shakespeare, Stevenson, Ogden Nash, David McCord, and Robert Francis. Some of the poems are humorous, as "The Umpire," some adulatory, as "To Lou Gehrig," and some serious, as "To an Athlete Dying Young" by A. E. Housman. These poems are distinguished and might be the means of introducing fine poetry to boys who claim to dislike it.

Three distinctive and unusual poetry collections for older readers have been made by Helen Plotz. In *Imagination's Other Place,* she has presented poems written about science and mathematics. The subject matter includes poems on dinosaurs, astronomy, physics, chemistry, biology, and medicine. The emphasis is on modern poetry, but well-known poets of other eras are represented. In *Untune the Sky,* Plotz has presented lovely poems of music and dance. The third book is *The Earth Is the Lord's: Poems of the Spirit,* drawn from the inspirational literature of many ages and places. The handsome wood engravings by Clare Leighton are as distinctive as the poetry in these anthologies. Most of the poems are for the discerning student of poetry and the mature child.

Recent years have witnessed a revival of interest in Oriental poetry, particularly haiku. Children in the middle grades can appreciate the simplicity and deep meaning of many of these poems. Richard Lewis has included fresh and profound haiku by Issa, Basho, and Buson in his superb collection of Japanese and Chinese poetry in *The Moment of Wonder.* Following this publication, Lewis edited a much briefer book containing only twenty-three haiku. This book, *In a Spring Garden,* has been beautifully illustrated in full color by Ezra Jack Keats. In *Cricket Songs,*

Harry Behn translated over eighty haiku. The accompanying pictures are chosen from the works of Japanese masters and add to the Oriental flavor of this book. All these collections would stimulate children in the middle grades to write their own haiku.

Quite different from the delicate haiku are the virile Eskimo poems collected by Knud Rasmussen for *Beyond the High Hills: A Book of Eskimo Poems.* Many of these poems were originally songs chanted to celebrate a hunt or the return of the caribou in the spring. Some were simply songs of praise, the joy of greeting a new day, or meeting new friends. The Eskimo's traditional struggle against the elements is the theme of many of these poems, for example:

> There is joy in
> Feeling the warmth
> Come to the great world
> And seeing the sun
> Follow its old footprints
> In the summer night.

> There is fear in
> Feeling the cold
> Come to the great world
> And seeing the moon
> —Now new moon, now full moon—
> Follow its old footprints
> In the winter night. (154)

Superb full-color photographs add greatly to the appeal of this book.

The frog
Is having a staring match
With me.
—Issa

With collage and sparkling colors, Ezra Jack Keats' illustrations capture the joy and delight of some twenty haiku collected by Richard Lewis in the book *In a Spring Garden*. Reprinted from *In a Spring Garden* edited by Richard Lewis, illustrated by Ezra Jack Keats. Text © 1965 Richard Lewis. Pictures copyright © 1965 Ezra Jack Keats. Used by permission of the publisher, The Dial Press, Inc. Haiku by permission of The Hokuseido Press.

Collections of Poems Written by Children Creative teachers have always appreciated the writing and art of their own students. They have recognized that age alone does not make a poet, and that some of the creative talents of boys and girls deserve recognition.

Richard Lewis, an elementary teacher in New York City, decided to go around the world and make an international collection of the poems of children. He collected over 3000 poems from which he selected some

200 for his book entitled *Miracles*. The poems do seem almost miraculous in their insight and imagination. An eleven-year-old child from Australia wrote *"Poems"*:

        · · ·

> A good poem must haunt the heart
> And be heeded by the head of the
>   Hearer.
>
> PETER KELSO (109)

"Poems are friends" another spoke, and then added, "Some last." One eleven-year-old Australian child described a breeze this way:

> ### BREEZE
> *Gentle as a feather*
> *Cat quiet*
> *Snow soft*
> *Gentle, gentle as a feather*
> *Softer than snow*
> *Quiet as a cat*
> *Comes*
> *The evening breeze.*
> MARIE HOURIGAN (109)

Completely different in mood and purpose is the heartbreaking poetry of the children of the Terezín Concentration Camp. Published under the title . . . *I Never Saw Another Butterfly*, these poems and drawings are all that remain of the more than 15,000 children who passed through this concentration camp on their way to death from 1942 to 1944. These poems and pictures are filled with the horror of dirt, disease, and death, yet courage and optimism shine through some of them as in the poem "Homesick":

> . . .
> *People walk along the street,*
> *You see at once on each you meet*
> *That there's a ghetto here,*
> *A place of evil and of fear.*
> *There's little to eat and much to want,*
> *Where bit by bit, it's horror to live.*
> *But no one must give up!*
> *The world turns and times change.*
>
> *Yet we all hope the time will come*
> *When we'll go home again.*
> *Now I know how dear it is*
> *And often I remember it.*
> ANONYMOUS (100)

Some will say these poems are too grim for children, yet they were written by children. If the function of poetry is to communicate to the heart, the mind, and the spirit, then these poems have fulfilled this purpose.

Single Poem Editions Traditionally, poetry books have had few illustrations in order to enable the reader to create vivid images on the screen of his imagination. This concept has changed, and today we have such books as the *Oxford Book of Poetry*, profusely illustrated with Wildsmith's brilliant pictures. It was inevitable that poetry should follow the trend established by the publishing of many beautifully illustrated single fairy tales or folk songs.

Paul Galdone has lead the way in illustrating many books of a single narrative poem. Beginning with Lear's amusing tale of *Two Old Bachelors*, Galdone then illustrated three patriotic poems: *Paul Revere's Ride* by Longfellow, *Barbara Frietchie* by Whittier, and *The Battle of the Kegs* by Hopkinson. The stirring tale of how the colonists were warned by Paul Revere's midnight message is appropriately illustrated by Galdone's vigorous drawings in moonlit blues and blacks. During the preparations for the illustrations of this book, Galdone made a special trip to New England in the spring, the time of the ride, and traced Paul Revere's route through the villages. In *The Battle of the Kegs*, he has captured the rollicking good humor of the old Revolutionary ballad that told of the colonists' plan to float kegs of gunpowder down the Delaware River in order to damage the English ships. His illustrations for *Barbara Frietchie* portray the courage of that intrepid old lady who waved the Union flag in defiance of Stonewall Jackson's orders. Oliver Wendell Holmes wrote *The Deacon's Masterpiece or The Wonderful One-Hoss Shay* over a hundred years ago; but unlike the remarkable shay that was built to last a hundred years to a day and then went to pieces all at once, the original humor of this poem endures. The amusing illustrations add to the fun of this poem that defies obsolescence. By way of contrast, Galdone's illustrations for *Three Poems of Edgar Allen Poe* seem quite melodramatic. Perhaps the haunting love ballad of "Annabel Lee,"

All at once the horse stood still,
Close by the meet'n'-house on the hill.

Illustrated books of a single poem, folk tale, or song represent a recent trend in publishing. Here Paul Galdone's amusing illustrations add to the humor of a familiar poem. From *The Deacon's Masterpiece or The Wonderful One-Hoss Shay* by Oliver Wendell Holmes. Illustrated by Paul Galdone. Copyright © 1965 by Paul Galdone. Used by permission of McGraw-Hill Book Company.

terrifying rhythms of "The Raven," and singing repetition of "The Bells" demand such interpretation. Emotion is more difficult to portray than action, however. With these books, Galdone has established a trend for illustrating books of a single poem. These editions are popular with both teachers and children who find that the illustrations increase their enjoyment of the poems.

In *The Charge of the Light Brigade*, Tennyson paid tribute to the courageous, but hopeless, charge of the British troops in the Crimean War in 1854. Alice and Martin Provensen have caught the rigidity, nobility, and futility of this bloody massacre in their handsome stylized illustrations. The cover of the book is cleverly fashioned after a newspaper report of the tragic event.

There are two illustrated editions of the popular "Casey at the Bat" by Ernest Thayer. Paul Frame interpreted this poem with broad humor in comical, orange and black illustrations portraying baseball players of the 1880s. *The First Book Edition of Casey at the Bat* has been illustrated in bold, black-and-white drawings by Leonard Everett Fisher. Boys thoroughly enjoy both books.

Both boys and girls in the middle grades will like Longfellow's haunting poem *The Skeleton in Armor*, with dramatic illustrations by Paul Kennedy. This would be an excellent poem to follow the reading of Polland's *Beorn the Proud* or *Hakon of Rogen's Saga* (see Chapter 6).

These illustrated single editions attract some children to poetry who would never think of reading an anthology. For this reason, they have a definite place on the library and classroom shelf. This kind of treatment tends to be appropriate for only the longer narrative poems, however. Children should continue to be exposed to the balanced kind of collection found in most of the recognized general anthologies.

SHARING POETRY WITH CHILDREN

Introducing Poetry to Children

The Place of Poetry in the Classroom   One sixth-grade boy recalled that he had not heard any poetry since an aunt had read him Mother Goose. Most Americans don't read poetry—in fact, all too often, anyone who does is viewed with some suspicion. Consequently, few children will be introduced to poetry at home. If they are to develop an appreciation for this form of literature, it would seem that they must do so at school. Yet the schools have failed miserably in their presentation of poetry! Teachers have probably done more to mitigate against it than they have ever done to promote a love for it.

There are several ways in which schools have alienated children from poetry. In the first place, they may have been victims of poorly selected verse; poems about childhood rather than for children. Poetry must be suited to the modern child's maturity, experience, and interests. Children like short poems rather than overly long ones, poems portraying action rather than abstract ideas, and poems that have a marked rhyme and rhythm.

Another way to create distaste for poetry is by requiring memorization of certain poems, usually selected by the teacher. When everyone has to learn the same poem, it is especially dull. By the time a child has heard a poem thirty times "around the room," he has little desire to hear it again.

One teacher was known to keep a record of the number of lines of poetry each child learned. When the class had an "extra" three minutes, a child would be called upon to recite. The recitation would end with the bell, not the end of the poem; the lines were tabulated; the class went to recess. No meaning, no comment, any poem—what an effective way to kill poetry! Some teachers have assigned a poem for memorization as punishment; the worse the misdeed, the longer the poem! Actually, many children enjoy memorizing favorite poems provided they may select the poem. But choosing to commit a certain poem to memory is quite different from being required to do so.

Another way to kill poetry is with elocution. If a teacher reads poetry in an artificial, unnatural manner, children will think of it in this way. Teachers all too frequently persist in dropping their voices to a hushed whisper whenever they read poetry. Others massacre it with a singsong rhythm. Poetry needs to be presented naturally and joyously.

Too detailed analysis of every poem is also detrimental to children's enjoyment of it. An appropriate question or comment to increase meaning is fine, but critical analysis of every word in a poem, every figure of speech, and every iambic verse is lethal! Everyone knows that if the point of a joke has to be explained, it is no longer funny. If one has to explain a poem, its beauty and resultant mood will vanish.

Finally, some younger teachers who have become disgusted with poetry forever through their own experiences with it in school, tend to neglect poetry. They prefer to ignore it, claiming they have no time in the curriculum for it. Children then progress from Mother Goose in their preschool days to Shakespeare and Tennyson in high school!

Providing Time for Poetry   How, then, may the schools promote interest in poetry? They must seek to make it a natural part of the daily program of living and learning. To make poetry-loving children, teachers must provide time for poetry and read it often. When children ask to hear a poem again, the teacher should take time to reread it. Modern teachers help children memorize poems by honoring their requests for the frequent reading of favorites, rather than through required memorizations. The youngsters should not receive an overdose of poetry at one time, however. An hour of poetry on Friday afternoon can be deadly. It is far better to read a poem or two daily, before story hour, after recess, or during sharing period, than to read too much of it. Capitalizing on "the teachable moment" will build interest. The first day of snow, Henry's birthday party, the arrival of a new baby brother, are examples of opportunities that call for the spontaneous sharing of poetry.

The teacher will also plan specific sharing times. This will be a period in which children can ask to hear their favorite poems. It may be a time for middle-grade children to bring in their own favorites to read or to record on the tape recorder for future sharing. Children might do some choral reading or dramatizing of poetry during this planned-poetry period. Children need time to share their enthusiasm for poetry.

Another time to share poetry is in relationship to other studies. Poetry should be a part of all children's learning activities. Sandburg's "Arithmetic" (165) or Eleanor Farjeon's "Geography" (65) may be read to fourth- and fifth-graders. The Benéts' biographical poems lend themselves well to social studies. There is hardly a subject that cannot be enriched by the inclusion of poetry.

Promoting a Climate for Poetry Poetry, then, should be a natural part of the children's day. It should not be presented under the pressure of limited time or a rushed schedule. Children should be able to relax and enjoy the humor and beauty that the sharing of poetry affords.

The physical environment of the classroom may be conducive to developing an interest in poetry. The teacher or children may set up simple poetry displays with real objects that will recall the mood or subject of a well-loved poem. Favorite poems may be transferred to charts for younger children. Attractive poetry bulletin boards may be arranged.

Every classroom should have several poetry books available for use by both the children and the teacher. Frequently, young people will want to read poems first introduced by the teacher. Some classes set up their own poetry collections, filing and categorizing their favorite poems in a card file or notebook. Groups of children may enjoy collecting poems about particular subjects and comparing them. Others may prefer to collect the poems of a favorite poet. These collections or anthologies should be readily available for all to use.

Presenting Poetry to Children Poetry was meant to be read aloud. Some children do not have the skill in reading or the background of experience to read poetry effectively; and so teachers must read it to them. Some poems need little or no introduction, others are more appreciated if children have some clue about what is to follow. Occasionally, they like to know the circumstances that surrounded the writing of a poem; knowing another poem by the same author may help build background.

In selecting a poem for presentation, a teacher should consider children's background of experience with poetry and their interests, rather than relying upon graded poetry lists. Many poems have a wide age appeal; for example, almost all ages enjoy Richard's "The Monkeys and the Crocodile" (6). Not all children enjoy nonsense poems, but humorous poems have an almost universal appeal. Poems to be read should appeal to the teacher. Enthusiasm is contagious, but so is dislike. Poems with dialect should

The Sad Shoes

My shoes are lying on the floor.
They are not very new,
And I can't wear them any more
Because the holes came through.

They had a lovely time today
Scrabbling up a tree:
Tomorrow they'll be thrown away
And cannot play with me.

They won't be here to lace or clean.
I wonder if they know.
I think perhaps they do—they lean
Upon each other so.   Dorothy Aldis

Write a story about a pair of shoes.

What kind of shoes were they?

What experiences did they have?

Children's interest in poetry may be aroused by the use of real objects in a simple table display. Department of Photography, The Ohio State University.

be read only if the teacher feels comfortable reading them. For instance, the Italian dialect in "Leetla Giorgio Washeenton" (66) by Daly can be very effective if it is read well. The teacher can gain skill in oral interpretation by making tape recordings and evaluating the presentation.

In presenting poetry to children, the emphasis should be placed on the meaning of the poem rather than the rhyme. In this way, the singsong effect that is characteristic of most children's reading of poetry is avoided. Generally, the appropriate pace for reading poetry is slower than for reading prose. It is usually recommended that a poem be read aloud a second time, perhaps to refresh children's memories, to clarify a point, or to savor a particular image. Most poetry, especially good poetry, is so concentrated and compact that few people can

grasp its meaning in one exposure. Following the reading of a poem, discussion should be allowed to develop. In certain instances, discussion is unnecessary or superfluous. Spontaneous chuckles may follow the reading of Mary Austin's "Grizzly Bear" (66)—nothing more is needed. Sometimes a moment of silence is the greatest applause. It is valuable to record children's reactions to poetry in order to guide future selections.

Children Share Poetry

Individual Reading   Children gain a feeling of satisfaction and accomplishment from reading poetry well enough to hold the attention of classmates. Some may *choose* to memorize their poems for presentation. In either case, children should be helped to read or recite their poems in a way that will be interesting to the others. The teacher may talk with them about how to read poetry, placing the emphasis upon the meaning of the poem and not the rhyming scheme, interpreting the mood and expressing its rhythm. The important point to remember is that poetry should be read well, whether it is read by the children or by the teacher.

Choral Reading Choral speaking or reading is the interpretation of poetry by several voices speaking as one. At first, young children *speak* it as they join in the refrains. Middle-grade children may prefer to *read* their poems. Poems are not always read in unison; in fact, this is one of the most difficult ways to present a poem. Four types of choral speaking are particularly suited for use in the elementary school. In the first, the "refrain" type, one person (teacher or child) reads the narrative and the rest of the class joins in the refrain. Another way, called antiphonal, is to divide the class into two groups. For example, when reading Rose Fyleman's poem "Shop Windows" (6), the boys may read the lines that tell what men like, and the girls may read of women's preferences. The whole group may join in on the last part that tells of a child's interest in a pet shop window displaying puppy dogs. An effective approach with young children is the "line-a-child" arrangement where different children say, or read, individual lines, with the class joining in unison at the beginning or end of the poem. "One, Two, Buckle My Shoe" is a good rhyme to introduce this type of choral reading. The dialogue of David McCord's "At the Garden Gate" (123) lends itself to this approach for children in the middle grades. A more difficult and formal version of this method is part speaking. The groups are divided according to the sound of their voices into high, middle, and low parts. The poem is then interpreted much as a song might be set to music. This is usually done with mature groups, and is the method utilized by verse-speaking choirs.

Another difficult method is to have children say the whole poem in unison, giving just one interpretation. Many variations to these approaches will be used by creative teachers and children. A certain sound that complements both rhythm and meaning of the poem may be an accompaniment; for example, "clickety clack" from the sound of Tippett's "Trains" (89). One group may repeat this phrase as another group says the words of the poem. Another poem that provides an interesting sound is "What the Gray Cat Sings" (139) by Guiterman. Alternate groups or solo voices could say the verses with the entire class joining in the cat's weaving song, "Pr-rrum, pr-rrum, thr-ree, thr-reads, in the thr-rum, Pr-rrum!"

The values of choral reading are many. Children derive much enjoyment from learning to respond as a group to the rhythm and melody of the poem. They learn much about the interpretation of poetry as they help plan various ways to read the poem. Shy children forget their fears in participating with the group, and all children learn to develop cooperation as they work together to present a poem. It is important to remember that the *process* of choral reading is much more important than the final product. Teachers must work for the enjoyment of poetry, not perfection of performance. Too frequently, choral reading becomes a "stunt," or a quick way to entertain a P.T.A. group, but children's interpretation of poetry should be natural. If teachers and children are pressured for a "production," interpretation of poetry will be exploited for unnatural ends.

Boys and girls should have many opportunities to share poetry in interesting and meaningful situations if they are to develop appreciation for the deep satisfactions that poetry brings. Appreciation for poetry develops slowly. It is the result of careful cultivation over a period of years. Children who are fortunate enough to have developed a love of poetry will always be the richer for it.

SUGGESTED ACTIVITIES

1. Begin a poetry collection for future use with children. Make your own system of filing. What categories will you include? Indicate possible uses for some poems.
2. Make a study of one poet. How would you characterize his work both as to style and usual content? What can you find out about his background? How are these experiences reflected in his poetry?
3. Bring your favorite children's poem to present to the class or to tape record. Class members should evaluate the selection and presentation.
4. Select three different kinds of poems and read them to a group of children. Record their reactions. What poems had the greatest appeal? Why?
5. Plan an interesting way to introduce a poem to a group of children. This might be a bulletin board display, a table exhibit, a mobile, or plans for pantomiming the poem.
6. Compare two general anthologies of poetry, using criteria suggested.
7. Select several poems that you think would lend themselves to choral reading. Work with a group of children or classmates in planning ways to present one of these poems. If possible, tape record these interpretations.
8. Interview several teachers to see how they utilize poetry in the classroom. How often do they read poetry? What are their favorite poems? What sources do they use?
9. Listen to some recordings of poetry read by authors and by interpreters. Contrast the presentations and appropriateness of the records for classroom use.

RELATED READINGS

1. Arbuthnot, May Hill. *Children and Books.* Third edition. Glenview, Ill.: Scott, Foresman, 1964.
   Chapters 5, 6, 7, and 8 present a comprehensive overview of children's poetry. Chapter 9 gives many suggestions for choral speaking and verse choirs.
2. Arnstein, Flora J. *Poetry in the Elementary Classroom.* New York: Appleton, 1962.
   This is a fascinating account of one teacher's techniques in encouraging children to create poetry. Many of the children's original poems are included and might inspire other children to try writing poetry. Arnstein's discussion of poetry will help an adult to recognize many of the qualities of fine poetry.
3. Perrine, Laurence. *Sound and Sense, an Introduction to Poetry.* Second edition. New York: Harcourt, 1963.
   This is a college text for the serious student of poetry. Separate chapters introduce the student to the elements of poetry, putting the emphasis on *how* and *why.*
4. Read, Herbert, Compiler. *This Way, Delight.* Illustrated by Juliet Kepes. New York: Pantheon, 1956.
   Sir Herbert Read discusses "What Is Poetry?" on pages 137–143 in this excellent anthology for young people. The author defines poetry and describes imagery, metaphors and the sounds of poetry. He gives suggestions for writing poetry.
5. Sandburg, Carl. *Early Moon.* Illustrated by James Daugherty. New York: Harcourt, 1930.
   In his "Short Talk on Poetry" in the introduction to this book, Carl Sandburg discusses what poetry is and why we like it. He suggests ways to develop an appreciation for poetry and to help children write poetry. Children in the middle grades would benefit from hearing this "Short Talk on Poetry." The poet recorded it on the Caedmon record, *Carl Sandburg Reads His Poems to Children.*
6. Walter, Nina Willis. *Let Them Write Poetry.* New York: Holt, Rinehart and Winston, 1962.
   This author feels that poetry appreciation may only be achieved as the child becomes the poet. Chapter 2 on "The Teaching of Poetry" gives excellent principles for the selection of poetry for children. Chapter 8, "Evaluating the Poetry of Children," lists characteristics against which a child's poem may be evaluated.

CHAPTER REFERENCES

1. Adshead, Gladys L., and Annis Duff, Compilers. *An Inheritance of Poetry.* Illustrated by Nora S. Unwin. Boston: Houghton Mifflin, 1948.
2. Aiken, Conrad. *Cats and Bats and Things with Wings.* Illustrated by Milton Glaser. New York: Atheneum, 1965.
3. Aldis, Dorothy. *All Together.* Illustrated by Marjorie Flack, Margaret Frieman, and Helen D. Jameson. New York: Putnam, 1925.
4. ————*Hello Day.* Illustrated by Susan Elson. New York: Putnam, 1959.
5. ————*Quick as a Wink.* Illustrated by Peggy Westphal. New York: Putnam, 1960.
6. Arbuthnot, May Hill, Editor. *Time for Poetry.* Illustrated by Arthur Paul. Glenview, Ill.: Scott, Foresman, 1952.
7. Association for Childhood Education, Literature Committee. *Sung Under the Silver Umbrella.* Illustrated by Dorothy Lathrop. New York: Macmillan, 1936.
8. Austin, Mary. *The Children Sing in the Far West.* Boston: Houghton Mifflin, 1928.
9. Austin, Mary C., and Queenie B. Mills, Compilers, *The Sound of Poetry.* Boston: Allyn and Bacon, 1963.
10. Baruch, Dorothy. *I Would Like to Be a Pony and Other Wishes.* Illustrated by Mary Chalmers. New York: Harper & Row, 1959.
11. Behn, Harry. *All Kinds of Time.* New York: Harcourt, 1950.
12. ————Compiler. *Cricket Songs.* New York: Harcourt, 1964.
13. ————*The Golden Hive.* New York: Harcourt, 1966.
14. ————*The House Beyond the Meadow.* New York: Pantheon, 1955.
15. ————*The Little Hill.* New York: Harcourt, 1949.
16. ————*Windy Morning.* New York: Harcourt, 1953.
17. ————*The Wizard in the Well.* New York: Harcourt, 1956.
18. Benét, Rosemary and Stephen Vincent. *A Book of Americans.* Illustrated by Charles Child. New York: Holt, Rinehart and Winston, 1933.
19. Blake, William. *Songs of Innocence.* Music and illustrated by Ellen Raskin. New York: Doubleday, 1966.
20. Blishen, Edward, Compiler. *Oxford Book of Poetry for Children.* Illustrated by Brian Wildsmith. New York: F. Watts, 1963.
21. Bogan, Louise, and William Jay Smith, Compilers. *The Golden Journey: Poems for Young People.* Illustrated by Fritz Kredel. Chicago: Reilly & Lee, 1965.
22. Brewton, Sara and John E., Compilers. *Birthday Candles Burning Bright.* Illustrated by Vera Bock. New York: Macmillan, 1960.
23. ————*Bridled with Rainbows.* Illustrated by Vera Bock. New York: Macmillan, 1949.
24. ————*Christmas Bells Are Ringing.* Illustrated by Decie Merwin. New York: Macmillan, 1951.
25. ————*Gaily We Parade.* Illustrated by Robert Lawson. New York: Macmillan, 1940.
26. ————*Laughable Limericks.* Illustrated by Ingrid Fetz. New York: Crowell, 1965.
27. ————*Sing a Song of Seasons.* Illustrated by Vera Bock. New York: Macmillan, 1955.
28. ————*Under the Tent of the Sky.* Illustrated by Robert Lawson. New York: Macmillan, 1937.
29. Brooks, Gwendolyn. *Bronzeville Boys and Girls.* Illustrated by Ronni Solbert. New York: Harper & Row, 1965.
30. Brown, Beatrice. *Jonathan Bing and Other Verses.* New York: Oxford, 1936.
31. Brown, Margaret Wise. *Nibble Nibble.* Illustrated by Leonard Weisgard. New York: W. R. Scott, 1960.
32. Browning, Robert. *The Pied Piper of Hamelin.* Illustrated by Harold Jones. New York: F. Watts, 1962.
33. Carroll, Lewis. *Alice's Adventures in Wonderland* and *Through the Looking Glass.* Illustrated by John Tenniel. New York: Macmillan, 1956, 1923, 1865.

34. Chute, Marchette. *Around and About.* New York: Dutton, 1957.
35. Ciardi, John. *I Met a Man.* Illustrated by Robert Osborn. Boston: Houghton Mifflin, 1961.
36. ———*The Man Who Sang the Sillies.* Illustrated by Edward Gorey. Philadelphia: Lippincott, 1961.
37. ———*The Monster Den.* Illustrated by Edward Gorey. Philadelphia: Lippincott, 1966.
38. ———*The Reason for the Pelican.* Illustrated by Madeleine Gekiere. Philadelphia: Lippincott, 1959.
39. ———*You Know Who.* Illustrated by Edward Gorey. Philadelphia: Lippincott, 1964.
40. ———*You Read to Me and I'll Read to You.* Illustrated by Edward Gorey. Philadelphia: Lippincott, 1962.
41. Coatsworth, Elizabeth. *Mouse Chorus.* Illustrated by Genevieve Vaughan-Jackson. New York: Pantheon, 1955.
42. ———*The Peaceable Kingdom.* Illustrated by Fritz Eichenberg. New York: Pantheon, 1958.
43. ———*Poems.* Illustrated by Vee Guthrie. New York: Macmillan, 1958.
44. ———*The Sparrow Bush.* Illustrated by Stefan Martin. New York: Norton, 1966.
45. ———*Summer Green.* Illustrated by Nora Unwin. New York: Macmillan, 1948.
46. Cole, William, Compiler. *Beastly Boys and Ghastly Girls.* Illustrated by Tomi Ungerer. Cleveland: World Publishing, 1964.
47. ———*The Birds and Beasts Were There.* Illustrated by Helen Siegl. Cleveland: World Publishing, 1963.
48. ———*Humorous Poetry for Children.* Illustrated by Ervine Metzl. Cleveland: World Publishing, 1955.
49. ———*I Went to the Animal Fair.* Illustrated by Colette Rosselli. Cleveland: World Publishing, 1958.
50. ———*Oh What Nonsense!.* Illustrated by Tomi Ungerer. New York: Viking, 1966.
51. ———*Poems of Magic and Spells.* Illustrated by Peggy Bacon. Cleveland: World Publishing, 1960.
52. ———*Poems for Seasons and Celebrations.* Illustrated by Johannes Troyer. Cleveland: World Publishing, 1961.
53. ———*Story Poems, New and Old.* Illustrated by Walter Buehr. Cleveland: World Publishing, 1957.
54. Colum, Padraic. *Roofs of Gold, Poems to Read Aloud.* New York: Macmillan, 1964.
55. Conkling, Hilda. *Poems by a Little Girl.* Philadelphia: Stokes, 1920.
56. De la Mare, Walter. *Bells and Grass.* Illustrated by Dorothy Lathrop. New York: Viking, 1963, 1942.
57. ———Compiler. *Come Hither.* Illustrated by Warren Chappell. New York: Knopf, 1957.
58. ———*Peacock Pie.* Illustrated by W. Heath Robinson. New York: Holt, Rinehart and Winston, 1929.
59. ———*Peacock Pie.* Illustrated by Barbara Cooney. New York: Knopf, 1961.
60. ———*Rhymes and Verses, Collected Poems for Young People.* Illustrated by Elinore Blaisdell. New York: Holt, Rinehart and Winston, 1947.
61. ———Compiler. *Tom Tiddler's Ground.* Illustrated by Margery Gill. New York: Knopf, 1961.
62. De Regniers, Beatrice Schenk. *Something Special.* Illustrated by Irene Haas. New York: Harcourt, 1958.
63. Dunning, Stephen, Edward Lueders, and Hugh Smith. *Reflections on a Gift of Watermelon Pickle . . . .* Glenview, Ill.: Scott, Foresman, 1966.
64. Farjeon, Eleanor. *The Children's Bells.* New York: Walck, 1960.
65. ———*Eleanor Farjeon's Poems for Children.* Philadelphia: Lippincott, 1951, 1926.
66. Ferris, Helen, Compiler. *Favorite Poems Old and New.* Illustrated by Leonard Weisgard. New York: Doubleday, 1957.

67. Field, Rachel. *Poems*. New York: Macmillan, 1951.
68. ————*The Pointed People*. New York: Macmillan, 1933.
69. ————*Taxis and Toadstools*. New York: Doubleday, 1926.
70. Fish, Helen Dean, Compiler. *Boys' Book of Verse, an Anthology*. Philadelphia: Lippincott, 1951.
71. Fisher, Aileen. *Cricket in a Thicket*. Illustrated by Feodor Rojankovsky. New York: Scribner, 1963.
72. ————*Going Barefoot*. Illustrated by Adrienne Adams. New York: Crowell, 1960.
73. ————*I Like Weather*. Illustrated by Janina Domanska. New York: Crowell, 1963.
74. ————*In the Middle of the Night*. Illustrated by Adrienne Adams. New York: Crowell, 1965.
75. ————*In the Woods, In the Meadow, In the Sky*. Illustrated by Margot Tomes. New York: Scribner, 1965.
76. ————*Like Nothing At All*. Illustrated by Leonard Weisgard. New York: Crowell, 1962.
77. ————*Listen, Rabbit*. Illustrated by Symeon Shimin. New York: Crowell, 1964.
78. ————*Runny Days, Sunny Days*. New York: Abelard-Schuman, 1933.
79. ————*That's Why*. Camden, N.J.: Nelson, 1946.
80. ————*Where Does Everyone Go?* Illustrated by Adrienne Adams. New York: Crowell, 1961.
81. Frost, Frances. *The Little Naturalist*. Illustrated by Kurt Werth. New York: Whittlesey, 1959.
82. ————*The Little Whistler*. Illustrated by Roger Duvoisin. New York: Whittlesey, 1949.
83. ————*Pool in the Meadow*. Boston: Houghton Mifflin, n.d.
84. Frost, Robert. *In the Clearing*. New York: Holt, Rinehart and Winston, 1962.
85. ————*You Come Too*. Illustrated by Thomas W. Nason. New York: Holt, Rinehart and Winston, 1959.
86. Fyleman, Rose. *Fairies and Chimneys*. New York: Doubleday, 1929.
87. Gasztold, Carmen Bernos de. *Prayers from the Ark*. Translated by Rumer Godden. Illustrated by Jean Primrose. New York: Viking, 1962.
88. Gay, Zhenya. *Jingle Jangle*. New York: Viking, 1953.
89. Geismer, Barbara Peck, and Antoinette Brown Suter. *Very Young Verses*. Illustrated by Mildred Bronson. Boston: Houghton Mifflin, 1945.
90. Graham, Harry. *Ruthless Rhymes for Heartless Homes and More Ruthless Rhymes for Heartless Homes*. New York: Dover, 1961, 1930, 1899.
91. Hannum, Sara, and Gwendolyn E. Reid, Compilers. *Lean Out of the Window*. Illustrated by Ragna Tischler. New York: Atheneum, 1965.
92. Hoberman, Mary Ann. *Hello and Good-by*. Illustrated by Norman Hoberman. Boston: Little, Brown, 1959.
93. Holmes, Oliver Wendell. *The Deacon's Masterpiece or the Wonderful One-Hoss Shay*. Illustrated by Paul Galdone. New York: McGraw-Hill: 1965, 1858.
94. Hopkinson, Francis. *The Battle of the Kegs*. Illustrated by Paul Galdone. New York: Crowell, 1964.
95. Howard, Coralie, Compiler. *The First Book of Short Verse*. Illustrated by Mamoru Funai. New York: F. Watts, 1964.
96. Hubbell, Patricia. *The Apple Vendor's Fair*. Illustrated by Julie Maas. New York: Atheneum, 1963.
97. ————*8 A.M. Shadows*. Illustrated by Julie Maas. New York: Atheneum, 1965.
98. Huffard, Grace T., *et al.*, Compilers. *My Poetry Book*. Illustrated by Willy Pogany. Revised edition. New York: Holt, Rinehart and Winston, 1956.
99. Hughes, Langston. *The Dream Keeper and Other Poems*. New York: Knopf, 1945.
100. . . . *I Never Saw Another Butterfly*. Children's Drawings and Poems from Theresienstadt Concentration Camp 1942–1944. New York: McGraw-Hill, 1964.

101. *Japanese Haiku.* Translated by Peter Beilenson. New York: Peter Pauper, 1955–1956.
102. Kuskin, Karla. *Alexander Soames, His Poems.* New York: Harper & Row, 1962.
103. ———*In the Middle of the Trees.* New York: Harper & Row, 1958.
104. ———*Sand and Snow.* New York: Harper & Row, 1965.
105. Larrick, Nancy, Compiler. *Piper, Pipe That Song Again!* Illustrated by Kelly Oechsli. New York: Random House, 1965.
106. Lear, Edward. *The Complete Nonsense Book.* New York: Dodd, Mead, 1946.
107. ———*The Two Old Bachelors.* Illustrated by Paul Galdone. New York: Whittlesey, 1962.
108. Lewis, Richard, Compiler. *In a Spring Garden.* Illustrated by Ezra Jack Keats. New York: Dial, 1965.
109. ———*Miracles, Poems by Children of the English-Speaking World.* New York: Simon & Schuster, 1966.
110. ———*The Moment of Wonder.* New York: Dial, 1964.
111. Livingston, Myra Cohn. *Happy Birthday.* Illustrated by Erik Blegvad. New York: Harcourt, 1964.
112. ———*I'm Hiding.* Illustrated by Erik Blegvad. New York: Harcourt, 1961.
113. ———*I'm Not Me.* Illustrated by Erik Blegvad. New York: Harcourt, 1963.
114. ———*I'm Waiting.* Illustrated by Erik Blegvad. New York: Harcourt, 1966.
115. ———*The Moon and a Star.* Illustrated by Judith Shahn. New York: Harcourt, 1965.
116. ———*See What I Found.* Illustrated by Erik Blegvad. New York: Harcourt, 1962.
117. ———*Whispers.* Illustrated by Jacqueline Chwast. New York: Harcourt, 1958.
118. ———*Wide Awake.* Illustrated by Jacqueline Chwast. New York: Harcourt, 1959.
119. Longfellow, Henry Wadsworth. *Paul Revere's Ride.* Illustrated by Paul Galdone. New York: Crowell, 1963.
120. ———*The Skeleton in Armor.* Illustrated by Paul Kennedy. Engelwood Cliffs, N.J.: Prentice-Hall, 1963.
121. Love, Katherine, Compiler. *A Little Laughter.* Illustrated by Walter Lorraine. New York: Crowell, 1957.
122. McCord, David. *All Day Long.* Illustrated by Henry B. Kane. Boston: Little, Brown, 1965.
123. ———*Far and Few.* Illustrated by Henry B. Kane. Boston: Little, Brown, 1952.
124. ———*Take Sky.* Illustrated by Henry B. Kane. Boston: Little, Brown, 1961.
125. McDonald, Gerald D., Compiler. *A Way of Knowing.* Illustrated by Clare and John Ross. New York: Crowell, 1959.
126. McEwen, Catherine Schaefer, Compiler. *Away We Go!* Illustrated by Barbara Cooney. New York: Crowell, 1956.
127. McGovern, Ann. *Arrow Book of Poetry.* Illustrated by Grisha Dotzenko. New York: Scholastic, 1965.
128. Merriam, Eve. *Catch a Little Rhyme.* Illustrated by Imero Gobbato. New York: Atheneum, 1966.
129. ———*It Doesn't Always Have to Rhyme.* Illustrated by Malcolm Spooner. New York: Atheneum, 1964.
130. ———*There Is No Rhyme for Silver.* Illustrated by Joseph Schindelman. New York: Atheneum, 1962.
131. Milne, A. A. *Now We Are Six.* Illustrated by E. H. Shepard. New York: Dutton, 1927.
132. ———*When We Were Very Young.* Illustrated by E. H. Shepard. New York: Dutton, 1924.
133. ———*The World of Christopher Robin.* Illustrated by E. H. Shepard. New York: Dutton, 1958.
134. Morrison, Lillian, Compiler. *A Diller, a Dollar, Rhymes and Sayings for the Ten O'clock Scholar.* Illustrated by Marjorie Bauernschmidt. New York: Crowell, 1955.
135. ———*Sprints and Distances, Sports in Poetry and Poetry in Sports.* Illustrated by Clare

and John Ross. New York: Crowell, 1965.

136. ———*Touch Blue.* Illustrated by Doris Lee. New York: Crowell, 1958.

137. ———*Yours Till Niagara Falls.* Illustrated by Marjorie Bauernschmidt. New York: Crowell, 1950.

138. Nash, Ogden, Compiler. *Everybody Ought to Know.* Illustrated by Rose Shirvanian. Philadelphia: Lippincott, 1961.

139. ———*The Moon Is Shining Bright as Day.* Philadelphia: Lippincott, 1953.

140. O'Neill, Mary. *Hailstones and Halibut Bones.* Illustrated by Leonard Weisgard. New York: Doubleday, 1961.

141. ———*People I'd Like to Keep.* Illustrated by Paul Galdone. New York: Doubleday, 1964.

142. ———*What Is That Sound!* Illustrated by Lois Ehbert. New York: Atheneum, 1966.

143. ———*Words Words Words.* Illustrated by Judy Piussi-Campbell. New York: Doubleday, 1966.

144. Parker, Elinor. *The Singing and the Gold, Poems Translated from World Literature.* Illustrated by Clare Leighton. New York: Crowell, 1962.

145. Petersham, Maud and Miska. *The Rooster Crows.* New York: Macmillan, 1945.

146. Peterson, Isabel J., Compiler. *The First Book of Poetry.* Illustrated by Kathleen Elgin. New York: F. Watts, 1954.

147. Plotz, Helen, Compiler. *The Earth Is the Lord's.* Illustrated by Clare Leighton. New York: Crowell, 1965.

148. ———, Editor. *Imagination's Other Place.* Illustrated by Clare Leighton. New York: Crowell, 1955.

149. ———, Editor. *Poems of Emily Dickinson.* Illustrated by Robert Kipniss. New York: Crowell, 1964.

150. ———, Editor. *Untune the Sky.* Illustrated by Clare Leighton. New York: Crowell, 1957.

151. Poe, Edgar Allen. *Three Poems of Edgar Allen Poe.* Illustrated by Paul Galdone. New York: McGraw-Hill, 1966.

152. Potter, Charles. *Tongue Tanglers.* Illustrated by William Wiesner. Cleveland: World Publishing, 1962.

153. ———*More Tongue Tanglers and a Rigmarole.* Cleveland: World Publishing, 1964.

154. Rasmussen, Knud. *Beyond the High Hills: a Book of Eskimo Poems.* Photos by Guy Mary-Roussilière. Cleveland: World Publishing, 1961.

155. Read, Herbert Edward, Compiler. *This Way, Delight.* Illustrated by Juliet Kepes. New York: Pantheon, 1956.

156. Reeves, James. *The Blackbird in the Lilac.* Illustrated by Edward Ardizzone. New York: Dutton, 1959.

157. ———*Prefabulous Animiles.* Illustrated by Edward Ardizzone. New York: Dutton, 1960.

158. ———*The Wandering Moon.* New York: Dutton, 1960.

159. Richards, Laura E. *Tirra Lirra.* Illustrated by Marguerite Davis. New edition. Boston: Little, Brown, 1955, 1932.

160. Rieu, E. V. *The Flattered Flying Fish and Other Poems.* Illustrated by E. H. Shepard. New York: Dutton, 1962.

161. Roberts, Elizabeth Madox. *Under the Tree.* Illustrated by F. D. Bedford. New York: Viking, 1930.

162. Rossetti, Christina. *Sing-Song.* Illustrated by Marguerite Davis. New York: Macmillan, 1924.

163. Sandburg, Carl. *The American Songbag.* New York: Harcourt, 1927.

164. ———*Early Moon.* Illustrated by James Daugherty. New York: Harcourt, 1930.

165. ———*Wind Song.* Illustrated by William A. Smith. New York: Harcourt, 1960.

166. Sechrist, Elizabeth Hough, Compiler. *One Thousand Poems for Children.* Illustrated by Henry C. Pitz. Philadelphia: Macrae, 1946.

167. Sheldon, William, Nellie Lyons, and Polly Rouault, Compilers. *The Reading of Poetry*. Boston: Allyn and Bacon, 1963.

168. Smith, William Jay. *Boy Blue's Book of Beasts*. Illustrated by Juliet Kepes. Boston: Little, Brown, 1956.

169. ———*Laughing Time*. Illustrated by Juliet Kepes. Boston: Little, Brown, 1953.

170. ———*Typewriter Town*. New York: Dutton, 1960.

171. Starbird, Kaye. *Don't Ever Cross a Crocodile*. Illustrated by Kit Dalton. Philadelphia: Lippincott, 1963.

172. ———*A Snail's a Failure Socially*. Illustrated by Kit Dalton. Philadelphia: Lippincott, 1966.

173. ———*Speaking of Cows*. Illustrated by Rita Fava. Philadelphia: Lippincott, 1960.

174. Stevenson, Robert Louis. *A Child's Garden of Verses*. Illustrated by Brian Wildsmith. New York: F. Watts, 1966.

175. ———*A Child's Garden of Verses*. Illustrated by Tasha Tudor. New York: Oxford, 1947.

176. Stoutenberg, Adrien. *The Things That Are*. Chicago: Reilly & Lee, 1964.

177. Teasdale, Sara. *Stars To-night*. Illustrated by Dorothy Lathrop. New York: Macmillan. 1954.

178. Tennyson, Alfred Lord. *The Charge of the Light Brigade*. Illustrated by Alice and Martin Provensen. New York: Golden Press, 1964.

179. Thayer, Ernest L. *Casey at the Bat*. Illustrated by Paul Frame. Engelwood Cliffs, N.J.: Prentice-Hall, 1964.

180. ———*The First Book Edition of Casey at the Bat*. Introduction by Casey Stengel. Illustrated by Leonard Everett Fisher. New York: F. Watts, 1964.

181. Thompson, Blanche Jennings, Compiler. *All the Silver Pennies*. New York: Macmillan, 1967.

182. Thompson, Jean McKee, Compiler. *Poems to Grow On*. Illustrated by Gobin Stair. Boston: Beacon, 1957.

183. Tippett, James. *I Go A-Traveling*. Illustrated by Elizabeth T. Wolcott. New York: Harper & Row, 1929.

184. ———*I Live in a City*. New York: Harper & Row, 1927.

185. ———*I Spend the Summer*. New York: Harper & Row, 1930.

186. Tudor, Tasha, Compiler. *Wings from the Wind*. Philadelphia: Lippincott, 1964.

187. Untermeyer, Louis, Compiler. *The Golden Treasury of Poetry*. Illustrated by Joan Walsh Anglund. New York: Golden Press, 1959.

188. ———*The Magic Circle: Stories and People in Poetry*. Illustrated by Beth and Joe Krush. New York: Harcourt, 1952.

189. ———*Rainbow in the Sky*. Illustrated by Reginald Birch. New York: Harcourt, 1935.

190. ———*Stars To Steer By*. Illustrated by Dorothy Bayley. New York: Harcourt, 1941.

191. ———*This Singing World*. New York: Harcourt, 1923.

192. Unternecker, John. *The Dreaming Zoo*. Illustrated by George Weinheimer. New York: Walck, 1965.

193. Welles, Winifred. *Skipping Along Alone*. New York: Macmillan, 1931.

194. Werner, Jane, Compiler. *The Big Golden Book of Poetry*. Illustrated by Gertrude Elliott. New York: Golden Press, 1949.

195. Whittier, John Greenleaf. *Barbara Frietchie*. Illustrated by Paul Galdone. New York: Crowell, 1965.

196. Withers, Carl, Compiler. *A Rocket in My Pocket*. Illustrated by Susanne Suba. New York: Holt, Rinehart and Winston, 1948.

197. Wood, Ray, Compiler. *The American Mother Goose*. Illustrated by Ed Hargis. Philadelphia: Lippincott, 1938.

198. ———*Fun in American Folk Rhyme*. Illustrated by Ed Hargis. Philadelphia: Lippincott, 1952.

INFORMATIONAL BOOKS

Students in the Children's Literature class were meeting in small groups and sharing books. As future elementary teachers and librarians, they were both enthusiastic and critical. One announced, "I have a beautifully illustrated science book to show. The call number is 595.7, p, and the title is *The Life of a Queen*. It tells about the ant, her marriage flight, the way she lays eggs, how the workers hatch and build the city. Aren't these illustrations cute? The queen is shown in an iron bed with a quilt of many colors, and the cocoons are in a cradle. The children will learn about the way ants use lice, and I think modern children would think it was really funny to read this part:

But one day a sweet fragrance floats up to the ants' doorway. It is the aroma of the blue plant-lice, from whose bodies drip an intoxicating juice. Out rush the ants. They round up the plant-lice, and herd them about like cattle. And they milk them. Then by the hour they sit and sip the intoxicating nectar. Their thirst cannot be satisfied. Even the guards at the gate get drunk, and soon there is wild disorder through all the tunnels and rooms of the realm.[1]

"Here they are carrying pails of nectar, just like milk-pails, here is the bar, and I think children would laugh at the guards falling down. The language is rather poetic fantasy, yet children would get facts, too."

---

[1]Colette Portal, *The Life of a Queen*, Translated by Marcia Nardi (New York: Braziller, 1964), unpaged.

445

"But wouldn't this confuse children?" questioned one of her friends. "I think it's a mixture of fantasy and fact, and surely more fantasy."

"I don't see how you could call it science when it portrays ants with such human qualities," commented another future teacher.

"This is what anthropomorphism really is!" exclaimed one of the fellows in the group.

"When illustrations are so filled with fantasy they are surely not teaching children to observe," added a future school librarian.

"Is this book even good fantasy?" queried another member of the group.

These students were engaged in a significant discussion of informational books. They were looking beyond the "cute" and "colorful" by applying criteria for informational books to titles in their library. By comparing the mediocre and poor with the good and outstanding, they were gaining the skills and understandings needed in their future work.

When the classroom teacher or librarian looks at the shelves of informational books now available, and thinks of the publications pouring from the presses each year, he feels overwhelmed by the immensity of the task of becoming familiar with these materials of instruction. The teacher is challenged to select new books, and to use a wide variety as he plans the teaching-learning activities. Before he begins to teach, he should become aware of criteria for evaluating informational books, be familiar with aids that will help him locate materials for a teaching-learning unit, learn to use reviewing sources, become acquainted with the types of informational books, and gain skill in evaluation by reading books on at least one topic.

GUIDES FOR EVALUATING INFORMATIONAL BOOKS

The following questions will help teachers and librarians evaluate informational books. No hierarchy of values is implied in the order of presentation, although accuracy may be deemed more important than criteria of organization. The reviewer will need to judge the various elements; there is no definite "scoring," for a book's major strengths may far outweigh the few weaknesses identified.

Accuracy and Authenticity

What Are the Qualifications of the Author? Informational books are written by people who are authorities in their fields, or they are written by writers who study a subject, interview specialists, and compile the data. A few are both specialists and writers; people who are interested in, and understand, children, know the subject, and have the ability to write in a clear and interesting style.

It is difficult for the teacher or librarian to judge the qualifications of an author. In writing of a foreign country, for example, who is best qualified—the person who travels there, and observes, and interviews; the person who lives there for several years; or the native who may be familiar with only one section or who may be biased by his own social class or viewpoint? The background of the traveler, his work in other countries, his general knowledge may make him an excellent observer and interpreter of that country. He also has knowledge of the audience for which he writes. If the work is prepared by a "writer," facts can be checked by authorities and the authority cited. Ravielli's

Elephants, the Last of the Land Giants was checked by the curator of mammals of the New York Zoological Park. For a series, *Natural Science Picture Books,* Dr. Gwynne Vevers, Curator of the Aquarium, The Zoological Society of London, is listed as the science advisor. One of this series, *The Big Cats,* by Morris, shows how the big cats feed and live in zoos, as contrasted with their natural environment. It should be recognized that authorities hold different views, especially regarding theoretical positions. Thus, a competent person might produce a book that would be held in error, in whole or part, by another. Competence in one field does not bring equal competence in another field. If the author has limited his book to what appears to be his field, it would seem the book should have a high degree of authenticity. For example, William E. Scheele, director of Cleveland's Museum of Natural History, has written a book, *The Mound Builders.* As he describes the Ohio mounds of the Hopewell Indians, he carefully limits his report to mounds and artifacts that have been found, shows how a theory has developed about these people, and indicates how little we know. This is an example of good science writing by a qualified person.

To a great degree, the teacher and librarian must rely upon reviews by competent science reviewers. Asimov, both a scientist and a writer, reviews science books for each issue of *The Horn Book Magazine,* but most of the reviews are for older readers, and comments are very brief. The books reviewed in the *Bulletin of the Center for Children's Books* are checked by subject-matter specialists. Books included in the *AAAS Science Book List for Children* and the monthly *Science and Children* have presumably been checked for scientific accuracy. An annual review by the staff of *Natural History* provides another source of critical evaluations by scientists. For example, in reviewing *Beyond he Solar System* by a respected science writer,

Willy Ley, the reviewer points out discrepancies:

> *. . . His historical accounts are interesting, but his discussion of stellar evolution is nearly fifteen years out of date, and poor editing is disturbing in some other places. For instance, we are told . . . Father Secchi found four spectral classes sufficient to account for most of the stars. Only three of the classes are enumerated. In another place we read that the eclipsing star system Algol consists of a GO star (yellow) and a B8 star (blue-white), four times brighter. But three pages farther on we read that "Algol is a binary consisting of two nearly identical Red Giants. . . ."*[2]

The alert teacher or science consultant might well observe the discrepancies cited, but probably would not be aware of what Franklin calls "very suspect scientific reasoning anent Rigel." His concluding comment to the effect that the book is "not bad if read by someone who already knows enough astronomy to detect its flaws for himself" indicates lack of awareness of the audience and the purpose of the book. Neither teachers nor children in upper grades or junior high school will have that kind of knowledge. There is a need for unequivocal reviews of science books that say clearly, "This book is not recommended." Teachers and librarians will need to draw upon their own knowledge of subject fields, make comparisons of books of one topic, use the available reviews, and, finally, evaluate the book according to the purposes of the book itself and the needs of the children in the particular school.

Are Facts Accurate?   Each book must be evaluated on its own merits, not merely as a part of a series or by author's reputation. Critical reading is essential to note discrep-

---

[2]K. L. Franklin, "Astronomy," *Natural History's 1965 Survey of Science Books for Young People* (New York: American Museum of Natural History, 1965), unpaged.

ancies. Historical "evidence" is often difficult to obtain; the writer must be especially careful in his presentation. For example, Lawson's account in *Watchwords of Liberty* quotes Colonel Parker at Lexington, "But if they mean to have a war, let it start here." Nolan reports in *The Shot Heard Round the World* that a sergeant *thought he heard* those words.

Within the book, discrepancies may reveal inaccuracy. In *Come Along to Thailand* by Prechtl, there is the statement that the people have food and clothing, "For one thing there is very little suffering among the Siamese."[3] Later the author states "There is an interesting story, a true one, told in connection with the distribution of food and clothing to the poor people in the Northeast who find it hard to make a living."[4] Perhaps the conflict hinges upon the word *suffering*, but certainly, two different impressions remain with the reader. When a Thai graduate student reviewed the book, she pointed out cultural discrepancies. She noted that a more accurate meaning for the bowl carried by the monks is an "accepting bowl" rather than a "begging bowl," for the people *ask* the monk to *accept* food from them.

Is the Book Realistic?   Content and style contribute to a realistic effect in the informational book. This criterion is closely related to selection of content and details, but should be considered in reviewing the book. McClung's life cycle books about animals, *Screamer* and *Possum*, for example, show the death of the young. Calmly, yet realistically, the author relates that a fox ate one possum, an owl pounced on another, a rattlesnake and a turtle took two more, and one was hit by a car. In the next generation, fifteen were born, but two never reached the pouch. He explains clearly and simply that the possum

had eleven nipples and "The last two babies had no place to go. They eventually starved to death."[5]

The First Book of the Early Settlers by Rich describes in realistic terms the early settlements of Plymouth, New Amsterdam, Delaware, and Jamestown. There is no mincing of words in Mrs. Rich's vivid telling of the hardships faced by the colonists at Jamestown:

> . . . *As the days grew shorter and colder, food became more and more scarce. They ate acorns, nuts, roots, fruits, whatever they could find. Then they ate the dogs. Then they caught frogs and snakes and toads and ate them.*
> *It was what has become known as the "Starving Time," and starve they really did. Jamestown became a settlement of walking skeletons and scarecrows, of bundles of skin and bones and rags, hardly able to crawl in and out of their miserable hovels. When Smith left, there had been over five hundred people in the colony. By Spring only about sixty of them were alive.*[6]

Are Facts and Theories Clearly Distinguished?   Children need guidance in developing skill to distinguish fact and theory, to become alert to such phrases as "scientists believe," "so far as we know," "according to this theory." To teach critical thinking, the materials themselves must distinguish fact and theory. Coombs makes it clear that he has presented one theory of the beginning of life, "This, of course, is an oversimplified version—and only one of several—of how the earth was formed, how the oceans came into being, and how life began."[7] Books dealing with evolution and human origins

---

[3]Louise Prechtl, *Come Along to Thailand*, Photographs by James Prechtl (Minneapolis: Denison, 1962), p. 17.
[4]Prechtl, p. 99.

[5]Robert McClung, *Possum* (New York: Morrow, 1963), p. 45.
[6]Louise Dickinson Rich, *The First Book of the Early Settlers*, Pictures by Douglas Gorsline (New York: F. Watts, 1959), p. 17.
[7]Charles Coombs, *Deep-Sea World, The Story of Oceanography* (New York: Morrow, 1966), p. 16.

have particular problems in stating theory. It may be difficult to deal with this topic in some communities, but children have a right to know of man's discoveries and theories regarding his origin. The point made by Friedman in *Man in the Making* is important:

> No anthropologist now or in the past, has ever claimed that man descended or developed from any of the living apes. Rather, these apes are our very distant cousins, descended with us from some common primate ancestor many millions of years ago.[8]

She goes on to point out that no one agrees on why this ancestor came to the ground or why he stood erect.

Do Text and Illustrations Avoid Stereotypes? Stereotyping, as defined in Chapter 5, should be avoided in informational books as well as fiction and picture books. A kind of subtle stereotyping is evident when science books do not show women in laboratories or when no Negro scientists are pictured. For example, in *The True Book of Energy* by Podendorf, only one illustration shows a girl or woman. That woman is ironing. The implication appears to be that women play no part in science related to energy.

Stereotyped characters appear more frequently in fiction or biography, but books about other countries may include such inaccurate writing. To write of the French as "excitable," the Germans as "steady," the Scot as "thrifty" is to write in generalizations.

Is the Book Up-to-Date? Recency of publication is a factor for evaluation if the informational book presents facts that may be changed by new discoveries or theories, or if it is about people of the world. For example, Jessup gives an excellent account of the development of the field of archeology

in *The Wonderful World of Archeology*, but recent theories about Stonehenge are needed to supplement this book, published in 1956. A book like *The Caves of the Great Hunters* by Baumann probably will not be outdated soon because it describes the discovery of the caves at Lascaux and summarizes previous discoveries. However, if a new theory regarding primitive man's reasons for the cave paintings were to develop as the result of new discoveries, the book would be outdated. It is particularly difficult to keep up-to-date with such topics as space exploration, DNA in biology, and emerging national governments. Teachers and librarians should examine copyright dates of books and be aware of new developments in the field as the text is evaluated.

Book lists about other countries that continue to include the one-hundred-year-old *Hans Brinker* for The Netherlands, *Heidi* for Switzerland, or *The Good Master* for Hungary are indeed invalid. Several bibliographies include the beautifully illustrated *Ola* by the d'Aulaires as a book to help children understand Norway. Actually, Ola's unusual adventures make this fantasy. What is learned in this book? The reader learns there are forests in Norway, Lapps live in the North, fishing is an industry, and eiderdown is gathered from nests. The story is delightful; the pictures are gay and bright; Ola wends his way about the country with joyous abandon. This is a book that can be used much like poetry to enrich a child's feeling and appreciation for a country, but the teacher will need to use other books, pictures, and displays to develop authentic concepts of the country and its people today. Perhaps peasant life has not changed appreciably in some regions of the world, but most countries have felt the impact of technology and industrialization.

If teachers take advantage of material in trade books, the curriculum itself can be more authentic. For example, studies of the

---

[8]Estelle Friedman, *Man in the Making,* Illustrated by Frederic Marvin (New York: Putnam, 1960), p. 45.

Indian often deal only with Indian life when the country was first explored and settled. Children need to become aware of the problems of various tribes today. In *The Navajo*, Bleeker gives anthropological concepts as facts about life are presented. In addition, she shows the forces creating cultural change as the white man came, as uranium was discovered, and as education and health were influenced by the white man's culture. She notes the difficulty of the Indians in getting jobs, but does not really discuss the prejudice they face. In some ways, then, this book is up-to-date; in other ways, it is partially inadequate.

Are Significant Details Omitted?   Writers of informational books must simplify and also limit the amount of material they include. If significant details are omitted, misconceptions will be the result. Science books about animals often give misconceptions by omission of some facts; for example, few deal with reproduction so that concepts are clarified. In some cases, publishing taboos continue to prevent use of correct terminology. McClung even avoids the word "mate" in the account of *Possum*. He states, "All night long the two of them wandered through the woods together. But at dawn each went his own way again. Possum's babies were born just twelve days later."[9] When he describes the birth, the author indicates the young are not born in the pouch, but are "licked off" by the mother. Then the creature who "wasn't much more than an embryo" climbs through the mother's fur to reach the pouch. The author does not answer the child's question, "Where do they come from?" There seems to be no good reason to omit information about the anatomical structure that delivers the young. Certainly the meaning of "embryo" should be explained in context. The illustration in

Dolphins by Compere shows the young at the moment of birth, and the text tells that the young appears tail first.

Omissions in books about history of a country or of a period also create misconceptions. Dreany's *A Child's Book of Mankind through the Ages* presents a pictorial survey of the history of man from the Stone Age to the development of the United Nations. The text is limited and sometimes oversimplified. For example, his description of the Middle Ages makes no mention of the role of the church or university in keeping learning alive, but flatly states: "The early Middle Ages, or dark ages, was a time of ignorance, cruelty, and disorder."[10] The establishment of the United States as a free nation is not included, and the reader is asked to leap from the exploration of the New World to the Westward Movement, and then to the development of world trade. The parent or teacher using this book would have to provide the needed interpolation.

Are There Supporting Facts for Generalizations?   The critical reader needs to become aware of generalizations made by the author. Some writers state the generalization; others give facts and assume the reader will generalize. Notice McClung's generalization at the end of this paragraph:

> *Rooting on the forest floor, she gobbled down beetle grubs and mushrooms, snails and tiny bulbs. Climbing another tree, she surprised a catbird in her nest. The catbird escaped, but the old opossum lapped up her four green eggs. Ambling along the creek, she caught a little green snake and ate it. Adult opossums eat all sorts of things.*[11]

In the book *California Harbors*, Huntington gives facts that would lead to a generalization for each chapter. For example, after

---

[9]McClung, p. 41.

[10]Joseph E. Dreany, *A Child's Book of Mankind through the Ages* (New York: Maxton, 1955), unpaged.
[11]McClung, p. 12.

reading Chapter 2, the child would understand "Lighthouses, beacons, and radar
serve as guides and warnings to ships." After
reading the entire book by Selsam, *You and
the World around You,* the generalization is
made clear that humans grow and change
just as do animals, plants and earth. The
author concludes, "Learn about yourself,
you are part of nature, too."[12]

Some generalizations are not in accord
with the facts. A 1963 book by Ravielli, *The
World Is Round,* is not accurate according to
the International Geophysical Year findings
that the earth is slightly pear-shaped. In
predicting the future, Vorwald and Clark, in
Computers! seem to be saying there is nothing
to fear from computers; yet, other specialists
today do warn us of dangers to individuality
and life as we know it. In *The First Book of
Mars,* Knight carefully avoids generalizing
beyond present knowledge when he discusses
the existence of life on that planet. His
look into the future, however, gives the
impression that colonies will be established
on Mars within a few hundred years. The
phrase, "it is highly possible" followed by the
statement of needs of an expanding population, gives the impression it is "highly
probable."

Are Differing Viewpoints Presented?
Controversial issues arise when there are
differing viewpoints regarding their solutions. The author who ignores other viewpoints is failing to help the reader learn
to examine issues. Children need the opportunity to study Communism, for example.
In *Communism, An American's View,* Johnson
writes:

> It is a mistake to think that one can learn all
> about Communism by reading one book. But it
> is also a mistake to think that one must know

everything about it in order to have a pretty
good idea of what it is. The commonest mistake,
though, is thinking that we know enough about
it without reading anything.[13]

Johnson gives children a lucid, objective account of the development of Communism,
and shows that from one point of view it has
brought progress. He also points out the
limitations of Soviet Communism as it has
developed.

A comparison of two books about the war
with Mexico illustrates the way different
writers present history. For example, in *The
War with Mexico,* Werstein comments in only
three sentences on the agreement that the
settlers from the United States were allowed
to have slaves.

> *Austin kept pressing the Mexicans to allow the
> settlers further privileges. By 1830, he wrested
> two important gains from them. The colonists
> were permitted to keep slaves—even though
> slavery had been abolished everywhere else in
> Mexico the previous year.*[14]

The paragraph in *Texas and the War with
Mexico,* one of the *American Heritage* series,
edited by Downey, gives a different interpretation:

> *On September 15, 1829, Guerrero's adminis-
> tration made more Mexican history by an-
> nouncing the abolition of slavery in Mexico
> —making Mexico one of the first countries in
> the Western Hemisphere to take this step.
> Although it is quite possible that the Guerrero
> administration sincerely disapproved of slavery,
> the action they took in freeing the slaves of
> Mexico and outlawing slavery in their country
> was specifically directed at the slave-owning
> Americans who had settled, by this time, in the
> northern province of the state of Coahuila
> which was known as Texas. For these Ameri-*

---

[12]Millicent Selsam, *You and the World around You,* Illustrated by Greta Elgaard (New York: Doubleday, 1963),
p. 4.

[13]Gerald Johnson, *Communism, An American's View* (New
York: Morrow, 1964), p. 21.
[14]Irving Werstein, *The War with Mexico* (New York:
Norton, 1965), p. 23.

cans were the only sizable group of slaveown-
ers in Mexico.[15]

The Werstein book summarizes the end of the war very briefly, and does not discuss the implications for the United States, the slavery issue, or future relationships with Mexico. However, the American Heritage editors point up criticism of the Mexican War by many Americans.

Teachers and children also need to be aware of the viewpoint from which the author writes. For example, a book by Trease describes events since 1900 in *This Is Your Century.* This is an excellent book, but children should be helped to see that his selection and interpretation of events reflect his English background. Not only must teachers be aware of the points of view being expressed, they must use these books to develop skills of critical reading.

In Geographical Books, Is Diversity Revealed? It is difficult indeed to portray a country or region accurately in all its diversity of people, industry, terrain, and so forth. The problem faced by many writers can be imagined by thinking of a book designed to give information about the United States. Even a region such as New England would represent wide diversities. By emphasizing village life of a country, for example, the Gidals in the *My Village* series overcome part of this problem by limiting their scope. *Sigemi, a Japanese Village Girl* by Kirk clearly illustrates the changing customs of modern Japan in one village. At the factory, father wears Western clothing, but at home, he is dressed in a kimono. At home, Sigemi sits on the floor, but at school she sits at a desk. An authentic picture may be presented by these specialized books. While a survey book cannot give such specific details, it should con-

vey a feeling for the diversity of life in a country.

In Science Books, Is Anthropomorphism Omitted? Anthropomorphism is the assignment of human feelings and behavior to animals, plants, or objects; it does not belong in the truly scientific book. In the book that purports to be an informational book, this seems to say to the child, "You really do not have the intelligence or interest to understand or accept straightforward information." For example, Arnold, in *Marvels of the Sea and Shore,* describes a starfish eating, and then writes, "After that it swims gaily off to search for another victim."[16] The starfish may actually be suffering from indigestion; "gaiety" is only the observer's interpretation.

The bluejays in *Ellen's Bluejays* by Sterling are given human characteristics in this manner: "They were trying to tell her that they could take care of their own babies."[17] An observer could only ascribe his feelings to the animals being observed, and say, "*It seems* they were saying . . . because that is what I would do if I were in that situation." Young children do give an emotional quality to animal behavior because they find it difficult to separate themselves from the object they observe. Wundheiler noted that children give feelings to plants, animals, and objects, not because they are imaginative, but because that is the only way they can perceive experience.[18]

Harking back to the didactic period, some authors continue to write in this style:

Meet Mr. and Mrs. Bob-o-link who live in a swamp meadow where cat-tails grow. Mrs.

[15]Fairfax Downey, and Editors of *American Heritage, Texas and the War with Mexico* (New York: Harper & Row, 1961), p. 29.

[16]Oren Arnold, *Marvels of the Sea and Shore,* Illustrated by J. Junge Bateman (New York: Abelard-Schuman, 1963), p. 86.

[17]Dorothy Sterling, *Ellen's Bluejays,* Illustrated by Winifred Lubell (New York: Doubleday, 1961), p. 34.

[18]L. Wundheiler, "The Child's View of Nature and Literature about Nature," *Library Quarterly,* vol. 37 (January 1967), pp. 23–31.

Bobby is sitting on five grayish, white, spotted eggs. Soon there will be five wee birds clamoring for food. . . . Mr. Bobby is a gay fellow in his summer coat. . . . Mr. and Mrs. Blue Jay are very pretty but oh so naughty! They think nothing of robbing.[19]

This is one form of "talking down" to children.

As he describes the territorial and alarm cries of the gulls in *The Gull's Way*, Darling uses the words *seemed* and *as if* to indicate that the birds do not have human feelings:

Usually the birds seemed to give this call for the sheer joy of being alive, for the joy of being gulls. But the call was clearly territorial, as if the birds were proclaiming, "I am a proud breeding gull. This is my spot on earth — a place for me and my mate alone."[20]

This is very different from saying, "The gull expressed his joy of being alive," or the gull cried, "This is my territory."

Selsam talks to her young readers about the problem of interpreting what animals do in the book, *Animals As Parents:*

It is hard to keep remembering that animals live in a different kind of world from our own. They see, hear, smell, and taste things differently. And they do not have human intelligence or emotions, so we must avoid interpreting their behavior in terms of our own feelings and thoughts. For example, it looks to us as though parent birds are devoted to their young in the same way that human parents are devoted to theirs. But only experimental work can show whether this interpretation is true.[21]

Talking animal stories have a place in the literature program as fantasy. However, a thinly disguised "story," designed to dis-

pense information, has little value. Usually, such books include information that is available elsewhere or actually give misconceptions. In *Cattail House* by Erickson for example, Muskrat says, "What a morning for adventure," as he sets forth to seek the forest. He talks with many animals on the way. A beaver gives a long reply when Muskrat asks, "Why do you build dams?" Conversation continues in this vein:

"What a broad tail you have," said the muskrat.
"I use it for a rudder when I swim and for slapping the water to warn my friends of danger."[22]

Many excellent animal-fiction stories do convey information, but the plot develops naturally, there is characterization, and the animal's behavior and habitat is authentic. Such a story is *The White Palace* by O'Neill. The description of "The Palace" illustrates the excellent prose, with its figurative language and appeal to the senses:

Sheathed in ice, a beautiful white palace stood in frozen perfection at the bottom of the stream. It had been created by the skeletons of two great fish lying next to each other. Each spine was a soaring central arch of heavy bone. From the lofty spines the ribs curved out and down, forming vaulted oval rooms striped in white coral and water crystal. From the roof, frozen fan-pennants flared.[23]

Chinook is the salmon who lives in the palace until "something spoke inside the silence of himself," and he left for a world of deeper waters. The ecstasy of the ocean is added to the realistic dangers he faces. It is interesting to compare the account of courtship behavior in this fiction and in Selsam's informational book, *The Courtship of Animals*. Actually,

---

[19]Luis Henderson, *A Child's Book of Birds* (New York: Maxton, 1946), unpaged.

[20]Louis Darling, *The Gull's Way* (New York: Morrow, 1965), p. 39.

[21]Millicent Selsam, *Animals as Parents*, Illustrated by John Kaufmann (New York: Morrow, 1965), p. 16.

[22]Phoebe Erickson, *Cattail House* (Chicago: Childrens Press, 1962), unpaged.

[23]Mary O'Neill, *The White Palace*, Illustrated by Nonny Hogrogian (New York: Crowell, 1966), unpaged.

O'Neill gives more information about the nest. The dramatic action of the story of Chinook ends with the knowledge that there will soon be another "white palace." Information is no less accurate, but there is a richer experience, and a deeper appreciation of the cycle of birth, life, and death is communicated. Other animal stories are described in Chapter 10.

Are Phenomena Given Teleological Explanations?   A teleological explanation of phenomena suggests that behavior of organic life and physical changes are caused by a design or purpose other than mechanical or natural causes. For example, Nature, capitalized, is considered purposeful or is given a supernatural or divine purpose. An example of a teleological explanation is seen in this statement following an account of causes of wind. Bethers, in *What Happens in the Sky* explains that warm air rises, and adds, "This is why winds blow—it is Nature's way of trying to keep a balance of air everywhere."[24] Nature viewed with some purpose is described by Hogner in *Conservation in America:* "Nature is ruthless, and one of her most effective methods of population control is by starvation. . . . Nature also thins overproduction by disease."[25] Although the manuscript was checked by scientists at the Scripps Institute of Oceanography, *Marvels of the Sea and Shore* includes this kind of explanation:

> *Whenever you come to the beach you enter the most important scientific laboratory in the world. Here in the sand and sea Nature herself is conducting the experiments. She is constantly mixing chemicals and testing forces. She works on microscopic bits and on objects huge in size. . . .*[26]

[24]Ray Bethers, *What Happens in the Sky* (New York: St. Martin's, 1963), p. 33.
[25]Dorothy Childs Hogner, *Conservation in America* (Philadelphia: Lippincott, 1958), p. 94.
[26]Oren Arnold, *Marvels of the Sea and Shore,* Illustrated by J. Yunge Bateman (New York: Abelard-Schuman, 1963), p. 17.

What image does such writing present? Does the child visualize a type of goddess in flowing gown presiding over a laboratory with microscopes and test tubes? Discussion of "Nature" and purposeful causation is more appropriately the province of philosophy than science.

Content

Is This a General Survey Book or One of Specific Interest?   There is a place for the general book and one for a specific topic. In evaluating these books, the teacher or librarian will need to consider the success of the book in achieving its purpose, as well as its value in the curriculum.

Books present general information about a topic, but should not try to cover too broad a field. Titles like *All About the Sea* or *All About Biology* are misleading. They only can introduce the reader to the general topic, but cannot be expected to give complete coverage. A title can also establish a theme for an informational book. *The Challenge of the Sea* by Clarke presents such challenges as navigation, exploring the depths, harvesting the sea, using its energy, exploring the past, and finding recreation in and under the sea. Other books about the sea give information on more specific topics such as underwater archeology, deep-sea diving, tides, and animal life.

Is the Coverage of the Book Adequate for Its Purpose?   Whether the book is designed to present a survey or to inform the reader about a specific topic, coverage should be extensive enough to clarify principles and prevent misconceptions. In forty-seven pages, Posell has answered most of the questions a primary child reading *The True Book of Whales* would ask. It tells how deep whales swim, how they breathe, how long they live, how they eat. Understanding the purpose of *Rain in the Woods and Other Small Matters* by Rounds, the reviewer would not expect all creatures of the woods to be described. The author's purpose is to encourage observation by citing examples of his discoveries. It is interesting to contrast Rounds' approach with Sanger's description of a day in a swamp, *Cypress Country.* Sanger notes birds, reptiles, amphibians, insects, mammals, and plants in this ecological study of one small area. The purpose of showing community relationships is achieved well.

A survey book is, of course, limited by space, but *significant* topics should not be omitted. In *Deep Sea World* by Coombs, there is a good chapter on the underwater living experiments of U.S. Navy divers and civilians, but no mention of the experiments of Cousteau is made. This is a glaring omission of an important scientific work.

A book about *The Department Store* by Hastings, for example, shows only the clothing and toy departments. Such limited coverage leads to misconceptions.

Coverage in a book of history is extremely important. Johnson's introduction to *America Is Born* expresses this need:

Part of the story is very fine, and other parts are very bad; but they all belong to it, and if you leave out the bad parts you never understand it all. Yet you must understand it if you are to make your part one of the fine parts.[27]

On the other hand, an author may underestimate the background of the child for whom the book is designed, and the content will not further his present understanding.

Explanations in an experiment book may be so general that understanding will be difficult. A comparison of two explanations of surface tension will illustrate the weakness of the first. The clarity of the metaphor and the lucid, step-by-step explanation of the second succeeds in explaining the reason why a pin or razor blade will float.

Dramatic scratchboard illustrations vividly recreate the purchase of Manhattan Island by the Dutch. From *America Is Born* by Gerald W. Johnson. Illustrated by Leonard Everett Fisher. Copyright © 1960. Reproduced by permission of William Morrow & Company, Inc.

This is because of the surface tension of the water. . . . What it is, exactly, and how surface tension occurs is a bit difficult to explain, but in practice it comes to this, that the surface of the water is very much like an elastic skin.[28]

---

[27]Gerald Johnson (in an introductory letter to Peter), *America Is Born*, Illustrated by Leonard Everett Fisher (New York: Morrow, 1958), pp. viii–ix.

[28]Leonard de Vries, *The First Book of Experiments*, Translated by Erie G. Briege, Illustrated by Joast van de Woestijne (New York: Macmillan, 1958), p. 69.

It acts as if it were fastened to the bowl and pulled tight. If something pushes down on a tight skin, the skin stretches. But the skin tries to stay as small as it can. It tries to keep from stretching. So it pushes back.

The pin pushes down in the water in the bowl. It makes a dent in the surface of the water. This makes the surface bigger. But the surface of the water is like a stretched skin. It tries to get as small as it can. So it pushes up against the pin. The pin is very light. The surface of the water pushes up against the pin just as hard as the pin pushes down. So the pin floats on top of the water.[29]

Is the Book within the Comprehension and Interest Range of the Age for Which Intended?

Book jackets or book reviews often indicate an age range according to reading level or interest. It is difficult to know whether one or both of these factors are reflected in the age recommended. Selection aids, such as the *Children's Catalog,* indicate approximate grade levels. The beginning teacher or librarian can develop skill in assessing approximate reading level, by examining basic readers for each grade level. Vocabulary, sentence length, size of type, and organization of the book are factors to be considered.

When children see crowded pages and relatively small type, they immediately think it is a book for the more gifted readers or adults. Books printed in a larger type-face and with wider margins have more appeal. Books printed in type that resembles manuscript writing, such as the *True Book* series and the *About* series, will probably be more appropriate for primary grades. The primary child need not be restricted to a narrow list of words, since he can discern meanings from context; however, vocabulary does have to be within his range. In *Moolack, Young Salmon Fisherman,* the author, Wor-

thylake, could have used another word without "writing down" as she stated, "Moolack rose reluctantly." New words can be explained in context as in one of the *I Can Read* series by Selsam. In her book, *Benny's Animals,* the museum professor says, "Another pile will be Amphibians—animals that live in the water when they are young and on land when they are grown up. Those are your frogs and toads."[30]

Some books are obviously too difficult for most elementary school children. The fine color photographs in the *Let's Travel* series would be appropriate, but the text is apparently an adult travelog narration. These phrases are in *Let's Travel in India* by Geis: "The abject poverty," "reflect the incredible opulence," "Fifty centuries of civilization have left a rich residue."

Another guide for determining the intended age level is the content of the book. Recognizing the egocentricity of the young child, authors should present information related to basic processes in which he is interested. He is concerned with play, eating, sleeping, elimination, and, to some extent, relating to others. He is curious about sex, birth, growth, death. Seeking mastery of his environment, he wants to know how things work, why they move or exert force as they do. A book that explains how birds digest food, for example, is intriguing to him. The text and diagrams of Williamson's *The First Book of Birds* clearly explain the function of *crop, gullet,* and *gizzard* in digesting food. The diagrams showing how an egg is made would be of interest.

Tony's Birds by Selsam is appropriate for young children who are ready for the *I Can Read* series. It is very realistic in that Tony goes for a walk and sees not one bird. The account of problems in using binoculars will be helpful, and the children will enjoy the humor of the book. Illustrating the use of a

[29]Irving and Ruth Adler, *Why? a Book of Reasons* (New York: John Day, 1961), pp. 22–23.

[30]Millicent Selsam, *Benny's Animals and How He Put Them in Order,* Illustrated by Arnold Lobel (New York: Harper & Row, 1966), p. 47.

guide book, it will lead the child to further bird-watching and discovery.

Many books about living things are, of necessity, more closely related to rural or suburban children, or to those who go to parks and camps. Where possible, books should provide information for the city child. For example, a good addition to *The First Book of Birds*, by Williamson, is the information about birds in the city.

The example chosen to illustrate a concept may affect the appeal of the book. *You and Your Amazing Mind* by Lewellen could be read by a good reader in sixth grade, but the anecdote used to illustrate the operation of the conscious, unconscious, and conscience is about a rivalry in which "your best girl walked off with him. . . ." This reference places the book in the teen category, although sixth-graders in a few schools do begin dating.

Many elements of style discussed below will influence the appeal and appropriateness of the book for an age group. However, both teachers and librarians will want to keep in mind the wide ability and interest range within one class.

Do Experiment Books Lead to Understanding of Science?   The science activity or "experiment" book should be designed to guide children in making their own discoveries. Open-ended questions, guides to observation, and suggestions for further study are strategies that lead to pupil problem solving. In some books, the author states a principle and then describes an activity that will "prove" it. Other writers lead the child through the activity and then give him clues to help him formulate his own generalization. If the author states it for the reader, he is not required to think.

Now Try This by the Schneiders, is a notable example of a book that guides the child to discover for himself the basic principles related to friction, levers, inclined planes, and wheels. Diagrams help the child as he

follows the pattern for each experiment: "Let's Find Out" (purpose of the experiment), "Try This" (procedure), "You Will Find" (observation of result), "Now You Know" (conclusion), and "You Found Out" (principle). As the child reads and carries out these activities, he is developing skill in using the scientific method.

The "cookbook" approach to science activity is illustrated by the "recipes" for a crystal garden and rock candy in *Crystal Magic* by David. Readers are told what to do, but not how to observe. No questions lead to discovery; no information is given. If the child asks why the crystals form, he will find no help in this book in which paper and string figures overshadow the slight content.

Selsam's books, *Play with Plants*, *Play with Seeds*, and *Play with Vines*, exemplify approaches that teach the method of science as the child engages in "play." In her clear style, she gives directions for observation:

> *Here is another thing to remember. When something changes, you have to know exactly how it looked before the change in order to be sure of the difference. You need "before" and "after" pictures. . . . Make a note of the time, the name of the plant, and what you do to it. Later, after something has happened, draw the tendril again, or take another picture, and note the time. . . .*[31]

In *Adventures with a String*, Milgrom does not give answers, but leads the child to observe and to draw his own conclusions. An example of his suggestions shows the process:

> *Make the string short.*
>   *Swing the key,*
> *Make the string longer.*
>   *Swing the key.*
> *Which time does the key swing faster?*[32]

---

[31]Millicent Selsam, *Play with Vines*, Illustrated by Fred F. Scherer (New York: Morrow, 1951), p. 37.
[32]Harry Milgrom, *Adventures with a String*, Illustrated by Tom Funk (New York: Dutton, 1965), pp. 18–19.

Milgrom also encourages the child to continue making discoveries on his own. "What else can YOU find out about a string. Think of what YOU want to do. Try it. See what YOU can discover."[33]

Some of the "experiment" books are more nearly activity books. For example, de Vries has published three books with similar titles, *The First Book of Experiments, The Second . . .,* and so forth. Many unusual activities are included, but emphasis seems to be more on manipulation than development of generalizations. There are excellent photographs of *active* children in *The World of Push and Pull* by Ubell, but the child is not led to try things for himself. The questions and conversational style of Schwartz in *It's Fun to Know Why* make the reader feel secure about carrying out the experiments. Children are guided to observe accurately through reading directions, such as the following, for an experiment with bread dough:

BREAD WITHOUT YEAST
Prepare another batch of dough in the same way, but this time do not put any yeast into the lukewarm water. Cover both dishes with a clean cloth. Look at them every fifteen minutes. What is happening? What one is rising? Do you see hundreds of tiny bubbles in one of your doughs?[34]

Previously, experiment books gave little attention to measurement and controls. Sootin emphasizes the skill of measurement in *Experiments with Machines and Matter,* and Wyler and Ames suggest scientific controls in their book, *Prove It!*

Some books lead to observation of living things by giving suggestions for study of plants and animals. An English writer has published a journal of his discoveries in *Small Creatures in My Garden.* Reynolds gives excellent clues for activities that could be carried out in gardens here. The text leads to further study by noting, "Someone—it might be you—has still to come along, with the patience and skill to study the larvae, to watch them grow, develop, and change."[35]

In *Fireflies in the Night,* Hawkes gives just the right amount of information for the age group intended in one of the *Let's-Read-and-Find-Out* series. Children do catch fireflies; this book will lead them to make their own observations by putting jars of fireflies first in cold, then warm, water. They can count and observe the rhythm of the flashes to see if they can distinguish males and females. The clear illustrations also lead to study of the insect. Writers who can develop ability to observe, relate facts, summarize, and generalize are contributing to the child's understanding of science concepts and skill in using methods and tools of science.

Are Experiments Feasible and Safe? Frequently, children carry out science experiments as independent projects. Thus, materials suggested should be available, and the text should include safety precautions. For example, in *The Crazy Cantilever and Other Science Experiments,* Kadesch warns the child to hold dry ice very briefly to avoid burns. It would seem far wiser to suggest a hot pad or tongs instead of handling it with bare hands. A book for children in second or third grade, *Let's Experiment,* by Straus, gives clear rules for safety after telling children how to make their own chemistry set:

Don't wear your best clothes.
Work in a room you can clean up easily. . .
Do your experiments on a tray. . .
Don't leave any mess for your Mother to clean up.
DON'T TAKE ANYTHING FROM THE KITCHEN OR BATHROOM UNLESS

---

[33]Milgrom, p. 32.

[34]Julius Schwartz, *It's Fun to Know Why* (New York: Whittlesey, 1952), p. 91.

[35]Christopher Reynolds, *Small Creatures in My Garden* (New York: Farrar, Straus, 1965), p. 109.

YOU ASK YOUR MOTHER IF YOU MAY HAVE IT. ASK HER EACH TIME.[36]

Care of materials as well as safety is taught in Podendorf's direction, "Perhaps you should put paper under them [candles] so that you do not get wax on the table."[37]

Materials suggested in the activities book should be easy to obtain. The authors of *Beginning Science with Mr. Wizard,* Herbert and Ruchlis, did not consider this factor when they suggested hammering a piece of wire with an object "such as an anvil." It's unlikely one could even borrow an anvil from a neighbor! These authors give no cautions about use of fire in their suggested activities.

Does the Book Show Interrelationships of Facts and Principles?   The style and organization of details should show the interrelationships of facts and principles. In a book about ecology, *The Living Community,* Hirsch states, "A poet once said that one could not pluck a flower without troubling a star. This is another way of saying that the living and the nonliving are linked together."[38] Information about behavior, properties of matter, and the earth should lead the child toward concepts of relatedness. A list of facts or descriptive accounts alone are not true science books. In *Animals As Parents,* Selsam presents many facts, but they are organized to show increasingly higher levels of parental behavior. She also shows the possible relationship of research in animal science to human life.

Man should be presented in relation to other species in the animal world. Zim does this effectively in *Your Heart and How It Works.* He traces the development of the heart in the earthworm, fish, and frog as well as that of the human. In *How Things Grow,* he describes growth by cell division in plants, animals, and man. The illustration of embryos of chicken, rabbit, monkey, and man show similarities in very early development.

The relationship of ocean currents, warmth, animals, and plants is shown in *Spring Comes to the Ocean* by Jean George. Responses of one-celled animals and behaviors of more complex animals are related to the seasonal change, and all are shown to have the instinct for self-preservation and reproduction.

Do Science Books Indicate Related Social Problems?   Where there are definite social problems related to scientific discoveries, it would seem that these relationships should be made clear. This criterion is especially important in conservation books. The rights of man and of animals should be presented. For example, Hogner presents the conflicting needs of the pileated woodpecker, a protected bird, and the utility companies whose poles the birds damage by drilling holes to store nuts. The author does not take sides on the basic issue of conservation versus private enterprise; she simply presents the problem. Russell's book, *Saving Wild Life for Tomorrow,* shows the conflict of interest as he describes the destruction of marsh areas when gravel is removed from streams. Man buys land, and surely has the right to use gravel for construction needs. What limits should be imposed? The author does not state the question, but the reader can infer the problem of use of resources by man and animals. In *Water and the Thirsty Land,* Jeanes and Carlsen describe the need for water for farming; yet, they omit the needs of West Coast cities. However, Archer gives a forthright presentation of the conflict between inland farmers and coastal cities of California in his book *Rain, Rivers and Reservoirs.*

---

[36]Jacqueline Harris Straus, *Let's Experiment,* Illustrated by Leonard Kessler (New York: Harper & Row, 1962), p. 10.

[37]Illa Podendorf, *101 Science Experiments,* Illustrated by Robert Borja (Chicago: Childrens Press, 1960), p. 74.

[38]S. Carl Hirsch, *The Living Community, a Venture into Ecology,* Illustrated by William Steinel (New York: Viking, 1966), p. 17.

This book is especially valuable because the conservation of water is viewed as a world problem.

Vorwald and Clark consider the social problems of man in a computer environment. In *Computers!*, they write:

> Computers, the elite machines of the second revolution, have completed the devaluation of the untrained mind just as certainly as the first industrial revolution devalued the brawny back. Thinking machines are making us think faster and clearer than we ever have before.[39]

This treatment oversimplifies the social problems of automation and cybernetics. However, Kenyon's book, *Calculators and Computers*, completely ignores the social implications.

Is the Book Fresh and Original? Many books seem to present content that has already been effectively presented by other titles. If the content is not organized in a new way, presented from a different point of view, or does not include new material, there would seem to be little reason to purchase the book for the well-stocked library. For example, there are numerous books about birds, but Kieran has provided an unusual organization in *An Introduction to Birds*. He describes birds as the ordinary bird-watcher might begin his study. This would be an excellent guide to precede use of Peterson's *A Field Guide to the Birds*.

There are now many books about the sea that include information about the ocean floor, tides, exploration of, and uses of the sea. Comparing books published before 1960 with those of the past five years, the reviewer finds new emphasis upon underwater archeology, living in sea labs, and life of the dolphins. New titles should be evalu-

ated in terms of new developments in the field.

Does the Book Help the Reader Understand the Methods of Science and Social Science? Informational books should illustrate the process of inquiry and convey the idea that discovery is fun. Experiment books promote inquiry by the child; books about living things or the earth should illustrate the approach of search; the history of scientific thought can be described; accounts of investigations that support the facts and generalizations can be included. Recently, some science writers have included information about the work of the scientist.

Bernice Kohn illustrates *The Scientific Method* by using an example of a boy deciding how and what to feed a puppy. This introduction shows the reader the steps of inquiry, but he is cautioned that scientists do not always take these steps in precise order. Following her illustration, the author describes the discoveries of Galileo, Harvey, Franklin, Fermi, and others. The role of imagination is emphasized.

The Crab That Crawled out of the Past, by the Milnes, provides a good example of scientific thinking. The book begins with the description of a crab as a man examines it. The reader feels he is standing by the side of the fisherman as he slowly and deliberately examines the tail, legs, eyes, and under parts. Then the behavior of the crab is observed as it sheds its shell. The hypothesis of changing direction according to light pattern is explained as a theory. One chapter is devoted to methods of study of the evolution of the crab. The reader is left with the realization that there is much more to learn about the horseshoe crab, and such knowledge will contribute to mankind.

Several books give accurate and interesting information about the work of the anthropologist. Friedman, in *Man in the Making*, gives clear details; for example, she

---

[39] Alan Vorwald and Frank Clark, *Computers! From Sand Table to Electronic Brain*, Illustrated by Frank Aloise (New York: McGraw-Hill, 1961), p. 157.

notes that a scientist would not look for fossils of man in rock layers of the age of the dinosaurs. She gives an excellent account of the contributions of geologists and anthropologists, citing names of the investigators. Mead's *Anthropologists and What They Do* is noteworthy because the author applies the method of the anthropologist in gathering data for the book. She describes anthropologists at their work, reports what they are actually doing at the moment, and what they considered their most interesting work. Then she gives an account of her own work in the field. Her previous book, *People and Places,* gives a better description of tools, questions, and methods of observing and recording. If one wants to learn about the work of a scientist in ethnology, he would find *The Shattered Skull* by Carol Perkins more illuminating. This book is a kind of journal of a visit to the site of the investigation of the Leakey prehistoric man. An original approach is used to describe the work of the archeologist in *Archeology, Exploring the Past* by Watts. By presenting the step-by-step record of the discovery and identification of one small pot, the author reveals the many tasks of the scientist. This book published by the Museum of Modern Art gives especially comprehensive information on "site."

If a book is to help children understand the method of science, it must show that present knowledge and current research is based upon previous investigation. Sometimes, a sentence or two expresses the idea; in other cases, the author will cite research or trace the development of knowledge. In *Birds With Bracelets,* Welty traces the development of bird-banding and shows how ideas used in Europe and America were exchanged. Thus, bird-banding is given both an historical and world setting. The theme of Grant's book, *Wonder World of Microbes,* is expressed in a quotation of Pasteur, "Chance only favors the mind that is prepared." In her account of the discoveries of ways to control microbes, the author emphasized the way one discovery is built upon previous knowledge. Teachers could read aloud the exciting story of the discovery of penicillin. The use of controls in experimentation is encouraged in the suggestions for readers. The search for answers to man's questions about natural causes is presented by Ludovici in *The Great Tree of Life,* a series of biographies of men and women who observed, made records, and were ahead of their time. How one scientist extended the work of another is shown in accounts of Buffon, Lamarck, Darwin, and Mendel.

If a book truly communicates the method of science, it will make the reader aware of new areas of investigation. After presenting current agreements and disagreements on archeological finds, Ludovici ends *The Great Tree of Life* commenting, "Oh, the waiting silence of these infinite spaces! What vast and wonderful new worlds they will reveal to us!"[40]

Inquiry begins with observation of behavior, of objects, or of reports of incidents. Books can help children "learn how to look." In a book for young children, *Let's Get Turtles,* Selsam illustrates the process of inquiry as two boys observe, read, consult authorities, and test hypotheses. The idea of controls is developed at the end of this *I Can Read* book. This same author adds humor to *How to Be a Nature Detective,* an "easy" book that teaches observation skills.

Few history books or geography books give any clue about the way scholars in these fields carry out their work. *History and Historians* by Boardman promised to fill the gap, but there is too much detail and no organizing theme. The section on materials the historian uses is good, but the dull accounts of historians of the ages will have little appeal or value in the elementary school curricu-

---

[40]L. J. Ludovici, *The Great Tree of Life; Paleontology, the Natural History of Living Creatures* (New York: Putnam 1963), p. 175.

lum. An example of historical research is presented by Palmer in *Quest for the Dead Sea Scrolls*. He gives information about early research, theories, and the value of the scrolls. For elementary schools, *The Big Dig, a Frontier Fort Comes to Life* by Gringhuis is one of the best examples of showing the historian at work in the field. This is the description of the excavation of the fort at Mackinac. The use of the grid system is explained, and the reader feels he is at the site as each three-inch layer of soil is removed, sifted, and studied.

Books should help children understand the differences between science and technology. Science relates to activity of the mind — questioning, observing, analyzing, interpreting, and generalizing. Technology utilizes facts and principles revealed by scientific investigation to solve individual and group problems. Many of the books about astronomy and space flight present a mixture of science and technology. Sasek's *This Is Cape Kennedy* is entirely concerned with the technology of space flight. It describes the area and the rockets, but is not a true science book. Well-written experiment books should contribute to the child's understanding of scientific method. Some special criteria for these books will be considered in a later section of this chapter.

Style

Is Information Given Directly or in Story Form? Books that present information through the veil of fiction with slight plots or didactic conversation continue to appear. *The Green Tree House* by Erdoes, for example, presents a thin plot with a country girl showing her friend from the city a tree where various animals were found. The trite, unchildlike language illustrates ineffective writing:

> *"That lovely old tree is full of life," said the girl. "I named it Green Tree House because*

many wild animals have made it their home. Have a little patience and keep your eyes open, then you can watch some of the lodgers."[41]

Thus, a priggish young lecturer seems to speak in 1965.

Information in *The Living Sea* by Lambert is presented through the device of magical qualities given to two children. Magic eyes and magic light enable them to see in the ocean depths, and magical strength makes it possible to swim for endless miles. This element of fantasy is unnecessary and is, in effect, a kind of "talking down" to children. The conversation is stilted indeed, as the boy lectures:

> *"If it were nighttime, we could see the polyps feeding with their tentacles out, like little anemones," Bill said. "They only feed at night. Then it's easy to see that corals are coelenterates, members of the phylum of the hollow tube and kin of the anemones, hydroids, and jellyfish."*[42]

Research has indicated that children want specific information. Straightforward presentation is the appropriate style for an informational book. Information about life on the shore is hidden midst the contrived plot of *Elizabeth, The Treasure Hunter* by Holman. The stilted language does sometimes reflect humor, but there is little information. In contrast, *Tide Pools and Beaches* by Clemons is a straightforward, but interesting, guide for collecting and identifying life of the sea.

Is the Text Interesting and Appropriate for the Age Level Intended? Discovery is exciting, and informational books should engender interest and communicate this excitement of learning. The content, as noted above, may be the first factor that draws the

[41]Richard Erdoes, *The Green Tree House* (New York: Dodd, Mead, 1965), unpaged.

[42]Elizabeth Lambert, *The Living Sea*, Illustrated by Elinor Jaeger (New York: Coward-McCann, 1963), p. 76.

reader's attention, but good writing style will maintain interest. When the author *tells* the reader he will find excitement or fun, it is unlikely that this will happen. In *About Creatures That Live Underground,* the child will probably disagree with the author, Uhl, who writes blithely, "It is fun to read about these underground creatures and find out how they live."[43] Adler commented that the goal of science writing should be "to present scientific ideas so simply that they can be followed and understood by an unsophisticated reader."[44] A "simple style" does not imply monosyllabic words, nor short, choppy, repetitive sentences. For example, in the first chapter of *O Canada!,* Barclay uses one-sentence paragraphs. The primer style of writing does not seem to flow.

> *Like most Stone Age people the Eskimo lived in tribes. In each tribe were several families. The men and boys did the hunting and fishing. Hunting was hard and dangerous. Sometimes the Eskimo had to travel many miles before they found game.*[45]

In the latter half of the book, the author's style will be more interesting to the child ready to read about the struggles of the French and English.

The author need not oversimplify his vocabulary, nor should he be a slave to a word list. However, he needs to be aware of the vocabulary level and background of understanding of the elementary school child. For example, *Birds in Flight* by Kirk presents attractive color photographs from *Arizona Highways Magazine,* but it gives no assistance with the meaning or pronunciation of *ingenious, agile, pterosaurs, pterodactyls,* or *deprived.*

Frequently, authors assume children possess understandings they do not have. For example, the authors of *The First Days of the World,* Ames and Wyler, assume children have concepts of atomic theory when they write, "specks and atoms crowded close." Consider all the meanings the child would need in order to understand this sentence from *Big Family of Peoples* by Eberle: "But the line of Ptolemy descendants has become decadent by this time."[46] Again, notice the number of concepts needed to visualize the country being described by Kaula in *The Land and People of New Zealand* for example: gorse, broom, weathered hills, sounds, and heavy forest.

> *Gorse and broom cover the weathered hills in the south but toward the west coast sounds, or Findland, alternating hills and mountains rise beyond canyons, carved by rapidly flowing rivers, until heavy forest is reached.*[47]

Terminology related to the subject being presented is best understood if explained in context. A glossary is helpful, but the reader is often unaware of it until he turns the last page. Young readers who are intent upon the content will often fail to use the glossary. In *You and Relativity,* Clark gives pronunciation in this way: "centrifugal force. (We pronounce it sen-TRIF-yuh-guhl.)"[48] In *Deep-Sea World* Coombs explains station, "At frequent intervals the scientist took a new station. *Station* is a term given by oceanographers to a known position in the ocean from which one or a series of experiments are conducted and tests made."[49]

An element of suspense in writing style contributes to interest. Dramatic action

---

[43]Melvin J. Uhl, *About Creatures That Live Underground,* Illustrated by Madalene Otteson (Chicago: Melmont, 1965), p. 5.

[44]Irving Adler, "On Writing Science Books for Children," *The Horn Book Magazine,* vol. 41 (October 1965), pp. 524–529.

[45]Isabel Barclay, *O Canada!,* Illustrated by Cecile Gagne (New York: Doubleday, 1964), p. 8.

[46]Eberle, Irmengarde, *Big Family of Peoples* (New York: Crowell, 1952), p. 29.

[47]Edna Kaula, *The Land and People of New Zealand* (Philadelphia: Lippincott, 1964), p. 15.

[48]Mary Lou Clark, *You and Relativity,* Illustrated by Bill Sanders (Chicago: Childrens Press, 1965), p. 19.

[49]Coombs, p. 40.

The tremendous rush of power and violent anger of two eagles is dramatized in this picture with effective shadings in soft green. Illustration by James Alexander is reproduced with the permission of Charles Scribner's Sons from *Young Eagle,* page 13, by Berniece Freschet. Copyright © 1965 James Alexander.

should not be so intense that it overshadows the information, however. The discovery of Schliemann, an amateur archeologist who followed a boyhood dream of finding ancient Troy, has been described by several writers. In *Digging Into Yesterday,* Friedman describes the excitement of his discovery. After months of digging, he caught a flash of light. Quickly, he told his wife to send the workmen home, and the two of them continued to dig alone. He held his breath as he removed:

> . . . *a layer of red ashes five feet thick.*
> . . . *at last, with a big knife, he began*

to unearth golden objects — one after another. Hastily, without examining them, he hid them in Sophia's shawl. The couple returned to their hut and locked the door.[50]

Action is also a factor in the writing style of an informational book. Although *Young Eagle* by Freschet contains some anthropomorphism, there is exciting action in the story of the eagle. In describing a battle of two males, the author created tension. "The two hung in space, swaying from side to side on their mighty wings. They screamed shrilly. . . . Beaks struck and talons tore."[51] Another example of the kind of action appropriate in books for children is Windle's description of research on bats, "They took off — and crash, slam, crunch — the 'deaf' bats bumped into walls, tables, and chairs."[52]

The beautiful color photographs in the *Our National Parks* series by Wood make the books worthwhile, but the text does not give a feeling of the beauty of the scenes. Space is wasted with detail that would not interest the child:

> *The cave is open all year. During the summer season, five guided tours go through the cave. The tours vary in length from three-quarters of a mile to seven miles, and usually take about an hour per mile. Not all of the tours are offered during the winter season.*[53]

The child would be more interested in how it feels to descend into the cave, the smell, the touch of the stones, the quiet, and the way the formations developed. The style in a book for primary children, . . . *If You Lived in Colonial Times,* by McGovern, is appropri-

[50]Estelle Friedman, *Digging into Yesterday* (New York: Putnam, 1958), p. 130.

[51]Berniece Freschet, *Young Eagle,* Illustrated by James Alexander (New York: Scribner, 1965), unpaged.

[52]Eric Windle, *Sounds You Cannot Hear,* Illustrated by John Kaufmann (Englewood Cliffs, N.J.: Prentice-Hall, 1963), p. 16.

[53]Frances Wood, *Great Smoky Mountains, Everglades, Mammoth Cave* (Chicago: Follett, 1964), p. 32.

ate. Questions related to their interests include "What were schools like?" "Did children have to worry about table manners?" and "What did you do on Sunday?" The question "How would you write a letter in colonial days?" was answered by comparing present forms with the past:

Suppose your father was away from home, and you wanted to write to him. How would you begin your letter?
You would never write, Dear Dad. *That wouldn't be polite.*
You would say Dear Sir *or* Honor'd Sir.
You would end your letter this way: I am with greatest respect, Dear Father, Your Dutiful Son *(or* Your Dutiful Daughter*).*[54]

Data may be included in an appendix, but inclusion in the text of such facts as "The area of New Brunswick is 28,354 square miles and the population is about 600,000"[55] contributes to dullness. These figures hold little meaning for a ten-year-old.

Do Vivid Language and Appropriate Metaphor Create Interest and Understanding? Scientific writing does not have to be dry, dull, or pedantic. Darling's prose in *The Gull's Way* exemplifies good use of sensory images in writing:

The gulls were perhaps the most beautiful then, with their plumage of gray and white against pearl-gray fog, silvered driftwood, dark ledges, and green plants beaded with fog moisture — the whole enclosed by the constant encircling boom of surf.[56]

Descriptive language stirs the imagination and stimulates re-creation of sensory experience. Rachel Carson's description of

shrimp cackle is an example. "One of the most extraordinarily wide-spread sounds of the undersea is the crackling, sizzling noise, like dry twigs burning or fat frying, heard near beds of the snapping shrimp."[57] The strange is related to the familiar in order that meanings become clear.

See Through the Jungle uses color, double-page spreads, and descriptive prose to help the child experience a walk through these regions:

We are in a dim green world. . . . A strange looking animal is waddling toward us on the trail. It has a nose like a nozzle, a tail like a huge brush, and legs that look like shaggy cowboy pants. This is the giant anteater. . . . [We turn the page to see bright yellow and green] Our jungle trail has led us to a clearing. . . . We are suddenly dazzled. . . . Swarms of insects are buzzing and whirring. Beetles shimmer with gold, emerald and ruby.[58]

Such a book helps the child experience the total environment. Writers tend to emphasize visual images, forgetting that other senses contribute to the child's awareness and understanding of the world. Sanger evokes multisensory responses in this descriptive prose:

The storm induced stillness was over. The swamp was loud with the shrilling of tree frogs and southern toads, the clamor of young wood storks, the intermittent bellowing of alligators, and the crying of limpkins. The night chorus had not yet begun in earnest, but it was ready to start.
The heat of afternoon dissolved into coolness. The air was lively, wafting many odors: wet flowers and ferns and moss, black muck and decay, brackish and fresh water, soaked nests

---

[54]Ann McGovern, . . . *If You Lived in Colonial Times,* Illustrated by Brinton Turkle (New York: Four Winds, 1964), p. 64.
[55]John Caldwell, *Let's Visit Canada* (New York: John Day, 1965), p. 24.
[56]Darling, p. 30.

[57]Rachel Carson, *The Sea Around Us,* Special edition for young readers adapted by Anne Terry White (New York: Simon and Schuster, 1958), p. 45.
[58]Millicent Selsam, *See through the Jungle* (New York: Harper & Row, 1957), pp. 23–24.

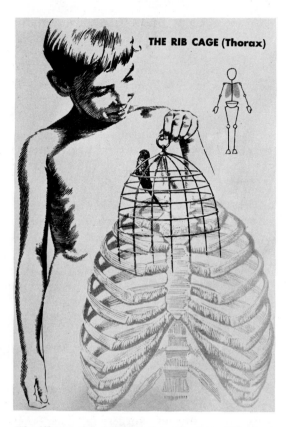

THE RIB CAGE (Thorax)

The illustration extends the metaphor of the text, "ribs like a bird cage," by relating the unknown to the known. From *Wonders of the Human Body* by Anthony Ravielli. Copyright 1954 by Anthony Ravielli. Reprinted by permission of the Viking Press, Inc.

and feathers, bark, roots, and leaves. Every questing animal knew these scents.[59]

Metaphors and similes can help a reader visualize and understand a situation or process. Corbett uses comparisons to explain *What Makes TV Work?* by beginning with the eyes receiving light. He illustrates the way single dots form a picture by showing a mosaic and magnifying newspaper photo-

graphs to show the dots of ink. These ideas are then related to the dots of light on the television screen. In Ravielli's classic, *Wonders of the Human Body*, the similes in text and diagram create interest as well as understanding: spine like a string of spools, ribs like a bird cage, thigh bone like a walking stick.

Using situations from the child's experience, a writer can often explain abstract concepts in familiar terms. In *A Fair World for All*, Dorothy Canfield Fisher explains each article of the *Declaration of Human Rights* by means of an everyday situation. Article 10 refers to "full equality" and "fair and public hearing by an independent and impartial tribunal." Such phrases remain "gobbledegook" unless dramatized in meaningful situations. The author describes a situation in which a big boy practicing with a ball inadvertently hits a small child who suddenly raced in front of him. The necessity for collecting evidence and presenting it to someone who was not emotionally involved is made clear. Another example of writing that helps clarify the "far away in time or space" is in Buehr's *Knights, Castles, and Feudal Life*. He relates medieval customs to modern life by explaining the law of the feudal days in these words:

> Now we are all subject to and protected by the same laws. It would be unthinkable for Chicago to declare war on Milwaukee over a piece of forest land, or for the Mayor of St. Louis to collect tolls from all Mississippi ships carrying freight by his city. . . .
> Yet such things happened every day in Medieval Europe and they were accepted as proper.[60]

Does the Style Invite Reader Involvement? The basic technique of creating a feeling of involvement is using the pronoun "you" and writing in a conversational tone.

---

[59]Marjorie Bartlett Sanger, *Cypress Country*, Illustrated by Christine Price (Cleveland: World Publishing, 1965), p. 60.

[60]Walter Buehr, *Knights, Castles and Feudal Life* (New York: Putnam, 1957), p. 8.

However, this is not the only approach; reader involvement can come as the writer develops a "you are there" atmosphere.

Children do seek adventure, but it should not appear too contrived. The opening lines of *Adventures in Living Plants* may be "over-drawn" for many children who want their science straight:

> *Would you like to go on some trips? I don't mean ordinary trips by car or train or plane. I mean special trips that are big adventures! The adventures I'm talking about aren't for softies, though. Do you still want to go? Good! I had hoped you would. Before we go on our first trip I think I should tell you a few things about plants. Then you will enjoy the thrills of the trip a lot more.*[61]

The author gives the child a reducing pill, suggests the child take his hand, and they swim or walk about inside plants. The child old enough to carry out the excellent activities will not want to take anyone's hand; neither will he appreciate this "talking down" approach. Another example shows how an introduction can create interest in a straight-forward manner:

> *There is excitement in the biology laboratories today. With trained minds and powerful research tools, scientists in every field related to the study of biology are closing in on the hitherto mysterious forces of life itself. The excitement centers around something far too small to be "seen" or photographed in detail through even the most powerful microscopes. But it is something that seems to hold the "key" to every form of life on earth. It is what makes the difference between a man, a mouse, or a mountain lion.*[62]

This book, too, offers adventure, but in a very different way!

An informational book appeals if it is a "true story." Two books about Monarch butterflies have good introductions for middle-grade readers. In the preface to *The Travels of Monarch X*, Hutchins begins, "This is the true story of a Monarch butterfly. It was one of thousands of Monarchs tagged by Dr. Fred Urquhart of the University of Toronto, Canada, in his interesting studies of butterfly migration."[63] The author of *Monarch Butterflies* indicated that other children are interested as she begins the book:

> *On the last Saturday of October, the children of Pacific Grove in California have a special holiday and parade that is celebrated nowhere else in the world. Dressed in homemade insect costumes, they welcome the arrival of some two million monarch butterflies, which come every year at this time to spend the winter on certain "butterfly trees."*[64]

One technique of writing that leads to a feeling of involvement is inclusion of questions. In *Bees, Bugs and Beetles*, Rood cites an incident in which a grasshopper is hanging with its head in a puddle:

> *Why hadn't the grasshopper drowned with its head under water? Because insects do not breathe the way we do. If you could look along the side of a grasshopper with a magnifying glass, you would see a row of tiny spots. A microscope would show that each spot is really a little hole. This is a breathing hole.*[65]

The pacing of the writing in Nathan's *The Building of the First Transcontinental Railroad* adds to the feeling that the reader is actually

[61]Edwin B. Kurtz, Jr. and Chris Allen, *Adventures in Living Plants* (Tucson: University of Arizona Press, 1965), p. 2.

[62]Carleen Maley Hutchins, *Life's Key—DNA, a Biological Adventure into the Unknown* (New York: Coward-McCann, 1961), p. 6.

[63]Ross E. Hutchins, *The Travels of Monarch X,* Illustrated by Jerome P. Connolly (Skokie, Ill.: Rand McNally, 1966), p. 2.

[64]Alice L. Hopf, *Monarch Butterflies,* Illustrated by Peter Burchard (New York: Crowell, 1965), p. 1.

[65]Ronald Rood, *Bees, Bugs and Beetles, the Arrow Book of Insects,* Illustrated by Denny McMains (New York: Four Winds, 1965), p. 9.

operating the telegraph key as the golden spike is ready to join the two sections. Telegraph wires are attached to the sledge hammers so the nation can hear. The reader "listens" intently as the operator taps out the messages:

> "All ready now," went out over the wire. "The last spike will soon be driven. The signal will be three dots for the commencement of the blow." An instant later the silver hammers came down.
> "Done!"
> The words flashed out. The last spike, the golden spike, had been driven home.
> The country was united from coast to coast by an unbroken band of iron rails.[66]

Clara Ingram Judson's clear prose style makes the reader feel he is mingling with the crowd watching the work on the *St. Lawrence Seaway*. He can almost hear the young salesman, turned canoe builder, direct the work as he reads, "Bring up the canoe, you, there! Take that end and climb in careful now!"[67] Again Mrs. Judson involves the reader as she describes the problems that would come when 18,000 acres would be flooded. She quotes one who has to move, "Would you think you had gained if you'd lived all your life by the canal and had to leave it? . . . Makes a man wonder. They tell us it's for the good of all. . . ."[68] Here is no collection of dry facts, but a lively story that has meaning for today.

Is the Language Pattern Clear and Simple, or Heavy and Pedantic?   Clarity is also related to the effectiveness of an informational book. It would be clear to say, "magnified one hundred times"; it is vague to say "highly magnified" as in the text of Kirk for the

photographic essay, *Birds in Flight*. In *Wonders of Hummingbirds*, Simon helps the reader recall his knowledge of light refraction, and then, helps him understand the effect of the construction of the bird's feathers. Bronowski and Selsam have written an accurate, clear explanation of a difficult concept, *Biography of an Atom*. Yet there is no heavy tone of the lecturer.

Is There an Appropriate Amount of Detail?   It has been noted previously that omission of some detail can lead to misconceptions. Irrelevant details that detract from the central purpose of the book have no place in the well-written informational book. This criterion will be evaluated according to the reader's purpose, and is related to the effectiveness of the table of contents and index in guiding the reader to the specific facts he seeks. Some books provide more detail than the average reader with general interest will want. *The Hunt for the Whooping Cranes, a Natural History Detective Story* by McCoy provides details of various searches for nesting places of the cranes. For most readers, there are too many details; however, a reader with special interest in cranes, will savor the information.

Extraneous details may merely clutter the account and occupy space that could have been used for more appropriate or more interesting content. In *The Deepest Hole in the World*, Wolfe includes a rather unnecessary chapter on science fiction and "crackpot theories" regarding the earth's core. Probably the details of problems of drilling the hole would be of concern only to the person interested in technicalities.

Does the Book Encourage Curiosity and Further Study?   Not only should the author communicate his own interest in the subject, he should convey his sense of wonder and help the reader see there is still more to learn. Clear directions are given for identif-

---

[66] Adele Nathan, *The Building of the First Transcontinental Railroad* (New York: Random House, 1950), p. 161.
[67] Clara Ingram Judson, *St. Lawrence Seaway*, Illustrated by Lorence V. Bjorklund (Chicago: Follett, 1959), p. 79.
[68] Judson, p. 111.

ication of bird nests in *Look for a Bird's Nest* by Scharff. The author points out the importance of recording information and labeling specimens carefully. Fisher's question in *The Wonderful World of the Sea* may stimulate future scientists:

> Who knows where these new and daring explorations will end? Someone already born may well see the world's greatest ocean depths, and bring back photographs of creatures unknown to science. . . . But we shall never learn the whole of the story of the sea's stormy surface or probe the last secret of the silent depths.[69]

The well-written informational book widens the child's vision and opens new vistas of beauty and mystery. As Rachel Carson describes the spawning of the grunion at the time of the highest tides, text and pictures create the scene:

> Now on these waves of the ebbing tide the fish begin to come in. Their bodies shimmer in the light of the moon as they are borne up the beach on the crest of a wave. . . . This strange, perfect link with the tides is something to fill us with wonder.[70]

Carthy points out the relationship of human mastery of environment to scientific investigation. He concludes the excellent book, *Animals and Their Ways*:

> In particular, we want to know more about the relationships between inborn and acquired behavior . . . and about the way learned behavior is stored. These are but a few of the fields open for further investigation. And, as in all scientific investigations, the more we discover, the more we shall be conscious of what remains to be discovered.[71]

Thus, informational books open doors to the future as the child reads about what is known today.

Format and Illustration

Do Illustrations Clarify and Extend the Text? Illustrations should blend with text, add interest, and create a pleasing artistic effect. However, the main purpose of photographs, diagrams, or drawings is to clarify or extend the information in the text. Mere decoration is not enough.

In recent years, photographs have been used more frequently in informational books. The photograph should be large enough to show all details clearly. It should focus upon one idea, one part, or one person. The photographs in *The World of The Living* by Ubell focus on one animal, or one part of his body. Strong, the photographer, utilized interesting shadows and textured backgrounds to create artistic effects. It is good to note that Negro as well as white children are at play in this book.

The photographs in the Sterling Nature series are outstanding examples of the effective use of the camera to give information. In Doering's *A Bee Is Born*, picture sequences show the development of larvae and emergence from the wax cells. Action photos show a guard bee attacking a wasp and illustrate the way a stinger is left as a bee flies away.

Photographs in books about cities or foreign countries should be up-to-date unless they are used for historical study. A photograph of a city in the United States that shows 1935 autos and streetcars would be out of date.

Closeups are preferable to distance shots because it is often difficult to distinguish features of terrain. A picture in *Greece* by Miller has tropical vegetation silhouetted in the foreground and a blurred image of buildings in the distance. Labeled "View across

---

[69] James Fisher, *The Wonderful World of the Sea* (New York: Garden City Books, 1957), p. 68.
[70] Carson, p. 24.
[71] J. D. Carthy, *Animals and Their Ways* (Garden City, N.Y.: Natural History, 1965), p. 149.

Accurate pictures for a science book can be beautiful, as shown by the fine composition of branches, soft night sky, and glowing luna moth. Illustration by Douglas Howland. Copyright 1965 by Douglas Howland, from the book *Moon Moth* by Carleen Maley Hutchins. Reprinted by permission of Coward-McCann, Inc.

harbor, Mykonas," this photograph gives little information.[72]

Do Different Types of Media Maintain Clarity of Concepts? When two or more media are used for illustration, each should be chosen because it serves a purpose; otherwise, a muddled effect may result. The combination of artistic drawings and photographs in *Birth of a Forest* by Selsam is effective. A diagrammatic sketch of the lake with its plants and animals is followed by a photo showing a closeup of a catfish. If different media are used, space should be planned to avoid a feeling of clutter.

---

[72] Helen Hill Miller, *Greece* (New York: Scribner, 1965), p. 151.

An excellent example of books profusely illustrated with many different types of pictures is the *American Heritage* series. It utilizes paintings, illustrations from books and newspapers, and photographs of artifacts to give information about one historical period. *The Erie Canal* by Andrist exemplifies the pattern of this excellent series. The cover picture in color is an 1884 painting of a scene on the Erie Canal, endsheets show a panoramic painting of the canal in the Mohawk Valley, and the title page includes a watercolor showing tow horses pulling a packet on the canal. On the first page of the table of contents is a photograph of an 1825 china plate showing the canal, and the index is decorated with a color swatch of wallpaper designed with a canal motif. There are several double-page spreads of paintings in full color. Children will learn much by reading the captions and studying the illustrations.

For some content, photographs would be better than drawings or paintings. *Look for a Bird's Nest* by Scharff, suggests ways to locate, collect, and display nests. Photographs would have been more helpful than drawings. In other books, the artist's sketch is more appropriate. For example, in *The Story of Ants* by Shuttlesworth the drawings accurately portray details of the various ants.

In *Wonders of Hummingbirds*, Simon used color and soft lines in order to convey the idea that the iridescence of the hummingbird's color results as light reflects through his feathers. Had she used harsh, brilliant color that would picture the bird at one moment, she would have lost this effect. The illustrations for Hutchins' *Moon Moth* evoke the night, and are beautiful in black and white. However, the realistic painting of the luna on the book jacket shows the importance of color.

Color and design can detract from illustrations. The heavy colors, sharp crests of stylized waves, and marblized pattern of ice in the illustrations for *At Home on the Ice* by

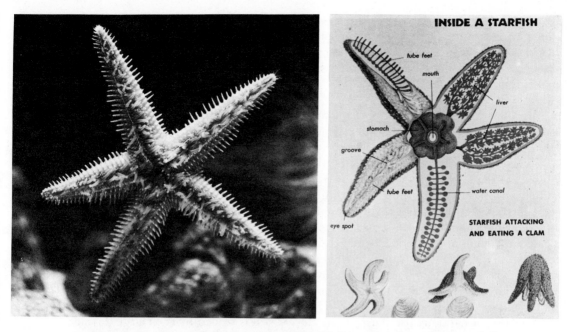

A photograph of a starfish gives one kind of information in a close-up of the underside of the animal. Further understandings are developed in diagrammatic form in another book. Children need both kinds of material for comparison. Photograph from *Let's Go to the Seashore* by Harriet Huntington, 1941. Reprinted by permission of Doubleday & Company, Inc. Diagram from "Inside a Starfish" from *What's Inside of Animals* by Herbert Zim, illustrated by Herschel Wartik. Copyright 1953. Reproduced by permission of William Morrow & Company, Inc.

Miller and Seligman draw attention away from the penguins, the main subject of the book. Although the artist can convey feeling and movement, the artistic effect should not dominate. For example, in Sherman's *You and the Oceans* the sketches are attractive but quite unrealistic. Dramatic illustration may be too intense. In *The First Book of Civil War Land Battles* by Dupuy, a dead soldier, mouth open, eyes staring, occurs in several chapters. It depicts the horror of war, but the repetition might be questioned.

Photographs or illustrations that are accurate in detail and color are necessary for identification books. The illustrations in *The First Book of Birds* by Williamson, for example, would not suffice for bird-watching.

Diagrams are essential to clarify processes or the abstract ideas explained in many books. For example, the illustrations are an integral part of Corbett's book, *What Makes a Light Go On?* Diagrams explain the theoretical structure of the atom and clearly show how electrons move through a wire, how static electricity is created, and the meaning of alternating current. When a diagram is used to illustrate steps in a process, space should be provided so each phase, part, or process can be clearly distinguished. The diagrams in *What Makes TV Work?* by Corbett, are so crowded it is difficult to distinguish the various parts. In Conklin's *I Like Caterpillars*, it is difficult to find the letter that identifies each caterpillar.

Although they do not have to be realistic in detail, the diagrams should not be fuzzy or vague. For example, the text in a book for young readers by Liss, *Heat*, says "Heat helps us run machines and engines." The illustration pictures some vague type of boiler or machine with dials, arrows, and a flame, but there is no explanation of the way heat makes the machine do work.

Are Illustrations Explained by Captions or Labels?   Parts of a diagram or illustration should be labeled and explained in the text or caption. One diagram in Corbett's *What Makes TV Work?* shows an amplifier, transmitter, and receiver, but these terms are not explained. A confusing diagram is presented in *Echoes* by Kohn, and the same idea is repeated throughout the book. Curved lines are used to illustrate the sound wave moving toward a reflecting object and then moving back. With an explanation in a caption or text, the idea could be clarified.

The use of captions for illustrations depends upon the purpose of the book. If additional information is given in the illustration, the caption is necessary. The text of *Sea Horses* by Hess really consists of expanded captions for the excellent photographs made by the author. Immediately above a clear picture of the head of a seahorse the text says:

> *The oxygen is extracted and the water flows out under the gill covers. Sea horses also breathe this way. If you look closely you can see that the edges of the gill covers look like the letter "C."*[73]

The picture shows the details clearly. Many books utilize this approach effectively; others use captions to give further information, while some may serve to emphasize information given in the text.

Are Size Relationships Made Clear? When illustrations show magnified parts or wholes, the diagram should make this clear. Some information should be given

regarding actual size. In *The First Book of Birds*, the diagram of the feather clearly shows there was magnification, but actual size is not presented. The illustration of feathers in *Birds* by Wasson does not indicate size, nor does it show the part of the bird from which the feather came.

The size of very small or very large objects is difficult to understand. The use of metaphor within the child's range of experience and illustrations will be helpful. Harris and Harris use an effective technique in *Flash, the Life Story of a Firefly* to develop understanding of the size of a firefly egg. They write that it is "only as large as the very tip of the lead in a pencil," and the illustration shows a pencil pointing to a small dot. A good example of size concept is in *The Story of Ants* by Shuttlesworth. A figure in actual size is placed by each large detailed drawing.

Does Size of Type and Space Contribute to Clarity?   Type should be easy to read and margins should give an effect of comfortable space. In some books, it is difficult to read the print on colored pages, as in Miller's *At Home on the Ice*. Another problem is the location of page numbers in books that omit numbers on several pages because photographs extend to the edge of the paper. The pages should be designed so that a number appears on at least one page of a double page spread. The size, kind, and placement of type contribute both to clarity and interest of the informational book.

Are Endpapers Used Effectively? Endpapers may be used to convey the general theme of the book, to show maps, or to give further illustration of the content. Unfortunately, many informational books do not utilize this space. The endpapers of *Animals and Their Ways* by Carthy, show colorful, childlike paintings that may well have been the work of the chimpanzee pictured on one of the pages in the text.

---

[73]Lilo Hess, *Sea Horses* (New York: Scribner, 1966), p. 21.

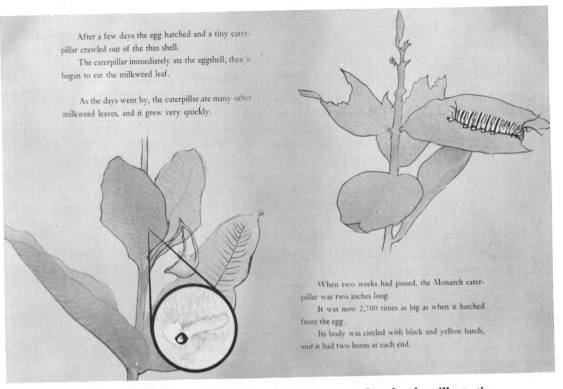

After a few days the egg hatched and a tiny caterpillar crawled out of the thin shell.

The caterpillar immediately ate the eggshell; then it began to eat the milkweed leaf.

As the days went by, the caterpillar ate many other milkweed leaves, and it grew very quickly.

When two weeks had passed, the Monarch caterpillar was two inches long.

It was now 2,700 times as big as when it hatched from the egg.

Its body was circled with black and yellow bands, and it had two horns at each end.

Text states the exact size of the caterpillar as it grows, but the clear illustration makes the changing size meaningful by showing magnification and relationship to the leaf. From *The Travels of Monarch X* by Ross E. Hutchins, illustrated by Jerome P. Connolly. Copyright 1966 by Rand McNally & Company, publishers.

Organization

Are Subheadings Utilized Effectively? The general, survey type of book should have subheadings that will help the reader get an overview of the content and locate information. For example, *Hawaii* by Swenson has no table of contents or index. Although it is a *Book-to-Begin On*, it should provide such help for younger readers. In contrast, another book for younger readers, *The True Book of Space* by Podendorf, has a very clear table of contents with important words printed in capital letters. Books on more specific topics frequently use subheadings, also. Chapter titles should reflect the content of the chapter or section, and should avoid the overly coy and clever. In *The First Book of Mars*, chapter titles give information, and are interesting. The author, Knight, includes: "Destination Mars—the Historic Flight of Mariner IV," "Those Martian Canals," and "But *Is* There Life on Mars?" A book that develops a concept, as *Biography of an Atom* by Bronowski and Selsam, does not require subheadings.

Does the Table of Contents and Index Help the Reader Locate Information Quickly? Usually a reader seeks specific information, but he often enjoys a more casual perusal of text and illustration. For example, he may enjoy browsing through a bird book; later he may seek specific information about one bird. An index is essential in an informational book, but it will be truly useful only if it is complete and has necessary cross-references. Perhaps every topic receiving mention will not be indexed, but certainly a discussion of a paragraph or more should be included. In *What Makes TV Work?* Corbett did not list "tuning" in the index, although two paragraphs discussed changes effected by tuning.

It is difficult to think of the possible words children might use to look up a topic or to answer a question, yet writers should consider as many possibilities as would seem reasonable. If one wanted to find out about "language," "talk," "sound," or "speech" of dolphins, he would probably look under l, s, or t. In Lauber's *The Friendly Dolphins,* the topic is finally found under "d" as "dolphin talk." In this same book the words "size," "eyes," and "baby" are omitted although there is information on these aspects of dolphin life.

Does the Bibliography Indicate Sources Used by the Author and Sources for Further Reading by Children?   If the child is to understand the method of inquiry, he needs to learn that a writer uses many sources of information, and he should be given a "recommended" list of materials for further study. Some authors include bibliographies in their informational books, but few separate books for children from the more technical resources used for their own research.

Do Appendixes Extend Information? Information can be extended by tabulating data, presenting charts or lists, or giving historical data in an appendix. The appendix of *Ships, Shoals, and Amphoras,* by de Borhegyi, for example, tells where to make archeological explorations and how to explore under the sea. Mead gives a list of the works of people she interviewed for *Anthropologists and What They Do* and gives information on scholarships. The appendix of Swinton's *Digging for Dinosaurs* gives a list, "Museums with Fossil Collections Worth Visiting." Folsom adds a reading list and

gives important dates in Russian history in *The Soviet Union.* When such materials are available, children should be taught to use them.

Summary of Criteria for Informational Books

Before a discussion of types of informational books, factors to be considered in their evaluation are summarized below.

ACCURACY AND AUTHENTICITY
- What are the qualifications of the author?
- Are facts accurate?
- Is the book realistic?
- Are facts and theories clearly distinguished?
- Do text and illustrations avoid stereotypes?
- Is the book up-to-date?
- Are significant details omitted?
- Do generalizations go beyond present knowledge?
- Are differing viewpoints presented?
- In geographic books, is diversity revealed?
- In science books, is anthropomorphism omitted?
- Are phenomena given teleological explanations?

CONTENT
- Is this a general survey book or one of specific interest?
- Is the coverage of the book adequate for its purpose?
- Is the book within the comprehension and interest range of the age for which intended?
- Do experiment books lead to understanding of science?
- Are experiments and activities safe and feasible?
- Does the book present interrelationships of facts and principles?
- Do science books indicate related social problems?

- Is the book fresh and original?
- Does the book help the reader understand the methods of science and social science?

STYLE
- Is information given directly or in story form?
- Is the text interesting and appropriate for the age level intended?
- Do vivid language and appropriate metaphor create interest and understanding?
- Does the style create the feeling of reader involvement?
- Is the language pattern clear and simple, or heavy and pedantic?
- Is there an appropriate amount of detail?
- Does the book encourage curiosity and further study?

FORMAT AND ILLUSTRATION
- Do illustrations clarify and extend the text?
- Do different types of media maintain clarity of concepts?
- Are illustrations explained by captions or labels?
- Are size relationships made clear?
- Do size of type and use of space contribute to clarity?
- Are endpapers used effectively?

ORGANIZATION
- Are subheadings utilized effectively?
- Do the table of contents and index help the reader locate information quickly?
- Does the bibliography indicate sources used by the author, and sources for further reading by children?
- Do appendixes extend information?

TYPES OF INFORMATIONAL BOOKS

Knowledge of the types of informational books now on library shelves and being published will help the teacher and librarian provide balanced and rich resources for learning. The types of informational books include concept books, informational picture books, life-cycle animal books, general surveys, experiment books, specialized content, documents, and reference books.

Concept Books

An understanding of the role of printed material in concept development is important for the librarian and teacher. Although first-hand experience and language development are primary in the process, books may play a part in this development of a generalized abstraction of a common characteristic or a relationship. Children develop mathematical concepts of size, weight, and number; concepts of time and space; scientific concepts of order, sequence, and cause in the physical environment; concepts of self; and such social concepts as family, community, slum, democracy, justice. Books that contribute to the young child's development through processes of naming objects and building such concepts as "roundness" were discussed in Chapter 3.

The titles of some books are concept statements: *A Map Is a Picture* by Rinkoff, *The World Is Round* by Ravielli, *I Live in So Many Places* by Hengesbaugh. Other books slowly build one fact upon another, from simple to more complex until the generalization is made. *The World Is Round,* for example, begins with a circle, then the edge of a coin; next, a sphere is related to a ball. Using the analogy of a fly on the ball and comparing it to a house, the author, Ravielli, builds the idea that we, as the fly, see only a very small part of the earth, so it appears flat to us. He follows this with the early observations of Pythagoras and Aristotle and the proof given by Columbus and Magellan. This book appears to be a picture book, yet it is not appropriate for the age group usually termed the "picture book age." It is a book that will help a middle-grade child develop concepts of time and space as he generalizes, "The world is round."

One of the *Let's Read and Find Out* series, *A Map Is a Picture* by Rinkoff, begins with children making a treasure map, thus relating the idea, again, to first-hand experience. Then a map of the neighborhood is followed by maps of the city, state, United States, continent, and world. Agricultural maps, a sea map, and star map are mentioned. No mention is made of the distortion of a flat map of the world.

Bits That Grow Big by Webber and *The Flower* by Downer are examples of books for preschool or kindergarten children that trace the development of a seed into a plant. *A Tree Is a Plant,* by Bulla, is one of the *Let's Read and Find Out* series that develops a concept of a tree growing and changing through the seasons. The book concludes by asking "When do you like apple trees best," but it shows the tree in spring, summer, winter, and fall, thus presenting an order that may lead to a misconception.

The series that begins "a fresh look at . . . " is intended to help the child recall his perceptions and build concepts. Some of the series are trite and fail to achieve the purpose, but *A Fresh Look at Night* by Bendick is original and will make the child more aware of the factors that contribute to the idea that "night is wonderful."

They Turned to Stone gives information that builds a concept of a fossil. By showing what might happen to a fish, May, the author, shows how a fossil is made. The book ends as it begins, with children looking at a stone, saying, "Maybe it was once alive."

How Far Is Far? is the intriguing title of a book by Tresselt. The collage illustrations are beautiful and essential in creating the concept through metaphors related to the child's experience. Similarly, *How Big Is Big?* by the Schneiders develops concepts of size

and distance. Relativity is a factor in the concept of speed developed by Froman in *Faster and Faster, a Book about Speed.* In series the author shows the speed of a glacier, snail, turtle, human, horse, fish, cheetah, car, tornado, rocket, and light. He ends with the speed of imagination.

What Is the World? by Miles brings to young children the concept of a round planet with land and sea, mountains, and rivers. In *I Live in So Many Places*, Hengesbaugh describes the world in which the child lives. Each page develops the idea of a place where the child lives—in a house on a street, in a town or city, in a state, a country, a continent, and a hemisphere. The simple line drawings help clarify the meaning of these words.

Although more facts are given in books for older children, some of them aim to develop one major generalization. *All about Us* by Evans illustrates the generalization that behavior is determined by culture. Cartoon-like drawings show how customs developed, for example, the handshake is derived from the action of a "Sir Bigglety" extending his right hand to show he has no weapons. Greetings in different cultures are then illustrated. The foundation for a concept of relativity is laid by Clark in *You and Relativity.* Relativity of "up" and "down," size, motion, and time is explained through very clear examples. The theories of Einstein, Nicholson, and Morley are presented briefly.

Processes as well as objects must be conceptualized by the child. For example, the process of classifying animals is explained in *Benny's Animals and How He Put Them in Order* by Selsam. This *I Can Read* book shows how pictures of animals were classified. Children could cut out pictures as Benny did and classify them according to animals with backbones and animals without backbones. An easy book by Miles, *A House for Everyone*, develops the concept that houses differ, but all of them provide shelter. Similar concepts are summarized by Burns in *A World Full of Homes:*

> *1. People live in homes because they need shelter. . . .*
> *2. They make their homes in ways that seem best to them. . . .*
> *3. We know that people were influenced by the country they lived in. . . .*[74]

Follow the Sunset presents the idea that the earth turns, bringing night to each part of the world. The soft pink glow of the sunset reflects on each page as the Schneiders describe the rhythm of life around the world as families return from work, eat, laugh together, and sing the little ones to sleep. Differences in environment, work, dress, home, food, and language are shown, but all are united in the need for rest and comfort in the family circle as the earth keeps turning. The recording of folk lullabies, under the same title, would enrich the experience of this book that is enjoyed by children in primary and middle grades.

Usually it will be wise to read concept books to children, giving them time to look at the pictures, to ask questions, and to relate the content of the book to their own experience. The child may not be able to verbalize the generalization, but books that help him discriminate and generalize are contributing to concept development.

Informational Picture Books

The picture book and picture story book as a type of literature were discussed in Chapter 3. The picture book as a literary experience is concerned with the emotional response to the environment or events. Gilberto plays with the wind, but there is no attempt to explain causes of the wind in *Gilberto and the Wind*, a picture book by Ets.

Tresselt's *Hide and Seek Fog* is not designed to give information about causes of fog nor economic problems of the lobster fisherman who cannot go out to his traps. Many books of pictures, especially photograph books, are designed to give information. A wide age range can enjoy the photographs, but the text requires middle-grade reading ability.

Examples of photographic informational picture books are *A Chipmunk Lives Here* and *Foxes Live Here* by Eberle, *Lion Island* by Bridges, and *Easter in November* by Hess. All use large, clear, interesting photographs and a brief text. The child who is losing his baby teeth will especially enjoy the information about the way chipmunks get permanent teeth. The book relates a full year in the chipmunk's life. *Lion Island* tells of two cubs born in the Bronx Zoo. The text must be read by the primary teacher, for it includes such sentences as, "But flop down she did in the most abject way that said as plainly as words, I know I shouldn't have done it."[75] *Easter in November* will interest all ages, for it tells about the Araucana chicken and how it is like and different from the other chickens. The title is understood when the reader sees the last color photo of a nest of pastel-colored eggs laid by the Araucana. The fine, uncluttered closeups give the details necessary for understanding. Although the text is beautifully written, and gives much information, the photographs in *The Gull's Way* make Darling's book a photographic essay. *The Sterling Nature* series includes such titles as *A Tree Is Born, A Fruit Is Born, A Bee Is Born,* and *A Butterfly Is Born.* The books really consist of captions for the excellent photographs. Guilcher and Noailles authored the first two, while Doering wrote the text about bees, and Eeckhoudt gave the captions about growth of butterflies. These books are appropriate for readers from eight to eighty.

---

[74]William A. Burns, *A World Full of Homes* (New York: Whittlesey, 1953), p. 114.

[75]William Bridges, *Lion Island,* Photographed by Emmy Haas and Sam Dunton (New York: Morrow, 1965), p. 60.

Amusing illustrations capture the tourists' view of London. From *This is London* by Miroslav Sasek, copyright © 1959 by Miroslav Sasek. Used with the permission of The Macmillan Company.

Artist's illustrations can also be essential for presentation of information. If the book depends in large part upon the illustration, it may be called an informational picture book rather than an illustrated informational book. For example, Ravielli's *Elephants* depends upon his fine drawings to give the information about the early ancestors and elephants today. The information of *Spider Silk* by Goldin is given in both text and illustration. Texture is skillfully used in these well-spaced drawings. However, such books as *Moon Moth* by Carleen Hutchins and *The Travels of Monarch X* by Ross Hutchins are enhanced by, but not dependent upon, the illustrations.

Sasek's picture books of cities and countries are in a class by themselves. These large, beautifully designed books reflect the interests of the traveler looking at the region through the eyes of a child. The series begins "This is . . ." and includes Paris, Munich, Rome, New York, Israel, Ireland, San Francisco, and Hong Kong. In *This Is Paris*, the well-known Czech painter has used the techniques of Monet and Seurat to express the reflections of the "City of Light" as tiny dots of color shimmer below the Eiffel Tower. The people's faces are reminiscent of Modigliani; for example, the lady carrying the long bread stick. Famous landmarks, such as Notre Dame, Pont de Neuf, and the Louvre, as well as every-day bus stops, book stalls, and letter boxes are pictured with an effective use of space. Wisely, he included the Monkey's Paradise at the zoo, French poodles, and a cemetery for dogs. Adults who have been in Paris may enjoy this book even more than children!

G. Warren Schloat has presented interesting photographic stories of children in other lands under such titles as *Junichi, A Boy of Japan; Uttam, A Boy of India; Propan, A Boy of Thailand;* and *Naim, A Boy of Turkey.* He includes information about daily life, food, clothing, games, work, and school. The reader is not given information about the place of the one village in the country, problems they face, or cultural values. There is much to learn by "reading" these photographs, however.

Girls will be pleased to find the picture book about *Sigemi, a Japanese Village Girl* by Kirk and Spring showing modern Japanese life. Carr's book is entitled *The Picture Story of Japan,* but the sketchy illustrations are almost too cluttered to give information effectively.

Information is extended to show changes in Japan and how it has achieved world status in finance, publishing, photography, and sports. The example of a letter written in Japanese will intrigue children in middle grades.

Children enjoy looking at picture books, and they do absorb much information in this way. However, if informational picture books are to serve their best purpose, children need guidance in comprehending and interpreting the information in each picture.

Identification Books

Identification books are books designed to help children classify and name living or nonliving things. The very first books for children are usually naming books. Teachers and librarians need to know identification books to help answer the question, "What kind is it?" when a child brings a stone, a leaf, or a wriggling snake. The *Golden Nature Guides* by Zim are very useful small pocketbooks crammed with information. The series includes stars, wildflowers, birds, and rocks and minerals. Another helpful series is *The First Book of . . .* series published by Watts. In this series, Cavanna wrote . . . *Wildflowers* and Beck wrote . . . *Weeds.* The illustrations for this series are clear, well spaced, and extend the text written for children in the middle grades. *The First Book of Birds* by Williamson and *Bird Watchers and Bird Feeders* by Blough both provide an introduction to birds. The clues for identification are perhaps better in the second book. The woodcuts by Clement Hurd are excellent in *Winter Birds*, but the slight text by Garelick gives little information. The pictures would be most useful for schools in the Central Plains and New England. There are few bird books for other regions. Peterson's *The Junior Book of Birds* is an authoritative reference, and middle-grade children can use his complete guide, *How to Know the Birds.*

Another series of identification books has been prepared by Pistorious under such titles as *What Butterfly Is It?*, *What Bird Is It?*, and *What Tree Is It?* Unusual questions are answered by the text and illustrations. In *What Dinosaur Is It?*, some of the questions are: "What dinosaur had 2000 teeth?" "What was the smallest dinosaur?" "What were the 'sail reptiles'?" Watts has written a very useful book titled *The Doubleday First Guide to Trees.* The trees are grouped according to areas where they would grow; sunny places, wet places, a shady forest. The leaf, flower, a fruit, and shape of the tree is shown on each page. This book is small enough to carry in pocket or knapsack on a field trip. Crayon rubbings were used by Lerner to make her illustrations for *I Found a Leaf.* It is a simple book, just right for the primary classroom when children are bringing leaves to identify. They could make their own books of crayon rubbings of leaves after looking at this book and hearing it read.

Clemons has organized her book about seaweed, crabs, starfish, shells, and coral

Books contribute to the thrill of discovering specific facts.

The next shells that we found
were scallop shells
with crimpy edges.
They were shaped like ladies' fans,
with little ridges
from top to bottom.

Delicately colored illustrations relate familiar objects to names of shells. With its accurate and imaginative pictures, this book was nominated runner-up for the 1960 Caldecott Award. Illustration by Adrienne Adams is reproduced with the permission of Charles Scribner's Sons from *Houses from the Sea*, page 13, by Alice Goudey. Copyright © 1959 Adrienne Adams.

very well. Both the common and scientific name is given in *Tide Pools and Beaches*. Her suggestion that animals be left in their natural habitat is a good one. Buck also gives helpful information about pond life and sea animals in her books. *In Ponds and Streams* and *Along the Seashore* include both plants and animals and would be excellent guides to use before and after a field trip.

Teachers will want books for identification of stars, planets, and constellations. A way of locating stars and constellations is explained in *The Stars by Clock and Fist*. This book by Neely will encourage children to establish bearings for locating stars by considering the Pole Star twelve o'clock on a clock face and by sighting a number of "fists" high, as the arm and closed fist become a sighting guide.

Children will enjoy the beautiful watercolors and the rhythmic text of *Houses from the Sea* by Goudey. Adrienne Adams' art work in this book about shells won a place as runner-up for the 1960 Caldecott award. This would be a good book to read aloud to the primary class. Much information is woven into the text, and the illustrations at the end will provide a quick guide for identification.

Life Cycle Animal Books

The cycle of life from the birth of one animal to the birth of its progeny is often the basis of the informational book. Several authors have used the technique of describing events in one year in an animal's life, or have traced the development of that animal through his life time. These factual books may give a name to the animal, but human emotions or the ability to talk have not been given to the creature (see Chapter 10). McClung has used this style in *Sphinx, the Story of a Caterpillar*. Sphinx, the caterpillar, eats tomato leaves, changes to a pupa beneath the ground, and emerges as a sphinx moth in the eternal mystery of metamorphosis, but he is never given human characteristics in this account of his habits. In *Screamer, Last of the Eastern Panthers*, McClung adds a postscript giving further information and conjecturing that there may be panthers in the eastern United States today. The Harrises also use this style effectively in *Little Red Newt*. This same writing team produced *Flash, the Life Story of a Firefly*. The information about body structure, changes in metamorphosis, enemies, and reproduction is presented by telling the story of one firefly. A contrived incident in which Flash is captured in a house, discussed in stilted language by parents and a boy, and finally released, detracts from the book.

Alice Goudey's series includes *Here Come the Beavers, Here Come the Seals,* and *Here Come the Bears.* Olive Earle is another writer who presents accurate, interesting information. *Crickets, Mice at Home and Afield, Swans of Willow Pond,* and *Robins in the Garden* are distinctive examples of her contribution to this type of literature for children. Both Goudey and Earle describe a cycle of life, showing the mating of adults, rearing the young, and the beginning of a new generation.

Longer life-cycle stories present the animal in such a way that courage, patience, curiosity, and skill are emphasized and character development is shown. But because the animal does not express feeling through language, he maintains his realistic animal nature. These are stories of survival against the elements and the enemies of the environment. John and Jean George have written and illustrated excellent stories of this type: *Masked Prowler, the Story of a Raccoon; Vison, the Mink; Vulpes, the Red Fox.* These books follow the pattern of the continued struggle for survival, finding food and shelter, selecting a mate, and defense against enemies. The skill, cunning, and determination of these animals is to be admired. They face death, often even dying violently, for this, too, is the way of life. The illustrations by Jean George portray their habitats with accuracy and beauty. Holling's beautifully illustrated books, *Minn of the Mississippi* and *Pagoo* trace the life history of a turtle, Minn, and a crawfish. The reader learns of the history of the environment created by man, industries in the area traversed by the animal, and many facts about the animals. O'Neill's *The White Palace* relates the life cycle of a Chinook salmon, giving more emotion to the animal than do some of the authors above.

Liers' story of Ottiga, a Michigan otter, follows a similar pattern. *An Otter's Story* tells how animals are often defeated by the jaws of the traps set by man. There is no conversation, but the otters are given human feelings. There is sorrow when an otter child is hurt. Pride, love, and tenderness are expressed by the animals in this fastmoving story.

An interesting comparison could be made of *Young Eagle* by Freschet and *The Golden Eagle* by Murphy. Murphy's novel of the eagle was written for adults but could be read by many fifth and sixth graders. The eagle, named Kira, is given human feelings. Kira is orphaned, learns to kill, faces and conquers the old man who captured her, finds ecstasy in soaring flights, and finally meets death through the poison left by a rancher. There is much information, but it is essentially the story of a brave, joyous eagle. The descriptions of the mountains are breathtaking.

The illustrations in *Young Eagle* are in sharper focus and show more movement. This is a well-written story with less emotion and character development than in *The Golden Eagle.* Admiring the eagle's courage, the hunters in this story put down their guns, and he lives on. *Hawk in the Sky* by Russell also might be compared with the books about eagles. The Hunter is the name given this red-tailed hawk who develops great courage and determination in meeting the challenges of his environment. As in most of the life-cycle stories, he achieves his purpose, to create new life.

Experiment and Activity Books

To many children, the word science is synonymous with experiment. Experiments to satisfy individual interests and to help children answer problems in broad unit studies may be found in three types of experiment books.

General Experiment Books   One type includes several experiments on varied topics. Illa Podendorf includes experiments to illustrate a number of principles in *The True Book* series, *Science Experiments* and *More Science Experiments.* In *More Science Experiments,* simple demonstrations help young children understand principles of light, work, inertia, and water. This author has also published *101 Science Experiments* for older readers. An oversize book, the large illustrations seem unnecessary, but the well-written text promotes scientific thinking.

In *The First Book of Science Experiments,* Wyler gives very clear directions for the middle grade reader. Wyler and Ames ask few "whys" in *Prove It!,* but explanations are clearly stated. The actual photographs in *Fun with Science* by the Freemans clearly show the young scientist what materials to use. The photograph of a stream of water being attracted to an electrically charged comb is an excellent example of this technique.

Applying his experience in television as Mr. Wizard, Don Herbert combines photographs, clear directions, and concise statements of the science principle being demonstrated in *Mr. Wizard's Science Secrets.* "How to Float Steel on Water," "The Strange Silver Egg Experiment," and "How to Show Why the Sky Looks Blue," exemplify the intriguing titles of experiments in *The Real Book of Science Experiments* by Leeming. Although these titles suggest magic, the author thoroughly explains the science principle demonstrated. Originally designed for teachers, the UNESCO book, *700 Science Experiments,* could be used by the advanced students in elementary schools.

The Adlers, a team of outstanding science writers, cover a wide variety of topics in their books, *Why? a Book of Reasons* and *Why and How? a Second Book of Reasons.* The questions range from "Why does a dog's tongue hang out . . . ?" to "Why can you skate on ice?" Their book, *Things that Spin* uses a unifying theme to present activities to help children understand tops, centrifugal force, gyroscopes, and motion in the universe. At first glance, this slim book may be considered a book for the primary child; instead, it is appropriate for middle and upper grades.

Science Teasers by Wyler and Baird would be an excellent book to encourage independent activity. Experiments are grouped under such titles as "Space Age Puzzles," "Magic—or So It Seems," "Weighty Problems," and "Trick or Tease." The style is interesting and leads the reader to think of an answer before he reads it. For example, the authors describe a theory of Jules Verne and conclude:

> *Verne had launched an idea, even though his cannon would not work. The concept was wrong. A bullet shot from the Earth would never reach space. Can you figure out why?*[76]

Then the authors give a simple, clear explanation.

Experiments Related to One Subject   A second type of experiment book presents experiments keyed to one subject. *The True Book of Weather Experiments* by Podendorf is an excellent book for children in primary grades. The author develops the idea of controls and helps the child to develop skills in observing and measuring:

> *Does water in the sun get warm, too? Put two pans the same size out of doors. Put one in the sun and one in the shade.*
> *Put the same amount of cold water in each pan.*

---

[76]Rose Wyler and Eva-Lee Baird, *Science Teasers,* Illustrated by Jerry Robinson (New York: Harper & Row, 1966), p. 4.

Two hours later take the temperature of the water in each pan.
Did you find that the sun will warm the water?[77]

Books about plants and animals also include experiments. Selsam suggests many demonstrations to help children understand plant growth in *Play with Seeds* and *Play with Vines.* In *Earthworms,* Hogner tells boys and girls how to set up an experiment to see earthworms make humus in sandy or clay soil in a mason jar. Although the fantasy element in *Adventures in Living Plants* is a detracting feature, the book by Kurtz and Allen includes some excellent "Things to Do and Think About." Measuring, recording data, and making graphs are kinds of activities that should be encouraged. Questions guide the observation and thinking of the pupil:

> *Do the plants in cup #1 change color? How long was it until you saw a color change in the seedlings in cup #1? What caused the seedlings to change color? Which seedlings grew taller, those in cup #1 or cup #2?*[78]

Sootin emphasizes measurement in his book, *Experiments with Machines and Matter.* Activities demonstrate principles related to pendulums, friction, and pulleys. Wisely, he utilizes open-ended questions. Wyler and Ames give machine-related experiments in *What Makes It Go?* There is a conversational approach, but no "talking down."

Experiments for Special Instruments   A third type of experiment book suggests activities with special instruments. *Fun with Your Microscope* by Yates, *Experiments with a Microscope* by Beeler and Branley, *Through the Magnifying Glass* by Schwartz, and *Andy's*

Wonderful Telescope by Schloat guide older boys and girls in using these tools of science. *Adventures with a Hand Lens* by Headstrom suggests many interesting activities. The Schneiders' *Science Fun with Milk Cartons* helps children understand basic principles through construction. An astronomer who writes fine books for children, Franklyn Branley, has written *Experiments in Sky Watching.* He shows how to make homemade instruments, how and what to record. His bibliography includes books for children.

Documents and Journals

An important contribution to literature for children in recent years has been the publication of books based upon original documents and journals. The series by Hoff, *Adventures in Eyewitness History* provides documentary reports for inquiry in history. These books give reports written by people who lived or traveled in the country. The series includes *Russia, America,* and *Africa* and provides excellent editorial comments in addition to the original sources of diaries, letters, and essays. In the introduction to the book about Russia, the editor makes an important comment:

> *The men and women who report on Russia in this book are all eyewitnesses. That means they are telling of something that they themselves have seen and heard and experienced. This is a vivid, exciting and rewarding branch of history but it is not always an entirely accurate one. For no matter how truthful a witness may be, his eyes may deceive him or his ears may play him false. And in any case, the eyewitness is an integral part of the picture he is describing and therefore cannot see all of it in just perspective. But eyewitness history comes to us "live." It has a warmth and an immediacy that the historian's history can never achieve.*[79]

---

[77]Illa Podendorf, *The True Book of Weather Experiments,* Illustrated by Felix Palm (Chicago: Childrens Press, 1961), pp. 16–17.

[78]Kurtz and Allen. p. 64.

[79]Rhoda Hoff, *Russia, Adventures in Eyewitness History* (New York: Walck, 1964), p. xii.

Reproductions of twenty-six documents of American history are included in *Freedom* by Hays. Explanatory information helps the reader understand the setting and the author of each document. A rough draft of the Declaration of Independence, Theodore Roosevelt's letter about Cuba, the German surrender statement of 1945 and part of the log of Old Ironsides are included.

An American Revolutionary War Reader edited by Sobol provides such original sources as a Minuteman Pledge, Washington's acceptance of command, and the journal of a Quaker woman. The material is indexed separately by author, title, and subject.

The series of books by Meredith and Smith provide excellent historical materials. *Pilgrim Courage* contains accounts from Governor Bradford's journal. An adaptation for younger children is presented under the title, *The Coming of the Pilgrims.* However, the reader is not sure when the *exact* words are used. Certainly, such passages as, "Being thus arrived in a good harbour and brought safe to land, they fell upon their knees and blessed the God of heaven, who had brought them over the vast and furious ocean to set their feet on the firm and stable earth,"[80] would seem to be from the original source, but only one selection was italicized. *Riding with Coronado* is based upon an eyewitness account of the Coronado exploration, and *The Quest of Columbus* is based upon the history written by the son of Columbus. Leonard Everett Fisher's illustrations enhance all of these documentaries.

The journal of a Venetian nobleman who accompanied Magellan is a primary source edited by Sanderlin in *First Around the World.* The introduction and commentaries for each selection provide continuity and further information. Magellan's contract with the Spanish king, his will, an order of the day that tells of his decision to sail on are some of the interesting materials included.

The Bayeux Tapestry is a unique documentary record of English history as interpreted by artists of the eleventh century. Color photographs of the 230-foot tapestry that tells the story of the conflict between Harold of England and William of Normandy are explained by Denny and Filmer-Sankey. The text describes the embroidered figures, and commentary explains historical data. This book provides an opportunity for critical comparisons of beliefs of the people in 1066 and 1966.

Background of current events is provided in three volumes by Meltzer, *In Their Own Words, a History of the American Negro.* The first volume includes letters, speeches, excerpts from books, testimony in courts for the period 1619–1865; the second volume gives records from 1865–1916; and the third volume continues the history to 1966.

To develop research skills, children need the opportunity to study primary sources. They can compare reproductions of original sources with biographies and historical interpretations. An interesting linguistic study could be made by noting the words and language patterns of these documents (see Chapter 6).

Geographic Series

There are few general books about geography; usually a book will deal with a region, a country, or a state. Many series books include books about single countries. Teachers and librarians should know the general format and reading level of series books, yet each book should be evaluated on its own merit. The following summary gives publishers and brief annotations of series books:

- *Enchantment of America* series. Childrens Press. By Alan Carpenter. Each book

---

[80]E. Brooks Smith and Robert Meredith, *The Coming of the Pilgrims Told from Governor Bradford's Firsthand Account,* Illustrated by Leonard E. Fisher (Boston: Little, Brown, 1964), p. 31.

Actual photographs of the beautiful Bayeux Tapestry acquaint children with this document that records the story of the Norman Conquest. Crude figures and symbols were embroidered on a strip of linen 230 feet long and 20 inches wide. Illustration reproduced from photographs supplied by Maison Combier, 4 Rue Agut, Macon, Saone-et-Loire, France. From *The Bayeux Tapestry* by Norman Deray and Josephine Filmer-Sarkey. Used by permission of Atheneum Publishers and by permission of William Collins Sons and Co. Ltd.

is about one state, gives history, industries, resources, famous people of the state, miscellaneous facts. Pedantic style. Study questions follow each section.

- *Getting to Know* . . . series. Coward-McCann. Each book written by a different person. Surveys geographical features, history, government. Gives pronunciations of foreign words.
- *Key to the City* series. Lippincott. Different author for each book. Includes Chicago, Boston, London, Moscow, and so forth, with descriptions of each city—industries, arts, and life.
- *Let's Travel In* . . . series. Childrens Press. Edited by Darlene Geis. Large color photos give a tourist's view of the

countries. Little information on social or cultural problems.

- *Let's Visit* . . . series. John Day. By Caldwell. Emphasis upon current problems, changes in each country.
- *Life World Library.* Time. A different writer for each volume. Outstanding color photography, full-page photos. Includes arts, politics, social problems. Text is difficult for many sixth graders.
- *Made In* . . . series. Knopf. Each book by a different author. Emphasis upon arts, crafts, history, and legend of Iceland, Thailand, Mexico, Japan, Italy. Above sixth-grade reading level.
- *My Village in* . . . series. Pantheon. By Sonia and Tom Gidal. Outstanding

black-and-white photography. Narration in first person tells of village life in European countries and Morocco.

- *Portraits of the Nations* series. Lippincott. Each book by a different author. Titled *Land and People of. . . .* More difficult reading level than other series books. Usually gives history with some discussion of current problems, emphasis on industries and products.
- *Rivers of the World* series. Garrard. Different author for each book. History of people along the rivers, people today, industries. Effect of the rivers on economy—Amazon, Nile, Congo, Rhone, Thames, Seine.

Survey Books

The survey book in a field of science or social science attempts to give an over-all view of trends, an introduction to methods of inquiry, or a sampling of facts or principles about a large topic. It is difficult to make a large topic comprehensible, but a few writers have been successful in this approach.

Children gain information about animal life in such general references as Parker's *Golden Treasury of Natural History* and *The Rainbow Book of Nature* by Peattie. These well-illustrated, concisely written volumes provide answers to many questions, but children who want more information will turn to books about specific plants or animals.

Wilfred Bronson writes of species such as *Turtles* and *Cats,* and surveys animal characteristics in *Horns and Antlers* and *Chisel-Tooth Tribe.* He especially emphasizes adaptations to environment. A naturalist of the American Museum of Natural History, George Mason, has communicated the fun of studying nature in his series of books, *Animal Weapons, Animal Tracks, Animal Tools,* and *Animal Homes.* Some chapter titles from the table of contents of *Animal Tools* indicate his interesting approach: "Feet as Tools," "The

Bee's Tool Kit," and "Goggles and Flashlights."

Informational survey books can be illustrated by noting three books about the ocean. One of the *Books to Begin On* series, *Ocean Wonders* by Holsaert, gives general information about divers, ocean life, currents, and resources. This is not a "beginning to read" book but it appears easier than one of the *You and . . .* series, *You and the Oceans.* The author, Sherman, includes theories of ocean formation, but there is little information on any one topic. An inexpensive series, *The How and Why* books includes *The How and Why Wonder Book of Oceanography* by Scharff. It gives quite complete information about tides, waves, life in the sea, and the future use of the sea.

A few books attempt to give children a survey of the important people, places, and events in the history of the world. Van Loon's *The Story of Mankind* was the first book to interpret world history to children in an interesting and informational fashion. This book, a pioneer in the field, received the first Newbery Award in 1922. Others have followed this courageous pattern.

Genevieve Foster has made notable and unique contributions to the interpretation of history for children. In two books, *Birthdays of Freedom,* Book One and Book Two, she has traced in a graphic story the growth of freedom from the time when man learned to use fire to the Fall of Rome. Her second book begins "On that small remote Roman Colony of Britain" and brings us thirteen centuries later to the shores of the new United States of America. These stories may be read in the pictures (one for each page), maps, and large type headings, or they may be followed more clearly in the text. In most instances, children will depend upon adults to use the books with them.

A horizontal treatment of history is presented in five other books by Mrs. Foster, *George Washington's World, Abraham Lincoln's*

World, Augustus Caesar's World, The World of Captain John Smith, 1580–1631, and *The World of Columbus and Sons.* Each of these books presents a time slice of history, a total picture of the world, historical, religious cultural, social, and economic in relationship to the span of one man's life. The many illustrations, maps, and charts give much information and graphically portray her theme of parallel events. Each story or event is well written and could be read separately from the others. For example, she uses the technique of writing a play for "The Tragedy of Italy" in *The World of Columbus and Sons.* Children could take parts and read this chapter aloud. Continuity is given to all episodes by frequent mention of the life of the one man who serves as the pivotal point of the book. Teachers will want to read parts of these books to children; more mature readers will read them independently. Two indexes are included in each book, one for characters and another general one of nations, places, and events.

Commager's *The First Book of American History* is exciting from the opening sentence, "Imagine discovering a new world!" He traces the history of the United States through World War II. Gerald Johnson's beautifully clear prose gives objective history

Text and detailed illustrations present parallel events during the lifetime of one person. Authentic sketches and explanations show architecture, costume, and artifacts of the period. From *Augustus Caesar's World 44 B.C. to 14 A.D.* written and illustrated by Genevieve Foster. Charles Scribner's Sons, 1947.

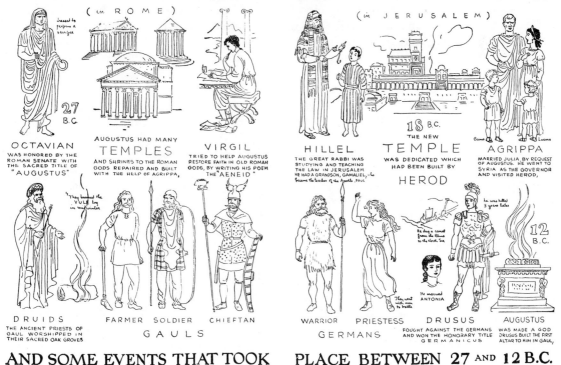

PEOPLE WHO WERE LIVING   WHEN HE BECAME AUGUSTUS

AND SOME EVENTS THAT TOOK   PLACE BETWEEN 27 AND 12 B.C.

in *America Is Born, America Grows Up,* and *America Moves Forward. The Rainbow Book of American History* by Earl S. Miers is a large, well-illustrated chronological history from the Norsemen to the Atomic Age. Each story is accompanied by a forceful illustration by James Daugherty. *The Golden Book of America,* adapted by Irwin Shapiro from the *American Heritage Mazazine,* is a miscellany of Americana including both legend and fact. Boys would particularly enjoy the colored photographs of old maps, ship pictures, and paintings. An index provides ready reference to such topics as the bicycle crazes and Daniel Boone. Descriptions of old valentines and the American country store give a flavor of the "olden days" that will intrigue many older boys and girls.

Varied survey books bring together information about a general topic. Wilcox's *Folk and Festival Costumes of the World* would be a useful reference for checking authenticity of historical fiction or in preparing plays. *The American Indian as Farmer* by Morris shows the ways farming was carried on in early America. Art and anthropology are served by *Masks and Mask Makers* by Hunt and Carlson. A collection of first person accounts of primitive life in different parts of the world is presented by Boer in *Igloos, Yurts, and Totem Poles.* This is a generalized anthropology book. Many authors have written books that are historical surveys of the United States. Frances Cavanah, in her book *Our Country's Story* has written an introduction to American history for boys and girls in the middle grades.

Specialized Books

Teachers and librarians will introduce children to survey books, or children will browse through them. However, children more frequently turn to the book on a special topic when seeking answers to their specific questions.

Living Things   There are books about animals, for example, Darling's well-written *Kangaroos* and *Turtles* and Zim's *Golden Hamsters, Owls,* and *Sharks.* Zim's books are organized so the child may find general information in the text and more details in the pages with illustrations of different animals of the species. This writer also established a unique pattern of presenting information in his *What's Inside?* series. A sequence of three pages gives data on one subject. The first page uses large print and an easy vocabulary. On the next page there are diagrams to explain the content. Printed in smaller type, the third page gives more detail for the teacher or advanced reader. Children are fascinated by the unusual, and will enjoy Olive Earle's *Strange Lizards* and *Strange Companions in Nature.* Her purpose is not only to present intriguing facts, but to illustrate biological relationships.

The series of books about plants, *The Amazing Seeds, This Is a Tree,* and *This Is a Leaf* by Hutchins exemplifies the kind of informational books that should be available for more mature readers. The author's excellent photographs give closeups, cross sections, and magnified views not found in other books.

People of the Past   Life of people in other times is described in many specialized books. The types of books about Indians, for example, include books about Indians of North America, such as *Indians* by Tunis, *Home of the Red Man* by Silverburg, and *Getting to Know American Indians Today* by Thompson. The latter is an accurate report of present-day conditions of the Navajo.

In *The North American Indians,* the paintings of author-artist Ernest Berke are outstanding. Each painting conveys a feeling about the Indians, as well as giving information. "Blackfoot Tracker" portrays a lone rider on a snow-covered plain; there is a haunting beauty in the painting of a woman

mourning a dead warrior, and in "The Em-
igrant Trail" two Indians view a chair and
rug left on a wagon trail. The artifacts of
Indians of each region of the United States
are clearly illustrated in this book.

Sonia Bleeker gives an anthropologist's
account of Indian life in single books about
each tribe. *The Chippewa Indians, The Cherokee,
The Crow Indians, The Apache Indians,* and *Indians of the Longhouse* are titles of some of
these semifictionalized stories. She objectively
describes both the good and cruel treatment of the Indians by the white man. Special aspects of Indian life are described in
Hofsinde's books, *Indian Sign Language, Indian Warriors and Their Weapons,* and *Indian
Picture Writing.* Information about the past is
given in an account of a modern-day tour at
Mesa Verde National Park, *Let's Go to an Indian Cliff Dwelling* by Williams. Museum exhibits are explained and the "you are there"
feeling is created as the ruins are described.

Factual books about explorers, early settlers, and pioneer life can provide for the
range of abilities within a group studying the
past. Leonard Everett Fisher's excellent illustrations give details of the work and
workers in his series about colonial life, *The
Papermakers, The Hatters, The Wigmakers.* A
Cornerstones of Freedom series by Miller describes *The Story of the Star-Spangled Banner,
The Story of the Statue of Liberty,* and *The Story
of the Liberty Bell.* These are picture books for
the middle-grade reader. The *Frontiers of
America* series written by McCall includes
books about *Pioneer Show Folk* and *Pioneer
Traders.* These books help give a picture of the
total life of the pioneer. The TV Western may
be questioned after children read *Overland
Stage* by Dines. Details of the coach construction, cost of the fare, how the drivers
worked, and the life at the stations are
given in a very readable style. For example,
we learn that the men laid their clothes on
an anthill so the ants would eat the lice
and bedbugs.

**A California Redwood provides the continuity
for the natural history of a region. Here, the big
tree witnesses the exciting fight between two
bucks.** From *Big Tree* by Mary and Conrad Buff.
Copyright 1946 by Mary Marsh Buff and Conrad
Buff. Reprinted by permission of The Viking
Press, Inc.

Boys, and a few girls, in the upper grades
become very much interested in wars. Some
become "Civil War buffs," for example, and
are thoroughly familiar with the deployment
of armies in the various battles. *Free Men
Must Stand* by Barnes gives many details of
the War for Independence and *The Battle of
Lake Erie* is described in full by Mason.
Dupuy has written *The First Book . . .* series
about *Civil War Land Battles, The Military
History of World War II,* and *The Naval War in
the Pacific.* With its usual fine collection of

landscapes, portraits, maps, and cartoons, the *American Heritage* series includes such titles as *The French Revolution* by Dowd and *Carrier War in the Pacific* by Sears. Colonel Reeder's war stories, such as *The Story of the Civil War* and *The Story of the War of 1812,* are authentic and dramatic.

The Arts   Information about the arts is available in many specialized books. Glubok has written an excellent series about art of different periods and different peoples. The photographs of paintings, sculpture, and artifacts are outstanding in these well-designed books. Titles include *The Art of Ancient Greece, The Art of Ancient Egypt,* and *The Art of the Eskimo.* The series published by Lerner includes *Kings and Queens in Art* by Coen, *Circuses and Fairs in Art* by Harkonen, and *The Horse in Art* by Zuelke. These books give information about techniques and artists.

The history of ballet as well as brief biographies of great dancers is given in *The Book of Ballet* by Audsley, while Goulden relates the story of well-known ballets in *The Royal Book of Ballet.* The illustrations convey the feeling of the dances in "The Nutcracker," "Swan Lake," "Giselle," and "Coppelia." Even more specialized are the books of a single ballet, such as *The Sleeping Beauty* and *Coppelia, the Girl with the Enamel Eyes* by Chappell.

Britten includes music of both East and West in his account of the development of music, *The Wonderful World of Music.* Shippen's *The Heritage of Music* is a more detailed history of music with definitions of terms. In his book, *Folk Instruments,* Gilmore describes the way such popular instruments as the guitar and harmonica developed (see Chapters 6 and 11).

Science and Technology   Trade books are especially useful in presenting information about new developments in science and technology. *Why the Mohole* by Cromie ex-plained the importance of the investigation of the earth's core and described the machines at work. There is the fascinating account of little-known *Camp Century, City Under the Ice* by Wagner, and *Century, Secret City of the Snows* by Hamilton. This experimental city, one hundred miles from Thule and twenty feet below the Greenland Ice Cap, is producing significant research related to atomic energy and future colonization of other planets. Mature readers will find Hutchins' book about *Life's Key—DNA* a report of exciting discovery. The interested child will find it challenging to compare Adler's *Sound and Ultrasonics,* written in 1959, with the 1963 *Sounds You Cannot Hear* by Windle. The latter book shows the application of ultrasonics in medicine and industry. A relatively unknown field of study is clearly described in Woodbury's *The Frigid World of Cryogenics.* The development of techniques to produce liquid oxygen and liquid hydrogen was based upon the "pure research" related to temperatures near absolute zero. The author communicates the excitement of discovery of new principles and their application to surgery and rocket propellants.

Books about space exploration quickly become outdated, although older books are useful to present principles of rocketry. For example, *Lift-Off, the Story of Rocket Power* by Coombs appeared in 1963, and continues to be useful because it gives information about types of rocket motors, and how they work. Coombs describes plans for the first moon landing in *Project Apollo.* His 1960 book, *Project Mercury,* could be compared with the records of the flights as they actually occurred. The *American Heritage* book by Dille, *Americans in Space* is one of the few that gives proper credit to Robert Goddard, as the pioneer of space flight. The color photos of historic flights will continue to be of interest.

Reading the new trade books about man's exploration and discoveries makes life today truly exciting for teachers and children.

Men Work Together Informational books also help children understand the ways men work together to provide food, clothing, houses, transportation, recreation, and laws for living together. Books can help boys and girls appreciate the wonders of their age that might be taken for granted. Goldwater's *Bridges and How They Are Built* and *Building Brooklyn Bridge* by Saunders tell of the challenges of building bridges; *Tunnels* by Bloch brings facts about their construction and an appreciation for the men who do such work; *About Roads* by Carlisle gives basic information about the men and machines who construct roads.

Children need to learn more about the concerns of our society such as the population explosion, urban changes, movement for civil rights, automation, and the role of government. In *Water Fit to Use,* the Carlsons present one of our serious national problems. This book tells of the research under way to make water reusable and to desalt water, and traces the development of government controls. *About the People Who Run Your City* by Newman and Sherman gives a clear picture of the structure of government. *What Does a Congressman Do?* by Levine and *The Congress* by Johnson give excellent background information. Although written in 1952, Dorothy Canfield Fisher's book *A Fair World for All* remains an inspiring statement of the Declaration of Human Rights. Goldman's *Civil Rights, the Challenge of the Fourteenth Amendment* describes the marches, sit-ins, and leaders in the Negroes' struggle.

Man Himself Perhaps children need to learn about themselves more than they need all the kinds of information cited in this chapter. Specialized books give understanding of human anatomy and senses. Zim's *What's Inside of Me?* presents a good beginning for this knowledge. In *You and Your Amazing Mind* by Lewellen, psychology is explained:

Many sources of information help children learn about ways men work together to build an expressway. Columbus, Ohio, Public Schools.

This new science turns an unflattering light on the drives and hates and loves and emotions that are in constant conflict in human minds. It interprets behavior. Its triumph is that it shows how to translate these energies and drives into constructive forms that lead to happiness and the good life. Self understanding is the first step.[81]

In *Who Do You Think You Are?* Lerner gives a lucid explanation of heredity. An understanding of how life begins and how characteristics are passed on will help the boy or girl understand himself. Virginia Burton's picture book, *Life Story, the Story of Life on Earth* gives an understanding of the

[81] John Lewellen, *You and Your Amazing Mind,* Illustrated by Winnie Fitch and Joe Phalen (Chicago: Childrens Press, 1952, 1965).

slow processes of change in animal and plant life. She concludes by saying, "The drama of Life is a continuous story—ever new, ever changing, and ever wondrous to behold."[82] She suggests the child develop his individual time line in order to see himself as a part of the life stream.

In this process of change, the effect of the machine upon man will be a major problem. Both Piper, in *The Story of Computers,* and Hirsch, in *This Is Automation,* hold the view that man is still the significant factor in the operation of the machines. An important, specialized book for children to read in elementary school is *The First Book of Ethics* by Black. The author describes this "study of how people treat each other and what it means to lead a good life" and stresses the idea that "you are the judge," "you must know your choices."

Informational books will make a tremendous contribution to the knowledge of the child; how he uses that knowledge will be influenced by his experiences with other types of fine literature.

---

[82]Virginia Burton, *Life Story, the Story of Life on Our Earth* (Boston: Houghton Mifflin, 1962), unpaged.

SUGGESTED ACTIVITIES

1. Evaluate books about one country. Ask a student from that country, or a recent traveler, to comment upon the books, noting stereotypes and inaccuracies. Compare the facts given about one nation in informational books and fiction.
2. Compare several books about one plant or animal species or one social process.
3. Evaluate several identification books on one topic, such as trees, birds, or rocks.
4. Select three or four current problems in the community, nation, or world. Locate materials that would help you and the children understand these problems.
5. Select a science or social-studies text for one grade level. Locate and evaluate trade books and other materials that would enrich one unit in the text.
6. Examine several books in each of three or four series. Compare style, content, reading level, and other pertinent factors.
7. Select passages from one informational book, or several, that could be used to develop skills of critical reading.

RELATED READINGS

1. Adler, Irving. "On Writing Science Books for Children," *The Horn Book Magazine,* vol. 61 (October 1965), pp. 524–529.
   The goals of the science writer are described. Examples of the author's problems and achievements in writing science books for children are included.
2. Eakin, Mary K. *Good Books for Children.* Chicago: University of Chicago Press, 1959.
   By using the index organized according to subject, the teacher can locate books related to the study of social processes and other lands. Each book is critically annotated.
3. Huus, Helen. *Children's Books to Enrich the Social Studies.* Revised edition. Washington, D.C.: National Council for the Social Studies, 1966.
   The annotations of the books in this bibliography present content concisely and indicate grade level placement. Fiction and nonfiction are included in the list organized according to the past, people today, the world's work, and living together.
4. Kenworthy, Leonard. *Introducing Children to the World.* New York: Harper & Row, 1956.

An outstanding book that presents the need for a planned program to develop international understanding. Many books for children and teachers are included. The themes for study at all levels will guide teachers in developing a good program for world understanding.

5. Larrick, Nancy. *A Teacher's Guide to Children's Books.* Columbus, Ohio: Merrill, 1960.
   Chapters 8, 9, and 10 deal with books and the content subjects, science, and social studies. Books for a unit on stars and a unit on the Westward Movement are listed and annotated briefly.

6. Selsam, Millicent. "Nature Writing: Scientific and Nonscientific" in *Readings about Children's Literature,* Evelyn Rose Robinson, Editor. New York: McKay, 1966.
   Criteria for science books are defined by an author who emphasizes observation, experiment, concepts, and principles.

7. Smith, Lillian. *The Unreluctant Years.* Chicago: American Library Association, 1953.
   The need for books of knowledge, and criteria for their selection are presented in Chapter 12.

8. Tooze, Ruth, and Beatrice Krone. *Literature and Music as Resources for Social Studies.* Englewood Cliffs, N.J.: Prentice-Hall, 1955.
   In Part II, "Growing Up as a Citizen of the World," the authors list books and music about many countries. Folk tales, fiction, and informational books are included. Annotations are brief.

CHAPTER REFERENCES*

Anthropology

1. Ames, Gerald, and Rose Wyler. *The First Days of the World.* Illustrated by Leonard Weisgard. New York: Harper & Row, 1958.
2. Baumann, Hans. *The Caves of the Great Hunters.* Revised edition. New York: Pantheon, 1962, 1954.
3. Boer, Frederick, Editor. *Igloos, Yurts, and Totem Poles.* Translated by Florence McHugh. New York: Pantheon, 1957.
4. De Borhegyi, Suzanne. *Ships, Shoals, and Amphoras, the Story of Underwater Archaeology.* Illustrated by Alex Schomberg. New York: Holt, Rinehart and Winston, 1961.
   5. Eberle, Irmengarde. *Big Family of Peoples.* New York: Crowell, 1952.
6. Friedman, Estelle. *Digging into Yesterday.* Illustrated by Leonard Everett Fisher. New York: Putnam, 1958.
7. —————*Man in the Making.* Illustrated by Frederic Marvin. New York: Putnam, 1960.
8. Hunt, Kari, and Bernice Wells Carlson. *Masks and Mask Makers.* New York: Abingdon, 1961.
9. Jessup, Ronald. *The Wonderful World of Archaeology.* Illustrated by Norman Battersill and Kenneth Symonds. Diagrams by Isotype Institute. New York: Garden City Books, 1956.
10. Ludovici, L. J. *The Great Tree of Life: Paleontology, the Natural History of Living Creatures.* Illustrated by Frank Aloise. New York: Putnam, 1963.
11. Mead, Margaret. *Anthropologists and What They Do.* New York: F. Watts, 1965.
12. —————*People and Places.* Illustrated by W. T. Mars and Jan Fairservis. Cleveland: World Publishing, 1959.
13. Perkins, Carol Morse. *The Shattered Skull.* New York: Atheneum, 1965.
14. Watts, Edith Whitney. *Archaeology, Exploring the Past.* New York: New York Graphic, 1965.

—————

*These chapter references are arranged alphabetically according to content.

The Arts

15. Audsley, James. *The Book of Ballet.* Illustrated by Grace Golden. Second revised edition. New York: Warne, 1964.
16. Britten, Benjamin, and Imogen Holst. *The Wonderful World of Music.* New York: Doubleday, 1958.
17. Burns, William A. *A World Full of Homes.* Illustrated by Paula Hutchison. New York: Whittlesey, 1953.
18. Chappell, Warren. *Coppelia, the Girl with the Enamel Eyes.* New York: Knopf, 1965.
19. ————*The Sleeping Beauty.* New York: Knopf, 1961.
20. Coen, Rena. *Kings and Queens in Art.* Minneapolis: Lerner, 1965.
21. Gilmore, Lee. *Folk Instruments.* Illustrated by George Overlie. Minneapolis: Lerner, 1962.
22. Glubok, Shirley. *The Art of Ancient Egypt.* Designed by Gerard Nook. New York: Atheneum, 1962.
23. ————*The Art of Ancient Greece.* Designed by Oscar Krauss. New York: Atheneum, 1963.
24. ————*The Art of the Eskimo.* Designed by Oscar Krauss. New York: Harper & Row, 1964.
25. Goulden, Shirley. *The Royal Book of Ballet.* Illustrated by Maraja. Chicago: Follett, 1962.
26. Harkonen, Helen B. *Circuses and Fairs in Art.* Designed by Robert Clark Nilson. Minneapolis: Lerner, 1965.
27. Miles, Betty. *A House for Everyone.* Illustrated by Jo Lowrey. New York: Knopf, 1958.
28. Shippen, Katherine B., and Anca Seidlova. *The Heritage of Music.* Illustrated by Otto Van Eersel. New York: Viking, 1963.
29. Wilcox, R. Turner. *Folk and Festival Costumes of the World.* New York: Scribner, 1965.
30. Zuelke, Ruth. *The Horse in Art.* Minneapolis: Lerner, 1965.

Biology

31. Buck, Margaret. *Along the Seashore.* New York: Abingdon, 1964.
32. ————*In Ponds and Streams.* New York: Abingdon, 1955.
33. Carthy, J. D. *Animals and Their Ways, the Science of Animal Behavior.* New York: Natural History, 1965.
34. Darling, Louis. *Kangaroos and Other Animals with Pockets.* Morrow, 1958.
35. Earle, Olive. *Strange Companions in Nature.* New York: Morrow, 1966.
36. Erdoes, Richard. *The Green Tree House.* New York: Dodd, Mead, 1965.
37. Erickson, Phoebe. *Cattail House.* Chicago: Childrens Press, 1962.
38. George, Jean Craighead. *Spring Comes to the Ocean.* Illustrated by John Wilson. New York: Crowell, 1965.
39. Glemser, Bernard. *All about Biology.* Illustrated by Eva Cellini. New York: Random House, 1964.
40. Hirsch, S. Carl. *The Living Community, a Venture into Ecology.* Illustrated by William Steinel. New York: Viking, 1966.
41. Hogner, Dorothy. *Earthworms.* Illustrated by Nils Hogner. New York: Crowell, 1953.
42. Hutchins, Carleen Maley. *Life's Key–DNA, a Biological Adventure into the Unknown.* New York: Coward-McCann, 1961.
43. Mason, George F. *Animal Homes.* New York: Morrow, 1947.
44. ————*Animal Tools.* New York: Morrow, 1951.
45. ————*Animal Tracks.* New York: Morrow, 1943.
46. ————*Animal Weapons.* New York: Morrow, 1949.

47. May, Julian. *They Turned to Stone*. Illustrated by Jean Zallinjer. New York: Holiday, 1965.
48. Parker, Bertha M. *Golden Treasury of Natural History*. New York: Simon and Schuster, 1952.
49. Peattie, Donald Culross. *The Rainbow Book of Nature*. Illustrated by R. Freund. New York: Harcourt, 1957.
50. Pistorious, Anna. *What Bird Is It?* Chicago: Follett, 1945.
51. ————*What Butterfly Is It?* Chicago: Follett, 1949.
52. ————*What Dinosaur Is It?* Chicago: Follett, 1958.
53. ————*What Tree Is It?* Chicago: Follett, 1955.
54. Reynolds, Christopher. *Small Creatures in My Garden*. New York: Farrar, Straus, 1965.
55. Sanger, Marjory Bartlett. *Cypress Country*. Illustrated by Christine Price. Cleveland: World Publishing, 1965.
56. Selsam, Millicent E. *Animals as Parents*. Illustrated by John Kaufmann. New York: Morrow, 1965.
57. ————*Benny's Animals and How He Put Them in Order*. Illustrated by Arnold Lobel. New York: Harper & Row, 1966.
58. ————*The Courtship of Animals*. Illustrated by John Kaufmann. New York: Morrow, 1964.
59. ————*You and the World Around You*. Illustrated by Greta Elgaard. New York: Doubleday, 1963.
60. Swinton, W. E. *Digging for Dinosaurs*. Illustrated by Barrie Driscoll. New York: Doubleday, 1962.
61. Ubell, Earl. *The World of the Living*. Photos by Arline Strong. New York: Atheneum, 1965.
62. Uhl, Melvin John. *About Creatures that Live Underground*. Illustrated by Madalene Otteson. Chicago: Melmont, 1965.
63. Zim, Herbert. *How Things Grow*. Illustrated by Gustav Schrotter. New York: Morrow, 1960.

Birds

64. Blough, Glenn. *Bird Watchers and Bird Feeders*. Illustrated by Jeanne Bendick. New York: McGraw-Hill, 1963.
65. Bosiger, E., and J. M. Guilcher. *A Bird Is Born*. Photos by E. Hosking and R. H. Noailles. Revised edition. New York: Sterling, 1963.
66. Darling, Louis. *The Gull's Way*. New York: Morrow, 1965.
67. Earle, Olive. *Robins in the Garden*. New York: Morrow, 1953.
68. ————*Swans of Willow Pond*. New York: Morrow, 1955.
69. Freschet, Berniece. *Young Eagle*. Illustrated by James Alexander. New York: Scribner, 1965.
70. Garelick, May. *Winter Birds*. Illustrated by Clement Hurd. New York: W. R. Scott, 1965.
71. Henderson, Luis M. *A Child's Book of Birds*. New York: Maxton, 1946.
72. Hess, Lilo. *Easter in November*. New York: Crowell, 1964.
73. Kieran, John. *An Introduction to Birds*. New York: Doubleday, 1965.
74. Kirk, Richard. *Birds in Flight*. Photos by Evan Davis. Illustrated by Dave Kenney. Chicago: Follett, 1962.
75. McCoy, J. J. *The Hunt for the Whooping Cranes, a Natural History Detective Story*. Illustrated by Ray Abruzzi. New York: Lothrop, 1966.
76. Miller, Patricia K., and Iran L. Seligman. *At Home on the Ice*. Illustrated by John Teppech. New York: Holt, Rinehart and Winston, 1963.
77. Murphy, Robert. *The Golden Eagle*. Illustrated by John Schoenherr. New York: Dutton, 1965.
78. Peterson, Roger Tory. *A Field Guide to the Birds*. Boston: Houghton Mifflin, 1934.

79. ————*How to Know the Birds.* Second edition. Boston: Houghton Mifflin, 1957.

80. ————*The Junior Book of Birds.* Boston: Houghton Mifflin, 1939.

81. Russell, Franklin. *Hawk in the Sky.* Illustrated by Fredric Sweney. New York: Holt, Rinehart and Winston, 1965.

82. Scharff, Robert. *Look for a Bird's Nest.* Illustrated by Valerie Swanson. New York: Putnam, 1958.

83. Selsam, Millicent. *Tony's Birds.* Illustrated by Kurt Werth. New York: Harper & Row, 1961.

84. Simon, Hilda. *Wonders of Hummingbirds.* New York: Dodd, Mead, 1964.

85. Sterling, Dorothy. *Ellen's Blue Jays.* Illustrated by Winifred Lubell. New York: Doubleday, 1961.

86. Wasson, Isabel B. *Birds.* Illustrated by William Barss. Chicago: Follett, 1963.

87. Welty, Susan F. *Birds with Bracelets, the Story of Bird Banding.* Illustrated by John Kaufmann. Engelwood Cliffs, N.J.: Prentice-Hall, 1965.

88. Williamson, Margaret. *The First Book of Birds.* New York: F. Watts, 1951.

89. Zim, Herbert. *Owls.* Illustrated by James Gordon Irving. New York: Morrow, 1950.

90. Zim, Herbert S., and Ira N. Gabrielson. *Birds.* Illustrated by James Gordon Irving. New York: Golden Press, 1956.

Documents

91. Denny, Norman, and Josephine Filmer-Sankey. *The Bayeux Tapestry, the Story of the Norman Conquest: 1066.* New York: Atheneum, 1966.

92. Hays, Wilma P., Editor. *Freedom.* New York: Coward-McCann, 1958.

93. Hoff, Rhoda. *Africa, Adventures in Eyewitness History.* New York: Walck, 1963.

94. ————*America, Adventures in Eyewitness History.* New York: Walck, 1962.

95. ————*Russia, Adventures in Eyewitness History.* New York: Walck, 1964.

96. Lawson, Robert. *Watchwords of Liberty, a Pageant of American Quotations.* Revised edition. Boston: Little, Brown, 1957.

97. Meltzer, Milton, Editor. *In Their Own Words, a History of the American Negro, 1865–1916.* New York: Crowell, 1965.

98. Meredith, Robert, and E. Brooks Smith. *Pilgrim Courage.* Illustrated by Leonard Everett Fisher. Boston: Little, Brown, 1962.

99. ————*The Quest of Columbus.* Illustrated by Leonard Everett Fisher. Boston: Little, Brown, 1966.

100. ————*Riding with Coronado.* Illustrated by Leonard Everett Fisher. Boston: Little, Brown, 1964.

101. Sanderlin, George. *First Around the World.* Illustrated by Alan E. Cober. New York: Harper & Row, 1964.

102. Smith, E. Brooks and Robert Meredith. *The Coming of the Pilgrims.* Illustrated by Leonard Everett Fisher. Boston: Little, Brown, 1964.

103. Sobol, Donald J., Editor. *An American Revolutionary War Reader.* Illustrated by Henry S. Gillette. New York: F. Watts, 1964.

Earth and Sky

104. Archer, Sellers G. *Rain, Rivers and Reservoirs.* New York: Coward-McCann, 1963.

105. Bendick, Jeanne, *A Fresh Look at Night.* New York: F. Watts, 1963.

106. Bethers, Ray. *What Happens in the Sky?* New York: St. Martin's, 1963.

107. Burton, Virginia Lee. *Life Story.* Boston: Houghton, Mifflin, 1962.

108. Carlson, Carl Walter and Bernice Wells Carlson. *Water Fit to Use.* Illustrated by Aline Hansens. New York: John Day, 1966.

109. Cromie, William J. *Why the Mohole, Adventure in Inner Space.* Illustrated by Arthur Knapp. Boston: Little, Brown, 1964.
110. Ets, Marie Hall. *Gilberto and the Wind.* New York: Viking, 1963.
111. Hengesbaugh, Jane R. *I Live in So Many Places.* Illustrated by Katherine Evans. Chicago: Childrens Press, 1957.
112. Hogner, Dorothy Childs. *Conservation in America.* New York: Illustrated by Nils Hogner. Philadelphia: Lippincott, 1958.
113. Jeanes, Charlotte, and Raymond Carlsen. *Water and the Thirsty Land.* Chicago: Follett, 1961.
114. Knight, David C. *The First Book of Mars.* New York: F. Watts, 1966.
115. Miles, Betty. *What Is the World?* Illustrated by Remy Charlip. New York: Knopf, 1958.
116. Neely, Henry M. *The Stars by Clock and Fist.* New York: Viking, 1956.
117. Ravielli, Anthony. *The World Is Round.* New York: Viking, 1963.
118. Russell, Solveig Paulson. *Saving Wild Life for Tomorrow.* Illustrated by Henry Lukes. Chicago: Melmont, 1960.
119. Schneider, Herman and Nina. *Follow the Sunset.* Illustrated by Lucille Corcos. New York: Doubleday, 1952.
120. ————*How Big Is Big? From Stars to Atoms.* Illustrated by Symeon Shimin. Revised edition. New York: W. R. Scott, 1950.
121. Tresselt, Alvin. *Hide and Seek Fog.* Illustrated by Roger Duvoisin. New York: Lothrop, 1965.
122. Wolfe, Louis. *The Deepest Hole in the World.* New York: Putnam, 1964.
123. Wood, Frances. *Great Smoky Mountains, Everglades, Mammoth Cave.* Chicago: Follett, 1964.
124. Zim, Herbert S., and Paul R. Shaffer. *Rocks and Minerals.* Illustrated by Raymond Perlman. New York: Golden Press, 1957.
125. Zim, Herbert S., and Robert H. Baker. *Stars.* Illustrated by James Gordon Irving. New York: Golden Press, 1957.

Energy, Matter, and Machines

126. Adler, Irving, pseud. (Robert Irving). *Sound and Ultrasonics.* Illustrated by L. E. Fisher. New York: Knopf, 1959.
127. Bronowski, J., and Millicent Selsam. *Biography of an Atom.* Illustrated by Weimer Pursell. New York: Harper & Row, 1965.
128. Clark, Mary Lou. *You and Relativity.* Illustrated by Bill Sanders. Chicago: Childrens Press, 1965.
129. Corbett, Scott. *What Makes a Light Go On?* Illustrated by Len Darwin. Boston: Little, Brown, 1965.
130. ————*What Makes TV Work?* Illustrated by Leonard Darwin. Boston: Little, Brown, 1965.
131. David, Eugene. *Crystal Magic.* Illustrated by Abner Graboff. Englewood Cliffs, N.J.: Prentice-Hall, 1965.
132. Froman, Robert. *Faster and Faster, a Book about Speed.* Illustrated by Arnold Spilka. New York: Viking, 1965.
133. Hamilton, Lee David. *Century, Secret City of the Snows.* New York: Putnam, 1963.
134. Hirsch, S. Carl. *This Is Automation.* Illustrated by Anthony Ravielli. New York: Viking, 1964.
135. Kenyon, Raymond G. *Calculators and Computers.* New York: Harper & Row, 1961.
136. Kohn, Bernice. *Echoes.* Illustrated by Albert Pucci. New York: Coward-McCann, 1965.

137. Liss, Howard. *Heat.* Illustrated by Abner Graboff. New York: Coward-McCann, 1965.

138. Piper, Roger. *The Story of Computers.* Illustrated by Felix Cooper. New York: Harcourt, 1964.

139. Podendorf, Illa. *The True Book of Energy.* Illustrated by George Wilde. Chicago: Childrens Press, 1963.

140. Ubell, Earl. *The World of Push and Pull.* Photos by Arline Strong. New York: Atheneum, 1964.

141. Vorwald, Alan, and Frank Clark. *Computers! from Sand Table to Electronic Brain* Illustrated by Frank Aloise. Revised edition. New York: McGraw-Hill, 1964.

142. Wagner, Walter. *Camp Century, City under Ice.* Philadelphia: Chilton, 1965.

143. Windle, Eric. *Sounds You Cannot Hear.* Illustrated by John Kaufmann. Englewood Cliffs, N.J.: Prentice-Hall, 1963.

144. Woodbury, David O. *The Frigid World of Cryogenics.* New York: Dodd, Mead, 1966.

145. Wyler, Rose, and Gerald Ames. *What Makes It Go?* Illustrated by Bernice Myers. New York: McGraw-Hill, 1958.

Experiments

146. Adler, Irving and Ruth. *Things That Spin.* New York: John Day, 1960.

147. ————*Why? a Book of Reasons,* New York: John Day, 1961.

148. ————*Why and How? a Second Book of Reasons.* New York: John Day, 1963.

149. Beeler, Nelson F., and Franklyn K. Branley. *Experiments with a Microscope.* Illustrated by Anne Marie Jauss. New York: Crowell, 1957.

150. Branley, Franklyn K. *Experiments in Sky Watching.* Illustrated by Helmut K. Wimmer. New York: Crowell, 1959.

151. Freeman, Ira M. and Mae B. *Fun with Science.* New York: Random House, 1943.

152. Headstrom, Richard. *Adventures with a Hand Lens.* Philadelphia: Lippincott, 1962.

153. Herbert, Don. *Mr. Wizard's Science Secrets.* Illustrated by Robert A. Barker. New York: Popular Mechanics, 1952.

154. Herbert, Don, and Hy Ruchlis. *Beginning Science with Mr. Wizard.* Illustrated by Mel Hunter. New York: Doubleday, 1960.

155. Kadesch, Robert R. *The Crazy Cantilever and Other Science Experiments.* New York: Harper & Row, 1961.

156. Leeming, Joseph. *The Real Book of Science Experiments.* Illustrated by Bette J. Davis. New York: Garden City Books, 1954.

157. Milgrom, Harry. *Adventures with a String.* Illustrated by Tom Funk. New York: Dutton, 1965.

158. Podendorf, Illa. *101 Science Experiments.* Illustrated by Robert Borja. Chicago: Childrens Press, 1960.

159. ————*The True Book of More Science Experiments.* Illustrated by Chauncey Maltman. Chicago: Childrens Press, 1956.

160. ————*The True Book of Science Experiments.* Illustrated by Mary Salem. Chicago: Childrens Press, 1954.

161. ————*The True Book of Weather Experiments.* Illustrated by Felix Palm. Chicago: Childrens Press, 1961.

162. Schloat, G. Warren. *Andy's Wonderful Telescope.* New York: Scribner, 1958.

163. Schneider, Herman and Nina. *Now Try This.* Illustrated by Bill Ballantine. New York: W. R. Scott, 1947.

164. ————*Science Fun with Milk Cartons.* Illustrated by Jeanne Bendick. New York: McGraw-Hill, 1953.

165. Schwartz, Julius. *It's Fun to Know Why.* Illustrated by Edwin Herron. New York: McGraw-Hill, 1952.

166. ————*Through the Magnifying Glass.* Illustrated by Jeanne Bendick. New York: McGraw-Hill, 1954.

167. Selsam, Millicent. *Play with Plants.* Illustrated by James MacDonald. New York: Morrow, 1949.

168. ————*Play with Seeds.* Illustrated by Helen Ludwig. New York: Morrow, 1957.

169. ————*Play with Vines.* Illustrated by Fred Scherer. New York: Morrow, 1951.

170. Sootin, Harry. *Experiments with Machines and Matter.* Illustrated by Frank Aloise. New York: Norton, 1963.

171. Straus, Jacqueline Harris. *Let's Experiment.* Illustrated by Leonard Kessler. New York: Harper & Row, 1962

172. United Nations Educational, Scientific, and Cultural Organization. *UNESCO Source Book for Science Teaching: 700 Science Experiments for Everyone.* Second edition. New York: UNESCO, 1962.

173. Vries, Leonard de. *The First Book of Experiments.* Translated by Eric G. Breeze. Illustrated by Joost van de Woestijne. New York: Macmillan, 1958.

174. ————*The Third Book of Experiments.* Translated by Eric G. Breeze. Illustrated by Joost van de Woestijne. New York: Macmillan, 1963.

175. Wyler, Rose. *The First Book of Science Experiments.* Illustrated by Ida Scheib. New York: F. Watts, 1952.

176. Wyler, Rose, and Gerald Ames. *Prove It!* Illustrated by Talivaldis Stubis. New York: Harper & Row, 1963.

177. Wyler, Rose, and Eva-Lee Baird. *Science Teasers.* Illustrated by Jerry Robinson. New York: Harper & Row, 1966.

178. Yates, Raymond. *Fun with Your Microscope.* New York: Appleton, 1943.

Explorers, Pioneers, the Past

179. Andrist, Ralph K., and Editors of *American Heritage. The Erie Canal.* New York: American Heritage, 1964.

180. Barnes, Eric Wollencott. *Free Men Must Stand.* Illustrated by W. N. Wilson. New York: McGraw-Hill, 1962.

181. Buehr, Walter. *Knights, Castles and Feudal Life.* New York: Putnam, 1957.

182. Cavanah, Frances. *Our Country's Story.* Illustrated by Julia Keats. Skokie, Ill.: Rand McNally, 1962.

183. Commager, Henry Steele. *The First Book of American History.* Illustrated by Leonard Everett Fisher. New York: F. Watts, 1957.

184. Dines, Glen. *Overland Stage.* New York: Macmillan, 1961.

185. Dowd, David L. *The French Revolution.* New York: American Heritage, 1965.

186. Downey, Fairfax, and Editors of *American Heritage. Texas and the War with Mexico.* New York: Harper & Row, 1961.

187. Dreany, E. Joseph. *A Child's Book of Mankind through the Ages.* New York: Maxton, 1955.

188. Dupuy, Trevor Nevitt. *The First Book of Civil War Land Battles.* Illustrated by Leonard Everett Fisher. New York: F. Watts, 1960.

189. ————*The Military History of World War II.* New York: F. Watts, 1962.

190. ————*The Naval War in the Pacific, the Rising Sun of Nippon.* New York: F. Watts, 1963.

191. Fisher, Leonard Everett. *The Hatters.* New York: F. Watts, 1965.

192. ————*The Papermakers.* New York: F. Watts, 1965.

193. ————*The Wigmakers.* New York: F. Watts, 1965.

194. Foster, Genevieve. *Abraham Lincoln's World.* New York: Scribner, 1944.

195. ————*Augustus Caesar's World.* New York: Scribner, 1947.

196. ————*Birthdays of Freedom, Book One.* New York: Scribner, 1952.

197. ————*Birthdays of Freedom, Book Two.* New York: Scribner, 1957.

198. ————*George Washington's World.* New York: Scribner, 1941.
199. ————*The World of Captain John Smith 1580–1631.* New York: Scribner, 1959.
200. ————*The World of Columbus and Sons.* New York: Scribner, 1965.
201. Gringhuis, Dick. *The Big Dig, a Frontier Fort Comes to Life.* New York: Dial, 1962.
202. Johnson, Gerald White. *America Grows up.* Illustrated by Leonard Everett Fisher. New York: Morrow, 1960.
203. ————*America Is Born.* Illustrated by Leonard Everett Fisher. New York: Morrow, 1959.
204. ————*America Moves Forward.* Illustrated by Leonard Everett Fisher. New York: Morrow, 1960.
205. McCall, Edith. *Pioneer Show Folk.* Illustrated by Carol Rogers. Chicago: Childrens Press, 1963.
206. ————*Pioneer Traders.* Illustrated by Felix Palm. Chicago: Childrens Press, 1964.
207. McGovern, Ann. . . . *If you Lived in Colonial Times.* Illustrated by Brinton Turkle. New York: Four Winds, 1964.
208. Mason, F. Van Wyck. *The Battle of Lake Erie.* Illustrated by Victor Mays. Boston: Houghton Mifflin, 1960.
209. Miers, Earl Schenck. *The Rainbow Book of American History.* Illustrated by James Daugherty. Cleveland: World Publishing, 1955.
210. Miller, Natalie. *The Story of the Liberty Bell.* Illustrated by Betsy Warren. Chicago: Childrens Press, 1965.
211. ————*The Story of the Star-Spangled Banner.* Illustrated by George Wilde. Chicago: Childrens Press, 1965.
212. ————*The Story of the Statue of Liberty.* Illustrated by John and Lucy Hawkinson. Chicago: Childrens Press, 1965.
213. Nathan, Adele. *The Building of the First Transcontinental Railroad.* Illustrated by Edward A. Wilson. New York: Random House, 1950.
214. Nolan, Jeanette. *The Shot Heard Round the World, the Story of Lexington and Concord.* New York: Messner, 1963.
215. Palmer, Geoffrey. *Quest for the Dead Sea Scrolls.* Illustrated by Peter Forster. New York: John Day, 1965.
216. Reeder, Red. *The Story of the Civil War.* Illustrated by Frederick Chapman. New York: Duell, Sloan, 1958.
217. ————*The Story of the War of 1812.* Illustrated by Frederick Chapman. New York: Duell, Sloan, 1960.
218. Rich, Louise Dickinson. *The First Book of the Early Settlers.* Illustrated by Douglas Gorsline. New York: F. Watts, 1959.
219. Sears, Stephen W. *Carrier War in the Pacific.* New York: American Heritage, 1966.
220. Shapiro, Irwin, Editor. *Golden Book of America.* Adapted from *American Heritage Magazine.* New York: Golden Press, 1957.
221. Trease, Geoffrey. *This Is Your Century.* New York: Harcourt, 1966.
222. Van Loon, Hendrik. *The Story of Mankind.* New York: Liveright, 1921, 1951.
223. Werstein, Irving. *The War with Mexico.* New York: Norton, 1965.

Fish, Reptiles, Amphibians

224. Bronson, Wilfred S. *Turtles.* New York: Harcourt, 1945.
225. Carson, Rachel Louise. *The Sea around Us.* Adapted by Anne Terry White. New York: Golden Press, 1958.
226. Clemons, Elizabeth. *Tide Pools and Beaches.* Illustrated by Joe Gault. New York: Knopf, 1964.
227. Darling, Lois and Louis. *Turtles.* New York: Morrow, 1962.
228. Earle, Olive L. *Strange Lizards.* New York: Morrow, 1964.

229. Goudey, Alice. *Houses from the Sea.* Illustrated by Adrienne Adams. New York: Scribner, 1959.
230. Harris, Louise and Norman. *Little Red Newt.* Illustrated by Henry B. Kane. Boston: Little, Brown, 1958.
231. Hess, Lilo. *Sea Horses.* New York: Scribner, 1966.
232. Holling, Holling C. *Minn of the Mississippi.* Boston: Houghton Mifflin, 1951.
233. ————*Pagoo.* Illustrated by author and Lucille Webster Holling. Boston: Houghton, Mifflin, 1957.
234. Holman, Felice. *Elizabeth the Treasure Hunter.* Illustrated by Erik Blegvad. New York: Macmillan, 1964.
235. Milne, Lorus and Margery. *The Crab that Crawled Out of the Past.* Illustrated by Kenneth Gosner. New York: Atheneum, 1965.
236. O'Neill, Mary. *The White Palace.* Illustrated by Nonny Hogrogian. New York: Crowell, 1966.
237. Selsam, Millicent. *Let's Get Turtles.* Illustrated by Arnold Lobel. New York: Harper & Row, 1965.
238. Žim, Herbert S. *Sharks.* Illustrated by Stephen Howe. New York: Morrow, 1966.

Geography

239. d'Aulaire, Edgar and Ingri Parin. *Ola.* New York: Doubleday, 1932.
240. Barclay, Isabel. *O Canada!* Illustrated by Cecile Gagnon. New York: Doubleday, 1964.
241. Caldwell, John C. *Let's Visit Canada.* New York: John Day, 1965.
242. Carr, Rachel. *The Picture Story of Japan.* Illustrated by Kazue Mizumura. New York: McKay, 1962.
243. Dodge, Mary Mapes. *Hans Brinker, or The Silver Skates.* Illustrated by George Wharton Edwards. New York: Scribner, 1943, 1865.
244. Folsom, Franklin. *The Soviet Union, a View from Within.* Camden, N.J.: Nelson, 1965.
245. Geis, Darlene, Editor. *Let's Travel in India.* Chicago: Childrens Press, 1965.
246. Gidal, Sonia and Tim. *My Village in France.* New York: Pantheon, 1965.
247. Huntington, Harriet. *California Harbors.* New York: Doubleday, 1964.
248. Kaula, Edna Mason. *The Land and People of New Zealand.* Philadelphia: Lippincott, 1964.
249. Kirk, Ruth, and Ira Spring. *Sigemi, a Japanese Village Girl.* New York: Harcourt, 1965.
250. Maxwell, Moreau S. *Eskimo Family.* Illustrated by Robert Glaubke. Chicago: Encyclopedia Britannica, 1962.
251. Miller, Helen Hill. *Greece.* New York: Scribner, 1965.
252. Prechtl, Louise. *Come along to Thailand.* Photos by James Prechtl. Minneapolis: Denison, 1962.
253. Rinkoff, Barbara. *A Map Is a Picture.* Illustrated by Robert Galster. New York: Crowell, 1965.
254. Sasek, Miroslav. *This Is Paris.* New York: Macmillan, 1959.
255. Schloat, G. Warren. *Junichi, a Boy of Japan.* New York: Knopf, 1964.
256. ————*Naim, a Boy of Turkey.* New York: Knopf, 1963.
257. ————*Propan, a Boy of Thailand.* New York: Knopf, 1963.
258. ————*Uttam, a Boy of Turkey.* New York: Knopf, 1963.
259. Seredy, Kate. *The Good Master.* New York: Viking, 1935.
260. Spyri, Johanna. *Heidi.* Translated by Helen B. Dole. Illustrated by William Sharp. New York: Grosset & Dunlap, 1945, 1884.
261. Sucksdorf, Astrid. *Chendru, the Boy and the Tiger.* English version by William Sansom. New York: Harcourt, 1960.

262. Swenson, Juliet Morgan. *Hawaii.* Illustrated by Ezra Jack Keats. New York: Holt, Rinehart and Winston, 1963.

Indians

263. Berke, Ernest. *The North American Indians.* New York: Doubleday, 1963.
264. Bleeker, Sonia. *The Apache Indians, Raiders of the Southwest.* Illustrated by Althea Karr. New York: Morrow, 1951.
265. ————*The Cherokee, Indians of the Mountains.* Illustrated by Althea Karr. New York: Morrow, 1952.
266. ————*The Chippewa Indians, Rice Gatherers of the Great Lakes.* Illustrated by Patricia Boodell. New York: Morrow, 1955.
267. ————*The Crow Indians, Hunters of the Northern Plains.* Illustrated by Althea Karr. New York: Morrow, 1953.
268. ————*Indians of the Longhouse, the Story of the Iroquois.* Illustrated by Althea Karr. New York: Morrow, 1950.
269. ————*The Navajo.* Illustrated by Patricia Boodell. New York: Morrow, 1958.
270. Hofsinde, Robert (Gray-Wolf). *Indian Picture Writing.* New York: Morrow, 1959.
271. ————*Indian Sign Language.* New York: Morrow, 1956.
272. ————*Indian Warriors and Their Weapons.* New York: Morrow, 1965.
273. Morris, Laverne. *The American Indian as Farmer.* Illustrated by Henry Lukes. Chicago: Melmont, 1963.
274. Scheele, William E. *The Mound Builders.* Cleveland: World Publishing, 1960.
275. Silverburg, Robert. *Home of the Red Man, Indian North America before Columbus.* Illustrated by Judith Ann Lawrence. New York: New York Graphic, 1963.
276. Thompson, Hildegard. *Getting to Know American Indians Today.* Illustrated by Shannon Stirnweiss. New York: Coward-McCann, 1965.
277. Tunis, Edwin. *Indians.* Cleveland: World Publishing, 1959.
278. Williams, Barbara. *Let's Go to an Indian Cliff Dwelling.* Illustrated by Robin King. New York: Putnam, 1965.
279. Worthylake, Mary M. *Moolack, Young Salmon Fisherman.* Illustrated by Ray Schroeder. Chicago: Melmont, 1963.

Insects

280. Conklin, Gladys. *I Like Caterpillars.* Illustrated by Barbara Latham. New York: Holiday, 1958.
281. Doering, Harold. *A Bee Is Born.* Translated by Dale Cunningham. New York: Sterling, 1962.
282. Earle, Olive L. *Crickets.* New York: Morrow, 1956.
283. Eeckhoudt, J. P. Vanden. *A Butterfly Is Born.* New York: Sterling, 1960.
284. Goldin, Augusta. *Spider Silk.* Illustrated by Joseph Low. New York: Crowell, 1964.
285. Harris, Louise and Norman. *Flash, the Life Story of a Firefly.* Illustrated by Henry B. Kane. Boston: Little, Brown, 1966.
286. Hawkes, Judy. *Fireflies in the Night.* Illustrated by Kazue Mizumura. New York: Crowell, 1963.
287. Hopf, Alice L. *Monarch Butterflies.* Illustrated by Peter Burchard. New York: Crowell, 1965.
288. Hutchins, Carleen Maley. *Moon Moth.* Illustrated by Douglas Howland. New York: Coward-McCann, 1965.
289. Hutchins, Ross E. *The Travels of Monarch X.* Illustrated by Jerome P. Connolly. Skokie, Ill.: Rand McNally, 1966.
290. McClung, Robert M. *Sphinx, Story of a Caterpillar.* New York: Morrow, 1949.

291. Portal, Colette. *The Life of a Queen.* Translated by Marcia Nardi. New York: Braziller, 1964.

292. Rood, Ronald. *Bees, Bugs and Beetles: The Arrow Book of Insects.* Illustrated by Denny McMains. New York: Four Winds, 1965.

293. Shuttlesworth, Dorothy. *The Story of Ants.* Illustrated by Su Tan N. Swain. New York: Doubleday, 1964.

Mammals

294. Bridges, William. *Lion Island.* Photos by Emmy Haas and Sam Drenton. New York: Morrow, 1965.

295. Bronson, Wilfrid S. *Cats.* New York: Harcourt, 1950.

296. ———*Chisel-Tooth Tribe.* New York: Harcourt, 1939.

297. ———*Horns and Antlers.* New York: Harcourt, 1942.

298. Compere, Mickie. *Dolphins.* Illustrated by Irma Wilde. New York: Four Winds, 1964.

299. Earle, Olive. *Mice at Home and Afield.* New York: Morrow, 1957.

300. Eberle, Irmengarde. *A Chipmunk Lives Here.* New York: Doubleday, 1965.

301. ———*Foxes Live Here.* New York: Doubleday, 1966.

302. George, John and Jean. *Masked Prowler, the Story of a Raccoon.* New York: Dutton, 1950.

303. ———*Vison, the Mink.* New York: Dutton, 1949.

304. ———*Vulpes, the Red Fox.* New York: Dutton, 1948.

305. Goudey, Alice E. *Here Come the Bears!* Illustrated by Garry MacKenzie. New York: Scribner, 1954.

306. ———*Here Come the Beavers!* Illustrated by Garry MacKenzie. New York: Scribner, 1957.

307. ———*Here Come the Seals!* Illustrated by Garry MacKenzie. New York: Scribner, 1957.

308. Lauber, Patricia. *The Friendly Dolphins.* Illustrated by Jean Simpson and Charles Gottlieb. New York: Random House, 1963.

309. Liers, Emil. *An Otter's Story.* Illustrated by Tony Palazzo. New York: Viking, 1953.

310. McClung, Robert. *Possum.* New York: Morrow, 1963.

311. ———*Screamer, Last of the Eastern Panthers.* Illustrated by Lloyd Sandford. New York: Morrow, 1964.

312. Morris, Desmond. *The Big Cats.* Illustrated by Barry Driscoll. New York: McGraw-Hill, 1965.

313. Posell, Elsa. *The True Book of Whales and Other Sea Mammals.* Illustrated by Arthur Warheit. Chicago: Childrens Press, 1963.

314. Ravielli, Anthony. *Elephants, the Last of the Land Giants.* New York: Parents Institute, 1965.

315. Rounds, Glen. *Rain in the Woods and Other Small Matters.* New York: Harcourt, 1964.

316. Selsam, Millicent. *How to Be a Nature Detective.* Illustrated by Ezra Jack Keats. New York: Harper & Row, 1958.

317. Zim, Herbert. *Golden Hamsters.* Illustrated by Herschel Wartik. New York: Morrow, 1951.

Man – Self

318. Evans, Eva Knox. *All about Us.* Illustrated by Vana Earle. New York: Capitol, 1957.

319. Lerner, Marguerite Rush. *Who Do You Think You Are? The Story of Heredity.* Illustrated by Polly Bolian. Engelwood Cliffs, N.J.: Prentice-Hall, 1963.

320. Lewellen, John. *You and Your Amazing Mind.* Illustrated by Winnie Fitch and Joe Phalen. Chicago: Childrens Press, 1952.

321. Ravielli, Anthony. *Wonders of the Human Body.* New York: Viking, 1954.

322. Zim, Herbert. *What's Inside of Me?* Illustrated by Herschel Wartik. New York: Morrow, 1952.

323. ————*Your Heart and How It Works.* Illustrated by Gustav Schrotter. New York: Morrow, 1959.

Men Work Together

324. Black, Algernon. *The First Book of Ethics.* Illustrated by Rick Schreiter. New York: F. Watts, 1965.

325. Fisher, Dorothy Canfield. *A Fair World for All, the Meaning of the Declaration of Human Rights.* Illustrated by Jeanne Bendick. New York: McGraw-Hill, 1952.

326. Goldman, Peter. *Civil Rights, the Challenge of the Fourteenth Amendment.* New York: Coward-McCann, 1965.

327. Hastings, Evelyn B. *The Department Store.* Photos by Lewis A. Ogan. Chicago: Melmont, 1956.

328. Johnson, Gerald. *Communism, an American's View.* New York: Morrow, 1964.

329. ————*The Congress.* Illustrated by Leonard Everett Fisher. New York: Morrow, 1963.

330. Levine, David. *What Does a Congressman Do?* Photos by Ira Mandelbaum. New York: Dodd, Mead, 1965.

331. Newman, Shirlee Petkin, and Diane Finn Sherman. *About the People Who Run Your City.* Illustrated by James David Johnson. Chicago: Melmont, 1963.

Oceanography

332. Arnold, Oren. *Marvels of the Sea and Shore.* Illustrated by J. Yunge-Bateman. New York: Abelard-Schuman, 1963.

333. Clarke, Arthur C. *The Challenge of the Sea.* Illustrated by Alex Schomburg. New York: Holt, Rinehart and Winston, 1960.

334. Coombs, Charles. *Deep-Sea World, the Story of Oceanography.* New York: Morrow, 1966.

335. Fisher, James. *The Wonderful World of the Sea.* New York: Garden City Books, 1957.

336. Holsaert, Eunice and Faith. *Ocean Wonders.* Illustrated by Leonard Kessler. New York: Holt, Rinehart and Winston, 1965.

337. Lambert, Elizabeth. *The Living Sea.* Illustrated by Elinor Jaeger. New York: Coward-McCann, 1963.

338. Lane, Ferdinand C. *All about the Sea.* Illustrated by Fritz Kredel. New York: Random House, 1953.

339. Scharff, Robert. *The How and Why Wonder Book of Oceanography.* Illustrated by Robert Doremus. New York: Grosset & Dunlap, 1964.

340. Sherman, Diane. *You and the Oceans.* Illustrated by Bill Sanders. Chicago: Childrens Press, 1965.

Plants

341. Beck, Barbara. *The First Book of Weeds.* Illustrated by Page Cary. New York: F. Watts, 1963.

342. Bulla, Clyde Robert. *A Tree Is a Plant.* Illustrated by Lois Lignell. New York: Crowell, 1960.

343. Cavanna, Betty. *The First Book of Wildflowers.* New York: F. Watts, 1961.

344. Downer, Mary Louise. *The Flower.* Illustrated by Lucienne Bloch. New York: Scott, 1955.

345. Grant, Madeleine P. *Wonder World of Microbes.* Illustrated by Clifford N. Geary. New York: McGraw-Hill, 1956.

346. Guilcher, J. M., and R. H. Noailles. *A Fruit Is Born.* New York: Sterling, 1960.

347. ————*A Tree Is Born.* New York: Sterling, 1960.

348. Hutchins, Ross E. *The Amazing Seeds.* New York: Dodd, Mead, 1965.

349. ————*This Is a Leaf.* New York: Dodd, Mead, 1962.

350. ————*This Is a Tree.* New York: Dodd, Mead, 1964.

351. Kurtz, Edwin B., Jr., and Chris Allen. *Adventures in Living Plants.* Tucson: University of Arizona Press, 1965.

352. Lerner, Sharon. *I Found a Leaf.* Minneapolis: Lerner, 1964.

353. Selsam, Millicent. *Birth of a Forest.* Illustrated by Barbara Wolff. New York: Harper & Row, 1964.

354. ————*See through the Jungle.* Illustrated by Winifred Lubell. New York: Harper & Row, 1957.

355. Watts, May Theilgaard. *The Doubleday First Guide to Trees.* Illustrated by Michael Bevans. New York: Doubleday, 1964.

356. Webber, Irma E. *Bits That Grow Big.* New York: W. R. Scott, 1949.

Science as Inquiry

357. Boardman, Fon Wyman. *History and Historians.* New York: Walck, 1965.

358. Kohn, Bernice. *The Scientific Method.* Illustrated by Ernest Crichlow. Engelwood Cliffs, N.J.: Prentice-Hall, 1964.

Space

359. Coombs, Charles. *Lift-Off, The Story of Rocket Power.* Illustrated by R. H. Foor. New York: Morrow, 1963.

360. ————*Project Apollo.* New York: Morrow, 1965.

361. ————*Project Mercury.* New York: Morrow, 1960.

362. Dille, John. *Americans in Space.* New York: Harper & Row, 1965.

363. Ley, Willy and Chesley Bonestell. *Beyond the Solar System.* New York: Viking, 1964.

364. Podendorf, Illa. *The True Book of Space.* Illustrated by Robert Borja. Chicago: Childrens Press, 1959.

365. Sasek, Miroslav. *This Is Cape Kennedy.* New York: Macmillan, 1964.

366. Tresselt, Alvin. *How Far Is Far?* Illustrated by Ward Brackett. New York: Parents Institute, 1964.

Transportation

367. Bloch, Marie Halun. *Tunnels.* Illustrated by Nelson Sears. New York: Coward-McCann, 1954.

368. Carlisle, Norman and Madelyn. *About Roads.* Illustrated by George Wilde. Chicago: Melmont, 1965.

369. Goldwater, Daniel. *Bridges and How They Are Built.* Illustrated by Harvey Weiss. New York: W. R. Scott, 1965.

370. Judson, Clara Ingram. *St. Lawrence Seaway.* Illustrated by Lorence F. Bjorklund. Chicago: Follett, 1959.

371. Saunders, F. Wenderoth. *Building Brooklyn Bridge.* Boston: Little, Brown, 1965.

Series

372. *All about* . . . . New York: Random House.
373. *The American Heritage Junior Library.* New York: American Heritage.
374. *Books to Begin on.* New York: Holt, Rinehart and Winston.
375. *Colonial American Craftsmen.* New York: F. Watts.
376. *Cornerstones of Freedom.* Chicago: Childrens Press.
377. *Enchantment of America.* Chicago: Childrens Press.
378. *The First Book of* . . . . New York: F. Watts.
379. *Frontiers of America.* Chicago: Childrens Press.
380. *Getting to Know* . . . . New York: Coward-McCann.
381. *Golden Nature Guides.* New York: Golden Press.
382. *Here Come the* . . . . New York: Scribner.
383. *How and Why Wonder Books.* New York: Grosset & Dunlap.
384. *I-Can-Read* Books. New York: Harper & Row.
385. *I Want to Be a* . . . . Chicago: Childrens Press.
386. *Key to the City.* Philadelphia: Lippincott.
387. *Let's Read and Find Out.* New York: Crowell.
388. *Let's Travel in* . . . . Chicago: Childrens Press.
389. *Let's Visit* . . . . New York: John Day.
390. *Life World Library.* New York: Time.
391. *Made in* . . . . New York: Knopf.
392. *My Village in* . . . . New York: Pantheon.
393. *Natural Science Picture Books.* New York: McGraw-Hill.
394. *Our National Parks.* Chicago: Follett.
395. *Portraits of the Nations* (titled *Land and People of* . . .). Philadelphia: Lippincott.
396. *Rivers of the World.* Chicago: Garrard.
397. *Sterling Nature Series.* New York: Sterling.
398. *This Is* . . . . New York: Macmillan.
399. *True Book of* . . . . Chicago: Childrens Press.
400. *True to Life.* Chicago: Encyclopedia Britannica.
401. *You and* . . . . Chicago: Childrens Press.

BOOKS FOR
SPECIAL INTERESTS

A blond pigtail switched as the chubby ten-year-old turned a page in the book she was reading. Miss Follett smiled as she watched Judy slip off one shoe, then another as she continued reading. Judy shifted her position in the comfortable chair in the reading corner. Only when her name was called by a classmate did she look up saying, "Is it time to get ready for lunch? This is really a neat book! Oh, I wish I could read a hundred books like *Misty!*"

"Can I have it next?" asked Nancy.

"Is your name next on the waiting list?" the teacher questioned. "I think we have a waiting list for *Misty.*"

"You can read my new Walter Farley book, Nancy," volunteered Betty, another lover of horse stories.

The girls walked out of the classroom discussing their favorite horse stories.

Children have special interests at each stage of development; some of these interests continue for several years. The older children grow, the more diversified their interests become. In the middle grades they begin to ask for "horse stories," "dog stories," "sports books," "mysteries," or other titles related to hobbies or activities. The vast numbers of special interest books make it necessary to select only a few examples to suggest the titles available and to present evaluative criteria.

ANIMAL STORIES

Appeals of Animal Stories

A high degree of interest in animals is found in studies of children's interests. The young child enjoys animals in picture books. Animals in fantasy and humorous stories contribute to interest in these types of books. When eight- to twelve-year-olds ask for an animal story, however, they want a story in which the animal is the hero, or one in which a child and animal share significant experiences. Dog stories or horse stories may be specified. Frequently, girls in the middle grades seem to have greater interest in horse and dog stories than do boys.

Animal stories appeal to children because they satisfy basic emotional needs. A child can identify with an animal who may be smaller, who is dependent, just as he is. Animals stand up against the forces of nature, the elements in the environment, yet they respond to the drive of instincts as the child would like to respond. The laws of nature do not always bring happiness; one would often wish the animal might behave like a human, but the honestly drawn animal character must obey the natural law. A sense of justice and "rightness" pervades the well-written animal story. It would be good if the animal would remain forever with the human who loved his pet, but it is *right* that he answer the call of a mate, that he receive freedom to face the problems of the natural world.

Animal heroes express intelligence, courage, patience, and loyalty; children find security in the consistent expression of these qualities they admire. In the well-written animal story, the animal hero may be endowed with such human qualities, as unusual persistence, perception, or devotion. But his behavior is consistent with that of his species. Just as human heroes possess attributes that set them apart, so animal heroes

are "common animals" with "uncommon powers."

In many of the animal stories, especially life-cycle stories, death is ever-present, is recognized, and is accepted as part of life. This honesty about death is not found in many other books for children, and it may be that an unspoken need for facing such shadows is expressed and satisfied in these books. Animal stories provide an outlet for release of tension, and may lead to understanding of man's conflicts with nature and himself. Frequently, the theme of the animal story is really the character development of the human protagonist.

Challenge, risk, and suspense are elements of the adventures children seek in books. Animal stories provide these ingredients in overcoming the obstacles and conflicts presented in the plot. Animals need love, respond to affection given by humans, and give back responses akin to human love. Through such stories, children may vicariously experience these responses of love and friendship.

Life-Cycle Stories

Life-cycle stories are also discussed in Chapter 9 because the purpose of many books of this type is to give information. Others are written to tell a good story about an animal character. For example, Kjelgaard emphasizes the life of the fox in *Haunt Fox*, but the reader also identifies with the boy who hunts the fox. The description of the outdoors and the details of the life of the fox and his care for his mate and cubs, are very ably handled. When the boy finds the fox in a trap, he frees the animal he has pursued, for he cannot take him unfairly.

Tarka the Otter was first published by the English writer, Henry Williamson, in 1927, and has recently been reissued. It is a slowly paced, realistic account of the life of an otter in North Devon, written for people of all ages who like to walk and *observe*. Children will find it difficult to read, and only parts should be read to introduce them to the book, and to the author's skill in writing. The introduction and the author's account of his work, in addition to the explanatory article about the unusual words, should be read before beginning the story. The linguistic study of such passages as the following would bring new insight into the English language:

> *At dimpsey, when day and night hunters see each other between the two lights.* . . .
> *They hunted and ragrowstered for many days under the high wooded hills, below which the river wound and coiled like a serpent.*
> *. . . With a yinny of anger she threw him off, and faced him with swishing rudder, tissing through her teeth.*[1]

Tarka does not talk, but is given feelings, as the observer thinks the animal must feel. Her mother "enjoyed the rage of the little cubs," Tarka "knew that hunted fish usually went upwater," and the fear of enemies, especially the man who hunts otters with dogs is described with keen emotion.

The life story of Runner, *The Frightened Hare,* by Russell, emphasizes the constant fear experienced by an animal. Runner can understand all the enemies he meets, except the plague. Although his existence is "an uneasy balancing of life and death," there are fine descriptions of joyous times when the rabbits leap and dance in the moonlight. It would be interesting to contrast the life story of the rabbit with that of the largest living mammal, *Bally the Blue Whale* by Arnov. Even this huge animal faces enemies as it migrates from warm waters to the Antarctic Ocean.

Aileen Fisher has written a suspenseful story of the struggle of a female shrew for existence in the *Valley of the Smallest.* The shrew's mountain environment is realistically and accurately described; for example, her first litter is eaten by a garter snake, but some of the second litter survive. True to the laws of nature, the little shrew falls prey to a stronger animal at the end of a year of life.

An unusual story is that of *Assateague Deer,* Beebe's account of a year in the life of Little Sika, a miniature deer from Japan. Scientists wonder whether these deer can survive on Assateague Island, where men give them no assistance. During a hurricane, the island literally disappears and Little Sika survives by clinging to a log. A hungry rat, mink, and raccoon share the safety of the log with Sika. The author presents a great deal of information about other animals on the island as she shows that instinct, as well as luck, save the small deer. Sika and a cinnamon fawn survive to begin a new herd, but the reader knows life will continue to be hazardous.

In the true life-cycle story, the animals have little or no contact with humans. Another of Beebe's fine stories, *Run Light Buck, Run,* tells of the pronghorns who live at the rim of the Grand Canyon. In this story, however, a prospector helps two of the herd survive.

Two authors have written fine stories about a Canada Goose. Robert Murphy's *Wild Geese Calling* is a gentle love story of a goose and gander and the warm relationship of a lonely boy with the gander he saved. Danny finally realizes he must give the gander his freedom, for nothing "can ever stay." In *Wild Voyageur,* Jones contrasts the responses of an Eskimo girl and a California boy to one young gander. Jones conveys the dangers of enemies and storms more vividly than does Murphy. This book includes a complete life cycle, with the courting and nesting of the gander's parents and gives more information about the long flights north and south. Mooshnuk, the Eskimo girl, is unu-

---

[1]Henry Williamson, *Tarka the Otter,* Illustrated by Barry Driscoll (New York: F. Watts, 1964), pp. 45, 65, 88.

sual in her sensitivity to beauty and concern for the young gander. She lies to her father in order to save the bird and bands it gently. At the refuge in America, Davey sees the bird Mooshnuk had named Chen, releases it from a trap, and writes to Aklavik, the name on the band. Mooshnuk's father understands when she reveals her guilt, and she and David correspond. In each case, the goose is portrayed as a brave, patient, loving animal with a spirit that goes beyond the response of instinct.

Children and Animals

Stories about pets provide the vicarious experience of giving love and receiving devotion and loyalty from an animal. *Bond of the Fire* by Fon Eisen tells how a Cro-magnon boy and a dog were bound by concern for each other. The boy learns how to give and accept love as he tames the dog and its wolf mate. Each chapter is an exciting incident imaginatively re-creating the life of a primitive people who have not developed a language. Ash is an unusually intelligent boy, but he is unable to communicate his knowledge of the danger of the ice jam, for example. Here is a boy-dog story that describes the early beginnings of the bond between children and pets.

Several authors have successfully conveyed the deep love and understanding of a pet. This bond is the theme of Morey's book, *Gentle Ben*. Ben was a brown bear, an unpredictable and possibly dangerous creature to have as a pet. Mark's mother understands this relationship:

> *I only know that sometimes something does happen between people and animals. There seems to be a bond that overcomes all fear, prejudice, everything objectionable. I suppose you might call it a perfect love, a sort of Biblical "lion and the lamb" kind of love.*[2]

---

[2]Walt Morey, *Gentle Ben*, Illustrated by John Schoenherr (New York: Dutton, 1965), p. 30.

Mark's father agrees to buy the bear after he has observed Mark and Ben playing together. A fish cannery manager helps Mark treat Ben when he was tormented by his former owner. As he reads this story of a boy's love for an animal that finally had to be taken away, the child will learn much about life in an Alaskan fishing village. The story of storms, fish pirates, and drunken men is not gentle; but the theme of the responsibility of love is woven into each exciting incident.

Dreams of taming a wild animal come true in *Coyote for Keeps* by Johnson and become a necessity for four Irish lads in *A Family of Foxes* by Dillon. The coyote pup was found by two city children spending a vacation with grandparents in Arizona. The foxes were washed ashore from a ship taking them to the Dublin Zoo. In each story, the children fear that adults will disapprove of their pets, and in each one, there is an ever-present danger that the bounty hunter or the entire village will kill the animals. Ecology and natural conservation is the theme of the first book. The Irish story presents the fallacy of superstitions about foxes and also reveals an understanding teacher. The villagers' hatred of foxes as devils or witches is not overcome despite the "sense" of Patsy, Seamus, Colin, and Peter. *Coyote for Keeps* moves at a slow pace in the beginning and dialogue is stilted. The ingenuity of the Irish boys and fine characterizations of children and adults make *A Family of Foxes* more worthwhile as literature.

A story of friendship with an animal can be a beautiful experience, and so it is with Guillot's tale, *Grishka and the Bear*. A Siberian boy tames a bear cub with his laughter, teaches it to fish and hunt, for it is adopted by the village as a symbol of good luck. Following tribal custom, the villagers plan to kill the bear, but Grishka escapes with it to the mountains. When Grishka falls into a pit, the bear leads humans to save the boy, somehow knowing it means the end of their friendship. The role of the woman in this culture is clearly portrayed as Yaku helps Grishka and shares his joys and sorrows.

Sterling North's book about his pet raccoon recalls life in a small town early in the twentieth century. The boy and his father are lonely, worry about the older boy serving in World War I, and share the joy of building a canoe. *Rascal, a Memoir of a Better Era* has been rewritten for younger readers under the title, *Little Rascal.*

Gay-Neck, the Story of a Pigeon by Mukerji received the Newbery Medal nearly fifty years ago.[3] Called an odyssey of a pigeon, it is the story of a bird's training, his travels, and his service with Indian soldiers in World War I. This story is told from three viewpoints: the pigeon's owner, the old hunter, and from Gay-Neck's point of view in "the grammar of fancy and the dictionary of imagination."[4] This technique of shifting narration sometimes makes the story difficult to follow. The theme of the book is as modern as the challenges of the moment, that courage and love may be communicated to others to overcome the hates and fears of life. The wisdom of Buddhist Lamas is incorporated as the humans pray for the bird and communicate their feeling of serenity through prayer:

> *Whatever we think and feel will colour what we say or do. He who fears, even unconsciously, or has his least little dream tainted with hate, will inevitably, sooner or later, translate these two qualities into his action. Therefore, my brothers, live courage, breathe courage and give courage. Think and feel love so that you will be able to pour out of yourselves peace and serenity as naturally as a flower gives forth fragrance.*
>
> *Peace be unto all!*[5]

---

[3]See the comparison of *Gay-Neck* and *Pigeon, Fly Home* by Thomas Liggett in "A New Look at Old Books," *Young Readers Review*, vol. 2 (September 1965), p. 12.

[4]Dhan Gopal Mukerji, *Gay-Neck, the Story of a Pigeon*, Illustrated by Boris Artzybasheff (New York: Dutton, 1927), p. 68.

[5]Mukerji, p. 197.

When wild animals become pets, it is difficult to give them freedom. Joel so longed for a pet that he was happy to care for an injured, wild goose. Sandburg adds humor to her story of *Joel and the Wild Goose* by including Joel's riddles and jokes. However, the serious theme of giving freedom to one you love is expressed when Joel allows the goose to be free. In *Miranda and the Cat* by Linell Smith, a city girl finds a proud, aggressive alley cat who has been badly injured in a fight. She takes him to a veterinarian and cares for this distrustful survivor of a battle-filled life. However, she never gives him a name, recognizing he will not stay with her. When Miranda is ill, the cat does return to give his love and cheer.

Hanno, a gorilla that escaped from the London Zoo was a "pet" of Ping, a Chinese refugee, for only two days, but a strange bond existed between the two. *A Stranger at Green Knowe* is one of L. M. Boston's stories about the mysterious English mansion and Mrs. Oldknow, the gracious owner who is unusually perceptive about children and life. The story begins in Africa with the early life and capture of the gorilla. Ping admired the gorilla in the zoo, and he learned a great deal about the animal as he talked with the keeper. The concrete walls and steel bars of Hanno's cage recalled Ping's life in refugee camps. Ping is captivated by the animal:

> *. . . for Ping had, as it were, fallen in love. The world contained something so wonderful to him that everything was altered. It was not only that Hanno existed, a creature with the strength of a bull, the pounce of a lion, and the dignity and grief of a man—too much to take in, all the animal creation in one—but somewhere there was a country of such size, power, and mystery, that gorillas were a sample of what it produced in secret, where everything else would be on the same scale.*[6]

---

[6]L. M. Boston, *A Stranger at Green Knowe*, Illustrated by Peter Boston (New York: Harcourt, 1961), p. 43.

The contrast of the huge animal, which does come to the Green Knowe forest, with the small boy is terrifying as Ping plays with the beast and tries to keep the police from discovering the "refugee." The boy is foolhardy, yet this mystical understanding between the two refugees protects him. An exciting climax brings death to the gorilla and hope that Ping has found a happy refuge.

More mature readers in sixth grade can appreciate the fine book by Marjorie Kinnan Rawlings, *The Yearling.* This story of a boy, his pet fawn, and his growth in the "big scrub" of Florida reveals the suffering that can come to all who give love. Rawlings writes with vigor, humor, and quiet beauty in words that capture the essence of the moment. In one episode, Jody has been enjoying a quiet play with a little fluttermill by the stream. At supper there is warmth and fun:

> *It was true. He was addled with April. He was dizzy with Spring. He was as drunk as Lem Forrester on a Saturday night. His head was swimming with the strong brew made up of the sun and the air and the thin gray rain. The flutter-mill had made him drunk, and the doe's coming, and his father's hiding his absence, and his mother's making him a pone and laughing at him. He was stabbed with the candlelight inside the safe comfort of the cabin; with the moonlight around it.*[7]

Jody's father realizes he will grow up and he tries to protect the boy's brief moments of pleasure with his fawn. When the deer continues to eat the corn, Jody's father says it must be killed. Jody refuses, and his mother must do the job because his father is ill. Jody runs away; after nearly starving, he returns to the woods near home. Even the flutter-mill brings no comfort. With his father's words Jody knows he has grown up to the responsibilities of the farm. "He did not believe he should ever love anything, man or woman or his own child, as he had loved the yearling. He would be lonely all his life. But a man took it for his share and went on."[8]

Horse Stories

Horse stories appeal to both boys and girls in the third grade, but by fourth or fifth grade, the girls often seem to adopt horses as kindred creatures. Boys will enjoy listening to a horse story and frequently read these books at home, but they do not discuss the horse books with as much enthusiasm for fear of being identified with the opposite sex.

A picture storybook series about Blaze is written and illustrated by C. W. Anderson. Easy to read, there is enough action in the stories of Billy and his horse to maintain interest. In *Billy and Blaze,* the little boy gets his pony. Blaze is stolen in *Blaze and the Gypsies,* and in *Blaze and Thunderbolt,* a wild horse becomes a friend of Blaze and his owner. Care of horses, kindness, and good feelings toward others are expressed.

Glen Rounds wrote and illustrated *The Blind Colt,* the story of a boy's devotion and care for a colt marked for death. A Dakota ranch is realistically portrayed in this story that emphasizes gentleness and kindness.

In *Blue Canyon Horse,* by Clark, an Indian boy waits patiently for the return of a mare who fled with the wild horses. Eventually she returns with her foal. The prose style of the author reflects the cadence of the Indian chants. Klose wrote *Benny, the Biography of a Horse,* a sensitive, spirited horse who grew old as a member of the Cline family in Michigan. Told in first person by the girl who understood him, trained him, and shared her joys and sorrows with him, it is also the autobiography of a girl who will be a good companion for ten-year-olds reading of her

---

[7]Marjorie Kinnan Rawlings, *The Yearling* (New York: Scribner, 1944), p. 13.

[8]Rawlings, p. 400.

life. Girls will also empathize with Tressa who dreamed of owning a white-starred chestnut horse. Priscilla Neff creates a lovable, natural little girl in *Tressa's Dream*. When the family moves to a rural area her father is developing as a subdivision, Tressa's dream seems possible. Accepting her own fears of large horses and recognizing the need of the family business, Tressa chooses a Shetland pony instead of her dream horse. Responsibility, patience, and growing confidence with horses bring the promise of a realization of her dream. None of these stories create high-pitched excitement, but girls who long to be with horses will enjoy these quiet, realistic stories.

A Dash of Pepper by Bell is a story of human relationships, although the horse, Pepper, is a central character. In a horse-loving community, Clyde is denied a horse because his sister was thrown and killed. Clyde and Pepper save another boy, who loves trains, when a locomotive runs wild, and Clyde's father changes his mind about Pepper. A child reviewer wrote, "Most of the problems were settled believably, but some were solved like T.V. shows. What I mean is that everything just 'happens' and solves the problem."

Walter Farley has written a favorite series about one horse, *The Black Stallion,* and his descendants. Alec Ramsey and a wild, black stallion are the only survivors of a shipwreck. When they are finally rescued the boy is determined to train the horse. After patient, secret training and night trials at the track, the Black is ready to run in the Derby. This famous race is recalled in *Son of the Black Stallion* when Alec receives Satan, the first foal of the Black. Training a horse that has the instinct to kill seems nearly impossible. The reader learns about the preliminary races that must be won before the attempt is made for the "Triple Crown" in *The Black Stallion's Filly*. Bonfire, sired by Black, becomes known for his harness racing in *The Blood Bay Colt*. In this story, there is better

characterization. Emphasis in all these books is on horse training and races. The people are merely shadows. Paced as fast as the races, the stories maintain high interest for readers who are absorbed in horse lore.

One of the first horse stories was the 1927 Newbery Award winner, *Smoky,* by Will James. It is difficult to read, and most children will wait until junior high school for this story of a horse who becomes a killer after being stolen and mistreated. After many cruel, painful times, Smoky is reunited with his first trainer, Clint. Although the horse does not speak his feelings, the reader is aware of a new spirit when Smoky finally recognizes Clint.

Marguerite Henry is one of the more skillful writers of horse stories. Careful research provides an authentic background for her accounts of horses and the people who train them. *Misty of Chincoteague* was the colt of Phantom, a descendant of the Spanish horses that struggled to Assateague Island when a ship was wrecked in a storm. Once each year, the wild horses are herded across the channel to Chincoteague Island where they are sold on Pony Penning Day. Paul and Maureen have their hearts set on buying Phantom and are delighted to learn they also can purchase her colt, Misty. Through Misty, they are able to gentle Phantom and win an exciting race. Phantom escapes to the island, but Misty remains with her human friends. A small horse named Misty really lived on Mrs. Henry's farm and was visited by many boys and girls. When she was returned to Chincoteague to find a mate, the event was recorded in news magazines and daily papers. *Stormy, Misty's Foal* continues the story. The foal overcomes the hazards of weather, and Misty is a laudable mother.

The dramatic, sad, yet noble story of an Arabian horse shipped from Morocco to France is told in *King of the Wind,* winner of the 1949 Newbery Award. Sham is not accepted by the French king, and is put out to

Wesley Dennis' horses are well proportioned and move with grace. The outstanding illustrations complement this well-written horse story. From *King of the Wind,* by Marguerite Henry, illustrated by Wesley Dennis. Copyright 1948 by Rand McNally & Company, publishers.

work. A series of owners leaves him bruised and worn, but the Earl of Godolphin finally recognizes his value and gives the small horse his true place. Sham becomes the sire of a new breed of fine horses. More than a horse story, this is the tale of the devotion of a deaf-mute Arabian boy, Agba, who stays with the horse until Sham dies. Agba's courage, patience, and unswerving loyalty are unequaled.

Loyalty is also a main theme in *Justin Morgan Had a Horse.* A poor schoolmaster accepts two horses as payment for a debt. Joel, his pupil, loves the runt colt who becomes a champion in the pulling matches. Bub, the horse, is sold and mistreated. After Joel and Bub are reunited, an exciting moment comes when President James Monroe

rides the horse. The famous Morgan line is descended from this indomitable little horse. *Brighty of the Grand Canyon* includes more humor, for this burro, who supposedly made the Bright Angel Trail, is amusing. Those who have visited the rim of the Grand Canyon especially enjoy the book.

In the foreword to *Gaudenzia,* Mrs. Henry tells how she gathered authentic details of the Palio, a horse race held each year in Siena, Italy, according to medieval customs. Giorgio Terni was a real boy, and he did ride the horse in three races through narrow city streets. Fate decreed that he should ride another horse in one race, and it was necessary to hurt his beloved Gaudenzia to try to win. The writing style creates the mounting tension with short sentences and pauses:

*From bleachers, from balconies, from all over
the Piazza Gaudenzia's enemies are shrieking
for blood. In full stride she goes up the incline.
A moment of terror! She stumbles, breaks gait.
Ivan, for Montone, tries to crowd her into the
posts. But Giorgio grasps her mane, squeezes
his right leg into her flanks. Squeezes tighter.
It works! She recovers; she's safe!*[9]

With *White Stallion of Lipizza* this author
tells another story based upon actual incidents in the training and protection of the
beautifully disciplined horses of the Spanish
Riding School in Vienna. The men who ride
these horses also must achieve a self-discipline
that is difficult and inspiring.

In *Mustang, Wild Spirit of the West*, Marguerite Henry writes in a different style, as
though Annie Bronn Johnston is telling her
story of the fight to protect the wild horses
of the western ranges. Based on a true story,
this narrative describes, in realistic detail, the
hunting of the mustangs by plane and truck,
and the torture before the animals are
slaughtered for dog food. The warm love of
her parents helps Annie overcome the effects of polio; her own love of her mustang,
Hobo, inspires her to fight by writing letters,
taking pictures of the cruelty, and by speaking to a Congressional committee. Horse
lovers of all ages will share the feelings of
Wild Horse Annie, and may be spurred to
write some letters to help in this continuing
struggle. The detailed history of the contributions of the mustang may be of less interest to young readers than to adults.

Without "humanizing" animals, Mrs.
Henry creates horses that are consistent with
their species yet have qualities of courage,
loyalty, and endurance. Plot does not take
precedence over characterization. Each
person is real, consistent, and fully developed. There is no lengthy descriptive prose,
for a few words create a picture. One horse
is described: "The Phantom ain't a hoss. She
ain't even a lady. She's just a piece of wind
and sky."[10] There is realism in Marguerite
Henry's writing; the pains of birth are described in *Black Gold*, yet the reader's senses
are not shocked. The slang or poor grammar of cowhands or trainers is authentically
used. Most of Henry's books have been illustrated by Dennis, whose work reflected
skill and knowledge of horses. These books
appeal to children in the middle years.

The Wild Heart by Griffiths is a well-
written novel of a wild horse on the Argentine
pampas and of the men who tried to subdue
her. La Bruja was an ugly mare, but she
could run with the speed of the wind so she
was desired by men. When a storm kills her
mother, the colt steals milk from other
mares and learns to survive alone, unloved
and unprotected. These seeds of anger and
distrust grow within the horse as men try to
catch her. She killed the soldier who rode
her because he beat her cruelly. A second
man rode her briefly before he was killed by
Indians. From an Indian captor the horse
received kindness, but the Indian is killed by
soldiers, and La Bruja escapes. Beautiful
descriptions of the pampas in North and
South are included with realistic details of
life in the herd guarded by the stallion. The
horse is given sanctuary by a priest when she
runs into a church. A crippled orphan boy at
the mission cares for the horse, and must
finally decide whether to give her the freedom she seeks or keep her in a small lot. An
alternative—to cripple La Bruja so she could
never run and thus never be hunted by
men—is suggested when a folk singer says,
"To let her free you must take away that
which makes her coveted by other men."[11]

[9]Marguerite Henry, *Gaudenzia, Pride of the Palio*, Illustrated by Lynd Ward (Skokie, Ill.: Rand McNally,
1960), p. 189.

[10]Marguerite Henry, *Misty of Chincoteague*, Illustrated by
Wesley Dennis (Skokie, Ill.: Rand McNally, 1947),
p. 54.

[11]Helen Griffiths, *The Wild Heart*, Illustrated by Victor G.
Ambrus (New York: Doubleday, 1963), p. 187.

The book closes on the note that to be kind one must sometimes be cruel. Was Angel's decision the wise one? Each reader will answer for himself. This is a horse story with substance and an unpredictable ending. It should appeal to many middle-graders.

Dog Stories

Many children ask for dog stories over and over again. Some well-known dogs from other groups of books have already been mentioned. Ruth and Latrobe Carroll's books about Tough Enough reflect life in the mountains today. In *Tough Enough's Trip,* the Tatum family goes to visit great-grandparents. Along the way, Beanie collects a kitten, a crow, a raccoon, a skunk, and a turtle. Fun, which is part of the Tatums' life, continues despite economic problems. The efforts of the family to make money by creating wildflower arrangements, acorn jewelry, and mica animals are rewarded. The little dog is a part of the story, but he is not the center. This series would be good to use in a study of the southeastern United States.

Ribsy is an important figure in Cleary's stories of Henry Huggins (see Chapter 5). In *Ribsy,* the dog is lost, but humor prevails. *Mishmash* as described by Cone causes many disturbances in his attempts to be helpful. Again, humor is the essence of this story of a boy and his dog.

Heroic Dogs   Several excellent books are based upon heroic dogs who overcome obstacles with little or no help from man. The courage and self-discipline of a dog left alone on an island when a volcano erupted is the theme of Coatsworth's book, *Jock's Island.* The sheep dog tries to keep the sheep together despite the confusion, the smell of danger, and the strange behavior of the animals left behind. Jock is found by a man who lived alone on the other end of the island. When he discovers the evacuation, he makes plans for the return of his beloved Mary, but the story ends without telling the reader whether the people ever return. This would provide an excellent opportunity for children to write a sequel to Jock's story.

Sheila Burnford's story of three runaway pets is an odyssey of courage and endurance as a young Labrador retriever, an old bull terrier, and a Siamese cat make *The Incredible Journey.* Left with a friend of their owner, the animals try to reach their home more than 250 miles away. Hunger, storms, dangerous river crossings, and fights are the nearly insurmountable problems of these three animals. Their survival and care for each other make a remarkable story. For younger readers, Lynd Ward tells a story of a house dog who survives in a forest environment, *Nic of the Woods.* Ward's dark, brooding illustrations of the forest create somber fear of the danger to the dog.

Another popular dog story, *Lassie Come-Home,* has been kept alive through the television series, but the original story may not be known to children. Eric Knight has written of a beautiful collie who goes every day to the school gate to meet her master, Joe. When the mines close, it is necessary to sell Lassie, but Lassie can recognize only one master. In late afternoon each day, Lassie becomes restless and escapes several times. Taken to Scotland, the dog finds her way back over 400 miles. Each time Lassie returns, Joe's father insists the dog must go back. The book conveys the theme of building honesty and self-respect.

The warmth of the relationship of a hen and a dog who became her self-appointed protector is the core of *Along Came a Dog* by DeJong. The dog was seeking a home, but the lonely man who managed the farm did not want a dog that might kill his chickens. After her toes are frozen, the little hen receives special care from the man. He tries repeatedly to get rid of the dog, but the dog returns, hides from him, and maintains vigilance over the hen. Suspense builds as the dog proves he is worthy of acceptance.

Dogs and Men   The reactions of dogs to the humans who give them love or cruel treatment are basic to the plots of several excellent books. DeJong's *Hurry Home, Candy* tells of a small dog's search for security. An impatient woman who really did not want the responsibility of a pet and did not know how to teach her children to give it love and discipline used a broom to punish him for puppy-like games and accidents. "After such an accident there was no pardon for him, no reprieve. He stayed in his corner. The evening had to ooze away in the corner. . . ."[12] When he pulled things and played with them, the mother put a broom across the corner. Finally, he would sleep, "A troubled broom-haunted sleep in which his paws twitched nervously because in his sleep he was fleeing from the fretful broom."[13] In a storm, Candy is separated from the family, and fear of a broom across the ditch prevents him from crossing to them. Alone, hungry, lost and sorrowful, he helps a farm woman and calls the attention of a passerby when her wagon tips over. The promise of security is lost when he runs from the hospital after seeing a man with a broom. At last he finds shelter with a man, a retired captain turned artist. One night, the artist interrupts some thieves, and Candy is caught in the police crossfire, while the man breaks a leg. The news story brings the original owners, but the children want only the reward, not the dog. Candy hides again, but is drawn to the house by hunger. Once more, a broom stands between the dog and love and security. The Captain discovers the source of the dog's fear; at the same time he gains understanding of his own fears: "Let me explain it

The three companions seek refuge for the night on their long trek home. The Siamese cat and the old bull terrier sleep, while the young Labrador retriever keeps watch. Copyright © 1960, 1961, by Sheila Burnford. From *The Incredible Journey* by Sheila Burnford, illustrated by Carl Burger, by permission of Atlantic-Little, Brown and Co.

to you—there are brooms in my life, too. I think that's the real explanation."[14] He tells how he hides from people because he is self-conscious about being an artist. He realizes an individual can deal with his own anxieties: "Who's to stop me but the brooms that have been rammed into my thin hide?"[15] The big man tosses the broom aside, and the dog edges his way to food, to love, and home.

---

[12]Meindert DeJong, *Hurry Home, Candy,* Illustrated by Maurice Sendak (New York: Harper & Row, 1956), p. 43.
[13]DeJong, p. 39.

[14]DeJong, p. 187.
[15]DeJong, p. 189.

Fergus was indeed *A Dog Like No Other,* for he was an ugly clown who is saved by a young Scot, Robbie Duncan. MacKellar's dog seems to have very unusual senses, for he finds a lucky white heather, wins the sheep dog trials by an uncanny awareness of the sheep behavior, and finally finds the lost sword of Bonnie Prince Charlie. Robbie is unusually aware of human needs as well as animal behavior. His treatment of the village simpleton, Lachie, provides an excellent model of compassion.

Diogenes was a perceptive dachshund hero who put *Four Paws into Adventure* when his Parisian master, a tramp named Clodomir had to enter a hospital. Realizing the tramp who promised to care for him planned to sell him, Diogenes escaped and found a new owner, a truck driver. The dog tells his own story, revealing cleverness in showing the family his real name so they wouldn't use the awful name "Squatty." Diogenes rescues a smuggler and comments on the foibles of humans. One young reviewer wrote, "The author proves that tramps can be good, and people that we think are bad, are really nice people." Cénac's book won the Prix Fantasia in 1961.

Chekhov's *Kashtanka* had two masters, first, a poor carpenter who drank and gave her little attention, and second, a circus trainer. Kashtanka learned to do tricks with a goose, a cat, and a pig. She is well fed, but life is boring and sad, with dreams of shadowy figures that smelt of glue, shavings, and varnish. When the goose dies, Kashtanka realizes anew the futility of life. One night in the theater Kashtanka is recognized and joyously responds to the call of the carpenter and his son. Children may evaluate the appeals of the harsher life that Kashtanka preferred.

Jack London's *The Call of the Wild* was written for adults, but is enjoyed by older boys and girls. The men in this book are ruthless, and the dog, Buck, returns to the wildness of nature just as the men revert to force and cruelty to survive.

Jim Kjelgaard communicates his knowledge of the wilderness and his love of animals through exciting dog stories. He uses words and phrases such as "thataway," "reckon," "this'n ain't friendly" to create characters of the woods and fields that are real and vivid. *Big Red* is the story of an Irish setter being groomed for championship dog shows. Danny, his seventeen-year-old trainer, shows patience and courage in holding back the dog in facing Old Majesty, the huge bear. *Snow Dog* is a wild puppy of the northern wilderness who finally finds a life with men. The story of Chiri continues in *Wild Trek.* Rescuing a naturalist and a flyer provides an exciting plot. A very different setting is described with the same clarity and attention to detail in *Desert Dog.* After his trainer dies, Tawny, a greyhound pup, runs away. His struggle for survival against heat, coyotes, thirst, and wild-dog packs provides most of the action. Finally, he meets a man to whom he can give his loyalty. Kjelgaard's dogs are consistently true to their nature. Through his descriptive prose, the reader can feel the wind and rain and smell the woods. The men who train the dogs exhibit patience, fortitude, and warmth.

The film based on Gipson's story, *Old Yeller,* brought to life another dog. Travis thinks the yellow dog that appears at the ranch one day is truly indispensable. Old Yeller saves Travis' brother from a mad animal. As a result, the dog must be shot. Travis takes one step toward maturity when he accepts this decision.

Some books are basically stories of human characters, although a dog is of special interest. In *Bristle Face,* Ball shows how a hound dog plays an important part in the lives of an orphan boy, a lonely man who gives the boy a home, and an aggressive widow who agrees to marry the man. The author adds humorous touches to his realistic picture of mountain life. The boy, Jase, courageously faces the knowledge that the dog must be returned to its owner and accepts the necessity for putting Bristle Face to death after he is blinded. The author does not reveal the dog's feelings; the dog does not emerge as a hero, but the reader who asks for a dog story will enjoy the exciting fox hunt and the resolution of the problems in which Bristle Face is involved.

The Greyhound by Griffiths is a dramatic story of a boy's love for a dog. Conflicts with family and society encountered after he purchases the dog and hides him in a bombed-out London basement make this a compellingly realistic story (see Chapter 5).

Older boys and girls will appreciate the unusual relationship shown among a boy, his uncle, and a Basenji hound in *Goodbye My Lady* by James Street. The poverty of Skeeter's life in a cabin at the edge of a swamp is enriched when he finds an amazing dog who laughs instead of barks, cries real tears, and achieves fame as a hunter. When his uncle and the neighbors read the advertisement for such a dog, they realize its value but leave the decision regarding her return to the boy. Skeeter makes his heartbreaking choice and joins the ranks of manhood. Symbolically, he downs the bitter cup of coffee offered by his Uncle's friend.

MYSTERIES

Appeals of the Mystery Book

An element of mystery, or suspense, is essential in all fiction for children. However, when children refer to "mystery books," they usually think of the book with "mystery" or "secret" in the title. When they ask for "mystery" books, they want a book in which there is a series of clues to solve a problem involving such elements as secret codes, lost treasures, or mysterious characters. Children

do seek action, suspense, and surprise in books. Because few juvenile "mysteries" are well written, and many inexpensive mystery series are available, teachers and librarians tend to discount the importance of the child's interest in these books and try to guide him away from *all* mysteries.

Little character development, stereotypes, lack of imagery in writing, trite or stilted dialogue, and failure to develop values do characterize many of the series books. The Nancy Drew mysteries, for example, merely provide repetitive plots with action the reader can predict. However, an examination of the appeals of the Nancy Drew books may serve to indicate qualities children will want in books suggested as substitutes. Nancy is eighteen, pretty, "becomingly dressed," virtuous, skillful, yet rather "a loner," so she wins sympathy. Her father gives her plenty of money, and she drives a convertible. She always knows exactly what to do; in her world there are no value decisions with "shades of gray," for characters are completely good or completely evil. Nancy moves into dangerous situations and usually is kidnapped or nearly hurt before help appears. Incident follows incident with no description of setting or character. The "young sleuth" is an oft-repeated phrase. Her thoughts are expressed in dialogue: "'I'll be caught!' flashed through her mind, 'And I won't be able to escape a second time,'"[16] is typical of the pattern. In *The Clue of the Tapping Heels*, Nancy is called "the Drew girl," but more serious is the use of the term "colored man" for an evil character. Conversation is stilted, indeed, in these poorly written Nancy Drew stories. Teachers and librarians ought to know better written mysteries and other books that contain elements of mystery in order to capitalize on children's interest and lead them to fine literature.

---

[16]Carolyn Keene, *The Secret of the Old Clock* (New York: Grosset & Dunlap, 1959), p. 130.

Evaluating Mystery Books

Plot The major appeal of the mystery is its fast action and suspense. Whereas the conflict is established quickly in many well-written stories, the mystery books frequently establish suspense by withholding the problem or mystery for several pages. In Fry's *The Riddle of the Figurehead,* for example, the figurehead does not appear until the second chapter, and the mystery is only hinted by page 27. At the end of the second chapter of *Secret of the Emerald Star* by Whitney, several questions have been raised, but no specific problem is identified. "There was still some answer here that escaped her—something that was a possible key to the puzzle. Until she discovered what it was, she would continue to be baffled and curious."[17] Other mysteries reveal the problem to the reader who becomes an omniscient viewer of the scenes in which the characters make the discoveries. Jean Bothwell uses this approach in *The Mystery Angel.* The opening lines of the first chapter, titled "How the Mystery Began," give clues:

> *It took ten years for the secret guarded by an angel in a little Nebraska town to be found out by several people, some children and a few grownups, and it began in a house in France, though perhaps the real beginning was in the little village church at Vimy-sur-Loire, where there was also the orphanage called La Petite Sainte. That house was the second part of the beginning.*[18]

The reader quickly learns that a Red Cross nurse takes a baby from the orphanage. The next chapter takes place in a Nebraska home where a mother and daughter discuss the importance of names. Not until the third chapter does the reader realize that it is an-other girl who probably is the baby stolen from the French orphanage. Whatever the approach, the reader must be intrigued and challenged. If the mystery is too obvious, the solution too apparent, it is not satisfying. The mystery book must pique the reader's curiosity, maintain suspense, and come to a quick conclusion.

The writer of mystery stories should have a plausible reason for introducing each character and incident. In *The Mystery of the Velvet Box* by Scherf, an antique dealer becomes a suspect through a plausible interest of buying an antique desk. However, his involvement in the plot was not fully explained in the denouement. All the strands of plot complication should be resolved or explained in the conclusion. *The Mystery of the Pilgrim Trading Post* by Molloy primarily revolves around Bart and the black market enterprise. A subplot describes the search for evidence that the old Maine homestead was an historic site to be preserved. The conclusion resolves both problems.

The mystery writer should give the reader the information that is accessible to the character. The character should not express knowledge in later scenes that the reader does not know this character possessed. Children realize the importance of details of characterization or setting, and they become alert to time sequences. The well-written mystery will create suspicion about more than one character or give false clues to provide further challenge to the reader. In *The Puss-in-the-Corner Mystery,* Mackenzie creates several suspicious characters who might be searching for the two valuable stencils.

The mystery book may focus upon one plot, or it may develop one or more subplots. Mysteries for younger children employ a single strand plot. *The Case of the Gone Goose* by Corbett has no secondary plots. It is concerned with the discovery of the person who killed two prize geese. Phyllis Whitney's

---

[17]Phyllis A. Whitney, *Secret of the Emerald Star,* Illustrated by Alex Stein (Philadelphia: Westminster, 1964), p. 31.
[18]Jean Bothwell, *The Mystery Angel,* Illustrated by Elinor Jaeger (New York: Dial, 1963), p. 9.

mysteries include subplots or developments related to a larger theme. Overcoming a physical handicap in *The Mystery of the Haunted Pool* and awakening a grandmother's interest in life in *The Mystery of the Angry Idol* are subplots in two of her books.

Children can develop skill in identifying significant details and foreshadowing as literary devices as they read mysteries. In Faulkner's *The Secret of the Simple Code,* information about testing hardness of minerals is presented naturally as Abby learns from the professor. The reason for this information is apparent later when she tests a "rock" to see if it might be a ruby. Details of a dusty painting in an attic are presented in a scene in *Private Eyes* by Kingman. Later, a boy's memory of this painting helps to solve a mystery. The inclusion of such detail should be plausible and natural for the characters and setting.

The interplay of the child's world and adult world should be reasonable and authentic. When children are solving problems, they should seek help from adults or the police so that the story is believable and represents wise action. Having established an atmosphere of good relationships between children and their parents, Orton's child characters are not believable when they fail to report to their parents their suspicions that someone was in the sugarhouse or that a stranger was inquiring about a cave. *Mystery in the Old Cave* continues implausibly, because Andy's father seems unconcerned when the children are frightened by someone in the sugarhouse. In *The Mystery of the Velvet Box* by Scherf, someone breaks into the attic, leaves a length of rope indicating escape through a window, but the parents do not notify the police. In the same story, Harriet hears someone in the coal bin and sees a person looking into the cellar, but does not tell the adults. The children in Mantel's *The Chateau Holiday* take risks without telling adults. The mystery that involves children should be one that could be plausibly solved by them. Of course, the characters may be unusually clever, as were Nina and Polly in solving the *Secret of the Unicorn,* Gottlieb's mystery about New York apartment dwellers. The clues to a valuable hidden tapestry are not plausible. The girls enjoy the tapestries at the Cloisters, share their fear of Great Aunt Augusta, and realize that their discovery has finally awakened the spirit of Nina's convalescent father.

Violence and murder are usually omitted in children's mystery books. In a story set in England, *The Mystery of Long Barrow House,* Faulkner allows violence by Georgie, an angry little man who seems determined to protect the "ancient ones." He tries to kill Derek when the children explore the barrow, or ancient burial ground. To save Derek, Pat hit Georgie with a stone. This strike restores Georgie's consciousness, for he had apparently suffered amnesia after an accident. In *The Black Tanker,* Howard Pease describes a boy's search for clues related to a murder on a ship carrying oil to the Japanese who are attacking China. Details of the murder are not given; it is only reported that a man is overboard. This book has historical interest, for it describes conditions at the beginning of World War II. Intelligence, patience, and logical deduction, rather than force, should be the source of the solution to the mystery for children.

Characterization Characters in the mystery books are too often one-dimensional or stereotyped, and little change in character is evident. Phyllis Whitney creates more realistic children. *Secret of the Emerald Star* concerns two girls who are portrayed with strengths and weaknesses. Stella Devery is a blind Cuban refugee who lives with her prejudiced, autocratic grandmother and timid mother, widow of old Mrs. Devery's son. Stella is obstinate, fearful, hostile, yet forgiving, brave, and friendly. Robin, who becomes her friend, also exhibits variation in character; she changes as she learns to persist in creating a sculpture and gradually to understand Stella's needs. The adults in this book—the sculptor, Robin's mother, and, especially, the grandmother—emerge as fully human characters. Each member of the Barker family, in Phipson's *Threat to the Barkers,* is believably drawn, showing such qualities as loyalty, courage, pride, and fear. Eleanor Estes also creates dimensional characters in *The Alley,* a story of thirty-three children who live in a secluded alley in a college housing area. Connie observes life in the alley from her swing until a burglary occurs at their house. The description of Connie includes physical appearance, interests, favorite books, as well as her thoughts.

The Witch's Daughter by Bawden includes several well-drawn characters. Perdita, daughter of a witch, is a lonely orphan shunned by the village children because of her odd clothes, strange green eyes, shy manner, and sensitivity to nature. She has never been to school, but has deep knowledge of the outdoors and expresses an awareness of the special sensitivities of the blind girl, Janey, who comes with her family to the Scottish island for a holiday. Perdita is treated kindly by the mysterious Mr. Smith who has rented a cottage and fishes for lobsters although he does not like lobster. Tim, Janey's brother, puts the pieces of the puzzle together, but the adults will not accept his theory of the stolen jewels. A strange visitor leaves the children in a cave, and blind Janey leads them to safety. Perdita's shyness is finally overcome in a moment of sharing with Janey. This is a haunting, exciting mystery.

Generalizing and stereotyping are weaknesses of many mysteries. Politicians are painted as the "bad guys" in *The Mystery of the Pilgrim Trading Post* by Molloy. Real estate developers are stereotyped in *The Mysterious Christmas Shell* by Cameron and *Private Eyes* by Kingman, although they are proved to be different from popular opinion.

Theme   Children who are learning to evaluate literature will look for a theme in their stories. Most of the mystery books are concerned with incident and action; some moralize through asides or through a monologue. Others provide a worthwhile theme in a natural manner. The theme that each individual has a talent that should be discovered and encouraged is presented by Whitney in *The Mystery of the Hidden Hand.* Set on the island of Rhodes, this mystery is about the possible revelation of the fact that Grandfather Thanos had kept an ancient marble hand from the authorities. Mias, his grandson, must decide how to protect his grandfather, yet clear the family name, and return the hand to the government. Amid the suspense involved with this plot, other action develops the theme. Tassovla finds she cannot become a ballerina in the image

The children discover a clue to the mystery —blood on the curtain! Typical Ardizzone figures capture the drama of the moment. From *The Alley* by Eleanor Estes, illustrated by Edward Ardizzone, © 1964, by Eleanor Estes. Reproduced by permission of Harcourt, Brace & World, Inc.

of her sister, but she can develop her talent in painting. Grandfather Thanos realizes Nicos should be allowed to manage the family pottery instead of being forced to be a sculptor. Gale, the American girl, learns that an understanding heart is a special gift. This book won the Mystery Writers "Edgar" for excellence in 1964. This same author's *Secret of the Emerald Star* is concerned with the respect for blind people, and all people, as individuals. The idea that the blind do not want pity is presented in many scenes, for example:

> *A real friend isn't someone who is sorry for you. I hate people who drool because I'm a poor little blind girl. Or the others who act as if I were a genius because I can walk across a room by myself. They're the ones who think about blindness all the time. And that's silly because I don't. Or anyway, I wouldn't if they didn't push it at me so much.*[19]

Whitney does attempt too much, however, for she includes discussion of the grandmother's prejudice toward Jews, a reference to causes of war, and develops a secondary theme about the importance of disciplined effort and study as well as creative talent in order to achieve works of art.

Style   Mystery writers utilize dialogue extensively and often employ a terse, staccato style to build suspense. The child who is eager for the next clue does not want to read lengthy description. Corbett's *The Cave above Delphi* is an exciting story based upon the search for a gold ring hidden in a cave by a Greek fighter during the Resistance. Some historical lectures are woven into the text as the American parents recall Greek life. Here is good information for the child who stops to read it, but many children will skip this part. An American boy and girl join a Greek

boy in the search, but they become unsure of Nicki's motives when the ring disappears again. "Cleverness was his great talent, but it was also his fatal flaw. Where would it lead him?"[20] Nicki is led in the direction of honesty, but the reader feels it may be only momentary. Hay, the American, grows up as he comes to understand the need for values. Unfortunately, the author generalizes about Greeks as he writes, "The boy turned and began asking questions in the forthright way of all Greeks. They think nothing of asking a stranger all sorts of personal questions, and they cheerfully answer any he may ask of them."[21] However, Nicki does not fit the stereotype because he does not answer questions.

Figurative language can be found in many mysteries. In *The Mystery of the Pilgrim Trading Post*, Molloy writes "lighthouses were carrying on their nightly conversations."[22] Unless a child plays bridge he would not understand the metaphor this author employs, "Lettie was able to produce her two new signatures at the 'Anti-Bridge Club' meeting that night as if they were trump cards."[23] "Bridge" refers to the bridge that was planned to "modernize" the Maine coastal village. Brief descriptions can enhance the feeling of suspense. In *The Mysterious Christmas Shell*, Cameron uses sensory imagery to reinforce the melancholy mood of Aunt Melissa. Sounds are included in the description of her walk by the shore as she ponders the search for the hidden will.

> *Over beyond the cypress grove, beyond the cliffs, the ocean thudded and sighed, and sud-*

---

[19]Phyllis Whitney, *Secret of the Emerald Star,* Illustrated by Alex Stein (Philadelphia: Westminister, 1964), p. 99.

[20]Scott Corbett, *The Cave above Delphi,* Illustrated by Gioia Fiammenghi (New York: Holt, Rinehart and Winston, 1965), p. 123.

[21]Corbett, p. 26.

[22]Anne Molloy, *The Mystery of the Pilgrim Trading Post,* Illustrated by Floyd James Torbert (New York: Hastings, 1964), p. 121.

[23]Molloy, p. 154.

denly a sea bird, high in the night sky, called once very sharp and clear. The call had a pleading, melancholy sound as if the bird were searching for something.[24]

The metaphor used by Emery to describe the setting of the final scene of *A Spy in Old West Point* is related to the military theme: "Along the range of hills the gold and scarlet colors of October draped the ranges like flaring banners."[25]

The criteria used for evaluating all fiction should be used in considering mystery stories, with the recognition that credible suspense and a challenging question receive greater emphasis. Children do develop skills in rapid reading, building vocabulary, and noting details as they read mysteries. Interest in reading as a pleasurable activity may begin with these books and be extended to other types of literature if children's choices are not criticized, if there is opportunity to select from a good collection, and if teachers introduce new books to the avid mystery fan.

Types of Mystery Books

Mystery as the Theme Influenced by television and adult interests, children as young as seven or eight ask for "mystery" books. The *I Can Read* series includes mystery titles. Bonsall's *The Case of the Hungry Stranger* and *The Case of the Cat's Meow* provide suspense and humor. Four young detectives, Snitch, Wizard, Skinny, and Tubby, cooperate and quarrel as they search for the lost cat. Snitch is younger, but allowed in the clubhouse, and Skinny is a Negro, accepted as a member of the gang. The facial expressions, clothing, and dialogue are delightfully realistic. The mysterious disappearance

of Mildred, Snitch's beloved cat, provides a simple plot, yet the author creates suspense, provides clues, and a good climax.

Elisabeth and the Marsh Mystery by Holman is an "informational" mystery for young readers. Elisabeth, her father, and Stewart Peebles enlist the aid of a museum director to solve the mystery of the strange call emanating from the marsh. Stewart gives the Latin names for the birds they see, and patiently explains to Elisabeth the meaning of the terms he uses. Elisabeth admires his erudition as well as the braces on his teeth, and the tone maintains humor so the facts do not seem dull. When the mysterious "exotic" is found to be a sandhill crane, both children learn about bird migration.

At the next reading level are Martin's books, *The Mystery at Monkey Run* and *The Mystery on Crabapple Hill.* Monkey Run is a cove where two boys observe a skin diver searching the waters with grappling hooks. The boys recover a heavy case, only to be surprised when their "suspect" is overpowered by the man who pretended to be a game warden. The incident in which the boys nearly drown seems contrived and overdrawn. In the Crabapple Hill story, clues lead the reader away from the person who was stealing, making a more believable mystery.

Phyllis Whitney received the Mystery Writers "Edgar" for *The Mystery of the Hidden Hand* and *The Mystery of the Haunted Pool.* This author develops a theme, but does not moralize in a didactic style. In *The Mystery of the Haunted Pool,* the development of a boy's attitude toward overtures of friendship is as important as the recovery of a diamond necklace. Her characters are multidimensional, and many settings give authentic information about life in other lands. Mystic, Connecticut, is the setting of *The Mystery of the Angry Idol,* and the author encourages readers to visit this historic site. Boastful Ned, Eddie, and Patrick, who has returned

---

[24]Eleanor Cameron, *The Mysterious Christmas Shell,* Illustrated by Beth and Joe Krush (Boston: Little, Brown, 1961), p. 78.

[25]Anne Emery, *A Spy in Old West Point,* Illustrated by Laurence F. Bjorklund (Skokie, Ill.: Rand McNally, 1965), p. 191.

from reform school, have exciting adventures as they recover a piece of jade hidden in the heart of the idol.

Children as Detectives   Some books feature boys or groups who imagine themselves detectives. These unusually bright children solve cases before the adults hardly realize there is a mystery. *The Alligator Case* by du Bois is one of the most amusing, and suspense is maintained until the final chapter explains all that happened during a hotel and circus theft. Written in first person, the young detective tells of his mistakes as well as his successes. "At first glance I took it to be a case for fishing poles, but I am a detective and must not make easy guesses."[26] Children will enjoy the slapstick and the gentle spoof of policemen. In *The Case of the Gone Goose,* Inspector Tearle, at age twelve, was known as a "boy bloodhound," "the noisiest kid in town," and "the Boy with a Thousand Interests." The amusing description of his morning mail reveals some of those interests:

> *The morning mailbag for the Tearle household was on the light side. For Roger there were a circular from a firm that made telescopes, a letter containing a set of Tanzanian commemoratives sent on approval by a stamp company, a weekly bulletin of nationwide contests, a letter from the Chief of Detectives in New York City in answer to a query concerning how his department handled certain routine investigations, a note from their Congressman saying how nice it was to hear from him again and enclosing a copy of a report he had asked for, a couple of advertising leaflets from a magicians' equipment firm and an outfit called Junior Electronics, and a postal chess card from two nuclear physics professors at the University of California at Berkeley, with whom he had been*

A circus theft is not easily solved when the suspects are "hidden" among some fifty circus "alligators." The illustrations have the same sophisticated humor that is characteristic of the text. Illustration by the author-artist, William Pène du Bois from *The Alligator Case.* Harper & Row, 1965.

> *playing chess by mail for over a year now. They played him as a team, and it was generally all he could do to beat them two games out of three.*[27]

Roger identifies the murderers of three prize geese, but his friendship for their owner seals his lips so no one ever knows of his success. Mr. Chadburn's exclamation, "Roger! What the devil are you doing prowling around at this hour?"[28] may be noted as realistic writing that will not harm young readers, though some adults may object to this mild profanity. In *Private Eyes,* Kingman presents the problems fishermen face when plans are made for a resort and marina. The "Saturday Gang" collect and analyze mysterious clues, and Teddy escapes his kidnappers in a most exciting scene. *Encyclopedia Brown, Boy Detec-*

---

[26]William Pène du Bois, *The Alligator Case* (New York: Harper & Row, 1965), p. 19.

[27]Scott Corbett, *The Case of the Gone Goose,* Illustrated by Paul Frame (Boston: Little, Brown, 1966), p. 25.
[28]Corbett, p. 127.

tive and *Encyclopedia Brown Strikes Again* relate the adventures of "America's Sherlock Holmes," the ten-year-old son of the Chief of Police. Sobol provides the solution to the cases at the back of each book so the reader can try to solve the mystery himself. Emil is an internationally known boy detective created by German writer Erich Kästner. Children in Europe and America enjoy *Emil and the Detectives* and *Emil and the Three Twins.* Kästner's comments on life, his wry humor, and details of German settings make these books interesting, but there is less suspense than in other books.

The Phantom of Walkaway Hill won Edward Fenton the "Edgar" award of the Mystery Writers of America as the best juvenile mystery of 1961. Ostensibly, this book and *The Riddle of the Red Whale* were written by James Smith, boy detective and author. In the first book, James solves the mystery of a phantom when he is snowbound with his cousins in the country. He describes the cousins: Olive, who is very logical; Amanda, who behaves according to the book she is currently reading; and Dee-Dee, the blond, spoiled tag-a-long. The easy visit to the Russian rest home seems rather coincidental. Several suspicious characters could have explained the meaning of the Red Whale, but the solution was more complex than might be expected. In this book, there is violence, and the children are truly in danger for a few moments. James, the "author" inserts jokes at the beginning of each chapter and uses many puns and literary allusions in his narrative. Middle-graders will appreciate the independence of these children and the way adults accept them in interesting conversations.

Mystery in Fantasy Two animal detectives solve mysteries with human wit, perseverance, and logic. Basil is a mouse created by Eve Titus. He became a detective in the image of Sherlock Holmes while living in the model mouse community he established in the Holmes cellar. In *Basil of Baker Street,* the mouse rescues two small white mice after a series of dangerous incidents. The story ends as he receives a caller at night, and the reader knows there will be a new case to solve. Basil's amazing deductions are apparent in this scene from *Basil and the Lost Colony:*

> "Good day," said the stranger. "You are Basil?"
> "I am, sir. Your studies at the British Mousemopolitan must be fascinating. But do you not long for the colder climate of your native Norway?"
> "I do indeed. We've never met—how did you know?"
> Basil smiled. "It's unseasonably cold for April. The mice outside wear coats. You do not, yet your paws are warm. Your slight accent is Norwegian, and the envelope you hold bears the Mousemopolitan imprint."
> The caller beamed. "What more did you deduce?"
> "That you are Edward Hagerup, from Tromso, near the Arctic, an author who writes about the cat family. Your hobby is our national game of cricket."
> "Amazing! Astounding! Astonishing!" cried Hagerup.
> "Elementary, my dear author. I observed, I analyzed, I deduced. Dangling from your watch chain is the award of the Golden Cheddar. In 1888 Edward Hagerup of Tromso won it for his fine book, Our Feline Foes. I perceive a pamphlet in your pocket, entitled The Sticky Wicket in Cricket. This tells me your hobby."[29]

The client brings a mysterious arrow dropped by the Adorable Snowmouse in the Swiss Alps. The arrow leads Basil to the Lost Colony, descendants of Tellmice who had

---

[29]Eve Titus, *Basil and the Lost Colony,* Illustrated by Paul Galdone (New York: Whittlesey, 1964), p. 15.

been hidden since the thirteenth century when William Tell led the fight for freedom. Although these books appear to be for younger children, the humor and understanding of much of the action depends upon the reader's sophistication and knowledge of Sherlock Holmes.

Freddy the Detective is one of the favorites in Brooks' series about a clever pig who is somewhat superior to the other animals because he can read. They live on the farm of Mr. Bean (Being) and effectively satirize human society with committee meetings and elections.

Secret of the Ron Mor Skerry by Fry takes place on the Scottish coast. When ten-year-old Fiona returns to the coast to live with her grandparents, the old gray seal tries to communicate with her. A flashback tells how her little brother, Jamie, floated out to sea in his cradle and was apparently cared for by a herd of seals. The chieftain of the seals brings Jamie to the land when Fiona returns with her grandparents to live on the island, Ron Mor. Love and loyalty are themes of this haunting mystery.

Mystery in Historical Fiction Spies made their contribution to American history, and books about them involve mystery and adventure. Lawrence's book, *A Spy in Williamsburg*, tells how Ben Budge, son of a smithy, discovers the secret of their apprentice, who was spying on Patrick Henry. Anne Emery has written several "historical mysteries" with authentic detail, including *A Spy in Old Detroit*, *A Spy in Old New Orleans*, and *A Spy in Old Philadelphia*. *A Spy in Old West Point* is based on events related to the treason of Benedict Arnold, commander of the West Point fort. The fictional character, Jack Fraser, finds himself drawn to Major André, a real spy for the British. Jack, the only one who can read, discovers André is carrying papers from Arnold. He must decide whether to let the spy go for ransom money

he desperately needs, or to turn him over to the Americans. Jack takes the course of patriotism, but joins others in respect for the man of honor who was hanged, while the man of dishonor, Arnold, went free.

One by Sea by Corbett portrays life in England and America early in the nineteenth century. Nye escapes the rigorous English school and his English grandfather's stern rules to return to his father, captain of a Boston merchant ship. On the way back to America, he is warned by the dying man who came for him that his father is to be killed. Nye survives a shipwreck and escapes a kidnapper in time to warn his father of the treachery of his mentally ill uncle.

A well-written mystery by Stephens, *The Perrely Plight*, takes place in Sturbridge Village, Massachusetts, in 1836. It concerns the identity of Philander Perrely, son of a peddler who is despised by the respected doctor, father of Gib, who tries to befriend the Perrely family. Gib discovers an old will that shows his father and the peddler are really brothers. When Gib is accused of setting a fire in a neighbor's barn, Perrely defends him. Descriptions of life on the farm, in the tavern, and in the meeting house are excellent. The author's writing is not trite; for example, "The bell of the meeting house was still wrecking the air with its clamor. . . ."[30] A clever and just sheriff solves the mystery with Gib's help, and Gib grows in understanding his father's values. A modern story is also set in the restored village of Sturbridge. Mahen's *Mystery at Old Sturbridge Village* is concerned with the search for a hidden will that will allow a paralyzed tenant to remain on a farm. The reader of this mystery may skip some of the details of colonial life, but he will gain some of the flavor of this period as he reads this book.

---

[30]Peter John Stephens, *The Perrely Plight, a Mystery at Sturbridge,* Illustrated by R. D. Rice (New York: Atheneum, 1965), p. 79.

Mystery in Realistic Stories Frequently, titles do not indicate the mystery in well-written, realistic fiction. Teachers and librarians, however, may suggest these stories to the reader who wants a "mystery book." *A Spell Is Cast* by Cameron is a story girls will enjoy, for it involves a mystery of identity of an orphan and her part in solving a broken engagement. Boys will like *The Minnow Leads to Treasure* by the English writer, Philippa Pearce. Two boys use a canoe, the Minnow, to explore a river in their search for clues to the hidden treasure of the Codling family. Several climactic points are reached, but the solution is slippery as a minnow. Even when the treasure is recovered, the reader must sort the events and infer his own explanation. Geoffrey Trease is another English author who wrote a good mystery, *No Boats on Bannermere*. Differences in the girls' school and boys' school from the public school in the United States will be of interest. Ancient treasure, bones from an old grave, the avaricious Sir Alfred, the headmistress of the "progressive" girls' school, and the headmaster of the "traditional" boys' school are entangled in the mystery discovered by the clever, brave children. *The Chateau Holiday* by Mantle is less than restful when some very self-possessed English children spend a holiday in a French village. The plot involving a kidnapping is skillfully developed; the characters of the children are believable, but the adults seem to be flat figures vanishing into another world. English phrases, as "booked rooms there" and "eat our elevenses," may need clarification.

Children who read *Threat to the Barkers* by Phipson will learn a great deal about life on a sheep ranch in New South Wales while they try to solve the problem of theft of the sheep. One of the Barker children, Edward, is drawn into the gang and threatened by them if he reveals their plans. The local expressions, such as "Half a tick" for "half a minute," and such language patterns as "They must of finished" and "Can I have me dog now?" offer opportunities for linguistic study. Family loyalty is the theme in this exciting story.

Older children will thoroughly enjoy Cameron's *The Terrible Churnadryne*, but the mystery is never really solved. Did they see a prehistoric monster along the shore? The play on words in Jennifer's creation of a "churnadryne" will appeal to nine- to twelve-year-olds.

October Treasure might suggest mystery, but Eva-Lis Wuorio's story may need to be introduced to children. The ancient castle in a village on the Isle of Jersey apparently held a treasure, for a strange visitor with a German accent is searching for something. He actually harms the children who investigate. Short chapters are about each character; then, one is titled, "They Meet," and the pace intensifies. Relationships of children and adults are portrayed realistically.

In *The Alley*, Eleanor Estes portrays life in a relatively quiet neighborhood in Brooklyn. After reading the entire story of a burglary, and apprehension of two policemen who were also burglars, children might reread the story to note the foreshadowing. For example, Connie thinks about burglars and recalls her father's reminder to keep the doors locked; Billy is described as unafraid to go away alone, but he is afraid of burglars. The children's dramatic play in a mock trial provides an excellent description of childhood society.

Good mysteries are available, although few rise to literary distinction. Interest in mysteries can be used to maintain interest in reading and lead to other types of books with strong elements of mystery, and, finally, to other types of literature.

BOOKS ABOUT SPORTS

In our society, sports are a significant part of life; it is especially necessary for boys in the middle grades to demonstrate ability to play and to be able to discuss sports events. The woman teacher and librarian may not be in full sympathy with this deep interest of many boys, but books are often a source of communication. Fiction, biography, and informational books about sports will satisfy the interests of many boys, and girls as well.

Sports in Fiction

It is difficult to find well-written sports stories. Most of the characters are flat, one-dimensional figures. The dialogue tends to be stilted and the plots predictable. Children persist in reading these stories because they describe activities in which they are participating and reflect their desire for success.

Sports stories by the Renicks meet the interests of second and third graders who are eager to play team sports. Basic information about the game that is the focus of each book is included. In *Steady, a Baseball Story,* two boys learn as Mike's father manages a ball team. A boy could improve his pitching by reading this description of a pitcher's action:

> . . . *Turning to the right on his right foot, he kicked his left foot forward and drew back his right arm for the throw, holding his left arm in front of him for balance. Then in one powerful movement his body and his pitching arm swung forward as he threw himself into a long step, shifting his weight to his left foot and sending the ball whizzing toward the catcher.*[31]

These detailed descriptions are incorporated in somewhat stilted dialogues that will be of interest only to the avid fan who is a novice to the game. When a girl cousin comes to live with the Dooleys, she learns from the boys and from a former ball player confined to a wheel chair. *The Dooleys Play Ball* would interest girls who like the game because

Linda wins a place on the team and acquits herself creditably. One boy is saved from involvement in a gang vandalism. Basketball information is presented in *David Cheers the Team* when the high school coach moves next door to David. Slight plot and little character development characterize these books that provide excitement with accounts of games. *Watch Those Red Wheels Roll* centers around a soap box derby. Vic "grows up" as he develops persistence in building his racer. The anxiety of younger boys caused by the "big boys" seemed overemphasized.

Matt Christopher's books depend upon accounts of games for their interest, but this writer also develops a problem theme. Kim was the *Basketball Sparkplug,* although he did make mistakes in the Small Fry League. His conflicting interest in singing in the church choir took valuable time from basketball practice and he foregoes a crucial game for a special Easter rehearsal. The song of the choir cheers the team in the tournament game. In *Touchdown for Tommy,* Tommy's problem is acceptance by foster parents, for he hopes they will adopt him. Tommy also has difficulty learning to play according to rules.

A mentally handicapped boy is given help and independence by his family, and he finally wins acceptance on the team in *Long Shot for Paul.* In this story, Christopher does not minimize the hardships the boy faces.

The activities and rules of Little League, the community-sponsored baseball club for boys, are described by Curtis Bishop in such titles as *Little Leaguer* and *Little League Double Play.* In *Little League Heroes,* a Negro boy wins a position on a Texas team, but Joel has to win a place for himself with the other boys. The wise guidance of his father, and their warm relationship make this more than a baseball story. *Little League Amigo* presents the problem of Cuban refugees. Strengths and weaknesses of the young brother of a famous rock 'n roll singer are portrayed in *Little League Visitor.* The brother, Sonny Bar-

---

[31]James and Marion Renick, *Steady, a Baseball Story,* Illustrated by Frederick Machetanz (New York: Scribner, 1942), p. 14.

ton, is shown to be the victim of his performing and publicity image. He proves his worth when he gives up a lucrative career to return to high school and give his brother a more stable home. Keith, the star of the team, is so "good" at home, school, and on the baseball field that boys will question his characterization. When Sonny, the singer, decides to remain in the city for the summer so he can play ball, he makes it possible for the team to have a topnotch pitcher. However, the "smart aleck" attitudes of his brother, Tom, cause problems with the team. The adults in Bishop's books are more convincing than in many sports stories.

Caary Jackson's stories also carry a theme of adjustment. In *Buzzy Plays Midget League Football,* a boy must learn to admit his mistakes. A junior high boy who "carried a chip on his shoulder" because of his size is the central figure in *Shorty at Shortstop.* In *Rookie First Baseman,* for older readers, Johnny Parr's resentment of his alcoholic father influences his relationships with others as he joins a major league team. The reader may dislike Johnny, but he will admire the rookie's skill and come to understand his behavior. Changing a "sissy" to a "regular guy," thus building his confidence as a pitcher, is the problem of the boys who play in *Little League Tournament.* Tips for young baseball players are included in a special section of this book and also appear in *Pee Wee Cook of the Midget League.* In *Midget League Catcher,* Beezie Hart faces conflicting demands. Should he go "all out" for golf and carry on the tradition of his grandfather and mother, or should he try to be a good ballplayer? He decides to *be himself.* Unsure of his skill, Beezie practices steadily and emulates the young coach. As Beezie learns, the reader will learn, and also share his disappointments and victories in the games described.

Elements of fantasy and humor make three books more than the typical baseball story that consists mainly of play-by-play accounts of games. Kerby, who appeared in other "trick" books by Corbett, seeks magic help for *The Baseball Trick.* Mrs. Graymalkin tells him how to mix a solution to make Kerby's team play better. The trick does not work out as Kerby planned, but they win the game and prove there were two illegal players on the other team. *The Iron Arm of Michael Glenn* developed fantastically when Michael became involved in a scientific experiment. The author, Lee, stereotypes the scientist with black suit, wild hair, and goatee. To avoid hurting others with his fast ball, Michael is not allowed to pitch in Little League and is soon a major league player. When his special strength is lost, his clever thinking saves the game. Beman Lord's *The Perfect Pitch* has a more tightly constructed plot and is more humorous. A mysterious Mr. Watts appears to grant Tommy's wishes. As a result of his ignorance of baseball, the wishes do not help. For example, when Tommy wished no one could hit his pitches, all of the pitches were out of reach, and the batters were walked. He uses the last wish to become a good pitcher.

Beman Lord's other books include *Bats and Balls, Guard for Matt,* and *Quarterback's Aim.* His humor enlivens these stories. *Rough Ice* presents the problem of a boy who tried to equal the skill of his father who was a champion hockey player. Eddie plays goalie instead of forward, accepting his weakness and building his strengths. *The Trouble with Francis* was his name, a "girl's" name that didn't help him play ball. Francis makes a winning play with his foot caught in a bucket and earns an unusual nickname. Second-and third-graders will enjoy the humor and predicament as well as the two ball games briefly described in easy-to-read style. The illustrations by Spilka for Lord's books are full of action and humor. *Monkey Shines, a Baseball Story* is also a humorous sports story by Miers. The struggle for community help in constructing a field and getting a coach is enlivened by the antics of three-year-old Mr. Trouble and a pet monkey who escaped from her owner.

Many sixth-graders will enjoy stories about high school players rather than characters their own age. Young has written *Carson at Second,* the story of a basketball hero who was urged to play baseball. He is not a good hitter, but develops great skill as a fielder. Jokes and locker-room banter are added to the usual story pattern. A subplot concerns the school election in which a disgruntled loser accuses Bill of unfair practices. *The Comeback Guy* was a high school senior who fully expected to be the lead cheerleader, but his snobbish behavior cost him friends and votes. Frick creates a character who changes as he loses his status and his girl, but he begins to learn about himself. Diligent practice, a job to earn money, and a new approach to people make it possible for him to achieve success as a pole vaulter and an award for popularity. Jeff's soliloquies may seem overdramatic to adults, but they are typical of adolescent thinking. Frequently, there are too many introspective comments to maintain the pace demanded of most sports stories. Yet, the need for popularity is so acute that this story of a boy who failed and rose again will be heartening to many preadolescents.

Mature sixth-graders will also enjoy the sports stories by John Tunis. In *All American,* racial prejudice and problems of adjustment to a new school are the themes. Ronald's defense of a Jewish boy he nearly killed in a game, and his insistence that the team refuse to play unless their Negro teammate is also allowed to play, dramatizes the cancerous problem of prejudice in our communities. The idea that the team is more important than the individual is stressed in *Keystone Kids. Yea! Wildcats* focuses upon a young coach whose principles create enemies in an Indiana town where basketball is called a

"disease." The plot of *Go, Team, Go,* published ten years later, is very much the same. Gambling, the attempt to "buy" a player by giving the father of a talented player from another school a better job in their town, and the powerful influence of a wealthy man are portrayed realistically. This author includes details of games only when the score is tied, or a player's decision will make a difference. Other plays are merely summarized. Tunis characters are often overdrawn, but the realism and action of the plots continue to appeal.

Biography

Sports enthusiasts will enjoy biographies of their heroes. Although too many facts are condensed into the last chapter, Van Riper's *Babe Ruth, Baseball Boy* will interest the young reader. The Babe's unsavory habits are handled with discretion. Shapiro's series about such famous players as Sal Maglie, Phil Rizzuto, and Roy Campanella may be suggested to the baseball fan. In *The Mel Ott Story,* for example, this author shows both strengths and weaknesses. Girls who are interested in sports will enjoy *Babe Didricksen* by the de Grummonds. The Epsteins' *Stories of Champions* is a good collection of biographical sketches of many great players. *Famous Negro Athletes,* a well-written volume by Bontemps, includes such winners as Jesse Owens, Sugar Ray Robinson, and Althea Gibson. Gelman's *Young Olympic Champions* describes the victories of eleven champions and includes excellent photographs. These books may be browsing books for some children; others will read them in entirety (see Chapter 6).

Informational Books about Sports

Informational books may describe the games and give tips on how to improve skills, or they may give data about people, statistics, or history of the sport. Information is included in most of the sports fiction, but the books designed to give facts are organized to meet specific interests and usually include clear photographs or illustrations. For example, Lindsay's *Figure Skating* presents the personal sacrifices, discipline, and joy of the sport. Basic ice skating skills are described clearly by the Ice Skating Institute.

The Game of Baseball by the Epsteins tells how the game has changed, and includes such interesting notes as the way old timers put balls on ice to make them "dead." Masin's books, *How to Star in Basketball* and *How to Star in Football* are very readable books with illustrative photographs and diagrams.

A series, *All-Star Sports* books, published by Follett, presents advice from outstanding coaches to beginners in many sports. *Track and Field for Boys* by Jordan describes different kinds of events and stresses the physical conditioning and mental attitude essential for track. Boys will enjoy the biographical notes about Kuharich, former Notre Dame coach, who wrote *Football for Boys*. Both boys and girls who begin to play golf will appreciate tips from Cromie, a literary editor who is a fine golfer and author of *Golf for Boys and Girls*. Photographs show boys and girls receiving instruction.

Photographic sequences in *How to Play Baseball* show specific movements of pitching, catching, and hitting. Iger and Fitzimmons give hints for practice, such as timing movements to the pronunciation of "Constan-ti-no-ple."

Interest in car racing as a sport is met by Robert Jackson in two books, *Grand Prix at the Glen* and *Road Race Round the World*. In a dry, rather pedantic style, information about the origin of the Grand Prix, car construction, and drivers' anecdotes is presented in the first book. Unfortunately, the dangers of the race are not mentioned. A background knowledge of cars would be necessary to enjoy this book. The second volume is an historical account of an actual event in1908 when six cars attempted to drive around the world. Photographs illuminate the text of both books.

Facts and figures about games and photographs of performers are in *The Junior Illustrated Encyclopedia of Sports* by Mullin and Kramm. Another kind of informational book is *Championship, the Complete NFL Title Story* by Izenberg. Critical games from 1933 to 1966 are described in terse style and illustrated with action photographs.

Probably more books of this type should be in the public library than in the school library, but the school needs such resources to build upon current interests and lead to reading of other books.

BOOKS OF ADVENTURE

When children ask for an "adventure story" or identify "adventure" as an element that makes a good story, what qualities are they seeking? The story of a hero facing dangers provides vicarious experience of achieving competence. Adventure implies a hazard, a danger, a peril. The hero may have to overcome nature, storms, or floods, for example; he may face the danger of being lost, or of starving; or he may be pitted against adversaries, evil characters who will limit or destroy his life or plans for doing good. Action, of course, is the first concern. Extraordinary events occur in rapid sequence, with suspense as to the outcome. The English critic, Margery Fisher, emphasizes character as a criterion for the adventure story:

Dominating the adventure story is the formula of good chap versus bad chap. We are not to look for changes of heart, as a rule; complexity in character might slow down the action. The most interesting thing about adventure stories is the way character, persistent as weeds or woodworm, pokes up its head when you think it is dead, says its say in the middle of the bang-

ing and crashing. The force of an interesting character comes stealing upon you, making a gradual but permanent impression. Though you may have been aware only of an exciting sequence of events, you realize in the end that character has been at the bottom of it all.[32]

It is not enough to have clashes of "good guys and bad guys"; the hero should have natural, human strengths and weaknesses. In order to portray child characters believably, it seems wise to follow Fisher's suggestion:

Far better, I believe, to put your young hero and heroine a little off centre, and give them attendant adults who at moments of crisis can produce common-sense or pistols as required, while the children face danger in their own way.[33]

However, the child hero can be unusually brave and clever, patient and strong. Adventure is a part of many books of all the types that have been described in this volume. The following examples illustrate books in which adventure, the survival of hazards, is the major theme.

Two widely different settings provide adventure in Kjelgaard's books, *Wildlife Cameraman* and *Boomerang Hunter*. In the first book, Jase Mason tries his skill in photographing wildlife. In the process, he helps capture an outlaw named Cat Bird, faces a renegade bear, and develops a great skill in photography. Through this adventure runs the theme of patience and courage in overcoming obstacles. *Boomerang Hunter* is the story of Balulu, an Australian aborigine. He refuses to let his doglike dingo, Warrigal, be killed, despite the hunger of the tribe. Balulu wins a contest when captured by another tribe and also wins access to their hunting

land. The theme here is the conflict of man against nature.

Stephen Meader's books present adventure through skillful prose. His settings authentically present regional or historical backgrounds. *River of the Wolves* tells of an escape from Indians and a dangerous trip back to a pioneer settlement. *Clear for Action* describes the impressment of seamen prior to the War of 1812. In *Trap Lines North* there is much information about Canada, but the pacing is slower than in his other books. Life in the late nineteenth century is vividly portrayed in *Jonathan Goes West*. Characterization is very good in this book. Boys interested in mechanics and construction will enjoy *Bulldozer*. Meader doesn't spare the details of hard life, death, cruelty, hangovers or brawls in his books. *The Voyage of the Javelin*, the story of a boy on a clipper ship, keeps this realism, yet shows good relationships among people. Middle-grade boys enjoy reading about such teen-agers as the heroes of these adventures.

Lapland Outlaw by Catherall gives much information about the people who live in the far reaches of Finland. Care of the herds of reindeer, customs of the tribes, woman's role, and the code of honor of these intelligent herdsmen are included as the details move the story forward. A trader and a tribal leader conspire to cheat a family by changing the agreement to sell 30 reindeer to 300. The greedy trader prefers a quick profit to the future needs. The family scarcely could exist the next year with such a decimated herd. When the father is burned and taken to a hospital, he cannot defend the truth. His son, Jouni, takes matters into his own hands and drives the herd away. The ensuing struggle against storms and the Sergeant who uses the modern radio and helicopter to capture the boy and his sister provide much excitement.

Another kind of enemy is presented in *The White Peril* by Falknor. Eagle Child joins

---

[32]Margery Fisher, *Intent upon Reading* (Leicester, England: Brockhampton, 1961), p. 197.
[33]Fisher, p. 209.

other Blackfoot scouts to learn how many white settlers have come. Enemy Indians are encountered in dangerous situations. He is rescued and taken aboard a steamboat where he learns more of the white man's strength. A white buffalo that Eagle Child had once known as a pet becomes a dangerous marauder and symbolizes the perils brought by white men. The ending is tragic, for Eagle Child can do nothing to fight the enemy that is coming to take his land, bring disease, and change his way of life.

A girl is the heroic figure of a novel set in Kenya, *The Bushbabies* by Stevenson. The "bushbabies" were Jacqueline, daughter of a game warden whose job has been taken over by a native, Kamau, her pet tarsier, and Tembo, a native who had been her father's assistant. Thinking she has time to return to the ship, Jackie decides she must leave her pet so Tembo can take it back to its bush home. The ship sails, leaving her alone. She finds Tembo and persuades him to help her travel nearly 300 miles. The descriptions of the African landscape and the animals encountered are intriguing and provide some exciting moments. Thinking the native has kidnapped the white girl, the police try to capture him. Jackie gains increasing respect for Tembo as a man, and she learns that the natives do have values and honor that should be accepted by whites. They survive a forest fire, a storm, and a perilous flood, and Jackie faces a wounded leopard in her attempt to help Tembo. This well-written book has the elements of a good adventure—a strange land, danger from nature and men, a theme of assuming responsibility and understanding needs of native peoples.

Big Tiger and Christian by Mühlenweg is a 593-page novel that may discourage readers by its very size. The complex plot and many characters would make it difficult for most sixth-graders. Christian, an English boy, and Tiger, Chinese, are two twelve-year-olds who become involved in the Chinese conflict among war lords that preceded the revolution. Taken to the lair of bandits in the Gobi desert, they observe important details, use their wits, and exhibit unusual courage and endurance. At the same time, adults offer protection and guidance. The Mongols are portrayed as men with very formal manners, deep loyalties, and ancient traditions, thus dispelling the idea that they were barbarians. Violence and death appear in this narrative, but the measured prose does not dwell upon sordid details. The intrigue of a wily merchant, dashing rides of a kind of Robin Hood bandit, the discovery of ancient treasure, a mysterious ring, and political affairs are elements in the adventure.

The well-written adventure story provides action, suspense, and a hero who is more than a "good guy in a white hat"—he is a *character* with a mission, a quest; the common man, perhaps, who develops uncommon, heroic qualities in meeting challenge.

Children's specialized interests are met by a wide variety of books. The fast action and suspense found in animal stories, mysteries, sports stories, and adventure stories will completely engross the interest of better readers and build their confidence in their reading ability. No matter what the child's special interest, there is a book that will enrich and deepen it.

SUGGESTED ACTIVITIES

1. Compare the mystery, adventure, or sports books written by two authors.
2. Compare two dog stories or two horse stories.
3. Compare the hero in an animal story, an adventure, a sports story, and a mystery.

4. Interview several children to assess their reading interests. Plan books you would suggest for them.

RELATED READINGS

1. Arbuthnot, May Hill. *Children and Books.* Third edition. Glenview, Ill.: Scott, Foresman, 1964.
Chapter 14, "Animal Stories," and "Mystery Tales," pages 459–463, present perceptive reviews according to author.
2. Broderick, Dorothy. "An Open Letter to Sports Writers," *School Library Journal,* vol. 8 (April 1962), pp. 27–28.
Critical comments suggest criteria for sports books.
3. Fisher, Margery. *Intent upon Reading.* Leicester, England: Brockhampton, 1961.
Chapter 11, "Good Chaps and Bad Chaps," gives criteria for adventure books.

CHAPTER REFERENCES

Adventure

1. Catherall, Arthur. *Lapland Outlaw.* Illustrated by Simon Jeruchim. New York: Lothrop, 1966.
2. Faulknor, Clifford. *The White Peril.* Illustrated by Gerald Tailfeathers. Boston: Little, Brown, 1966.
3. Kjelgaard, Jim. *Boomerang Hunter.* Illustrated by W. T. Mars. New York: Holiday, 1960.
4. ———*Wildlife Cameraman.* Illustrated by Sam Savitt. New York: Holiday, 1957.
5. Meader, Stephen W. *Bulldozer.* Illustrated by Edwin Schmidt. New York: Harcourt, 1951.
6. ———*Clear for Action!* Illustrated by Frank Beaudouin. New York: Harcourt, 1940.
7. ———*Jonathan Goes West.* Illustrated by Edward Shenton. New York: Harcourt, 1946.
8. ———*River of the Wolves.* Illustrated by Edward Shenton. New York: Harcourt, 1948.
9. ———*Trap Lines North.* Illustrated with photos. New York: Dodd, Mead, 1936.
10. ———*The Voyage of the Javelin.* Illustrated by John O'Hara Cosgrave II. New York: Harcourt, 1959.
11. Mühlenweg, Fritz. *Big Tiger and Christian.* Translated by Isabel and Florence McHugh. Illustrated by Rafaello Busoni. New York: Pantheon, 1952.
12. Stevenson, William. *The Bushbabies.* Illustrated by Victor Ambrus. Boston: Houghton Mifflin, 1965.

Animal Stories

13. Anderson, C. W. *Blaze and the Gypsies.* New York: Macmillan, 1937.
14. ———*Blaze and Thunderbolt.* New York: Macmillan, 1955.
15. ———*Billy and Blaze.* New York: Macmillan, 1936.

16. Arnov, Boris. *Bally the Blue Whale*. Illustrated by John Mack. New York: Criterion, 1964.

17. Ball, Zachary. *Bristle Face*. New York: Holiday, 1962.

18. Beebe, B. F. *Assateague Deer*. Illustrated by James Ralph Johnson. New York: McKay, 1965.

19. ———*Run Light Buck, Run!* Illustrated by James Ralph Johnson. New York: McKay, 1962.

20. Bell, Thelma Harrington. *A Dash of Pepper*. Illustrated by Corydon Bell. New York: Viking, 1965.

21. Boston, L. M. *A Stranger at Green Knowe*. Illustrated by Peter Boston. New York: Harcourt, 1961.

22. Burnford, Sheila. *The Incredible Journey*. Illustrated by Carl Burger. Boston: Little, Brown, 1961.

23. Carroll, Ruth and Latrobe. *Tough Enough's Trip*. New York: Oxford, 1956.

24. Cénac, Claude. *Four Paws into Adventure*. Translated by Sarah Chokla Gross. Illustrated by Brinton Turkle. New York: F. Watts, 1965.

25. Chekhov, Anton. *Kashtanka*. Illustrated by William Stobbs. New York: Walck, 1961.

26. Clark, Ann Nolan. *Blue Canyon Horse*. Illustrated by Allan Houser. New York: Viking, 1954.

27. Cleary, Beverly. *Ribsy*. Illustrated by Louis Darling. New York: Morrow, 1964.

28. Coatsworth, Elizabeth. *Jock's Island*. Illustrated by Lilian Obligado. New York: Viking, 1963.

29. Cone, Molly. *Mishmash*. Illustrated by Leonard Shortall. Boston: Houghton Mifflin, 1962.

30. DeJong, Meindert. *Along Came a Dog*. Illustrated by Maurice Sendak. New York: Harper & Row, 1958.

31. ———*Hurry Home, Candy*. Illustrated by Maurice Sendak. New York: Harper & Row, 1956.

32. Dillon, Eilís. *A Family of Foxes*. New York: Funk & Wagnalls, 1964.

33. Farley, Walter. *Black Stallion*. Illustrated by Keith Ward. New York: Random House, 1941.

34. ———*The Black Stallion's Filly*. Illustrated by Milton Menasco. New York: Random House, 1952.

35. ———*The Blood Bay Colt*. Illustrated by Milton Menasco. New York: Random House, 1950.

36. ———*Son of the Black Stallion*. Illustrated by Milton Menasco. New York: Random House, 1947.

37. Fisher, Aileen. *Valley of the Smallest*. Illustrated by Jean Zallinger. New York: Crowell, 1966.

38. Fon Eisen, Anthony. *Bond of the Fire*. Illustrated by W. T. Mars. New York: Harcourt, 1966.

39. Gipson, Frederick B. *Old Yeller*. Illustrated by Carl Burger. New York: Harper & Row, 1956.

40. Griffiths, Helen. *The Greyhound*. New York: Doubleday, 1966.

41. ———*The Wild Heart*. Illustrated by Victor Ambrus. New York: Doubleday, 1963.

42. Guillot, René. *Grishka and the Bear*. Illustrated by Joan Kiddell-Monroe. Translated by Gwen Marsh. New York: Criterion, 1959.

43. Henry, Marguerite. *Black Gold*. Illustrated by Wesley Dennis. Skokie, Ill.: Rand McNally, 1957.

44. ———*Brighty of the Grand Canyon*. Illustrated by Wesley Dennis. Skokie, Ill.: Rand McNally, 1954.

45. ———*Gaudenzia, Pride of the Palio*. Illustrated by Lynd Ward. Skokie, Ill.: Rand McNally, 1960.

46. ————*Justin Morgan Had a Horse.* Illustrated by Wesley Dennis. Skokie, Ill.: Rand McNally, 1954.

47. ————*King of the Wind.* Illustrated by Wesley Dennis. Skokie, Ill.: Rand McNally, 1948.

48. ————*Misty of Chincoteague.* Illustrated by Wesley Dennis. Skokie, Ill.: Rand McNally, 1947.

49. ————*Mustang, Wild Spirit of the West.* Illustrated by Robert Lougheed. Skokie, Ill.: Rand McNally, 1966.

50. ————*Stormy, Misty's Foal.* Illustrated by Wesley Dennis. Skokie, Ill.: Rand McNally, 1963.

51. ————*White Stallion of Lipizza.* Illustrated by Wesley Dennis. Skokie, Ill.: Rand McNally, 1964.

52. James, Will. *Smoky.* New York: Scribner, 1926.

53. Johnson, Burdetta. *Coyote for Keeps.* Illustrated by James Ralph Johnson. Chicago: Follett, 1965.

54. Jones, Adrienne. *Wild Voyageur, Story of a Canada Goose.* Illustrated by Louis Darling. Boston: Little, Brown, 1966.

55. Kjelgaard, Jim. *Big Red.* Illustrated by Bob Kuhn. New York: Holiday, 1956.

56. ————*Desert Dog.* New York: Holiday, 1956.

57. ————*Haunt Fox.* Illustrated by Glen Rounds. New York: Holiday, 1954.

58. ————*Snow Dog.* Illustrated by Jacob Landau. New York: Holiday, 1948.

59. ————*Wild Trek.* New York: Holiday, 1950.

60. Klose, Norma Cline. *Benny, the Biography of a Horse.* Illustrated by Gloria Gaulke. New York: Lothrop, 1965.

61. Knight, Eric. *Lassie Come-Home.* Illustrated by Marguerite Kerinse. New York: Holt, Rinehart and Winston, 1940.

62. London, Jack. *The Call of the Wild.* Illustrated by Karel Kezer. New York: Macmillan, 1963, 1903.

63. MacKellar, William. *A Dog Like No Other.* New York: McKay, 1965.

64. Morey, Walt. *Gentle Ben.* Illustrated by John Schoenherr. New York: Dutton, 1965.

65. Mukerji, Dhan Gopal. *Gay-Neck, the Story of a Pigeon.* Illustrated by Boris Artzybasheff. New York: Dutton, 1927.

66. Murphy, Robert. *Wild Geese Calling.* Illustrated by John Kaufmann. New York: Dutton, 1966.

67. Neff, Priscilla Holton. *Tressa's Dream.* Illustrated by Marcia Howe. New York: McKay, 1965.

68. North, Sterling. *Little Rascal.* Illustrated by Carl Burger. New York: Dutton, 1965.

69. ————*Rascal, a Memoir of a Better Era.* Illustrated by John Schoenherr. New York: Dutton, 1963.

70. Rawlings, Marjorie Kinnan. *The Yearling.* Illustrated by N. C. Wyeth. New York: Scribner, 1944.

71. Rounds, Glen. *The Blind Colt.* New York: Holiday, 1941.

72. Russell, Franklin. *The Frightened Hare.* Illustrated by Fredric Sweney. New York: Holt, Rinehart and Winston, 1965.

73. Sandburg, Helga. *Joel and the Wild Goose.* Illustrated by Thomas Daly. New York: Dial, 1963.

74. Smith, Linell. *Miranda and the Cat.* Illustrated by Peggy Bacon. Boston: Little, Brown, 1963.

75. Street, James. *Goodbye, My Lady.* Philadelphia: Lippincott, 1954.

76. Ward, Lynd. *Nic of the Woods.* Boston: Houghton Mifflin, 1965.

77. Williamson, Henry. *Tarka the Otter.* Illustrated by Barry Driscoll. New York: F. Watts, 1964, 1927.

Mystery

78. Bawden, Nina. *The Witch's Daughter*. Philadelphia: Lippincott, 1966.
79. Bonsall, Crosby. *The Case of the Cat's Meow.* New York: Harper & Row, 1965.
80. ———*The Case of the Hungry Stranger*. New York: Harper & Row, 1964.
81. Bothwell, Jean. *The Mystery Angel*. Illustrated by Elinor Jaeger. New York: Dial, 1963.
82. Brooks, Walter. *Freddy the Detective*. Illustrated by Kurt Wiese. New York: Knopf, 1963, 1932.
83. Cameron, Eleanor. *The Mysterious Christmas Shell*. Illustrated by Beth and Joe Krush. Boston: Little, Brown, 1961.
84. ———*A Spell Is Cast*. Illustrated by Beth and Joe Krush. Boston: Little, Brown, 1964.
85. ———*The Terrible Churnadryne*. Illustrated by Beth and Joe Krush. Boston: Little, Brown, 1959.
86. Corbett, Scott. *The Case of the Gone Goose*. Illustrated by Paul Frame. Boston: Little, Brown, 1961.
87. ———*The Cave above Delphi*. Illustrated by Gioia Fiammenghi. New York: Holt, Rinehart and Winston, 1965.
88. ———*One by Sea*. Illustrated by Victor Mays. Boston: Little, Brown, 1965.
89. Du Bois, William Pène. *The Alligator Case*. New York: Harper & Row, 1965.
90. Emery, Anne. *A Spy in Old Detroit*. Skokie, Ill.: Rand McNally, 1963.
91. ———*A Spy in Old New Orleans*. Skokie, Ill.: Rand McNally, 1960.
92. ———*A Spy in Old Philadelphia*. Skokie, Ill.: Rand McNally, 1958.
93. ———*A Spy in Old West Point*. Illustrated by Lorence F. Bjorklund. Skokie, Ill.: Rand McNally, 1965.
94. Estes, Eleanor. *The Alley*. Illustrated by Edward Ardizzone. New York: Harcourt, 1964.
95. Faulkner, Nancy. *The Mystery at Long Barrow House*. Illustrated by C. Walter Hodges. New York: Doubleday, 1960.
96. ———*The Secret of the Simple Code*. Illustrated by Mimi Korach. New York: Doubleday, 1965.
97. Fenton, Edward. *The Phantom of Walkaway Hill*. New York: Doubleday, 1961.
98. ———*The Riddle of the Red Whale*. New York: Doubleday, 1966.
99. Fry, Rosalie. *The Riddle of the Figurehead*. New York: Dutton, 1963.
100. ———*Secret of the Ron Mor Skerry*. New York: Dutton, 1959.
101. Gottlieb, Robin. *Secret of the Unicorn.* Illustrated by Mimi Korach. New York: Funk & Wagnalls, 1965.
102. Holman, Felice. *Elisabeth and the Marsh Mystery*. Illustrated by Erik Blegvad. New York: Macmillan, 1966.
103. Kästner, Erich. *Emil and the Detectives*. Illustrated by Walter Trier. New York: Doubleday, 1930.
104. ———*Emil and the Three Twins*. Translated by Cyrus Brooks. London: J. Cape, 1958, 1935.
105. Keene, Carolyn. *The Clue of the Tapping Heels*. New York: Grosset & Dunlap, 1939.
106. ———*The Secret of the Old Clock*. New York: Grosset & Dunlap, 1959.
107. Kingman, Lee. *Private Eyes, Adventures with the Saturday Gang*. Illustrated by Burt Silverman. New York: Doubleday, 1964.
108. Lawrence, Isabelle. *A Spy in Williamsburg*. Illustrated by Manning Lee. Skokie, Ill.: Rand McNally, 1955.
109. Mackenzie, Jeanette Brown. *The Puss in the Corner Mystery*. New York: Washburn, 1964.

110. Mahen, Julia C. *Mystery at Old Sturbridge Village.* Illustrated by Sidney Rafilson. Racine, Wis.: Whitman, 1966.
111. Mantle, Winifred. *The Chateau Holiday.* Illustrated by Kurt Werth. New York: Holt, Rinehart and Winston, 1965.
112. Martin, Frederic. *The Mystery at Monkey Run.* Illustrated by Ned Butterfield. Boston: Little, Brown, 1966.
113. ————*The Mystery on Crabapple Hill.* Illustrated by Nathan Goldsteen. Boston: Little, Brown, 1965.
114. Molloy, Anne. *The Mystery of the Pilgrim Trading Post.* Illustrated by Floyd James Torbert. New York: Hastings, 1964.
115. Orton, Helen. *Mystery in the Old Cave.* Philadelphia: Lippincott, 1950.
116. Pearce, A. Philippa. *The Minnow Leads to Treasure.* Illustrated by Edward Ardizzone. Cleveland: World Publishing, 1955.
117. Pease, Howard. *The Black Tanker.* New York: Doubleday, 1950.
118. Phipson, Joan. *Threat to the Barkers.* Illustrated by Margaret Horder. New York: Harcourt, 1965.
119. Scherf, Margaret. *The Mystery of the Velvet Box.* New York: F. Watts, 1963.
120. Sobol, Donald J. *Encyclopedia Brown.* Illustrated by Leonard Shortall. Camden, N.J.: Nelson, 1963.
121. ————*Encyclopedia Brown Strikes Again.* Illustrated by Leonard Shortall. New York: Scholastic, 1965.
122. Stephens, Peter John. *The Perrely Plight, a Mystery at Sturbridge.* Illustrated by R. D. Rice. New York: Atheneum, 1965.
123. Titus, Eve. *Basil and the Lost Colony.* Illustrated by Paul Galdone. New York: McGraw-Hill, 1964.
124. ————*Basil of Baker Street.* Illustrated by Paul Galdone. New York: McGraw-Hill, 1958.
125. Trease, Geoffrey. *No Boats on Bannermere.* Illustrated by Richard Kennedy. New York: Norton, 1965.
126. Whitney, Phyllis A. *Mystery of the Angry Idol.* Illustrated by Al Fiorentino. Philadelphia: Westminster, 1965.
127. ————*The Mystery of the Haunted Pool.* Philadelphia: Westminster, 1960.
128. ————*The Mystery of the Hidden Hand.* Philadelphia: Westminster, 1963.
129. ————*Secret of the Emerald Star.* Illustrated by Alex Stein. Philadelphia: Westminster, 1964.
130. Wuorio, Eva-Lis. *October Treasure.* Illustrated by Carolyn Cather. New York: Holt, Rinehart and Winston, 1966.

Sports

131. Bishop, Curtis. *Little League Amigo.* Philadelphia: Lippincott, 1964.
132. ————*Little League Double Play.* Philadelphia: Lippincott, 1962.
133. ————*Little League Heroes.* Philadelphia: Lippincott, 1960.
134. ————*Little League Visitor.* Philadelphia: Lippincott, 1966.
135. ————*Little Leaguer.* Austin, Tex.: Steck-Vaughn, 1956.
136. Bontemps, Arna. *Famous Negro Athletes.* New York: Dodd, Mead, 1964.
137. Christopher, Matt. *Basketball Sparkplug.* Illustrated by Ken Wagner. Boston: Little, Brown, 1957.
138. ————*Long Shot for Paul.* Illustrated by Foster Caddell. Boston: Little, Brown, 1966.
139. ————*Touchdown for Tommy.* Illustrated by Foster Caddell. Boston: Little, Brown, 1959.

140. Corbett, Scott. *The Baseball Trick*. Illustrated by Paul Galdone. Boston: Little, Brown, 1965.

141. Cromie, Robert A. *Golf for Boys and Girls*. Chicago: Follett, 1965.

142. De Grummond, Lena Young, and Lynne de Grummond Delaune. *Babe Didriksen*. Illustrated by James Porter. Indianapolis: Bobbs-Merrill, 1963.

143. Epstein, Sam and Beryl. *The Game of Baseball*. Illustrated by Hobe Hays. Chicago: Garrard, 1965.

144. ———*Stories of Champions*. Illustrated by Ken Wagner. Chicago: Garrard, 1965.

145. Freeman, S. H. *Basic Baseball Strategy*. New York: Doubleday, 1965.

146. Frick, C. H. *The Comeback Guy*. New York: Harcourt, 1961.

147. Gelman, Steve. *Young Olympic Champions*. Illustrated with photos. New York: Norton, 1964.

148. Ice Skating Institute of America. *Skating on Ice*. New York: Sterling, 1963.

149. Iger, Martin and Robert Fitzimmons. *How to Play Baseball*. New York: Doubleday, 1962.

150. Izenberg, Jerry. *Championship, the Complete NFL Story*. New York: Four Winds, 1966.

151. Jackson, Caary Paul. *Buzzy Plays Midget League Football*. Illustrated by Kevin Royt. Chicago: Follett, 1956.

152. ———*Little League Tournament*. Illustrated by Charles Geer. New York: Hastings, 1959.

153. ———*Midget League Catcher*. Chicago: Follett, 1966.

154. ———*Pee Wee Cook of the Midget League*. Illustrated by Frank Kramer. New York: Hastings, 1965.

155. ———*Rookie First Baseman*. New York: Crowell, 1950.

156. ———*Shorty at Shortstop*. Illustrated by Kevin Royt. Chicago: Follett, 1951.

157. Jackson, Robert. *Grand Prix at the Glen*. New York: Walck, 1965.

158. ———*Road Race Round the World*. New York: Walck, 1965.

159. Jordan, Payton, and Marshall McClelland. *Track and Field for Boys*. Chicago: Follett, 1960.

160. Kuharich, Joe, and Marshall McClelland. *Football for Boys*. Chicago: Follett, 1960.

161. Lee, Robert C. *The Iron Arm of Michael Glenn*. Illustrated by Al Fiorentino. Boston: Little, Brown, 1965.

162. Lindsay, Sally. *Figure Skating*. Skokie, Ill.: Rand McNally, 1963.

163. Lord, Beman. *Bats and Balls*. Illustrated by Arnold Spilka. New York: Walck, 1962.

164. ———*Guard for Matt*. Illustrated by Arnold Spilka. New York: Walck, 1961.

165. ———*The Perfect Pitch*. Illustrated by Harold Berson. New York: Walck, 1965.

166. ———*Quarterback's Aim*. Illustrated by Arnold Spilka. New York: Walck, 1960.

167. ———*Rough Ice*. Illustrated by Arnold Spilka. New York: Walck, 1963.

168. ———*The Trouble with Francis*. Illustrated by Arnold Spilka. New York: Walck, 1958.

169. Masin, Herman. *How to Star in Basketball*. New York: Four Winds, 1966.

170. ———*How to Star in Football*. New York: Four Winds, 1966.

171. Miers, Earl Schenck. *Monkey Shines, a Baseball Story*. Illustrated by Paul Galdone. Cleveland: World Publishing, 1952.

172. Mullin, Willard, and Herbert Kramm, Editors. *The Junior Illustrated Encyclopedia of Sports*. Revised edition. Indianapolis: Bobbs-Merrill, 1963.

173. Renick, James and Marion. *David Cheers the Team*. Illustrated by Frederick Machetanz. New York: Scribner, 1941.

174. ———*Steady, a Baseball Story*. Illustrated by Frederick Machetanz. New York: Scribner, 1942.

175. Renick, Marion. *The Dooleys Play Ball*. Illustrated by Dwight Logan. New York: Scribner, 1950.

176. ———*Watch Those Red Wheels Roll.* Illustrated by Leonard Shortall. New York: Scribner, 1965.
177. Shapiro, Milton J. *The Mel Ott Story.* New York: Messner, 1959.
178. Tunis, John R. *All American.* Illustrated by Hans Walleen. New York: Harcourt, 1942.
179. ———*Go, Team, Go!* New York: Morrow, 1954.
180. ———*The Keystone Kids.* New York: Harcourt, 1943.
181. ———*Yea! Wildcats.* New York: Harcourt, 1944.
182. Van Riper, Guernsey. *Babe Ruth, Baseball Boy.* Illustrated by William B. Ricketts. Indianapolis: Bobbs-Merrill, 1954.
183. Young, I. S. *Carson at Second.* Chicago: Follett, 1966.

3

DEVELOPING
A LITERATURE
PROGRAM

11

CREATING THE LEARNING ENVIRONMENT

*T*here was a child went forth every day
And the first object he looked upon,
*   that object he became*
And that object became part of him
*   for the day or a certain part of the day,*
Or for many years or stretching cycles of years. . . .

WALT WHITMAN

The child "becomes," and self is created as he responds to the environments surrounding him in school and out of school. His intelligence is a product of interaction of biological and environmental factors. Personal qualities are developed as others respond to him. Home, community, and school provide both tangible and intangible environments as resources for the child's growth. The school is challenged to supply needed material resources and to manage the use of time, talent, and energy to fullest capacity. Each teacher creates an atmosphere of respect, encouragement, and challenge that leads the child to reach his own potential.

The school has the responsibility not only to teach children to read, but to create an environment that will make them want to read. The long-range goal of developing readers who appreciate fine literature should serve as a beacon for the objectives of instruction in reading skills. The school staff will express commitment to this goal of lifetime reading interests and development of tastes as it plans the environment and use of time. The adage, "We find time for the things we hold important," holds true as teachers plan for experiences of boys and girls.

THE SCHOOL ENVIRONMENT

Commitment to Literature

The school that is committed to the long range goals of adult reading interests and lifetime appreciation of a wide variety of literature will provide libraries to make fine books available to children. The faculty will also plan a literature program that rests on the foundation of knowledge of literature, learning, and child development. Teachers will not rely upon an incidental literature program as a mere adjunct to the reading instructional program, and the study of literature will receive planned time in the weekly schedule. Children's progress in understanding literature and methods of studying literature will be evaluated as well as progress in mathematics, science, and other areas.

The school will be committed to the use of many books in all of the content areas. Whether one textbook or several texts are recommended for science and social studies, many trade books and a wide variety of instructional materials will be used for individualized and group instruction. The principles of self-selection and individualized instruction are not new; they have been accepted at the level of theory for twenty-five years; it is time to implement these principles in planning the environment for use of books and teaching literature in the elementary school.

Provision of Time and Space

Space Space needed for a literature program differs little from the space needs of other subjects. However, a literature program does require many books, and books require space in a central instructional materials center and in the classroom. Children need space to read comfortably—this means a library and a quiet area in the classroom. Carrels in new schools provide space for independent reading. Space for small group discussions is necessary if teachers are to implement the findings of research regarding effective size of groups. Discussion areas may be created by rearranging classroom furniture, by utilizing such space as storage areas or the unused stage in the auditorium. Some schools utilize outdoor space effectively when weather is satisfactory. Many schools use outdoor patios and theaters for storytelling, discussions, or dramatizations.

Children need free space—space for movement to avoid bumping the work of others, space to provide a feeling of comfort and freedom. When activity areas, discussion areas, and study areas are separated by space, results of each activity are improved.

Space is needed for storage and display of pupils' writing, paintings, models, dioramas, and other creative products related to books.

Teachers can create a feeling of space by selecting a few samples of children's work and changing the display in two or three days. The teacher will want to make sure all children have their work displayed at some time, but it is not necessary to have twenty-five or thirty book reports, or dust jackets, or mobiles displayed at one time. Children need some space free of color, design, and symbols; children and adults need space to give their eyes a rest from the bombardment of the busyness of many schoolrooms.

Time Some aspects of a literature program are already a part of the regular school program for many children; for many others, literature is only a small part of a reading program. At all levels, listening should be a major part of the literature program. Time for listening to the teacher tell stories or read should be planned for each day. Wise choices of material and challenging follow-up discussion make the story hour more than a time for fun and teacher ease! There should be time each day for individuals to select and read books. Time for conferences with the teacher and time for small group discussion should also be planned. It is not necessary for a child to have a conference every day, but at least two conferences a week should be arranged. Many children, and parents, have come to feel they have not "had reading" if they have not sat in a group and "taken turns" reading aloud. This notion of "reading class" could be supplanted with the idea that the teacher works with a group needing similar instruction in reading skills, discusses a book several have read, or works with individuals.

Children can learn without the immediate presence of the teacher. They can learn from programmed materials, films, tapes, records, and from books. They can learn to work in small groups in areas outside the classroom. Time can be planned for several groups to meet concurrently to share book reports. Children may tape record group discussions, and then evaluate them with the teacher. Time for sharing books and creative activities based upon books can be found in the language arts schedule and the art programs. For example, creative writing and book reviews provide excellent material for developing language skills. Only by evaluating the worth of the activity can the teacher decide its time value. With a strong commitment to the value of literature, the school staff will plan time for a balanced program.

School Organization Patterns

Literature in a Self-contained Classroom

Children may be grouped in a multigrade or single-grade pattern and assigned to one teacher. Although the teacher is primarily responsible for the learning activities, consultants may assist in planning, and teach some lessons. The self-contained classroom also provides for individualized instruction and work in small and large groups. Continuity and integration of all learning experiences are basic characteristics made possible by this pattern of organization. A visit to a classroom indicates the kind of literature environment provided for the children.

In Miss Holt's room the visitor is immediately aware of the children's reading interests and opportunities for literature study. A large map of the United States has been mounted over the shelf where books about pioneer life are displayed. Ribbons lead from each book to the location on the map representing the setting of the story. Caddie Woodlawn, Little House on the Prairie, Hello the Boat!, The Matchlock Gun, *and* Carolina's Courage *are on the shelf. On another shelf are evidences of children's interpretations of books. A diorama representing* Mary Poppins, *a model of Homer Price's doughnut machine, and a clay figure of the Black Stallion show the children's reading interests are not limited to books about pioneers.*

On the reading table is a large notebook labeled, "Books We Have Liked." Sections are devoted to mysteries, adventure, sports, and animals. Children place their written reports here so others can read the critical reviews and recommendations.

The news bulletin board includes a picture of Marguerite Henry and Misty. A letter from Mrs. Henry to one of the pupils is placed beside the pupil's report on the life of this favorite author. The news bulletin board also includes the announcement of two new book

Children can organize books for their classroom library where independent choices may be made easily. West Lafayette, Indiana, Public Schools.

Children have illustrated a chart of favorite book characters which is fastened to the wall near the comfortable reading corner. Here extra book shelves have been used to create a quiet reading area and to conveniently house the current collection of approximately two hundred books.

A chart naming pupil librarians for the week indicates that the children are responsible for care of the library and for the circulation of books. Games related to children's literature are on one of the shelves. A puzzle chart on a bulletin board illustrates several book titles in rebus picture writing.

The pupil secretary of the room has written the plans for the day on the chalkboard. Time had been planned for a literature lesson. Names of children were listed for a reading skills lesson. Individual reading was planned for the rest of the class at that time. At story-time they would hear Miss Holt read a part of the book, The Tree in the Trail.

arrivals. Their shiny new dust covers are displayed along with a sheet of paper for a waiting list of readers.

The following account of a day in a third grade illustrates the opportunities for teaching literature in a self-contained classroom:

LITERATURE IN A SELF-CONTAINED CLASSROOM

Tentative Time	Activity	Literature Opportunities
8:20	*Individual Work Period*	Browse in reading center . . . Work on book reports . . . Play book games . . . Art activities involving book interpretation . . . Reading for information . . . Reading for fun . . . Work in instructional materials center.
8:45	*Sharing Time*	Betty shows illustrations in a birthday gift book . . . Teacher introduces two new library books . . . John and Bill have children guess the title of their peep show, *The Sword in the Tree.*
9:10	*Science — work on committee reports about prehistoric life*	Children using many references for information. Some go to the materials center to see filmstrip, some preview a film, others prepare a transparency for use with the overhead projector.

9:45	*Outdoor Play*	
10:10	*Rest — story hour*	Teacher reads a chapter from *The Land of the Forgotten Beasts* by Wersba.
10:25	*Language Skills — spelling, oral book reports,*	Ed explained his diorama of *The Castle of Yew.*
	independent activities,	
	teacher works with one group on word-perception skills	Sally and Lissa compare *The Courage of Sarah Noble* with *Carolina's Courage* for a class report.
11:30	*Lunch*	
12:45	*Reading*	Self-selection of books to read. Teacher confers with several children.
1:15	*Mathematics*	
1:50	*Outdoor Play*	
2:10	*Directed Art Period — teacher introduces mobiles*	Several mobiles are based on favorite book characters or the themes of one book.
2:50	*Literature Study*	Teacher leads study of techniques of writing fantasy, using *The Land of the Forgotten Beasts.*
3:10	*Evaluation and Planning*	

Literature in a Team-Teaching, Nongraded Elementary School Kennedy Elementary School has organized multigrade units at primary, intermediate, and upper levels. Children of a three-year age span are grouped in large units of approximately ninety. Continuous progress, flexible grouping, individualization, and use of teacher specialists are basic characteristics of the program. Teaching teams for each unit include a team leader who works with the elementary school for two trimesters and with a college for one trimester. Other members of the team are three interns, two teachers, and one clerk. The elementary school has consultants available in mathematics, science, social studies, literature, communication skills, art, music, and physical education. The two teachers and three interns are "homeroom teachers" each of whom works with small groups of sixteen children. Each teacher has an area of specialization and works with the consultants in developing plans and materials for this field.

The instructional materials center is also a center for independent study; discussion centers provide the "home base" for room groups; art, and music studios, and science laboratories are also available.

The "home group" of sixteen has a morning sharing time in which a display may be explained, information about an author may be shared, a favorite poem may be read. Literature is an important part of the weekly "assembly" when the large unit meets. But these are only incidental aspects of the literature program. The daily schedule provides time for the room teacher to read to the small group of children each day. There is much emphasis upon independent reading in the daily communication skills period. Children select their own books to read. Conferences with the teacher provide opportunity to discuss understanding of the theme, character development, and enjoyment of particular aspects of the book as well as time to check word attack skills. Each room teacher works with a small group of sixteen now grouped according to reading ability level. On one day each week the literature specialist meets with the large group. A film may be shown; folk tales may be presented by a story teller; children may meet in discussion groups. Just as in science, mathematics, and social studies, the specialist teacher or consultant leads the team in planning for the study of literature.

Regardless of the organizational plan of the school, time for listening, reading, and discussing literature can be arranged.

THE INSTRUCTIONAL MATERIALS CENTER

New school designs often place classrooms so they radiate from a central laboratory for learning. This instructional materials center becomes the hub of school activity.

The center will contain books, films, tapes, machinery for duplicating, microfilm readers and devices for information retrieval. It may be connected to a central materials center with a dial system, whereby the local librarian may dial for an article that will be sent to the school. Encyclopedias, for example, may be on discs, and pages will be quickly duplicated as needed. A revolution in printing and copying processes is in the beginning stages.

Books will continue to be important sources of information and recreation. Gaver's study showed the effectiveness of a centralized library collection:

> *Children who have had continuing [sic] access to good school library collections administered by qualified library personnel generally read two to three times as many items in a greater variety of literary forms and interest areas, read more magazines more frequently, and also include fewer nonreaders than do children who have had access only to classroom collections or centralized collections with no professional personnel.*[1]

Books in the Center

Trade Books   Books will continue to be a major source of learning in the instructional materials center. In 1963, sixty-six per cent of the elementary schools had no libraries. Ten million children went to schools where there was no school library. Seventy-four per cent of the new schools were built without libraries. Although $40 million dollars was spent for school libraries in 1963, $180 million would have been spent if schools had met the minimum standards suggested by the American Library Association in 1960. The recognition of the need for instructional materials centers led to federal grants in 1965 and made possible the beginning of these essential resources for learning.

---

[1] Mary Virginia Gaver, "Research on Elementary School Libraries," *ALA Bulletin* (February 1962), p. 121.

The standards suggested by the American Library Association in 1960 were *minimum* and outdated quickly. New Standards[2] developed cooperatively in 1967–1968 by the American Association of School Librarians and the NEA Department of Audio-visual Instruction (presented in *Standards for Media Programs* published jointly by the AASL and DAVI) reflect the philosophy that audio-visual material and books should be unified in an instructional materials center in each school. The new version of the *National School Library Standards* shows some striking differences from the old *Standards*. Instead of a suggested flat sum of $4 to $6 per student, it is now suggested that at least 6 per cent of the total cost be spent on printed material and audio-visual materials. These recommendations are made:

- *Books:* The new *Standards* recommends a core of resources of 6000–10,000 books, or 15 per pupil, whichever is greater. An initial collection would include some 6000–7500 titles.
- *Magazines:* 50–75 titles for the elementary school.
- *Professional collection:* 200–1000 books, 40–50 magazines.
- *Films:* "Ready access" to one 16 mm. film title per teaching station, with a component of 3000 titles "available" in the school and district. A basic collection of 500 titles of 8 mm.
- *Filmstrips:* An initial collection of 500 titles per school, increasing eventually to a collection of 1500–2000 titles.
- *Tapes and discs* (recordings): At least 500 titles per school.

One professional person and one media aid for each 250 students up to 1000 are recommended. Most importantly, provision for change has been built into the *Standards*; it is recommended that they be updated every two years. The explosion of knowledge must be controlled if students are to benefit from its potential. The new *Standards* will assure that information in all forms will be made readily available to all students.

Textbooks The use of multiple texts rather than a single textbook creates the need for a central storage place for these materials. Housing texts with the trade books and nonprint media helps the teacher see the textbook as only one of many sources for learning. Central housing of these books allows for a wider variety of texts and avoids the duplication of purchasing one set for each class. Teachers can become better acquainted with many texts and select those that meet needs of a particular group. Easy access to these books allows changing collections for all classrooms.

Recently, some textbook materials have been developed for the elementary school literature program. One type presents short selections from longer works in order to promote interest in reading the book and to develop skill in analysis. Unless the child is encouraged to read the entire book, he is denied the complete literary experience. Other books, called literary readers, contain short stories, poems, and selections from longer works. Some new reading programs include a complete work of literature in the basic reader, supplementary books that emphasize literature of high quality, and "packaged libraries" of hardbound trade books. Accompanying these materials are guides that aid the teacher in planning literature lessons. Although these materials are helpful, no single anthology or literary reader can substitute for a rich literature program (see Chapter 13).

Paperbound Books Paperbacks have now found their place on the bookshelves in the elementary school and are here to stay.

[2]This report is based on the provisional draft of these standards published in *School Library Journal* (September 1967), pp. 47–48 and notes from the editorial committee on standards, AASL and DAVI (February 1968).

A paperback bookrack in the hall encourages reading interest. Children learn to make wise choices when they buy their own books. West Lafayette, Indiana, Public Schools.

However, they do not remain long on the shelves since children enjoy their compactness and light weight. Frequently, a child will select a paperback book in preference to a hardbound copy of the same title. In most instances, the paperbacks present original, unabridged versions. Their relatively low cost makes it possible to use multiple copies of a title for literature study. It has been found that paperbacks are durable and last for approximately four to ten readings.[3] A paperback bookstore or display racks in the school make it easy for children to purchase

books for their own libraries. Pride of ownership motivates wide reading and encourages the rereading of books. Children learn to make choices as they select books from an attractive display. They may also order paperbacks through various book clubs, but it is more difficult to select a book from a catalog. On the other hand, when teachers send children's orders there may be greater opportunity to guide selection.

Nonprint Materials in the Center

Nonprint materials are essential resources for extending and enriching the literature program as well as other areas of the curriculum. Films, filmstrips, or recordings may be used to introduce a book or poem, to develop meaning, or as a presentation of literature in another form. The resource center should make these materials easily accessible to children and teachers. Only a few of the many materials available can be reviewed in this volume. Catalogs of film and record companies should be consulted (see Appendix D). Films may be rented from commercial firms or certain state universities.

Audio-visual materials should be previewed and evaluated before purchase. Faithfulness to the story and interpretation of theme should be considered as well as the artistic quality of the material. Since many of the films, filmstrips, and recordings are based on traditional literature, there is no exact version, but the characters and theme should follow familiar interpretations. For example, the SVE[4] filmstrip and record, *Little Red Riding Hood*, moralizes at the conclusion when Red Riding Hood says it was wrong to wander from the path, and now, she would always mind her mother. This ending does not provide the justice of the traditional tale nor leave the moral to the listener. An inquisitive neighbor is an addi-

---

[3]Max Bogart, *Paperback Books in New Jersey Schools* (Trenton, N.J.: Department of Instruction, 1965), p. 34.

[4]SVE—Society for Visual Education, Inc.

tional character added to the filmstrip, *Elves and the Shoemaker,* by SVE, presenting a different theme from many versions. In *King Midas,* an EBEC[5] filmstrip, the familiar character, Marigold, is not included. The EBEC version of *The Pied Piper* shows the mayor of Hamelin keeping the money for himself; neither the usual version of the legend nor Browning's poem includes this incident.

The language of captions and recordings should be evaluated for literary quality. Short captions cannot provide the experience of good writing, but they should avoid colloquialisms and phrases that seem inappropriate for the traditional tale. The coordination of the narrator's text with the illustration, the pacing of narration, and the dramatic quality of the voice should be evaluated. The artistic quality of the pictures, puppets, or costumes and setting for films of live dramatizations is an important factor to consider when evaluating a film or filmstrip. Each audio-visual presentation should provide some value that could not be obtained by use of the printed book. Entertainment should not be the sole purpose of the audio-visual material used for literature.

Filmstrips   Filmstrips can be viewed by one child using an individual viewer, by small interest groups, or used to present literature to an entire class. With the filmstrip, the child can move each frame at his own pace, whereas the film moves at a predetermined rate. If there is a recording with the filmstrip, even primary children can learn to move the filmstrip in conjunction with the recording as a signal is given. Filmstrips are especially helpful for individualized instruction. For example, children in primary grades could read the captions of the J 'm Handy series that includes *The Three Bears, Three Billy Goats Gruff,* and *Three Little Pigs.*

---

[5]EBEC—Encyclopedia Britannica Educational Corporation.

The filmstrip pictures may be explained by captions under the picture, by separate captions presented in a frame preceding or following the picture, or a record may accompany the filmstrip. The SVE sound-filmstrip, *The Little Engine That Could,* includes easy-to-read captions within the frame, and the record presents the story with clear, crisp diction. Interesting sound effects do not overpower the story. A single frame of text precedes one to three picture illustrations in the EBEC filmstrip, *The Lady of Staveren.* This technique is appropriate for older children. Activities are suggested at the close of the folk tale. However, the introduction refers to the Hanseatic League without giving adequate information about it. This filmstrip, one of a series by EBEC, *Stories from Other Lands,* follows the pattern of including discussion questions after the story frames. For example, in *Dick Whittington,* the viewer is asked if Dick Whittington was the kind of person he would like as a friend. *Pheidippedes, The Marathon Runner, Robert Bruce, Joan of Arc,* and *William Tell* are titles in this series.

A good story comes alive as a child reads picture and text of a filmstrip at his own pace. Allisonville Public Schools, Indiana. Photograph by Donald Sellmire.

Many filmstrips are based on drawings that resemble cartoons. Disney cartoons are the basis of an EBEC series, *Fantasy Stories.* These filmstrips, including such titles as *Cinderella, Ben and Me, Alice in Wonderland,* and *Ferdinand the Bull,* might be used effectively for critical comparison of text and film version. Adapted from Disney motion pictures, these and several other series in the Disney version should be carefully evaluated.

With only sixty frames for such a story as *Hans Brinker,* for example, it is apparent that only a very condensed version of this classic could be presented. The child may learn something of the plot and characters in a story, but a longer book cannot be faithfully presented in this way. A similar criticism could be made of the SVE series, *Hero Legends of Many Lands.* In *Robin Hood,* for example, only a few incidents are presented in a cartoon style. The romance of Allan-A-Dale is emphasized, and other characters and events are mentioned so briefly there can be little understanding of the story. *Ulysses and Circe* would require background knowledge of the epic. Such a brief filmstrip does not seem appropriate for an introduction to this tale, and the narration is too limited to be considered a substitute for reading or listening to a well-illustrated book version.

Another series of filmstrips and records has been made available to homes and schools by General Electric. A record player fits on top of a viewing screen designed to resemble a television set. Strips of color slides are inserted and move automatically as the record plays. Unfortunately, there are only a few frames for such long stories as *Heidi, Hans Brinker,* and *Tom Sawyer.* Perhaps this good technical idea will be improved in the future.

A cartoon style is used for the illustrations of an SVE series of Hans Christian Andersen stories. The coarse features of *The Little Match Girl* and the almost grotesque appearance of the child in *The Emperor's New Clothes* are examples of art work that should be compared to fine illustrations available in books. However, Danish artists Helga and Beate Neergaard created interesting figures and settings with collage techniques for the Andersen stories by EBEC. Each story is summarized at the beginning of the filmstrip, and the children are urged to "tell the story ourselves while looking at the pictures." This would be a good filmstrip to follow the reading of Andersen's fairytales.

Two filmstrips by SVE, *Three Billy Goats Gruff* and *Town Mouse and Country Mouse,* are delightfully illustrated by Burridge and Smith, respectively. These productions are not in cartoon style, and the text is well written. Details of the house, cupboard, and costumes in the SVE *Elves and the Shoemaker* provide an authentic old German setting for this tale by Grimm. Dutch artists created the drawings for the EBEC series that includes *The Lady of Staveren, The Wild Swans,* and *Gulliver among the Lilliputians.* In *The Wild Swans,* an effect of tapestry is created, with interesting details of flowers and foliage in a pleasing design. The record that accompanies *The Four Musicians,* a well-illustrated SVE filmstrip, has rather distracting sound effects.

Older children who have difficulty reading mythology will enjoy two of the Jam Handy series, *Heroes of Greek Mythology* and *Myths of Greece and Rome.* Such filmstrips as *Pegasus and Bellerophon* and *Prometheus and Pandora* will provide a good introduction to these myths.

Fine filmstrips are produced by the Weston Woods Studios by photographing the well-designed picture book itself. Such books as McCloskey's *Make Way for Ducklings,* Gág's *Millions of Cats* and Yashima's *Crow Boy* are available, with the original text read by excellent narrators. Children will join in singing with the records as they enjoy the Weston Woods' folk song series, including *Over in the Meadow* and *The Fox Went out on a Chilly Night.*

Films   Some films provide background information or enriching visual experiences related to literature. *Glooscap's Country,* produced by the Canadian Travel Film Library, shows the beautiful rivers and hills of Nova Scotia and tells some of the Indian legends of the creation of these natural features. The excellent narration describes the power struggle of beaver and frog against Glooscap. *The Loon's Necklace* uses authentic masks of Indians of the Northwest to tell the story of how the bird received his white neck markings. An explanation of the technique should be made before the children see the film, and it may be wise to note that eerie sound effects and dramatic close-ups of the masks are used to show how the Indians feared their gods. Another excellent film is *The Eskimo in Life and Legend,* by EBEC. This film opens with a scene inside an igloo where a storyteller is telling a tale in the native language. The narrator interposes an English translation. The film continues as a man makes a stone carving of the sea goddess who keeps all the seals at the bottom of the sea. A boy's first catch, tribal customs, and a dance show modern life, as well as the myths of the people. Superb photography makes this film excellent in itself, but it would enrich the literature about Eskimo life.

Films can give information about book production and introduce authors and illustrators. *Story of a Book,* by Churchill films, for example, shows how H. C. Holling, author of *Pagoo,* did research in a library and made observations of ocean life before illustrating his story. *Robert McCloskey* by Weston Woods shows this author-artist at work in his barn studio. McCloskey talks to the audience in a friendly manner as he explains the way he creates books. In some schools, librarians have made their own films of local authors and illustrators in their homes. *The Lively Art of Picture Books* by Weston Woods is too long for young children to enjoy at one sitting, but parts could be shown at different times.

One section deals with various artists' interpretations of life and a story; for example, many different illustrations of trees, villages, and cats are shown. Another part of the film shows Barbara Cooney, Robert McCloskey, and Maurice Sendak in their homes and in their studios as they discuss their work in a very informal manner. A third part of the film presents the book *Time of Wonder.*

Several films have been produced to give children instruction in literature. For example, *Preparing Your Book Report,* Coronet, shows a boy enthusiastically telling about a book before class and later giving a dull "report" in class. His friend decides to give an interesting book report, and the viewers observe him making an outline, practicing before his family, and giving a formal report. This kind of film would be useful for teachers, but children who are having enjoyable experiences in sharing books informally may not need such a presentation. *Poems Are Fun,* Coronet, is a contrived episode of a sixth-grade class sharing poetry at a party, which may turn children away from poetry rather than create interest in it.

An understanding of the unique qualities of poetry is presented through beautiful color photography in the motion picture entitled *Poetry for Me,* Grover-Jennings Production. For example, the principle that some words sing to movement is illustrated by the camera focusing upon a small boy riding on a carousel while the narrator recites "The Merry-Go-Round." The bobbing motion of "Mrs. Peck-Pigeon" is matched to the rhythm of Farjeon's poem about her. A sequence of sea poems is photographed against the changing mood of the ocean and illustrates the principle that poems help one to see more and to discover what has never really been "seen" before. This same company has produced a film for middle-graders titled *Poetry to Grow On.*

Films may enrich the interpretation of individual poems, too. Longfellow's poem is illustrated by the fine color photography of Boston and the restored village of Sturbridge in Coronet's *Midnight Ride of Paul Revere.* Old North Church, authentic buildings, the colonial figure galloping under a dark sky, the British man-of-war, and the stirring drum-and-fife parade will add meaning to the poem. *Hailstones and Halibut Bones,* Sterling, is a six-minute animated film showing shapes and lines in glowing color. Celeste Holm's reading of selections from O'Neill's poem will introduce the book or add to children's interest in this original concept. This film omits the aspect of the poem that deals with the emotional quality of each color. Before reading poems about rain, the teacher might show the film *Rainshower,* produced by Churchill. After the narrator introduces the film with its simple presentation of rain on a farm and in a town, there is no further sound except that of the rain. Later, children might make tape recordings of appropriate poems to accompany the beautifully photographed rainshower.

Filmed versions of folk tales and fables might be compared in terms of language, art techniques, and theme. There are three *Rumplestiltskin* films; puppets are used in the Coronet version, adult actors dramatize the story in the Sterling production, and live action plus narration is utilized in the Encyclopedia Britannica presentation. Coronet has two Paul Bunyan films: *Paul Bunyan and the Blue Ox* utilizes a large wooden puppet, while *Paul Bunyan Lumber Camp Tales* is based on cartoon-like drawings. The narration and the content of the latter film are superior, despite the somewhat "feminine" appearance of Paul Bunyan's face. Seeing the stacks of 137 bunkhouse beds, the gigantic griddle, and the straightening of the Big Onion River will increase enjoyment of these tall tales.

Sound films of stories and fables, just as the filmstrips, may utilize live characters, puppets, or animated drawings. The Gakken films produced in Japan for Coronet use collage and color very effectively; for example, *The Ant and the Dove* and *The Country Mouse and City Mouse.* Abstract designs and good musical effects create the color and movement of the city where the city mouse lives in a sewer pipe. Children will enjoy the Japanese labels on trunks and cartons on the train that the country mouse rides to the city. Narration is also important in film presentation. In *Lion and Mouse* by Coronet, the dialogue seems unnaturally pitched, and there are too many "Oh! Ho, Ho!" exclamations. The rhythm of the narration of *The Little Engine that Could,* Coronet, fits the animated story appropriately. Young children will enjoy the dialogue of the toys carried by the train. *The Ugly Duckling,* Coronet, is presented through color film of live animals in the Danish countryside. The "duckling" encounters the other animals, enters a charming thatched-roof cottage, and leaves when the cat and hen seem to communicate their disgust. Winter scenes do not include the growing swan, so he does not appear until he sees his own reflected beauty in a pond. This film would provide an excellent introduction to the story, or enrich children's experiences with it. The fable, *Hare and the Tortoise,* is presented by EBEC by showing live animals as they move through the woods, over stones, around roots. The narration tells the story in an excellent style. Live bears are also used in the Coronet film, *Goldilocks and the Three Bears.* A little girl dreams a cabin in the woods becomes a "real bear's house," and she becomes Goldilocks. Kindergarten and first-grade children will enjoy the bears who sit in storybook chairs, eat steaming porridge when they return, and amble gently toward Goldilocks. Unfortunately, the child actress appears overdramatic. Weston Woods has produced *The Doughnuts,* recreating one of the most amusing episodes from *Homer Price* by McCloskey. By using real children in integrated scenes, a 35-year-old doughnut machine, and some

12,000 doughnuts, the film adheres faithfully to the original text.

The National Film Board of Canada has produced a beautifully colored film based on Holling's book, *Paddle-to-the-Sea,* distributed by Contemporary Films.

Full-length films based on literature may be rented, or purchased for a school system. *Misty, Lassie Come Home,* and *Johnny Tremain* are among the titles available. *And Now Miguel,* a sixty-minute film based on Krumgold's book, can be rented for about eight dollars. The scenes of life on the New Mexico sheep ranch and Miguel's search for acceptance as an adult are faithfully portrayed.

Video tapes and kinescopes of educational television programs may be obtained from the National Education Television film library at Indiana University. For example, in The Friendly Giant series there are films showing the giant reading *Cowboy Small* by Lenski, *Raindrop Splash* by Tresselt, and *Springtime for Jeanne Marie* by Francoise.

Under the direction of Morton Schindel, the Weston Woods studios have produced outstanding films based on picture books. The camera is used skillfully to focus on part of the picture as the narrator reads the story. For example, in *The Camel Who Took a Walk,* the viewer feels that he is walking down the path as the camera "pans" slowly over the page. When the tiger's eyes are described, there is a good closeup, and when the bird is mentioned, the camera eye moves up the tree to the bird. Such films make it possible for all children to see the pictures easily, and their attention can be focused upon the particular object or character being discussed. The text is read clearly, with excellent timing. This iconographic technique has been used to make films of many picture books.

Recordings The wide range of recordings based upon children's literature available today makes it essential to select the best. The story should be appropriate for adaptation to storytelling (see Chapter 13).

The narrator should possess a pleasant, natural voice. Clear enunciation is especially important, for the listeners cannot receive clues from facial expressions. Variation in voice tone is also necessary. The story should be well paced for the understanding and interest of the age group for which it is intended. Pacing can indicate speed of action such as "he clomped slowly" or "the dog ran, and ran—and ran." The words in the narration should create a visual image. The language should tell how the dog ran, or how the man walked. A simple production usually creates the best result; there should be more solo parts than choruses. Overdramatization, modern colloquialisms, and overemphasis on sound limit the literary worth of the recorded folk tale.

The elementary school library should stock several types of literature records. Mother Goose is available in many forms. A gay, rollicking Caedmon disc of *Mother Goose* verse has been made by Celeste Holm, Cyril Ritchard, and Boris Karloff. The music enriches the setting of this record, and the variation of voices and the excellent pacing maintain interest. The Young People's record, *Muffin and Mother Goose,* presents the rhymes in song. Judith Anderson's beautiful voice is delightful in *A Child's Garden of Verses* by Columbia, although she seems aloof, and the recording lacks a certain warmth.

Music is an integral part of many fairy-tale records. The background music from *Bambi* and songs from *Sleeping Beauty* are based upon the Walt Disney films of these stories. Music is used also to create the mood for an RCA presentation, *Cinderella, Pinocchio, and Other Great Stories for Boys and Girls.* Each story in Audio Education's record, *Once upon a Time,* is introduced by a song that the children can join in singing. Several characters dramatize Cinderella, Robin Hood, Peter Pan, and Alice in Wonderland through song and narrative in Bravo Records' *Children's Hour of Songs and Stories.* Music and sound effects are very good. In the opera version of *The Emperor's New Clothes*, recorded by Young People's Records, George Rasely is a delightful emperor. A musical adaptation of the *Just So Stories* was made by Columbia. Garry Moore narrates *The Elephant's Child* with gay humor, excellent expression, and effective pacing. The songs by the chorus sometimes seem too long, but the narration uses most of Kipling's wonderful prose. Several songs were added to the presentation of *The Tale of Benjamin Bunny,* which was narrated by Vivien Leigh. This additional material in the Riverside record seems to detract from the original story.

Recordings of stories by one narrator can serve as listening experiences for children, and also, can help the teacher become a better storyteller. A series produced by RCA for the American Library Association brings to children such famous storytellers as Ruth Sawyer, Frances Clarke Sayers, Jack Lester, and Gudrun Thorne-Thomsen. The selections are of special interest. Harold Courlander brings wit and humor in the Folkways record, *Folk Tales from West Africa.* He also recorded *Folk Tales from Indonesia* and *Ashanti Folk Tales from Ghana* for Folkways. An authentic collection of *Jack Tales* is available from the Library of Congress. Augusta Baker is another good storyteller who recorded Folkways' *Uncle Bouqui of Haiti.* Anne Pellowski's very precise narration may give the impression she is reading rather than telling the fairy tales and Indian folklore in her series of CMS records. *The Seventh Princess and Other Fairy Tales* includes "Cinderella" and "The Goose Girl" as well as an unfamiliar Kipling story, "The Potted Princess." Pellowski's smooth style, effective pauses, and authentic phrasing are also evident in *The Star Maiden and Other Indian Tales.* Sources of the *American Indian Tales for Children* are given on the record holder. Ruth Sawyer's *Joy to the World* is a beautiful album of Christmas legends recorded by

Weston Woods. Unusual tales from Arabia, Serbia, and Ireland are told in Sawyer's inimitable style.

Children will especially enjoy poetry read by the poet himself. John Ciardi brings delight in his verse in the Spoken Arts recordings of *You Read to Me, I'll Read to You* and *You Know Who.* For the first time, children may hear David McCord, Harry Behn, Karla Kuskin, and Aileen Fisher present their favorite poems in the Weston Woods album entitled *Poetry Parade.* Hearing these poets read their own poems gives children a special sense of identity with the poet. Arna Bontemps reads *An Anthology of Negro Poetry for Young People* for Folkways, and Carl Sandburg reads *Poems for Children* in a Caedmon recording. Upper-grade children will enjoy T. S. Eliot's Spoken Arts recording of his poems, *Old Possum's Book of Practical Cats* and the selections read by Robert Frost in a Caedmon title, *Robert Frost Reads His Poetry.* Folkways has produced a lovely recording of *Prayers from the Ark* written by Carmen de Gasztold and read by Marian Seldes.

Longer stories may be presented effectively by recording selections, or by narrating a part and then dramatizing a part of a story. The Gloria Chandler Recordings of the radio program, "Books Bring Adventure," are outstanding. *Trap Lines North, Gift of the Forest, Miss Hickory, The Singing Tree,* and *Homer Price* are among the titles available. *Many Moons* is another story that is dramatized effectively. Boris Karloff creates a delightful story as he portrays the king, the voices of the wise men, jester, and princess. Karloff's reading of *The Jungle Book* and *Just-So Stories,* Caedmon, is excellent also. The sound effects of the animals, recorded at the Dublin Zoo, and the Indian music enrich, but do not overwhelm, the story "Rikki-Tikki-Tavi" of *The Jungle Book* recorded by Spoken Arts. Michael Redgrave's reading of *Tales of Hans Christian Andersen* is appropriate to the fine style of the

Keigwin translation. This Caedmon recording includes "The Tinder Box," "The Emperor's New Clothes," and "The Emperor's Nightingale."

Eve Watkinson and Christopher Casson maintain the traditional style in their Spoken Arts recordings, *Best Loved Fairy Tales by Perrault* and *Grimms' Fairy Tales.* Harp music, the sound of sea gulls, and sound of waves contribute to the effect of "The Fisherman and His Wife." In "The Goose Girl," the verse of the horse, Falada, is sung to a haunting melody. Some educators may not like the grim version of "Little Red Riding Hood"; others will question the musical moral that modern "wolves ogle and prance after young ladies." The Disney version of *Emil and the Detectives*, narrated by Walter Slezak, would interest middle graders in this story by Kästner. Excitement and mystery are maintained in this fast-paced retelling, which is faithful to Kästner's style.

Two recordings of *The Wind in the Willows* might be compared before purchasing. The London recording by Toby Robertson keeps much of the original text; yet, the dialogue is presented by several voices. Sound effects of the river add to the realism, and they sing such songs as the "Ducks Ditty." Pathway of Sound presents "Dulce Domum" and "The Piper at the Gates of Dawn." Robert Brooks, Hume Cronyn, and Jessica Tandy read each chapter. Their pacing, intonation, and fine interpretation provide an excellent model of oral reading. The first record would serve well as an introduction to the book, while the latter album would be an excellent source for children and teacher to hear after part of the book had been read and discussed.

Wheel on the School by Newbery Award Records brings to children a lively dramatization of DeJong's book. The clear dialogue will help children with pronunciation of difficult Dutch names. The text and characterizations are true to the original story.

The Weston Woods records prepared to

A **listening center enables a child to hear any story he wishes, as many times as he desires. Following the printed text in the book while he listens will improve his skills in reading.** Picture published with the permission of Scott, Foresman and Company.

accompany their filmstrips could be used for listening experiences. *Stone Soup, The Five Chinese Brothers*, and *Madeline's Rescue* are but a few of the recordings available.

Large-sized, color photographs have been published by the Society for Visual Education to accompany recorded poetry. The narration introduces a group of poems; for example, *It's Raining* suggests children look at a picture while such poems as "U for Umbrellas," "Raining," and "Brooms" are read. The poems are printed on the back of each print so the child could read as he listens. The themes of the prints include city, pets, boats, autumn, and wind. All the poems do not relate to the pictures. For example, the poem "Sunning" by Tippett refers to an old dog, but the picture shows a perky pup.

Tape recordings of interviews with authors, prepared by Norton, are available from the University of Michigan. Authors answer questions written by children. Among the tapes available are interviews with Rebecca Caudill and Marguerite de Angeli. The authors tell how they get ideas for books, how they write, and give glimpses into their personal lives.

Many records enhance the science and social studies programs. Enrichment Records have been prepared to accompany the *Landmark* series of books and filmstrips. Somewhat typical of the books, these records rely upon incident, quick action, and contrived conversations. However, they do create interest and can lead to further reading. *Sounds of the Sea* is a Folkways record of actual sounds of fish recorded in the ocean at varying depths and in isolated tanks. Unfortunately, there is no narration to identify the sound with the name of the fish, but this is a very outstanding, realistic record. Bird-song records are included with the National Geographic Society book, *Song and Garden Birds of North America*. Droll Yankees Recordings is the name of a firm releasing such titles as *Birds on a May Morning, Songs of the Forest, The Brook,* and *The Swamp in June.* On one side of the record, a narrator identifies the sounds and comments on the setting, while on the other side, the sound is presented as though the listeners were actually in the forest or swamp.

Radio and Television Contrary to the dire predictions concerning reading habits that accompanied the introduction of television programs for children, research has indicated that children continue to read widely. Some television programs stimulate reading. Following the television production of *Peter Pan,* there was a resurgence of interest in this older classic. A few producers plan programs to stimulate reading interest. One network featured well-known personalities who read their favorite books to their children or grandchildren. Another included children's book reviews once each week. One television network made available a selected bibliography for each of the programs in the *Discovery* series.

It is essential that the teacher keep informed of television and radio programs that can stimulate reading. To capitalize on those based upon children's literature, a calendar might be kept in the classroom to alert children to these forthcoming programs. Discussion preceding and following the programs will help children evaluate the presentations. The televised version can be compared with the original story. For example, one class discussed the television presentation of *Stuart Little* by reading aloud parts of the book that were illustrated or omitted. The teacher should anticipate new interests that may be developed by special programs in such fields as adventure, history, travel, and science. Related books may be displayed, and discussions of these programs may develop further reading interests.

The teacher or librarian will need to plan for an introduction to the audio-visual material and some follow-up activity. Nonprint materials should be used when such material is more effective than firsthand experience, to provide individual instruction, or to extend literary experiences.

Role of the School Librarian

The librarian in the instructional materials center works with children, teachers, and parents and is a very important member of the elementary school faculty. Special training provides background knowledge of children's books and all media for instruction, library procedures, knowledge of children, and teaching methods. A description of a day in an instructional materials center will serve to illustrate the role of the librarian working with children and teachers.

The elementary school librarian is busy all day serving children. When the school

ONE DAY IN AN INSTRUCTIONAL

MATERIALS CENTER

8:00 — An intern teacher works with the librarian to select materials appropriate for study of developing nations in Africa. Magazines, pamphlets, and newspapers are used as well as books, films, and tapes. The file of TV tapes in the central school center reveals an interview with a visitor from Nigeria filmed the previous year.

8:15 — The library is open so children may come in to return and check out books, to look at displays, to read, to use the carrels. If a pupil missed a television lesson, he may see it by presenting a card from the teacher indicating the number of the lesson he should see. Some children work·on reports in study carrels. These activities continue throughout the day. The library clerk is present to assist.

9:10 — Two fifth-graders ask for help in locating information about a boundary dispute with Canada.

9:20 — Three fourth graders want material about Elizabeth Coatsworth, a favorite author. The vertical file contains information, material from the publisher, and a copy of a letter written by the author to another child.

9:25 — Ten children go to the listening area for a filmstrip and record presentation of *Blueberries for Sal.* They will compare the Weston Woods presentation with the book.

9:30 — The librarian goes to a second-grade classroom for a book-sharing period. She listens to a program about bear characters in books. Paddington, Pooh, August, Sal, Goldilocks, the Bears on Hemlock Mountain are some of the "characters" who tell of their adventures, their authors, and illustrators. This was a culminating experience after the librarian had introduced "Bears in Books." In the library six children listen to a tape recording of a folk tale. Three boys study "slide tape" material on astronomy.

9:40 — A committee from the intermediate unit comes to preview filmstrips on life in the sea. The clerk gives them viewers — each sees a filmstrip and takes notes. The committee will discuss important points to bring out when they show the filmstrips to classmates.

10:00 — A first grade comes for a story hour. The librarian tells a story in the listening area.

10:15 — The music consultant checks out recordings for a lesson in appreciation. The librarian has left a new biography of Leonard Bernstein on the table so he may use it or call it to the attention of the children.

10:45 — The librarian meets with a third-grade group for a planned lesson on use of the card catalog. The lesson was reinforced with programed materials.

11:30 — The librarian has a luncheon meeting with a parent committee and the public librarian to plan a program on books for children.

1:45 — The entire group of ninety children in the intermediate team-teaching unit hears the librarian present a lecture about various editions of Aesop's fables through the centuries. In the library, fifth-graders compare reviews of books in *The Horn Book Magazine* and *Young Readers Review.*

3:00 — The librarian meets with the other members of the team-teaching group to evaluate the presentation and to plan further activities.

door opens, the librarian is there to guide selection of books before classroom work begins. The library is open all day. When questions arise in the classroom, when there is research to be done, the consultant is there to guide children in effective use of books.

All children should think of the library as a ready source of information. After talking about the new hamster in the kindergarten, one five-year-old suggested, "Let's take it to the library to find out if it's a boy or girl."

A modern library provides a comfortable atmosphere for groups of children to study and do independent research. Casis School, Austin, Texas. Page, Sutherland, Page—architects. Photograph by Dewey G. Mears.

On some days, the librarian must allow some office time for work in becoming familiar with new materials; the never-ending task of selecting materials is most significant. In the large system, technical processes are centralized; in small schools, time is needed for processing books and library administration. The teaching librarian needs time to prepare the lessons requested by teachers.

Special Services of the Librarian The librarian may plan workshops for teachers to acquaint them with new materials. A professional bulletin board may call attention to interesting articles in current periodicals. The librarian might be the leader of monthly meetings in which teachers review new books for children. Such meetings make it possible to keep informed and provide a forum to compare evaluation of books.

The librarian has the unique opportunity of serving the same children for six or seven years. Each year, the child meets a new teacher, but the librarian remains as a familiar friend who is ready to help with his reading. The librarian sees each child's developing interests, abilities, and needs. When new books come across the desk, individuals who would enjoy them are remembered. Frequently, children reveal their problems to the librarian who may also play a counseling role.

A service club may be organized to help the entire school through giving assistance in the library. Children in such a club will serve by checking books in and out, shelving them, arranging displays, checking overdue books, delivering notices, and housekeeping. Care should be taken to avoid exploiting children in custodial tasks. The librarian may help members of the service club prepare stories to tell younger children. They might make posters, write announcements for the school paper, and plan other ways to advertise new books. They could make booklets recommending titles in special-interest areas such as horses, space, "funny books," mysteries, and sports. With appropriately illustrated covers, these booklets would attract the interest of other children.

The librarian also plans for activities with special-interest groups. Some librarians have established a book club for particularly interested readers. The librarian in one school challenged such a group of gifted children to extend their literary-appreciation skills and reading.[6] Such a club can provide the opportunity for enthusiastic readers from several grade levels to participate in stimulating "book talk," which may not be possible in the regular classroom. Some librarians have worked with such groups in furthering interest in literature through creative writing. In these ways, the librarian can make a unique contribution to the development of an enriched curriculum for gifted children.

The librarian guides individual children in book selection, serves as a resource for teachers and parents, and is involved in direct teaching of library skills and literature. The well-qualified school librarian is truly a key person in the laboratory for learning.

Relation of School and Public Library

The problem of duplication of effort of the school and public library is one that must be resolved. Several questions need to be answered: Who shall pay for library services? Where do students go to read in after-school hours? Why isn't the school library open during the summer months? Many elementary schools have relied upon room col-

The library becomes a center of learning where children use a variety of materials to seek information. Cleveland Public Schools. Photograph used by permission of Elnora Portteus.

lections from the public library, but this arrangement is unsatisfactory. The public library should not be the agency to provide instructional materials for the schools. The purposes of the public library and school library are different; each is needed. Some public libraries have established branches in the elementary school, but this pattern is a poor substitute for a library as an integral part of an instructional materials center. Furthermore, the elementary school librarian has been especially trained to work with teachers and children in the instructional program.

Fenwick's survey of school and public library relationships revealed a low level of communication. For example, many public libraries are overwhelmed when teachers make assignments and give the librarian no warning.[7] Teachers and school librarians need to work closely with the public library,

---

[6]Audrey Carpenter, "More than Plot," *Elementary English*, vol. 34 (October 1957), p. 383–385.

[7]Sara I. Fenwick, "School and Public Library Relationships," *Library Quarterly*, vol. 30 (January 1960), pp. 63–74.

recognizing each has a purpose in providing for educational needs of boys and girls.

CLASSROOM READING ENVIRONMENT

The classroom in most elementary schools will continue to be the center for planning, discussion, study, and evaluation. Creating a stimulating environment that encourages children to read and to use many materials for learning remains the teacher's responsibility.

The Classroom Collection

Sources of Books   The teacher will use many resources to obtain the books needed in the classroom. Extensive classroom collections of books are needed so children will have immediate access to them. Children may work in the instructional materials center and bring books back to the classroom. The librarian may provide a rolling cart of materials related to a unit of study in science or social studies. Paperback books may aug-

Children enjoy sharing a story written by their friends for the classroom library. West Lafayette, Indiana, Public Schools.

ment this changing collection from the materials center. If the central school library cannot provide enough books, teachers may obtain books from the local public library or from a bookmobile. Some state libraries will send boxes of books to the teacher who describes the needs of her group. Federal funds are available for the purchase of books for the elementary school.

Children may share their own books; however, these books seldom provide for informational needs, and often, they represent inferior quality. Books from the attic and basement may be of historical interest but old, frayed copies and poorly written books should not be brought to the classroom even when establishing a library.

Pupil Participation   The involvement of children in the process of selecting, obtaining, and arranging books for the room library can become a significant learning experience. Children may review new books and share in their selection. Excitement mounts as they unpack boxes of books, whether they come from the library or directly from the publisher. They may help with book arrangement and display. Orderly book shelves are more inviting than dusty shelves in disorder. A room library committee can function effectively by planning procedures for use of the classroom library. Sometimes, children's classifications of books will not be in agreement with the Dewey decimal system, but the arrangement they develop will be meaningful to them. At least once a month, the book collection should be changed in the room library. When children share in creating a reading environment, their interest in reading is increased.

Classroom Arrangement

The physical arrangement of the classroom is a factor in enticing children to read. Space should be planned for a reading center in each classroom. If possible, this area should be somewhat secluded and away from the general traffic pattern. Teacher and children should experiment with different arrangements to provide for a library corner. Shelves or bulletin boards may be used as dividers to create a separate area for quiet library reading. Comfortable and colorful chairs may make this a more inviting corner. Frequently, primary grades will have small reading chairs or gaily decorated benches in their reading centers. Children enjoy sitting on the floor. Squares of carpeting samples make good mats. One fifth-grade teacher provided two brightly colored, canvas sling chairs that delighted her gangling pre-adolescents. Inexpensive bookshelves may be constructed from salvaged materials such as boards and bricks. If a library table is not available, the teacher might use a card table or cut a free form of plywood or masonite and place it on a school desk.

Children will gain respect for books when they share in the planning of a reading center. One third-grade class utilized an unused cloak room for their room library. With the aid of the custodian, a committee built and painted bookshelves and a bench. Another committee designed unbleached muslin curtains that were decorated with crayon drawings of their favorite book characters. A rug on the floor completed the homey aspect of this reading center. The children shared in the selection and purchase of their books. The creation of a comfortable, attractive reading center did much to stimulate enthusiasm for reading.

Enticing Children to Read

Bulletin Boards Although the emphasis should be upon *children's* interpretations of literature (see Chapter 12), the teacher and librarian may create some bulletin boards and displays to excite children's interest in reading.

A teacher-prepared bulletin board using pictures plus captions may interest children in one book. Yvonne Meyers, student, Ohio State University.

Initially, the teacher may prepare "participation bulletin boards." This type of bulletin board provides an opportunity for children to identify characters in books, to see relationships between authors and titles, and to develop new reading interests. A riddle bulletin board titled "Do You Know These People?" could be created by the teacher and several children. The viewer must match the picture and the clues of both titles and characters. Another type of participation bulletin board can be made by placing a large map of the United States under a sheet of acetate. Using a wax pencil, similar to grocers' marking pencils, children mark on the map the setting of books that have been listed on a sheet of paper at the right. *Cotton in My Sack, Little House in the Big Woods, The Empty Schoolhouse, The Nickel-Plated Beauty,* and *Island of the Blue Dolphins* are some of the titles that could be included. The pencil marks are easily removed from the acetate by rubbing with a soft cloth. After one child's work is checked, the lines are erased and another child may take his turn.

Information and pictures obtained from a publisher may create interest in the work of one author. Jean Jones and Norma Ahlers, students, Purdue University.

The children may also use maps to trace routes followed by the characters in such books as *Carolina's Courage* by Yates, *Odyssey of Courage* by Wojciechowska, *The Tree in the Trail* by Holling, *Retreat to Glory* by Latham, *African Traveler, the Story of Mary Kingsley*

Imaginative teachers and librarians collect posters and objects to illustrate books.

by Syme, *The Road to Agra* by Sommerfelt, or the route of David in *North to Freedom* by Holm.

A bulletin board may be arranged to show the theme of one book, books of one author, or books on one topic. New books may be introduced and titles may be suggested for summer or holiday reading through the use of interesting bulletin boards. Pictures and dust jackets alone will not interest children in reading; captions, slogans, and questions in eye-catching style are needed to entice children to read.

Displays Alert teachers and librarians collect objects, models, and figurines related to children's literature. Intrigued by these objects, the child may become interested in reading the accompanying books. A display of a blue willow plate and a caption about the book, *Blue Willow*, would capture the attention of middle-grade children. Younger children may be introduced to the characters of Peter Rabbit and Jemima Puddleduck through the delightful Beatrix Potter figurines. The setting of a story may be suggested by arranging objects in a display. Rocks, sand, and a seashell might develop interest in reading McCloskey's *Time of Wonder*, or other books about the sea. To stimulate children's interest in reading, the teacher may make a diorama for the book display shelf (see Chapter 12). A shadow box could be constructed to provide an attractive display setting. The wooden box in the picture on this page is 28 by 18 by 15 inches and lighted from the top by a bulb hidden behind the 3-inch frame. To attract the attention of children and to stimulate further reading, bulletin boards and displays should be changed frequently. Teacher-made displays encourage children to create their own.

The Calendar, a useful quarterly publication of the Children's Book Council,[8] lists sources of material for display. For Book Week each year, well-known illustrators create posters and streamers. *The Calendar* lists free illustrative material from publishers, which may be used to create interest in new books.

Knowing Authors and Illustrators To develop a concept of books as living literature, children need to learn about authors and

_____
[8]*The Children's Book Council, 175 Fifth Avenue, New York, 10010.*

Teachers, librarians, and children may use a shadow box to display favorite books and objects. Here a small doll and old sampler replicate a picture in *Hitty, Her First Hundred Years* by Rachel Field.

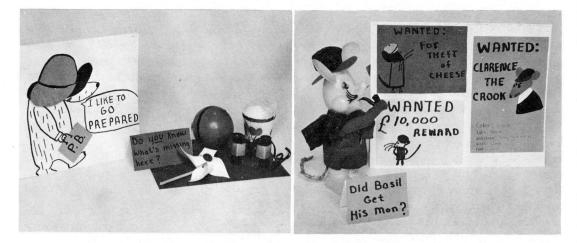

Teachers may interest children in particular books through a variety of classroom displays. Two table displays advertise *A Bear Called Paddington* **by Bond and** *Basil of Baker Street* **by Titus.** Kathleen Lubs, student, Purdue University.

illustrators. Even young children should be told the names of the author and illustrator of the book the teacher is reading. Increased interest in the story will be aroused as the teacher supplies additional information about the way the story came to be written. The following description by Marjorie Flack could be read to the children after they had heard *Walter, the Lazy Mouse:*

New books may be announced with a Town Crier display board. Margaret Thompson, student, Purdue University.

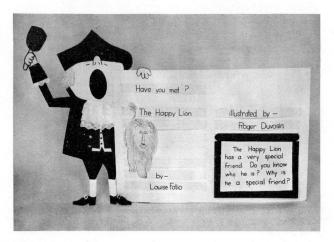

When you read my new book Walter, the Lazy Mouse, *I can just hear you say, "Surely Walter is not real. He must be a make-believe mouse because he wears overalls and goes skating and everything." But Walter is not all make-believe, nor is Mouse Island, where he lives.*

One day I was sketching some frogs by a lily pond, and what do you think I saw? I saw a little white-footed mouse scamper over the lily pads to a tiny island in the pond. That island was this mouse's home, and he lived there alone with the frogs for friends. And he seemed very happy.

I got to thinking about this little mouse, and I began to make up stories about him, make-believe stories (just as you do sometimes about things you see). I named the little mouse Walter in my stories, and I dressed him up in overalls because a mouse looks funny in overalls. Then, I made pictures to go with the stories (just as you do sometimes, I am sure). Soon I had a whole book about Walter, and now it is printed for you to enjoy.[9]

[9]Marjorie Flack, "Even Walter Is Not All Make-Believe," in *Writing Books for Boys and Girls*, Helen Ferris, Editor (New York: Doubleday, 1952), p. 38.

After reading the description of McCloskey's detailed research on Mallard ducks, the teacher could tell the children of the painstaking hours he spent drawing hundreds of sketches. They would be much more excited about the illustrations in *Make Way for Ducklings*[10] if they knew the artist once kept six ducklings in the bathtub of his New York apartment.

Recognizing the need for young children's reading materials about authors and artists, one teacher wrote brief biographical sketches of her first graders' favorite authors and illustrators. These were printed in primary type for the children to read. The story about Maurice Sendak is reproduced below:

MAURICE SENDAK

Maurice Sendak has a dog named Jennie. Jennie is the terrier that you see Max chasing

A five-foot paper sculpture of Mary Poppins calls attention to new books. Victoria Morman, student, Purdue University.

[10]See report of McCloskey's work in creating *Make Way for Ducklings* in Nancy Larrick, *A Teacher's Guide to Children's Books* (Columbus, Ohio: Merrill, 1960), pp. 188–191.

Fourth-graders displayed their letters to authors with the answers and pictures received. Barbara Friedberg, teacher, Washington School, Evanston, Illinois, Public Schools.

3

a new story. It is about my dog. Her name is Jennie. She is Max's dog too — and the Queen's dog in Health Protectu. Here's how she looks.

hello!

Thank you so much for writing to me & I wish you all a very merry Christmas!

Sincerely,
Maurice Sendak

Part of a letter sent by Maurice Sendak to a first grade is reproduced above. The artist graciously answered the children's questions about his illustrations and his childhood. Carol Kowalik, student teacher, Mishawaka, Indiana.

with a fork in the book, Where the Wild Things Are. *Jennie lives in Mr. Sendak's apartment on a quiet Manhattan street in New York City. Mr. Sendak has put Jennie in almost every book he has illustrated in the past eleven years.*

Maurice Sendak was born in 1928. His parents came to this country from Poland. He has a big sister, Natalie, and a big brother, Jack. Maurice began writing his own stories when he was nine or ten. He wrote the stories by hand and drew his own pictures. Now he illustrates his own books and also illustrates books for many other authors.

ADA MCINTOSH, Teacher, Brookline, Mass.

The teacher and librarian can develop a file of biographical information, pictures, and anecdotes about authors and illustrators. Many sources may be used to build such a file. In *The Story behind Modern Books,* Montgomery has collected authors' accounts of the way they were inspired to write and work. Similarly, Ferris compiled brief autobiographies of modern children's authors in *Writing Books for Boys and Girls. The Junior Book of Authors* edited by Kunitz and Haycraft and *More Junior Authors* edited by Fuller are comprehensive resources. These books contain much biographical data, but fewer anecdotes. *Newbery Medal Books, 1922–1955* edited by Miller and Field provides background material about the winners of these awards, while *Caldecott Books 1938–1957* gives similar information on the artists. *Newbery and Caldecott Medal Books, 1956–1965* edited by Kingman updates the series. Biographies of illustrators of children's books are included in the two companion volumes titled, *Illustrators of Children's Books.* The Walck monographs give teachers biographical sketches of such English authors as Potter, de la Mare, Grahame, and Sutcliff.

Several magazines provide current information about authors and illustrators. Frequently *Elementary English* features an article about the work of an author or illustrator. *The Horn Book Magazine* regularly publishes essays about writers and artists of children's literature.

Publishing companies also provide information about authors and illustrators of their books. Biographical data and pictures may be obtained by writing to publishers.

Teachers and librarians will find an author-illustrator file very useful. Publishers' materials, news clippings, magazine articles, teacher's notes, pictures of authors and illustrators, and book jackets may be included in the file for use by children and teacher. This material can be used by children in giving reports about authors or in arranging bulletin boards.

It is sometimes possible to obtain authors or illustrators as speakers for programs, book fairs, or teachers' meetings. At this time, an author may autograph library copies of his book. One school prepared for a visit by Louis Slobodkin by reading all of his works and interpreting them through art activities. The children contributed to a large notebook of pictures and essays, which was presented to their guest. Slobodkin was welcomed by a huge newspaper displayed in the hall. The headline announced his arrival, and all articles were related to his books.

Children may write letters to authors and illustrators to express their appreciation and enjoyment of books. These should be sent in care of the publisher. Some groups might even suggest sequels of a book. One class wrote Walt Disney suggesting Lawson's *The Fabulous Flight* as film material. Sometimes,

children can send their own illustrations of an author's works. Occasionally, letters may request clarification, further information, or biographical material. Children should be taught the value of the author's time and usually, their letters should not require time-consuming answers. Here is an opportunity to teach business courtesy and appreciation.

The teacher or librarian herself may become an author or illustrator. Having day-to-day contact with children, the teacher is sensitive to their interests and preferences. Many teachers have untapped resources of good story material and creative abilities that have not been released. Writing stories and trying them out in classroom laboratories can be an exciting and fascinating experience.

Creative activities described in Chapter 12 will also motivate children's reading. Chapter 13, "Teaching Literature to Children," includes many other ways to entice children to read: the story hour, book reporting, and discussion of books.

BOOKS IN THE ELEMENTARY CURRICULUM

Books in the Reading Instructional Program

"Reading," as part of the language arts, has usually given major emphasis to development of skills. If a child is to find success in reading for information and recreation, he will need many reading skills, such as word recognition, comprehension, and skill in critical reading. Whether they are reading content in social studies, mathematics, science, or literature, children need instruction throughout their reading activities. In order that literature receives its proper emphasis, this volume proposes a definite time for literature as well as time for teaching reading skills. Many books are needed for both the literature and the reading program.

One school prepared for a visit of an author by making an enormous newspaper heralding his arrival. Maryland Avenue School, Bexley, Ohio. Used by permission of Sue Scatterday, principal, and Judith Rosenfeld, librarian.

Beginning Reading Instruction   The initial teaching of reading skills is rapidly changing as new approaches are developed. Materials using an initial teaching alphabet (i/t/a) are now available. Other materials for initial teaching of reading are based upon linguistic patterns. Following the "language experience approach," many teachers use children's own sentences and stories as the basis for beginning reading instruction. Basal readers, too, have changed their content and approaches for developing· initial reading skills. In some classrooms, children are learning to read through use of trade books. Research regarding the "best" method for initial reading instruction gives only tentative findings. Whatever the plan for the beginning phase of reading skill instruction, the goal of reading many materials for information and recreation should be uppermost in the minds of teachers and administrators. From the very beginning, children should have access to books and encouragement to read independently.

The Basal Reading Program   A basal reading program is characterized by a basic text, workbooks, ability groups, and sequential development of skills as suggested in a teacher's manual. Usually all children move through the same steps of the program, although time and rate may be varied. Most basal reading programs recommend use of supplementary texts and trade books for enjoyment and development of further skill.

The Individualized Reading Program   The individualized reading program is based upon principles of seeking, self-selection, and pacing. In this program, instruction is given in a pupil-teacher conference or a skills group organized for a specific purpose. These groups are temporary, lasting only long enough to teach the skill.

A major emphasis of the individualized program is the child's selection of his own reading material. However, it must be recognized that the teacher has already selected a rich and worthwhile collection of books. Discarded, old books or books of poor quality should not be used for the reading instructional program. In order to provide for adequate selection, there should be six to ten books per child. Both text and trade books on many levels should be available. As the child selects a book, it is helpful to suggest that he sample one or two pages before making his choice. If he can read a page and needs assistance with only four to six words, the book probably will be appropriate. Records have shown that children will often read a difficult book, then select an easier one, later returning to a more difficult level.

Individual conferences are essential to provide for diagnosis, instruction, and evaluation. Through the one-to-one relationship, the teacher builds a sense of security by encouraging the child, by showing him specific ways he is improving, by helping him learn how to learn. Usually, teachers will plan for six or seven conferences plus a skills group during an hour reading period. By utilizing other study periods during the day, the teacher will be able to confer with each child twice a week.

Activities in the conference will vary. The child may read a part of the story he especially liked, the funniest part, or the most exciting part. He may read orally a part he has just finished reading silently. The teacher may note the way he solves problems, specific difficulties with word recognition skills, problems of comprehension and interpretation. The child's ability to read familiar as well as unfamiliar material also may be evaluated. Discussion of the book he has completed may center upon plot, theme, characterization, style, or other aspects of critical reading. *The Taxonomy of Literary Skills* (see pages 688–691) provides suggestions for evaluation of reading. During the conference, the teacher and child will check the

A sixth-grader reads her favorite part of *The Borrowers* to her teacher in an individual conference. Jeanne Hilson, teacher, Columbus, Ohio.

reading record kept by the child. Plans for a report to the class or creative activities based upon the book may be discussed.

To conduct a meaningful conference, it is not imperative that the teacher read every book being read by the children. A quick glance at the book, clues from the child, and knowledge of methods of study of literature enable the teacher to guide the child. However, there is much greater opportunity for a meaningful evaluation and sharing of the child's responses if the teacher has read the book. The danger in an individualized program is that children will not be challenged to go beyond a literal understanding of the book. Questions that ask "why," "how," "because of," "in what way," "what do you think" lead to higher levels of thinking than questions that begin with "who, what, when, where." In some schools, teachers have worked together to review and annotate books. Fact and inference questions related to content and literary analysis were written

on cards that would enable the teacher to guide the child's evaluation of the book with greater sensitivity.

Meeting individual differences in rate of learning, in levels of achievement, in interests is only one aspect of the teaching that is concerned with individuality. The individual is more than his scores, more than these ability differences; he is a unique person to be respected for all his qualities. Individualized instruction is a method; concern for individuality is expressed in a total atmosphere, an intangible environment of friendliness, encouragement, respect, freedom, discipline, support, and commitment to holding each child to his best. Respect for individuality means recognition and acceptance of different rates of growth and different styles of learning. Individuals may learn in very large groups and very small groups, but it is always *individual learning.*

Developing Language Skills through Literature

Listening Skills   Children's first literature experiences are derived from auditory images, and listening to stories and poems should continue to be an important part of the literature program. Literature that provides drama, interesting word sounds, and content that stretches the mind in realism and fantasy helps children develop the ability to listen attentively.

However, listening skill is required to go beyond the superficial pleasure of the poem or story. Children need guidance in listening to apprehend literal meaning, to infer deeper meanings, and to appreciate the literary effect of the writing. A planned program of literary study as described in Chapter 13 provides many opportunities to develop listening skill.

Oral Language Skills   As the child talks about books he has enjoyed, there are opportunities to develop vocabulary, to learn to speak so that he maintains the interest of an audience, and to enjoy the sounds of words. Retelling a story to a small group or to children in another class, puppet plays, dramatizations, choral speaking are types of presentation experiences that develop language skill. Sharing books by giving reviews, discussing one book in a small group, reporting to a large group, conducting real or imaginary interviews with authors and illustrators give further oral language experience.

Language Study   Linguistics, the study of speech and language, is a relatively new development in the language arts curriculum for the elementary school. Although scholars study language from different viewpoints, and there is disagreement about theories, linguists do agree that children should study language as it is spoken—as a living, changing thing. Linguists focus on many specialities; some study biological aspects of sound and speech, anthropological linguists study the relationships of language and culture; others emphasize the study of phonology (analysis of sound), structure (word arrangement or syntax), and semantics (meaning and relationship of words to behavior). New approaches to the teaching of grammar and to initial reading instruction have resulted from the influence of linguistic scholars. It has been suggested that children should have experiences that lead to development of such concepts as the following:

- *Language and culture are intimately related. Each shapes the other.*
- *The* sounds *of a language are its basic features, not the words or the grammar.*
- *"Correct" language is the current spoken tongue of the people who use it. There are* non-*standard words and phrases at a given time, but there are no* sub-*standard ones.*
- *Dialects may in time lead to standard languages . . . .*

- *Language is in a constant state of change . . . .*
- *Language functions as a system of interrelated patterns or structures, not as isolated sounds strung together. No language item, linguistically speaking, has any significance out of the context of a language system.*[11]

Materials and guides for study of phonology (sound of language), morphology (study of word forms), form classes (similar to parts of speech), syntax (meaningful combinations of words), history of the language, and dialect have been produced by the Nebraska Curriculum Development Center and other publishers.[12] Knowledge about the language we use was formerly limited to knowledge of prescriptive grammar based upon Latin. As new approaches are tried, it should be remembered that language study in the elementary school should provide for "exploration" and should avoid memorization of terms and analysis of literature that destroys appreciation of literary experience. The Nebraska Curriculum for English points out that:

> *The function of such analysis is not to make children linguists but to make them aware of the unique character of and unique possibilities in our language—to give them some tools for expanding their repertory of linguistic resources or for using consciously and in composition the repertory they already command.*[13]

Through literature, children can become aware that language changes from time to time, from place to place, and from situation

[11]Cited by Harold G. Shane, *Linguistics and the Classroom Teacher* (Washington, D.C.: Association for Supervision and Curriculum Development, 1967), from an article by Charles C. Fries, "Advances in Linguistics," *College English*, vol. 25 (October 1961), pp. 30–37.
[12]Nebraska Curriculum Development Center, "Language Explorations for the Elementary Grades," *A Curriculum for English* (Lincoln, Neb.: University of Nebraska Press, 1966).
[13]Nebraska Curriculum Development Center, p. 1.

to situation; they can compare foreign words and phrases; they can become aware of word meanings and the influence of words upon behavior. (See also Chapter 1, "Style," and Chapter 12, "Developing Sensitivity to Language. ')

Awareness of Language Children become aware of figurative language, symbolism, colloquialism, and sentence patterns as they experience good writing. After a story has been finished, the teacher and children may read and relish particularly enjoyable words, phrases, or paragraphs. Teachers and librarians who value children's language development will select stories that will make a rich contribution to the child's developing language.

Contrast the listening experiences of children who hear the two translations of Hans Christian Andersen's, *The Ugly Duckling*.

a. *Once upon a time there was a proud Mama Duck. She was sitting on four eggs, waiting for them to hatch.*
Every day she said, "Quack! Quack! Just wait till my babies come out of their shells. I always have such beautiful ducklings!"
One day the shells began to go Crack. *One by one three baby ducks stuck their heads out of their shells.*
"Quack! Quack!' the Mama Duck said "Look at them! How beautiful!'
"Peep! Peep!' the baby ducks said. "Look at us!' [14]

b. *Summer-time! How lovely it was out in the country, with the wheat standing yellow, the oats green, and the hay all stacked down in the grassy meadows! And there went the stork on his long red legs, chattering away in Egyptian, for he had learnt that language from his mother. The fields and meadows had large*

woods all around, and in the middle of the woods there were deep lakes.
Yes, it certainly was lovely out in the country. Bathed in sunshine stood an old manor-house with a deep moat round it, and growing out of the wall down by the water were huge dock-leaves; the biggest of them were so tall that little children could stand upright underneath The place was as tangled and twisty as the densest forest, and here it was that a duck was sitting on her nest. It was time for her to hatch out her little ducklings, but it was such a long job that she was beginning to lose patience. She hardly ever had a visitor; the other ducks thought more of swimming about in the moat than of coming and sitting under a dock-leaf just for the sake of a quack with her.
At last the eggs cracked open one after the other—"peep! peep!"—and all the yolks had come to life and were sticking out their heads. [15]

The adapted version is a mere shell of the original by Andersen. Action and conversation have replaced the detailed picture-making qualities of the original. What new words will children learn from hearing the first selection? Yet, how many they may learn from the second!

Young children enjoy the sound and meaning of new words. One six-year-old was heard chanting the words, "humiliated, humiliated" after he had heard it used in Lynd Ward's *The Biggest Bear*. After a group of kindergarten children had enjoyed the story and large photographs of Wright's *The Lonely Doll*, their teacher asked them what *lonely* meant. The children gave various definitions, when finally one small, serious boy said, "To be lonely is to have no one to walk beside you." Who could give a more descriptive definition?

Children of all ages find pleasure in playing with words. They enjoy the sound of

[14]Jean Lee Latham, *The Ugly Duckling*, Illustrated by José Correas and Pablo Ramirez (Indianapolis: Bobbs-Merrill, 1962), unpaged.

[15]Hans Christian Andersen, *The Ugly Duckling*, Illustrated by Johannes Larsen, Translated by R. P. Keigwin, (New York: Macmillan, n.d.), pp. 5–6.

the zany words in the sophisticated ABC book, *I Love My Anteater with an A*. Each letter is represented by an animal who is loved, hated, and named by words beginning with the letter. The animal's home, food, and activities are also described by words beginning with the same sound. The pattern is easy to memorize, and middle-grade children delight in making their own versions.

I love my Dalmatian with a D because he is delightful.
I hate him with a D because he is disagreeable.
His name is Dalrymple. He comes from Denmark.
He lives on dates and dumplings,
And he is a deep sea diver.[16]

With the development of language maturity, children begin to understand the multiple meanings of words. They appreciate making and reading puns, and can laugh with Johnny when his Grandfather Orchard recounts the time that he ran away from a bear and says, "Better to have a bear in the orchard than an Orchard in the bear."[17] The idiosyncrasy of the English language is fully exploited in Sage's book *If You Talked to a Boar*. Homonyms are grouped together by such verse as:

If a tree was BARE/Would it look like a BEAR?
If you had a HARE. . ./Would he comb his HAIR?[18]

In *My Great-Grandfather and I*, Krüss gives children nonsense, serious poems, and stories told by an old seaman in Helgoland. After composing a poem about the foolish cockroaches who had a newspaper bearing only the word "Raestaetae," he explained

that the word has no meaning. The old man and the boy compose rhymes involving word meanings and nonsense.

The multiple meanings of some words produce different images, and the results may be ludicrous. Clifford's story *A Bear Before Breakfast* is based upon children's attempts to understand why their father insists he is a "bear" early in the morning. Children love Parrish's literal-minded housekeeper *Amelia Bedelia* who misinterprets notes regarding her duties. Told to "change the towels," she cuts holes in them; upon reading "draw the drapes," she sketches a picture; and while she does not see why she has to dress the chicken, she does make a pair of trousers for him! Children are quick to think of other possible perplexing situations for Amelia Bedelia such as "switch the light," "poach the egg," or "whip the cream." The animals in Welty's fantasy, *The Shoe Bird*, misinterpret a boy's comment, "Shoes are for the birds." Giving the phrase a literal meaning, Gloria, the goose, plans a party and invites the birds to the store where Arturo, the helpful parrot, "reduces shoes" to a proper size for the birds. There is a moral in this tale, but full appreciation is derived from awareness of subtle word meanings.

Humor in *The Phantom Tollbooth* by Juster is also derived from awareness of words and phrases. When Milo, a bored boy, drives through a phantom toll booth he comes to the land of Expectations, where he is then urged to go Beyond Expectations. Because he "wasn't thinking" he stopped in the Doldrums, but soon came to Dictionopolis when he started thinking. In this strange land, synonyms are given for most of the words used.

"Well, then," said Milo, not understanding why each one said the same thing in a slightly different way, "wouldn't it be simpler to use one? It would certainly make more sense."
"Nonsense."

[16]Dahlov Ipcar, *I Love My Anteater with an A* (New York: Knopf, 1964), unpaged.

[17]Lynd Ward, *The Biggest Bear* (Boston: Houghton Mifflin, 1952), p. 10.

[18]Michael Sage, *If You Talked to a Boar*, Illustrated by Arnold Spilka (Philadelphia: Lippincott, 1960), unpaged.

"Ridiculous."
"Fantastic."
"Absurd."
"Bosh," they chorused again, and continued.[19]

Probably, the teacher will have to help children become aware of the humor by explaining many meanings, such as "short shrift." The children will find the "light meal" and "square meal" very amusing. When other words are given, Milo said, "I didn't know I was going to have to eat my words." The banquet food includes a rigmarole, ragamuffin, just desserts, and a synonym bun.

Appreciation for the well-chosen word or phrase or a rich, descriptive passage is best accomplished by reading and discussing excellent literature. Even young children can appreciate fine writing that creates vivid word pictures. The poetic prose of Tresselt's *White Snow Bright Snow* is thoroughly enjoyed by six- and seven-year-olds. It can help older boys and girls identify and recognize similes and metaphors.

In the morning a clear blue sky was overhead and blue shadows hid in all the corners.
Automobiles looked like big fat raisins buried in snow drifts.
Houses crouched together, their windows peeking out from under great white eyebrows.
Even the church steeple wore a pointed cap on its top.[20]

After reading a picture-story book, the teacher may reread a part to call attention to use of the descriptive details such as those of Jay's walk in *A Pocketful of Cricket* by Caudill.

Queen of the meadow grew on the hillside below the lane. The great pinkish crowns nodded on tall stalks.
A gray spider slept in a web between two of the stalks.

A yellow butterfly sucked nectar from one of the pink flowers. Jay stood and watched it fan its wings—open and shut, open and shut.[21]

Awareness of a variety of style and sentence patterns may contribute to a beginning understanding of linguistics. In the same book, children in primary grades can note the sentences in the text do not follow the usual noun-verb pattern so frequently found in their readers. A lesson about movables could be developed. For example, children could listen to the differences between "He waded across the creek" and "Across the creek he waded."

He gathered the cricket in both hands. Carrying it gently, he hurried after the cows.
Across the creek he waded.
Along the lane he trudged in the dust.
Into the barn he drove the cows. His father was waiting to milk them.[22]

If the teacher is reading *Secret of the Andes* children in the middle grades may take time to discuss the beauty and meaning of such passages as: "The boy's thoughts were whirling like the foaming rapids on the far side of the valley," or "Curiosity can leap the highest wall: an open gate is better."[23]

The writings of Virginia Sorensen contain many descriptive phrases, particularly the book *Miracles on Maple Hill*. In the passage which follows, Marly ponders the multiplicity of feelings that can be associated with one sound, sight, or word:

How so many things could be in a few words was something else Marly didn't know. But it was the same way the whole feel of school can be in the sound of a bell ringing. Or the way the whole feeling of spring can be in one robin on a fence post.[24]

[19]Norton Juster, *The Phantom Tollbooth*, Illustrated by Jules Feiffer (New York: Epstein & Carroll, 1961), p. 40.
[20]Alvin Tresselt, *White Snow, Bright Snow* (New York: Lothrop, 1947), p. 20.
[21]Rebecca Caudill, *A Pocketful of Cricket*, illustrated by Evaline Ness (New York: Holt, Rinehart and Winston, 1964), unpaged.
[22]Caudill.
[23]Ann Nolan Clark, *Secret of the Andes* (New York: Viking, 1952), pp. 14–15.
[24]Virginia Sorensen, *Miracles on Maple Hill* (New York: Harcourt, 1956), p. 4.

Mrs. Sorensen's vivid description of the beauty of the changing seasons at Maple Hill should be savored with children. Her ability to evoke a visual image is clearly shown in this description of Marly's first impression of a frosty morning in the country:

When Marly woke up the next morning, there was another miracle right outside her window. The sun was coming up, and it was clear and frosty out. And there were ten million little crystals shining on every single branch of every single tree, down to the littlest twig. The tree right next to her window was a wilderness of shining threads, as if every branch, every twig, was spun from ice. Among the threads hopped the cold little black figures of birds. Marly felt as if she could never in the world look at it long enough.[25]

The rich prose of Laura Ingalls Wilder recreates the shimmering beauty and terror of the endless prairie in her book, *The Long Winter.* She describes Laura and Carrie's walk through the tall slough grass in words that prompt images of sight, smell, sound, and touch:

Laura pushed ahead between the thick clumps of grass-stems that gave way rustling and closed again behind Carrie. The millions of coarse-grass stems and their slender long leaves were greeny-gold and golden-green in their own shade. The earth was crackled with dryness underfoot, but a faint smell of damp lay under the hot smell of the grass. Just about Laura's head the grass-tops swished in the wind, but down at their roots was a stillness, broken only where Laura and Carrie went wading through it.[26]

After children have experienced the humor and pathos of the story, *Charlotte's Web,* they may take time to appreciate the author's ability to impart the sense of smell in the following description of Wilbur's barnyard:

The barn was very large. It was very old. It smelled of hay and it smelled of manure. It smelled of the perspiration of tired horses and the wonderful sweet breath of patient cows. It often had a sort of peaceful smell—as though nothing bad could happen ever again in the world.[27]

While dialect and colloquial language make difficult reading for children, they enjoy hearing it read. Children in the middle grades can learn to appreciate the regional variations of language patterns. They recognize that the characters in Lenski's *Strawberry Girl* do not use correct grammar, but they enjoy the color and flavor of such idiomatic phrases as "gettin' biggety," "totin' water," "right purty," and "plumb good." They can discuss the meanings and origins of such idioms and look for idiomatic expressions in their own speech. Carl Sandburg captured the flavor of the "wilderness lingo" in describing the speech of young Abe Lincoln and his family:

His folks talked like other folks in the neighborhood. They called themselves "pore" people. A man learned in books was "eddicated." What was certain was "sartin." . . .
A man silent was a "say-nothin." They asked "Have ye et?" There were dialogues, "Kin ye?" "No, I cain't." And if a woman had an idea of doing something she said, "I had a idy to." They made their own words. Those who spoke otherwise didn't belong, were "puttin on." This was their wilderness lingo; it had gnarled bones and gaunt hours of their lives in it.[28]

Only as children are led to enjoy the well-chosen phrase, rich descriptive prose, or poetry, will they become aware of the power of words. Too much discussion and analysis may disgust children forever. Teachers should remember that enjoyment of literature should be the primary goal. Apprecia-

[25]Sorensen, p. 50.
[26]Laura Ingalls Wilder, *The Long Winter* (New York: Harper & Row, 1953, 1940), p. 20.
[27]E. B. White, *Charlotte's Web* (New York: Harper & Row, 1952), p. 13.
[28]Carl Sandburg, *Abe Lincoln Grows Up* (New York: Harcourt, 1926), pp. 40–41.

tion of fine writing can enhance enjoyment; it should never be forced.[29]

Books about Words   Children may also develop a sensitivity to the sound and meaning of words by discussing some of the books that make "words" their major theme. One of the most familiar books about words and their meanings is *A Hole Is to Dig* by Ruth Krauss. This book is a collection of definitions given by nursery-school children. In keeping with their stage of language development, the children define common words in terms of their function. "A nose is to blow," "Snow is to roll in," "Hands are to hold," and "A hole is to dig." The capering, gay figures by Maurice Sendak make this an entertaining book. Six- and seven-year-olds enjoy making their own definitions after they have heard these.

Karen's Opposites helps children understand antonyms through humorous illustrations by the Provensens. This book shows two little girls in a *shallow* puddle and looking at a *deep* well; asking why are there *none* when looking at a hen's nest, and seeing her friend has them *all* in a basket. As Karen and her friend greet each other, the picture caption is "one *Beginning*"; the last page shows the two girls glumly tugging a doll, and the caption says "one *End*." Children enjoy making their own books of opposites. One second-grader pictured a United States flag and a flag of the Soviet Union with the captions, "Free" and "Slave."

Word Twins by White is a less interesting book, but Palczak's illustrations for ball-bawl, bare-bear, eight-ate, pane-pain would also stimulate children to make their own books of homonyms. Homonyms are also the subject for a clever book titled *Monkeys Have Tails* by Van Gelder. Using a question and rhyme approach, the author asks:

Windows have panes/Do they come from a cold?
Monkeys have tails/Can they be told?[30]

Sparkle and Spin by Ann and Paul Rand is an imaginative book about words. With colorful pictures and simple, rhythmic prose, the authors talk about different kinds of words. The introductory page gives this description:

What are words?
Words are how what you think inside
Comes out.
And how to remember what you might
forget about.

This book also gives examples of onomatopoetic words, homonyms, and descriptive words. The title of the book is derived from these gay lines:

Some words are gay and bright
And full of light
like tinsel and silver
and sparkle and spin,
while lurk and murk
or moan and groan
are just as dark as night.[31]

Older boys and girls will delight in the amusing collection of odd words found in Alastair Reid's *Ounce Dice Trice*. The author suggests that the reader should get the feel of the words by beginning with a sound and letting it grow. The title of the book is taken from the first three numbers of an imaginary counting vocabulary. Lists of "light words" and "heavy words" are included. Names for elephants and names for cats are suggested. Among the "Odds and Ends" is this descriptive list:

A Blunder of Boys
A Giggle of Girls

---

[29]See Chapter 12 for suggestions about language development through children's writing.

[30]Rosalind van Gelder, *Monkeys Have Tails* (New York: McKay, 1966), unpaged.

[31]Ann and Paul Rand, *Sparkle and Spin* (New York: Harcourt, 1957), unpaged.

A Consternation of Mothers
A Grumbling of Buses[32]

This book calls attention to the many different sounds of words and invites further experimentation by the reader.

Eve Merriam has written two books about relatively unfamiliar names for groups of animals and the young of animals. In *A Gaggle of Geese*, Galdone has illustrated groups as a lepe of leopards, a bale of turtles, a skulk of foxes, a pride of lions. The introduction notes that all the category groupings are to be found in the Oxford English Dictionary, and it leads the reader to explore further, "Bevies and swarms and flights galore:/So many, many words to explore!" *Small Fry* by Merriam follows this same pattern by introducing unusual, but true, names of baby animals, birds, and fish.

Fifth- and sixth-graders who are studying the Greek and Roman myths will be interested in Asimov's *Words from the Myths*. By exploring the traditional myths, the author points out the roots of hundreds of words that are a part of our daily language. For example, he tells the story of how Achilles was dipped in the River Styx to make him immortal. However, since his mother held him by the heel, this remained a vulnerable spot. Since that time, the term "Achilles heel" has meant a weak point in an otherwise solid defense. This is a very readable book and a fascinating one. Pronunciations of all the Greek gods and goddesses are given in context.

Mary O'Neill has written a book of poems about our language titled *Words Words Words*. Some of the poems tell of the dark unknown days before man had a written language; others present the history of our language; still others, describe the function of certain words; while the last group define the dimensions of words like "Hope," "Happi-

ness," and "Patience." Part of the closing poem follows:

THE WONDERFUL WORDS
Never let a thought shrivel and die
For want of a way to say it,
For English is a wonderful game
And all of you can play it.
All that you do is match the words
To the brightest thoughts in your head
So that they come out clear and true
And handsomely groomed and fed—
For many of the loveliest things
Have never yet been said. . . .[33]

These books about words may call attention to the many and varied uses and meanings of the words in our language. Only as children read words in context can they appreciate the depth of meaning and the beauty that can be conveyed through the appropriate use of words.

Books about Language Several books present the history of our language in readable form for primary children. Alexander's *The Magic of Words* and Waller's *Our American Language* explain briefly the origin of written and spoken language. *The Magic of Words* presents the various means of communication by which man expresses his ideas and feelings. *Our American Language* emphasizes the many sources from which our language is derived, and the fact that the American language is now spreading back throughout the countries of the world from which it came.

The First Book of Words by the Epsteins gives a thorough overview of our changing language. Not only is the history of the language traced, but sources for the creation of new words are identified. The fact that some words such as victrola, icebox, and cookstove are disappearing is also pointed out. Middle-

[32]Alastair Reid, *Ounce Dice Trice* (Boston: Little, Brown, 1958), p. 18.

[33]Mary O'Neill, *Words Words Words* (New York: Doubleday, 1966), p. 63.

grade children would be interested in the description of slang words and the meanings of first and last names.

Teachers and junior high school students will find the Lairds' *The Tree of Language* a useful reference. This book includes the derivations of many words with fascinating histories.

Many of these books *about* language develop a respect *for* language. After Mauree Applegate has described language and how to use it, she has this to say about it:

> Our language is the story of America itself. It is a glorious mixture from many nations. The words of kings, of freemen, and of slaves are in it. It has been fashioned from the sweat and dreams of farmers, sailors, cowboys, steelworkers, weavers, traders. It wears the mark of doctors, of teachers, of men of God, of lawyers, of scientists.
> It is so rich a language that it can express the great thoughts of great men, yet it is so simple that it can whisper the dreams of a child.
> It is so beautiful a language that it can conjure up the sound of the wind in the pines, and catch the happiness of a summer day.
> It is the voice of democracy. It is your language, yours to have and to hold, yours to enrich, yours to respect, yours to protect, and above all, yours to use as well as you know how.[34]

Books for Science Education

Trends in Teaching Science   From the nature study movement of the thirties to the organized science program emphasizing acquisition of information in the physical sciences as well as biological sciences, science education has moved toward emphasis on methods of science. Inquiry training,[35] processes of discovery, and science skills are currently stressed in science curricula. Concepts once held too difficult for children are included in primary grades. Scholars in science, especially physics and astronomy, worked with educators and psychologists as they tried out materials and teaching methods with children.[36]

Textbooks, too, place emphasis on creating situations through which children discover structure. Thus, science is now more concerned with observing, classifying, measuring, recording, experimenting, and generalizing. These major objectives of science cannot be achieved through reading of texts or trade books. However, many of the projects and texts have swung the pendulum too far from the use of books. A few textbook guides suggest use of trade books. For example, one manual notes, "These annotated bibliographies remind the pupil that reading is truly a part of the scientist's work."[37] A limited number of books is listed for each unit. Books are mentioned as a possible source of information in a text based upon the AAAS skills approach,[38] but the suggested lists are very brief. Reports of most curriculum projects have not included use of books.

Contribution of Books to Science   Trade books can contribute to the total science program if they are written with accuracy and understanding of the nature of science. As an author presents facts, the young child should sense the curiosity and excitement about discovery that is an integral aspect of

---

[34]Mauree Applegate, *The First Book of Language and How to Use It* (New York: F. Watts, 1962), p. 60.

[35]J. R. Suchman, "Inquiry Training: Building Skills for Autonomous Discovery," *Merrill-Palmer Quarterly* (July 1961).

[36]See Educational Services Incorporated, *Quarterly Report* (Watertown, Mass.: ESI); Commission on Science Education, *Science, a Process Approach, Commentary for Teachers* (Washington, D.C.: American Association for the Advancement of Science, 1964); University of California, Elementary School Science Project, Berkeley, Calif., 1963–1966.

[37]John Navarra and Joseph Zaffroni, *Today's Basic Science* (New York: Harper & Row, 1964), Book 4.

[38]George Mallinson, *et al.*, *Science* (Morristown, N.J.: Silver Burdett, 1965).

science. The well-written trade book can provide extended, up-to-date information not found in textbooks. Many trade books make it possible for the child to perceive relationships or make generalizations after he has had firsthand experience. Trade books can provide questions and guide him in planning experiments. Topics such as evolution and reproduction are frequently avoided in textbooks but may be included in trade books. The social problems resulting from scientific or technological advances may be considered in trade books, whereas the text frequently omits such concepts. Biography, fiction, or an informational book can present the history of science. Trade books can encourage hobbies related to science, and help children interpret the environment they explore on camping trips or vacations. More than this, the trade book can encourage individual study of living things in schools where the new science curricula tend to emphasize only the development of skills in methods of science. Examples of science trade books and criteria for their evaluation are presented in Chapter 9.

Books for the Social Studies Curriculum

Trends in Teaching Social Studies In the past, the term "social studies" has referred to history and geography. The typical social studies curriculum began with a study of the home and family and extended outward to "old world neighbors" in sixth grade. "Social education" was included through room activities, student councils, and "current events" reports. Recently, scholars have begun to work with educators to identify concepts from all social sciences that can be taught in the elementary school. Anthropology, economics, sociology, and political science are included in the elementary school curriculum projects. The development of modes of inquiry that are characteristic of the discipline is a new emphasis.

"Social study" is perhaps the more appropriate term. Children engage in social study when they study evidences of human variety, change, or pattern. More non-Western studies are being emphasized. Instead of studying several countries, children will research one country in depth in order to learn a method of study.

In many of the programs, problems for study are selected by the scholars, and do not emerge from children's life experience. For example, McCauley found that twenty-one of sixty-eight supervisors in five eastern states reported emphasis had moved away from social living, international understanding, and social education.[39] Prepackaged materials will include tapes, films, artifacts, picture cards, and materials for game theory activities.

Current projects indicate a trend toward the teaching of separate subjects. To some leaders, citizenship education should be achieved through instruction in the basic social sciences. Others hold the view that attention should be given to citizenship skills and attitudes through study of current life problems in school and community.

Citizenship education, broadly defined, is basically concerned with the development of decent human beings who respect the rights of others. Viewing imaginative literature as a source for learning about the diversity of humanity, the needs of humans, and ways of solving the human problems of birth, growth, love, hate, and death, the curriculum-makers may recognize the value of a planned literature curriculum in the elementary school.

Implications of Trends for Use of Books Teachers and librarians face four tasks in using the newer social studies programs. Some of the programs and text series in-

---

[39]J. D. McCauley, "Brush Fires in the Social Studies," *Education*, vol. 84 (January 1964), pp. 266–270.

clude suggestions of trade books; many do not provide this help. The first task is to examine the books suggested by the scholars and educators who have prepared texts or unit materials. In some cases, only superior readers could gain information from the books. For example, the Greater Cleveland program suggests *The First Book of the American Revolution* by Morris and *You and the Constitution of the United States* by Witty for third grade; both would be difficult for most children of this age group. Even more questionable was this suggestion in a project guide for first-grade anthropology: "Utilize a scheduled library period to look for information about the Arunta, Kazuk, and American families."[40] *Igloos, Yurts and Totem Poles* by Boer and the *National Geographic* magazine were suggested for first graders. The program for Economic Education, *Our Working World,* for second grade includes the text of *The Little House* by Burton, but the illustrations are omitted.[41] If the teacher follows the discussion guide, and emphasizes economic changes, the total impact of the book, including the emotional content, may be lost. The guide also suggests *Crow Boy* by Yashima, and says, "The teacher might suggest, for discussion, Crow Boy's talents could later turn toward scientific work where careful observation and recordings are important."[42] In this instance, the entire meaning of the story is distorted because this character was portrayed as a boy who could not learn language skills and was taunted by his peers. Although an understanding teacher helps Chibi (Crow Boy) gain a feeling of success, Chibi's lonely life of poverty continues after he leaves school at sixth grade. "Scientific work" would be impossible for this boy, but he is respected for his steadfastness, integrity, and his one talent, imitating crows. Thus, the first task of the teacher is to check the books suggested in texts and programs to see if they are appropriate for ability levels within the class and if the total effect of the book is limited or distorted by discussion from one viewpoint only.

The second task of the teacher in planning for the social studies is to find books that will extend textbook understandings. An examination of social studies texts and teachers guides revealed that suggestions for further reading are very limited. For example, one text for sixth grade listed three books about Africa, two gave no titles related to the units, and one gave an annotated list. Also, new books should be purchased each year to enrich the social studies content. Many resources are available to help the teacher locate informational books, fiction, biography, and poetry related to the topic to be studied (see Appendix B).

A third task of the teacher is to select books related to current events. The demands upon the time in the elementary school day seem to preclude time for discussion of current events, and the trend in experimental programs seems to be away from use of current problems to initiate study. However, children are part of these times; they need guidance in understanding people and events. The weekly schedule could allow time for discussion, and a special shelf of books and magazines could be provided for materials related to current problems. During the Viet Nam war, there were headlines about Buddhists. Children asked, "What is Buddhism?" *Their Search for God* by Fitch, *The Story of Religion* by Pyne, and *The World's Great Religions,* adapted by Watson from the *Life* edition, were made available. When a Peace Corps volunteer spoke at a school, the book by Lavine and Mandelbaum, *What Does a Peace Corps Volunteer Do?* was dis-

---

[40] *Anthropology Curriculum Project, University of Georgia, Publication No. 1* (Athens, Ga.: University of Georgia, 1965).

[41] Lawrence Senesh, *Our Working World, Families at Work,* Resource Unit (Chicago: Science Research Associates, 1963).

[42] Senesh, p. 63.

played alongside *Beyond the Sugar Cane Field, UNICEF in Asia* by Shotwell. These books may be used for browsing and for special reports during the current events period. In this way, current events becomes more than a show and tell time.

A fourth task of the teacher is to identify books that provide information and concepts related to the teaching-learning units.[43] If a study of cultural change in developing countries is being planned, for example, the book *Meeting with A Stranger* by Bradley might be analyzed. Books for the social studies include such original sources as documents, diaries and journals, biography, fiction and nonfiction written in particular periods of time, informational books, historical fiction, and modern realistic fiction. Historical fiction and biography is presented in Chapter 8, realistic fiction in Chapter 7, and informational trade books in Chapter 9.

Books and Mathematics

Trade books can contribute to children's understanding of mathematics. Counting books in primary grades aid in building number concepts; they are especially important in schools in culturally disadvantaged areas (see Chapter 3). Aliki has illustrated two books by Kohn that introduce geometry, *Everything Has a Shape* and *Everything Has a Size*. The same artist adds humor to information in two books by Jonas, *New Ways in Math* and *More New Ways in Math*. Children in fifth and sixth grades will enjoy the well-designed illustrations of Bell in the book, *String, Straightedge and Shadow, the Story of Geometry*, by Diggins. This is really a history of man's thinking about forms in nature, their use in construction, and finally, the abstract rules of geometry. Although modern textbooks provide background in the "new math," children often can gain insights through a well-written trade book such as *Numerals, New Dresses for Old Numbers* by the Adlers. The diagrams would help the child to understand bases other than ten. Hogben's *The Wonderful World of Mathematics* is a book to use many times. Children pore over the pictures showing the history of mathematics; some read it for themselves, but the teacher may find it wise to read parts of this book when appropriate in the mathematics class.

A guide published by the National Council of Teachers of Mathematics provides an extensive list and includes books that develop concepts of size, space, and time.[44] The author of the guide points out concepts of comparison in such books as *The Carrot Seed* by Krauss and *Farther and Faster* by McCullough. For intermediate grades, it is suggested that concepts of time and size are developed in *Big Tree* by the Buffs, and that the idea of scale drawing is shown in *Understanding Maps* by Tannenbaum and Stillman. As children read or hear stories, they do build concepts of number, but teachers should avoid overemphasizing this aspect. *Many Moons*, by Thurber, does indeed use ideas of number when the various men of the court describe the moon. However, it certainly would destroy the literary quality of the book if the teacher placed too much emphasis upon the number ideas expressed.

Books in Art Education

Art education that aims to develop perception and facilitate expression of meanings in many forms will make use of children's literature. Children's experiences in creating

---

[43]For an excellent description of utilization of a book in an anthropology unit, read Taba's analysis of concepts regarding learning in Mirsky's *Thirty-One Brothers and Sisters* in Hilda Taba, *Curriculum Development: Theory and Practice* (New York: Harcourt, 1962), p. 368–378.

[44]Clarence Hardgrove, *The Elementary and Junior High School Mathematics Library* (Washington, D.C.: National Council of Teachers of Mathematics, 1960).

their own responses to the environment are enriched and extended as they learn of art history. The photographs and drawings of prehistoric art in the caves at Altamira and Lascaux in *The Caves of the Great Hunters* by Baumann communicate the drama of art of ages past. Art in household artifacts is illustrated in *The Art of Ancient Egypt* and *The Art of Lands in the Bible* by Glubok. *Famous Paintings* and *Looking at Art* by Chase are examples of books that give children excellent reproductions of paintings and interpretative comments about composition and the way the artist expresses his ideas. Teachers should also be aware of information on the development of art reported in encyclopedias. *Compton's Encyclopedia* includes numerous excellent reproductions, for example. Art in other lands is discussed by Price in *The Story of Moslem Art* and by Glubok in *The Art of the Eskimo* and others of her series. Gracza utilizes a most interesting approach in presenting *The Ship and the Sea in Art*. She writes, "The artist has recorded, interpreted and symbolized man and his bond with the sea. He has taken us all out to sea to share in its wonder and glory."[45] As she discusses mosaics, sculpture, and paintings, she gives information on technique. The process of making Winslow Homer's *etching*, the technique of Monet's *impression* and Signac's *pointillism*, and the process of *abstraction* by Feininger are explained in the clear and interesting text. Unfortunately, color reproductions were not included, so the impact is often diminished. The author asks, "If you stand alone on a long, quiet beach and look out at the ocean and up at the sky, what do you see? Does the sky have a limit? Does the sea have an end? What do you wonder? What do you feel?"[46] Literature and visual art are integrated, and children learn the ways many artists have answered.

Books can serve to sharpen awareness and to awaken sensitivity. The titles of Borten's books, *Do You See What I See?* and *A Picture Has a Special Look,* suggest the development of ideas about lines, colors, and patterns in the visual world. Spilka's *Paint All Kinds of Pictures* shows the relationship of color and line to mood and feeling. For children in middle and upper grades, Downer's books are rich sources of art experience. In *Discovering Design,* the author uses photographs of leaves, webs, and waves to show rhythm, balance, and pattern. *The Story of Design* illustrates design through the ages. Kirn's book of rubbings, *Full of Wonder,* makes the child aware of the tactile quality of things around him.

The classroom teacher or art teacher will find many of the technique books useful. *Masks and Mask Makers* by Hunt would be very helpful after viewing the film, *The Loon's Necklace.* In this outstanding film, a legend is told through artistic movement of authentic masks. *Print Making with a Spoon* by Gorbarty and *Printing for Fun* by Ota are examples of two how-to-do-it books that open doors to creativity instead of holding children in conformity.

Biographies of artists convey the human problems, trials, and successes of artists of the ages. *Picasso, Durer, Michelangelo, Van Gogh,* and *Gainsborough* are among the biographies by Ripley. Not only does she tell of the artist, she shows the influences of his time. Full-page reproductions face the page of explanatory text.

More importantly, art and literature are integrated as children are exposed to a wide variety of illustrations and guided in developing awareness of color, design, texture, use of space, balance, and rhythm. The total *image* communicates meanings through form, color, and design.

Influences of artists upon illustrators of children's books can be noted as books are enjoyed. Sasek's dots of color in *This Is Paris* reflect the technique of the impressionists,

[45]Margaret Gracza, *The Ship and the Sea in Art,* designed by Robert Clark Nelson (Minneapolis: Lerner, 1965), p. 6.
[46]Gracza, p. 22.

while the flat planes of color in a double-page painting of the Valley of Jezrul in *This Is Israel* are reminiscent of Cezanne's work. In *The White Land*, Raymond Briggs creates a field glowing in warm sunshine, very similar to Van Gogh's field with crows. The influence of cubism is evident in Rand's illustrations for *I Know a Lot of Things*. Abstract design as expressed by painters of the twentieth century has influenced many illustrators of children's books. Look at the brilliant color blobs and design of Tinkelman's two red owls under a cold moon in *Who Says Hoo?* The surrealistic influence is noted in one picture in which the branch is not attached to a tree. When Burt Dow splashes paint and grease on the pink lining of the whale's stomach, McCloskey creates a design that might be traced directly back to Kandinsky. The collage of Braque and others has recently been used by Lionni in *Inch by Inch*, Keats in *The Snowy Day*, and Wynants for *Noah's Ark*. Wildsmith's brilliant, merging color is arranged in geometric figures. The small squares of color in costumes, furniture, and houses are similar to the effects in many of Klee's paintings. In one of the Provensens' illustrations for *Aesop's Fables*, a bouquet of flowers on a table is similar in design to some of the paintings by Matisse. The influence of pop art is seen in *Kangaroo & Kangaroo* by Braun and illustrated by McMullan.

The influence of art of a period or a country is often reflected in illustration. Chinese art qualities are integrated in Burkert's richly colored illustrations for Andersen's *The Nightingale*, and delicate brush paintings decorate the sides of each page. In *Tico and the Golden Wings*, Lionni has adapted motifs of art of India. The folk art of Sweden is used in *Sven's Bridge* by Anita Lobel.

Illustrations may be studied in the art class to learn more about materials and ways artists have expressed ideas and emotions. *The Lively Art of Picture Books* might be shown to help teachers and children "learn to look." This Weston Woods film portrays different ways artists have illustrated trees, cats, churches, and villages. In the same way, children might compare illustrations for the same fairy tale, stories such as "The Three Bears," or for Aesop's fables. They might look for ways animals have been portrayed—from Ylla's photographs, to Newberry's charcoal drawings, to Marcia Brown's woodcuts.

Knowledge of literature is needed to understand some art, especially sculpture. Figures from mythology are frequently sources of art or become part of the symbols used in the work.

Librarians and classroom teachers will need to work with art teachers to help them realize there are rich resources in children's books for art appreciation. All are concerned with perception of new relationships, balances, textures, meanings in life.

Books for the Music Program

There is a wide range of materials for music, just as for art education. Song books, particularly books of folk songs, can supplement the material in textbooks. *Folk Songs of China, Japan, Korea* was edited by Dietz and Park. This book includes an authentic recording of the songs and gives the pronunciation of words in the original language. A single Christmas carol, *Bring a Torch, Jeanette Isabella*, is beautifully portrayed by Adrienne Adams. *The Fox Went Out on a Chilly Night* by Spier, *Frog Went A-Courtin'* by Langstaff, and *Mommy, Buy Me a China Doll* by the Zemachs are three folk songs depicted in rich color and design. Nonny Hogrogian's misty, heathery pictures capture the droll humor of the Scottish folk song *Always Room for One More* by Nic Leodhas (see Chapter 4, folk songs).

Numerous books give information about instruments of the orchestra and the composition of music. *The First Book of Music* by Norman and *All About the Symphony and What It Plays* by Commins are examples of books from series that give interesting information. Kettelkamp's book, *Horns,* is the fourth in his series about instruments. These small books would be especially useful as children make decisions about the instruments they want to learn to play. Also, the author shows how to make simple instruments.

Chappell has designed beautiful books based on the theme and music of *The Sleeping Beauty, The Nutcracker,* and *The Magic Flute.* A German version of Prokofieff's *Peter and the Wolf,* illustrated delightfully by Frans Haacken, is now available in the United States. The scratchboard illustrations show white, green, or red lines on black pages. Action is vigorous as the duck is caught in the wide-open mouth, as Peter climbs the tree, and as the bird flies near the wolf. A proud Peter heads the hunters and captured wolf in a grand finale. Bulla has written good background stories for the Wagner opera, *The Ring and the Fire; Stories from the Nibelung Operas Retold.*

Biographies of musicians, composers, and conductors can play an important part in the music classes. Ewen's biographies, *Leonard Bernstein, The Story of George Gershwin,* and *The Story of Arturo Toscanini* have a livelier style than do the biographies of Wheeler and Duecher, *Ludwig Beethoven and the Chiming Tower Bells, Mozart, the Wonder Boy,* and others. Older children will enjoy *Famous Negro Music Makers* by Hughes. However, this book was published in 1955, and children will miss the contemporary musicians.

WORKING WITH PARENTS AND THE COMMUNITY

Parents and Children's Reading

The Parent's Role   The teacher's responsibility in education includes parent education. An important task is to help parents recognize their own role in guiding their children's reading. The teacher can help the parent to assist the child in finding books he can read, to encourage regular home reading, and to understand the child and his level of reading achievement. Parents can be urged to take preschool and primary children to the library, allow them to browse and select some books independently, while guiding selection of others. The school can provide information about library story hours and encourage parents to take their young children to the library for this weekly experience.

Parents often are not aware of the values of building the child's own library. Space should be provided in the home for each child's books. Book gifts should be encouraged among family and friends, and children enjoy making lists of books they would like to own. Money received for a birthday or Christmas gift can be taken by the child to the bookstore where he can select volumes for his personal library.

In busy family life, it is difficult for parents to find time for family reading activities. Through P.T.A. meetings, study groups, and individual conferences, the teacher can suggest ways of planning a quiet time at home for the child's individual reading, and encourage family read-aloud sessions. Just as adults accept book suggestions from others and enjoy discussing their reading with friends and family, children need companionship in reading experiences.

Book Lists for Parents   Another way teachers and librarians can help parents guide children's reading is by providing book lists. They can send home a list of good books on the child's interest level for the parents to read aloud. A list of inexpensive paperbacks could be sent for purchase for the home library. As a unit of study is developed, the classroom teacher can send a brief note to the parents explaining the study and suggesting books to read. Books for Christmas and other holidays may be listed in the school news bulletin for parents. Suggestions for summer reading can be sent home before the summer vacation. Parents will appreciate information from the teacher regarding children's magazines, weekly newspaper subscriptions, and book clubs. Also, a list of suggested television and radio programs may be supplied.

In many schools, a special bookshelf provides material to guide parents in studying children and in dealing with the problems of rearing them. Among these books, parents should find Duff's *Bequest of Wings* and Larrick's *A Parent's Guide to Children's Reading.* Such books will provide additional suggestions to guide selection of books for children. A competent speaker or study-group consultant can help parents consider criteria of good literature. Well-known authors and illustrators of children's books may be invited to describe their work. Children's book editors, the local librarian, and managers of bookstores also may serve as resource people for parent-study programs.

Parent Conferences The individual conference is an effective means of helping parents with children's reading. Here, the teacher listens and learns more about the child. In turn, he may assist the parent in finding techniques for observing the child in different ways to discover his special needs and interests. As the parent senses the teacher's acceptance of him and his problems, he feels free to express his concerns for the child. The teacher and the parent then can cooperate to plan ways to guide the child's reading.

Through this informal conference, the teacher can communicate his enthusiasm for books. In some communities, this will mean stressing the value of borrowing books from the library. In other socio-economic groups, the discussion may center upon improving the child's literary tastes, extending his reading interests, and suggesting titles to be

purchased for the child's library. Regardless of the level of these conferences, it is the teacher's personal interest in the child's growth and enthusiasm for learning and books that are the crucial factors in improving parent-child-school relationships.

Parents in the School In a democratic society, the schools recognize the importance of involving parents in solving school problems. If schools desire to establish a library or increase the mediocre supply of books they currently have, they should ask for the aid of the people most directly concerned, the parents of the children who will be reading the books. Parent groups may contribute money from a recent benefit to purchase books, but the schools would do better to make an effort to obtain tax funds for a library and a trained librarian. If this is not possible, fathers can make shelves for a little-used storage room, or even for the halls of the school. Mothers may solicit books and money or participate in mending and arranging library materials. Parents may supervise and help children unpack and shelve books. When they have the opportunity to observe children eagerly waiting for a new book or joyously rereading a favorite one, no one will need to convince them of the vital role that books can play in the lives of their children. If given an opportunity to participate, parents will become firm supporters of the library program.

Extending Community Interests

Book Fairs Parents may also become interested in children's books by participating in planning for a book fair (see Appendix E). This is a display of new children's books that is usually a representative sampling of several publishing firms, sent out on a loan basis. Book fairs may be organized by the local bookseller, but more frequently, they are the result of widespread community

Browsing at a book fair is fun and creates interest in new books. The Ohio State University School.

participation. Planning may be initiated by a state or public library, the school, or other agency. It is especially important that librarians or teachers work with the parent committees in selecting books. Unaware of the need for quality, some parents have accepted the selections of book jobbers, only to find few good books available for display. Books may be purchased or ordered, and the sponsoring group usually receives a small percentage of the profits. Groups of children may visit the fair and make lists of the books most desired. Teachers have a responsibility for planning with children as they go to a book fair. Children should bring paper and pencil to list books they would like for the home or school library. Before going to the fair, they might discuss ways of learning about a book very quickly, such as scanning chapter headings, looking at a few illustrations, reading a page to see if it seems too easy or too difficult. Children may look

for new titles by favorite authors and illustrators. This is also a good time to discuss a balance of reading—biography, fiction, informational books and poetry.

Resource People In every community, there are people with interesting backgrounds, hobbies, or talents who could share their accomplishments with school children. Frequently, such people can serve to promote further interest in children's literature. The fabric of our children's literary heritage is woven with strands from many countries. If a community is fortunate enough to have someone who can recall the tales of his old country, children will enjoy hearing them. The local community may have a chapter of the National Story League. Its members tell stories in community centers, libraries, and at parties. Some citizens will have hobbies that may be connected with children's literature. In one community, a woman who collected dolls had many that were replicas of well-known storybook characters displayed in the school library. An archeologist shared some of his early relics and small digging tools for a book display on early civilizations. Book artists, editors, or authors may be willing to discuss their work. Faculty members might cooperate with parent groups in setting up a file of resource people in the community who will share their interests with children.

Concern for the development of lifetime reading habits is not the sole responsibility of the school or library. One of the best radio programs about children's books was initially sponsored by a large department store whose book buyer made many people increasingly aware of the importance of good children's books. Local newspapers can be encouraged to give publicity to book fairs, lectures, and children's activities during Book Week and throughout the year. Reviews of the latest children's books should be included in the book review sections of the newspaper, with, perhaps, special emphasis given to them during Book Week and Christmas. Local librarians or interested teachers could review the new Caldecott and Newbery Award books following their announcements in March.

Service clubs may take the responsibility for bringing children and books together through such projects as reading to hospitalized children, establishing story hours in community centers, and encouraging children's theatrical activities.

All of these suggestions grow out of the philosophy that the home, school, and community should work cooperatively to create an effective reading environment.

SUGGESTED ACTIVITIES

1. Prepare a plan for introducing an author or illustrator to one class. You might write a publisher for information, read speeches or articles of the author or illustrator, and use biographical references.
2. Begin a file of anecdotes and information about authors and illustrators that can be used with elementary school children.
3. Spend a day in an elementary classroom. Observe the children's responses to materials and teacher's questions and comments that promote thinking. Note the way literature is taught and opportunities that need further development.
4. Spend a day in an instructional materials center. Observe the ways individual children select books and use materials. Notice the ways teachers and librarians work together. Become familiar with the types of equipment available.
5. Learn to operate a tape recorder, filmstrip, movie, opaque, and overhead projectors. Prepare transparencies that might be used in a literature program.
6. Prepare a bulletin board that would introduce children to books by one author or illustrator, books on one theme, or that would create interest in reading.
7. Bring to class examples of selections from literature that could be used to develop children's appreciation for language.
8. Examine several textbooks in science or social studies. Become familiar with content at different grade levels and prepare an annotated bibliography of appropriate trade books.
9. Examine several textbooks for teaching reading and language arts. Become familiar with the kind of material included at different grade levels.
10. Examine paperback books available for children. Note the range of content, types of literature, and authors whose works are available. If possible, observe children buying books in a school paperback store.
11. If you plan to be a teacher, talk with a school librarian about her work. Find out about the various roles she plays in serving children and teachers. What are her expectations? If you plan to be a school librarian, talk with a teacher, using a similar approach.
12. Attend a community book fair. Observe the children's reactions as you look at the books.
13. Listen to children's radio and television programs and evaluate their effectiveness in stimulating reading.
14. Preview some of the films and filmstrips related to children's literature. Plan the introductory and follow-up activities for one of them.
15. Listen to several recordings based upon children's books. Compare them with the original text.
16. Plan a section of a handbook for parents that would give suggestions for ways to encourage children's reading.

17. Discuss children's reading with the parent of a school-age child. What is the reading environment of the home? What are the parents' expectations of the school?

RELATED READINGS

1. Baker, Augusta. *Recordings for Children.* New York: The New York Public Library. Using sound criteria for evaluation, a committee selects musical recordings and recordings of poetry and prose. Brief annotations are included.

2. Blough, Glenn, and Julius Schwartz. *Elementary School Science and How to Teach It.* Third edition. New York: Holt, Rinehart and Winston, 1964.
"Helping Children Learn Science," Chapter 3, includes a discussion of "Reading to Find the Answers." Criteria for selecting science books are presented, pp. 70–71. Trade books for children and teachers are listed according to science topics. A list of magazines for science will be especially helpful.

3. Brown, James W., Richard Lewis, and Fred Harcleroad. *A-V Instruction, Materials and Methods.* Second edition. New York: McGraw-Hill, 1964.
Techniques for selection and use of filmstrips, films, tape recordings, radio, and television are given in addition to good bibliographies of sources for further information.

4. Burns, Paul C., and Alberta L. Lowe. *The Language Arts in Childhood Education.* Skokie, Ill.: Rand McNally, 1966.
This college text emphasizes the "guided discovery" method in the teaching of language arts from oral composition and listening, to linguistics, semantics, and literature.

5. Children's Book Council, Inc. *Speakers List.* New York: CBC, 175 Fifth Avenue.
A list of authors and illustrators who will speak to school, professional, and community groups is made available for each region of the United States.

6. Clements, H. Millard, William Fielder, and B. Robert Tabachnick. *Social Study, Inquiry in Elementary Classrooms.* Indianapolis: Bobbs-Merrill, 1966.
The inquiry approach applied to social studies is illustrated with examples of classroom practices. The use of books, documents, and observation and survey techniques illustrates interrelationships of fields of study when children are engaged in study of social problems.

7. Dale, Edgar. *Audio-Visual Methods in Teaching.* Revised edition. New York: Holt, Rinehart and Winston, 1954.
A comprehensive work on theory of audio-visual instruction. The "cone of experience" is a significant concept. Classroom suggestions for English and reading include procedures and sources of materials.

8. Draper, Marcella K., and Louise H. Schwietert. *A Practical Guide to Individualized Reading.* New York: Board of Education, City of New York, Bureau of Educational Research, Publication No. 40, 1960.
One of the most useful guides on individualized reading, this bulletin gives suggestions for organizing the classroom, conducting the teacher-pupil conference, keeping records, and evaluating progress of children's reading skills.

9. Educational Film Library Association. *Film Evaluation Guide.* New York: Educational Film Library Association, 250 West 57th Street, 1965.
Evaluation of films available in 1965, published 1946–1964, are made by committees of the association. The evaluation gives subject, age level, price, distributor, and a rating of its merit.

10. *Educational Leadership,* "Centers for Learning," vol. 21 (January 1964).
The articles in this issue of the Journal of the Association for Supervision and Curriculum Development describe the function of the learning center and role of the librarian in such a center.

11. Fleming, Robert S., Editor. *Curriculum for Today's Boys and Girls.* Columbus, Ohio: Merrill, 1963.
Purposes of the elementary school curriculum are clearly stated and examples of classroom practices that foster creativity, critical thinking, and values are described. The discussion of unit teaching expands ideas in this volume.

12. Gega, Peter. *Science in Elementary Education.* New York: Wiley, 1965.
Examples of science units illustrate development of hypotheses and science skills.

13. Horn, George F. *Bulletin Boards.* New York: Reinhold, 1962.
Clever cartoons and succinct captions demonstrate good bulletin board display. The section about three-dimensional display is especially good.

14. Kambly, Paul E., and John E. Suttle. *Teaching Elementary School Science.* New York: Ronald, 1963.
Methods of teaching science and a valuable list of resources for children and teachers.

15. Lowrie, Jean E. *Elementary School Libraries.* New York: Scarecrow Press, 1961.
A report of a study of ten school libraries describes the work of the librarian for curriculum enrichment, reading guidance, library instruction. Practices related to work with teachers and the community are also reported.

16. Manolakes, George. *The Elementary School We Need.* Washington, D. C.: Association for Supervision and Curriculum Development, 1965.
The concise statement of guidelines for the organization of classes, use of time, and instructional procedures provides a sound foundation for planning the elementary program.

17. Minor, Ed. *Preparing Visual Instructional Materials.* New York: McGraw-Hill, 1962.
Mounting techniques and lettering techniques will help the teacher or librarian prepare good bulletin boards. Suggestions for making transparencies may be very useful.

18. Muessig, Raymond H., and Vincent R. Rogers. *Social Science Seminar Series.* Columbus, Ohio: Merrill, 1965.
Scholars in the fields of history, geography, anthropology, economics, sociology, and political science have written separate volumes that present major concepts of each field. Classroom activities and related literature are suggested by specialists in education.

19. *National Tape Recording Repository.* Boulder, Colo.: Bureau of A-V Instruction, Stadium Building, Room 348.
This catalog lists programs taped by university A-V centers, public schools, junior leagues, and the U.S. Office of Education.

20. Nebraska Curriculum Development Center. *A Curriculum for English, Language Explorations for Elementary Grades.* Lincoln, Neb.: University of Nebraska Press, 1966. Also distributed by NCTE, Champaign, Ill.
One of a series of guides for the teaching of English, this book gives basic information about linguistic study in meaningful terms. Linguistic study based upon literature is presented in examples for each grade level.

21. Norton, Eloise. *Authors on Tape.* Ann Arbor: Michigan Audio-Visual Center, Frieze Building, 720 East Huron.
Authors, illustrators, and editors answer questions that have been suggested by children.

22. Pearson, Mary D. *Recordings in the Public Library.* Chicago: American Library Association, 1963.
School librarians and teachers will find the chapter about record selection, with its bibliography of selection aids, very useful.

23. Phillips, Ward H., and John O'Lague. *Successful Bulletin Boards.* Dansville, N.Y.: Owen, 1966.
Photographs illustrate bulletin boards designed for such purposes as providing

information, stimulating curiosity, and displaying children's work. Ideas for suspended bulletin boards are included.

24. Randall, Arne. *Murals for Schools.* Worcester, Mass.: Davis, 1956.
    Numerous photographs of murals in many media will give the teacher or librarian ideas for development of murals. Evaluation suggestions are included.

25. Schultz, Morton J. *The Teacher and Overhead Projection.* Englewood Cliffs, N.J.: Prentice-Hall, 1965.
    The value of the overhead projector for effective visual communication in each subject area is presented. Suggestions for use of transparencies for oral storytelling, poetry, and analysis of writing are included.

26. Smith, Nila Banton. *Reading Instruction for Today's Children.* Englewood Cliffs, N.J.: Prentice-Hall, 1963.
    A comprehensive and sound discussion of the teaching of reading. Nearly one-third of the book deals with the basic skills of word identification and comprehension. Part 3 is devoted to "Developing Interest and Taste in Reading Literature."

27. Taba, Hilda. *Curriculum Development, Theory and Practice.* New York: Harcourt, 1962.
    Sources of the curriculum and the teacher's role in relating learning theory to classroom practice are discussed in this book. Use of trade books to develop concepts in a discipline is described. The discussion of teaching units is excellent.

28. Tannenbaum, Harold E., and Nathan Stillman. *Science Education for Elementary School Teachers.* Boston: Allyn and Bacon, 1960.
    In Chapter Four, "Using Reference Materials," the authors illustrate development of reference skills by describing classroom situations. The librarians in this anecdote guide development of skill in using encyclopedias and other references.

29. Walck *Monographs.* New York: Walck.
    A biographical series about well-known writers of children's books including *Walter de la Mare, Beatrix Potter, E. Nesbit, Rudyard Kipling, Kenneth Grahame, R. L. Stevenson,* and others. Information about the author's life, quotations from diaries and letters, and critical comments about the works of the author are given.

CHAPTER REFERENCES

1. Adams, Adrienne. *Bring a Torch, Jeannette Isabella.* New York: Scribner, 1963.
2. Adler, Irving and Ruth. *Numerals, New Dresses for Old Numbers.* New York: John Day, 1964.
3. Aesop. *Aesop's Fables.* Selected and adapted by Louis Untermeyer. Illustrated by A. and M. Provensen. New York: Golden Press, 1965.
4. Alexander, Arthur. *The Magic of Words.* Illustrated by R. S. Alexander. Englewood Cliffs, N.J.: Prentice-Hall, 1962.
5. Andersen, Hans Christian. *The Nightingale.* Translated by Eva Le Gallienne. Illustrated by Nancy Ekholm Burkert. New York: Harper & Row, 1965.
6. ————*The Ugly Duckling.* Translated by R. P. Keigwin. Illustrated by Johannes Larsen. New York: Macmillan, n.d.
7. Applegate, Mauree. *The First Book of Language and How to Use It.* Illustrated by Helen Borten. New York: F. Watts, 1962.
8. Asimov, Isaac. *Words from the Myths.* Illustrated by William Barss. Boston: Houghton Mifflin, 1961.
9. Baumann, Hans. *The Caves of the Great Hunters.* Revised edition. New York: Pantheon, 1962.
10. Beatty, Patricia. *The Nickel-Plated Beauty.* Illustrated by Liz Dauber. New York: Morrow, 1964.
11. Boer, Friedrich, Editor. *Igloos, Yurts and Totem Poles.* New York: Pantheon, 1957.

12. Bond, Michael. *A Bear Called Paddington.* Illustrated by Peggy Fortnum. Boston: Houghton Mifflin, 1960.
13. Borten, Helen. *Do You See What I See?* New York: Abelard-Schuman, 1959.
14. ———*A Picture Has a Special Look.* New York: Abelard-Schuman, 1961.
15. Boston, L. M. *The Castle of Yew.* Illustrated by Margery Gill. New York: Harcourt, 1965.
16. Bradley, Duane. *Meeting with a Stranger.* Illustrated by E. Harper Johnson. Philadelphia: Lippincott, 1964.
17. Braun, Kathy. *Kangaroo & Kangaroo.* Illustrated by Jim McMullan. New York: Macmillan, 1965.
18. Briggs, Raymond. *The White Land.* New York: Coward-McCann, 1963.
19. Brink, Carol Ryrie. *Caddie Woodlawn.* Illustrated by Kate Seredy. New York: Macmillan, 1936.
20. Buff, Mary and Conrad. *Big Tree.* New York: Viking, 1963, 1946.
21. Bulla, Clyde Robert. *The Ring and the Fire.* Illustrated by Clare and John Ross. New York: Crowell, 1962.
22. ———*The Sword in the Tree.* Illustrated by Paul Galdone. New York: Crowell, 1956.
23. Burton, Virginia Lee. *The Little House.* Boston: Houghton Mifflin, 1942.
24. Caudill, Rebecca. *A Pocketful of Cricket.* Illustrated by Evaline Ness. New York: Holt, Rinehart and Winston, 1964.
25. Chappell, Warren. *The Nutcracker.* New York: Knopf, 1958.
26. ———*Sleeping Beauty.* New York: Knopf, 1961.
27. Chase, Alice Elizabeth. *Famous Paintings.* Revised edition. New York: Platt & Munk, 1964.
28. ———*Looking at Art.* New York: Crowell, 1966.
29. Clark, Ann Nolan. *Secret of the Andes.* Illustrated by Jean Charlot. New York: Viking, 1952.
30. Clifford, Eth. *A Bear Before Breakfast.* New York: Putnam, 1962.
31. Commins, Dorothy B. *All About the Symphony and What It Plays.* Illustrated by Warren Chappell. New York: Random House, 1961.
32. Crawford, Phyllis. *Hello, the Boat!* Illustrated by Edward Laning. New York: Holt, Rinehart and Winston, 1938.
33. Dalgliesh, Alice. *The Bears on Hemlock Mountain.* Illustrated by Helen Sewell. New York: Scribner, 1952.
34. ———*The Courage of Sarah Noble.* Illustrated by Leonard Weisgard. New York: Scribner, 1954.
35. Dietz, Betty Warner, and Thomas Choonbai Park, Editors. *Folk Songs of China, Japan, Korea.* New York: John Day, 1964.
36. Diggins, Julia. *String, Straightedge and Shadow, the Story of Geometry.* New York: Viking, 1965.
37. Downer, Marion. *Discovering Design.* New York: Lothrop, 1947.
38. ———*The Story of Design.* New York: Lothrop, 1963.
39. Edmonds, Walter D. *The Matchlock Gun.* Illustrated by Paul Lantz. New York: Dodd, Mead, 1941.
40. Epstein, Sam and Beryl. *The First Book of Words, Their Family Histories.* Illustrated by Laszlo Roth. New York: F. Watts, 1954.
41. Ewen, David. *Leonard Bernstein.* Philadelphia: Chilton, 1960.
42. ———*Story of Arturo Toscanini.* New York: Holt, Rinehart and Winston, 1960.
43. ———*Story of George Gershwin.* New York: Holt, Rinehart and Winston, 1943.
44. Farley, Walter. *The Black Stallion.* Illustrated by Keith Ward. New York: Random House, 1941.
45. Ferris, Helen, Editor. *Writing Books for Boys and Girls.* New York: Doubleday, 1952.
46. Fitch, Florence Mary. *Their Search for God, Ways of Worship in the Orient.* Photos

selected by Edith Bozyan, Beatrice Creighton, and the author. New York: Lothrop, 1947.

47. Flack, Marjorie. *Walter the Lazy Mouse.* Illustrated by Cyndy Szekeres. New York: Doubleday, 1963.

48. Fuller, Muriel, Editor. *More Junior Authors.* New York: H. W. Wilson, 1963.

49. Gates, Doris. *Blue Willow.* Illustrated by Paul Lantz. New York: Viking, 1940.

50. Glubok, Shirley. *The Art of Africa.* New York: Harper & Row, 1965.

51. ————*The Art of Ancient Egypt.* Designed by Gerard Nook. New York: Atheneum, 1962.

52. ————*The Art of Lands in the Bible.* Designed by Gerard Nook. New York: Atheneum, 1963.

53. ————*The Art of the Eskimo.* Designed by Oscar Krauss. Special photos by Alfred H. Tamarin. New York: Harper & Row, 1964.

54. Gorbarty, Norman. *Print Making with a Spoon.* New York: Reinhold, 1960.

55. Gracza, Margaret. *The Ship and the Sea in Art.* Designed by Robert Clark Nelson. Minneapolis: Lerner, 1965.

56. Henry, Marguerite. *Misty of Chincoteague.* Illustrated by Wesley Dennis. Skokie, Ill.: Rand McNally, 1962, 1947.

57. Hogben, Lancelot. *The Wonderful World of Mathematics.* Illustrated by André Charles Keeping and Kenneth Symonds. Maps by Marjorie Saynor. New York: Doubleday, 1955.

58. Holling, Holling C. *The Tree in the Trail.* Boston: Houghton Mifflin, 1942.

59. Holm, Ann. *North to Freedom.* New York: Harcourt, 1965.

60. Hughes, Langston. *Famous Negro Music Makers.* New York: Dodd, Mead, 1955.

61. Hunt, Kari, and Bernice Wells Carlson. *Masks and Mask Makers.* New York: Abingdon, 1961.

62. Ipcar, Dahlov. *I Love My Anteater with an A.* New York: Knopf, 1964.

63. Jonas, Arthur. *More New Ways in Math.* Illustrated by Aliki. Englewood Cliffs, N.J.: Prentice-Hall, 1964.

64. ————*New Ways in Math.* Illustrated by Aliki. Englewood Cliffs, N.J.: Prentice-Hall, 1962.

65. Juster, Norton. *The Phantom Tollbooth.* Illustrated by Jules Feiffer. New York: Random House, 1961.

66. Keats, Ezra Jack. *The Snowy Day.* New York: Viking, 1962.

67. Kettelkamp, Larry. *Horns.* New York: Morrow, 1964.

68. Kingman, Lee, Editor. *Newbery and Caldecott Medal Books, 1956–1965.* Boston: Horn Book, 1965.

69. Kirn, Ann. *Full of Wonder.* Cleveland: World Publishing, 1959.

70. Kohn, Bernice. *Everything Has a Shape.* Illustrated by Aliki. Englewood Cliffs, N.J.: Prentice-Hall, 1964.

71. ————*Everything Has a Size.* Englewood Cliffs, N.J.: Prentice-Hall, 1964.

72. Krauss, Ruth. *The Carrot Seed.* Illustrated by Crockett Johnson. New York: Harper & Row, 1945.

73. ————*A Hole Is to Dig.* Illustrated by Maurice Sendak. New York: Harper & Row, 1952.

74. Krüss, James. *My Great-Grandfather and I.* Translated by Edelgard von Heydekampf Bruhl. Illustrated by Jochen Bartsch. New York: Atheneum, 1964.

75. Kunitz, Stanley J., and Howard Haycraft, Editors. *The Junior Book of Authors.* Second edition, revised. New York: H. W. Wilson, 1951.

76. Laird, Helene and Charlton. *The Tree of Language.* Illustrated by Ervine Metzl. Cleveland: World Publishing, 1957.

77. Langstaff, John. *Frog Went A-Courtin'.* Illustrated by Feodor Rojankovsky. New York: Harcourt, 1955.

78. Latham, Jean Lee. *Retreat to Glory*. New York: Harper & Row, 1965.
79. ————*The Ugly Duckling*. Illustrated by José Correas and Pablo Ramirez. Indianapolis: Bobbs-Merrill, 1962.
80. Lavine, David, and Ira Mandelbaum. *What Does a Peace Corps Volunteer Do?* Introduction by Sargent Shriver. New York: Dodd, Mead, 1964.
81. Lawson, Robert. *The Fabulous Flight*. Boston: Little, Brown, 1949.
82. Lenski, Lois. *Cotton in My Sack*. Philadelphia: Lippincott, 1949.
83. ————*Strawberry Girl*. Philadelphia: Lippincott, 1945.
84. Leodhas, Sorche Nic. *Always Room for One More*. Illustrated by Nonny Hogrogian. New York: Holt, Rinehart and Winston, 1965.
85. *Life* Magazine. *The World's Great Religions*. New York: Golden Press, 1958.
86. Lionni, Leo. *Inch by Inch*. New York: Obolensky, 1960.
87. ————*Tico and the Golden Wings*. New York: Pantheon, 1964.
88. Lobel, Anita. *Sven's Bridge*. New York: Harper & Row, 1965.
89. McCloskey, Robert. *Blueberries for Sal*. New York: Viking, 1948.
90. ————*Burt Dow, Deep-Water Man*. New York: Viking, 1963.
91. ————*Homer Price*. New York: Viking, 1943.
92. ————*Make Way for Ducklings*. New York: Viking, 1941.
93. ————*Time of Wonder*. New York: Viking, 1957.
94. McCullough, John, and Leonard Kessler. *Farther and Faster*. New York: Crowell, 1954.
95. Mahony, Bertha *et al.*, Compilers. *Illustrators of Children's Books, 1744–1945*. Boston: Horn Book, 1961, 1947.
96. Merriam, Eve. *A Gaggle of Geese*. Illustrated by Paul Galdone. New York: Knopf, 1965.
97. ————*Small Fry*. Illustrated by Garry MacKenzie. New York: Knopf, 1965.
98. Miller, Bertha E. *et al.*, Compilers. *Illustrators of Children's Books, 1946–1956*. Boston: Horn Book, 1958.
99. Miller, Bertha Mahony and Elinor Whitney Field, Editors. *Caldecott Medal Books: 1938–1957*. Boston: The Horn Book, 1957.
100. Miller, Bertha Mahony and Elinor Whitney Field, Editors. *Newbery Medal Books, 1922–1955*. Boston: Horn Book, 1955.
101. Milne, A. A. *Winnie the Pooh*. Illustrated by Ernest H. Shepard. New York: Dutton, 1926.
102. Mirsky, Reba Paeff. *Thirty-one Brothers and Sisters*. Illustrated by W. T. Mars. Chicago: Follett, 1952.
103. Montgomery, Elizabeth Rider. *The Story behind Modern Books*. New York: Dodd, Mead, 1949.
104. Morris, Richard B. *The First Book of the American Revolution*. Illustrated by Leonard Everett Fisher. New York: F. Watts, 1956.
105. Norman, Gertrude. *First Book of Music*. Illustrated by Richard Gackenbach. New York: F. Watts, 1954.
106. O'Dell, Scott. *Island of the Blue Dolphins*. Boston: Houghton Mifflin, 1960.
107. O'Neill, Mary. *Words Words Words*. New York: Doubleday, 1966.
108. Ota, Koshi, *et al. Printing for Fun*. New York: Obolensky, 1960.
109. Parrish, Peggy. *Amelia Bedelia*. Illustrated by Fritz Siebel. New York: Harper & Row, 1963.
110. Potter, Beatrix. *The Tale of Jemima Puddle-Duck*. New York: Warne, 1936, 1908.
111. ————*The Tale of Peter Rabbit*. New York: Warne, 1902.
112. Price, Christine. *Story of Moslem Art*. New York: Dutton, 1964.
113. Prokofieff, Serge. *Peter and the Wolf*. Illustrated by Frans Haacken. New York: F. Watts, 1961.
114. Provensen, A. and M. *Karen's Opposites*. New York: Golden Press, 1963.

115. Pyne, Mable. *The Story of Religion.* New York: Houghton Mifflin, 1954.
116. Rand, Ann and Paul. *I Know a Lot of Things.* Illustrated by Paul Rand. New York: Harcourt, 1956.
117. ————*Sparkle and Spin.* Illustrated by Paul Rand. New York: Harcourt, 1957.
118. Reid, Alastair. *Ounce Dice Trice.* Illustrated by Ben Shahn. Boston: Little, Brown, 1958.
119. Ressner, Phil. *August Explains.* Illustrated by Crosby Bonsall. New York: Harper & Row, 1963.
120. Ripley, Elizabeth. *Durer.* Philadelphia: Lippincott, 1958.
121. ————*Gainsborough.* Philadelphia: Lippincott, 1964.
122. ————*Michelangelo.* New York: Walck, 1953.
123. ————*Picasso.* New York: Lippincott, 1959.
124. ————*Vincent Van Gogh.* New York: Walck, 1954.
125. Rojankovsky, Feodor. *The Three Bears.* New York: Golden Press, 1948.
126. Sage, Michael. *If You Talked to a Boar.* Illustrated by Arnold Spilka. Philadelphia: Lippincott, 1960.
127. Sandburg, Carl. *Abe Lincoln Grows Up.* Illustrated by James Daugherty. New York: Harcourt, 1956, 1928.
128. Sasek, M. *This Is Israel.* New York: Macmillan, 1962.
129. ————*This Is Paris.* New York: Macmillan, 1959.
130. Shotwell, Louisa. *Beyond the Sugar Cane Field, UNICEF in Asia.* Cleveland: World Publishing, 1964.
131. Sommerfelt, Aimée. *The Road to Agra.* Illustrated by Ulf Aas. New York: Criterion, 1961.
132. Sorensen, Virginia. *Miracles on Maple Hill.* Illustrated by Beth and Joe Krush. New York: Harcourt, 1956.
133. Spier, Peter. *The Fox Went out on a Chilly Night.* New York: Doubleday, 1961.
134. Spilka, Arnold. *Paint All Kinds of Pictures.* New York: Walck, 1963.
135. Syme, Ronald. *African Traveler, the Story of Mary Kingsley.* Illustrated by Jacqueline Tomes. New York: Morrow, 1962.
136. Tannenbaum, Beulah, and Myra Stillman. *Understanding Maps, Charting the Land, Sea, and Sky.* Illustrated by Rus Anderson. New York: McGraw-Hill, 1957.
137. Thurber, James. *Many Moons.* Illustrated by Louis Slobodkin. New York: Harcourt, 1943.
138. Tinkelman, Murray. *Who Says Hoo?* New York: Golden Press, 1963.
139. Travers, Pamela L. *Mary Poppins.* Illustrated by Mary Shepard. New York: Harcourt, 1934.
140. Tresselt, Alvin. *White Snow, Bright Snow.* Illustrated by Roger Duvoisin. New York: Lothrop, 1956.
141. Updike, John. *The Magic Flute.* Adapted and illustrated by John Updike and Warren Chappell. New York: Knopf, 1962.
142. Van Gelder, Rosalind. *Monkeys Have Tails.* New York: McKay, 1966.
143. Waller, Leslie. *Our American Language, a Book to Begin On.* New York: Holt, Rinehart and Winston, 1961.
144. Ward, Lynd. *The Biggest Bear.* Boston: Houghton, Mifflin, 1952.
145. Welty, Eudora. *The Shoe Bird.* New York: Harcourt, 1964.
146. Wersba, Barbara. *The Land of Forgotten Beasts.* Illustrated by Margot Tomas. New York: Atheneum, 1964.
147. Wheeler, Opal. *Ludwig Beethoven and the Chiming Tower Bells.* Illustrated by Mary Greenwalt. New York: Dutton, 1942.
148. Wheeler, Opal, and Sybil Deucher. *Mozart, the Wonder Boy.* Illustrated by Mary Greenwalt. New York: Dutton, 1941.
149. White, E. B. *Charlotte's Web.* Illustrated by Garth Williams. New York: Harper & Row, 1952.

150. White, Mary Sue. *Word Twins*. New York: Abingdon, 1961.

151. Wilder, Laura Ingalls. *The Little House in the Big Woods*. Illustrated by Garth Williams. New York: Harper & Row, 1953, 1932.

152. ————*Little House on the Prairie*. Illustrated by Garth Williams. New York: Harper & Row, 1953, 1935.

153. ————*The Long Winter*. Illustrated by Garth Williams. New York: Harper & Row, 1953, 1940.

154. Witty, Paul, and Julilly Kohler. *You and the Constitution of the United States*. Illustrated by Lois Fisher, Chicago: Childrens Press, 1948.

155. Wojciechowska, Maia. *Odyssey of Courage*. Illustrated by Alvin Smith. New York: Atheneum, 1965.

156. Wright, Dare. *The Lonely Doll*. New York: Doubleday, 1957.

157. Wynants, Miche. *Noah's Ark*. New York: Harcourt, 1965.

158. Yashima, Taro. *Crow Boy*. New York: Viking, 1955.

159. Yates, Elizabeth. *Carolina's Courage*. Illustrated by Nora S. Unwin. New York: Dutton, 1964.

160. Zemach, Harve and Margot. *Mommy, Buy Me A China Doll*. Chicago: Follett, 1966.

12

STIMULATING CREATIVE ACTIVITIES THROUGH LITERATURE

The following stories grew out of a discussion subsequent to the reading of *Burt Dow: Deep Water Man* by McCloskey. The children had identified the type of story and the incidents that introduced the element of fantasy. In order to help the children to better understand the difference between fantasy and realistic writing, the teacher suggested that they create a story beginning at the point at which Burt Dow feels a heavy tug on his line. Their stories could be either realistic or another version of fantasy. Creative thinking was developed as the children used a book as a springboard for writing stories.

Just then Burt felt a tug on his line. He pulled at it, but it wouldn't budge. "Maybe it's stuck on a branch," he thought.

He gave one great pull and something landed with a SLOP on the deck. Burt looked at it. It was only a big, black boot!

"He—hee-he," laughed the giggling gull.

Burt looked in the boot. Something pinched his nose.

"Ouch!" he cried, and he reached into the boot. Out came a crab! He put the crab in the trap and chuckled softly, "So that's what scared the fish. I'd a' been scared, too, if I'd a' seen a boot hoppin' round 'thout a master."

Burt laughed and the gull giggled all the way home.

NANCY SCHAEFFER, Fourth Grade

600

"All hands down to Davey Jones' locker!" yelled Burt.

Giggling gull just giggled.

Burt held his breath and went down, down, down.

When Burt opened his eyes he saw an old sunken ship. Over the hatch were letters the color of the floor and door of Doc Walton's waiting room that read, "Davey Jones Locker."

In a minute the hatch opened and out walked a short fat man with silver hair. "I've been expectin' you," he said. "Come on in."

Burt followed silently.

"Oh don't tell me an old sea dog like you could be tongue'tied," cried Davey. "Oh well, never mind talk, and follow me." Davey led Burt into the ship. They went through a long winding passage and into a room full of treasure.

"Oh!" exclaimed Burt. "May I take something home for Leela?"

"Sure, take as much as you want," said Davey.

Burt picked out a pearl necklace.

Then they went into the Captain's quarters and talked about the sea. In this way Burt spent a happy afternoon.

Then all of a sudden, Davey clapped his hands and a great many fish appeared and fell at Burt's feet.

"You will need something for supper, Burt," said Davey, "and here it is."

"Oh, thank you," cried Burt. "How can I ever repay you?"

"You're repaying me right now by entertaining me. But now you must go home," said Davey.

"Yes," said Burt, "but how am I going to get home?"

"Hold your breath

Close your eyes

And when they open

You'll have a surprise."

So Burt got into the Tidely-Idely and

Held his breath

Closed his eyes

And when he opened them

He had a big surprise!

HE WAS OUT ON THE COVE.

He pumped all the water out. Slish-slosh. He started the make and break engine, and went chudite-bang, firm hand on the tiller, giggling gull flying along behind, home to Leela.

MELISSA CURTIN, Fourth Grade

Some of the factors in creative thinking are flexibility, fluency, originality, association of ideas, and openness. Children need many experiences in using different materials in a variety of ways. Literature may provide a rich background that can be tapped for original interpretations.

Children respond differently to different media. Mary may find it easy to express her understanding of a book in a written report, while Betty may communicate her interpretation through painting a picture; yet, each child may adequately comprehend the book. When teachers extend their concepts of acceptable ways of reporting and sharing books, children will be encouraged to read more widely, more thoughtfully, and with greater joy. The activities and experiences suggested in this chapter will help the teacher guide children's interpretation of their reading and foster creative activities.

CREATIVE WRITING AND LITERATURE

Children's appreciation of the writing of others increases as they read widely and have many opportunities to create their own stories and poems. They will be motivated to write if they have interesting, exciting, and rich sensory experiences that bring a depth of feeling about people, places, and things. Literature affords many opportunities for the motivation of creative writing.

Developing Sensitivity to Language

Skill in descriptive writing may be developed by helping children become aware of the power of words to convey sensory images. After a story has been finished, the teacher and children may read and relish particularly enjoyable words, phrases, or paragraphs. Boys and girls can be taught to identify figurative language, respond to symbolism, and enjoy colloquialisms (see pages 576–580).

Creative writing requires many first-hand experiences of touching and feeling and savoring textures, sounds, colors, shapes, rhythms and patterns. Literature, too, can sharpen sensitivity to nature, people, and relationships. Rich sensory imagery helps children "see" the world around them in new perspectives. For example, in *A Fresh Look at Night*, Jeanne Bendick presents various night scenes in lovely descriptive language a child could understand:

A city full of lights and windows is like frozen fireworks on the Fourth of July.

Rainy nights are like silk and satin. Snowy nights are like feathers and fur.[1]

Children's delight in a fog-shrouded village has been captured by Tresselt in *Hide and Seek Fog*. Vivid imagery characterizes his descriptions. The children

. . . spoddled in the lazy lapping waves on the beach, . . . But out of doors the fog twisted about the cottages like slow-motion smoke. It dulled the rusty scraping of the beach grass. It muffled the chattery talk of the low tide waves. And it hung wet and dripping, from the bathing suits and towels on the clothesline.[2]

Good poetry is replete with sensory images. In the first two stanzas of her poem "Feet," Dorothy Aldis conveys the joy of going barefoot:

There are things
Feet know
That hands never will:
The exciting
Pounding feel
Of running down a hill;

The soft cool
Prickliness
When feet are bare
Walking in
The summer grass
To most anywhere. . . .[3]

---

[1]Jeanne Bendick, *A Fresh Look at Night* (New York: F. Watts, 1963), unpaged.
[2]Alvin Tresselt, *Hide and Seek Fog* (New York: Lothrop, 1965), unpaged.
[3]Dorothy Aldis, *All Together* (New York: Putnam, 1925).

If primary children have been exposed to this kind of poetry, they will be ready for the implied imagery of haiku in the middle grades.

> *What happiness*
> *Crossing this summer river,*
> *Sandals in hand!*[4]
>
> — BUSON

Eve Merriam's poem "A Cliché" will help boys and girls become alert to overworked expressions and unimaginative responses.

> A CLICHÉ
> *is what we all say*
> *when we're too lazy*
> *to find another way*
>
> *and so we say*
>
> warm as toast,
> quiet as a mouse,
> slow as molasses,
> quick as a wink.
>
> *Think.*
>
> *Is toast the warmest thing you know?*
> *Think again, it might not be so.*
> *Think again: it might even be snow!*
> *Soft as lamb's wool, fleecy snow,*
> *a lacy shawl of new-fallen snow.*
>
> *Listen to that mouse go*
> *scuttling and clawing,*
> *nibbling and pawing.*
> *A mouse can speak*
> *if only a squeak.*
>
> *Is a mouse the quietest thing you know?*
> *Think again, it might not be so.*
> *Think again: it might be a shadow.*
> *Quiet as a shadow,*
> *quiet as growing grass,*
> *quiet as a pillow,*
> *or a looking glass.*

> *Slow as molasses,*
> *quick as a wink.*
> *Before you say so,*
> *take time to think.*
>
> *Slow as time passes*
> *when you're sad and alone;*
> *quick as an hour can go*
> *happily on your own.*[5]

After hearing this poem, children may be directed to look for fresh, creative metaphors or create their own. One fourth-grade class wrote the following comparisons: "Slow as a moving glacier," "slow as a six-week spelling test," and "lonely as an ant in orbit." Two other poems by Merriam, "Metaphor" and "Simile: Willow and Ginkgo," might help children understand figurative language.

Mary O'Neill's *Hailstones and Halibut Bones* gives children new dimensions of meaning for color words. These thirteen poems describe color in terms of objects, feelings, taste, and sound. After hearing these poems, children have found delight in creating their own responses to color. One blind child described "Blue" in this way:

> BLUE
> *Blue is the sky high over your head.*
> *Blue is the blanket that's on a bed.*
> *It's blueberry pie and juicy sweet plums.*
> *It's the ink with which you write your sums.*
> *It's water lapping the distant shore.*
> *It's fresh new paint on the front door.*
> *The air in spring is the smell of blue.*
> *What scent brings forth this color to you?*
> *Anchors Aweigh is a blue song to me,*
> *I think of a sailor's uniform you see.*
> *It's the loyalty I owe a friend,*
> *Steadfast and true to the very end.*[6]

---

[4]Richard Lewis, Editor, *The Moment of Wonder* (New York: Dial, 1964), p. 78.

[5]Eve Merriam, *It Doesn't Always Have to Rhyme*, Illustrated by Malcolm Spooner (New York: Atheneum, 1964), pp. 48–50.

[6]Mary Joyce Pritchard, in *Elementary English*, vol. 40 (May 1963), p. 543.

In *Words Words Words*, Mary O'Neill uses a similar technique to present facets of meaning in such words as "mean," "sloppy," "happiness," and "forget." It might be interesting to compare O'Neill's poem, "Feelings about Words," in the above book with McCord's "Take Sky" in his book of the same title.

Younger children may be encouraged to explore the various possibilities or functions of a single object in *See What I Found* by Myra Cohn Livingston. When the child hears the lines about a key, his imagination may open doors with "a silver key to secret places." Creative uses of a rubber band, a piece of clay, a little bug, or a seashell may be discovered through reading this book.

An individual or class notebook of interesting passages and picturesque speech provides another way to develop awareness of language. One sixth-grade boy selected his favorite passages from *Hakon of Rogen's Saga:*

> Still I believe I know now what courage is: it is to smile, when fear has locked all smiles within your breast.[7]
> Ships are to men, as infants are to women, they cannot pass one by without examining it — one eye filled with tenderness, the other looking sharply, ready to criticize.[8]

A fifth-grade girl copied the following passage describing the oppressive heat of the San Joaquin Valley in the book, *Blue Willow*.

> It was noon and the sun hung white and fierce almost directly overhead. It beat down upon Janey, the shack, and all the wide flat country stretching away for miles and miles in every direction. It was hot, so terribly hot that when Janey cupped her hands and blew into her sweaty palms her warm breath seemed cooler than the air she was breathing.[9]

This description of heat might be compared to that used in *Bristle Face* by Ball: *"sun on my back was digging in its claws like a scared tomcat."*[10]

Literature as Model

Literature may be used as a model to teach different forms of writing. Primary children can write stories using the repetition, talking animals, magic, or enchantment, characteristic of folk tales. After one first-grade teacher read and discussed "The Three Little Pigs" and "The Story of the Little Red Hen," a group of children dictated "a talking animal story." Next, the class heard "The Sleeping Beauty" and "Snow White and the Seven Dwarfs." Following the discussion of the enchantment of sleep in these tales, the group composed a story, "The Sleeping Prince," in which a witch casts a spell on a birthday cake to win the friendship of the princess who had not been invited to the party. One bite of the cake causes Prince Jonathan to sleep for ten years. The spell is broken when the witch breaks her bottle of witchcraft and dies. The story ends:

> As soon as the witch was dead, the spell came off the Prince. He sat up in bed and stretched. He ran to his Mother and Father. They were so happy that they planned·a party for the whole kingdom. The Queen herself made a beautiful white cake for the big party. The cake had ten layers and was covered with pink flowers. The King and Queen invited Princess Alice and Jonathan and the Princess became friends again. Prince Jonathan grew up to be King and lived happily ever after.

> *Suzanne Heinmiller, Teacher*
> *Columbus Public Schools, Ohio*

One sixth-grade class studied fables in much the same way, and then composed their own. The following modern fables were written by two of the children:

---

[7]Erik Haugaard, *Hakon of Rogen's Saga,* Illustrated by Leo and Diane Dillon (Boston: Houghton Mifflin, 1963), p. 37.
[8]Haugaard, p. 67.
[9]Doris Gates, *Blue Willow,* Illustrated by Paul Lantz (New York: Viking, 1940), p. 1.
[10]Zachary Ball, *Bristle Face* (New York: Holiday, 1962), p. 7.

Once there was a girl named Lily who thought she was the pink of perfection. She wore Paris model dresses, twelve-dollar shoes, and had her hair done at the beauty parlor.

The day of the fair she was all decked out in her best clothes. She was having the time of her life — eating, going on the ferris wheel — when it started to rain. He hair uncurled and, believe it or not, under her make-up was the ugliest, freckled face ever known!

Beauty is only skin deep.

PAM GREENWOOD

One day my mother told me to go to the store to get a gallon of milk. It cost 96 cents. She gave me a dollar and said that I could keep the money that was left over.

While I was riding down to the store, I told myself what I was going to buy: a 4-cent candy bar, then I would sell it for 5 cents, buy a pack of gum, trade it for some Cracker Jack, and at last I would trade it for a 40-cent bag of M & M Fruit Chewies.

When I put the milk on the counter the clerk said, "96 cents, 4 cents tax, that will be one dollar."

Don't count your chickens before they hatch.

CRAIG LEICHNER
Allaire Stuart, Teacher
Boulder Public Schools, Colorado

Other forms of prose such as the tall tale, the essay, myth, or biography may serve as models for children's writing. It is essential that many examples of the literary form be presented and discussed in order that children understand its pattern and elements.

Different forms of poetry, too, may serve as models for creative writing. Haiku frequently releases children from the problem of rhyme, and focuses on the idea of the poem. This form of poetry is deceptively simple in that it requires a high level of abstraction. Frequently, the reader must sense the relationship between two disparate ideas. The strict structure of the seventeen syllables also imposes a discipline upon the writer. However, writing this form of poetry is a challenge to many middle-grade children. The examples below illustrate two twelve-year-olds' success in writing haiku:

The cabin is small
in the vast whiteness. Only
the smoke reveals it.

CAROL BARTLETT

The leaves on a tree
Rustle, impatient, restless,
Waiting to fall off.

PATTI KROG
Allaire Stuart, Teacher
Boulder Public Schools, Colorado

A variant of the form of cinquain is easy enough for children to write. This brief poem consists of five lines in which a one-word title forms the first line. Two words describe the title in the second line, while the third line of three words expresses an action. The fourth line contains four words expressing a feeling. The last line is again one word, a synonym for the title. In the following cinquain, one child expresses feelings for his small village, while another shows his consuming interest in racing cars:

Harrisburg
Sleepy village
Busy and growing
Nice place to be —
Home.

JERRY HARRIS (AGE 12)
Joann Mason, Teacher
Harrisburg Public Schools, Ohio

Tires
Black devils
Fast take-off
Clouds of blue smoke
Slicks.

JOHN CALLADINE (AGE 13)
Art Prowant, Teacher
Columbus Public Schools, Ohio

The limerick is another form of poetry that children especially enjoy writing. David McCord describes this short verse form in his limerick about the limerick:

> The limerick's lively to write:
> Five lines to it—all nice and tight.
>   Two long ones, two trick
>   Little short ones; then quick
> As a flash here's the last one in sight.[11]

After reading *The Limerick Trick* by Corbett, children in the middle grades would have fun pretending to place some of Mrs. Graymalkin's liquid chemical on their foreheads to enable them to write limericks. Their magic would be confined to writing limericks, whereas Kerby, the hero of the story, always spoke in limerick form. When a friend asks for a hammer, Kerby says "Try using your bean, instead! It's big and it's thick, and it's hard as a brick—so bang in the nails with your head!"[12]

Literature to Motivate Creative Writing

Literature develops sensitivity to language, provides models for good writing in different forms, and may serve as a springboard to creative writing. When the teacher finishes reading a good story, the children may exclaim, "Oh! Isn't there any more?" This is the cue to suggest that they write further adventures to the story. "What do you suppose Mrs. Piggle Wiggle would do next? How would she cure a giggler?" Such leading comments will direct children to create an original sequel to MacDonald's delightfully humorous book for children. The ending of *Chitty-Chitty-Bang-Bang* by Fleming invites children to continue the adventures of the Pott family and their fantastic car:

> . . . the great green car soared up into the sky.
> . . . "I can't control her, she's taken off. Where in heavens is she taking us?"
> And to tell you the truth, even I haven't been let into the secret.[13]

Nine- to eleven-year-olds would have fun following up Lawson's provocative ending of *McWhinney's Jaunt:*

> That was a month or two ago and Mr. Purslane is still eagerly awaiting the arrival of the Z-gas, for he has thought of a great many amusing things that could be done with such a remarkable substance.
> It is probable that the Professor has been too busy with his new classes to get around to it. It is also possible that, being somewhat absentminded, he has forgotten all about it.[14]

The teacher could ask the children, "What do you think happened?" "How will Mr. Purslane use his gas?" "How would *you* use Z-gas if you could obtain it?"

Another book that provides an interesting basis for writing is L. M. Boston's *The Castle of Yew.* Following the advice of the old lady who told Joseph, "You can go anywhere you want if you really want to," eight- or nine-year-olds can pretend they become small and visit the castle built in the hedge of yew.

Primary children might write about an imaginary friend who helps them in the same way as *My Friend Charlie* by Flora. For example, Charlie "borrowed" a dream and returned it five days later beautifully embellished with added details.

New incidents may be created in relation to a particular theme. After hearing several of Kipling's *Just So Stories*, young authors can experiment with animal stories entitled "How the Giraffe Got Its Long Neck," "Why a Cat Has Nine Lives," or "How the Skunk

---

[11]David McCord, "Write Me a Verse" in *Take Sky* (Boston: Little, Brown, 1961), p. 55.

[12]Scott Corbett, *The Limerick Trick*, Illustrated by Paul Galdone (Boston: Little, Brown, 1964), p. 32.

[13]Ian Fleming, *Chitty-Chitty-Bang-Bang, the Magical Car*, Illustrated by John Burningham (New York: Random House, 1964), pp. 112–113.

[14]Robert Lawson, *McWhinney's Jaunt* (Boston: Little, Brown, 1951), p. 76.

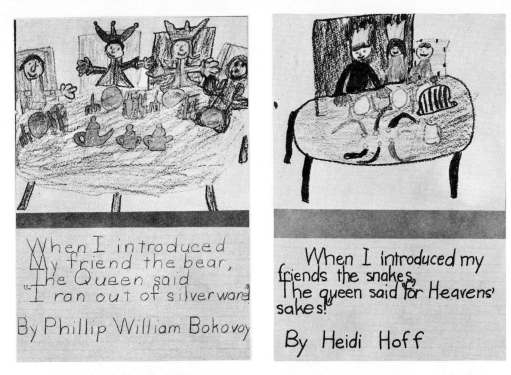

When I introduced
My friend the bear,
"The Queen said
"I ran out of silverware"

By Phillip William Bokovoy

When I introduced my
friends the snakes,
The queen said "for Heavens'
sakes!"

By Heidi Hoff

Second-graders wrote additional verses about friends they invited to visit the king and queen after hearing *May I Bring a Friend?* **by de Regniers.** Nancy Sawrey, teacher, West Lafayette, Indiana, Public Schools.

Received Its Aroma." A sixth-grader wrote the following interpretation of the origin of the lion's roar:

HOW THE LION GOT ITS ROAR

One day many years ago in southern India there came through the jungle a kitten. It was the smallest kitten you could ever imagine. This made the kitten very upset. All the animals in India had heard about the poor, poor, poor little tinsy, tinesy kitten, and all of them were laughing hysterically.

Once someone laughed at him and he decided that it was the last time he was going to be laughed at. He set out to see the cruel world in which he thought he lived. At that time, to him, the world was cruel. He was walking along a trail seldom used. He was crying so very, very pitifully, that if you'd been there, you just couldn't have stood it. Then suddenly he no-

ticed what he was walking in. At first he thought it was powder (which is just what it was) but then he changed his mind. It couldn't possibly be snow. Or could it? You see he had never seen any really, real live snow in his life. But no it couldn't be that. Could a falling star have whisked by? No, it couldn't have. Well then what was it?

"It is fairy powder," said a small voice. "I just couldn't stand there and listen to you cry like that. If you'd listen to yourself you'd see how impossible it is."

"I'm sorry if I disturbed you," said the little kitten. "But if you were me you'd be crying, too."

"Well, what reason would you have for crying so much?" asked the fairy.

"Me, just me, me, me," cried the little kitten, and started crying all over again.

"Why, what's supposed to be wrong with you?" she asked.

"I'm little," he said.

   "Well so am I," said the fairy.

"But you're supposed to be," he said, starting to cry again.

"Very well, if you'll stop crying, you can be very, very big."

"Really," asked the kitten, sniffing back the tears.

"Certainly," she said. And with a wave of her magic wand, he was as big as a full grown lion, today.

"Thank you," he said. And then he noticed his voice, and started crying harder than ever.

Well the fairy was sure that these tears were not tears of joy, so she tried to calm him. (You've heard of elephant tears?) (Well these were even larger.) Well finally the fairy gave in. She simply couldn't bear to hear him cry. "O.K.," she said, "if you really want it, you can have a voice, almost the largest in the jungle."

"Oh, please," he said, "I—I mean thank you—or—or—oh you know what I mean, you're a fairy."

Yes, the fairy knew what he meant. So she gave him a roar.

That's why today we say that the kitten is related to the lion. And that's how we came to have lions. He and his descendants were the lions.

PATRICIA DERBY, Columbus Public Schools, Ohio

Younger children may relate events that could happen on their streets, similar to those which occurred to the lad in Dr. Seuss' *And To Think that I Saw It on Mulberry Street.* The pattern of the book *Fortunately* by Remy Charlip could stimulate children to create their own contrasts of fortunate and unfortunate circumstances. For example, Ned, the hero, is fortunate to receive an invitation to a party, but unfortunately, it was in Florida. "Fortunately a friend loaned him an airplane. Unfortunately the motor exploded. Fortunately. . . ."[15] After hearing this book,

one second grade had a good time continuing the fortunate and unfortunate sequence. One child would write a fortunate incident on part of a roll of wallpaper, roll it up, and pass it on to another child to write an unfortunate event. After each child added an incident, the completed story was revealed. Another book that follows this same pattern and could be used in a similar way is *That's Good, That's Bad* by Joan Lexau.

Creative writing enables the teacher to learn more about the children's needs. Just as projective tests reveal inner thoughts, so children's writings reflect their concerns and desires. After hearing the following poem, read by the teacher in a friendly, receptive atmosphere, children will be ready to write their three wishes:

> ### I KEEP THREE WISHES READY
> *I keep three wishes ready*
> *Lest I should chance to meet,*
> *Any day a fairy*
> *Coming down the street.*
>
> *I'd hate to have to stammer*
> *Or have to think them out*
> *For it's very hard to think them up*
> *When a fairy is about.*
>
> *And I'd hate to lose my wishes*
> *For fairies fly away*
> *And perhaps I'd never have a chance*
> *On any other day.*
>
> *So I keep three wishes ready*
> *Lest I should chance to meet*
> *Any day a fairy*
> *Coming down the street.*

ANNETTE WYNNE[16]

Stories or poems may be written to explain incidents preceding the situation described in a poem. For example, the children might write what happened before the opening of this poem:

---

[15]Remy Charlip, *Fortunately* (New York: Parents Magazine, 1964), unpaged.

[16]Annette Wynne, "I Keep Three Wishes Ready," in *Time for Poetry*, May Hill Arbuthnot, Editor (Glenview, Ill.: Scott, Foresman, 1952).

BAD

I've been bad and I'm in bed
For all the naughty things I said.
I'm in bed, I wish I had
Not said those things that were so bad.
I wish that I'd been good instead,
But I was bad, and I'm in bed.

DOROTHY ALDIS[17]

Some highly improbable wishes appear in the book *Someday* by Zolotow. For example, one double-page spread shows a little girl's dream as she practices the piano and says, "Someday . . . the lady across the street will call and say 'Please play that beautiful piece again.'"[18] Children can make their own "Someday" books. Two other books reflect young children's wishes to participate in adult activities that are now forbidden: *When I Have a Little Girl* by Zolotow and *When I Am Big* by Smith. In contrast to these books portraying secret desires, the story of *Do You Know What I'll Do?* by Zolotow is filled with promises of all the good things a little girl wants to do for her baby brother.

In order to help the child see himself as a part of the continuity of life, the children may write autobiographies or trace the history of their families. After reading *The Sky Was Blue* by Zolotow, primary children could prepare a picture album of their ancestors. *Life Story* by Burton and Lawson's *They Were Strong and Good* might introduce older children to the idea of writing autobiographies.

Books can provide the stimulus for children's writing about their own joys, fears, and problems. After hearing about the fun that was planned by the four Melendy children for *The Saturdays* by Enright, a class might describe their "ideal" Saturday. Children could identify their fears after reading Urmston's description of the first day at school of *The New Boy*. Older boys and girls might write of their own decision-making experiences after reading such books as Sterling's *Mary Jane* and Beim's *Trouble after School*. All ages enjoy books of the pattern of Schulz's *Happiness Is a Warm Puppy* and Anglund's *A Friend Is Someone Who Likes You*.

Many children have secret places where they go to be alone with their problems. Discussing family relations in the poem, "Keziah," will help children realize that such feelings are common to all.

KEZIAH

I have a secret place to go
Not anyone may know.

And sometimes when the wind is rough
I cannot get there fast enough.

And sometimes when my mother
Is scolding my big brother,

My secret place, it seems to me,
Is quite the only place to be.

GWENDOLYN BROOKS[19]

Other poems and stories may stimulate writing about secret places. For example, the story of a baby Hippo who found a place to be alone, yet not too far away, is told in *The Secret Hiding Place* by Bennett. Poems that describe different hiding places are "Hideout" from Fisher's *In the Woods, in the Meadow, in the Sky*, "Solitude" in *Now We Are Six* by Milne, and "This Is My Rock" in *Far and Few* by McCord.

After hearing Rumer Godden's translation of de Gasztold's *Prayers from the Ark*, a group of gifted fifth-grade children composed prayers of other animals:

PRAYER OF THE RAT

Dear God,
Why am I so ugly?
How come people must
scream when I'm around?
Why do I have to live in
a dirty leftover spot?

---

[17] Dorothy Aldis, *All Together*, Illustrated by Marjorie Flack (New York: Putnam, 1925).

[18] Charlotte Zolotow, *Someday*, Illustrated by Arnold Lobel (New York: Harper & Row, 1965), unpaged.

---

[19] Gwendolyn Brooks, *Bronzeville Boys and Girls*, Illustrated by Ronni Solbert (New York: Harper & Row, 1956), p. 6.

What reason did you have
To make me so hated?
I'm just a little different than the pretty white
mouse
Who lives in luxury,
Why then, should he be
Cared for and not I?
        I do not understand
        Do I have to be the one
        To carry germs and make
        Children dislike picking me up?
        Grease and grime and hate.
        Undernourishment. That's what
        My life adds up to.
        Dear Lord, Why???
            Amen

BARBARA HAMMER

PRAYER OF THE MOUNTAIN LION
Oh Lord,

Why must I always be feared by everyone who
    comes out in the mountains
Why must I make such an ugly sound.
You have made me how I am, and I must accept,
But please make people understand
It's not my fault I'm wild and it's not me who
    makes me kill for food.
I'd like to be friendly, but since people fear and
    dislike me I am not able to control myself.
I wish you could do something so someone under-
    stands my feelings.
Oh Lord, give me a friend.
        Amen

BRADLEY POLAKOW
Barbara Friedberg, Teacher
Evanston Public Schools, Illinois

Creative Reporting

Book reports can become creative-writing experiences when children are given suggestions to write the story from another point of view. To understand this approach, the picture book, *It Looks Like This,* by Web-

ber might be read. Similar to *The Blind Man and the Elephant,* retold by Quigley, the different animals in this book give their impressions of the cow in a barn. Older children could learn much about techniques of writing as well as causes of behavior when they compare the different perspectives of Stolz's *A Dog on Barkham Street* and *The Bully of Barkham Street.* The same events are related in these books, but from different viewpoints. To write of *Carolina's Courage* by Yates, a child might pretend to be the little Indian girl who played with Carolina, exchanged dolls, and observed the wagon train moving westward. A report of *The Courage of Sarah Noble* by Dalgliesh might be written from the viewpoint of the Indians who kept Sarah while her father returned to the white settlement. Older readers would find it interesting to report the story of *Towappu, Puritan Renegade* by Stephens from the viewpoint of Panchuk, the Indian boy who befriended the Puritan lad.

It would also be challenging to write an account of the incidents in Carlson's *The Letter on the Tree* from the viewpoint of the American boy who found the Canadian boy's letter on a Christmas tree. Another report might be written by pretending to be the Boy who met Arrietty in Norton's *The Borrowers.* He could give his impressions of the tiny creatures, tell how he helped them, and how they nearly lost their lives. It would require deep understanding of the theme of the book, *The Superlative Horse,* by Jean Merrill to write the story as though you were the Prime Minister. Children might enjoy using Robert Lawson's device of telling a story from the viewpoint of an animal. Lawson uses a humorous approach in *Ben and Me;* one might report the story of the surrender at Appomattox, as told by Traveller, Lee's horse.

Imagining themselves reporters for a local paper, children could prepare news articles based upon events in literature. An interview with a professor who just returned from a trip in his twenty-one balloon flying ship might be reported after reading *The Twenty-One Balloons* by du Bois. A series of news accounts of Merrill's *The Pushcart War* of 1976 could present the amusing battles between the mighty trucks and puny push-carts of New York City. A report could be made of the discovery of oil at the Amory home by General De Gaulle, the mole hero of *Mr. Twigg's Mistake* by Lawson. Charlie's day in the chocolate factory as related by Dahl would make interesting "news copy." By pretending they were witnesses to a famous historical event, children could write an "I was there" story. Such a story could be motivated by reading historical fiction or biography.

An entire group could contribute ideas for a class newspaper based upon events related to literature. The paper could include news stories, editorials on book reading, and announcements of book awards. For example, a headline might herald the arrival of *The Cricket in Times Square;* the society column could give a report of Eeyore's birthday party; the sports page could report the results of the race between the hare and the tortoise, and the race for the silver skates of Hans Brinker; the death of Charlotte, the spider, could be recorded in the obituary column. A creative want ad written in the same code as that used by the Boggart in *Magic to Burn* by Fritz might be found in the want-ad section. A sample follows:

Do *Throw This Advertisement in Your Wastebasket*
     You *May Be the Familiar for a Boggart*
(To decode the message, circle every tenth word.)

A sixth-grader used the code in *Magic to Burn* by Fritz in an imaginative report of her reactions to the book.

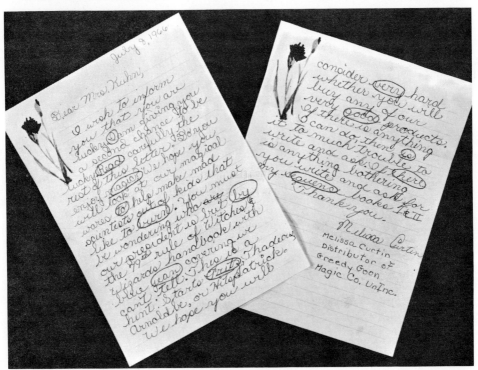

We want to tell you about a new product for your home. This machine will make your garden work much easier. It will cut grass and give you much fun at the same time. As you drive, you can read the newspaper or a new book for children. Turn about and you can dry your hair while you cook the dinner. We guarantee the durability of this new and mysterious machine for completing many jobs. Invented by young Jeffrey Boggart, it is practically indestructible. You can leave it outdoors in all kinds of weather. The inventor has made a magic touch control which enables the owner to work and to use the telephone simultaneously. It is guaranteed not to burn out for five years. Call us for a demonstration by one of our agents. He'll come in a blue jean uniform. "Nothing in this machine will go on the fritz," says the inventor. Ask your librarian for the number.

The teacher might suggest that the children write the diary of a particular character, or create imaginary correspondence between characters. Girls would enjoy recording Carolina's travel in a covered wagon as described in Yates' *Carolina's Courage*. They might complete the diary of Ann Hamilton in *The Cabin Faced West* by Fritz. Boys could report David's story in Holm's *North to Freedom* by writing an imaginary journal of his adventures following his flight from a concentration camp. A middle-grade reader might continue Harriet's notebook from *Harriet, the Spy* by Fitzhugh. The following questions could stimulate ideas for correspondence between characters:

- What would Little Bear write to his grandparents after spending a day with them? (*Little Bear's Visit* by Minarik)
- How would *Pippi Longstocking* by Lindgren write about her first day at school in a letter to her father?
- What would Jethro write to his teacher friend about events at home? (*Across*

Five Aprils by Irene Hunt)
- How would Tom describe his adventures in the midnight garden to his brother? (*Tom's Midnight Garden* by Pearce)

Another kind of report is based upon the idea of a social-distance scale. A book that involves several characters who are clearly delineated may be evaluated in this way:

WHO WOULD YOU LIKE FOR FRIENDS?

The following children lived on The Alley *in the book by Eleanor Estes. Read the descriptions below. Then write the number of the description that tells how you feel about each character opposite his name. You may use any number as many times as you wish. For example, you might want two or three characters for very, very best friends.*

Characters from the book, The Alley

Connie Ives_____   *Stephen Carroll* _____
Bully Vardeer_____   *Billy Maloon* _____
Hugsy Goode _____   *Judy Fabadessa* _____
Katy Starr _____   *Arnold Trickman* ___
Anthony Bigelow ___   *Jonathan Stuart* _____
Ray Arp _____   *June Arp*_____

Descriptions:

1. *I would like this person for my very, very best friend. I could tell this person my secrets. I would invite this person to my house to stay overnight.*
2. *I would like this person for a good friend. I would like to play games with this person and I would like to work on committees at school with this person. I would invite this person to a party at my house.*
3. *I would talk to this person. This person is all right to play with in a group. I don't know this person very well.*
4. *I would not want to play with this person. I would not want this person to sit near me at school. I do not like this person very much.*

Write on another sheet of paper the reasons for choosing characters to be best *friends.*

Various materials including yarn, paperclips, buttons, cloth, and colored paper, were used by a third-grader to depict *The Man Who Didn't Wash His Dishes.*

ART ACTIVITIES AND LITERATURE

Exciting stories, sensitive descriptions of beauty, and vivid characterizations are the "stuff" of the creative environment that motivates children's responses in writing, creative dramatics, and art activities. Children of all ages need opportunities to express understandings of some of the books they read by using varied art media. The usual crayons and manila paper, yes—but chalk, textured paper, paint, *pâpier maché*, yarn, cloth, and clay should also be available to help children interpret feelings and meanings.

Flat Pictures
and Three-Dimensional Construction

A teacher's rather vague direction, "Make a picture of a book you like," fails to engender enthusiasm and may hinder fullest realization of the child's creative potential. Children must be "filled to overflowing" be-

fore they can create. The teacher's role is to set an environment for creativity by providing materials and suggesting questions:

- What does the main character look like?
  How old was he?
  What did he wear?
- Where did the story take place?
- Did this story take place in the past, or today?
- Can you show the funniest, or saddest, or most exciting incident?
- Can you make a map of the story setting (for example, the map of the "100 Aker Wood" in *Winnie the Pooh*)?
- What time of year is it?
- Does the story make you think of another picture (for example, do you have a secret place as in *The Secret Garden* by Burnett or *The Hole in the Tree* by George)?
- What do you think happened next?

A "Seuss-inspired" animal with two heads was created by a second grader. Mary Pastor, teacher, Morton School, Hammond, Indiana, Public Schools.

Children's illustrations of books may be used for many purposes. A bulletin board display of drawings and paintings may enhance the attractiveness of the room. One picture on a small display board in the reading corner may call attention to a particular book. Paper dust-jackets may be designed and displayed on a bulletin board. Posters advertising Book Week or a book fair create interest. After the children have made illustrations for a story, the pictures may be bound in a booklet and placed on a library table. Interested children may make individual booklets of illustrations of favorite books, sequential episodes, or storybook characters.

Books might stimulate the creation of new characters. For example, one fifth-grade group wrote and illustrated their own book titled "On Beyond Dr. Seuss" following the idea established in *On Beyond Zebra*. They used scraps of cloth to make their imaginary animals. In a second grade, sculptures of Dr. Seuss animals were fashioned from boxes, foil paper, cloth, buttons, and metal scraps. Another book by Seuss, *And To Think that I Saw It on Mulberry Street*, was used by a first-grade teacher to stimulate children's illus-

trations of imaginary events on their own street. Their bulletin board titled "And To Think We Saw It on Forest Parkway" revealed many hilarious and imaginative pictures.

Teachers could stop reading a book at an appropriate place and have children anticipate the ending. One second-grade teacher interrupted the reading of *Leopold, the See-Through Crumbpicker* by Flora just at the point where Minerva started to paint Leopold in order to make him visible. The children's pictures revealed highly imaginative concepts. A similar technique could be used with *Lion* by du Bois or the story *The Four Fur Feet* by Brown, in which the reader sees only the little black feet of the animal who walks around the world.

Book illustration can provide opportunities for children to experiment with different art media. One primary group used potato prints, paper-lace doilies, and other materials to create underwater effects similar to that of *Swimmy* by Lionni. After sharing Keats' *The Snowy Day*, children could make their own collage pictures. Girls would enjoy constructing hats of snippets of ribbons, valentines, gift paper, and flowers from seed catalogues, as in *Jennie's Hat* by Keats.

Dioramas

A diorama is a three-dimensional scene made by arranging objects or figures in front of a scenic background. Frequently used in museums to illustrate habitat groups, the technique can be adapted for children's illustration of scenes from literature. A large cardboard carton placed on one side can serve as a background for the scene. Clay or pâpier mâché models or paper cutouts may be placed in the foreground. Lights may be added at the back. Plastic wrap, placed over the open side, will protect the scene. Children have constructed dioramas of such books as Heyward's *The Country Bunny*,

Collage and crayon were used by fourth-graders as they visualized *Leopold, the See-Through Crumbpicker,* **by Flora.** Barbara Friedberg, teacher, Evanston, Illinois, Public Schools.

Front and rear views of a four-section diorama constructed so that a small electric motor causes the turntable to revolve. Four scenes from a book may be shown. Constructed by John Price, student, Purdue University. Settings by Harriet Aleksick, student, Purdue University.

It's fun to give a book report when you have a diorama to share. West Lafayette, Indiana, Public Schools.

The Borrowers' **kitchen and living room are illustrated in a diorama that shows the pipes, wallpaper made from a letter, postage-stamp pictures, bottlecap dishes, thimble pails, gauze hand towels, half of a manicure scissor used to cut raw potato, and a supply of pins used by Pod for climbing.** Constructed by Phyllis Morales, student, The Ohio State University.

McElligot's Pool by Seuss and Wilder's *Little House in the Big Woods*. Sequence of events can be shown by dividing the diorama into two or more sections. For example, *The Little House* by Burton could be shown in the country and after the city "mushroomed" around it.

A teacher constructed a diorama of the barnyard scene of *Charlotte's Web* to introduce the book to her children. A curved background gave perspective as they looked in the barn door to see Wilbur, the pig, and Templeton, the rat. Tiny farm tools and a lantern added realism. Charlotte, the spider, was painted on a piece of plexiglass designed to resemble a web in the corner of the door. Another diorama illustrated the materials "borrowed" by the tiny Clock family to furnish their home. The following description was used to create this diorama:

> *Homily was proud of her sitting room: the walls had been papered with scraps of old letters out of wastepaper baskets, and Homily had arranged the handwriting sideways in vertical strips which ran from floor to ceiling. On the walls . . . hung several portraits of Queen Victoria as a girl; these were postage stamps, . . . a chest of drawers made of match boxes. There was a round table with a red velvet cloth, which Pod had made from the wooden bottom of a pill box supported on the carved pedestal of a knight from the chess set. . . . The floor of the sitting room was carpeted with deep red blotting paper. . . .*[20]

Older children enjoy constructing peep shows in shoe boxes. A miniature scene representing an incident or book setting is arranged in the box. Light can be admitted through a narrow opening cut across the box lid and covered with tissue paper. In the end of the box, a peephole is cut for viewing the scene. *Beauty and the Beast, Tom's Midnight Garden* by Pearce, *Mary Poppins* by Travers,

[20] Mary Norton, *The Borrowers* (New York: Harcourt, 1953), p. 15.

and numerous others may be interpreted in this way. Poems and nursery rhymes can also be represented by peep shows. The "Old Woman in the Shoe," Fyleman's "The Best Game the Fairies Play," and de la Mare's "The Old Stone House" are examples of poems that are suitable for this treatment.

Guessing boxes can be made by constructing a peep show and covering the open side. Questions or words on the outside serve as clues to the title of the book. For Book Week, the peep shows may be numbered, but not titled. As children throughout the school view the displays, they may write titles on numbered sheets. Each child can check his responses with an answer sheet posted nearby. The peep-show game pictured consists of cardboard boxes labeled with clues related to the miniature scene inside the box. If the child does not guess the name of the book from the clues, he can open the box and see a scene from *Mei Li* by Handforth.

Older children may have fun constructing guessing boxes with clues on the outside and miniature scenes on the inside. Books represented above are *Mei Li, Song of the Swallows,* and *Many Moons.* Constructed by Carol Gattner, student, The Ohio State University.

Table Displays

Table scenes and models help children recall incidents in books; for example, the Pilgrim homes described by Meadowcroft's

The First Year can be built in miniature. A group of second-graders arranged figures for the scene from *Make Way for Ducklings* depicting the swan boats on the pond in the

Children can make interesting table displays using simple materials and mysterious questions. *No Name Man of the Mountain* arranged by Kathleen Lubs, student, Purdue University. *The Enormous Egg* arranged by Rosalie Kinney, student, University of Maine.

Boston Public Garden. Michael, the policeman, was shown blowing his whistle as Mrs. Mallard and her ducklings crossed Beacon Street. Models of early autos can be displayed to illustrate Bendick's *The First Book of Automobiles.*

Descriptions in some books may suggest specific displays. For example, children may create *Miss Hickory* after reading this description:

> As a matter of fact Miss Hickory had difficulty in turning her head. It was a hickory nut that had grown with an especially sharp and pointed nose. Her eyes and mouth were inked on. Her body was an applewood twig formed like a body. . . . She wore a blue-and-white checked gingham dress. . . . Miss Hickory's house was made of corncobs, notched, neatly fitted together and glued.[21]

Enright's book, *Zeee,* could be illustrated by a table display of the many homes of this bad fairy who was one hundred years old, but always appeared to be eight-and-one-half. There was a pagoda tent of dock leaves, a sand pail, a fisherman's boat, the deserted wasps' nest, and an empty pickle jar one summer. At other times, she had made her home in a sea shell, an oriole's nest, and a watering can. When Zeee finally found a home in a doll's house, she was especially happy because at least one human could see her. Children would read carefully to discover how to make the furniture: a bed of a milkweed pod, a hammock of woven grass, a chair made of a walnut shell, a clam shell bathtub, and a sequin mirror. The purpose of such activity is not just for the sake of construction, but to cause children to check details of the story, to make the story memorable, and to develop creativity in using many materials for different purposes.

In one school, a tradition has grown from the reading of *The Egg Tree* by Milhous; each

spring, children from all the rooms decorate egg shells and hang them on a large tree in the central hall.

Time Lines

Since it is difficult for children to develop time concepts, it is helpful for them to prepare a calendar of the major events of one person's life. Some boys and girls enjoy making a time-line with real string or twine from which descriptive markers may be strung. This type of project can be presented for a book report of a particular biography. Children will need to learn how to represent equal periods of time by equal spaces on the chart or line.

Children may construct a chart of the major world events occurring during the lifetime of one person. This might be motivated by reading any of Genevieve Foster's *The World of —— Books.* A chart might be made, for example, for the lifetime of Benjamin Franklin. Major events can be indicated by single years, or decades.

A similar kind of composite time-line can be devised for a group of leaders who lived during the same period. Taking the period 1700–1800, it would be interesting to mark the lives of the various Revolutionary leaders. Children could see that Benjamin Franklin was twenty-six years old when George Washington was born; but that he died only nine years before Washington died. Who else lived during this time? How old were they when the Revolution began? Such a time-line might be developed into a mural with representative pictures for each leader.

Murals

Books may serve as springboards to cooperatively planned murals. After choosing the theme, teacher and children discuss the scenes or characters to be portrayed in the

[21]Carolyn Sherwin Bailey, *Miss Hickory,* Illustrated by Ruth Gannett (New York: Viking, 1946), p. 9.

Following the reading of *The Land of Forgotten Beasts*, sixth-graders cut and pasted a mural of their own "concocted beasts." Allaire Stuart, teacher, Boulder, Colorado, Public Schools.

mural. Each child may make a sketch of one part, or small groups may meet to plan one section. These preliminary drawings may be fastened to the chalkboard with masking tape or pinned to the bulletin board and easily moved as children plan the total effect of the mural.

A variety of material may be used for murals. Crayon drawings may be cut out, pinned in place, and then glued to a large sheet of wrapping paper. This type of an assembled mural is made easily and quickly. Chalk or tempera paint is effective in creating large murals. Older children may enjoy using small bits of paper to produce a mosaic design. A mural of paper sculpture creates an interesting three-dimensional effect when the figures or objects are fastened to the mural with small rolls of masking tape. Chalk, paint, crayon, and other materials

Fifth-graders painted a mural of the fearsome tropical island of the man-eaters and captured an exciting moment in *Call It Courage*. Cornelia Downs, teacher, Bexley, Ohio, Public Schools.

may also be combined in making murals. A collage mural may be made of yarn, various scraps of papers, seeds, twigs, cloth, bits of sponge for trees, wire, ribbons, and so forth.

Planning these murals provides the opportunity for discussing themes, characters, types of illustrations, and kinds of books. Through such discussions, children grow in their appreciation of literature.

The events in one story may be illustrated in a mural. Children in kindergarten can easily make a mural of *The Three Bears.* Pagoo's journey, from Holling's book, could be the basis of a delightful mural. A mural based on one theme, such as horse stories, could be developed by children in the middle grades. *Misty, Black Gold,* and *Brighty* by Henry; *The Black Stallion,* by Farley; and *Smoky* by James might be represented. The adventures of Freddy and his friends provide an example of a mural based on a series of books by Brooks. *McElligot's Pool* by Seuss might be the basis for creating three-dimensional paper sculptures of imaginary fish placed on a marine background designed by finger painting.

Constructing Box Movies

A simple box movie may be constructed by attaching dowel rods or pieces of broom handles for rollers at either side of a suit box, carton, or wooden apple box. A strip of shelf paper or an old window shade may be used for the children's illustrations of the sequence of events in the story. Each end of the strip is fastened to a roller. One child rolls the paper by turning the rod as the narrator relates the story. If window shades are not available, edging the shelf paper with masking tape will make the "film strip" more durable.

The same principle can be carried out with older children who wish to make individual "movies." Drawings or pictures in a series may be made on a strip of adding-machine tape and pulled through slits cut in an envelope.

Some good stories for box movies include Gramatky's *Little Toot,* Flack's *Ask Mr. Bear,* Seuss' *And To Think that I Saw It on Mulberry Street,* and Paul Bunyan tales. It is wise to select fantasy that would be difficult to portray through creative dramatics, yet provides action.

Flannel-Board Stories

After the teacher presents a flannel-board story, children love to create their own. Small groups can plan and construct figures to portray the story. If the number of children in a group is limited to four or five, the storytellers will not block the view of the audience, and each child can present his own character. A small group of third-graders told the folk tale, *No Room,* by Dobbs. They made the outline of the house that was considered too small by the old woman. Following the advice of the wise man of the village, her husband brought in several animals. After he finally removed the animals, the old woman was satisfied with her "large house." Flannel-board stories may be told by individuals. A fourth-grader held the attention of his classmates as he related the story of *The Five Chinese Brothers,* by Bishop, and manipulated the figures on the flannel board.

Some informational books can be portrayed graphically by using a flannel board. The animals that lived in *The Hole in the Tree* by George could be drawn and placed on the flannel board to present information about their habits. The diagrams in Haber's *Our Friend, the Atom* become more meaningful when represented on a flannel board.

Children develop language skills as they tell stories using the felt or flannel board. A shy child may tell a felt story with confidence because attention is focused upon the figures he manipulates, and these tangibles help him to recall the sequence of events.

Bulletin Boards

Teacher-planned bulletin boards direct children's interests in reading (see Chapter 11). Children, too, may plan bulletin boards to share the fun and information they find through reading. Their paintings, dust jackets, and murals will be displayed in the classroom where literature is used to widen and deepen interests and understandings.

A "participation" bulletin board provides an opportunity for children to identify characters. For example, a group of ten-year-olds drew pictures of favorite book characters. Brief descriptions were written on cards and placed in an envelope pocket at the lower right-hand corner. The cards contained such statements as "I started a doughnut machine and couldn't get it stopped," "I wanted the moon to wear on a chain around my neck," "I put the hot beans in my hat," "My tail was used as a bell-pull." When a child played the game, he fastened the correct statement card beside the matching picture. The teacher or a member of the bulletin board committee checked his responses before the cards were returned to the envelope for the next player.

Story sequences may also be utilized for a participation bulletin board. Pictures can be matched to written descriptions numbered in order. Children may arrange pictures illustrating events in the proper order, or they may arrange both caption and picture according to sequence. Such activities help children become more aware of plot development. For example, events in *Journey Cake, Ho!* by Sawyer were illustrated by a group of first-graders. Mounted on oak tag, the pictures were stacked in random order on a shelf near the bulletin board. During the activity period, a child could arrange the pictures in sequential order on the bulletin board.

Children may also participate in the planning and arranging of special bulletin

One child holds her classmates spellbound as she tells an interesting story. John D. Rockefeller School, Cleveland, Ohio, Public Schools.

A participation bulletin board attracts children's attention. On the reverse side of each felt coin is a question about the Pippi Longstocking books. Kathleen Lubs, student, Purdue University.

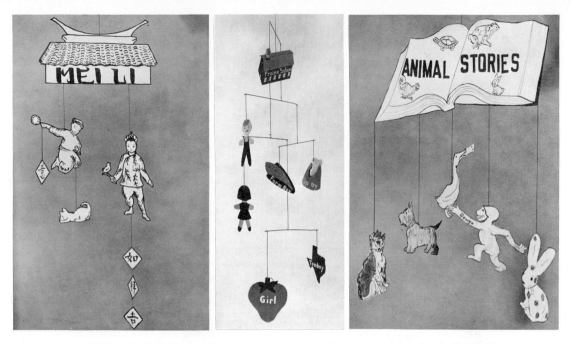

Mobiles may be constructed to represent the characters of one book, books by one author, or books of one type: *Mei Li*, **Maxine Priest; Lois Lenski's regional books, Ardis Hanish; animal stories, Ruth Seidel.** Students, The Ohio State University.

boards. Books for seasons of the year, books related to certain subjects, such as sports stories, or the books written by one author, may form the theme. One group of sixth-graders designed a "haunted house" display of mystery stories. Children who are studying their state may make an outline map of yarn and place appropriate book jackets around it. Some third-graders displayed their favorite animal stories under the caption "Tales of Tails." Seasonal themes may be utilized for literature bulletin boards; for example, "A Fall of Favorites," showing leaves and acorns with book titles; the caption, "Right down Your Line" could be illustrated by favorite book jackets strung on a clothesline. Children will enjoy thinking of other intriguing possibilities. Bulletin board space should also be provided for children's advertisements and recommendations of favorite books. A display of interesting book reports will motivate further reading.

Mobiles

To make a mobile, cutouts or objects representing a book theme or characters are balanced and suspended on thread or fine wire attached to rods. The objects or figures must be hung so that they move freely. Wire coat hangers may be cut with tin shears or pliers for the balancing pieces. Black thread attached to each end with airplane glue will suspend the next figure or rod. Very simple mobiles may be made by hanging objects from the cut branch of a tree or a coat hanger. Since the mobiles turn freely, the figures must be painted on both sides.

Individuals or groups of three or four children may plan a mobile. Guidance by the teacher or librarian is essential in developing appreciation of literature as boys and girls participate in this activity. The values of children's creative efforts in planning and constructing *their own* mobiles far outweigh the artistic effect of those produced commercially.

Wall Hangings

Wall hangings are another form of art activity that may be motivated by literature. Varied materials, such as old sheets and colored or natural burlap, may be used as background for figures and objects that represent book characters, titles, books by one author, poetry, or Mother Goose rhymes. A dowel rod, flat stick, or hanger may serve to support the hanging. Making wall hangings does not require a particular skill in sewing,

since the figures may be made of felt or textured cloth and glued to the background. Also, "iron-on" material may be used. Both boys and girls enjoy this activity.

Children can make a wall hanging or a hooked rug cooperatively. One group made a rug depicting *Winnie the Pooh* by Milne. The teacher copied a child's design on the rug backing, and the children used a simple tool to attach the wool thread.

Dolls

It is far better for children to create their own figures for dioramas and displays than to use commercial toys. Small figures may be

Real objects may be used in a mobile. Authentic Pennsylvania Dutch designs were painted on egg shells to illustrate *The Egg Tree*. Constructed by Barbara Glancy, student, The Ohio State University.

A wall hanging representing *Crow Boy, Umbrella*, and *The Village Tree* by Yashima has been made with figures cut from "iron-on" material. Josephine Scott, student, The Ohio State University.

Scraps of upholstery material, felt, toweling, and paper tissue were used by a fourth-grader to create a wall hanging of her favorite character from _Winnie the Pooh_. Barbara Friedberg, teacher, Evanston, Illinois, Public Schools.

The figure of Karana was made of a stocking body with clay head and limbs. This authentic doll combined interest in reading and doll making.

made from pipe cleaners, clothespins, or modeled in clay; larger dolls can be made from socks. Characters from books should be portrayed authentically. Children also enjoy making animal dolls such as characters from _Charlotte's Web_ by E. B. White or _The Cricket in Times Square_ by Selden.

Using Projectors

The opaque projector can be used effectively to present children's interpretations of their reading to an audience. Used in conjunction with a tape-recorded narration, a Book Week program could be presented. The overhead projector offers opportunities for creative book reporting. A child may make transparencies of characters, book settings, or illustrations of poems. By using a map, he could trace the route taken by characters in a story such as _Walk the World's Rim_ by Baker.

MUSIC AND RHYTHMIC ACTIVITIES

Identifying Background Music for Literature

The process of identifying appropriate background music for prose selections and poetry would help children appreciate the mood and changes in mood. A second-grade group discussed the kind of music that would portray the action of _Where the Wild Things Are_ by Sendak. They recognized the increasing tempo, volume, and quiet conclusion of the story. Older children might enjoy reading de la Mare's poem "Silver" or Tennyson's "The Charge of the Light Brigade" to music of their own choosing.

Composing Music

Poetry can be set to music as children create melody, and identify the rhythmical elements. Frequently, music teachers or parents cooperate with this work. Rhythm instruments could accompany choral speaking.

Rhythmic Activities

Basic rhythmical movements might be introduced through Mother Goose rhymes. For example, children could walk to "Tommy Snooks and Bessie Brooks," gallop to "Ride a Cock Horse," jump to "Jack Be Nimble," and run to "Wee Willie Winkie." Nursery rhymes could also motivate dramatic action such as "Hickory Dickory Dock," "Three Blind Mice," and "Jack and Jill."

As children learn basic movements, they can use them in different areas of space, at different levels, and at different tempos. Swinging, bending, stretching, twisting, bouncing, and shaking are kinds of body movements that may be made by standing tall, at a middle position, or by stooping low. For example, "The Swing" by Allingham could be interpreted by swinging, pushing motions that vary in speed according to the words in the poem. Other poetry that suggests movement includes "The Merry-Go-Round" by Baruch, "The Giant Shoes" by Fallis, "The African Dance" by Hughes, and "The Potatoes' Dance" by Lindsay.

Children who have had this kind of experience are ready to create a rhythmical interpretation of a longer story. *May I Bring a Friend?* by de Regniers, *Where the Wild Things Are* by Sendak, and *The Moon Jumpers* by Udry are examples of books that are appropriate for rhythmic activity.

INTERPRETING BOOKS THROUGH CREATIVE DRAMATICS

Creative Dramatics Defined

Books become more real to children as they identify with the characters through creative dramatics. Young children begin this identification with others through dramatic play. A five-year-old engaged in his impromptu play may become an airplane zooming to the airport built of blocks; another assumes the role of mother in the play house; others take the part of milkman or postman. Sometimes, children of this age will play a very familiar story without adult direction. For example, *The Three Billy Goats Gruff* is often a favorite. Dramatic play represents this free response of children as they interpret experience.

Creative dramatics, structured and cooperatively planned playmaking, is usually based on literature or an actual event. Plays may be developed from a simple story, folk tale, poem, incidents, or scenes from longer books. In beginning creative dramatics, the teacher may guide pantomimed interpretations of well-known characters. For example, the scene in which Goldilocks comes into the bears' house and samples the porridge may be pantomimed by several children. The scenes to be played should be relatively short and require limited action. Many children should have an opportunity to "play" the scene. Extemporaneous dialogue is added as children have more experience in developing belief in characters and setting. Staging is simple, props are negligible, and additional characters may be added as the play is developed. After playing each scene, the children are guided in evaluating the characterization and plot development. A new cast is chosen and the scene is played again.

Children play out the story as they "believe" in the roles they assume. The teacher's major concern is with the process and values for the children involved. While occasionally a play developed creatively may be shared with another classroom, the value of creative dramatics lies in the process of playing and does not require an audience. A more formal production may grow out of creative

A second-grade "Max" tames the "wild things." Wearing their own fantastic masks, the children danced the "wild rumpus." Nancy Sawrey, teacher, West Lafayette, Indiana, Public Schools.

dramatics, but its primary purpose will be entertainment, not expression. For such a production, children plan more elaborate settings, acquire props, and wear costumes. Although the lines may become "finalized" as the scenes are rehearsed, they are neither written nor memorized.

Formal plays requiring memorization of written scripts have no place in the elementary school. When the child is limited by preplanned dialogue, there is little or no opportunity for him to think through the reactions of the character to the situation. Creativity is further limited when elementary school children attempt to write scripts. Usually their writing skill is not equal to the task of writing natural dialogue. Also, the length of time required to compose scripts

often becomes so frustrating that interest in the play is killed.

Even though formal productions are developed creatively, there are several cautions to be considered. The child may have developed a sincere belief in his role, but when costumed he may become overly concerned with the trappings of his part. The regal queen who gracefully mounted the throne during a creative rehearsal, may remain a chubby nine-year-old fussing with her mother's long skirt in an audience situation. Rehearsing for a perfect play for a P.T.A. program produces tense teachers and tense children. There is a real danger in exploiting children to entertain and gratify parents.

The many values of creative dramatics suggest its significance for the elementary curriculum. The child broadens living and learning experiences by playing the roles of people in the past, in other places, and in different situations. In creating plays, children obtain information and utilize their understandings from social studies and science classes. Language skills are developed through this form of creative expression. Tensions may be released and emotional and social adjustment can be fostered through creative dramatics. For example, the child who consistently seeks attention through "show off" behavior, may gain attention legitimately. The child who identifies with characters who are alone, or cold, or scorned, gains new insights and understandings of human behavior and becomes more sensitive to the needs of others. Since there is no written script in creative drama, the player is forced to "think on his feet" and draw on his inner resources. Skills of democratic living are developed through cooperative planning of action and characterization. Developing the ability to accept and give criticism in the informal evaluation period which should follow each playing, is an important concomitant of learning. Finally, interpretation of literature through creative dramatics brings children joy and zest in learning.

AN ACCOUNT OF CREATIVE DRAMATICS

An illustration of children's interpretation of a book through creative dramatics is included here to clarify purposes and methods. The *marginal* notes identify the teacher's role and procedural steps used in presenting the material.

CLASS DEVELOPMENT

Mrs. Stein read the Thurber story, *Many Moons,* to the fourth-grade class. The main character is a little princess who becomes ill of a "surfeit of raspberry tarts." When she is ill the Princess Lenore demands the moon to wear around her neck. The Lord Chamberlain, the Royal Wizard, and the Royal Mathematician are unable to agree on the facts about the moon or a method of obtaining it for her. Only the Court Jester discovers her ideas and is wise enough to solve the problem.

On the day following the teacher's reading, the children participated in retelling the story. The teacher's questions led them to a clear delineation of character:

- What kind of a little girl is Lenore?
- How does she treat the servants?
- Why does she behave in this way?

All the children pantomimed Lenore entering the throne room. After developing the character of

IDENTIFICATION OF TEACHING TECHNIQUES

The story selected for creative dramatics should have action, tight plot, and natural, interesting characters. A quick, satisfying ending, and sufficient dialogue are essential.

The teacher reads the story with enthusiasm and dramatic emphasis.

Children are involved in summarizing the story.

Teacher's questions guide children's understanding of the characters and setting.

the King and his three wise men, small groups pantomimed their movements and suggested a few phrases of greeting for the king. These questions guided the pantomime:

- How does the old Mathematician walk?
- What does he carry?
- What does he do when he approaches the king?
- How does he greet the King?

In the third class session, the children listed the major events in sequence and selected one incident they wanted to play.

This was the scene in which the worried King calls for his advisors to solve the problem of getting the moon for Lenore.

MRS. STEIN: Whom does the King call first?

CHILDREN: The Lord High Chamberlain.

MRS. STEIN: Let's talk about the Chamberlain. What kind of man is he?

BILL: He is short and fat.

SALLY: And he wears thick glasses.

JERRY: He thinks he know more than anyone else.

MRS. STEIN: What are some of the things he has done for the King?

CHILDREN: He has brought ivory, peacocks, pink elephants, blue poodles and—and—

MRS. STEIN: Perhaps we should hear the list again. Why does the Lord Chamberlain say he can't get the moon?

ANNE: It is made of melted metal of some kind and 30,000 miles away.

BRUCE: Melted copper!

[*The teacher leads a similar discussion of the Royal Wizard and the Royal Mathematician.*]

MRS. STEIN: (*Placing two chairs in front of the room.*) Here is the throne—it has a high back—is covered with soft red velvet. Who would like to play King? All right, Mike. (*She then selects the other characters for the scene.*)

The use of pantomime in the initial stages encourages children to use their bodies and helps them develop belief in the characters. It avoids mere verbalization.

The total class is involved in character development. Each child participates. The teacher may select a few children to demonstrate their interpretation of character. The teacher's questions stimulate creative responses.

The addition of one or two lines of conversation makes it possible to evaluate brief units of action. Also, many children can participate before an entire scene is planned.

It is not necessary to begin with the first scene in the story—children may choose to first "play" the most exciting scene or the one with the most characters. This process often strengthens the introductory scene if the entire story is to be developed as a play.

The teacher directs attention to sequence of events in the scene.

Characterization is reviewed. Physical characteristics and personality patterns are discussed. Children may want to return to the word pictures in the text and look at the illustrations as they imagine the appearances of the major characters.

The teacher suggests the setting by mapping areas necessary to the action. Only a few pieces of furniture are used. In the beginning, no props are needed. Later, such simple items as crown and scepter may be added if the children suggest them.

In selecting volunteers for the first playing, it is wise to choose children who will "carry the scene." Avoid typing characters. The fat boy usually should not play the part of the fat chamberlain, for example. Some child other than the dainty little blond in the class could play the part of Princess Lenore.

Sometimes children may suggest having a child play the part of an animal or tree. Unless the animal

MRS. STEIN: King—where are you sitting? Royal Advisors—take your places.

Audience—remember, we will talk about the scene *after* our imaginary curtain comes down. Be ready to tell how to make the scene better.

MRS. STEIN: When the scene opens, who is the first person to speak? Do you know what you are going to say, King? All ready, places! Curtain! [*The children play the scene which ends when the teacher says, "Cut."*]

MRS. STEIN: What did you especially like about this scene?

HANK: The Lord Chamberlain and all the others really bowed down to the King.

MARY: They forgot all the things they had done for the King.

MRS. STEIN: We'll come to that suggestion later, Mary. Let's talk about the things we liked first.

TOM: I liked it when the Chamberlain pretended to read his grocery list.

SUZY: The Royal Wizard really seemed old and fussy.

BILL: I didn't know when to come in.

MRS. STEIN: How could we help the advisers know when to appear?

MIKE: The King could tell the palace guard to send them in.

CHILDREN: That's neat—good idea!

is personified with human qualities of character, this is not recommended. There is little value in pretending to be a tree.

In creating the mood and giving directions, the teacher uses the name of the character rather than the name of the child playing that character.

The teacher emphasizes the responsibility of the audience for the evaluation. When beginning creative dramatics, it should be stressed that the audience does not participate during the scene.

The teacher briefly reviews the action before giving an agreed upon stage direction for beginning play.

Although she may be tempted to add comments or suggestions, the teacher joins the audience and refrains from giving any stage directions until the scene has been played. If the players are "floundering," it may be necessary to stop the action and replan. In case one player resorts to buffoonery, the teacher may temporarily halt the action and quietly but firmly assign another child to the part.

The scene is ended when the teacher gives an agreed upon terminating phrase. "Curtain," "finish," or "cut" are words that might be used.

The players return to their seats for the evaluation period.

The evaluation period begins with positive comments.

Children and teacher continue to refer to names of characters instead of using the name of the child who played the part.

Negative comments are accepted, but held in abeyance for the suggestion period.

The players themselves recognize difficulties.

Rather than giving answers, the teacher asks leading questions to guide children in solving the problem.

MRS. STEIN: What other suggestions do you have for improving the scene? Mary, you were concerned about remembering what the advisers had done for the King.

BILL: Well, I was the Mathematician and I couldn't remember all that stuff.

MARY: Mrs. Stein, couldn't we just write those funny things on a sheet of paper like they do in the story?

MRS. STEIN: Yes, I think that would help. We would want to use Thurber's exact words because they are so funny.

LARRY: I thought the Court Jester was really funny.

MRS. STEIN: Yes, he was. What things did he do that we enjoyed?

LARRY: He made silly faces and he imitated the fat old Chamberlain.

BRUCE: He did too much — I thought it was too silly.

MRS. STEIN: Would a Court Jester do anything to try to make the King laugh while he was talking to one of his advisers?

MARILYN: I don't think so. He's supposed to help. The King wouldn't like being interrupted.

MRS. STEIN: When would the Jester try to entertain the King? What would he do? Yes, Jim, he could imitate them as they leave the throne room. This illustration in the book shows him playing his lute.

SUZY: The Royal Wizard turned his back to the audience and we couldn't hear him.

MRS. STEIN: Is there another way to arrange the furniture on the stage so this won't happen?

SUZY: If we put the throne at the side of the stage the advisers wouldn't have to turn their backs.

MRS. STEIN: Good idea! Let's try it that way. Let's play the scene again now. We've added the palace guard. Who would like to be King? (*She continues to select a new cast.*)

MRS. STEIN: (*Aware of need for guidance.*) Let's remember the suggestions we've made. The King is really worried about Lenore's illness. He orders the guard to summon his advisers. Tomorrow the advisers can read from a list. For this time, just remember as many items as you can. The Jester

The teacher encourages the children to suggest ways to improve the play.

In certain circumstances, a part of the story could actually be read.

All comments are accepted. If the teacher withholds her views for a time, more perceptive children will usually recognize distracting elements and inadequate character portrayal.

Further questions help the children discover relationships between characters and predict behavior in the existing situation. They recognize inadequacies in the first playing, and plan for improvements.

The book is used to aid in planning.

Stage techniques receive less emphasis than plot and character development. However, such suggestions are accepted. The teacher's questions will lead children to improve stage techniques.

Whenever possible, children's ideas are tried out.

Children indicate their willingness to participate in many ways. A hand tentatively extended, or shining eyes may reveal a desire for a part. Try to give parts so children will experience a measure of success. A shy child cannot be expected to play the part of an aggressive King in the initial playing.

The teacher's descriptive phrases continuously emphasize characterization.

Once again, the teacher summarizes suggestions and the play begins.

will do funny things only after each adviser leaves. All right, let's play! Be ready to evaluate as soon as the scene is ended. Curtain!

In later sessions, the same techniques were used to develop the next scenes. One scene was created to explain why the Princess was sick. The children decided she had been greedy at her own birthday party. This new scene made it possible to add a number of characters as the guests who came to the royal birthday party. The children planned ways in which the Princess would further reveal her selfish character when she opened her gifts. For example, one gift was a mirror. The princess vainly exclaimed how pretty she was.

Some scenes were telescoped in order to preserve continuity of the plot.

New scenes may be created. Other characters may be added. Every opportunity to develop creativity is utilized.

The play might end with the development of only one scene. If the entire story is dramatized, the scenes are planned and played over a longer period of time. When the playing no longer produces creative responses, it is time to try another story.

DRAMATIZATION THROUGH PUPPETRY

Puppetry is another form of playmaking that provides experiences in interpreting literature. Beginning in the kindergarten with the construction of paper-bag puppets or simple stick puppets, this activity can bring satisfaction to children throughout elementary school. Materials and types of puppets will range from the simple to the complex, depending on the skill and age of the children.

The techniques of creative dramatics should be followed as puppet plays are created cooperatively by children and teacher. It is highly recommended that children "play out" stories prior to using their puppets. Written scripts are not necessary. Playing the story creatively will allow the child to identify with the characters before becoming involved with the mechanical manipulation of his puppet.

Value of Puppetry

Many children will "lose themselves" in the characterization of a puppet while hidden behind the stage; whereas, they may hesitate to express ideas and feelings on the open stage before an audience. Through puppetry, children learn to project their voices and develop facility in varying voice quality to portray different characters. For example, a rather quiet, shy child may use a booming voice as he becomes the giant in *Jack and the Beanstalk.* Puppetry also facilitates development of skills in arts and crafts. Problems of stage construction and the modeling of characters provide opportunities for development of creative thinking.

Selecting Stories for Puppetry

The techniques of puppetry are especially appropriate for certain stories. For

Students give rapt attention to a puppet show produced by their peers. Mrs. Cochrane, teacher, Washington School, Evanston, Illinois, Public Schools.

example, a group of second-graders presented a puppet show based on Rudyard Kipling's story of *The Elephant's Child.* At the appropriate moment, the crocodile pulled the elephant's short, stocking nose into the familiar elongated trunk. Such action would be nearly impossible for live actors to portray. Another group of ten-year-olds used marionettes to capture the hilarious action of the laughing-gas birthday party described in Travers' *Mary Poppins.* This scene would be difficult to portray in any other dramatic form.

Constructing Puppets and Marionettes

Numerous books are available that tell children how to make puppets, marionettes, and stages. Young children enjoy making simple cardboard figures that can be stapled to sticks or to tongue depressors. Paper bags stuffed with old stockings or newspaper may be tied to represent a puppet head and body. Ears, hair, aprons, and so on may be attached to create animals or people. By placing his hand in a sock or paper bag, the child can make the puppet appear to talk by moving his fingers and thumb.

A very simple puppet may be created by using a ping pong ball for a head and a plain handkerchief. The index finger may be inserted in a hole in the ball; the handkerchief slit and slipped over the puppeteer's hand. Two rubber bands may secure the handkerchief to the thumb and second finger, thereby making the arms of the puppet. Children may be taught to move their fingers and the puppet's head. Puppets that are somewhat more complex to construct may have heads of *pâpier maché,* potatoes, styrofoam balls, or other material. Cloth bodies can be cut and sewn by the children. Cardboard cylinders and small boxes may be used to create animal puppets. Yarn, fuzzy cloth, or old mittens make good cover materials for animals.

Marionettes require a degree of skill usually possessed by older elementary children. These figures are manipulated by moving strings attached to parts of the body and a board held aloft. A clothesline marionette is one of the most simple to make. Loops of clothesline form the framework of the body. Limbs and body may be covered with *pâpier maché*. Two strings fastened to screw eyes placed on either side of the head can be used to move the figure. Arms and legs can be made to move by attaching other strings to the elbow and knee joints. A marionette body can also be made by stuffing the foot of a sock and cutting and sewing arms and legs. One group of fifth-graders made animal marionettes by folding strips of paper into springs for legs and body. A special string on the giraffe made him stretch his neck in a most believable fashion. Wooden marionettes may be made by children who are able to remain interested for a long period of time while they construct the complex figures.

Most books on puppetry give directions for constructing stages. A simple stage for stick or hand puppets can be made by turning a table on its side. The puppeteer sits or kneels behind the table top. Another simple stage may be made by hanging curtains so they cover the lower and upper part of a doorway. A table, cardboard, or side of a large box could also be placed in a doorway. This type of stage is particularly good because children waiting their turns at the side of the stage are hidden from view. Older children can construct a framework for more durable puppet stages. Permanent stages that can be moved from room to room should be available in the school. Here is a way to involve parents in school activities. Screens or hinged wings may be placed at the side of such a puppet stage. Cloth, paper, or old window shades can be used for background material.

GAMES BASED ON LITERATURE

Games provide another means for reinforcing children's knowledge of books and authors. They capitalize upon the child's natural inclination for play and bring teacher and child together in the mutual enjoyment of books.

Book games can be played when there are brief waiting periods between scheduled activities. Educationally sound games are also needed for quiet indoor play.

Guessing Games and Riddles

Children enjoy "acting out" real-life situations and scenes from books. Many guessing games utilize pantomime in some form. Young children may try to guess the Mother Goose character being pantomimed. Older children divide into groups to play charades based upon literature. One group might choose to portray a title by actions representing words or syllables. The first audience group that guesses the title correctly has the privilege of presenting the next charade. In another version, two teams alternate in presenting timed charades. The team that names the most dramatized books in the shortest time wins the game. Teams may pantomime characters and scenes from stories as well as book titles.

Riddles are fun for all ages. They can be based upon several types of questions. Samples of these types of riddles follow:

WHO AM I?

- I rescued the big ocean liner. Who am I? (Answer: *Little Toot*)
- I am a house painter who longs to go exploring. I keep penguins in the ice box. Who am I? (Answer: Mr. Popper)
- I am a Hungarian tomboy who went to live with my uncle on a farm. Who am I? (Answer: Kate in *The Good Master*)

WHO LIVED HERE?

- Who lived on a boat in the Yangtze River? (Answer: Ping in *The Story About Ping*)
- Who lived neither in the Highlands of Scotland nor the Lowlands, but half way between? (Answer: *Wee Gillis*)
- Who lived in a school with eleven other little girls? (Answer: *Madeline*)

WHAT IS IT?

- What did *Little Leo* take to Italy? (Answer: his Indian suit)
- With what did Pecos Bill capture lightning? (Answer: a tornado)
- What one thing did Janey Larkin cherish on all of her moves? (Answer: her *Blue Willow* plate)

"Find the Missing Color" is a game that can be played by writing the correct color word from the titles of stories the children have read. The game might include:

Island of the _____ Dolphins (Blue)
The _____ Stallion (Black)
The Children of _____ Knowe (Green)
The Little Rabbit Who Wanted Wings (Red)
_____ Willow (Blue)
Hans Brinker or the _____ Skates (Silver)
_____ Mystery (Blue)
The _____ Bow (Bronze)

Similarly, with words representing foods, such titles as the following could be given in a game called "What Food?"

_____ Girl (Strawberry)
On the Banks of _____ Creek (Plum)
Space Ship Under the _____ Tree (Apple)
The _____ Trick (Lemonade)
The Enormous _____ (Egg)
_____ John (Onion)
Wonderful Flight to the _____ Planet (Mushroom)
Miracles on _____ Hill (Maple)

A group of children might create their own book of riddles. One class might exchange riddles with another group. A new riddle could be displayed on the library bulletin board each week. Sometimes, riddles may be composed in verse. The riddle below was written about Langstaff's *Frog Went A-Courtin'*.

> *I am a little creature*
> *And I'm as happy as can be;*
> *The reason why I'm happy*
> *Is Miss Mouse will marry me.*[22]

Children can make "Guess Who?" games and puzzles that can be duplicated for individual use. Examples of completion and scrambled-name puzzles follow:

SCRAMBLED CHARACTERS SUPER[23]

1. *I had adventures with the white rabbit and Cheshire cat.*   ELICA
2. *My story takes you to the Alps.*   DEIHI
3. *I am the* angel *burro of Grand Canyon.*   GHTYBRI
4. *I wore an Indian suit to Italy.*   LELTTI OLE
5. *I was a princess who wanted the moon.*   ENELRO
6. *I grew watermelons in China so I'd have money to buy a bracelet for my mother.*   TTLLIE UW
7. *Jane, Michael, and I had tea on the ceiling one afternoon.*   YRMA PPPINOS
8. *I'm a doll but had adventures in a boy's pocket.*   YMPIUINT EJNA
9. *My father left me in Indian country, but I had courage.*   SRAHA NBLEO
10. *I pretended I had 100 dresses.*   WNDAA
11. *I am the man of the family who borrows odd objects.*   ODP
12. *I wrote a composition about storks*   NAIL

[22] Joy Cramer, student, The Ohio State University.
[23] Created by Jeanette Sexton, student, Michigan State University.

13. *Benjamin Franklin took the credit for all my inventions.*   **SOAM**

14. *My dream came true when I went up the mountains with the sheep.*   **LEUGIM**

15. *I had a famous descendant named Man-of-War.*   **MASH**

BOOK TITLE QUIZ[24]

1. *I convinced the Baron that I am big, fast, and furious. I am a daschund and my name is _____.* (Maxie)

2. *Johnny Orchard's bear cub outgrew his welcome on their farm and ended up in the zoo because he was the _____.* (The Biggest Bear)

3. *I was rather lazy after all my meals and soon there was not room for me in my house because I am _____.* (The Man Who Didn't Wash His Dishes)

4. *A little old man set out to find a kitten for his wife, but he just couldn't decide which he liked best. Soon he had _____.* (Millions of Cats)

5. *Mr. and Mrs. Mallard were able to raise their family in Boston's Public Garden because the people did not hesitate to _____.* (Make Way for Ducklings)

6. *I am a little dog who was adopted by Madeline and her friends because I was responsible for _____.* (Madeline's Rescue)

7. *Katy and Carl had an Easter Egg hunt. Then their grandma helped them make _____.* (The Egg Tree)

8. *I was built on a hill in the country, but I was soon surrounded by the big city. One spring morning, I was moved from the city to the country by the great-great-granddaughter of the builder of _____.* (The Little House)

9. *I am a dog who is white but usually rather dirty.*

[24]Created by Cleone McNamara, student, The Ohio State University.

I am _____. (Harry, the Dirty Dog)

10. *I grew tired of working in the city and living in a house, so I went away to the country. However, I soon decided to return to the city because I really did not mind being _____.* (The Horse Who Lived Upstairs)

Crossword puzzles devised by the boys and girls in the middle grades provide for fun in interpreting literature. Before making their own puzzles, children need guidance from the teacher. This guidance may be given simply by constructing a puzzle with the entire class.

Another type of puzzle may be constructed by making a story using book titles. Children enjoy developing these individually or in small groups. The following is an example of such a story:

FIND THE TITLES

One morning in Maine, Mr. Revere and I decided to go with Jane and Jane's father to visit Mrs. Piggle Wiggle's farm. We didn't know how we were all going to get in his little auto, but it was not too small after all; it was just the right size.

"Wake up farm," we chanted all together as we rode along toward the farm. "Look out the window," Jane called. "There's a dead bird." But Father rounded the corner and started down, down the mountain. "When we were very young there used to be bears on Hemlock Mountain," said Mr. Revere. "I can remember when Miss Hickory saw the biggest bear—she ran into Mike's house, took his Matchlock gun and made the loudest noise in the world."

We saw the little house in the distance. It was a very special house—for when Mr. Peaceable paints, he uses 900 buckets of paint. The first animals to greet us were millions of cats and then along came a dog.

We went down to the barnyard where Onion John was examining an enormous egg. "Un-

less Horton hatches the egg, we're going to have scrambled eggs super," he said. Onion John showed us the clean pig, the black stallion, and Chanticleer, his prize rooster. Above the door in the wall hung Charlotte's web. This is the happy place I thought. Perhaps I'll be a farmer in many moons to come. As we follow the sunset home, we know this has been a time of wonder.

The above story contains forty titles. How many did you find? You may check your answers with those listed below.

One Morning in Maine	*The Loudest Noise in the World*
Mr. Revere and I	*The Little House*
Jane's Father	*The First Animals*
Mrs. Piggle-Wiggle's Farm	*Millions of Cats*
Little Auto	*Along Came a Dog*
Not Too Small after All	*Onion John*
Just the Right Size	*The Enormous Egg*
Wake up Farm	*Horton Hatches the Egg*
All Together	*Scrambled Eggs Super*
Look out the Window	*Clean Pig*
The Dead Bird	*The Black Stallion*
Down, down the Mountain	*Chanticleer*
When We Were Very Young	*Door in the Wall*
The Bears on Hemlock Mountain	*Charlotte's Web*
Miss Hickory	*Happy Place*
The Biggest Bear	*Perhaps I'll Be a Farmer*
Mike's House	*Many Moons*
The Matchlock Gun	*Follow the Sunset*
	Time of Wonder
	A Very Special House
	Mr. Peaceable Paints
	900 Buckets of Paint

Older children have fun writing sets of clues on paper shaped like footprints for the game, "Book Detective." Different groups could compose four clues for each book numbered in order of their difficulty. If the group cannot guess the name of the book with the first clue, the children can ask the leader for another clue. The group that identifies the most books with the fewest footprint clues wins the game.

"Twenty Questions" is a game that can be played by small groups or the entire class. In one room, we might observe five fourth-graders questioning a classmate who is thinking of a book. The questions can be answered only by responding "yes" or "no." Children quickly learn to ask categorical questions. Some of the questions may include:

- Is it a fairy tale?
- Does it take place in modern times?
- Is it an animal book?
- Do the animals actually exist?
- Are they farm animals?

The questioning continues until all twenty questions are asked or the title is guessed.

A "Tic Tac Toe" game can be constructed by writing literature categories on a board as shown in the diagram. With the guidance of the teacher, the children will have previously submitted appropriate questions for each category. These will be written on cards and placed in labeled envelopes. There are two players in this game. The first player chooses the category with which he would like to start; for example, science books. He then draws a question from the envelope pertaining to his category. If he answers the question correctly, he may place his mark in the square. The players continue in the usual Tic Tac Toe fashion until one player or "the cat" wins.

"Book Baseball" is another way of utilizing children's knowledge of literature. Four bases are designated in the room. The teacher "pitches" questions based on authors, titles, or characters to each player in turn. If the question is answered correctly, "the batter" moves to first base; if not, he makes an out. The player progresses from base to base as other teammates answer correctly. Following baseball rules, the opposing team takes its turn at bat when the other team makes three outs.

A book version of "Hot Potato" is played as any number of children sit in a circle. The leader, who stands in the center, gives a book to a player and calls, "Book." By the count of five, the player must give the title of a book and return the "hot book" to the leader or be eliminated. The game may be varied by calling for an author, a poem, or favorite character.

Table Games

Resourceful teachers can construct a variety of board or table games. The basic patterns may be designed for two to four players who move numbers or figures along marked spaces in a pathway or channel to reach a desired goal. A player can move forward by selecting a question card from a pile and giving the correct answer. The game may be made more interesting by adding chance cards which would govern the number of question cards to be drawn or spaces to be moved forward.

Using similar procedures, a table game may be devised that uses the characters and events in one book. "Call It 100-Point Courage"[25] was based on Sperry's *Call It Courage.* The game is played by throwing dice in order to move markers around a course. When the marker stops on certain squares, the player must draw a card from the center pack. Cards of courage, with such labels as "Direction pointed by Kivi the Albatross" or "Mafatu's knife," give the player ten additional points. The player loses ten points if he draws a card of fear with such titles as "mast and sail broken by typhoon" or "noise from eater-of-men's drums." The game continues until one player accumulates 100

Science	Biography	Fiction
Poetry	Horse Stories	Myths and Legends
Humor	Fairy Tales and Fantasy	Sports Stories

Literature "Tic Tac Toe."

points taking Mafatu back to the island of Hikueri.

"Go with Anatole" is a table game devised by a teacher to be played on a board marked in four sections similar to a parcheesi board. Each of the four players starts his miniature mouse from the hole at position one and moves in twelve spaces to his cheese. The player uses a spinner to determine the number of cards he may draw. Each correct answer allows him to move one space forward. If the spinner stops on "lucky mouse," the player gets another turn. Questions may be based on familiar books and current reading in the classroom.

---

[25]Game created by Sharlene Polk, The Ohio State University.

Children can develop an awareness of types of books by playing a game in which it is necessary to classify titles. In a game entitled "Katy-No-Pockets," a board is constructed by folding plastic-coated paper so each player has twelve pockets. Forty-eight cards of one color are labeled with titles of books; five to eight category cards are placed in the center. Title cards are dealt to the players who place them in the pockets. Each child in turn draws a category card. Suppose he draws the category card, *Horse Stories*. If he has title cards of *King of the Wind* and *The Black Stallion*, he removes these cards from the pockets and replaces the category card at the bottom of the center pile. The game ends when a player removes all his cards.

The game of *Authors*, always popular with children, may be made by using familiar book titles and well-known authors of children's literature. Cards can be designed so that there are three title cards for each author selected. Children take turns "calling" or "drawing" for cards until they complete their "books" of four title cards. The following authors and titles of their books could be used for sets of cards:

- Marguerite de Angeli
  The Door in the Wall
  Thee, Hannah
  Bright April
  Skippack School
- Robert Lawson
  Rabbit Hill
  Mr. Twigg's Mistake
  McWhinney's Jaunt
  Ben and Me
  The Fabulous Flight
- William Pène du Bois
  The Twenty-One Balloons
  The Alligator Case
  The Great Geppy
  Lion
- Carolyn Haywood
  Little Eddie
  Eddie and His Big Deals
  "B" Is for Betsy
  Betsy's Busy Summer
- Marguerite Henry
  Misty of Chincoteague
  King of the Wind
  Brighty of the Grand Canyon
  The White Stallion of Lippiza
- Meindert DeJong
  The House of Sixty Fathers
  Along Came a Dog
  Hurry Home, Candy
  The Wheel on the School
- Dr. Seuss
  The 500 Hats of Bartholomew Cubbins
  And To Think that I Saw It on Mulberry Street
  Horton Hatches the Egg
  The Cat in the Hat
- Robert McCloskey
  Homer Price
  Centerburg Tales
  Lentil
  Burt Dow
- Lois Lenski
  Strawberry Girl
  Shoo-Fly Girl
  Judy's Journey
  San Francisco Boy
- Beverly Cleary
  The Mouse and the Motorcycle
  Henry Huggins
  Beezus and Ramona
  Ribsy
- Laura Ingalls Wilder
  Little House in the Big Woods
  The Long Winter
  On the Banks of Plum Creek
  These Happy Golden Years
- William Steele
  The No-Name Man of the Mountain
  The Perilous Road
  The Lone Hunt
  Winter Danger

Variations of lotto or bingo games may be made for children's use. Titles, authors, characters, and places in children's literature are written on "Book-O" cards. A caller reads matching identification cards, and the players place markers over the proper squares. A winner is declared when a player has one horizontal, diagonal, or vertical row covered. The game may be played until a winner has all squares on his card covered. Each card in the set must be different.

Young children enjoy working picture puzzles made from book covers pasted on heavy cardboard. The pieces may be stored in small boxes labeled with the title and placed in the reading corner.

Electric quiz games made by the teacher or older children themselves provide another source of entertainment and education. These boards have questions and answers placed by metal hooks or brads which are connected in pairs. Dry cells provide electric current so a light flashes when the questioner touches the wire to the proper answer to complete the circuit. Specific directions for wiring such boards are given in Parker's *Science Experiences Elementary*

School.[26] The train lamp in the quiz board (pictured here) is lighted when the player successfully matches the name of the book character and symbolic object. One free wire is held to touch the screw under the title, *Mary Poppins*. When the other free wire is held to the screw under the umbrella symbol, the electric circuit is completed and the bulb is lighted.

Commercially prepared games are also available for activities related to children's literature.[27] However, children derive many values through the process of constructing games. When boys and girls plan puzzles, riddles, and games, they recall characters from literature, titles, authors, and situations. If the complete group is to enjoy the games, each child needs to read widely. It is important to remember that the purpose of all these games is to stimulate reading, not to master isolated details of children's litera-

[26]Bertha Parker, *Science Experiences Elementary School* (New York: Harper & Row, 1953).
[27]The Children's Book Council, 175 Fifth Avenue, New York 10010, is one source.

An electric quiz board may be adapted for children's literature games. When the question is answered correctly, the train's headlight flashes. Constructed by Jean Neale, student, Purdue University.

ture. The elementary school should provide opportunities for children to enjoy educationally sound leisure-time activities.

Through games, pantomime, creative dramatics, puppetry, and use of varied art media, children interpret and share their understandings of children's literature. Valuable in their own right, these activities lead to deeper insights and lasting appreciations. Creativity does not develop in a vacuum; a book or poem may provide the stimulus for creative expression. For example, the poem below may lead to creative expression through writing, dramatics, music, or art media.

IMAGINE

IMAGINE!
  A tiny door that leads under a hill,
  Beneath roots and bright stones — and pebbly rills.

IMAGINE!
  A quaint little knocker and shoe scraper too,
  A curious carved key — waiting for you.
IMAGINE!
  Tiptoe on the doormat — you're turning the key.
  The red door would open — and there you'll be.
IMAGINE!
  Shut the door tightly — so no one should see,
  And no one would know then — where you would be!
    IMAGINE!

ANONYMOUS

If the classroom environment includes a rich variety of literature, interesting art materials, and teacher guidance and stimulation, children will interpret their reading in many ways. The creativity of children will extend the ideas given in this chapter.

SUGGESTED ACTIVITIES

1. Make a list of poems and stories that could be used to motivate creative writing.
2. Make a list of books and poems that could be interpreted in a peep show, wall hanging, model, diorama, or table display.
3. Illustrate one book using different media; for example, painting and a clay model.
4. Prepare a peep show, model, diorama, wall hanging, or table display to illustrate the title, character, or scene in a well-known book or poem.
5. List several themes for murals. Work with a group and develop one.
6. Construct a box movie, flannel-board story, puppet, or doll.
7. Work with a small group of children or peers to dramatize a scene from children's literature.
8. Pantomime Mother Goose rhymes.
9. Prepare a list of stories that could be told appropriately by using a flannel-board.
10. Make a mobile illustrating your favorite book characters.
11. Construct a participation bulletin board or one to introduce particular books.
12. Prepare one table game and one group game using characters, titles, and situations from children's literature.
13. Construct a literary crossword puzzle for middle-grade children.

RELATED READINGS

1. Andersen, Harold, Editor. *Creativity and Its Cultivation.* New York: Harper & Row, 1959.
   Basic viewpoints of such leaders as Erich Fromm, Rollo May, Carl Rogers, J. P. Guilford, and Margaret Mead are presented in papers included in this volume. A good reference for the nature of creativity and its relation to educational processes.

2. Applegate, Mauree. *Freeing Children to Write.* New York: Harper & Row, 1963.
The author's creativeness, enthusiasm, and joy in writing are shared with her excellent suggestions for guiding and evaluating children's writing.

3. Arnstein, Flora J. *Poetry in the Elementary Classroom.* New York: Appleton, 1962.
This author believes that children must write poetry to enjoy poetry written by others. Many examples of children's poems illustrate approaches to "teaching poetry." Chapter 11 gives suggestions for criticism of children's works that will foster growth.

4. Burrows, Alvina, Doris C. Jackson, and Dorothy Saunders. *They All Want to Write.* Third edition. New York: Holt, Rinehart and Winston, 1964.
Distinguishing children's practical writing and personal writing, the authors provide suggestions to stimulate original responses and guide development of children's writing skills. Case studies provide examples of children's work.

5. East, Marjorie. *Display for Learning.* New York: Holt, Rinehart and Winston, 1952.
"How to Make Posters and Charts" and "The Bulletin Board" are two chapters that will provide the teacher and librarian with effective suggestions for display.

6. Jagendorf, Moritz Adolf. *The First Book of Puppets.* Illustrated by Jean Michener. New York: F. Watts, 1952.
Clear descriptions of different kinds of puppets such as push, rod, and hand puppets, as well as marionettes are included. Information about stages, sets, and lighting will help teacher and pupils.

7. Johnson, Lillian. *Pâpier-Maché.* New York: McKay, 1958.
A book for children that shows how to create dolls, figures, and varied displays.

8. Kelley, Marjorie, and Nicholas Roukes. *Let's Make a Mural.* San Francisco: Fearon, 1959.
The authors of this booklet stress the idea that murals are the result of intellectual and emotional activity. Planning and organizing techniques are helpful. They suggest murals using fingerpaints, mosaics, ceramics, paper sculpture, and collage.

9. Kelley, Marjorie, and Nicholas Roukes. *Matting and Displaying the Work of Children.* San Francisco: Fearon, 1957.
This booklet provides creative ideas for effective display of children's art work. The varied mat treatments are especially interesting. The ideas for table displays and three dimensional displays are excellent.

10. Petty, Walter T., and Mary E. Bowen. *Slithery Snakes and Other Aids to Children's Writing.* New York: Appleton, 1967.
This paperback gives excellent suggestions for motivating children's creative writing. It uses literature as a model for children's writing and as a springboard for their creative expression.

11. Siks, Geraldine Brain. *Creative Dramatics, an Art for Children.* New York: Harper & Row, 1958.
The elementary teacher can obtain a thorough understanding of creative dramatics through this excellent book. Many examples and questions to be used in setting the stage, interpreting the story, and planning the dramatization illustrate creative dramatics at its best. Specific helps are presented by relating stories, motivation, and development to the interests and needs of different age levels. An annotated list of poems and stories to dramatize will be especially useful.

12. Thomas, R. Murray, and Sherwin G. Swartout. *Integrated Teaching Materials.* New York: McKay, 1960.
Chapter 20, "Models and Puppets," gives many ideas for preparing dioramas, models, and puppets. The photographs of children and their work are outstanding.

13. Torrance, E. Paul. *Guiding Creative Talent.* Englewood Cliffs, N.J.: Prentice-Hall, 1962.
A leader in the field writes about identification of creativity and suggests ways to maintain and guide creativity through classroom activities.

14. Ward, Winifred. *Playmaking with Children.* New York: Appleton, 1947.

Written by a pioneer in the field, this book describes creative dramatics as a process, shows its relation to the total program, and suggests stories to dramatize.

15. Williams, Catharine. *The Diorama as a Teaching Aid.* Columbus, Ohio: Bureau of Educational Research, The Ohio State University, 1956.

A supplement to the filmstrip also produced at Ohio State University, this pamphlet shows many ways of constructing a diorama.

16. Williams, Catharine. *How to Make and Use the Felt Board.* Columbus, Ohio: Bureau of Educational Research, The Ohio State University, 1956.

This pamphlet supplements a filmstrip by the same title and gives clear directions for making a felt board, constructing figures, and using the board in the classroom.

17. Wilt, Miriam E. *Creativity in the Elementary School.* New York: Appleton, 1959.

The author presents a philosophy of creativity that is implemented with examples. "Words are the Colors of my Palette" suggests ways of stimulating creative writing.

18. Yates, Elizabeth. *Someday You'll Write.* New York: Dutton, 1962.

Originally written for a twelve-year-old who was interested in the career of writing, this book gives worthwhile suggestions for anyone who wishes to write. Examples from well-known books of children's literature are given as models. Fine to read to a class or small group of middle-graders.

CHAPTER REFERENCES

1. Aldis, Dorothy. "Bad" and "Feet" in *All Together.* Illustrated by Marjorie Flack, Margaret Freeman, and Helen D. Jameson. New York: Putnam, 1925.

2. ———*Jane's Father.* Illustrated by Mary Stevens. New York: Putnam, 1954.

3. Allingham, William. "A Swing Song" in *Favorite Poems Old and New,* Helen Ferris, Editor. Illustrated by Leonard Weisgard. New York: Doubleday, 1957.

4. Anglund, Joan Walsh. *A Friend Is Someone Who Likes You.* New York: Harcourt, 1958.

5. ———*Look out the Window.* New York: Harcourt, 1959.

6. Asbjørnsen, P. C., and J. E. Moe. *The Three Billy Goats Gruff.* Illustrated by Marcia Brown. New York: Harcourt, 1957.

7. Atwater, Richard and Florence. *Mr. Popper's Penguins.* Illustrated by Robert Lawson. Boston: Little, Brown, 1938.

8. Bailey, Carolyn S. *The Little Rabbit Who Wanted Red Wings.* Illustrated by Dorothy Grider. New York: Platt & Munk, 1945.

9. ———*Miss Hickory.* Illustrated by Ruth Gannett. New York: Viking, 1962, 1946.

10. Baker, Betty. *Walk the World's Rim.* New York: Harper & Row, 1965.

11. Ball, Zachary. *Bristle Face.* New York: Holiday, 1962.

12. Baruch, Dorothy. "The Merry-Go-Round" in *Time for Poetry,* May Hill Arbuthnot, Editor. Glenview, Ill.: Scott, Foresman, 1952.

13. Becker, Edna. *900 Buckets of Paint.* New York: Abingdon, 1949.

14. Beim, Jerrold, *Trouble After School.* Illustrated by Don Sibley. New York: Harcourt, 1957.

15. Bemelmans, Ludwig. *Madeline.* New York: Viking, 1939.

16. ———*Madeline's Rescue.* New York: Viking, 1953.

17. Benary-Isbert, Margot. *Blue Mystery.* Translated by Richard and Clara Winston. Illustrated by Enrico Arno. New York: Harcourt, 1957.

18. Bendick, Jeanne. *The First Book of Automobiles.* New York: F. Watts, 1955.

19. ———*A Fresh Look at Night.* New York: F. Watts, 1963.

20. Bennett, Rainey. *The Secret Hiding Place.* Cleveland: World Publishing, 1960.

21. Bethers, Ray. *Perhaps I'll Be a Farmer.* New York: Aladdin, 1950.

22. Bishop, Claire Huchet. *The Five Chinese Brothers.* Illustrated by Kurt Wiese. New York: Coward-McCann, 1938.

23. Boston, L. M. *The Castle of Yew*. Illustrated by Margery Gill. New York: Harcourt, 1965.

24. ———*The Children of Green Knowe*. Illustrated by Peter Boston. New York: Harcourt, 1955.

25. Brooks, Gwendolyn. *Bronzeville Boys and Girls*. Illustrated by Ronni Solbert. New York: Harper & Row, 1956.

26. Brooks, Walter R. *Freddy, the Detective*. Illustrated by Kurt Wiese. New York: Knopf, 1932.

27. Brown, Margaret Wise. *The Dead Bird*. Illustrated by Remy Charlip. New York: W. R. Scott, 1958.

28. ———*Four Fur Feet*. Illustrated by Remy Charlip. New York: W. R. Scott, 1961.

29. Burnett, Frances Hodgson. *The Secret Garden*. Illustrated by Tasha Tudor. Philadelphia: Lippincott, 1938, 1909.

30. Burton, Virginia. *Life Story*. Boston: Houghton Mifflin, 1962.

31. ———*The Little House*. Boston: Houghton Mifflin, 1942.

32. Butterworth, Oliver. *The Enormous Egg*. Illustrated by Louis Darling. Boston: Little, Brown, 1956.

33. Cameron, Eleanor. *The Wonderful Flight to the Mushroom Planet*. Illustrated by Robert Henneberger. Boston: Little, Brown, 1954.

34. Carlson, Natalie Savage. *The Letter on the Tree*. Illustrated by John Kaufmann. New York: Harper & Row, 1964.

35. Carroll, Lewis, pseud. (Charles Dodgson). *Alice's Adventures in Wonderland and Through the Looking-Glass*. Illustrated by John Tenniel. New York: Macmillan, 1963 (first published separately, 1865 and 1872).

36. Charlip, Remy. *Fortunately*. New York: Parents Institute, 1964.

37. Cleary, Beverly. *Beezus and Ramona*. Illustrated by Louis Darling. New York: Morrow, 1955.

38. ———*Henry Huggins*. Illustrated by Louis Darling. New York: Morrow, 1950.

39. ———*The Mouse and the Motorcycle*. Illustrated by Louis Darling. New York: Morrow, 1965.

40. ———*Ribsy*. Illustrated by Louis Darling. New York: Morrow, 1964.

41. Clymer, Eleanor. *Not Too Small After All*. Illustrated by Tom O'Sullivan. New York: F. Watts, 1955.

42. Cooney, Barbara. *Chanticleer and the Fox*. New York: Crowell, 1958.

43. Corbett, Scott. *The Lemonade Trick*. Boston: Little, Brown, 1960.

44. ———*The Limerick Trick*. Boston: Little, Brown, 1964.

45. Credle, Ellis. *Down, Down the Mountain*. Camden, N.J.: Nelson, 1934.

46. Dalgliesh, Alice. *Bears on Hemlock Mountain*. Illustrated by Helen Sewell. New York: Scribner, 1952.

47. ———*The Courage of Sarah Noble*. Illustrated by Leonard Weisgard. New York: Scribner, 1954.

48. De Angeli, Marguerite. *Bright April*. New York: Doubleday, 1946.

49. ———*The Door in the Wall*. New York: Doubleday, 1949.

50. ———*Thee, Hannah!* New York: Doubleday, 1949.

51. ———*Skippack School*. New York: Doubleday, 1961.

52. De Gasztold, Carmen Bernos. *Prayers from the Ark*. Translated by Rumer Godden. Illustrated by Jean Primrose. New York: Viking, 1962.

53. DeJong, Meindert. *Along Came a Dog*. Illustrated by Maurice Sendak. New York: Harper & Row, 1958.

54. ———*The House of Sixty Fathers*. Illustrated by Maurice Sendak. New York: Harper & Row, 1956.

55. ———*Hurry Home, Candy*. Illustrated by Maurice Sendak. New York: Harper & Row, 1956.

56. ———*The Wheel on the School*. Illustrated by Maurice Sendak. New York: Harper & Row, 1954.

57. De la Mare, Walter. *Jack and the Beanstalk.* Illustrated by Joseph Low. New York: Knopf, 1959.

58. ————"The Old Stone House" in *Rhymes and Verses: Collected Poems for Young People.* Illustrated by Elinore Blaisdill. New York: Holt, Rinehart and Winston, 1947.

59. ————"Silver" in *Time for Poetry,* May Hill Arbuthnot, Editor. Glenview, Ill.: Scott, Foresman, 1952.

60. De Regniers, Beatrice Schenk. *May I Bring a Friend?* Illustrated by Beni Montresor. New York: Atheneum, 1964.

61. Dobbs, Rose. *No Room.* Illustrated by Fritz Eichenberg. New York: McKay, 1966.

62. Dodge, Mary Mapes. *Hans Brinker: or The Silver Skates.* Illustrated by George Wharton Edwards. New York: Scribner, 1915, 1865.

63. Du Bois, William Pène. *The Alligator Case.* New York: Harper & Row, 1965.

64. ————*The Great Geppy.* New York: Viking, 1940.

65. ————*Lion.* New York: Viking, 1956.

66. ————*The Twenty-One Balloons.* New York: Viking, 1947.

67. Edmonds, Walter D. *The Matchlock Gun.* Illustrated by Paul Lantz. New York: Dodd, Mead, 1941.

68. Elkin, Benjamin. *The Loudest Noise in the World.* Illustrated by James Daugherty. New York: Viking, 1954.

69. Enright, Elizabeth. *The Saturdays.* New York: Holt, Rinehart and Winston, 1941.

70. ————*Zeee.* Illustrated by Irene Haas. New York: Harcourt, 1965.

71. Estes, Eleanor. *The Alley.* Illustrated by Edward Ardizzone. New York: Harcourt, 1964.

72. ————*The Hundred Dresses.* Illustrated by Louis Slobodkin. New York: Harcourt, 1944.

73. Fallis, Edwina. "The Giant Shoes" in *Let's Read-Together Poems* (Book 3), Helen A. Brown and Harry J. Helt, Editors. New York: Harper & Row, 1954.

74. Farley, Walter. *The Black Stallion.* Illustrated by Keith Ward. New York: Random House, 1941.

75. Fisher, Aileen. *In the Woods, in the Meadow, in the Sky.* Illustrated by Margot Tomes. New York: Scribner, 1965.

76. Fitzhugh, Louise. *Harriet, the Spy.* New York: Harper & Row, 1964.

77. Flack, Marjorie. *Ask Mr. Bear.* New York: Macmillan, 1932.

78. ————*The Story about Ping.* Illustrated by Kurt Wiese. New York: Viking, 1933.

79. Fleming, Ian. *Chitty-Chitty-Bang-Bang.* Illustrated by John Burningham. New York: Random House, 1964.

80. Flora, James. *Leopold, the See-Through Crumbpicker.* New York: Harcourt, 1961.

81. ————*My Friend Charlie.* New York: Harcourt, 1964.

82. Foster, Genevieve. *Abraham Lincoln's World.* New York: Scribner, 1944.

83. ————*Augustus Caesar's World.* New York: Scribner, 1947.

84. ————*George Washington's World.* New York: Scribner, 1941.

85. ————*The World of Captain John Smith.* New York: Scribner, 1959.

86. ————*The World of Columbus and Sons.* New York: Scribner, 1965.

87. Fritz, Jean. *The Cabin Faced West.* Illustrated by Feodor Rojankovsky. New York: Coward-McCann, 1958.

88. ————*Magic to Burn.* Illustrated by Beth and Joe Krush. New York: Coward-McCann, 1964.

89. Fyleman, Rose. "The Best Game the Fairies Play" in *Time for Poetry,* May Hill Arbuthnot, Editor. Glenview, Ill.: Scott, Foresman, 1952.

90. Gág, Wanda. *Millions of Cats.* New York: Coward-McCann, 1928.

91. Gates, Doris. *Blue Willow.* Illustrated by Paul Lantz. New York: Viking, 1940.

92. George, Jean. *The Hole in the Tree.* New York: Dutton, 1957.

93. Godden, Rumer. *Impunity Jane.* Illustrated by Adrienne Adams. New York: Viking, 1954.

94. Gramatky, Hardie. *Little Toot*. New York: Putnam, 1939.
95. Haber, Heinz, Editor. *Our Friend the Atom*. Illustrated by Walt Disney Productions. New York: Golden Press, 1956.
96. Handforth, Thomas. *Mei Li*. New York: Doubleday, 1938.
97. "The Hare and the Tortoise" in *Aesop's Fables*, Joseph Jacobs, Editor. New York: Macmillan, 1950.
98. Haugaard, Erik. *Hakon of Rogen's Saga*. Illustrated by Leo and Diane Dillon. Boston: Houghton Mifflin, 1963.
99. Haywood, Carolyn. *"B" Is for Betsy*. New York: Harcourt, 1939.
100. ———*Betsy's Busy Summer*. New York: Harcourt, 1956.
101. ———*Eddie and His Big Deals*. New York: Morrow, 1955.
102. ———*Little Eddie*. New York: Morrow, 1947.
103. Henry, Marguerite. *Black Gold*. Illustrated by Wesley Dennis. Skokie, Ill.: Rand McNally, 1957.
104. ——— *Brighty of the Grand Canyon*. Illustrated by Wesley Dennis. Skokie, Ill.: Rand McNally, 1953.
105. ———*King of the Wind*. Illustrated by Wesley Dennis. Skokie, Ill.: Rand McNally, 1948.
106. ———*Misty of Chincoteague*. Illustrated by Wesley Dennis. Skokie, Ill.: Rand McNally, 1947.
107. ———*White Stallion of Lipizza*. Illustrated by Wesley Dennis. Skokie, Ill.: Rand McNally, 1964.
108. Heyward, DuBose. *The Country Bunny and the Little Gold Shoes*. Illustrated by Marjorie Flack. Boston: Houghton Mifflin, 1939.
109. Holling, Holling C. *Pagoo*. Boston: Houghton Mifflin, 1956.
110. Holm, Anne. *North to Freedom*. New York: Harcourt, 1965.
111. Hughes, Langston. "The African Dance" in *Favorite Poems Old and New*, Helen Ferris, Editor. Illustrated by Leonard Weisgard. New York: Doubleday, 1957.
112. Hunt, Irene. *Across Five Aprils*. Chicago: Follett, 1964.
113. James, Will. *Smoky, the Cow Horse*. New York: Scribner, 1965, 1926.
114. Kahl, Virginia. *Maxie*. New York: Scribner, 1956.
115. Keats, Ezra Jack. *Jennie's Hat*. New York: Harper & Row, 1966.
116. ———*The Snowy Day*. New York: Viking, 1962.
117. King, Robin and Billie. *Just the Right Size*. Illustrated by Robin King. New York: Dutton, 1957.
118. Kipling, Rudyard. *Just So Stories*. Illustrated by J. M. Gleeson. New York: Doubleday, 1952, 1902.
119. Krasilovsky, Phyllis. *The Man Who Didn't Wash His Dishes*. Illustrated by Barbara Cooney. New York: Doubleday, 1950.
120. Krauss, Ruth. *A Very Special House*. Illustrated by Maurice Sendak. New York: Harper & Row, 1953.
121. Krumgold, Joseph. . . . *And Now Miguel*. Illustrated by Jean Charlot. New York: Crowell, 1953.
122. ———*Onion John*. Illustrated by Symeon Shimin. New York: Crowell, 1959.
123. Langstaff, John. *Frog Went A-Courtin'*. Illustrated by Feodor Rojankovsky. New York: Harcourt, 1955.
124. Lawson, Robert. *Ben and Me*. Boston: Little, Brown, 1939.
125. ———*The Fabulous Flight*. Boston: Little, Brown, 1949.
126. ———*McWhinney's Jaunt*. Boston: Little, Brown, 1951.
127. ———*Mr. Revere and I*. Boston: Little, Brown, 1953.
128. ———*Mr. Twigg's Mistake*. Boston: Little, Brown, 1947.
129. ———*Rabbit Hill*. New York: Viking, 1945.
130. ———*They Were Strong and Good*. New York: Viking, 1940.
131. Leaf, Munro. *Wee Gillis*. Illustrated by Robert Lawson. New York: Viking, 1938.
132. Lenski, Lois. *Judy's Journey*. Philadelphia: Lippincott, 1947.

133. ———*The Little Auto.* New York: Walck, 1934.

134. ———*San Francisco Boy.* Philadelphia: Lippincott, 1955.

135. ———*Shoo-Fly Girl.* Philadelphia: Lippincott, 1963.

136. ———*Strawberry Girl.* Philadelphia: Lippincott, 1945.

137. Lewis, Richard, Editor. *The Moment of Wonder.* New York: Dial, 1964.

138. Lexau, Joan. *That's Good, That's Bad.* Illustrated by Aliki. New York: Dial, 1963.

139. Lindgren, Astrid. *Pippi Longstocking.* Translated by Florence Lamborn. Illustrated by Louis S. Glanzman. New York: Viking, 1950.

140. Lindsay, Vachel. "The Potatoes' Dance" in *Favorite Poems Old and New,* Helen Ferris, Editor. Illustrated by Leonard Weisgard. New York: Doubleday, 1957.

141. Lionni, Leo. *Swimmy.* New York: Pantheon, 1963.

142. Liu, Beatrice. *Little Wu and the Watermelons.* Illustrated by Graham Peck. Chicago: Follett, 1954.

143. Livingston, Myra Cohn. *See What I Found.* Illustrated by Erik Blegvad. New York: Harcourt, 1962.

144. McCloskey, Robert. *Burt Dow, Deep-Water Man.* New York: Viking, 1963.

145. ———*Centerburg Tales.* New York: Viking, 1951.

146. ———*Homer Price.* New York: Viking, 1943.

147. ———*Lentil.* New York: Viking, 1940.

148. ———*Make Way for Ducklings.* New York: Viking, 1941.

149. ———*One Morning in Maine.* New York: Viking, 1952.

150. ———*Time of Wonder.* New York: Viking, 1957.

151. McCord, David. *Far and Few.* Illustrated by Henry B. Kane. Boston: Little, Brown, 1952.

152. ———*Take Sky.* Illustrated by Henry B. Kane. Boston: Little, Brown, 1962.

153. MacDonald, Betty. *Mrs. Piggle-Wiggle.* Revised edition. Illustrated by Hilary Knight. Philadelphia: Lippincott, 1957.

154. ———*Mrs. Piggle-Wiggle's Farm.* Illustrated by Maurice Sendak. Philadelphia: Lippincott, 1954.

155. McGinley, Phyllis. *The Horse Who Lived Upstairs.* Illustrated by Helen Stone. Philadelphia: Lippincott, 1944.

156. Meadowcroft, Enid LaMonte. *The First Year.* Illustrated by Grace Paull. New York: Crowell, 1946.

157. Merriam, Eve. *It Doesn't* Always *Have to Rhyme.* Illustrated by Malcolm Spooner. New York: Atheneum, 1964.

158. Merrill, Jean. *The Pushcart War.* Illustrated by Ronni Solbert. New York: W. R. Scott, 1964.

159. ———*The Superlative Horse.* Illustrated by Ronni Solbert. New York: W. R. Scott, 1961.

160. Milhous, Katherine. *The Egg Tree.* New York: Scribner, 1950.

161. Milne, A. A. *Now We Are Six.* Illustrated by E. H. Shepard. New York: Dutton, 1927.

162. ———*When We Were Very Young.* Illustrated by E. H. Shepard. New York: Dutton, 1924.

163. ———*Winnie the Pooh.* Illustrated by E. H. Shepard. New York: Dutton, 1926.

164. Minarik, Else Holmelund. *Little Bear's Visit.* Illustrated by Maurice Sendak. New York: Harper & Row, 1961.

165. Norton, Mary. *The Borrowers.* Illustrated by Beth and Joe Krush. New York: Harcourt, 1953.

166. O'Dell, Scott. *Island of the Blue Dolphins.* Boston: Houghton Mifflin: 1960.

167. O'Neill, Mary. *Hailstones and Halibut Bones.* Illustrated by Leonard Weisgard. New York: Doubleday, 1961.

168. ———*Words, Words, Words.* Illustrated by Judy Piussi-Campbell. New York: Doubleday, 1966.

169. Payne, Emmy. *Katy No-Pocket.* Illustrated by H. A. Rey. Boston: Houghton Mifflin, 1944.
170. Pearce, Philippa. *Tom's Midnight Garden.* Illustrated by Susan Einzig. Philadelphia: Lippincott, 1959.
171. Politi, Leo. *Little Leo.* New York: Scribner, 1951.
172. Quigley, Lillian. *The Blind Men and the Elephant.* Illustrated by Janice Holland. New York: Scribner, 1959.
173. Rojankovsky, Feodor. *The Three Bears.* New York: Golden Press, 1948.
174. Sauer, Julia L. *Mike's House.* Illustrated by Don Freeman. New York: Viking, 1954.
175. Sawyer, Ruth. *Journey Cake, Ho!* Illustrated by Robert McCloskey. New York: Viking, 1953.
176. Schneider, Herman and Nina. *Follow the Sunset.* Illustrated by Lucille Corcos. New York: Doubleday, 1952.
177. Schulz, Charles M. *Happiness Is a Warm Puppy.* New York: Determined Productions, 1962.
178. Selden, George. *The Cricket in Times Square.* Illustrated by Garth Williams. New York: Farrar, Straus, 1960.
179. Sendak, Maurice. *Where the Wild Things Are.* New York: Harper & Row, 1963.
180. Seredy, Kate. *The Good Master.* New York: Viking, 1935.
181. Seuss, Dr., pseud. (Theodor S. Geisel). *And To Think That I Saw It on Mulberry Street.* New York: Vanguard, 1937.
182. ————*The Cat in the Hat.* New York: Random House, 1957.
183. ————*The 500 Hats of Bartholomew Cubbins.* New York: Vanguard, 1938.
184. ————*Horton Hatches the Egg.* New York: Random House, 1940.
185. ————*McElligot's Pool.* New York: Random House, 1947.
186. ————*On Beyond Zebra.* New York: Random House, 1955.
187. ————*Scrambled Eggs Super.* New York: Random House, 1953.
188. Slobodkin, Louis. *The Space Ship Under the Apple Tree.* New York: Macmillan, 1952.
189. Smith, Robert Paul. *When I Am Big.* Illustrated by Lillian Hoban. New York: Harper & Row, 1965.
190. Sorensen, Virginia. *Miracles on Maple Hill.* Illustrated by Beth and Joe Krush. New York: Harcourt, 1956.
191. Speare, Elizabeth George. *The Bronze Bow.* Boston: Houghton Mifflin, 1961.
192. Sperry, Armstrong. *Call It Courage.* New York: Macmillan, 1941.
193. Spyri, Johanna. *Heidi.* Translated by Helen B. Dole. Illustrated by William Sharp. New York: Grosset & Dunlap, 1945, 1884.
194. Steele, William O. *The Lone Hunt.* Illustrated by Paul Galdone. New York: Harcourt, 1956.
195. ————*The No-Name Man of the Mountain.* Illustrated by Jack Davis. New York: Harcourt, 1964.
196. ————*The Perilous Road.* Illustrated by Paul Galdone. New York: Harcourt, 1958.
197. ————*Winter Danger.* Illustrated by Paul Galdone. New York: Harcourt, 1954.
198. Stephens, Peter John. *Towappu: Puritan Renegade.* New York: Atheneum, 1966.
199. Sterling, Dorothy. *Mary Jane.* New York: Doubleday, 1959.
200. Stolz, Mary. *The Bully of Barkham Street.* New York: Harper & Row, 1963.
201. ————*A Dog on Barkham Street.* New York: Harper & Row, 1960.
202. Tennyson, Alfred, Lord. *The Charge of the Light Brigade.* Illustrated by Alice and Martin Provensen. New York: Golden Press, 1964.
203. Thurber, James. *Many Moons.* Illustrated by Louis Slobodkin. New York: Harcourt, 1943.
204. Titus, Eve. *Anatole.* Illustrated by Paul Galdone. New York: McGraw-Hill, 1956.
205. Travers, Pamela L. *Mary Poppins.* Illustrated by Mary Shepard. New York: Harcourt, 1934.

206. Tresselt, Alvin. *Hide and Seek Fog.* Illustrated by Roger Duvoisin. New York: Lothrop, 1965.

207. ———*Wake Up, Farm!* Illustrated by Roger Duvoisin. New York: Lothrop, 1955.

208. Udry, Janice May. *The Moon Jumpers.* Illustrated by Maurice Sendak. New York: Harper & Row, 1959.

209. Urmston, Mary. *The New Boy.* Illustrated by Brinton Turkle. New York: Doubleday, 1950.

210. Ward, Lynd. *The Biggest Bear.* Boston: Houghton Mifflin, 1952.

211. Webber, Irma E. *It Looks Like This.* New York: W. R. Scott, 1949.

212. Weisgard, Leonard. *The Clean Pig.* New York: Scribner, 1952.

213. ———*Mr. Peaceable Paints.* New York: Scribner, 1956.

214. White, E. B. *Charlotte's Web.* Illustrated by Garth Williams. New York: Harper & Row, 1952.

215. Wilder, Laura Ingalls. *The Little House in the Big Woods.* Illustrated by Garth Williams. New York: Harper & Row, 1953, 1932.

216. ———*The Long Winter.* Illustrated by Garth Williams. New York: Harper & Row, 1953, 1940.

217. ———*On the Banks of Plum Creek.* Illustrated by Garth Williams. New York: Harper & Row, 1953, 1937.

218. ———*These Happy Golden Years.* Illustrated by Garth Williams. New York: Harper & Row, 1953, 1943.

219. Wynne, Annette. "I Keep Three Wishes Ready" in *Time for Poetry,* May Hill Arbuthnot, Editor. Glenview, Ill.: Scott, Foresman, 1952.

220. Yates, Elizabeth. *Carolina's Courage.* Illustrated by Nora S. Unwin. New York: Dutton, 1964.

221. Zion, Gene. *Harry the Dirty Dog.* Illustrated by Margaret Bloy Graham. New York: Harper & Row, 1956.

222. Zolotow, Charlotte. *Do You Know What I'll Do?* Illustrated by Garth Williams. New York: Harper & Row, 1958.

223. ———*The Sky Was Blue.* Illustrated by Garth Williams. New York: Harper & Row, 1963.

224. ———*Someday.* Illustrated by Arnold Lobel. New York: Harper & Row, 1964.

225. ———*When I Have a Little Girl.* Illustrated by Hilary Knight. New York: Harper & Row, 1965.

13

TEACHING LITERATURE IN THE ELEMENTARY SCHOOL

As teachers gathered for a meeting about a new literature program, fragments of conversation indicated their concern about the topic for discussion:

"How can we add another subject to a crowded schedule?"
"But I already have literature in my reading program!"
"The new readers have fine literary material."
"And the supplementary books give even more!"
"I certainly don't want children to pull literature apart as I did in high school."
"We have a good library reading program now."
"My gifted children are already reading the classics."
"Will it mean a required reading list for all children?"
"What is a literature program, anyway?"
"I teach literature in my story hour. . . ."

The majority of elementary schools in the United States have no planned literature program; usually literature is subsumed under the "reading" or "English" program. Some of the basic readers do include literary selections and teaching suggestions for literary criticism. An examination of curriculum guides for the language arts reveals little attention is given to literature. In a statewide study of Wisconsin schools in 1964, Pooley found that primary children had been exposed to literature but that no time *whatsoever* was devoted to the study of literature in the intermediate grades.[1] Thus, the relatively new

---

[1] As cited by James Squire in *Source Book on English Institutes for Elementary Teachers* (Champaign, Ill.: National Council of Teachers of English, 1965), p. 9.

idea of a planned literature curriculum in the elementary school generates the kinds of questions cited in the introductory anecdote.

Recent research would indicate that schools cannot afford to postpone the study of literature until the junior high school. Bloom maintains that children have obtained at least seventy-five per cent of their total general achievement by the time they have reached age thirteen. He points out that "the first period of elementary school (grades one–three) is probably the most crucial period available to the public schools for the development of general learning patterns."[2] An increasing awareness of the ability of children to grasp ideas once considered too complex for the elmentary school child also suggests that literature is an appropriate subject for the elementary school. Furthermore, curriculum planners have given close attention to the concepts stated by Bruner in his much quoted book, *The Process of Education*,[3] that every subject has a structure, and that teaching it involves *progressive* emphasis upon basic concepts underlying that structure. Some of the basic concepts of literature can be taught in the kindergarten.

While the entire elementary school curriculum contributes to the appreciation of literature, a planned literature program should be a part of an integrated language arts curriculum. Through experiencing literature, the child's natural curiosity is extended as he is helped to see his world in a new light. Hyde Cox describes the way a question by Robert Frost made him see education in a new light.

> *"How many things have to happen to you," he [Frost] asks his young friends, "before something occurs to you?" Things that happen to you, of course, are only events. Things that occur to you are ideas; and he is saying that ideas are more important. That is the kind of question he asks that I would not have thought to ask myself, and it leads to one of the best things he ever taught me: to entertain ideas. We all speak of having ideas but entertaining them is an art. You have to invite them in and*

> *make them feel at home—as you do company—while you get to know them, to see if you want to know them better. Entertaining ideas is almost the heart of education.*[4]

WHAT LITERATURE DOES FOR CHILDREN

Teaching literature is the process of guiding children to enjoy, interpret, and evaluate the writing they encounter. This teaching should be guided by recognition of the values that literature holds for children.

Enjoyment

First, and foremost, literature provides enjoyment. The child delights in the rhythm of "My Shadow" or "The Highwayman"; he responds to the imagery of such lines as "Slowly, silently, now the moon/Walks the

[2]Benjamin Bloom, *Stability and Change in Human Characteristics* (New York: Wiley, 1964), p. 110.

[3]Jerome S. Bruner, *The Process of Education* (Cambridge, Mass.: Harvard University Press, 1960).

[4]Hyde Cox, "Foreword," in Robert Frost, *You Come Too, Favorite Poems for Young Readers,* with wood engravings by Thomas W. Nason (New York: Holt, Rinehart and Winston, 1959), p. 9.

night in her silver shoon,"; he chuckles at the ridiculous Pippi Longstocking as she says, "I like policemen as well as I like rhubarb pudding"; he shivers as Tolly unravels mysteries at Green Knowe; he is breathless with suspense as Mafatu faces the dangerous octopus. The literature program should intensify and expand the child's enjoyment of many types of literature.

New Perspectives

Literature brings children new perspectives. Good writing will pique curiosity. "Have you ever thought of a hill, or a mouse, or a relationship in this way?" it will ask. The title of Ciardi's poem, "The River Is a Piece of the Sky" may give the child a new way of looking at a reflection in the water. In concluding the poem, the poet separates his metaphor with the idea that "The river has splashes./The sky hasn't any." Literature may also provide new viewpoints on social problems of today's world. The child who reads Lenski's *Shoo-Fly Girl* gains a new insight into the problems of children of a minority group. By reading *Mine for Keeps* by Little, a ten-year-old may gain understanding and compassion for a handicapped child.

Vicarious Experience

New perspectives are derived as the child has vicarious experiences through literature. Good writing transports the reader to other places and other periods of time. Identification with others is experienced as the reader enters an imaginary situation with his emotions tuned to those of the story. He may feel he *is* Ishi as he reads Kroeber's *Ishi, Last of His Tribe*, and actually sense some of the pain that gripped this Indian who was a lone survivor of his tribe. The young reader sits tensely as he imagines he is bumping along in a covered wagon by the side of Carolina in the story of *Carolina's Courage* by Yates. Identification with a character in a book is a unique experience. Some individuals do not feel emotions as they read, for they seem unable to move from imagination to empathy to identification. Although little is known about the process of identification, it seems likely that the reader who is able to experience problems, feelings, and attitudes of book characters will be more ready to identify with people he meets in life. For example, the reader who shares Jenny's experience of alienation from her mother in Little's *Home from Far*, may be better prepared to face a similar situation in his own life.

Through literature, a reader may vicariously observe nature. The text and illustrations of *Moon Moth* by Hutchins, provide unusual glimpses of an insect. Vistas of the universe await the child who reads widely.

Literature provides vicarious experiences of adventure, excitement, and struggle against the elements or other obstacles. In fantasy, Tolkien's hobbit faces the unknown with uncommon bravery. In *Banner in the Sky* by Ullman, Rudi meets many dangers, but must choose between responsibility to his fellow men and his consuming desire to scale the mountain peak where his father died. Often the adventure of the spirit is found in biography such as portrayed in Simon's story of Albert Schweitzer, titled *All Men Are Brothers*. The achievements of Hakon in Haugaard's *Hakon of Rogen's Saga* were difficult and tragic. This book makes the reader aware of the adventure of living and the common heritage of humanity. For example, fear of being alone comes to all men. Hakon, a Viking who lived centuries in the past, commented,

If you have learned to be alone without fear, then no man can call you weak, though your arms be unfit to wield a sword or an axe. Many a strong man trembles when night has

*made him a small island in the ocean of dark-
ness and the hooting owl is heard.*[5]

Insight into Human Behavior

Literature develops insight into human
behavior. All books for children may not tell
why the characters behaved as they did, but
the reader is led to think about the causes of
behavior. The good writer presents a conflict
and characters who make choices. Scenes are
framed as the writer selects details, focuses
upon elements, and reveals subtle meanings;
thus, the reader may examine human motives and feelings. In *The Bully of Barkham
Street,* Stolz provides for this reflection on
human behavior. As the reader is made
aware of the reasons for the bully's actions,
he develops empathy for the character.

Wisdom of Mankind

Literature transmits the accumulated
wisdom of mankind, and continues to ask
universal questions about the meaning of life
and man's relationships with nature and
other men. Wondriska's allegory, *The Tomato
Patch,* asks why men cannot find ways to live
in peace. Gregor's biography, *Galileo,* brings
to the modern child the ever-present question of conformity or conflict of an individual with his religious faith. C. S. Lewis poses
problems concerning reality and truth in *The
Lion, the Witch, and the Wardrobe.* In the myths
of Greece and Rome, Norway and North
America, the child learns of early man's explanations of the mysteries of life. Literature
provides a record of man's experience and
imagination through the ages.

Beauty and Inspiration

Literature that gives boys and girls enjoyment, new perspectives, vicarious experi-

---

[5]Erik Haugaard, *Hakon of Rogen's Saga,* Illustrated by
Leo and Diane Dillon (Boston: Houghton Mifflin,
1963), p. 79.

ence, insight into human behavior and wisdom, also provides beauty and inspiration. A
concept of beauty is ever-growing and expanding—from the infant's cries of "pretty,
pretty" at a shiny bauble, or gay, tinkling
verse to the beauty of language and pattern
that conveys a deep meaning or portrays a
scene of imagined or remembered delight. In
North to Freedom, Holm describes a boy who
grew up in a prison camp knowing only
grays, browns, and blacks in a world of bitterness, evil, and hatred. David was taught
by one man who told him of other qualities
of life. When he is allowed to escape, David
awakens on his first morning in Italy to a
world of color; blue sea, blue sky, green and
gold of trees and fields. Suddenly he has a
meaning for the word *beauty!* He had heard
Johannes speak the word; he could read the
word, but he had no experience to give it
meaning. So it is with words and experiences: a word may signify nothing until life
or literature gives it "body" and "spirit"; experience can be synthesized and expressed,
made clear, through words. Literature provides for children encounters with life that
bring enjoyment, meaning, and inspiration.

PURPOSES OF THE LITERATURE PROGRAM

Each school staff will want to develop its
own literature program in terms of the
background and abilities of the children it
serves. The following nine purposes of a
good literature program can be achieved
through varied methods and materials.

Experiencing Literature

The major purpose of a literature program is to provide opportunities for children
to experience and enjoy literature through
listening, reading, and discussing. The full
measure of literature is not experienced by
merely reading prose and poetry. The child

may gain pleasure, insight, new perspectives, and beauty through his reading, but he needs skilled guidance to derive deeper values from the experience. Often, we do not "see" until we have learned to "look." Although the total school program contributes to development of sensitivity, an adequate self-concept, understanding of others, critical thinking and values, yet, all these factors are consciously planned for in a literature program.

Developing Taste

A planned literature program is essential if the school is to meet the challenge of developing children's tastes. Taste is valuing works of artistic merit; it is discriminating according to knowledge of criteria. Children need to know the basis for their value judgments. The process of making judgments concerning the worth of a work involves:

- Reading the words for their literal comprehension
- Interpreting meanings
- Analyzing ways the author achieved his effect
- Comparing this work with others
- Considering standards that have been established by the individual.

Children cannot be *given* tastes or values, but teachers can lead them to discover the sources of their present values. Opportunities can be provided for children to learn criteria for good writing and to experience good writing. Although research related to development of taste is limited, there is evidence that the tastes of the teacher influence the level of taste of the students. Enjoyment of a variety of good writing develops as children have opportunities to hear, read, and share reactions to many types of materials. However, teachers need to accept the level of taste that currently exists in the classroom while working to improve the chil-

dren's values. Belittling or ridiculing the child's preference for *The Happy Hollisters* may alienate him from free exploration of the wider world of literature.

The teacher who asks in a sugared tone, "Isn't that lovely?" as the reading of a poem or selection of prose is completed, is not helping children to develop their own values, nor are those children learning criteria for judging. Such a question merely asks children to agree with the teacher's opinion. Sometimes, it is wise to say nothing, and wait for children's comments about the selection. Questions such as those suggested in the Guide for Evaluating Children's Literature will be helpful (see Chapter 1). The psychological environment should also make it possible to express dislike as well as liking for a selection. Is it the content, or the form, or pattern that is disliked? Does the poem call up memories that are unpleasant? If the child hears the comment, "Good!" when he gives a response with which the teacher agrees, and if the teacher's response to another child seems to be noncommittal or in a tone that indicates the teacher thinks it is of little worth, the child is not learning to make his own judgments. He may be learning only to please the teacher. In discussing values, the response by each child should be considered worthy.

Developing Knowledge

Another purpose of the literature program is concerned with developing knowledge of the literary heritage, authors and illustrators, history of children's literature, types of literature, standards for judging, and methods of studying literature.

Reading comprehension is the foundation for interpretation and appreciation. The total curriculum contributes to development of scientific, historical, and social concepts that provide the background for understanding a selection. Another part of the essential base for appreciation is the reader's maturity and life experiences. Literal meaning of a selection precedes literary analysis. General knowledge and reading skills are needed, but the literature program is more concerned with other types of knowledge.

Literary Classics Familiarity with "time-tested" works of prose and poetry is essential for comparison and development of standards. Knowledge of heroes of mythology, morals from fables, Biblical references, and other literary situations and symbols is necessary for comprehension of literary allusions. "Don't count your chicks before they hatch," "Just sour grapes," "Midas touch" are examples of oft-used expressions derived from literature. Common reference points are drawn from familiarity with classics. Situations like "Tom Sawyer white-washing the fence," characters similar to "an old Scrooge," a "Lilliputian," and "a friend like Charlotte," frequently are used in modern books or conversation. The child who does not recognize the mythical figure of Pan would miss the meaning of E. E. Cummings' poem, "Chanson Innocente," also titled, "In Just." By comparing the balloonman to the goat-footed Pan, the poet describes the spirit of spring in his concluding stanza:

> . . .
> its
> spring
> and
>   the
>   goat-footed
> balloonMan   whistles
> far
> and
> wee.
>
> E. E. CUMMINGS[6]

Pan also is an important figure in *The Wind in the Willows* by Grahame; in this story, he symbolizes the little animals' deity.

[6]E. E. Cummings, "Chanson Innocente" in *Poems 1923–1954* (New York: Harcourt,), p. 21.

Authors and Illustrators Children learn about authors and illustrators as they are introduced to books, and as they share reaction to books. The teacher may say, "Here is a new book by Leo Politi, *Lito the Clown.* Do you remember any other books he has written? Are these illustrations similar to those in *Song of the Swallows?* How do they seem alike to you? Is the setting of this story also in California?" A child in the middle grades who has enjoyed reading Steele's *The Lone Hunt* may be encouraged to seek other books by this author.

Knowledge of a writer's life, and information about the background of the work being read may add enjoyment and understanding. Knowing that Marguerite Henry actually owned a pony named Misty, and seeing photographs of the small pony in the family living room would add another dimension to reading the books about Misty (see Chapter 11, pp. 567–571).

History of Children's Literature Knowledge of the historical development of children's literature helps children place the book they are discussing in a definite period. To fully appreciate *Black Beauty,* a child needs to realize that it was written as a protest at a time when there was much cruelty to horses. No child should read the one-hundred-year-old *Hans Brinker, or The Silver Skates* expecting a picture of life as it is in The Netherlands today. Children in the elementary school can begin to understand that today's literature reflects modern social problems just as the books of the past reflect the societal concerns of the period. When children study the Westward Expansion, for example, they could become aware of the literature available for children of that period. Facsimiles of a horn book, the *New England Primer*, and chapbooks are available, and might well be a part of the school library. Children would enjoy comparing copies of McGuffey Readers to modern readers, or such books as *Little Rollo* and

LITERATURE FOR CHILDREN

Picture Books	Prose		Poetry
Fiction	*Fiction*	*Nonfiction*	Mother Goose
Nonfiction	Realistic — contemporary	Informational	Narrative
	and historical	Biography	Lyrical
	Fantasy		Specialized Forms
	Modern		Haiku
	Traditional — folk and fairy tales		Cinquain
	Fable		Limericks
	Myth		Sonnet
	Legend		

Little Prudy to current books of travel and realistic fiction.

Types of Literature   For centuries, critics have held that literature fitted into genres or types. Classification according to tragic, comic, epic, and lyric is now difficult because there are many overlapping works. Some categories commonly used for adult literature are:

- *Fiction (a tale, long or short, in verse or prose, chiefly narrated, although often with some dialogue);*
- *Drama (again, long or short, verse or prose, but presented entirely in dialogue by impersonators);*
- *Lyric (the versified expression of an emotion).*[7]

Today, it appears that genres are descriptive, and rules are not prescribed for authors to follow. Within the discipline of literature, different genre theories have been developed. Generally, the literature for children has been classified by types derived from both content and form. Children are expected to be able to differentiate between

prose and poetry, between fiction and nonfiction. Within the classification of fiction are books whose content might be described as realistic or fantasy. Nonfiction includes both informational books and biography. For the purpose of this text, however, juvenile biographies are discussed with historical fiction, since the majority of biographies for children are fictionalized. Books that make use of both picture and word symbols to convey meaning, story, and mood were placed in a separate category. These classifications frequently agree with children's descriptions of their books and seem discrete and teachable.

Children need to have some classification pattern for their literature for two reasons. First, the ability to identify the type of book that they have enjoyed will enable them to pursue this particular preference. Second, knowledge of the kind of book they are reading helps children apply the appropriate criteria for evaluation. For example, a reader does not analyze fantasy in the same way that he considers a book of realistic fiction. He does not look for character development in a fairy tale, because he knows that the characters in fairy tales are frequently symbolic representations of good and evil. Knowledge of different types of literature helps him understand and value the purpose and the form of the selection.

[7]Sylvan Barnet, Morton Berman, and William Burto, *The Study of Literature* (Boston: Little, Brown, 1960), p. 91.

Standards for Evaluation   Children need knowledge about criteria for evaluating literature. One group studied the episodic events and characterization in *The Happy Hollisters*, one of a series by West. They discovered many incidents had no relationship to the plot development. For example, there is a sudden storm as two girls row toward an island. While the storm created momentary excitement, it had no real significance for the plot. They reach the shore and discover some shells that do relate to the plot; however, there is another contrived incident in which one child falls into quicksand. Little description is included to create the setting or atmosphere. There is no theme, no character change, no development of values. One child said, "They are all goody-goody; real people just aren't like this." A comparison with *The Alley* by Estes revealed differences in writing, and showed the quality of writing. Teachers and librarians must do more than decry the poor quality of fictional series books; they could help children discover the weaknesses in these books.

Methods of Study   Another type of knowledge necessary for a higher level of appreciation is knowledge of the process of literary criticism—how one goes about interpreting a story or poem. What questions should the reader ask himself about the content and the form of expression? What factors should be considered in making judgments? In the past, emphasis has been upon the question, "What does the selection mean?" Teachers also should ask, "How did the author or poet create meaning?"

Children can begin to understand that they can read for literal meaning and for symbolic meaning; a reader can study a selection by analyzing plot, characterization, and theme; he can compare a work with others; he can evaluate a work according to criteria of good writing. The guides for evaluation, pages 17 to 18 and 109 to 110, give suggestions for the study of literature.

Developing Skills of Literary Criticism

Literary criticism involves discussion and analysis of both the content and the form of prose and poetry; what is said, and how it is said. Overemphasis on one to the neglect of the other leads to impoverishment of experience. The aim of literary criticism is to extend meaning, heighten appreciation, and relate literature to life. In the elementary school, literary criticism simply means the ordered inquiry into the writing that children are reading.

Literary criticism requires skills of identification, analysis, comparison, and evaluation. Children need to be able to identify types of literature such as realistic fiction, biography, or fantasy. They also must recognize such constants as plot, theme, setting, point of view, style, characterization, and techniques of writing, including figurative language, symbolism, use of flashbacks, and dialogue. Literary criticism requires skill in analysis of relationships within the selection, effect of language, form, and author's intent or purpose. Children need to develop the skill of comparing and contrasting one selection with others by the same author, other works having similar content or theme, and with the whole body of literature. Evaluative skills include ability to select appropriate criteria, to withhold judgment, consider alternatives, and determine how well the selected writing meets the criteria.

Applying these skills of literary analysis to *The Empty Schoolhouse* by Natalie Carlson, children could be asked to identify the point of view from which the story is told. They could discuss the effect of having Emma tell the story of her sister; they could identify and analyze the theme of the story and its social implications. Study of the figurative language will reveal its relationship to the rural Southern setting. Children could then compare this book with Baum's *Patricia Crosses Town* or Sterling's *Mary Jane* to discover similarities and differences in the treatment of racial prejudice. This study could be extended to include some of the first books that openly discussed racial prejudices; for example, Marguerite de Angeli's *Bright April* and Jesse Jackson's *Call Me Charley*. After identifying, analyzing, and comparing various aspects of this book, students could be asked to evaluate its worth as a personal experience, as a presentation of a social problem, and as a piece of literature.

Fostering Language Skills

As an integral part of the language arts program, the literature curriculum fosters development of skills in listening, oral reading, storytelling, writing, reporting, and discussing. Literature increases sensitivity to, and enjoyment of, language. Words are the tools used to create literature, and words are the instruments used by children to express responses to literature. Composition skills are improved as literature provides models of good writing. Literature related activities suggested in this chapter and Chapters 11 and 12 contribute to such language skills.

Enriching Content of Curriculum

Literature leads the child to new meanings in all areas of the curriculum. Biography and historical fiction cannot serve as the core of a social studies program, but these literary materials offer much information and frequently develop greater understanding than factual accounts presented in textbooks. For example, a class studying new nations of Africa may read of the geographical features and economical and historical development in a factual account; yet, such books as *Thirty-one Brothers and Sisters* and its sequel, *Nomusa and the New Magic*, by Mirsky give a meaningful understanding of the changes and problems as seen through the eyes of a member of an African tribe. Biographies of scientists help boys and girls un-

derstand the achievements of science. *Gull 737* by George is the fictional account of a biologist and his son who are engaged in "pure research." This book also will help students understand the method of science.

Literature also enriches the music and art programs. As children learn about illustrations and become aware of art techniques, they may gain a greater understanding of visual arts. Musical themes relate to some of the classics and to folk tales. Legends of the Firebird, Sleeping Beauty, and references to the Valkyries are examples of literary allusions in music. Biographies of such musicians as Marian Anderson and Leonard Bernstein contribute to enjoyment of music.

Stimulating Creative Activities

The literature program serves to stimulate creative activities in writing, telling stories, using art media to convey ideas based upon books, rhythmic movement, and in creative dramatics. The stimulating discussion of a favorite book or poem may, in itself, be a creative experience (see Chapter 12).

Memorizing Worthwhile Selections

Through the literature program children will be encouraged to memorize worthwhile selections. Hundreds of children have turned away from poetry because of the drudgery involved in memorizing a specific number of lines. Yet, there is an inner satisfaction in learning poetry that has meaning to the individual.

It is easy for most children to memorize; witness their singing of "popular" songs, recitals of football players, and baseball scores. As children request their favorite poems over and over, they will learn easily and with pleasure. Instead of reading poetry in a sharing period, the children could be encouraged to recite their favorites. Choral speaking of poetry also facilitates memorization. The assignment of one poem for all to memorize is unwise, for each poem should have meaning for the child memorizing it.

Teachers who read good poetry with enthusiasm will encourage children to memorize the best. Children become more interested in memorizing poetry when their teacher has memorized a repertoire of poems they enjoy. A poem selected for memorization should be worthy of the time spent in learning it. This means that good anthologies and collections of works by worthy poets should be easily accessible. Through memorization, poetry becomes part of the personal heritage of literature.

Developing Appreciation

The long-term goal of a literature program is development of a lifetime pattern of preference for reading of fine books in contrast to a steady diet of television, spectator sports, and listless sitting. Short-term goals of skill development are important, but reading instruction that produces negative attitudes toward reading seems of questionable value.

Interest in different literary genres is another aspect of appreciation. A higher level of appreciative interest is evidenced when a reader can view a selection as an interesting work of art, regardless of his own preferences. He is "open" to new or different forms. A child may disdain poetry until an enthusiastic teacher provides an enjoyable poetry experience for him. The balanced curriculum introduces a child to many forms of literature.

Knowledge, skills, and emotional and imaginative responses are components of appreciation. These components do not always occur simultaneously. A reader who can assess literary merit on the basis of knowledge is not necessarily reaching a higher level of appreciation than one who has keen emotional and sensory responses. A higher level of appreciation does encompass

more of the components, yet each facet of appreciation is balanced against the others. Rosenblatt cited the danger of emphasis upon abstract verbalization:

> . . . *Acquaintance with formal qualities in literature will not in itself insure esthetic sensitivity. . . . The only way in which he will be able to refine his primary reactions to literature will be through a sharpening of his senses, a greater knowledge of himself, and an increasing refinement and enlargement of his scheme of values. Growth in human understanding is a necessary basis for literary understanding.*[8]

Appreciation is further derived from creative activities of the reader. Attempts to write poetry in the haiku form lead to awareness of the order, the structure, and the beauty of such poems. Writing a story on the same theme in a different form heightens awareness of the author's skill. Taking the role of a character in the dramatization of a scene provides opportunity for deepened empathy. Moving to the rhythm of a poem sharpens awareness of meter. These activities have value in themselves, but they also greatly enhance the child's appreciation of literature.

In summary, these nine purposes provide guidelines for the development of the literature curriculum in the elementary school. Ultimately, such a curriculum would lead to the development of citizens who view reading as a significant part of their lives.

PRESENTING LITERATURE TO CHILDREN

From the time of the earliest primitive fire circle, to the middle ages when minnesingers and troubadours sang their ballads, to the modern age of television, people have

---

[8]Louise Rosenblatt, *Literature as Exploration* (New York: Appleton, 1938), pp. 63, 78.

found delight in hearing stories and poems. Since literature serves many educational purposes in addition to entertainment and enjoyment, teachers should give an important place to the presentation of literature. Children at all grade levels should have the opportunity to hear good literature every day.

Reading to Children

One of the best ways to interest children in books is to read to them. Teachers accept the idea of reading to the young child who has not attained independent reading skills. Unfortunately, the practice too often ceases in the middle grades, when children still need this experience. In these middle grades, many children still do not have the ability to read the books in which they are interested. Most modern television-reared children have developed interests and appreciation levels above their reading ability levels. Once a child has heard a good book read aloud, he can hardly wait to savor it again. Reading aloud thus generates further interest in books. Good oral reading should develop a taste for fine literature.

Effective oral reading by the teacher will help develop sensitivity to beautiful and descriptive language, fine characterization, and appreciation of plot structure. Enjoying books together heightens interests and deepens appreciation. After one group of fourth-graders had heard E. B. White's *Charlotte's Web*, their teacher evaluated the experience:

The group lived together (vicariously, to be sure, but eights are beginning to be quite able to live some life vicariously) through some of the major problems of life. We laughed till we wept, together, and we struggled to hold back tears of sadness with pride that we all could do so. Then, together, we faced death and accepted it maturely, recognizing the continuity of life.

Finally at the end of the book, the members of the group were closer to one another than they had ever been.[9]

The teacher will read parts of books for specific purposes such as dramatization, creative writing, and promotion of interest in the book. To provide a basis for discussion, the teacher will present prose or poetry that is appropriate for literary study. Parts of informational books and difficult materials may be read aloud to provide answers to questions and to enrich study in any area.

Books to Read Aloud   Some books are more appropriate than others for reading aloud. Usually, the teacher will not select books that the children in the group are reading avidly. The story hour is the time to stretch their imaginations, to extend interests, and to develop appreciation of finer writing. For example, if the children are reading series books about horses, the teacher might select Henry's well-written *King of the Wind* to upgrade their taste in literature.

In the writers' experience, children tend to enjoy fantasies if they are read aloud. The subtle humor of Milne's *Winnie the Pooh* may be completely lost when the child is reading alone; when shared by an appreciative teacher-reader, the awkward but well-meaning Pooh and the dismal Eeyore become real personages to fourth-graders. The difficult vocabulary used by Father Rabbit, the Southern gentleman of *Rabbit Hill* created by Lawson, may prevent the intermediate-grade child from finding pleasure in this book. The rather slow pace of Norton's *The Borrowers* might deter some nine- and ten-year-old readers; yet, they will enjoy this delightful book when read aloud by the teacher.

Some of the newer picture books for older children may be overlooked, as their size may require shelving with books for younger

[9]Lucy Nulton, "Eight-Year-Olds Tangled in 'Charlotte's Web,'" *Elementary English*, vol. 31 (January 1954), p. 16.

A picture book should be held so that all children have an opportunity to see the pictures. Nancy Sawrey, teacher, West Lafayette Indiana, Public Schools.

children. *Chanticleer and the Fox*, by Cooney, is more appropriately read to the middle-grade child. Unless the teacher shares this book with the children, however, it may be neglected. Few middle-grade children will select *Big Tree* from the shelf; however, they will listen with rapt interest to the Buffs' account of dramatic events surrounding the life of the big California redwood.

The teacher can read relatively few books aloud during the year, and for this reason, they should be selected carefully. A "List of Books for Literary Study" may be found on pages 668 to 670 and would be appropriate for reading aloud.

Techniques of Reading Aloud Reading aloud requires skill; it is not just an activity to fill time or give information. In the classroom, children should be seated close to the teacher so that all may see the pictures easily and enjoy the twinkle in the teacher's eye. If children are seated on the floor or on chairs close to each other, they seem to identify

more easily with the characters and action of the story. Proximity to neighbors who suppress giggles or hold their breath in anticipation enhances enjoyment.

A picture book should be held so the children can see the pictures at all times. If the teacher knows the text, the book may be held directly in front of the body. When reading the book, it is easier to hold it perpendicularly at one side and turn the head sufficiently to read the words. The book should be held at the child's eye level and moved slowly so that all children will have an opportunity to see the pictures. Also, eye contact with the children should be maintained by looking away from the book at frequent intervals.

The teacher's voice is an instrument for communicating the author's meanings and moods. Distinct articulation is one foundation stone of effective oral reading. Another important element is the voice tone and pitch. Conversation should be read naturally, and volume should be varied with the content of the story. Humor, mystery, disgust, and other feelings can be communicated through the voice. Although poetry should be read somewhat more slowly than prose, a "sugary, poetry voice" should be avoided. It is wise to practice reading poetry or dialect before presenting it to children.

An introduction to the selection will set the stage for enjoyment and appreciation. The dust jacket of a book may be displayed, and the children may discuss the author, possible meanings of the title, and predictions about the story. From the very beginning of the school years, the author and illustrator should be noted. Very unusual words may be explained before the reading. Knowing that "abeles" are birch trees in Hopkins' poem, "The Starlight Night," helps the listener visualize the scene. Introductions should be brief and serve to lead into the selection itself.

The length of the unit selected for reading

should vary with age level. Stories for children under the age of seven should be short, so that they may be completed in one reading period. Middle-grade children enjoy continued stories, but an incident or chapter should be completed in one period. Older children can accept the rigid adherence to a time schedule that requires the cessation of reading regardless of events in the story, but a flexible approach allows for more enjoyment.

Instead of interrupting continuity of the story, discussion should follow the reading of one chapter or incident or entire poem. Frequently, it is helpful if a poem is read twice. After completing a story, the teacher may call attention to a particularly effective description, colloquial expressions, or characterization, by rereading sentences or paragraphs. Children first enjoy the development of plot, but many well-written lines deserve to be reread and savored. In Kenneth Grahame's chapter, "The Piper at the Gates of Dawn," Rat and Mole have been searching through the night for little Portly. Rat has heard the rapturous music of Pan's pipes as they glided down the river. Grahame's rich description evokes the sounds, sights, and smells of the river:

> On either side of them, as they glided onwards, the rich meadow-grass seemed that morning of a freshness and a greenness unsurpassable. Never had they noticed the roses so vivid, the willow-herb so riotous, the meadow-sweet so odorous and pervading. Then the murmur of the approaching weir began to hold the air, and they felt a consciousness that they were nearing the end, whatever it might be, that surely awaited their expedition.
> A wide half-circle of foam and glinting lights and shining shoulders of green water, the great weir closed the backwater from bank to bank, troubled all the quiet surface with twirling eddies and floating foam-streaks, and deadened all other sounds with its solemn and soothing rumble. In midmost of the stream, braced in the weir's shimmering armspread, a small island lay anchored, fringed close with willow and silver birch and alder. Reserved, shy, but full of significance, it hid whatever it might hold behind a veil, keeping it till the hour should come, and with the hour, those who were called and chosen.[10]

The Wind in the Willows is an excellent example of a book that is enjoyed best when read aloud. Each chapter is a complete incident conveying humor, adventure, and beauty in the life of these river animals. Some children may not enjoy its slow pace, but effective reading by the teacher contributes to the development of a taste for this imaginative prose. However, the teacher who does not find pleasure in reading *The Wind in the Willows* should not attempt to share it with children. Enthusiasm and dislike are equally contagious. As teachers free themselves to read naturally, with joy and enthusiasm, children will find increasing satisfaction in books.

Storytelling

A five-year-old said to his teacher, "Tell the story from your face." His preference for the story *told* by the teacher or librarian instead of the story that is read directly from the book is echoed by boys and girls everywhere. The art of storytelling is frequently neglected in the elementary school today. There are many beautiful books, and our harried life allows little time for learning stories. Yet children should not be denied the opportunity to hear well-told stories. Through storytelling the teacher helps transmit our literary heritage.

Storytelling provides for intimate contact and rapport with the children. No book separates the teacher from the audience. The story may be modified to fit group needs. A

---

[10]Kenneth Grahame, *The Wind in the Willows* (New York: Scribner, 1940, 1908), pp. 133–134.

difficult word or phrase may be explained in context. For example, in telling a Mexican folktale, the meaning of the word *mesa* may be interpolated. Stories can be personalized for very young children by substituting their names for those of the characters. Such a phrase as "and, David, if you had been there you would have seen the biggest Billy Goat Gruff. . . ." will redirect the child whose interest has wandered. The pace of the story can be adapted to the children's interests and age level.

Guides for Telling Stories   From the time of the early minstrels, storytelling has been considered an art. For this reason, many teachers have been afraid to attempt it. However, the classroom teacher is an artist in working with children and should have no fear in telling stories to them. Enjoyment of the tale and knowledge of children will help to convey enthusiasm and appreciation for

Young children are entranced as the storyteller weaves her art. They like to be close to the storyteller for moments of excitement and wonder. Polly Paxton, teacher, Punahou School, Honolulu, Hawaii.

the story. All life experiences enrich the interpretation of the story. Sensitivity to textures, line, pattern, color, and rhythm helps the storyteller to convey details and images. Skill in storytelling requires a rich vocabulary and enjoyment of words and language patterns. The teacher must be able to identify with the setting and characters of the story in order to communicate the spirit and feelings expressed in the tale.

If the teacher knows and enjoys the story, techniques will come naturally. The story, however, should be carefully prepared. The teacher needs to be thoroughly familiar with its plot, characters, and the flavor of its language, but it should not be memorized. Memorization often results in a stilted, artificial presentation. There is the added danger of being completely confused when a line is forgotten. The storyteller should first visualize the setting, imagine the appearance of characters, their age and costume, plan an introduction that will set the mood of the story. It may be wise to learn the pattern of some introductions such as "Once there was, and once there wasn't. . . ." If there are repeated chants or songs, these should be memorized. Outline the sequence of events including major incidents, the climax, and conclusion. The importance of good diction and a pleasant, natural voice cannot be overemphasized. Sincerity rather than an artificial, condescending manner is essential.

The good storyteller does not call attention to himself, but to the story. Voice and, perhaps, a few gestures transport the child to storyland. Many storytellers believe sound effects should be omitted. If the lion roars, the narrator should not attempt an imitation of a roar, but the idea can be conveyed as the word "roared" is given a deeper tone and increased volume. The *r* sound may be exaggerated so the lion "urroarrd." Writers and such well-known storytellers as Ruth Sawyer and Gudrun Thorne-Thomsen suggest variations in pitch, tone, and volume of voice in accordance with the mood of the story to make it more effective. Well-timed pauses may help the listeners anticipate a climax. No amount of study of these techniques will substitute for actual practice. With experience comes assurance and a willingness to experiment. Tape recordings can be made to evaluate storytelling skills. These tapes may be compared with the recordings of such artists as Ruth Sawyer, Gudrun Thorne-Thomsen, and Harold Courlander. By learning a few stories at first, and adding to the repertoire each year, the teacher will soon have a rich resource for literature.

Selecting Stories   Stories that are to be told should be selected with care. Stories worth the telling have special characteristics that include a quick beginning, action, a definite climax, natural conversation, and a satisfying conclusion. It is best to select stories with only three or four speaking characters. Such folk tales as *The Three Billy Goats Gruff, Chicken Little,* and *Cinderella* are particular favorites of younger children. The repetitive pattern of these tales makes them easy to tell. Originally passed down from generation to generation by word of mouth, these tales were polished and embellished with each retelling. *Gone Is Gone* by Gàg, *Ask Mr. Bear* by Flack, and "Elsie Piddock Skips in her Sleep" from Colwell's collection, *A Storyteller's Choice,* exemplify modern tales to tell. Middle-grade children will enjoy folk tales from other lands such as Batchelor's *A Cap for Mul Chand,* Babbit's *Jataka Tales, The Cow Tail Switch* collected by Courlander, and *Heather and Broom* by Sorche Nic Leodhas. Incidents from biographies and longer books may be adapted for storytelling. Stories of such American folk heroes as Paul Bunyan, Pecos Bill, and John Henry delight eight- to twelve-year-olds.

If the exact words are necessary to convey the humor or mood, the story should be read rather than told. Kipling's story of *The Elephant's Child* would lose much of its charm without the inclusion of such phrases as "the great grey-green, greasy, Limpopo River all set about with fever-trees" or "the bi-colored python rock snake with its scalesome flailsome tail." Since these phrases require memorization, it is recommended that the teacher read this story.

Just as books with rich language should be read to children, so should the picture books in which the illustrations form an integral part of the whole. The pictures of *Madeline* by Bemelmans add much humor and delight to this story, and children should not be denied the beauty and charm of Burton's rhythmical illustrations of *The Little House.*

Flannel-Board Stories   Storytelling may be varied by using a flannel or felt board. To tell a flannel-board story, the scenery or characters of a story may be made of flannel, felt, pellon, or paper. As the story is told, the figures are placed in the proper positions on the board. If the figures are made of paper, strips of flannel attached to the reverse side will cause them to adhere to the flannel board. A commercial Hook-'N-Loop board may be used in the same way as the flannel board.

Some tales are more suitable for flannel-board presentation than others. The stories should be simple and have few characters. Detailed settings are too difficult to re-create. While rapid changes can be portrayed, physical action is better dramatized. The accumulative tale, or one in which elements are added, is usually quite appropriate for a felt story presentation. For example, in what other way could Gàg's *Nothing at All* complete his metamorphosis from a round ball, to the shape of a dog, to a live dog with spots, tongue, ears, and tail that wags? Similarly, children delight in watching the appearance and disappearance of the red wings on the little rabbit in Bailey's *The Little Rabbit Who Wanted Red Wings.* One group of

The story, *The Man Who Didn't Wash His Dishes*, is told by adding figures and objects to the flannel board. Demonstrated by Sheila Johnston, Purdue University student, prepared by Barbara Friedberg, student, The Ohio State University.

second-graders listened with rapt attention as the different figures from the story of *Magic Michael* by Slobodkin appeared. *The Man Who Didn't Wash His Dishes* by Krasilovsky, *Always Room for One More* by Sorche Nic Leodhas, *The Three Wishes* illustrated by Paul Galdone, and *House of Four Seasons* by Duvoisin are stories that make effective flannel-board presentations. Such stories will help build rapport in the first weeks of a school year. Also, children will enjoy making their own flannel-board stories. (see page 620).

Storytelling Devices Young children will enjoy a "story bag" that may be used in several ways. As the teacher begins the story of *The Gingerbread Man*, for example, a gingerbread cookie could be taken from the story bag. A bow and arrow might be "discovered" for *The Mighty Hunter* by the Haders. In telling Flack's *Ask Mr. Bear*, an egg, a feather, wool, and a butter carton could be drawn from a bag. These objects could symbolize the suggestions made by the animals in the story for Danny's birthday present to his mother. A hat with miniature objects on it could be used to introduce the folk tales in *The Story Hat* by Aardema.

A hand puppet may be used to announce storytime, or the puppet may become the protagonist of the story. A Cinderella puppet might relate her own story. Antique dolls could be used to tell the stories of *Hitty* by Field or *Impunity Jane* by Godden. A tiny artificial Christmas tree might relate Andersen's tale of "The Fir Tree."

One teacher interested a third grade in *Appolonia's Valentine* by showing examples of the cut-paper valentines described by Milhous. Appolonia's story came alive as the children saw the intricately cut, Pennsylvania Dutch designs.

Whether or not one uses devices, it is the enthusiasm and sincerity of the storyteller that capture children's attention and develop appreciation of literature.

Using Audio-Visual Media

Television and Radio   Instructional television or radio offers the possibility of bringing excellent presentations of good writing to classrooms where libraries are limited or the school has not planned a literature program. Television lessons could also provide more challenge for gifted children. Dramatization of the books and background information on the authors and illustrators could enrich the literature program. Interviews with authors and illustrators would develop further interest. One librarian interested the educational television station in making taped films of authors in their homes. Children have been able to listen to skilled interpretations of classics as read on radio. Television instruction depends upon effective introduction and follow-up by the classroom teacher. If the television teacher suggests reading poems after the lesson, the classroom teacher must make time available, find the poems, and carry out the suggested lesson.

Program sheets and teacher guides may help the teacher evaluate programs emanating from educational radio and television centers. However, the teacher should judge all programs carefully in terms of the needs of the particular group. The merits of each

program need to be weighed and contrasted with the values of a more intimate literature experience with the classroom teacher. Radio and television programs should not be used as "pupil-sitter" devices without adequate preparation or follow-up.

Out-of-school television can also contribute much to the literature program. Often, there is a resurgence of interest in a book after its television presentation. The teacher may capitalize on this interest and encourage children to read and compare the original version with the one televised. For example, the television production of *Stuart Little* could be compared with the book of the same name by E. B. White. A calendar might be kept in the classroom to alert children to forthcoming programs. Discussion preceding and following the program will guide evaluation.

Telephone Interviews   It is now possible to arrange an interview by telephone with anyone in the country. A regular telephone and loudspeaker are connected to the telephone system so the teacher may dial an author, illustrator, or editor and children may conduct an interview. Preplanning includes arrangements with the person to be interviewed regarding time of call, fee to be paid, and questions that might be asked. In planning for the interview, a committee of children might select the most important questions submitted by the class. This kind of activity provides a good opportunity for children to learn how to conduct an interview, evaluate important questions, and show their appreciation. A follow-up activity might well provide a real purpose for writing thoughtful letters of appreciation.

Filmed Materials, Tapes, and Records   Using the library as a laboratory for learning, as described in Chapter 11, makes it possible to individualize presentation of literature.

One child, or a small group, may view a film or a filmstrip, or listen to a tape recording. If such experiences are to have maximum value, the teacher should give some guidance. The teacher may prepare a tape with an introduction and follow-up suggestions, or these instructions may be typed on a card. In a conference with the teacher, or in a small group, the child should evaluate his listening experiences.

Films may be used effectively to introduce a book, a theme, or a particular selection of poetry. For example, the beautiful color film prepared by the Nova Scotia Information Service titled *Glooscap's Country* makes an excellent introduction to these legends of Canada. *The Loon's Necklace* is another fine film using authentic masks of the Indians of Alaska to portray the legend. This film might be used to introduce other myths explaining animal characteristics and earth formations (see Chapter 11).

Comparisons of filmed versions with the original book provide opportunities for literary criticism. One third-grade class compared the movie version of *Mary Poppins* with P. L. Travers' book of the same name. They identified omissions and changes in characterization and story line. Two examples follow:

MARY POPPINS

I think the book was better, because the book had more effort in it. The book was probably harder to do because of the tones. The tones of the voices were harder to do with words.
Mary Poppins was too easy-going in the movie. She was strict in the book, and I liked the book better. She had more character, I mean, she had more interest that way.
There was too much flying around in the movie. And the children were always saying they were sorry, you know, like when they ran away. In the book, Michael would say, if Mary Poppins scolded him, "So?" Michael didn't care about

other people as much in the book as in the movie. It makes Michael seem to have more character. It was more interesting. Like for instance, I don't try to be naughty, but when I do get into mischief and then get out, it's not all that bad. Because you can't be good all the time, because you have to face situations. And it wouldn't be life if everything was good all the time.
And also the movie was so mixed-up; it was like a hodge-podge, because Bert appeared in a lot of odd places in the movie, which didn't happen in the book.

DICTATED BY FREDERIC OLDFIELD
TO MISS TWAY

MARY POPPINS

I think Walt Disney made a good improvement. I liked it because it had more action than the book. I sat through the movie, with my coat on, without getting hot. I liked it when Mr. Banks was raving when he tore up the children's note [asking] for a nanny after Katey Nanna left.

WRITTEN BY SARA ANASTAPLO[11]

GUIDING LITERARY CRITICISM

The Process of Literary Criticism

The process of literary criticism is one in which teachers and children share their discoveries as they inquire about the content and the form of literature. An inductive approach will encourage children's active exploration of the material. Some lessons will begin with the general question "What did you discover about this book?" Usually, children will begin with the literal level and give an account of the story. Sometimes, the teacher or the children will suggest re-

---

[11]Shared by Eileen Tway, teacher, University of Chicago Laboratory Schools.

reading the text to clarify interpretations. The teacher may continue to reiterate the questions, "What else did you discover?" "Can you tell anything else about——?" If children have not explored particular aspects of the selection, the teacher can ask leading questions to direct attention to those elements. For example, if children have not yet mentioned the theme, the teacher might ask such a specific question as "What do you think is the 'big idea' of this story? What do you think the author was trying to tell us?" or "What was the theme of this story?" Other lessons may begin with such questions as "What kind of story is this?" or "How did the author reveal the characters in this story?" These kinds of questions help the teacher and children focus on a particular aspect of literary analysis. By participation in many literature lessons, children will begin to ask questions, and will learn what kinds of questions are significant.

The teacher will accept responses given in childlike language and will avoid molding ideas to fit adult terminology. If the children cannot grasp certain understandings, the teacher will not give the answer or push for further analysis. A brief summary at the end of the lesson will help children to order their learnings and become aware of the process of literary inquiry.

If each child is to be actively involved in the process of literary criticism, it is preferable to arrange for small group discussions of six to eight children. However, the selection may be presented to the large group by the teacher or via record or a film. While one group is engaged in discussion, the other children may be reading or carrying out independent activities. It is best to avoid lengthy discussions and stop while interest is still high. Worthwhile lessons can be very short; for example, a lesson on the poem, "On a Night of Snow," required only fifteen minutes. A study of a book may continue over several discussion periods but, certainly, would not extend for a period of weeks. It is important to know that every book does not have to be "completely analyzed." Lessons using a variety of materials and emphasizing different skills of literary criticism will better serve the literature program.

Selecting Materials for Literary Study

A balanced program will provide for a variety of materials and experiences. Impoverished indeed were the fourth-grade children whose teacher read one page a day from the same book for the entire year! The quality of the selections to be used for literary study is a major consideration in planning the lesson. A book from the *Bobbsey Twins* series would hardly be appropriate for discussion of fine character development. (It could, however, be used to contrast with a book in which the characters are carefully drawn.) In planning a lesson on symbolism, the teacher will search for those books that make obvious use of this literary device, such as *The Cabin Faced West*, by Fritz, *Hurry Home, Candy*, by DeJong, and *Call It Courage*, by Sperry. The selection of books or poems to be read to the entire class for literary study is even more important because only the best writing will provide a significant literary experience. As schools plan their literature programs, they may wish to develop a list of books for literary study. Many selections could be used for this kind of study, provided they represent fine writing and can be read for several layers of meaning. The following list may serve as a guide in selecting books for literary study. Wise use of this list must provide for flexibility; books suggested for second grade, for example, may well be used in first or third grade. Knowledge of the background of your children also determines selection.

BOOKS FOR LITERARY STUDY WITH CHILDREN

Kindergarten

Bailey, Carolyn S. *The Little Rabbit Who Wanted Red Wings.* New York: Platt & Munk, 1931.
Du Bois, William Pène, Illustrator. *Three Little Pigs.* New York: Viking, 1962.
Flack, Marjorie. *Ask Mr. Bear.* New York: Macmillan, 1932.
Gág, Wanda. *Millions of Cats.* New York: Coward-McCann, 1928.
Gramatky, Hardie. *Little Toot.* New York: Putnam, 1939.
Keats, Ezra Jack. *The Snowy Day.* New York: Viking, 1962.
McCloskey, Robert. *Make Way for Ducklings.* New York: Viking, 1941.
Minarik, Else H. *Little Bear.* Illustrated by Maurice Sendak. New York: Harper & Row, 1957.
Potter, Beatrix. *The Tale of Peter Rabbit.* New York: Warne, 1903.
Sendak, Maurice. *Where the Wild Things Are.* New York: Harper & Row, 1963.
Seuss, Dr. *And to Think That I Saw It on Mulberry Street.* New York: Vanguard, 1937.
Slobodkina, Esphyr. *Caps for Sale.* New York: W. R. Scott, 1947.

First Grade

d'Aulaire, Ingri and Edgar Parin. *Abraham Lincoln.* New York: Doubleday, 1957, 1939.
Bemelmans, Ludwig. *Madeline.* New York: Viking, 1939.
Burton, Virginia Lee. *The Little House.* Boston: Houghton Mifflin, 1942.
————*Mike Mulligan and His Steam Shovel.* Boston: Houghton Mifflin, 1939.
Duvoisin, Roger, *Petunia.* New York: Knopf, 1950.
Fatio, Louise. *The Happy Lion.* Illustrated by Roger Duvoisin. New York: Whittlesey, 1954.
Fisher, Aileen. *Listen, Rabbit.* Illustrated by Symeon Shimin. New York: Crowell, 1964.
La Fontaine. *The North Wind and the Sun.* Illustrated by Brian Wildsmith. New York: F. Watts, 1964.
Lindgren, Astrid. *The Tomten.* Illustrated by Harald Wiberg. New York: Coward-McCann, 1961.
McCloskey, Robert. *Blueberries for Sal.* New York: Viking, 1948.
Tresselt, Alvin. *Hide and Seek Fog.* Illustrated by Roger Duvoisin. New York: Lothrop, 1965.
Tworkov, Jack. *The Camel Who Took a Walk.* Illustrated by Roger Duvoisin. New York: Dutton, 1951.

Second Grade

Andersen, Hans Christian. *The Emperor's New Clothes.* Illustrated by Virginia Lee Burton. Boston: Houghton Mifflin, 1949.
Bishop, Claire Huchet. *The Five Chinese Brothers.* Illustrated by Kurt Wiese. New York: Coward-McCann, 1938.
Brown, Marcia. . . .*Once a Mouse.* New York: Scribner, 1961.
Cooney, Barbara, Illustrator. *Chanticleer and the Fox.* New York: Crowell, 1958.
Dalgliesh, Alice. *The Bears on Hemlock Mountain.* Illustrated by Helen Sewell. New York: Scribner, 1952.
————*The Courage of Sarah Noble.* Illustrated by Leonard Weisgard. New York: Scribner, 1954.

Freeman, Don. *Dandelion*. New York: Viking, 1964.

Hunter, Edith Fisher. *Child of the Silent Night*. Illustrated by Bea Holmes. Boston: Houghton Mifflin, 1963.

Lionni, Leo. *Swimmy*. New York: Pantheon, 1963.

McCloskey, Robert. *Burt Dow, Deep-Water Man*. New York: Viking, 1963.

Ward, Lynd. *The Biggest Bear*. New York: Houghton, Mifflin, 1952.

Yashima, Taro. *Crow Boy*. New York: Viking, 1955.

Third Grade

Artzybasheff, Boris, Editor-Illustrator. *Aesop's Fables*. New York: Viking, 1933.

Edmonds, Walter D. *The Matchlock Gun*. Illustrated by Paul Lantz. New York: Dodd, Mead, 1941.

Hawthorne, Nathaniel. *The Golden Touch*. Illustrated by Paul Galdone. New York: McGraw-Hill, 1959.

Kipling, Rudyard. *Just So Stories*. Illustrated by J. M. Gleeson. New York: Doubleday, 1946.

Lawson, Robert. *Ben and Me*. Boston: Little, Brown, 1939.

Lionni, Leo. *Tico and the Golden Wings*. New York: Pantheon, 1964.

Seuss, Dr. *The 500 Hats of Bartholomew Cubbins*. New York: Vanguard, 1938.

Thurber, James. *Many Moons*. Illustrated by Louis Slobodkin. New York: Harcourt, 1943.

Travers, Pamela. *Mary Poppins*. Illustrated by Mary Shepard. New York: Harcourt, 1934.

Wersba, Barbara. *Land of the Forgotten Beasts*. Illustrated by Margot Tomes. New York: Atheneum, 1964.

Wilder, Laura Ingalls. *The Little House on the Prairie*. Illustrated by Garth Williams. New York: Harper & Row, 1953, 1935.

Yates, Elizabeth. *Carolina's Courage*. Illustrated by Nora S. Unwin. New York: Dutton, 1964.

Fourth Grade

Andersen, Hans Christian. *The Nightingale*. Translated by Eva Le Gallienne. Illustrated by Nancy Burkert. New York: Harper & Row, 1965.

Brink, Carol Ryrie. *Caddie Woodlawn*. Illustrated by Kate Seredy. New York: Macmillan, 1935.

Chase, Richard. *The Jack Tales*. Illustrated by Berkeley Williams. Boston: Houghton Mifflin, 1943.

DeJong, Meindert. *Hurry Home, Candy*. Illustrated by Maurice Sendak. New York: Harper & Row, 1956.

Fritz, Jean. *The Cabin Faced West*. Illustrated by Feodor Rojankovsky. New York: Coward-McCann, 1958.

Henry, Marguerite. *King of the Wind*. Illustrated by Wesley Dennis. Skokie, Ill.: Rand McNally, 1947.

Little, Jean. *Home from Far*. Boston: Little, Brown, 1965.

Milne, A. A. *Winnie the Pooh*. Illustrated by E. H. Shepard. New York: Dutton, 1926.

Norton, Mary. *The Borrowers*. Illustrated by Beth and Joe Krush. New York: Harcourt, 1953.

Peare, Catherine Owens. *The Helen Keller Story*. New York: Crowell, 1959.

Seredy, Kate. *The Good Master*. New York: Viking, 1935.

White, E. B. *Charlotte's Web*. Illustrated by Garth Williams. New York: Harper & Row, 1952.

Fifth Grade

Colum, Padraic. *Children of Odin.* Illustrated by Willy Pogany. New York: Macmillan, 1920.

De Angeli, Marguerite. *The Door in the Wall.* New York: Doubleday, 1949.

Du Bois, William Pène. *The Twenty-One Balloons.* New York: Viking, 1947.

Estes, Eleanor. *The Alley.* Illustrated by Edward Ardizzone. New York: Harcourt, 1964.

Forbes, Esther. *Johnny Tremain.* Illustrated by Lynd Ward. Boston: Houghton Mifflin, 1943.

Grahame, Kenneth. *The Wind in the Willows.* Illustrated by E. H. Shepard. New York: Scribner, 1908.

Haugaard, Erik. *Hakon of Rogen's Saga.* Illustrated by Leo and Diane Dillon. Boston: Houghton Mifflin, 1963.

Lewis, C. S. *The Lion, the Witch, and the Wardrobe.* Illustrated by Pauline Baynes. New York: Macmillan, 1950.

Merrill, Jean. *The Pushcart War.* Illustrated by Ronni Solbert. New York: W. R. Scott, 1964.

O'Dell, Scott. *Island of the Blue Dolphins.* Boston: Houghton Mifflin, 1960.

Sandburg, Carl. *Abraham Lincoln Grows Up.* Illustrated by James Daugherty. New York: Harcourt, 1928.

Stolz, Mary. *Belling the Tiger.* Illustrated by Beni Montresor. New York: Harper & Row, 1961.

Sixth Grade

Ish-Kishor, Sulamith. *A Boy of Old Prague.* Illustrated by Ben Shahn. New York: Pantheon, 1963.

Krumgold, Joseph. *. . . And Now Miguel.* Illustrated by Jean Charlot. New York: Crowell, 1953.

L'Engle, Madeleine. *A Wrinkle in Time.* New York: Farrar, Straus, 1962.

Rawlings, Marjorie Kinnan. *The Yearling.* Illustrated by N. C. Wyeth. New York: Scribner, 1939.

Speare, Elizabeth George. *The Bronze Bow.* Boston: Houghton Mifflin, 1961.

Sperry, Armstrong. *Call It Courage.* New York: Macmillan. 1941.

Sutcliff, Rosemary. *The Lantern Bearers.* Illustrated by Charles Keeping. New York: Walck, 1954.

Tolkien, J. R. R. *The Hobbit.* Boston: Houghton Mifflin, n.d.

Watson, Jane. *The Iliad and the Odyssey.* Illustrated by Alice and Martin Provensen. New York: Simon and Schuster, 1956.

Weir, Ester. *The Loner.* Illustrated by Christine Price. New York: McKay, 1963.

Wojciechowska, Maia. *Shadow of a Bull.* Illustrated by Alvin Smith. New York: Atheneum, 1964.

Yates. Elizabeth. *Amos Fortune: Free Man.* Illustrated by Nora Unwin. New York: Dutton, 1950.

The Teacher's Preparation

Although literature lessons are informal, preplanning is necessary to help the teacher guide children's learning. Planning begins with selection of the poem, story, or book to determine what elements are teachable, or it may begin with a specific purpose such as development of sensitivity to imagery, identifying cues that reveal genre, or development of ability to recognize theme. The teacher needs to be thoroughly familiar with the book or poem to be used for literary study. The written plan will begin with ways to introduce the selection, possible questions and anticipated reactions of the children, a summary, and suggested follow-up activities.

The plan should include more material, ideas and questions than may be used. All of the teacher's knowledge will not be imparted to children, but will serve as a rich background for the development of the lesson in process.

PLANNING LITERATURE LESSONS

The following illustrations suggest possible approaches to literature study. The teacher will adjust these plans as boys and girls respond. It is best to work with small groups of six to eight children when exploring literature.

Studying a Picture Storybook

WHERE THE WILD THINGS ARE
by MAURICE SENDAK

Most primary children love this particular book and ask to have it read again and again. A teacher might well increase children's enjoyment of this story by helping them to discover the layers of meaning in it and how the author-illustrator conveyed these meanings. After reading the story and sharing the awesome pictures, the following questions might guide children's discoveries about this book:

- *What kind of story is this?*
  Children will probably respond with such expressions as "funny," "scary," "make-believe."
- *Could this story really happen? Where?*
  Most of the action in this story took place in Max's imagination. While it is a make-believe story or fantasy, children might well say that it could have happened in Max's mind but not in "real life."

- *What kind of boy is Max? How do you know? Is he like other children you know?*
  Children will give their varied impressions. Some will think he is naughty, that he has a vivid imagination, and a good sense of humor. One child may call attention to the expression on Max's face in the fifth picture in the book. Another may point out that Max is enjoying making up this story.
- *How did Max treat the Wild Beasts? Why do you suppose he treated them this way?*
  Children will remember that Max tamed the wild beasts by "the magic trick of staring into their yellow eyes without blinking" and then led them in their "wild rumpus." Finally, he sent them off to bed without their supper. Children will recognize that Max just did to the wild beasts the very same things that had happened to him.
- *Was Max happy with the wild beasts?*
  The wild beasts all went to sleep and Max became lonely. Most of all he "wanted to be where someone loved him best of all" so he went home.
- *What did Max find waiting for him in his room? Who brought it? What did the supper tell us about Max's mother?*
  Most children infer that Max's mother brought him his supper, but they do not always see that by this action, she is conveying her love and forgiveness. Actually, the warm supper symbolizes her continuing love.
- *What did you notice about the size of the pictures in this story? Why do you think the illustrator made them this way? What happens to the size of the pictures after Max returns to his room?*
  Children may notice that the pictures become larger and larger as Max's dream becomes more fantastic. They become smaller after Max returns home, but never as small as the first pictures; just as Max will never be quite the same little boy after his fantasy.

- *What did you notice about the color of the pictures? Why do you suppose Sendak used these colors?*

  Most of the colors used are greens and blues. Children may decide these convey the idea of a jungle, or a dream, or night.

The teacher will want to summarize or have a child summarize the important learnings that they discovered by discussing this story. Some observations might be the way the author-illustrator paints his pictures to convey characterization and exaggeration in this story. They might include the fact that authors sometimes use one object to represent something of greater importance; namely, that a warm supper can stand for a mother's love.

Comparing Picture Storybooks with Similar Themes

DANDELION   by DON FREEMAN

HARRY THE DIRTY DOG   by GENE ZION

Illustrated by Margaret Bloy Graham

These two books have a similar theme, that is, the importance of being true to one's own nature. Their plots are quite different, however. *Dandelion* is the story of a lion who is invited to a party. To prepare for the party, he does, in fact, become a "dandy lion," having his mane curled, buying a new checked sports coat, new cap, and cane, and even a bouquet of dandelions for his hostess. He dresses up so much that Miss Giraffe does not recognize him and refuses to let him into the party.

Harry the Dirty Dog is quite the opposite of *Dandelion,* as one might suspect from the title. Harry is a white dog with black spots who gets so dirty that he becomes a black dog with white spots and his family doesn't recognize him. When Harry digs up the scrubbing brush that he had carefully buried, takes it upstairs, and jumps into the bathtub, the children get his message, give him a bath, and discover their dog! After a violent wind and rain storm unfurls Dandelion's curls and soaks his new sports jacket so he must take it off to dry, Dandelion once again tries to go to Miss Giraffe's party, and this time, he is recognized. Dandelion laughs at himself and promises never to turn himself into a dandy again: "From now on I'll always be just plain me." Harry, however, does not reform so completely. For a while, he was glad to be bathed so that his family recognized him. However, the last page pictures him clean and asleep, but the scrubbing brush is hidden under his pillow!

After the teacher has read these two books to the children, the plots and themes could be compared by asking such questions as follow:

- *How are these two stories alike?*

  Both have animals as characters. As a result of foolish behavior, both main characters are not recognized by their families and friends. Both Dandelion and Harry decide they'll never act that way again, although the reader is less sure of Harry's reform.
- *How are these stories different?*

  Dandelion is bathed and dressed in fine clothes to go to a party. Harry gets very dirty playing by himself.
- *What is the big idea (or theme) that the authors are telling in both these stories?*

  You are happier being yourself. You shouldn't try to be something you are not.
- *Do people ever act as Harry or Dandelion did? Have you ever acted this way?*

  Children will give examples from their experience.
- *Have you read any other books that have this same theme?*

Children may have read *The Unhappy Hippopotamus* by Nancy Moore, *Veronica* by Roger Duvoisin, *Robbut, a Tale of Tails* by Lawson. *The Little Rabbit Who Wanted Red Wings* by Bailey, or *You Look Ridiculous* by Waber. All these books have a similar theme.

- *Make up a story with a different plot than* Dandelion *or* Harry the Dirty Dog *but use the same theme.*

If children develop a story with a conclusion similar to the one portrayed in these two books, it can be assumed that they have an initial understanding of theme.

Identifying Form and Setting of Books

Using the opening paragraphs from the following three books, upper-grade children may be helped to surmise the form of the literature and determine the time or place setting of each selection.

I am a peasant and the son of peasants; my name is Tomas, and I was born in the year 1540 on the domains of the Great Bohemian lord, near the city of Prague.[12]

Once upon a time and a long long time ago the tiger was king of the forest. At evening when all the animals sat together in a circle and talked and laughed together, Snake would ask,
"Who is the strongest of us all?"
"Tiger is the strongest," cried the dog. "When Tiger whispers the trees listen. When Tiger is angry and cries out, the trees tremble."[13]

When Manolo was nine he became aware of three important facts in his life. First: the

He rang the bell.

A debonair "dandy-lion" is ready for Miss Giraffe's party. From *Dandelion* written and illustrated by Don Freeman. Copyright © 1964 by Don Freeman. Reprinted by permission of The Viking Press, Inc.

older he became, the more he looked like his father. Second: he, Manolo Olivar, was a coward. Third: everyone in the town of Arcangel expected him to grow up to be a famous bullfighter, like his father.[14]

What kind of story do they anticipate from the opening paragraph? The following questions might be used to guide children's comparisons of these selections.

- *In the first selection, who is telling the story? What has he revealed about himself?*
- *What kind of book do you think this will be? How do you know?*
- *What kind of story is the second one?* (folk tale)

[12]S. Ish-Kishor, *A Boy of Old Prague* (New York: Pantheon, 1963), p. 3.

[13]Philip M. Sherlock, *Anansi the Spider Man, Jamaican Folk Tales,* Illustrated by Marcia Brown (New York: Crowell, 1957), pp. 3–4.

[14]Maia Wojciechowska, *Shadow of a Bull,* Illustrated by Alvin Smith (New York: Atheneum, 1964), p. 3.

- *What clues do you find to help you decide?* (the beginning, talking animals, language patterns)
- *How much do you find out about the story by reading the last selection?*
- *In what country could it take place?* (Spain, Mexico, wherever there are bullfights)
- *When do you think it takes place?* (The text does not tell. It could be in the present or the past.)
- *Could this story really have happened? How would you find out?*

The students may discover other contrasts among these selections. Generally, they should be helped to see that different kinds of literature use different forms. A folk tale easily can be differentiated from historical fiction or realistic fiction. The setting will provide the clue to help children distinguish between historical fiction and realistic fiction. While the word "fiction" indicates that the stories are not true, they could conceivably happen. Historical fiction must be true to its time and place in history just as realistic fiction of today should present a believable slice of reality.

Character Delineation and Development

CALL IT COURAGE by ARMSTRONG SPERRY

After children have enjoyed this well-written and exciting story, the teacher could plan a literature lesson to identify ways the author revealed the character of Mafatu. In the first chapter, the reader learns that Mafatu fears the sea and the reason for this fear. He is told what the older members of the tribe think about Mafatu and particularly how his father feels about him. Mafatu is taunted and jeered at by the boys and laughed at by the girls. The text explains what Mafatu thinks, and what he is finally forced to do. Seldom does an author use as

many different ways to reveal character as Sperry does in this book. A sixth-grade teacher planned the following lesson on techniques of character development:

INTRODUCTION
- *Ask the children how they get to know a person.*
- *Have them imagine that a new pupil came to the class. How would they find out about him?*
- *List suggestions on the board.* Possible responses might be: "Look at him — describe him," "Listen to what he says," "Notice how he talks," "Ask somebody about him," "See how he plays," "Find out how he treats you."
- *Help children realize the limitations of surface impressions.* Children will recognize that you need to see a person in many situations over a period of time to really know him.
- *Ask the children how an author might reveal character to the reader.*

PROCEDURE Use paperback books of *Call It Courage.* Ask children to reread Chapter 1, and find passages in which the character of Mafatu is described. Number each passage by writing lightly in the book. On a separate sheet of paper, indicate the various ways the author helps the reader see Mafatu. The following passages are illustrative of what the children might identify:

> *It was the sea that Mafatu feared. He had been surrounded by it ever since he was born. The thunder of it filled his ears; the crash of it upon the reef, the mutter of it at sunset, the threat and fury of its storms — on every hand, wherever he turned — the sea. (p. 2)*

[Telling about the character]

> *They worshiped courage, those early Polynesians. The spirit which had urged them across the Pacific in their sailing canoes, before the dawn of recorded history, not knowing where they were going nor caring what*

their fate might be, still sang its song of danger in their blood. There was only courage. A man who was afraid—what place had he in their midst? And the boy Mafatu—son of Tavana Nui, the Great Chief of Hikueri —always had been afraid. (p. 1)

[Describing the character in his surroundings]

"That will be fun, won't it?" Kana insisted, watching Mafatu closely. But the boy made no answer. Kana started to speak; he stopped, turned impatiently, and walked away. Mafatu wanted to cry out after him: "Wait, Kana! I'll go! I'll try—" But the words would not come. Kana had gone. (p. 9)

[Letting the character talk—showing what others say to the character]

He knew in that instant what he must do: he must prove his courage to himself, and to the others, or he could no longer live in their midst. He must face Moana, the Sea God— face him and conquer him. He must. (p. 11)

[Revealing the character's thoughts]

Mafatu, standing tense in the shadows, heard a scornful laugh. "Not all of us will go," he heard Kana scoff. "Not Mafatu!"
"Ha! He is afraid."
"He makes good spears," offered Viri generously.
"Ho! That is woman's work. Mafatu is afraid of the sea. He will never be a warrior." Kana laughed again, and the scorn of his voice was like a spear thrust through Mafatu's heart. "Aia!" Kana was saying. "I have tried to be friendly with him. But he is good only for making spears. Mafatu is a coward." (pp. 10, 11)

[Showing what others say about the character]

The older people were not unkind to the boy, for they believed that it was all the fault of the tupapau—the ghost-spirit which possesses every child at birth. But the girls laughed at him, and the boys failed to include him in their games. . . .
Mafatu's stepmother knew small sympathy for

Mafatu has conquered his fear of Moana the sea god and triumphantly returns home. Reprinted with permission of The Macmillan Company from *Call It Courage* written and illustrated by Armstrong Sperry. Copyright 1940 by The Macmillan Company.

him, and his stepbrothers treated him with open scorn. . .
The boy learned to turn these jibes aside, but his father's silence shamed him. He tried with all his might to overcome his terror of the sea. (p. 6)

[Showing the reactions of others to the character]

The boy's hands tightened on his paddle. Behind him lay safety, security from the sea. What matter if they jeered? For a second he almost turned back. Then he heard Kana's voice once more saying: "Mafatu is a coward."

The canoe entered the race formed by the ebbing tide. It caught up the small craft in its churn, swept it forward like a chip on a millrace. No turning back now. . . . (p. 13)[15]
[Showing the character in action]

In a later lesson, students might look at the character *development* of Mafatu. The following questions could be used to guide this discussion:

- *How did Mafatu change?* (He overcame fear.)
- *What were events that caused Mafatu to develop courage?* (Left home, faced storm, defied *tabu*, fought shark, killed pig, overcame octopus, escaped man-eaters.)
- *How did Mafatu feel toward Uri? How do you know?* (He loved Uri and saved his life.)
- *When does Mafatu finally begin to have some confidence in himself? What gave this to him?* (When he had forced himself to take the spear from the *tabu* platform.)
- *The story ends with the same paragraph with which it begins, with the exception of one line. How does the omission of that line show the change in Mafatu's character?*
- *Do you know anyone whose character has changed?*
- *Do you know the reasons for that change?*

Discovering Figurative Language in Poetry

Young children can become sensitive to the imaginative use of language. It is not important that primary children be able to identify various figures of speech, but they should understand that a poet can describe one object by comparing it to another one. One teacher developed the following lesson based on the poems, "Brooms" and "The Moon's the North Wind's Cooky."

INTRODUCTION
- *The title of this poem is "Brooms." What do you think it will be about?*
  Children might anticipate such content as brooms, Halloween, sweeping, witches riding brooms.
- *Then the teacher reads the poem.*

BROOMS
On stormy days
When the wind is high
Tall trees are brooms
Sweeping the sky.

They swish their branches
In buckets of rain
And swash and sweep it
Blue again.
        DOROTHY ALDIS[16]

DISCUSSION
- *What did you discover about this poem?*
  It is about stormy weather. It rained and then stopped raining. The trees blow in the wind. The trees look like brooms. It rhymes.
- *Why is the poem called "Brooms"?*
  One child might respond that the branches catch the rain. Another might say the trees sweep the sky.
- *The poet knows the trees are* not *brooms. In what other way are they like brooms?*
  The response, "Trees look like upside-down brooms," could be expected.
- *What are some other objects that may look like trees?*
  Children might suggest umbrellas, soldiers, people with arms and fingers extended.
- *Reread the poem. What do the sounds of the words remind you of?*
  Children might respond that the words

---

[15]Armstrong Sperry, *Call It Courage* (New York: Macmillan, 1951).

[16]Dorothy Aldis, "Brooms" in *Everything and Anything* (New York: Minton, Balch, 1927), p. 73.

"swish," "swash," "sweep" sound like the wind in the trees, or the rain, or the action of sweeping.

THE MOON'S THE NORTH WIND'S COOKY

The Moon's the North Wind's Cooky,
He bites it day by day,
Until there's but a rim of scraps
That crumbles all away.

The South Wind is a baker,
He kneads clouds in his den,
And bakes a crisp new moon—that greedy
North . . . Wind . . . eats . . . again!
                    VACHEL LINDSAY[17]

- *Read the title of "The Moon's the North Wind's Cooky." What do you think the poet means by this title?*
- *Does the moon ever look as though it has been eaten? Who eats the moon, according to the poet?*
- *Why does the poet make the South Wind a baker?*
- *What does he make?*
- *How are these poems alike?*

Children might recognize that both these poems compare objects in nature to man-made objects. Both of them produce a vivid picture in the reader's mind.

Studying a Poem

In contrast to the previous lesson that taught a specific literary skill, this lesson focuses upon the form and meaning of a single poem. It offers many possibilities for middle-graders to develop skills in studying poetry.

ON A NIGHT OF SNOW

Cat, if you go outdoors you must walk in the snow.
You will come back with little white shoes on your feet,
Little white slippers of snow that have heels of sleet.

Stay by the fire, my Cat. Lie still, do not go.
See how the flames are leaping and hissing low,
I will bring you a saucer of milk like a marguerite,
So white and so smooth, so spherical and so sweet—
Stay with me Cat. Outdoors the wild winds blow.

Outdoors the wild winds blow, Mistress, and dark is the night.
Strange voices cry in the trees, intoning strange lore;
And more than cats move, lit by our eye's green light,
On silent feet where the meadow grasses hang hoar—
Mistress, there are portents abroad of magic and might,
And things that are yet to be done. Open the door!
                    ELIZABETH COATSWORTH[18]

Introduce the poem by reading the title and asking students to listen to discover who is talking and where the characters are on "the night of snow."

- *Show the poem on the overhead projector so all children can read it while discussion is in progress.*
- *See if they discover:*
  (a) The poem tells a story. It is a narrative poem.
  (b) The poet contrasts the warmth of the inside of the house with the cold, mysterious outside.
  (c) The two characters express different feelings toward the wild night of snow.
  (d) The mistress and cat represent conflicting desires of security and adventure.
  (e) The sound effects of the words heighten and create mood: the hissing of the flame; the soothing, coaxing sound of the repetitive *s*, line seven; alliteration of "wild winds"; the weird sound of long vowels, $\bar{o}\bar{a}\bar{o}$, (assonance).

---

[17]Vachel Lindsay, "The Moon's the North Wind's Cooky" in *The Golden Treasury of Poetry*, Louis Untermeyer, Editor (New York: Golden Press, 1959.), p. 258.

[18]Elizabeth Coatsworth, "On a Night of Snow" in *The Golden Treasury of Poetry*, Louis Untermeyer, Editor (New York: Golden Press, 1959), p. 48.

(f) Word meanings: may have to explain *portents, hoar*; relate cats to things magical and eerie.

(g) Use of figurative language: metaphors—little white shoes, white slippers, heels of sleet; simile—"milk like a marguerite" (explain that a marguerite is a white daisy).

(h) Rhyme pattern and form: stanza 1—abba, abba (8 lines); stanza 2 —cdcdcd (6 lines). This arrangement of fourteen lines is called a sonnet.

* *Summarize the factors that have been discussed.*
  They would probably include: content—what the poem is about; effect of dialogue; sound-effect words; metaphor and simile; form of sonnet; ideas and feelings created by poem.

Children may not identify all of the elements of this poem. They should not be pushed into analysis for which they are not ready, nor should the teacher give them his interpretation as the final answer.

One Child's Analysis of a Book

HOME FROM FAR by JEAN LITTLE

The following account of a teacher-pupil conference reveals the way one fifth-grader gained awareness of deeper meanings and the structure of a book.

* *What did the title of the book mean to you?*
  I thought the title meant a girl would travel away from home. The house (pictured on the cover) looks old so she might have gone to her grandmother's. It could be a mystery. When I read it, I knew the title meant something else.
* *Can you tell more about it?*
  Well, it meant she was far away in sadness because her twin died, and then,

later she felt better, and more at home. The other two children, Mike and Hilda, came to a new home, too, only they didn't come from far away.
* *How did the author reveal, or tell you about, the setting of the story?*
  It was fairly modern because they had cars and swing sets. I think it was a small town because there were lots of trees and bushes. There would have to be a tree for a tree-house. They went swimming at a quarry, and you wouldn't do that in a city; you would go to a pool. If they lived in the country they wouldn't have had neighbors to go to the circus. And there might not be bushes with caterpillars in the city.
* *How is the story told?*
  Most of it is Jenny thinking. Then the writer tells what happens.
* *What did happen in the story?*
  Jenny is sad because her twin died in a car accident. But she doesn't like it when her parents take in two foster children. One is named Michael, like her twin. Jenny sneaks into Mike's hideout. She knocks over a candle, and there is a fire. She is even sadder. Her father makes her and Mike build a playhouse for the little kids. Mike, the new one, doesn't want to stay because he would rather be with his father. But he likes his new father because he protects him when some boys accuse him of stealing. After the fire, Jenny and Mike sort of like each other. They decide to get even with Alec because he told and was a sneak. Jenny puts caterpillars on him and they leave him tied up, and it nearly scares him to death because he can't stand caterpillars. Jenny is sorry, and they decide to have a circus. She goes to the attic and gets things for a costume.
* *Is there a happy ending?*
  Yes, and no. Jenny and Mike are

friends, and Alec is, too, but Michael is still dead, and that's sad.

- *Do you remember how we knew Jenny was unhappy with her mother?*
She didn't like it because they gave Michael's watch to Mike. (Used the book to find the scene she wanted to describe.) This was the time in the attic when Jenny admitted she was angry at her mother for forgetting Michael by putting his things away. She didn't want Mike to take Michael's place.

- *What would you consider the climax, the turning point, of the story?*
One was when Jenny found out her mother put Michael's things away because she wanted them to have happy memories. And then, when Mike found out he could still love his real father and stay with the new family.

- *How did the author tell us about the characters?*
You see Jenny on the cover, and then she described her. I have a different picture in my mind than the one on the cover. I think the illustrator just drew pictures of people, and didn't make it like the book. You know about Jenny from what she did—like at the accident, she was thoughtful and picked up her mother's purse. And she helped Hilda learn to swim. She was afraid in the fire, but she didn't cry.

- *Did the characters change? If they did, how can you tell?*
Jenny changed—to like Mike, and I think to understand her mother. Mike changed his feelings. Alec learned to stand caterpillars, and he probably won't be such a sneak.

- *Are the characters natural, are they like people you know?*
Yes, they're sort of usual—maybe Jenny *thinks* more.

- *What would you say about the way the author wrote?*

She didn't have long, complicated sentences. It was just like people talking. (She turned to the part about the fire and read: "The sharp smell of wet smoke stung her nostrils. He looked very big, bigger than she had ever seen him before. Then, all in one instant, Jenny's pipe-cleaner legs caved in under her. She felt herself folded up; the world tipped sideways and everything swam in a bright blue before her. Dad caught her as she started to fall." p. 77) That was really good! I read the author was once blind, so I think she adds more description than others.

- *Did the author create a mood? Can you tell how?*
I liked the hot afternoon when Jenny tried to read *Mary Poppins*, and when she read so she could cry. This was a sad-happy book.

- *Do you have any other ideas now about the meaning of the title?*
Yes, the home was not the house. Jenny was far away from her family in her thoughts, and Mike and Hilda came from an unhappy home to a happy home.

- *Do you think the author had a purpose beyond entertainment?*
Not to mourn (her word) over Michael's death—and she should have talked with her mother.

Although this intelligent child had read voraciously, she had little guidance in studying literature. For example, she could recall no symbols, nor could she interpret the symbol of Jenny's being called the willful lamb. After the discussions, she reported to her mother that she had never talked so much about one book, but it was really fun. It is evident that she moved from recollection of plot toward deeper understanding. A rereading of the book after such discussion may lead to further understanding.

CHILDREN REPORT THEIR READING

For many years, teachers have devised various means to interest children in books and to evaluate their reading. Book trees, book clubs, and required weekly book reports have been used to stimulate children's reading. *A gold star by any other name still tarnishes!* Too frequently, these motivational devices have brought about results that were in conflict with the desired purposes of well-meaning teachers. Competent readers may come to enjoy the smug satisfaction of winning competitions rather than finding the longlasting pleasure in books for their own sake. They may select five "thin" books in order to achieve more rockets placed after their names, instead of one book that challenges their reading ability. Meanwhile, a slow reader feels defeated before he begins, and turns away from books as sources of pleasure and information. When competition is stressed, emphasis is placed on quantity of books read, rather than on the quality of the reading experience.

Book reports should serve to further enjoyment in reading, extend interests, and guide evaluation of literature. The book report should help the child recall the setting, characters, and sequence of events. Reviewing a book reinforces understandings, develops skills of analysis and promotes critical thinking. It helps him contrast the literary experience with real life experience. The purpose of the book report is not to prove to the teacher that the child has read the words and knows the plot. The process of book reporting should help develop children's tastes through establishing individual and group standards. The review of the book should also lead to understanding of methods of study.

Oral Reports

A good book deserves to be shared; it is enjoyed again, and new insights are developed as the book is discussed. When a child gives a report he does just that; he tells about the book and his discoveries about it as literature. When he gives a review he may compare it with other books of similar content, with a similar theme, or with other books by the same author. Classmates are motivated to read the book as one child gives a well-organized, enthusiastic talk about his current favorite.

There should be no rigid pattern for oral book reports. It can become very dull to have a series of brief reports in which each child follows the same routine: "The author was . . . the publisher . . . the story is about . . . the characters are . . . I like it because. . . ." After ten or fifteen of these talks, often given in hesitating and mumbling fashion, the class is ready to forego reading forever!

It is not necessary for a child to give an oral report for every book he reads. His reading record would include the titles of the books read and indicate each follow-up activity. He may discuss the book with the teacher in a conference; he may give a report to the entire class or to a small group; he may make a display or device to interest others; he may write about the book. Occasionally, a book may make such an impact on a child that he does not even want to discuss it; he only wishes to experience it again. One fourth-grade boy was observed reading *The Matchlock Gun* by Edmonds six times in one year. Each time, he read it with absorption and enjoyment. This deep interest pleased his teacher, and no formal report was necessary.

Informal reports may be given in the daily show-and-tell, or sharing, period. The teacher may guide such reports and reviews by asking some of the following questions:

- Show us your favorite pictures.
- Tell us about the most exciting part.
- What is the setting of this book?
- Who is your favorite character?

- Tell us about the part you thought was funniest.
- What other books has this author written?
- Do you think this story could have happened in our town today?
- Have you ever had an experience like this?
- Have you read any other books like this story?

In this sharing time, when children talk about many areas of interest, dioramas, displays, and bulletin boards may be presented and described.

A part of the literature program should be planned for book-sharing periods. There may be a panel discussion of one book, or of books on similar themes. A few children may present a program about the work of one author or illustrator. One third-grade group discussed bear stories, including Ward's *The Biggest Bear*, Dalgliesh's *The Bears on Hemlock Mountain*, Monsell's *Paddy's Christmas*, Minarik's *Little Bear*, Goudey's *Here Come the Bears*, and Milne's *Winnie the Pooh*. In this situation, children with varying reading abilities shared similar interests by comparing plots, incidents, and illustrations.

Children who have read the same story may tell it from the point of view of various characters. For example, the story of *Home from Far* by Little could be told from Jenny's point of view, Jenny's mother's, Michael's, and even Alec's. Misunderstandings and conflicts could be brought out by such a discussion. Only books with fully developed characters are suitable for this kind of presentation.

It is educationally unsound to waste the time of a group by requiring them to listen to an unprepared report, a report of a book of poor quality, or a book that is inappropriate for most of the children in the group. The form of the report should also be appropriate to the book. In one classroom, a second-grade child attempted a chalk talk to report *The Pushcart War* by Merrill. The child giving the report was mature, and understood some of the satire in this book; another child had read it, and helped with the interpretation. However, it was most difficult to present the complex events in this story by a chalk talk. The other children in the room were soon disinterested by the lengthy and confusing presentation of a book that was much too advanced for most of them to understand. This situation could have been prevented if the teacher had planned with the child and guided his report to the entire class, or simply discussed this book with him individually.

The pupil-teacher conference is one of the most significant reporting times because the child receives the teacher's full attention, and they may share their reactions to the book. In the conference, reading skills should not be overemphasized to the neglect of the literary experience. Some of the guide questions presented in Chapter 1 could be used by the teacher to help the child understand the book. At this time, the teacher will also be alert to the child's interest in books and make recommendations for future reading. Longer discussion may be delayed until several children have read the same book. Then, the teacher may meet with this small group for a discussion and suggest ways they might prepare a group report.

Individual pupil-teacher conferences are time-consuming, so other ways need to be devised to give all the children many opportunities to share their enthusiasm about particular books. Several reports may be given simultaneously. For example, children may place their names on the chalkboard or in a pocket on the bulletin board labeled, "We Have Books to Share." Before dividing the class into groups for such a book-sharing period, the teacher could say, "Today we have three book reports. You may decide which group you wish to join. Who would like to hear about a dinosaur that hatched from a chicken egg? Who would like to hear

A small group of sixth graders discuss favorite biographies. Jeanne Hilson, teacher, Columbus, Ohio, Public Schools.

a good baseball story? Who wants to hear about another Miss Pickerell adventure?" Thus, choices are made according to interest in books rather than individual popularity. The children meet in small groups in various parts of the room, and the teacher circulates from one group to the next to enjoy the reviews and to guide the discussions.

On another day, every child could have an opportunity to share one book with a small group of five or six children. Such small groups can be planned so they meet at the same time, or one group can meet while the remainder of the class is engaged in other learning activities.

Book Clubs

Many schools have organized special-interest clubs for discussion of books. Parent groups and church groups have also developed programs designed to acquaint children with the classics and to provide opportunities to develop skill in literary criticism. Several follow the "Great Books" pattern for

adult programs of reading and discussion. Unfortunately, many of the programs are quite rigid and allow no choice of reading material. There is a danger that children will merely develop patterns of verbalization without real understanding. Informal book clubs sponsored by school and community agencies can bring enjoyment and the satisfaction of sharing inquiry if they are directed by leaders who understand children and books.

Written Reports

Purpose of Written Reports Records of the reading of an individual pupil and of the class are necessary in order to evaluate the child's total reading progress and the attitude of the class toward books. The child should maintain a record of his own reading, noting title and author of books completed. He may indicate the type of follow-up activity, including his conference with the teacher. It seems unnecessary to keep a cumulative total of number of pages read. This simply promotes competition, and does not indicate level of reading or the quality of the child's response.

Teachers should consider the child's developmental skill in writing before asking him to prepare a written account of his reading. If young children are required to write book reports before they have achieved a measure of writing facility, their interest in reading may be permanently damaged. The assignment of the same number of reports from all children, regardless of ability, may produce similar unhappy results.

Children should be encouraged to write about books for different purposes. A major purpose of a book report is to develop skill in literary criticism. The child also reviews a book in order to share his thinking about it with others. The following well-written report was prepared by a sixth-grader and appeared in the literary magazine published by the class. She gives an interesting summary of the action, identifies the type of literature, and gives her own opinion of the story.

THE PUSHCART WAR by JEAN MERRILL

The war was fought in New York City in the year of 1976 between the pushcart peddlers and the truck drivers. It got really out of hand when the pushcart peddlers started using peashooters that shot pea pins to flatten tires. A Peace March was held on three streets. The pushcarts went, in rows, down West Street, Broome Street and Greene Street. They were holding banners and signs that said, "Peace March," "Pushcarts for Peace," "Don't Push the Pushcarts Around," etc.

On the first and second streets, everything went exactly as planned, but on Greene Street, there was trouble. Albert P. Mack, a Mighty Mammoth Truck driver, tried to drive through the pushcarts. Many pushcarts were ruined and Mack smashed a cafeteria window, but no one was killed. Mack was arrested for reckless driving.

The next part of the War was a war of words. Thousands of people wrote letters to newspapers concerning the Pushcart War.

The trucks finally surrendered but still another war occurred on Bleeker Street. Here at least thirty puchcarts were doing business in the fruit and vegetable line. Half a dozen trucks drove up, and customers and peddlers alike began hurling fruits and vegetables at them. When an officer said to a lady, "Hey, lady the war's over. Haven't you heard?" she replied, "Certainly, we're just celebrating."

This book is both humor and fantasy. It is fantasy because it occurs in the future. The author is poking fun at New York City's traffic situation.

I think this is a very funny book.

ANN TWEED

Allaire Stuart, Teacher
Boulder Public Schools, Colorado

Book Report Forms   The use of prepared forms for book reports should be considered in terms of the purposes of the activity. If a form is used as a guide, the children should participate in planning the form and the information to be recorded. Usually, forms are planned in terms of providing information for another reader who might want to know about the book. Thus, the form will include title, author, what the book is about, and the degree of enjoyment experienced. Older children will include character names, and, perhaps, a part that was especially amusing or interesting. A cumulative file may be developed for one book. Each child who reads the book adds his comments on the large card or sheet in a loose-leaf notebook. Other children can note names of children who read the book and their reactions. At the end of the year, the teacher will have a record of all the children who have read a particular book and their comments on it. A form may be useful in this situation in order to conserve space.

Book report forms that provide limited space for each response tend to force the child into a pattern instead of leading him to a more creative approach. If Katy, in second grade, had been required to use a form giving brief comments, the following interesting account would not have been possible. Spelling can be corrected later; Katy has communicated her ideas about the book.

STORY CARIVAN

I liked Story Carivan for the playn resane (plain reason) it was funny. But it was not jast funny it had stories that made your spin tingkl (spine tingle). In other words it was a spin tingkling (spine tingling) book. The very very best story was: the Saving Sneeze. There was this girl and she lived in a log house in a little clering in the woods. It was about in the middel of the war betwen the red coats and amrecans (Americans). This is the time they found an american soldger (soldier) in the woods. She took him home and they took cary of him till the red coat came. He got under the covers in the bed. But they stock (stuck) up to much and so the little girl got in to (too) so the red coats thot (thought) he was not there. Until he snzesed (sneezed). But the little girl snezed a geain (again) and so the red coats weant away.

KATY DALY, Evanston Public Schools, Illinois

If the purpose of a report is to give the teacher information quickly and easily, a form may be desirable. However, is this the purpose for which children should be writing book reports? The teacher may ask the child to complete a reaction card when he finishes a book and place it in his own file or folder. This reaction card will be very helpful in the conference period. These cards clearly state the reader's feelings:

The Conquest of the North Pole and South Pole by Russel Owen

Illustrated by Lynd Ward

I did not like this book because I do not know and do not care to know about the north and south poles. I am sure that I made a wrong selection.

Written by Dick Bowers
Wickliffe School, Upper Arlington, Ohio

An Otter's Story by Emil E. Liers

Illustrated by Tony Palazzo

I just hated it when I quit this book. It was so good that it will ring in my ears forever. It was full of sorrow happiness and laughter. And I can label this book as the best I've ever read.

Written by Roberta Price
Wickliffe School, Upper Arlington, Ohio

It is possible that the child will omit some aspects of the book as he writes a report if he does not have a form at hand to guide him. A chart on the wall may list guides for re-

ports, or the teacher may duplicate a page of guide questions that have been developed with the children. The child may then refer to these guides as he writes the report. An evaluation of the report written without the exact form will provide evidence of his growing ability to ask important questions about the selection.

Varied Kinds of Written Reports Teachers and children should explore the possibility of writing various kinds of book reports. Children in kindergarten and the primary grades may develop group lists of favorite books. Reporting may be extended as they dictate captions for illustrations or brief summaries for storybook murals. After hearing the teacher read *A Very Special House* by Krauss, one first grade dictated a group book report. This experience chart provided an opportunity to develop beginning reading skills and the ability to summarize books.

Periodically, children in the middle grades may develop lists of their favorite books. A group list of the class favorites might be compiled and sent home as a possible Christmas list or exchanged with other classes for purposes of comparison.

One sixth-grade teacher encouraged the students to select quotations from their favorite books. Sometimes, these were selected for the beauty of the language; at other times they were selected to show interesting descriptions of settings or methods of revealing character. These quotations could be published in a class newspaper, posted on the bulletin board, or used in a book review.

Children may write comparisons of their reactions with those of other reviewers, both adult and child. After studying books intensively for one year, a group of third graders prepared a booklet entitled *Book Notes, a Children's Literary Review.* One child wrote a review of *Stuart Little* by E. B. White. Another child reacted to this review and an adult's review of the book from *The Horn Book Magazine.* He then compared both re-

TOP. Book reporting may begin with simple lists of favorite stories. Second grade, Kenilworth, Illinois, Public Schools.
MIDDLE. First-grade children dictated a group book report of a favorite story. Virginia Kessler, teacher, Clarfield School, Columbus, Ohio, Public Schools.
BOTTOM. Children contributed their colorful illustrations for this first-grade group book report. Sandra Isolampi, student teacher, Hammond, Indiana, Public Schools.

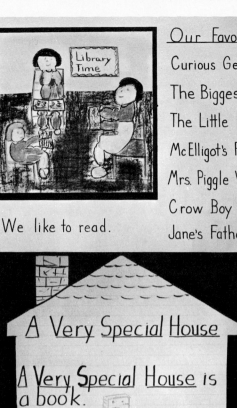

views and gave his opinion of the book. Certainly, this experience called for much critical analysis on the part of a third-grade child! All three reviews were included in a section of the booklet called "Criticizing the Critics." They appeared as follows:

STUART LITTLE by E. B. WHITE

I think it was a good book (besides the ending). It was also funny, like when Stuart had to go into the drain. When Stuart was born, he looked like a mouse, and his family thought he really was a mouse. And that was why he could go into drains and places like that.

It was sad in some parts, too, like when Margalo left Stuart. Margalo was a bird that Stuart liked.

The whole book would be good if it had a better ending. I think the author should tell if Stuart found Margalo. I feel that Stuart just went on and on. I don't think it ended like other books.

JED ROBERTS
Eileen Tway, Teacher
The Laboratory Schools, University of Chicago

STUART LITTLE (An Adult Review)

Pictures by Garth Williams. A children's book by E. B. White will be greeted with undisguised joy by many readers who know the wise and salty touch of **One Man's Meat.** *Stuart Little* *is a mouse, two inches long, a gentle and heroic human figure. Of course, his size made him likely to be mislaid at times, but from the first he was quite able to cope with dilemmas. The Littles live in New York and some of Stuart's experiences have to do with getting about in a city. He sails in a sailboat in Central Park and wins a race, gives sound advice to a class he taught in school, and finds a lasting friend in Margalo, an enchanting brown bird. This is an endearing book for young and old, full of wit and wisdom and amusement, and Garth Williams' drawings make a perfect accompaniment.*

THE HORN BOOK MAGAZINE, vol. 21
(November 1945), p. 455

STUART LITTLE (A Comparison
of a Child's Review and an Adult Review)

What I didn't like about the Horn Book Review was that it didn't mention the ending, and I think that was one of the points that most people should recognize — people trained in writing.

Also, I think that they were both trying to say the same thing in the beginning about how it was funny and how Stuart had to go in the drain and do odd things.

It seems strange how two reviewers can disagree about an ending so much different. Whoever it was must have thought the ending wasn't an important point, because it wasn't mentioned in the adult review. I think when the adult reviewer said Margalo was an enchanting, lasting friend, they meant that Stuart always remembered her, but I agree with Jed's review — because I've read the book and I think that Stuart just kept searching and searching in his little car and I don't really know whether he ever found Margalo. I wonder if the author had the idea to write a second book.

Both reviews didn't mention how everybody did

things for Stuart, and they didn't mention the real highlight of the book about how Stuart saved Margalo from two cats.

AARON PARZEN
Eileen Tway, Teacher
The Laboratory Schools, University of Chicago

Book reviews may be printed in a room newspaper, a school magazine, a bulletin board display, or a class file or notebook. Riddles, advertisements, and dust jackets with summaries are other forms that may be utilized in writing about books. Suggestions in Chapter 12 provide further opportunities for creative writing about books. Teachers will want to encourage children to try a variety of ways to share their interest in books with others.

Evaluating Book Reports

Evaluation of book reports should be based upon the purposes of the report and individual differences. The quality of the child's reading is more important than the quantity of book reports. As suggested earlier, standards for oral and written reports should be developed through group discussion. Continued reference to a chart that lists these standards will help children develop an awareness of areas where improvement is needed. One third grade composed this guide for oral reports:

WHEN WE GIVE A BOOK REPORT
- Tell the title of the book.
- Tell about the author.
- Tell enough of the story to interest others.
- Don't give the story away!
- Tell what you liked best.
- Keep to the point.
- Show a picture you like.
- Talk loud enough.

- You may read a part you liked.
- Compare with other books.

After an individual has given a report, evaluation should emphasize positive comments. Evaluation sessions should not diminish the self-concept of the child giving the report. Instead of asking the entire class to react to each standard, the child may choose one or two children to serve as an evaluation team. Later, they may discuss the report with him. After several children have given reports, the teacher may meet with them to evaluate their presentation. A tape recording of the oral report could be evaluated by the pupil himself. The child may write a brief summary of his strengths and needs after listening to his own tape.

When children write reports that are to be displayed or to be duplicated, they should be expected to extend the reader the common courtesies of accurate spelling, correct punctuation, and legible handwriting. Although proofreading and recopying develop skills of writing and expression, adult standards of perfection should not be imposed.

The teacher may duplicate copies of several book reports about the same book. An adult review might be included. The children could read these reports by different people, comparing the content, the aspects of the book considered, and the writing style. The opaque or overhead projector may be used to display a report on the screen. The children may discuss its completeness, clarity, and quality of interest. By analyzing models of good reports, boys and girls develop standards for well-written reviews.

PLANNING THE LITERATURE CURRICULUM

The literature program is conceived as a continuous plan that provides for gradual development of understanding and appreciation. One teacher may provide a rich literature program within a classroom, but children need balanced, sequential experiences throughout their school years. Thus, a curriculum guide for literature is needed to identify purposes, suggest materials and methods, and establish scope and sequence. The values of literature for children, the needs and characteristics of children, knowledge of the learning process, and the structure of the discipline provide the foundation for curriculum development. The purposes of the literature program as identified in this chapter were:

- Experiencing literature
- Developing taste
- Developing knowledge
- Developing skills of literary criticism
- Fostering language skills
- Enriching content of curriculum
- Stimulating creative activities
- Memorizing worthwhile literary selections
- Developing appreciation

Literary Understandings and Skills

Over-all purposes need to be translated into statements of pupil behaviors. Generalized objectives such as "Recognize style" are difficult to achieve and impossible to evaluate. Perhaps, literature programs have not been developed in the elementary school because of the failure to come to grips with the problem. Only recently have scholars from the fields of education and English worked cooperatively to plan a sequential program. The following taxonomy of literary understandings and skills is suggestive of the kind of behavioral goals that should be achieved in the elementary school.

A TAXONOMY OF LITERARY UNDERSTANDINGS AND SKILLS

Understands Types of Literature

- Differentiates fiction from nonfiction
- Differentiates prose from poetry
- Recognizes folk tale
    - Identifies traditional beginnings and endings
    - Can locate repetition of phrases and episodes
    - Realizes characters are usually stereotypes symbolizing extremes — good and evil, pretty and ugly, wise and foolish, timid and brave
    - Recognizes that folk tales communicate values: loyalty, faithfulness, courage
- Recognizes fable
    - Identifies talking animals as representative of human characters
    - Recognizes that a fable states a moral
- Recognizes myth
    - Recognizes that characters are supernatural beings interacting with each other or men
    - Recognizes that myths were early man's explanations for natural phenomena or human behavior
    - Recognizes that plight of mankind is expressed in myths
- Identifies realistic fiction
    - Compares characters and events with his knowledge to determine if story could happen
    - Looks for evidence of modern life (housing, transportation)
- Identifies historical fiction
    - Finds date if mentioned in text
    - Establishes period of history through associating way of life, people, or events
- Identifies fantasy
    - Recognizes the ways in which an author creates fantasy
        - Gives animals the power of speech and thought
        - Gives inanimate objects the power of speech and thought
        - Endows human beings with magical power or powers
        - Manipulates time patterns
        - Changes sizes of humans
        - Creates new worlds

Understands Components of Fiction

- Recognizes structure of plot
    - Summarizes sequence of events
    - Identifies conflict or problems
        - Conflict of one character with another
        - Conflict between man and his environment
        - Conflict of values
        - Conflict within the individual
    - Looks for the interrelatedness of characters and events
    - Identifies contrivance in structure
    - Recognizes climax of story
        - Identifies details and events that build toward climax
        - Identifies methods author uses to build suspense
            - Finds examples of foreshadowing
            - Notices when conflict is first introduced
            - Recognizes author's use of "cliff-hangers"
    - Recognizes subplot or parallel plot
    - Recognizes flashback as a literary device

      Distinguishes episodic and unified plots

      Recognizes details of denouement

- Recognizes character delineation and development

      Can describe important traits of main characters

      Seeks character clues in illustrations

      Recognizes techniques author uses to reveal character

          Describing character in his surroundings

          Showing him in action

          Listening to him talk

          Revealing his thoughts and reactions to people and events

          Showing what others say and think about him

          Telling how others act toward him

      Seeks causes of behavior of characters

      Looks for consistency in characterization

          Consistency of age, period of history, setting

          Internal consistency of character, language, behavior

      Looks for many facets of character other than a stock figure

      Recognizes what changes occur in the character

      Looks for causes of change in character development

- Recognizes theme of story

      Infers meaning beyond the literal account of story

      Looks for clues to meaning in title

- Recognizes setting—both time and place

      Looks for clues in text and pictures that reveal place settings

          Descriptions of places, landmarks, activities, or people

      Looks for clues in text and pictures that reveal time settings

          Period of history

          Season of the year

      Identifies influence of setting on characters and events

      Recognizes significance of changes in setting

- Describes author's style or use of words

      Distinguishes between straightforward and figurative use of words

      Identifies consistency of an individual's style in writing and illustrating

      Recognizes function of repetition

      Observes balance of narration and dialogue

      Notices descriptive language, figurative language, and allusions

          Identifies metaphor, simile, and personification

          Recognizes meaning of symbols

          Notices play on words or puns

      Recognizes variety of sentence patterns

      Recognizes authentic speech patterns of character

      Recognizes language patterns that relate mood

- Recognizes point of view

      Distinguishes third person narrator (author is telling the story), first person narrator (usually main character telling the story), and omniscient narrator (author telling story and thoughts of all characters, adding analytical comment)

      Recognizes influence of point of view on interpretation of story

Understands Components of Poetry

- Interprets meaning

      Looks for key words, images, symbols for meaning

      Recognizes multiple meanings and ambiguity

      Recognizes point of view

      Recognizes theme

- Looks for imagery in poem
    Sensory appeal
    Simile
    Metaphor
    Allusion
    Symbol
    Personification
- Can describe diction (poet's choice of words)
    Direct, straightforward
    Conversational
    Ornate or simple
- Recognizes sound effects of poetry
    Recognizes words that make the rhyme
    Identifies rhyme scheme
    Looks for words and phrases that create special effects
        Alliteration
        Assonance
        Onomatopoeia
- Identifies various forms of poetry
    Recognizes story element in narrative form
    Recognizes rhythmical and descriptive form of a lyric
    Recognizes nonsense content and line pattern of limerick
    Recognizes stanza form of sonnet
    Recognizes form and content of free verse

Evaluates Literature

- Understands authors write to achieve purpose
    Recognizes different criteria apply to different types of literature
    Recognizes that details are selected to contribute to effect
    Recognizes that form contributes to effect
    Recognizes that theme, plot, characterization, and style all contribute to a unified whole
- Evaluates setting
    Considers effectiveness of setting
        Descriptions appeal to five senses
        Influence of setting on plot and characters clearly shown
    Considers authenticity of setting
        True to facts of history and spirit of the times
        Reflects accurate geographical locale
        True to cultural and social attitudes
- Evaluates plot
    Recognizes significance of plot
    Recognizes fresh, unusual plot
    Identifies trite or overworked plot
    Recognizes well-constructed plot
        Evaluates plausibility of plot
        All events contribute to total purpose of story
        Events are significant for forward movement of the plot
        Events occur logically and naturally as a result of action and characters
        Suspense is maintained believably
        Logical and believable events build up to climax

      Economy of incident follows climax
      Structure and pacing of plot appropriate for content
- Evaluates characterization
    Recognizes convincing characterization
      Reveals true emotions
      Shows both strengths and weaknesses
      Language and knowledge consistent with background, environment, and age
      Main character described fully
    Evaluates character change
      Characters changed by life events
      Author shows reason for change
      Change consistent with personality of character
    Evaluates worthiness of characters themselves
- Evaluates style of writing
    Recognizes appropriateness of style for purpose, character, total effect
    Recognizes quality of description and sensory impressions
    Recognizes originality in use of language
      Interesting, fresh metaphor
      Colloquial language used appropriately
    Evaluates use of symbol
      Symbol made clear in context
      Symbol appropriate to character, setting, plot
- Evaluates point of view
    Recognizes effectiveness of point of view used
    Decides if choice of point of view was a good one
- Evaluates theme
    Considers effectiveness of presentation
      Easily identified in prose or poetry
      Logically developed from plot
      Does not overpower story
    Considers worthiness of theme
      Universal application to life
      Real significance for human behavior

Applies Knowledge of Literary Criticism

- Uses criteria appropriate for type of literature
    Emphasizes criteria of authenticity of setting to evaluate historical fiction
    Evaluates techniques used to create believable fantasy
      Grounds fantasy in reality
      Gradual introduction to the fantastic
      Detailed descriptions of settings and characters
      Characters in story express belief in their situation
    Emphasizes image and sound to evaluate poetry
- Asks appropriate questions to analyze writing technique
- Sees relationships among literary selections
    Recognizes similarity in themes, plots, settings, characters, style
- Recognizes similarities and differences in works of one author or illustrator
- Asks appropriate questions for understanding larger meanings
- Recognizes that literature gives insight into human thought and action
- Applies insights gained through literature to his own life
- Continues to seek new understandings

Balance in the Literature Curriculum

To achieve the purposes of the literature curriculum, the school staff will plan for balance in the program. There will be a balance among individual, small-group, and large-group activities. Children will experience literature by listening, reading, and discussing. The child will interpret literature in a variety of ways, including oral and written expression and creative art and dramatics.

Throughout the school year, there will be experiences emphasizing enjoyment, and experiences designed to instruct. However, discussion of books should be pleasurable and increase children's enjoyment of literature. Literary understandings may be developed by both incidental and planned instruction. Literature lessons will provide a balance between analysis of the craft of writing and consideration of the meaning of the selection for the lives of the children.

The literature curriculum for the school should provide for a balance in literature between the old and the new, prose and poetry, fiction and nonfiction, realism and fantasy, and fiction with historical and contemporary settings. In planning the curriculum, some agreement should be made by the staff concerning a basic list of material that provides these balances.

Planning the Curriculum Guide

The first step in planning a literature curriculum in the elementary school is the development of the commitment of the faculty to the importance of teaching literature. As teachers and supervisors recognize the values of literature for children, they will come to see the importance of a planned program. A curriculum guide for literature is needed to identify purposes and experiences.

The process of planning a curriculum guide is as important as the completed document. When teachers and supervisors are actively involved in planning, they find satisfaction in cooperative efforts, gain new insights about children, and increase their understandings of literature. Although this process is time-consuming, teachers will find it worthy of their efforts. They should be given released time during the school year, and groups might be employed during the summer for this activity. While the actual writing of the guide should be the responsibility of a small group of interested teachers and supervisors, the entire staff should participate in various aspects of the planning. For example, when scholars from the disciplines of Education, English, and Psychology are invited to consult with the working committee, they might also present their views to the entire faculty.

The curriculum guide should be based upon evidence from research. Studies of children's interests and factors related to development of interests will provide significant guides for planning the program. Research related to the analysis of children's literature will also be useful. Methods of study and findings of investigations of children's responses to literature will suggest procedures for local studies. Research and evaluation are part of curriculum development.

The curriculum guide provides suggestions for the program, but each teacher implements it in terms of the needs and interests of the children. Continuous evaluation of the program and new developments in the field will challenge the staff to make frequent revisions in the guide. Such a planned program of teaching literature in the elementary school will assure children the opportunity of getting to know books and developing an understanding of literature.

The introduction to this book invited the reader to explore the world of books for children. The entire volume has been concerned with this exploration and with ways to guide children's discoveries in that world.

The teacher is granted the opportunity to become the piper who leads children into that wonderful world of books. It is both exciting and deeply satisfying to become such a piper, "piping down the valleys wild," for the way is only partially explored.

SUGGESTED ACTIVITIES

1. Look at state and local curriculum guides to determine the place of literature in the curriculum. Find out about suggestions given for teaching literature. Literature may be included in the guides for reading or language arts or may have its own section. For example, see *Teaching Literature in Wisconsin*, the *Nebraska Curriculum Project in English* and *Handbook for Language Arts* from New York City.
2. Examine literature readers, sample kits of literature, and published units based upon literature. Note purposes, content, and activities.
3. Plan a literature lesson for a small group or entire class.
4. Analyze a book or poem to determine what literary skills and understandings might be taught from this selection.
5. Listen to children giving book reviews or discussing books. If possible, make a tape recording that could be analyzed to note children's understandings of literature.
6. Analyze several written book reports by children to note their understandings.
7. Prepare several reports on one book by using different patterns; for example, a first person account, dialogue between characters, a sales talk.
8. Find examples in a work of fiction that illustrate ways an author revealed character.
9. Make a file of passages from literature that represent rich language and use of figurative language.
10. Select several poems on one subject or theme and plan ways to guide children's comparisons of these poems.
11. Make a tape recording of a group discussion of a book read by you and your peers. Analyze the discussion to discover the factors that were considered and those that were omitted.
12. Plan a lesson that moves from identification skills to interpretation to evaluation and application. The Taxonomy of Literary Understandings and Skills should prove useful in making such a plan.

RELATED READINGS

1. Barnet, Sylvan, Morton Berman, and William Burto. *The Study of Literature*. Boston: Little, Brown, 1960.
   A collection of essays by writers from Aristotle to T. S. Eliot. The dictionary of literary terms will be especially useful.
2. Bloom, Benjamin, *et al. Taxonomy of Educational Objectives. Handbook I: Cognitive Domain*. New York: McKay, 1956.
   A classification of goals defined as behavior that reflects knowlege and intellectual skill. Of particular value in developing a curriculum.
3. Brooks, Cleanth, *et al. An Approach to Literature*. New York: Appleton, 1952.
   A general discussion of critical reading of literature.
4. Ciardi, John. *How Does a Poem Mean?* Boston: Houghton Mifflin, 1959.
   Emphasis is upon experiencing the poem as the reader learns to identify elements that give a poem meaning. Sections on words in poetry, images, motion and countermotion include poems and discussion of their meanings.
5. Daiches, David. *Critical Approaches to Literature*. Engelwood Cliffs, N.J.: Prentice-Hall, 1956.

The nature of imaginative literature gives a philosophical basis for "practical criticism." Criticism as related to psychology and sociology will be of special interest.

6. Early, Margaret, and Norine Odland. "Literature in the Elementary and Secondary Schools," *Review of Educational Research*, vol. 37 (April 1967), pp. 178–85.
   Gives a comprehensive review of the research in literature for the past three years.

7. Frye, Northrop. *Anatomy of Criticism*. Princeton, N.J.: Princeton University Press, 1957.
   Types of criticism are identified as Historical, Ethical, Archetypal, and Rhetorical. Theory of myths and genres will be of interest to advanced students.

8. ————*The Educated Imagination*. Toronto, Canada: Canadian Broadcasting Corporation, n.d.
   Six lectures help define criticism as a process of interpreting one work in the range of the whole. The author suggests literature is the source of the "educated imagination."

9. Huus, Helen. "Development of Taste in Literature in the Elementary Grades," *Elementary English*, vol. 39 (December 1962), pp. 78–89.
   This article summarizes the investigations of factors affecting children's tastes and methods for improving literary appreciation.

10. Krathwohl, David, *et al. Taxonomy of Educational Objectives. Handbook II: Affective Domain*. New York: McKay, 1964.
    This classification points out the need for clearly defined behavioral goals, relates the cognitive and affective domain, and establishes a continuum from receiving and responding to valuing, organizing, and internalizing attitudes, interests, appreciations.

11. Perrine, Laurence. *Sound and Sense*. New York: Harcourt, 1956.

12. ————*Story and Structure*. New York: Harcourt, 1959.
    These guides to understanding poetry and fiction will be especially useful to those who are inexperienced in criticism. Practical aids to understanding poetry and prose can be applied to children's literature.

13. Rosenheim, Edward W., Jr. *What Happens in Literature*. Chicago: University of Chicago Press, 1960.
    Written for undergraduate humanities classes, this small volume provides an excellent introduction to the discovery of elements of prose, poetry, and drama that create enjoyment. Chapter 2 gives a good explanation of "point of view" and elements of plot and characterization.

14. Sawyer, Ruth. *The Way of the Storyteller*. Revised edition. New York: Viking, 1962.
    A great storyteller shares her experience and pictures storytelling as an art. A classic in the field, it includes helpful advice on selection and eleven stories often told by the author. Weston Woods Studios has produced a record album entitled *Ruth Sawyer, Storyteller*, which includes her comments on storytelling and her rendition of four stories.

15. Tooze, Ruth. *Storytelling*. Englewood Cliffs, N.J.: Prentice-Hall, 1959.
    The teacher will find help in developing the skill and art of storytelling in this readable book. Several stories are included, and an extensive bibliography lists stories to tell children in three age groups. Also included are holiday and seasonal material.

16. University of Nebraska. *A Curriculum for English*. Lincoln, Neb.: University of Nebraska Press, 1966.
    An analysis of children's literature is included in this description of an integrated literature composition program for the elementary grades. Six bulletins (one for each grade level) contain many units for literary study. Another bulletin on *Poetry for the Elementary Grades* gives many suggestions for teaching poetry.

17. Wellek, René, and Austin Warren. *Theory of Literature*. New York: Harcourt, 1956.
    A book for the advanced student, this volume discusses the nature of literary study and approaches to study.

18. Wisconsin English-Language Arts Curriculum Project. *Teaching Literature in Wisconsin.* Madison, Wis.: Department of Public Instruction, 1965.
This guide outlines a balanced, sequential program, gives examples of lessons, and provides suggested titles for basic study for kindergarten through grade twelve.

CHAPTER REFERENCES

1. Aardema, Verna. *Tales from the Story Hat.* Illustrated by Elton Fax. New York: Coward-McCann, 1960.
2. Aldis, Dorothy. "Brooms" in *Time for Poetry.* May Hill Arbuthnot, Editor. Revised edition. Glenview, Ill.: Scott, Foresman, 1961.
3. Andersen, Hans Christian. "The Fir Tree" in *Seven Tales.* Translated by Eva Le Gallienne. Illustrated by Maurice Sendak. New York: Harper & Row, 1959.
4. Asbjørnsen, P. C., and J. E. Moe. *The Three Billy Goats Gruff.* Illustrated by Marcia Brown. New York: Harcourt, 1957.
5. Babbitt, Ellen C. *Jataka Tales.* Illustrated by Ellsworth Young. New York: Appleton, 1940, 1912.
6. Bailey, C. S. *The Little Rabbit Who Wanted Red Wings.* Illustrated by Dorothy Grider. New York: Platt & Munk, 1945.
7. Batchelor, Julie Forsyth. *A Cap for Mul Chand.* Illustrated by Corinne V. Dillon. New York: Harcourt, 1950.
8. Baum, Betty. *Patricia Crosses Town.* Illustrated by Nancy Grossman. New York: Knopf, 1965.
9. Bemelmans, Ludwig. *Madeline.* New York: Viking, 1939.
10. Boston, L. M. *The Children of Green Knowe.* Illustrated by Peter Boston. New York: Harcourt, 1955.
11. Brown, Marcia. *Cinderella.* New York: Scribner, 1954.
12. Buff, Mary and Conrad. *Big Tree.* New York: Viking, 1963, 1946.
13. Burton, Virginia Lee. *The Little House.* Boston: Houghton Mifflin, 1942.
14. Carlson, Natalie Savage. *The Empty Schoolhouse.* Illustrated by John Kaufmann. New York: Harper & Row, 1965.
15. Cooney, Barbara. *Chanticleer and the Fox.* New York: Crowell, 1958.
16. Ciardi, John. "The River Is a Piece of the Sky" in *The Reason for the Pelican.* Illustrated by Madeleine Gekiere. Philadelphia: Lippincott, 1959.
17. Coatsworth, Elizabeth. "On a Night of Snow" in *The Golden Treasury of Poetry.* Louis Untermeyer, Editor. Illustrated by Joan Walsh Anglund. New York: Golden Press, 1959.
18. Colwell, Eileen. *A Storyteller's Choice.* Illustrated by Carol Barker. New York: Walck, 1963.
19. Courlander, Harold, and George Herzog. *The Cow-Tail Switch and Other West African Stories.* Illustrated by Madye Lee Chastain. New York: Holt, Rinehart and Winston, 1947.
20. Cummings, E. E. "Chanson Innocente" in *Favorite Poems Old and New.* Helen Ferris, Editor. Illustrated by Leonard Weisgard. New York: Doubleday, 1957.
21. Dalgliesh, Alice. *The Bears on Hemlock Mountain.* Illustrated by Helen Sewell. New York: Scribner, 1952.
22. De Angeli, Marguerite. *Bright April.* New York: Doubleday, 1946.
23. DeJong, Meindert. *Hurry Home, Candy.* Illustrated by Maurice Sendak. New York: Harper & Row, 1956.
24. De la Mare, Walter. "Silver" in *Time for Poetry.* May Hill Arbuthnot, Editor. Revised edition. Glenview, Ill.: Scott, Foresman, 1961.
25. Dodge, Mary Mapes. *Hans Brinker, or the Silver Skates.* Illustrated by George Wharton Edwards. New York: Scribner, 1915, 1865.
26. Duvoisin, Roger A. *The House of Four Seasons.* New York: Lothrop, 1956.
27. ———*Veronica.* New York: Knopf, 1961.

28. Edmonds, Walter D. *The Matchlock Gun.* Illustrated by Paul Lantz. New York: Dodd, Mead, 1941.

29. Estes, Eleanor. *The Alley.* Illustrated by Edward Ardizzone. New York: Harcourt, 1964.

30. Field, Rachel. *Hitty, Her First Hundred Years.* Illustrated by Dorothy Lathrop. New York: Macmillan, 1929.

31. Flack, Marjorie. *Ask Mr. Bear.* New York: Macmillan, 1932.

32. Freeman, Don. *Dandelion.* New York: Viking, 1964.

33. Friskey, Margaret. *Chicken Little, Count-to-Ten.* Illustrated by Katherine Evans. Chicago: Childrens Press, 1946.

34. Fritz, Jean. *The Cabin Faced West.* Illustrated by Feodor Rojankovsky. New York: Coward-McCann, 1958.

35. Frost, Robert. *You Come Too, Favorite Poems for Young Readers.* Illustrated by Thomas Nason. New York: Holt, Rinehart and Winston, 1959.

36. Gág, Wanda. *Gone Is Gone.* New York: Coward-McCann, 1935.

37. ————*Nothing at All.* New York: Coward-McCann, 1941.

38. George, Jean. *Gull 737.* New York: Crowell, 1964.

39. Godden, Rumer. *Impunity Jane.* Illustrated by Adrienne Adams. New York: Viking, 1954.

40. Goudey, Alice. *Here Come the Bears!* Illustrated by Garry MacKenzie. New York: Scribner, 1954.

41. Grahame, Kenneth. *The Wind in the Willows.* Illustrated by E. H. Shepard. New York: Scribner, 1908.

42. Gregor, Arthur S. *Galileo.* Illustrated by George Giusti. New York: Scribner, 1965.

43. Hader, Berta and Elmer. *The Mighty Hunter.* New York: Macmillan, 1943.

44. Haugaard, Erik. *Hakon of Rogen's Saga.* Illustrated by Leo and Diane Dillon. Boston: Houghton Mifflin, 1963.

45. Henry, Marguerite. *King of the Wind.* Illustrated by Wesley Dennis. Skokie, Ill.: Rand McNally, 1962, 1948.

46. ————*Misty of Chincoteague.* Illustrated by Wesley Dennis. Skokie, Ill.: Rand McNally, 1962, 1947.

47. Holm, Anne. *North to Freedom.* New York: Harcourt, 1965.

48. Hope, Laura Lee (pseud.). *The Bobbsey Twins.* New York: Grosset & Dunlap, 1910.

49. Hopkins, G. M. "The Starlight Night" in *Modern British Poetry.* Louis Untermeyer, Editor. New York: Harcourt, 1950.

50. Hutchins, Carleen. *Moon Moth.* Illustrated by Douglas Howland. New York: Coward-McCann, 1965.

51. Ish-Kishor, S. *A Boy of Old Prague.* Illustrated by Ben Shahn. New York: Pantheon, 1963.

52. Jackson, Jesse. *Call Me Charley.* Illustrated by Doris Spiegel. New York: Harper & Row, 1945.

53. Jacobs, Joseph. *The Three Wishes.* Retold and illustrated by Paul Galdone. New York: McGraw-Hill, 1961.

54. Kipling, Rudyard. "The Elephant's Child" in *Just So Stories.* Illustrated by Nicolas. New York: Doubleday, 1952, 1912.

55. Krasilovsky, Phyllis. *The Man Who Didn't Wash His Dishes.* Illustrated by Barbara Cooney. New York: Doubleday, 1950.

56. Krauss, Ruth. *A Very Special House.* Illustrated by Maurice Sendak. New York: Harper & Row, 1953.

57. Kroeber, Theodora. *Ishi, Last of His Tribe.* Illustrated by Ruth Robbins. New York: Parnassus, 1964.

58. Lawson, Robert. *Rabbit Hill.* New York: Viking, 1945.

59. ————*Robbut, A Tale of Tails.* New York: Viking, 1949.

60. Lenski, Lois. *Shoo-Fly Girl.* Philadelphia: Lippincott, 1963.

61. Leodhas, Sorche Nic. *Always Room for One More.* Illustrated by Nonny Hogrogian. New York: Holt, Rinehart and Winston, 1965.

62. ———*Heather and Broom: Tales of the Scottish Highlands.* Illustrated by Consuelo Joerns. New York: Holt, Rinehart and Winston, 1960.

63. Lewis, C. S. *The Lion, the Witch, and the Wardrobe.* Illustrated by Pauline Baynes. New York: Macmillan, 1950.

64. Liers, Emil. *An Otter's Story.* New York: Viking, 1953.

65. Lindgren, Astrid. *Pippi Longstocking.* Translated by Florence Lamborn. Illustrated by Louis Glanzman. New York: Viking, 1950.

66. Lindsay, Vachel. "The Moon's the North Wind's Cooky" in *Time for Poetry.* May Hill Arbuthnot, Editor. Revised edition. Glenview, Ill.: Scott, Foresman, 1961.

67. Little, Jean. *Home from Far.* Boston: Little, Brown, 1965.

68. ———*Mine for Keeps.* Illustrated by Lewis Parker. Boston: Little, Brown, 1962.

69. Merrill, Jean. *The Pushcart War.* Illustrated by Ronni Solbert. New York: W. R. Scott, 1964.

70. Milhous, Katherine. *Appolonia's Valentine.* New York: Scribner, 1954.

71. Milne, A. A. *Winnie the Pooh.* Illustrated by Ernest H. Shepard. New York: Dutton, 1926.

72. Minarik, Else Holmelund. *Little Bear.* Illustrated by Maurice Sendak. New York: Harper & Row, 1957.

73. Mirsky, Reba. *Nomusa and the New Magic.* Illustrated by W. T. Mars. Chicago: Follett, 1962.

74. ———*Thirty-one Brothers and Sisters.* Illustrated by W. T. Mars. Chicago: Follett, 1952.

75. Monsell, Helen. *Paddy's Christmas.* New York: Knopf, 1942.

76. Moore, Nancy. *The Unhappy Hippopotamus.* Illustrated by Edward Leight. New York: Vanguard, 1957.

77. Nolte, Nancy. *The Gingerbread Man.* Illustrated by Richard Scarry. New York: Golden Press, 1961, 1953.

78. Norton, Mary. *The Borrowers.* Illustrated by Beth and Joe Krush. New York: Harcourt, 1953.

79. Noyes, Alfred. "The Highwayman" in *The Golden Treasury of Poetry.* Louis Untermeyer, Editor. Illustrated by Joan Walsh Anglund. New York: Golden Press, 1959.

80. Owen, Russell. *The Conquest of the North and South Pole.* Illustrated by Lynd Ward. New York: Random House, 1952.

81. Politi, Leo. *Lito the Clown.* New York: Scribner, 1964.

82. ———*Song of the Swallows.* New York: Scribner, 1949.

83. Sendak, Maurice. *Where the Wild Things Are.* New York: Harper & Row, 1963.

84. Sewell, Anna. *Black Beauty.* Illustrated by John Beer. New York: Dodd, Mead, 1941, 1877.

85. Sherlock, Philip M. *Anansi the Spider Man: Jamaican Folk Tales.* Illustrated by Marcia Brown. New York: Crowell, 1954.

86. Simon, Charlie May. *All Men Are Brothers, a Portrait of Albert Schweitzer.* New York: Dutton, 1956.

87. Slobodkin, Louis. *Magic Michael.* New York: Macmillan, 1944.

88. Sperry, Armstrong. *Call It Courage.* New York: Macmillan, 1941.

89. Steele, William O. *The Lone Hunt.* Illustrated by Paul Galdone. New York: Harcourt, 1956.

90. Sterling, Dorothy. *Mary Jane.* New York: Doubleday, 1959.

91. Stevenson, Robert Louis. "My Shadow" in *A Child's Garden of Verses.* Illustrated by Tasha Tudor. New York: Oxford, 1947, 1885.

92. Stolz, Mary. *The Bully of Barkham Street.* Illustrated by Leonard Shortall. New York: Harper & Row, 1963.

93. Tolkien, J. R. R. *The Hobbit.* Boston: Houghton Mifflin, 1938.

94. Travers, Pamela L. *Mary Poppins.* Illustrated by Mary Shepard. New York: Harcourt, 1934.

95. Ullman, James Ramsey. *Banner in the Sky.* Philadelphia: Lippincott, 1954.

96. Waber, Bernard. *You Look Ridiculous.* Boston: Houghton Mifflin, 1966.

97. Ward, Lynd. *The Biggest Bear.* Boston: Houghton Mifflin, 1952.

98. West, Jerry. *The Happy Hollisters.* New York: Doubleday, 1953.

99. White, E. B. *Charlotte's Web.* Illustrated by Garth Williams. New York: Harper & Row, 1952.

100. ————*Stuart Little.* Illustrated by Garth Williams. New York: Harper & Row, 1945.

101. Wojciechowska, Maia. *Shadow of a Bull.* New York: Atheneum, 1964.

102. Wondriska, William. *The Tomato Patch.* New York: Harper & Row, 1963.

103. Yates, Elizabeth. *Carolina's Courage.* Illustrated by Nora S. Unwin. New York: Dutton, 1964.

104. Zion, Gene. *Harry the Dirty Dog.* Illustrated by Margaret Bloy Graham. New York: Harper & Row, 1956.

APPENDIXES

A

CHILDREN'S BOOK AWARDS

GENERAL AWARDS

THE JOHN NEWBERY MEDAL is named in honor of John Newbery, a British publisher and bookseller of the eighteenth century. He has frequently been called the father of children's literature since he was the first to conceive the idea of publishing books expressly for children.

The Award is presented each year to "the author of the most distinguished contribution to American literature for children." To be eligible for the award, the author must be an American citizen or a permanent resident of the United States. The selection of the winner is made by a committee of the Children's Services Division of the American Library Association. There are twenty-three members on this committee. The winning author is presented a bronze medal designed by René Paul Chambellan and donated by Frederick G. Melcher. The announcement is made in the spring. Later at the summer conference of the American Library Association, a banquet is given in honor of the Award winners.

The following list of books includes the Award winners (capitalized and listed first) and the run-ners-up for each year. The date in the left-hand column indicates the year in which the Award was conferred. All books were necessarily published the preceding year. The name of the present publisher, if not the same as when the book was originally published, is given in parentheses.

1922 *THE STORY OF MANKIND* by Hendrik Van Loon. Boni & Liveright.
The Great Quest by Charles Boardman Hawes. Little, Brown.
Cedric the Forester by Bernard G. Marshall. Appleton.
The Old Tobacco Shop by William Bowen. Macmillan.
The Golden Fleece by Padraic Colum. Macmillan.
Windy Hill by Cornelia Meigs. Macmillan.

1923 *THE VOYAGES OF DOCTOR DOLITTLE* by Hugh Lofting. Stokes (Lippincott).
[No record of the runners-up.]

1924 *THE DARK FRIGATE* by Charles Boardman Hawes. Little, Brown.
[No record of the runners-up.]

1925 *TALES FROM SILVER LANDS* by Charles

J. Finger. Illustrated by Paul Honoré. Doubleday.

Nicholas by Anne Carroll Moore. Putnam.

Dream Coach by Anne and Dillwyn Parrish. Macmillan.

1926 *SHEN OF THE SEA* by Arthur Bowie Chrisman. Illustrated by Else Hasselriis. Dutton.

The Voyagers by Padraic Colum. Macmillan.

1927 *SMOKY, THE COWHORSE* by Will James. Scribner.

[No record of the runners-up.]

1928 *GAY NECK* by Dhan Gopal Mukerji. Illustrated by Boris Artzybasheff. Dutton.

The Wonder-Smith and His Son by Ella Young. Longmans, Green (McKay).

Downright Dencey by Caroline Dale Snedeker. Doubleday.

1929 *TRUMPETER OF KRAKOW* by Eric P. Kelly. Illustrated by Angela Pruszynska. Macmillan.

The Pigtail of Ah Lee Ben Loo by John Bennett. Longmans, Green (McKay).

Millions of Cats by Wanda Gág. Coward-McCann.

The Boy Who Was by Grace T. Hallock. Dutton.

Clearing Weather by Cornelia Meigs. Little, Brown.

The Runaway Papoose by Grace P. Moon. Doubleday.

Tod of the Fens by Eleanor Whitney. Macmillan.

1930 *HITTY, HER FIRST HUNDRED YEARS* by Rachel Field. Illustrated by Dorothy P. Lathrop. Macmillan.

Pran of Albania by Elizabeth C. Miller. Doubleday.

The Jumping-Off Place by Marian Hurd McNeely. Longmans, Green (McKay).

A Daughter of the Seine by Jeanette Eaton. Harper (Harper & Row).

1931 *THE CAT WHO WENT TO HEAVEN* by Elizabeth Coatsworth. Illustrated by Lynd Ward. Macmillan.

Floating Island by Anne Parrish. Harper (Harper & Row).

The Dark Star of Itza by Alida Malkus. Harcourt.

Queer Person by Ralph Hubbard. Doubleday.

Mountains Are Free by Julia Davis Adams. Dutton.

Spice and the Devil's Cave by Agnes D. Hewes. Knopf.

Meggy McIntosh by Elizabeth Janet Gray. Doubleday.

1932 *WATERLESS MOUNTAIN* by Laura Adams Armer. Illustrated by Sidney Armer and the author. Longmans, Green (McKay).

The Fairy Circus by Dorothy Lathrop. Macmillan.

Calico Bush by Rachel Field. Macmillan.

Boy of the South Seas by Eunice Tietjens. Coward-McCann.

Out of the Flame by Eloise Lounsbery. Longmans, Green (McKay).

Jane's Island by Marjorie Hill Alee. Houghton Mifflin.

Truce of the Wolf by Mary Gould Davis. Harcourt.

1933 *YOUNG FU OF THE UPPER YANGTZE* by Elizabeth Foreman Lewis. Illustrated by Kurt Wiese. Winston (Holt, Rinehart and Winston).

Hepatica Hawks by Rachel Field. Macmillan.

Romantic Rebel by Hildegarde Hawthorne. Appleton.

Auntie by Maude and Miska Petersham. Doubleday.

Tirra Lirra by Laura E. Richards. Little, Brown.

Little House in the Big Woods by Laura Ingalls Wilder. Harper (Harper & Row).

1934 *INVINCIBLE LOUISA* by Cornelia Meigs. Little, Brown.

Forgotten Daughter by Caroline Dale Snedeker. Doubleday.

Swords of Steel by Elsie Singmaster. Houghton Mifflin.

ABC Bunny by Wanda Gág. Coward-McCann.

Winged Girl of Knossos by Erick Berry. Appleton.

New Land by Sarah L. Schmidt. McBride.

Apprentices of Florence by Anne Kyle. Houghton Mifflin.

1935 *Dobry* by Monica Shannon. Illustrated by Atanas Katchamakoff. Viking.

The Pageant of Chinese History by Elizabeth Seeger. Longmans, Green (McKay).

Davy Crockett by Constance Rourke. Harcourt.

A Day on Skates by Hilda Van Stockum. Harper (Harper & Row).

1936 *CADDIE WOODLAWN* by Carol Ryrie Brink. Illustrated by Kate Seredy. Macmillan.

Honk the Moose by Phil Stong. Dodd, Mead.

The Good Master by Kate Seredy. Viking.

Young Walter Scott Elizabeth Janet Gray. Viking.

All Sail Set by Armstrong Sperry. Winston (Holt, Rinehart and Winston).

1937 *ROLLER SKATES* by Ruth Sawyer. Illustrated by Valenti Angelo. Viking.

Phoebe Fairchild: Her Book by Lois Lenski. Stokes (Lippincott).

Whistler's Van by Idwal Jones. Viking.

The Golden Basket by Ludwig Bemelmans, Viking.

Winterbound by Margery Bianco. Viking.

Audubon by Constance Rourke. Harcourt.

The Codfish Musket by Agnes D. Hewes. Doubleday.

1938 *THE WHITE STAG* by Kate Seredy. Viking.

Bright Island by Mabel L. Robinson. Random House.

Pecos Bill by James Cloyd Bowman. Whitman.

On the Banks of Plum Creek by Laura Ingalls Wilder. Harper (Harper & Row).

1939 *THIMBLE SUMMER* by Elizabeth Enright. Farrar & Rinehart (Holt, Rinehart and Winston).

Leader by Destiny by Jeanette Eaton. Harcourt.

Penn by Elizabeth Janet Gray. Viking.

Nino by Valenti Angelo. Viking.

"Hello, the Boat!" by Phyllis Crawford. Holt (Holt, Rinehart and Winston).

Mr. Popper's Penguins by Richard and Florence Atwater. Little, Brown.

1940 *DANIEL BOONE* by James H. Daugherty. Viking.

The Singing Tree by Kate Seredy. Viking.

Runner of the Mountain Tops by Mabel L. Robinson. Random House.

By the Shores of Silver Lake by Laura Ingalls Wilder. Harper (Harper & Row).

Boy with a Pack by Stephen W. Meader. Harcourt.

1941 *CALL IT COURAGE* by Armstrong Sperry. Macmillan.

Blue Willow by Doris Gates. Viking.

Young Mac of Fort Vancouver by Mary Jane Carr. Crowell.

The Long Winter by Laura Ingalls Wilder. Harper (Harper & Row).

Nansen by Anna Gertrude Hall. Viking.

1942 *THE MATCHLOCK GUN* by Walter D. Edmonds. Illustrated by Paul Lantz. Dodd, Mead.

Little Town on the Prairie by Laura Ingalls Wilder. Harper (Harper & Row).

George Washington's World by Genevieve Foster. Scribner.

Indian Captive by Lois Lenski. Stokes (Lippincott).

Down Ryton Water by E. R. Gaggin. Viking.

1943 *ADAM OF THE ROAD* by Elizabeth Janet Gray. Illustrated by Robert Lawson. Viking.

The Middle Moffat by Eleanor Estes. Harcourt.

"Have You Seen Tom Thumb?" by Mabel Leigh Hunt. Stokes (Lippincott).

1944 *JOHNNY TREMAIN* by Esther Forbes. Illustrated by Lynd Ward. Houghton Mifflin.

These Happy Golden Years by Laura Ingalls Wilder. Harper (Harper & Row).

Fog Magic by Julia L. Sauer. Viking.

Rufus M. by Eleanor Estes. Harcourt.

Mountain Born by Elizabeth Yates. Coward-McCann.

1945 *RABBIT HILL* by Robert Lawson. Viking.

The Hundred Dresses by Eleanor Estes. Harcourt.

The Silver Pencil by Alice Dalgliesh. Scribner.

Abraham Lincoln's World by Genevieve Foster. Scribner.

Lone Journey by Jeanette Eaton. Harcourt.

1946 *STRAWBERRY GIRL* by Lois Lenski. Lippincott.

Justin Morgan Had a Horse by Marguerite Henry. Wilcox & Follett (Follett).

The Moved-Outers by Florence Crannell Means. Houghton Mifflin.

Bhimsa, the Dancing Bear by Christine Weston. Scribner.

New Found World by Katherine B. Shippen. Viking.

1947 *MISS HICKORY* by Carolyn Sherwin Bailey. Illustrated by Ruth Gannett. Viking.

The Wonderful Year by Nancy Barnes. Messner.

Big Tree by Mary and Conrad Buff. Viking.

The Heavenly Tenants by William Maxwell. Harper (Harper & Row).

The Avion My Uncle Flew by Cyrus Fisher. Appleton.

The Hidden Treasure of Glaston by Eleanore M. Jewett. Viking.

1948 *THE TWENTY-ONE BALLOONS* by William Pène du Bois. Viking.

Pancakes-Paris by Claire Huchet Bishop Viking.

Li Lun, Lad of Courage by Carolyn Treffinger. Abingdon-Cokesbury (Abingdon).

The Quaint and Curious Quest of Johnny Longfoot by Catherine Besterman. Bobbs-Merrill.

The Cow-Tail Switch by Harold Courlander and George Herzog. Holt (Holt, Rinehart and Winston).

Misty of Chincoteague by Marguerite Henry. Rand McNally.

1949 *KING OF THE WIND* by Marguerite Henry. Illustrated by Wesley Dennis. Rand McNally.

Seabird by Holling Clancy Holling. Houghton Mifflin.

Daughter of the Mountains by Louise Rankin. Viking.

My Father's Dragon by Ruth S. Gannett. Random House.

Story of the Negro by Arna Bontemps. Knopf.

1950 *THE DOOR IN THE WALL* by Marguerite de Angeli. Doubleday.

Tree of Freedom by Rebecca Caudill. Viking.

Blue Cat of Castle Town by Catherine Coblentz. Longmans, Green (McKay).

Kildee House by Rutherford Montgomery. Doubleday.

George Washington by Genevieve Foster. Scribner.

Song of the Pines by Walter and Marion Havighurst. Winston (Holt, Rinehart and Winston).

1951 *AMOS FORTUNE, FREE MAN* by Elizabeth Yates. Illustrated by Nora Unwin. Aladdin (Dutton).

Better Known as Johnny Appleseed by Mabel Leigh Hunt. Lippincott.

Gandhi, Fighter without a Sword by Jeanette Eaton. Morrow.

Abraham Lincoln, Friend of the People by Clara I. Judson. Wilcox & Follett (Follett).

The Story of Appleby Capple by Anne Parrish. Harper (Harper & Row).

1952 *GINGER PYE* by Eleanor Estes. Harcourt.

Americans before Columbus by Elizabeth Chesley Baity. Viking.

Minn of the Mississippi by Holling Clancy Holling. Houghton Mifflin.

The Defender by Nicholas Kalashnikoff. Scribner.

The Light at Tern Rock by Julia L. Sauer. Viking.

The Apple and the Arrow by Mary Buff. Houghton Mifflin.

1953 *SECRET OF THE ANDES* by Ann Nolan Clark. Illustrated by Jean Charlot. Viking.

Charlotte's Web by E. B. White. Harper (Harper & Row).

Moccasin Trail by Eloise J. McGraw. Coward-McCann.

Red Sails for Capri by Ann Weil. Viking.

The Bears on Hemlock Mountain by Alice Dalgliesh. Scribner.

Birthdays of Freedom by Genevieve Foster. Scribner.

1954 *. . . AND NOW MIGUEL* by Joseph Krumgold. Illustrated by Jean Charlot. Crowell.

All Alone by Clarie Huchet Bishop. Viking.

Shadrach by Meindert DeJong. Harper (Harper & Row).

Hurry Home, Candy by Meindert DeJong. Harper (Harper & Row).

Theodore Roosevelt, Fighting Patriot by Clara I. Judson. Follett.

Magic Maize by Mary Buff. Houghton Mifflin.

1955 *THE WHEEL ON THE SCHOOL* by Meindert DeJong. Illustrated by Maurice Sendak. Harper (Harper & Row).

The Courage of Sarah Noble by Alice Dalgliesh. Scribner.

Banner in the Sky by James Ramsy Ullman. Lippincott.

1956 *CARRY ON, MR. BOWDITCH* by Jean Lee Latham. Houghton Mifflin.

The Golden Name Day by Jennie D. Lindquist. Harper (Harper & Row).

The Secret River by Marjorie Kinnan Rawlings. Scribner.

Men, Microscopes, and Living Things by Katherine B. Shippen. Viking.

1957 *MIRACLES ON MAPLE HILL* by Virginia Sorensen. Illustrated by Beth and Joe Krush. Harcourt.

Old Yeller by Fred Gipson. Harper (Harper & Row).

The House of Sixty Fathers by Meindert DeJong. Harper (Harper & Row).

Mr. Justice Holmes by Clara I. Judson. Follett.

The Corn Grows Ripe by Dorothy Rhoads. Viking.

The Black Fox of Lorne by Marguerite de Angeli. Doubleday.

1958 *RIFLES FOR WATIE* by Harold Keith. Illustrated by Peter Burchard. Crowell.

The Horsecatcher by Mari Sandoz. Westminster.

Gone-away Lake by Elizabeth Enright. Harcourt.

The Great Wheel by Robert Lawson. Viking.

Tom Paine, Freedom's Apostle by Leo Gurko. Crowell.

1959 *THE WITCH OF BLACKBIRD POND* by Elizabeth George Speare. Houghton Mifflin.

The Family under the Bridge by Natalie S. Carlson. Harper (Harper & Row).

Along Came a Dog by Meindert DeJong. Harper (Harper & Row).

Chucaro by Francis Kalnay. Harcourt.

The Perilous Road by William O. Steele. Harcourt.

1960 *ONION JOHN* by Joseph Krumgold. Illustrated by Symeon Shimin. Crowell.

My Side of the Mountain by Jean George. Dutton.

America Is Born by Gerald Johnson. Morrow.

The Gammage Cup by Carol Kendall. Harcourt.

1961 *ISLAND OF THE BLUE DOLPHINS* by Scott O'Dell. Houghton Mifflin.

America Moves Forward by Gerald Johnson. Morrow.

Old Ramon by Jack Schaefer. Houghton Mifflin.

The Cricket in Times Square by George Selden. Farrar (Farrar, Straus).

1962 *THE BRONZE BOW* by Elizabeth George Speare. Houghton Mifflin.

Frontier Living by Edwin Tunis. World Publishing.

The Golden Goblet by Eloise J. McGraw. Coward-McCann.

Belling the Tiger by Mary Stolz. Harper & Row.

1963 *A WRINKLE IN TIME* by Madeleine L'Engle. Farrar (Farrar, Straus).

Thistle and Thyme by Sorche Nic Leodhas. Holt, Rinehart and Winston.

Men of Athens by Olivia Coolidge. Houghton Mifflin.

1964 *IT'S LIKE THIS, CAT* by Emily Neville. Illustrated by Emil Weiss. Harper & Row.

Rascal by Sterling North. Dutton.

The Loner by Ester Wier. McKay.

1965 *SHADOW OF A BULL* by Maia Wojciechowska. Illustrated by Alvin Smith. Atheneum.

Across Five Aprils by Irene Hunt. Follett.

1966 *I, JUAN DE PAREJA* by Elizabeth Borten de Treviño. Farrar, Straus.

The Black Cauldron by Lloyd Alexander. Holt, Rinehart and Winston.

The Animal Family by Randall Jarrell. Pantheon.

The Noonday Friends by Mary Stolz. Harper & Row.

1967 *UP A ROAD SLOWLY* by Irene Hunt. Follett.

The King's Fifth by Scott O'Dell. Houghton Mifflin.

Zlateh the Goat and Other Stories by Isaac Singer. Harper & Row.

The Jazz Man by Mary Hays Weik. Atheneum.

1968 *FROM THE MIXED-UP FILES OF MRS. BASIL E. FRANKWEILER* by E. L. Konigsburg. Atheneum.
Jennifer, Hecate, Macbeth, William McKinley, and Me, Elizabeth by E. L. Konigsburg. Atheneum.
The Black Pearl by Scott O'Dell. Houghton Mifflin.
The Fearsome Inn by Isaac Bashevis Singer. Scribner.
The Egypt Game by Zilpha Keatley Snyder. Atheneum.

THE CALDECOTT MEDAL is named in honor of Randolph Caldecott, a prominent English illustrator of children's books during the nineteenth century. This Award is presented each year to "the artist of the most distinguished American picture book for children." The winner is selected by the same committee that chooses the Newbery winner.

The following list of books includes the Award winners (capitalized and listed first) and the runners-up for each year. The date in the left-hand column indicates the year in which the Award was conferred. If the illustrator's name is not cited, the author illustrated his own book. The Caldecott Award is given to the illustrator, not to the author of these books.

1938 *ANIMALS OF THE BIBLE, A PICTURE BOOK.* Text selected from the King James Bible by Helen Dean Fish. Illustrated by Dorothy O. Lathrop. Stokes (Lippincott).
Seven Simeons by Boris Artzybasheff. Viking.
Four and Twenty Blackbirds compiled by Helen Dean Fish. Illustrated by Robert Lawson. Stokes (Lippincott).

1939 *MEI LI* by Thomas Handforth. Doubleday.
The Forest Pool by Laura Adams Armer. Longmans, Green (McKay).
Wee Gillis by Munro Leaf. Illustrated by Robert Lawson. Viking.
Snow White and the Seven Dwarfs translated and illustrated by Wanda Gág. Coward-McCann.
Barkis by Clare Turlay Newberry. Harper (Harper & Row).
Andy and the Lion by James Daugherty. Viking.

1940 *ABRAHAM LINCOLN* by Ingri and Edgar Parin d'Aulaire. Doubleday.

Cock-a-Doodle-Doo by Berta and Elmer Hader. Macmillan.
Madeline by Ludwig Bemelmans. Simon and Schuster.
The Ageless Story by Lauren Ford. Dodd, Mead.

1941 *THEY WERE STRONG AND GOOD* by Robert Lawson. Viking.
April's Kittens by Clare Turlay Newberry. Harper (Harper & Row).

1942 *MAKE WAY FOR DUCKLINGS* by Robert McCloskey. Viking.
An American ABC by Maud and Miska Petersham. Macmillan.
In My Mother's House by Ann Nolan Clark. Illustrated by Velino Herrera. Viking.
Paddle-to-the-Sea by Holling Clancy Holling. Houghton Mifflin.
Nothing at All by Wanda Gág. Coward-McCann.

1943 *THE LITTLE HOUSE* by Virginia Lee Burton. Houghton Mifflin.
Dash and Dart by Mary and Conrad Buff. Viking.
Marshmallow by Clare Turlay Newberry. Harper (Harper & Row).

1944 *MANY MOONS* by James Thurber. Illustrated by Louis Slobodkin. Harcourt.
Small Rain text arranged from the Bible by Jessie Orton Jones. Illustrated by Elizabeth Orton Jones. Viking.
Pierre Pidgeon by Lee Kingman. Illustrated by Arnold Edwin Bare. Houghton Mifflin.
Good-Luck Horse by Chih-Yi Chan. Illustrated by Plato Chan. Whittlesey.
Mighty Hunter by Berta and Elmer Hader. Macmillan.
A Child's Good Night Book by Margaret Wise Brown. Illustrated by Jean Charlot. W. R. Scott.

1945 *PRAYER FOR A CHILD* by Rachel Field. Pictures by Elizabeth Orton Jones. Macmillan.
Mother Goose compiled and illustrated by Tasha Tudor. Oxford.
In the Forest by Marie Hall Ets. Viking.
Yonie Wondernose by Marguerite de Angeli. Doubleday.
The Christmas Anna Angel by Ruth Sawyer. Illustrated by Kate Seredy. Viking.

1946 *THE ROOSTER CROWS* by Maud and

Miska Petersham. Macmillan.

Little Lost Lamb by Margaret Wise Brown. Illustrated by Leonard Weisgard. Doubleday.

Sing Mother Goose music by Opal Wheeler. Illustrated by Marjorie Torrey. Dutton.

My Mother Is the Most Beautiful Woman in the World by Becky Reyher. Illustrated by Ruth C. Gannett. Lothrop.

You Can Write Chinese by Kurt Wiese. Viking.

1947 THE LITTLE ISLAND by Golden MacDonald. Illustrated by Leonard Weisgard. Doubleday.

Rain Drop Splash by Alvin R. Tresselt. Illustrated by Leonard Weisgard. Lothrop.

Boats on the River by Marjorie Flack. Illustrated by Jay Hyde Barnum. Viking.

Timothy Turtle by Al Graham. Illustrated by Tony Palazzo. Robert Welch (Viking).

Pedro, Angel of Olvera Street by Leo Politi. Scribner.

Sing in Praise by Opal Wheeler. Illustrated by Marjorie Torrey. Dutton.

1948 WHITE SNOW, BRIGHT SNOW by Alvin Tresselt. Illustrated by Roger Duvoisin. Lothrop.

Stone Soup told and illustrated by Marcia Brown. Scribner.

McElligot's Pool by Theodor S. Geisel (Dr. Seuss). Random House.

Bambino the Clown by George Schreiber. Viking.

Roger and the Fox by Lavinia R. Davis. Illustrated by Hildegard Woodward. Doubleday.

Song of Robin Hood edited by Anne Malcolmson. Illustrated by Virginia Lee Burton. Houghton Mifflin.

1949 THE BIG SNOW by Berta and Elmer Hader. Macmillan.

Blueberries for Sal by Robert McCloskey. Viking.

All around the Town by Phyllis McGinley. Illustrated by Helen Stone. Lippincott.

Juanita by Leo Politi. Scribner.

Fish in the Air by Kurt Wiese. Viking.

1950 SONG OF THE SWALLOWS by Leo Politi. Scribner.

America's Ethan Allen by Stewart Holbrook. Illustrated by Lynd Ward. Houghton Mifflin.

The Wild Birthday Cake by Lavinia R. Davis. Illustrated by Hildegard Woodward. Doubleday.

Happy Day by Ruth Krauss. Illustrated by Marc Simont. Harper (Harper & Row).

Henry-Fisherman by Marcia Brown. Scribner.

Bartholomew and the Oobleck by Theodor S. Geisel (Dr. Seuss). Random House.

1951 THE EGG TREE by Katherine Milhous. Scribner.

Dick Whittington and His Cat told and illustrated by Marcia Brown. Scribner.

The Two Reds by Will (William Lipkind). Illustrated by Nicolas (Mordvinoff). Harcourt.

If I Ran the Zoo by Theodor S. Geisel (Dr. Seuss). Random House.

T-Bone the Baby-Sitter by Clare Turlay Newberry. Harper (Harper & Row).

The Most Wonderful Doll in the World by Phyllis McGinley. Illustrated by Helen Stone. Lippincott.

1952 FINDERS KEEPERS by Will (William Lipkind). Illustrated by Nicolas (Mordvinoff). Harcourt, Brace.

Mr. T. W. Anthony Woo by Marie Hall Ets. Viking.

Skipper John's Cook by Marcia Brown. Scribner.

All Falling Down by Gene Zion. Illustrated by Margaret Bloy Graham. Harper (Harper & Row).

Bear Party by William Pène du Bois. Viking.

Feather Mountain by Elizabeth Olds. Houghton Mifflin.

1953 THE BIGGEST BEAR by Lynd Ward. Houghton Mifflin.

Puss in Boots told and illustrated by Marcia Brown. Scribner.

One Morning in Maine by Robert McCloskey. Viking.

Ape in a Cape by Fritz Eichenberg. Harcourt.

The Storm Book by Charlotte Zolotow. Illustrated by Margaret Bloy Graham. Harper (Harper & Row).

Five Little Monkeys by Juliet Kepes. Houghton Mifflin.

1954 *MADELINE'S RESCUE* by Ludwig Bemelmans. Viking.
Journey Cake, Ho! by Ruth Sawyer. Illustrated by Robert McCloskey. Viking.
When Will the World Be Mine? by Miriam Schlein. Illustrated by Jean Charlot. W. R. Scott.
The Steadfast Tin Soldier translated by M. R. James. Adapted from Hans Christian Andersen. Illustrated by Marcia Brown. Scribner.
A Very Special House by Ruth Krauss. Illustrated by Maurice Sendak. Harper (Harper & Row).
Green Eyes by Abe Birnbaum. Capitol.

1955 *CINDERELLA* by Charles Perrault. Illustrated by Marcia Brown. Harper (Harper & Row).
Book of Nursery and Mother Goose Rhymes compiled and illustrated by Marguerite de Angeli. Doubleday.
Wheel on the Chimney by Margaret Wise Brown. Illustrated by Tibor Gergely. Lippincott.

1956 *FROG WENT A-COURTIN'* by John Langstaff. Illustrated by Feodor Rojankovsky. Harcourt.
Play with Me by Marie Hall Ets. Viking.
Crow Boy by Taro Yashima. Viking.

1957 *A TREE IS NICE* by Janice May Udry. Illustrated by Marc Simont. Harper (Harper & Row).
Mr. Penny's Race Horse by Marie Hall Ets. Viking.
1 Is One by Tasha Tudor. Oxford (Walck).
Anatole by Eve Titus. Illustrated by Paul Galdone. Whittlesey.
Gillespie and the Guards by Benjamin Elkin. Illustrated by James Daugherty. Viking.
Lion by William Pène du Bois. Viking.

1958 *TIME OF WONDER* by Robert McCloskey. Viking.
Fly High, Fly Low by Don Freeman. Viking.
Anatole and the Cat by Eve Titus. Illustrated by Paul Galdone. Whittlesey.

1959 *CHANTICLEER AND THE FOX* edited and illustrated by Barbara Cooney. Crowell.
The House That Jack Built by Antonio Frasconi. Crowell.
What Do You Say, Dear? by Sesyle Joslin. Illustrated by Maurice Sendak. W. R. Scott.

Umbrella by Taro Yashima. Viking.

1960 *NINE DAYS TO CHRISTMAS* by Marie Hall Ets and Aurora Labastida. Viking.
Houses from the Sea by Alice E. Goudey. Illustrated by Adrienne Adams. Scribner.
The Moon Jumpers by Janice May Udry. Illustrated by Maurice Sendak. Harper (Harper & Row).

1961 *BABOUSHKA AND THE THREE KINGS* by Ruth Robbins. Illustrated by Nicolas Sidjakov. Parnassus.
Inch by Inch by Leo Lionni. Obolensky.

1962 *ONCE A MOUSE* by Marcia Brown. Scribner.
The Fox Went Out on a Chilly Night by Peter Spier. Doubleday.
Little Bear's Visit by Else Minarik. Illustrated by Maurice Sendak. Harper (Harper & Row).
The Day We Saw the Sun Come Up by Alice Goudey. Illustrated by Adrienne Adams. Scribner.

1963 *THE SNOWY DAY* by Ezra Jack Keats. Viking.
The Sun Is a Golden Earring by Natalia Belting. Illustrated by Bernarda Bryson. Holt, Rinehart and Winston.
Mr. Rabbit and the Lovely Present by Charlotte Zolotow. Illustrated by Maurice Sendak. Harper & Row.

1964 *WHERE THE WILD THINGS ARE* by Maurice Sendak. Harper & Row.
Swimmy by Leo Lionni. Pantheon.
All in the Morning Early by Sorche Nic Leodhas. Illustrated by Evaline Ness. Holt, Rinehart and Winston.
Mother Goose and Nursery Rhymes by Philip Reed. Atheneum.

1965 *MAY I BRING A FRIEND?* By Beatrice Schenk de Regniers. Illustrated by Beni Montresor. Atheneum.
Rain Makes Applesauce by Julian Scheer. Illustrated by Marvin Bileck. Holiday.
The Wave by Margaret Hodges. Illustrated by Blair Lent. Houghton Mifflin.
A Pocketful of Cricket by Rebecca Caudill. Illustrated by Evaline Ness. Holt, Rinehart and Winston.

1966 *ALWAYS ROOM FOR ONE MORE* by Sorche Nic Leodhas. Illustrated by Nonny Hogrogian. Holt, Rinehart and Winston.

Hide and Seek Fog by Alvin Tresselt. Illustrated by Roger Duvoisin. Lothrop.
Just Me by Marie Hall Ets. Viking.
Tom Tit Tot edited by Joseph Jacobs. Illustrated by Evaline Ness. Scribner.

1967 *SAM, BANGS AND MOONSHINE* by Evaline Ness. Holt, Rinehart and Winston.
One Wide River to Cross by Barbara Emberley. Illustrated by Ed Emberley. Prentice-Hall.

1968 *DRUMMER HOFF* by Barbara Emberley. Illustrated by Ed Emberley. Prentice-Hall.
Frederick by Leo Lionni. Pantheon.
Seashore Story by Taro Yashima. Viking.
The Emperor and the Kite by Jane Yolen. Illustrated by Ed Young. World Publishing.

THE MILDRED L. BATCHELDER AWARD is named for a former executive secretary of the American Library Association's Children's Services Division, who worked toward international understanding through the interchange of children's books. First presented in 1968 for a book published two years earlier, the citation goes to an American publisher for the most outstanding juvenile book originally published abroad in another language. Selection is made from nominees of an Award Committee by members of the ALA Children's Services Division.

1968 *The Little Man* by Erich Kästner (Knopf).

THE SPRING FESTIVAL BOOK WEEK AWARDS were established in 1937 by the New York *Herald Tribune* in order to balance the output of new books between fall and spring. These Awards carry a cash prize of $200 and are given annually to the best books for children published during the first half of the year. Four Honor Books are chosen for each of three age levels. Two judges are chosen each year for each of the three divisions. Awards are announced in *Book Week*, a special Sunday supplement of the Washington *Post* and Chicago *Sun-Times*.

PICTURE BOOK

1937 *Seven Simeons* by Boris Artzybasheff. Viking.

1938 *The Hobbit* by J. R. R. Tolkien. Houghton Mifflin.

1939 *The Story of Horace* by Alice M. Coats. Coward-McCann.

1940 *That Mario* by Lucy H. Crockett. Holt (Holt, Rinehart and Winston).

1941 *In My Mother's House* by Ann Nolan Clark. Viking.

1942 *Mr. Tootwhistle's Invention* by Peter Wells. Winston (Holt, Rinehart and Winston).

1943 *Five Golden Wrens* by Hugh Troy. Oxford.

1944 *A Ring and a Riddle* by M. Ilin and E. Segal. Lippincott.

1945 *Little People in a Big Country* by Norma Cohn. Oxford.

1946 *Farm Stories* by Kathryn and Bryan Jackson. Simon and Schuster.

1947 *Oley, the Sea Monster* by Marie Hall Ets. Viking.

1948 *My Father's Dragon* by Ruth Stiles Gannett. Random House.

1949 *Bonnie Bess: The Weathervane Horse* by Alvin Tresselt and Marilyn Hafner. Lothrop.

1950 *Sunshine: A Story about New York* by Ludwig Bemelmans. Simon and Schuster.

1951 *Jeanne-Marie Counts Her Sheep* by Francoise. Scribner.

1952 *Looking-for-Something* by Ann Nolan Clark. Viking.

1953 *Pet of the Met* by Lydia and Don Freeman. Viking.

1954 *Alphonse: That Bearded One* by Natalie Savage Carlson. Harcourt.

1955 *Frog Went A-Courtin'* by Feodor Rojankovsky and John Langstaff. Harcourt.

1956 *Lion* by William Pène du Bois. Viking.

1957 *Madeline and the Bad Hat* by Ludwig Bemelmans. Viking.

1958 *Crictor* by Tomi Ungerer. Harper (Harper & Row).

1959 *Sia Lives on Kilimanjaro* by Astrid Lindgren. Macmillan.

1960 *The Secret Hiding Place* by Rainey Bennett. World Publishing.

1961 *Gwendolyn the Miracle Hen* by Nancy Sherman. Golden Press.

1962 *Adam's Book of Odd Creatures* by Joseph Low. Atheneum.

1963 *The Seven Ravens* by the Brothers Grimm. Harcourt.

1964 *The Coconut Thieves* by Catharine Fournier.

Scribner.

1965 *Salt* by Margot Zemach. Follett.

1966 *Nothing Ever Happens on My Block* by Ellen Raskin. Atheneum.

1967 *Moon Man* by Tomi Ungerer. Harper & Row.

MIDDLE AGE (8–12)

1941 *Pete* by Tom Robinson. Viking.

1942 *"I Have Just Begun to Fight"* by Edward Ellsberg. Dodd, Mead.

1943 *These Happy Golden Years* by Laura Ingalls Wilder. Harper (Harper & Row).

1944 *They Put Out to Sea: The Story of the Map* by Roger Duvoisin. Knopf.

1945 *The Gulf Stream* by Ruth Brindze. Dutton.

1946 *The Thirteenth Stone* by Jean Bothwell. Harcourt.

1947 *Pancakes-Paris* by Claire Huchet Bishop. Viking.

1948 *Daughter of the Mountains* by Louise Rankin. Viking.

1949 *Bush Holiday* by Stephen Fennimore. Doubleday.

1950 *Windfall Fiddle* by Carl Carmer. Knopf.

1951 *Ginger Pye* by Eleanor Estes. Harcourt.

1952 *The Talking Cat* by Natalie Savage Carlson. Harper (Harper & Row).

1953 *Captain Ramsay's Daughter* by Elizabeth Fraser Torjesen. Lothrop.

1954 *Winter Danger* by William O. Steele. Harcourt.

1955 *Crystal Mountain* by Belle Dorman Rugh. Houghton Mifflin.

1956 *Beaver Water* by Rutherford G. Montgomery. World Publishing.

1957 *Gone-away Lake* by Elizabeth Enright. Harcourt.

1958 *Chucaro, Wild Pony of the Pampa* by Francis Kalnay. Harcourt.

1959 *The Long-Nosed Princess* by Priscilla Hallowell. Viking.

1960 *The Trouble with Jenny's Ear* by Oliver Butterworth. Atlantic-Little (Little, Brown).

1961 *Norwegian Folk Tales* by Peter C. Asbjørnsen and Jorgen E. Moe. Viking.

1962 *The Orphans of Simitra* by Jacques Bonzon. Criterion.

1963 *A Dog So Small* by Philippa Pearce. Lippincott.

1964 *The Family Conspiracy* by Joan Phipson. Harcourt.

1965 *Dorp Dead* by Julia Cunningham. Pantheon.

1966 *Boy Alone* by Reginald Ottley. Harcourt.

1967 *The Egypt Game* by Zilpha K. Snyder. Atheneum.

OLDER AGE

1937 *The Smuggler's Sloop* by Robb White, III. Doubleday.

1938 *The Iron Duke* by John R. Tunis. Harcourt.

1939 *The Hired Man's Elephant* by Phil Stong. Dodd, Mead.

1940 *Cap'n Ezra, Privateer* by James D. Adams. Harcourt.

1941 *Clara Barton* by Mildred Mastin Pace. Scribner.

1942 *None But the Brave* by Rosamond Van Der Zee Marshall. Houghton Mifflin.

1943 *Patterns on the Wall* by Elizabeth Yates. Knopf.

1944 *Storm Canvas* by Armstrong Sperry. Winston (Holt, Rinehart and Winston).

1945 *Sandy* by Elizabeth Janet Gray. Viking.

1946 *The Quest of the Golden Condor* by Clayton Knight. Knopf.

1947 *The Twenty-One Balloons* by William Pène du Bois. Viking.

1948 *The Crimson Anchor* by Felix Riesenberg, Jr. Dodd, Mead.

1949 *Start of the Trail* by Louise Dickinson Rich. Lippincott.

1950 *Amos Fortune, Free Man* by Elizabeth Yates. Aladdin (Dutton).

1951 *Americans Before Columbus* by Elizabeth Chesley Baity. Viking.

1952 *Big Mutt* by John Reese. Westminster.

1953 *The Ark* by Margot Benary-Isbert. Harcourt.

1954 *Engineers' Dreams* by Willy Ley. Viking.

1955 *The Buffalo Trace* by Virginia S. Eifert. Dodd, Mead.

1956 *Cold Hazard* by Richard Armstrong. Houghton Mifflin.

1957 *Because of Madeline* by Mary Stolz. Harper (Harper & Row).

1958 *Sons of the Steppe* by Hans Baumann. Walck.

1959 *An Edge of the Forest* by Agnes Smith. Viking.

1960 *The Walls of Windy Troy* by Marjorie Braymer. Harcourt.

1961 *Adventures in the Desert* by Herbert Kaufmann. Obolensky.

1962 *Dawn Wind* by Rosemary Sutcliff. Walck.

1963 *The Cossacks* by B. Bartos-Hoppner. Walck.

1964 *The Story of Design* by Marion Downer. Lothrop.

1965 *Jazz Country* by Nat Hentoff. Harper & Row.

1966 *This Is Your Century* by Geoffrey Trease. Harcourt.

1967 *The Little Fishes* by Erik C. Haugaard. Houghton Mifflin.

FIFTY BOOKS OF THE YEAR EXHIBITION

The Children's Book Shows are sponsored by the American Institute of Graphic Arts to honor books on the basis of design, typography, manufacture, and concept. Each year the Fifty Books of the Year are chosen by a jury of the American Institute of Graphic Arts for their excellence of design and manufacture in bookmaking. The books are selected from all books published that year, not just children's books. However, a proportionate number of juvenile titles are always included. In 1966, ten were juveniles.

Periodically, this same institute selects books to be exhibited in their Children's Book Show. Again, total format of the book is the single criterion. The jury agreed on ninety-five titles for the 1961–1962 show and ninety-six titles for the 1963–1964 show. Up to one hundred books may be selected. Obviously, all these books cannot be listed here, but the reader should know of these shows which feature the best-designed children's books. A catalog is available that describes the winning book for each year (see page 729).

SPECIAL INTEREST AWARDS

THE JANE ADDAMS CHILDREN'S BOOK AWARD was established in 1953 by the Women's International League for Peace and Freedom. The purpose of this Award is "to encourage publication of books for children which are of literary merit and contain constructive themes." The Award is given annually. The following books have won:

1953 *People Are Important* by Eva Knox Evans. Capitol (Golden Press).

1954 *Stick-in-the-Mud* by Jean Ketchum. W. R. Scott.

1955 *Rainbow Round the World* by Elizabeth Yates. Bobbs-Merrill.

1956 *Story of the Negro* by Arna Bontemps. Knopf.

1957 *Blue Mystery* by Margot Benary-Isbert. Harcourt.

1958 *The Perilous Road* by William O. Steele. Harcourt.

1959 [No award.]

1960 *Champions of Peace* by Edith Patterson Meyer. Little, Brown.

1961 *What Then, Raman?* by Shirley A. Arora. Follett.

1962 *The Road to Agra* by Aimée Sommerfelt. Criterion.

1963 *The Monkey and the Wild, Wild Wind* by Ryerson Johnson. Abelard-Schuman.

1964 *Profiles in Courage* by John F. Kennedy. Young Readers' Memorial Edition. Harper & Row.

1965 *Meeting with a Stranger* by Duane Bradley. Lippincott.

1966 *Berries Goodman* by Emily Cheney Neville. Harper & Row.

1967 *Queenie Peavy* by Robert Burch. Viking.

THE AURIANNE CHILDREN'S BOOK AWARD was administered by the Children's Service Division of the American Library Association from a bequest to ALA by Augustine Aurianne, a former New Orleans school librarian. The bequest provided that, for several years, annual Awards be given to writers of books for children of eight to fourteen years, "which develop humane attitudes towards animal life (fiction or nonfiction)." Only books published two years previous to the giving of the Awards were considered. Thus, the first Award was made in 1958 to the best animal story published in 1956. The final Award was presented in 1966.

1958 *Dipper of Copper Creek* by Jean and John George. Dutton.

1959 [No award; no 1957 book judged worthy enough to qualify]

1960 *Along Came a Dog* by Meindert DeJong. Harper (Harper & Row).

1961 *An Edge of the Forest* by Agnes Smith. Viking.
1962 *Old Ramon* by Jack Shaefer. Houghton Mifflin.
1963 *The Incredible Journey* by Sheila Burnford. Little, Brown.
1964 *A Black Bear's Story* by Emil Liers. Viking.
1965 *Rascal* by Sterling North. Dutton.
1966 *Big Blue Island* by Wilson Gage. World Publishing.

THE CHILD STUDY ASSOCIATION AWARD   has been given annually since 1943 to a "book for young people which deals realistically with problems in their contemporary world." A special committee is appointed by the Child Study Association of America to select the book. Some of the winners are for younger boys and girls while others are for high school students. A list of the honor books and their years of publication follows:

1943 *Keystone Kids* by John R. Tunis. Harcourt.
1944 *The House* by Marjorie Hill Allee. Houghton Mifflin.
1945 *The Moved-Outers* by Florence Crannell Means. Houghton Mifflin.
1946 *Heart of Danger* by Howard Pease. Doubleday.
1947 *Judy's Journey* by Lois Lenski. Lippincott.
1948 *The Big Wave* by Pearl Buck. John Day.
1949 *Paul Tiber* by Maria Gleit. Scribner.
1950 *The United Nations and Youth* by Eleanor Roosevelt and Helen Ferris. Doubleday.
1951 [No award.]
1952 *Twenty and Ten* by Claire Huchet Bishop. Viking.
1953 *In a Mirror* by Mary Stolz. Harper (Harper & Row).
1954 *High Road Home* by William Corbin. Coward-McCann.
         The Ordeal of the Young Hunter by Jonreed Lauritzen. Little, Brown.
1955 *Crow Boy* by Taro Yashima. Viking.
         Plain Girl by Virginia Sorensen. Harcourt.
1956 *The House of Sixty Fathers* by Meindert DeJong. Harper (Harper & Row).
1957 *Shadow Across the Campus* by Helen R. Sattley. Dodd, Mead.
1958 *South Town* by Lorenz Graham. Follett.

1959 *Jennifer* by Zoa Sherburne. Morrow.
1960 *Janine* by Robin McKown. Messner.
1961 *The Road to Agra* by Aimée Sommerfelt. Criterion.
1962 *The Trouble with Terry* by Joan Lexau. Dial.
1963 *The Rock and the Willow* by Mildred Lee. Lothrop.
         The Peaceable Revolution by Betty Schecter. Houghton Mifflin.
1964 *The High Pasture* by Ruth Harnden. Houghton Mifflin.
1965 *The Empty Schoolhouse* by Natalie Carlson. Harper & Row.
1966 *Queenie Peavy* by Robert Burch. Viking.

THE EDGAR ALLAN POE AWARD, established in 1961, is given each spring by the Mystery Writers of America to honor the best juvenile mystery of the previous year, if one is considered worthy. The award itself, a ceramic bust of Poe, is known as an "Edgar."

1961 *Mystery of the Haunted Pool* by Phyllis A. Whitney. Westminster.
1962 *The Phantom of Walkaway Hill* by Edward Fenton. Doubleday.
1963 *Cutlass Island* by Scott Corbett. Little, Brown.
1964 *Mystery of the Hidden Hand* by Phyllis A. Whitney. Westminster.
1965 *Mystery at Crane's Landing* by Marcella Thum. Dodd, Mead.
1966 *The Mystery of 22 East* by Leon Ware. Westminster.

MASS MEDIA AWARDS: THOMAS ALVA EDISON FOUNDATION. Four of these Awards are made annually to children's books in the following categories:

- The Best Children's Science Book
- The Best Science Book for Youth
- For Special Excellence in Portraying America's Past
- For Special Excellence in Contributing to the Character Development of Children

These awards give a cash prize of $250 for each category and an honorary scroll. The winners since the inception of the awards in 1955 are:

THE BEST CHILDREN'S SCIENCE BOOK

1956 *The Boy Scientist* by John Lewellen. Simon and Schuster.

1957 *Exploring the Universe* by Roy A. Gallant and Lowell Hess. Garden City Books.

1958 *The Wonderful World of Energy* by Lancelot Hogben. Garden City Books.

1959 *Science in Your Own Back Yard* by Elizabeth K. Cooper. Harcourt.

1960 *Experiments in Sky Watching* by Franklyn M. Branley. Crowell.

1961 *Animal Clocks and Compasses* by Margaret Hyde. McGraw-Hill.

1962 *Experiments in Sound* by Nelson Beeler. Crowell.

1963 *Knowledge and Wonder* by Victor Weisskopf. Doubleday.

1964 *The Globe for the Space Age* by S. Carl Hirsch. Viking.

1965 *The Universe of Galileo and Newton* by William Bixby and Giorgio de Santillana. American Heritage.

1966 *Biography of an Atom* by J. Bronowski and Millicent E. Selsam. Harper & Row.

1967 *The Living Community* by Carl S. Hirsch. Viking.

THE BEST SCIENCE BOOK FOR YOUTH

1958 *Building Blocks of the Universe* by Isaac Asimov. Abelard-Schuman.

1959 *Elements of the Universe* by Glenn T. Seaborg and Evans G. Valens. Dutton.

1960 *IGY: Year of Discovery* by Sidney Chapman. University of Michigan Press.

1961 *Saturday Science* edited by Andrew Bluemle. Dutton.

1962 *The Atoms within Us* by Ernest Borek. Columbia University Press.

1963 *Stars, Men, and Atoms* by Heinz Haber. Golden Press.

1964 *You and Your Brain* by Judith Groch. Harper & Row.

1965 *The Earth Beneath Us* by Kirtley Mather. Random House.

1966 *Explorations in Chemistry* by Charles A. Gray. Dutton.

1967 *The Language of Youth* by George and Muriel Beadle. Doubleday.

FOR SPECIAL EXCELLENCE
IN PORTRAYING AMERICA'S PAST

1956 *The Buffalo Trace* by Virginia S. Eifert. Dodd, Mead.

1957 *The Story of the "Old Colony" of New Plymouth* by Samuel Eliot Morison. Knopf.

1958 *Colonial Living* by Edwin Tunis. World Publishing.

1959 *The Americans* by Harold Coy. Little, Brown.

1960 *The Great Dissenters: Guardians of Their Country's Laws and Liberties* by Fred Reinfeld. Crowell.

1961 *Peter Treegate's War* by Leonard Wibberley. Farrar (Farrar, Straus).

1962 *The Fight for Union* by Margaret Coit. Houghton Mifflin,

1963 *Westward Adventure: The True Stories of Six Pioneers* by William Steele. Harcourt.

1964 *Voices from America's Past* edited by Richard Morris and James Woodress. Dutton.

1965 *Yankee Doodle Boy* edited by George F. Scheer. W. R. Scott.

1966 *In Their Own Words: A History of the American Negro 1865–1916* edited by Milton Meltzer. Crowell.

1967 *Introduction to Tomorrow* by Robert G. Abernethy. Harcourt.

BEST CHILDREN'S BOOK
FOR CHARACTER DEVELOPMENT

1956 *His Indian Brother* by Hazel Wilson. Abingdon.

1957 *Mr. Justice Holmes* by Clara Ingram Judson. Follett.

1958 *Armed with Courage* by May McNeer and Lynd Ward. Abingdon.

1959 *That Dunbar Boy* by Jean Gould. Dodd, Mead.

1960 *Willie Joe and His Small Change* by Marguerite Vance. Dutton.

1961 *Touched with Fire* by Margaret Bell. Morrow.

1962 *Thomas Jefferson: His Many Talents* by Johanna Johnston. Dodd, Mead.

1963 *Seeing Fingers: The Story of Louis Braille* by E. DeGering. McKay.

1964 *The Peaceable Revolution* by Betty Schechter. Houghton Mifflin.

1965 *The White Bungalow* by Aimée Sommerfelt. Criterion.

1966 *The Summer I Was Lost* by Philip Viereck. John Day.

1967 *Boy Alone* by Reginald Ottley. Harcourt.

LASTING CONTRIBUTIONS TO CHILDREN'S LITERATURE

THE LAURA INGALLS WILDER AWARD is given "to an author or illustrator whose books published in the United States, have over a period of years made a substantial and lasting contribution to literature for children." This Award was established in 1954 by the Children's Services Division of the American Library Association and was presented first to Laura Ingalls Wilder, herself, for her well-loved "Little House" books. A committee of six determines the winner of this Award which is given every five years. A medal designed by Garth Williams has been presented to the following authors:

1954 Laura Ingalls Wilder
1960 Clara Ingram Judson
1965 Ruth Sawyer

THE REGINA MEDAL was presented for the first time in 1959 by the Catholic Library Association for a "lifetime dedication to the highest standards of literature for children." The Regina Medal "is not limited to one creed, nor to one country, nor to one criterion other than excellence." It may be given to a publisher, editor, writer, or illustrator who has given unstintingly of individual genius to the field. A children's literature committee of five members selects the winner. The Award is made annually. Its recipients are:

1959 Eleanor Farjeon
1960 Anne Carroll Moore
1961 Padraic Colum
1962 Frederic G. Melcher
1963 Ann Nolan Clark
1964 May Hill Arbuthnot
1965 Ruth Sawyer
1966 Leo Politi
1967 Bertha Mahony Miller

THE LEWIS CARROLL SHELF AWARD was established in 1958 by the University of Wisconsin School of Education and cooperating state organizations. The purpose of this annual Award is "to select those books worthy enough to sit on the shelf with *Alice in Wonderland.*" Publishers select those books which they feel should receive the Award. These are then submitted to a committee of five representing librarians, teachers, parents, and writers. A unanimous vote from this committee is necessary to qualify for the Award. The following books have been selected:

1958 *Millions of Cats* by Wanda Gág. Coward-McCann, 1928.
The 397th White Elephant by René Guillot. Criterion, 1957.
The World of Pooh by A. A. Milne. Dutton, 1957.
The Little House in the Big Woods by Laura Ingalls Wilder. Harper, 1932, 1953 (Harper & Row).
Ol' Paul, the Mighty Logger by Glen Rounds. Holiday, 1949.
The Story of Dr. Dolittle by Hugh Lofting. Lippincott, 1920.
Mr. Popper's Penguins by Richard Atwater. Little, Brown, 1938.
The Blue Cat of Castle Town by Catherine C. Coblentz. Longmans, Green, 1949 (McKay).
Prayer for a Child by Rachel Field. Macmillan, 1944.
The Little Engine That Could by Watty Piper. Platt & Munk, 1930.
Horton Hatches the Egg by Dr. Seuss. Random House, 1940.
Caps for Sale by Esphyr Slobodkina. W. R. Scott, 1947.
The Wind in the Willows by Kenneth Grahame. Scribner, 1908.
The Little Bookroom by Eleanor Farjeon. Walck, 1956.
The Tale of Peter Rabbit by Beatrix Potter. Warne, 1903.
Pecos Bill by James C. Bowman. Whitman, 1937.

1959 *The Five Chinese Brothers* by Claire Huchet Bishop. Coward-McCann, 1938.
Charlotte's Web by E. B. White. Harper, 1952 (Harper & Row).
The Secret Garden by Frances Hodgson Burnett. Lippincott, 1910.

The Courage of Sarah Noble by Alice Dalgliesh. Scribner, 1954.

The White Stag by Kate Seredy. Viking, 1937.

The Little House by Virginia Lee Burton. Houghton Mifflin, 1942.

Tirra Lirra by Laura E. Richards. Little, Brown, 1932.

Caddie Woodlawn by Carol Ryrie Brink. Macmillan, 1935.

The Story of Babar by Jean de Brunhoff. Random House, 1933.

This Boy Cody by Leon Wilson. F. Watts, 1950.

Snipp, Snapp, Snurr and the Red Shoes by Maj Lindman. Whitman, 1932.

The Minnow Leads to Treasure by Philippa Pearce. World Publishing, 1958.

Li Lun, Lad of Courage by Carolyn Treffinger. Abingdon, 1947.

1960 *The Blind Colt* by Glen Rounds. Holiday, 1941.

The Borrowers by Mary Norton. Harcourt, 1953.

Curious George Takes a Job by Hans A. Rey. Houghton Mifflin, 1947.

Johnny Crow's Garden by L. Leslie Brooke. Warne, 1903.

The Jungle Book by Rudyard Kipling. Doubleday, 1894.

Lavender's Blue compiled by Kathleen Lines. F. Watts, 1954.

The Matchlock Gun by Walter D. Edmonds. Dodd, Mead, 1941.

Onion John by Joseph Krumgold. Crowell, 1959.

Young Fu of the Upper Yangtze by Elizabeth Lewis. Winston, 1932 (Holt, Rinehart and Winston).

1961 *And to Think That I Saw It on Mulberry Street* by Dr. Seuss. Vanguard, 1937.

Ben and Me by Robert Lawson. Little, Brown, 1939.

Blue Willow by Doris Gates. Viking, 1940.

Grishka and the Bear by René Guillot. Criterion, 1960.

The Door in the Wall by Marguerite de Angeli. Doubleday, 1949.

Hitty by Rachel Field. Macmillan, 1929.

Island of the Blue Dolphins by Scott O'Dell.

Houghton Mifflin, 1960.

Misty of Chincoteague by Marguerite Henry. Rand McNally, 1947.

The Moffats by Eleanor Estes. Harcourt, 1941.

A Roundabout Turn by Robert Charles. Warne, 1930.

When I Was a Boy by Erich Kästner. F. Watts, 1961.

1962 *The Adventures of Huckleberry Finn* by Mark Twain. Harper, 1884 (Harper & Row).

A Penny a Day by Walter de la Mare. Knopf, 1960.

Daughter of the Mountains by Louise Rankin. Viking, 1948.

Inch by Inch by Leo Lionni. Obolensky, 1960.

Paddle-to-the-Sea by Holling C. Holling. Houghton Mifflin, 1941.

Padre Porko, the Gentlemanly Pig by Robert Davis. Holiday, 1939.

The Dark Frigate by Charles Hawes. Little, Brown, 1924.

The Lion, the Witch and the Wardrobe by C. S. Lewis. Macmillan, 1950.

The Tailor of Gloucester by Beatrix Potter. Warne, 1903.

The World of Christopher Robin by A. A. Milne. Dutton, 1958.

Thistle and Thyme by Sorche Nic Leodhas. Holt, Rinehart and Winston, 1962.

Thumbelina by Hans Christian Andersen. Scribner, 1961.

Winter Danger by William O. Steele. Harcourt, 1954.

1963 *Annuzza: A Girl of Romania* by Hertha Seuberlich. Rand McNally, 1962.

The Art of Ancient Egypt by Shirley Glubok. Atheneum, 1962.

The Cricket in Times Square by George Selden. Farrar, Straus, 1960.

Dwarf Long-Nose by Wilhelm Hauff. Random House, 1960.

The Griffin and the Minor Canon by Maurice Sendak and Frank R. Stockton. Holt, Rinehart and Winston, 1963.

Invincible Louisa by Cornelia Meigs. Little, Brown, 1933.

The Man Who Was Don Quixote by Rafaello Busoni. Prentice-Hall, 1958.

Moccasin Trail by Eloise McGraw. Coward-McCann, 1952.

Rabbit Hill by Robert Lawson. Viking, 1945.

The Reluctant Dragon by Kenneth Grahame. Holiday, 1938.

The Superlative Horse by Jean Merrill. W. R. Scott, 1961.

Tom's Midnight Garden by Philippa Pearce. Lippincott, 1959.

Uncle Remus: His Songs and His Sayings by Joel Chandler Harris. Appleton, 1881.

Water Babies by Charles Kingsley. F. Watts, 1961 (1863).

The Wheel on the School by Meindert De-Jong. Harper, 1954 (Harper & Row).

The Yearling by Marjorie K. Rawlings. Scribner, 1939.

1964 *A Little Princess* by Frances H. Burnett. Scribner, 1963 (1914).

Old Wind and Liu Li-San by Aline Glasgow. Harvey House, 1962.

Rascal by Sterling North. Dutton, 1963.

Rifles for Watie by Harold Keith. Crowell, 1957.

Roller Skates by Ruth Sawyer. Viking, 1936.

Roosevelt Grady by Louisa Shotwell. World Publishing, 1963.

Where the Wild Things Are by Maurice Sendak. Harper & Row, 1963.

1965 *Bond of the Fire* by Anthony Fon Eisen. World Publishing, 1965.

The Cock, the Mouse, and the Little Red Hen by Felicite Lefèvre. Macrae, 1945.

Joel and the Wild Goose by Helga Sandburg. Dial, 1963.

My Side of the Mountain by Jean George. Dutton, 1959.

The Nightingale by Hans Christian Andersen. Translated by Eva Le Gallienne. Harper & Row, 1965.

The Pushcart War by Jean Merrill. W. R. Scott, 1964.

The Return of the Twelves by Pauline Clarke. Coward-McCann, 1964.

Smoky by Will James. Scribner, 1926.

The Story About Ping by Marjorie Flack. Viking, 1933.

The Wolves of Willoughby Chase by Joan Aiken. Doubleday, 1963.

A Wrinkle in Time by Madeleine L'Engle. Farrar, Straus, 1962.

1966 *Across Five Aprils* by Irene Hunt. Follett, 1964.

Banner in the Sky by James Ramsey Ullman. Lippincott, 1954.

A Child's Garden of Verses by Robert Louis Stevenson. F. Watts, 1966 (1885).

An Edge of the Forest by Agnes Smith. Viking, 1959.

Jed by Peter Burchard. Coward-McCann, 1960.

Once a Mouse by Marcia Brown. Scribner, 1961.

Papa Pellerin's Daughter by Maria Gripe. John Day, 1966.

AWARDS BASED ON CHILDREN'S CHOICES

THE BOYS' CLUB OF AMERICA JUNIOR BOOK AWARDS are presented to five or more books published in the past year that received the highest recommendations from club members throughout the country. A committee makes the final selection from those books which were given the best reviews by member of the Boys' Clubs over the nation. The purpose of giving the awards is to encourage children to read widely and more selectively. The books that have won the award are listed below:

1948 *Big Red* by Jim Kjelgaard. Holiday.

The Black Stallion Returns by Walter Farley. Random House.

Joe Mason, Apprentice to Audubon by Charlie May Simon. Dutton.

Mystery Island by Enid Blyton. Macmillan.

Fun with Puzzles by Joseph Leeming. Lippincott.

Guns over Champlain by Leon W. Dean. Rinehart (Holt, Rinehart and Winson).

1949 *Great Men of Medicine* by Ruth Fox. Random House.

Heart of Danger by Howard Pease. Doubleday.

How Much and How Many by Jeanne Bendick. Whittlesey.

King of the Stallions by Edward B. Tracy. Dodd, Mead.

Prairie Colt by Stephen Holt. Longmans,

Green (McKay).

The Rain Forest by Armstrong Sperry. Macmillan.

Wild Animals of the Five Rivers Country by George Cory Franklin. Houghton Mifflin.

1950   *Albert Einstein* by Elma Ehrlich Levinger. Messner.

Chains for Columbus by Alfred Powers. Westminster.

Cruise of the Jeanette by Captain Edward Ellsberg. Dodd, Mead.

Fourth Down by Robert Sidney Bowen. Lothrop.

George Washington by Genevieve Foster. Scribner.

The Green Ginger Jar by Clara Ingram Judson. Houghton Mifflin.

Hearts Courageous by William Herman. Dutton.

Peter's Pinto by Mary and Conrad Buff. Viking.

Snakes by Herbert S. Zim. Morrow.

You and Atomic Energy by John Lewellen. Childrens Press.

1951   *Bay of the North* by Ronald Syme. Morrow.

The Ben Lilly Legend by J. Frank Dobie. Little, Brown.

The Big Sky by A. B. Guthrie, Jr. Sloane.

Hot Rod by Gregor Felsen. Dutton.

Lost Horse by Glenn Balch. Crowell.

Mahatma Gandhi by Catherine Owens Peare. Holt (Holt, Rinehart and Winston).

The Shining Shooter by Marion Renick. Scribner.

The Sky River by Chang Fa-Shun. Lothrop.

Son of the Hawk by Thomas H. Raddell. Winston (Holt, Rinehart and Winston).

1952   *Johnny Wants to Be a Policeman* by Wilber J. Grandberg. Aladdin (Dutton).

The Cowboy and His Horse by Sydney E. Fletcher. Grosset (Grosset & Dunlap).

A Long Way to Frisco by Alfred Powers. Little, Brown.

Phil Sterling, Salesman by Michael Gross. Dodd, Mead.

Passage to America by Katherine B. Shippen. Harper (Harper & Row).

The Official Encyclopedia of Baseball by Hy Turkin and S. C. Thompson. Barnes.

The Kid Who Batted 1.000 by Bob Allison and F. E. Hill. Doubleday.

Bullard of the Space Patrol by Malcolm Jameson. World Publishing.

Minn of the Mississippi by Holling C. Holling. Houghton Mifflin.

Bucky Forrester by Leland Silliman. Winston (Holt, Rinehart and Winston).

1953   *Buffalo Bill* by Ingri and Edgar Parin d'Aulaire. Doubleday.

Benjie and His Family by Sally Scott. Harcourt.

A Place for Peter by Elizabeth Yates. Coward-McCann.

Marooned on Mars by Lester del Rey. Winston (Holt, Rinehart and Winston).

The Trap by Kenneth Gilbert. Holt (Holt, Rinehart and Winston).

True Tales of Buried Treasure by Edward Rowe Snow. Dodd, Mead.

1954   *. . . And Now Miguel* by Joseph Krumgold. Crowell.

Fast Iron by Victor Mays. Houghton Mifflin.

Fast Is Not a Ladybug by Miriam Schlein. W. R. Scott.

The Golden Geography by Elsa Jane Werner. Pictures by Cornelius De Witt. Simon and Schuster.

Mr. Revere and I by Robert Lawson. Little, Brown.

1955   *Alphonse, That Bearded One* by Natalie Savage Carlson. Harcourt.

High Road Home by William Corbin. Coward-McCann.

Hound Dog Moses and the Promised Land by Walter D. Edmonds. Dodd Mead.

The Little Horse Bus by Graham Greene. Lothrop.

The Secret of the Two Feathers by Ivo Duka and Helena Kolda. Harper (Harper & Row).

Squanto, Friend of the White Man by Clyde Robert Bulla. Crowell.

1956   *Eddie and His Big Deals* by Carolyn Haywood. Morrow.

Great Discoverers in Modern Science by Patric Pringle. Roy.

Switch on the Night by Ray Bradbury. Pantheon.

Wheels by Edwin Tunis. World Publishing.

Wings Against the Wind by Natalie Savage Carlson. Harper (Harper & Row).

1957 *Beaver Water* by Rutherford G. Montgomery. World Publishing.

The First Lake Dwellers by Chester H. Osborne. Follett.

Quest of the Snow Leopard by Roy Chapman Andrews. Viking.

The Story of Albert Schweitzer by Jo Manton. Abelard-Schuman.

Trail Blazer of the Seas by Jean Lee Latham. Houghton Mifflin.

1958 *The Earth Satellite* by John Lewellen. Knopf.

Prehistoric Man and the Primates by William E. Scheele. World Publishing.

Hokahey by Edith Dorian and W. N. Wilson. Whittlesey.

The Wonderful World of the Sea by James Fisher. Garden City Books.

Faint George by Robert E. Barry. Houghton Mifflin.

The Valiant Sailor by C. Fox Smith. Criterion.

1959 *The Golden Impala* by Pamela Ropner. Criterion.

Avalanche! by A. Rutgers van der Loeff. Morrow.

All Aboard by Mary Britton Miller. Pantheon.

The Adventure of Light by Frank Jupo. Prentice-Hall.

Digging into Yesterday by Estelle Friedman. Putnam.

Simba of the White Mane by Jocelyn Arundel. Whittlesey.

1960 *The Byzantines* by Thomas Caldecot Chubb. World Publishing.

Dinosaurs and Other Prehistoric Animals by Darlene Geis and R. F. Peterson. Grosset & Dunlap.

The First Book of Color by Herbert P. Paschel. F. Watts.

Jets and Rockets and How They Work by William P. Gottlieb. Garden City Books.

The Silver Sword by Ian Serraillier. Criterion.

The Snow Party by Beatrice de Regniers and Reiner Zimnik. Pantheon.

1961 *The Challenge of the Sea* by Arthur Clarke. Holt, Rinehart and Winston.

Devil's Hill by Nan Chauncy. F. Watts.

Grishka and the Bear by René Guillot. Criterion.

Map-Making by Lloyd Brown. Little, Brown.

Rasmus and the Vagabond by Astrid Lindgren. Viking.

This Is New York by Miroslav Sasek. Macmillan.

1962 *Digging Up America* by Frank Hibben. Hill and Wang.

Elsa, the Story of a Lioness by Joy Adamson. Pantheon.

The Man Who Sang the Sillies by John Ciardi. Lippincott.

Next Please by Robert Barry. Houghton Mifflin.

The Road to Agra by Aimée Sommerfelt. Criterion.

The Wonderful World of Communication by Lancelot Hogben. Doubleday.

1963 *America's First Army* by Burke Davis. Holt, Rinehart and Winston.

Robert Boyle: Founder of Modern Chemistry by Harry Sootin. F. Watts.

The Early Eagles by Frank Donovan. Dodd, Mead.

Owls in the Family by Farley Mowat. Little, Brown.

Stars, Mosquitoes and Crocodiles edited by Millicent Selsam. Harper (Harper & Row).

The Tide in the Attic by Aleid Van Rhijn. Criterion.

1964 *The Boundary Riders* by Joan Phipson. Harcourt.

The Bully of Barkham Street by Mary Stolz. Harper & Row.

By the Great Horn Spoon! by Sid Fleischman. Atlantic Monthly.

Coyote, Come Home by B. F. Beebe. McKay.

The North American Indians by Ernest Berke. Doubleday.

1965 *The Pushcart War* by Jean Merrill. W. R. Scott.

Communism: An American's View by Gerald Johnson. Morrow.

Rain in the Woods: And Other Small Matters by Glen Rounds. World Publishing.

The Two Reigns of Tutankhamen by William Wise. Putnam.

Powder and Steel by Albert Orbaan. John Day.

1966 *North to Freedom* by Anne Holm. Translated by L. W. Kingsland. Harcourt.
Ramlal by A. T. W. Simeons. Atheneum.
Jack Holburn by Leon Garfield. Pantheon.
I Had Trouble Getting to Solla Sollew by Dr. Seuss. Random House.
The Quest: A Report on Extraterrestrial Life by Tom Allen. Chilton.

THE DOROTHY CANFIELD FISHER CHILDREN'S BOOK AWARD is offered by the Parent Teachers Association and Vermont Free Library Commission to the book that is the most popular with boys and girls in grades four through eight in the Vermont schools. The Award-winning book is chosen from a master list of some thirty books that have previously been approved by a group of Vermont specialists in children's literature and reading. These books are then made accessible for reading by gifts of local P.T.A. units to schools and libraries. The children may vote for their favorite on this list. The Award is made annually. Its purpose is "to encourage children to read more and better books and to read with discrimination." The books that have won the Award are listed below:

1957 *Old Bones, the Wonder Horse* by Mildred Mastin Pace. McGraw-Hill.
1958 *Fifteen* by Beverly Cleary. Morrow.
1959 *Comanche of the Seventh* by Margaret Carver Leighton. Ariel (Farrar, Straus).
1960 *Double or Nothing* by Phoebe Erickson. Harper (Harper & Row).
1961 *Captain Ghost* by Thelma Bell. Viking.
1962 *The City under the Back Steps* by Evelyn Lampman. Doubleday.
1963 *The Incredible Journey* by Sheila Burnford. Little, Brown.
1964 *Bristle Face* by Zachary Ball. Holiday.
1965 *Rascal* by Sterling North. Dutton.
1966 *Ribsy* by Beverly Cleary. Morrow.
1967 *The Summer I Was Lost* by Philip Viereck. John Day.

THE NENE AWARD is an annual Award, first given in 1964, for a book of fiction suitable for grades four through eight. Titles are nominated and voted upon by the school children of Hawaii. This Award is sponsored by the Children's Section of the Hawaii Library Association and the Hawaii Association of School Librarians.

1964 *Island of the Blue Dolphins* by Scott O'Dell. Houghton Mifflin.
1965 *Mary Poppins* by P. L. Travers. Harcourt.
1966 *Old Yeller* by Fred Gipson. Harper & Row.

THE PACIFIC NORTHWEST YOUNG READER'S CHOICE AWARD is given annually to a book chosen by children of the Pacific Northwest states as a favorite book published some two or three years earlier. Each year, a list of titles is compiled from suggestions sent by teachers and librarians and then distributed to schools and libraries. Polling of the favorite title is conducted in children's and school libraries in Idaho, Montana, Oregon, Washington, and in the Canadian provinces of Alberta and British Columbia. The decision to limit the selection to books published two or three years earlier was made in order that there should be time for the books to be purchased and read, and to establish their popularity.

1940 *Paul Bunyan Swings His Axe* by Dell McCormick. Caxton, 1936.
1941 *Mr. Popper's Penguins* by Florence and Richard Atwater. Little, Brown, 1938.
1942 *By the Shores of Silver Lake* by Laura Ingalls Wilder. Harper, 1938 (Harper & Row).
1943 *Lassie Come-Home* by Eric Knight. Winston, 1940 (Holt, Rinehart and Winston).
1944 *Black Stallion* by Walter Farley. Random House, 1941.
1945 *Snow Treasure* by Marie McSwigan. Dutton, 1942.
1946 *The Return of Silver Chief* by John S. O'Brien. Winston, 1943 (Holt, Rinehart and Winston).
1947 *Homer Price* by Robert McCloskey. Viking, 1943.
1948 *Black Stallion Returns* by Walter Farley. Random House, 1945.
1949 *Cowboy Boots* by Shannon Garst. Abingdon, 1946.
1950 *McElligott's Pool* by Dr. Seuss. Random House, 1947.
1951 *King of the Wind* by Marguerite Henry. Rand McNally, 1948.
1952 *Sea Star* by Marguerite Henry. Rand McNally, 1949.

1953 [No award.]
1954 [No award.]
1955 [No award.]
1956 *Miss Pickerell Goes to Mars* by Ellen Mac-Gregor. McGraw-Hill, 1951.
1957 *Henry and Ribsy* by Beverly Cleary. Morrow, 1954.
1958 *Golden Mare* by William Corbin. Coward-McCann, 1955.
1959 *Old Yeller* by Fred Gipson. Harper, 1956 (Harper & Row).
1960 *Henry and the Paper Route* by Beverly Cleary. Morrow, 1957.
1961 *Danny Dunn and the Homework Machine* by Jay Williams and Raymond Abrashkin. McGraw-Hill, 1958.
1962 *Swamp Fox of the Revolution* by Stewart Holbrook. Random House, 1959.
1963 *Danny Dunn on the Ocean Floor* by Jay Williams and Raymond Abrashkin. McGraw-Hill, 1960.
1964 *The Incredible Journey* by Sheila Burnford. Little, Brown, 1961.
1965 *John F. Kennedy and PT 109* by Richard Tregaskis. Random House, 1962.
1966 *Rascal* by Sterling North. Dutton, 1963.
1967 *Chitty-Chitty-Bang-Bang* by Ian Fleming. Random, 1964.

THE SEQUOYAH CHILDREN'S BOOK AWARD was first presented in 1959. The school children of Oklahoma from the fourth grade through the ninth grade vote on the "best book" from a master list chosen by a special committee.

1959 *Old Yeller* by Fred Gipson. Harper (Harper & Row), 1956.
1960 *Black Gold* by Marguerite Henry. Rand McNally, 1957.
1961 *Have Space Suit—Will Travel* by Robert Heinlein. Scribner, 1958.
1962 *The Helen Keller Story* by Catherine Owens Peare. Crowell, 1959.
1963 *Mystery of the Haunted Pool* by Phyllis Whitney. Westminster, 1960.
1964 *Where the Panther Screams* by William Robinson. World Publishing, 1961.
1965 *A Wrinkle in Time* by Madeleine L'Engle. Farrar (Farrar, Straus), 1962.

1966 *Rascal* by Sterling North. Dutton, 1963.
1967 *Harriet the Spy* by Louise Fitzhugh. Harper & Row, 1964.

THE WILLIAM ALLEN WHITE CHILDREN'S BOOK AWARD is chosen by the annual vote of the Kansas school children in grades four through seven. A committee of Kansas specialists in children's literature or education select the master list. The purpose of the Award is to encourage the Kansas school children to read more and better books. The Award was named in honor of the famous editor of the *Emporia Gazette*.

1953 *Amos Fortune, Free Man* by Elizabeth Yates. Dutton, 1950.
1954 *Little Vic* by Doris Gates. Viking, 1951.
1955 *Cherokee Bill* by Jean Bailey. Abingdon, 1952.
1956 *Brighty of the Grand Canyon* by Marguerite Henry. Rand McNally, 1953.
1957 *Daniel 'Coon* by Phoebe Erickson. Knopf, 1954.
1958 *White Falcon* by Elliot Arnold. Knopf, 1955.
1959 *Old Yeller* by Fred Gipson. Harper (Harper & Row), 1956.
1960 *Flaming Arrow* by William O. Steele. Harcourt, 1957.
1961 *Henry Reed, Inc.* by Keith Robertson. Viking, 1958.
1962 *The Helen Keller Story* by Catherine Owens Peare. Crowell, 1959.
1963 *Island of the Blue Dolphins* by Scott O'Dell. Houghton Mifflin, 1960.
1964 *The Incredible Journey* by Sheila Burnford. Little, Brown, 1961.
1965 *Bristle Face* by Zachary Ball. Holiday, 1962.
1966 *Rascal* by Sterling North. Dutton, 1963.

CHILDREN'S BOOK AWARDS IN OTHER COUNTRIES

Australia

THE BOOK OF THE YEAR AWARD for Australia is announced each year by the Australian Children's Book Council to usher in the national observance of Book Week. First given in 1946, the Award was intended to promote the idea of more and better books for children. A panel of judges from the Council chooses the winner and labels the runners-up "highly commended" or "commended"; in some years two books have shared the top Award. A list of the winners follows, with United States publishers indicated where available in this country:

1946   *Karrawingi the Emu* by L. C. Rees.
1947   [No award.]
1948   *Shackelton's Argonauts* by F. Hurley.
1949   *Whalers of the Midnight Sun* by Alan Villiers.
1950–1951   *Verity of Sydney Town* by R. C. Williams.
1952   *The Australia Book* by Eve Pownall (Tri-Ocean).
1953   *Good Luck to the Rider* by Joan Phipson.
        Aircraft of Today and Tomorrow by H. J. Martin.
1954   *Australian Legendary Tales* by Langloh-Parker. Selected by H. Drake-Brockman.
1955   *The First Walkabout* by N. B. Tindale and H. A. Lindsay.
1956   *The Crooked Snake* by P. Wrightson.
1957   *Boomerang Book of Legendary Tales* by E. M. Heddle.
1958   *Tiger in the Bush* by Nan Chauncy (F. Watts).
1959   *Devil's Hill* by Nan Chauncy (F. Watts).
        Sea Menace by John Gunn.
1960   *All the Proud Tribesmen* by Kylie Tennant (St. Martin's).
1961   *Tangara* by Nan Chauncy (F. Watts, titled *The Secret Friends*).
1962   *The Racketty Street Gang* by L. H. Evers.
        Rafferty Rides a Winner by Joan Woodberry.
1963   *The Family Conspiracy* by Joan Phipson (Harcourt).
1964   *The Green Laurel* by Eleanor Spence (Roy).
1965   *Pastures of the Blue Crane* by H. F. Brinsmead (Coward-McCann).
1966   *Ash Road* by Ivan Southall (St. Martin's).

Canada

THE BOOK OF THE YEAR MEDAL is presented each year by the Canadian Library Association. It consists of two bronze medals for the best children's books written either in English or French. There is both an English Language Award (established in 1946) and a French Language Award (established in 1950). Both may be given in the same year or one may be given without the other. The author must be a Canadian citizen. The winners are selected by a committee of the Canadian Association of Children's Librarians, a division of the Canadian Library Association. This award was first given in 1947. Since many of these books are available to American school children, a list of the winners will be included:

1947   *Starbuck Valley Winter* by Roderick L. Haig-Brown. Collins.
1948   *Kristli's Trees* by Bertha Mabel Dunham. McClelland & Stewart.
1950   *Franklin of the Arctic* by Richard Stanton Lambert. McClelland & Stewart (Hale).
1952   *The Sun Horse* by Catherine Anthony Clark. Macmillan.
1954   *Monseigneur de Laval* by S. J. Emile Gervais. Comité des Fondateurs.
1956   *Train for Tiger Lily* by Louise Riley. Macmillan.
1957   *Glooskap's Country* by Cyrus Macmillan. Oxford (Walck).
1958   *Lost in the Barrens* by Farley Mowat. Little, Brown.
1959   *The Golden Phoenix* by Marius Barbeau and Michael Hornyansky. Oxford (Walck).
1960   *The St. Lawrence* by William Toye. Oxford (Walck).
1961   No English award.
1962   *The Incredible Journey* by Sheila Burnford. Little, Brown.
1963   *The Whale People* by Roderick Haig-Brown. Collins (Morrow).
1964   *Tales of Nanabozho* by Dorothy Reid. Oxford (Walck).
1965   *The Double Knights: More Tales from Round the World* by James McNeill. Oxford (Walck).
1966   *Tiktá Liktak* by James Houston. (Harcourt).

England

THE CARNEGIE MEDAL, an annual Award since 1937, has been presented by the Library Association of England to the outstanding children's book written by a British author and published in England during the year prior to the award. In two of the war years, the award was withheld for lack of a book of suitable quality. Many of these books are republished by American publishers and are well known to American children. American publishers are given in parentheses. A list of the winners follows:

1937 *Pigeon Post* by Arthur Ransome. Cape.
1938 *The Family from One End Street* by Eve Garnett. Muller (Vanguard).
1939 *The Circus Is Coming* by Noël Streatfeild. J. M. Dent.
1940 *The Radium Woman* by Eleanor Doorly. Heinemann.
1941 *Visitors from London* by Kitty Barne. J. M. Dent.
1942 *We Couldn't Leave Dinah* by Mary Treadgold. Cape.
1943 *The Little Grey Men* by D. J. Watkins Pitchford. Eyre & Spottiswood.
1944 [No award.]
1945 *The Wind on the Moon* by Eric Linklater. Macmillan.
1946 [No award.]
1947 *The Little White Horse* by Elizabeth Goudge. University of London (Coward-McCann).
1948 *Collected Stories for Children* by Walter de la Mare. Faber.
1949 *Sea Change* by Richard Armstrong. J. M. Dent.
1950 *The Story of Your Home* by Agnes Allen. Faber (Transatlantic).
1951 *The Lark on the Wing* by Elfrida Vipont. Oxford.
1952 *The Wool-Pack* by Cynthia Harnett. Methuen.
1953 *The Borrowers* by Mary Norton. J. M. Dent (Harcourt).
1954 *A Valley Grows Up* by Edward Osmond. Oxford.
1955 *Knight Crusaders* by Ronald Welch. Oxford (Walck).
1956 *The Little Bookroom* by Eleanor Farjeon. Oxford (Walck).
1957 *The Last Battle* by C. S. Lewis. Bodley Head (Macmillan).
1958 *A Grass Rope* by William Mayne. Oxford (Dutton).
1959 *Tom's Midnight Garden* by Philippa Pearce. Oxford (Lippincott).

1960 *The Lantern Bearers* by Rosemary Sutcliff. Oxford (Walck).
1961 *The Making of Man* by Ian W. Cornwall and Howard M. Maitland. Phoenix (Dutton).
1962 *A Stranger at Green Knowe* by L. M. Boston. Faber (Harcourt).
1963 *The Twelve and the Genii* by Pauline Clarke. Faber (Coward-McCann, titled *Return of the Twelves*).
1964 *Time of Trial* by Hester Burton. Oxford (World Publishing).
1965 *Nordy Bank* by Sheena Porter. Oxford.
1966 [No award].

THE KATE GREENAWAY MEDAL is an Award that was established by the Library Association of England in 1955 for the most distinguished illustrated book for children published in Great Britain. The award was withheld the first year and awarded for the first time in 1957 for a book published in 1956. American publishers are given in parentheses.

1957 *Tim All Alone* by Edward Ardizzone. Oxford (Walck).
1958 *Mrs. Easter and the Storks* by Violet H. Drummond. Faber (Barnes).
1959 [No award.]
1960 *Kashtanka* by Anton Chekhov. Illustrated by William Stobbs. Oxford (Walck).
A Bundle of Ballads edited by Ruth Manning-Sanders. Illustrated by William Stobbs. Oxford (Lippincott).
1961 *Old Winkle and the Seagulls* by Elizabeth and Gerald Rose. Faber (Barnes).
1962 *Mrs. Cockle's Cat* by Philippa Pearce. Ilustrated by Antony Maitland. Constable (Lippincott).
1963 *Brian Wildsmith's ABC* by Brian Wildsmith. F. Watts.
1964 *Borka* by John Burningham. Cape (Random House).
1965 *Shakespeare's Theatre* by C. Walter Hodges. Oxford (Coward-McCann).
1966 *The Three Poor Tailors* by Victor Ambrus. Oxford (Harcourt).
1967 *The Mother Goose Treasury* by Raymond Briggs. Lund, Humphries (Coward-McCann).

THE ELEANOR FARJEON AWARD is given annually by the Children's Book Circle of England for "distinguished services to children's books in the past year." First given in 1966, this cash prize is not restricted to one profession or nationality.

1966 Margery Fisher
1967 Jessica Jenkins

Other Countries

Many European countries have established awards similar to those given in this country. Some prizes are sponsored by government agencies, others by publishing houses, still others by various private associations. Among the countries where these awards are given are Austria, Belgium, Finland, France, Germany, Italy, The Netherlands, Norway, Spain, Sweden, and Switzerland.

INTERNATIONAL CHILDREN'S BOOK AWARD

Hans Christian Andersen Prize

In 1956, the first international children's book award was established. It is given every two years to a living author of a book of fiction for children. It can also be awarded for the complete works of an author. A committee of five, each from a different country, judges the selections recommended by the board or library association in each country. The award is given by the International Board on Books for Young People. In 1966, the award was expanded to honor an illustrator as well as an author. The following have won the Hans Christian Andersen Prize:

1956 Eleanor Farjeon for *The Little Bookroom.* Illustrated by Edward Ardizzone. Oxford (Walck).

1958 Astrid Lindgren for *Rasmus pa Luffen.* Illustrated by Eric Palmquist. Rabén and Sjögren (Viking, titled *Rasmus and the Vagabond*).

1960 Erich Kästner "for his complete work for children and young people." Germany.

1962 Meindert DeJong. United States.

1964 René Guillot. France.

1966 Tove Jansson (author). Finland.
Alois Carigiet (illustrator). Switzerland.

B

BOOK SELECTION AIDS

GUIDES TO BOOK SELECTION AIDS

1. *Aids to Choosing Books for Your Children.* Prepared by Alice Dalgliesh and Annis Duff. Children's Book Council, 175 Fifth Avenue, New York 10010. $0.15 each, fifty or more $0.10 each.

   This leaflet lists books and booklists about children's books. It is excellent for quantity distribution in children's literature classes. Revised frequently.

2. *Book Selection Aids for Children and Teachers in Elementary and Secondary Schools.* Milbrey L. Jones. Washington, D.C.: U.S. Government Printing Office, 1966. 16 pp. $0.15.

   Includes references to some fifty book selection aids for teachers in elementary and secondary schools. Brief annotations are given.

3. *Book Selection Media.* Ralph Perkins. National Council of Teachers of English, 508 South Sixth Street, Champaign, Illinois 61820. 1966. 188 pp. $2.00.

   A descriptive guide to 175 aids for selecting library materials. Includes guides for all ages from elementary school students to adults, and guides to specific subject matter from atomic energy to materials for retarded readers. This bulletin is well-organized, includes all bibliographic materials, cost, addresses, and evaluation of the specific book selection aids.

4. *Children's Literature, a Guide to Reference Sources.* Prepared under the direction of Virginia Haviland. Washington, D.C.: Library of Congress, U.S. Government Printing Office, 1966. 341 pp. $2.50.

   A comprehensive guide to many reference sources in children's literature, this annotated bibliography describes books, articles, and pamphlets concerned with the study of children's books in this country and throughout the world. It has an especially useful section on the historical development of children's literature. An invaluable bibliography for the serious student of children's literature.

5. *Guides to Newer Educational Media.* Margaret I. Rufsvold and Carolyn Guss. American Library Association, 50 East Huron Street,

Chicago, Illinois 60611. 1961. 74 pp. $1.50. A bibliography of bibliographies of all nonprint material. Includes annotations of media catalogs, periodicals, and professional organizations concerned with the newer media of films, filmstrips, slides, radio, television, phonorecords, phonodiscs, and phonotapes. In process of revision.

REFERENCE BOOKS

1. *A Basic Book Collection for Elementary Grades.* Seventh edition. Edited by Miriam Snow, *et al.* American Library Association, 50 East Huron Street, Chicago, Illinois 60611. 1960. $2.00.
A selective, annotated, classified list of children's books. Compiled by library and educational authorities, it provides a well-balanced list for libraries in elementary schools. Fiction, picture, and easy books are grouped separately. Grade levels are indicated. Over 1000 titles are included. Designed to serve as a buying guide for smaller or medium-sized schools that may not have a trained librarian.

2. *Children's Catalog.* Eleventh edition. Edited by Rachel and Estelle A. Fidell. H. W. Wilson Company, 950 University Avenue, Bronx, New York 10452. 1966. 1024 pp. $17.00.
New edition every five years. Kept up-to-date by four annual paper supplements. One of the most useful and comprehensive lists in the field of children's literature. This list contains some 4274 titles. Part I is a classified list giving author, title, publisher, date, price, approximate grade level, and brief synopsis. Titles suggested for first purchase are double-starred, and those suggested for second purchase are single-starred. Part II is an alphabetical author, title and subject index to all the books. Separate sections classify books by grade level, and a directory of publishers and distributors is included.

3. *Children's Books for Schools and Libraries.* 1966–1967 edition. Edited by Phyllis B. Steckler. R. R. Bowker Company, 1180 Avenue of the Americas, New York 10036. $4.95 postpaid.
Lists information on 18,000 in-print editions including bindings, current prices, and recommendations from *ALA Basic Book Collection for Elementary Grades, Children's Catalog, The Elementary School Library Collection, Best Books for Children,* and *School Library Journal.* No annotations are given.

4. *The Elementary School Library Collection.* Second edition. Edited by Mary Virginia Gaver, *et al.* The Bro-Dart Foundation, 113 Frelinghuysen Avenue, Newark, New Jersey 07114. 1967–1968 edition. $20.00
Annual supplement. A collection of some 5000 titles designed as a guide for the acquisition of a balanced elementary school collection of good quality. Phase 1 represents a minimum collection for the smallest school library. Phases 2 and 3 include professional and audio-visual materials as well as children's books. Arranged in Dewey Decimal call number sequence, entries consist of a reproduction of an actual catalog card for each title in the collection.

5. *Index to Children's Poetry.* 1965 supplement. Compiled by John E. and Sara W. Brewton. H. W. Wilson Company, 950 University Ave., Bronx, New York 10452. $10.00.
Indexes some 15,000 poems in 130 collections by title, subject, author, and first line. Estimated grade levels are indicated through grade twelve.

6. *Index to Fairy Tales, Myths and Legends.* Compiled by Mary Eastman. Boston, Mass.: Faxon, 1952. $7.50.
Title index to stories in many collections, with cross references from variant titles to known titles.

7. *Junior High School Library Catalog.* H. W. Wilson Company, 950 University Avenue, Bronx, New York 10452. 1966. $20.00.
Includes four annual supplements. Lists some 3278 titles of fiction and nonfiction appropriate for use at the junior high school level. Full bibliographic information is given and descriptive and critical annotations. Teachers and librarians need to know this reference book, since some mature readers in the elementary school will be ready for titles in this list.

8. *Subject and Title Index to Short Stories for Chil-*

dren. Compiled by a subcommittee of the American Library Association, 50 East Huron Street, Chicago, Illinois 60611. 1955. $5.00.

Indexes some 5000 stories from 372 books and anthologies. The stories are categorized under more than 2000 subject headings. This is an indispensable tool for locating the hard-to-find stories. Age levels are approximately eight to fourteen years.

9. *Subject Index to Books for Primary Grades.* Second edition. Prepared by Mary K. Eakin and Eleanor Merritt. American Library Association, 50 East Huron Street, Chicago, Illinois 60611. 1961. $4.50.

An index to the content of both trade and textbooks. Subject headings are common to study in primary grades. Poetry and folk tales are omitted. Grade levels are designated and also the levels at which the book might be appropriately read aloud.

10. *Subject Index to Books for Intermediate Grades.* Third edition. Edited by Mary K. Eakin. American Library Association, 50 East Huron Street, Chicago, Illinois 60611. 1963. 308 pp. $7.50.

About 1800 titles are classified by subjects that are commonly taught in grades four to six. Makes reference to fiction, nonfiction, and school texts. Gives estimate of age level.

11. *Subject Index to Poetry for Children and Young People.* Compiled by Violet Sell, *et al.* American Library Association, 50 East Huron Street, Chicago, Illinois 60611. 1957. $9.00. This index of 592 pages with references to 157 poetry collections is a result of more than ten years of work by the compilers. A comprehensive range of subject headings is employed, and cross-references are used.

GENERAL BOOKLISTS

1. *Adventuring with Books: A Book List for Elementary Schools.* Edited by Elizabeth Guilfoile, Editorial Chairman, and the Committee on the Elementary School Book List, National Council of Teachers of English. A Signet Book published by The New American Library, 1301 Avenue of the Americas, New York 10019. 1966. 256 pp. $0.75.

Revised periodically. A classified bibliography of over 1000 old favorites and books of recent publication. Books are briefly annotated; price, date, and age levels are included. Listings are organized under thirty-two subject categories.

2. *Best Books for Children.* 1967 edition. Edited by Ann Currah. R. R. Bowker Co., 1180 Avenue of the Americas, New York 10036. $3.00.

Published annually. Over 4000 approved titles are included in this booklist. Annotations are arranged by grade and subject; there is an author-illustrator index and a title-series index. Three grade ranges are included: preschool to third grade; grades four to six; grades seven and up. Books recommended by *ALA Booklist, School Library Journal* and the *Children's Catalog* are specially coded. Indispensable.

3. *Bibliography of Books for Children.* Edited by Association for Childhood Education International, 3615 Wisconsin Ave., N.W., Washington, D.C. 20016. 1965. 130 pp. $1.50.

This list presents the best books reviewed by *Childhood Education* during the preceding two years. It covers a wide range of interests and reading abilities. Includes over 1700 entries that are annotated, priced, and grouped by age levels. This booklist is well indexed, and cross-references are included.

4. *Books of the Year for Children.* Edited by the Child Study Association of America, 9 East 89th Street, New York 10028. 1965. 32 pp. $0.50.

A classified, annotated bibliography of about 2000 books for children and books about children, parents, and family life. Titles are grouped by age from preschool through early teens. Within each age group are topical groupings and books for easy reading. Books of outstanding quality are starred.

5. *Books for Children 1960–1965.* The American Library Association, 50 East Huron Street, Chicago, Illinois 60611. 1966. 447 pp. $10.00.

Reviews of over 3000 titles originally recommended for purchase in the Children's Section of *The Booklist and Subscription Books Bulletin.* Titles are arranged according to a modified Dewey Decimal classification. Complete bibliographic and ordering information is given for each book, plus an evaluative review. Grade levels are indicated.

6. *Books for Children 1965–1966.* The American Library Association, 50 East Huron Street, Chicago, Illinois 60611. 1966. $2.00.

This first annual compilation lists the 770 new titles from the Children's Books section of *The Booklist* from September 1965–August 1966. Following the same plan as the previously listed five-year volume, this supplement is also annotated, classified, and indexed.

7. *Children's Books: Awards and Prizes.* 1966–1967 edition. Children's Book Council, Inc., 175 Fifth Avenue, New York 10010. $0.75. Copies of previous *Awards and Prizes* booklets, first issued in 1961, available at $0.25 each.

Revised annually. Lists the most recent winners of over forty honors for children's books. Brief explanation of each award is given. Books are not annotated.

8. *Children's Books—1966.* Compiled by Virginia Haviland and Lois Watt. LC#65–60014. Washington, D.C.: Superintendent of Documents, U.S. Government Printing Office, 1967, 16 pp. $0.15.

Annual. An annotated list of about 200 books for preschool through junior high school. Arranged by subject and age groups. Reading levels are indicated.

9. *Children's Books . . . for $1.25 or Less.* Edited by Siddie Joe Johnson, *et al.* Association for Childhood Education International, 3615 Wisconsin Avenue, N.W., Washington, D.C. 20016. 1965. 35 pp. $0.75.

Lists over 300 worthwhile but inexpensive books for children through grade six. Arranged alphabetically, classified, and briefly annotated.

10. *Children's Book Shelf.* 1965 edition. Child Study Association of America, 9 East 89th Street, New York 10028. $0.95.

Lists about 2000 books under subject headings about children and family life. Complete bibliographic material is given and good annotations; includes pamphlets, paperbacks, publishers' directory, author-title index, and introductory article.

11. *Children's Books Too Good to Miss.* Fifth edition. May Hill Arbuthnot, Margaret Clark, and Harriet Long. Western Reserve University Press, 2029 Adelbert Road, Cleveland, Ohio 44106. 1966. 72 pp. Paperback $1.75 (also hardbound).

A small, but excellent, booklist of about 260 titles that include the "classics" of today and yesterday. The annotations are excellent, as is a fine sixteen-page section on "The Artist and Children's Books." Entries are classified as to age groups, and within age groups as to type of book.

12. *Current Books, Junior Booklist.* Compiled by Committee on Junior Booklist, National Association of Independent Schools, 4 Liberty Square, Boston, Massachusetts 02109. 1966. 118 pp. $0.50.

Published annually. An annotated bibliography of current books for recreational reading for the youngest through grade nine. Includes family reading.

13. *Fanfare: The Horn Book's Honor List, 1961–1965.* Edited by The Horn Book Committee. *The Horn Book Magazine,* 585 Boylston Street, Boston, Massachusetts, 02116. 1967. $0.10.

A classified list of books for preschool—twelfth grade, chosen by the reviewing editors for *The Horn Book Magazine* as the best books for this five-year period.

14. *Good Books for Children.* Second edition. Edited by Mary K. Eakin. University of Chicago Press, 5750 Ellis Avenue, Chicago, Illinois 60637. 1962. Paperback $1.95.

In this book, Mary K. Eakin selected the best of the books that had been reviewed in the *Bulletin of the Center for Children's Books.* Includes over 1000 evaluative reviews of both fiction and nonfiction. Titles are arranged alphabetically by author. Approximate grade level from kindergarten through high school is indicated. The topical index that helps locate books for special interests is very useful.

15. *Growing Up with Books.* Revised edition. Edited by R. R. Bowker Company, 1180 Avenue of the Americas, New York 10036. 1966. 36 pp. $4.15 per 100 copies.

Lists "250 books every child should have a chance to enjoy." Entries are classified by age and interest and include brief annotations. Prepared for quantity distribution to P.T.A.'s, libraries, bookstores, and civic clubs.

16. *Notable Children's Books of 1966.* Edited by the ALA Committee on Notable Children's Books. American Library Association, 50 East Huron Street, Chicago, Illinois 60611. 1967. One copy free; quantity rates.

Each year, an ALA committee selects what it considered to be the distinctive books of the preceding year. List first appears in the April issue of the *ALA Bulletin.*

17. *Notable Children's Books, 1940–1959.* American Library Association, 50 East Huron Street, Chicago, Illinois 60611. 1966. $1.50. The annual Notable Children's Books lists provide the basis for this selection of nearly 300 children's books. Each of the titles has been reevaluated after at least a five-year period of use. Those of enduring worth and interest to children are included in this twenty-year reappraisal.

18. *Paperbound Book Guide for Elementary Schools.* R. R. Bowker Company, 1180 Avenue of the Americas, New York 10036. 1966. $0.50. An annotated catalogue of available paperbacks appropriate for use in the elementary school. Lists 730 titles in two age groups, kindergarten through grade three and grades four through six. Subject categories are included in each age group. Includes a list of paperback aids for teachers and librarians and a section of i/t/a publications.

19. *A Parents' Guide to Children's Reading.* Revised edition. Nancy Larrick. Sponsored by the National Book Committee. 1964. Paperback (New York: Pocket Books) $0.50 plus $0.10 per copy mailing charges. Hardback (New York: Doubleday) $3.95.

An excellent handbook for parents suggesting appropriate titles for children at each stage of their development. Special chapters on poetry, reference books, television, and comics are useful. A section on how reading is taught today will answer many parental questions.

20. *Recommended Children's Books of ———.* Reprinted from *School Library Journal.* R. R. Bowker Company, 1180 Avenue of the Americas, New York 10036. Single copies $3.00, five or more $2.00 each. Old editions $2.00 each.

Published annually. A complete listing of the "best" in children's literature each year. The reviews are reprinted from the *School Library Journal* section of the *Library Journal.* About 1000 titles are evaluated for literary quality, appeal, suitability to age, interest level versus reading level, curriculum applications, illustrations, and format. Reviews are arranged in four age groups from the youngest to teenage.

21. *Treasure for the Taking.* Revised edition. Prepared by Anne Thaxter Eaton. New York: Viking, 1957. $4.00.

This book lists some 1580 titles. It summarizes the basic story of each book, classifies it by subject, and suggests the appropriate age level. Books listed range from picture books to those that would interest high school age. Useful for both parents and teachers; needs another revision.

SPECIALIZED BOOKLISTS

1. *The AAAS Science Booklist for Children.* Second edition. Compiled by Hilary J. Deason. American Association for the Advancement of Science. 1963. 201 pp. Paperback $1.50. Hardback $2.50.

An annotated bibliography of nearly 1300 science and mathematics books for grades one–eight arranged by Dewey classification. Reading level is indicated, and some high-interest, low vocabulary materials are included.

2. *About 100 Books, a Gateway to Better Intergroup Understanding.* Fifth edition. Ann G. Wolfe. The American Jewish Committee, Institute of Human Relations, 165 East 56th Street, New York 10022. 1965. 43 pp. $0.35.

An annotated bibliography of books,

1962–1965, divided by ages five–nine, eight–thirteen, eleven–sixteen to promote better understanding of various ethnic and cultural groups.

3. *American History in Juvenile Books.* Seymour Metzner. H. W. Wilson Company, 950 University Avenue, Bronx, New York 10452. 1966. 329 pp. $7.00.

A graded bibliography arranged chronologically beginning with grade three and continuing through grade seven. A useful reference.

4. *Behavior Patterns in Children's Books: A Bibliography.* Clara J. Kircher. Washington, D.C.: Catholic University Press of America, 1966. 132 pp. Paperback $1.95. Hardback $3.75.

An annotated bibliography of over 500 books organized under twenty-two different headings such as Honesty, Intercultural Understanding, and Kindness to Animals.

5. *A Bibliography of Children's Art Literature.* Edited by Kenneth Marantz. National Education Association, 1201 Sixteenth Street, N.W., Washington, D.C. 20036. 1965. 24 pp. $0.45.

A classified, annotated bibliography of about 165 books related to art for grades kindergarten–twelve.

6. *Books about Negro Life for Children.* Third edition. Prepared by Augusta Baker. New York Public Library, 5th Avenue at 42nd Street, New York 10018. 1963. 33 pp. $0.35.

The books selected for this list are those "that give an unbiased, accurate, well-rounded picture of Negro life in all parts of the world." Criteria for language, theme, and illustrations have been established and choices made accordingly. The entries are briefly annotated, classified, and age groupings have been assigned. This is an excellent and useful list.

7. *Books for Beginning Readers.* Elizabeth Guilfoile. National Council of Teachers of English, 508 South Sixth Street, Champaign, Illinois 61822. 1962. 73 pp. $1.00.

A comprehensive list of over 300 titles providing material for children beginning to read on their own. Reading levels include grades one–three; books are arranged by subject and author. A 1963 supplement of one hundred more titles is included.

8. *Books for Brotherhood.* Edited by National Conference of Christians and Jews Committee, 43 West 57th Street, New York 10019. 1965. One copy free; quantity rates.

Printed annually, this annotated bibliography includes thirty-seven titles appropriate for children.

9. *Books for Friendship.* Third edition. Edited by Mary Esther McWhirter. American Friends Service Committee and Anti-Defamation League of B'nai B'rith. 1962. 63 pp. $0.50. *1966 Supplement.* American Friends Service Committee, 160 North 15th Street, Philadelphia, Pennsylvania 19102. 1966. 11 pp. $0.15.

A classified, annotated bibliography of books for ages six–fifteen. Supplement updates.

10. *Children's Books, 1965–1966; Children's Books, 1963–1964; Children's Books, 1961–1962; Children's Books, 1958–1960.* American Institute of Graphic Arts, 5 East 40th Street, New York 10016. Catalogs of the biennial Children's Book Shows. $1.50 each.

These catalogs reproduce a page from each of the books selected by the judges to appear in these shows sponsored by the American Institute of Graphic Arts. The type of media used, number of colors, platemaker, typeface, composition, paper, printing, and binding are noted for each picture. A synopsis of the book is not given, since selection for the show is based on format only. Comments by the judges on the quality of each show are most interesting.

11. *Children's Books to Enrich the Social Studies.* Revised edition. Compiled by Helen Huus. Bulletin No. 32, National Council for the Social Studies, 1201 Sixteenth Street, N.W., Washington, D.C. 20036. 1966. $2.50.

Fiction and nonfiction are categorized under five major areas: our world, times past, people today, the world's work, living together. Complete annotations summarize content and give suggestions for use of books. Each book is graded. Especially useful for teachers.

12. *Children's Books Suggested as Holiday Gifts.* Edited by New York Public Library Committee, 5th Avenue at 42nd Street, New York 10018. 1965. 47 pp. $0.25. Annual.

Each year, during November and December, an exhibition of children's books suggested as holiday gifts has been held in the central Children's Room of the New York Public Library. A catalog of annotated titles is available.

13. *Educational Materials Laboratory Report.* OE-14031-31. Washington, D.C.: U.S. Office of Education.

Schools and libraries may be placed on the mailing list to receive single copies without charge. Write to the Educational Materials Laboratory. (For specific back issues or quantity orders, write to the Publications Distribution Unit, U.S. Office of Education.) Back issues include: "Western Europe," OE-14031-23 — March 15, 1963; "Eastern Europe," OE-14031-25 — June 26, 1963; "The Far East," OE-14031-28 — December 11, 1963; "The Near East and North Africa," OE-14031-29 — March 20, 1964; "Early Civilizations," OE-14031-31 — July 1, 1964. These include textbooks, nonfiction trade books, fiction with grade level designations. Some descriptive annotations are included. Teacher resources are listed.

14. *The Elementary and Junior High School Mathematics Library.* Compiled by Clarence E. Hardgrove. National Council of Teachers of Mathematics, 1201 Sixteenth Street, N.W., Washington, D.C. 20036. 1960. 32 pp. $0.35.

Fiction and nonfiction for primary, intermediate grades, and junior high school are listed as means for enriching the instructional program in mathematics. Titles are annotated.

15. *Good Reading for Poor Readers.* Fourth edition. Compiled by George Spache. Reading Laboratory and Clinic, University of Florida, Gainesville, Florida. 1964. $1.50.

An excellent listing of easy books for the reluctant reader in the elementary school. Each title is graded and a special reading level is given for each book. Complete annotations are given. Special listings are arranged around boys' interests and girls' interests in alphabetical order by author. Includes trade books, series, magazines, newspapers, programed materials, and textual materials. Especially useful for teachers of grades four through seven.

16. *Growing Up with Science Books.* Compiled with the assistance of Julius Schwartz. R. R. Bowker Company, 1180 Avenue of the Americas, New York 10036. 1966. $3.75 per 100 copies.

Revised every two years. Similar to the little booklet *Growing Up with Books,* this booklist identifies 300 titles that are of interest for today's scientific child. The entries are annotated, priced, and classified within five different age groupings. These booklets are excellent for distribution by P.T.A.'s, libraries, or booksellers.

17. *A Guide to Science Reading.* Revised edition. Edited by Hilary J. Deason. Signet P2283 — New American Library. 1964. 239 pp. $0.60.

An annotated bibliography of about 1000 paperbacks for kindergarten — grade twelve. Entries are keyed to four reading and comprehension levels: upper elementary and junior high, upper secondary, superior secondary and college undergraduate, and advanced college or specialist.

18. *Guide to Children's Magazines, Newspapers, Reference Books.* Revised edition. Nancy Nunnally. Association for Childhood Education International, 3615 Wisconsin Avenue, N.W., Washington, D.C. 20016. 1966. 8 pp. $0.10 each; quantity rates.

Annotated bibliography arranged by kinds of material. Criteria for selection are stated.

19. *Human Relations: A Basic Booklist.* Edited by Madison Public Schools Committee, 545 West Dayton Street, Madison, Wisconsin 53703. 1965. 21 pp. $2.00.

An annotated bibliography of over 200 titles for kindergarten through grade twelve. Titles are arranged under age groups.

20. *I Can Read It Myself.* Edited by Frieda M. Heller. The Ohio State University Publications Office, 242 West 18th Avenue, Columbus, Ohio 43210. 1965. 46 pp. $1.00.

An annotated bibliography for grades one — three and beginning readers, arranged by reading levels.

21. *Let's Read Together: Books for Family Enjoyment.* Edited by Committee of National Congress of Parents and Teachers, and Children's Services Division, American Library Association, 50 East Huron Street, Chicago, Illinois 60611. 1964. 91 pp. $1.50.

An annotated bibliography of about 750 titles for children from the youngest to fifteen years old. Arranged by categories of reader interest and age level. Intended as an aid to parents in selecting books for their children, for family reading aloud, individual reading, and a child's own library.

22. *Library Materials for Elementary Science.* Albert C. Haman and Mary K. Eakin. Cedar Falls, Iowa: State College of Iowa, 1964. $1.00.

Lists 710 titles under three categories: physical sciences, biological science, and biographies of scientists. Would help a teacher supplement a unit study in science.

23. *Light the Candles!* Compiled by Marcia Dalphin. Revised by Anne Thaxter Eaton. Boston, Mass.: Horn Book, 1960. 22 pp. $1.00.

This is an annotated listing of poetry, stories, legends, carols, and plays about Christmas. It includes many suggestions for family reading.

24. *Literature and Music as Resources for Social Studies.* Ruth Tooze and Beatrice Krone. Englewood Cliffs, N.J.: Prentice-Hall, Inc., 1955. 457 pp. $7.95.

This book suggests references to both books and music as a means of enriching the social studies curriculum. The references are about the history of our country and the other countries of the world. This useful book needs to be updated, but the music and history references are still very helpful.

25. *Magazines for Elementary Grades.* Revised edition. Madison Public Schools, Department of Curriculum Development, 545 West Dayton Street, Madison, Wisconsin 53703. 1965. 27 pp. $3.00.

Annotated list of magazines appropriate for use in the elementary school.

26. *Mathematics Library: Elementary and Junior High School.* Clarence E. Hardgrove. National Council of Teachers of Mathematics, 1201 Sixteenth Street, N.W., Washington, D.C. 20036. 1962. 32 pp. $0.35.

Suggests books that may enrich the mathematics instructional program. Books are listed alphabetically by author under primary, intermediate, and junior high schools. In some instances, the content is stretched to fit mathematics.

27. *Natural History's 1965 Survey of Science Books for Young People.* Evelyn Shaw. Natural History Reviews, Central Park West at 79th Street, New York 10024. 1965. 8 pp. $0.20; free to teachers and librarians for a stamped, self-addressed envelope.

Critical evaluations of science books of the past year for junior and senior high schools. A useful service.

28. *The Negro in Schoolroom Literature.* Edited by Minnie W. Koblitz. Center for Urban Education, 33 West 42nd Street, New York 10036. 1967. Single copies $0.25; orders over fifty, $0.15 each.

A comprehensive bibliography of over 350 books "that contribute to the understanding and appreciation of the Negro American Heritage." Listings include full bibliographic information, grade levels, and critical annotations of books for kindergarten through sixth grade.

29. *Once upon a Time.* Revised edition. Prepared by Augusta Baker and committee. The New York Public Library, Library Sales Office, Fifth Avenue at 42nd Street, New York 10018. 1964. 16 pp. $0.50.

This leaflet includes a discussion of methods and techniques for planning the library story hour. Some suggested programs are given and a bibliography of recommended stories for telling is included.

30. *Reading Ladders for Human Relations.* Fourth revised edition. Edited by Muriel Crosby, *et al.* American Council on Education, 1785 Massachusetts Avenue, N.W., Washington, D.C. 20036. 1964. 242 pp. Paperback $2.50, Hardback $4.00.

A classified, annotated bibliography of over 1000 books for kindergarten – grade twelve. Titles are grouped under six headings: (1) How It Feels to Grow Up; (2) The Individual and the Group; (3) The Search for Values; (4) Feeling at Home; (5) Living with Change; (6) Living as a Free People. Under each thematic heading, books are arranged in order of difficulty providing the "reading ladders."

31. *Resources for Teaching about the United Nations.* Edited by Elizabeth M. Thompson. National Education Association, 1201 Sixteenth Street, N.W., Washington, D.C. 20036. 1962. 90 pp. $1.50.
Annotated bibliography of books and audiovisual materials about the United Nations. Grades kindergarten–twelve.

32. *Stories.* Sixth revised edition. A List of Stories to Tell and to Read Aloud. Compiled by Ellin Greene. New York Public Library, Fifth Avenue at 42nd Street, New York, New York 10018. 1965. 78 pp. $1.00.
A list of proven stories and poems to tell to children. The entries are briefly annotated; age level is not suggested.

33. *Studying the World: Selected Resources.* Revised edition. Edited by Leonard S. Kenworthy. New York: Bureau of Publications, Teachers College, Columbia University, 1965. 71 pp. $1.50.
Annotated bibliography of books, films, periodicals, pamphlets, and other materials. Grades one–twelve. Arranged by geographical areas and world concerns. Kenworthy has also edited special lists for *Studying Africa, South America,* and the *Middle East.* These titles are available from the same source at $1.50 each.

34. *We Build Together, A Reader's Guide to Negro Life and Literature for Elementary and High School Use.* Third revision. Edited by Charlemae Rollins. National Council of Teachers of English, 508 South Sixth Street, Champaign, Illinois 61822. 1967. 77 pp. $1.50.
This new edition contains perceptive and complete annotations of children's books that portray the Negro. Shows the changing role of the Negro in literature, and discusses stereotypes and language.

PERIODICALS

1. *Bookbird.* A quarterly published by the International Board on Books for Young People. Edited by Dr. Richard Bamberger. U.S.

Subscriptions: Package Library of Foreign Children's Books, Inc., 119 Fifth Avenue, New York, New York 10003. $3.80.
An international periodical on literature for children and young people. Includes papers about books and authors in many countries, prize-winning books, and books recommended for translation.

2. *The Booklist and Subscription Books Bulletin.* American Library Association, 50 East Huron Street, Chicago, Illinois 60611. Issued semimonthly. $8.00 per year.
Reviews both adult and juvenile books, some before publication. Comprehensive reviews are annotated, graded by age levels and grades. Includes reviews of encyclopedias and reference books, also. Suggests the kind of library for which the books are recommended. It is the library profession's own reviewing medium and is a recognized authority in the field.

3. *Book Review Digest.* H. W. Wilson Company, 950 University Avenue, Bronx, New York 10452.
Sold to libraries on service basis. Evaluates about 4000 adult and children's books each year. Provides for comparison as several reviews of a book are listed in one source. Reviews are taken from English and American periodicals devoted to reviewing current literature.

4. *The Bulletin of The Center for Children's Books.* Graduate Library School, University of Chicago, 5750 Ellis Avenue, Chicago, Illinois 60637. Issued monthly except August. $4.50 per year.
An authoritative reviewing service concerned with the critical evaluation of current juvenile books. Reviews include adverse as well as favorable comments. Each entry is graded and fully annotated with heavy emphasis on the use of the book. December issue contains list of recommended books for the year.

5. *Calendar.* Children's Book Council, 175 Fifth Avenue, New York 10010. Issued four times a year. $1.00 per year.
This leaflet lists days to observe that directly concern children's books, and also those which offer especially good possibilities for

book displays. Titles of prize-winning books and coming television programs that are based upon children's books are noted. A list of recent and available material concerning children's literature is presented. An amazing amount of information is included in this little bulletin.

6. *Childhood Education.* Association for Childhood Education International, 3615 Wisconsin Avenue, N.W., Washington, D.C. 20016. Issued monthly, September – May. $5.50 per year.

This professional magazine includes a monthly column on children's books that contains a dozen or more reviews of books for children from age two – twelve. Reviews are written by a committee of librarians and subject specialists and are edited by the chairman. Occasionally, special categories of books are considered such as science books, books on other lands, and so forth.

7. *Elementary English.* National Council of Teachers of English, 508 South Sixth Street, Champaign, Illinois 61822. Issued monthly, October – May. $7.00 per year.

This professional magazine regularly includes reviews of children's books with indications of grade levels, curriculum use, and prices, etc. Shelton Root is the current editor of this "Books For Children" section. Articles on children's interests in reading, authors, illustrators, and research are frequent features of this most popular journal.

8. *The Grade Teacher.* Teachers Publishing Corporation, 23 Leroy Avenue, Darien, Connecticut 06820. $5.50 per year.

The "Books for Children" column edited by Anne Izard, a children's librarian, reviews some nine or ten titles each month.

9. *The Horn Book Magazine.* Horn Book, Inc., 585 Boylston Street, Boston, Massachusetts, 02116. Published six times yearly. $6.00 per year.

Devoted wholly to children's books and reading, this magazine includes detailed reviews of current children's books. Emphasis is placed on the literary quality of the books. Entries are classified by subject and age level. Articles about authors, illustrators, award books, and the history of chil-

dren's literature are frequently featured. The acceptance papers by the winners of the Newbery and Caldecott Medals, together with biographical pieces about the winners, appear in the August issue each year. In October, there is a "Fanfare" list of outstanding books of the preceding year.

10. *The Instructor.* Dansville, N.Y.: F. A. Owen Publishing Company. Ten issues per year. $6.00 per year.

This popular magazine for teachers has a section devoted to "Books for Children." Phyllis Fenner is the book-review editor for this column that includes annotations, grades, and priced entries. Occasionally, articles concerning children's literature are featured.

11. *Library Journal.* R. R. Bowker and Company, 1180 Avenue of the Americas, New York 10036. Issued monthly, September – May. $10.00 per year for *Library Journal.* $5.00 per year for *School Library Journal.*

School Library Journal appears each month as a special section of the *Library Journal,* or it may be subscribed to separately. It includes appraisals of approximately 1500 new children's books yearly. Reviews are written by practicing school and public librarians and teachers. Single and double stars indicate better-than-average and exceptional-quality books, respectively. Entries are arranged by different grade levels and subject categories.

12. *Monthly Selection Guide for the Children's Department.* Detroit Public Library, Book Selection Department, 5201 Woodward Avenue, Detroit, Michigan 48202. $5.00 per year.

A compilation of signed annotations of recommended books. Includes a second list of "Books considered but not included." Bulletin is about twenty-five pages in length.

13. *Publishers' Weekly* – Children's Book Number. R. R. Bowker and Company, 1180 Avenue of the Americas, New York 10036. $15.00 per year.

Twice a year (spring and fall) this "Publishers' Bible" devotes huge issues to children's books. It lists juveniles of all types for all ages and tastes and includes an index of children's books by author, title, and illustrator. Dates of publication, including forthcoming books, are indicated. Feature articles on children's books are always included in these special issues.

14. *Saturday Review.* 25 West 45th Street, New York 10036. Weekly. $8.00 per year.

About once a month, an issue of the *Saturday Review* includes a section on children's books, currently edited by Zena Sutherland. Special children's book issues appear in the spring and fall of each year. An occasional feature article will discuss some phase of children's literature.

15. *Science Books.* A Quarterly Review. American Association for the Advancement of Science, 1515 Massachusetts Avenue, N.W., Washington, D.C. 20005. Published quarterly. $4.50 per year.

Reviews trade books, textbooks, and reference works in the pure and applied sciences for students in elementary, junior high, secondary schools, and college, and for those in professional work. Gives three levels for elementary, very simple, intermediate, and advanced; double-starred books are highly recommended. Each book is reviewed by a qualified specialist. The published annotations are prepared by the editorial staff from the notes and comments of the reviewers.

16. *Science and Children.* National Science Teachers Association, 1201 Sixteenth Street, N.W., Washington, D.C. 20036. Eight issues per year. $4.00 per year.

Includes a monthly column that reviews recent science books and audio-visual materials.

17. *Wilson Library Bulletin.* H. W. Wilson Company, 950 University Avenue, Bronx, New York 10452. Issued monthly, September–June. $4.00 per year.

This bulletin includes discussions and reviews of all types of books, adult and children's. Features include a monthly review of current library reference books, news of literary awards, biographical sketches of authors, and a section devoted to displays of the month.

18. *Young Readers Review.* Box 137, Wall Street Station, New York 10005. Published monthly, September–June. $5.00 per year. Presents extensive and definitive reviews of children's books, including both fiction and nonfiction. Each review compares the book with the author's previous work or with other similar books. Suggested age levels are given. A comparatively new reviewing service but one that has brought real literary criticism to the field of children's books.

NEWSPAPER BOOK SUPPLEMENTS

1. *Book Week.* 125 Barclay Street, New York 10015. Published weekly. $7.00 per year. Originally part of the old New York *Herald Tribune*, *Book Week* was syndicated and is now a part of the Washington *Post* and Chicago *Sun Times.* In addition to the weekly page, there are large fall and spring children's issues. Now awards the Book Week (Spring Book Festival) Awards.

2. *Book World.* 230 West 41 Street, New York 10036. Published weekly. $7.00 per year. Children's books are reviewed each week in this section of the Chicago *Sunday Tribune.* Polly Goodwin is editor of the column titled "Children's Book World." During Book Week in the fall, a large special edition of the book section features children's books, authors, and illustrators. Again in the spring a special edition features new children's books.

3. The New York *Times Book Review.* Published weekly. $7.50 per year.

Book reviews of the latest children's books are presented each week in a special column of the New York *Times* entitled "For Younger Readers." During Book Week in the fall, and in mid-May, an entire issue of the *Book Review* section is devoted to children's books. In the November issue, also, a jury of art experts selects its choice of the ten best-illustrated children's books of the year. Before Christmas, the editor's choice of "100 Outstanding Books" is included.

GUIDE
TO PRONUNCIATIONS

The names associated with children's literature—characters and place names from many books, as well as the names of some authors and illustrators—often cause difficulties in pronunciation. For this reason, the following guide has been prepared. Most of the pronunciations were obtained from children's book editors.

Except for the general rules that lone vowels have their short sound and the letter "g" always has its hard value, the following guides are meant to be phonetic and self-explanatory. Some names, of course, have subtle nuances of stress and alternate pronunciations that are not given here.

AUTHORS AND ILLUSTRATORS

AAS, ULF   ahs
ALIKI   ah *lee* ki
APPEL, BENJAMIN   ah *pel*
ARDIZZONE, EDWARD   ar dit *zoh* nee
ARTZYBASHEFF, BORIS   art zee *bash* eff
ARUNDEL, JOCELYN   *air* un del
ASBJØRNSEN, P. C.   *ahs* byern sen

ASIMOV, ISAAC   *a* si mov
D'AULAIRE, EDGAR   doh *lair*

BACMEISTER, RHODA   *bahk* mice ter
BEHN, HARRY   bane
BEIM, JERROLD   bime
BENARY-ISBERT, MARGOT   *mahr* go
  ben *air* ee *iz* bert
BENET, ROSEMARY AND STEPHEN   ben *ay*
BETTINA   be *teen* ah
BJORKLUND, LORENCE   *byork* lund
BOBRI, VLADIMIR   *vlad* i mir *boh* bree
BOLOGNESE, DON   boh loh *na* zee
BONTEMPS, ARNA   bon *tawmp*
BONZON, PAUL   bohn *zoh*
BRUNHOFF, JEAN DE   zhahn duh broo *noff*
BUEHR, WALTER   byoor

CARIGIET, ALOIS   al *wah* cah ree *jyay*
CAUDILL, REBECCA   *kaw* d'l
CAVANAH, FRANCES   *kav* uh nah
CHARLIP, REMY   *reh* mee *shar* lip
CHARLOT, JEAN   zhahn shar *loh*
CHASTAIN, MADYE LEE   *maid* ee lee *chas* tayne
CHERMAYEFF, IVAN   chair *my* ef

CHÖNZ, SELINA   se *lee* nah shŏonz
CHUTE, MARCHETTE   mar *shet* choot
CIARDI, JOHN   chee *ar* dee
COLUM, PADRAIC   *paw* drik *cahl* um
CREDLE, ELLIS   cradle

DALGLIESH, ALICE   *dal* gleesh
DAUGHERTY, JAMES   *daw* er tee
DE BORHEGYI, SUZANNE   duh bor *hay* gee
DE GASZTOLD, CARMEN   duh *gaz* tol
DEJONG, MEINDERT   *mine* dert de *yung*
DE LA MARE, WALTER   duh lah mair
DELEEUW, CATEAU   cat oo de *lay* oo
DE REGNIERS, BEATRICE   duh *rayn* yay
DILLON, EILÍS   eye leesh dill un
DOISNEAU, ROBERT   dwahz *noh*
DRUON, MAURICE   droo *ohn*
DU BOIS, WILLIAM PÈNE   pen doo *bwah*
DUHEME, JACQUELINE   doo *aym*
DUVOISIN, ROGER   dyoo vwah *zahn*

EBERLE, IRMENGARDE   *ebb* er li
ECONOMAKIS, OLGA   ee kon o *mah* kis
EICHENBERG, FRITZ   *ike* en berg

FEA, HENRY   fay
FIAMMENGHI, GIOIA   *joy* ah fee ah *men* jee
FONSECA, GEORGE   fon sek eh
FOURNIER, CATHARINE   foor *nyay*
FRANCHERE, RUTH   frahn *shair*
FRANCOIS, ANDRE   frahn *swah*
FRANCOISE   frahn *swahz*
FREUCHEN, PIPALUK   *pip* a luk *froy* ken
FRIIS, BABBIS   *bah* bis frees
FUNAI, MAMORU   mah moh roo foo nah ee

GAEDDERT, LOU ANN   *ged* ert
GAER, JOSEPH   gare
GAG, WANDA   gahg
GEISEL, THEODOR SEUSS   soos *geye* z'l
GERGELY, TIBOR   *tee* bor *gair* ge lee
GIDAL, SONIA   *soh* nyah gi *dahl*
GOUDEY, ALICE   *gou* dee (ou as in loud)
GRAMATKY, HARDIE   gra *mat* kee
GRIFALCONI, ANN   *gree* fal koh nee
GRINGHUIS, DIRK   *grin* gus
GUILFOILE, ELIZABETH   *gill* foil
GUILLOT, RENÉ   ruh nay gee *yoh*

HAAS, IRENE   hahs
HÁMORI, LÁSZLÓ   *laz* loh *ham* oh ree
HAUGAARD, ERIK   *how* gard
HEILBRONER, JOAN   *hile* bron er

HEYERDAHL, THOR   *heye* er dahl
HOFSINDE, ROBERT   *hoff* sin duh
HOGROGIAN, NONNY   hoh *groh* gi an
HOSOE, EIKOH   eye koh hoh soy

IPCAR, DAHLOV   *dah* luff *ip* car

JANSSON, TOVE   *toh* vay *yahn* son

KEPES, JULIET   *kep* esh
KJELGAARD, JIM   *kyell* gard
KOCH, DOROTHY   kotch
KRASILOVSKY, PHYLLIS   kraz i *luv* ski

LABASTIDA, AURORA   lah bah *stee* dah
LAMORISSE, ALBERT   ahl *bair* lah moh *rees*
LANIER, SIDNEY   lah *neer*
LATHAM, JEAN LEE   *lay* thum
LEODHAS, SORCHE NIC   sawr ah nik ly *oh* us
LE SUEUR, MERIDEL   luh *soor*
LEXAU, JOAN   *lex* ou (ou as in loud)
LIANG, YEN   lee *ang*
LIERS, EMIL   lirs
LIONNI, LEO   lee *oh* nee
LIU, BEATRICE   leeyou

MACHETANZ, FREDERICK   *mak* eh tanz
MATSUNO, MASAKO   mah sah koh maht soo noh
MILHOUS, KATHERINE   *mil* house
MINARIK, ELSE   *min* ah rik
MITSUI, EIICHI   ay ee chee meet soo ee
MOE, JORGEN   *yor* gun moh
MONTRESOR, BENI   *bay* nee *mohn* tre sor
MOWAT, FARLEY   *moh* ut
MUNARI, BRUNO   moo *nah* ree

OBLIGADO, LILIAN   oh bli *gah* do
OECHSLI, KELLY   ox lee
OLSCHEWSKI, ALFRED   all *shev* ski

PALAZZO, TONY   pah *laht* zoh
PAPASHVILY, HELEN   pa pash vi li
PERRAULT, CHARLES   pair *oh*
PETRIDES, HEIDRUN   *hide* run puh *tree* deez
PIATTI, CELESTINO   sel les *tee* noh pee *ah* tee
PLASENCIA, PETER   plah *sen* see ah
POLITI, LEO   poh *lee* tee

RAILLON, MADELEINE   ray *ohn*
RASMUSSEN, KNUD   nood *rahs* muh sen
RHIJN, ALEID VAN   *ay* leed van *reen*
RIWKIN-BRICK, ANNA   *riv* kin brik
ROJANKOVSKY, FEODOR   *fee* oh dawr
    roh jahn *koff* skee
RUCK-PACQUET, GINA   ruck pa *kay*

SAINT EXUPERY, ANTOINE DE   an *twahn* duh
san ex ew pair ee
SANDOZ, MARI   *ma* ree *san* doze
SASEK, MIROSLAV   *meer* oh slahf *sah* sek
SAUER, JULIA   sour
SAVIOZZI, ADRIANA   sav i *ot* zee
SCHEELE, WILLIAM E.   *shee* lee
SCHLEIN, MIRIAM   shline
SCHOENHERR, JOHN   *show*en hair
SEGAWA, YASUO   yah soo oh seg ah wah
SELLEW, CATHERINE   sel *looh*
SEREDY, KATE   *shair* uh dee
SERRAILLIER, IAN   ee an se *rahl* yay
SHIMIN, SYMEON   *sim* ee un *shi* min
SIDJAKOV, NICOLAS   *sid* juh koff
SIEBEL, FRITZ   *see* b'l
SIMONT, MARC   si *mahnt*
SLOBODKIN, LOUIS   sloh *bod* kin
SLOBODKINA, ESPHYR   ess fer sloh bod *keen* ah
SOLBERT, RONNI   *soll* bert
SOMMERFELT, AIMEE   *ay* mee *sum* mer felt
SPENDER, STEPHEN   *spen* der
SPONSEL, HEINZ   hines *spon* sell
SPYRI, JOHANNA   yo *hah* nah *shpee* ree
STRACHAN, MARGARET   strawn
STREATFEILD, NOËL   *noh* el *stret* feld
SURANY, ANICO   ah *nee* koh soo *rah* nee
SYME, RONALD   sime

TASHJIAN, VIRGINIA   *tas* jun
TENGGREN, GUSTAF   *goo* stahf *teng* gren
TENNIEL, SIR JOHN   *ten* yell
TOLKIEN, J. R. R.   *tall* ken
TREGASKIS, RICHARD   tre *gas* kiss
TRESSELT, ALVIN   *treh* selt

UCHIDA, YOSHIKO   yoh shee koh oo chee dah
UDRY, JANICE   *yoo* dri
UNGERER, TOMI   *toh* mee *ung* ger er
UNNERSTAD, EDITH   *oon* er stad

VAN DER LOEFF, A. RUTGERS   *van* der luff
VIERECK, PETER   *veer* ek

WABER, BERNARD   *way* ber
WEIL, LISL   *lee* s'l wile
WEISGARD, LEONARD   *wise* gard
WIER, ESTER   weer
WIESE, KURT   *vee* zuh
WOJCIECHOWSKA, MAIA   *meye* ah voy che *hov* skah
WUORIO, EVA-LIS   *ay* vuh lis *woor* yoh

YAMAGUCHI, MARIANNE   yah mah goo chee

YASHIMA, TARO   tar oh yah shee mah
YLLA   eel ah

ZEMACH, MARGOT   *zee* mak
ZOLOTOW, CHARLOTTE   *zol* uh tou (rhymes with how)

CHARACTERS AND SETTINGS

- *Beorn the Proud* by Madeleine Polland
  BEORN   byorn
- *The Big Wave* by Pearl S. Buck
  KINO   kee no
  JIYA   jee yah
- *A Black Bear's Story* by Emil Liers
  KODA   koh dah
  KABATO   kah bah toh
- *The Borrowers* by Mary Norton
  ARRIETTY   *air* i eh tee
  HOMILY   *hom* i lee
- *The Bronze Bow* by Elizabeth George Speare
  MALTHACE   *mawl* thess
  THACIA   *thay* shuh
- *Call It Courage* by Armstrong Sperry
  HIKUERU   hee koo *ay* roo
  KIVI   *kee* vee
  MAFATU   *mah* fah too
  TAVANA NUI   tah *vah* nah *noo* ee
  URI   *oo* ree
- *Carry on, Mr. Bowditch* by Jean Lee Latham
  BOWDITCH   *bow* ditch ("bow" rhymes with "how")
- *Chronicles of Prydain* by Lloyd Alexander
  ACHREN   *ahk* ren
  ADAON   ah *day* on
  ANNUVIN   ah *noo* vin
  ARAWN   ah *rawn*
  CAER CADARN   *keye* r *kah* darn
  CAER COLUR   *keye* r *koh* loor
  CAER DALBEN   *keye* r *dahl* ben
  CAER DATHYL   *keye* r *dah* thil
  COLL   kahl
  DALBEN   *dahl* ben
  DOLI   *doh* lee
  DYRNWYN, SWORD OF   *duhrn* win
  EIDDILEG, KING   eye *dill* eg
  EILONWY, PRINCESS   eye *lahn* wee
  ELLIDYR, PRINCE OF PEN-LLARCAU   el *lee* der pen *lar* cow
  FFLEWDDUR FFLAM   *flew* der flam

GURGI   *gher* ghi
GWYDION, PRINCE   *gwih* dyon
GWYTHAINTS   *gwih* thaints
ISLIMACH   iss *lim* ahk
LLAWGARDARN MOUNTAINS   law *gah* darn
LLUNET, MIRROR OF   *loo* net
LLYAN, THE CAT   lee *ahn*
LLYR, CASTLE OF   leer
MELYNGAR   *mehlin* gahr
MELYNLOS   *mehlin* lass
OETH-ANOETH, CASTLE OF   eth *ahn* eth
ORDDU   *or* doo
ORGOCH   *or* gahk
ORWEN   *or* wen
PRYDAIN   prih *dane*
RHUDDLUM, KING   *rud* lum
RHUN, PRINCE   roon
SMOIT, KING   smoyt
TARAN   *tah* ran
TELERIA, QUEEN   tel *ehr* ya

- *Chúcaro* by Francis Kalnay
  CHÚCARO   *choo* car roh
- *The Family Under the Bridge* by Natalie Savage Carlson
  ARMAND POULY   ahr *mahn* poo lee
  CALCET   kahl *say*
- *Felice* by Marcia Brown
  FELICE   fay *lee* chay
- *The Good Master* by Kate Seredy
  JANSCI   *yahn* see
- *The Green Ginger Jar* by Clara Ingram Judson
  AI-MEI   *eye* may
- *Hakon of Rogen's Saga* by Erik Haugaard
  HAKON   *hah* ken
  ROGEN   *roh* gen
- *Honk the Moose* by Phil Stong
  IVAR   *eye* var
  WAINO   *way* noh
- *The House of Sixty Fathers* by Meindert DeJong
  TIEN PAO   tyen pou
- *Island of the Blue Dolphins* by Scott O'Dell
  KARANA   kah *rah* nah
  RAMO   *rah* moh
  TUTOK   *too* tock
  ULAPE   oo *lah* pay
- *The Jungle Book* by Rudyard Kipling
  MOWGLI   *mou* glee
  KAA   kah

- *The Lantern Bearers* by Rosemary Sutcliff
  AQUILA   a *kwill* uh
  FLAVIA   *flay* vee ah
- *Mei Li* by Thomas Handforth
  MEI LI   may lee
- *Minou* by Francoise
  MINOU   mee *noo*
- *Misty of Chincoteague* by Marguerite Henry
  CHINCOTEAGUE   *ching* kuh teeg
  ASSATEAGUE   *ass* uh teeg
- *Nkwala* by Edith Sharp
  NKWALA   nuh *kwah* lah
- *Pelle's New Suit* by Elsa Beskow
  PELLE   *pel* lee
- *Pippi Longstocking* by Astrid Lindgren
  PIPPI   *pip* i
- *Pitschi* by Hans Fischer
  PITSCHI   *pit* chee
- *The Poppy Seed Cakes* by Margery Clark
  ANDREWSHEK   ahn *droo* shek
  ERMINKA   er *ming* kah
  KATUSHKA   kah *toosh* kah
- *The Promised Year* by Yoshiko Uchida
  KEIKO   kay *ee* koh
- *Secret of the Andes* by Ann Nolan Clark
  CHUTO   *choo* toh
  CUSI   *koo* zee
- *The Spettecake Holiday* by Edith Unnerstad
  SPETTECAKE   *speh* ti cake
  PELLE-GORAN   *pel* lee goh run
- *The Story of Babar* by Jean de Brunhoff
  BABAR   bah *bar*
- *Takao and Grandfather's Sword* by Yoshiko Uchida
  TAKAO   tah *kah* oh
- *Viollet* by Julia Cunningham
  VIOLLET   vee oh *lay*
- *Vison the Mink* by John and Jean George
  VISON   *veye* zun
- *Vulpes the Red Fox* by John and Jean George
  VULPES   *vul* peez
- *The Wheel on the School* by Meindert DeJong
  AUKA   *awk* ah
  EELKA   *eel* kah
  JANUS   *yah* nus
  JELLA   *yell* ah
  LINA   *leye* nah
  PIER   peer
- *White Stallion of Lipizza* by Marguerite Henry
  LIPIZZA   *lip* it zah

NAMES FROM MYTHS
AND FOLK TALES

ACHILLES   a *kill* eez
ACRISIUS   uh *kris* ee us
AGAMEMNON   ag a *mem* non
ANANSI   ah *nahn* see
ATTILA   uh *till* uh

BABA YAGA   *bah* bah *yah* gah
BAUCIS   *baw* sis
BELLEROPHON   beh *lair* oh fawn
BEOWULF   *bay* oh wulf
BRYNHILD   *broon* hilt

CHARYBDIS   kah *rib* dis
CIRCE   *sir* see
CUCHULAIN   koo *kull* in

DAEDALUS   *ded* uh lus
DEMETER   dee *mee* tur
DILILI   duh luh luh
DOBRYNA   daw *bree* nah

EPAMINONDAS   i pam i *non* dus

FAFNIR   *fahv* nir

GAWAIN   *gah* wayn
GRENDEL   *gren* d'l
GUDRUN   *good* roon

HILILI   huh luh luh

ICARUS   *ik* uh rus
ILYA   *eel* yah
ISIS   *eye* sis
ISUN BASHI   ee soon bah shee

JATAKA   *jah* tah kah

MAGARAC   maj a *rak*

MAGYAR   *mag* yahr
MAUI   *mou* ee
MEDEA   mee *dee* ah
MEDUSA   mee *doo* sah
MENELAUS   men ee *lay* us

NIBELUNGENLIED   *nee* buh *loong* un *leet*

ODIN   *oh* din
ODYSSEUS   odd *iss* ee us

PAKA'A   *pah* kah ah
PANCHATANTRA   *pun* chuh *tun* truh
PERSEPHONE   per *sef* oh nee
PERSEUS   *per* see us
PETIT JEAN   puh tee zhahn
PHAETHON   *fay* uh thun
PHILEMON   fee *lee* mon
PRIAM   *preye* um
PUNIA   poo nee ah
PYTHIAS   *pith* ee us

RAMA   *rah* mah

SCHEHERAZADE   shuh *hair* uh *zahd*
SCYLLA   *skill* ah
SIGURD   *zee* goort
SITA   *see* tah

THESEUS   *thee* see us
TIKTÁ LIKTAK   *tik* ta *lik* t'k

URASHIMA TARO   oo rah shee mah tah roh

VAINAMOINEN   *veh* na *moy* nen
VLADIMAR   *vlad* i mahr
YMIR   *ee* mir

ZLATEH   *zlah* teh
ZEUS   zoos

D

PUBLISHERS' ADDRESSES

ABELARD-SCHUMAN LTD.
6 West 57th Street
New York, New York 10019

ABINGDON PRESS
201 Eighth Avenue, South
Nashville, Tennessee 37023

ALADDIN
(See E. P. Dutton & Co., Inc.)

ALLYN AND BACON, INC.
150 Tremont Street
Boston, Massachusetts 02111

AMERICAN HERITAGE PUBLISHING CO., INC.
551 Fifth Avenue
New York, New York 10017

APPLETON-CENTURY-CROFTS
440 Park Avenue South
New York, New York 10016

ATHENEUM PUBLISHERS
122 East 42nd Street
New York, New York 10017

BARNES & NOBLE, INC.
105 Fifth Avenue
New York, New York 10003

THE BEACON PRESS
25 Beacon Street
Boston, Massachusetts 02108

THE BOBBS-MERRILL COMPANY, INC.
3 West 57th Street
New York, New York 10019

GEORGE BRAZILLER, INC.
1 Park Avenue
New York, New York 10016

CAPITOL PUBLISHING COMPANY, INC.
850 Third Avenue
New York, New York 10022

CHILDRENS PRESS, INC.
1224 West Van Buren
Chicago, Illinois 60607

CHILTON COMPANY, BOOK DIVISION
227 South Sixth Street
Philadelphia, Pennsylvania 19106

COWARD-McCANN, INC.
200 Madison Avenue
New York, New York 10016

CRITERION BOOKS, INC.
6 West 57th Street
New York, New York 10019

THOMAS Y. CROWELL COMPANY
201 Park Avenue South
New York, New York 10003

THE JOHN DAY COMPANY, INC.
62 West 45th Street
New York, New York 10036

T. S. DENISON & CO., INC.
321 Fifth Avenue South
Minneapolis, Minnesota 55415

THE DIAL PRESS, INC.
750 Third Avenue
New York, New York 10017

DODD, MEAD & COMPANY, INC.
432 Park Avenue South
New York, New York 10016

DOUBLEDAY & COMPANY, INC.
277 Park Avenue
New York, New York 10017

DOVER PUBLICATIONS, INC.
180 Varick Street
New York, New York 10014

DUELL, SLOAN & PEARCE-MEREDITH PRESS
60 East 42nd Street
New York, New York 10017

E. P. DUTTON & CO., INC.
201 Park Avenue South
New York, New York 10003

ENCYCLOPEDIA BRITANNICA, INC.
Britannica Educational Corp.
1000 North Dearborn Street
Chicago, Illinois 60610

FARRAR, STRAUS & GIROUX, INC.
19 Union Square West
New York, New York 10003

FOLLETT PUBLISHING CO.
1010 West Washington Boulevard
Chicago, Illinois 60607

THE FOUR WINDS PRESS
(See Scholastic Book Services)

GARDEN CITY BOOKS
(See Doubleday & Co., Inc.)

GARRARD PUBLISHING COMPANY
2 Overhill Road
Scarsdale, New York 10583

GOLDEN GATE JUNIOR BOOKS
8344 Melrose Avenue
Los Angeles, California 90069

GOLDEN PRESS, INC.
850 Third Avenue
New York, New York 10022

GROSSET & DUNLAP, INC.
51 Madison Avenue
New York, New York 10010

HARCOURT, BRACE & WORLD, INC.
757 Third Avenue
New York, New York 10017

HARPER & ROW, PUBLISHERS
49 East 33rd Street
New York, New York 10016

HARVARD UNIVERSITY PRESS
79 Garden Street
Cambridge, Massachusetts 02138

HARVEY HOUSE, INC.
12 Parkside Drive
Great Neck, New York 11023

HASTINGS HOUSE, PUBLISHERS, INC.
151 East 50th Street
New York, New York 10022

HOLIDAY HOUSE, INC.
18 East 56th Street
New York, New York 10022

HOLT, RINEHART AND WINSTON, INC.
383 Madison Avenue
New York, New York 10017

THE HORN BOOK, INC.
585 Boylston Street
Boston, Massachusetts 02116

HOUGHTON MIFFLIN COMPANY
2 Park Street
Boston, Massachusetts 02107

INTERNATIONAL TEXTBOOK COMPANY
Scranton, Pennsylvania 18515

ALFRED A. KNOPF
501 Madison Avenue
New York, New York 10022

LERNER PUBLICATIONS COMPANY
133 First Avenue North
Minneapolis, Minnesota 55401

J. B. LIPPINCOTT COMPANY
E. Washington Square
Philadelphia, Pennsylvania

LITTLE, BROWN & COMPANY
34 Beacon Street
Boston, Massachusetts 02106

LIVERIGHT PUBLISHING CORPORATION
386 Park Avenue South
New York, New York 10016

LONGMANS, GREEN & CO.
(See David McKay Company, Inc.)

LOTHROP, LEE & SHEPARD CO.
381 Park Avenue South
New York, New York 10016

THE MACMILLAN COMPANY
866 Third Avenue
New York, New York 10022

MACRAE SMITH CO.
225 South 15th Street
Philadelphia, Pennsylvania 19102

McGRAW-HILL, INC.
330 West 42nd Street
New York, New York 10036

DAVID McKAY COMPANY, INC.
750 Third Avenue
New York, New York 10017

MAXTON PUBLISHING CORPORATION
1012 West Washington Boulevard
Chicago, Illinois 60607

MELMONT PUBLISHERS, INC.
1224 West Van Buren Street
Chicago, Illinois 60612

JULIAN MESSNER
8 West 40th Street
New York, New York 10018

MINTON, BALCH & CO.
(See G. P. Putnam's Sons)

WILLIAM MORROW & COMPANY, INC.
425 Park Avenue South
New York, New York 10016

NATURAL HISTORY PRESS
American Museum of Natural History
Central Park West at 79th Street
New York, New York 10024

THOMAS NELSON & SONS
Copewood & Davis Streets
Camden, New Jersey 08103

NEW AMERICAN LIBRARY OF WORLD LITERATURE, INC.
1301 Avenue of the Americas
New York, New York 10019

NEW YORK GRAPHIC SOCIETY
95 East Putnam Avenue
Greenwich, Connecticut 06831

W. W. NORTON & COMPANY, INC.
55 Fifth Avenue
New York, New York 10003

IVAN OBOLENSKY, INC.
1117 First Avenue
New York, New York 10021

OXFORD UNIVERSITY PRESS
200 Madison Avenue
New York, New York 10016

PANTHEON BOOKS
501 Madison Avenue
New York, New York 10022

THE PARENTS' INSTITUTE, INC.
52 Vanderbilt Avenue
New York, New York 10017

PARNASSUS PRESS
2422 Ashby Avenue
Berkeley, California 94705

PETER PAUPER PRESS
629 North McQuesten Parkway
Mount Vernon, New York 10552

S. G. PHILLIPS, INC.
Great Meadows
New Jersey 07838

THE PLATT & MUNK COMPANY, INC.
200 Fifth Avenue
New York, New York 10010

POPULAR MECHANICS PRESS
575 Lexington Avenue
New York, New York 10022

PRENTICE-HALL, INC.
Englewood Cliffs
New Jersey 07632

G. P. PUTNAM'S SONS
200 Madison Avenue
New York, New York 10016

RAND MCNALLY & COMPANY
8255 Central Park Avenue
Skokie, Illinois

RANDOM HOUSE, INC.
501 Madison Avenue
New York, New York 10022

THE REILLY & LEE CO.
114 West Illinois Street
Chicago, Illinois 60610

ROW, PETERSON
(See Harper & Row)

ROY PUBLISHERS
30 East 74th Street
New York, New York 10021

ST. MARTIN'S PRESS, INC.
175 Fifth Avenue
New York, New York 10010

SCHOLASTIC BOOK SERVICES
50 West 44th Street
New York, New York 10036

WILLIAM R. SCOTT, INC.
333 Avenue of the Americas
New York, New York 10014

SCOTT, FORESMAN AND COMPANY
1900 East Lake Avenue
Glenview, Illinois 60025

CHARLES SCRIBNER'S SONS
597 Fifth Avenue
New York, New York 10017

THE SEABURY PRESS, INC.
815 Second Avenue
New York, New York 10017

SIMON AND SCHUSTER, INC.
630 Fifth Avenue
New York, New York 10020

STERLING PUBLISHING CO., INC.
419 Park Avenue South
New York, New York 10016

FREDERICK A. STOKES COMPANY
(See J. B. Lippincott Co.)

TIME, INC., BOOKS DIVISION
Time & Life Building
Rockefeller Center
New York, New York 10020

TRANSATLANTIC ARTS, INC.
565 Fifth Avenue
New York, New York

TRI-OCEAN BOOKS
44 Brannan Street
San Francisco, California 94107

CHARLES E. TUTTLE CO., INC.
28 South Main Street
Rutland, Vermont 05701

UNIVERSITY OF ARIZONA PRESS
Box 3398 College Station
Tucson, Arizona 85700

VANGUARD PRESS, INC.
424 Madison Avenue
New York, New York 10017

D. VAN NOSTRAND COMPANY, INC.
120 Alexander Street
Princeton, New Jersey 08541

THE VIKING PRESS, INC.
625 Madison Avenue
New York, New York 10022

HENRY Z. WALCK, INC.
19 Union Square West
New York, New York 10003

FREDERICK WARNE & CO., INC.
101 Fifth Avenue
New York, New York 10003

IVES WASHBURN, INC.
750 Third Avenue
New York, New York 10017

FRANKLIN WATTS, INC.
575 Lexington Avenue
New York, New York 10022

THE WESTMINSTER PRESS
Witherspoon Building
Philadelphia, Pennsylvania 19107

ALBERT WHITMAN & COMPANY
560 West Lake Street
Chicago, Illinois 60606

WHITMAN PUBLISHING CO.
1220 Mound Avenue
Racine, Wisconsin 53404

WHITTLESEY HOUSE
(See McGraw-Hill, Inc.)

THE WORLD PUBLISHING COMPANY
2231 West 110 Street
Cleveland, Ohio

YALE UNIVERSITY PRESS
149 York Street
New Haven, Connecticut 06511

THOMAS YOSELOFF, INC.
8 East 36th Street
New York, New York 10016

FILM SOURCES

AMERICAN LIBRARY ASSOCIATION
50 East Huron Street
Chicago, Illinois 60611

CHURCHILL FILMS
662 North Robertson Boulevard
Los Angeles, California

CORONET
65 East Water Street
Chicago, Illinois 60601

ENCYCLOPEDIA BRITANNICA EDUCATIONAL
CORPORATION
425 North Michigan Avenue
Chicago, Illinois 60611

GROVER FILM PRODUCTIONS
P.O. Box 303
Monterey, California 93942

JAM HANDY ORGANIZATION
2821 East Grand Boulevard
Detroit, Michigan 48211

NATIONAL EDUCATIONAL TELEVISION, FILM LIBRARY
Indiana University
Bloomington, Indiana 47401

SOCIETY FOR VISUAL EDUCATION, INC.
1345 Diversey Parkway
Chicago, Illinois 60614

STERLING FILMS
316 West 57th Street
New York, New York

WESTON WOODS
Weston, Connecticut 06880

SOURCES OF RECORDINGS

AMERICAN LIBRARY ASSOCIATION
50 East Huron Street
Chicago, Illinois 60611

CAEDMON RECORDS
461 Eighth Avenue
New York, New York 10001

CHILDREN'S READING SERVICE
1078 St. John's Place
Brooklyn, New York

CMS RECORDS, INC.
14 Warren Street
New York, New York 10007

DROLL YANKEES, INC.
Box 2447
Providence, Rhode Island 02906

EDUCATIONAL RECORD SALES
153 Chambers Street
New York, New York

ENRICHMENT TEACHING MATERIALS
246 Fifth Avenue
New York, New York 10001

FOLKWAYS RECORDS
121 West 47th Street
New York, New York

LONDON RECORDS, INC.
539 West 25th Street
New York, New York 10001

NATIONAL COUNCIL OF TEACHERS OF ENGLISH
508 South Sixth Street
Champaign, Illinois 61822

PATHWAYS OF SOUND, INC.
102 Mt. Auburn Street
Cambridge, Massachusetts 02188

RIVERSIDE RECORDS
Bill Grauer Productions, Inc.
233 West 46th Street
New York, New York

SPOKEN ARTS, INC.
95 Valley Road
New Rochelle, New York 10804

BOOK EXHIBITS
AND BOOK CLUBS

BOOK EXHIBITS

Recent years have seen an increasing number of book fairs and book exhibits. A well-planned book fair can be a most rewarding community project. Two helpful references for those planning book fairs are "Seven ALA Criteria for Book Fairs" published by the Children's Services Division of the American Library Association (single copy free), and "Recipe for a Book Fair" published by the Children's Book Council, Inc., at $1.25.

Books for exhibits and for book fairs are available from the following sources. In many cases, selection of the titles may be made by the sponsor of the exhibits. Those wishing to select quality books are referred to Appendix B (Book Selection Aids). Some exhibitors encourage sale of books, while others exhibit only. Advance arrangements should be made. Inclusion on this list does not represent endorsement of any of the exhibits; the sponsor must ask how many publishers are represented, how many books are available, who selects the books, and what the terms are.

AMERICAN PUBLISHERS CORPORATION
 1024 West Washington Boulevard
 Chicago, Illinois 60607
Sends the number of books requested. The exhibit is accompanied by a salesman. Sponsor pays the transportation for one way.

BOOK FAIRS, INC.
 162 Atlantic Avenue
 Lynbrook, New York 11563
Provides an extensive exhibit of books from all publishers for schools and libraries.

BOOK FAIR ASSOCIATES
 1200 North Branch Street
 Chicago, Illinois 60622
Exhibits books for elementary book fairs, schools, and libraries.

BOOK FAIR DISTRIBUTORS
 Mear Road
 Holbrook, Massachusetts 02343
Exhibits new trade books for schools and libraries.

BOOK MAIL SERIVE
 8229 164th Street
 Jamaica, New York 11432
Exhibits paperbound books only.

BOOKS ON EXHIBIT
North Bedford Road
Mount Kisco, New York 10549

An exhibit of over 1000 new books from some fifty cooperating publishers. Two exhibits a year are organized in each grade range: kindergarten–six, seven–nine, ten–twelve. Graded catalogues are provided. Arrangements must be made six months to a year in advance of exhibit.

COLEMAN BOOK SERVICE, INC.
23 East 22nd Street
New York, New York 10010

Sells paperbacks to schools only. Will send books on consignment for book fairs. Transportation is paid.

THE COMBINED PAPERBACK EXHIBIT IN SCHOOLS
Scarborough Park
Albany Post Road
Briarcliff Manor, New York 10510

Organizes and places exhibits of paperbacks in schools for faculty inspection. Prints catalogues of each exhibit for use of faculty and libraries.

CONFERENCE BOOK SERVICE, INC.
201 South Washington Street
Alexandria, Virginia 22313

Cooperative book exhibits with schools and libraries. All fields are represented.

COSMO BOOK DISTRIBUTING COMPANY
Institutional Division
33–49 Whelan Road
East Rutherford, New Jersey 07073

These books are selected from major publishers' lists and include from 200–2000 books. The sponsor pays the transportation one way if the gross sales are under $250.

EDUCATIONAL READING SERVICE, INC.
64 East Midland Avenue
Paramus, New Jersey 07652

Loans books for fairs and library exhibits all over U.S.

FOLLETT LIBRARY BOOK CO.
1018 West Washington Boulevard
Chicago, Illinois 60607

The books are selected by the dealer who sends a representative. The sponsor pays for the transportation one way.

THE H. R. HUNTTING CO., INC.
Burnett Road and First Avenue
Chicopee Falls, Massachusetts 01020

Any number of books are sent for exhibits to schools only. Sponsor is asked to pay transportation for one way.

JEAN KARR AND CO.
5656 Third Street, N.E.
Washington, D.C. 20011

Five hundred books will be sent for a P.T.A. exhibit, and 750 will be sent for exhibits for teachers. The sponsor pays for the transportation.

LORD ASSOCIATES
115 East 92nd Street
New York, New York 10028

Offers assistance to groups planning book fairs. Represents eight large book companies and will set up an exhibit of their books. Also, will lead and direct discussion for groups of librarians and teachers.

A. C. M^cCLURG AND CO.
2121 Landmeier Road
Elk Grove Village, Illinois 60007

Will send up to 1,000 books to school exhibits. Sometimes, a representative accompanies the exhibit. The sponsor pays for the transportation for one way.

MARCO BOOK CO., INC.
577 Albany Avenue
Brooklyn, New York 11203

Given advance notice, this company will loan books for book fairs or exhibits.

MATERIALS FOR LEARNING, INC.
1376 Coney Island Avenue
Brooklyn, New York 11230

Will loan books for book fairs for parent-teacher groups and for book exhibits for schools and libraries.

MELTON BOOK COMPANY
1901 Levee Street
Dallas, Texas 76207

Write for information about special exhibits. Will set up exhibits if given advance notice.

NEW METHOD BOOK BINDERY, INC.
West Morton Road
Jacksonville, Illinois 62650

As many prebound books as required are sent in this exhibit. The sponsor is asked to pay the transportation both ways.

THE NEW ENGLAND MOBILE BOOK FAIR
1980 Centre Street
West Roxbury, Massachusetts 02132

Will exhibit up to 400 juveniles; new titles, classics, and award books are included. Sponsor group gets a percentage of sales.

MARY GRIFFIN NEWTON
  4095 West Buena Vista
  Detroit, Michigan 48238
Exhibits for book clubs, churches, libraries, schools. Annual book show of adult and juveniles is prepared.

NORTH SHORE BOOK FAIRS
  814 Glenwood Lane
  Glenview, Illinois 60025
Some 800 books are sent to exhibits in the Midwest only. The sponsor pays the transportation.

PILGRIM BOOK SOCIETY, INC.
  82 Pembroke Road
  Akron, Ohio 44313
Approximately 450 books from kindergarten through junior high school are selected by an editorial board. Books are arranged by age and interest level and booklists are included. More than 200 paperbacks for the young adult are also included.

RUTH TOOZE
  Santa Coloma Farm, Rt. #1
  Chapel Hill, North Carolina 27514
Ruth Tooze presents a selective exhibit of children's books representing many publishers and a wide range of reading levels. She will discuss the books with parents, teachers, and children.

SCHOLASTIC BOOK SERVICES
  900 Sylvan Avenue
  Englewood Cliffs, New Jersey 07632
Will send an exhibit of their paperback books. Catalogues provided.

ST. PAUL BOOK AND STATIONERY CO.
  6th and Cedar Streets
  St. Paul, Minnesota 55101
The number of books required for any particular exhibit in the upper Midwest will be sent by this company. The sponsor is asked to pay the transportation.

PERC B. SAPSIS INC.
  1795 Del Monte Boulevard
  Seaside, California 93955
Provides exhibits for schools and libraries that are west of the Mississippi. A representative will be sent or not depending on the preference of the sponsor.

SATHER GATE BOOK SHOP, WHOLESALE DIVISION
  6355 Hollis Street
  Emeryville, California 94608
Some 350 books are mailed to any sponsor west of the Mississippi. Sponsor or dealer will select the books.

JUVENILE BOOK CLUBS

The number of book clubs has increased in the past five years. Terms and arrangements vary with each club—some sell only to schools, others to individual children. Inclusion on this list does not represent endorsement. Circulars and other advertising should be studied to determine who selects the books, criteria used, age level, and financial terms.

ARROW BOOK CLUB
  (Scholastic Book Services)
  904 Sylvan Avenue
  Englewood Cliffs, New Jersey 07632
Publishes *Arrow Book Club News* and *Memo: To Teachers.* Paperbound reprints and originals for grades four–six.

BEST-IN-CHILDREN'S BOOKS
  Garden City
  New York 11530
A division of Doubleday, offers books for boys and girls ages five–ten.

BEST LOVED GIRLS' BOOKS
  Garden City
  New York 11530
A division of Doubleday, offers books for girls ages eleven–fifteen.

THE BOOKPLAN
  921 Washington Avenue
  Brooklyn, New York 11225
Personalized service that chooses books for enrolled children and young people through their histories and descriptions kept on file. Ages eight months–eighteen years (founded 1943).

CAMPUS BOOK CLUB
  (Scholastic Book Services)
  904 Sylvan Avenue
  Englewood Cliffs, New Jersey 07632
Publishes *Campus Book Club News* and *Memo: To Teachers.* Paperbound reprints of classics and contemporary books for grades nine–twelve.

JUNIOR DELUXE EDITIONS CLUB
Garden City
New York 11530

A division of Doubleday, provides "DeLuxe" editions of classics and well-loved books.

JUNIOR LITERARY GUILD
177 Park Avenue
New York, New York 10017

A book club for boys and girls ages five – sixteen.

LUCKY BOOK CLUB
(Scholastic Book Services)
904 Sylvan Avenue
Englewood Cliffs, New Jersey 07632

Publishes *Lucky Book Club News* and *Memo: To Teachers.* Paperbound reprints and originals for grades two – three.

PARENTS' MAGAZINE'S READ-ALOUD BOOK CLUB FOR LITTLE LISTENERS AND BEGINNING READERS
Divison of Parents' Magazine Enterprises
52 Vanderbilt Avenue
New York, New York 10017

Books for boys and girls ages three – eight.

SEE-SAW BOOK PROGRAM
(Scholastic Book Services)
904 Sylvan Avenue
Englewood Cliffs, New Jersey 07632

Publishes *See-Saw Book Club News* and *Memo: To Teachers.* Paperbound reprints and originals for kindergarten and first grade.

TEEN-AGE BOOK CLUB
(Scholastic Book Services)
904 Sylvan Avenue
Englewood Cliffs, New Jersey 07632

Publishes *TAB Book Club News* and *Memo: To Teachers.* Paperbound originals and reprints for grades seven – nine.

THE WEEKLY READER CHILDREN'S BOOK CLUB
1250 Fairwood Avenue
Columbus, Ohio 43216

Offers current selections from all leading publishers in two age groups: four-seven and seven-ten.

YOUNG AMERICA BOOK CLUB
1250 Fairwood Avenue
Columbus, Ohio 43216

Offers current selections from all leading publishers for ages ten-fourteen.

YOUNG FOLKS BOOK CLUB
1376 Coney Island Avenue
Brooklyn, New York 11230

Operates through schools to distribute books to young people in kindergarten – grade six.

YOUNG PEOPLE'S BOOK CLUB
226 North Cass Avenue
Westmont, Illinois 60559

Books for boys and girls ages eight – thirteen.

INDEXES

SUBJECT INDEX

A

Adaptations of books, 40
Adopted children in juvenile literature, 221–222
Adventure
  in eighteenth century children's books, 62
  in fiction, 532
  in nineteenth century children's books, 73–74
  poetry of, 413
  stories, 533–534
Aesop, 185, il. 186, 187
Africa
  fiction, 248–249, 534
  folk tales, 160, 164, 165, 167, 175
  informational books, 483
Ages and stages, books suggested, 30–36
Allegory, 262, 344, 350, 361
Alphabet books, 104–106
  criteria for evaluation, 104
Amish, 236
Andersen, Hans Christian, Award, 22, 23; Appendix A,
  722–723
Animals
  appeals of stories, 508
  dog stories, 516–519
  fanciful, in picture books, 135–136
  in fantasy, 346–351
  in folk tales, 175, 178
  horse stories, 512–516
  in humorous books, 373–374

  informational books, 448, 450, 452, 453, 454, 456,
    459, 460, 462, 463, 465, 467, 468, 469, 470, 472,
    476, 477, 478, 479, 480, 481, 486, 488
  life-cycle books, 480–481, 508–510
  nineteenth century stories, 74
  pets as major characters, 218, 227, 239, 510–512,
    516–519
  poems of, 407
  realistic, in picture books, 134
  talking, 178, 453
  twentieth century stories, 86
Anthologies, poetry, 426–431
Anthropology in informational books, 447, 450, 488
Anthropomorphism, 446, 452–454, 464
Appreciation, components of, 658
Archeology, 449, 461
Archetype, 158
Argonauts, 194
Art, 586–587
  activities based upon literature, 613–624
  and literature curriculum, 587
  informational books of, 490
Audio-visual material; *see* Non-print material
Australia, fiction, 219, 253, 533
Authors
  biographical information, 567–571
  letters to, 571
  qualifications for informational books, 446–447
  taped interviews, 559–560
Automation, 460

Awards, children's book, 21–23; Appendix A, 701–723
  Hans Christian Andersen Award, 22, 23, 722–723
  John Newbery Medal, 21, 701–705
  Laura Ingalls Wilder Award, 22, 713–714
  Randolph J. Caldecott Medal, 21, 706–708
  Regina Medal, 22, 714

B

Ballads, 396–397
Basal reading program, 573
Battledore, 63, il. 64
"Beginning-to-read" books, 109
  biographies, 279, 291
  defined, 6
Bestiaries, 60
Bible
  in literature curriculum, 198–203
  poetry of, 416
  selections for teaching, 199, 203
  teaching as literature, 199
Bibliotherapy
  in classroom, 264
  defined, 264
Biography, 274–295
  of artists, 586
  authenticity, 278
  beginning-to-read biographies, 279, 291
  biographers of juvenile literature, 283–289
  characterization in, 275
  choice of subject, 274–275
  criteria for evaluation, 274–278
  documentary biographies, 294–295
  illustrations in, 278
  of musicians, 588
  nineteenth century, 68, 71
  picture books of, 283, 289
  poems of, 413–415
  series, 278–282
  sportsmen, 531
  style of, 276–277
  theme in, 277
  types of, 289–295
Blindness in children's literature, 239, 522
Block prints, linoleum, 115
Book clubs, Appendix E, 747–748
  as discussion groups, 682
Book exhibits, Appendix E, 745–747
Book fairs, 589–590
Book reports, 680–687
  as creative writing, 610–612
  evaluation, 686–687
  forms, 683
  group, 684
  informal sharing, 680–682
  oral, 680–682
  purposes of, 680, 682
  written, 682–687
Book selection, 38–45
  aids, 43–45, 447; Appendix B, 724–734
  curriculum needs, 41
  need for, 38–39
  policy statement, 40, 43
  principles of, 39
  responsibility for, 39
Book Week, 83, 591
Box movies, 620
Britain
  epics, 189–190, 191–192
  fiction, 227, 240, 245, 247, 519, 521, 528
  folk tales, 165, 171, 179–180, 182, 184
  historical fiction, 316–317
Bulletin boards, 565–566, 621

C

Caldecott Award, 21, 22; Appendix A, 706–708
Canada
  fiction, 219, 533
  informational books, 463
Cardboard cuts, 115
Catch tale, 159
Cats
  in picture books, 131, 134
  in poetry, 409
Censorship, 39, 42–43
Chain tale, 159
Chapbooks, 60, 62, 78
Characterization
  in biography, 275
  consistency, 11
  criteria for evaluating, 11
  delineation, 19
  in folk tales, 163
  growth and development, 12
  in literature lesson, 674–676
  in mystery books, 521–522, 533
  in picture books, 112–113
  in realistic fiction, 217, 218, 226, 238
  ways of revealing character, 11
China
  fiction, 246, 534
  in picture books, 144
Child development, 23–27
  books for ages and stages, 30–36
  characteristics of age groups, 29–36
  child study, 36–38
  cognition, 25
  influence of environment, 25
  physical growth, 24
  related to socio-economic background, 40
Childhood, poets of, 416, 420
Children's literature
  content, 8, 40–41
  definition, 7
  related to adult literature, 7
Choral reading, 437
Cinquain, 605
Circulation of books, 5

City life
  in picture books, 131
  poems of, 418
Civil War
  fiction, 309–312
  informational books, 471, 489
Classics, 18–20, 654
  defined, 22
  evaluation, 19
  in literature curriculum, 654
  readiness for reading, 20
  required reading of, 20
  use in elementary school, 20
Colloquialisms, 167
Colonial America
  children's books available in, 59, 60–64
  fiction, 301–305
  informational books, 484
Communism
  in fiction, 238
  in informational books, 451
Community resources, 589–591
Concept books
  informational books, 475–477
  picture books, 133
Conferences
  with parents, 38, 589
  pupil-teacher, 573–574, 681
Conservation, informational books, 454, 459, 468
Counting books, 106–108
  criteria for evaluating, 106
Country life, in picture books, 130
Creation myths, 193
Creative dramatics, 625–631
  defined, 625
  process, 625–631
  values of, 626–627
Creative writing
  based on fables, 186, 188
  book reports, 610–612
  examples of children's, 600–601, 603, 604, 605, 607,
    609, 610, 666, 683, 684, 685, 686
  motivated by books, 604–608
  motivated by poetry, 602, 603, 605, 608, 609
Creativity
  defined, 26
  factors in, 601
Criteria for evaluation
  adventure story, 533, 534
  alphabet books, 104
  animal stories, 508, 515
  appropriate content, 40–41
  biography, 274–278
  characterization, 11
  fantasy, 339
  fiction, 9–18
  films, filmstrips, recordings, 552, 557
  format, 15
  historical fiction, 295–296
  informational books, 446–475
  media of illustrations, 118

mystery books, 519–524
picture books, 109–110
plot, 9
realistic fiction, 217, 220, 221, 230, 233
setting, 10
style, 14
theme, 11
Cultural change, theme in children's books, 247–250
Cumulative records, 37
Cumulative tales, 160
Curriculum guide, for literature, 693

D

Dance, 625
Deafness in children's literature, 240
Death
  in picture books, 129–130
  as theme in fiction, 64, 68, 252, 253–255
Developmental tasks, 26
Dialect, 10, 11, 167, 579
Didacticism, 65, 66, 67, 70, 79, 452
Dioramas, 614–616
Dime novel, 74, 82
Discovery, process in literary criticism, 666, 667
Displays, 566–567
  table 617–618
Documentary biographies, 294–295
Documents and journals, 483–484
Dog stories, 227, 516–519
Dolls
  in fantasy, 351–353
  to interpret literature, 623–624
Dramatic play, 625
Dreams in fantasy, 343
Dwarfs, 179–180

E

"Edgar" Award, 523, 526; Appendix A, 712
Eighteenth century children's books, 59–66
Emblem books, 60–61
Enchantment
  in fantasy, 359–360
  folk tale motif, 169–170
Endless story, 159
Endpapers, 122–123, 472
Epics, 188–192
Eskimo
  fiction, 250–251
  poems of, 431
Evolution, informational books, 448–449
Experiment books, 457–459, 481–483
Explorers in historical fiction, 301

F

Fables, 185–188
  comparison, 185–186

Fables (*continued*)
  defined, 185
  films, 556
  filmstrips, 554
  modern, 187–188
  origin, 185
  single fables, 186–187
Fairies, in folk tales, 179–180
Fairy tale, defined, 159
Fairy tale, modern
  defined, 332
  single editions of, 333–334
Family life
  fiction, 217–224, 230, 231, 232, 233, 235, 236, 237, 242, 259
  future trends in children's books, 89
  nineteenth century books, 72, 73
  in picture books, 126
  in poetry, 400
Fantasy, 338–367
  animals in, 346–351
  criteria for evaluation, 339
  eighteenth century, 65
  fabulous flights, 356–358
  imaginary kingdoms, 343, 346
  lilliputian worlds, 353, 356
  magical powers, 359–360
  in mystery books, 526–527
  nineteenth century, 75–76
  overcoming evil, 360–362
  in picture books, 135–141
  poems of 409, 422
  strange and curious worlds, 339–342
  time magic, 362, 366
  toys and dolls, 351–353
  twentieth century, 85–86
Feltboard stories; *see* Flannelboard stories
Fiction, criteria for evaluating, 9–18
"Fiction factories," 82
Fictionalized biography, defined, 276
Films, 555–557
Filmstrips, 553–554
Finland
  epic, 190
  fiction, 533
"First books," 96
Flannelboard stories, 620, 663–664
Flashback in plot structure, 227, 237, 243
Folk song books, 184–185
Folk tales
  characterization, 161, 163
  collections, 180–181
  defined, 159
  eighteenth century collections, 62
  films, 556
  filmstrips, 553–554
  motifs, 169–180
  in musical form, 184–185
  nineteenth century collections, 72
  plot structure, 160–163
  recordings, 558

  single editions, 181–182
  style, 164–168
  style in picture books, 141
  themes, 168
  twentieth century collections, 85
  types, 159–160
  types of books, 180–185
Folklore, defined, 156
Fools and simpletons, folk tale motif, 173–174
Format
  criteria for evaluation, 15–16
  defined, 15
  factor in children's interest, 29
  in informational books, 469–472
  of picture books, 121–125
Formula tale, 159
France
  epic, 191
  fiction, 221, 243, 245, 518
  in picture books, 143
Free verse, 399

G

Games
  based on literature, 633–640
  in nineteenth century books, 76
Gangs, in children's literature, 226–228
Genre, in children's literature, 655, 658
Geographic series, 484–486
Geography books, 65, 70, 71, 84, 452
Germany, fiction, 247
Ghost stories, 179–180
Government reflected in literature, 238–239
Greece
  epics, 188–189
  fiction, 246, 522, 523
  myths, 193, 196
Guides for evaluating fiction, 17–18

H

Haiku, 399–400, 431
Halftone printing process, 79
Harlequinades, 76
Historical fiction, 295–322
  American frontier, 305–309
  American Indians, 297–300
  ancient times, 313–315
  Civil War, 309–312
  colonial America, 301–305, 524, 527
  criteria for evaluating, 295–296
  defined, 295
  early Britain, 316–317
  European, 313–322
  explorers, 301
  medieval times, 317
  modern Europe, 321
  prehistoric times, 296–297

twentieth century beginnings, 85
U.S. through 1900, 312, 313
Vikings, 315
History, American
  informational books, 448, 452, 462, 467, 470, 484,
    486, 487, 488, 489
History books, 71
Horn book, 63, il. 63
Horse stories, 512–516
Humor, 370–376
  amusing animals, 373–374
  children's concepts of, 370
  fun in everyday happenings, 374–376
  in mystery books, 525
  nineteenth century, 76
  in picture books, 137–139
  in poetry, 411–412, 423
  strange and amusing characters, 370–373
  twentieth century, 85, 86

I

Iconographic process, 557
Identification books, 479–480
Illustrations
  children's interpretations of books, 614
  in informational books, 469–472
  media of illustrations, 114–118
  in picture books, 110–124
Illustrators, biographical information, 567–571
Imagery
  in folk tales, 166
  in informational books, 465
  in poetry, 392–393, 602, 603
  teaching of, 578–579
India
  epics, 192
  fiction, 243–244, 250
  informational books, 456, 478
Indians, American
  fiction, 248, 253, 256, 533
  historical fiction, 297–300
  informational books, 447, 450, 488–489
  myths and folk tales, 161, 162, 169, 170, 179, 181,
    193
Individualized instruction, 546, 547, 549, 550,
    573–574, 665–666
Individualized reading, 573–574
Informational books
  accuracy, 447–448
  authenticity, 446–454
  author qualifications, 446–447
  concept books, 475–477
  controversial issues, 451
  criteria for content, 454–456
  distinguishing fact and theory, 448
  documents and journals, 483–484
  eighteenth century books, 64, 65
  experiment books, 457–459
  facts related to principles, 459

format and illustration, 469–472
generalizations, 450–451
geographical, 452, 484–486
identification books, 479
life-cycle stories, 480–481
nineteenth century books, 69–71
picture books, 477–479
realistic content, 448
recency of, 449–450
science and social problems related, 459–460
seventeenth century books, 60, 63, 64
sports, 531–532
survey books, 486–488
teleological explanations, 454
twentieth century developments, 84–85
types, 475–492
Initial Teaching Alphabet, 573
Instructional materials center, 550–563
Intaglio printing, 79
Interests, children's, 27–29, 67, 507
  age and sex, 28
  ages and stages, 30–36
  defined, 27
  as factor in selection, 40
  factors determining, 28–29
  format, as factor in, 29
  identifying reading interests, 36–37
  in informational books, 456, 463–464
  mental age, related, 28
Ireland, epic, 190
Italy
  fiction, 228
  picture books, 142

Japan
  fiction, 254
  folk tales, 159, 168, 169, 170, 171, 178, 183, 184
  informational books, 452, 478
  picture books, 140
Jews
  in fiction, 218, 237–238
  folk tales, 173
  historical fiction, 321
"Journey-novel," 160
Juvenile books published, 5

K

King Arthur, epic hero, 191
Korea, fiction, 233, 247

L

Language, authenticity of, in biographies, 278
Language awareness, 576–580
  books about history of language, 581

Language awareness (*continued*)
  books about words, 580–581
  in fiction, 235, 253, 509
  in folk tales, 166–167, 180
  sensitivity through literature, 602–604
Language experience approach, 573
Language patterns, 14–15
Language skills
  listening, 574
  in literature curriculum, 657
  oral language, 574–575
Learning
  discovery in, 26
  principles, 27
  theories, 25
Learning environment
  bulletin boards, 565
  classroom management, 564–565
  defined, 545
  displays, 566
Legends, 176–178
Librarian
  censorship, 42–43
  responsibility in book selection, 39
  studying children, 36
Librarian, school
  roles, 560–563
  special services, 562
Library
  activities in, 561
  classroom, 564
  service clubs, 562
Life-cycle animal stories, 480–481, 508–510
Limericks, 398–399, 423
  creative writing, 606
Lincoln biographies, 289–295
Linguistics, 164, 166, 198, 202–203, 575–582
Listening
  materials, 576
  skills, 574
Literary criticism, 656–657
  analysis by child in a conference, 678–679
  examples, 671–680
  process, 666–667
  psychological, 158
  selections for study, 667–670
Literary readers, 551
Literary study, 671–680
  character delineation and development, 674–676
  comparing picture books, 672–673
  fiction analysis, one book, 678–679
  identifying form and setting, 673–674
  poetry, 676–678
Literary understandings, 653–656
  of authors and illustrators, 654
  of classics, 654
  of history of children's literature, 654
  methods of study, 656
  standards of evaluation, 656
  types of literature, 655
Literature
  appreciation, 658

  beauty and inspiration, 652
  children's, defined, 7
  classics, 18–20, 654
  defined, 7
  of "despair," 232
  as enjoyment, 650
  function, 7, 216, 650–652
  influence on child development, 263
  lesson plans, 670–680
  model for creative writing, 604–606
  motivation for creative writing, 602–608
  types, 655
  values to child, 4, 650–652
Literature curriculum
  balances, 692
  faculty planning, 687, 693
  need for, 546, 649–650
  purposes, 652–658, 687–692
  related to art, 586–587
  related to elementary curriculum, 571–582, 650, 657
  relation to language skills, 657
  space needs, 546
  stimulating creative activities, 657
  teaching literature, defined, 650
  time needs, 547
Lithography, 79, 82
  stone, 115
Locke, John, influence on literature, 68
Loneliness theme in children's literature, 250–253
Lyrical poetry, 398

M

Magazines for children, 78–79
Magic objects, folk tale motif, 171
Magical transformation, folk tale motif, 170
Mathematics, trade books, 585
Media of illustration, 114–118
  cardboard cuts, 115
  collage, 116
  crayons, 117
  evaluating media, 118
  linoleum block prints, 115
  opaque paints, 117
  photography, 117
  scratchboard, 116
  stone lithography, 115
  watercolors, 116
  woodcuts, 115
  wood engravings, 115
  use of color, 118
Media programs *Standards,* 550–551
Medieval history
  fiction, 317
  informational books, 484
Melcher, Frederick, 83
Memorization, 657–658
Mennonites, 236
Migrant workers, 240–243, 252
Minority groups, 229–239
Mobiles, 622

Mother Goose
  appeals of, 98
  criteria for evaluation, 104
  editions of, 100–103
  historical background, 61–62
Motif, folk tale, 169–180
Murals, 618–620
Music
  background for selections, 624
  books in curriculum, 587–588
  creating melodies, 624
  folk songs, 184–185
  informational books, 484
  recordings, 557
Mysteries, 519–528
  appeals of, 519
  characterization, 521–522
  criteria, 519
  in fantasy, 526–527
  in historical fiction, 527
  plot development, 520–521
  realistic stories, 528
  style, 523, 524
  theme in, 522–523
  types, 524–528
Myth, definition, 157
Mythic heroes, 193–195
Mythology, 157
Myths
  collections, 197–198
  films, 555
  filmstrips, 554
  gods punish men, 195
  Greek and Roman, 193–196
  Norse, 196
  origin of, 157, 192
  relationships among gods, 196
  selection for children, 192, 195, 196, 197
  teaching of, 192, 196
  types, 193–196

N

National Council of Teachers of English, 83
Nature
  myths, 193
  poets of, 420–422
Nebraska Curriculum Development Center, 575
Negro
  in biography, 286–287, 289
  in children's literature, 87, 529
  in fiction for children, 229–233, 240, 520
  in informational books, 484
  in poetry, 418
Netherlands
  fiction, 218, 245, 258
  in picture books, 143
Newbery Award, 21–22; Appendix A, 701–705
  biographies, award-winning, 289
Nineteenth century books for children, 66–81
Non-graded organization, 549–550

Non-print materials, 552–560
  use of audio visual media, 665–666
Norse myths, 193, 196
Norway
  in informational books, 449
  in picture books, 143

O

Onomatopoeia, 388
Opaque projector, 624
Other lands in picture books, 142–143
Overhead projector, 624

P

Paperbound books, 551–552
Parents
  book lists for, 588–589
  characterization in fiction for children, 217–224
  conferences, 38, 589
  resources for school, 589
  role in children's reading, 588
"Participation" books, 97
Peep shows, 616–617
Peer group in realistic fiction, 224, 228
Personification
  in picture books, 131, 140
  in poetry, 405–407
Photo-offset, 115
Photographs, criteria for informational books, 469, 470, 471, 477
Physical handicaps in children's fiction, 239–240
Picture books, 108–144
  authenticity in, 113
  beginning reading books, 107
  color in, 118–119
  comparison of, 125–126
  consistency in, 110–114
  criteria for evaluation, 109–110
  definition of, 108
  format, 121–125
  foreign settings of, 113
  historical development, 60, 63, 70, 76, 79–80, 83–84
  illustrations in, 110–124
  informational, 477–481
  readability, 109
  style, 119–121
  techniques in reading to children, 660
  types and themes, 126–144
  values of, 96, 108
Picture storybook
  defined, 108
  literature lesson, 671–672, 672–673
Pioneers
  fiction, 305–309
  informational books, 489
Planographic printing, 79
Plot
  contrivance, 226, 231, 233, 242

Plot (*continued*)
  criteria for evaluating, 9
  episodic structure, 218, 255
  flashback, 227, 237, 243
  in mysteries, 520–521
  structure in folk tales, 160
  sub-plot, 224
Poetry
  of adventure and accomplishment, 413
  animal poems, 407
  anthologies
    general, 426
    specialized, 429
    written by children, 431
  ballads, 396–397
  of beauty and wisdom, 415
  biographical, 413–415
  childhood poets, 416–420
  choral reading, 437
  climate for, 435
  content of children's, 400–416
  defined, 386
  discovery lessons, 676–678
  eighteenth century, 66
  emotional response to, 394–395
  everyday happenings, 403–404
  of family and self, 400
  of fantasy and make believe, 409, 422
  figures of speech, 388
  films about, 555–556
  forms of, 396–400
  free verse, 399
  haiku, 399–400
  humorous, 411–412, 423
  imagery in, 392–393
  limerick, 398–399, 423
  lyrical, 398
  narrative, 395, 397
  nature, 420–422
  nineteenth century, 77–78
  nonsense verse, 423
  place in classroom, 434
  poets and their books, 416–427
  presenting poetry to children, 435–436
  Psalms, 416
  recordings, 558, 559
  rhyme and sound, 391
  rhythm in, 389–391
  satisfactions of, 389
  seventeenth century, 60
  sharing poetry with children, 434–437
  single poem editions, 432–434
  sixteenth century, 60
  to stimulate creative writing, 602, 603
  symbolism in, 388
  time for, 435
  twentieth century developments, 87–88
  values of, 386
  war, 414
  weather and seasons, 404
Point of view, 15, 226
  in informational books, 452
Pourquoi story, 160, 162, 178–179, 193

Poverty in realistic fiction, 219, 222, 224, 225, 227, 228, 232, 240–244, 260, 519
Prehistoric period, fiction, 296–297
Prejudice, as theme in children's books, 229–234, 237–238, 321, 523, 531
Printing process, 79–80, 82
Pronunciation guide, Appendix C, 735–739
Proverbs, 202
Psalms, 416
Public library, relation to school library, 563
Publishers' addresses, Appendix D, 740–744
Puerto Ricans in fiction, 233
Puppetry
  construction, 632–633
  selection of stories, 631–632
  values, 631

Q

Quakers, 236

R

Racial problems in children's books, 87, 89, 229–234, 531
Radio, 560
Reading
  basal reading program, 573
  beginning instruction, 573
  individualized program, 573–574
  Initial Teaching Alphabet, 573
  interests of children, 27–29
  language experience approach, 573
  records of children's reading, 37
  skills, 511
Reading aloud, by teacher, 659–661
  books to read aloud, 659
  purposes, 659
  techniques, 660
Realism
  in informational books, 448, 456
  in literature, 216
  in writing, 261
Realistic fiction, 87
  defined, 217
Realistic motif in folk tales, 176
Recordings, 557–560
  dramatization of fiction, 558–559
  poetry, 558, 559
  science, 560
Regina Medal, 22; Appendix A, 714
Regional fiction, 234–236
  defined, 234
Relief printing, 79
Religion in books for children
  eighteenth century, 59, 60, 66
  nineteenth century, 67–69
  prejudice reflected in literature, 236–238
  in realistic fiction, 218
  seventeenth century, 60, 63
  twentieth century development, 86

Revolutionary War
  in biography, 277, 289
  in fiction, 304, 305
  in informational books, 448, 484
Rhyme in poetry, 391
Rhythm in poetry, 389, 391
Rhythmic movement, 625
Riddles, based on literature, 633–635
Robin Hood, 191
Romance, as folk tale pattern, 160

S

Satire, 366, 374
School library
  ALA *Standards*, 550–551
  Bill of Rights, 42
Science books
  eighteenth century, 64
  nineteenth century, 70, 71
  twentieth century developments, 84, 88
Science education, 582–583
  contributions of books, 582–583
  trends, 582
Science fiction, 367–370
  beginnings, 74
  defined, 367
  values of, 367
Scientific method in informational books, 457–458,
    460–462
Scratchboard technique, 116
Selection of books; *see* Book selection
Self concept, 26, 255–263, 457, 491, 530, 545
Self-contained classroom, 542–549
Series books
  biography, 84–85, 278–282
  defined, 6
  evaluation, 17
  family life, 72–73
  fiction, 73–74, 527
  geographical, 71, 84, 87, 484–486
  horse stories, 512, 513
  I Can Read mysteries, 524
  science, 84
  stock characters, 11
Service clubs
  community, 591
  library, 562
Setting
  criteria for evaluation, 10
  in folk tales, 161
  in picture books, 113
Seventeenth century books for children, 59–65
Single editions
  of fairy tales, 333–334
  of folk tales, 181–185
  of Mother Goose rhymes, 103
  of poems, 432, 434
Social-distance scale, as form of book report, 612
Social studies
  books for the curriculum, 583–584

informational books; *see* specific topics
  trends, 583
Society, influences on literature
  eighteenth century, 59–60
  nineteenth century, 66
  seventeenth century, 59
  twentieth century, 81
Spain
  fiction, 258
  folk tales, 170
Sports stories, 528–532
Standards, ALA School Library, 550–551
Stars, informational books, 480
Stereotypes, 87
  in fiction, 229
  in folk tales, 160
  in informational books, 449
  in mysteries, 522
  in sports stories, 530
Story League, National, 590
Storytelling, 661–665
  devices, 664–665
  preparation for, 662–663
  selection of stories, 663
  values of, 661–662
Studying children, 36–38
Style
  in biography, 276
  criteria for evaluating, 14–15
  in folk tales, 164–168
  of illustration, 119–121
  in informational books, 448, 451, 453, 455, 462–469,
    487
  in mystery books, 523–524, 525, 527
  in myths, 198
  of poets, 416–425
  in realistic fiction, 221, 222, 234, 235, 241, 246, 248,
    253, 258, 261
Supernatural creatures, in folk tales, 179–180
Survey books, 454, 455
Switzerland
  fiction, 224, 246, 262–263
  in picture books, 142
Symbolism, 61
  defined, 14
  in folk tales, 163
  in poetry, 388
  in realistic fiction, 223, 231, 241, 245, 253, 517, 519

T

Table games, 637
Taboos, publishing, 450
Tall tales
  modern, 337–338
  traditional, 176–177, 179, 181, 184
Tasks and trials, folk tale motif, 171–172
Taste, development of, 653
Taxonomy of literary understandings and skills,
    688–691
Team teaching, 549–550

Technology, in children's books, 490
Teleological explanations, 454
Telephone interviews, 665
Television, 557, 560, 665
Theme
  in biography, 277–278
  criteria for evaluation, 11
  in folk tales, 168–169
Time, in fantasy, 362–366
Time lines, 618
Toys, dolls in fantasy, 351–353
Trade books
  defined, 6
  for instruction, 6
  minimum recommended, 551
Traditional literature defined, 156
Translations, foreign children's books, 88, 89
Transparencies, 624
Trees, 470, 477, 479, 488
Trickery, folk tale motif, 175
Twentieth century developments in children's books, 81–89

U

USSR
  censorship of Russian books, 42, 43
  epic, 192

fiction, 238
folk tales, 161, 166, 169, 171, 172, 182, 183
informational books, 483

V

Vikings, fiction, 315

W

Wall hangings, 623, il. 623
War
  in children's fiction, 244–247
  historical fiction, 304, 305, 309–312
  poems of, 414
Weather and seasons
  in informational books, 482
  in picture books, 131–133
  poems of, 404
Wilder, Laura Ingalls, Award, 22; Appendix A, 713–714
Wise beast-foolish beast pattern, 160
Wishes, folk tale motif, 173–174
Wit, folk tale motif, 172
Wood engravings, 115
Woodcuts, 115
World history, informational books, 450, 452, 461, 483, 486–487

AUTHOR, ILLUSTRATOR, TITLE INDEX

Numbers in **bold** type indicate an evaluative or descriptive annotation of a book; starred numbers indicate a quoted poem. The abbreviation "il." marks the pages on which an illustration is reproduced in the text. Titles in quotes are poems or stories. The color section is found between pages 136 and 137.

A for the Ark, **106**
A Is for Annabelle, 106
AAAS Science Book List for Children, 447, 728
ABC An Alphabet Book, **104**
ABC Book, An, 83, 104
ABC Bunny, 104
ABC of Buses, 106
ABC of Cars and Trucks, 106
"Aaron Burr," 413
Abbott, Jacob, 71
Abe Lincoln, Frontier Boy, 276
Abe Lincoln Gets His Chance, **292**
Abe Lincoln Grows Up, **292**, 579, 670
Abe Lincoln's Birthday, 291
Abigail Adams and Her Times, 85
About Creatures That Live Underground, 463
About 100 Books, a Gateway to Better Intergroup Understanding, 266
About Roads, 491
About Series, 456
About the People Who Run Your City, 491
"Abraham Lincoln," 397, 414*

Abraham Lincoln (d'Aulaire), 34, 109, 116, 278, 283, **290**, il. 290, 668
Abraham Lincoln (Daugherty), **294**
Abraham Lincoln (Judson), 279, 291
Abraham Lincoln (Martin), 279, 291
Abraham Lincoln for the People, **291**
Abraham Lincoln, Friend of the People, 276, 284, 285, **292**
Abraham Lincoln in Peace and War, 282, **294**, 295
Abraham Lincoln, the Prairie Years, 292
Abraham Lincoln's World, 281, 486
Across Five Aprils, 35, **311**, 612
Adam and the Golden Cock, **304**
Adam of the Road, **320**
Adams, Adrienne, 132, 181, il. 182, 333, 420, 480, il. 480, 587
Adams, William Taylor, 74
Adler, Irving, 463, 490, 492
Adler, Irving and Ruth, 456, 482, 585
Adshead, Gladys, 428
Adventure into Poetry, 438
Adventures in Eyewitness History Series, 483

Adventures in Living Plants, **467**, 483
Adventures of a Naval Officer . . ., 73
Adventures of Huckleberry Finn, The, 19, 75
"Adventures of Isabel, The," 424, 426
Adventures of Pinocchio, The, 76, **351**
Adventures of Rama, The, 192
Adventures of Spider, The, 160, 165
Adventures of Tom Sawyer, The, 75
Adventures of Ulysses, The, 198
Adventures with a Hand Lens, 483
Adventures with a String, 457
Adventures with Abraham's Children, **202**
Adventures with the Gods, 198
Aesop: Five Centuries of Illustrated Fables, 90, 204
Aesop's Fables, 33, 587
Aesop's Fables (Artzybasheff), 115, 186, il. 186, 669
Aesop's Fables (Caxton), 60
Aesop's Fables (Provensen), il. 187
Aesop's Fables (Rackham), 84
Africa: Adventures in Eyewitness History, 483
"African Dance, The," 625

African Traveler: The Story of Mary Kingsley, **285**, 566
African Wonder Tales, 180
"After My Bath," 418
"After the Party," 413
Age of Fable or Beauties of Mythology, The, 203
Age of Fables, The, 197
Agle, Nan, 33
Aiken, Conrad, 408, il. 408
Akino, Fuku, 178
ALA Bulletin, 500
Alain, 107
Alcock, Gudrun, 222
Alcott, Louisa May, 73, 79
Aldis, Dorothy, 88, 389, 392, 394, 397, 400, 401, 402, 403, 404, 405, 406, 409, 418, 419, 426, 436, 602, 608, 676
Alexander, Anne, 106
Alexander, Arthur, 581
Alexander, Beatrice, 197
Alexander, James, il. 464
Alexander, John T., 413
Alexander, Lloyd, 34, 344, 365, 376
Alexander Soames: His Poems, 419
Alexander the Great, 282
Alger, Horatio, 73, 82
Alice in Wonderland, 19, 20, 58, il. 75, 76, filmstrip 554
Alice's Adventures in Wonderland, il. 75, 76, **339**, 423
Alice's Adventures Underground, il. 74, 76
Aliki, 32, 283, 585
All Aboard, 74
All about Biology, 454
All about Books, 84
All about Eggs, 32
All about the Sea, 454
All about the Symphony and What It Plays, 587
All about Us, 476
All American, 531
All Around the Town, **106**
All Day Long, 424
All Except Sammy, **219**, il. 220
All Falling Down, **133**
All in a Suitcase, **106**
All in the Morning Early, **182**
All Men Are Brothers, a Portrait of Albert Schweitzer, 36, 651
All-of-a-Kind Family, 218
All-of-a-Kind Family Uptown, 218
All the Principal Nations of the World . . ., 64
All the Silver Pennies, **426**
All Together, 418, 602, 636
Allen, Chris, 467, 483
Allen, Mary Louise, 406
Alley, The, 522, il. 522, **528**, 612, 656, 670

Alligator Case, The, 34, 525, il. 525, 638
"Alligator on the Escalator," 413, 425
Allingham, William, 78, 410, 625
All-Star Sports Books Series, 532
Almedingen, E. M., 191, 192
Almy, Millie, 46
Aloise, Frank, 184
"Alone," 418
Along Came a Dog, **516**, 636, 638
Along the Hill, 84
Along the Seashore, 480
Alphabet Tale, The, 30, **105**
Altsheler, Joseph, 85
Alvin's Secret Code, 34
Always Room for One More, color section, 117, **184**, 587, 664
Amazing Seeds, The, 488
Ambrus, Victor, il. 227
Amelia Bedelia, 32, **371**, 577
America: Adventures in Eyewitness History, 483
America Grows Up, 488
America Is Born, 455, il. 455, 488
America Moves Forward, 488
American Children through Their Books 1700–1835, 90
American Folk Songs for Children, 185
American Heritage Junior Library, **282**
American Heritage Series, The, 451, 470, 490
American Indian as Farmer, The, 488
American Indian Tales for Children, recording 558
American Mother Goose, The, 411
"American Names," 413
American Practical Navigator, The, 286
American Primer, The, 70
American Revolutionary War Reader, An, 484
American Songbag, The, 397
American Universal Geography, 65
Americans in Space, 490
America's Abraham Lincoln, 34, 276, 284, **293**, il. 293, 295
America's Mark Twain, 284
Ames, Gerald, 458, 463, 482, 483
Amiable Giant, The, **335**
Amos Fortune: Free Man, 10, 35, 275, **288**, 670
Amy and the New Baby, 126
"Anansi and the Old Hag," 175
Anansi, the Spider Man: Jamaican Folk Tales, 673
Anatole, 136
Anatomy of Criticism, 694
"Ancient History," 428
And Forever Free . . ., **311**
And Now Miguel, 35, 234, **257**, 557, 670

And the Waters Prevailed, 297
And to Think That I Saw It on Mulberry Street, 139, 608, 614, 620, 638, 668
Andersen, Hans Christian, 33, 72, 79, 159, 169, 171, 180, 332, 333, il. 333, 334, il. 334, 347, 351, 353, 554, 576, 665, 668, 669
Anderson, C. W., 86, 512
Anderson, Harold, 640
"Andre," 402
Andrew Carnegie, 285
"Andrew Jackson," 413
Andrew Jackson, Frontier Statesman, 284
Andrews, Jane, 71
Andrist, Ralph K., 470
"Androcles and the Lion," 188
Andy and the Lion, 120, 140, 188
Andy Jackson's Water Well, 337
Andy's Wonderful Telescope, 483
Anglund, Joan Walsh, 102, 202, 427, il. 427, 609
Angus and the Ducks, 30
Angus Stories, The, 134
Animal Babies, 117
"Animal Crackers," 403
Animal Family, The, 350, **351**
Animal Homes, 486
Animal Tools, 486
Animal Tracks, 486
Animal Weapons, 486
Animals and Their Ways, 469, 472
Animals as Parents, 35, 453, 459
Animals for Sale, 97
Animals of the Bible, 86, **202**
"Annabel Lee," 427, 432
Annotated Mother Goose, The, 61
Ant and the Dove, The, film 556
Anthology of Negro Poetry for Young People, An, recording 558
Anthropologists and What They Do, 461, 474
Anthropology Curriculum Project, 584
Anybody at Home?, 97
Apache Indians, The, 489
Ape in a Cape, 104
Appel, Benjamin, 275
Apple Vendor's Fair, The, 419
Applegate, Mauree, 582, 641
Appleton, Victor, 82
Appolonia's Valentine, 665
Approach to Literature, An, 694
"April," 406
"April Rain Song," 399, 406
April's Kittens, 134, il. 135
Arabian Nights, The, 62, 85, 171, 175
Araminta, 87
Arbuthnot, May Hill, 46, 90, 203, 265, 323, 376, 427, 438, 535
Archaeology, Exploring the Past, 461

Archer, Sellers, 459
Archetypal Patterns in Poetry, 158
Ardizzone, Edward, 116, 422, il. 522, 620
Are You Square?, 133
"Arithmetic," 435
Arithmetic, 65
Ark, The, 247
Arkhurst, Joyce Cooper, 160, 165
Armed Vision, The, 158
Armed with Courage, **284**
Armer, Laura, 253
Army and Navy Series, The, 74
Arnold, Oren, 452, 454
Arnov, Boris, 509
Arnstein, Flora J., 438, 641
Arora, Shirley, 250
Around the World in Eighty Days, 75
Arrow Book of Poetry, **427**
Art of Ancient Egypt, The, 490, 586
Art of Art for Children's Books, The, 145
Art of Greece, The, 490
Art of Lands in the Bible, The, 586
Art of the Eskimo, The, 490, 586
Arthur, Ruth, 224
Artzybasheff, Boris, 83, 115, 186, il. 186, 669
Asbjørnsen, P. C., color section, 163
Ashanti Folk Tales from Ghana, recording 558
"Ashes my burnt hut," 400*
Asimov, Isaac, 189, 198, 202, 447, 581
Ask Mr. Bear, 31, 141, 620, 663, 664, 668
"Asleep," 394*
Asquith, Herbert, 390, 409
"Ass in the Lion's Skin, The," 185
Assateague Deer, **509**
At Home on the Ice, 470, 472
"At Josephine's House," 403
At the Back of the North Wind, 76
"At the Garden Gate," 424, 437
"At the Seaside," 417
At the Seven Stars, 278
Atwater, Richard and Florence, 34, 86, 373
Auden, W. H., 7
Audio-Visual Methods in Teaching, 592
Audsley, James, 490
August Explains, 32
Augustus Caesar's World, 487, il. 487
Aulaire, Ingri and Edgar Parin d', 34, 84, 109, 116, 143, 198, 275, 278, 283, 290, il. 290, 449, 668
Aunt America, **238**
Aunt Judy's Magazine, 78, 80
Austin, Mary, 391, 403, 408, 412, 414, 421, 426, 436
Authors on Tape, 593

Away Goes Sally, 85
Away We Go, 426
"Aziza," 193

"B" *Is for Betsy*, 638
"B" *Is for Betsy* Series, 33
Baba Yaga, 168, **182**
Babbitt, Ellen, 85, 663
Babe Didrikson, 531
Babe Ruth, Baseball Boy, 531
Baboushka and the Three Kings, 117, 125
Baby Beebee Bird, The, 31, 135
Baby Is Born, A, 35
Baby Sister for Frances, A, 135
Baby's First Book, 96
Bach, 283
Backbone of the King, 14, 15, **194**, il. 195
Backward Day, The, 138
Bacmeister, Rhoda W., 391
"Bad," 394, 418, 609*
"Bad Old Woman, The," 171
"Bad Sir Brian Botany," 395, 413
Bailey, Carolyn, 137, 353, 618, 663, 668, 673
"Bailiff's Daughter of Islington, The," 397
Baird, Eva-Lee, 482
Baker, Augusta, 265, 558, 592
Baker, Betty, 26, 298, 299, 301, 624
Baker, Karle Wilson, 388
Balboa, Discoverer of the Pacific, 281
Baldwin, James, 191
Ball, Zachary, 177, 518, 604
Ballad Book, 78
"Ballad of the Green Beret, The," 397
"Ballad of the Harp-Weaver, The," 397
Ballantyne, Robert, 73
Bally the Blue Whale, 509
"Bam Bam Bam," 425
Bambi, 19, recording, 557
Bangs, John, 410
Banner in the Sky, **262**, 651
Bannerman, Helen, 76
"Barbara Frietchie," 413
Barbara Frietchie, 432
Barbauld, Mrs., 65
"Barber's Clippers," 402
Barclay, Isabel, 463
"Barefoot Boy, The," 388
Baring-Gould, William S. and Ceil, 61
Barnes, Eric Wollencott, 489
Barnet, Sylvan, 157, 655, 694
Barnhart, Nancy, 200
Barrie & Daughter, **313**
Barrie, J. M., 85

Barringer, D. Moreau, 297
Bartholomew and the Oobleck, 336
Baruch, Dorothy, 391, 402, 404, 625
Baseball Trick, The, 530
Basho, 399, 430
Basil and the Lost Colony, **526**
Basil of Baker Street, 526, il. 568
Basket in the Reeds, A, **201**
Basketball Sparkplug, 529
Bat Poet, The, **350**
Batchelor, Julie, 663
Bats and Balls, 530
Battery and the Boiler . . ., The, 73
"Battle of Blenheim, The," 414
Battle of Lake Erie, The, 489
Battle of the Kegs, The, **432**
Baum, Betty, 231, 656
Baum, L. Frank, 86, 340
Baumann, Hans, 314, 449, 586
Bawden, Nina, 522
Bayeux Tapestry, The, 484, il. 485
Baynes, Pauline, 670
Bayou Boy, **235**
"Be Like the Bird," 416
Beach Before Breakfast, The 32, **128**
"Beach Fire," 403
Bear Before Breakfast, A, 577
Bear Called Paddington, A, **373**, 568
"Bear Goes Fishing, The," 179
Bears on Hemlock Mountain, The, 636, 668, 681
Beastly Boys and Ghastly Girls, 429
Beatrix Potter, 594
Beatty, John and Patricia, 278, 323
Beatty, Patricia, 312
Beaumont, Madame, 78
"Beauty and the Beast," 163, 170
Beauty and the Beast, 78, 168, 616
Beck, Barbara, 479
Becker, John, 229
"Bedtime," 403, 419
Bedtime for Frances, 30, 135
Bee Is Born, A, 469, 477
Beebe, B. F., 509
Beeler, Nelson F., 483
Bees, Bugs and Beetles, 467
Beethoven, 282
Beezus and Ramona, 35, **375**, 638
Beginning Science with Mr. Wizard, 459
Beginning to Read Series, The, **279**
Beginnings: Earth, Sky, Life, Death, 193
Behavior Patterns in Children's Books: A Bibliography, 265, 729
"Behind the Water Fall," 410, 422
Behn, Harry, 297, 392, 393, 394, 398, 400, 402, 405, 406, 410, 411, 420, 421, 422, 423, 431, 558
Beim, Jerrold, 32, 224, 227, 609

Beim, Lorraine and Jerrold, 87, 129, 229
Bell, Corydon, 585
Bell for Ursli, A, 142
Bell, Thelma Harrington, 513
Belling the Tiger, **349**, 670
"Bells, The," 433
Bells and Grass, 422
Belting, Natalia, 193
Bemelmans, Ludwig, color section, 31, 112, 113, 116, 143, 662, 668
Ben and Me, 276, 554, 610, 638, 669
Benary-Isbert, Margot, 247
Bendick, Jeanne, 476, 602, 618
Benét, Rosemary and Stephen Vincent, 397, 413, 414, 435
Benét, Stephen Vincent, 395, 413
Benjamin Bunny, 86
Benjamin Franklin, 283
Benjie, 31, 128
Benjy's Bird, 129
Benjy's Blanket, 128
Bennett, Rainey, 135, 609
Bennett, Rowena, 404
Benny, The Biography of a Horse, 512
Benny's Animals and How He Put Them in Order, 456, 476
Benson, Sally, 198
Beorn the Proud, **315**, 433
Beowulf, 189, 190
Beowulf the Warrior, 189
Bequest of Wings, 589
Berke, Ernest, 488
Berman, Morton, 157, 655, 694
Berries Goodman, 10, 35, 43, **237**
"Best Game the Fairies Play, The," 410, 617
Best Little House, 134
Best-Loved Doll, The, 33
Best-Loved Fairy Tales by Perrault, recording, 559
"Beth Gêlert," 397
Bethers, Ray, 454
Betsy Series, The, 374
Betsy-Tacy Series, The, 33
Betsy's Busy Summer, 638
Bettina, 142
Between Planets, 370
Bewick, Thomas, 66
Beyond the Gorge of Shadows, **297**, 367
Beyond the High Hills: A Book of Eskimo Poems, **431**
Beyond the Solar System, 447
Beyond the Sugar Cane Field: UNICEF in Asia, 585
Big Blue Island, **221**
Big Brother, **127**
Big Cats, The, 447
Big City, A, **106**
Big Dig, A Frontier Fort Comes to Life, The, 462
Big Family of Peoples, 463

Big Golden Book of Poetry, The, **426**
Big Little Davy, **126**
Big Rain, The, 132
Big Red, 518
Big Snow, The, 22, 132
Big Tiger and Christian, **534**
Big Tree, il. 489, 585, 660
Big Wave, The, **254**
Biggest Bear, The, 11, 109, **111**, il. 111, 118, **135**, 576, 577, 635, 636, 669, 681, 685
Bileck, Marvin, 137
Billy and Blaze, 512
Billy Boy, 184
Billy the Kid, **134**
Biography for Girls . . ., 68
Biography of an Atom, 468, 473
Bird Watchers and Bird Feeders, 479
Birds, 472
Birds and the Beasts Were There, The, 429, il. 429
Birds in Flight, 463, 488
Birds on a May Morning, recording 560
Birds Will Come to You, 88
Birds with Bracelets, 461
Birth of a Forest, 470
Birthday Candles Burning Bright, 429
Birthday Present, The, 98
Birthdays of Freedom, 486
Bishop, Claire Huchet, 31, 141, 245, 295, 529, 620, 668
Bits That Grow Big, 476
Bixby, William, 282
Black, Algernon, 492
Black Beauty, 19, 58, 74, 654
Black Cauldron, The, **345**
Black Gold, 515, 620
Black Heart of Indri, The, **162**, il. 163
Black Stallion, The, **513**, 620, 634, 636, 638
Black Stallion Series, The, 35, 86
Black Stallion's Filly, The, 513
Black Tanker, 521
Blackbird in the Lilac, The, 422
Blake, William, 66, 394, 398, 408, 416, 427
Blanck, Jacob, 90
Blaze and the Gypsies, 512
Blaze and Thunderbolt, 512
Blaze Stories, The, 86
Bleeker, Sonia, 450, 489
Blegvad, Erik, 333, 419
Blind Colt, The, 512
Blind Man and the Elephant, The, 610
Blishen, Edward, 427
"Blizzard of '98," 181
Bloch, Marie Halun, 36, 238, 491
"Block City," 417
Blood Bay Colt, The, 513
Bloom, Benjamin, 650, 694
Blough, Glenn, 479, 592

"Blue," 603
Blue Backed Speller, Simplified and Standardized American Spelling, 65
Blue Canyon Horse, 512
Blue Fairy Book, The, 72, 180
Blue in the Seed, **233**
Blue Mystery, 634
Blue Willow, 38, 87, **241**, 566, 604, 634
Blueberries for Sal, **111**, 118, 121, 561, il. 566, 668
Boardman, Fon Wyman, 461
Boat Club Series, The, 74
"Boats sail on the rivers," 398, 420
"Bobbily Boo and Wollypotump," 412
Bobbsey Twins, The, 38, 58, 82, 667
Bodkin, Maud, 158
Bodley Family, The, 71
Boer, Frederick, 488
Bogan, Louise, 428, il. 429
Bogart, Max, 553
"Bogles from the Howff, The," 179
Boileau, D., 77
Bond, Michael, 373, 568
Bond of the Fire, 254, **510**
Bonham, Frank, 228
Bonsall, Crosby, 524
Bontemps, Arna, 184, 229, 531, 558
Bonzon, Jacques, 221
Book for Boys and Girls or Country Rhymes for Children, A, 60
Book of Americans, A, 413
Book of Astronauts for You, A, 31
Book of Ballet, The, 490
Book of Children's Literature, A, 204
Book of Courtesye, The, 60
Book of Dwarfs, A, 180
Book of Good Tidings, A, 202
Book of Greek Myths, **198**
Book of Martyrs, 65
Book of Myths, A, 197
Book of Nursery and Mother Goose Rhymes, The, color section, **102**
Book of Three, The, 34, **344**
Booke in Englysh Metre . . ., A, 60
Booklist and Subscription Books Bulletin, The, 44, 732
Bookman, The, 83
Books about Negro Life for Children, 265, 729
Books Bring Adventure Series, recording 558
Books Children and Men, 11, 59, 90
Books to Begin On Series, 473, 486
Boomerang Hunter, 533
Borrowers, The, il. 12, 16, 20, 108, 339, **353**, il. 354, 610, 616, 659, 669
Borrowers Afield, The, 354
Borrowers Afloat, The, 354
Borrowers Aloft, The, 354

Borrowers Series, The, 16
Borten, Helen, 586
Boston, L. M., 35, 342, 343, 361, 363, 511, 606
Bothwell, Jean, 520
Botticelli, 282
Boundary Riders, The, 219
Bourne, Miriam, 131
Bowker Annual, 5
Boxes, 31
Boy Alone, **253**
"Boy and the Water-Sprite, The," 162
Boy Blue's Book of Beasts, 423
Boy of Old Prague, A, 35, **321**, 670, 673
Boy Who Discovered the Earth, The, **367**
"Boy Who Laughed at Santa Claus, The," 424
Boyd, Jennemary, 265
Boyden, Polly Chase, 393
Boy's King Arthur The, 191
Boys of '61, 71
Boys of '76, 71
Boys Will Be Boys, 91
Bradley, Duane, 35, 249, il. 249, 585
Brady, **310**
Brahms, 282
Branley, Franklin, 31, 483
Braun, Kathy, 116, 587
"Brave Little Tailor, The," 175
Braymer, Marjorie, 275
Bread and Butter Indian, **298**
Bread and Jam for Frances, 135
Breakthrough Books, **281**
Breakthrough to the Big League, The Story of Jackie Robinson, 281
Brean, Herbert, 203
"Breeze," 432*
Breman, Thomas, 65
Brewster, Benjamin, 34
Brewton, Sara and John, 429
Brian Wildsmith's ABC, **105**
Brian Wildsmith's Mother Goose, color section, **101**
Brian Wildsmith's 1, 2, 3's, **107**
"Briar Rose," 169
Bridges and How They Are Built, 491
Bridges, William, 477
Bridled with Rainbows, 429
Briggs, Raymond, 100, 101, 587
Bright April, 87, 229, **230**, 638, 657
Brighty of the Grand Canyon, 514, 620, 638
Bring a Torch, Jeanette Isabella, 587
Brink, Carol Ryrie, 12, 35, 296, 307, 669
Bristle Face, **518**, 604
Britten, Benjamin, 490
"Brittle World," 406*

Broderick, Dorothy, 535
Bronowski, J., 468, 473
Bronson, Wilfred, 486
Bronze Bow, The, 35, **314**, 634, 670
Bronzeville Boys and Girls, **418**
Brook, The, recording 560
Brooke, Leslie, 30, 72, 84, 100, il. 101, 101, 102
Brooklyn Girl, **256**
Brooks, Cleanth, 694
Brooks, Gwendolyn, 394, 401, 402, 404, 418, 609
Brooks, Walter, 527, 620
"Brooms," recording 559, 676*
"Brother," 394
Brother for the Orphelines, A, 221
Brown, Beatrice, 412
Brown Cow Farm, 107
Brown, James W., 592
Brown, Marcia, color section, 6, 14, 22, 30, 31, 85, 113, 115, 117, 118, 119, 121, 123, 125, 142, 143, 166, 181, 187, 194, il. 195, 277, 333, 587, 668
Brown, Margaret Wise, 30, 31, 129, il. 130, 131, 134, 136, 614
Brown, Myra, 126, 127, 128
Brown, Palmer, 412
Brownies, The, il. 80
Browning, Robert, 38, 397, 553
Bruner, Jerome, 8, 9, 25, 157, 650
Bruno Munari's ABC, **105**, il. 105, 108
Bryant, Sara Cone, 184
Buck, Margaret, 480
Buck, Pearl S., 8, 254, 281
"Buckingham Palace," 417
Buckley, Helen, 30, 31, 127, 132
Budney, Blossom, 30, 133
Buehr, Walter, 466
Buff, Mary and Conrad, il. 489, 585, 660
Buffalo Bill, 283
"Buffalo Dusk," 421
Buffalo Knife, The, 308
"Bugle-Billed Bazoo," 412
Building Brooklyn Bridge, 491
Building of the First Transcontinental Railroad, The, 467
Bulfinch, Thomas, 196, 197, 203
Bulla, Clyde, 28, 34, 273, 288, 301, 315, 317, 476, 588
Bullard, Asa, 69
Bulldozer, 533
Bulletin Boards, 593
Bulletin of the Center for Children's Books, 44, 447, 732
Bully of Barkham Street, The, 35, **226**, 610, 652
Bundle Book, The, **126**
Bunyan, John, 60
Burch, Robert, 35, 221, 224, 259,

260
Burchard, Peter, il. 13, 288
Burger, Carl, il. 517
Burgess, Gelett, 87, 412
Burkert, Nancy Ekholm, 334, il. 334, 357, 587, 669
Burnett, Frances Hodgson, 5, 73, 79, 247
Burnford, Sheila, 516, il. 517
Burning Rice Fields, The, 126, 184
Burningham, John, il. 358
Burns, Paul C., 592
Burns, William A., 477
Burrows, Alvina, 641
Burt Dow: Deep Water Man, 139, il. 139, 600, 638, 669
Burto, William, 157, 655, 694
Burton, Hester, 322
Burton, Virginia Lee, 30, 31, 116, il. 123, 125, 131, 140, 184, 192, 491, 584, 609, 663, 668
Bushbabies, The, **534**
Buson, 430, 603
"But they that wait upon the Lord . . .," 416
Butterfly Is Born, A, 477
"Butterfly Tongues," 420
Butterfly's Ball and the Grasshopper's Feast, The, 77, il. 77
Butterworth, Oliver, 20, 374, 375
Buzzy Plays Midget League Football, 530
By Secret Railway, 310
By the Great Horn Spoon!, 312
By the Shores of Silver Lake, 307

Cabin Faced West, The, 14, 15, 33, **303**, 612, 667, 669
Caddie Woodlawn, 12, 22, 35, 58, 296, **307**, 547, 669
Caesar, 282
Calculators and Computers, 460
Caldecott Medal Books: 1938–1957, 46, 118, 146, 570
Caldecott, Randolph, color section, 80
Caldwell, John, 465
Calendar, The, 567, 732
Calico Bush, 298
Calico Captive, **298**
"Calico Pie," 411
California Harbors, 450
Call It Courage, 9, 11, 17, 19, 35, **251**, 637, 667, 670, il. 675, 674–676
Call Me Charley. 87, 229, **230**, 657
Call of the Wild, The, 86, 518
Camel Who Took a Walk, The, 139, 557, 668
Cameron, Eleanor, 368, 522, 523, 528

Camp Century: City under the Ice, 490
Campion, Nardi, 289
Camus, Albert, 82
Canalboat to Freedom, **310**
Candita's Choice, 233
Candy Floss, 352
Canterbury Tales, 113, 187
Cap for Mul Chand, A, 663
Cappa, Dan, 29
Caps for Sale, 97, 141, 668
Captain of the Planter, **287**
Carey, Ernestine, 215
Carey, Matthew, 70
Carigiet, Alois. il. 23, 23, 143
Carlisle, Norman and Madelyn, 491
Carlsen, Raymond, 459
Carlson, Bernice Wells, 488, 491
Carlson, Carl Walter, 491
Carlson, Natalie, 10, 33, 34, 40, 219,
    221, 231, il. 231, 243, 248, 610,
    656
Carolina's Courage, **305**, il. 306, 547,
    549, 566, 610, 612, 651, 669
Caroline and Her Kettle Named Maud,
    305
Carpenter, Audrey, 563
Carpenter, Frances, 163, 180
Carpet of Solomon, The, 202
Carr, Rachel, 478
Carrier War in the Pacific, 490
Carroll, Lewis, il. 74, il. 75, 411,
    423, 427, 429
Carroll, Ruth, 30, 97
Carroll, Ruth and Latrobe, 516
Carrot Seed, The, 585
Carry On, Mr. Bowditch, **286**
Carryl, Charles, 412
Carson at Second, 531
Carson, Rachel, 465, 469
Carthy, J. D., 469, 472
Cary, Barbara, 280, 291
Cary, Phoebe, 397
Case of the Cat's Meow, The, 524
Case of the Gone Goose, The, 520, **525**
Case of the Hungry Stranger, The, 524
"Casey at the Bat," 395, 433
Castaways in Lilliput, **353**
Castle of Llyr, The, **345**
Castle of Yew, The, 549, 606
Castle on the Border, 247
"Cat," 409
"Cat and the Moon, The," 409
"Cat Heard the Cat-Bird, The,"
    412*
Cat in the Hat, The, 31, 107, 638
"Catalog," 409
Catch a Cricket, 88
Catch a Little Rhyme, **425**
Catherall, Arthur, 533
Cats, 486

Cats and Bats and Things with Wings,
    408, il. 408
Cattail House, 453
Caudill, Rebecca, 32, 33, 121, il.
    122, 128, 234, 305, 313, 560, 578
Cavanah, Frances, 292, 295, 488
Cavanna, Betty, 479
Cave, The, **258**
Cave above Delphi, The, **523**
Caves of the Great Hunters, The, 449,
    586
Caxton, William, 60, 185
Celestino Piatti's Animal ABC, **105**
Celtic Fairy Tales, 72
Cénac, Claude, 518
Centerburg Tales, 375, il. 566, 638
"Centers for Learning," 592
"Centipede, The," 424
Century: Secret City of the Snows, 490
Certain Small Shepherd, A, 234
Chafetz, Henry, 166
Challenge of the Sea, The, 454
Chalmers, Mary, 127
*Championship, The Complete NFL Title
    Story,* 532
Chancy and the Grand Rascal, **337**
Chang Liang-Ch'en, 407
"Chanson de Roland," 191
"Chanson Innocente," 654*
Chanticleer and the Fox, **113**, il. 114,
    116, 121, 123, 187, 636, 660, 668
Chappell, Warren, 490, 588
"Charge of the Light Brigade, The,"
    397, 624
Charge of the Light Brigade, The, **433**
"Charles," 394*
Charlie and the Chocolate Factory, 35,
    341
Charlip, Remy, il. 130, 159, 608
Charlot, Jean, 84, 670
Charlotte's Web, 5, 10, 15, 16, 20, 21,
    34, 338, **346**, il. 346, 347, 370,
    579, 616, 624, 636, 659, 669
Charm, The, 78
Chase, Alice Elizabeth, 586
Chase, Richard, 157, 167, 181, 184,
    203, 669
Chateau Holiday, The, 521, 528
Chaucer, Geoffrey, 187
Chauncy, Nan, 363
Cheaper by the Dozen, 215
"Check," 405
Chekhov, Anton, 518
Cherokee, The, 489
Chicago Tribune, 45, 734
Chicken Little, 663
Chicken World, The, 84
Chie and the Sports Day, 144
Child Life, A Collection of Poems, 78
Child, Lydia, 76

Child of the Silent Night, 669
Childhood and Adolescence, 47
Childhood and Society, 26
Childhood Education, 44
Childhood of Famous Americans Series,
    85, 273, **280**
Children and Books, 46, 90, 203, 265,
    323, 376, 438, 535
Children, Books and Reading, 28
Children Learn to Read, 29
Children of Green Knowe, The, **363**,
    634
Children of Odin, 34, 191, 196, 670
Children of the Red King, **318**
"Children of the Wind, The," 164
Children Sing in the Far West, The, **421**
"Children When They're Very
    Sweet," 424*
Children's Bells, The, 417
Children's Book Council, Inc., 592
*Children's Books in England and
    America in the Seventeenth Century,*
    59, 91
*Children's Books in England: Five Cen-
    turies of Social Life,* 90
*Children's Books to Enrich the Social
    Studies,* 492
Children's Catalog, 45, 456, 725
Children's Classics, 18
Children's Homer, The, 189
"Children's Hour, The," 388, 427
Children's Hour of Songs and Stories,
    recording 557
Child's Book of Birds, A, 453
*Child's Book of Mankind Through the
    Ages, A,* 450
Child's Garden of Verses, A, 78, **417**,
    recording 557
Chipmunk Lives Here, A, 477
Chippewa Indians, The, 489
Chisel-Tooth Tribe, 486
Chissell, Joan, 283
Chitty-Chitty-Bang-Bang, **357**, il. 358,
    606
Chönz, Selina, il. 23, 142
"Choosing Shoes," 385, 386, 403
Chopin, 283
Christ Child, The, 86
Christian Science Monitor, The, 199
Christmas Bells Are Ringing, 429
Christmas on the Mayflower, 301
Christopher Columbus, 279
Christopher, Matt, 529
Chukovsky, Kornei, 98, 100
Church, Alfred, 189
Church, Joseph, 47
Chute, Marchette, 320, 402
Chwast, Jacqueline, il. 401
Cianciolo, Patricia, 264, 265

Ciardi, John, 187, 389, 406, 412, 424, 427, 558, 651, 694
"Cinderella," 61, 166, 169, recording 558
Cinderella, 6, 22, 62, filmstrip 554, 663
Cinderella (Brown), color section, 31, 85, 118, 121, 181
Cinderella, Pinocchio, and Other Great Stories for Boys and Girls, recording 557
Circle of the Sciences, The, 65
"Circles," 416*, 421
Circuses and Fairs in Art, 490
"City," 494*
City-Country ABC, The, **106**
City Noisy Book, The, 131
"City Rain," 405, 418
City under Ground, The, 35, **367**
Civil Rights, The Challenge of the Fourteenth Amendment, 491
Civil War Land Battles, 489
Clark, Ann Nolan, 257, 512, 578
Clark, Eleanor, 191
Clark, Frank, 451, 460
Clark, Mary Lou, 463, 476
Clarke, Arthur, 454
Clarke, Pauline, 339, 352
Clarke, Rebecca, 73
Clean Pig, The, 636
Clean the Air!, 85
Clear for Action, 533
Cleary, Beverly, 20, 33, 35, 86, 374, 375, 516, 638
Clements, H. Millard, 592
Clemons, Elizabeth, 462, 479
Clever Bill, 83
"Clever Elsie," 174
"Cliché, A" 425, 603*
Clifford, Eth, 577
"Clipper Ships and Captains," 413
Cloud Forest, The, **361**
Clue of the Tapping Heels, The, 519
Coal Camp Girl, 235
Coatsworth, Elizabeth, 34, 85, 258, 387, 391, 394, 395, 405, 407, 413, 415, 421, 427, 516, 561, 677
Cock and the Ghost Cat, The, **178**
Coconut Thieves, The, **175**
Coen, Rena, 490
Coffin, Charles, 71
"Coin, The," 415
Colby, Jean Poindexter, 145
"Cold Winter Now Is in the Wood," 407
Cole, William, 429, il. 429
Collodi, C., 76, 351
Colum, Padraic, 34, 85, 189, 191, 194, 196, 204, 428, 670
"Columbus," 413

Columbus, 283
Columbus Story, The, 32, 284
Colver, Anne, 291, 298
Colwell, Eileen, 663
Combs, Arthur, 25, 265
Come along to Thailand, 448
Come Hither, 427
Comeback Guy, The, **531**
Comenius, John, 60
Comic Adventures of Old Mother Hubbard and Her Dog, The, 62
"Coming American, The," 413
Coming of the Pilgrims, The, 85, 484
Commager, Henry Steele, 487
Commins, Dorothy B., 587
Commodore Perry in Japan, 282
Communism: An American's View, 451
Company's Coming to Dinner, 128
Compere, Mickie, 450
Complete Nonsense Book, The, il. 423
Complete Tales of Uncle Remus, The, 167
Computers: From Sand Table to Electronic Brain, 451, 460
Cone, Molly, 33, 237, 516
Congress, The, 491
Conklin, Gladys, 471
Conkling, Hilda, 393, 399
Connolly, Jerome P., il. 473
Conquest of the North and South Pole, The, 684
Conroy, Jack, 184
Conservation in America, 454, 459
"Contes de ma Mere l'Oye" (Tales of Mother Goose), 61
"Conversation," 424
Coolidge, Olivia, 191
Coombs, Charles, 448, 455, 463, 490
Coombs, Patricia, 34
Cooney, Barbara, color section, 103, 106, 113, il. 114, 116, 121, 123, 187, 422, 426, 555, 660, 668
Cooper, James Fenimore, 73
Cooper, Paul Fenimore, 331
Cooper, Susan, 362
Cooper's History of America . . ., 65
Coppelia, The Girl with the Enamel Eyes, 490
Corbett, Scott, 33, 375, 466, 471, 472, 474, 520, 523, 525, 527, 530, 606
Cormack, M. B., 33
Corn Farm Boy, 235
Cornerstones of Freedom Series, 489
Cortés of Mexico, 285
Costain, Thomas, 281
Cothran, Jean, 181
Cotton in My Sack, 565

Cotton, John, 63
Country Bunny, The, 614
Country Mouse and City Mouse, The, film 556
Country Noisy Book, The, 131
Courage of Sarah Noble, The, 38, **302**, 304, 549, 610, 668
Courlander, Harold, 160, 164, 181, 558, 663
Course of Geography, by means of instructive games . . ., A, 76
Courtship of Animals, The, 453
Courtship . . . of Cock Robin . . ., The, color section, **103**
Cousins, Margaret, 281
"Cow, The," 409
Cow Tail Switch and Other West African Stories, The, 663
Cow Who Fell in the Canal, The, 143
Cowboy Small, 120, film 557
Cox, Hyde, 650
Coyote for Keeps, **510**
Crab That Crawled Out of the Past, The, 460
"Crafty Crab," 175
Craig, M. Jean, 31, 139
Crane, Walter, 80
Crazy Cantilever and Other Science Experiments, The, 458
Creative Dramatics, An Art for Children, 641
Creativity and its Cultivation, 640
Creativity in the Elementary School, 642
Credle, Ellis, 181, 234
"Crescent Moon," 420
Cretan, Gladys, 219, il. 220
Crichlow, Ernest, 230, il. 232
Cricket in a Thicket, 420
Cricket in Times Square, The, **347**, 611
Cricket Songs, 430
Crickets, 34, 481
Crictor, 136
Critical Approaches to Literature, 694
Critical History of Children's Literature, A, 59, 91
Cromie, Robert A., 532
Cromie, William J., 490
Crone, Ruth, 277
Crosby, Muriel, 265
Crouch, Nathaniel, 65
Crouse, Anna and Russel, 275
Crow Boy, 33, **112**, 117, 123, il. 124, 125, 144, filmstrip 554, 584, 669, 685
Crow Indians, The, 489
Cruikshank, George, 80, il. 80
Crystal Magic, 457
Cuchulain, 190
Cummings, E. E., 654
Cunningham, Allan, 398

Cunningham, Julia, 261, il. 261, 348, 361

Cunningham, Ruth, 46

"Cupboard, The," 402

Curcija-Prodanovic, Nada, 180

Curious George, 136, 685

Curious George Gets a Medal, 32

Curriculum Development: Theory and Practice, 585, 594

Curriculum for English, Language Explorations for Elementary Grades, 575, 593, 695

Curriculum for Today's Boys and Girls, 592

Curry, Jane Louise, 162, 193

"Custard the Dragon," 397

Cypress Country, 455, 465

Cyrano, the Crow, 137

D. J.'s Worst Enemy, 35, **224**

"Daddy Fell into the Pond," 402, 426

"Daffodils," 427

Dahl, Roald, 35, 341, 357, 359, il. 359, 611

Daiches, David, 694

Daisy Chain, The, 73

Dale, Edgar, 592

Dalgliesh, Alice, 32, 38, 284, 302, 304, 610, 668, 681

Daly, Thomas Augustine, 436

Dancing in the Moon, 107

Dancing Kettle, The, 171

"Dancing Princesses, The," 170

Dandelion, 109, 118, 137, 669, **672**, il. 673, 673

Daniel Boone, 85, **287**, il. 288

Daniel Boone's Echo, 337

Daniell, David, 199

Danny and the Dinosaur, 31

Danny Dunn, Time Traveler 33

Dark of the Cave, The, **239**

Dark Pilgrim: The Story of Squanto, 288

Darling, Louis, 453, 465, 477, 488

Darton, F. J. Harvey, 90

Dasent, Sir George, 72

Dash of Pepper, A, **513**

Daugherty, James, 85, 120, 140, 177, 281, 287, il. 288, 294, 488, 670

"Daughter of the Dragon King, The," 163

d'Aulaire, Ingri and Edgar; *see* Aulaire, Ingri and Edgar Parin d'

David, 202

David and Goliath, **201**

David Cheers the Team, 529

David, Eugene, 457

David in Silence, **240**

Davies, William Henry, 415

Davy Crockett's Earthquake, 337

Dawn Wind, **317**

"Day Dreams," 410*

Day the Sun Danced, The, 132

Day, Thomas, 66

"Days," 388*

Deacon's Masterpiece or The Wonderful One-Hoss Shay, The, 432, il. 433

Dead Bird, The, 123, **129**, il. 130, 254, 636

De Angeli, Marguerite, color section, 12, 16, il. 16, 87, 102, 116, 167, 200, il. 200, 229, 236, 240, 303, 309, 317, 560, 638, 657, 670

Dear Rat, **348**

"Death of the Hired Man, The," 422

De Borhegyi, Suzanne, 474

De Brunhoff, Jean, 120, 136

De Brunhoff, Laurent, 136

"December Leaves," 388*, 419

Deep-Sea World, The Story of Oceanography, 448, 455, 463

Deepest Hole in the World, The, 468

"Deer, The," 408

Defoe, Daniel, 19, 62

De Gasztold, Carmen Bernos, 409, 558, 609

De Grummond, Lena Young, 531

DeJong, Meindert, 14, 17, 23, 34, 36, 41, 218, 246, 258, 343, 516, 517, 559, 638, 667, 669

De la Mare, Walter, 87, 166, 200, 394, 400, 402, 410, 422, 426, 427, 571, 617, 624

De la Ramee, Louise, 72, 75

Delaune, Lynne de Grummond, 531

"Demeter and Persephone," 193

Denney, Reuel, 263

Dennis, Wesley, 134, il. 514, 515, 669

Denny, Norman, 484, il. 485

"Dentist, The," 402

Department Store, The, 455

De Regniers, Beatrice Schenk, color section, 30, 32, 137, 201, 419, 625

De Selincourt, Aubrey, 189

Description of a Great Variety of Animals and Vegetables . . ., A, 65

Desert Dog, 518

De Treviño, Elizabeth Borten, 289

Deucher, Sybil, 282, 588

Deutsch, Babette, 190

Developing Permanent Interest in Reading, 29

Development in and through Reading, 266

Developmental Psychology of Jean Piaget, The, 25

Developmental Tasks and Education, 26

De Vries, Leonard; *see* Vries, Leonard de

De Worde, Wynken, 60

Diamond in the Window, The, **362**

Diary of Anne Frank, The, 39, 256

"Dick Whittington and His Cat," 176

Dick Whittington and His Cat, 85, 115, 181, filmstrip 553

Dickens, Charles, 72

Dickinson, Emily, 386, 389, 405, 416

"Did You Ever Pet a Baby Goat?," 409

Dietz, Betty Warner, 587

Digging for Dinosaurs, 474

Digging into Yesterday, 464

Diggins, Julia, 585

Dillar, a Dollar, A, 430

Dille, John, 490

Dillon, Eilís, 510

Dillon, Leo and Diane, il. 315, 670

Dines, Glen, 489

Diorama as a Teaching Aid, The, 642

"Dirge for a Bad Boy, A," 424

Discovering Design, 586

Discovering the Bible, **199**

"Discovery," 406*

"Discovery, The," 413

Discovery Books, The, **279**

Discovery, television series 560

"Disobedience," 392

Display for Learning, 641

Divine Songs Attempted in Easy Language for the Use of Children, 66

Do You Know What I'll Do?, 30, 121, **127**, 609

Do You Know What I'm Going to Do Next Saturday?, 31

Do You See What I See?, 586

Dobbs, Rose, 620

Dobry, **256**

Doctor, 72

"Dr. Foster," 100

Dodge, Mary Mapes, 71, 79

Dodgson, Charles, 76

Doering, Harald, 469, 477

Dog Like No Other, A, **518**

Dog of Flanders, A, 75

Dog on Barkham Street, A, **226**, 610

Dog So Small, A, **343**

"Dog's Cold Nose, The," 409

Dolls' House, The, 352

Dolphins, 450

Domanska, Janina, il. 163

Donovan, Frank R., 282

Don't Be Scared Book, The, 32

Don't Ever Cross a Crocodile, 419

Dooleys Play Ball, The, 529

Doone, Radko, 250

Door in the Wall, The, 12, 16, il. 16, 240, **317**, 636, 638, 670

"Doorbells," 402

Dorp Dead, **261**, il. 261, **361**

Dorrie's Magic, 34
Dorson, Richard, 158
Dos Passos, John, 281
Dotty Dimple Series, 73
Doubleday First Guide to Trees, The, 479
Dowd, David L., 490
Down, Down the Mountain, **234**, 636
Down from the Lonely Mountain, 162, 193
Down to Earth, **369**
Downer, Marion, 586
Downer, Mary Louise, 476
Downey, Fairfax, 451
Downing, Charles, 181
Downing, Joseph, 59
Dragon in the Clock Box, The, 31, **139**
Dragon Slayer, The, 169
Dragons, Unicorns and Other Magical Beasts, 179
"Drakestail," 178
Draper, Marcella K., 592
Dreaming Zoo, The, 408
"Dreams," 395*, 428
Dreany, E. Joseph, 450
Druon, Maurice, 360
Du Bois, William Pène, 34, 35, 86, 347, 358, 359, il. 359, 371, 373, 525, il. 525, 611, 614, 638, 668, 670
Duchess Bakes a Cake, The, 32, 120, 141
"Duck and the Kangaroo, The," 423
Duckett, Alfred, 281
"Duel, The," 78, 397
Duff, Annis, 428, 589
"Dunkirk," 414*
Dunning, Stephen, 428
Dupuy, Trevor Nevitt, 471, 489
Durango Street, **228**
Durer, 586
Durkin, Dolores, 25
"Dust of Snow," 415*, 422
Duvoisin, Roger, color section, 31, 84, 106, 107, 118, 119, 123, 130, 131, 132, 136, 143, il. 162, 664, 668, 673
Dwarf Pine Tree, The, **168**

E. Nesbit, 594
Eager, Edward, 20, 352, 359, 360
Eagle of the Ninth, 316
Eakin, Mary K., 492
Earle, Olive L., 34, 481, 488
Early, Margaret, 694
Early Moon, 387, 389, 421, 438
Earth for Sam, The, 84
Earth Is the Lord's: Poems of the Spirit, The, 430
Earthfasts, 179, 339, **365**
Earthworms, 483
East, Marjorie, 641

"East of the Sun and West of the Moon," 170
East of the Sun and West of the Moon and Other Tales, 163
East O' the Sun and West O' the Moon, 85
Easter in November, 477
Easy Lessons, 68
Easy Lessons for Children, 65
Easy Puppets, 641
"Eat-It-All Elaine," 419
Eaton, Jeannette, 289
Eberle, Irmengarde, 463, 477
Echoes, 472
Eclectic Readers, 70
Economakis, Olga, 143
Eddie and His Big Deals, 374, 638
Edge of April: A Biography of John Burroughs, The, 287
Edge of the Forest, An, **350**
Edgeworth, Maria, 68
Edmonds, Walter, 273, 298, 303, 308, 669, 680
Educated Imagination, The, 199, 204, 377, 694
Educational Film Library Association, 592
Eeckhoudt, J. P. Vanden, 477
"Eel, The," 424
Egg and I, The, 371
Egg Tree, The, 618, 635
Eichenberg, Fritz, 84, 104, 106
8 A.M. Shadows, **419**
Ekrem, Selma, 166, 181
Eleanor Farjeon's Poems for Children, 417
Eleanor Roosevelt, Courageous Girl, 280
Elementary and Junior High School Mathematics Library, The, 585
Elementary English, 29, 44, 204, 265, 266, 563, 571, 603, 659, 694, 733
Elementary School Science and How to Teach It, 592
Elementary School We Need, The, 593
"Elephant, The," 408
Elephants, 478
Elephant's Bathtub, Wonder Tales from the Far East, The, 180
"Elephant's Child, The," 632, 663
Elephant's Child, The, **373**, recording 558
Elephants, The Last of the Land Giants, 447
"Eletelephony," 392, 412
"Elf and the Dormouse, The," 397, 410
Elgin, Kathleen, 198
Elin's Amerika, 303
Eliot, T. S., 409, 558
Elisabeth and the Marsh Mystery, **524**
Elizabeth, the Treasure Hunter, 462

Elkin, Benjamin, 108
Ellen Tebbits, 33
Ellen's Bluejays, 452
Elsie Dinsmore Series, 73
"Elsie Piddock Skips in Her Sleep," 663
"Elves and the Shoemaker, The," 72, 166
Elves and the Shoemaker, The, 166, filmstrip 553, 554
Emberley, Barbara and Ed, 133, 134, 184
Emery, Anne, 524, 527
Emil and the Detectives, 88, 526, 559
Emil and the Three Twins, 526
Emile, 27
Emilio's Summer Day, **131**
Emma in Winter, **360**
Emperor and the Drummer Boy, The, **321**
Emperor's New Clothes, The, 333, filmstrip 554, recordings 558 and 559, 668
"Emperor's Nightingale, The," recording 559
Empty Schoolhouse, The, 10, 41, **231**, il. 231, 565, 656
Enchantment of America Series, 484
Encyclopedia Brown, Boy Detective, 525
Encyclopedia Brown Strikes Again, 526
Enemy at Green Knowe, An, **361**
English Children's Books 1600 to 1900, 91
English Fairy Tales, 72
Enormous Egg, The, **374**, 634, 636
Enright, Elizabeth, 33, 217, 343, il. 344, 609, 618
"Epitaph for a Concord Boy," 414
Epstein, Sam and Beryl, 34, 90, 280, 531, 532, 581
Erdoes, Richard, 462
Erickson, Phoebe, 453
Erie Canal, The, 470
Erikson, Erik H., 26
Escape to King Alfred, 316
Eskimo in Life and Legend, The, film 555
Estes, Eleanor, 33, 87, 217, 225, 522, il. 522, 528, 612, 656, 670
Ets, Marie Hall, 30, 118, 121, 132, 140, 141, 143, 477
Evans, Eva Knox, 87, 476
"Evening," 405*
Everybody Ought to Know, 430
"Everybody Says," 400*
Everything Has a Shape, 585
Everything Has a Size, 585
Evslin, Bernard, 198
Ewen, David, 588
Ewing, Mrs., 71, 78, il. 80
Experiment in Criticism, An, 216, 264, 266

Experiments in Sky Watching, 483
Experiments with a Microscope, 483
Experiments with Machines and Matter, 458, 483
Exploring Reading in the Primary Grades, 28
"Extraordinary Black Coat, The," 178

FDR Story, The, 286
Faber, Doris, 36
Fables from Aesop, 185
Fables of Bidpai, The, 185
Fables of La Fontaine, The, 186
Fabulous Flight, The, **356**, 357, 571, 638
Fabulous Histories, 65
Fahs, Sophia Lyn, 193
Fair World for All, A, 466, 491
Fairchild Family, The, 68
"Fairies, The," 410
"Fairy and the Bird, The," 422
Fairy Doll, The, 352
Fairy Elves: A Dictionary of the Little People . . ., 179
Fairy Shoemaker and Other Poems, The, 84
Fairy Tales, 159, il. 333
Fall, Thomas, 310
"Falling Star, The," 405, 421
Fallis, Edwina, 625
"Fallow Deer, The," 408
"Fallow Deer at the Lonely House, The," 408
Falls, C. B., 83, 104
Family Conspiracy, The, 219
Family of Foxes, A, **510**
Family under the Bridge, The, 243
Famous Myths of the Golden Age, 197
Famous Negro Athletes, 531
Famous Negro Music Makers, 588
Famous Paintings, 586
Fantasy Stories, filmstrip series 554
Far and Few, 424, 609
"Far and Near,", 393*
Far Out the Long Canal, 17, 34, **218**
Faraway Lurs, The, **297**
Farewell to Arms, A, 8
Farjeon, Eleanor, 386, 389, 390, 394, 395, 403, 409, 412, 417, 418, 435, 555
Farley, Walter, 35, 86, 507, 513, 620
Farm Book, The, 84
"Farmer Grigg's Boggart," 179
Farmer, Penelope, 35, 360
Farther and Faster, 585
Fast Is Not a Ladybug, 133
Fast Sooner Hound, The, 183
Faster and Faster, a Book about Speed, 476

"Father William," 411, 423
Fatio, Louise, 123, 143, 668
Faulkner, Georgene, 229
Faulkner, Nancy, 521
Faulknor, Clifford, 533
Faun and the Woodcutter's Daughter, The, 181
Favorite Fairy Tales Told in Czechoslovakia, 164, il. 180
Favorite Fairy Tales Told in France, 162, il. 162
Favorite Fairy Tales Told in Germany, 180
Favorite Fairy Tales Told in Italy, 180
Favorite Fairy Tales Told in Russia, 180
Favorite Fairy Tales Told in Sweden, 162
Favorite Poems Old and New, 427
"Fawn," 408
Fax, Elton, 230
"Feelings about Words," 604
"Feet," 602
Felice, color section, 114, 123
"Feller I Know, A," 403, 421
Felsen, Gregor, 367
Felt, Sue, 31, 128, 131
Fenner, Carol, 140
Fenner, Phyllis, 46
Fenton, Carroll, 84
Fenton, Edward, 526
Fenwick, Sara, 563
Ferdinand the Bull, filmstrip 554
"Fern Hill," 428
Ferris, Helen, 427, 570
"Ferry-Boats," 418
Feuerlecht, Roberta, 176
Field, Elinor Whitney, 46, 146, 323, 570
Field, Eugene, 78, 389, 397
Field Guide to the Birds, A, 460
Field, Rachel, 88, 298, 353, 401, 402, 404, 405, 407, 418, 426, 427, il. 567, 665
Fielding, Sarah, 65
Fifth Reader, 70
Fifty Years of Children's Books 1910–1960: Trends, Backgrounds, Influences, 91
Figure Skating, 532
"Figures of Speech," 424
Fillmore, Parker, 85
Film Evaluation Guide, 592
Filmer-Sankey, Josephine, 484, il. 485
Finders Keepers, 141
Finley, Martha, 73
"Fir Tree, The," 351, 665
"Fire-Bird, the Horse of Power, and the Princess Vasilissa, The," 172
Fire Hunter, 297

Fire on the Mountain, The, 164
Fireflies in the Night, 31, 458
First Animals, The, 636
First around the World, 484
First Bible, A, 86
First Book Edition of Casey at the Bat, The, 433
First Book Edition of the Gettysburg Address, The Second Inaugural, The, 294
First Book of American History, The, 487
First Book of Automobiles, The, 618
First Book of Baseball, The, 34
First Book of Birds, The, 456, 457, 471, 472, 479
First Book of Civil War Land Battles, The, 471
First Book of Codes and Ciphers, The, 34
First Book of Ethics, The, 492
First Book of Experiments, The, 455, 458
First Book of Language and How to Use It, The, 582
First Book of Mars, The, 451, 473
First Book of Music, The, 587
First Book of Mythology, The, 198
First Book of Poetry, The, 426
First Book of Printing, The, 90
First Book of Puppets, The, 641
First Book of Science Experiments, The, 482
First Book of Short Verse, The, **426**
First Book of Stones, The, 33
First Book of Swimming, The, 34
First Book of Tales of Ancient Araby, The, 176
First Book of Tales of Ancient Egypt, The, 181
First Book of the American Revolution, The, 584
First Book of the Early Settlers, The, 448
First Book of Weeds, The, 479
First Book of Wildflowers, The, 479
First Book of Words, The, 581
First Book Series, The, 84, 479, 489
First Days of the World, The, 463
First Delights, **133**
First Night Away from Home, **127**
First of May, The, 80
First Seven Days, The, 201
"First Snow, The," 406
First Year, The, 301, 617
Fischer, Hans, 165
Fish, Helen, 202
Fisher, Aileen, color section, 31, 88, 128, 132, 134, 295, 383, 401, 404, 405, 406, 407, 420, 426, 509, 558, 609, 668

Fisher, Dorothy Canfield, 8, 281, 466, 491
Fisher, James, 469
Fisher, Leonard Everett, 143, 294, 433, il. 455, 484, 489
Fisher, Margery, 46, 377, 532, 533, 535
Fisherman and His Wife, The, 174, recording, 559
Fitch, Florence Mary, 86, 584
Fitzhugh, Louise, 41, 225, 234, 312, 612
Fitzimmons, Robert, 532
Five Chinese Brothers, The, 31, 141, 559, 620, 668
500 Hats of Bartholomew Cubbins, The, **336**, 638, 669
Five Little Peppers, The, 58
Five Little Peppers Series, The, 73
Flack, Marjorie, 5, 30, 31, 32, 126, 134, 141, 144, 568, 620, 663, 668
Flaming Arrows, 308
Flash, The Life Story of a Firefly, 472, 480
Flattered Flying Fish and Other Poems, The, 424
Flavell, John, 25
"Flaxen Thread, The," 170
Fleet, Thomas, 62
Fleischman, Sid, 312, 337, 338
Fleming, Ian, 357, il. 358, 606
Fleming, Robert S., 592
Flip, 134
Flip and the Cows, 134
Flora, James, 139, 606
Florian, 198
Florina and the Wild Bird, 142
Flower, The, 476
Flowers of Delight, il. 77, 77, 90
Fly High, Fly Low, 113
"Flying Ship, The," 171
"Fog," 399
Fog Magic, 339, **363**
Folk and Festival Costumes of the World, 488
Folk Instruments, 490
Folk Songs of China, Japan, Korea, 587
Folk Tales from Indonesia, recording 558
Folk Tales from West Africa, recording 558
"Folk Who Live in Backward Town, The," 419
Folktale, The, 159, 169, 204
Follow My Black Plume, 322
Follow My Leader, **239**
Follow the Sunset, 477, 636
Folmsbee, Beulah, 90
Folsom, Franklin, 474
Fon Eisen, Anthony, 254, 510
Football for Boys, 532

Forbes, Esther, 240, 305, 670
"Foreign Children," 417
"Forget," 604
"Forgiven," 397
Forgotten Door, The, **368**
Forman, James, 246, 254
Forsee, Aylesa, 289
Fortnum, Peggy, 373
Fortunately, 159, 608
Fortune Magazine, 82
Foss, Sam Walter, 413
Foster, Genevieve, 280, 281, 486, il. 487, 618
Foster, Joanna, 145
Four Fur Feet, The, 614
"Four Little Foxes," 406, 407
Four Musicians, The. filmstrip and record, 554
Four Paws into Adventure, **518**
Fox, Charles P., 88
Fox and the Fire, The, 135
Fox Went Out on a Chilly Night, The, filmstrip 554, 587
Foxe, John, 65
Foxes Live Here, 477
Frame, Paul, 433
Francis, Robert, 405, 430
Francoise, 30, 96, 107, 120, 132, 143, 557
Frankenberg, Robert, 293
Franklin, K. L. 447
Frasconi, Antonio, 103, il. 115, 115
Frazer, Sir James, 158
Freddy the Detective, 527
Free Men Must Stand, 489
Freedom, 484
Freedom Train, The Story of Harriet Tubman, **287**
Freeing Children to Write, 641
Freeman, Don, 109, 113, 118, 137, 138, 669, 672, il. 673
Freeman, Ira M. and Mae B., 84, 482
French Revolution, The, 490
Freschet, Berniece, 464, il. 464, 481
Fresh Look at Night, A, 476, 602
Freud, Sigmund, 158
Freund, Philip, 158
Frick, C. H., 531
Friedman, Estelle, 449, 460, 464
Friend Is Someone Who Likes You, A, 609
Friendly Dolphins, The, 474
"Friendly Giant, The," television film series 557
Fries, Charles C., 575
Frigid World of Cryogenics, The, 490
Frightened Hare, The, 509
Friskey, Margaret, 97, 134, 295
Fritz, Jean, 14, 33, 179, 303, 309, 310, 354, 355, 611, 612, 667, 669

"Frog Prince, The," 170
Frog Went A-Courtin', 117, 184, 587, 634
"From a Railway Carriage," 390
From Primer to Pleasure: An Introduction to the History of Children's Books in England . . ., 91
From Rollo to Tom Sawyer, 90
From the Eagle's Wing, **287**
From Two to Five, 98
Froman, Robert, 476
Frontiers of America Series, 489
Frost, Frances, 171, 403, 407, 420, 488
Frost, Robert, 386, 387, 388, 389, 392, 406, 407, 409, 414, 415, 421, 422, 426, 427, 558, 650
Fruit Is Born, A, 477
Fry, Rosalie, 520, 527
Frye, Northrop, 158, 199, 204, 377, 694
Full of Wonder, 586
Fuller, Muriel, 570
Fun with Science, 482
Fun with Your Microscope, 483
Funai, Mamoru, 126
"Funny the Way Different Cars Start," 404
Fyleman, Rose, 394, 402, 410, 422, 437, 617

Gaelic Ghosts, 180, 181
Gág, Wanda, 30, 83, 85, 104, 110, il. 110, 118, 141, 164, 166, 181, 554, 663, 668
Gage, Wilson, 221, 372
Gaggle of Geese, A, **581**
Gaily We Parade, 429
Gainsborough, 586
Galdone, Paul, 84, 103, 127, 201, 432, il. 433, 581, 664, 669
Galileo, 652
Gallant, Roy A., 84
"Galoshes," 391
Galumph, **131**
Game of Baseball, The, 532
Gammage Cup, The, **355**
Gannett, Ruth, 353
"Garden at Night, A," 422
Garelick, May, color section, 112, 117, 479
Garfield, James, 239
Garis, Howard, 82
Garis, Roger, 82, 90
Garnett, Richard, 336
Garten, Jan, 30, 105
Garthwaite, Marion, 242
Gate of Worlds, The, **365**
Gates, Doris, 38, 87, 241, 604
Gatty, Mrs. Margaret, 71, 78
Gaudenzia, **514**

Gaver, Mary Virginia, 550, 725
Gay-Neck, The Story of a Pigeon, **511**
Gay, Zhenya, 394, 409
Gega, Peter, 593
Geis, Darlene, 456
Geisel, Theodor; *see* Seuss, Dr.
Geismer, Barbara, 426
Gelman, Steve, 531
"General Store," 418
Gentle Ben, **510**
"Geography," 435
George and the Cherry Tree, 283
George, Jean, 20, 36, 223, 251, 252, 459, 481, 620
George, John and Jean, 481
George Washington (d'Aulaire), 283
George Washington (Judson), 279
George Washington Carver, 280
George Washington: Frontier Colonel, 281
George Washington, Leader of the People, 284
George Washington's World, 281, 486
"Get Up and Bar the Door," 396
Getting to Know American Indians Today, 488
Getting to Know Series, 485
Getzels, Jacob W., 29
Ghost of Peg-Leg Peter, The, **177**
Ghosts Go Haunting, **180**
"Giant Shoes, The," 625
Gidal, Sonia and Tim, 452
Gift of the Forest, recording 558
"Gift Outright, The," 414
"Gift to Be Simple, The," 414
Gilbert, W. S., 395
Gilberto and the Wind, 118, 121, **132,** 477, 490
Gilbreth, Frank, 215
Gingerbread Man, The, 664
Gipson, Fred, 518
Girl's Own Book, The, 76
Gladstone, William, 79
Glaser, Milton, il. 408
Gleazer, Nathan, 263
Gleeson, J. M., 669
Glemser, Bernard, 454
Glooscap's Country, film 555 and 666
"Glowworm," 412
Glubok, Shirley, 490, 586
"Gnome, A," 422
Go, Team, Go, 531
"Goblinade, A," 410
Godden, Rumer, 8, 33, 347, 352, 609, 665
"Godfrey Gordon Gustavus Gore," 391
"God's Grandeur," 392
Going Barefoot, 133, 420
"Going to Sleep," 418
Golden Bible, The, **200**

Golden Book of America, The, 488
Golden Bough, The, 158
Golden Crane, The, **183**
Golden Eagle, The, 481
Golden Fleece, The, 194
Golden Goblet, The, **314**
Golden Hamsters, 34, 488
Golden Hive, The, **420**
Golden Journey, The, **428,** il. 429
"Golden Journey to Samarkan," 428
Golden Nature Guides, 479
"Golden Phoenix, The," 172
Golden Phoenix, The, 167
Golden Touch, The, 195, 669
Golden Treasury of Myths and Legends, The, 189, 191, 198
Golden Treasury of Natural History, The, 486
Golden Treasury of Poetry, The, 427, il. 427
Goldilocks and the Three Bears, 30, film 556
Goldin, Augusta, 478
Goldman, Peter, 491
Goldsmith, Oliver, 63
Goldwater, Daniel, 491
Golf for Boys and Girls, 532
Gone Is Gone, 663
Gone with the Wind, 39
Good Bird, The, 97
Good Books for Children, 492, 727
"Good Boy, A," 417
Good Master, The, 22, 35, 58, **255,** 449, 633, 669
Good Night Moon, 30
"Good or Bad?," 159
"Good Play," 78
Goodbye My Lady, **519**
Goodrich, Samuel, 70
"Goody O'Grumpity," 403
Goody Two Shoes, 61
Goops and How to Be Them, 87
"Goose Girl, The," recordings 558 and 559
Goose Girl, The, 167
"Goose Hans," 174
Gorbarty, Norman, 586
Gordon, Ira J., 24
Gorey, Edward, 424
Gorgon's Head, The, 194
Gottlieb, Gerald, 198
Gottlieb, Robin, 521
Goudey, Alice, 480, il. 480, 481, 681
Goulden, Shirley, 490
Goya, 282
Gracza, Margaret, 586
Graham, Harry, 424
Graham, Lorenz, 35, 231, il. 232
Graham, Margaret Bloy, 672
Grahame, Kenneth, 8, il. 20, 85, 336, 349, 350, 571, 654, 661, 670

Gramatky, Hardie, 30, 140, il. 140, 620, 668
Grand Prix at the Glen, 532
Grandfather and I, 30, 127
Grandmother and I, 127
Grandpa's Farm, 139
Grant, Madeleine, 461
Grass Rope, A, **342**
"Grasshopper, The," 424
Graves, Robert, 194
Gray, Elizabeth Janet, 320
Great Composers Series, 282
Great Geppy, The, **373,** 638
Great Quillow, The, 335
Great Rebellion, The, 349
Great Smoky Mountains, Everglades, Mammoth Cave, 464
Great Tree of Life, The, 461
Great Wheel, The, **312**
"Greatest Hoax in New York City," 177
Greece, 469
Greek Gods, The, 198
Greek Gods and Heroes, 194
Green Fairy Book, The, 72
"Green Hill Neighbors," 407
"Green Moth, The," 392*, 422
Green, Mary, 134
Green, Roger L., 193
Green Tree House, The, 462
Greenaway, Kate, 78, 80, il. 81, 100, 102
Gregor, Arthur, 117, 652
Greyhound, The, **227,** il. 227, 519
Grifalconi, Ann, il. 233
Griffiths, Helen, 9, 227, il. 227, 515, 519
Grimm, Jacob and Wilhelm, 41, 58, 72, 80, 157, 169, 170, 171, 174, 180, 182, il. 182, il. 183, 332, 554
Grimms' Fairy Tales, recording 559
Gringhuis, Dick, 462
Grishka and the Bear, **510**
Grizzly, The, 222
"Grizzly Bear," 412, 421, 426, 436
Growing Story, The, 30
Growth of Logical Thinking, The, 25
Grossbart, Francine, 106
Gruenberg, Sidonie, 32
Grund, Josef, 228
Guard for Matt, 530
"Gudbrund on the Hillside," 172
Guiding Creative Talent, 641
Guilcher, J. M., 477
Guilfoile, Elizabeth, 109
Guillot, René, 164, 510
Guillot's African Folk Tales, 164
Guiterman, Arthur, 409, 428, 437
Gull 737, 36, **223,** 657
Gulliver among the Lilliputians, filmstrip 554

Gulliver's Travels, 62, 84, 353
Gull's Way, The, 453, 465, 477
Gunther, John, 194
Gurko, Miriam, 289
Guy of Warwick, 60
Gwynne, John, 201

Haachen, Frans, color section, 116, 588
Haas, Irene, 344, il. 344, 419
Haber, Heinz, 620
Hader, Berta and Elmer, 22, 132, 664
Hailstones and Halibut Bones, **425**, il. 425, film 556, 603
"Hairy Dog, The," 409
Hakon of Rogen's Saga, 8, 14, 15, **315**, il. 315, 433, 604, 651, 670
Hale, Lucretia, 79, 371
Half Magic, **359**
"Halfway Down," 391, 417
Hall, Donald, 428
"Halloween," 419
Halmi, Robert, 6
Hamilton, Edith, 204
Hamilton, Lee David, 490
Handforth, Thomas, 144
Hannah Elizabeth, **236**
Hannum, Sara, 428
Hans and Peter, 32, **131**
Hans Brinker, or The Silver Skates, 19, 58, 71, 449, filmstrip and recording 554, 634, 654
"Hansel and Gretel," 160, 175
"Happiness," 417, 581, 604
Happiness Is a Warm Puppy, 609
Happy Birthday, 419
Happy Day, The, 132
Happy Days, The, **247**
Happy Hollisters, The, 653, 656
Happy Lion, The, 123, **136**, 668
Happy Orpheline, The, 33, 221
Happy Owls, The, color section, **118**
Happy Place, The, 636
Happy Prince, The, **334**
Hardgrove, Clarence, 585
Hardison, O. B., Jr., 158
Hardy Boys, The, 38
Hardy, Thomas, 402, 408
"Hare and the Tortoise, The," 175
Hare and the Tortoise, The, film 556
Harkonen, Helen B., 490
Harnden, Ruth, 35, 254
Harold and the Purple Crayon, 137
Harriet, the Spy, **225**, 234, 312, 612
Harris, Christie, 298, 300, il. 300
Harris, Joel Chandler, 72, 167, 180
Harris, John, 70
Harris, Louise Dyer, 472, 480
Harris, Norman, 472, 480

Harry, the Dirty Dog, 635, **672**, 673
Harvey, James O., 296, 367
Hastings, Evelyn, 455
Hatters, The, 489
Haugaard, Erik, 8, 14, 311, 315, il. 315, 316, 604, 651, 670
Haunt Fox, 508
Havelock the Dane, **192**
Havighurst, Robert J., 26
Haviland, Virginia, 162, il. 162, 164, 180, il. 180
Hawaii, 473
Hawes, Judy, 31
Hawk in the Sky, 481
Hawkes, Judy, 458
Hawthorne, Nathaniel, 72, 195, 197, 669
Haycraft, Howard, 570
Haydn, 282
Hayes, Florence, 229, 230
Hays, Wilma Pitchford, 291, 301, 304, 484
"Haystacks," 421
Haywood, Carolyn, 33, 374, 638
Hazard, Paul, 11, 59, 90
Headstrom, Richard, 483
Hearn, Lafcadio, 184
Heat, 471
Heather and Broom, 171, 181, 663
Heaton, Margaret M., 264
Heavy Is a Hippopotamus, 133
Hector Protector and *As I Went Over the Water*, **103**
Heffernan, Helen, 145
Heidi, 19, 58, 71, 449, filmstrip and recording 554
"Heifer Hide, The," 167
Heilbroner, Joan, 280
Heilman, Robert B., 7
Heinlein, Robert, 35, 370, 377
Helen Keller Story, The, ·**286**, 669
"Hello and Good-by," 390*
Hello and Good-by, **419**
Hello Day, 418
Hello-Goodbye, **131**
Hello the Boat!, 547
Hemingway, Ernest, 8
Henderson, Luis, 453
Hengesbaugh, Jane R., 475, 476
Henry and Beezus, **374**
Henry-Fisherman: A Story of the Virgin Islands, 143
Henry Huggins, 20, 86, 638
Henry Huggins Series, 33, 374
Henry, Marguerite, 34, 35, 86, 513, 514, il. 514, 515, 547, 620, 638, 654, 659, 669
Henry Reed, Inc., **375**
Henry Reed's Baby-Sitting Service, 376
Henry Reed's Journey, 35, 376
Henry's Lincoln, **291**, 295

"Hens, The," 409, 420
Henty, George, 71, 82
Herbert, Don, 459, 482
Herbert Hoover Story, The, 286
Hercules, 140
Here and Now Story Book, 84
Here Come the Bears, 481, 681
Here Come the Beavers, 481
Here Come the Seals, 481
"Heredity," 402*
Herford, Oliver, 388, 410
Heritage of Music, The, 490
Hero Legends of Many Lands, filmstrip series 554
Heroes, The, 194, 198
Heroes in American Folklore, 177
Heroes of Greek Mythology, filmstrip series 554
Hess, Lilo, 472, 477
"Hi, Mr. Robin!," 132
Hicks, Clifford, 34
Hide and Seek Fog, 132, 477, 602, 668
"Hideout," 609
"Hiding," 397, 418, 419
Higginson, Thomas, 71
"High Flight," 415
High Pasture, The, 35, **254**
"Highwayman, The," 395, 397, 650
Hilili and Dilili, 166, 174
Hill, W. M., 194
"Hills," 399
Hirsch, S. Carl, 459, 492
History and Historians, 461
History of America, The, 65
History of Cajanus, the Swedish Giant, The, 62
History of Children's Literature, The, 91
History of Cock Robin and Jenny Wren, 80
"History of Dwarf Long Nose, The," 169
History of Four-Footed Beasts, The, 60
History of Little Goody Two Shoes, The, 63
History of Little Henry and His Bearer, The, 68
History of Sandford and Merton, The, 66
History of Simple Simon, The, 103
History of the Newbery and Caldecott Medals, A, 47
Hitler From Power to Ruin, 275
Hitty, Her First Hundred Years, 353, 567, 665
Hoban, Russell, 30, 32
Hoban, Russell and Lillian, 135
Hobbit, The, **356**, 670
Hoberman, Mary Ann, 390, 392, 394, 404, 412, 419
Hodges, Elizabeth, 165

Hodges, Margaret, 115, 184
Hoff, Rhoda, 483
Hoff, Syd, 31
Hoffman, Felix, 182, il. 183
Hoffman, Heinrich, 424
Hofsinde, Robert, 489
Hogan, Inez, 87
Hogben, Lancelot, 585
Hoge, Dorothy, 162, il. 163
Hogner, Dorothy, 454, 459, 483
Hogrogian, Nonny, color section, 117, il. 175, 184, 587
Hokushi, 400
Hole in the Tree, The, 613, 620
Hole Is to Dig, A, **580**
Holl, Adelaide, 30
Holland, Crossley, 192
Hollander, John, 339, 345
Holling, Holling C., 481, 555, 566, 620
Hollowell, Lillian, 204
Holm, Anne, 260, 566, 652
Holman, Felice, 462, 524
Holmes, Bea, 669
Holmes, Oliver Wendell, 79, 432, il. 433
Holsaert, Eunice and Faith, 486
Holst, Imogen, 283
Home from Far, 10, 224, 254, 651, 669, **678**, 681
Home Is the Sailor, **352**
Home of the Red Man, 488
Homer, 188
Homer Price, 20, 86, **375**, 558, il. 566, 638
"Homesick," 432*
Honk the Moose, 22
"Hope," 581
"Hope is the thing with feathers," 416
Hopf, Alice, 467
Hopkins, Gerard Manley, 389, 392, 660
Hopkinson, Francis, 432
"Hoppity," 417
Horizon Caravel Books, **282**
Horn Book Magazine, The, 44, 72, 83, 126, 266, 278, 323, 361, 376, 377, 410, 447, 463, 492, 561, 571, 684, 686, 733
Horn Book Sampler, A, 20
Horn, George F., 593
Horns, 588
Horns and Antlers, 486
Hornyansky, Michael, 167
Horse in Art, The, 490
Horse Who Lived Upstairs, The, 635
Horsemen of the Plains, The, 85
Horton Hatches the Egg, 112, 136, 636, 638
Hosford, Dorothy, 191, 196
Hound of Ulster, The, 190

Hourigan, Marie, 432
House at Pooh Corner, The, **351**
House Beyond the Meadow, The, 422
House for Everyone, A, 476
"House of a Mouse, The," 407
House of Four Seasons, 664
House of Sixty Fathers, The, 22, 36, 41, **246**, 638
House on East 88th Street, The, 136
"House That Jack Built, The," 160
House That Jack Built, The (Frasconi), **103**, il. 115
House That Jack Built, The (Galdone), 80, 103
Houses from the Sea, 480, il. 480
Housman, A. E., 430
Houston, James, 36, il. 177, 251
How and Why Series, 486
How and Why Wonder Book of Oceanography, The, 486
How Big Is Big?, 476
How Does a Poem Mean?, 694
"How Doth the Busy Bee," 423
"How doth the little crocodile," 423
"How Duck Got His Bill," 193
"How Far," 392*
How Far Is Far?, 476
"How Frogs Lost Their Tails," 193
"How Rabbit Deceived Fox," 175
"How Rabbit Lost His Tail," 179
"How Spider Got a Bald Head," 160
"How Spider Got a Thin Waist," 160
"How the Birds Came to Have Many Colors," 193
How the Camel Got His Hump, 373
How the Leopard Got His Spots, 373
How Things Grow, 35, 459
How to Be a Nature Detective, 461
"How to Eat a Poem," 425
How to Know the Birds, 479
How to Make and Use the Felt Board, 642
How to Make Flibbers, 34
How to Play Baseball, 532
How to Star in Basketball, 532
How to Star in Football, 532
"How to Tell the Wild Animals," 412
Howard, Coralie, 426
Howitt, Mary, 72, 423
Howland, Douglas, il. 470
Hubbell, Patricia, 419
Hughes, Langston, 42, 395, 399, 404, 406, 427, 428, 588, 625
Hughes, Thomas, 74
Hugo, Victor, 416
Humorous Poetry for Children, 429
Hundred Dresses, The, 33, 87, **225**
Hunt for the Whooping Cranes, The, 468
Hunt, Irene, 35, 311

Hunt, Kari, 488, 586
Hunter, Edith Fisher, 669
Huntington, Harriet, 450
Hurd, Clement, color section, 115, 132, 479
Hurd, Edith and Clement, 132
Hurry Home, Candy, 14, 17, 34, **517**, 638, 667, 669
Hutchins, Carleen, 467, il. 470, 470, 478, 490, 651
Hutchins, Ross, 467, il. 473, 478, 488
Huus, Helen, 28, 492, 694
Hyman, Stanley E., 158
Hyman, Trina Schart, il. 180

I, Adam, **309**
I Can Read Series, 456, 461, 476, 524
I Found a Leaf, 479
I Go A-Traveling, 418
"I heard a bird sing," 388*
"I Held a Lamb," 409
I, Juan de Pareja, **289**
"I Keep Three Wishes Ready," 608*
I Know a Lot of Things, 30, 587
"I Know-Not-What of I Know-Not-Where," 172
I Like Caterpillars, 471
I Like Weather, 420
I Like Winter, 132
I Live in So Many Places, 475, 476
I Live in the City, 418
I Love My Anteater with an A, 577
"I loved my friend," 395*
I Marched with Hannibal, **314**
I, Mary, 295
I Met a Man, 424
. . . I Never Saw Another Butterfly, **432**
I Sailed on the Mayflower, **301**
I Saw a Rocket Walk a Mile, 159
I Went to the Animal Fair, 429
I Will Adventure, **320**
I Wish, I Wish, 142
"The Ice-Cream Man," 402
"Ichabod Paddock," 170
If It Weren't for You, **127**
"If once you have slept on an island," 418
. . . If You Lived in Colonial Times, 464
If You Talked to a Boar, 577
Iger, Martin, 532
Igloos, Yurts and Totem Poles, 488, 584
Ik, Kim Yong; *see* Kim Yong Ik
Iliad, The, **188**
Iliad and the Odyssey, The, 6, 189, il. 197, 198, 670
Iliad of Homer, The, 189
"I'll tell you how the sun rose," 405

Illustrating Children's Books, 91, 146
Illustrators of Children's Books:
1744–1945, 61, 90, il. 145
Illustrators of Children's Books:
1946–1956, 119, 146, 571
I'm Hiding, 419
I'm Not Me, 419
I'm Waiting, 419
Imagination's Other Place, **430**
"Imagine," 640*
Immortals of History and Science
Series, The, 283
Important Book, The, 108, 134
Impunity Jane, 352, 665
In a Pumpkin Shell, **102**
In a Spring Garden, 430, il. 431
"In Just," 654*
In Ponds and Streams, 480
"In Spring in Warm Weather," 409
In the Clearing, 422
"In the Dark of Night," 407
In the Middle of the Night, 31, 128,
420
In the Middle of the Trees, 419
In the Woods, In the Meadow, In the
Sky, 420, 609
In Their Own Words: A History of the
American Negro, 484
Inch by Inch, 116, 121, 587
Incredible Journey, The, 7, 57, 516, il.
517
"Indian," 413*
Indian Captive: The Story of Mary Jem-
ison, **298**
"Indian Children," 413
Indian Fairy Tales, 72
Indian Picture Writing, 489
Indian Sign Language, 489
Indian Warriors and Their Weapons,
489
Indians, 488
Indians of the Longhouse, 489
Individual Behavior, 25
"Infant Joy," 417, 427
Inhelder, Bärbel, 25
Inheritance of Poetry, An, 428
Initial Biographies, **280**
"Inside a Poem," 390*
Instruction, Materials, and Methods,
592
Integrated Teaching Materials, 641
Intent upon Reading, 46, 377, 532,
535
Intergroup Education in Kindergarten-
Primary Grades, 266
Introducing Children to the World, 492
Introduction to Arithmetic, 65
Introduction to Birds, An, 460
Invincible Louisa, 276
Ipcar, Dahlov, 107, 577
"Irish Airman Foresees His Death,
An," 414

Iron Arm of Michael Glenn, The, 530
Iron Charm, The, **314**
"Ironing Day," 418
Irving, Washington, 70, 72
Is It Hard? Is It Easy?, 134
Isenberg, Irwin, 282
Ish-Kishor, S., 35, 202, 321, 670,
673
Ishi, Last of His Tribe, 298, **300**, 651
Island of the Blue Dolphins, 14, 15, 20,
251, 254, 565, 634, 670
Issa, 430
"Isun Bashi, the One-Inch Lad,"
169
It Doesn't Always Have to Rhyme, 390,
425, 603
It Looks Like This, 610
It's Fun to Know Why, 458
It's Like This, Cat, 35, 223
It's Raining, recording 559
Izenberg, Jerry, 532

"Jabberwocky," 411, 423
"Jack and His Comrades," 178
"Jack and Jill," 61
"Jack and the Beanstalk," 171
Jack and the Beanstalk, 631
Jack Dandy's Delight . . ., 65
"Jack in the Giant's Newground,"
175
Jack of Dover, **336**
Jack Tales, The, 167, 181, recording
558, 669
Jack the Giant Killer, 60
Jackson, Caary, 530
Jackson, Jacqueline, 313
Jackson, Jesse, 87, 229, 230, 657
Jackson, Robert, 532
Jacobs, Joseph, 72, 180, 332
Jagendorf, Moritz, 641
James and the Giant Peach, **357**
James and the Rain, 132
James, Will, 12, 86, 513, 620
Jane's Father, 636, 685
Janeway, James, 64
Jansson, Tove, 341
"January," 421
Janus, Grete, 30, 96
Japanese Twins, The, 84
Jaques, Florence Page, 410
Jarolimek, John, 323
Jarrell, Randall, 350
Jataka Tales, 85, 663
Jatakas, 185
Jazz Man, The, **232**, il. 233
Jeanes, Charlotte, 459
Jeanne-Marie Books, 120
Jeanne-Marie Counts Her Sheep, 107
Jemima Puddleduck, 86
Jennie's Hat, **116**, 614
Jessup, Ronald, 449

Jesus, 202
Joan of Arc, filmstrip 553
Jock's Island, **516**
"Joe Magarac," 177
Johann Sebastian Bach, 282
John Billington, Friend of Squanto,
288, **301**
John Darling, 176
"John Henry," 177
John J. Plenty and Fiddler Dan, 187
John Smith of Virginia, 285
John Tabor's Ride, color section, 115,
139
John Treegate's Musket, **304**
John Wesley, 284
"Johnny-Cake," 160
Johnny Crow's Garden, 30, 58, 84
Johnny Tremain, 17, 240, **305**, 557,
670
Johnson, Annabel and Edgar, 222
Johnson, Burdetta, 510
Johnson, Crockett, 137
Johnson, E. Harper, il. 249
Johnson, Gerald, 451, 455, il. 455,
487, 491
Johnson, Lillian, 641
Joel and the Wild Goose, 511
Joji and the Dragon, 141
Joji and the Fog, 141
Jon the Unlucky, 34
"Jonathan Bing," 412
Jonathan Goes West, 533
Jonas, Arthur, 585
Jones, Adrienne, 509
Jones, Cordelia, 247
Jones, Elizabeth Orton, 86
Jones, Harold, 100
Jordan, Alice, 18, 90
Jordan, Payton, 532
Josefina February, 115, 143
Joseph, 202
Joseph Haydn, the Merry Little Peasant,
282
Josie and the Snow, **132**
Joslin, Sesyle, 32, 137
Journey Cake, Ho!, 31, 184, 621
Joy to the World, recording 558
Joyce, James, 7, 393
Juanita, 234
Judson, Clara Ingram, 22, 36, 276,
279, 284, 285, 291, 292, 468
Judy's Journey, **240**, 243, 638
"*Julian Messner Shelf of Biogra-*
phies," 283
Juline, Ruth, 242
"Jumblies, The," 411, 423
Jung, Carl C., 158
Jungle Book, The, 19, 75, recording
558
Junichi, a Boy of Japan, 478
Junior Book of Authors, The, 570
Junior Book of Birds, The, 479

Junior Illustrated Encyclopedia of Sports, The, 532
Junior Libraries, 275
Junior Research Books Series, 84, 283
Just Like Everyone Else, 32, **138**
Just Me, 30
Just Say Hic!, **173**
"Just simply alive," 394*
Just So Stories, 85, **373**, recording 558, 606, 669
Just the Right Size, 636
Juster, Norton, 20, 341, 577
Justin Morgan Had a Horse, 514
Justus, May, 184, 230
Juvenile Miscellany, The, 78
Juvenile Rambles, 65

Kadesch, Robert, 458
Kahl, Virginia, 32, 120, 141
Kalevala, 190
Kambly, Paul E., 593
Kangaroo & Kangaroo, **116**, 587
Kangaroos, 488
Kantor, MacKinlay, 281
Kappas, Katherine H., 377
Karen's Opposites, **580**
Kashtanka, **578**
Kästner, Erich, 88, 526, 559
Kate Greenaway's Birthday Book, 5
Katy and the Big Snow, 140
Katy No-Pocket, 136
Kauffman, Lois, 31
Kaufmann, John, il. 231
Kaula, Edna, 463
Kay, Helen, 290
Keating, Bern, 281
Keats, Ezra Jack, 30, 32, 81, 116, il. 117, 128, 131, 177, 427, 430, il. 431, 587, 614, 668
Keene, Carolyn, 519
"Keep a poem in your pocket," 419*
Keeping, Charles, 670
Keigwin, R. P. 576
Keith, Harold, 311
Kelley, Marjorie, 641
Kelso, Peter, 431
Kendall, Carol, 355
Kennedy, Paul, 433
Kenneth Grahame, 594
"Kentucky Belle," 414
Kenworthy, Leonard, 492
Kenyon, Raymond, 460
Kepes, Juliet, 103, 106
Kessler, Ethel and Leonard, 133
Kettelkamp, Larry, 34, 588
Key, Alexander, 368
Key Out of Time, 370
Key to Knowledge, A, 70
Key to the City Series, 485
Keystone Kids, 531

"Keziah," 404, 609*
Kiefer, Monica, 90
Kieran, John, 460
Killer-of-Death, 298, **299**
Killilea, Marie, 239
Kim Yong Ik, 233, 247
Kindergarten Teacher, The, 145
Kinder-und Hausmärchen (Household Stories), 72
King Arthur, 190
King Arthur and His Knights, 191
"King John and the Abbot of Canterbury," 397
"King John's Christmas," 397, 413
King Midas, filmstrip 553
King of the Golden River, The, 72
King of the Wind, 34, **513**, il. 514, 638, 659, 669
Kingman, Lee, 46, 121, 145, 521, 522, 525, 571
Kings and Queens in Art, 490
"King's Breakfast, The," 395, 397, 413
King's Fifth, The, **301**
Kingsley, Charles, 40, 75, 194, 198
Kingston, W.H.G., 73
Kingston's Magazine for Boys, 73
Kipling, Rudyard, 19, 75, 79, 85, 373, 558, 606, 632, 663, 669
Kircher, Clara J., 265
Kirk, Richard, 463, 468
Kirk, Ruth, 452, 478
Kirn, Ann, 108, 586
Kiss Is Round, A, 30, 133
Kitchen Knight, The, 191
"Kite," 398
Kites, 34
"Kitten, A," 409
Kjelgaard, Jim, 281, 297, 508, 518, 533
Klemin, Diana, 145
Klose, Norma Cline, 512
Kluckhohn, Clyde, 158
Knight, Damon, 367
Knight, David C., 451
Knight, Eric, 516
Knight, Hilary, 126
Knight's Castle, **352**
Knights, Castles and Feudal Life, 466
Knight's Fee, **320**
Knights of the Golden Table, The, 192
Knowledge of the Heavens and the Earth . . ., The, 64
Kohn, Bernice, 460, 472, 585
Korzybski, Alfred, 273
Kramm, Herbert, 532
Krasilovsky, Phyllis, 32, 128, 143, 664
Krathwohl, David, 694
Krauss, Ruth, 30, 126, 132, 137, il. 138, 138, 580, 585, 684
Kredel, Fritz, il. 429

Kroeber, Theodora, 298, 300, 493, 651
Krumgold, Joseph, 22, 35, 223, 257, 557, 670
Krush, Beth and Joe, il. 12, 16, 108, 184, 354, il. 354, 669
Kruss, James, 107, 577
"Kubla Khan," 428
Kugelmass, J. Alvin, 36
Kuharich, Joe, 532
Kumin, Maxine, 32, 128
Kunhardt, Dorothy, 30, 97
Kunitz, Stanley, J., 570
Kurtz, Edwin B., 467, 483
Kuskin, Karla, 32, 132, 138, 419, 558

Lad: A Dog, 86
Lady Bird, Quickly, **103**
Lady of Staveren, The, filmstrips 553 and 554
La Fontaine, Jean de, 118, 185, 186, 668
Lagerlöff, Selma, 85
Laird, Helene and Charlton, 582
"Lake, The," 420
Lambert, Elizabeth, 462
Lamorisse, Albert, 118
Lampe, G. W. H., 199
Land and People of New Zealand, The, 463
Land and People of . . . Series, 486
"Land of Counterpane," 417
Land of Forgotten Beasts, The, 331, il. 332, 549, 669
Land of the Right Up and Down, The, 116
Landmark Series, The, **281**, 560
Lane, Ferdinand C., 454
Lang, Andrew, 72, 157, 163, 171, 180
Langstaff, John, 107, 123, 184, 587
Langton, Jane, 362
Language Arts in Childhood Education, The, 592
Language of Flowers, The, 80
Lanier, Sidney, 191
Lansdown, Brenda, 131
Lantern Bearers, The, **316**, 670
Lantz, Paul, 669
Lapland Outlaw, **533**
Larrick, Nancy, 266, 426, 493, 569, 589
Larson, Jean, 181
Lassie Come-Home, **516**, film 557
Last Battle, The, 25, 344
Last of the Mohicans, The, 73
"Last Word of a Bluebird, The," 407, 422
Latham, Jean Lee, 277, 286, 302, 566, 576

Lathrop, Dorothy, 86, 202, 422
Lathrop, Harriet, 73
Lauber, Patricia, 474
Laughable Limericks, 429
"Laughing Song, The," 394, 417
Laughing Time, 423
Lavender's Blue, **100**, 102
Lawrence, Isabelle, 527
Lawson, Robert, il. 12, 20, 22, 34, 39, 86, 118, 137, 143, 276, 277, 312, 342, 347, 356, 372, 448, 571, 606, 609, 610, 611, 638, 659, 669, 673
"Lazy Days," 394
Lazy Tommy Pumpkinhead, **371**
Leach, Maria, 181
Leaf, Munro, 87, 118, 137, 143
Lean Out of the Window, 428
Lear Alphabet: ABC, 104
Lear, Edward, 78, 104, 121, 399, 411, 423, il. 423, 427, 429, 432
Learning and Mental Health in the School, 24, 25
Leekley, Thomas B., 161
Leeming, Joseph, 482
"Leetla Giorgio Washeenton," 436
Le Gallienne, Eva, 669
"Legend of Knockmany, A," 172
"Legend of Sleepy Hollow, The," 72
"Legend of the Northland, A," 397
Legends of Paul Bunyan, The, 176
Legends of the North, 191
Legends of the United Nations, 171
Le Hibou et La Poussiquette, 121
Leif, the Lucky, 283
Leighton, Clare, 430, il. 430
"Leisure," 415
Lemonade Trick, The, 33, **375**, 634
L'Engle, Madeleine, 17, 34, 35, 39, 216, 219, 256, 369, 670
Lenski, Lois, 12, 30, 33, 87, 120, 126, 132, 234, 235, 236, il. 237, 240, 241, 298, 557, 579, 638, 651
Lent, Blair, color section, 115, 125, 139, 143, 184
Lentil, 375, il. 566, 638
Leodhas, Sorche Nic; *see* Nic Leodhas, Sorche
Leonard Bernstein, 588
Leonardo da Vinci, 282
Leopold, the See-Through Crumb-Picker, 614
Lerner, Marguerite Rush, 491
Lerner, Sharon, 479
Leslau, Wolf, 164
Lessons for Children from Two to Four Years Old, 70
Lester, Jack, 558
Le Sueur, Meridel, 295
Let Them Write Poetry, 439
Let's Be Enemies, 32, **129**
Let's Experiment, 458

Let's Feed the Animals, 97
Let's Get Turtles, 461
Let's Go to an Indian Cliff Dwelling, 489
Let's Make a Mural, 641
Let's Read and Find Out Series, 84, 458, 476
Let's Travel in India, 456
Let's Travel Series, 456, 485
Let's Visit Canada, 465
Let's Visit . . . Series, 485
Letter on the Tree, The, 34, **219**, 610
Levine, Milton, 35
Lewellen, John, 84, 457, 491
Lewis, Alfred, 85
Lewis, C. S., 8, 25, 35, 216, 264, 266, 344, 377, 652, 670
Lewis, Helen B., 264
Lewis, Richard, 231, 430, 431, il. 431, 603
Lewis, Roger, 88
Lewiton, Mina, 233
Lexau, Joan, 31, 33, 72, 128, 491, 608
Ley, Willy, 84, 447
Liers, Emil, 481, 684
Life and Strange and Surprising Adventures of Robinson Crusoe, The, 62
Life of a Queen, The, **445**
Life Story: The Story of Life on Earth, 491, 609
Life Treasury of American Folklore, The, 203
Life World Library, 485
Life's Key—DNA, A Biological Adventure into the Unknown, 467, 490
Lift Every Voice, 287
Lift-Off, the Story of Rocket Power, 490
Lifton, Betty, 141, 178
Light in the Forest, The, **299**
Light Princess, The, **335**
Like Nothing at All, 420
"Limerick shapes to the eye, A," 398*
Limerick Trick, The, 375, 606
Lincoln: A Big Man, **290**
Lincoln's America, 294
Lincoln's Animal Friends, **292**
Lindbergh, Charles, 284
Lindgren, Astrid, color section, 34, 88, 141, 222, 371, 668
Lindsay, Sally, 532
Lindsay, Vachel, 409, 625, 677
Lines, Kathleen, 40, 100
"Lines to Dr. Ditmars," 414
Linguistics and the Classroom Teacher, 575
Lion, 614, 638
"Lion, The" (Aiken), 408
"Lion, The" (Smith), 408
Lion and Mouse, film 556
"Lion and the Mouse, The," 188

Lion and the Rat, The, 187
Lion in the Gateway, The, 281
Lion Island, 477
Lion, the Witch, and the Wardrobe, The, 35, **344**, 652, 670
Lionni, Leo, color section, 33, 116, 118, 119, 121, 188, 587, 614, 669
Liss, Howard, 471
Listen, Rabbit, color section, 134, 420, 668
Listen to My Seashell, 30
"Listeners, The," 422
Listening Walk, The, 30
Literature and Music as Resources for Social Studies, 493
Literature as Exploration, 658
Lito and the Clown, 143, 654
"Little," 402, 418
Little Auto, 636
"Little Bear," 170
Little Bear, 31, 109, 668, 681
Little Bear Series, 31
Little Bear's Visit, 612
Little Blue and Little Yellow, 116, 121
Little Boy and the Birthdays, The, 31, 127
"Little Boy Blue," 389
"Little Brother," 394
Little Eddie, 638
Little Eddie Series, 33, **374**
"Little Elf, The," 410
Little Engine That Could, The, 140, record and filmstrip 553, film 556
"Little Fan," 422
"Little Fox Lost," 420
Little Frightened Tiger, The, 31
Little History of the Horn Book, A, 90
Little House, The, 31, 116, il. 123, 125, **131**, 140, 584, 616, 635, 636, 663, 668, 685
Little House Books, 22, 58, **306**
Little House in the Big Woods, 306, il. 307, 307, 565, 616, 638
Little House of Your Own, A, 32
Little House on the Prairie, 306, 547, 669
Little Island, The, 117
Little, Jean, 10, 224, 239, 254, 266, 651, 669, 678, 681
"Little John Bottlejohn," 412
Little League Amigo, 529
Little League Double Play, 529
Little League Heroes, 529
Little League Tournament, 530
Little League Visitor, **529**
Little Leaguer, 529
Little Leo, 142, il. 142, 634
Little Lord Fauntleroy, 73
Little Lost Lamb, 117, **119**
"Little Match Girl, The," 333
Little Match Girl, The, filmstrip 554
Little Men, 73

"Little Mermaid, The," 333
"Little Minnie Mystery," 412
"Little Miss Muffet," 62
Little Naturalist, The, 420
Little Old Automobile, 121, 140
Little Old Woman Who Used Her Head, The, 31
"Little One-Eye, Two-Eyes, and Three-Eyes," 171
"Little One Inch," 169
Little One Inch, 156
"Little Orphant Annie," 78
Little Pretty Pocketbook, A, 62
Little Prince, The, **336**
Little Prudy, 655
Little Prudy Series, 73
Little Prudy's Captain Horace, 73
Little Rabbit Who Wanted Red Wings, The, 137, 634, 663, 668, 673
Little Rascal, 511
Little Red Lighthouse and the Great Gray Bridge, The, 140
Little Red Newt, 480
"Little Red Riding Hood," 168, recording 559
Little Red Riding Hood, 62, filmstrip and recording 552
Little Rollo, 654
"Little Things," 408
Little Tim Books, 116
Little Tiny Rooster, The, 134, 143
Little Toot, 30, 140, il. 140, 620, 668
Little Town on the Prairie, 306
"Little Turtle, The," 397
Little Whistler, The, 420
Little Women, 12, 19, 58, 73
Lively Art of Picture Books, The, film 125, 555, 587
Lives to Remember Series, **281**
Living Community, The, 459
Living Sea, The, 462
Livingston, Myra Cohn, 394, il. 401, 406, 418, 419, 604
"Llama Who Had No Pajama, The," 419
Lobel, Anita, 587
"Lobster Quadrille, The," 423
Locke, John, 68
Lofting, Hugh, 86, 373
Lois Lenski: An Appreciation, 235
London, Jack, 86, 518
"Lone Dog, The," 398*
Lone Hunt, The, 35, **307**, 638, 654
Lonely Crowd, The, 263
Lonely Doll Series, The, 118, 576
Loner, The, 234, **252**, 254, 670
Long and Dangerous Journey, The, 139
Long Secret, The, 41
Long Shot for Paul, 529
Long-Tailed Bear, The, 193
Long Winter, The, 579, 638

Longfellow, H. W., 388, 413, 427, 432, 433, 555
Look, 422
Look for a Bird's Nest, 469, 470
Look Out the Window, 636
Looking at Art, 586
Loon's Necklace, The, film 555, 586, 666
Loopy, 140
Lopshire, Robert, 34
Lord, Beman, 33, 530
Lord Is My Shepherd, The, **200**, 202
Lord of the Rings, 356
Lord, Walter, 281
Lorenzini, Carlo, 76
Lost John, **319**
Lost Little Cat, The, 17
Lotte's Locket, **224**
Loudest Noise in the World, The, 120, 636
Lovelace, Maud Hart, 33
"Loveliness," 393*
Lowe, Alberta L., 592
Lowrie, Jean E., 593
Lucretia Mott, Gentle Warrior, **287**
Ludovici, L. J., 461
Ludwig Beethoven and the Chiming Tower Bells, 588
Lueders, Edward, 428
Lyle, Lyle, Crocodile, 136

Macaroon, **348**
"Macavity," 409
McBroom Tells the Truth, 338
McCall, Edith, 489
McCauley, J. D., 583
McCleod, Irene Rutherford, 398
McCloskey, Robert, color section, 15, 20, 22, il. 22, 32, 86, 111, 112, 113, 116, 118, 121, 128, 134, il. 139, 139, 181, 184, 375, 554, 555, il. 566, 567, 569, 587, 600, 638, 668, 669
McClung, Robert, 34, 448, 450, 480
McCord, David, 391, 398, 403, 404, 412, 424, 427, 430, 437, 558, 604, 606, 609
McCoy, J. J., 468
McCullough, John, 585
MacDonald, Betty, 31, 371, 606
MacDonald, George, 40, 76, 335
McDonald, Gerald, 427
MacDonald, Golden, 31, 119
McElligot's Pool, 139, 614, 616, 620, 685
McEwen, Catherine, 426
McGinley, Phyllis, 106, 335
McGovern, Ann, 427, 464
McGraw, Eloise, 299, 313, 314
MacGregor, Ellen, 34, 368

MacGregor, Mary, 85
McGuffey Readers, 654
McGuffey, William H., 70
McKay, Donald, 177
MacKellar, William, 518
McKendry, John J., 90, 204
Mackenzie, Jeanette Brown, 520
MacKinstry, Elizabeth, 410
McKown, Robin, 182
McLeod, Emilie, 107
MacLeod, Mary, 191
McMullan, Jim, 116, 587
McNeer, May, 34, 276, 281, 284, 293, il. 293, 294, 295
McSwigan, Marie, 244, 295
McWhinney's Jaunt, **372**, 606, 638
Made In . . . Series, 485
Madeline, 31, **112**, **113**, 116, 143, 634, 663, 668
Madeline in London, 143
Madeline's Rescue, color section, 113, 143, recording 559, 635
Magasin des infants, 78
Magee, John Gillespie, 415
Maggie Rose, Her Birthday Christmas, **243**
Magic Finger, The, **359**, il. 359
Magic Fishbone, The, 72
Magic Flute, The, 588
"Magic Lamp, The," 171
Magic Michael, 664
Magic of Words, The, 581
"Magic Ring, The," 171
Magic Stone, The, **360**
Magic To Burn, 179, **354**, 611
Magic Top, The, **183**
Magician's Nephew, The, 344
Mahen, Julia C., 527
Mahony, Bertha E., il. 61, 90, 145, 146
"Maia," 180
"Maid on the Glass Mountain, The," 172
Make Way for Ducklings, il. 22, 113, 116, 118, 134, filmstrip 554, 569, 617, 635, 668
Makers of America Series, 283
Making of Myth, The, 157, 204
Malaeska, the Indian Wife of the White Hunter, 74
Malcolmson, Anne, 181, 192
Mallinson, George, 582
Malory, Sir Thomas, 191
Man in the Making, 449, 460
"Man in the wilderness, The," 100
Man Named Lincoln, A, **291**
Man Named Washington, A, 279
"Man Who Didn't Believe in Ghosts, The," 180
Man Who Didn't Wash His Dishes, The, 32, 138, 635, 664

"Man Who Helped Carry the Coffin, The," 180
"Man Who Hid His Own Front Door, The," 410
Man Who Sang the Sillies, The, 424
Mandel, R. L., 266
Manhood of Humanity, 273
Manners Can Be Fun, 87
Manolakes, George, 593
Mantle, Winifred, 521, 528
Manual of Manners for Polite Infants . . ., A, 87
Many Moons, 109, 116, 120, **335,** recording 558, 585, **627,** 636, 669
Many Worlds of Benjamin Franklin, The, 282
Map Is a Picture, A, 475, 476
Mara, Daughter of the Nile, **313**
Marco Polo's Adventures in China, 282
Margin for Surprise, About Books, Children and Librarians, 47
Maria, 33
Marigold Garden, 78, 80
Mario, **242**
Marmaduke Multiply's Merry Method . . ., 70
Marryat, Captain Frederick, 73
Marshmallow, 134
Martel, Suzanne, 35, 367
"Martin and the Peasant's Son," 171
Martin, Fran, 275
Martin, Frederic, 524
Martin Luther, 284
Martin, Patricia Miles, 279, 291
Martin, Sarah, 62
Martin, Stefan, 421
Martin, William B., 266
Marvels of the Sea and Shore, 452, 454
Mary Jane, 87, **230,** 609, 656
Mary McLeod Bethune, 286
Mary Poppins, il. 12, 20, 34, 370, **372,** 547, 616, 632, 639, 666, 669
Mary Poppins Comes Back, 372
Mary Poppins in the Park, 372
Mary Poppins Opens the Door, 372
Mary Poppins Series, 86
Mary's Meadow, 71
Masefield, John, 398, 427
"Masie," 419
Masin, Herman, 532
Masked Prowler, The Story of a Raccoon, 481
Masks and Mask Makers, 488, 586
Mason, F. Van Wyck, 281, 489
Mason, George, 486
Mason, Miriam E., 280, 305
Massie, Diane, 31, 135
Masterman Ready, 73
Matchlock Gun, The, 273, 298, **303,** 547, 636, 669, 680
Mather, Cotton, 64

Matsuno, Masako, 33, 144, il. 144
Matthiesen, Thomas, 104
Matting and Displaying the Work of Children, 641
Maxie, 141, 635
Maximilian's World, 349
May I Bring a Friend?, color section, 30, 117, **137,** 625
May, Julian, 476
May, Sophie, 73, 82
Mayne, William, 179, 339, 342, 365
Mayo, Betty D., 199
"Me Myself and I," 401*
Mead, Margaret, 461, 474
Meader, Stephen, 35, 533
Meadowcroft, Enid, 301, 310, 617
"Mean," 604
Meanest Squirrel I Ever Met, The, 32
Means, Florence, 247
Medals for Morse, 286
Meet Abraham Lincoln, 280, 291
Meet George Washington, 280
Meet John F. Kennedy, 280
Meet the Austins, 17, **219,** 254
Meeting with a Stranger, 35, **249,** il. 249, 585
Mei Li, 144, il. 617
Meigs, Cornelia, 58, 65, 72, 79, 91, 276
Mel Ott Story, The, 531
Melindy's Medal, **229**
Meltzer, Milton, 484
"Mending Wall," 387, 422
Mercer, Charles, 282
Meredith, Robert, 484
Merriam, Eve, 387, 390, 391, 392, 401, 402, 412, 413, 424, 425, 581, 603
Merrill, Jean, 31, 168, 338, 339, 366, il. 366, 610, 611, 670, 683
Merry Adventures of Robin Hood, The, 192
"Merry-Go-Round, The," 391, 555, 625
"Metaphor," 425, 603
"Mice," 422
Mice at Home and Afield, 481
Michaelis, John U., 323
Michelangelo, 282, 586
"Mick," 409
Middle Moffat, The, **217**
Midget League Catcher, 530
Midnight Ride of Paul Revere, film 556
Miers, Earl Schenk, 282, 294, 295, 488, 530
Mighty Hunter, The, 664
Mike Mulligan and His Steam Shovel, 30, 140, 668
Mike's House, 31, 636
Miles, Betty, 476

Miles, Miska, 87, 135, 231
"Miles Standish," 413
Milgrom, Harry, 457
Milhous, Katherine, 618, 665
Military History of World War II, The, 489
"Milkmaid and Her Pail, The," 185
Millay, Edna St. Vincent, 397, 403, 408
Miller, Bertha Mahony, 46, 146, 323, 570
Miller, Helen Hill, 469
Miller, James E., 158, 204
Miller, Joaquin, 413
Miller, Mary Britton, 409
Miller, Natalie, 489
Miller, Patricia K., 470, 472
Millions of Cats, 30, 83, **110,** il. 110, 118, 141, filmstrip 554, 635, 636, 668
Milne, A. A., 15, 86, 88, 338, 351, 388, 391, 395, 397, 404, 409, 413, 417, 609, 659, 669, 681
Milne, Lorus and Margery, 460
Minarik, Else, 31, 109, 668, 681
Mine for Keeps, **239,** 651
Minn of the Mississippi, 481
"Minnie Morse," 419
Minnow Leads to Treasure, The, 528
Minor, Ed, 593
Minou, 143
Miracles, **431**
Miracles on Maple Hill, 22, 34, 218, **578,** 634
Miranda and the Cat, 511
Miriam, 35
Mirsky, Jeannette, 281
Mirsky, Reba, 36, 248, 282, 585, 657
Mish-Mash, 33, 516
Miss Bianca, 34, **348,** il. 349
Miss Bianca in the Salt Mines, 349
Miss Happiness and Miss Flower, 33
Miss Hickory, **353,** recording 558, 618, 636
Miss Osborne-the-Mop, 372
Miss Pickerell and the Geiger Counter, 368
Miss Pickerell Goes to Mars, **368**
Miss Pickerell Goes to the Arctic, 368
Miss Pickerell Goes Undersea, 368
Miss Pickerell Series, 34, 368
"Missing," 397, 417
Mississippi Possum, 87, **135,** 231
"Mist and All, The," 407
Mr. Bass's Planetoid, 368
Mr. Justice Holmes, 22, 36, **285**
Mr. Lincoln Speaks at Gettysburg, 294
Mr. Midshipman Easy, 73
Mr. Mysterious and Company, **312**
Mr. Peaceable Paints, 636
Mister Penny, 141

Mister Penny's Race Horse, 121, 141
Mr. Popper's Penguins, 21, 34, 86, **373**
Mr. Rabbit and the Lovely Present, color section, 120
Mr. Revere and I, 277, 636
Mr. T. W. Anthony Woo, 141
Mr. Twigg's Mistake, 34, **372**, 611, 638
Mr. Wizard's Science Secrets, 482
"Mrs. Gilfillan," 412
"Mrs. Golightly," 412
"Mrs. Peck-Pigeon," 390*, 418, 555
Mrs. Piggle-Wiggle, 31, **371**, 685
Mrs. Piggle-Wiggle's Farm, 636
"Mrs. Snipkin and Mrs. Wobble-chin," 412
Mrs. Teachem's School for Girls, 65
Misty of Chincoteague, 35, 507, **513**, 515, film 557, 620, 638
Mitchell, Lucy Sprague, 84, 407
Mitsui, Eiichi, 141
Mitten, The, 32, 134, **182**
"Mix a pancake," 78
Mizumura, Kazue, 144, il. 144
Moccasin Trail, 298, **299**
Modern Continental Literary Criticism, 158
Moe, Jorgen E., color section, 163
Moffats, The, **217**
Molloy, Anne, 520, 522, 523
"Molly Whuppie," 172
Moment of Wonder, The, 430, 603
Mommy, Buy Me a China Doll, 587
Monarch Butterflies, 467
Monkey Shines, a Baseball Story, 530
"Monkeys and the Crocodile, The," 397, 413, 423, 435
Monkeys Have Tails, 580
Monro, Harold, 410
Monsell, Helen, 681
Monster Den, The, 424
Montgomery, Elizabeth Rider, 570
Monthly Packet, The, 78
Montresor, Beni, color section, 108, 117, 137, 670
Moolack: Young Salmon Fisherman, 456
Moon and a Star, The, 419
Moon by Night, The, 35, **256**
Moon Is Shining Bright as Day, The, 430
Moon Jumpers, The, 120, 129, 420, 625
Moon Moth, 470, il. 470, 478, 651
"Moon's the North Wind's Cooky, The," 676, 677*
Moore, Anne Carroll, 83
Moore, Clement, 77, 397
Moore, Lilian, 107
Moore, Nancy, 137, 673
Moore, Roselle, 409

Mop Top, 138
Mordvinoff, Nicolas, 84
More about Paddington, 373
More All-of-a-Kind Family, 218
More Junior Authors, 570
More New Ways in Math, 585
More Nonsense, 78
More Science Experiments, 482
More Silver Pennies, 426
More Tales From Grimm, 166
Morey, Walt, 510
Morley, Christopher, 393
"Morning and Afternoon," 405*
"Morning in Winter," 406
Morris, Desmond, 447
Morris, Laverne, 488
Morrison, Chester, 422
Morrison, Lillian, 411, 430
Morse, Jedediah, 65
Morse, Samuel, 106
Morte d'Arthur, 191
Moses, 202
Most Beautiful Place, The, **262**
Mother Goose, 30, 61, recording 557
Mother Goose (Tudor), color section, **102**
Mother Goose and Nursery Rhymes, **102**
Mother Goose and Other Nursery Rhymes, il. 103
Mother Goose Nursery Rhymes, color section
Mother Goose, Old Nursery Rhymes, 84, **100**
Mother Goose, or The Old Nursery Rhymes, il. 81, **100**
Mother Goose Treasury, The, **101**
"Mother's Party," 401
Motif Index of Folk-Literature, 169
Motor Boys, The, 82
"Motor Cars," 404
Mound Builders, The, 447
Mountain Born, 10, 234, **256**
"Mountain Whipporwill, The," 395
"Mouse," 399
Mouse and the Motorcycle, The, 638
"Mouse Bride, The," 170
Mouse Chorus, 421
"Mouse Whose Name Is Time, The," 405
Mousewife, The, **347**
Moved Outers, The, **247**
Mozart, 282
Mozart, The Wonder Boy, 282, 588
Mozley, Charles, 176
"Mud," 393*
Muessig, Raymond H., 593
Muffin and Mother Goose, recording 557
Mühlenweg, Fritz, 534
Muir, Percy, 91
Mukerji, Dhan, 192, 511
Mullin, Willard, 532

Mulready, William, il. 77
Multiplication Table, The, 70
Munari, Bruno, 30, 97, 98, 105, il. 105
Murals for Schools, 593
Mure, Eleanor, 72
Murphy, Robert, 481, 509
Murray, Henry A., 158
Murray, Thomas R., 641
"Musetta of the Mountains," 410
Musgrave, Florence, 234, 248
"Musicians of Bremen, The," 178
Mustang, Wild Spirit of the West, **515**
"My Bed Is a Boat," 78
"My Brother," 418
My Cousin, Abe, 295
My Daughter, Nicola, **224**
My Dog Is Lost, 131
My Father Was Uncle Wiggly, The Story of the Remarkable Garis Family, 82, 90
My First Counting Book, 107
My Friend Charlie, 606
"My Friend, Leona," 403*
My Great-Grandfather and I, 577
"My Inside-Self," 401
"My Last Duchess," 38
My Mother Is the Most Beautiful Woman in the World, 33, 42, 43
"My Mother's Cross Afternoon," 402
My Name Is Pablo, **244**
"My Shadow," 78, 650
My Side of the Mountain, 20, **251**
My Sister and I, 127
My Teacher's Gem, 68, 69
My Village Series, 452, 485
"My-what," 170
Myrick, Mildred, 32
"Mysterious Cat, The," 409
Mysterious Christmas Shell, The, 522, 523
Mystery Angel, The, **520**
Mystery at Monkey Run, The, 524
Mystery at Old Sturbridge Village, 527
Mystery for Mr. Bass, A, 368
Mystery in the Old Cave, 521
Mystery of Long Barrow House, The, 521
Mystery of the Angry Idol, The, 521, 524
Mystery of the Haunted Pool, The, 521, 524
Mystery of the Hidden Hand, The, **522**, 524
Mystery of the Pilgrim Trading Post, The, 520, 522, 523
Mystery of the Velvet Box, The, 520, 521
Mystery on Crabapple Hill, The, 524
Myth and Method, Modern Theories of Fiction, 158, 204

Myth of the Birth of the Hero and Other Writings by Otto Rank, 158
Mythology, 204
Myths of Greece and Rome, filmstrip series 554
Myths of the World, 204

"Nail Soup," 172
Nail Soup, 125
Naim, a Boy of Turkey, 478
Nancy Drew Books, 38, 82, **519**
"Nancy Hanks," 397
Nancy Hanks of Wilderness Road, 295
Nash, Ogden, 397, 412, 413, 424, 426, 430
Nathan, Adele, 294, 467
Nathan, Robert, 414
National School Library Standards, 551
National Tape Recording Repository, 593
Natural History's 1965 Survey of Science Books for Young People, 447
Natural Science Picture Books, 447
Navajo, The, 450
Naval War in the Pacific, The, 489
Navarra, John, 582
"Nazar the Brave," 175
Nebraska Curriculum Development Center, 575, 593
Neely, H. M., 480
Neergaard, Helga and Beate, 554
Neff, Priscilla, 513
Nesbit, E., 85
Ness, Evaline, 115, il. 122, 128, 132, 143, 165, 182, 348
Neville, Emily, 10, 35, 43, 216, 226, 237, 238
New Boy, The, **225,** 609
New Boy in School, **230**
"New Clothes and Old," 417
New England Primer, 64, il. 65, 69, 654
"New Little Boy, The," 402*
"New Neighbor, The," 402
New Pet, The, 32, 126
"New Shoes," 385*
"New Song to Sing about Jonathan Bing, A," 412
New Ways in Math, 585
New York Herald Tribune, 83, 87
New York Times, 45
Newberry, Clare, 134, il. 135, 587
Newbery and Caldecott Medal Books: 1956–1965, 46, 108, 125, 145, 570
Newbery, John, 62, 63, 65, 66
Newbery Medal Books: 1922–1955, 46, 323, 570
Newbery, Thomas, 60
Newell, E., 266
Newell, Hope, 31

Newman, Shirlee Petkin, 491
Neyhart, Louise, 291
Nibelungenlied, The, 191
Nic of the Woods, **135,** 516
Nicholson, William, 83
Nickel-Plated Beauty, The, **312,** 565
Nicky's Football Team, 34
Nic Leodhas, Sorche, color section, 165, 171, 180, 182, 184, 663, 664
Nicodemus and the Gang, 87
Nigerian Pioneer, The Story of Mary Slessor, 285
"Night," (Sandburg) 421*
"Night," (Teasdale) 405, 415*, 421
Night before Christmas, The, 77
Night of Masks, The, 370
"Night of the Wind," 407, 408
"Night Song," 392
"Night Will Never Stay, The," 395*, 418
Nightingale, The, 333, 334, il. 334, 587, 669
Night's Nice, 134
"Niilo and the Wizard," 170
Nine Days to Christmas, 121, **143**
900 Buckets of Paint, 636
Nine in a Line, **108**
Nkwala, **256**
No Boats on Bannermere, 35, 528
No-Name Man of the Mountain, The, **337,** 638
No Room, 620
Noah's Ark, **201,** il. 201, 587
Noailles, R. H., 477
Nobody Listens to Andrew, 109
Nobody's Garden, **247**
"Noise of Waters, The," 393
Nolan, Jeannette, 277, 448
Nomusa and the New Magic, 36, **248,** 657
Noonday Friends, The, **225**
Norman, Gertrude, 279, 291, 587
North American Indians, The, 488
North, Joan, 361
North Star Books, **281**
North, Sterling, 281, 511
North to Freedom, **260,** 566, 612, 652
North Town, 232
North Wind and the Sun, The, 118, 187, 668
Norton, Andre, 362, 370
Norton, Eloise, 593
Norton, Mary, il. 12, 16, 20, 86, 108, 339, 353, il. 354, 610, 616, 659, 669
"Not That," 403
Not Too Small after All, 636
"Nothing," 410*, 422
Nothing at All, 141, 663
Nothing to Do, 135
"Now I Lay Me Down to Sleep," 64
Now It's Fall, 132

Now Try This, 457
Now We Are Six, 609
Noyes, Alfred, 395, 397, 402, 426
Nulton, Lucy, 659
Numerals: New Dresses for Old Numbers, 585
Nürnberg Stove, The, 72
Nursery Rhyme Picture Book, Number Two, il. 101
Nutcracker, The, 588
Nutshell Library, 6, 121
Nuvat the Brave, **250**

O Canada!, 463
Oakley, Graham, 336
Oasis of the Stars, **143**
Ocean Wonders, 486
October Treasure, **528**
"Octopus, The," 412
O'Dell, Scott, 14, 20, 251, 301, 670
Odland, Norine, 694
Odysseus the Wanderer, 189
Odyssey, **188**
Odyssey of Courage, 301, 566
Odyssey of Homer, The, 189
Oh What Nonsense!, 429
Ohrmann, Richard M., 157, 158, 204
Ol' Paul the Mighty Logger, 176
Ola, 116, 143, 449
O'Lague, John, 593
"Old Bluebeard," 172
"Old Man's Comforts, The," 423
Old Mother Hubbard and Her Dog, 103
Old Old Teakettle, The, 171
Old Possum's Book of Practical Cats, recording 558
"Old silent pond, An," 400*
"Old Stone House, The," 617
Old Stormalong, 176
Old Testament, The, **200,** il. 200
"Old Wife and the Ghost, The," 422
"Old Woman and Her Pig, The," 159
Old Woman and Her Pig, The, 103
Old Yeller, 22, 518
"On a Night of Snow," 667, 677*
On a Summer Day, 132
On Beyond Zebra, 614
On the Banks of Plum Creek, 307, 634, 638
Once a Mouse, color section, 85, 115, 119, 121, **187,** 668
Once There Was and Was Not, il. 175
Once Upon a Time, recording 557
Once Upon a Totem, 181
One by Sea, **527**
One God: The Ways We Worship Him, 86
"One Horned Mountain Goat, The," 181

101 Science Experiments, 459, 482
1 Is One, 107
One Is One, **319**
One Man's Meat, 685
"One misty, moisty morning," 99
One Morning in Maine, 32, **128**, 636
One Small Blue Bead, **296**
One Snail and Me, 107
One Step, Two . . ., 107
"One, Two, Buckle My Shoe," 62
One, Two, Three, Going to Sea, 107
One Was Johnny, 107
O'Neill, Mary, 403, 425, il. 425, 453, 454, 481, 556, 581, 603, 604
Onion John, 35, **223**, 634, 636
"Onomatopoeia," 425
Opie, Iona and Peter, 61
Optic, Oliver, 74, 82
Orbus Pictus, 60
Oregon at Last!, **309**
Original Poems for Infant Minds, 77
Ormondroyd, Edward, 364
Orphans of Simitra, The, **221**
Orphans of the Sky, 35
Orphans of the Wind, **311**
Orton, Helen, 521
Osborne Collection of Early Children's Books, The, 68, il. 69, 80, 91
Ota, Koshi, 586
Otter's Story, An, 481, 684
Ottley, Reginald, 253
"Otto," 394*
Ounce Dice Trice, **580**
Our American Language, 581
Our Country's Story, 488
Our Friend, the Atom, 620
Our National Parks Series, 464
Our Working World, Families at Work, 584
"Outlandish Knight, The," 397
Outward Bound, 74
Over and Over, 32, 121, **133**
"Over and Under," 423
Over in the Meadow, **107**, 123, filmstrip 554
Over Sea, Under Stone, **362**
"Over the Garden Wall," 418
"Overheard on a Saltmarsh," 410
Overland Stage, 489
Overstreet, Bonaro, 266
Owen, Russell, 684
"Owl and the Pussy Cat, The," 121, 411, 423
Owls, 488
Oxford Book of Poetry for Children, **427**, 432
Oxford Nursery Rhyme Book, The, 61
"Ozymandias," 428

Paddington at Large, 373
Paddington Helps Out, 373

Paddington Marches On, 373
Paddy's Christmas, 681
Pages, Pictures, and Print, 145
Pagoo, 481, 555
Paint All Kinds of Pictures, 586
Pair of Red Clogs, A, **144**, il. 144
Palace in Bagdad, 181
Palazzo, Tony, 202, 684
Palmer, Geoffrey, 462
Palmer, Helen, 31
Palmer, Mary B., 340
Palmer, Robin, 179
"Pancake, The," 184
Pancakes-Paris, **245**
Panchatantra, 185
Pantaloni, 142
"Panther, The," 412*, 424
Papa Small, 30
Papashvily, Helen, 281
Paperback Books in New Jersey Schools, 552
Papermakers, The, 489
Pâpier-Maché, 641
Papyroplastics, or The art of modelling in paper; . . ., 77
Parables from Nature, Worlds Not Realized, 71
Parent's Assistant: or Stories for Children, The, 68
Parent's Guide to Children's Reading, A, 589, 728
Parish, Peggy, 32, 371, 577
Park, Thomas Choonbai, 587
Parker, Bertha M., 486, 639
Parker, Elinor, 428
"Pasture, The," 409, **421**, 422
Pat the Bunny, 30, 97
"Patience," 581
Patricia Crosses Town, **231**, 656
Patrick Henry, Firebrand of the Revolution, **289**
"Pat's Fiddle," 422
Patten, William S., 74
"Paul Bunyan," 179
Paul Bunyan, 176
Paul Bunyan and the Blue Ox, film 556
Paul Bunyan Lumber Camp Tales, 556
Paul Revere, 279
"Paul Revere's Ride," 413
Paul Revere's Ride, 397, **432**
Pavel, Frances, 166
Payne, Emmy, 136
Peaceable Kingdom, The, 421
Peacock Pie, 88, 422
Pearce, Philippa, 343, 364, 528, 616
Peare, Catherine Owens, 286, 669
Pearson, Mary D., 593
Peary to the Pole, 281
Pease, Howard, 521
Peattie, Donald Culross, 486
Pecos Bill, 176, 179

Pedro, the Angel of Olvera Street, 113, 234
Pee Wee Cook of the Midget League, 530
Pegasus and Bellerophon, filmstrip 554
Pellowski, Anne, 558
Pels, Gertrude, 641
Penny Whistles, 78
People and Places, 461
"People keep saying it's not good." 422*
Pepper and Salt, 72
Perceiving, Behaving, Becoming, 265
Perfect Pancake, The, 141
Perfect Pitch, The, 530
Perhaps I'll Be a Farmer, 636
Perilous Road, The, 10, 35, **310**, 638
Perkins, Carol, 461
Perkins, Lucy Fitch, 84
Perrault, Charles, color section, 61, 62, 169
Perrely Plight, The, **527**
Perrine, Laurence, 438, 695
Personn, Lisa-Christina, 91
Personnel and Guidance Journal, 264, 265
Peter and the Wolf, color section, 116, 588
Peter Pan, 19
Peter Pan and Wendy, 85
Peter Parley to Penrod, 90
Peter Parley's Farewell, 70
Peter the Whaler, 73
Peter Treegate's War, 304
Peterkin Papers, The, 371
Peter's Long Walk, 121
Petersham, Maud and Miska, 84, 86, 202, il. 411, 411
Peterson, Isabel, 426
Peterson, Roger, 460, 479
Petrides, Heidrun, 32, 131
Petry, Ann, 302
Petunia, 31, 136, 668
Phantom of Walkaway Hill, The, **526**
Phantom Tollbooth, The, 20, **341**, 577
Pheidippedes, the Marathon Runner, filmstrip 553
Phelan, Mary Kay, 294
Phillips, Ward H., 593
Phipson, Joan, 219, 522, 528
"Phizzog," 421
Piaget, Jean, 25
Piatti, Celestino, color section, 105, 118
Picard, Barbara Leonie, 181, 189, 191, 319
Picasso, 586
Piccolo's Prank, 113
"Pickety Fence, The," 391*
"Picnic, The," 403
Picture Has a Special Look, A, 586
Picture Story of Japan, The, 478

Pied Piper, The, filmstrip 553
"Pied Piper of Hamelin, The," 397, 427
Pike, Nicholas, 65
Pilgrim Courage, 85, 484
Pilgrim Thanksgiving, 301
"Pilgrims and Puritans," 413
Pilgrim's Progress, 60
Pilkington, Mary, 68
Pilkington, Roger, 301
Pioneer Show Folk, 489
Pioneer Traders, 489
Piper, Pipe That Song Again!, **426**
Piper, Roger, 492
Piper, Watty, 140
"Piping Down the Valleys Wild," 398, 417
Pippi Goes on Board, 371
Pippi in the South Seas, 371
Pippi Longstocking, 34, 88, **371**, 612
"Pirate Don Durk of Dowdee," 397
Pistachio, 115
Pistorious, Anna, 479
Pitz, Henry C., 91, 146
Place for Johnny Bill, A, **242**
Plain Girl, **236**
Plain Princess, The, **335**
"Plaint of the Camel, The," 412
Play with Me, 118, 121
Play with Plants, 457
Play with Seeds, 457, 483
Play with Vines, 457, 483
Playmaking with Children, 641
Pleasant Surprises . . ., il. 77
Plenty to Watch, 117, 144
"Plop!," 160
Plotz, Helen, 430, il. 430
Plum Pudding for Christmas, 141
Pocahontas (d'Aulaire), 116, 283
Pocahontas (Martin), 279
Pocketful of Cricket, A, 32, il. 122, 122, **128, 578**
Podendorf, Illa, 449, 459, 473, 482
Poe, Edgar Allan, 427
"Poem of Praise," 415*, 421
Poems (Coatsworth), 421
Poems (Field), 418
"Poems" (Kelso), 431*
Poems Are Fun, film 555
Poems for Children, recording 558
Poems for Seasons and Celebrations, 429
Poems of Childhood, 78
Poems of Emily Dickinson, 386
Poems of Magic and Spells, 429
Poems to Grow On, **426**
"Poetry," 386
Poetry for Me, film 555
Poetry in the Elementary Classroom, 641
Poetry Parade, recording 558
Pogany, Willy, 189, 670
Pointed People, 418

Poky Little Puppy, The, 5
Policeman Small, 120
Politi, Leo, 22, 113, 117, 120, 142, il. 142, 143, 234, 284, 654
Polland, Madeleine, 315, 318, 433
"Pontius Pilate," 179
Popular Tales from the North, 72
"Porcupine, The," 412
Portal, Colette, 445
"Portrait," 402
"Portrait by a Neighbor," 403
Portraits of the Nations Series, 486
Posell, Elsa, 454
Possum, 448, 450
"Potatoes' Dance, The," 625
"Potted Princess, The," recording 558
Potter, Beatrix, color section, 31, 86, 121, 566, 571, 668
Potter, Charles, 411
Powers, Richard, 202
Practical Guide to Individualized Reading, A, 592
"Prairie-Dog Town," 421
Prairie School, **235**
Prairie Years, The, 294
"Prayer of the Cock, The," 409*
"Prayer of the Dog," 409
"Prayer of the Foal," 409
Prayers from the Ark, 408, 409, recording 558, 609
Prechtl, Louise, 448
Prefabulous Animiles, **422**
Preep, The Little Pigeon of Trafalgar Square, 143
Preparing Visual Instructional Materials, 593
Preparing Your Book Report, film 555
Present to Children, A, 66
Pretty Book of Pictures for Little Masters and Misses . . ., A, 66
Pretty Poems for Children Three Feet High, 66
Price, Christine, 586, 670
"Primer Lesson," 416*
"Princess and the Pea, The," 72, 333
Print Making with a Spoon, 586
Printing for Fun, 586
Pritchard, Mary Joyce, 603
Private Eyes, 521, 522, 525
Process of Education, The, 25, 650
Prodigal Son Sifted, The, 61
Project Apollo, 490
Project Mercury, 490
Prokofieff, Serge, color section, 116
Prometheus and Pandora, filmstrip 554
Promise Is a Promise, A, **237**
Proof of the Pudding, What Children Read, The, 46
Propan, A Boy of Thailand, 478
Properties of Things, 60

Prove It!, 458, 482
Provensen, Alice and Martin, 6, il. 187, 189, il. 197, 198, 433, 580, 587, 670
"Ptarmigan," 424
"Pumpkin Child, The," 168
Punctuation Personified, 70
Punia and the King of the Sharks, 176
"Puppy and I," 407
Puptents and Pebbles, 106
"Purple Cow," 412
Pushcart War, The, 338, 339, **366**, il. 366, 611, 670, 681, 683
"Puss in Boots," 61
Puss in Boots, 62
Puss in Boots (Brown), 85, 117, 167, 178, 181
Puss in Boots (Fischer), 165, 178
Puss-in-the-Corner Mystery, The, 520
"Pussy Willows," 420*
"Pussycat, Pussycat," 61
Putnam, Peter, 281
Pyle, Howard, 72, 80, 161, 166, 191, 192
Pyne, Mable, 584

"Quangle Wangle's Hat, The," 423
"Quarreling," 394
Quarreling Book, The, 33, **129**
Quarterback's Aim, 33, 530
Quarterly Report, 582
Queen Elizabeth, 277
Queenie Peavy, 35, **259**
"Queer Things," 422
Quest for Myth, 157, 203
Quest for the Dead Sea Scrolls, 462
Quest of Columbus, The, 484
Quest of the Gole, The, 339, **345**
Quick As a Wink, 418
Quiet Boy, 248
Quigley, Lillian, 610

R. L. Stevenson, 594
Rabbit Hill, il. 12, 20, 39, **347**, 638, 659
"Rabbit in the Moon, The," 178
Rabbits' Wedding, The, 121
Rackham, Arthur, color section, 84, 100
Ragged Dick, 73
"Raggedy Man, The," 78
"Raggle Taggle Gypsies," 397
Rain Drop Splash, 132, film 557
Rain in the Woods and Other Small Matters, 454
Rain Makes Applesauce, 32, **137**
Rain Puddle, The, 30
Rain, Rivers and Reservoirs, 459
"Rain Sizes," 405, 406, 424
Rainbow Book of American Folk Tales and Legends, The, 181

Rainbow Book of American History, The, 488
Rainbow Book of Bible Stories, The, 201
Rainbow Book of Nature, The, 486
Rainbow in the Sky, 427
"Raining," recording 559
Rainshower, film 556
Rakoto and the Drongo Bird, 182
Ralph J. Bunche, Fighter for Peace, 36
Rama, the Hero of India, 192
Ramirez, Carolyn, 133
Rand, Ann and Paul, 30, 580
Rand, Paul, 587
Randall, Arne, 593
Randall, Ruth Painter, 292, 295
Randolph Caldecott Picture Book Number One, color section
Rank, Otto, 158
Rapunzel, 182
Rascal: A Memoir of a Better Era, 7, 511
Raskin, Ellen, 417
Rasmus and the Vagabond, 88, **222**
Rasmussen, Knud, 431
"Rats of Nagasaki, The" 159
"Raven, The," 433
Raven's Cry, The, 298, **300**, il. 300
Ravielli, Anthony, 446, 451, 466, il. 466, 475, 478
Rawlings, Marjorie Kinnan, 11, 343, 512, 670
Read, Herbert, 428, 438
Reading Instruction for Today's Children, 594
Reading Ladders for Human Relations, 263, 264, 265, 731
Readings about Children's Literature, 377, 493
Real Book of Science Experiments, The, 482
Real Mother Goose, The, **102**
Real Personages of Mother Goose, The, 61
"Real Princess, The," 333
Reason for the Pelican, The, 424
Recent Trends in Reading, 29
Recordings for Children, 592
Recordings in the Public Library, 593
Red Balloon, The, 118
Red Bantam, 143
Red Fairy Book, The, 72, 163, 180
Red Planet: A Colonial Boy on Mars, 370
"Red Riding Hood," 61
"Redchicken," 178
Reed, Philip, 102, il. 103, 115
Reed, W. Maxwell, 84
Reeder, Red, 490
Reeves, James, 181, 185, 186, 409, 410, 412, 422
Reflections on a Gift of Watermelon

Pickle, **428**
Reid, Alastair, 580
Reid, Bill, il. 300
Reid, Gwendolyn, 428
Reisman, David, 263
Reluctant Dragon, The, **336**
Rembrandt, 282
Renault, Mary, 281
Renick, James and Marion, 529
Renick, Marion, 34, 529
Rescuers, The, 348
Ressner, Phil, 32
Retreat to Glory: The Story of Sam Houston, 57, 277, 286, 566
Return of the Twelves, The, 339, **352**
Rey, H. A., 30, 32, 97, 120, 136
Reyher, Becky, 33, 42, 43
Reynolds, Christopher, 458
Reynolds, Robert L., 282
Rhymes and Verses: Collected Poems for Young People, 422
Rhymes of Childhood, 78
Ribsy, 516, 638
Rich Cat, Poor Cat, 131
Rich, Elaine, 236
Rich, Louise Dickinson, 448
Rich Man and the Shoemaker, The, 187
Richards, Laura E., 79, 85, 392, 397, 412, 413, 423
Richter, Conrad, 299
Riddle of the Figurehead, The, 520
Riddle of the Red Whale, The, **526**
"Ride-by-Nights," 422
Ride on the Wind, 284
Ride the Cold Wind, **143**
Ride with the Sun, 181
"Riding to Poughkeepsie," 412
Riding with Coronado, 484
Rieu, E. V., 424
Rifles for Watie, **311**
"Rikki-Tikki-Tavi," 19, 558
Riley, James Whitcomb, 78
Ring and the Fire: Stories from the Nibelung Operas, The, 588
Ring O' Roses, **100**
Ring the Judas Bell, 246
Rinkoff, Barbara, 475, 476
"Rip Van Winkle," 72
Ripley, Elizabeth, 282, 586
"Rise, Sun!," 409
Riswold, Gilbert, 334
Ritchie, Jean, 185
River at Green Knowe, The, 363
"River Is a Piece of Sky, The," 424, 651
"River Moons," 421
River of the Wolves, 35, 533
Rivers of the World Series, 486
"River's Song," 420*
Road Not Taken, The," 388, 422
Road Race Round the World, 532

Road to Agra, The, **243**, 566
Road to Miklagard, The, 316
"Roads," 418
Robbins, Ruth, 321
Robbut, A Tale of Tails, 137, 673
Robert Bruce, filmstrip 553
Robert E., 234, **248**
Robert Frost, America's Poet, 36
Robert Frost Reads His Poetry, recording 558
Robert McCloskey, film 555
"Robert, Who Is Often a Stranger to Himself," 401
Roberts, Elizabeth Madox, 400, 409, 420, 426
Robertson, Keith, 35, 376
Robin Hood, 190, filmstrip 554
"Robin Hood and Allan-a-Dale," 397
"Robin Hood and the Widow's Sons," 397
Robins in the Garden, 481
Robinson, Barbara, 308
Robinson Crusoe, 19, 20, 58, 61
Robinson, Jackie, 281
Robinson, Mabel L., 191
Robinson, Veronica, 240
Rocket in My Pocket, A, 396, 411
Rodin, 282
Rogers, Vincent R., 593
Rojankovsky, Feodor, color section, 84, 101, 102, 107, 117, 123, 184, 200, 634, 669
Roller Skates, **312**
Rollo, 71
Rollo in Holland, 71
Romeo and Juliet, 320
Rood, Ronald, 467
Roofs of Gold, Poems to be Read Aloud, 428
Rookie First Baseman, 530
Roosevelt Grady, il. 13, 87, **242**
Rooster Crows, The, 411, il. 411
Rosa, 143
Rosa-Too-Little, 31, 128
Rosamund and the Purple Jar, 68
Roscoe, William, 77, il. 77
Rose, Karen, 256
Rosenblatt, Louise, 658
Rosenheim, Edward W. 695
Rosselli, Colette, 429
Rossetti, Christina, 78, 398, 405, 420, 426
Rough Ice, 530
Roukes, Nicolas, 641
Rounds, Glen, 176, 184, 221, 454, 512
Rousseau, J. J., 27
Rover Boys, The, 82
Rowan Farm, 247
Royal Book of Ballet, The, 490

Rubens, 282
Ruchlis, Hy, 459
Ruck-Pauquet, Gina, 262
"Rudolph Is Tired of the City," 404*
Rudyard Kipling, 594
Rufus M., **217**
Rugoff, Milton, 282
"Rum Tum Tugger, The," 409
"Rumplestiltskin," 72, 171, film 556
Run, Light Buck, Run, 509
Run, Westy, Run, **222**
"Runaway, The," 409, 422
Runaway Bunny, The, 31, **136**
Runny Days, Sunny Days, 420
Ruskin, John, 72
Russell, David, 28, 264
Russell, Franklin, 481, 509
Russell, Solveig, 457
Russia: Adventures in Eyewitness History, 483
Russian Wonder Tales, 166
"Rusty Jack," 174
Ruth, 202
Ruthless Rhymes for Heartless Homes, 424
Rydberg, Ernie, 239

Sad-Faced Boy, **229**
"Sad Shoes, The," 436*
Sage, Michael, 577
"Saginsack, The," 412, 424
Saint-Exupéry, Antoine de, 336
St. John, Judith, 68, 91
St. Lawrence Seaway, 468
St. Nicholas Magazine, 58, 79, 80
Salt, 179, il. 179
Salten, Felix, 19
San Francisco Boy, 638
Sand and Snow, 419
Sandburg, Carl, 289, 292, 294, 386, 387, 389, 391, 397, 399, 415, 416, 421, 426, 435, 439, 558, 579, 670
Sandburg, Helga, 511
Sanderlin, George, 484
"Sandhill Crane, The," 421
Sandys, E. V., 189
Sanger, Marjorie, 455, 465
Saporta, Raphael, 201
Sara Crewe, 73
Sarett, Lew, 406, 407
Sartre, Jean Paul, 82
Sasek, Miroslav, 462, 478, il. 478, 586
"Satellite, Satellite," 402
Saturdays, The, **217**, 609
Sauer, Julia, 31, 339, 363
Saunders, F. Wenderoth, 491
Savage, Steele, 201
Saving Wild Life for Tomorrow, 459

Sawyer, Ruth, 22, 31, 184, 243, 312, 558, 662, 663, 693
Saxon, Gladys, 279
Sayers, Frances Clarke, 7, 47, 558
"Says Tom to Me," 424
Scarlet Badge, The, **304**
Scarry, Richard, 185
Scenes, 71
Scenes in Africa, 71
Scenes of Commerce . . ., 71
Schackburg, Richard, 122
Scharff, Robert, 469, 470, 486
Schatz, Esther, 28
Scheele, William E., 447
Scheer, Julian, 32, 137
"Schenectady," 412
Scherf, Margaret, 520, 521
Scherman, Katharine, 191
Schiffer, Don, 34
Schiller, Barbara, 191
Schlein, Miriam, 133
Schloat, G. Warren, 478, 483
"Schmat-Razum," 172
Schneider, Herman and Nina, 84, 457, 476, 477, 483
School Library Journal, 44, 535, 551
Schreiber, Georges, 284
Schultz, Morton J., 594
Schulz, Charles, 609
Schwartz, Julius, 458, 483, 592
Schweitzer, Byrd Baylor, 296
Schwietert, Louise, 592
Science, a Process Approach, 582
Science Education for Elementary School Teachers, 594
Science Experiences Elementary School, 639
Science Experiments, 482
Science Fun with Milk Cartons, 483
Science in Elementary Education, 593
Science in Your Back Yard, 57
Science Teasers, 482
Scientific Method, The, 460
Scrambled Eggs Super, 636
"Scrapefoot," 72
Screamer, Last of the Eastern Panthers, 480
Scudder, Horace, 71, 78
Sea around Us, The, 465, 469
Sea Captain from Salem, 304
Sea Egg, The, **342**
"Sea-Fever," 398
"Sea Gull, The," 391*
Sea Horses, 472
Sears, Stephen W., 490
Secret Friends, The, **363**
Secret Garden, The, 5, 19, 58, 73, 247, 613
Secret Hiding Place, The, **135**, 609
Secret of the Andes, 21, **257,** 578
Secret of the Emerald Star, 520, **521,**

523
Secret of the Old Clock, The, 519
Secret of the Ron Mor Skerry, **527**
Secret of the Simple Code, The, 521
Secret of the Unicorn, 521
"Secret Place, The," 404, 418
Secret River, The, **343**
Secret Three, The, 32
See Again, Say Again, 115
See and Read Beginning to Read Biographies, **279**
See and Read Biographies, **279**
"See, I Can Do It," 403
See Through the Jungle, 465
See What I Found, 419, 604
Seeger, Ruth, 185
Selden, George, 347
"Selfish Giant, The," 334
Seligman, Iran L., 470
Sellew, Catharine, 198, 202
Selsam, Millicent, 32, 35, 84, 451, 453, 456, 457, 459, 461, 465, 468, 470, 473, 476, 483, 493
Sendak, Maurice, color section, 6, 41, 103, 107, 117, 120, 121, 129, 137, il. 138, 139, 173, 351, 555, 569, 580, 624, 625, 668, 669, 671
Senesh, Lawrence, 584
"September," 420
Seredy, Kate, 35, 195, 243, 255, 669
Serraillier, Ian, 189, 194, il. 194, 245
Seton, Ernest Thompson, 75
Seuss, Dr., 31, 86, 109, 112, 119, 120, 136, 139, 336, 397, 608, 614, 620, 638, 668, 669
Seven-Day Magic, **360**
Seven Diving Ducks, 97, 134
700 Science Experiments, 482
Seven Little Sisters Who Live on the Big Round Ball . . ., 71
"Seven Little Tigers and the Aged Cook, The," 423
Seven Queens of England, The, 277
Seven Ravens, The, 41, 168, **171**, 182, il. 183, 332
Seven Silly Wise Men, 174
Seven Wonders of the World, The, 71
Seventeenth-Street Gang, The, **227**
Seventh Princess and Other Fairy Tales, The, recording 558
Sewell, Anna, 19, 75
Sewell, Helen, 86, 195, 197, 198, 668
"Sh," 418
Shadow of a Bull, 26, 36, **258**, il. 259, 670, 673
Shadrach, 17, **218**, 343
Shadrach, Meshach and Abednego, **201**
Shahn, Ben, 670
Shakespeare, William, 70, 389, 427, 430

Shane, Harold, 575
Shannon, Monica, 256
Shapiro, Irwin, 177, 488
Shapiro, Milton J., 531
Sharks, 488
Sharp, Edith, 256
Sharp, Margery, 34, 348, il. 349, 349
Sharpe, Stella, 87, 229
Shattered Skull, The, 461
Shelley, Percy, 427
Shepard, Ernest, il. 20, 336, 417, 669, 670
Shepard, Mary, il. 12, 669
Shephard, Esther, 176
"Shepherd, The," 419
"Shepherd Who Laughed Last, The," 174
Shepherd's Psalm, The, 202
Sherlock, Philip, 180, 673
Sherman, Diane, 471, 486, 491
Sherwood, Martha, 67
Sherwood, Mary, 68
Sherwood, Merriam, 191
Shimin, Symeon, color section, il. 220, 420, 668
Ship and the Sea in Art, The, 586
"Ship That Sailed by Land and Sea, The," 171
Shippen, Katherine B., 490
Ships, Shoals, and Amphoras, 474
Shoe Bird, The, 577
Shoemaker and the Elves, The, 181, 182
Shoo-Fly Girl, 33, **236**, il. 237, 638, 651
"Shop Windows," 437
Shorter Oxford English Dictionary on Historical Principles, The, 278
Shorty at Shortstop, 530
Shot Heard Round the World, The, 448
Shotwell, Louisa, il. 13, 87, 242, 585
Showers, Paul, 30
Shrodes, Caroline, 264
Shulman, Milton, 143
Shuttlesworth, Dorothy, 106, 470, 472
Sidjakov, Nicolas, 22, 117, 125, 321
Sidney, Margaret, 73
Siegl, Helen, il. 429
Sigemi, A Japanese Village Girl, 452, 478
Sigurd, 190
Siks, Geraldine Brain, 641
Silence over Dunkerque, **245**
Silent Storm, The, **277**
"Silly Jean," 173
"Silver," 391, 422, 624
Silver Branch, The, 316
Silver Pennies, 426
Silver Sword, The, **245**
Silverberg, Robert, 365, 488

"Simile: Willow and Ginkgo," 425, 603
Simon, Charlie May, 36, 651
Simon, Hilda, 468
Simon, Irving B., 146
Simon, Norma, 129
Simont, Marc, 84, 132, 134
Sing a Song of Seasons, 429
Sing Song, 78, **420**
Singer, Isaac, 173, il. 173
Singing and the Gold: Poems Translated from World Literature, The, **428**
"Singing Time," 394
Singing Tree, The, recording 558
Sir Gibbie, 40
"Sir Patrick Spens," 397
Siri the Conquistador, 349
Six Foolish Fishermen, **108**
"Six Servants," 170
"Skating," 390
Skeleton in Armor, The, 433
Sketch Book, 72
Skid, 229, 230
Skies of Crete, The, 254, **246**
Skinny, **221**
"Skins," 393*
Skippack School, 236, **303**, 638
"Skipping Along Alone," 403
Skipping Along Alone, **422**
Sky Was Blue, The, **127**, 609
"Skyscrapers," 404, 418
Slave's Tale, A, 315, **316**
"Sleeping Beauty," 61, 161, 604
Sleeping Beauty, 62, recording 557
Sleeping Beauty, The, 182, 490, 588
"Sleeping Beauty in the Wood, The," 169
"Sleeping Tsarevna and the Seven Giants, The," 169
Sleepy Little Lion, The, 117
"Sleet Storm," 406
Sloane, William, 59, 91
Slobodkin, Louis, 33, 84, 116, 120, 335, 367, 571, 572, 664, 669
Slobodkina, Esphyr, 97, 141, 668
"Sloppy," 604
"Slovenly Peter," 424
Small as a Raisin Big as the World, 133
Small Creatures in My Garden, 458
Small, Ernest, 168
Small Fry, 581
Small Rain, 86
Smallest Boy in the Class, The, 224
"Smells (Junior)," 394
Smith, Agnes, 350
Smith, Alvin, il. 259, 670
Smith, Dora V., 29, 91
Smith, E. Boyd, 84
Smith, E. Brooks, 85, 484
Smith, Elva S., 91
Smith, George Harmon, 235, 242

Smith, Hugh, 428
Smith, Irene, 47
Smith, Lillian, 47, 146, 204, 323, 493
Smith, Linell, 511
Smith, Nila Banton, 594
Smith, Robert Paul, 126, 609
Smith, William Jay, 106, 399, il. 399, 408, 423, 428, il. 429
Smoky, the Cowhorse, 11, 86, **513**, 620
Snail's a Failure Socially, A, 419
"Snare, The," 408*
"Sneezles," 397, 417
"Snow" (Aldis), 392*, 406
"Snow" (Wilkins), 406
"Snow Color," 406
Snow Dog, 518
"Snow Drop," 169
"Snow in the City," 418
"Snow Queen, The," 333
Snow Treasure, 244, 295
"Snow White," 72
"Snow White and Rose Red," 170
Snow White and Rose Red, 182, il. 182
"Snow White and the Seven Dwarfs," 169, 604
Snow White and the Seven Dwarfs, 181
"Snowman's Resolution, The," 406
Snowstorm, The, il. 23, 142
Snowy Day, The, 30, 87, 116, il. 117, 131, 587, 614, 668
Snyder, Zilpha, 243
Snygg, Donald, 25
Sobol, Donald J., 484, 526
Social Science Seminar Series, 593
Social Studies for Children in a Democracy, 323
Social Studies in Elementary Education, 323
Social Study, Inquiry in Elementary Classrooms, 592
Solbert, Ronni, il. 366, 670
"Solitary Reaper, The," 428
"Solitude," 404, 417, 609
"Some Cook," 424
"Some Day," 395*
Some Merry Adventures of Robin Hood, 192
Someday, 32, 127, 609
Someday You'll Write, 642
"Someone," 410, 422
Something Special, **419**
"Something Told the Wild Geese," 407*, 418
Sommerfelt, Aimée, 35, 36, 243, 244, 566
Son of the Black Stallion, 513
Song and Garden Birds of North America, recording 560
"Song of Greatness, A," 414, 421
Song of Roland (Baldwin), 191

Song of Roland (Clark), 191
Song of Roland (Sherwood), 191
"Song of the Rabbits Outside the Tavern, The," 407
Song of the Swallows, 117, 654
"Song to Night," 405*
Songs for Childhood, 87
Songs for the Nursery; or Mother Goose's Melodies, 62
Songs from the Nursery Collected by the Most Renowned Poets, 62
Songs of Innocence, 66, 398, **417**
Songs of Robin Hood, 192
Songs of the Forest, recording 560
"Sonic Boom," 428
Sons of the Volsungs, 191
Sootin, Harry, 458, 483
Sorely Trying Day, The, 32
Sorensen, Virginia, 34, 218, 224, 236, 578
Sound and Sense, an Introduction to Poetry, 438, 695
Sound and Ultrasonics, 490
Sounds of a Summer Night, 117
Sounds of the Sea, recording 560
Sounds You Cannot Hear, 464, 490
Source Book on English Institutes for Elementary Teachers, 649
South Town, 35, 230, **231**, il. 232
Southey, Robert, 72, 414, 423
Soviet Union, The, 474
Space Alphabet, 106
Space Ship Returns to the Apple Tree, The, 367
Space Ship Under the Apple Tree, The, 33, 367, 634
Spaghetti for Breakfast, 137
Spanfeller, James, il. 261
"Spangled Pandemonium, The," 412
"Spark in the sun, A," 400*
Sparkle and Spin, **580**
Sparrow Bush, The, 387, 421
Speakers List, 592
Speaking of Cows, 419
Speare, Elizabeth, 22, 35, 299, 302, 314, 670
Speevack, Yetta, 233
Spell Is Cast, A, 528
Spencer, William, 397
Sperry, Armstrong, 9, 11, 17, 19, 35, 251, 281, 637, 667, 670, 674, il. 675, 676
Sphinx, The Story of a Caterpillar, 34, 448, 480
"Spider and the Fly, The," 423
Spider Plant, The, **233**
Spider Silk, 478
Spier, Peter, 587
Spilka, Arnold, 530, 586
"Spin, Weave, Wear," 171
Spirit of St. Louis, The, 284

Spiritual Milk for Boston Babes . . ., 63
Spoerl, Dorothy, 193
Spooky Thing, The, 34, **337**
"Spotted Rug, The," 164
Sprague, Rosemary, 323
"Spring," 419
Spring Comes to the Ocean, 459
Spring, Ira, 478
Spring Is Here, 132
"Spring Rain," 405
Springtime for Jeanne Marie, film 557
Sprints and Distances, Sports in Poetry and Poetry in Sports, **430**
Spy in Old Detroit, A, 527
Spy in Old New Orleans, A, 527
Spy in Old Philadelphia, A, 527
Spy in Old West Point, A, 524, **527**
Spy in Williamsburg, A, 527
Spyri, Johanna, 71
Squanto, Friend of the White Man, 288
"Squares," 417
Squire, James, 649
Squire, John Collings, 413
"Squirrels," 419
Stability and Change in Human Characteristics, 650
Stamm, Claus, 184
Stamp Collecting, 88
Standards, 551
Standards for Media Programs, 550–551
Standards for School Library Programs, 42
Star Maiden and Other Indian Tales, The, recording 558
Starbird, Kaye, 388, 407, 419
Starry Flag Series, The, 74
"Starlight Night, The," 660
"Stars," 421
Stars by Clock and Fist, The, 480
Stars To-Night, **421**
Stars to Steer By, 427
"Steadfast Tin Soldier, The," 351
Steadfast Tin Soldier, The, 85, 332, 333
Steady, A Baseball Story, **529**
Steel Flea, The, 176
Steel Magic, **362**
Steele, William O., 10, 19, 34, 35, 272, 298, 307, 308, 311, 337, 638, 654
Steiner, Charlotte, 30
Stendler, Celia B., 266
Step-Up Books, The, **280**
Stephens, Ann S. W., 74
Stephens, James, 405, 408, 427
Stephens, Peter John, 527, 610
Sterling, Dorothy, 87, 230, 286, 452, 609, 656
Sterling Nature Series, The, 469, 477
"Stern Parent, The," 424*

Stevens, Carla, 88
Stevenson, Augusta, 276, 280
Stevenson, Robert Louis, 75, 78, 79, 389, 390, 398, 405, 409, 417, 420, 426, 427, 430
Stevenson, William, 534
Stillman, Myra, 585
Stillman, Nathan, 594
Stobbs, William, il. 194, 285
"Stocking Fairy," 410
Stolz, Mary, 35, 39, 225, 226, 349, 610, 652, 670
Stone, Helen, 106
Stone, L. Joseph, 47
Stone Soup, 85, 125, 172, 181, recording 559
"Stop-Go," 404
"Stopping by Woods on a Snowy Evening," 392, 406
Stories from Other Lands, filmstrip series 553
Stories from the Bible, **200**
Stories of Champions, 531
Stories of King Arthur and His Knights, 191
Stories of the Gods and Heroes, 198
"Storm," 405*
"Storm, The" (Aldis), 405
"Storm, The" (Behn), 405, 420
Storm Book, The, 132
Stormy, Misty's Foal, 513
Story about Ping, The, 5, 144, 634
Story and Structure, 693
Story behind Modern Books, The, 570
Story Hat, The, 664
Story of a Book, film 555
Story of Ants, The, 470, 472
Story of Arturo Toscanini, The, 588
Story of Babar, The, **136**
Story of Computers, The, 492
Story of Design, The, 586
Story of Dr. Dolittle, The, 86, 373
Story of Ferdinand, The, 118, 137
Story of George Gershwin, The, 588
Story of Greece, 85
Story of Holly and Ivy, The, 352
Story of Johnny Appleseed, The, 283
Story of King Arthur and His Knights, The, 191
Story of Little Black Sambo, The, 76
"Story of Little Mukra, The," 176
Story of Mankind, The, 85, 486
Story of Moslem Art, The, 586
Story of Printing, The, 146
"Story of Red Chicken, The," 604
Story of Religion, The, 584
Story of Roland, The, 191
Story of the Civil War, The, 490
Story of the Liberty Bell, The, 489
Story of the Star Spangled Banner, The, 489

Story of the Statue of Liberty, The, 489
Story of the Three Bears, The, 72
Story of the War of 1812, The, 490
Story of William Penn, The, 283
Story Poems New and Old, 429
Storyteller's Choice, A, 663
Storytelling, 693
Stoutenberg, Adrian, 405
Stowaway to the Mushroom Planet, 368
Strange Companions in Nature, 488
Strange Lizards, 488
Stranger at Green Knowe, A, **511**
Stratemeyer, Edward, 82
Straus, Jacqueline, 458
"Straw Ox, The," 161
Strawberry Girl, 12, 235, 579, 634, 638
"Stray Cat, The," 425
Street, James, 519
String, Straightedge and Shadow, 585
Struggling Upward, 73
Stuart Little, il. 13, 346, 560, 665, 684, 686
Study of Literature, The, 157, 655, 694
Sturton, Hugh, 166, 167
Successful Bulletin Boards, 593
Suchman, J. R., 582
Sue Barton Stories, 38
"Sugar Plum Tree, The," 78
"Summer" (Behn), 420
"Summer" (Starbird), 407
Summer Adventure, A, **231**
Summer Birds, The, 35, **360**
Summer Green, 421
"Summer Morning, A," 407
Summoned by Books, 7, 47
Sun Up, 130
Sung Under the Silver Umbrella, 426
"Sunning," recording 559
Superlative Horse, The, **168**, 610
Surany, Anico, 143
Surprise for a Cowboy, 28
Sutcliff, Rosemary, 39, 190, 297, 316, 317, 320, 571, 670
Suter, Antoinette, 426
Suttle, John E., 593
Sven's Bridge, 587
Swamp in June, The, recording 560
Swans of Willow Pond, 481
Swapping Boy, The, 184
Swapping Song Book, 185
Swartout, Sherwin G., 641
"Sweet Misery," 160
Swenson, Juliet Morgan, 473
Swift, Hildegarde, 140, 287
Swimmy, color section, 118, 121, 614, 669
Swineherd, The, 333, 334
"Swing, The" (Allingham), 625
"Swing, The" (Stevenson), 390, 398, 417

Swing in the Summerhouse, The, 362
Swinton, W. E., 474
Swiss Family Robinson, 19, 58, 73
Sword in the Tree, The, 28, 34, **317**, 548
Sword in the Wilderness, 298
Sword of Siegfried, The, 191
Syme, Ronald, 285, 566
"System," 417

Taba, Hilda, 585, 594
Tad Lincoln and the Green Umbrella, 295
"Take Sky," 604
Take Sky, 398, 424, 606
Tale of a Pig, 184
"Tale of Bat," 179
Tale of Benjamin Bunny, The, recording 558
"Tale of Custard the Dragon, The," 413
Tale of Peter Rabbit, The, color section, 5, 31, 38, 58, 86, 121, 668
Tales from Grimm, 164
Tales from Moominvalley, **341**
Tales from the Story Hat, 164
Tales of a Chinese Grandmother, 163, 180
Tales of Hans Christian Andersen, recording 558
Tales of Peter Parley about America, 70
Tales of the Genii, The, 62
Tales of the Hodja, 181
Tales the Muses Told, 193
Tales Told Again, 166
Tall Book of Mother Goose, The, color section, **101**
Tall Tales from the High Hills, 181
Tamarindo!, 142
Tanglewood Tales, 72
Tannenbaum, Beulah, 585
Tannenbaum, Harold E., 594
Tappan, Eva March, 85
Taran Wanderer, **345**
Tarka the Otter, **508**
Taro and the Tofu, 33
Tashjian, Virginia, il. 175
Taste of Spruce Gum, The, **313**
Tatsinda, **343**, il. 344
"Tattercoats," 169
"Taxis," 404, 418
Taxis and Toadstools, 418
Taxonomy of Educational Objectives Handbook I, 694
Taxonomy of Educational Objectives Handbook II, 694
Taylor, Ann and Jane, 77
Taylor, Edgar, 72
Taylor, Isaac, 71
Taylor, Jane, 77
Taylor, Sidney, 218

"Tea Party," 392*
Teacher and Overhead Projection, The, 594
Teacher's Guide to Children's Books, A, 493, 569
Teaching Elementary School Science, 593
Teaching Literature in Wisconsin, 695
Teasdale, Sara, 405, 406, 415, 421
Teaspoon Tree, The, **340**
Teddy, 30, 96
"Teevee," 413, 425
Tell about the Cowbarn, Daddy, 31
"Tell me, tell me everything," 395
Ten Big Farms, 107
Ten Boys Who Lived on the Road from Long Ago to Now, 71
Tenggren, Gustaf, 102
Tenggren Mother Goose, The, **102**
Tenniel, Sir John, 75, il. 75
Tennyson, Alfred, Lord, 79, 389, 397, 427, 433, 624
Terhune, Albert Payson, 86
Terrible Churnadryne, The, 528
Texas and the War with Mexico, 451
Texas Tomboy, **235**
Thackeray, William, 427
Thank You, Amelia Bedelia, 371
That Bad Carlos, **233**
That Eager Zest, 47
That's Good, That's Bad, 608
Thayer, Ernest, 433
Thee, Hannah, 236, **309**, 638
"Theft of Dawn, The," 162
Their Search for God, 584
Theodore Roosevelt, Fighting Patriot, 284
Theory of Literature, 216, 695
There Is a Bull on My Balcony, 137
There Is a Dragon in My Bed, 137
"There is joy in . . .," 431*
There Is No Rhyme for Silver, 425
"There Once Was an Owl," 424
These Happy Golden Years, 306, 638
They All Want to Write, 641
They Knew Abe Lincoln, 295
They Turned to Stone, 476
They Were Strong and Good, 609
Thidwick, the Big-Hearted Moose, 136
Thimble Summer, 21
Things I Like, The, 30, 96
Things That Spin, 482
Third Part, 65
13 Clocks, The, **333**
Thirty-One Brothers and Sisters, 248, 585, 657
This Boy Cody, **235**
This Dear Bought Land, **302**
"This Happy Day," 394
This Is a Leaf, 488
This Is a Tree, 488

This Is Automation, 492
This Is Cape Kennedy, 462
This Is Israel, 587
This Is London, il. 478
"This Is My Rock," 403*, 404, 609
This Is Paris, 478, 586
This Is Your Century, 452
This Singing World, 427
This Way, Delight, 428, 438
Thistle and Thyme, 165, 181
Thomas, Isaiah, 61, 65
"Thomas Jefferson," 413
Thomas Jefferson, Champion of the People, 284
Thomas, Katherine Elwes, 61
Thompson, Blanche Jennings, 426
Thompson, Hildegard, 488
Thompson, Jean, 426
Thompson, Stith, 159, 169, 204
Thompson, Vivian, 193, 194
Thorne-Thomsen, Gudrun, 85, 558, 662, 663
Thought and Language, 25
Thousand Lights and Fireflies, A, **130**
Threat to the Barkers, 219, 522, **528**
Three Bears, The, 72, filmstrip 553, 587, 620
"Three Billy Goats, The," 161
Three Billy Goats Gruff, The, color section, 30, 121, 181, filmstrips 553 and 554, 625, 663
Three Boys Series, 33
3 X 3 Three by Three, **107**
"Three Golden Oranges," 170
"Three Little Pigs, The," 604
Three Little Pigs, filmstrip 553, 668
"Three Little Puffins," 412
"Three Owls, The," 83
Three Owls, Third Book, 332
Three Poems of Edgar Allen Poe, **432**
Three Princes of Serendip, The, 165
"Three Sneezes, The," 174
Three Strong Women, 184
Three Tall Tales, 181
"Three Wise Men of Gotham," 61
"Three Wishes, The," 174
Three Wishes, The, 664
Through the Looking-Glass, 423
Through the Magnifying Glass, 483
"Thumbelina," 169, 180
Thumbelina, 33, 333, 353
"Thumbprint," 401*
Thunder of the Gods, 196
Thunderbird and Other Stories, 166
Thurber, James, 109, 335, 585, 627, 669
Thwaite, M. F., 91
Tickle the Pig, 30, 97
Tico and the Golden Wings, 33, **188**, 587, 669
Tide Pools and Beaches, 462, 480

"Tiger, The," 408
Tiger Called Thomas, A, 32
Tigers in the Cellar, **140**
"Tiger's Minister of State, The," 173
Tiger's Whisker and Other Tales and Legends from Asia and the Pacific, The, 164
Tiktá Liktak: An Eskimo Legend, 36, **177**, il. 177, 251
Time, 82
Time and Mr. Bass, 368
Time at the Top, **364**
Time Cat, **365**
Time for All Things, A, **202**
Time for Fairy Tales Old and New, 203
Time for Poetry, 427
Time for the Stars, 370
Time of Trial, 322
Time of Wonder, color section, 15, il. 22, **112**, 116, 119, 125, 555, il. 566, 567, 636
"Tinder Box, The," 72, recording 559
Tinkelman, Murray, 587
Tippett, James, 404, 406, 418, 437, 559
"Tired Tim," 394*
Tirra Lirra, **423**
Tistou of the Green Thumbs, **360**
Titian, 282
Tituba of Salem Village, **302**
Titus, Eve, 136, 526, il. 568
"To an Athlete Dying Young," 430
To Kill a Mockingbird, 39
"To Lou Gehrig," 430
"Toadstool Wood, The," 422
Tobe, 87, **229**
Today's Basic Science, 582
Todd, Vivian E., 145
Token for Children . . ., A, 64
Told Under the Green Umbrella, 72, 166
Tolkien, J. R. R., 356, 377, 651, 670
"Tom-Tit-Tot," 171
Tom Tit Tot, 165
Tom Brown's School Days, 74
Tom Sawyer, 19, 20, 40, 58, filmstrip 554
Tom Swift, 82
Tom Thumb, 60
Tom Tiddler's Ground, 427
Tom, Tom the Piper's Son, 103
Tomahawk Family, The, **248**
Tomahawks and Trouble, 308
Tomato Patch, The, 652
Tomes, Margot, il. 332, 669
Tommy Trip, 62
Tommy Trip's History of Beasts and Birds, 65
Tom's Midnight Garden, **364**, 612, 616
Tomten, The, color section, 141, 668

Tomten and the Fox, The, 141
Tongue Tanglers, 411
Tony Beaver, 176
Tony's Birds, 456
"Toomai of the Elephants," 19
Tooze, Ruth, 493, 695
Torrance, E. Paul, 641
Touch Blue, 411, 430
Touchdown for Tommy, 529
Tough Enough's Trip, **516**
Tough Winter, The, **347**
Towappu: Puritan Renegade, 610
Towle, George, 71
Town Mouse and Country Mouse, filmstrip 554
Trace through the Forest, **308**
Track and Field for Boys, 532
"Tragic Story, A," 413
Trail Blazer of the Seas, 286
Trail through Danger, 308
"Trains," 404, 437
"Trains, The," 418
Translations of Children's Books, 91
Trap Lines North, 533, recording 558
Traveler in Time, A, **365**
Travels of Monarch X, The, 467, il. 473, 478
Travers, P. L., il. 12, 20, 34, 370, 372, 616, 632, 666, 669
Trease, Geoffrey, 35, 277, 316, 322, 452, 528
Treasure Island, 19, 20, 58, 75
Treasure of Green Knowe, The, 35, 339, **363**
Treasure of Siegfried, The, 191
Treasure Seekers, The, 86
Tree and Leaf, 377
Tree for Peter, A, **243**
Tree Is a Plant, A, 476
Tree Is Born, A, 477
Tree of Freedom, **305**
Tree of Language, The, 582
Tree in the Trail, 548, 566
Tree Is Nice, A, 6, 121, 134
Treece, Henry, 316
Treegate's Raiders, 304
Tressa's Dream, 513
Tresselt, Alvin, color section, 32, 130, 131, 132, 182, 476, 477, 557, 578, 602, 668
Trimmer, Mrs. Sarah, 65
Triumph of the Seeing Eye, The, 281
Trouble After School, **227**, 609
Trouble with Francis, The, 530
Trouble with Jenny's Ear, The, **375**
True Book of Energy, The, 449
True Book of Space, The, 473
True Book of Weather Experiments, The, 482
True Book of Whales, The, 454
True Book Series, The, 84, 456, 482

Tudor, Tasha, color section, 6, 102, 106, 107, 119, 120, 133, 417, 427, il. 428
Tunis, Edwin, 488
Tunis, John, 245, 531
Tunnels, 491
Turkish Fairy Tales, 166, 181
Turnabout Trick, The, 375
Turner, E. S., 91
Turret, The, 349
Turtles, 486, 488
Twain, Mark, 40, 75, 79
"'Twas the Night before Christmas," 397
"Twelve Months, The," 163
Twenty and Ten, 245, 295
Twenty-One Balloons, The, 35, **358**, 611, 638, 670
Twenty Thousand Leagues under the Sea, 58, 75
"Twinkle Twinkle Little Star," 77
"Twins, The," 413
Twins Series, 84
"Two Bears, The," 193
Two Brothers, The, 169
Two Is a Team, 32, 87, **129**, 229
Two Little Bears, 117
Two Logs Crossing, John Haskell's Story, **308**
Two Lonely Ducks, 107
Two Old Bachelors, 432
"Two People," 424
Two Reds, The, **131**
Two Worlds of Damyan, The, 36, **238**
Tworkov, Jack, 139, 668
Typewriter Town, 399, il. 399, 423

"U for Umbrellas," recording 559
UNESCO, 482
Ubell, Earl, 458, 469
Udry, Janice, 6, 32, 121, 129, 134, 420, 625
"Ugly Duckling, The," 72
Ugly Duckling, The, 332, 333, film 556, 576
Uhl, Melvin J., 463
Ullman, James Ramsey, 262, 651
Ulysses and Circe, filmstrip 554
Umbrella, 30, **132**
"Umpire, The," 430
Uncle Bouqui of Haiti, recording 558
Uncle Remus, His Songs and Sayings, 72
Uncle Remus Stories, 175
Under the Tent of the Sky, 429
Under the Tree, **420**
Under the Window, 78
Understanding Group Behavior of Boys and Girls, 46
Understanding Maps, 585

Ungerer, Tomi, 136, 429
Unhappy Hippopotamus, The, 137, 673
Universe of Galileo and Newton, The, 282
University of Nebraska, 693
Untermeyer, Louis, 427, il. 427
Unternecker, John, 408
Unreluctant Years, The, 47, 146, 204, 323, 493
"Until We Built a Cabin," 404*
Untune the Sky, 430, il. 430
Unwin, Nora S., il. 306, 669, 670
Updike, John, 428
"Urashima Taro and the Princess of the Sea," 170
Urmston, Mary, 225, 609
Uttam, a Boy of India, 478
Uttley, Alison, 365

Valens, Evans G., color section, 109, 115
"Valentine," 428
Valley of the Smallest, 509
Vance, Marguerite, 289
Van der Loeff, A. Rutgers, 309
Van Gelder, Rosalind, 580
Van Gogh, 282, 586
Van Loon, Hendrik, 85, 486
Van Riper, Guernsey, Jr., 280, 531
Van Stockum, Hilda, 245
Vasco da Gama, **285**
"Vasilissa the Beautiful," 171
Velvet Room, The, **243**
"Velvet Shoes," 406
Velveteen Rabbit, The, **141**
Verne, Jules, 75, 367
Veronica, 136, 673
"Very Early," 419
Very Special House, A, 30, **137**, 138, 139, 636, 684
Very Young Verses, 426
"Vespers," 388
Victory at Valmy, **322**
Viguers, Ruth Hill, 47
Viking Adventure, 34, **315**
Viking's Dawn, 316
Viking's Sunset, 316
"Village Blacksmith, The," 396, 427
Village Tree, 117, 144
Viollet, **348**
Virgil, 430
"Visit from St. Nicholas, A," 77, 397
Visit to a Chief's Son, 6
Vison, the Mink, 481
Vogel, Ilse-Margaret, 32
"Voice of the Sky," 405
Vorwald, Alan, 451, 460
Voyage of the Javelin, The, 533
Vries, Leonard de, 77, il. 77, 90, 455, 458

Vulpes, the Red Fox, 481
Vygotsky, L. S., 25

Waber, Bernard, 131, 136, 137
Wagner, Walter, 490
Wait for William, 32
Wait Till the Moon Is Full, 121
Wake Up, City!, 130
Wake Up, Farm!, 130, 636
Walck *Monographs,* 594
Walk the World's Rim, 26, **301**, 624
Walker, Barbara K., 166
Waller, Leslie, 581
Walls of Windy Troy, The, 275
"Walrus and the Carpenter, The," 411
Walsh, Frances, 47
Walter de la Mare, 594
Walter, Nina Willis, 439
Walter, the Lazy Mouse, 31, 568
Walters, Marguerite, 106
Waltrip, Lela and Rufus, 248
Wanderers of the Field, **242**
Wandering Moon, The, 422
War with Mexico, The, 451
War Years, The, 294
Ward, Lynd, 11, 109, 111, il. 111, 118, 135, 140, 284, 287, 293, il. 293, 294, 516, 576, 577, 669, 670, 681, 684
Ward, Winifred, 641
Warren, Austin, 216, 695
Warrior Scarlet, **297**
Wartik, Herschel, il. 471
Wasson, Isabel B., 472
Watch Those Red Wheels Roll, 529
Watchwords of Liberty, 448
Water and the Thirsty Land, 459
Water Babies, The, 40, 58, 75
Water Fit to Use, 491
"Water Noises," 420
"Water of Life, The," 161
Waterless Mountain, **253**
Watson, Jane Werner, 189, 198, 584, 670
Watts, Edith, 461
Watts, Isaac, 64, 66, 423
Watts, May Theilgaard, 479
Wave, The, 115, 126, **184**
Way of Danger, The, 194, il. 194
Way of Knowing, A, **427**
Way of the Storyteller, The, 695
Wayah of the Real People, **298**
Ways of Studying Children, 46
Webber, F. E., 204
Webber, Irma E., 476, 610
Webster, Daniel, 70
Webster, Noah, 65
Wee Gillis, 118, 143, 634
Weed Is a Flower, A, 283

Weik, Mary, 232, il. 233
Weil, Eleanor, 280
Weil, Lisl, 142
Weisgard, Leonard, color section, 108, 112, 117, 119, 125, 128, 134, 301, 343, 420, il. 425, 668
Wellek, René, 216, 695
Welles, Winifred, 392, 393, 403, 410, 422
Wells, Carolyn, 412
Welty, Eudora, 577
Welty, Susan, 461
Werner, Elsa, 200
Wersba, Barbara, 331, il. 332, 549, 669
Werstein, Irving, 451, 452
West Indian Folk Tales, 180
West, Jerry, 656
"Western Wagons," 413
"Wet Sheet and a Flowing Sea, A," 398
Wezel, Peter, 97
What Bird Is It?, 479
What Butterfly Is It?, 479
What Dinosaur Is It?, 479
What Do You Do, Dear?, 137
What Do You Say, Dear?, 32, 137
What Does a Congressman Do?, 491
What Does a Peace Corps Volunteer Do?, 584
What Happens in Literature, 695
What Happens in the Sky, 454
"What happiness," 603
"What Is Pink?," 420
What Is That Sound!, 425
What Is the World?, 476
What Makes a Light Go On?, 471
"What makes a poem?," 387*
What Makes It Go?, 483
What Makes TV Work?, 466, 471, 472, 474
"What the Gray Cat Sings," 437
What Then, Raman?, **250**
What Tree Is It?, 479
What Whiskers Did, 30, 97
What's Inside of Animals, il. 471
What's Inside of Me?, 491
What's Inside? Series, 488
What's That Noise?, 31
"Whatsoever things are true . . .," 416
Wheel on the School, The, **258**, recording 559, 638
Wheeler, Opal, 282, 588
"When Candy Was Chocolate," 423
When I Am Big, 126, 609
When I Have a Little Girl, **126**, 609
When Knights Were Bold, 85
When We Were Very Young, 636
Where Does Everyone Go?, 133, 420
Where Does the Butterfly Go When It Rains?, color section, **112**
"Where Go the Boats?," 398*, 417
Where Have You Been?, 30
Where the Wild Things Are, color section, 41, 117, 120, 121, 123, 139, 570, 624, 625, 668, **671**
Where's My Baby?, 30, 97
"Which Loved Best," 389
Whim Wham . . ., The, 77
Whisper of Glocken, The, 355
"Whispers," 419*
Whispers and Other Poems, il. 401, 418
"Whistle," 404
Whistle for Willie, 32, 116, 128
White, Ann Terry, 189, 191, 198
"White Bird, The," **160**
White Bungalow, The, 36, **244**
White, E. B., 5, 10, 11, 13, 15, 16, 20, 34, 338, 346, il. 346, 370, 579, 659, 665, 669, 684, 685
White Land, The, 100, 587
White Marble, The, 32, **129**
White, Mary Sue, 580
White, Nancy B., 280
White Palace, The, 453, 481
White Peril, The, **533**
"White Season," 407*
White Snow, Bright Snow, color section, 118, 131, 578
White Stag, The, **195**
White Stallion of Lipizza, 515, 638
"Whither No One Knows," 172
Whitman, R. S., 204
Whitman, Walt, 545
Whitmore, W. H., 61
Whitney, Phyllis, 520, 521, 522, 523, 524
Whittier, John Greenleaf, 78, 388, 389, 413, 432
Who Do You Think You Are?, 491
"Who has seen the wind?," 78, 398, 405, 420
Who Says Hoo?, 587
"Whole Duty of Children," 417
Who's There? Open the Door!, 30, 98
"Whose are this pond and house?," 407*
Why? A Book of Reasons, 456, 482
Why and How? A Second Book of Reasons, 482
"Why Spider Lives in Ceilings," 160
Why the Mohole, 490
"Why the Sea Is Salt," 179
"Why Wisdom Is Found Everywhere," 178
Wibberley, Leonard, 304
Wiberg, Harald, color section, 668
"Wicked House of Duncan Mcbain, The," 180
Wide Awake, 419
Wier, Ester, 252, 253, 670
Wiese, Kurt, 668
Wiggin, Kate Douglas, 85
Wigmakers, The, 489
Wilcox, R. Turner, 488
Wild Animals I Have Known, 75
Wild Geese Calling, 509
Wild Heart, The, 9, **515**
Wild Swans, The, 171, 332, 333, filmstrip 554
Wild Trek, 518
Wild Voyageur, **509**
Wilde, Oscar, 334
Wilder, Laura Ingalls, 21, 22, 306, il. 307, 579, 638, 669
"Wilderness Is Tamed, The," 413
Wildfire, 115
Wildlife Cameraman, 533
Wildsmith, Brian, color section, 6, 101, 105, 107, 118, 186, 192, 417, 427, 432, 587, 668
Wilkins, Alice, 385, 406
Will and Nicolas, 22, 131, 134, 141, 143
William Penn, 32
William Tell, filmstrip 553
Williams, Barbara, 489
Williams, Berkeley, 669
Williams, Catharine, 642
Williams, Garth, il. 13, 16, 96, 107, 121, 127, 298, 307, il. 307, il. 346, 348, 349, il. 349, 669, 685
Williams, Jay, 33
Williams, Margery, 141
Williamson, Henry, 508
Williamson, Joanne, 311, 314
Williamson, Margaret, 456, 457, 471, 479
Willson, Dixie, 407
Wilson, Leon, 235
Wilson, Maurice, 186
Wilt, Miriam E., 642
"Wind," 405
"Wind, The," 398
Wind in the Willows, The, 8, 19, il. 20, 20, 58, 85, **349**, 350, 559, 654, 661, 670
Wind Song, **421**
Windle, Eric, 464, 490
Windy Morning, 422
"Windy Nights," 78, 390*, 398, 405, 417
"Windy Wash Day, The," 418
Wing on a Flea, The, 133
Winged Watchman, The, **245**
Wingfin and Topple, color section, 109, 115
Wings from the Wind, **427**, il. 428
Winnie the Pooh, 15, 19, 20, 58, 86, 338, **351**, 613, 659, 669, 681
'Winning of the TV West, The,' 413

Winslow Homer, 282
Winstanly, Henry, 64
"Winter and Summer," 406*
Winter at Valley Forge, The, 281
Winter Birds, 479
Winter Danger, 19, 308, 638
"Winter Night," 406, 420
Winterfeld, Henry, 353
Wisconsin English-Language Arts Curriculum Project, 695
Witch of Blackbird Pond, The, **302**
Witch's Daughter, The, **522**
With a Wig, With a Wag, 181
Withers, Carl, 159, 396, 411
Wizard in the Well, The, 422
Wizard of Oz, The, 19, 58, 86, **340**
Wojciechowska, Maia, 26, 36, 258, il. 259, 301, 566, 670, 673
"Wolf and the Seven Little Kids, The," 169
"Wolf Who Knew How to Be a Friend, The," 172
"Wolf Wisdom," 161
Wolfe, Ann G., 166
Wolfe, Ffrida, 385
Wolfe, Louis, 468
Wonder Book, The, 195
Wonder Book and Tanglewood Tales, A, **197**
Wonder Clock, The, 72, 161, 166
Wonder World of Microbes, 461
Wonderbook for Boys and Girls, The, 72
Wonderful Adventures of Nils, The, 58, 85
Wonderful Flight to the Mushroom Planet, 368, 634
Wonderful O, The, 335, **336**
Wonderful Stories for Children, 72
Wonderful Story of How You Were Born, The, 32
Wonderful Winter, The, **320**
"Wonderful Words, The," 581
Wonderful World of Archeology, The, 449
Wonderful World of Mathematics, The, 585
Wonderful World of Music, The, 490
Wonderful World of the Sea, The, 469
Wonders of Hummingbirds, 468, 470
Wonders of the Human Body, 466, il. 466
Wonders of the Telescope, The, 71
Wondriska, William, 652
Wood, Frances, 464
Wood, Ray, 411
Wood, Samuel, 71
Woodbury, David O., 490
"Woodpecker, The," 400, 420
Woodrow Wilson Story, The, 286
Woolf, Virginia, 7
Woolson, Constance Fenimore, 414

"Word, A," 416*
Word Twins, 580
Words from the Myths, 189, **198**, **581**
Words in Genesis, 202
Words, Words, Words, 425, **581**, 604
Wordsworth, William, 427
World Full of Homes, A, 477
"World is full of wonderful smells, The," 394
World Is Round, The, 451, 475
World of . . . Books, The, 618
World of Captain John Smith: 1580–1631, The, 487
World of Christopher Robin, The, **417**
World of Columbus and Sons, The, 487
World of Manabozho, The, 161
World of Push and Pull, The, 458
World of the Living, The, 469
"World turns softly, The," 399*
World's Great Religions, The, 584
Worlds to Come, 367
Worthington, Kim, 409
Worthylake, Mary, 456
Wren, **239**
Wright, Blanche Fisher, 102
Wright, Dare, 118, 576
Wrightson, Patricia, 369
Wrinkle in Time, A, 34, **369**, 670
"Write Me a Verse," 424, 606
Writing Books for Boys and Girls, 568, 570
Writing, Illustrating and Editing Children's Books, 145
Wundheiler, L., 452
Wuorio, Eva-Lis, 116, 528
Wyeth, N. C., 670
Wyler, Rose, 458, 463, 482, 483
Wylie, Elinor, 406
Wynants, Miche, 201, il. 201, 587
Wynne, Annette, 413, 608
Wyss, J. H., 73

Yamaguchi, Tohr, 183
Yankee Doodle, 122, 184
Yankee Doodle's Cousins, 181
"Yarn of the 'Nancy Bell,' The," 395
Yaroslava, 182
Yashima, Taro, 30, 33, 84, 112, 117, 123, il. 124, 125, 128, 132, 144, 554, 584, 669
Yasu and the Stranger, 120
Yates, Elizabeth, 8, 10, 35, 40, 256, 275, 288, 305, il. 306, 566, 610, 612, 642, 651, 669, 670
Yates, Raymond, 483
Yea! Wildcats, 531
"Year Later, A," 404
Year of the Bloody Sevens, The, **308**
Yearling, The, 11, **512**, 670
Yeats, William Butler, 409, 414

Yellow Fairy Book, The, 72, 180
Ylla, 117, 587
Yonge, Charlotte, 72, 78
You and Relativity, 463, 476
You and . . . Series, 486
You and the Constitution of the United States, 584
You and the Oceans, 471, 486
You and the World around You, 451
You and Your Amazing Mind, 457, 491
You Better Come Home with Me, **342**
You Come Too, **421**, 650
You Have a Friend, Pietro, **228**
You Know Who, 424, recording 558
"*You Look Ridiculous*," **137**, 673
You Read to Me and I'll Read to You, 424, recording 558
Young Buglers, The, 71
Young Christians Library, The, 59
Young, Clarence, 82
Young Eagle, 464, il. 464, 481
Young Folk's Heroes of History, 71
Young Folk's History of the United States, A, 71
Young Fur Trader, The, 73
Young, I. S., 531
Young Man in a Hurry, 277, 286
Young Man's Calling, The, 65
Young Mike Fink, 177
Young Olympic Champions, 531
Young Readers Review, 44, 511, 561
Youngest One, 128
Your Heart and How It Works, 459
Yours Till Niagara Falls, 430
Youth's Behavior, 60
Youth's Companion, The, 79
Yugoslav Folk Tales, 180

Zacks, Irene, 106
Zaffroni, Joseph, 582
Zebulon Pike: Young America's Frontier Scout, 281
Zeee, 33, 618
Zemach, Harve, 125, 179, il. 179, 587
Zemach, Margot, il. 179, 587
"Zero Weather," 393*
Zim, Herbert, 34, 35, 84, 459, il. 471, 479, 488, 491
Ziner, Feenie, 288
Zion, Gene, 32, 133, 672
Zlateh the Goat, **173**, il. 173
"Zlatovlaska the Golden-Haired," 172
Zolotow, Charlotte, color section, 30, 32, 107, 120, 121, 126, 127, 129, 132, 133, 609
Zomo the Rabbit, 166, 167
Zuelke, Ruth, 490